Key to map pages

Shetland Islands **160**
Lerwick

Orkney Islands
Fair Isle
Kirkwall **159**

Lewis
Stornoway
154 155
Harris

Thurso
Wick
Scourie
156 157 **158**

North Uist
Skye
148 149
South Uist
Kyle of Lochalsh

Ullapool
Dornoch
A835
150 151
Inverness

Elgin
Fraserburgh
152 153
A96 A90

A87 A82 A95
136 137 138 139
Aberdeen
140 141

Mallaig
A830 A86
Fort William
A9
130 131 132 133
134 135
A90

Coll Tiree
146 147
Mull
A828
Oban
Dundee
124 125
A85
126 127
Perth
St Andrews
Colonsay
A83 A82
Stirling
M90 A92
144 145
128 129
Jura

Islay
Glasgow
Edinburgh
122 123
142 143
118 119 120 121
Berwick-upon-Tweed
M74 A702
Arran
Campbeltown
Ayr A76
Hawick
A68
112 113
114 115
Alnwick
A77
116 117
A74(M) A7 A1

Stranraer
A75
Dumfries
Newcastle upon Tyne
104 105
106 107
110 111
Carlisle A69
Sunderland
108 109
Durham
A19
Middlesbrough
Whitehaven
A66
A1(M)
102 103
A591 M6
100 101
A19 A171
98 99
Kendal
Scarborough
A595
A1

Coleraine
Isle of Man
Barrow in Furness
Lancaster
Harrogate
York A64
A165
Derry/Londonderry
84
92 93
94 95
96 97
Ballymena
Douglas
Blackpool
Bradford
Leeds
Hull
Belfast
Preston
86 87
88
M62 A63
Enniskillen
Portadown
M62
Manchester
Doncaster
Grimsby
Sligo
Newry
85
89 90 91
Liverpool
Sheffield
Lincoln
M53
Holyhead
Llandudno Chester
Macclesfield
Mansfield
Skegness
Drogheda
Anglesey A55
82 83
74 75
A6
78 79
A16
Bangor A487
Wrexham
Hanley
Derby
Nottingham
Boston
Galway
Athlone
A5
76 77
A17
Dublin
70 71
Stoke
A50
Dun Laoghaire
Dolgellau
Stafford
80 81
Cromer
Shrewsbury
Leicester
A148
A458
62 63
A1
King's Lynn
Great Yarmouth
Limerick
Aberystwyth
60 61
64
66 67
Norwich
68 69
58 59
Telford
A47
Peterborough
Kilkenny
Newtown
Wolverhampton
A17 A1(M)
A10
45 46 47 48 49
Birmingham
A43
56 57
Killarney
Wexford
Builth Wells
Worcester
Coventry
Kettering
Newmarket
Bury St Edmunds
XIX
Waterford
A470
Stratford-upon-Avon
Northampton
A14
Ipswich
Cork
Rosslare
Hereford
50 51 52 53 54 55
Cambridge
A12
A484 A44
Banbury
Milton Keynes
M11
Felixstowe
Fishguard
Merthyr Tydfil
Gloucester
Cheltenham
Luton
Colchester
44
32 33 34 35 36 37 38 39 40 41 42 43
Southend-on-Sea
Pembroke
Llanelli
Newport
Swindon
Oxford
Chelmsford
Lundy
Swansea
A34 London
31
M4
Cardiff Bristol
Bath
Reading
Windsor
Croydon
Canterbury
20 21
22 23 24 25 26 27 28 29 30
Dover
Ilfracombe
Newbury
Gatwick
Maidstone
A37 A36
Winchester
M2
Bideford
Taunton
Salisbury
Southampton
Ashford
A361
M27
Lewes
A259
8 9 10 11 12 13 14 15 16 17 18 19
A39 A386
Dorchester
Poole
Portsmouth
Chichester
Brighton
Exeter
A35
A303
A30
Weymouth
Bournemouth
Isle of Wight
Newquay
Plymouth
Torquay
4 5 6 7
Isles of Scilly
Penzance
Truro
2 3
A30 A38

Channel Islands
Guernsey
Jersey

◆ Town plan and urban approach map
● Town plan

XVIII

PHILIP'S

COMPLETE ROAD ATLAS
Britain
and Ireland

www.philips-maps.co.uk
First published in 2009 by Philip's
a division of Octopus Publishing Group Ltd
www.octopusbooks.co.uk
Endeavour House, 189 Shaftesbury Avenue
London WC2H 8JY
An Hachette UK Company
www.hachette.co.uk

Second edition 2010
First impression 2010

ISBN 978-1-84907-108-6 (spiral)
ISBN 978-1-84907-109-3 (hardback)

Cartography by Philip's
Copyright © 2010 Philip's

OS Ordnance Survey® This product includes mapping data licensed from Ordnance Survey® with the permission of the Controller of Her Majesty's Stationery Office. © Crown copyright 2010. All rights reserved. Licence number 100011710.

The map of Ireland on pages XVIII–XIX is based on Ordnance Survey Ireland by permission of the Government Permit Number 8621 © Ordnance Survey Ireland and Government of Ireland and

OS ORDNANCE SURVEY OF NORTHERN IRELAND Ordnance Survey Northern Ireland on behalf of the Controller of Her Majesty's Stationery Office © Crown copyright 2010 Permit Number 90158.

Data for the speed cameras provided by PocketGPSWorld.com Ltd.

Information for National Parks, Areas of Outstanding Natural Beauty, National Trails and Country Parks in Wales supplied by the Countryside Council for Wales.

Information for National Parks, Areas of Outstanding Natural Beauty, National Trails and Country Parks in England supplied by Natural England. Data for Regional Parks, Long Distance Footpaths and Country Parks in Scotland provided by Scottish Natural Heritage.

Gaelic name forms used in the Western Isles provided by Comhairle nan Eilean.

Data for the National Nature Reserves in England provided by Natural England. Data for the National Nature Reserves in Wales provided by Countryside Council for Wales. Darparwyd data'n ymwneud â Gwarchodfeydd Natur Cenedlaethol Cymru gan Gyngor Cefn Gwlad Cymru.

Information on the location of National Nature Reserves in Scotland was provided by Scottish Natural Heritage.

Data for National Scenic Areas in Scotland provided by the Scottish Executive Office. Crown copyright material is reproduced with the permission of the Controller of HMSO and the Queen's Printer for Scotland. Licence number C02W0003960.

Printed in China

*Independent research survey, from research carried out by Outlook Research Limited, 2005/06.
**Estimated sales of all Philip's UK road atlases since launch.

Road map symbols

M6 — Motorway, toll motorway

4 — 5 — Motorway junction – full, restricted access

S — S — Motorway service area – full, restricted access

Motorway under construction

A453 — Primary route – dual, single carriageway

S — Service area, roundabout, multi-level junction

4 — 5 — Numbered junction – full, restricted access

Primary route under construction

Narrow primary route

Derby — Primary destination

A34 — A road – dual, single carriageway

A road under construction, narrow A road

B2135 — B road – dual, single carriageway

B road under construction, narrow B road

Minor road – over 4 metres, under 4 metres wide

Minor road with restricted access

2 — Distance in miles

Scenic route

40 — 40 — Speed camera – single, multiple

TOLL — Toll, steep gradient – arrow points downhill

Tunnel

National trail – England and Wales

Long distance footpath – Scotland

Railway with station

Level crossing, tunnel

Preserved railway with station

National boundary

County / unitary authority boundary

Car ferry, catamaran

Passenger ferry, catamaran

Hovercraft

Ferry destination, journey time – hrs : mins

CALAIS 1:30

Ferry — Car ferry – river crossing

Principal airport, other airport

National park

Area of Outstanding Natural Beauty – England and Wales **National Scenic Area** – Scotland

forest park / regional park / national forest

Woodland

Beach

Linear antiquity

Roman road

1066 — Hillfort, battlefield – with date

795 — Viewpoint, nature reserve, spot height – in metres

Golf course, youth hostel, sporting venue

Camp site, caravan site, camping and caravan site

P&R — Shopping village, park and ride

29 — Adjoining page number – road maps

Road map scale 1: 200 000 or 3·15 miles to 1 inch

0 1 2 3 4 5 6 miles

0 1 2 3 4 5 6 7 8 9 10 km

Approach map symbols

M6 — Motorway

Toll motorway

6 — 5 — Motorway junction – full, restricted access

S — Service area

Under construction

A6 — Primary route – dual, single carriageway

S — Service area

Multi-level junction

roundabout

Under construction

A195 — A road – dual, single carriageway

B1288 — B road – dual, single carriageway

Minor road – dual, single carriageway

Ring road

3 — Distance in miles

COSELEY — Railway with station

LOXDALE — Tramway with station

M — Underground or metro station

Congestion charge area

Uncharged road in congestion charge area

Town plan symbols

Motorway

Primary route – dual, single carriageway

A road – dual, single carriageway

B road – dual, single carriageway

Minor through road

one-way street

Pedestrian roads

Shopping streets

Railway with station

City Hall — Tramway with station

Bus or railway station building

Shopping precinct or retail park

Park

Building of public interest

Theatre, cinema

P — Parking, shopmobility

Bank — Underground station

West St — Metro station

H — Hospital, Police station

PO — Post office

Tourist information

Abbey, cathedral or priory

Ancient monument

Aquarium

Art gallery

Bird collection or aviary

Castle

Church

Country park England and Wales Scotland

Farm park

Garden

Historic ship

House

House and garden

Motor racing circuit

Museum

Picnic area

Preserved railway

Race course

Roman antiquity

Safari park

Theme park

Tourist information centre
i open all year
i open seasonally

Zoo

Other place of interest

Relief

Feet	metres
3000	914
2600	792
2200	671
1800	549
1400	427
1000	305
0	0

Speed Cameras

Fixed camera locations are shown using the 40 symbol.

In congested areas the 40 symbol is used to show that there are two or more cameras on the road indicated.

Due to the restrictions of scale the camera locations are only approximate and cannot indicate the operating direction of the camera. Mobile camera sites, and cameras located on roads not included on the mapping are not shown. Where two or more cameras are shown on the same road, drivers are warned that this may indicate that a SPEC system is in operation. These cameras use the time taken to drive between the two camera positions to calculate the speed of the vehicle.

Save £1000 off your annual motoring costs

Seven Top Tips from motoring journalist Andrew Charman

In today's cost-conscious motoring environment, is it possible to slice serious money from the cost of running a car? With the right preparation, it could well be.

Jonathan Maddock / iStockphoto.com

Ask any motorist whether they get good value from their driving and most will likely say no – many argue that motoring has never been more expensive. Drivers fight a constant battle against many enemies including fluctuating fuel prices, aggressive tax rates and an ever-expanding epidemic of safety cameras that many believe are present to generate revenue from fines first, and slow speeds second.

Some 60% of the drivers recently questioned for the Annual Report on Motoring compiled by the RAC believed that rising costs were the biggest minus of running a car in Britain today. Those drivers will be surprised to hear that, in fact, motoring is getting cheaper – the report concluded that even rocketing fuel prices have not stopped the overall cost of motoring falling in the past two decades.

The RAC research concluded that such factors as cheaper purchase and maintainance prices for cars have resulted in motoring costs decreasing in real terms by about 20% since the late 1980s, despite fuel costs more than doubling. Ignore fuel price rises and motoring today is approximately 30% less expensive than 20 years ago.

This little bit of good news, however, does not mean that you can't save money on your motoring – and I intend to show you how some simple moves could put significant cash back into your pocket each year – possibly more than £1000.

Different cars, different homes

Saving big money on your motoring costs starts even before you buy the car. The vehicle you choose and how you buy it can make a difference of thousands of pounds, as shown in the panel on page V. But have no fear, because whether you've just bought a brand-new car or have used the same vehicle for many years, you can still save a packet on your motoring costs.

Of course, I can't say exactly what you will save by following the advice in these pages – so many varying factors affect one's motoring expenses. For example, I used to live in commuter-belt Surrey. Every morning I drove my children 8 miles to school, a journey of around half an hour on congested roads. Now I live in Mid-Wales and drive my wife to work, coincidentally also around 8 miles; it takes less than 15 minutes and I use 10–15% less fuel.

Similarly, potential savings in such areas as tyre life will be affected by your car, the way you drive and the roads you drive on. What I can confidently predict, however, is that by following even some of the advice on these pages, you will leave a noticeable amount of cash in your pocket.

In order to calculate these savings, we've devised 'Mr Average Motorist'. He drives a petrol-powered car – because, despite diesel soaring in popularity in recent times, the majority of cars on today's roads still run on petrol. Our man owns a Ford Mondeo family car, which is regularly one of the UK's top ten most popular buys and averages 35mpg in fuel consumption. So, if he clocks up the national average of around 12,000 miles a year, he will use 1558 litres of fuel costing, at current prices, around £1760.

Preparation is everything

Fuel prices are the most visible and most obvious indicator of the cost of motoring today. At the time of writing, the price of a litre of unleaded petrol has risen over the past twelve months by 25% to an average of about 113 pence. By the time you read this, prices could be soaring again and generally they are on the rise – remember that they have doubled within 20 years. We can't change fuel prices – but we can make the best use of every litre we buy.

You might think, then, that the first obvious move is to buy fuel from the cheapest source – but it's not. Before you put any fuel in your tank, you need to check that your car is in the best condition, both mechanically and otherwise, to stretch those litres. Skimping on servicing is NOT a way to save money on motoring. If your engine is not correctly tuned, it uses more fuel. In particular, clean fresh oil not only helps reduce fuel consumption but also wear caused by the friction of moving engine parts. Allow such parts to keep wearing and you could end up with a failure – and all your savings will be wiped out by an expensive repair bill. Ideally, on a petrol car you should change the oil at least once a year, and a diesel engine benefits from a change every six months.

But by far the biggest mechanical influence on fuel economy comes courtesy of what the car stands on – its tyres. Incorrectly inflated tyres, particularly containing too little pressure, leads to less mpg – and, incredibly, research by the tyre industry suggests that half of all tyres running on today's roads are under-inflated. Tyre manufacturers have calculated that for every 6psi a tyre is under-inflated, an extra 1% is added to consumption, and in roadside checks many cars have been found to have tyres under-inflated by as much as 20%.

◄ **Checking your tyre pressures is simple, and could greatly improve fuel economy.**
killerb10/iStockphoto.com

▼ **Under-inflated or damaged tyres could end up costing you more than a bigger fuel bill.**
ZavgSG /iStockphoto.com

Rocter/iStockphoto.com

Seven Top Tips to save money

1 SLOWING DOWN
average annual saving: up to £665

The first, most obvious area to watch is speed. We are always being told to slow down, but apart from the risk of paying out big money in fines having been caught by a safety camera, there's a far more obvious reason to ease back on that right-hand pedal – it saves money!

The effect is most noticeable on motorways. The national speed limit in Britain is 70mph, but on many a motorway that seems to be treated as a minimum, with traffic charging along at 80mph-plus. However, above 70mph aerodynamic drag becomes a serious issue, really eating into your fuel. If you adopt a more radical attitude, though, cruising along at 50mph instead of 70mph, your fuel costs will plummet, by an astonishing 38% in the average car.

Of course, many drivers will consider slowing down that much, particularly on a clear motorway, as a step too far, but even keeping firmly within speed limits will greatly influence your fuel costs. And there is much more you can do.

Smooth is good – don't, for example, floor the throttle the moment you see a clear stretch of road open up ahead of you. Harsh acceleration, and the resultant equally harsh braking, burns up those litres. Keep a good distance back from the car in front, so you can slow down gently when they do.

Powering around to the red line on your rev counter is another no-no – today's engines work most efficiently at speeds between 1500–2000rpm, and on modern petrol cars changing up a gear at around 2500rpm (2000rpm on a diesel) is both safe, smooth and fuel-friendly.

2 FUEL'S GOLD
average annual saving: up to £420

Find a bargain. Fuel prices charged by garages vary enormously – within a 20-mile radius of my home the differences add up to 5p per litre. And at the time of writing prices are changing almost daily. Clearly the trick is to buy from the cheapest source, but don't drive around looking for cheap prices – you could use as much as you save. Online resources, such as www.petrolprices.com, are a good way of finding out where fuel costs the least in your area, and while prices change constantly, the cheapest garages tend to remain cheapest.

When you've found your cheap supplier, try not to make a special trip to fill up – it's an unnecessary journey that uses fuel. Plan your motoring, factoring in a visit to the garage on the way to or from somewhere else. It's also prudent to visit the garage more often and only run on half a tank instead of a full one, if doing so suits your schedule, because all that extra liquid in a full tank is extra weight.

Myth buster

A few motoring savings that are not always true....

? **Buy your fuel from a busy garage** because the fuel is used quicker, so has no time to age and lose quality

Not necessarily so – The big issue affecting fuel quality is water getting into the tanks through, for example, condensation. Garages periodically remove this water and busier garages may have less chance to do so compared to quieter rural outlets. Fuel quality depends on an individual garage's 'housekeeping' standards and there is no general standard. Also, by going to a busy garage you may lose any potential tiny saving from better-quality fuel while sitting in the queue with your engine running.

? **When buying fuel in the early morning or evening,** you get more for your money because in cooler conditions each litre of liquid becomes denser

False – Most garages keep their fuel in underground tanks, where temperature changes throughout the day are miniscule.

? **Coasting down hills** with the car in neutral saves fuel

False – At least with modern cars. Modern fuel systems cut off the supply to the engine the moment you come off the accelerator, but whether you are in gear or not a tiny amount is still used to ensure the engine does not stall. And without a gear, you have no engine braking, and less control.

? **It's cheaper to** get your car serviced at an independent

Not necessarily so – While independents might appear cheaper than a franchised dealer, because they don't specialize in a particular brand they don't know that brand so well, and crucially often don't possess the same level of diagnostic equipment as a franchised dealer. Therefore, tracing any faults can take significantly longer, which will be charged in service hours.

? **A fast-fit supplier** is the cheapest place to buy new tyres

Not necessarily so – Many franchised dealers are actively price-matching tyres to fast-fit opposition, and if you are told new tyres are needed during a service at the dealer, driving to a fast-fit supplier to find what you expect to be cheaper tyres can be an unnecessary, fuel-using journey.

▼ Recent on the scene are low-rolling-resistance tyres that extend fuel economy by causing less drag on the road surface.
Photo courtesy Mercedes-Benz

▲ Nice luggage, but leave the bags in the boot when you don't need them and you are simply adding fuel-using weight.
ZavgSG/iStockphoto.com

▶ Roof racks are useful, but left atop the car when not in use, they simply ruin the aerodynamics, and the fuel economy.
Photo courtesy GM UK

3 CUTTING DRAG
average annual saving: up to £175

Surely we can't change a car's aerodynamics? Oh yes, we can. Did you fit a roof rack to take all the extras for the family holiday last summer? Is it still bolted to the roof? The extra drag from such a large, anything-but-aerodynamic item could be costing you as much as 30% in fuel consumption.

The same goes for bike racks hung on the back of a car – they don't have the same dramatic effect as a roof rack, but they will unsettle the air ahead of them, thus affecting the aerodynamics of the rear end. Even running with your windows open harms the aerodynamics, interrupting the flow along the sides of the car. Do you tow a caravan and use those wing-mirror extensions to see around it? Well, if you haven't got the van hitched behind, take them off – they act like a couple of airbrakes.

4 AVOID THE CON
average annual saving: up to £175

Remember how it was advised to keep your windows closed for the best aerodynamics? Well, this next tip will go against the grain. Most modern cars have air-conditioning and many drivers leave it permanently switched on. But in doing so they can use up to 10% more fuel. Use the fans on cool without the system switched on, or have the window open just a little. If it's really hot, use the air-con for short periods instead of leaving it switched on and forgetting about it.

5 CLEVER FUELLING
average annual saving: up to £98

Planning ahead saves fuel and first you need to ask, 'Do I really need to make this trip?' Cars take a while to warm up during which they use the most fuel, which is why you should drive gently, avoiding stressing the engine, for the first few miles of any journey. But if said trip is merely nipping down to the shops for, say, a pint of milk, the car never has a chance to warm up, and your fuel economy suffers greatly. So for such short journeys consider walking, or perhaps cycling – it will benefit your health, as well as your car and your wallet. Alternatively, why not combine a number of short journeys in the week – visiting the family one night and doing the shopping on another – into one longer trip, perhaps popping into the garage for fuel at the same time.

Planning ahead comes into its own on longer journeys, especially if travelling to somewhere unfamiliar – you need to know exactly where you are going, to avoid driving around trying to find a destination and eating up extra miles in the process.

Try to avoid congestion hotspots, because sitting in traffic queues not only wastes fuel but also tries one's patience, and when the jam clears we then drive more aggressively, and less fuel-efficiently, to try and make up time. Check where the problems are likely to be – Traffic England, the Highways Agency's website (www.trafficengland.com), carries constantly updated information on traffic issues and even has a facility where one can look at the view from the roadside CCTV cameras to see how heavy the traffic is. Once in the car, listen out for traffic reports on the radio so you can plan ahead and avoid the hot spots. Don't forget to take this road atlas with you so you can use it to detour around problems.

6 PRESSURE POINTS
average annual saving: up to £53

Under-inflated tyres cause increased wear, which as well as becoming dangerous (a bald tyre will harm grip in anything but totally dry conditions, as well as further increasing fuel consumption) reduces the life of the tyre by as much as 30%. You should also check the alignment of your wheels – simply hitting a pothole or a kerb can knock the alignment out, which again will increase tyre wear.

A recent advance in tyre technology, used extensively on the new breed of 'eco' cars, is to cut the tyre's rolling resistance, which is basically the force required to move the rubber over the road. Lower-rolling-resistance tyres require less force and so aid fuel economy, by around 2.5%. Now, less rolling resistance would suggest less grip, which is not very desirable, but these tyres use silica in their construction which effectively puts the grip back. And, surprisingly, such tyres do not generally carry a big price premium over traditional counterparts.

7 CAR WEIGHTWATCHERS
average annual saving: up to £44

Of all the battles fought by motorsport car designers, two areas stand out – reducing the weight of their cars by as much as possible, and making them as smooth as possible, so they slice more efficiently through the air. Exactly the same principles apply to road cars, not for speed, but for economy, and while we would not advocate slicing bits from your car, or trying to add wings and things to a body shape honed over many hours in a wind tunnel by professionals, there are distinct steps one can take that will have major effects on efficiency.

Have you looked in the back of your car recently? Do you know what is in there? Carrying around a lot of unnecessary weight greatly affects fuel economy, and thus your motoring costs – in some cases by as much as 10%. So if you play golf and your clubs and bag live in the boot, or you've been for a day out and left the deckchairs in the car, along with the picnic basket, that weight is squeezing your wallet. Go through the car looking for those pounds that can be shed. You might not think, for example, that a glovebox full of CDs weighs very much, but it all adds up.

Out on the road

There are still big savings to be made, but the onus is now firmly on you and the way you drive the car. So, if you are a bit of a speed merchant, like to use your throttle and brakes, can't remember the last time you checked your tyre pressures, and throw your cases on the roof rack because there's no room left in the boot, following the economy regime above could save you at least £1000 in a year! But even if you are a conscientious motorist who only needs to follow a couple of these Top Tips, you could still save significant money.

▲ Whether filling up with petrol, diesel or the latest biofuels, a little preparation will make the most of your visit to the garage.
1001nights/iStockphoto.com

◀ Neglecting regular servicing can be a false economy.
Mlenny/iStockphoto.com

Road warrior approximately 40,000 miles per year

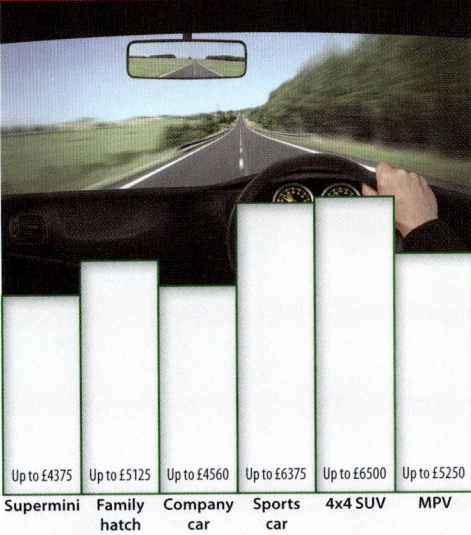

Supermini	Family hatch	Company car	Sports car	4x4 SUV	MPV
Up to £4375	Up to £5125	Up to £4560	Up to £6375	Up to £6500	Up to £5250

Professional driver approximately 22,000 miles per year

Supermini	Family hatch	Company car	Sports car	4x4 SUV	MPV
Up to £2300	Up to £2840	Up to £2500	Up to £3500	Up to £3625	Up to £2875

Family runabout approximately 12,000 miles per year

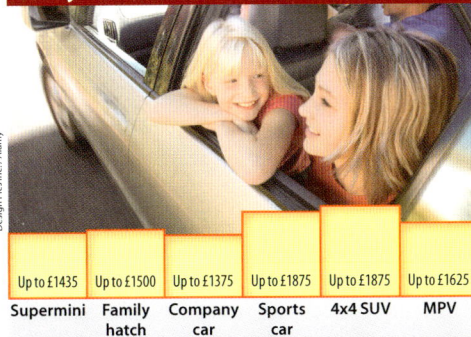

Supermini	Family hatch	Company car	Sports car	4x4 SUV	MPV
Up to £1435	Up to £1500	Up to £1375	Up to £1875	Up to £1875	Up to £1625

Just for shopping approximately 6000 miles per year

Supermini	Family hatch	Company car	Sports car	4x4 SUV	MPV
Up to £700	Up to £775	Up to £675	Up to £940	Up to £975	Up to £790

Buying a car

Most of us don't buy a new car every year, but when we do, there are thousands of pounds we can potentially save, as long as we do our homework first. Recent research by the AA found that a person spending up to £10,000 on a car could end up with a vehicle returning anything from 33 to almost 70mpg. Over a year, the difference in fuel costs for our average driver would add up to more than £700. When the AA compared the mpg figures for cars costing between £20,000 and £30000, the potential fuel savings came close to £2000! In addition, smaller, greener cars attract lower insurance premiums, and cheaper annual road tax – depending on your model, the cost of a tax disc can vary from £0 to £405 a year.

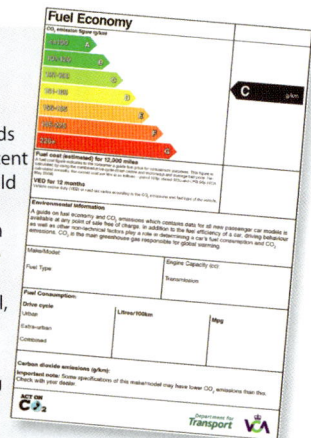

- **Think carefully before making your choice.** Do you really need a seven-seat people carrier? It might be useful on the few occasions your children bring friends home from school, but most of the time you will be carrying around extra, fuel-burning weight. Do you really want that sporty convertible? Folding roof mechanisms add weight, and as well as being less mpg-friendly to start with, performance engines encourage 'performance' driving, which gobble up those litres.

- **Many manufacturers are now producing new 'eco' versions** of their most popular models, with such refinements as low-rolling-resistance tyres, remapped engine electronics and reshaped aerodynamics to further stretch that fuel economy, and slash CO₂ emissions to levels that qualify for free road tax. But they can sometimes cost significantly more to buy than traditional counterparts.

- **The most economical cars will generally be diesel-powered.** Diesel engines travel a lot further on each litre of fuel and they produce less CO₂. But diesel fuel is usually more expensive than the equivalent unleaded petrol – and the majority of diesel-powered cars come with a price premium over their petrol counterparts.

- **Spend time working out your annual mileage** and how far you will need to drive a diesel before you start saving money. Used-car specialist Parkers Guide recently launched a very useful fuel-cost calculator on its website (www.parkers.co.uk), which enables an instant check on how much individual car models will cost you in a year, and it can throw up surprises – for example, at recent fuel prices and car list prices, a BMW 318d diesel would take close to 300,000 miles to recoup the £2790 more that it costs over the 318i petrol version.

- **Consider depreciation** when buying. Be sure to check the 'residual value' – which is an industry-quoted figure, easily found on internet sites such as Parkers, predicting how much the car will be worth after three years' use. Many factors influence such values – the make of car, its reliability, additional equipment installed, even in some cases the colour – so it's worth checking carefully to save money down the line.

- **Do you need to buy new?** New cars lose a significant amount of their value – sometimes 20-25% – the moment they are driven off the showroom forecourt. Yet there are many buyers who change their car every year, which adds excellent vehicles to a dealer's nearly-new selection. Many have at least a year of the manufacturer's warranty remaining – some substantially more

with several makers moving to five-year and, in the case of Hyundai, seven-year warranties.

- **If you do buy used**, it's crucial to spend a little money, usually no more than £30–£40, on a vehicle data check, which will show up any irregularities in the car's history – whether it has outstanding finance owing on it, for example. This could avoid costing you a big bill, or even your car, later on.

- **Whether you buy new or used**, never accept the price stated at face value. With car sales having plummeted in the second half of 2008, dealers are desperate to sell – which puts the buyer in a very strong position to haggle over the price. Even persuading the dealer to fill the car with a tank of fuel is a significant saving at today's prices. And if you have hard cash available, this can encourage the dealer to offer you savings.

- **Shopping around for car insurance is essential**, and made easier these days thanks to a number of well-advertised internet price-comparison sites, but don't take these at face value – do your own research too. The choice of car is crucial to how much it will cost you in premiums, but insurers also like cars that are kept off the road, even better if you have a garage available. So if you have a garage full of junk with the car parked outside, why not have a clear out?

- **Also, think beyond the obvious.** If your eldest offspring has reached 17, passed their test and bought themselves an old banger to run around in, do they really need to be on the family car insurance too? If they are, it will send the premium rocketing. You might also consider taking an advanced driving course. While this will cost you money in the first place, insurers tend to give discounts to drivers with advanced qualifications, and along the way you learn driving techniques that will also help your overall economy.

- **Keeping your licence clean** can make a big difference to your insurance costs. You don't want penalty points, so don't use a handheld mobile phone at the wheel, and keep within speed limits – doing so offers a potential double saving, in fuel and insurance costs.

▲ All new cars on display in showrooms now include this chart giving the potential buyer a guide to their annual motoring cost.

Wasted fuel...

You could be using more than double the amount of fuel you need to! This chart shows how much cash you could be wasting by not attending to basic economy measures. Excess speed, for example, can increase fuel use by more than a third.

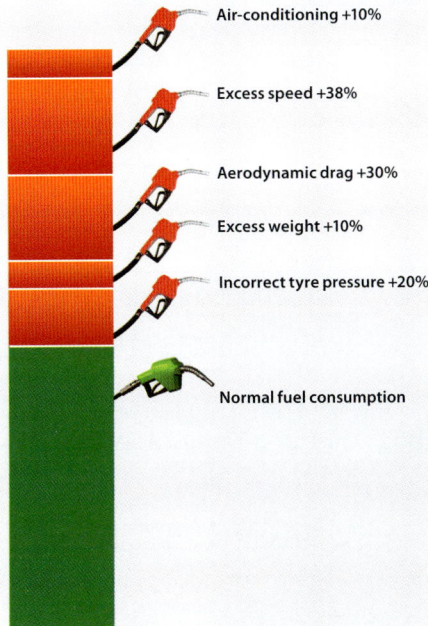

- Air-conditioning +10%
- Excess speed +38%
- Aerodynamic drag +30%
- Excess weight +10%
- Incorrect tyre pressure +20%
- Normal fuel consumption

▼ Careful driving really does save fuel. In the annual MPG challenge 400-mile endurance marathon, this Toyota Yaris diesel recorded 84.66mpg, almost 35% higher than its official combined fuel consumption figure.
Photo courtesy Toyota GB

V

Our Top 10 Tips
to avoid
speeding penalties

The good news for motorists is that, in the year ending March 2007, the money raised from speeding fines in England and Wales fell by 9%. But it's not all good news. The number of tickets sent out to motorists in that period fell by just 2% – most of the benefit for motorists came from the smaller chance of the fines actually being collected. At the same time, the responsibility for speed cameras has been devolved to a local level – which could make getting a ticket even more of a lottery. And there still remains the big question – is the time and money spent on speed cameras the best way to reduce road deaths?

We asked Stephen Mesquita, our speed camera expert, to give us an update on the whole thorny subject – and to give us his Top 10 Tips about what you can do to keep penalty points off your licence.

- It's four years since Philip's atlases first started its Speed Camera campaign. In that time, we've worked hard to bring to your attention the fact that speed camera fines are a regional lottery.
- I'm not a speed merchant. I don't regard it as the motorist's right to drive fast or to break the law. But the more research I've done on speed cameras, the less convinced I've become that this is an effective way to do what we all want to do – reduce the appalling total of nearly 3,000 killed on our roads every year.
- And in the past 12 months, there has been more sinister news on the future of speed cameras. Speed cameras have been 'devolved'. That means that each local authority decides its own policy (on what basis?) and runs its own camera bureaucracy. It can pretty much do what it wants both to raise the money and to spend it. This has had mixed results, including the much-publicised refusal of Swindon to pay for cameras.

- And there's another consequence of speed camera devolution. It's become almost impossible to collect consistent figures on fines from around the UK. It's as if central government has decided that speed cameras are too much trouble. The decision on whether they do or do not improve road safety is now to be taken at a local level.
- Nearly 1.75 million motorists had 3 points put on their licence in 2006/07 and paid a fixed penalty of £60. Here are my Top 10 Tips to avoid speeding fines in 2011.

1 Understand the system

If you are caught speeding, you can agree to pay a fixed £60 fine and get three points on your licence. The points normally stay on your licence for 4 years (11, if the conviction was drink or drug related or you failed to provide a specimen for analysis). In some cases, breaking a temporary speed limit where there are roadworks will only trigger the fine, not the points on your licence. If you get 12 points on your licence within a three-year period – or just 6 in your first two years as a driver – you will be banned from driving.

If you go over the speed limit by too much, you'll get an automatic summons. Then, at the discretion of the court, the fines will be higher and the points could go up to 6 or even a ban. You can challenge the penalty in court. But if you lose, it's likely to prove expensive.

2 Where you're most likely to get NIP-ped

When you're caught speeding on camera, you will be issued with a Notice of Impending Prosecution. In 2006/07, 3.02 million were sent out (2% down on 2005/06). Here were England and Wales' top 10 counties (with the number of NIP's sent out to motorists)

London	359 798
Mid and South Wales	242 473
Avon, Somerset	149 315
Thames Valley	143 525
Essex	137 802
Greater Manchester	108 533
Lancashire	103 872
West Yorkshire	90 008
Hertfordshire	84 835
Kent	84 774

Not surprisingly, these are some of the busiest parts of the country.

3 Will 'they' catch up with you?

Once you've received a Notice of Intended Prosecution, you can either accept it and agree to pay a Fixed Penalty Notice or contest it.

But, in 2006/07, 2.24 million Fixed Penalty Notices were sent out, compared with 3.02 million NIP's. That means that 28% of 'camera flashes' were not converted into requests for your £60. It's unlikely that nearly 840,000 people contested their NIP's – so you've immediately got a chance that the Fixed Penalty Notice will never even reach you.

Some counties claim 100% conversion from NIP to FPN – so here were the 10 worst conversion rates in England and Wales in 2006/07 (where, in theory, you're least likely to receive a Fixed Penalty Notice if you've been flashed):

Avon and Somerset	41%
London	44%
Essex	51%
Thames Valley	60%
Merseyside	61%
West Midlands	63%
Wiltshire	64%
Hampshire and Isle of Wight	65%
Derbyshire	66%
Warwickshire	67%

And then there's a further stage in the process – the collection of the money. And here, the record of the Safety Camera Partnerships seems to be getting worse. In 2006/07, only 80% of Fixed Penalty Notices issued were actually paid. That's compared with 85% in 2005/06. It seems that the authorities are finding it harder to collect your money.

More Cash, less flash

Here are the 10 worst counties in England and Wales in 2006/07 at collecting the fixed penalty fines:

	%fixed penalties collected
West Yorkshire	48%
Lancashire	57%
Herts	59%
Mid and South Wales	59%
Leicestershire	63%
Northamptonshire	65%
Kent	72%
West Mercia	73%
Staffordshire	77%
Cheshire	77%

(All 2006/07 figures are taken from the Safety Camera Partnership Fixed Penalty Notice Hypothecation returns on the DfT website)

4 Understand the regional lottery

It is clear from all these figures why we are talking about the system as being a regional lottery. Just to prove the point finally, here are the Top 10 counties in England and Wales in 2006/07 for cash raised in speeding fines per person of population:

Beds	£5.18
North Wales	£4.88
Wiltshire	£4.78
Dorset	£4.00
Northamptonshire	£3.88
Warwickshire	£3.78
Cumbria	£3.73
Notts	£3.06
Suffolk	£2.74
Mid/North Wales	£2.59

You can't say we didn't warn you.

Speed limits (mph)	Built-up area	Single carriageway	Dual carriageway	Motorway
Cars and motorcycles	30	60	70	70
Cars towing caravans and trailers	30	50	60	60
Buses and Coaches	30	50	60	60
Goods vehicles under 7.5 tonnes	30	50	60	70 (60 if articulated or towing)

5 Drive like a woman (it's safer)

More than 80% of all speeding penalties are given to men.

There are two types of speeder – the deliberate speeder and the accidental speeder.

If you are interested in the camera locations in this atlas so that you can break the speed limit between them, you're a deliberate speeder, and almost certainly a man. Read on. Our Top 10 Tips might make you more conscious of the chances – and consequences – of being caught.

Who are the accidental speeders? Almost everyone at some time. We've all done it. You're in an area that you're not familiar with. It's dark. You're quite alert but you're caught up in the rush hour and the traffic is moving fast. You've gone from a 40 zone to a 30 but you haven't seen the sign. Flash!

The truth is – most of us speed both deliberately and accidentally at some stage in our driving careers. The message is – cameras are widespread and they're not very forgiving.

So if you don't want the fine or the endorsement, you need to concentrate as much on your speed as you concentrate on not having an accident.

If you are a conscientious driver who feels the need to develop your skills of concentration in particular and defensive driving in general, then I'd recommend The Institute of Advanced Motorists (IAM) tel: 020 8996 9600.

6 Know your speed limit rules

Street lights = 30mph, unless it says otherwise. It's a horrible rule. Lots of people who should know about it don't. Lots of people who do know about it would like to see it changed.

Add to that the apparently arbitrary definition of 30mph and 40mph limits, and the frequency with which they change, and you have a recipe for confusion. Again, lots of inconsistencies to baffle the motorist.

…done for speeding at 31mph in a 30mph zone

The round white sign with a black diagonal flash through it means 60mph max, except on dual carriageways and motorways.

How much leeway do you have? Is it zero tolerance? Is it the ACPO guidelines of +10%+2mph (that's the Association of Chief Police Officers, by the way)? Or is it somewhere in between? Well, the law is this – you can be done for speeding at 31mph in a 30mph zone. As to the complicated equation, the police stress that guidelines are just that and they do not alter the law. But they probably would admit that they would be inundated if they stopped every motorist who is driving a couple of mph over the limit.

You are probably getting a bit of help from your speedometer. It's the clever idea of the car makers to set our speedometers 2–3mph faster than we are actually going. Now that so many of us have GPS in the car, this is getting more widely known. Now you know, it might be wiser to use the extra mph as air between you and a ticket.

7 Learn to tell your Gatso from your Digital Specs

Here's a concise guide to cameras. There are loads of different species, so we're only going to describe the main families.

Gatso – the most common ones. Generally in yellow boxes, they flash you from the back and store your number plate on film. As the film only has 400 exposures, don't assume, if you see the flash in your rear-view mirror, that you've been done. In fact it's reckoned that you have a three in four chance that the one you've just passed is not working. And there's now a new type of digital Gatso called a Monitron that is starting to spring up in our cities. No film needed here. The data automatically creates a Notice of Intended Prosecution ready to post in 30 minutes.

Truvelo – pink-eyes. The pink eye gives you an infrared flash from the front, after sensors in the road have registered your speed. Unlike the GATSO, which can't identify the driver (worth remembering if you want to argue) the TRUVELO gets a mug-shot.

Digital Specs – pairs of video cameras set some distance apart to create a no-speeding zone between them. If your average speed over the distance exceeds the limit, you are snapped with an infrared flash. So they are much more testing for the driver. It's one thing slowing down when you see a camera, it's another thing maintaining an average speed over a distance of several miles. They are sprouting fast and likely to be used more and more.

DS2s – strips in the road detect your speed and pass the information to an innocent-looking post at the side of the road. Look out for the detector van nearby, because that's what does the business.

Red light cameras – the UK total is creeping up towards 1,000. If you drive through a traffic light when it's at red, sensors in the road tell the camera to flash you.

All of the above can be detected using GPS devices for fixed cameras but not these -

Lasers – most mobile cameras are Lasers. You normally see a tripod in a van with the backdoors open and facing you; or on a motorway bridge or handheld by the side of the road. They work – although rumour has it not in very bad weather – and they can't be detected by any of the GPS devices. If you happen to see a local villager touting a laser gun, you may get a letter asking you to drive more carefully but not a fine or penalty points.

8 Know where the cameras are

If you are serious about not getting caught speeding, there are some obvious precautions you can take before setting out.

- Check in this atlas whether there are fixed cameras on the route you are planning to take. They are marked on the map by the 40 symbol, with the figures inside the red circle indicating the speed limit in mph (see the key to map symbols for further details).

- Check in the listings whether there are 'located' mobile sites on your route.

- Use a camera detector, such as those marketed by Road Angel, Road Pilot or Cyclops. These are perfectly legal, if expensive; they just tell you where the cameras are. Devices that detect and jam police laser detectors are about to be banned. Many sat-navs now include this information but you pay for updates.

- Use the websites for up-to-date information, including guidelines (but only guidelines) about where the police are locating their mobile vans each week. Each Safety Camera Partnership has a website (search for the county name followed by Safety Camera Partnership). Don't use the Department for Transport listings, which were 18 months out of date at the time we went to press.

9 Don't challenge a penalty without good reason

Check your ticket carefully: make sure it is your car and that you were driving it at the time and place recorded. The cameras aren't perfect and mistakes have been made. My favourite is the tractor caught speeding in Wales at 85mph. It turned out there was 'a confusion about the number plate' – the tractor had never been to Wales and could only do a max of 26mph.

Once you've checked the ticket, you have two choices. Pay the £60 and accept the three points. It's humiliating and irritating but then that's the idea. Or contest it.

If you do decide to fight, do as much research and get as much information about the circumstances as you can; and get as much case-study information as you can about the camera involved. The more witnesses and information you have, the more a good lawyer can build a case on your behalf.

Again, www.speed-trap.co.uk has some interesting case studies.

But don't expect success with a fabricated defence. The safety camera partnerships know the scams to look out for and lies can turn a simple speeding fine into something much more serious. In fact, you can be prosecuted for trying to pervert the course of justice. A criminal record can cost you much more than the £60 fixed penalty.

10 Avoid the points by going back to school

In a few areas, the police are giving drivers who are caught speeding another option. They can go on a Speed Awareness Scheme. These normally last half a day, you have to pay for them (probably more than £60) but you don't get the penalty points. So, if you like the sound of this as an option, it's worth considering.

Your alternative is to ask for your case to go forward for prosecution (see Top Tip No. 9)

And finally…

If you've got this far, you're obviously a bit of an aficionado on the subject of speeding, so I'm going to allow myself just one bit of preaching.

The 'Speed Kills' slogan has become much used. But here are three pieces of information that certainly make me think twice about letting the needle stray over the prescribed limit:

1 Every year we kill over 3,000 of our fellow-citizens on our roads and we seriously injure 35,000. If you happen to live in a reasonable-sized town, just work that out as a percentage of the population of where you live. Road deaths have not fallen substantially since the proliferation of speed cameras – but the evidence seems to be reasonably conclusive that speed cameras reduce the number of deaths and serious injuries at the sites themselves.

2 The argument rages about whether speed is the cause of accidents or not. But that's all rather academic (isn't it?). A car that's not moving is not likely to injure someone. If the accident happens when the car is in motion, speed is at least part of the cause.

But here's the point. This is the 'if I hit a pedestrian, will I kill them?' chart ➤

So if you hit a pedestrian in a 30mph area and you're doing just 35mph (just on the 10%+2mph

Right The probability that a pedestrian will be killed when struck by a vehicle travelling between 20mph and 40mph

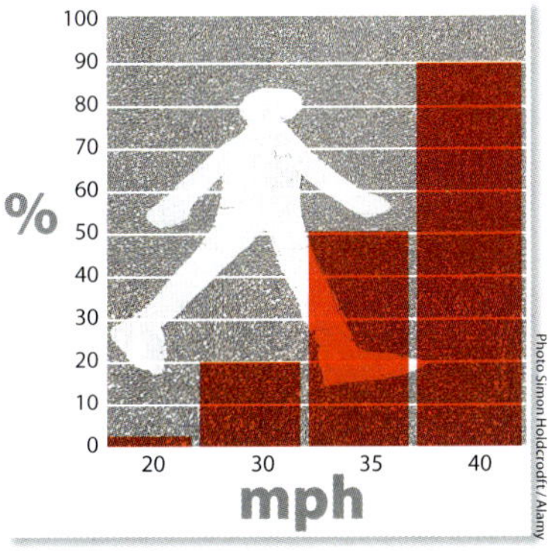

Top Gantry-mounted SPECS cameras in Cornwall
Above Truvelo camera
Below Mobile camera unit

Websites for further information

Official

Safety Camera Partnerships (use Google and put in Safety Camera Partnership plus the area you want)

- www.safetycamera.org.uk • www.dvla.gov.uk
- www.thinkroadsafety.gov.uk • www.dft.gov.uk
- www.road-safe.org

Safety pressure groups

- www.rospa.com • www.transport2000.com
- www.roadpeace.org • www.brake.org.uk

Anti-camera pressure groups and websites

- www.speed-trap.co.uk • ukgatsos.com
- www.ukspeedcameras.co.uk
- www.abd.org.uk • www.ukspeedtraps.co.uk
- www.speedcam.co.uk
- www.speedcamerasuk.com

leeway) you're more than twice as likely to kill them. Not a nice thought. Maybe I should have called that the 'if I am hit by a car while on foot, will I be killed by it?' chart.

3 Every death costs us, as taxpayers, £1.5m and every serious injury £100,000. And that's doesn't take into account the human cost.

So, at the end of all this, my 11th Top 10 Tip is

11 Don't press the pedal to the metal

St. George's Channel

Bristol Channel

45 **46** **47** **48**

44 **32** **33** **34**

20 **21** **22**

8 **9** **10**

4 **5** **6** **7**

2 **3**

Rosslare 3:30
Rosslare 3:45
Cork 10:00
Roscoff 6:00
Santander 20:00

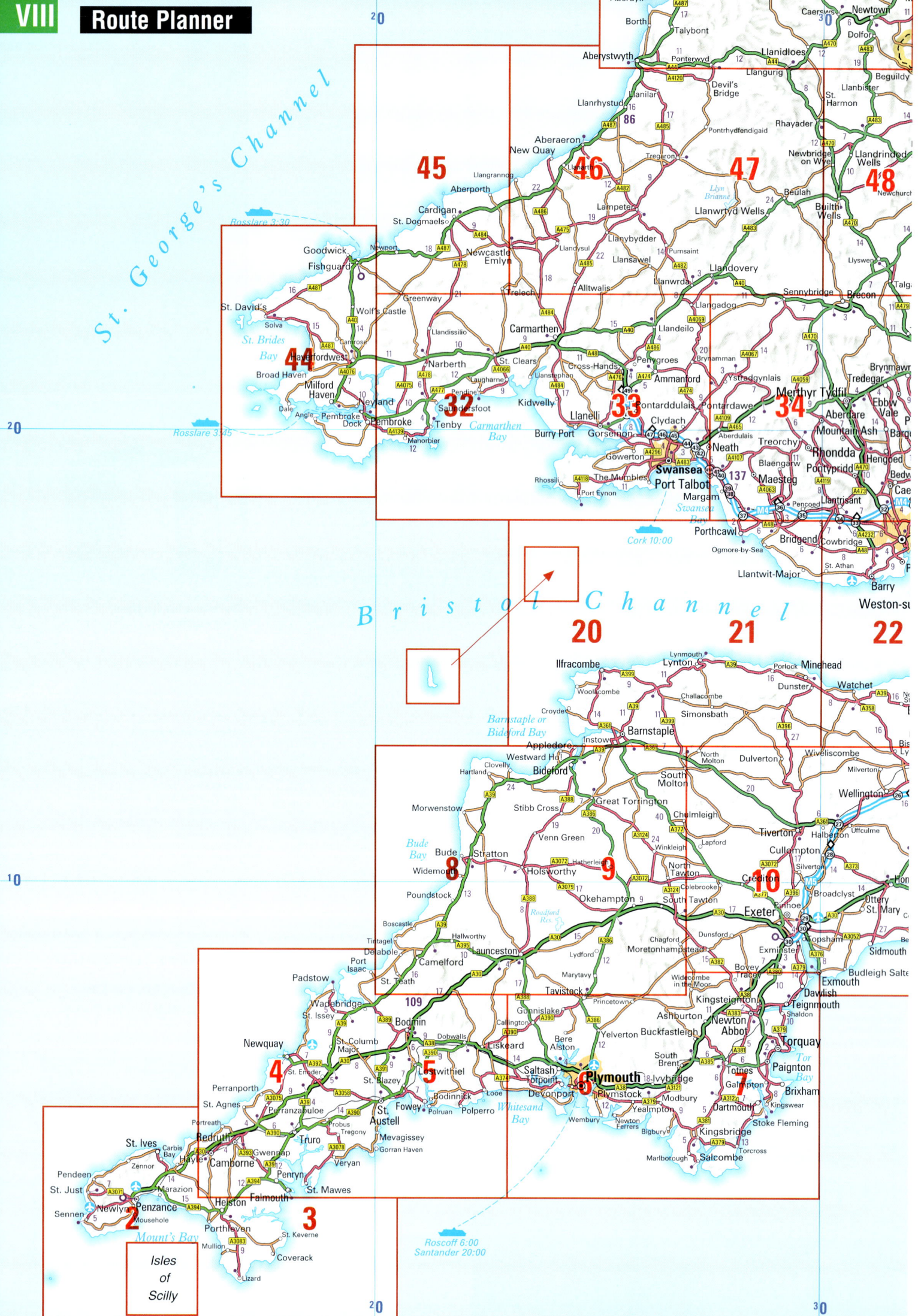

Isles of Scilly

St. Brides Bay
Carmarthen Bay
Swansea Bay
Mount's Bay
Barnstaple or Bideford Bay
Bude Bay
Whitesand Bay
Tor Bay

Aberdyfi, Borth, Talybont, Aberystwyth, Ponterwyd, Devil's Bridge, Llangurig, Llanidloes, Caersws, Newtown, Dolfor, Llanbister, Beguildy, St. Harmon, Rhayader, Newbridge on Wye, Llandrindod Wells, Newchurch

Goodwick, Fishguard, St. David's, Solva, Wolf's Castle, Haverfordwest, Broad Haven, Milford Haven, Neyland, Pembroke Dock, Pembroke, Angle, Dale, Manorbier, Tenby, Saundersfoot, Narberth, Laugharne, Kidwelly, Llanelli, Burry Port, Gorseinon, Gowerton, Swansea, The Mumbles, Port Eynon, Rhossili, Port Talbot, Margam, Porthcawl, Ogmore-by-Sea, Bridgend, Cowbridge, Llantwit-Major, Barry, Weston-super-Mare

Newport, Cardigan, St. Dogmaels, Aberporth, Llangrannog, New Quay, Aberaeron, Newcastle Emlyn, Lampeter, Llanybydder, Llandysul, Llansawel, Tregaron, Llanwrtyd Wells, Beulah, Builth Wells, Brecon, Sennybridge, Llandovery, Llandeilo, Carmarthen, St. Clears, Cross Hands, Ammanford, Ystradgynlais, Merthyr Tydfil, Aberdare, Tredegar, Ebbw Vale, Mountain Ash, Rhondda, Pontypridd, Maesteg

Ilfracombe, Lynmouth, Lynton, Porlock, Minehead, Dunster, Watchet, Woolacombe, Croyde, Challacombe, Simonsbath, Barnstaple, Appledore, Instow, Dulverton, Wiveliscombe, Milverton, Wellington, Westward Ho!, Bideford, South Molton, North Molton, Tiverton, Cullompton, Hartland, Clovelly, Great Torrington, Chulmleigh, Lapford, Crediton, Broadclyst, Morwenstow, Stibb Cross, Venn Green, Holsworthy, Hatherleigh, North Tawton, Colebrooke, Exeter, Bude, Stratton, Widemouth, Poundstock, Okehampton, South Tawton, Dunsford, Topsham, Boscastle, Hallworthy, Lydford, Chagford, Moretonhampstead, Bovey Tracey, Sidmouth, Budleigh Salterton, Exmouth, Dawlish, Teignmouth

Tintagel, Delabole, Port Isaac, Camelford, Launceston, Marytavy, Tavistock, Princetown, Widecombe in the Moor, Ashburton, Kingsteignton, Newton Abbot, Shaldon, Padstow, Wadebridge, St. Issey, Camborne, St. Teath, Bodmin, Dobwalls, Callington, Gunnislake, Bere Alston, Yelverton, Buckfastleigh, South Brent, Totnes, Torquay, Paignton, Newquay, St. Columb Major, St. Enoder, Lostwithiel, Liskeard, Saltash, Torpoint, Plymouth, Plymstock, Ivybridge, Modbury, Brixham, Dartmouth, Kingswear, Perranporth, St. Agnes, Perranzabuloe, Probus, Tregony, St. Austell, Mevagissey, Gorran Haven, Fowey, Bodinnick, Polruan, Looe, Polperro, Devonport, Yealmpton, Newton Ferrers, Wembury, Bigbury, Kingsbridge, Salcombe, Torcross, Stoke Fleming, Marlborough, Pendeen, St. Ives, Carbis Bay, Hayle, Zennor, St. Just, Sennen, Newlyn, Penzance, Marazion, Mousehole, Redruth, Gwennap, Truro, Penryn, Falmouth, St. Mawes, Helston, Porthleven, Mullion, Coverack, Lizard, St. Keverne

Channel Islands

Legend

Motorway (M6)	Primary route (A519)	Distances - in miles
junctions - full, restricted	single/dual carriageway	120 major
Toll motorway	A Road (A519)	12 minor
Services	B Road	Railway
Ferry route	Airport	National boundary

Scale 1:1 000 000 1cm = 10km 1 inch = 15.78 miles

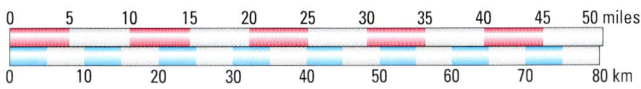

0 5 10 15 20 25 30 35 40 45 50 miles

0 10 20 30 40 50 60 70 80 km

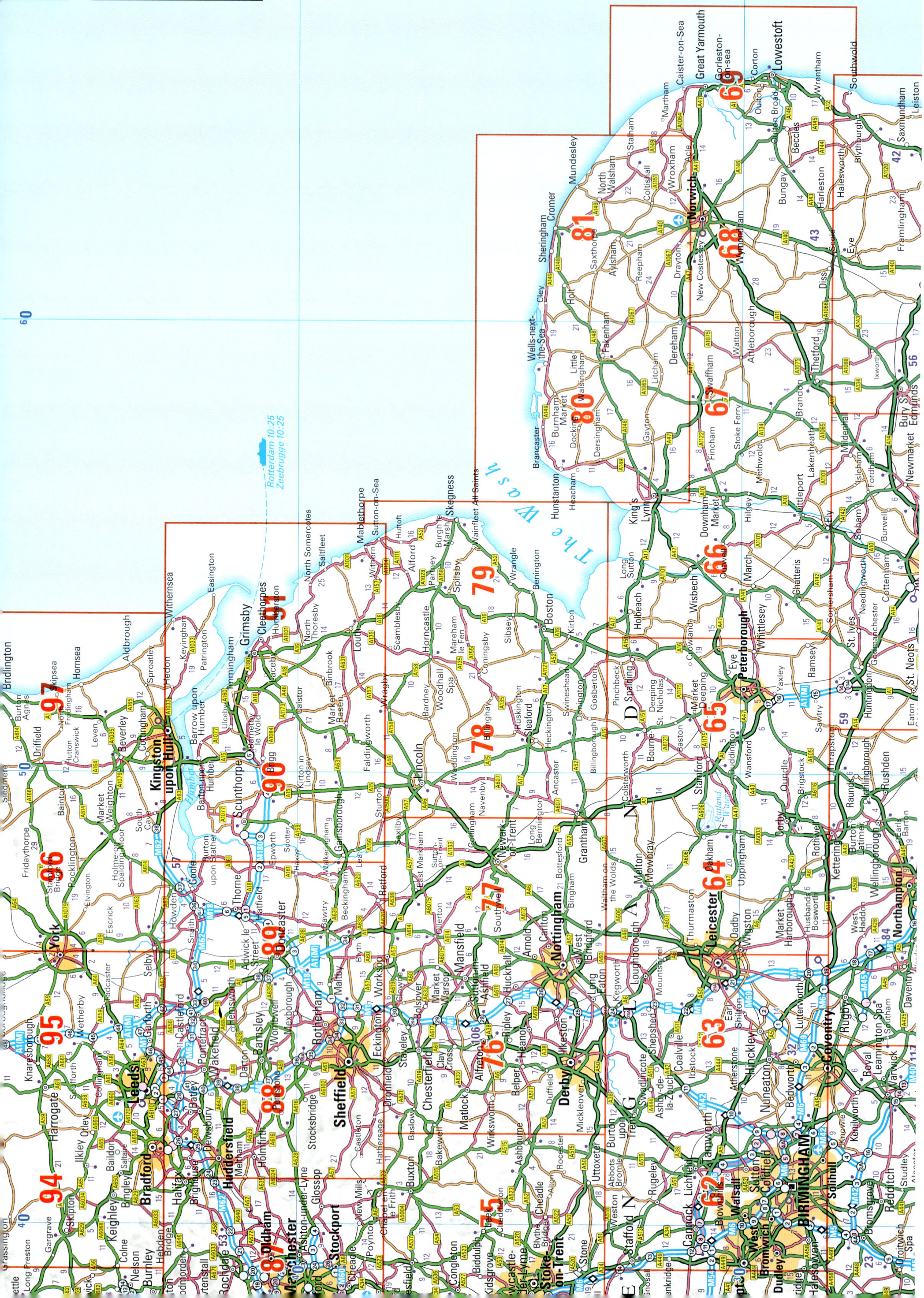
The Wash
Rotterdam 10:25
Zeebrugge 10:25
York
Leeds
Bradford
Huddersfield
Manchester
Oldham
Stockport
Sheffield
Rotherham
Doncaster
Barnsley
Wakefield
Harrogate
Kingston upon Hull
Grimsby
Cleethorpes
Scunthorpe
Lincoln
Boston
Skegness
Louth
Nottingham
Derby
Mansfield
Chesterfield
Leicester
Coventry
Birmingham
Walsall
Solihull
Northampton
Peterborough
King's Lynn
Norwich
Great Yarmouth
Lowestoft
Cromer
Wisbech
Grantham
Newark-on-Trent
Stoke-on-Trent
Stafford
Lichfield
Tamworth
Nuneaton
Rugby
Kettering
Corby
Melton Mowbray
Loughborough
Stamford
Spalding
Thetford
Ely
Dereham
Swaffham
94
95
96
97
87
88
89
90
91
75
76
77
78
79
80
81
62
63
64
65
66
67
68
69

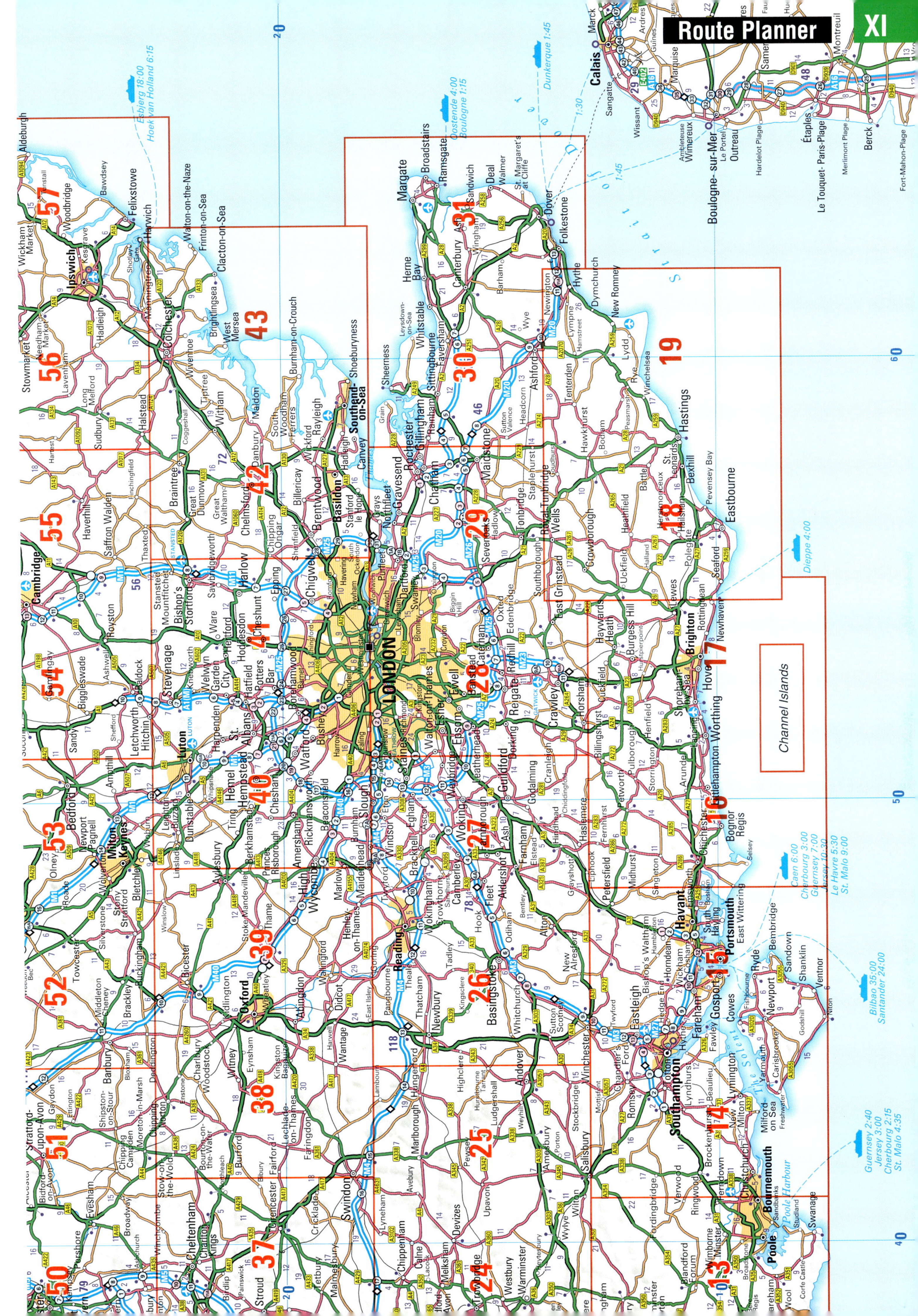
LONDON
Channel Islands
Calais
Boulogne-sur-Mer
Dunkerque 1:45
Dieppe 4:00
Oostende 4:00
Boulogne 1:15
Esbjerg 18:00
Hoek van Holland 6:15
Caen 6:00
Cherbourg 3:00
Guernsey 7:00
Jersey 10:30
Le Havre 5:30
St. Malo 9:00
Bilbao 35:00
Santander 24:00
Guernsey 2:40
Jersey 3:00
Cherbourg 2:15
St. Malo 4:35
Cambridge
Ipswich
Colchester
Chelmsford
Southend-on-Sea
Basildon
Margate
Ramsgate
Canterbury
Dover
Folkestone
Ashford
Maidstone
Hastings
Eastbourne
Brighton
Worthing
Chichester
Portsmouth
Southampton
Bournemouth
Poole
Salisbury
Winchester
Basingstoke
Reading
Oxford
Swindon
Cheltenham
Milton Keynes
Bedford
Luton
Stevenage
Watford
Slough
Guildford
Crawley
Gatwick
Heathrow
Stansted
Le Touquet-Paris-Plage
Étaples
Berck
50
51
52
53
54
55
56
57
37
38
39
40
41
42
43
24
25
26
27
28
29
30
31
13
14
15
16
17
18
19

IRISH SEA
Isle of Man
Solway Firth
Luce Bay
Wigtown Bay
Morecambe Bay
Liverpool Bay
Conwy Bay
Holyhead Bay
Caernarfon Bay
Tremadog Bay
Cardigan Bay
Bardsey Sd.
Belfast 2:55
Dublin 2:55
Larne 8:00
Belfast 8:00
Dublin 7:00
Dublin 1:49
Dun Laoghaire 1:59
3:30
2:30
104
105
106
107
108
109
98
99
84
92
93
85
86
82
83
72
73
74
70
71
58
59
60
61
Stewart
Kirkcowan
Glenluce
Lochans
Portpatrick
Sandhead
Port William
Port Logan
Drummore
Whauphill
Wigtown
Creetown
Gatehouse of Fleet
Garlieston
Whithorn
Isle of Whithorn
Kirkcudbright
Borgue
Dundrennan
Castle Douglas
Dalbeattie
New Abbey
Laurieston
Caulkerbush
Ruthwell
Annan
Gretna
Kirkbean
Silloth
Kirkbride
Newton Arlosh
Carlisle
Smithfield
Brampton
Gilsland
Greenhead
Haltwhistle
Lambley
Wetheral
Thursby
Dalston
Wigton
Abbey Town
Beckfoot
Aspatria
High Hesket
Croglin
Alston
Maryport
Bothel
Caldbeck
Lazonby
Langwathby
Flimby
Workington
Cockermouth
Greystoke
Penrith
Temple Sowerby
Appleby-in-Westmorland
Distington
Thornthwaite
Threlkeld
Keswick
Hackthorpe
Whitehaven
Frizington
Buttermere
Derwent Water
Ullswater
Patterdale
Shap
Hoff
St. Bees
Borrowdale
Haweswater
Kirkby Stephen
Egremont
Grasmere
Orton
Gosforth
Wast Water
Ambleside
Tebay
Seascale
Windermere
Coniston
Torver
Bowness-on-Windermere
Kendal
Grayrigg
Garsdale Head
Ravenglass
Broughton-in-Furness
Coniston Water
Oxenholme
Sedbergh
Bootle
Newby Bridge
Grizebeck
Millom
Milnthorpe
Arnside
Kirkby Lonsdale
Askam-in-Furness
Ulverston
Dalton-in-Furness
Grange-over-Sands
Burton
Barrow-in-Furness
Carnforth
Ingleton
Vickerstown
Rampside
High Bentham
Morecambe
Caton
Heysham
Lancaster
Galgate
Slaidburn
Fleetwood
Garstang
Cleveleys
Clitheroe
Poulton-le-Fylde
Longridge
Blackpool
Kirkham
Preston
Padiham
Blackburn
Lytham St. Anne's
Leyland
Darwen
Southport
Chorley
Horwich
Ormskirk
Skelmersdale
Formby
Bolton
Bury
Wigan
Maghull
Worsley
Crosby
Kirkby
Leigh
Bootle
St. Helens
Wallasey
Liverpool
Hoylake
Birkenhead
Widnes
Warrington
Bebington
Heswall
Speke
Runcorn
Prestatyn
Rhyl
Rhuddlan
Holywell
Ellesmere Port
Helsby
Northwich
Flint
Connah's Quay
Kelsall
Knutsford
Chester
Winsford
Middlewich
Queensferry
Mold
Buckley
Sandbach
Hope
Crewe
Wrexham
Rossett
Holt
Nantwich
Malpas
Audlem
Madeley
Whitchurch
Market Drayton
Overton
Llangollen
Corwen
Chirk
Ellesmere
Prees
Wem
Whittington
Oswestry
Hodnet
Baschurch
Shawbury
Newport
Llanymynech
Crudgington
Shrewsbury
Wellington
Oakengates
Telford
Welshpool
Westbury
Minsterley
Cressage
Much Wenlock
Ironbridge
Wolverhampton
Chirbury
Montgomery
Church Stretton
Bridgnorth
Bishop's Castle
Highley
Clun
Craven Arms
Kidderminster
Leintwardine
Ludlow
Cleobury
Stourport
Ramsey
Andreas
Kirk Michael
Peel
Laxey
Foxdale
Douglas
Ballasalla
Port Erin
Port St. Mary
Castletown
Cemaes
Amlwch
Moelfre
Benllech
Llanerchymedd
Holyhead
Valley
Anglesey
Pentraeth
Llangefni
Menai Bridge
Beaumaris
Rhosneigr
Aberffraw
Bangor
Bethesda
Newborough
Y Felinheli
Caernarfon
Llanberis
Waunfawr
Penygroes
Llandudno
Conwy
Llanfairfechan
Colwyn Bay
Abergele
St. Asaph
Trefnant
Denbigh
Llansannan
Dolgarrog
Llanrwst
Capel Curig
Betws-y-Coed
Ruthin
Dolwyddelan
Cerrigydrudion
Rhosllanerchrugog
Blaenau Ffestiniog
Ffestiniog
Penrhyndeudraeth
Beddgelert
Llanaelhaiarn
Nefyn
Porthmadog
Criccieth
Tudweiliog
Pwllheli
Llanbedrog
Abersoch
Aberdaron
Rhiw
Harlech
Trawsfynydd
Bala
L. Bala
Llandrillo
Llanbedr
Llanuwchllyn
Dolgellau
Barmouth
Llwyngwril
L. Vyrnwy
Penybontfawr
Llanwddyn
Llanfyllin
Guilsfield
Foel
Mallwyd
Tal-y-llyn
Corris
Aberangell
Llanfair Caereinion
Bryncrug
Tywyn
Machynlleth
Llanbrynmair
Berriew
Aberdyfi
Carno
Caersws
Newtown
Borth
Talybont
Dolfor
Aberystwyth
Llanidloes
Ponterwyd
Llangurig
Beguildy
Llanbister
Devil's Bridge
Llanilar
WALES
M6
M55
M58
M61
M65
M62
M53
M56
M54
20
30
40
50

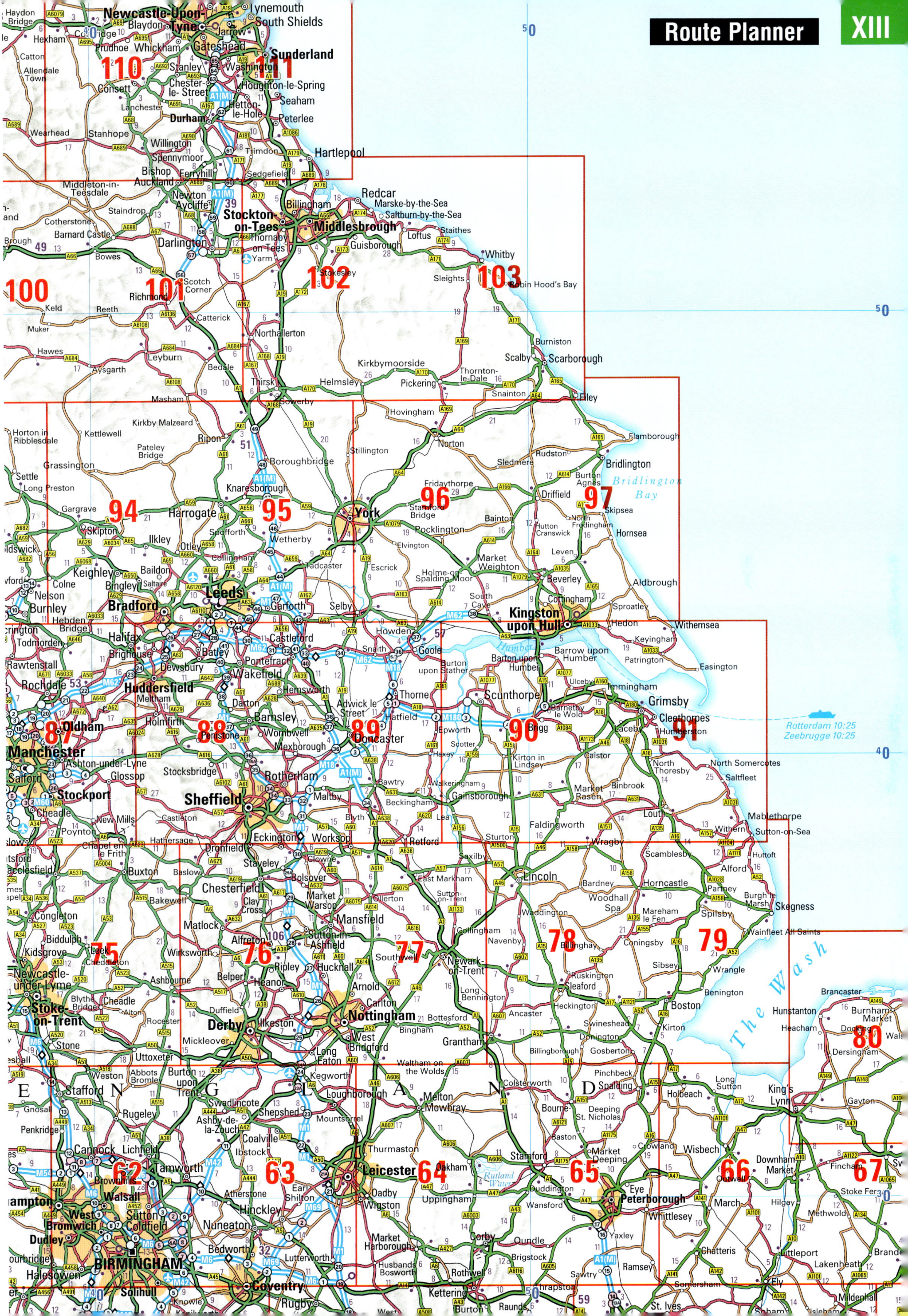
Newcastle-Upon-Tyne
Tynemouth
South Shields
Gateshead
Sunderland
Hexham
Consett
Durham
Hartlepool
Bishop Auckland
Stockton-on-Tees
Middlesbrough
Redcar
Darlington
Whitby
Robin Hood's Bay
Richmond
Northallerton
Scarborough
Thirsk
Helmsley
Pickering
Filey
Flamborough
Bridlington
Bridlington Bay
Ripon
Harrogate
Knaresborough
York
Driffield
Skipton
Ilkley
Keighley
Bradford
Leeds
Beverley
Hornsea
Kingston upon Hull
Withernsea
Halifax
Huddersfield
Wakefield
Castleford
Pontefract
Goole
Scunthorpe
Grimsby
Cleethorpes
Rotterdam 10:25
Zeebrugge 10:25
Rochdale
Oldham
Manchester
Stockport
Barnsley
Doncaster
Rotherham
Sheffield
Worksop
Gainsborough
Louth
Mablethorpe
Lincoln
Skegness
Chesterfield
Mansfield
Newark-on-Trent
Boston
The Wash
Hunstanton
Stoke-on-Trent
Derby
Nottingham
Grantham
King's Lynn
Stafford
Loughborough
Melton Mowbray
Spalding
Wisbech
Leicester
Stamford
Peterborough
Walsall
Birmingham
Coventry
Nuneaton
Kettering
Ely
ENGLAND
100
101
102
103
110
111
94
95
96
97
87
88
89
90
91
75
76
77
78
79
80
62
63
64
65
66
67

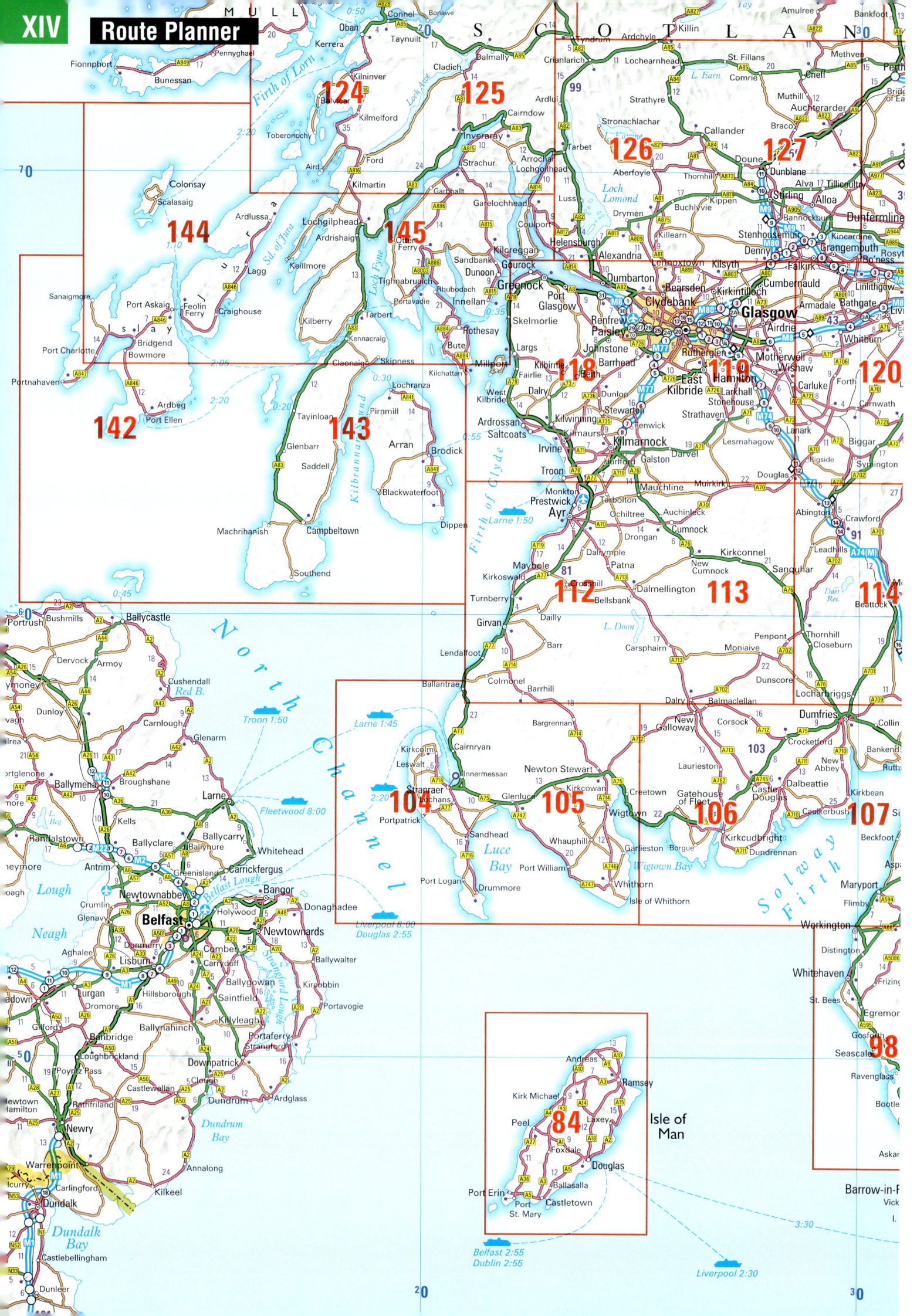

MULL SCOTLAND

Grid reference numbers: 124, 125, 126, 127, 144, 145, 118, 119, 120, 142, 143, 112, 113, 114, 104, 105, 106, 107, 84, 98

Oban · Kerrera · Taynuilt · Connel · Bonawe · Tyndrum · Ardchyle · Killin · Amulree · Bankfoot
Fionnphort · Pennyghael · Bunessan · Kilninver · Kilmelford · Dalmally · Cladich · Lochearnhead · St. Fillans · Comrie · Crieff · Methven · Perth
Toberonochy · Ford · Aird · Inveraray · Strachur · Cairndow · Ardlui · Crianlarich · Strathyre · Callander · Braco · Auchterarder · Bridge of Earn
Colonsay · Scalasaig · Kilmartin · Garbhallt · Arrochar · Lochgoilhead · Tarbet · Stronachlachar · Doune · Dunblane · Muthill
Ardlussa · Lochgilphead · Ardrishaig · Otter Ferry · Garelochhead · Luss · Aberfoyle · Thornhill · Stirling · Alva · Tillicoultry
Port Askaig · Feolin Ferry · Craighouse · Kilberry · Tarbert · Sandbank · Dunoon · Helensburgh · Alexandria · Lennoxtown · Kilsyth · Falkirk · Grangemouth · Bo'ness
Portnahaven · Port Charlotte · Bowmore · Bridgend · Kennacraig · Rhubodach · Portavadie · Innellan · Gourock · Greenock · Port Glasgow · Dumbarton · Bearsden · Kirkintilloch · Cumbernauld · Linlithgow
Port Ellen · Ardbeg · Claonaig · Skipness · Rothesay · Bute · Largs · Clydebank · Glasgow · Airdrie · Whitburn
Tayinloan · Lochranza · Pirnmill · Millport · Kilbirnie · Beith · Renfrew · Paisley · Rutherglen · Motherwell · Wishaw
Glenbarr · Arran · Brodick · West Kilbride · Dalry · Johnstone · Barrhead · East Kilbride · Hamilton · Larkhall · Carluke · Forth
Saddell · Blackwaterfoot · Ardrossan · Saltcoats · Kilwinning · Stewarton · Stonehouse · Lanark · Biggar
Machrihanish · Campbeltown · Dippen · Irvine · Kilmarnock · Galston · Strathaven · Lesmahagow · Rigside · Symington
Southend · Troon · Mauchline · Darvel · Muirkirk · Douglas · Abington · Crawford
Prestwick · Ayr · Tarbolton · Ochiltree · Auchinleck · Cumnock · Kirkconnel · Sanquhar · Leadhills
Maybole · Dalrymple · Drongan · Patna · New Cumnock · Thornhill · Closeburn · Beattock
Kirkoswald · Crosshill · Dalmellington · Bellsbank · Penpont · Moniaive · Dunscore · Lochmaben
Turnberry · Girvan · Dailly · Barr · Carsphairn · Lochanbriggs · Dumfries · Collin
Lendalfoot · Colmonel · Barrhill · Bargrennan · Dalry · Balmaclellan · New Galloway · Corsock · Crocketford · New Abbey
Ballantrae · Cairnryan · Newton Stewart · Laurieston · Castle Douglas · Dalbeattie · Kirkbean
Kirkcolm · Leswalt · Innermessan · Glenluce · Kirkcowan · Creetown · Gatehouse of Fleet · Caulkerbush
Stranraer · Portpatrick · Sandhead · Wigtown · Whithorn · Kirkcudbright · Dundrennan · Beckfoot · Maryport
Port Logan · Drummore · Port William · Isle of Whithorn · Workington

Isle of Man: Andreas · Ramsey · Kirk Michael · Laxey · Peel · Foxdale · Douglas · Port Erin · Ballasalla · Castletown · Port St. Mary

North Channel · Firth of Clyde · Solway Firth · Wigtown Bay · Luce Bay

Northern Ireland: Portrush · Bushmills · Ballycastle · Dervock · Armoy · Cushendall · Carnlough · Glenarm · Ballymena · Broughshane · Larne · Ballyclare · Carrickfergus · Antrim · Randalstown · Whitehead · Newtownabbey · Greenisland · Bangor · Belfast · Holywood · Newtownards · Lisburn · Comber · Ballywalter · Lurgan · Hillsborough · Saintfield · Ballygowan · Portavogie · Banbridge · Ballynahinch · Killyleagh · Portaferry · Downpatrick · Dundrum · Ardglass · Castlewellan · Newry · Warrenpoint · Annalong · Kilkeel · Dundalk · Castlebellingham

Ferry routes: Troon 1:50 · Larne 1:45 · Larne 1:50 · Fleetwood 8:00 · Liverpool 8:00 · Douglas 2:55 · Belfast 2:55 · Dublin 2:55 · Liverpool 2:30

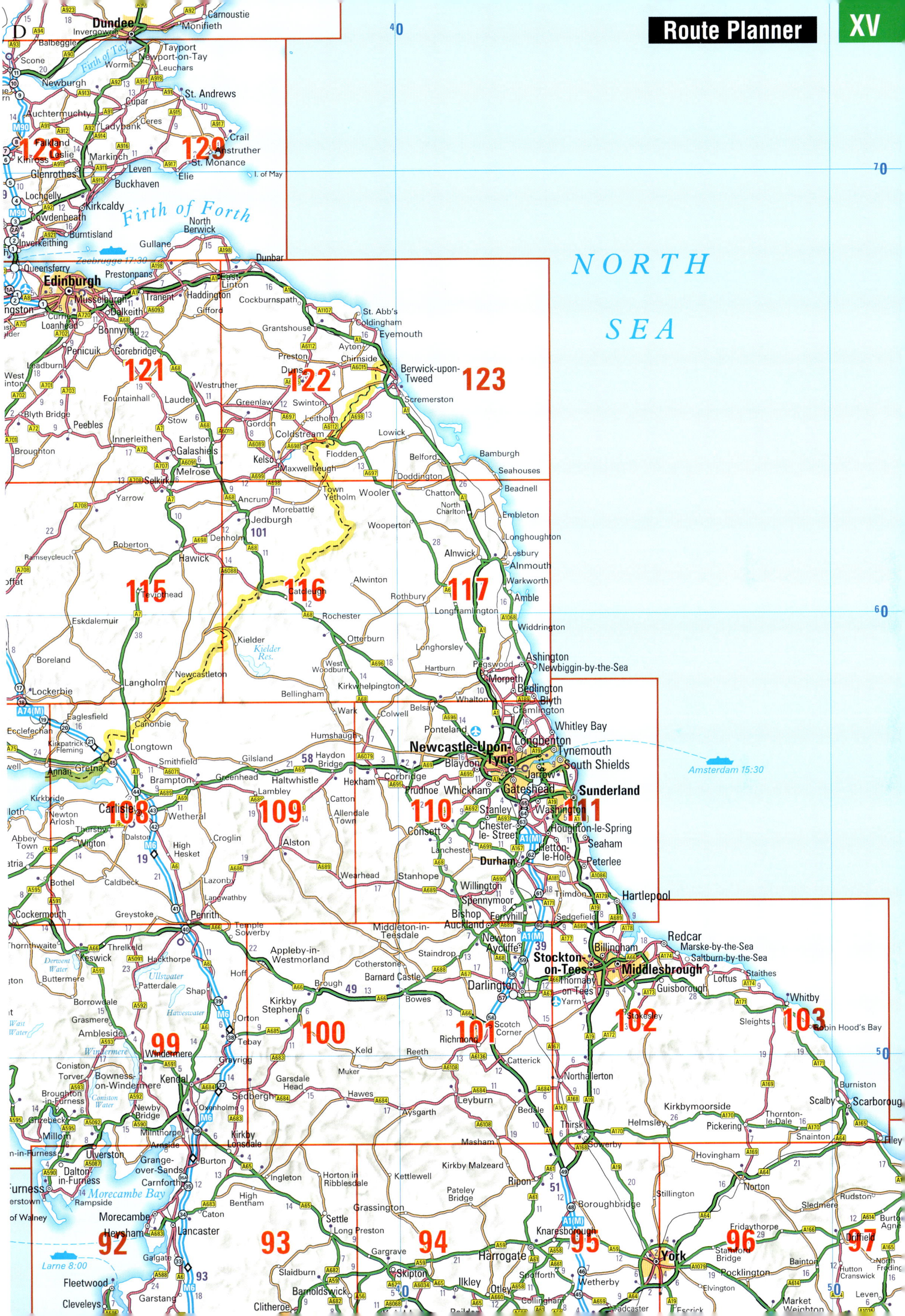

N O R T H   S E A

Grid reference numbers: 128, 129, 121, 122, 123, 115, 116, 117, 108, 109, 110, 111, 99, 100, 101, 102, 103, 92, 93, 94, 95, 96, 97, 101

Dundee, Invergowrie, Carnoustie, Monifieth, Balbeggie, Scone, Newburgh, Auchtermuchty, Falkland, Leslie, Kinross, Glenrothes, Markinch, Leven, Elie, Buckhaven, Kirkcaldy, Cowdenbeath, Inverkeithing, Burntisland, North Berwick, Gullane, Queensferry, Edinburgh, Musselburgh, Dalkeith, Loanhead, Bonnyrigg, Gorebridge, Penicuik, Leadburn, Peebles, Innerleithen, Galashiels, Melrose, Selkirk, Hawick, Denholm, Jedburgh, Ancrum, Newtown, Wormit, Tayport, Newport-on-Tay, Leuchars, St. Andrews, Cupar, Ladybank, Ceres, Crail, Anstruther, St. Monance, I. of May

Firth of Tay, Firth of Forth

Prestonpans, Tranent, Haddington, Gifford, East Linton, Dunbar, Cockburnspath, Grantshouse, Coldingham, Eyemouth, Ayton, Chirnside, Preston, Duns, Swinton, Berwick-upon-Tweed, Scremerston, Lowick, Westruther, Lauder, Stow, Greenlaw, Gordon, Leitholm, Earlston, Coldstream, Kelso, Maxwellheugh, Flodden, Belford, Bamburgh, Seahouses, Yarrow, Roberton, Morebattle, Town Yetholm, Wooler, Doddington, Chatton, North Charlton, Embleton, Beadnell, Wooperton, Alnwick, Alnmouth, Warkworth, Amble, Ramseycleuch, Eskdalemuir, Teviothead, Catcleugh, Rochester, Alwinton, Rothbury, Longframlington, Widdrington, Otterburn, Longhorsley, Boreland, Kielder Res., Newcastleton, Langholm, West Woodburn, Bellingham, Hartburn, Pegswood, Ashington, Newbiggin-by-the-Sea, Lockerbie, Kirkwhelpington, Wark, Morpeth, Bedlington, Blyth, Eaglesfield, Ecclefechan, Canonbie, Longtown, Humshaugh, Haydon Bridge, Colwell, Belsay, Ponteland, Cramlington, Whitley Bay, Annan, Gretna, Kirkpatrick Fleming, Smithfield, Brampton, Gilsland, Greenhead, Haltwhistle, Hexham, Corbridge, Newcastle-Upon-Tyne, Blaydon, Tynemouth, South Shields, Kirkbride, Newton Arlosh, Carlisle, Wetheral, Lambley, Catton, Prudhoe, Whickham, Gateshead, Jarrow, Sunderland, Abbey Town, Wigton, Dalston, High Hesket, Allendale Town, Stanley, Washington, Houghton-le-Spring, Seaham, Bothel, Caldbeck, Croglin, Alston, Consett, Lanchester, Chester-le-Street, Hetton-le-Hole, Peterlee, Cockermouth, Greystoke, Penrith, Lazonby, Langwathby, Wearhead, Stanhope, Durham, Willington, Spennymoor, Trimdon, Hartlepool, Thornthwaite, Keswick, Threlkeld, Hackthorpe, Temple Sowerby, Middleton-in-Teesdale, Bishop Auckland, Newton Aycliffe, Ferryhill, Sedgefield, Buttermere, Borrowdale, Patterdale, Shap, Orton, Appleby-in-Westmorland, Hoff, Cotherstone, Barnard Castle, Staindrop, Billingham, Redcar, Marske-by-the-Sea, Saltburn-by-the-Sea, Grasmere, Ambleside, Tebay, Brough, Bowes, Darlington, Stockton-on-Tees, Thornaby-on-Tees, Middlesbrough, Guisborough, Loftus, Staithes, Whitby, Coniston, Torver, Bowness-on-Windermere, Windermere, Kendal, Grayrigg, Kirkby Stephen, Keld, Muker, Reeth, Richmond, Scotch Corner, Catterick, Stokesley, Sleights, Robin Hood's Bay, Broughton-in-Furness, Newby Bridge, Oxenholme, Sedbergh, Garsdale Head, Hawes, Leyburn, Northallerton, Kirkbymoorside, Thornton-le-Dale, Pickering, Scalby, Scarborough, Millom, Arnside, Kirkby Lonsdale, Aysgarth, Bedale, Thirsk, Helmsley, Hovingham, Snainton, Filey, Ulverston, Grange-over-Sands, Carnforth, Burton, Ingleton, Kettlewell, Kirkby Malzeard, Ripon, Boroughbridge, Stillington, Norton, Sledmere, Rudston, Morecambe, Heysham, Lancaster, Caton, High Bentham, Horton in Ribblesdale, Pateley Bridge, Knaresborough, York, Stamford Bridge, Fridaythorpe, Kirkham, Fleetwood, Cleveleys, Garstang, Galgate, Slaidburn, Long Preston, Settle, Gargrave, Skipton, Harrogate, Wetherby, Pocklington, Market Weighton, Clitheroe, Barnoldswick, Ilkley, Otley, Spofforth, Collingham, Tadcaster, Escrick, Leven

Morecambe Bay, Windermere, Ullswater, Derwent Water, Haweswater, Coniston Water

Zeebrugge 17:30, Amsterdam 15:30, Larne 8:00

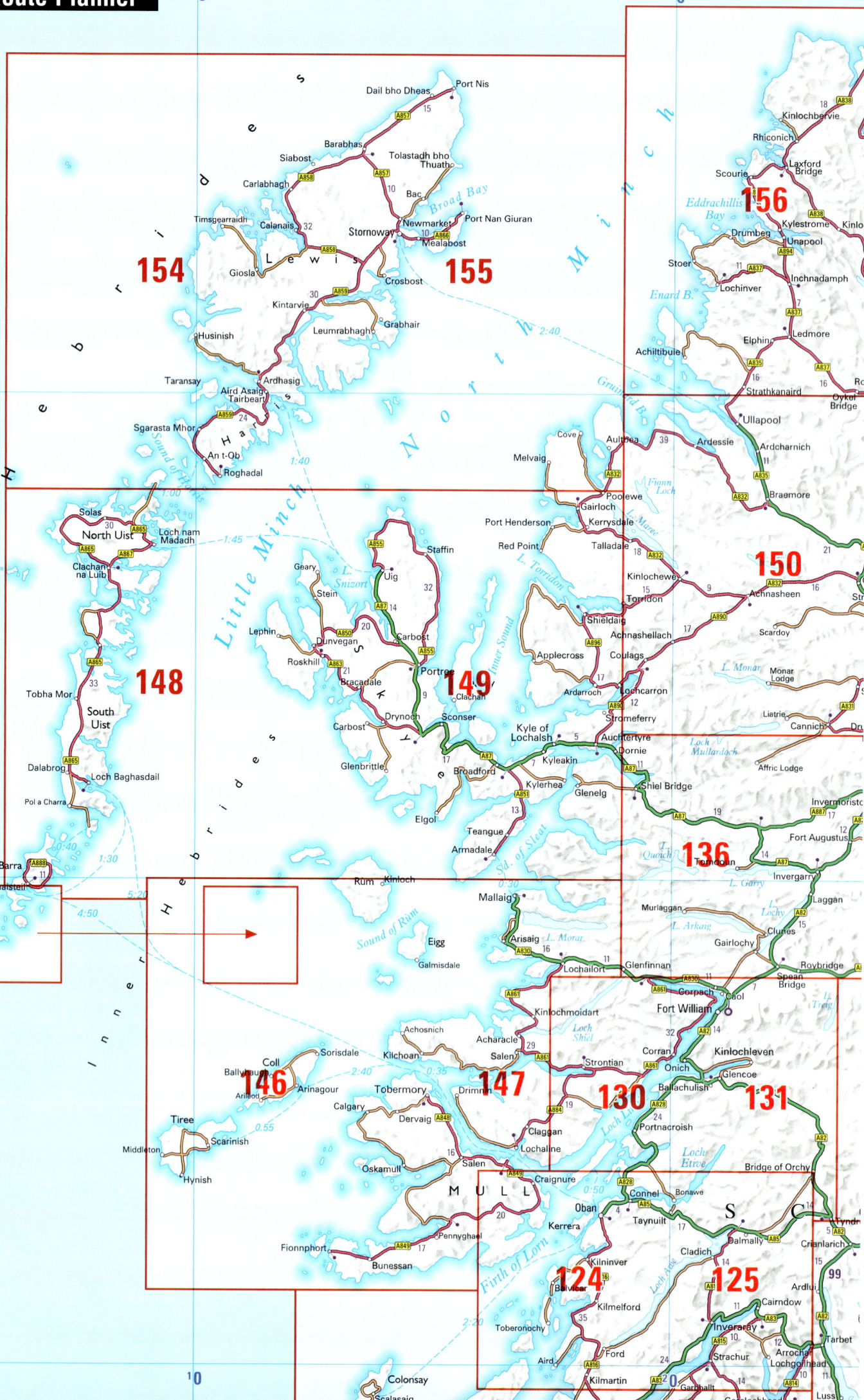

154 155 156

150

148 149

136

146 147 130 131

124 125

99

Lewis, Harris, North Uist, South Uist, Barra, Skye, Mull, Coll, Tiree

Stornoway, Tarbert, Portree, Broadford, Kyle of Lochalsh, Fort William, Oban, Mallaig, Ullapool, Gairloch, Lochinver, Kinlochbervie

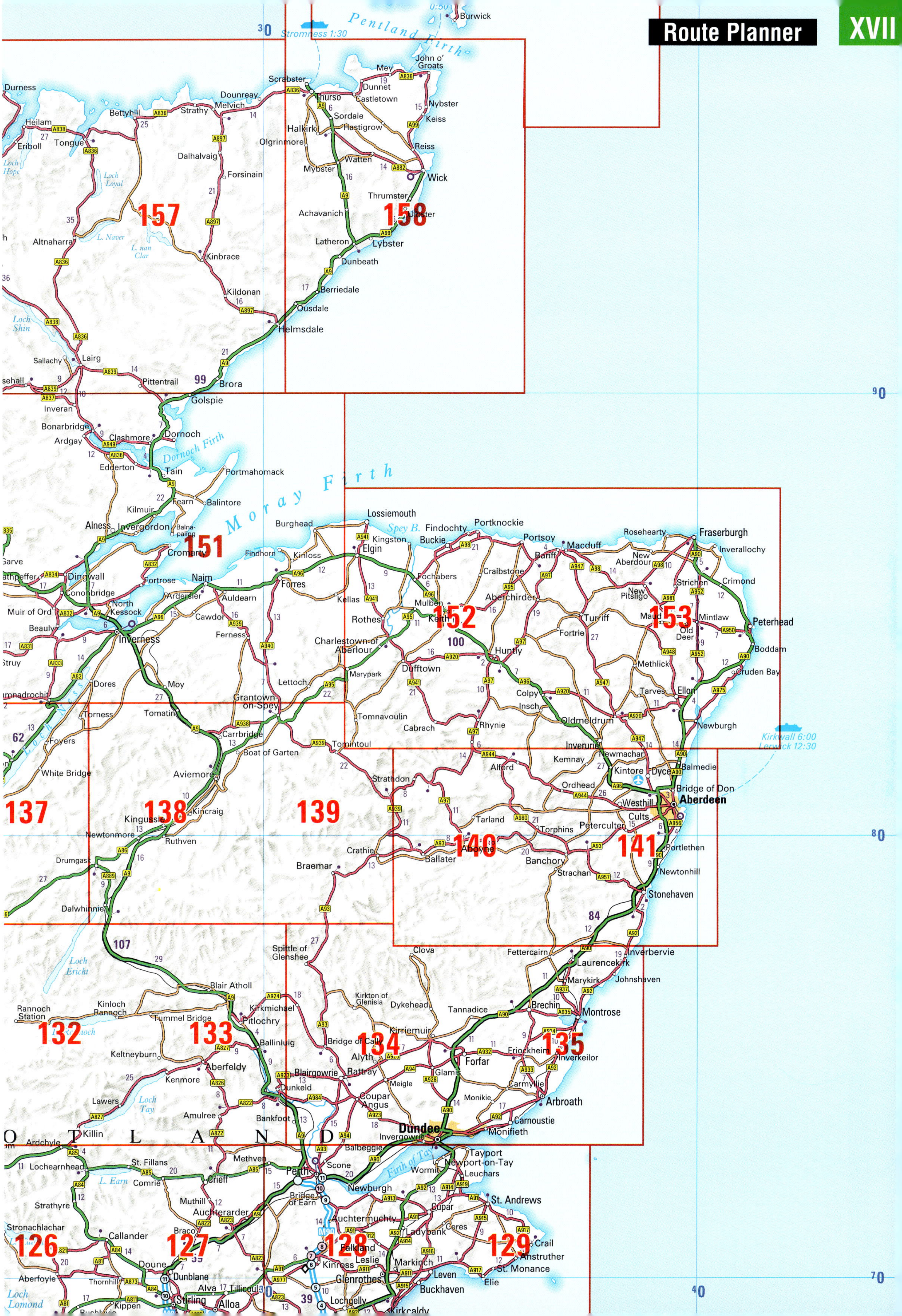
Pentland Firth
Stromness 1:30
Burwick
John o' Groats
Mey
Dunnet
Scrabster
Thurso
Castletown
Nybster
Keiss
Durness
Dounreay
Melvich
Bettyhill
Strathy
Heilam
Eriboll
Tongue
Loch Hope
Sordale
Halkirk
Hastigrow
Olgrinmore
Reiss
Watten
Mybster
Wick
Dalhalvaig
Forsinain
Loch Loyal
Thrumster
157
158
Achavanich
Ulbster
Altnaharra
L. Naver
L. nan Clar
Kinbrace
Latheron
Lybster
Dunbeath
Berriedale
Kildonan
Ousdale
Loch Shin
Helmsdale
Sallachy
Lairg
Pittentrail
Brora
Golspie
Inveran
Bonarbridge
Ardgay
Clashmore
Dornoch
Dornoch Firth
Edderton
Tain
Portmahomack
Moray Firth
Fearn
Balintore
Kilmuir
Alness
Invergordon
Balnapaling
Cromarty
151
Burghead
Lossiemouth
Spey B.
Findochty
Portknockie
Kingston
Buckie
Elgin
Findhorn
Kinloss
Forres
Portsoy
Macduff
Banff
Rosehearty
Fraserburgh
Inverallochy
New Aberdour
Crimond
Strichen
New Pitsligo
Dingwall
Conon Bridge
Fortrose
Nairn
Ardersier
Auldearn
North Kessock
Muir of Ord
Beauly
Cawdor
Inverness
Ferness
Kellas
Fochabers
Mulben
Craibstone
Aberchirder
Turriff
Fortrie
Maud
153
Mintlaw
Old Deer
Peterhead
Boddam
Rothes
Keith
152
Charlestown-of-Aberlour
Huntly
Dufftown
Methlick
Cruden Bay
Marypark
Lettoch
Dores
Moy
Grantown-on-Spey
Tarves
Ellon
Colpy
Insch
Newburgh
Tomnavoulin
Cabrach
Rhynie
Oldmeldrum
Loch Ness
Torness
Tomatin
Carrbridge
Boat of Garten
Tomintoul
Inverurie
Newmachar
Kemnay
Kirkwall 6:00
Lerwick 12:30
Foyers
White Bridge
Aviemore
Strathdon
Alford
Kintore
Dyce
Balmedie
Bridge of Don
Aberdeen
Westhill
Ordhead
137
138
139
Kingussie
Kincraig
Tarland
Torphins
Cults
Peterculter
Newtonmore
Ruthven
Crathie
140
Aboyne
Ballater
Banchory
141
Portlethen
Braemar
Drumgask
Strachan
Newtonhill
Stonehaven
Dalwhinnie
Loch Ericht
Spittle of Glenshee
Clova
Fettercairn
Inverbervie
Laurencekirk
Johnshaven
Marykirk
Blair Atholl
Kirkton of Glenisla
Dykehead
Tannadice
Brechin
Montrose
Rannoch Station
Kinloch Rannoch
Tummel Bridge
Kirkmichael
Pitlochry
132
133
Kirriemuir
Ballinluig
Bridge of Cally
134
135
Alyth
Forfar
Friockheim
Inverkeilor
Keltneyburn
Aberfeldy
Blairgowrie
Rattray
Glamis
Kenmore
Dunkeld
Meigle
Carmyllie
Lawers
Loch Tay
Coupar Angus
Monikie
Arbroath
Amulree
Bankfoot
Carnoustie
Killin
Dundee
Invergowrie
Monifieth
SCOTLAND
Ardchyle
Balbeggie
Tayport
Newport-on-Tay
Methven
Scone
Lochearnhead
St. Fillans
Perth
Firth of Tay
Wormit
Leuchars
L. Earn
Comrie
Crieff
Newburgh
Bridge of Earn
St. Andrews
Strathyre
Muthill
Auchterarder
Auchtermuchty
Cupar
Stronachlachar
Braco
Ladybank
Ceres
126
Callander
127
128
Falkland
129
Crail
Doune
Kinross
Leslie
Markinch
Anstruther
St. Monance
Aberfoyle
Thornhill
Dunblane
Glenrothes
Leven
Elie
Loch Lomond
Stirling
Alva
Tillicoultry
Alloa
Kippen
Lochgelly
Buckhaven
Kirkcaldy

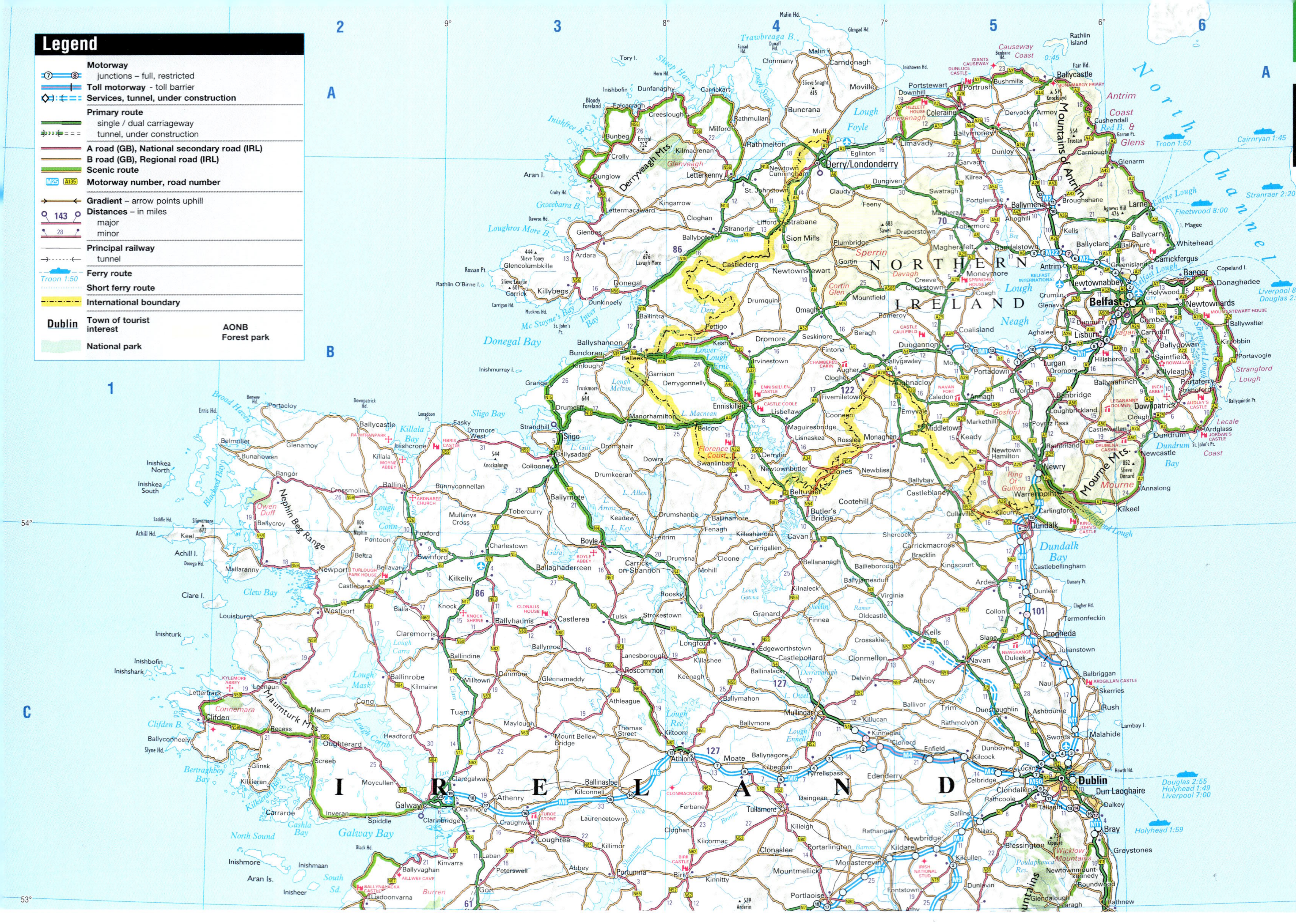
Legend
Motorway
junctions – full, restricted
Toll motorway - toll barrier
Services, tunnel, under construction
Primary route
single / dual carriageway
tunnel, under construction
A road (GB), National secondary road (IRL)
B road (GB), Regional road (IRL)
Scenic route
Motorway number, road number
Gradient – arrow points uphill
Distances – in miles
major
minor
Principal railway
tunnel
Ferry route
Short ferry route
International boundary
Dublin Town of tourist interest
AONB
Forest park
National park
North Channel
NORTHERN IRELAND
IRELAND
Belfast
Dublin
Derry/Londonderry
Galway Bay
Donegal Bay
Dundalk Bay

George's Channel

St. George's Channel

Wicklow Mts

Knockmealdown Mts

Galtee Mts

Boggeragh Mts

Macgillycuddy's Reeks

Dingle Bay

Brandon Bay

Tralee Bay

Castlemaine Harbour

Kenmare River

Bantry Bay

Dunmanus Bay

Roaringwater Bay

Clonakilty Bay

Courtmacsherry Bay

Kinsale Harbour

Cork Harbour

Youghal Bay

Dungarvan Harbour

Tramore Bay

Waterford Harbour

Wexford Harbour

Mouth of the Shannon

Shannon

Mal Bay

Liscannor Bay

Cliffs of Moher

Scale ● 1 : 1280000   1cm = 12.8km   1 inch = 20 miles

0   10   20   30 miles

0   10   20   30   40   50 km

Fishguard 18:30   Pembroke 3:45

Cherbourg 17:30   Rosslare Harbour   Le Havre 22:00

Roscoff 14:00   Swansea 10:00

Index to Ireland

Distance table

John o' Groats
Kyle of Lochalsh
Inverness
Aberdeen
Braemar
Fort William
Dundee
Oban
Edinburgh
Glasgow
Berwick-upon-Tweed
Ayr
Stranraer
Newcastle upon Tyne
Carlisle
York
Kingston upon Hull
Blackpool
Leeds
Manchester
Doncaster
Holyhead
Liverpool
Sheffield
Lincoln
Nottingham
Norwich
Great Yarmouth
Shrewsbury
Leicester
Birmingham
Aberystwyth
Cambridge
Fishguard
Gloucester
Harwich
Swansea
Oxford
Cardiff
Bristol
London
Dover
Southampton
Brighton
Exeter
Bournemouth
Portsmouth
Plymouth
Land's End

Supporting

THINK!

Travel safe – Don't drive tired

How to use this table

Distances are shown in miles and kilometres with estimated journey times in hours and minutes.

For example: the distance between Dover and Fishguard is 331 miles or 533 kilometres with an estimated journey time of 6 hours, 20 minutes.

Estimated driving times are based on an average speed of 60mph on Motorways and 40mph on other roads. Drivers should allow extra time when driving at peak periods or through areas likely to be congested.

Dover					
Dundee					523 842 9:10
Edinburgh				56 90 1:30	462 744 8:10
Exeter			450 724 8:00	518 834 9:10	248 399 4:40
Fishguard		230 370 4:30	399 642 7:30	460 740 8:30	331 533 6:20
Fort William	486 782 9:30	560 901 10:20	144 232 3:30	127 204 3:10	596 959 11:00

London																																																
Aberdeen																																																517 832 11:20
Aberystwyth																																															445 716 8:40	211 340 4:40
Ayr																																														317 510 6:10	183 295 4:20	394 634 7:20
Berwick-upon-Tweed																																													134 216 3:00	311 501 6:20	182 293 4:40	352 567 7:30
Birmingham																																												274 441 5:30	289 465 5:30	114 183 2:50	420 676 8:30	117 188 2:50
Blackpool																																											123 198 2:40	181 291 3:50	180 290 3:30	153 246 3:20	308 496 6:20	226 364 4:30
Bournemouth																																										270 435 5:00	147 237 3:10	412 663 7:50	436 702 8:00	207 333 4:30	564 908 10:20	107 172 2:40
Braemar																																									524 843 9:30	281 452 5:20	385 620 7:10	148 238 3:20	143 230 3:00	405 652 7:50	59 95 1:30	482 776 10:30
Brighton																																								534 859 9:40	92 148 2:10	286 460 5:20	163 262 3:20	409 658 7:40	446 718 8:00	253 407 5:10	573 922 10:30	52 84 1:50
Bristol																																							147 237 4:10	477 768 8:40	82 132 2:30	204 328 3:50	81 130 2:00	362 583 6:50	370 595 6:40	125 201 3:00	493 793 9:10	122 196 2:50
Cambridge																																						169 272 3:10	116 187 2:20	438 705 7:50	154 248 3:00	208 335 3:50	100 161 2:10	306 493 5:40	357 575 6:20	214 344 4:20	471 758 10:00	54 87 1:30
Cardiff																																					190 306 3:30	45 72 1:20	182 293 3:40	483 778 8:40	117 188 3:00	209 336 4:00	103 166 2:20	368 592 7:00	382 615 7:00	105 169 2:40	505 813 9:20	157 253 3:20
Carlisle																																				289 465 5:20	264 425 4:40	277 446 5:00	370 596 6:40	196 316 3:50	343 552 6:20	87 140 1:50	196 315 3:50	87 140 2:10	93 150 2:00	224 360 4:30	221 356 4:30	301 484 5:40
Doncaster																																			142 229 3:00	209 336 4:00	116 187 2:10	175 282 3:20	236 380 4:30	310 499 5:40	235 378 4:20	94 151 1:50	94 151 2:00	184 296 3:50	235 378 4:20	176 283 3:40	344 554 6:50	171 275 3:30
Dover																																		242 390 4:30	389 626 7:00	238 383 4:30	125 201 2:30	202 325 3:50	82 132 2:20	553 890 9:50	174 280 4:30	312 502 5:40	194 312 3:50	424 683 7:50	478 769 8:30	297 478 5:50	588 947 10:40	71 114 2:00
Dundee																																	523 842 9:10	275 443 5:00	152 245 3:00	441 710 8:00	406 654 7:10	430 692 7:40	517 832 9:10	52 84 1:20	495 797 8:50	239 385 4:30	349 562 6:20	113 182 2:40	117 188 2:30	376 605 7:10	67 108 1:50	448 721 8:40
Edinburgh																																56 90 1:30	462 744 8:10	219 352 4:00	96 154 2:00	385 620 7:00	345 555 6:10	373 600 6:50	456 734 8:20	91 146 2:10	439 707 8:00	183 295 3:30	292 470 5:30	57 92 1:40	73 117 1:50	320 515 6:20	125 201 3:10	390 628 7:20
Exeter																															450 724 8:00	518 834 9:10	248 399 4:40	251 404 4:30	353 568 6:20	121 195 2:30	249 401 4:30	76 122 1:40	184 296 5:00	550 885 9:40	82 132 2:20	282 454 5:10	157 253 3:10	428 689 7:50	446 718 7:50	201 323 4:10	569 916 10:20	181 291 3:40
Fishguard																														230 370 4:30	399 642 7:30	460 740 8:30	331 533 6:20	247 398 4:50	297 478 5:40	112 180 2:40	270 435 5:10	154 248 3:20	291 468 5:40	493 794 9:10	222 357 4:40	209 336 4:10	170 274 3:40	371 597 7:20	373 600 7:00	56 90 1:30	504 811 10:10	260 418 5:20
Fort William																													486 782 9:30	560 901 10:20	144 232 3:30	127 204 3:10	596 959 11:00	357 575 7:00	206 332 4:30	485 781 9:10	479 771 9:00	486 782 9:10	575 926 10:50	125 201 3:10	539 867 10:10	296 476 6:00	392 631 7:40	190 306 4:40	133 214 3:20	430 692 8:40	149 240 3:50	510 821 9:50
Glasgow																												101 163 2:50	376 605 7:10	449 723 8:00	44 71 1:20	83 134 2:00	488 786 8:40	249 401 4:40	96 154 2:10	385 620 7:00	372 599 6:40	373 600 6:50	468 753 8:30	110 177 2:30	439 707 8:00	183 295 3:40	292 470 5:30	101 163 2:40	33 53 1:10	320 515 6:20	145 233 3:30	397 639 7:30
Gloucester																											346 557 6:10	454 731 8:30	153 246 3:10	111 179 2:10	349 562 6:10	410 660 7:10	191 307 3:30	150 241 2:50	247 398 4:20	56 90 1:20	123 198 2:20	35 56 1:00	159 256 3:10	443 713 8:00	99 159 2:40	174 280 3:10	56 90 1:20	318 512 6:00	330 531 5:50	102 164 2:30	468 753 8:30	109 175 2:30
Great Yarmouth																										225 362 4:40	419 674 8:00	527 848 10:20	366 589 7:20	335 539 6:30	386 621 7:30	484 779 9:00	185 298 4:00	167 269 3:40	320 515 6:20	284 457 5:50	82 132 2:10	275 443 5:40	180 290 4:10	477 768 9:10	240 386 5:00	252 406 5:10	180 290 4:10	345 555 7:00	402 647 7:40	294 473 6:20	517 832 10:50	128 206 3:40
Harwich																									82 132 2:10	196 316 4:00	432 695 8:10	543 874 10:30	337 542 6:40	279 449 5:20	413 665 7:40	469 755 8:40	125 201 2:50	194 312 4:00	336 541 6:20	246 396 5:00	67 108 1:50	217 349 4:30	128 206 3:00	504 811 9:20	187 301 4:00	275 443 5:20	167 269 3:40	372 599 7:20	425 684 8:00	281 452 5:50	535 861 11:20	76 122 2:20
Holyhead																								349 562 7:10	334 538 7:00	191 307 4:00	330 531 6:40	438 705 8:50	167 269 4:00	282 454 5:40	333 536 6:40	394 634 7:30	360 580 7:00	181 291 3:50	231 372 4:50	216 348 5:40	270 435 5:20	206 332 4:30	334 538 6:40	426 686 8:20	288 463 5:50	141 227 3:20	148 238 3:30	311 501 6:30	305 491 6:10	111 179 2:50	439 707 8:40	269 433 5:40
Inverness																							474 763 9:40	569 916 11:00	553 890 11:00	504 811 9:30	166 267 4:00	66 106 1:40	542 872 10:30	618 995 11:30	158 254 3:50	132 212 3:20	622 1001 11:30	383 617 7:30	262 422 5:30	549 884 10:20	505 813 9:30	539 867 10:10	617 993 11:30	75 121 2:00	597 961 11:20	348 560 7:00	458 737 9:00	215 346 5:10	199 320 4:30	486 782 9:40	105 169 2:50	550 885 10:40
John o' Groats																						129 208 3:20	603 970 12:40	693 1116 14:00	677 1090 14:00	628 1011 12:30	295 475 7:10	195 314 5:00	671 1080 13:40	744 1197 14:30	285 459 7:00	259 417 6:30	746 1201 14:40	507 816 10:30	391 629 8:40	680 1094 13:30	630 1014 12:30	668 1075 13:20	741 1193 14:40	202 325 5:00	724 1165 14:20	478 769 10:00	574 924 11:50	342 550 8:10	328 528 7:40	601 967 12:40	232 373 5:50	663 1067 13:30
Kingston upon Hull																					518 834 10:50	394 634 7:50	231 372 4:50	196 316 4:10	207 333 5:20	169 272 3:10	254 409 4:50	369 594 7:20	280 451 5:30	309 497 5:40	234 377 4:30	295 475 5:30	256 412 4:50	47 76 1:10	158 254 3:00	244 393 4:40	139 224 3:10	233 375 4:20	245 394 4:40	327 526 6:10	264 425 5:00	127 204 2:30	134 216 2:50	185 298 3:50	251 404 4:40	223 359 4:40	364 586 7:20	184 296 3:50
Kyle of Lochalsh																				445 716 9:00	189 304 4:40	84 135 2:10	514 827 10:40	611 983 12:10	602 969 12:10	528 850 10:20	179 288 4:40	79 127 2:00	567 913 11:20	628 1011 12:00	216 348 5:20	186 299 4:40	671 1080 12:50	432 695 8:40	275 443 6:10	564 908 11:10	555 893 10:50	552 888 10:50	651 1048 12:40	159 256 4:00	618 995 12:10	372 599 7:50	471 758 9:40	263 423 6:20	212 341 5:10	499 803 10:20	189 304 4:50	586 943 11:40
Land's End																			763 1228 15:10	421 678 8:20	868 1397 17:20	741 1193 14:20	405 652 8:30	390 628 8:00	446 718 9:10	235 378 5:00	573 922 10:50	686 1104 13:20	353 568 7:20	123 198 3:20	574 924 10:50	642 1033 12:00	381 613 7:40	374 602 7:20	477 768 9:10	245 394 5:20	374 602 7:20	200 322 4:40	308 496 7:50	665 1070 12:30	205 330 5:20	405 652 8:00	281 452 6:00	552 888 10:40	570 917 10:50	313 504 6:50	692 1114 13:10	297 478 6:30
Leeds																		405 652 8:00	394 634 8:20	55 89 1:30	487 784 10:20	360 579 7:10	176 283 4:00	223 359 4:30	196 315 4:20	174 280 3:20	215 346 4:10	329 530 6:40	237 381 4:40	270 435 5:00	202 325 4:00	258 415 4:50	260 418 4:50	29 47 0:50	119 192 2:30	232 373 4:20	145 233 2:50	194 312 3:50	260 419 5:00	293 472 5:30	255 410 4:50	72 116 1:40	113 182 2:30	156 251 3:20	212 341 4:00	169 272 3:40	327 526 6:50	189 304 3:50
Leicester																	95 153 2:00	320 515 6:30	500 805 9:50	102 164 2:10	588 947 11:50	461 742 8:50	190 306 4:00	147 237 3:10	140 225 3:20	85 137 1:40	314 505 5:40	422 679 8:00	209 336 4:10	196 315 3:40	296 476 5:20	349 562 6:20	185 298 3:30	74 119 1:30	206 332 3:50	154 248 3:00	68 109 1:20	120 193 2:30	166 267 3:20	389 626 7:00	158 254 3:10	140 225 2:40	39 63 1:10	252 406 5:00	299 481 5:20	153 246 3:20	414 666 7:40	97 156 2:20
Lincoln																51 82 1:20	68 109 1:50	371 597 7:30	476 766 9:40	44 71 1:20	554 892 11:30	427 687 8:30	216 348 4:40	155 249 3:30	128 206 3:20	159 256 3:10	291 468 5:30	399 642 7:50	272 438 5:30	247 398 4:40	258 415 5:00	314 505 5:50	202 325 4:00	39 63 1:10	191 307 3:40	208 335 4:10	85 137 2:20	183 295 3:40	197 317 4:00	357 575 6:40	209 336 4:10	128 206 2:40	90 145 2:10	224 360 4:40	274 441 5:10	199 320 4:20	383 616 7:20	131 211 3:10
Liverpool															129 208 2:50	130 209 2:40	75 121 1:50	361 581 7:20	407 655 8:30	130 209 2:40	511 822 10:40	382 615 7:40	102 164 2:40	265 427 5:20	240 386 5:00	140 225 2:40	216 348 4:10	329 530 6:40	160 257 3:30	237 381 4:30	216 348 4:10	286 460 5:20	299 481 5:30	86 138 1:50	120 193 2:30	169 272 3:20	194 312 3:40	161 259 3:10	272 438 5:10	318 512 6:00	234 377 4:30	49 79 1:20	93 150 2:10	219 352 4:30	213 343 4:10	104 167 2:40	341 549 6:40	202 325 4:10
Manchester														35 56 1:10	84 135 2:00	92 148 2:00	40 64 1:10	361 581 7:20	406 654 8:30	95 153 2:10	500 805 10:30	373 600 7:30	124 200 3:00	228 367 4:40	212 341 4:30	126 203 2:30	215 346 4:10	329 530 6:40	197 317 4:00	236 380 4:20	215 346 4:10	285 459 5:20	276 444 5:10	61 98 1:30	119 192 2:30	183 295 3:40	165 266 3:10	161 259 3:10	257 414 4:50	318 512 6:00	227 365 4:20	48 77 1:20	80 129 2:00	196 315 4:00	212 341 4:00	129 208 3:00	340 547 6:30	185 298 3:50
Newcastle upon Tyne													132 212 2:50	168 270 3:20	159 256 3:20	187 301 3:40	92 148 2:10	498 802 9:40	318 512 7:00	132 212 2:50	395 636 8:50	268 431 5:40	272 438 5:40	308 496 6:00	281 452 5:40	266 428 4:50	148 238 3:10	253 407 5:20	329 529 6:20	364 586 6:30	110 177 2:20	166 267 3:20	358 576 6:30	114 183 2:20	57 92 1:50	325 523 6:00	241 388 4:20	299 481 5:30	352 567 6:30	201 323 4:00	347 558 6:30	129 208 2:40	207 333 4:10	64 103 1:50	149 240 3:00	257 414 5:20	235 378 4:50	286 460 5:40
Norwich												264 425 5:20	185 298 4:30	220 354 4:40	105 169 2:50	119 192 3:20	176 283 3:50	421 678 8:40	582 937 11:50	149 240 4:00	654 1053 13:30	529 852 10:30	311 501 6:40	73 117 2:00	20 32 0:40	204 328 4:10	385 620 9:00	504 811 10:00	343 552 7:00	308 496 6:00	366 589 7:00	422 679 8:00	174 280 3:50	147 237 3:20	289 465 5:40	262 422 5:20	62 100 1:50	252 406 5:10	175 282 4:00	457 735 8:40	214 344 4:40	232 373 4:50	166 267 3:50	328 528 6:40	382 615 7:20	276 444 6:00	496 798 9:40	114 183 3:30
Nottingham											130 209 3:40	157 253 3:10	73 118 1:40	98 158 2:10	35 56 1:10	25 40 0:50	70 113 1:40	345 555 7:00	479 771 9:40	90 145 2:00	557 896 11:30	430 692 8:20	185 298 4:00	150 241 3:20	153 246 3:30	110 177 2:10	293 472 5:30	401 646 7:50	220 354 4:30	221 356 4:10	262 422 4:50	328 528 6:00	205 330 3:50	43 69 1:10	194 312 3:40	172 277 3:20	83 134 1:40	145 233 3:00	193 311 3:50	353 568 6:30	183 295 3:40	111 179 2:20	50 80 1:20	221 356 4:30	274 441 5:10	164 264 3:40	393 633 7:30	122 196 2:40
Oban										390 628 7:30	492 792 9:40	233 375 4:50	307 494 6:00	308 496 6:10	387 623 7:30	419 674 7:50	307 494 6:00	665 1070 12:50	128 206 3:10	346 557 6:40	244 393 6:10	117 188 3:00	427 687 8:30	524 843 10:00	515 829 10:00	441 710 8:10	92 148 2:30	49 79 1:20	481 774 9:10	549 884 10:00	123 198 3:00	117 188 2:50	585 942 10:40	346 557 6:40	188 303 4:00	477 768 9:00	468 753 8:40	465 748 8:40	565 910 10:30	141 227 3:30	530 853 9:50	285 459 5:40	384 618 7:30	180 290 4:20	94 151 2:20	412 663 8:10	178 286 4:20	499 803 9:30
Oxford									462 744 8:30	109 175 2:10	145 233 3:50	260 418 4:50	144 232 2:50	172 277 3:20	137 221 2:50	73 117 1:30	168 270 3:10	274 441 5:40	550 885 10:40	192 309 3:40	656 1056 13:00	532 856 10:00	238 383 4:50	145 233 3:10	200 322 4:20	52 84 1:30	356 573 6:30	472 760 9:00	205 330 4:10	156 251 3:00	372 599 6:40	433 697 7:40	141 227 2:50	145 233 2:40	260 418 4:40	108 174 2:20	83 134 1:40	74 119 1:40	108 174 2:20	465 749 8:20	90 145 2:00	187 301 3:30	64 103 1:30	324 521 6:10	353 568 6:20	154 248 3:20	483 777 8:50	57 92 1:40
Plymouth								199 320 4:00	587 945 11:00	267 430 5:10	343 552 7:00	410 660 7:40	283 455 5:30	283 455 5:30	293 472 5:50	242 389 4:40	316 509 6:00	89 143 2:20	674 1085 13:10	355 571 6:40	790 1271 15:40	664 1069 12:30	328 528 6:40	309 497 6:10	365 588 7:20	157 253 3:20	495 797 9:10	595 958 11:20	264 425 5:30	46 74 1:30	496 798 9:00	552 888 10:00	300 483 5:50	297 478 5:40	399 642 7:20	167 269 3:40	293 472 5:30	122 196 2:50	224 361 6:00	587 945 10:40	128 206 3:30	328 528 6:10	203 327 4:20	474 763 9:00	492 792 9:00	237 382 5:10	615 990 11:20	218 351 4:40
Portsmouth							176 283 4:50	77 124 1:40	545 877 10:00	191 307 3:40	207 333 4:20	337 542 6:10	236 380 4:30	254 409 4:50	201 323 4:00	162 261 3:10	257 414 4:50	259 417 5:40	633 1019 12:10	269 433 5:00	737 1186 14:30	613 987 11:30	311 501 6:10	166 267 3:40	221 356 4:40	119 192 3:00	448 721 8:10	555 893 10:20	251 404 5:00	135 217 2:40	453 729 8:10	514 827 9:00	130 209 2:50	234 377 4:20	348 560 6:10	142 229 3:00	144 232 2:50	97 156 2:10	48 77 1:40	547 881 9:50	52 84 1:30	264 425 4:50	141 227 3:00	401 645 7:30	430 692 7:40	222 357 4:40	560 901 10:10	70 113 2:00
Sheffield						230 370 4:20	283 455 5:30	135 217 2:40	339 546 6:30	37 60 1:00	146 235 3:20	125 201 2:40	38 61 1:00	72 116 1:40	46 74 1:20	62 100 1:20	33 53 1:00	361 581 7:10	427 687 8:40	65 105 1:30	520 837 10:50	393 632 7:40	168 270 3:40	187 301 3:50	166 267 3:40	126 203 2:20	248 399 4:40	348 560 6:50	215 346 4:20	237 381 4:20	235 378 4:20	291 468 5:20	245 394 4:30	18 29 0:40	152 245 3:00	194 312 3:40	120 193 2:20	161 259 3:10	226 364 4:20	320 515 6:00	216 348 4:10	86 138 1:50	76 122 1:50	190 306 4:00	245 394 4:30	159 256 3:30	360 579 6:50	159 256 3:20
Shrewsbury					82 132 2:10	207 333 3:50	225 362 4:40	106 171 2:10	364 586 7:00	93 150 2:00	205 330 4:20	201 323 3:50	69 111 1:40	58 93 1:50	133 214 2:50	84 135 1:40	109 175 2:20	303 488 6:10	451 726 9:00	169 272 3:10	567 912 11:30	438 705 8:20	113 182 2:50	240 386 4:40	225 362 4:40	77 124 1:30	272 438 5:00	382 615 7:20	145 233 3:10	179 288 3:20	274 441 5:00	330 531 6:00	251 404 4:30	109 175 2:10	176 283 3:20	111 179 2:20	159 256 3:00	103 166 2:50	226 364 4:20	371 597 6:50	185 298 3:40	98 158 2:00	45 72 1:20	265 426 5:10	269 433 5:00	77 124 2:10	399 642 7:30	160 258 3:20
Southampton				185 298 4:10	199 320 3:40	21 34 0:50	151 243 4:10	64 103 1:30	530 853 9:40	176 283 3:20	206 332 4:20	324 521 5:50	221 356 4:10	239 385 4:30	204 328 4:00	137 220 2:40	232 373 4:20	228 367 5:00	618 995 12:00	256 412 4:40	723 1164 14:10	598 963 11:10	293 472 5:50	164 264 3:30	220 354 4:40	105 169 2:40	433 697 7:40	541 871 10:00	233 375 4:40	105 169 3:00	438 705 7:50	500 805 8:50	143 230 2:50	209 336 3:50	324 521 5:50	121 195 2:30	148 238 2:50	76 122 2:20	61 98 1:50	532 856 9:30	31 50 1:00	251 404 4:40	128 206 2:40	388 624 7:10	417 671 7:30	201 323 4:10	547 880 10:00	77 124 2:00
Stranraer			445 716 8:20	277 446 5:30	263 423 5:20	461 742 8:40	500 805 9:40	379 610 7:10	148 238 3:40	290 467 5:50	403 649 8:10	158 254 3:40	220 354 4:40	221 356 4:40	298 480 6:00	330 531 6:20	220 354 4:40	585 942 11:30	263 423 6:30	259 417 5:20	379 610 9:00	262 422 6:00	338 544 7:00	410 660 8:10	426 686 8:40	343 552 6:30	84 135 2:30	195 314 4:50	392 631 7:50	454 731 8:30	124 200 3:00	167 269 3:40	496 798 9:10	257 414 5:10	101 163 2:40	390 628 7:30	379 610 7:10	378 608 7:20	475 765 9:00	194 312 4:20	444 715 8:30	188 303 4:00	297 478 6:00	170 274 4:10	51 82 1:20	325 523 6:50	228 367 5:10	402 647 7:50
Swansea		417 671 7:50	161 259 3:00	118 190 2:20	217 349 4:00	182 293 3:30	206 332 4:10	141 227 2:40	506 815 9:20	192 309 3:40	301 485 6:00	347 559 6:20	187 301 3:30	195 314 3:40	233 375 4:30	177 285 3:20	248 399 4:40	285 459 6:00	594 956 11:30	264 425 4:50	696 1120 13:40	572 921 10:40	184 296 4:50	267 430 5:10	329 530 6:30	89 143 1:50	409 658 7:20	496 798 9:20	67 108 1:50	161 259 3:00	412 663 7:20	473 761 8:20	274 441 5:00	232 373 4:10	309 497 5:30	41 66 1:10	227 365 4:10	85 137 1:50	222 357 4:20	505 813 9:00	167 269 3:20	216 348 4:00	119 192 2:30	383 616 7:10	379 610 6:50	73 117 2:00	507 816 9:20	194 312 4:00
York	272 438 5:10	222 357 4:40	258 415 5:10	133 214 2:40	52 84 1:20	278 448 5:10	333 536 6:20	181 291 3:20	309 497 6:00	77 124 1:40	181 291 4:20	84 135 2:20	64 103 1:30	99 159 2:10	75 121 1:50	108 174 2:10	24 39 0:50	411 661 8:00	407 655 8:20	37 60 1:10	479 771 10:10	352 566 7:00	204 328 4:20	228 367 4:40	201 323 4:20	189 304 3:30	217 349 4:10	330 531 6:30	261 420 5:10	287 462 5:10	194 312 3:40	250 402 4:40	282 454 5:10	34 55 1:00	121 195 2:30	244 393 4:40	165 266 3:10	222 357 4:10	275 443 5:10	285 459 5:20	269 433 5:00	96 154 2:00	130 209 2:40	148 238 3:10	214 344 4:00	195 314 4:10	319 513 6:10	207 333 4:10

Key to 3-mile map pages

Shetland Islands
160
Lerwick
Fair Isle
Orkney Islands
Kirkwall
159
Thurso
Wick
158
Lewis
Stornoway
154
155
Harris
Scourie
156
157
A9
Ullapool
Dornoch
A835
150
151
Inverness
North Uist
Skye
A87
148
149
South Uist
Kyle of Lochalsh
Elgin
Fraserburgh
152
153
A96
A90
A87
A82
A95
136
137
138
139
A830
A86
Aberdeen
140
141
Mallaig
Fort William
A9
A90
Coll
Tiree
146
147
130
131
132
133
134
135
Mull
Dundee
A828
Oban
124
125
A83
A85
126
127
Perth
St Andrews
M90
A92
128
129
Colonsay
M9
Stirling
144
145
A82
Jura
Glasgow
Edinburgh
M8
122
123
Islay
118
119
120
121
Berwick-upon-Tweed
142
143
M74
A702
Arran
Campbeltown
Ayr
A76
Hawick
A68
A1
Alnwick
112
113
114
115
A77
A74(M)
A7
116
117
Newcastle upon Tyne
Stranraer
A75
Dumfries
110
111
104
105
106
107
Carlisle
A69
Sunderland
Durham
108
109
A19
Whitehaven
A66
Middlesbrough
A591
M6
A1(M)
98
99
100
101
102
103
A595
Kendal
A1
A19
A171
Scarborough
Isle of Man
84
Douglas
Barrow in Furness
Lancaster
Harrogate
York
A64
A165
92
93
A59
94
95
96
97
Blackpool
Bradford
Leeds
M62
A63
Hull
Preston
86
87
Grimsby
M180
85
Manchester
M62
88
89
90
91
Liverpool
M62
Doncaster
M53
Sheffield
Lincoln
A16
82
83
Holyhead
A55
Anglesey
Llandudno
Chester
A49
Macclesfield
M1
A46
Skegness
Bangor
A487
74
M6
75
A6
Mansfield
72
73
Hanley
76
77
A17
78
79
80
81
Wrexham
A483
Stoke
A50
Derby
Nottingham
Boston
Cromer
A5
70
71
A1
A16
A17
A148
Great Yarmouth
Dolgellau
Shrewsbury
Stafford
Leicester
King's Lynn
A47
Norwich
A458
60
61
M54
62
63
64
A47
65
A47
66
67
68
69
Telford
M69
Birmingham
Peterborough
58
59
Wolverhampton
Coventry
A43
A1(M)
A10
A11
A12
Aberystwyth
A49
Stratford-upon-Avon
M1
Kettering
Cambridge
Newmarket
A44
Worcester
Northampton
A14
A14
45
46
47
48
49
50
51
52
53
54
55
56
57
Builth Wells
A470
Hereford
A44
Ipswich
A487
A483
M50
M5
Banbury
A43
Milton Keynes
M11
A12
Felixstowe
Fishguard
A40
A49
Cheltenham
M40
Luton
A1(M)
Colchester
44
Gloucester
M1
Chelmsford
32
33
34
35
36
37
A40
38
39
40
41
42
43
Pembroke
Llanelli
A470
M4
Newport
Swindon
A34
Oxford
M25
London
Southend-on-Sea
Swansea
Cardiff
M40
M4
Reading
30
31
Lundy
20
21
22
Bristol
Bath
Newbury
Windsor
28
29
M2
Canterbury
23
24
25
26
27
Croydon
Maidstone
Ilfracombe
M5
A37
A36
M3
A3
Dover
Winchester
Bideford
A361
Taunton
Salisbury
M27
Southampton
A23
Ashford
A259
A303
Brighton
8
9
A386
10
11
12
13
14
15
Chichester
16
A27
17
18
19
A39
A30
Exeter
Dorchester
Poole
Portsmouth
A35
Bournemouth
Weymouth
Isle of Wight
Torquay
Newquay
Plymouth
A38
4
5
6
7
Penzance
A30
Truro
2
3
Isles of Scilly
Channel Islands
Guernsey
Jersey

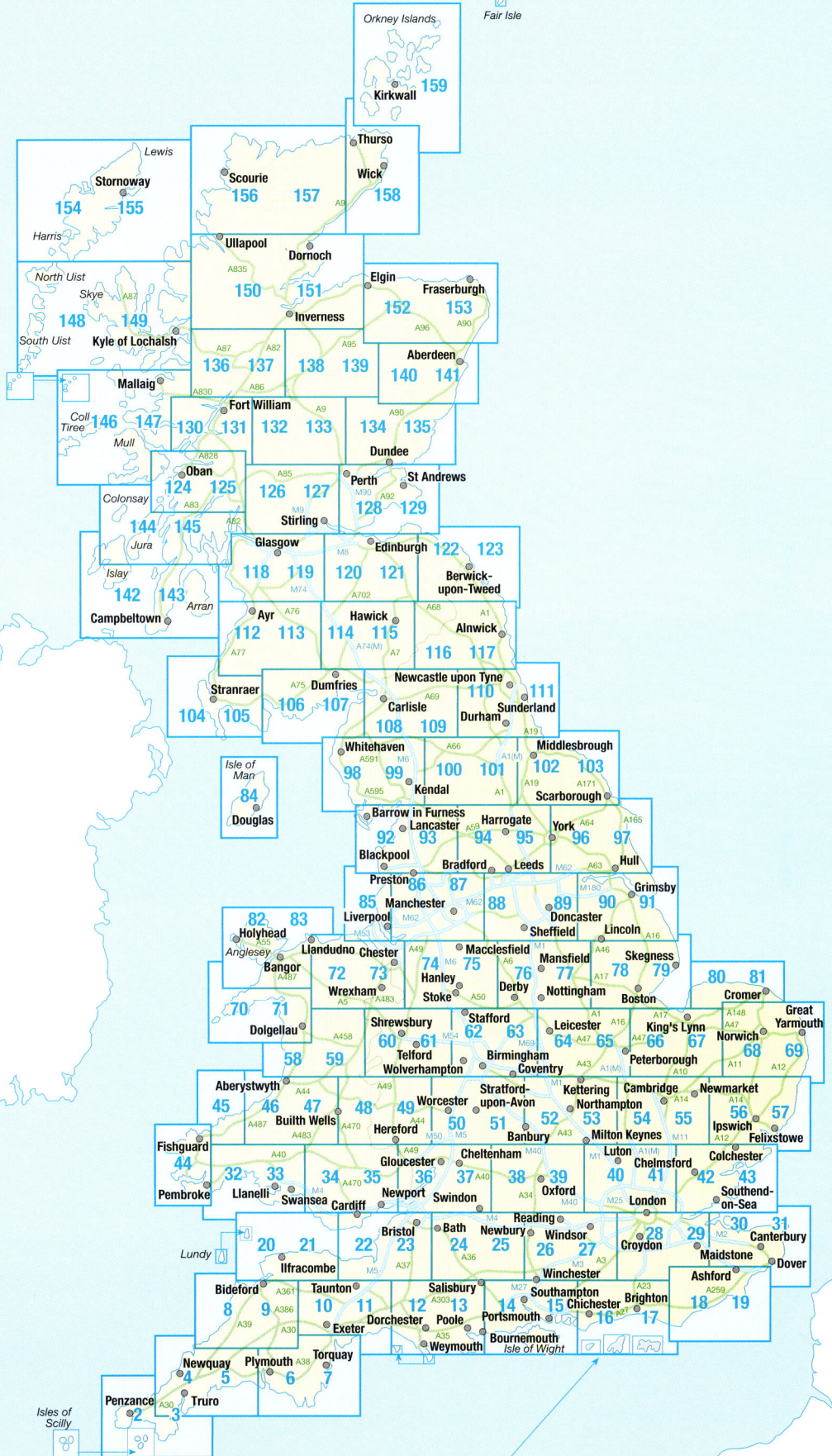

1
2
3
4
5
A
B
C
D
E
F
CORNWALL
SW
Godrevy Island
Godrevy Pt.
Navax Pt.
The Carracks
Clodgy Pt.
TATE ST IVES
The Island
St Ives Bay
BARBARA HEPWORTH MUSEUM
St Ives
SOUTH WEST COAST PATH
Gwithian
Kehelland
A30
A3047
B3306
Carbis Bay
Phillack
Connor Downs
Roseworthy
TREVITHICK COTTAGE
TEHIDY
Gurnard's Head
Zennor
247
Halsetown
A3074
B3301
Lelant
Copperhouse
Barripper
Carnhell Green
Porthmeor
Towednack
WAYSIDE FOLK MUSEUM
Cripplesease
PARADISE PARK
Hayle
Praze-an-Beeble
B3303
B3306
252
Morvah
Bojewyan
Pendeen
GEEVOR TIN MINE MUSEUM
Trewellard
Higher Boscaswell
CHYSAUSTER ANCIENT VILLAGE
Nancledra
Canon's Town
B3302
St Erth
Fraddam
B3280
Crowan
Leedstown
Newmill
B3311
Hayle
Drym
B3303
Botallack
Carnyorth
Cape Cornwall
B3318
PENZANCE HELIPORT
Ludgvan
B3309
Crowlas
Townshend
Nancegollan
St Just
A3071
TRENGWAINTON
Madron
Gulval
A3077
Relubbus
B3280
GODOLPHIN HOUSE
Godolphin Cross
The Bisons
BALLOWALL BARROW
LAND'S END
Newbridge
Heamoor
PENZANCE
Chyandour
A394
St Hilary
Trescowe
Crowntown
Bosavern
Marazion
ST MICHAEL'S MOUNT
Goldsithney
Kelynack
224
Sancreed
Res.
Penzance
Perranuthnoe
Germoe
Ashton
Sithney
B3306
CARN EUNY ANCIENT VILLAGE
Tredavoe
NEWLYN ART GALLERY
B3302
LAND'S END
Lower Drift
Newlyn
SOUTH WEST COAST PATH
Praa Sands
Breage
Whitesand Bay
Brane
Paul
Catchall
12
A394
Sennen Cove
A30
Crows-an-wra
B3283
Kerris
Mousehole
Cudden Pt.
Rinsey
B3304
Longships
Sennen
St Buryan
St Clement's Island
Trewavas Hd.
Porthleven
The Loe
LAND'S END
Trewoofe
SOUTH WEST COAST PATH
B3315
B3315
Lamorna
MOUNTS BAY
Porthleven Sands
Polgigga
TREGIFFIAN BURIAL CHAMBER
Porthcurno
Boskenna
Lamorna Cove
ISLES OF SCILLY 2:40 (Apr-Nov)
Treen
St Levan
MINACK OPEN AIR THEATRE
Gwennap Hd.
Runnel Stone
Isles of Scilly
White Island
St Helens
KING CHARLES CASTLE
St Martin's
Bryher
41
47
CROMWELL'S CASTLE
New Grimsby
Higher Town
Bryher
Tresco
TRESCO ABBEY GARDENS
Crow Sound
Eastern Isles
Samson
The Road
BANT'S CARN
51
INNISIDGEN CAIRNS
North West Passage
Newford
Maypole
LONGSTONE HERITAGE CEN
St Mary's
A3110
Hugh Town
ST MARY'S
GARRISON WALLS
Old Town
Broad Sound
Smith Sound
St Mary's Sound
Annet
St Agnes
Gugh
PENZANCE 2:40 (Apr-Nov)
St Agnes
0 1 2 3 4 5 6 miles
0 1 2 3 4 5 6 7 8 9 10 km

Grid reference numbers

5 6 7 8 9

A B C D E F

Penhale Pt. HOLYWELL BAY FUN PARK Kestle Mill St Columb Road Indian Queens Trezaise Bugle

Holywell Carines St Newlyn East TRERICE Gummow's Shop St Enoder Fraddon St Dennis Hensbarrow Stenalees Penwithick

Ligger or Perran Bay Cubert LAPPA VALLEY STEAM RAILWAY DAIRY LAND FARM WORLD Penhale Whitemoor Downs CHINA CLAY Nanpean Carthew Trethurgy EDEN PROJECT

Rejerrah St Enoder Summercourt Treviscoe Foxhole WHEAL MARTYN CHINA CLAY HERI CENTRE Carclaze Boscoppa

Perran Sands Mount Rose PERRAN ROUND Newlyn Downs Mitchell Brighton Trethosa St Stephen High Street St Austell Holmbush

Perranporth PERRANPORTH Goonhavern MINIATURA PARK Carland Cross Trelassick St Stephen Trewoon ST AUSTELL HERITAGE Charlestown ST AUSTELL BREWERY

St Agnes Hd. Bolingey Perranzabuloe Trevellas Zelah St Allen Trispen St Erme New Mills Coombe St Mewan Sticker Polgooth Porthpean

St Agnes Mithian Callestick Marazanvose Ladock Grampound Road Hewas Water TORTOISE GARDEN Trenarren

Goonbell Allet Shortlanesend Tresillian Probus Grampound TREWITHEN Creed St Ewe Polmassick Pentewan THE LOST GARDENS OF HELIGAN Black Hd. Mevagissey Bay

Porthtowan Mount Hawke Three Burrows Blackwater Kenwyn Truro CATHEDRAL Merther Tresawle Kestle Gorran Churchtown Mevagissey

Portreath Mawla P&R Threemilestone ROYAL CORNWALL MUS St Clement Tregony Trevarrick Portmellon Chapel Pt.

TOLGUS MILL CORNISH GOLD Scorrier Chacewater Baldhu Kea Malpas Ruan Lanihorne Lamorran St Michael Caerhays Gorran Haven

PORTREATH Illogan CORNISH MINES & ENGINES St Day Twelve Heads Bissoe Playing Place Old Kea St Michael Penkevil Treworga Veryan Portholland Boswinger Penare

Roscroggan Redruth GWENNAP PIT Carharrack Carnon Downs Penpol Feock Trelissick Philleigh Treworlas Carne Dodman Pt.

CAMBORNE Pool Carn Brea Gwennap Devoran FERRY TRELISSICK Trelissick Phillelgh Gerrans Bay Portloe SOUTH WEST COAST PATH Veryan Bay

SHIRE HORSE FARM Troon Lanner Ponsanooth Burnthouse St Just in Roseland Trewithian Nare Hd.

Four Lanes Penhalvaen Stithians Mylor Bridge Gertans Portscatho

Burras Carnkie Stithians Res. Longdowns Mabe Burnthouse Flushing Penryn Falmouth Greeb Pt. Greeb Pt.

Penmarth Carnkie Rame ART GALLERY NATIONAL MARITIME St Mawes Zone Pt.

Releath Porkellis Treverva Budock Water PENDENNIS CASTLE Bohortha

Wendron Seworgan Penjerrick Pendennis Pt. Zone Pt.

POLDARK MINE Constantine Porth Navas Mawnan Smith Rosemullion Hd.

Helston Trewennack GLENDURGAN TREBAH Mawnan Falmouth Bay

FLAMBARDS EXPERIENCE Gweek NATIONAL SEAL SANCTUARY Helford Passage Helford River

Garras NATIONAL SEAL SANCTUARY Helford St Anthony-in-Meneage Nare Pt. SW

Berepper HALLIGGYE FOGOU TRELOWARREN Mawgan Manaccan SOUTH WEST COAST PATH

Gunwalloe Cury Cross Lanes St Martin Tregidden Porthallow CORNWALL

Mullion FUTUREWORLD @ GOONHILLY Newtown Traboe St Keverne Porthoustock Manacle Pt. The Manacles

Mullion Cove THE LIZARD Trelan Penhale Lowland Pt.

Mullion Island Gwenter Goonhilly Downs Coverack COVERACK Chynhalls Pt.

Predannack Wollas Kuggar Black Hd.

Vellan Hd. St Ruan Ryan Minor Cadgwith

Grade SOUTH WEST COAST PATH

Kynance Cove Lizard Hot Pt.

LIZARD POINT LIZARD

WORLD OF MODEL RAILWA

SOUTH WEST COAST PATH

CORNWALL
Tintagel Hd.
CASTLE
POST OFFICE
TINTAGEL
Start Pt.
SOUTH WEST COAST PATH
Port Isaac Bay
Port Isaac
Port Quin Bay
Port Quin
Port Gaverne
Pendoggett
Pentire Pt.
New Polzeath
Polzeath
Padstow Bay
LONG CROSS
Trelights
St Endellion
Trelill
Gulland Rock
Trebetherick
St Minver
Gunver Hd.
TREVOSE HEAD
Crugmeer
PRIDEAUX PLACE
Pityme
Trewethern
St Kew
Chapel Amble
St Kew Highway
Trevone
Rock
NATIONAL LOBSTER HATCHERY
Constantine Bay
Constantine Bay
TREYARNON
Treyarnon
St Merryn
Padstow
Camel
Bodieve
St Mabyn
Shop
Trevanson
Wadebridge
SOUTH WEST COAST PATH
Porthcothan
Little Petherick
Whitecross
St Breock
Egloshayle
PENCARROW HOUSE
St Issey
Park Hd.
Penrose
St Ervan
Rumford
Tredinnick
Burlawn
Washaway
St Jidgey
CREALY GREAT ADVENTURE PARK
ST BREOCK DOWNS MONOLITH
208
St Eval
Trenance
CORNISH BIRDS OF PREY CENTRE
SPIRIT OF THE WEST
Nanstallon
Berryl's Pt.
Trevarrian
St Mawgan
Rosenannon
Ruthernbridge
St Lawrence
Withiel
Talskiddy
WATERGATE BAY
St Wenn
Tregurrian
NEWQUAY
St Columb Major
Tregonetha
Lanivet
Towan Hd.
Newquay Bay
Fistral Bay
Porth
St Columb Minor
227
CASTLE AN DINAS
Belowda
Victoria
Pentire
NEWQUAY ZOO
Trebudannon
SPRINGFIELDS FUN PARK & PONY CENTRE
Kelsey Hd.
BLUE REEF AQUARIUM
Newquay
Quintrell Downs
Colan
Mountjoy
Ruthvoes
Tregoss
Lockengate
West Pentire
Crantock
Lane
Trevarren
GOSS MOOR
Roche
Bilberry
HOLYWELL BAY FUN PARK
Kestle Mill
St Columb Road
Indian Queens
Trezaise
Penhale Pt.
Holywell
Carines
DAIRY LAND FARM WORLD
Fraddon
Penhale
Bugle
TRERICE
St Dennis
Hensbarrow
Ligger or Perran Bay
Cubert
St Newlyn East
Gummow's Shop
St Enoder
Retew
Whitemoor
Downs
312
CHINA CLAY
Stenalees
Penhale Sands
Rejerrah
LAPPA VALLEY STEAM RAILWAY
Treviscoe
Nanpean
Penwithick
SOUTH WEST COAST PATH
Mount
Summercourt
Carthew
Rose
PERRAN ROUND
Newlyn Downs
Brighton
Trethosa
Foxhole
WHEAL MARTYN CHINA CLAY HERITAGE CENTRE
Trethurgy
Perranporth
EDEN PROJECT
PERRANPORTH
Goonhavern
MINIATURA PARK
Mitchell
High Street
Carclaze
Bolingey
Carland Cross
St Austell
Boscoppa
Perranzabuloe
Zelah
Trelassick
St Stephen
Holmbush
St Agnes Hd.
Trevellas
SW
New Mills
Coombe
Trewoon
St Agnes
Mithian
St Allen
St Erme
St Mewan
Charlestown
Callestick
Ladock
Grampound Road
ST AUSTELL BREWERY
192
Trispen
Polgooth
Porthpean
Goonbell
CORNISH CYDER FARM
Marazanvose
Sticker
Hewas Water
TORTOISE GARDEN
Allet
Trenarren
Mount Hawke
Probus
Grampound
TREWITHEN
Black Hd.
Porthtowan
Shortlanesend
Pentewan
Three Burrows
Tresillian
THE LOST GARDENS OF HELIGAN
Mevagissey Bay
Blackwater
P&R
Creed
St Ewe
Portreath
Mawla
Truro
Kenwyn
Tresawle
Polmassick
Kestle
WORLD OF MODEL RAILWAYS
TOLGUS MILL
CORNISH GOLD
CATHEDRAL
Merther
Mevagissey
PORTREATH
Scorrier
Threemilestone
Tregony
Illogan
Chacewater
ROYAL CORNWALL MUS
Portmellon
CORNISH MINES & ENGINES
St Day
Baldhu
Truro
Kea
St Clement
Trevarrick
Chapel Pt.
Twelve Heads
Ruan Lanihorne
St Michael Caerhays
Gorran Churchtown
Redruth
Bissoe
Malpas
Pool
225
Cambrea
Carharrack
Playing Place
St Michael Penkevil
Lamorran
Gorran Haven
Tuckingmill
Carnkie
GWENNAP PIT
Carnon Downs
Old Kea
Portholland
Boswinger
BOSWINGER
CAMBORNE
Gwennap
Treworga
Penare
Lanner
Penpol
Trelissick
Philleigh
Veryan Bay
114
SHIRE HORSE FARM
Four Lanes
Perranarwothal
Veryan
Portloe
Dodman Pt.
Troon
Devoran
Feock
TRELISSICK
SOUTH WEST COAST PATH
Ponsanooth
Treworlas
Carne
Penhalvaen
Gerrans Bay
252
Stithians
Burnthouse
Mylor Bridge
Trewithian
Nare Hd.
Stithians Res.
St Just in Roseland
Carrick Roads
Penmarth
Burras
Gerrans
Portscatho
Crowan
Carnkie
Penryn
Flushing
Greeb Pt.
St Mawes
Falmouth
NATIONAL MARITIME
Bohortha
PENDENNIS CASTLE
Pendennis Pt.
Zone Pt.
Wendron
Seworgan
Treverva
Crowntown
Nancegollan
Releath
0 1 2 3 4 5 6 miles
0 1 2 3 4 5 6 7 8 9 10 km
A30
A39
A392
A389
A391
A390
A3058
A3059
A3075
A3076
A3078
A393
A394
A3047
B3276
B3274
B3314
B3267
B3275
B3279
B3285
B3284
B3277
B3298
B3287
B3273
B3289
B3291
B3297
B3280
B3303
B3301

BODMIN MOOR

TAMAR VALLEY

Launceston
Bodmin
Camelford
Liskeard
Saltash
Torpoint
Devonport
Looe
Fowey
Lostwithiel

Tintagel
Treknow
Trewarmett
Trebarwith
Treligga
Delabole
Valley Truckle
Helstone
St Teath
Treveighan
Michaelstow
St Tudy
St Breward
Row
Wenfordbridge
Blisland
Helland
Bodmin Forest
Cardinham
Warleggan
Mount
St Neot
Ley
Millpool
Maidenwell
Bradford
Temple
Colliford Lake
Dozmary Pool
Brown Willy
Garrow Tor
Kilmar Tor
Codda
Bolventor
High Moor
Altarnun
Trewint
Davidstow
Crowdy Res.
Hallworthy
Trewassa
Tremail
Cold Northcott
Laneast
St Clether
Polyphant
Lewannick
Congdon's Shop
Trebartha
North Hill
Henwood
Rilla Mill
Upton Cross
Minions
Caradon Hill
Darite
Tremar
St Cleer
Commonmoor
Golitha Falls
Siblyback Lake
The Hurlers Stone Circles
King Doniert's Circles
Trethevy Quoit
Carnglaze Slate Caverns
Dobwalls
Doublebois
St Pinnock
Liskeard
Merrymeet
Pensilva
St Ive
Gang
Newbridge
Callington
Kelly Bray
Golberdon
Haye
Trevigro
Kit Hill
St Ann's Chapel
Gunnislake
Chilsworthy
Luckett
Latchley
Downgate
South Hill
Linkinhorne
Stoke Climsland
Bray Shop
Coad's Green
Trebullett
Treburley
Rezare
Dunterton
Sydenham Damerel
Horsebridge
Milton Abbot
Lezant
Lawhitton
Kelly
Bradstone
South Petherwin
Launceston
Dutson
Liftondown
Lifton
Tinhay
Portgate
Chillaton
Stowford
Thrushelton
Broadwoodwidger
Cross Green
Werrington
North Petherwin
Yeolmbridge
St Stephen's
Egloskerry
Langore
Daw's House
Tregadillett
Piper's Pool
Trewen
Tresmeer
Tregeare
Treneglos
Tremaine
St Dominick
Cotehele
Calstock
Bere Alston
Cargreen
Landulph
Botusfleming
Saltash
St Stephens
St Germans
Tideford
Trematon
Landrake
Hatt
Pillaton
Quethiock
Menheniot
Tideford Cross
Blunts
St Mellion
Pengover Green
Trewidland
St Keyne
Duloe
Herodsfoot
Sandplace
Morval
Widegates
Hessenford
Polbathic
Sheviock
Crafthole
Portwrinkle
Downderry
Seaton
St Martin
East Looe
West Looe
Looe
Polperro
Porthallow
Talland Bay
Polruan
Fowey
Bodinnick
Lansallos
Lanteglos Highway
Trenewan
Pelynt
Muchlarnick
Lanreath
Bocaddon
Lanreath
Couch's Mill
Milltown
East Taphouse
West Taphouse
Braddock
Lerryn
St Veep
Penpoll
Golant
Tywardreath
Par
St Blazey
Penpillick
St Austell Bay
Gribbin Hd.
Menabilly
Polkerris
Luxulyan
Lanlivery
Sweethouse
Redmoor
Trebyan
Lanhydrock House
Restormel Castle
Bodmin
Torpoint
Antony
St John
Freathy
Whitsand Bay
Millbrook
Kingsand
Cawsand
Rame
Rame Hd.
Penlee Pt.
Devonport
Cremyll
Mount Edgcumbe

ROSCOFF 6:00
SANTANDER 20:00
(Mar-Nov)

DARTMOOR

DARTMOOR NATIONAL FOREST PARK

Broadwoodwidger, Bridestowe, BLACK-A-TOR COPSE, HIGH WILLHAYS, Gidleigh, Murchington, Easton, Sandypark, Teign

Cross Green, Thrushelton, Lewdown, Shortacombe, OKEMENT HILL, Teigncombe, Chagford

Stowford, 262, 585, HANGINGSTONE HILL, Frenchbeer, Lettaford

DINGLE'S FAIRGROUND HERITAGE CENTRE, Lewtrenchard, Lydford, LYDFORD, SITTAFORD TOR, THE MINIATURE PONY CENTRE, North Bovey

LAUNCESTON STEAM RAILWAY, Liftondown, Portgate, Coryton, LYDFORD GORGE, CUT HILL, Widecombe in the Moor, HOUND TOR, Bonehill

Lifton, Tinhay, Chillaton, North Brentor, Willsworthy, 604, 537, GRIMSPOUND, 529, HAMELDOWN TOR, B3387

Lawhitton, Kelly, Mary Tavy, Horndon, POSTBRIDGE INFORMATION CENTRE, Postbridge, RIPPON TOR, 473

Bradstone, Milton Abbot, Cudliptown, 546, ROUGH TOR, Bellever, 431, Ponsworthy

Dunterton, Lamerton, Peter Tavy, 539, GT. MIS TOR, BELLEVER (Dartmoor), WISTMAN'S WOOD, E. Dart

Trekenner, Rezare, Wilminstone, Merrivale, PREHISTORIC SETTLEMENT, Two Bridges, Dartmeet, Buckland in the Moor

Sydenham Damerel, Horsebridge, Whitchurch, Rundlestone, HIGH MOORLAND VISITOR CENTRE, Princetown, Hexworthy, Poundsgate

Stoke Climsland, Luckett, Latchley, Tavistock, Grenofen, Sampford Spiney, Whiteworks, Holne, RIVER DART ADVENTURES

Downgate, Chilsworthy, Gunnislake, St Ann's Chapel, Higher Walreddon, Walkhampton, 515, RYDER'S HILL, BUCKFAST ABBEY, Buckfast

Kelly Bray, KIT HILL, Drakewalls, Horrabridge, Buckland Monachorum, PAPERWEIGHT CENTRE, Dousland, Sheepstor, Burrator Res., Buckfastleigh

Callington, Harrowbarrow, Calstock, THE GARDEN HOUSE, Crapstone, Yelverton, Meavy, 493, Dean

DUPATH WELL HOUSE, COTEHELE, St Dominick, BUCKLAND ABBEY, Milton Combe, Clearbrook, UPPER PLYM VALLEY, 475, SHELL TOP, Dean Prior

Newbridge, St Mellion, Bere Alston, Lopwell, Shaugh Prior, DENDLES WOOD, 464, Didworthy, PENNYWELL FARM & WILDLIFE CENTRE

TAMAR VALLEY, Weir Quay, Tamerton Foliot, Bickleigh, Wotter, Lee Moor, 311, Rattery

Pillaton, Cargreen, Roborough, Cornwood, South Brent, 371, Lincombe

Hatt, Landulph, SALTASH SERVICES, CROWNHILL FORT, PLYMOUTH CITY, Plym Forest, Drakeland Corner, Lutton, Harford, UGBOROUGH BEACON, Avonwick

Botusfleming, Tideford, Trematon, Saltash, St Budeaux, Eggbuckland, Sparkwell, Bittaford, Diptford

St Erney, St Stephens, MARY NEWMAN'S COTTAGE, PLYM VALLEY RAILWAY, Lee Mill, Ivybridge, Ugborough, North Huish

St Germans, ANTONY HOUSE, MERCHANT'S HOUSE, Plympton, Westlake, Curtisknowle

Sheviock, Torpoint, Devonport, Plymouth, SALTRAM, ROYAL CITADEL, Ermington, Modbury, Brownston

Crafthole, Antony, Cremyll, MOUNT EDGCUMBE, Plymstock, Elburton, Brixton, Yealmpton, Loddiswell, Woodleigh

Portwrinkle, St John, Millbrook, Hooe, Down Thomas, Knighton, Battisborough Cross, St Ann's Chapel, Aveton Gifford

SOUTH WEST COAST PATH, Freathy, Kingsand, Staddiscombe, Wembury, Newton Ferrers, Mothecombe, Bigbury, SORLEY TUNNEL ADVENTURE WORLDS

Whitsand Bay, Cawsand, Rame, The Sound, Bovisand Bay, Heybrook Bay, Wembury Bay, Noss Mayo, Kingston, Ringmore, West Alvington, Churchstow

Rame Hd., Penlee Pt., Great Mew Stone, Worswell, Stoke Pt., Bigbury on Sea, Burgh I., Bantham, Buckland, South Milton, Kingsbridge

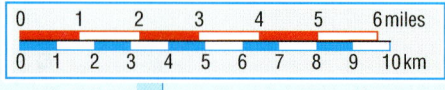

ROSCOFF 6:00, SANTANDER 20:00 (Mar-Nov), SOUTH WEST COAST PATH, BIGBURY BAY, Thurlestone, Woolston

Galmpton, Hope, Bolt Tail, Bolberry, Soar, Malborough, Salcombe, East Portlemouth

SOUTH, Bolt Hd., OVERBECKS MUSEUM & GARDEN

0 1 2 3 4 5 6 miles
0 1 2 3 4 5 6 7 8 9 10km

Dunsford Shillingford St George Topsham Clyst St George Salterton Newton Poppleford Sidmouth

Doccombe 315 Bridfordmills Exminster Ebford Woodbury wkerland Colaton Raleigh Cotmaton

Moretonhampstead Bridford Christow Doddiscombsleigh Kennford Exton BICTON PARK Yettington Otterton OTTERTON MILL

Higher Ashton Kenn Powderham BLACK HILL 167 East Budleigh Ladram Bay

Lustleigh Lower Ashton Kenton Lympstone Withycombe Raleigh Knowle Budleigh Salterton Danger Pt.

Manaton Hennock Trusham POWDERHAM CASTLE Starcross A-LA-RONDE Littleham FAIRLYNCH ARTS CENTRE AND MUSEUM

Water EAST DARTMOOR WOODS & HEATHS Cockwood Exmouth WORLD OF COUNTRY LIFE

Bovey Tracey Ashcombe DAWLISH WARREN EXMOUTH MODEL RAILWAY Straight Pt.

HAYTOR INFORMATION CENTRE Chudleigh Knighton IGBROOKE HOUSE Dawlish Warren

Haytor Vale Brimley Ilsington CRAFT CENTRE Ideford Luton Little Haldon Dawlish

Liverton Coldeast STOVER TRAGO MILLS Preston Holcombe 247

Sigford Bickington Teigngrace Bishopsteignton Teignmouth

Kingsteignton Highweek NEWTON ABBOT BRADLEY Sheldon SHALDON WILDLIFE TRUST

Ashburton West Ogwell Wolborough Combeinteignhead Netherton SOUTH WEST COAST PATH

Woodland East Ogwell PRICKLY BALL HEDGEHOG HOSPITAL Abbotskerswell Stokeinteignhead

Forder Grn. Denbury DECOY PLANT WORLD Coffinswell Maidencombe BABBACOMBE BAY

Landscove Torbryan Ipplepen Kingskerswell Watcombe SX SY

BUCKFAST BUTTERFLIES & DARTMOOR OTTER SANCTUARY North Whilborough Barton Babbacombe MODEL VILLAGE

Staverton Broadhempston Shiphay Torquay KENT'S CAVERN PREHISTORIC CAVES

Dartington Compton COMPTON CASTLE Cockington TORRE ABBEY Wellswood Hope's Nose

DARTINGTON CIDER PRESS CENTRE Shinner's Bridge DARTINGTON HALL Marldon OLDWAY MANSION LIVING COASTS

Cott BERRY POMEROY CASTLE Hollicombe

Totnes SOUTH DEVON RAILWAY Blagdon Torbay Paignton

Tigley CASTLE Berry Pomeroy KIRKHAM PAIGNTON & DARTMOUTH STEAM RAILWAY

Belsford Collaton St Mary ZOO TORBAY TOR BAY

Harberton Ashprington Goodrington GOLDEN HIND Brixham BERRY HEAD

Harbertonford Tuckenhay Stoke Gabriel Churston Ferrers Berry Head BERRY HEAD

Crabadon Washbourne Cornworthy Galmpton St Mary's Bay

Halwell Allaleigh Dittisham Capton RIVER DART Sharkham Pt.

Moreleigh WOODLANDS LEISURE PARK Hillhead

Woodford Blackawton Dartmouth NEWCOMEN ENGINE HOUSE Scabbacombe Hd.

Millcombe Ferry Kingswear COLETON FISHACRE

East Allington BAYARDS COVE FORT Warfleet DARTMOUTH CASTLE Mew Stone

Bowden Stoke Fleming

Goveton Strete Blackpool

Harleston SOUTH WEST COAST PATH

Sherford Slapton

Frogmore SLAPTON LEY Slapton Sands

Charleston Chillington Stokenham

Kernborough Torcross DEVON

South Pool Beeson

Kellaton Beesands

Hallsands

South Allington START POINT

East Prawle Lannacombe Bay

Prawle Pt.

Rivers: Exe, Teign, Dart, Kenn

Roads: A382, A38, A380, A379, A381, A383, A385, A384, A3022, A3121, A376, A381

1
2
3
4
5
A
B
C
D
E
F
NORTH
BIDEFORD
HARTLAND POINT
Windbury Pt.
Titchberry
HARTLAND ABBEY
Stoke
Hartland Quay
Hartland
CLOVELLY VILLAGE
Clovelly
Higher Clovelly
SOUTH WEST COAST PATH
DOCTON MILL
Philham
Milford
Eddistone
ELMSCOTT
Elmscott
Tosberry
THE MILKY WAY ADVENTURE PARK
Buck's Cross
Woolfardisworthy
South Hole
Hartland Forest
Alminstone Cross
Knaps Longpeak
Welcombe
235
Meddon
Ashmansworthy
Woolley
Gooseham
156
Eastcott
Youlstone
Morwenstow
Dinworthy
Higher Sharpnose Pt.
Shop
A39
Woodford
Bradworthy
BROCKLANDS ADVENTURE PARK
Bradworthy Cross
Lower Sharpnose Pt.
14
Alfardisworthy
Coombe
Kilkhampton
Sutcombe
Stibb
Soldon Cross
Strat
CORNWALL
BUDE
Poughill
DUNSDON
Flexbury
Hersham
Grimscott
Bude Haven
1643
Stratton
Chilsworthy
Bude
A3072
Pancrasweek
BAY
Launcells
9
Tamar
Holsworthy
SS
Upton
B3254
Derril
Marhamchurch
Bridgerule
Derriton
Widemouth Bay
Pyworthy
162
Chasty
Widemouth Sand
Budd's Titson
Leworthy
Coppathorne
Millook
Dizzard Pt.
Poundstock
Whitstone
SOUTH WEST COAST PATH
Treskinnick Cross
Tregole
St Gennys
Week St Mary
North Tamerton
Trewint
Deer
Claw
PENHALLAM
Cambeak
Crackington Haven
Rosecare
Tetcott
Jacobstow
Lana
Wainhouse Corner
SX
Luffincott
Tresparrett Posts
West Curry
B3263
South Wheatley
Fire Beacon Pt.
260
A39
Beeny
Maxworthy
Marshgate
Bennacott
Northcott
Tresparrett
Boyton
BOSCASTLE
Canworthy Water
Brazacott
Boscastle
Otterham
256
Lesnewth
Warbstow
TAMAR OTTER & WILDLIFE CENTRE
Trevalga
Trelash
Langdon
CASTLE
Tintagel Hd.
Tremaine
Ottery
Bridgetown
OLD POST OFFICE
Bossiney
North Petherwin
TINTAGEL
B3266
B3262
Tintagel
Hallworthy
Treneglos
Werrington
Yeolmbridge
308
Treknow
Davidstow
Tresmeer
Trewarmett
13
Egloskerry
Langore
B3263
Tremail
Trewassa
THE ARTHURIAN CENTRE
Tregeare
St Stephen's
Dutson
Start Pt.
Davidstow Moor
Cold Northcott
Trebarwith
CORNWALL AT WAR
B3314
A395
Piper's Pool
HIDDEN VALLEY DISCOVERY PARK
Treligga
Launceston
SOUTH WEST COAST PATH
Tregadillett
A30
CASTLE
Delabole
St Clether
Laneast
Camelford
Trewen
Valley Truckle
Crowdy Res.
TRETHORNE LEISURE FARM
Daw's House
B3254
Port Isaac Bay
A388
B3314
B3267
Polyphant
70
South Petherwin
Helstone
Inny
Port Quin Bay
Port Isaac
High Moor
Altarnun
Lewannick
Port Quin
400 ROUGH TOR
Port Gaverne
B3267
St Teath
Trewint
B3257
LONG CROSS
Pendoggett
5
420 BROWN WILLY
A30
Trelights
5
Lezant
Polzeath
369
Michaelstow
Congdon's Shop
Trekenner
331 GARROW TOR
Codda
St Breward
BODMIN
Trebartha
Trebullett
MUSEUM OF SMUGGLING
Coad's Green
Treburley
18
Bolventor
North Hill
St Kew
Chapel Amble
MOOR
B3254
B3257
0 1 2 3 4 5 6 miles
0 1 2 3 4 5 6 7 8 9 10 km

Barnstaple

LUNDY 2:00
Braunton Burrows
Chivenor
Goodleigh
Brayford
High Bray
North Heasley
Gunn
Charles
Heasley Mill
South Radwort

Pilt
MUSEUM OF NORTH DEVON
Westacott
West Buckland
East Buckland
North Molton

Fremington
Yelland
Bickington
Newport
Landkey
Swimbridge Newland
NORTH DEVON FARM PARK
Swimbridge
Filleigh

NORTH DEVON MARITIME MUSEUM
Instow
Bishops Tawton
QUINCE HONEY FARM
Mole
Yeo

Appledore
NORTHAM BURROWS
Tawstock
Herner
Cobbaton
East Stowford
COBBATON COMBAT COLL
Chittlehampton
South Molton
Bish Mill

Westward Ho!
Northam
Orchard Hill
Westleigh
Horwood
Newton Tracey
Ensis
Chapelton
Fishleigh Barton
Clapworthy
Bishops Nympton

THE BIG SHEEP
Bideford
East-the-Water
Handy Cross
Eastleigh
Hiscott
Umberleigh
Warkleigh
Satterleigh
Chittlehamholt
George Nympton
Alswear
Marian

Abbotsham
Buck's Mills
Horns Cross
Ford
Woodtown
Landcross
BURTON ART GALL & MUS
ATLANTIC VILLAGE
Alverdiscott
Yarnscombe
Atherington
High Bickington
King's Nympton
Romansleigh

Fairy Cross
Goldworthy
Parkham
Monkleigh
Weare Giffard
Langridge Ford
Sherwood Green
Week

Parkham Ash
Buckland Brewer
Frithelstock
DARTINGTON CRYSTAL
High Bullen
St Giles in the Wood
Burrington
Elstone
Cadbury Barton

West Putford
East Putford
Tythecott
Frithelstock Stone
Taddiport
Great Torrington
Kingscott
Roborough
Ashreigney
Chulmleigh
Cheldon
West Worling

Langtree
R.H.S. GARDEN ROSEMOOR
Little Torrington
Beaford
Riddlecombe
Chawleigh

Bulkworthy
Stibb Cross
Peters Marland
Woollaton
Winswell
Merton
Huish
Dolton
Hollocombe
Ashley
Filleigh
Easting

Abbots Bickington
Newton St Petrock
Buckland Filleigh
Petrockstow
Meeth
Dowland
Winkleigh
Wembworthy
Lapford

Venn Green
Milton Damerel
Shebbear
Bradford
Iddesleigh
Broadwood Kelly
Coldridge
Nymet Rowland
Nymet

Holsworthy Beacon
Thornbury
Sheepwash
Monkokehampton
Bondleigh
West Leigh
East Leigh
Zeal Monachorum
Down St Mary

Woodacott
Cookbury
Black Torrington
Holemoor
Highampton
Hatherleigh
Honeychurch
North Tawton
Bow
Colel

Whimble
Hollacombe
Brandis Corner
Chilla
Graddon Moor
WINSFORD WALLED GARDEN
Exbourne
Jacobstowe
Sampford Courtenay
Nymet Tracey
Colebro

Clawton
Quoditch
Halwill Junction
Beaworthy
Northlew
Inwardleigh
DARTMOOR RAILWAY
Itton
Spreyton
Hillerton

Ashwater
Henford
Halwill
Patchacott
Ashbury
Oak Cross
Taw Green
Ettisleigh

Chapmans Well
Virginstow
Germansweek
Boasley Cross
Thorndon Cross
Folly Gate
Okehampton
Sticklepath
FINCH FOUNDRY
South Tawton
South Zeal
Whiddon Down
Cheriton Bis

East Panson
St Giles on the Hth.
Grinacombe Moor
Bratton Clovelly
SOURTON CROSS SERVICES
CASTLE
OKEHAMPTON (Dartmoor)
Okehampton Camp
BRACKEN TOR
Belstone
Drewsteignton

Gridley Corner
Broadwoodwidger
Eworthy
Meldon
Okehampton Common
COSDON HILL
Throwleigh
Wonson
CASTLE DROGO
Sandypark
Easton

Stowford
BLACK-A-TOR COPSE
YES TOR
HIGH WILLHAYS
Bridestowe and Sourton Common
Gidleigh
Murchington
Chagford

Cross Green
DINGLE'S FAIRGROUND HERITAGE CENTRE
Thrushelton
Bridestowe
Sourton
Teigncombe
Frenchbeer

Liftondown
Lifton
Tinhay
Portgate
Lewdown
Shortacombe
DARTMOOR NATIONAL PARK
OKEMENT HILL
HANGINGSTONE HILL
SITTAFORD TOR
Teigncombe
THE MINIATURE PONY CENTRE

Lawhitton
Kelly
Bradstone
Coryton
LYDFORD
LYDFORD GORGE
Willsworthy
Black Down
CUT HILL
Lettaford
North Bovey

North Brentor
DARTMOOR FOREST
GRIMSPOUND
HAMELDOWN TOR
Manaton

Milton Abbot
Dunterton
Mary Tavy
Horndon
Cudliptown
ROUGH TOR
POSTBRIDGE INFORMATION CENTRE
Postbridge
Widecombe in the Moor
HOUND TOR

Rezare
Sydenham Damerel
Lamerton
Wilmington
Peter Tavy
Merrivale
GT. MIS TOR
WISTMAN'S WOOD
CLEAVE (Dartmoor)
Bellever
Haytor V

PREHISTORIC SETTLEMENT
Merrivale
Bonel

Barnstaple Bay
DEVON
Torridge
Taw
A39
A361
A377
A386
A388
A3072
A3079
A30
A3124
B3232
B3217
B3227
B3226
B3096
B3042
B3220
B3215
B3212
B3206
B3387

1   2   3   4   5

A West Buckland · East Buckland · Charles · High Bray · Brayford · Radworthy · North Heasley · Heasley Mill · South Radworthy · Winsford · Liscombe · Bridgetown · Exton · Withiel Florey · B3224

B 21 · Filleigh · ast Stowford · QUINCE HONEY FARM · South Molton · B3226 · B3227 · Clapworthy · 173 · Satterleigh · tlehamholt · Bish Mill · Bishops Nympton · Newtown · Alswear · George Nympton · Ash Mill · Mariansleigh · Rose Ash · Knowstone · 17 · Molland · West Anstey · East Anstey · Twitchen · Molland Common · Anstey Common · Dane's Brook · Tarr Steps · Hawkridge · Dulverton · Nightcott · Battleton · Brushford · Oldways End · Exebridge · Bampton · Morebath · Bury · Skilgate · Brompton Regis · HADDON HILL · 355 · Cove · Petton · Shillingford · Clayhanger · Huish Champflower · HEYDON HILL 338 · Chipstable · Upton · Wimbleball Lake · B3227 · 267 · A396

C King's Nympton · Cadbury · 9 · Elstone · Chulmleigh · B3096 · B3042 · Cheldon · West Worlington · East Worlington · Drayton · Thelbridge Barton · Chawleigh · Meshaw · 238 · Creacombe · Rackenford · Witheridge · Nomansland · SS · Templeton Bridge · Templeton · B3137 · Cruwys Morchard · Withleigh · Loxbeare · 60 · Washfield · Calverleigh · Bolham · KNIGHTSHAYES COURT · TIVERTON CASTLE · Tiverton · Cowleymoor · GRAND WESTERN CANAL · Cotteylands · 23 · Chevithorne · East Mere · Uploman · Whitnage · Halberton · Sampford Peverell · A361 · 28

D Coldridge · B3220 · Brushford · West Leigh · East Leigh · Zeal Monachorum · Nymet Rowland · Lapford · A377 · Morchard Bishop · 174 · Oldborough · Kennerleigh · Ash Bullayne · Down St Mary · Newbuildings · Copplestone · Sandford · East Village · Stockleigh English · Cheriton Fitzpaine · East Village · Upton Hellions · Stockleigh Pomeroy · Cadeleigh · Butterleigh · BICKLEIGH MILL · Bickleigh · BICKLEIGH CASTLE · DEVON RAILWAY CENTRE · FURSDON HOUSE · Cadbury · 8 · Thorverton · Up Exe · Silverton · Hele · V · Ellerhayes · Nether Exe · Rewe · Budlake · Westwood · Colebrook · Bradninch · 261 · Mutterton · Westcott · Clyst Hydon · Langford · B3181 · 164 · Clyst St Lawrence · Cullompton · CULLOMPTON SERVICES · DIGGERLAND · A373 · Willand · S · A361 · M5

E North Tawton · A3072 · Itton · Bow · Nymet Tracey · Colebrooke · Yeoford · Hillerton · Knowle · Coleford · Crediton · THE COLLEGIATE CHURCH OF THE HOLY CROSS · Shobrooke · Efford Shute · Brampford Speke · Stoke Canon · Poltimore · Pinhoe · Dog Village · Whimple · Jack in the Green · Rockbeare · Spreyton · Hittisleigh · Tedburn St Mary · Whitestone · Venny Tedburn · Hookway · Newton St Cyres · Upton Pyne · Cowley · A377 · Exwick · Whipton · EXETER · Clyst Honiton · EXETER INTERNATIONAL · A30 · Marsh Green · SX · 70 · Longdown · B3212 · Wheatley · St Thomas · Ide · CATHEDRAL · Heavitree · EXETER SERVICES · Sowton · Clyst St Mary · 29 · 30 · Farringdon · Aylesbeare · South Tawton · South Zeal · Whiddon Down · 9 · A30 · Cheriton Bishop · Crockernwell · A382

F South Zeal · Throwleigh · Gidleigh · Wonson · Murchington · Drewsteignton · CASTLE DROGO · Sandypark · Easton · Teign · Dunsford · B3193 · Bridfordmills · Shillingford St George · Alphington · P&R · COUNTESS WEAR · ADVENTURE PARK · Topsham · MUS. · Clyst St George · Woodbury Salterton · Ebford · Woodbury · A376 · Exton · BLACK HILL 167 · Teigncombe · Frenchbeer · Chagford · 356 · Doccombe · 315 · Bridford · Christow · Higher Ashton · Lower Ashton · Doddiscombsleigh · Kenn · Kennford · Exminster · Powderham · POWDERHAM CASTLE · Kenton · Starcross · Lympstone · A LA RONDE · Withycombe Raleigh · B3178 · THE MINIATURE PONY CENTRE · Lettaford · North Bovey · Moretonhampstead · B3212 · 40 · 31 · Exe River · 70 · 10 · 30 · Exmouth · 30 · A380

GRIMSPOUND · 529 · HAMELDOWN TOR · Manaton · Lustleigh · Water · Bovey · EAST DARTMOOR HEATHS · 7 · Hennock · Bovey Tracey · Chudleigh · Chudleigh Knighton · Trusham · CANONTEIGN FALLS · A38 · EXETER · A38 · Ashcombe · Cockwood · 7 · DAWLISH WARREN · EXMOUTH MODEL RAILWAY · Exmouth · Straight Pt. · Littleham · B3192

Postbridge · B3212 · B338 · Brimley · HAYTOR INFORMATION CENTRE · Ilsington · Heathfield · Luton · Ideford · Little Haldon · Dawlish Warren · Dawlish · DAWLISH WARREN

0 1 2 3 4 5 6 miles
0 1 2 3 4 5 6 7 8 9 10 km

VALE OF TAUNTON DEANE

BLACKDOWN HILLS

BLACKDOWN HILLS

EAST DEVON

Taunton

Wellington

Wiveliscombe

Honiton

Axminster

Chard

Crewkerne

Ilminster

South Petherton

Merriott

Ottery St Mary

Sidmouth

Budleigh Salterton

Seaton

Beer

Lyme Regis

Charmouth

Bridport

Langport

Wrantage

Curry Rivel

LYME BAY

South West Coast Path

A303 A30 A35 A358 A38 A361 A372 A378 M5

5 6 7 8 9

A B C D E F G

King's Sedge Moor
SOMERSET LEVELS
Middlezoy
Othery
Pathe
High Ham
Henley
Dundon
Compton Dundon
Butleigh
Baltonsborough
Southwood
Barton St David
West Lydford
East Lydford
Hornblotton Green
Sutton
Alford
Lovington
Ansford
Castle Cary
Cole
Pitcombe
Redlynch
Hardway
Stoney Stoke
ALFRED'S TOWER
Shepton Montague
HADSPEN GARDEN
Bratton Seymour
Charlton Musgrove
Leigh Common
Bayford
Wincanton
Stoke Trister
Yarlington
Galhampton
Keinton Mandeville
Lydford-on-Fosse
Kingweston
Littleton
Somerton
Charlton Adam
Charlton Mackerell
Babcary
North Barrow
South Barrow
HAYNES MOTOR MUS
North Cadbury
Holton
Maperton
Lattiford
North Cheriton
South Cheriton
Horsington
Sparkford
Cary Fitzpaine
LYTES CARY MANOR
Kingsdon
STEMP
TOWER MILL
Low Ham
Pitney
Aller
Burrowbridge
Stathe
Athelney
Stoke St Gregory
West Sedge Moor
Langport
LANGPORT & R PARRETT VISITOR CENTRE
Huish Episcopi
Long Sutton
Muchelney
Curry Rivel
Drayton
ABBEY
Fivehead
Isle Brewers
Isle Abbotts
Hambridge
Kingsbury Episcopi
Long Load
Stapleton
Ash
Coat
Martock
TREASURER'S HO
Westport
East Lambrook
West Lambrook
E. LAMBROOK MANOR
BARRINGTON COURT
Barrington
South Petherton
Bower Hinton
Hurst
Stoke sub Hamdon
STOKE-SUB-HAMDON PRIORY
Montacute
MONTACUTE HOUSE
Tintinhull
TINTINHULL GARDEN
Chilthorne Domer
Ilchester
Yeovilton
FLEET AIR ARM MUS
Limington
Podimore
Northover
Bridgehampton
West Camel
Queen Camel
Chilton Cantelo
Ashington
Marston Magna
Sutton Montis
South Cadbury
Compton Pauncefoot
Blackford
Corton Denham
Charlton Horethorne
Abbas Combe
Templecombe
Yenston
Henstridge
Henstridge Marsh
Henstridge Ash
Stowell
Milborne Wick
Milborne Port
Stalbridge
Purse Caundle
Stalbridge Weston
Stourton Caundle
Bishop's Caundle
Lydlinch
Rimpton
SANDFORD ORCAS MANOR HOUSE
Sandford Orcas
Adber
Mudford
Trent
Nether Compton
Over Compton
Poyntington
Oborne
SHERBORNE OLD CASTLE
Goathill
Sherborne
SHERBORNE CASTLE
North Wootton
Haydon
Alweston
Folke
Longburton
Yeovil Marsh
Yeovil
YEOVIL
Preston Plucknett
Brympton
Odcombe
HAM HILL
Norton sub Hamdon
Chiselborough
West Chinnock
West Coker
North Coker
East Coker
Barwick
Stoford
Bradford Abbas
Thornford
Lillington
Ryme Intrinseca
Beer Hackett
Yetminster
East Chinnock
HARDINGTON MOOR
Hardington Mandeville
Closworth
Haselbury Plucknett
Ilminster
Donyatt
PERRYS CIDER
Kingstone
Dowlish Wake
Cricket Malherbie
Hinton St George
Dinnington
Seavington St Mary
Seavington St Michael
Over Stratton
Lopen
Merriott
Chillington
Cudworth
HORNSBURY MILL
Chaffcombe
Cricket St Thomas
WILDLIFE PARK
Crewkerne
Hewish
Misterton
North Perrott
Hardington Marsh
Pendomer
Puckington
Ilton
Stocklinch
Ashwell
Shepton Beauchamp
Holnest
Holwell
King's Stag
Woodbridge
Crouch Hill
Glanvilles Wootton
Pulham
Hazelbury Bryan
Leigh
Chetnole
Hermitage
Middlemarsh
Westfields
Mappowder
Dunttish
Whatley
Winsham
Wayford
Clapton
Seaborough
South Perrott
Halstock
Melbury Osmond
Melbury Sampford
West Chelborough
Corscombe
Mosterton
Chedington
Drimpton
Evershot
Melbury Bubb
Hilfield
Lyon's Gate
Buckland Newton
Minterne Magna
MINTERNE HOUSE & GARDENS
Batcombe
Holywell
Frome St Quintin
Up Cerne
Alton Pancras
Plush
Up Sydling
CERNE ABBAS GIANT
Cerne Abbas
Chard
FORDE ABBEY AND GARDENS
Thorncombe
Holditch
Burstock
Broadwindsor
THE CRAFT AND DESIGN CENTRE
HOLM PARK
Birdsmoorgate
Beaminster
Rampisham
Hawkchurch
Marshalsea
Bettiscombe
Stoke Abbott
Netherbury
Marshwood
Pilsdon
Mapperton
MAPPERTON
Hooke
Wraxall
Cattistock
Chilfrome
Toller Porcorum
Maiden Newton
Sydling St Nicholas
Nether Cerne
Godmanstone
Piddletrenthide
White Lackington
Piddlehinton
Melplash
North Poorton
Toller Fratrum
HOG CLIFF
Wootton Fitzpaine
Whitchurch Canonicorum
Ryall
Broad Oak
Salwayash
Dottery
West Milton
Powerstock
Nettlecombe
Eggardon Down
Wynford Eagle
Frampton
Forston
Charlton Down
Grimstone
Stratton
Muckleford
Charminster
HARDY'S COTTAGE GARDEN
Stinsford
Kingston Maurward
Morcombelake
Charmouth
CHARMOUTH HERITAGE COAST CENTRE
Symondsbury
Bridport
Bradpole
Loders
Uploders
D O R S E T
Dorset
West Compton
Askerswell
Compton Valence
Bradford Peverell
Dorchester
THE TUTANKHAMUN EXHIBITION
Lyme Regis
AQUARIUM
DINOSAURLAND
Chideock
Seatown
Eype
SOUTH WEST COAST PATH
West Bay
Walditch
Bothenhampton
Shipton Gorge
Chilcombe
Litton Cheney
LITTON CHENEY
Kingston Russell
Long Bredy
POOR LOT BARROWS
Winterbourne Abbas
NINE STONES
MILITARY MUSEUM
THE DINOSAUR MUSEUM
West Stafford
Whitcombe
Winterborne Herringston
West Knighton
Broadmayne
Winterbourne Steepleton
Martinstown
MAIDEN CASTLE
Winterborne Monkton
Black Down
HARDY MONUMENT
Portesham
SOUTH WEST COAST PATH
Littlebredy
VALLEY OF STONES
KINGSTON RUSSELL STONE CIRCLE
Burton Bradstock
Puncknowle
Swyre
West Bexington
Abbotsbury
ABBOTSBURY CHILDREN'S FARM
SUB TROPICAL GARDENS
ST CATHERINES CHAPEL
SWANNERY
Rodden
Upwey
Bincombe
WHITE HORSE
Poxwell
Broadwey
Littlemoor
Preston
Upton
Osmington
Osmington Mills
Nottington
Overcombe
JORDAN HILL ROMAN TEMPLE
Radipole
BENNETTS WATER GARDENS
SEA LIFE
Melcombe Regis
Chickerell
Langton Herring
CHESIL BEACH
Charlestown
Westham
Weymouth
NOTHE FORT
BREWER'S QUAY AND TIMEWALK
Rodwell
Wyke Regis
Portland Harbour
WEYMOUTH
Chestown
Weymouth
BREWER'S QUAY AND TIMEWALK
Rodwell
Wyke Regis
Portland Harbour
GUERNSEY 2:10
JERSEY 3:25
ST. MALO 5:15
WEYMOUTH & PORTLAND NATIONAL SAILING ACADEMY
PORTLAND
PORTLAND CASTLE
Fortuneswell
West Bay
Grove
Easton
Weston
PORTLAND
MUSEUM
Southwell
Bill of Portland
SY
ST
A303
A37
A30
A3088
A35
A354
A356
A359
A372
A361
A378
A371
A352
A351
A3030
A3066
A353
B3151
B3153
B3165
B3168
B3162
B3164
B3163
B3148
B3145
B3146
B3143
B3142
B3157
B3159
B3081
B3092
0 1 2 3 4 5 6 miles
0 1 2 3 4 5 6 7 8 9 10 km

A map of Dorset and south Wiltshire, including grid references and place names.

Major towns and places:

Mere, Gillingham, Shaftesbury, Sturminster Newton, Blandford Forum, Wimborne Minster, Ringwood, Fordingbridge, Salisbury, Wilton, Verwood, Ferndown, Bournemouth, Poole, Wareham, Swanage, Corfe Castle

A-roads labelled:

A303, A350, A30, A357, A354, A31, A35, A338, A348, A349, A352, A351, A36, A3094

Place names (selection):

Stourton, Zeals, Penselwood, Bourton, Queen Oak, Milton on Stour, Cucklington, Wyke, Buckhorn Weston, Kington Magna, West Stour, Fifehead Magdalen, Stour Provost, Stour Row, Guy's Marsh, Cann, Cann Common, Ludwell, Charlton, Melbury Abbas, Compton Abbas, Ashmore, Fontmell Magna, Sutton Waldron, Iwerne Minster, Iwerne Courtney or Shroton, Child Okeford, Okeford Fitzpaine, Shillingstone, Durweston, Stourpaine, Pimperne, Bryanston, Blandford St Mary, Tarrant Rawston, Tarrant Monkton, Tarrant Hinton, Tarrant Gunville, Tarrant Launceston, Tarrant Rushton, Tarrant Keyneston, Tarrant Crawford, Spetisbury, Charlton Marshall, Thorncombe, Winterborne Stickland, Winterborne Clenston, Winterborne Houghton, Whatcombe, Winterborne Whitechurch, Winterborne Kingston, Winterborne Zelston, Anderson, Milborne St Andrew, Milton Abbas, Cheselbourne, Dewlish, Bere Regis, Turners Puddle, Affpuddle, Tolpuddle, Burleston, Athelhampton, Puddletown, Tincleton, Woodsford, Moreton, Crossways, Warmwell, Owermoigne, Holworth, Chaldon Herring or East Chaldon, Winfrith Newburgh, East Knighton, Coombe Keynes, Wool, East Stoke, East Burton, Stokeford, Northport, Wareham, Stoborough, Ridge, Arne, Studland, Corfe Castle, Church Knowle, Steeple, Kimmeridge, Tyneham, Kingston, Langton Matravers, Worth Matravers, Acton, Swanage, Peveril Pt, Durlston Head

Bournemouth/Poole area:

Corfe Mullen, Broadstone, Canford Heath, Upton, Hamworthy, Parkstone, Branksome, Westbourne, Boscombe, Southbourne, Pokesdown, Moordown, Kinson, Ensbury, Bearwood, Merley, Oakley, Canford Magna, Hampreston, Longham, West Parley, Stapehill, Three Legged Cross, St Leonards, St Ives, Ashley Heath, West Moors, Holt, Mannington, Horton, Woodlands, Cranborne, Edmondsham, Alderholt, Verwood

Water features:

POOLE BAY, Poole Harbour, Brownsea Island, Sandbanks, Studland Bay, Swanage Bay, Kimmeridge Bay, Worbarrow Bay, Ringstead Bay, Durdle Door, Lulworth Cove

Ferry times (bottom right):

GUERNSEY 2:40 — JERSEY 3:00 — ST. MALO 4:35 — CHERBOURG 2:15 (Apr-Oct) (May-Sept)

Grid references (top): 5, 6, 7, 8, 9
Grid references (bottom): 5, 6, 7, 8, 9
Side letters: A, B, C, D, E, F, G

Regional labels: CRANBORNE CHASE AND WEST WILTSHIRE DOWNS, DORSET, ISLE OF PURBECK, PURBECK HILLS, VALE OF WARDOUR

14

Salisbury 25

Wilton

Bournemouth

CHRISTCHURCH

Ringwood

Verwood

Ferndown

LYMINGTON

Totton

SOUTHAMPTON

Romsey

Fordingbridge

Brockenhurst

Blackfield

Dibden Purlieu

Hythe

Lyndhurst

New Milton

Highcliffe

Barton on Sea

Milford on Sea

HAMPSHIRE

NEW FOREST NATIONAL PARK

POOLE BAY

Christchurch Bay

THE SOLENT

Studland Bay

The Foreland

Swanage Bay

SU

SZ

THE ISLE OF WIGHT

Yarmouth

Totland

Freshwater

The Needles

Brighstone Forest

Needs Ore Pt.

Thorness Bay

Newtown Bay

Atherfield Pt.

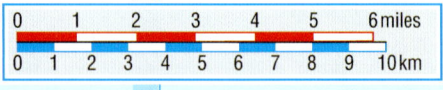

GUERNSEY 2:40
JERSEY 3:00 } (Apr-Oct)
ST. MALO 4:35
CHERBOURG 2:15 } (May-Sept)

0 1 2 3 4 5 6 miles
0 1 2 3 4 5 6 7 8 9 10km

Alresford
Dighton Solbridge
Four Marks
Selborne
Whitehill
Standford
GILBERT WHITE'S HOUSE & THE OATES MUSEUM
Blackmoor
Conford
A

Kings Worthy
Martyr Worthy
Itchen Abbas
New Alresford
Bishop's Sutton
Gundleton
Ropley
Kitwood
North Street
East Tisted
Newton Valence
Longmoor Camp
Liphook

Littleton
Headbourne Worthy
Easton
Avington
Ovington
MID-HANTS RAILWAY
Ropley Dean
Monkwood
Colemore
Greatham
A3
Langley

Weeke
Winnall
Winchester
CATH
P&R
Chilcomb
ST CATHERINE'S HILL
INTECH SCIENCE CENTRE & PLANETARIUM
Tichborne
New Cheriton
Cheriton
Bramdean
West Tisted
Hawkley
Froxfield Green
West Liss
East Liss
Liss
Rake
B2070
Milland

Stanmore
Oliver's Battery
Compton
Twyford
Shawford
Otterbourne
Beauworth
Kilmeston
Hinton Ampner
Brockwood
Privett
High Cross
Stoner Hill
Steep Marsh
Steep
Sheet
Liss Forest
Petersfield
Rother
Rogate
A272
Chithurst
Iping
B

Fisher's Pond
EASTLEIGH
Bishopstoke
Fair Oak
Morestead
Lane End
West Meon
East End
East Meon
Langrish
Ramsdean
Weston
ST PETER'S CHURCH
THE BEAR MUS
Nursted
Dumpford
Nyewood
Trotton
Minsted

SOUTH DOWNS WAY
BEACON HILL
Warnford
OLD WINCHESTER HILL
Coombe
BUTSER HILL
QUEEN ELIZABETH
UPPARK
North Marden
East Harting
South Harting
Elsted
Didling
Treyford
Bepton
C

Upham
Lower Upham
Dean
Exton
Corhampton
Meonstoke
Brockbridge
Chidden
Clanfield
Chalton
Compton Up Marden
East Marden
Chi Cove
West Dean

West End
Hedge End
Botley
Curdridge
Shirrell Heath
Soberton
Hambledon
Catherington
Blendworth
West Marden
Stoughton
KINGLEY VALE
WEST DEAN GARDENS
BOW HILL

Thornhill
Sholing
Horton Heath
Durley
Long Common
Waltham Chase
Swanmore
Hoe Gate
Soberton Heath
Anthill Common
Lovedean
Horndean
Finchdean
Forestside
Rowlands Castle
STANSTED PARK
Walderton
Woodend
West Stoke
Lavant
East Ashling
Summersdale
Mid

Old Netley
Bursledon
Lower Swanwick
Shedfield
Newtown
Hundred Acres
Denmead
Cowplain
STAUNTON PARK
Leigh Park
Stockheath
Westbourne
Hambrook
West Ashling
Nutbourne

ROYAL VICTORIA
Hamble-le-Rice
HOLLY HILL WOODLAND PARK
Park Gate
Funtley
Boarhunt
SOUTHWICK BREWHOUSE
Southwick
Waterlooville
Purbrook
Bedhampton
HAVANT
Warblington
Emsworth
Southbourne
Broadbridge
Fishbourne
Chichester
CATH
D

WHITELEY VILLAGE
Locks Heath
Warsash
Titchfield
Wallington
FORT NELSON
Ports Down
Wymering
Drayton
Cosham
Langstone
Northney
North Hayling
Chidham
Bosham
FISHBOURNE PALACE
Apuldram
A

Fawley
Ashlett
CALSHOT CASTLE
CALSHOT ACTIVITY CENTRE
Calshot
Hill Head
Lee-on-the-Solent
Stubbington
Peel Common
Bridgemary
PORTCHESTER CASTLE
Fleetlands
Portchester
Hilsea
FARLINGTON MARSHES
Stoke
North Hayling
Thorney
CHICHESTER HARBOUR
West Thorney
West Itchenor
Donnington
Huston
SUSSEX FALCONR

TITCHFIELD HAVEN
FORT BROCKHURST
Brockhurst
Hardway
HMS VICTORY MARY ROSE
1642 LIVING HISTORY VILLAGE
Portsea
Portsmouth
Portsmouth Harbour
EXPLOSION
GUNWHARF QUAYS
DICKENS BIRTHPLACE
Fratton
Langstone Harbour
Fleet
HAYLING ISLAND
Chichester Harbour
HARBOUR
Shipton Green
Birdham

GOSPORT
SUBMARINE
BLUE REEF AQUARIUM
CATHEDRAL
Milton
Eastney
ROYAL MARINES MUSEUM
FORT
SOUTHSEA CASTLE
Southsea
West Town
South Hayling
Eastoke
West Wittering
Acre Street
Somerley Highleigh
EARNLEY BUTTERFLIES AND GARDENS

Stone Pt.
Stokes Bay
Alverstoke
Gilkicker Pt.
PORTSMOUTH
Fort Cumberland
EAST HAYLING LIGHT RAILWAY
East Wittering
Earnley
Bracklesham
Ch
E

SOLENT
Cowes
Gurnard Bay
MARITIME MUSEUM
East Cowes
Gurnard
Osborne Bay
OSBORNE HOUSE
SPITHEAD
16
Selsey
SELSEY BILL
Norton

Rew Street
Northwood
Whippingham
Wootton Bridge
Fishbourne
RYDE
Nettlestone Pt.
TOLL
SEAVIEW WILDLIFE ENCOUNTER
Seaview
Nettlestone

Isle
Parkhurst
Wootton Common
Havenstreet
ISLE OF WIGHT STEAM RAILWAY
Binstead
BRICKFIELDS
Elmfield
WALTZING WATERS
St Helens
F

COLEMANS FARM PARK
Gunville
Carisbrooke
Glatterford
NEWPORT
ROMAN VILLA
ROBIN HILL ADVENTURE PARK
BUTTERFLY WORLD
Staplers
Downend
Brading
Steyne Cross
BEMBRIDGE
Bembridge
Foreland
Lane End
WINDMILL
Hillway
Whitecliff Bay

Hunny Hill
Shide
CARISBROOKE CASTLE
Bowcombe
Blackwater
ARRETON MANOR
Arreton
ISLE OF WIGHT (SANDOWN)
Newchurch
Alverstone
Yar
MORTON MANOR
DINOSAUR ISLE
Yaverland
Culver Cliff

Gatcombe
Chillerton
Merstone
Rookley
AMAZON WORLD
Horringford
Winford
ISLE OF WIGHT ZOO
Sandown
SZ

Shorwell
Godshill
Branstone
NATURAL HISTORY CENTRE
Sandford
Apse Heath
Lake
Sandown Bay

Kingston
MODEL VILLAGE
Whiteley Bank
Shanklin
SHANKLIN CHINE
GUERNSEY 7:00
JERSEY 10:30

Little Atherfield
Chale Green
Roud
APPULDURCOMBE HOUSE
Luccombe Village
Luccombe Chine

Pyle
Stenbury Down
HERITAGE MUSEUM
Wroxall
Dunnose

Chale Bay
Blackgang Chine
Whitwell
Niton
BOTANIC GARDEN & VISITOR CENTRE
Ventnor
Bonchurch

BLACKGANG CHINE
ST CATHERINE'S ORATORY
St Lawrence
The Undercliff
G

Guernsey
3½ miles to 1 inch

Alderney
3½ miles to 1 inch

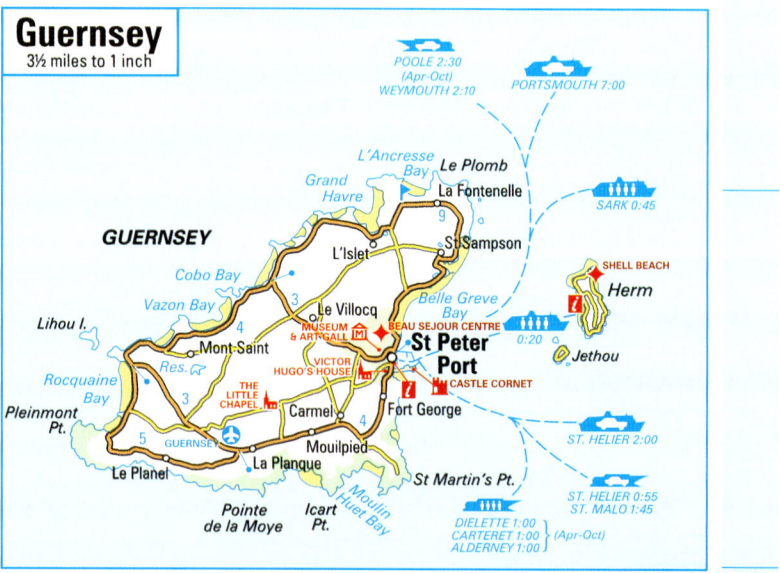

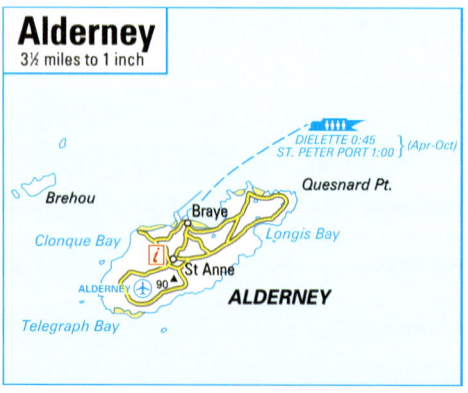

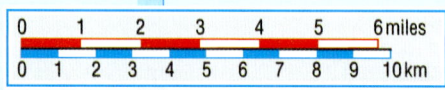

17
Horsham
Crowborough
Haywards Heath
Cuckfield
Burgess Hill
Uckfield
Lewes
Brighton and Hove
HOVE
BRIGHTON
Shoreham-by-Sea
Southwick
Worthing
Lancing
Newhaven
Seaford
Peacehaven
Henfield
Steyning
Hassocks
Ditchling
Rottingdean
Ashdown Forest
St Leonard's Forest
Balcombe
Lindfield
Dieppe 4:00
Jersey
3½ miles to 1 inch
St Helier
St Aubin
Gorey
St Ouen's Bay
St Brelade's Bay
St Aubin's Bay
Royal Bay of Grouville
St Clements Bay
St Catherine's Bay
Bouley Bay
TQ
TV

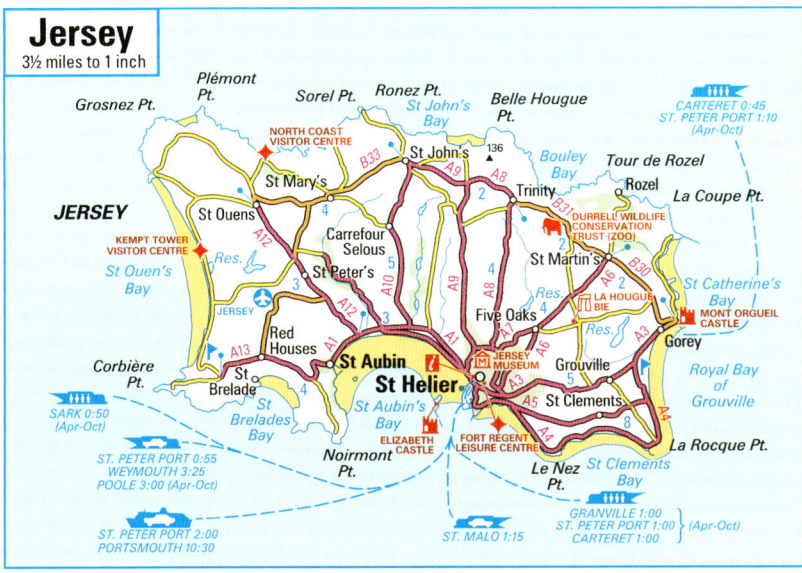

ROYAL TUNBRIDGE WELLS
Southborough
Bidborough
Penshurst
Speldhurst
Rusthall
Langton Green
Groombridge
Pembury
Paddock Wood
Matfield
Brenchley
Horsmonden
Lamberhurst
Frant
Eridge Green
Crowborough
Mayfield
Wadhurst
Ticehurst
Flimwell
Hawkhurst
Cranbrook
Staplehurst
Headcorn
Marden
Goudhurst
Kilndown
Bewl Water
Bedgebury Forest
Burwash
Etchingham
Robertsbridge
Bodiam
Northiam
Sandhurst
Newenden
Hurst Green
Heathfield
Uckfield
Maresfield
Nutley
Hartfield
Withyham
Ashdown Forest
Buxted
Framfield
Blackboys
Halland
Horam
Hailsham
Herstmonceux
Battle
Bexhill
St Leonards
Hastings
Ore
Hollington
Catsfield
Ninfield
Sedlescombe
Brede
Westfield
Pevensey
Pevensey Bay
Polegate
Willingdon
Eastbourne
Beachy Head
East Dean
Friston
Birling Gap
Seaford
Newhaven
Alfriston
Berwick
Glynde
Ringmer
Laughton
Chiddingly
Arlington
Norman's Bay
Cooden
TQ
TV
HIGH WEALD
East Sussex
Rother
DIEPPE 4:00
0 1 2 3 4 5 6 miles
0 1 2 3 4 5 6 7 8 9 10 km

A B C D E F G

5 6 7 8 9

Pluckley
Thorne
GODINTON HOUSE
KENNINGTON
Brook
Hastingleigh
Elham
Sw
Lymbridge Green
Rhodes Minnis
Ottinge
BUTTERFLY CENTRE
Swingfield Minnis
Densole

HEADCORN
Smarden Bell
Smarden
Maltman's Hill
Great Chart
Ashford
Willesborough Lees
Brabourne
Stowting
KENT BATTLE OF BRITAIN MUSEUM
Drellingore
West Hougham

Haffenden Quarter
Wissenden
Willesborough
Sevington
Kingsnorth
Mersham
Smeeth
Sellindge
Postling
Lyminge
Etchinghill
Paddlesworth
Hawkinge
Capel le Ferne

Standen
Bether A28 30
Stubbs Cross
Cheeseman's Green
Sellindge Lees
Stanford
STOP 24 SERVICES
Beachborough
30
CHANNEL TUNNEL
Biddenden
Tanden
Shadoxhurst
Bromley Green
Aldington Frith
Clap Hill
Aldington
Newingreen
Newington
FOLKESTONE
M20
11A
12
13
Folkestone

BIDDENDEN VINEYARD
High Halden
Henghurst
Shirkoak
Orlestone
HAM STREET WOODS
Bilsington
Bonnington
Lympne
PORT LYMPNE WILD ANIMAL PARK AND GARDENS
West Hythe
Pedling
BROCKHILL
ELHAM VALLEY RLY MUS
Cheriton
Saltwood
Sandgate
ROTUNDA
CLIFF LIFT

KENT & EAST SUSSEX RAILWAY
St Michael's
Woodchurch
Kenardington
Warehorne
Ruckinge
Hamstreet
Newchurch
Burmarsh
Palmarsh
Hythe
31

Parkgate
Tenterden
COLONEL STEPHENS RAILWAY MUSEUM
Leigh Green
Brook Street
Reading Street
Appledore Heath
HORNE'S PLACE CHAPEL
Snave
ROMNEY MARSH
St Mary in the Marsh
ROMNEY, HYTHE AND DYMCHURCH LIGHT RAILWAY
A259

Small Hythe
SMALLHYTHE PLACE
Appledore
Snargate
Brenzett
AERONAUTICAL MUSEUM
Ivychurch
ROMNEY-WARREN
Dymchurch
MARTELLO TOWER

Rolvenden Layne
ISLE OF OXNEY
Peening Quarter
Stone
Brookland
Old Romney
New Romney
St Mary's Bay

ROTHER LEVELS
Wittersham
Ham Green
The Stocks
Walland Marsh
Littlestone on Sea
Romney Sands
Greatstone on Sea

FARM WORLD
Four Oaks
Iden
Houghton Green
A259
East Guldeford
Lydd
LYDD (LONDON ASHFORD)
Lydd on Sea

Beckley
Peasmarsh
Rye Foreign
Playden
Rye
Camber
Denge Marsh
LYDD INTERNATIONAL RACEWAY
DUNGENESS
Denge Beach

Udimore
RYE HERITAGE CENTRE
Rye Harbour
CAMBER CASTLE
Rye Bay
DUNGENESS POWER STATION & INFORMATION CENTRE
THE OLD LIGHTHOUSE
DUNGENESS

Winchelsea
WINCHELSEA COURT HALL MUSEUM
Winchelsea Beach
A259
Icklesham
Pett
Guestling Green
Cliff End
Fairlight
Fairlight Cove
HASTINGS CAVES
WATER WORLD

ENGLISH CHANNEL

1 2 3 2 3 4 5

A

¹8

B

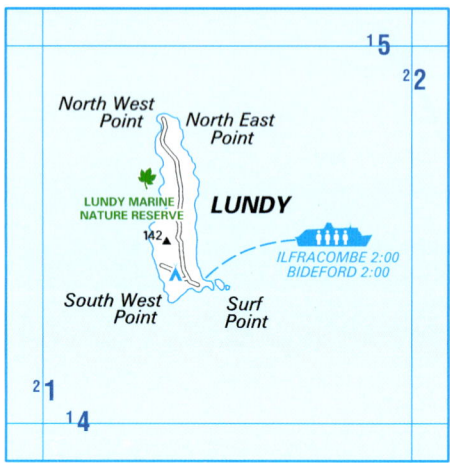

¹5
²2

North West
Point
North East
Point

LUNDY

LUNDY MARINE
NATURE RESERVE

142

ILFRACOMBE 2:00
BIDEFORD 2:00

C

South West
Point
Surf
Point

²1
¹4

D

SS

SWANSEA 0:50

LUNDY 2:00

Rillage Pt.
OLD CORN MILL
Combe Martin
Bay
Trentishoe

ILFRACOMBE
MUSEUM
WATERMOUTH CASTLE
Girt Down
349
Heale

Ilfracombe
Hele

Bull Pt.
Rockham Bay
Lee
Whitestone
Slade
206
Berrynarbor
Sterridge
Combe
Martin
10

Morte Point
Mortehoe

Trimstone
Cheglinch
269
Berry
Down
Bittadon
Berry Down
Cross
Patchole
Kentisbury
Ford
Kentisbury

E

Woolacombe

MORTE
BAY

Woolacombe Sand
SOUTH WEST
COAST PATH
Pickwell
210
Dean
West
Down
East Down
Churchill
Arlington
ARLINGTON
COURT

Baggy Pt.
Putsborough
North
Buckland
Milltown
Muddiford
Loxhore

Georgeham
Nethercott
Halsinger
Marwood
Guineaford
198
Shirwell
Bratton
Fleming

Croyde Bay
Croyde
158
Lobb
Darracott
Knowle
Pippacott
Kingsheanton
Prixford
Shirwell
Cross
Stoke
Rivers

Saunton
14
BROOMHILL
MARWOOD
HILL GARDENS

F

Saunton
Sands
ELLIOT GALLERY
Braunton
Heanton
Punchardon
Ashford
Burridge
Goodleigh
Gunn

Wrafton
TOLL
Chivenor
40
Pilton
Barnstaple
Westacott

Braunton
Burrows
LUNDY 2:00
Taw
Fremington
MUSEUM OF
NORTH DEVON
P&R
Newport
Landkey
Swimbridge
Newland
NORTH DEVON
FARM PARK
Swimbridge
10

BIDEFORD BAY
NORTH DEVON
MARITIME MUSEUM
Yelland
Bickington
Bishops
Tawton

¹3
NORTHAM BURROWS
Instow
Bickleton

Appledore
Westward Ho!
Northam
Tapeley
PARK GDNS
Westleigh
Newton
Tracey
Herner
Cobbaton

THE BIG SHEEP
Orchard
Hill
Bideford
Eastleigh
Horwood
Ensis
COBBATON
COMBAT COLL.
East
Stowford

Abbotsham
BURTON ART
GALL & MUS
East-the-
Hiscott
Chapelton

CLOVELLY VILLAGE
Woodtown

0 1 2 3 4 5 6 miles
0 1 2 3 4 5 6 7 8 9 10km

MÔR HAFREN
BRISTOL CHANNEL
SS
Kenfig
Mawdlam
Kenfig Burrows
KENFIG POOL AND DUNES
Pyle (Y Pîl)
North Cornelly
South Cornelly
Cefn Cribbwr
Cefn Cross
Aberkenfig
Tondu
Sarn
SARN PARK SERVICES
Bryncethin
Pencoed
Coity
COITY CASTLE
Bridgend (Pen-y-bont ar Ogwr)
Laleston
Coychurch
Tythegston
Merthyr Mawr
OGMORE CASTLE
Ogmore
Ogmore-by-Sea
St Brides Major
Southerndown
GLENMORGAN HERITAGE COAST CENTRE
ROYAL PORTHCAWL
Nottage
Newton
Hutchwns
Clevis
Porthcawl
CONEY BEACH
MERTHYR MAWR WARREN
Tusker Rock
Ewenny
Corntown
Treoes
St Mary Hill
Llangan
Craig Penllyn
Llansannor
Penllyn
Pentre Meyrick
Colwinston
Llysworney
Penuchadre
Wick
Broughton
Monknash
Marcross
St Donat's
Nash Pt. Trwyn yr As
Llantwit Major (Llanilltud Fawr)
Boverton
Llanmaes
Eglwys-Brewis
Sigingstone
Llanmihangel
St Mary Church
Llandow
Cowbridge (Y Bont-Faen)
Llanblethian
Llandough
Aberthin
Maendy
Ystradowen
Welsh St Donats
St Hilary
OLD BEAUPRE CASTLE
Flemingston
Llanbethery
St Athan
East Aberthaw
Rhoose (Y Rhws)
Breaksea Pt. Trwyn Breaksea
Vale of Glamorgan (Bro Morgannwg)
Brynna
Llanharan
Bryncae
Llanilid
Llanharry
Brynsadler
Dolau
Pontyclun
Talygarn
LLANERCH VINEYARD
Highveer Pt.
Woody Bay
Lynmouth
Lynmouth Bay
CLIFF RAILWAY
Foreland Pt.
Countisbury
Lynton
Martinhoe
WATERSMEET HOUSE
LYNTON AND BARNSTAPLE RLY
Barbrook
Cheriton
East Ilkerton
Martinhoe Cross
Furzehill
Shallowford
Parracombe
Brendon
Malmsmead
Oare
CULBONE HILL
Brendon Common
EXMOOR FOREST
EXMOOR NATIONAL PARK
Blackmoor Gate
Challacombe Common
Pinkworthy Pond
PINKERY
Exe Plain
Challacombe
EXMOOR ZOO
Shoulsbarrow Common
Knightacott
Leworthy
Simonsbath
Edgcott
Exford
Lydcott
Benton
North Radworthy
Withypool Common
Withypool
HORSEN HILL
WINSFORD HILL
Winsford
Brayford
High Bray
North Heasley
Heasley Mill
South Radworthy
Charles
West Buckland
East Buckland
Liscombe
TARR STEPS
Hawkridge
Molland Common
Twitchen
Dane's Brook
Anstey Common
West Anstey
East Anstey
Molland
Dulverton
Battleton
Nightcott
Yeo Mill
Filleigh
QUINCE HONEY FARM
South Molton
Hurlstone Pt.
Porlock Bay
Porlock Weir
Porlock
Bossington
EXMOOR FALCONRY
SOUTH WEST COAST PATH
SELWORTHY BEACON
Allerford
Selworthy
Woodcombe
Minehead
WEST SOMERSET RAILWAY
BUTLINS
Alcombe
Periton
Marsh Street
DOLL MUS.
MILL & YARN MARKET
Dunster
DUNSTER CASTLE
Carhampton
Blue Anchor Bay
Blue Anchor
Old Cleeve
West Luccombe
Luccombe
HAWKCOMBE WOODS
Holnicote Estate
DUNKERY BEACON
THE DUNKERY & HORNER WOOD
Wootton Courtenay
DUNKERY VINEYARD
Cowbridge
Timberscombe
BRENDON FOREST
CROYDON HILL
Withycombe
Bilbrook
CLEEVE ABBEY
Washford
Rodhuish
Roadwater
Luckwell Bridge
Cutcombe
Wheddon Cross
LYPE HILL
Luxborough
Kingsbridge
Treborough
BRENDON HILLS
Exton
Bridgetown
Brompton Regis
Withiel Florey
Clatworthy Res.
Wimbleball Lake
HADDON HILL
Upton
Huish Champflower
HEYDON HILL
Chipstable
Bury
Skilgate
Waterrow

Pencoed
Llanharan
Talbot Green
Llantrisant
Pontyclun
Cross Inn
Creigiau
Pentyrch
Taff's Well
Tongwynlais
Llanishen
Rhiwbina
Whitchurch
Radyr
Lisvane
Llanedeyrn
Cyncoed
Castleton
Coedkernew
Marshfield
Blacktown
St Brides Wentlooge
Peterstone Wentlooge
Rumney
Llanrumney
St Mellons
Nash
Cardiff
(Caerdydd)
CARDIFF
(CAERDYDD)
Birchgrove
Heath
Cathays
Roath
Llandaff
Canton
Ely
Caerau
St Fagans
MILLENNIUM STADIUM
NAT MUS OF WALES
NATIONAL HISTORY MUSEUM
Butetown
Grangetown
CARDIFF BAY VISITOR CENTRE
TECHNIQUEST
CARDIFF BAY BARRAGE
TURNER HOUSE GALLERY
Newton
Llandough
Cogan
PENARTH
Leckwith
Michaelston-le-Pit
Wenvoe
St Andrew's Major
Dinas Powys
Cadoxton
COSMESTON LAKES
MEDIEVAL VILLAGE
Lower Penarth
Lavernock Pt.
Trwyn Larnog
Sully
Sully Island
Ynys Sili
Flat Holm
Steep Holm
Vale of Glamorgan (Bro Morgannwg)
Brynsadler
Llanharry
Dolau
Bryncae
Llanilid
Talygarn
LLANERCH VINEYARD
Groes-faen
Capel Llanilltern
CARDIFF WEST SERVICES
St Brides super Ely
Peterston super-Ely
St George's
Michaelston-super-Ely
Ystradowen
Welsh St Donats
Pendoylan
Craig Penllyn
Llansannor
Llangan
St Mary Hill
Pentre Meyrick
Penllyn
Maendy
Aberthin
Cowbridge
(Y Bont-Faen)
Llanblethian
Llwyworney
Llandow
Llandough
St Hilary
Llantrithyd
Bonvilston
St Nicholas
Wallston
St Lythans
DYFFRYN GARDENS
OLD BEAUPRE CASTLE
Llanmihangel
St Mary Church
Sigingstone
Walterston
Flemingston
Moulton
Llanmaes
Eglwys-Brewis
Llanbethery
Llancarfan
Penmark
WELSH HAWKING CENTRE
Colcot
Merthyr-Dyfan
BARRY
(Y BARRI)
Barry Island
BARRY ISLAND PLEASURE PARK
Llantwit Major
(Llanilltud Fawr)
Boverton
St Athan
Gileston
East Aberthaw
Rhoose
(Y Rhws)
Porthkerry
PORTHKERRY
CARDIFF
(MAES AWYR CAERDYDD)
Breaksea Pt.
Trwyn Breaksea
MÔR HAFREN
BRISTOL CHANNEL
ABER HAFREN
MOUTH OF THE SEVERN
ST
BRIDGWATER BAY
Sand Pt.
Sand Bay
Kewstoke
Milton
NORTH SOMERSET MUS
Weston-super-Mare
Weston Bay
SEAQUARIUM
HELICOPTER MUS
Uphill
Hutton
Brean Down
Bleadon
Brean
BERROW FLATS
BREAN LEISURE PARK
Eastertown
Lympsham
Gore Sands
Berrow
East Brent
Brent Knoll
Burnham-on-Sea
Edithmead
STERT FLATS
Highbridge
Watchfield
BRIDGWATER BAY
Stolford
Steart
Huntspill
SECRET WORLD
Bason Bridge
East Huntspill
HUNTSPILL RIVER
Stretcholt
Stockland Bristol
Otterhampton
Combwich
Pawlett
Woolavington
Dunball
Puriton
Bawdrip
Chilton Trinity
BLAKE MUS
BRIDGWATER AND TAUNTON CANAL AND DOCKS
Chedzoy
Wembdon
Bridgwater
Durleigh
Four Forks
Enmore
Goathurst
North Petherton
BRIDGWATER SERVICES
Huntworth
TEMPLE OF HARMONY
FYNE COURT
Broomfield
Northmoor Green or Moorland
North Newton
BRIDGWATER & TAUNTON CANAL MAUNSEL LOCKS
Thurloxton
Lyng
Hedging
West Lyng
Durston
Creech Heathfield
Meare Green
North End
WILLOWS & WETLANDS VISITOR CENTRE
Knapp
Minehead
Woodcombe
WEST SOMERSET RAILWAY
BUTLINS
Alcombe
Periton
Marsh Street
MINEHEAD
DOLL MUS
DUNKERY VINEYARD
Dunster
DUNSTER CASTLE
MILL & YARN MARKET
Blue Anchor Bay
Carhampton
Timberscombe
Withycombe
BRENDON FOREST
CROYDON HILL
Luxborough
Roadwater
LYPE HILL
Kingsbridge
Treborough
BRENDON HILLS
Blue Anchor
Old Cleeve
Bilbrook
Rodhuish
CLEEVE ABBEY
Washford
TROPIQUARIA
MARKET HOUSE MUS
Watchet
West Quantoxhead
Williton
Sampford Brett
Yard
Monksilver
COMBE SYDENHAM
Elworthy
Vellow
Stogumber
WEST SOMERSET RAILWAY
East Quantoxhead
Staple
Kilve
Kilton
Lilstock
Burton
Shurton
Stringston
Stogursey
Holford
Nether Stowey
Fiddington
COLERIDGE COTTAGE
Over Stowey
CANNINGTON COLLEGE
Rodway
Cannington
Charlynch
Spaxton
Bicknoller
QUANTOCK FOREST
QUANTOCK HILLS
Crowcombe
Flaxpool
Lower Vexford
Lower Aisholt
Courtway
West Bagborough
Willett
Lydeard St Lawrence
Tolland
GAULDEN MANOR
Combe Florey
East Combe
Cothelstone
Cushuish
Tarr
Withiel Florey
Clatworthy Res.
Brompton Ralph
Clatworthy
Brompton Regis
Wimbleball Lake
Upton
Champflower
Langley Marsh
Wiveliscombe
Fitzhead
Ash Priors
Bishops Lydeard
Fulford
Pickney
Kingston St Mary
West Monkton
Nailsbourne
Monkton Heathfield
Cheddon Fitzpaine
Halse
VALE OF TAUNTON DEANE
Preston Bowyer
Milverton
Heathfield
Hillcommon
Norton
Staplegrove
Bathpool
Bury
Waterrow
0 1 2 3 4 5 6 miles
0 1 2 3 4 5 6 7 8 9 10 km

North Somerset

Bath and N.E. Somerset

Bristol

KEYNSHAM

Bath

Somerset

Goldcliff
Whitson
Avonmouth
Portishead
West Hill
Redcliff Bay
Sheepway
Clapton-in-Gordano
Weston-in-Gordano
Walton-in-Gordano
Clevedon
Tickenham
Nailsea
West End
East End
Farleigh
Kingston Seymour
North End
Yatton
Cleeve
Claverham
Brockley
Chelvey
West Town
Backwell
Wick St Lawrence
Bourton
Hewish
Puxton
Congresbury
Wrington
Redhill
Worle
West Wick
Brinsea
Lower Langford
Cowslip Green
Ridgehill
Butcombe
Churchill
Sandford
Banwell
Burrington
Blagdon
Ubley
Compton Bishop
Locking
Christon
Cross
Lower Weare
Axbridge
Weare
Badgworth
Winscombe
Sidcot
Shipham
Charterhouse
Compton Martin
West Harptree
East Harptree
Blagdon Lake
Blackford
Chapel Allerton
Cocklake
Cheddar
Draycott
Rodney Stoke
Priddy
Wedmore
Latcham
Westbury-sub-Mendip
Easton
Mark
Mark Causeway
West Stoughton
Blackford
Theale
Wookey Hole
West Horrington
East Horrington
Westham
Heath House
Mudgley
Wookey
Wells
Dinder
Croscombe
Burtle
Westhay
Meare
Godney
Coxley
Polsham
Worminster
West Compton
Pilton
Downside
Stoke St Michael
Gossington
Chilton Polden
Edington
Catcott
Shapwick
Ashcott
Northover
Glastonbury
Edgarley
West Pennard
Pylle
Evercreech
Milton Clevedon
Bruton
Stawell
Sutton Mallet
Moorlinch
Greinton
Pedwell
Walton
Overleigh
Street
Compton Dundon
Dundon
Butleigh Wootton
Butleigh
Baltonsborough
Ham Street
West Bradley
Parbrook
Wraxall
Alhampton
Ditcheat
Lamyatt
Cole
Castle Cary
Middlezoy
Othery
Henley
High Ham
Dundon
Kingweston
Lydford
Ansford
Pitcombe
Redlynch
Stoney Stoke
Bayford
Wincanton
Burrowbridge
Stathe
Aller
Pitney
Somerton
Charlton Adam
Charlton Mackrell
Babcary
North Barrow
South Barrow
North Cadbury
Hadspen
Charlton Musgrove
Athelney
Stoke St Gregory
Langport
Huish Episcopi
Curry Rivel
Kingsdon
Keinton Mandeville
Lydford-on-Fosse
Alford
Lovington
Galhampton
Sparkford
Holton
Maperton
North Cheriton

MENDIP HILLS

POLDEN HILLS

King's Sedge Moor

West Sedge Moor

Iron Acton
Chipping Sodbury
Old Sodbury
Yate
Wickwar
Nibley
Wapley
Codrington
Dodington
Hinton
Pucklechurch
Dyrham
Abson
Doynton
Wick
Cold Ashton
Mangotsfield
Kingswood
Hanham
Oldland
Bitton
Saltford
Corston
Newton St Loe
Twerton
Keynsham
Queen Charlton
Chewton Keynsham
Burnett
Compton Dando
Chelwood
Hunstrete
Marksbury
Farmborough
Timsbury
High Littleton
Camerton
Carlingcott
Peasedown St John
Radstock
Midsomer Norton
Clandown
Paulton
Writhlington
Chilcompton
Ston Easton
Emborough
Holcombe
Coleford
Vobster
Kilmersdon
Charlton
Stratton on the Fosse
Nettlebridge
Oakhill
Leigh upon Mendip
Downhead
Chantry
Nunney
Shepton Mallet
Doulting
Cranmore
Chesterblade
Batcombe
Wanstrow
Witham

Filton
Patchway
Easter Compton
Hallen
Catbrain
Henbury
Stoke Gifford
Winterbourne
Frenchay
Downend
Westerleigh
Horfield
Westbury on Trym
Stapleton
Fishponds
Eastville
Redland
Clifton
Bedminster
Knowle
Brislington
Whitchurch
Dundry
Bishopsworth
North Wick
Norton Malreward
Norton Hawkfield
Chew Magna
Chew Stoke
Stanton Drew
Stanton Wick
Pensford
Publow
Woollard
Stanton Prior
Englishcombe
Combe Hay
Dunkerton
Wellow
Hinton Charterhouse
Norton St Philip
Tellisford
Rode
Beckington
Berkley
Frome

Acton
Nibley
Yate
Little Sodbury
Old Sodbury
A46
Little Badminton
Luckington
Norton
Corston
Brinkworth
Callow Hill

Watley's End
Coalpit Heath
Chipping Sodbury
36
Badminton
Littleton Drew
Hullavington
Startley
Lower Stanton St Quintin
Great Somerford
Lower Seagry
Dauntsey
Grittenham

Winterbourne
Wapley
Codrington
Tormarton
Burton
Leigh Delamere
Stanton St Quintin
Upper Seagry
37
Tockenham Wick

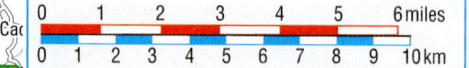

MANGOTSFIELD
Hinton
West Kington
Nettleton
Castle Combe
LEIGH DELAMERE SERVICES
Kington St Michael
A350
Sutton Benger
Christian Malford
Foxham
Church End
Tockenham

KINGSWOOD
Pucklechurch
Dyrham
West Littleton
Slaughterford
North Wraxall
Ford
Biddestone
CASTLE MANOR
Hardenhuish
CHIPPENHAM MUS
Kington Langley
West Tytherton
Bradenstoke
Lyneham
Preston Goatacre

Hanham
Siston
Bridge Yate
Doynton
Marshfield
Cold Ashton
Thickwood
SHELDON MANOR
Chippenham
Studley
Bremhill
Hilmarton
Highway

A4174
Warmley
Wick
Colerne
Corsham
CORSHAM COURT
Easton
Notton
A4
Derry Hill
BOWOOD HOUSE
Calne
Compton Bassett
Cherhill

Oldland
Upton Cheyney
St Catherine
Alcombe
Hawthorn
LACKHAM
Gastard
LACOCK ABBEY
FOX-TALBOT MUS
Bowden Hill
Mile Elm
Sandy Lane
Quemerford
Calstone Wellington

KEYNSHAM
North Stoke
Langridge
Northend
Batheaston
Box
Neston
Lacock
Chittoe
Blackland
Stockley
MORGAN'S HILL

Saltford
Kelston
Charlcombe
Swainswick
Bathford
Whitley
Shaw
Norrington Common
Sandridge
Bromham
Heddington
ROUNDWAY HILL

Chewton Keynsham
Weston
Bath
Bathampton
Monkton Farleigh
Atworth
Beanacre
A350
Bowerhill
Rowde
Roundway
Bishops Cannings

Corston
Newton St Loe
Twerton
ROYAL CRESCENT
Claverton
AMERICAN MUS
South Wraxall
Broughton Common
Melksham
A365
Sells Green
Coate

Compton Dando
Stanton Prior
Englishcombe
Odd Down
Combe Down
Bradford Leigh
Broughton Gifford
GREAT CHALFIELD MANOR
Holt
Seend Cleeve
Seend
Poulshot
Devizes
BROADLEAS GARDENS

Marksbury
Inglesbatch
PRIOR PARK
Monkton Combe
Winsley
Bradford-on-Avon
THE COURTS
Kennet & Avon Canal
Semington
Potterne
Stert
CANAL

Priston
PRISTON MILL
Southstoke
Combe Hay
Limpley Stoke
Turleigh
Staverton
Hilperton
Great Hinton
Worton
Potterne Wick
Urchfont

Farmborough
Dunkerton
Twinhoe
Freshford
TITHE BARN
THE BARN
WESTWOOD MANOR
Trowle Common
Ashton Common
Keevil
Bulkington
Marston

Timsbury
Carlingcott
Wellow
Hinton Charterhouse
Westwood
Barton Farm
PETO
Earleigh Hungerford
Trowbridge
Bulkington
A361
West Ashton
Steeple Ashton
ST

High Littleton
Hallatrow
Camerton
NORWOOD FARM
LONG BARROW
Norton St Philip
Wingfield
Yarnbrook
Great Cheverell

Paulton
Clandown
Shoscombe
Tellisford
Southwick
West Ashton
Heywood
Coulston
Erlestoke
Little Cheverell
Market Lavington

RADSTOCK MUSEUM
Radstock
Writhlington
Faulkland
RODE BIRD GARDENS
North Bradley
Coulston
Edington
West Lavington
Eastcott
Easterton

Midsomer Norton
Kilmersdon
Hemington
Hardington
Rode
BROKERSWOOD
Hawkeridge
Bratton
BRATTON CAMP & WHITE HORSE
B3098
Littleton Pannell

Charlton
Stratton on the Fosse
Buckland Dinham
Woolverton
Laverton
Beckington
Rudge
Westbury Leigh
Westbury
Summer Down
West Lavington Down

Holcombe
Nettlebridge
Coleford
Highbury
Mells
Great Elm
Oldford
Dilton Marsh
A350
Littleton Down
Gore Cross

Vobster
Little Green
Clink
Berkley
Upton Scudamore
Tilshead

Oakhill
Stoke St Michael
Leigh upon Mendip
Whatley
Frome
NUNNEY CASTLE
Chapmanslade
Corsley
WARMINSTER SERVICES
Warminster
SALIS

Downhead
Chantry
Nunney
The Butts
Corsley Heath
A36
Boreham
WARMINSTER DEWEY MUSEUM
Chitterne
B390

Heale
East Cranmore
Tytherington
West Woodlands
Bugley
Bishopstrow
Norton Bavant
Heytesbury
PLA

EAST SOMERSET RAILWAY
Trudoxhill
LONGLEAT
Crockerton
Shear Cross
Sutton Veny
Tytherington
Upton Lovell
Codford St Peter
Codford St Mary
PARSONAGE DOWN

Doulting
West Cranmore
Chesterblade
Wanstrow
Witham Friary
Horningsham
Longbridge Deverill
Knook
Corton
A36
Boyton
Sherrington

Evercreech
Westcombe
Batcombe
Upton Noble
Bruton Forest
Maiden Bradley
Monkton Deverill
Brixton Deverill
Stockton
Stapleford
Steeple Langford

Milton Clevedon
Gare Hill
Kilmington
Kingston Deverill
A350
CRANBORNE
Great Ridge
Wylye
WYLYE VALLEY
Little Langford

Lamyatt
Bruton
North Brewham
Norton Ferris
Keysley Down
Pertwood
Chicklade
Hanging Langford
A36
WYLYE DOWN

Ansford
Hardway
South Brewham
Stourton
ALFRED'S TOWER
STOURHEAD
STOURTON HOUSE
WHITE SHEET HILL
Berwick St Leonard
Fonthill Bishop
Chilmark
VALE OF WAR
Grovely

Castle Cary
Redlynch
Stoney Stoke
Penselwood
Zeals
West Knoyle
Hindon
Fonthill Gifford
Teffont Magna
Baverstock

Shepton Montague
WINCANTON
Charlton Musgrove
Bayford
Queen Oak
The Green
East Knoyle
Ridge
Chilmark
Teffont Evas
Dinton

HADSPEN GARDEN
Bratton Seymour
Leigh Bourton Common
13
BUSH FARM BISON CENTRE
Mere
Barrow Street
Fonthill Gifford
Tisbury
13
A303

Galhampton
Yarlington
Huntingford
Milton on Stour
Sedgehill
Newtown
Hatch
Sutton Mandeville
Fovant

North Cadbury
Lattiford
North Cheriton
Wyke
Gillingham
Ham Common
Elm
Swallowcliffe
OLD WARDOUR CASTLE
Ansty
Fifield

A303
Blackford
Compton
Bayford
Semley
PRESCOMBE DOWN
Broad Chalke

Scale: 0 1 2 3 4 5 6 miles
0 1 2 3 4 5 6 7 8 9 10km

M4

Swindon A419 A419

Wootton Bassett
The Marsh
16
B4553
B4005
North Wroughton
Great Western (Maize) Maze
Coate
Coate Water
A259
Wanborough
Liddington
Hinton Parva
Idstone
Ashbury
Kingston Warren
Bassett
238

LAMBOURN DOWNS

Farnborough
Cat

Broadtown Lane
Broad Town
Bushton
Clyffe Pypard
Clyffe Pypard 215
Clevancy
Winterbourne Bassett
Berwick Bassett

Vroughton
37
B4005
Chiseldon
Elcombe
Badbury
277
15
Upper Upham
Woodsend
Aldbourne
Baydon
12
Membury Services 216
38
Upper Lambourn
Lambourn
Eastbury
East Garston
South Fawley
Fawley
Brightwalton
Chaddleworth
Leckhampstead Thicket
Leckhampstead
Lilley
P
Fanborough

MARLBOROUGH DOWNS
272
HACKPEN HILL
Southend
Ogbourne St George
Ogbourne St Andrew
Rockley
Ogbourne Maizey
Preston
Whittonditch
Ramsbury
A346
NORTH WESSEX
Woodlands St Mary
Great Shefford
Shefford Woodlands
Weston
Welford
Winterbourne
Westbrook
Boxford
Snelsmore Common
Bagnor
B4494

Windmill Hill
Avebury Manor
Yatesbury
Avebury
THE RIDGEWAY
FYFIELD DOWN
Mildenhall
Axford
Kennet
14
Hungerford Newtown
Chilton Foliat
Wickham
M4

Beckhampton
A4
West Kennett
Silbury Hill
STONE CIRCLE
W KENNETT AVENUE
LONG BARROW
East Kennett
THE SANCTUARY
Fyfield
Manton
Lockeridge
West Overton
Marlborough
Savernake Forest
Cadley
Froxfield
CHISBURY CHAPEL
Chisbury
Little Bedwyn
Bagshot
Hungerford
A4
Halfway
Avington
Kintbury
Laylands Green
Hamstead Marshall
26
Enborne
A34
Newbury
Speer
30
Stockcross
Donnington
164

A4361

DOWNS
294 TAN HILL
294 MILK HILL
Huish
Clench Common
Durley
Great Bedwyn
Shalbourne
Ham
West Woodhay
Inkpen
Upper Green
Walbury Hill 297
North End
Woolton Hill
East Woodhay
Broad Laying
HIGHCLERE CASTLE
Highclere

Horton
Allington
Stanton St Bernard
Alton Priors
All Cannings
Honey Street
Wilcot
289
Wootton Rivers
Oare
New Mill
Crofton
Stibb Green
Eastcourt
CROFTON BEAM ENGINES
WILTON WINDMILL
Wilton
Rivar
Buttermere
Combe
East Woodhay
East End
B4192

VALE OF PEWSEY
Beechingstoke
Woodborough
Bottlesford
Pewsey
Easton Royal
Milton Lilbourne
Burbage
West Grafton
East Grafton
Marten
Wexcombe
Oxenwood
Linkenholt
Vernham Street
Netherton
Ashmansworth
Crux Easton
261
HIGHCLERE CASTLE

Patney
Wedhampton
Chirton
Marden
HENGE
Wilsford
North Newnton
Manningford Bruce
Southcott
238
Manningford Bohune
Charlton
Pewsey Down
Aughton
Brunton
Collingbourne Kingston
Sunton
Tidcombe
262 HAYDOWN HILL
Vernham Dean
Upton
Faccombe
Fosbury
SU
A342

Rushall
Upavon
Lower Everleigh
Everleigh
Cadley
Collingbourne Ducis
Collingbourne Forest
Upper Chute
Chute Standen
Lower Chute
Tangley
Ibthorpe
Hurstbourne Tarrant
Woodcott
Dunley
Binley
18
A343

Black Heath
Compton Down
West Chisenbury
East Chisenbury
Compton
Enford
Fifield
Coombe
Haxton
Haxton Down
224
A338
Ludgershall
Wildhern
Doles Wood
Stoke
St Mary Bourne

West Down
Enford Down
Orcheston Down
Fittleton
Netheravon
30
A3026
North Tidworth
Tidworth
Hatherden
Clanville
Enham Alamein
Little London
Smannell
Picket Piece
Hurstbourne Priors
Whitchurch

BURLEY
DOVECOTE
Figheldean
Ablington
Milston
South Tidworth
Shipton Bellinger
Kimpton
Fyfield
Appleshaw
Penton Mewsey
Charlton
A303
Weyhill
FINKLEY DOWN FARM PARK
Andover Down
A3093
Andover
Middleton
Longparish

Orcheston
B3086
Elston
Shrewton
Larkhill
Knighton Down
Durrington
WOODHENGE
Bulford Camp
204 BEACON HILL
THRUXTON
Thruxton
THE HAWK CONSERVANCY TRUST
WEYHILL SERVICES
Monxton
Amport
Abbotts Ann
Anna Valley
Upper Clatford
B3420
Harewood Forest
26
Forton
TIDBURY RING
Bullington
Barton Stacey
S

A344
STONEHENGE
Countess
Bulford
70
CHOLDERTON RARE BREEDS
CHOLDERTON
Cholderton
Quarley
Grateley
172
Goodworth Clatford
Wherwell
Newton Stacey
SUTTON SCOTNEY SERVICES

B3083
40
A303
Winterbourne Stoke
West Amesbury
Amesbury
Wilsford
Palestine
Newton Tony
B3084
A343
Chilbolton
10
A30
A272

Berwick St James
Stapleford
Little Wishford
Great Wishford
Lake
Great Durnford
Upper Woodford
Boscombe
Allington
A338
Over Wallop
MUSEUM OF ARMY FLYING
Middle Wallop 143
Nether Wallop
Longstock
Leckford
158
A3057
Crawley
Worthy Down
B3049

Wood
Stoford
South Newton
30
Middle Woodford
Lower Woodford
Idmiston
Porton
Gomeldon
Winterbourne Dauntsey
Lopcombe Corner
East Winterslow
Stockbridge
158
Little Somborne
Up Somborne
Ashley
H

DOUR
Barford St Martin
Wilton
Quidhampton
Bemerton
A36
Ditchampton
WILTON HOUSE
Chilhampton
Stratford Sub Castle
OLD SARUM
New Sarum
P&R
SALISBURY
Winterbourne Earls
Winterbourne Gunner
158
A30
Firsdown
Middle Winterslow
162
West Winterslow
151 WHITESHOOT HILL
Broughton
Houghton
Horsebridge
King's Somborne
Little Somborne
Sparsholt
FLOWERDOWN BARROWS
174
FARLEY MOUNT
Week

Burcombe
Netherhampton
West Harnham
East Harnham
SALISBURY CATH
14
P&R
Milford
Laverstock
Pitton
Farley
West Tytherley
East Tytherley
WEST DEAN
Brook
14
FARLEY MOUNT

Stra 5rd Tony
Coombe Bissett
A354
Bishopstone
Ebble
Homington
Odstock
Nunton
Bodenham
Whaddon
Alderbury
Britford
157 PEPPERBOX HILL
West Grimstead
East Grimstead
East Dean
West Dean
Lockerley
Butt's Green
Mottisfont
MOTTISFONT ABBEY
8
Michelmersh
Standon
Braishfield
Olive
A30
G

West Ilsley
East Ilsley
Farnborough
Moulsford
South Stoke
Checkendon
Stoke Row
Highmoor Cross
Satwell
Shepherd's Green
Rotherfield Greys
Rotherfield Peppard
Woodcote
Fawley
South Fawley
Catmore
Compton
Streatley
Goring
Cray's Pond
Goring Heath
Sonning Common
Cane End
Kidmore End
Binfield Hth
Lilley
Stanmore
Aldworth
Streatley on Thames
Lower Basildon
St Bartholomew's
Beale Park
Whitchurch Hill
Basildon Park
Whitchurch
Mapledurham
Tokers Green
Dunsden Green
Emmer Green
Play Hatch
Caversham
Brightwalton
Leckhampstead Thicket
Peasemore
Beedon
World's End
The Living Rainforest
Hampstead Norreys
Ashampstead
Quicks Green
Upper Basildon
Pangbourne
Purley
Maple-Durham
Chaddleworth
East Garston
Woodlands St Mary
Great Shefford
Leckhampstead
West Berkshire
Downend
Yattendon
Tidmarsh
Reading
Shefford Woodlands
Weston
Welford
Chieveley
Hare Little
Hungerford
Hermitage
Frilsham
Bradfield
Sulham
Tilehurst
Winterbourne
Chieveley Services
Longlane
Stanford Dingley
North Street
Englefield
Hungerford Newtown
Wickham
Westbrook
Boxford
Snelsmore Common
Curridge
Bucklebury
Clay Hill
Tutts Clump
Theale
Calcot Row
Mus. of English Rural Life
Whitley
Foliat
Hungerford
Berkshire
Southend
Bagnor
Donnington Castle
Cold Ash
Upper Bucklebury
Chapel Row
Ufton Nervet
Sheffield Bottom
Reading Services
Burghfield
Shinfield
Halfway
Stockcross
Donnington
Shaw
Thatcham
Beenham
Sulhamstead
Burghfield Hill
Threemile Cross
Arborfield
Avington
Speen
Midgham
Woolhampton
Aldermaston Wharf
Burghfield Common
Grazeley
Kintbury
Laylands Green
Enborne
Newbury
Kennet
Padworth
Wokefield Park
Spencers Wood
Farley Hill
Hamstead Marshall
Greenham
Brimpton
Aldermaston
Mortimer
Swallowfield
Inkpen
Upper Green
Wash Common
Crookham
Wasing
Stratfield Mortimer
Beech Hill
Riseley
West Woodhay
Ball Hill
North End
Newtown
Ashford Hill
Mortimer West End
Roman Town
Stratfield Saye House
Wellington
Walbury Hill
Woolton Hill
Broad Laying
Headley
Plastow Green
Ashford Hill
Heath End
Pamber Heath
Silchester
Stratfield Saye
West End Green
East Woodhay
Burghclere
Sandham Memorial Chapel
Tadley
Fair Oak Green
Bramshill
Buttermere
Combe
East End
Highclere
Tothill Services
Ecchinswell
Baughurst
Pamber Green
Little London
Heckfield
Stratfield Turgis
Turgis Green
Hazeley
Linkenholt
Faccombe
Highclere Castle
Whitway
Kingsclere
Wolverton Common
West Heath
Pamber End
Bramley
Hound Green
Mattingley
Netherton
Sydmonton
Wolverton
Charter Alley
Sherfield on Loddon
Hartley Westpall
Ashmansworth
Old Burghclere
Ramsdell
The Vyne
Lyde Green
Crux Easton
Hannington
Monk Sherborne
Sherborne St John
Church End
Rotherwick
West Green
Upton
Woodcott
North Oakley
Milestones
Chineham
Newnham
Hook
Ibthorpe
Hurstbourne Tarrant
Dunley
Binley
Litchfield
Ibworth
Upper Wootton
Popley
Daneshill
Wootton St Lawrence
Winklebury
Oakridge
Basingstoke
Old Basing
Doles Wood
Stoke
Newfound
Worting
South View
North Warnborough
Cole Henley
Quidhampton
Deane
Oakley
Buckskin
South Ham
Hatch
Up Nately
St Mary Bourne
Overton
Ashe
Kempshott
Mapledurwell
Greywell
Odiham
Little London
East Oakley
Brighton Hill
Enham Alamein
Smannell
Laverstoke
Steventon
Cliddesden
Tunworth
Upton Grey
Picket Piece
Whitchurch
Winslade
Long Sutton
Charlton
Finkley Down Farm Park
Hurstbourne Priors
Broadmere
South Warnborough
Andover
Andover Down
Tufton
North Waltham
Dummer
Farleigh Wallop
Ellisfield
Herriard
Weston Patrick
Anna Valley
Upper Clatford
Harewood Forest
Middleton
Longparish
Micheldever Services
Nutley
Southrope
Forton
Tidbury Ring
Popham
Axford
Goodworth Clatford
Hampshire
Woodmancott
Golden Pot
Lasham
Wherwell
Newton Stacey
Bullington
Micheldever Forest
Preston Candover
Bradley
Shalden
Holybourne
Barton Stacey
West Stratton
Lower Wield
Ansty
Chilbolton
Sutton Scotney Services
Wonston
East Stratton
Curtis Museum
Alton
Fullerton
Sutton Scotney
Micheldever
Brown Candover
Holt End
Bentworth
Beech
Wilsom
Stoke Charity
Upper Wield
Flying
Longstock
Leckford
Micheldever Wood
Northington
Hattingley
Wivelrod
Medstead
Jane Austen's House
West Worldham
Chawton
Mid-Hants Railway
South Wonston
Northington Grange
South Town
Lower Farringdon
Upper Farringdon
Stockbridge
Crawley
Worthy Down
Winchester Services
Old Alresford
Bighton
Soldridge
Four Marks
Selborne
Little Somborne
Kings Worthy
Martyr Worthy
Itchen Abbas
Itchen Stoke
New Alresford
Gundleton
North Street
Newton Valence
All Saints Church
Up Somborne
Littleton
Bishop's Sutton
Ropley
Kitwood
Gilbert White's House & The Oates Museum
Flowerdown Barrows
Headbourne Worthy
Easton
Avington
Ovington
Mid-Hants Railway
Ropley Dean
Monkwood
East Tisted
King's Somborne
Ashley
Sparsholt
Farley Mount
Weeke
Winchester
Winnall
Tichborne
West
Colemore
Hawkley
Brook
Intech Science Centre & Planetarium
Cheriton
Bramdean
Chilcomb
New Cheriton
Hinton Ampner
High Cross
Ashford Hangers
St Catherine's Hill
Longwood Warren
Beauworth
Brockwood
Privett
Stoner Hill
Michelmersh
Braishfield
Kilmeston
North
South
M4
M3
A34
A303
A339
A31
A33
A4
P&R
0 1 2 3 4 5 6 miles
0 1 2 3 4 5 6 7 8 9 10 km

Uxbridge
Hillingdon
Yeading
Southall
Cowley
Yiewsley
Hayes
West Drayton
Heston
Brentford
Isleworth

Windsor
Burnham
Maidenhead
Slough
SLOUGH
Langley
Richings Park
Harmondsworth
Sipson
Cranford
HOUNSLOW

Henley-on-Thames
Warren Row
Pinkneys Grn.
Bray
Dorney
Eton Wick
Eton
Datchet
Colnbrook
Poyle
Longford
HEATHROW AIRPORT
Feltham

Maidenhead
Waltham St Lawrence
Holyport
WINDSOR
Old Windsor
Wraysbury
Stanwell
Ashford
Hampton
Teddington

Woodley
Twyford
Shurlock Row
Hawthorn Hill
FOREST
Cranbourne
Winkfield
EGHAM
Staines
Littleton
Sunbury-on-Thames
West Molesey
East Molesey

Earley
Winnersh
Binfield
Popeswood
Bullbrook
Ascot
Englefield Green
Virginia Water
Thorpe
Shepperton
Walton-on-Thames
Esher

WOKINGHAM
Bracknell
BRACKNELL FOREST
Easthampstead
Sunninghill
Sunningdale
Broomhall
CHERTSEY
Addlestone
WEYBRIDGE
Hersham
Claygate

Crowthorne
Bagshot
Windlesham
Lightwater
West End
Chobham
Woodham
Byfleet
Whiteley Village
Cobham
Oxshott

Finchampstead
Little Sandhurst
Sandhurst
CAMBERLEY
York Town
Donkey Town
Bisley
Knaphill
Horsell
WOKING
Old Woking
Ripley
Downside
Leatherhead

Eversley
Yateley
Frogmore
Blackwater
Hawley
Cove
Frimley
Frimley Green
Deepcut
Brookwood
St John's
Mayford
Pyrford
Wisley
Martyr's Green
Fetcham

Fleet
Church Crookham
ALDERSHOT
FARNBOROUGH
Ash Vale
Pirbright
Fox Corner
Sutton Green
East Horsley
Effingham
Great Bookham
Westhumble

Crookham Village
Ash
Tongham
Normandy
Wood Street
Stoughton
Burpham
West Clandon
East Clandon
Ranmore Common

Farnham
Seale
Puttenham
Wanborough
Compton
Guildford
Shalford
Albury
Shere
Gomshall
Abinger Hammer
Westcott
Wotton

Runfold
The Sands
Shackleford
Farncombe
Bramley
Wonersh
Blackheath
Farley Green
Abinger Common

Rowledge
Tilford
Elstead
Milford
Godalming
Thorncombe Street
Grafham
Shamley Green
Hurt Wood
Peaslake
Holmbury St Mary

Frensham
Thursley
Witley
Wormley
Hambledon
Cranleigh
Ewhurst
Walliswood
Oakwoodhill

Hindhead
Grayshott
Shottermill
Haslemere
Chiddingfold
Dunsfold
Alfold Crossways
Rudgwick
Warnham

Liphook
Camelsdale
Ramsnest Common
Fisherstreet
Plaistow
Ifold
Loxwood
Slinfold

Fernhurst
Northchapel
Mackerel's Common
Roundstreet Common
Itchingfield

Uxbridge
Hillingdon
Yiewsley
Hayes
Southall
EALING
Acton
Willesden
Harlesden
Camden
Islington
Bethnal Green
Shoreditch
Stratford
East Ham
Barking
West Ham
Poplar
Finsbury
Holborn
City
Paddington
Kensington
Westminster
Southwark
Bermondsey
Blackwall Tunnel
North Woolwich
Woolwich Ferry
Woolwich
Greenwich
Charlton
Deptford
LAMBETH
Peckham
Camberwell
New Cross
Lewisham
Catford
Eltham
New Eltham
Mottingham
Chislehurst
BROMLEY
Bickley
Petts Wood
Chiswick
Hammersmith
Fulham
Chelsea
Battersea
Kew Br.
Brentford
Heston
Harlington
Cranford
Sipson
West Drayton
Longford
HEATHROW AIRPORT
Stanwell
Stanwell Moor
East Bedfont
West Bedfont
HOUNSLOW
Isleworth
Richmond
Mortlake
Roehampton
Putney
Clapham
Wandsworth
Brixton
Dulwich
Balham
Streatham
Tooting
Wimbledon
Merton
Norwood
Sydenham
Penge
Beckenham
Elmers End
Eden Park
West Wickham
Hayes
Bromley Common
Keston
Farnborough
Shirley
Addiscombe
Croydon
South Croydon
Addington
New Addington
Selsdon
Sanderstead
Hamsey Green
Farleigh
Warlingham
Biggin Hill
Cudham
South Street
Tatsfield
Woldingham
Titsey
Limpsfield
Westerham
Oxted
Limpsfield Chart
Crockham Hill
Tandridge
Godstone
South Godstone
Bletchingley
Nutfield
South Nutfield
Redhill
Earlswood
Reigate
Merstham
Caterham
Chaldon
Old Coulsdon
Coulsdon
Whyteleafe
Kenley
Purley
Wallington
Sutton
Carshalton
Hackbridge
Mitcham
Morden
St. Helier
Cheam
Ewell
EPSOM
Banstead
Woodmansterne
Burgh Heath
Chipstead
Kingswood
Tadworth
Walton on the Hill
Lower Kingswood
Headley
Ashtead
Leatherhead
Fetcham
Great Bookham
Little Bookham
Effingham
Mickleham
Westhumble
Ranmore Common
Dorking
Pixham
Brockham
Betchworth
Buckland
Westcott
Wotton
Abinger Hammer
Abinger Common
Gomshall
Shere
Albury
Chilworth
Newlands Corner
East Clandon
West Clandon
West Horsley
East Horsley
Ockham
Ripley
Pyrford
Wisley
West Byfleet
Byfleet
New Haw
WEYBRIDGE
CHERTSEY
Hersham
Walton-on-Thames
Whiteley Village
Cobham
Oxshott
Stoke D'Abernon
Claygate
Esher
Hook
Chessington
Tolworth
Surbiton
Kingston upon Thames
New Malden
Worcester Park
Thames Ditton
Long Ditton
East Molesey
West Molesey
Sunbury-on-Thames
Hampton
Teddington
Twickenham
Hanworth
Feltham
Ashford
Staines
Laleham
Littleton
Shepperton
Kingston Vale
Raynes Park
Thornton Heath
Selhurst
South Norwood
Upper Tooting
Holmwood
North Holmwood
South Holmwood
Coldharbour
Holmbury St Mary
Peaslake
Sutton
Farley Green
Brook
Hurt Wood
Ewhurst
Ewhurst Green
Cranleigh
Rowly
Forest Green
Ockley
Walliswood
Oakwoodhill
Ellen's Green
Rowhook
Rudgwick
Alfold
Tisman's Common
Bucks Green
Park Street
Slinfold
The Haven
Roundstreet Common
Warnham
Strood Green
Broadbridge Heath
Horsham
Roffey
Kingsfold
Rusper
Capel
Clark's Green
Beare Green
Newdigate
Parkgate
Charlwood
Norwood Hill
Strood Green
Leigh
Sidlow
Salfords
Doversgreen
Ridge Green
Nalderswood
Meath Green
Hookwood
Horley
Weatherhill
Smallfield
Outwood
Horne
Burstow
GATWICK AIRPORT
Copthorne
Felbridge
East Grinstead
Crawley Down
Three Bridges
Pound Hill
Worth
Crawley
County Oak
Ifield
Lambs Green
Broadfield
Faygate
Tilgate
Pease Pottage
Colgate
St Leonard's Forest
Tilgate Forest Row
Balcombe
Balcombe Lane
Handcross
Staplefield
Slaugham
Ashfold Crossways
Monk's Gate
Lower Beeding
Warninglid
Southwater
Brook Street
Slough Green
Whitemans
Ardingly
Highbrook
Horsted Keynes
Danehill
Chelwood Gate
Chelwood Common
Nutley
Wych Cross
Sharpthorne
West Hoathly
Selsfield Common
Turners Hill
Saint Hill
Sunnyside
Ashurstwood
Forest Row
Blackwell
Hammerwood
Lullenden
Dormansland
Lingfield
Felcourt
Newchapel
Marsh Green
Edenbridge
Crouch House Green
Crowhurst
Crowhurst Lane End
Blindley Heath
Marlpit Hill
Surrey
Greater London
M25
M23
M3
M4
A3
A22
A23
A24
A25
A264
0 1 2 3 4 5 6 miles
0 1 2 3 4 5 6 7 8 9 10 km

THAMES ESTUARY

Thurrock

CANVEY ISLAND

Dagenham
Rainham
Creekmouth
Thamesmead
Belvedere
Erith
Abbey Wood
Plumstead
Welling
Bexleyheath
Sidcup
Crayford
DARTFORD
Bexley
Wilmington
Swanley
Orpington
Chelsfield

South Ockendon
Aveley
Purfleet
Dartford Crossing
West Thurrock
Grays
Tilbury
Chadwell St Mary
West Tilbury
East Tilbury
Stanford-le-Hope
Corringham
Coryton
Leigh Beck

Greenhithe
Swanscombe
NORTHFLEET
GRAVESEND
Betsham
Southfleet
Singlewell
Shorne
Higham
Chalk
Cliffe
Cooling
High Halstow
St Mary Hoo
Allhallows
Lower Stoke
Stoke
North Street
Grange

Strood
ROCHESTER
CHATHAM
Gillingham
Rainham
Medway
Hoo St Werburgh
Upnor
Frindsbury
Brompton
Luton
Wayfield
Walderslade
Hempstead
Wigmore
Breach
Newington
Hartlip
Upchurch

Sevenoaks
Otford
Kemsing
Borough Green
Wrotham
Ightham
Platt
West Malling
East Malling
Ditton
Maidstone
Bearsted
Leeds
Broomfield
Langley
Kingswood
Sutton Valence
Headcorn
Staplehurst

Kent

TONBRIDGE
ROYAL TUNBRIDGE WELLS
Southborough
Pembury
Paddock Wood
Marden
Cranbrook
Hawkhurst
Goudhurst
Sissinghurst
Benenden

Crowborough
Mayfield
Wadhurst
Ashdown Forest
Hartfield
Withyham
Groombridge
Frant
Lamberhurst
Flimwell
Ticehurst
Etchingham
Bodiam

HIGH WEALD

CANVEY ISLAND
Coryton
Leigh Beck
Thames Haven
Shoeburyness
Cambridge Town
THAMES ESTUARY
Halstow Marshes
St Mary's Marshes
Allhallows-on-Sea
Allhallows
St Mary Hoo
Lower Stoke
Isle of Grain
Grain
Cliffe
Cooling
High Halstow
Stoke
North Street
Medway
Cliffe Woods
Medway
Chattenden
Hoo St.Werburgh
Upnor
HISTORIC DOCKYARD
Frindsbury
Brompton
Grange
RIVERSIDE
ROCHESTER
CHATHAM
Gillingham
Luton
Wayfield
Rainham
Upchurch
Lower Halstow
Ham Green
Breach
Bobbing
Iwade
Moor Street
Wigmore
Hempstead
Walderslade
Newington
Hartlip
Sheerness
West Minster
Halfway Houses
Minster
Queenborough
Rushenden
Chetney Marshes
Eastchurch
Warden Pt.
Warden
Leysdown-on-Sea
ISLE OF SHEPPEY
ELMLEY
Isle of Harty
THE SWALE
Shell Ness
WHITSTABLE
Tankerton
Swalecliffe
Seasalter
Chestfield
South Street
Yorkletts
Kemsley
The Swale
Milton Regis
SITTINGBOURNE
Conyer
Uplees
Borden
Bapchild
Barrow Green
Teynham
Oad Street
Rodmersham
Lynsted
Bredhurst
Stockbury
Tunstall
Highsted
Oare
Graveney
Faversham
Goodnestone
Ospringe
Preston
Dargate
Hernhill
Honey Hill
Tyler Hill
Blean
Rough Common
Boughton Street
Dunkirk
Harbledown
South Green
Bredgar
Swanton Street
Milstead
Bicknor
Hucking
Thurnham
Detling
Boxley
Sandling
Maidstone
Broad Street
Fristed
Wormshill
Doddington
Newnham
Eastling
Sheldwich
North Street
Selling
Oversland
Chartham Hatch
Thanington
Chartham
Roseacre
Bearsted
Hollingbourne
Eyhorne Street
Wichling
Throwley
Badlesmere
Shottenden
Old Wives Lees
Shalmsford Street
Chilham
Street End
Tovil
East Farleigh
Shepway
Otham
West Street
Warren Street
Stalisfield Green
Leaveland
Molash
Garlinge Green
Petham
Loose
Boughton Monchelsea
Langley
Leeds
Broomfield
Harrietsham
Lenham
Langley Heath
Kingswood
Sandway
Lenham Heath
Challock
Godmersham
Sole Street
Crundale
Waltham
Linton
Chart Corner
Chart Sutton
Sutton Valence
Warmlake
Ulcombe
Grafty Green
Boughton Malherbe
Charing
Charing Heath
Westwell Leacon
Westwell
Boughton Aluph
Bilting
Boughton Lees
Wye
Hassell Street
Bodsham
Elmsted
Stelling Minnis
Rabbit's Cross
Cross-at-Hand
Milebush
Marden
Egerton
Egerton Forstal
Little Chart
Ram Lane
Goat Lees
Southernden
Headcorn
Hawkenbury
Pluckley
Pluckley Thorne
Hothfield
Kennington
Brook
Hastingleigh
Staplehurst
Sinkhurst Green
Smarden
Smarden Bell
Maltman's Hill
Great Chart
Ashford
Willesborough
Hinxhill
Willesborough Lees
Brabourne
Lymbridge Green
Stowting
Marden Beech
Marden Thorn
Knox Bridge
Frittenden
Lashenden
Haffenden Quarter
Wissenden
Sevington
Brabourne Lees
Winchet Hill
Curtisden Green
Standen
Bethersden
Kingsnorth
Mersham
Smeeth
Postling
Collier's Green
Cranbrook Common
Three Chimneys
Biddenden
Tanden
Stubbs Cross
Shadoxhurst
Cheeseman's Green
Sellindge
Sellindge Lees
Beach
Stanford
Wilsley Pound
Sissinghurst
High Halden
Bromley Green
Aldington Frith
Clap Hill
Aldington
Newingreen
Cranbrook
East End
St Michael's
Henghurst
Shirkoak
Orlestone
Bonnington
Court-at-Street
Lympne
Pedlinge
Hartley
Parkgate
Woodchurch
Ham Street
Bilsington
West Hythe
Tenterden
Benenden
Brook Street
Kenardington
Ruckinge
Hamstreet
Royal Military Canal
Palmarsh
Gill's Green
Iden Green
Leigh Green
Warehorne
Newchurch
Burmarsh
High Street
Hawkhurst
Dingleden
Rolvenden
Small Hythe
Reading Street
Appledore Heath
Snave
Four Throws
Rolvenden Layne
ISLE OF OXNEY
Appledore
ROMNEY MARSH
Dymchurch
The Moor
Sandhurst
Peening Quarter
Stone
Snargate
St Mary in the Marsh
Wittersham
The Stocks
Brenzett
Ivychurch
St Mary's Bay
Hurst Green
Ham Green
Bodiam
0 1 2 3 4 5 6 miles
0 1 2 3 4 5 6 7 8 9 10 km

5　　6　　7　　8　　6 5　9

A

1 8

B

THE SHELL GROTTO

Margate ▲MARGATE　Cliftonville　Foreness Pt.

Westgate on Sea　Kingsgate
B2052　**NORTH**
Northdown　**FORELAND**
LIGHTHOUSE

RECULVER
RECULVER TOWERS
AND ROMAN FORT
Reculver　Minnis Bay　Birchington　St Peter's

HERNE BAY　Hillborough
Beltinge　A299　QUEX HOUSE　Northwood　**BROADSTAIRS**
Greenhill　Broomfield　St Nicholas at Wade　A28　Acol　Isle of Thanet　BLEAK HOUSE
Herne　A299　SPITFIRE AND HURRICANE MEM　Newington　DICKENS HOUSE MUSEUM
Hoath　Boyden Gate　A299　B2190　KENT INTERNATIONAL　Manston　Dumpton
Calcott　Chislet　Sarre　WINDMILL　A253　Monkton　Way　Cliffsend　**Ramsgate**
Broadoak　Upstreet　Hersden　A28　West Stourmouth　**Minster**　MARITIME MUSEUM
Sturry　Westbere　Grove　STODMARSH　Preston　East Stourmouth　Cliffsend　Pegwell
Fordwich　Stodmarsh　Elmstone　Hoaden　Ware　SANDWICH & PEGWELL BAY
Canterbury　P&R　Wickhambreux　Ickham　Guilton　RICHBOROUGH CASTLE　ST. AUGUSTINE'S CROSS　Pegwell Bay
ST. AUGUSTINE'S ABBEY　CANTERBURY　AMPHITHEATRE　A256
HOWLETTS WILD ANIMAL PARK　Littlebourne　Wingham　A257　Great Stonar
A2　Bramling　WINGHAM BIRD PARK　**Sandwich**　Sandwich Bay
Nackington　Bekesbourne　Goodnestone　Ash　Marshborough　Woodnesborough　Stone Cross　Royal St. George's
Patrixbourne　Adisham　Staple　Gore　Worth　TOLL
Bridge　GOODNESTONE PARK　**Eastry**　Ham　Finglesham
Lower Hardres　Chillenden　Knowlton　A258
Bishopsbourne　Aylesham　Easole Street　Northbourne　Sholden　MARITIME AND LOCAL HISTORY MUSEUM
Kingston　Nonington　Snowdown　Betteshanger　**Deal**
Upper Hardres Court　Barham　Womenswold　Tilmanstone　Elvington　Great Mongeham　DEAL CASTLE
Bossingham　Derringstone　Barfrestone　EAST KENT RLY　**Walmer**
ELHAM VALLEY VINEYARD　Woolage Green　**Eythorne**　West Langdon　Ripple　WALMER CASTLE AND GARDENS
Denton　A2　Coxhill　Shepherdswell　East Studdal　Sutton
Wingmore　LYDDEN　Coldred　East Langdon　Ringwould　**Kingsdown**
Wootton　LYDDEN TEMPLE EWELL　Martin　A258
Elham　Selsted　Lydden　**Whitfield**　Guston　Martin Mill
Rhodes Minnis　ST JOHN'S COMMANDERY　Ewell Minnis　Temple Ewell　**St Margaret's at Cliffe**
Ottinge　BUTTERFLY CENTRE　Swingfield Street　CRABBLE CORN MILL　West Cliffe　THE BAY MUSEUM
Lyminge　Swingfield Minnis　A256　Buckland　A2　THE PINES GARDEN　St Margaret's Bay
Paddlesworth　Densole　Alkham　ROMAN PAINTED HOUSE　WHITE CLIFFS　**SOUTH FORELAND**
KENT BATTLE OF BRITAIN MUSEUM　Drellingore　Maxton　CASTLE & HELLFIRE CORNER
Etchinghill　Hawkinge　West Hougham　Farthingloe　**DOVER**
CHANNEL TUNNEL　Capel le Ferne　A20　Aycliff　DE BRADELEI WHARF
Newington　A20　B2011　SAMPHIRE HOE
ELHAM VALLEY RLY MUS　Cheriton　13　12　11A　East Wear Bay
Saltwood　**Folkestone**　ROTUNDA　CLIFF LIFT
Hythe　Sandgate

19

THE DOWNS

TR

OOSTENDE 4:00
BOULOGNE 1:15

CALAIS 1:30
DUNKERQUE 1:45

BOULOGNE 1:45

CHANNEL TUNNEL

C

D

E

F

1 3

G

5　　6　　7　　8　　6 5　9

MYNYDD PRESELI
Pontfaen
Crymych
Tegryn
Cwmorgan
Tanglwst
Bryn-Iwan
Cwmduad
Hermon
Pentre-galar
Mynachlog-ddu
Llanfyrnach
Hen-feddau fawr
Dinas
Trelech
New Inn
Rosebush
Puncheston
Castlebythe
Tufton
Henry's Moat
Maenclochog
Llangolman
Glandy Cross
Glandwr
Hebron
Blaen-waun
Cynwyl Elfed
Blaen-y-coed
Pen-y-bont
Woodstock
Wallis
New Moat
Efailwen
Pant-y-Caws
Llanglydwen
Cefn-y-pant
WELSH CHOCOLATE FARM
Cwmbach
Llanwinio
Talog
Bwlchnewydd
LLYS-Y-FRAN RESERVOIR
Llys-y-frân
Walton East
Llanycefn
Pen-ffordd
Maesgwynne
Cross-hands
Login
Cwmfelin Mynach
Llanboidy
Gellywen
Ty-hen
Abernant
Newchurch
Dyffryn
Tre-vaughan
Clarbeston
Clarbeston Road
Bletherston
Llandissilio
Hiraeth
Henllan Amgoed
Meidrim
Merthyr
Carmarthen (Caerfyrddin)
Llanfallteg
Clunderwen
Cwmfelin Boeth
Llangynin
Sarnau
Gelli
Wiston
LLAWHADEN CASTLE
Bethesda
Bancyfelin
CORS GOCH, LLANLLWCH
Llanllwch
Llawhaden
Robeston Wathen
Narberth (Arberth)
Llanddewi Velfrey
Whitland
Trevaughan
Pwll-trap
Backe
Afon Taf
St Clears (Sanclêr)
Llangynog
Llangain
The Rhos
Blackpool
WILSON MUSEUM
Crinow
Lampeter Velfrey
Llwyn-y-brain
Llanddowror
PICTON CASTLE & GARDENS
BLUE LAGOON
HERONS BROOK
Minwear
OAKWOOD
Cross Hands
Cold Blow
Princes Gate
Tavernspite
Halfpenny Furze
Llanybri
Morfa Bach
Afon Tywi
Landshipping
Templeton
Red Roses
Llandawke
DYLAN THOMAS BOATHOUSE
Llansteffan
Landshipping Quay
Martletwy
Ludchurch
Longstone
Llanteg
Llansadurnen
Laugharne
CASTLE
Ferryside
Black Tar
Yerbeston
FOLLY FARM
Reynalton
Marros
Brook
Broadway
Broadlay
Port Lion
Loveston
Thomas Chapel
Stepaside
COLBY WOODLAND GARDEN
MUSEUM OF SPEED
Pendine
East Marsh
Llansaint
Cresswell Quay
Lawrenny
Begelly
Jeffreyston
Kilgetty
Amroth
Pendine Sands
Traeth Pentywyn
Cresselly
West Williamston
Broadmoor
Carew Newton
East Williamston
Saundersfoot
PEMBROKESHIRE COAST
ARFORDIR PENFRO
Cosheston
CAREW CASTLE
Redberth
Carew
Broadfield
Milton
Sageston
New Hedges
Pembrey Forest
Pembroke (Penfro)
Carew Cheriton
TENBY DINOSAUR PARK
TUDOR MERCHANT'S HOUSE
LAMPHEY BISHOP'S PALACE
MANOR HOUSE WILDLIFE PARK
Tenby (Dinbych-y-Pysgod)
St Florence
Gumfreston
CARMARTHEN BAY
BAE CAERFYRDDIN
Lamphey
Hodgeston
Jameston
Penally
Freshwater East
Lydstep
Giltar Pt.
Caldey Sound
Cheriton or Stackpole Elidor
Trewent Pt.
Trwyn Trewent
MANORBIER CASTLE
Manorbier
MANORBIER
Old Castle Hd.
Caldey Island
Ynys Bŷr
Chapel Pt.
Trwyn Capel
Stackpole Hd.
Pen Stackpole
SN
SS
Burry Holms
Rhossili Bay
Bae Rhossili
Worms Head
Penrhyn-Gŵyr
A40
A477
A478
A4066
A484
B4313
B4329
B4299
B4333
B4298
B4328
B4314
B4315
A4115
A4075
B4586
B4316
B4318
B4584
A4139
B4312
PEMBREY
0 1 2 3 4 5 6 miles
0 1 2 3 4 5 6 7 8 9 10 km

Carmarthenshire
(Sir Gaerfyrddin)
Swansea
(Abertawe)
Llandovery
Llandeilo
Ammanford (Rhydaman)
Llanelli
Burry Port (Porth Tywyn)
Kidwelly (Cydweli)
Pontarddulais
Gorseinon
Clydach
Pontardawe
Ystalyfera
Ystradgynlais
Neath (Castell-Nedd)
Port Talbot
Margam
Baglan
Aberavon
Swansea (Abertawe)
The Mumbles (Y Mwmbwls)
Mumbles Hd.
Trwyn yr Mwmbwls
SWANSEA BAY
BAE ABERTAWE
Oxwich Bay
Bae Oxwich
Port Eynon Bay
Bae Port Eynon
Port Eynon Pt.
Trwyn Port Eynon
Pwlldu Hd.
Pen Pwlldu
Whiteford Pt.
Trwyn Whiteford
Llanrhidian Sands
Traeth Llanrhidian
GOWER
Brechfa Forest
BLACK MOUNTAIN
Y MYNYDD DU
VALE OF TYWI
DYFFRYN TYWI
SWANSEA VALLEY
CWM ABERTAWE
Mynydd y Gwair
Mynydd March-Hywel
Carmarthen
Pembrey
Brynamman
Llandybie
Cross Hands
Tumble
Llangennech
Loughor
Gowerton
Morriston
Skewen
Glais
Rhossili
Llangennith
Port-Eynon
Oxwich
Horton
Penmaen
Parkmill
Bishopston
Killay
Dunvant
Llandovery
Llangadog
Talley
Brechfa
Abergorlech
Bethlehem
Trapp
Garnant
Glanaman
Cwmgors
Gwaun-Cae-Gurwen
Tairgwaith
Felindre
Pontlliw
Penllergaer
Llangyfelach
CORK 10:00
ILFRACOMBE 0:50
SN
SS
46
47
34
5
6
7
8
A
B
C
D
E
F
G

Llandovery

A40 Llanwrda
Cilgwyn
Myddfai
Halfway

Llanddeusant
Llangadog
Talsarn
Trecastle
Cwmwysg
Llywel
Sennybridge (Pont Senni)
Penpont
Llanspyddid

Brecon (Aberhonddu)

Myrtle Hill
Twynllanan
Llanddeusant
Crai
Defynnog
Heol Senni
Tai'r-Bull
Libanus
Llanfrynach
Pencelli

BRECON BEACONS

BLACK MOUNTAIN / MYNYDD DU

SN

Glas Fynydd Forest

FFOREST FAWR

FAN BRYCHEINIOG 802
FAN GIHIRYCH 575
FAN FAWR 734
PEN Y FAN 886
DANYWENALLT 769

Brynamman
Rhosaman
Cwmllynfell
Ystradowen
Abercraf
Cwmgiedd
Penrhos
Caehopkin
Coelbren
Ystradfellte
Nant-ddu

THE NATIONAL SHOWCAVES FOR WALES
DAN-YR-OGOF
Craig-y-nos
Penwyllt
OGOF FFYNNON DDU
Glyntawe

Ystradgynlais
Ystalyfera
Seven Sisters
Dyffryn Cellwen
Onllwyn
Penderyn
Hirwaun
Garwnant Visitor Centre

Pontardawe
Clydach
Resolven
Glyn-neath (Glynedd)
Rhigos
Aberdare (Aberdâr)
Merthyr Tydfil (Merthyr Tudful)
Dowlais

VALE OF NEATH / CWM NEDD

Neath (Castell-Nedd)

Rhondda

Neath

Port Talbot (Castell-Nedd Port Talbot)

Cynon Taff

Mountain Ash (Aberpennar)
Treharris
Abercynon
RHONDDA
Treherbert
Treorchy (Treorci)
Ferndale
Maerdy
Tonypandy
Porth
Pontypridd

Baglan
Maesteg
Pontycymer
Blaengarw
Nantyffyllon

Port Talbot
Margam
MARGAM ABBEY AND STONES MUSEUM

Bridgend (Pen-y-bont ar Ogwr)

(Rhondda Cynon Taf)

Tonyrefail
Llantrisant
Beddau

SWANSEA BAY / BAE ABERTAWE

SS

Porthcawl
Pyle (Y Pîl)
North Cornelly
South Cornelly
Kenfig
Coychurch
Laleston
Ewenny
Ogmore
St Brides super Ely

M4

Scale: 0 1 2 3 4 5 6 miles / 0 1 2 3 4 5 6 7 8 9 10 km

Map — South East Wales (Cardiff, Newport, Monmouthshire)

BLACK MOUNTAINS / Y MYNYDDOEDD DUON

Monmouthshire (Sir Fynwy)

Torfaen (Tor-faen)

Caerphilly (Caerffili)

Newport (Casnewydd)

CARDIFF (Caerdydd)

Key places:
Llanfilo, Talgarth, Tredustan, Trefecca, Tredomen, Llandefaelog-tre'r-graig, Llanfihangel Tal-y-llyn, Talyllyn, Llangors, Llangasty Talyllyn, Cathedine, Scethrog, Cross Oak, Llansantffraed, Talybont-on-Usk, Aber-Village, Bwlch, Tretower, Pen Cerig-calch, Llanbedr, Crickhowell, Llangattock, Llangenny, Cwrt-y-gollen, Glangrwyney, Bettws, Llanfihangel-Crucorney, Pandy, Tre-wyn, Stanton, Llanthony, Longtown, Oldcastle, Cwmyoy, Walterstone, Ewyas Harold, Pontrilas, Rowlestone, Abbey Dore, Howton, Grosmont, Hoaldalbert, White Rocks, Cross Ash, Skenfrith, Norton, Garway, Broad Oak, Llangua, Monmouth Cap, Kentchurch, Orcop, Garway Hill, Michaelchurch, Pencoy.

Abergavenny (Y Fenni), Govilon, Gilwern, Llanelly, Clydach, Blackrock, Brynmawr, Nantyglo, Blaenavon, Blaina, Ebbw Vale (Glyn Ebwy), Tredegar, Rhymney (Rhymni), New Tredegar (Tredegar Newydd), Bargoed (Bargod), Blackwood (Coed Duon), Oakdale, Crumlin (Crymlyn), Newbridge, Pontypool (Pont-y-pwl), Griffithstown, Abersychan, Abertillery (Abertyleri), Cwmbran (Cwmbrân), Pontnewydd, Crosskeys, Risca (Rhisga), Caerleon (Caerllion), Christchurch, Newport (Casnewydd), Caerphilly (Caerffili), Machen, Bedwas, Bassaleg, Rogerstone, Duffryn, Castleton, Marshfield, St Brides, Peterstone Wentlooge, Rumney, Whitchurch, Llanishen, Radyr, Llandaff, Cardiff (Caerdydd), Ely, St Fagans.

Raglan, Usk (Brynbuga), Llangwm, Llangybi, Tredunnock, Llanvaches, Penhow, Caerwent, Caldicot, Rogiet, Magor, Redwick, Goldcliff, Whitson, Nash, Llanwern, Llandevenny, Undy, Portishead, Redcliff Bay, Avonmouth, Sheepway.

SECOND SEVERN CROSSING

Roads: A470, A465, A40, A449, A4042, A4043, A48, M4, M48, A466, A4137, A4233, B4233, B4521, B4598, B4246, B4251, B4600, A472.

Monmouthshire (Sir Fynwy)

FOREST OF DEAN

GLOUCESTERSHIRE

South Gloucestershire

Ross-on-Wye

Monmouth (Trefynwy)

Chepstow (Cas-gwent)

Newent

Cinderford

Lydney

Coleford

Caldicot

Thornbury

Yate

Chipping Sodbury

Wotton-under-Edge

Dursley

Frampton on Severn

Berkeley

Filton

Patchway

Mangotsfield

Severn Beach

Almondsbury

River Severn

The Noose

Tintern Abbey

Raglan

Grosmont

Kilpeck

Skenfrith

Tewkesbury · Bishop's Cleeve · Winchcombe · Stow-on-the-Wold · Bourton-on-the-Water · Cheltenham · Charlton Kings · Gloucester · Hucclecote · Churchdown · Northleach · Stroud · Stonehouse · Chalford · Cirencester · Fairford · Lechlade-on-Thames · Nailsworth · Tetbury · South Cerney · Cricklade · Highworth · Malmesbury · Wootton Bassett · Swindon · Stratton St Margaret · Purton

M5 · M4 · A40 · A417 · A419 · A429 · A433 · A436 · A435 · A46 · A38 · A424 · A44 · A346 · A361 · A3102 · A4259

COTSWOLD · GLOUCESTERSHIRE · WILTSHIRE

Moreton-in-Marsh
Batsford
Bourton on the Hill
Lemington
Great Wolford
Whichford
Hook Norton
Wigginton
South Newington
Milton
Barford St John
Barford St Michael
Deddington
Clifton
Hempton
Cutsdean
Ford
Sezincote
Barton on the Heath
Long Compton
Little Compton
Great Rollright
Swerford
Worton
Great Tew
Over Worton
Duns Tew
North Aston
Somerton
Middle Aston
Upper Heyford
Condicote
Temple Guiting
Longborough
Donnington
Evenlode
Chastleton
Salford
Over Norton
Little Tew
Heythrop
Ledwell
Sandford St Martin
Middle Barton
Steeple Aston
Kineton
Upper Swell
Lower Swell
Stow-on-the-Wold
Broadwell
Adlestrop
Cornwell
Oddington
Daylesford
Maugersbury
Chipping Norton
Church Enstone
Enstone
Westcott Barton
Gagingwell
Steeple Barton
Lower Heyford
Lidstone
Cleveley
Kiddington
Over Kiddington
Glympton
Naunton
Upper Slaughter
Lower Slaughter
Wyck Rissington
Icomb
Kingham
Churchill
Bledington
Sarsden
Chadlington
Spelsbury
Taston
Bourton-on-the-Water
Notgrove
Cold Aston
Westcote
Bruern Abbey
Lyneham
Idbury
Upper Rissington
Little Rissington
Clapton-on-the-Hill
Fifield
Chilson
Ascott-under-Wychwood
Charlbury
Tackley
Wootton
Milton under Wychwood
Shipton-under-Wychwood
Stonesfield
Fawler
Woodstock
Bunkers Hill
Shipton on Cherwell
Turkdean
Great Rissington
Farmington
Finstock
Combe
Thrupp
Leafield
Ramsden
Blenheim Palace
Sherborne
Great Barrington
Taynton
Fordwells
Whiteoak Green
East End
North Leigh
Bladon
Begbroke
Kidlington
Northleach
Windrush
Little Barrington
Burford
Fulbrook
Asthall Leigh
Hailey
Long Hanborough
Church Hanborough
Freeland
Yarnton
Eastington
Lodge Park
Swinbrook
Minster Lovell
Crawley
New Yatt
Fossebridge
Coln St Dennis
Asthall
Witney
Barnard Gate
Cassington
Aldsworth
Westwell
Signet
Charterville Allotments
Cogges
South Leigh
High Cogges
Eynsham
Wolvercote
Coln Rogers
Winson
Holwell
Shilton
Bradwell Grove
Curbridge
Brize Norton
Ducklington
Swinford
Wytham
Farmoor
Ablington
Arlington
Bibury
Carterton
Lew
Hardwick
Sutton
Stanton Harcourt
Botley
Eastleach Turville
Eastleach Martin
Coln St Aldwyn's
Hatherop
Filkins
Alvescot
Black Bourton
Kencot
Broadwell
Yelford
Brighthampton
West End
Cumnor
North Hinksey
Quenington
Fyfield
Broughton Poggs
Southrop
Aston
Cote
Standlake
Northmoor
Eaton
Chawley
Langford
Bampton
Weald
Little Faringdon
Clanfield
Shifford
Bessels Leigh
Appleton
Wootton
Boars Hill
Poulton
Milton End
Fairford
Horcott
Grafton
Radcot
Chimney
Duxford
Lamborough Hill
Foxcombe Hill
Sunningwell
Meysey Hampton
Lechlade-on-Thames
Kelmscot
Carswell Marsh
Hinton Waldrist
Longworth
Netherton
Fyfield
Tubney
Cothill
Whelford
Inglesham
Eaton Hastings
Buckland
Kingston Bagpuize
Southmoor
Shippon
Marston Meysey
Dunfield
Buscot
Littleworth
Pusey
Frilford
Garford
Marcham
Caldecott
Down Ampney
Kempsford
Upper Inglesham
Faringdon
Latton
Castle Eaton
Hannington Wick
Hatford
Charney Bassett
Lyford
Drayton
Cricklade
Hannington
Coleshill
Great Coxwell
Shellingford
Little Coxwell
Stanford in the Vale
East Hanney
West Hanney
Milton
Highworth
Fernham
Goosey
Denchworth
Steventon
Broad Blunsdon
Baulking
Longcot
Stanton Fitzwarren
Blunsdon St Andrew
Sevenhampton
Watchfield
Uffington
Grove
Milton Hill
Rowstock
Harwell
Shrivenham
West Challow
East Challow
West Hendred
East Hendred
Ardington
Widham
Haydon Wick
Penhill
South Marston
Kingston Lisle
Sparsholt
Childrey
Wantage
Lockinge
Purton
Stratton St Margaret
Upper Stratton
Woolstone
Compton Beauchamp
Bourton
Letcombe Regis
West Ginge
East Ginge
Lydiard Millicent
Pinehurst
Rodbourne Cheney
Gorse Hill
Walcot
Rodbourne
Swindon
Ashbury
Idstone
Bishopstone
Hinton Parva
Letcombe Bassett
Chilton
Coate
Wanborough
Liddington
West Ilsley
East Ilsley
North Wroughton
Wroughton
Badbury
Fawley
Farnborough
Upper Lambourn
Catmore
Broadtown Lane
Chiseldon
South Fawley
Lilley
Stanmore
Lambourn
Brightwalton
Beedon
Baydon
Eastbury
East Garston
Chaddleworth
Leckhampstead Thicket
Peasemore
Woodsend
Aldbourne
World's End
VALE OF WHITE HORSE
LAMBOURN DOWNS
Kingston Warren
Oxford
SP
SU
Thames or Isis
Farmoor Reservoir
Evenlode
Windrush
Leach
Coln
Ock
Akeman Street
Oxford Canal
Glyme
Dorn
ARBORETUM
SEZINCOTE
WELLINGTON AVIATION MUSEUM
CHASTLETON HOUSE
ROLLRIGHT STONES
HOOK NORTON BREWERY VISITOR CENTRE
COTSWOLD FARM PARK
STOW-ON-THE-WOLD
THE OLD MILL
MODEL VILLAGE
BIRDLAND PARK & GARDENS
ROUSHAM HOUSE
NORTH LEIGH ROMAN VILLA
MINSTER LOVELL HALL AND DOVECOTE
COTSWOLD WILDLIFE PARK
COGGES MANOR FARM MUS
ARLINGTON MILL
ARLINGTON ROW
LODGE PARK
OXFORD SERVICES
CONDUIT HOUSE
THE THAMES PATH
CHIMNEY MEADOWS
KELMSCOTT MANOR
BUSCOT PARK
KINGSTON BAGPUIZE
BADBURY HILL
GREAT BARN
SWINDON AND CRICKLADE RAILWAY
STANTON PARK
GWR MUS
UFFINGTON CASTLE
WHITEHORSE HILL
WAYLAND'S SMITHY
THE RIDGEWAY
ARDINGTON HO
ASHDOWN PARK
COATE WATER
GREAT WESTERN (MAIZE) MAZE
LONDON OXFORD
ASHMOLEAN MUS
COUNTY HALL
0 1 2 3 4 5 6 miles
0 1 2 3 4 5 6 7 8 9 10 km

B u c k i n g h a m SP

o r d

Oxford, Cowley, Bicester, Aylesbury, Buckingham, Bletchley, Thame, Wendover, Princes Risborough, Prestwood, Great Missenden, High Wycombe, Marlow, Henley-on-Thames, Maidenhead, Windsor, Didcot, Wallingford, Abingdon, Goring

Croughton, Aynho, Souldern, Fritwell, Fewcott, Ardley, Bucknell, Caversfield, Woodfield, Highfield, Chesterton, Kirtlington, Weston-on-the-Green, Bletchingdon, Hampton Poyle, Charlton on Otmoor, Islip, Noke, Oddington, Beckley, Elsfield, Woodeaton, Marston, Headington, Wheatley, Horspath, Cuddesdon, Garsington, Denton, Toot Baldon, Marsh Baldon, Nuneham Courtenay, Radley, Culham, Clifton Hampden, Burcot, Dorchester, Berinsfield, Drayton St Leonard, Newington, Chalgrove, Pyrton, Watlington, Cuxham, Brightwell Baldwin, Britwell Salome, Ewelme, Benson, Roke, Warborough, Shillingford, Long Wittenham, Little Wittenham, Appleford, Sutton Courtenay, Didcot, East Hagbourne, South Moreton, North Moreton, Aston Upthorpe, Aston Tirrold, Blewbury, Upton, West Hagbourne, Hampstead Norreys, Ashampstead, Aldworth, Streatley, Goring, Cleeve, Whitchurch, Mapledurham, Pangbourne, Purley, Upper Basildon, Lower Basildon, Woodcote, Checkendon, Stoke Row, Satwell, Highmoor Cross, Greys Court, Shepherd's Green, Rotherfield Greys, Rotherfield Peppard, Sonning Common, Kidmore End, Cane End, Binfield Heath, Shiplake, Wargrave, Hare Hatch, White Waltham, Maidenhead

Buckingham, Tingewick, Radclive, Mixbury, Water Stratford, Finmere, Barton Hartshorn, Chetwode, Preston Bissett, Hillesden, Gawcott, Padbury, Adstock, Addington, Steeple Claydon, Middle Claydon, East Claydon, Botolph Claydon, Winslow, Granborough, North Marston, Oving, Pitchcott, Quainton, Whitchurch, Creslow, Hoggeston, Dunton, Swanbourne, Stewkley, North End, South End, Wing, Cublington, Aston Abbotts, Hardwick, Weedon, Bierton, Aylesbury, Weston Turville, Aston Clinton, Buckland, Halton, Wendover, Ellesborough, Great Kimble, Little Kimble, Meadle, Askett, Monks Risborough, Princes Risborough, Saunderton, Bledlow, Loosley Row, Lacey Green, Speen, Hughenden Valley, Naphill, Bradenham, West Wycombe, Downley, High Wycombe, Loudwater, Flackwell Heath, Bourne End, Cookham, Maidenhead

Linslade, Soulbury, Burcott, Wing, Ledburn, Mentmore, Wingrave, Rowsham, Long Marston, Wilstone, Drayton Beauchamp, The Lee, Dunsmore, Ballinger Common, Little Hampden, Great Hampden, Prestwood, Great Missenden, Kingshill, South Heath, Cryers Hill, Widmer End, Hazlemere, Tylers Green, Penn, Beaconsfield, Wooburn Green, Bourne End, Cookham Rise, Cookham, Cookham Dean

A421, A43, A413, A41, A418, A4010, A413, A34, A40, M40, A4074, A404, A4130, A329, A418

The Ridgeway, Ridgeway Path, The Thames Path, Chiltern

Waddesdon Manor, Claydon House, Quainton Windmill, Buckinghamshire Railway Centre, Boarstall Tower, Brill Windmill, Waterperry Gardens, Rycote Chapel, Stonor, Chinnor & Princes Risborough Railway, Didcot Railway Centre, Cholsey and Wallingford Railway, West Wycombe Caves, Hughenden Manor, River & Rowing Museum, Greys Court, Maharajah's Well, Beale Park, The Living Rainforest, St Bartholomew's, Maple-durham, Pendon Museum, Dorchester Abbey

Central Bedfordshire
Luton
Hertfordshire
Chiltern Hills
Windsor and Maidenhead
Bletchley
Woburn
Leighton Buzzard
Dunstable
Houghton Regis
Aylesbury
Tring
Berkhamsted
Wendover
Princes Risborough
Great Missenden
Chesham
Amersham
Hemel Hempstead
St Albans
Harpenden
Hitchin
Watford
Rickmansworth
Borehamwood
High Wycombe
Beaconsfield
Marlow
Maidenhead
Slough
Windsor
Eton
Uxbridge
Ruislip
Harrow
Wembley
Ealing
Hayes
Southall
Brentford
Isleworth
Heston
Edgware
Stanmore
Bushey
Elstree
London Colney
Kings Langley
Abbots Langley
Chalfont St Giles
Chalfont St Peter
Gerrards Cross
Burnham
Datchet
Twyford
Kimpton
Redbourn
Wheathampstead
Markyate
Whipsnade
Stopsley
Toddington
Barton le Clay
Shillington
Stewkley
Wing
Cheddington
Ivinghoe
Bovingdon
Chorleywood
Northwood
Pinner
Yiewsley
West Drayton
Langley
0 1 2 3 4 5 6 miles
0 1 2 3 4 5 6 7 8 9 10 km

LETCHWORTH • Baldock • Wallington • Norton • Sandon • Buckland • Chipping • Langley Lower Green • Upper Green • Newport • Debden • Howlett End

Walsworth • Willian • Clothall • Rushden • Weston • Throcking • Buntingford • Wyddial • Hare Street • Anstey • Meesden • Brent Pelham • Starlings Green • Clavering • Wicken Bonhunt • Rickling • Priors Hall Barn • Widdington • Hamperden End • Cutler's Green

Great Wymondley • Little Wymondley • Graveley • Cromer Windmill • Cottered • Ardeley • Aspenden • Westmill • Hay Street • Furneaux Pelham • East End • Manuden • Farnham Green • Henham • Elsenham • Molehill Green • Brick End • Duton Hill

Stevenage • Benington Lordship Gardens • Benington • Haultwick • Levens Green • Wellpound Green • Little Hadham • Birchanger • Stansted Mountfitchet • STANSTED AIRPORT • Bambers Green • Takeley

Langley • Knebworth • Aston End • Shephall • Broadwater • Aston • Datchworth • Watton at Stone • Dane End • Collier's End • Standon • Much Hadham • Hadham Ford • Bury Green • BISHOP'S STORTFORD • Takeley Street • Smith's Green • Hope End Green

Old Knebworth • Codicote • Woolmer Green • Datchworth Green • Bull's Green • Sacombe • Barwick • High Cross • Hadham Cross • Spellbrook • Allens Green • Hatfield Heath • Gt. Hallingbury • Lit. Hallingbury • Hatfield Broad Oak • Great Canfield

Welwyn • Ayot St Peter • Oaklands • Burnham Green • Bramfield • Chapmore End • Tonwell • Thundridge • Wareside • Widford • Perry Green • Sawbridgeworth • High Wych • Sheering • White Roding • Abbess Roding • Beauchamp Roding

WELWYN GARDEN CITY • Hertford • Hertford Heath • St Margarets • Great Amwell • Stanstead Abbotts • Eastwick • Gilston • Churchgate Street • Matching • Matching Green

Hatfield • Letty Green • Hertingfordbury • Ware • Hunsdon • Hailey • Netteswell • HARLOW • Potter Street • High Laver • Little Laver • Fyfield • Willingale

HODDESDON • Brickendon • Bayford • Little Berkhamsted • Broxbourne • Roydon • Gt. Parndon • Tye Green • Foster Street • Magdalen Laver • Moreton • Norton Mandeville

Hatfield Garden Village • The Ryde • Essendon • Wildhill • Wormley West End • Brookmans Park • Wormley • Lower Nazeing • Broadley Common • Thornwood Common • Epping Green • Epping Upland • North Weald Bassett • Toot Hill • Greensted • Chipping Ongar • High Ongar • Nine Ashes

Colney Heath • Welham Green • Northaw • Cuffley • Goff's Oak • Turnford • CHESHUNT • Waltham Cross • Epping • Ivy Chimneys • Coopersale Common • Fiddlers Hamlet • Stanford Rivers • Little End • Stondon Massey • Doddinghurst

POTTERS BAR • Botany Bay • Enfield Chase • Forty Hill • Enfield Wash • Sewardstone • WALTHAM ABBEY • Upshire • Theydon Bois • Stapleford Tawney • Navestock Heath • Navestock Side • Pilgrims Hatch

Monken Hadley • BARNET • East Barnet • Cockfosters • Winchmore Hill • ENFIELD • Sewardstonebury • High Beach • Debden • Loughton • Abridge • Stapleford Abbotts • Lambourne End • Havering-atte-Bower • Noak Hill • BRENTWOOD • Great Warley

Mill Hill • Finchley • Friern Barnet • Southgate • Edmonton • Wood Green • Ponders End • Chingford • Buckhurst Hill • Chigwell • Chigwell Row • Grange Hill • Hainault • Collier Row • Harold Hill • Harold Wood • Gidea Park

Hendon • Golders Green • Hampstead • Highgate • Hornsey • Tottenham • Walthamstow • Woodford • Woodford Bridge • Barkingside • Newbury Park • ROMFORD • Hornchurch • Upminster

Cricklewood • Willesden • Camden • Stoke Newington • Leytonstone • Leyton • Wanstead • Seven Kings • ILFORD • Manor Park • Becontree • Elm Park • North Ockendon

Harlesden • Kilburn • Regents Park • Islington • Hackney • Forest Gate • East Ham • BARKING • DAGENHAM • South Hornchurch • Rainham • South Ockendon

Acton • Paddington • Kensington • Hyde Park • LONDON • Finsbury • Shoreditch • Bethnal Green • Stratford • West Ham • Poplar • Beckton • Creekmouth • Wennington • Aveley • North Stifford

Chiswick • Hammersmith • Fulham • Chelsea • Westminster • LAMBETH • Southwark • Bermondsey • Blackwall Tunnel • North Woolwich • Woolwich Ferry • Thamesmead • Purfleet • THURROCK SERVICES • Grays

Kew Br. • Battersea • Camberwell • Peckham • New Cross • Deptford • Greenwich • Charlton • Woolwich • Plumstead • Abbey Wood • Erith • Belvedere • Dartford Crossing • South Stifford

Putney • Kidbrooke • Welling • Bexleyheath • Slade Green • Swanscombe

ESSEX

Major towns and places:

BISHOP'S STORTFORD, Stansted Mountfitchet, STANSTED AIRPORT, Great Dunmow, Halstead, BRAINTREE, Coggeshall, Kelvedon, Tiptree, Witham, Maldon, Heybridge, Chelmsford, Great Baddow, Danbury, Writtle, Ingatestone, Chipping Ongar, North Weald Bassett, BRENTWOOD, Billericay, Wickford, RAYLEIGH, Rochford, Hockley, Hawkwell, South Woodham Ferrers, Hullbridge, Basildon, Laindon, Pitsea, Thundersley, Hadleigh, Leigh on Sea, Westcliff-on-Sea, SOUTHEND-ON-SEA, Canvey Island, Romford, Hornchurch, Upminster, Dagenham, Rainham, Aveley, Thurrock, South Ockendon, Stanford-le-Hope, Corringham, Tilbury, Chadwell St Mary, West Tilbury, East Tilbury

Places (selection):

Newport, Howlett End, Wimbish Green, Little Sampford, Finchingfield, Sible Hedingham, Maplestead, Alphamstone, Wicken Bonhunt, Ricklin, Debden, Debden Cross, Thaxted, Wethersfield, Blackmore End, Gosfield, Colne Engaine, Wakes Colne, Quendon, Ugley, Henham, Monk Street, Lindsell, Great Bardfield, Shalford, Church End, Beazley End, High Garrett, Earls Colne, Greenstead Green, Chappel, Great Tey, Ugley Green, Elsenham, Broxted, Duton Hill, Bardfield Saling, Shalford Green, Jasper's Green, Bocking Churchstreet, Stisted, Pattiswick, Broad Green, Molehill Green, Brick End, Great Easton, Bran End, Stebbing, Great Saling, Panfield, Bocking, Bradwell, Tye Green, Cressing, Coggeshall Hamlet, Silver End, Feering, Gore Pit, Messing, Inworth, Takeley, Smith's Green, Hope End Green, Little Dunmow, Bannister Green, Rayne, Great Notley, Black Notley, White Notley, Faulkbourne, Rivenhall End, Great Braxted, Great Totham, Hatfield Forest, Great Canfield, Bishop's Green, Hounslow Green, North End, Hartford End, Great Leighs, Little Leighs, Fairstead, Terling, Chipping Hill, Wickham Bishops, Little Totham, Broad Street Green, Heybridge, Hatfield Broad Oak, Aythorpe Roding, Leaden Roding, High Easter, Howe Street, Pleshey, Great Waltham, Little Waltham, Flack's Green, Langford, Sheering, Hatfield Heath, Matching, White Roding, Margaret Roding, Good Easter, Chignall Smealy, Broomfield, Nounsley, Hatfield Peverel, Woodham Walter, Matching Tye, Abbess Roding, Mashbury, Chignall St James, Parsonage Green, Boreham, Little Baddow, Maldon, Matching Green, Beauchamp Roding, Boyton Cross, Roxwell, Springfield, Chelmer Village, Heybridge Basin, Northey I., Foster Street, High Laver, Little Laver, Shellow Bowells, Writtle, Chelmsford, Runsell Green, Magdalen Laver, Moreton, Willingale, Great Oxney Green, Widford, Saltcote, Woodham Mortimer, Bovinger, Bobbingworth, Shelley, Norton Mandeville, Norton Heath, Loves Green, Galleyend, Danbury, Cock Clarks, Rudley Green, Mundon, North Weald Bassett, Greensted, Chipping Ongar, Nine Ashes, Blackmore, Mill Green, Galleywood, Howe Green, Bicknacre, Purleigh, Cold Norton, Latchingdon, Stanford Rivers, Little End, Stondon Massey, Fryerning, West Hanningfield, East Hanningfield, Stapleford Tawney, Kelvedon Hatch, Doddinghurst, Swallows Cross, Ingatestone, Stock, Reservoir, Woodham Ferrers, Stow Maries, Navestock Heath, Mountnessing, Coalhill, Rettendon, South Hanningfield, Downham, Navestock Side, Heybridge, Queen's Park, Norsey Wood, Ramsden Heath, Rettendon Place, Battlesbridge, South Fambridge, Canewdon, Stanford Rivers, Pilgrims Hatch, Hutton, Ramsden Bellhouse, Runwell, Hullbridge, Ashingdon, Havering-atte-Bower, Shenfield, South Weald, Little Burstead, South Green, Shotgate, Rawreth, Hockley, Stroud Green, Harold Hill, Ingrave, Great Warley, Herongate, Dunton Waylets, Great Burstead, Grays Hill, Nevendon, North Benfleet, Hadleigh Castle, Rochford, Harold Wood, Little Warley, North Benfleet, Bowers Gifford, Daws Heath, Eastwood, Prittlewell, Gidea Park, West Horndon, Langdon Hills, Vange, Hope's Grn., Leigh on Sea, Winter Gardens, Romford, Cranham, Bulphan, South Benfleet, Wat Tyler, Canvey Island, Westcliff-on-Sea, Rush Green, Elm Park, Hacton, Corbets Tey, Horndon on the Hill, Fobbing, Corringham, Leigh Beck, South Hornchurch, North Ockendon, Baker Street, Orsett, Mucking, Thames Haven, Belhus Woods, South Ockendon, North Stifford, Coryton, Wennington, Linford, THAMES ESTUARY, Chadwell St Mary, West Tilbury, East Tilbury, Halstow Marshes, St Mary's Marshes, Allhallows-on-Sea, Slade Green, Tilbury, Cliffe, East Tilbury, Cooling, High Halstow, St Mary Hoo, Allhallows, Lower Stoke, Isle of Grain, Belvedere

Roads: M11, M25, A120, A131, A12, A130, A414, A127, A13, A128, A176, A132, A129, A130, A1014, A1013, A282, A126, A124, A118, B1051, B1383, B1256, B1018, B1022, B1024, B1026, B1010, B1012, B1021, B1008, B1019, B183, B184, B1060, B1335, B148, B186, B187, B1421, B186

Junctions: 55, 56, 41, 40, 8, 8A, 29, 30, 31, 13, 12, 14, 15, 16, 17, 18, 19, 20A, 20B, 21, 22, 23, 24

Features: PRIORS HALL BARN, MOLE HALL WILDLIFE PARK, HOUSE ON THE HILL TOY MUS, ST MARY'S CHURCH, GLENDALE FORGE, WINDMILL, LONDON STANSTED, HATFIELD FOREST, DUNMOW SERVICES, MALTINGS, FLITCH WAY, FREEPORT BRAINTREE, GRANGE BARN, PAYCOCKES, LOCAL HISTORY MUSEUM, CRESSING TEMPLE, ST JAMES THE LESS CHURCH, COMBINED MILITARY SERVICES MUSEUM, HYTHE QUAY, CATH, MOULSHAM MILL, P&R, BARLEYLANDS FARM MUS, ST MARY MAGDALENE, HYDE HALL (RHS), TROPICAL WINGS AND BIRD GARDENS, MARSH FARM, OLD MACDONALD'S, WEALD, THORNDON, QUEENS PARK, SECRET NUCLEAR BUNKER, KELVEDON HATCH, GREENSTED CHURCH, TOOT HILL, EPPING ONGAR RLY, ST MARY AND ST HELEN'S CATH, ST MARY AND ST HELEN'S, HADLEIGH CASTLE, PLANETARIUM, ADVENTURE ISLAND, SEA LIFE CENTRE, CHERRY ORCHARD, OLD HOUSE, BELHUS WOODS, THURROCK SERVICES, SWANSCOMBE SKULL SITE, TOLL

Scale:
0 1 2 3 4 5 6 miles
0 1 2 3 4 5 6 7 8 9 10km

Bures
Nayland
Street
Stratford St Mary
A12
Brantham
STOUR VALLEY
Upper Street
Harkstead
Shotley Gate
NATURE RESERVE
Shop Corner
Shotley Gate

Wormingford
Mount Bures
Little Horkesley
Roxted
Boxted Heath
Boxted Cross
Langham
Dedham
BRIDGE COTTAGE
Dedham Heath
Cattawade
Holbrook Bay
Stour
HARWICH

SIR ALFRED MUNNINGS ART MUSEUM
Lawford
Mistley
MISTLEY TOWERS
Bradfield
Wrabnes
Parkeston
HARWICH REDOUBT FORT
Dovercourt

EAST ANGLIAN RAILWAY MUSEUM
Great Horkes
56
Manningtree
A120
Upper Dovercourt
Dovercourt

A134
WESTON HOMES COMMUNITY STADIUM
Ardleigh
Bradfield Heath
A120
Little Oakley

ESBJERG 18:00
HOEK VAN HOLLAND 6:15

Fordham
Horkesley Heath
29
Horsleycross Street
Horsley Cross
Wix
Great Oakley

West Bergholt
A12
Mile End
Little Bromley
Stone's Green

Fordstreet
HIGHWOODS
Parson's Heath
Fox Street
Great Bromley
Little Bentley
Tendring Green
Beaumont

Eight Ash Green
Aldham
ST BOTOLPH'S PRIORY
Crockleford Heath
A120
Horsey Island
HAMFORD WATER
The Naze

Marks Tey
27
Lexden
Colchester
Elmstead Market
Hare Green
Little Bentley
Tendring
Thorpe Green
Kirby-le-Soken
MARITIME MUSEUM

26
Beacon End
Stanway
EARTH WORKS
Abbey Field
Old Heath
Balls Green
Frating Green
Thorpe-le-Soken
Walton-on-the-Naze

Copford Green
Shrub End
Maypole Green
BOURNE MILL
Wivenhoe Cross
BETH CHATTO GDNS
Great Bentley
Weeley
Thorpe Green
Kirby Cross
Frinton-on-Sea

Easthorpe
Birch
COLCHESTER ZOO
Heckfordbridge
Layer de la Haye
Blackheath
Rowhedge
Wivenhoe
Alresford
Aingers Green
Weeley Heath
Great Holland

Hardy's Green
Smythe's Green
Birch Green
Malting Green
Fingringhoe
Thorrington
Row Heath
Little Clacton
CLACTON VILLAGE
HOLLAND HAVEN

Layer Marney
Layer Breton
LAYER MARNEY TOWER
Abberton
ABBERTON RESERVOIR
Langenhoe
St Osyth Heath
A133

Oxley Green
Paternoster Heath
Salcott
Peldon
Great Wigborough
Mersea Island
East Mersea
CUDMORE GROVE
Point Clear
ST OSYTH PRIORY
St Osyth
Great Clacton
Holland-on-Sea

Tolleshunt D'Arcy
B1023
Tolleshunt Major
Tollesbury
Goldhanger
COPT HALL MARSHES
Blue Row
COLNE ESTUARY
Brightlingsea
Jaywick
Clacton-on-Sea

BLACKWATER ESTUARY
West Mersea
MERSEA ISLAND MUSEUM
Colne Pt.
The Nass
Virley Channel

Blackwater
Osea I.
Sales Pt.
ST PETERS ON THE WALL
Bradwell Waterside
Bradwell on Sea
TM
D

Ramsey Island
St Lawrence
Tillingham
DENGIE

Steeple
B1021
Asheldham
Dengie

Mayland
Southminster
Ray Sand

Althorne
B1018
Stoneyhills
MANGAPPS RAILWAY MUS
Montsale
Deal Hall
Foulness Sand
Foulness Pt.
TR
E

Ostend
B1010
Creeksea
Burnham-on-Crouch
MUS
Crouch
Courtsend
Churchend
WALLASEA WETLANDS

Paglesham Churchend
Paglesham Eastend
Ballards Gore
Potton Island
FOULNESS ISLAND
MAPLIN SANDS

Barling
Little Wakering
Great Wakering
Havengore Island

Bournes Green
North Shoebury
B1017
Shoeburyness
Thorpe Bay
B1016
Cambridge Town
Shoeburyness
F

5 6 7 8
G

44

A Strumble Head
Pen Caer

ROSSLARE 3:30

ROSSLARE 1:50
(May-Sept)

Dinas Head

Tresinwen

Llanwnda

Fishguard
Bay
Bae
Abergwaun

Brynhenllan

A487

PWLL
DERI
213

Goodwick
(Wdig)
191

Lower
Town

Dinas
Cross

45

Trefasser

PEMBROKESHIRE COAST ARFORDIR PENFRO

Penbwchdy

Dyffryn

Fishguard
(Abergwaun)

B Manorowen

St Nicholas

Llanychaer

Pontfaen

PEMBROKESHIRE
COAST PATH
LLWYBR ARFORDIR
PENFRO

Scleddau

A40

A487

Llanychaer

B4313

TREGWYNT
WOOLLEN MILL

Abercastle

Granston

Trecwn

Ynysduellyn

Newbridge

Little
Newcastle

Castlebythe

Porthgain

Trefin

Mathry

CORSYDD
LLANGLOFFAN

Penclegyr

B4329

Tufton

16

Castlemorris

St Dogwells

Abereiddy

Llanrhian

Penparc

164

Treddiog

Letterston

Welsh
Hook

Wolf's
Castle

Ambleston

Woodstock

Croes-goch

B4330

B4331

14

Treffynnon

Treglemais

Llanreithan

Pont-yr-hafod

Rinaston

Wallis

LLYS-Y-FRAN
RESERVOIR

C St DAVID'S
HEAD
PENMAEN DEWI

181

Tretio

Carnhedryn

Llandeloy

Trefgarn
Owen

Hayscastle

Hayscastle
Cross

Mountain
Water

Treffgarne

Triffleton

Spittal

Walton
East

Whitesand Bay
Porth-mawr

ST DAVID'S

Rhodiad

Caerfarchell

Middle Mill

Brimaston

SCOLTON
MANOR

Treddiog
178
DUDWELL MT.

Leweston

BISHOP'S PALACE

Whitchurch

CATHEDRAL

St David's
(Tyddewi)

Nine
Wells

Solva

A487

P e m b r o k e s h i r e

Clarbeston
Road

Ramsey
Island
Ynys Dewi

Rhosson

RAMSEY
ISLAND

Ramsey Sound

Penycwm

Newgale

Wolfsdale

(S i r   B e n f r o)

Wiston

A40

Rudbaxton

Tangiers

Leechpool

D Roch
Gate

Roch

Camrose

Keeston

Pelcomb
Cross

Crundale

S T .   B R I D E S

B A Y

B A E   S A I N   F F R A I D

SM

Nolton
Haven

Simpson
Cross

PEMBROKE
MOTOR MUSEUM

Pelcomb

Haverfordwest
(Hwlffordd)

B4330

Druidston

Nolton

Lambston

Pelcomb
Bridge

Slade

A487

CASTLE MUSEUM AND
ART GALLERY

The
Rhos

PEMBROKESHIRE
COAST PATH
LLWYBR ARFORDIR
PENFRO

BROAD HAVEN

Haroldston
West

Portfield Gate

Dreenhill

Merlin's
Bridge

Millin
Cross

Uzmaston

PICTON CASTLE
& GARDENS

B4327

Broad Haven

Broadway

Pope
Hill

Boulston

Minwear

B4341

Landshipping

Little Haven

Walton West

North
Johnston

Hook

Langwm

Landshipping
Quay

Talbenny

12

Martletwy

Tower Point
Trwyn Twr

82

Walwyn's
Castle

8

Black Tar

Tiers
Cross

Johnston

West
Williamston

E Wooltack Point
Trwyn Wooltack

St Bride's

Robeston
Cross

A4076

Rosemarket

Port Lion

Houghton

NATIONAL
NATURE RESERVE

79

Marloes

B4327

Hasguard

Thornton

Steynton

Hill
Mountain

Lawrenny

Skomer
Island
Ynys Skomer

SKOMER
ISLAND

MARLOES
SANDS

St
Ishmael's

Sandy
Haven

Herbrandston

A471

10

Honeyborough

Burton

UPTON
CASTLE
GARDENS

Broad Sound

Gateholm
Island
Ynys Gateholm

Dale

Milford Haven
(Aberdaugleddau)

Waterston

Neyland

Coston

CAREW CASTLE

32

Skokholm
Island
Ynys Skokholm

Hakin

MILFORD HAVEN
ABERDAUGLEDDYF

Llanstadwell

B4325

Pembroke Dock
(Doc Penfro)

Milton

PEMBROKESHIRE COAST PARFORDIR PENFRO

71

St Ann's Hd.
Pentir St. Ann

ROSSLARE 3:45

Angle
Bay
Bae Angle

Angle

Pwllcrochan

PEMBROKE DOCK
SUNDERLAND TRUST

B4322

TOLL

Pembroke
(Penfro)

LAMPHEY
BISHOP'S
PALACE

Sheep
Island
Ynys y Defaid

Rhoscrowther

Pennar

Monkton

Lamphey

Freshwater
West

Hundleton

B4320

Maiden
Wells

71

B4584

Hodgeston

F Linney Hd.
Pentir Linney

B4319

Castlemartin

B4319

Warren

St
Twynnells

St
Petrox

Merrion

Stackpole

Chenton or East
Stackpole
Elidor

Trewent Pt.
Trwyn Trewent

ELEGUG
STACKS

Bosherston

STACKPOLE

Stackpole Hd.
Pen Stackpole

The Wash

PEMBROKESHIRE
COAST PATH
LLWYBR ARFORDIR
PENFRO

St Govan's Hd.
Pen St Gofan

SR

G

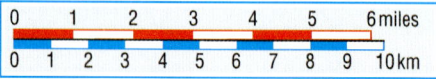

A

B

C

D

E

F

G

1 2 3 4 5

CARDIGAN

BAY

BAE

CEREDIGION

SN

46

Cwmtudu
Cwmtydu

Ynys-Lochtyn

Blaencelyn
Llangrannog
Pontgarreg
Plwm
Penbryn
Penmorfa
Pent

Cardigan I.
Ynys
Aberteifi

Cemaes Head
Pen Cemaes

MWNT
151
Gwbert

Parcllyn
Tresaith
Felinwynt
Aberporth
Brynhoffnant
Sarnau

Y Ferwig
Blaenannerch
ABERPORTH
WEST WALES
AIRPORT
A487
Tan-y-groes
Glynarthen
Rhydlewis

POPPIT SANDS
Cippyn
B4546
Cardigan
(Aberteifi)
CASTLE
Tremain
16
Blaenporth
Bettws
Ifan
Hawen
Beulah

St-Dogmaels
ABBEY
Bridgend
Penparc
Pantgwyn
Ponthirwaun
Bryngwyn
Penrhi
Coed

PEMBROKESHIRE COAST
ARFORDIR PENFRO
Moylgrove
Llangoedmor
185
Capel
Tygwydd
Troe
aur
Maesllyn

PEMBROKESHIRE
COAST PATH
LLWYBR ARFORDIR PENFRO
Monington
COEDMOR
Llechryd
Llandygwydd
46

Newport Bay
Croft
Pen-y-bryn
CILGERRAN
CASTLE
Cilgerran
Carreg-wen
11
Cwm-cou
Llandyfriog
Aber-banc

Dinas Head
Glanrhyd
197
Bridell
CORACLE CENTRE
& FLOURMILL
Cenarth
Newcastle
Emlyn
(Castell Newydd
Emlyn)
Pentrecagal
TREFI V

Fishguard Bay
Bae Abergwaun
Berry
Hill
Pontgareg
Llantood
Rhos-hill
Abercych
6

Brynhenllan
NEWPORT
Nevern
B4582
Felindre
Farchog
Newchapel
B4332
Penrherber
Aber
Arad
NATIONAL
WOOL
MUSEUM

Lower
Town
Parrog
PENGELLI
FOREST
Eglwyswrw
CLYNFYW
Boncath
Cilwendeg
CHEESE
FARM
Cwmhiraeth
Dre

Fishguard
(Abergwaun)
Dinas
Cross
Newport
(Trefdraeth)
CASTELL
HENLLYS FORT
DYFED SHIRES &
LEISURE FARM
BRO MEIGAN
GARDENS
Llanfair-
Nant-Gwyn
Blaenffos
Capel Iwan
335
MOELFRE

Lla Fychaer
347
CARNINGLI
TY CANOL
Afon Nevern
Bwlchygroes
Cwmcych
Cwmorgan

44
Cilgwyn
Crosswell
Pontyglasier
Eglwyswen
Star
Clydey
Tanglwst
Hermon

Trecwn
Pontfaen
Brynberian
Penygroes
395
Tegryn
Hen-feddau
fawr
247
Bryn-Iwan

B4313
MYNYDD   PRESELI
468
Crymych
Llanfyrnach
Dinas
Trelech

536
FOEL-
CWMCERWYN
Pentre-galar
Hermon
B4299

Little
Newcastle
Puncheston
Castlebythe
32
New Inn
Rosebush
Mynachlog-ddu
20
32
Pen-y-bont

0 1 2 3 4 5 6miles
0 1 2 3 4 5 6 7 8 9 10km
enclochog
Glandwr
289
Blaen-
waun
Gy-
ed

Ambleston
Woodstock
Glandy
Cross
3
Hebron
Llanglydwen
Llanwinio
Talo

New Moat
Pant-y-
Caws
WELSH
CHOCOLATE
FARM
Cwmbach
Cefn-y-pant

Aberystwyth
ARTS CENTRE
NATIONAL LIBRARY
CLIFF RAILWAY
Clarach
Bow Street
Penrhyn-coch
Gogerddan
Comins Coch
Capel Dewi
Llanbadarn Fawr
Trefechan
CASTLE
Penparcau
Southgate
Glanrafon
Rhydyfelin
Moriah
Capel Seion
Llanfarian
Gors
Chancery
New Cross
Blaenplwyf
Llanilar
Pentre-llyn
Rhos-y-garth
Llanddeiniol
Llangwyryfon
Llanrhystud
Lledrod
Trefenter
Rhyd-Rosser
Rhydfudr
LLYN EIDDWEN
MYNYDD BACH
Bronnant
Bontnewydd
Llansantffraed
FANTASY FARM PARK
Llanon
Nebo
Cross Inn
Blaenpennal
Bethania
Ceredigion (Sir Ceredigion)
Tyncelyn
Penuwch
Aberarth
Aberaeron
Monachty
Pennant
Crynfryn
Ffos-y-ffin
LLANERCHAERON
New Quay (Ceinewydd)
Cei-bach
Cilcennin
Llangeitho
Llwyncelyn
Newbridge
Bwlch-Llan
Capel Betws Lleucu
Maen-y-groes
Gilfachrheda
Oakford
Ciliau Aeron
Afon Aeron
Cwmtudu Cwmtydu
Cross Inn
Llanarth
Trefilan
Llundain-fach
Commins Capel Betws
Nanternis
Caerwedros
Ystrad Aeron
Tal-sarn
Gartheli
Abermeurig
Llwyn-y-groes
Ynys-Lochtyn
Dihewyd
Felinfach
Olmarch
Llangrannog
Blaencelyn
Llwyndafydd
Mydroilyn
Felindre
Temple Bar
Synod Inn
Pontgarreg
Caledrhydiau
Ffynnon-oer
Llangybi
Penbryn
Plwmp
Tresaith
Penmorfa
Pentregat
Llanfair Clydogau
Aberporth
Brynhoffnant
Gorsgoch
Cribyn
Silian
Betws Bledrws
Sarnau
Talgarreg
ABERPORTH WEST WALES AIRPORT
Tan-y-groes
Glynarthen
Capel Cynon
RHOS LLAWR CWRT
Bwlch-y-fadfa
Castell-Howell
Aber
Cwrt-newydd
Maestir
Olwen
Cellan
Lampeter (Llanbedr Pont Steffan)
Pentrefelin
Blaenporth
Rhydlewis
Ffostrasol
Llanwnnen
Cwmann
Bettws Ifan
Hawen
Pont-siân
Cwmsychpant
Pentre-bach
Beulah
Maesymeillion
Pantgwyn
Penrhiw-pâl
Alltyblaca
Ram
Ponthirwaun
Coed-y-bryn
Llanwenog
Dre-fach
Parc-y-rhôs
Llanycrwys
Bryngwyn
Brongest
Troedyraur
Tregroes
Rhydowen
Pencarreg
Llandygwydd
Capel Tygwydd
Maesllyn
Croes-lan
Llanybydder
Ffaldybrenin
Prengwyn
Brynteg
Mynydd Pencarreg
Rhuddlan
Glan-Duar
Ty Mawr
Harford
Horeb
Capel Dewi
Cwm-cou
Llandyfriog
Aber-banc
Penrhiw-llan
ROCK MILL WOOLLEN MILL
Maesycrugiau
TEIFI VALLEY RAILWAY
Llandysul
Esgairdawe
Newcastle Emlyn (Castell Newydd Emlyn)
Cenarth
Pentrecagal
Henllan
Llanfihangel-ar-arth
Aber-Giâr
Aber-Arad
NATIONAL WOOL MUSEUM
Llangeler
Drefach
Llanllwni
CLYNFYW
Penrherber
Felindre
Pentre-cwrt
Bancyffordd
Rhydcymerau
CHEESE FARM
Saron
Drefelin
Llidiad Nenog
Cwmhiraeth
Cwmpengraig
Capel Iwan
Cwmcych
Pencader
New Inn
Llansawel
MOELFRE
Rhôs
Gwyddgrug
Cwmorgan
Tanglwst
Carmarthenshire (Sir Gaerfyrddin)
Dolgran
MYNYDD RHOS-WEN
Gwernogle
Forest
Abergorlech
Edwinsford
TALLEY ABBEY
Afon Cothi
Talley
CYNROS
Cwm-byr
Nant-y-ffin
Pen-y-garn
Brechfa
Bryn-Iwan
Cwmduad
Alltwalis
Hen-feddau fawr
Hermon
Halfway
Cwmdu
Trelech
Dinas
Llanpumsaint
Llanllawddog
Soar
Pontarsais
Horeb
Llanfynydd
Capel Isaac
Blaen-waun
Llanwinio
Pant-glas
Salem
Rhydargaeau
Afon Duad
A44
A487
A485
A4577
A482
A486
A475
A484
B4576
B4575
B4577
B4337
B4342
B4339
B4334
B4321
B4338
B4578
B4343
B4333
B4571
B4459
B4476
B4336
B4310
B4299
B4301
B4302
45
58
32
33
SN
0 1 2 3 4 5 6 miles
0 1 2 3 4 5 6 7 8 9 10 km

Grid references (top): 5 6 7 8 9

Llanidloes
Glynbrochan
Cwmbelan
New Chapel
GLYNDWR'S WAY
A

Pen-bont Rhydybeddau
Dyffryn Castell
Pant Mawr
Llanifyny
A44
Llangurig
Lliwch
David's Well
Llaithd

Capel Bangor
Dollwen
Goginan
LLYWERNOG SILVER LEAD MINE
Cwmbrwyno
58
Ponterwyd
Ysbytycynfyn
564
59
584
Nantgwyn
Pant-y-dwr
B4518
RED LION INN
493
B

VALE OF RHEIDOL RAILWAY
Aberffrwd
Ystumtuen
RHEIDOL HYDRO ELECTRIC STATION
COED RHEIDOL
Ysbytycynfyn
Pisgah
A4120
Mynydd Bach
Devil's Bridge
Trisant
PEN Y GARN 610
Blaenycwm
Wye (Gwy)
498
St Harmon
Bwlch-y-sarnau
Cnwch-coch
New Row
B4574
Cwmystwyth
MOEL HYWEL 505
Abermagwr
Crosswood
Llanafan
HAFOD ESTATE
Pont-rhyd-y-groes
571 GEIFAS
Craig-goch Res.
Llansantffraed Cwmdeuddwr
WELSH ROYAL CRYSTAL
Gaufron
A44
Nantmel
Wenallt
Mynydd Bach 371
Tanyrhydiau
572 TRAWSALLT
CLAERWEN
Penygarreg Res.
Elan Village
THE GIGRIN RED KITE FEEDING CENTRE
Nant-glas
C

Tynygraig
Ystradmeurig
Ffair-Rhos
530 DIBYN DU
Claerwen Reservoir
Garreg-ddu Res.
Rhayader (Rhaeadr Gwy)
48
Llanwrthwl
Argoed
Llandrindod Wells (Llandrindod)
Llanyre

Swydd-ffynnon
Pontrhydfendigaid
STRATA FLORIDA ABBEY
Afon Claerwen
Caban-coch Res.
P o w y s
537 DRUM-DDU
Newbridge on Wye
Howe
Cross

d i g i o n (eredigion)
CORS CARON
249
Ty'n-yr-eithin
B4343
WELSH GOLD CENTRE
Tregaron
508 Y DRUM
532 BRYN CRWN
DOLGOCH
645 DRYGARN FAWR
SN
Llanafan-fawr
Disserth
A483

Llanddewi-Brefi
Pentre-rhew
484 ESGAIR CERRIG
TYNCORNEL
500
NANT IRFON
Pentre-llwyn-llwyd
Troed-rhiwdalar
Cwmbach
CORS Y LLYN
Builth Road
Llanelw
D

463
484 BRYN BRAWD
Soar-y-Mynydd
Llyn Brianne Res.
456
Abergwesyn
487
Cwm Irfon
Beulah
Llanfechan
A483
Cilmery
Oaklands

ALLT RHYD Y GROES
Ystradffin
Mynydd Trawsnant
CAMBRIAN WOOLLEN MILL
Llanwrtyd
Garth
Tyn-y-graig
Builth Wells (Llanfair-ym-Muallt)

440
Nant-y-Bai
459
Rhandirmwyn
Llanwrtyd Wells (Llanwrtud)
Cefn-gorwydd
Llangammarch Wells
441 Maesmynis
Llanddewi'r Cwm
Alltm

Ffarmers
Mynydd Mallaen
Cwrt-y-cadno
434 ESGAIR FERCHON
Nant-y-groes
474 DRUM-DDU
B4519
E P Y N T
48
Gwenddwr

Llandre
Pumsaint
DOLAUCOTHI GOLD MINES
Cilycwm
Crychan Forest
Tirabad
463 BRYN DU
Pentre Dolau-Honddu
433
Upper Chapel

Caio
341
Llanfair-ar-y-bryn
Cynghordy
11
Babel
Blaendyryn
Merthyr Cynog
Llaneglwys
456

Crugybar
B3002
A482
Porthyrhyd
Siloh
Divlyn
Pentre-ty-gwyn
442 Mynydd Bwlch-y-groes
Llandeilo'r Fan
Llanfihangel Nant Bran
Lower Chapel
F

i r e
16
A40
Llandovery (Llanymddyfri)
Halfway
Llywel
Pentre'bach
Pont-faen
Pwllgloyw
B4520
Garthbre

Waunclunda
Llansadwrn
Cwmdwr
Llanwrda
A4069
Myrtle Hill
440
Usk Reservoir
12
A40
Trecastle
Cwmwysg
Pentre'r-felin
Trallong
34
Aberyscir
Battle
Llanfaes
Brecon (Aberhonddu)
G

Hermon
Felindre
33
Cilgwyn
Myddfai
Pont ar Hydfer
Defynnog
Sennybridge (Pont Senni)
Penpont
Llanspyddid
BRECON GAER ROMAN FORT
CATHEDRAL
BRECKNOCK MUS

Manordeilo
Ashfield
Llangadog
Talsarn
Tai'r-Bull
Mynydd Illtyd
MOUNTAIN CENTRE
A4067

Grid references (bottom): 5 6 7 8 9

48

A483 B4355

New Chapel
GLYNDWR'S WAY
584 59 thddu
David's Well
Tylwch
Nantgwyn
Pant-y-dwr
Bwlch-y-sarnau
St Harmon
498
MOEL HYWEL 505
Nant-glas
Llanwrthwl
Argoed
Llanafan-fawr
Llanfechan
Garth
DRUM-DDU 474

Anchor
528 CILFAESTY HILL
Hall of the Forest
BLACK MT 448
Newcastle
Whitcott Keysett
Bicton
Lower Down
Felindre
Bettws-y-crwyn
Quabbs
Clun Mill CASTLE Clun B4368 Clunton
Llwyn Churchbank
Beguildy 60 Redlake
Llanbadarn Fynydd
Black Mountain
BEACON HILL 547
Rhydmoelddu
RED LION HILL 493
Llanbister 393
Crug
Llangunllo
Knucklas
Dutlas Upper Treverward
Llanfair Waterdine Purlogue New Invention
Skyborry Green Stowe
Knighton (Tref-y-Clawdd) A4113 Milebrook
Hobarris
Chapel Lawn
OFFA'S DYKE PATH

Abbey-cwm-hir
450
Llandewi Ystradenny
Dolau
Llanfihangel Rhydithon
RADNOR FOREST
Bleddfa Monaughty 1402 Pilleth
Rhos-y-meirch
Whitton Norton
Dolley Green Discoed
Maes-Treylow
Cascob
Beggar's Bush
Presteigne (Llanandras) JUDGES LODGING
Stapleton
Rodd Combe
Lugg

Rhayader (Rhaeadr Gwy)
WELSH ROYAL CRYSTAL
Llansantffraed Cwmdeuddwr
Gaufron
B4518
47 A44
Nantmel
THE GIGRIN FARM RED KITE FEEDING CENTRE
Gwystre Fron Crossgates
Penybont
Llandegley
Llandrindod Wells (Llandrindod)
RADNORSHIRE MUSEUM
Ridgebourne
NATIONAL CYCLE COLLECTION
411 436
New Radnor
Kinnerton Evenjobb Knill
P O W Y S
DRUM-DDU 537
Newbridge on Wye
Disserth
Crossway
Howey
CORS Y LLYN
Cwmbach
Builth Road
Llanelwedd
Oaklands
Frank's Bridge
Llansantffraed-in-Elvel
Hundred House
Cregrina
Glascwm
GWAUNCESTE HILL 542
Colva
Hengoed
Michaelchurch on Arrow
Newchurch
Gladestry
Old Radnor
Yardro Dolyhir Burlingjobb
STANNER ROCKS 391
Flintsham
Upper Hergest
Hergest Ridge
HERGEST CROFT GDNS
Kington Headbrook
Lower Hergest
OAKLANDS SMALL BREEDS FARM
Kingswood
Huntington
Lyonshall
Holme Marsh
Hopley's Green
Wootton
Almeley
Upcott
B4355

Pentre-llwyn-llwyd
Troed-rhiwdalar
Cilmery
Tyn-y-graig
Builth Wells (Llanfair-ym-Muallt)
Llanfaredd
451
Rhulen
RED HILL 509
Bryngwyn
Rhos-goch 389
RHOS GOCH
Brilley
Dol-y-cannau
Rhydspence TOLL
Whitney-on-Wye
Winforton
Willersley
Ailey
Eardisley
Kinnersley
Letton
GARDENS & GALLERY
Brobury
441 Maesmynis
Llanddewi'r Cwm
Aberedw
Alltmawr
A470
Llandeilo Graban
Llanbadarn-y-Garreg
Llanbedr
Painscastle
Clyro
Clifford Priory Wood Merbach
Bredwardine
Hay-on-Wye (Y Gelli Gandryll)
Bronydd
The Bage
Hardwicke
ARTHUR'S STONE
Dorstone
A4350
B4352
463 RYN DU
Pentre Dolau-Honddu 47
Gwenddwr
Crickadarn
Erwood
Llanstephan
Rhydness
Boughrood
Cwmbach
Glasbury Pipton
Llowes A438
Cusop
Llanigon
Tregoyd
Velindre
HAY BLUFF 677
Craswall
Peterchurch
Hinton
Llanrosser
Urishay Common
Upper Maes-coed
Michaelchurch Escley
Middle Maes-coed
Newton
Lower Maes-coed
Blaendyryn
Merthyr Cynog
456 Lower Chapel
Llaneglwys
Three Cocks
A4079
Llyswen
Glangammarch Wells
B4519
Upper Chapel
433
Pont-faen
Pwllgloyw
Garthbrengy Talachddu
Sarnau
Llandefalle
Bronllys BRONLLYS
A479
Boughrood
Tredomen
Trefecca HOWELL HOUSE
Talgarth
Tredustan
Pengenffordd
THE TUMPA 690 703
Llanfihangel Nant Bran
Llandefaelog Fach
Llanddew
Llandefaelog-tre'r-graig
Llanfilo Felinfach
A470
TREFEINON OPEN FARM
Pengenffordd
BLACK MOUNTAINS
Y MYNYDD DUON
Longtown
Llanveynoe
Battle CATHEDRAL
BRECON GAER ROMAN FORT
34 Brecon (Aberhonddu)
Llanywern
Llanfihangel Tal-y-llyn
35
Llanelieu
Mynydd Troed
B4560 609
Clodock
PRIORY
OFFA'S DYKE PATH
CLAWDD OFFA
400
Bull MOUNTAIN CENTRE
Aberyscir
Llanfaes
Llechfaen
Llanfrynach
Llangorse LLANGORSE LAKE
Llannamlach
Llangasty Talyllyn
A479
Usk (Wysg)
Honddu

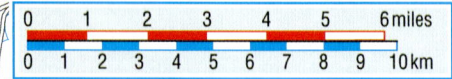

0 1 2 3 4 5 6 miles
0 1 2 3 4 5 6 7 8 9 10km

Craven Arms · Ludlow · Leominster · Hereford · Bromyard · Tenbury Wells · Ledbury

A49 · A44 · A438 · A4103 · A4112 · A456 · A417 · A449 · A465 · A44 · A4110

Herefordshire

Wyre Forest

Major places:
Craven Arms, Stokesay Castle, Ludlow, Ludford, Leintwardine, Wigmore, Croft Castle, Leominster, Kingsland, Pembridge, Weobley, Dilwyn, Bromyard, Tenbury Wells, Burford, Cleobury Mortimer, Mamble, Clows Top, Hereford, Holmer, Lugwardine, Mordiford, Fownhope, Woolhope, Much Marcle, Ledbury, Eastnor, Bromsberrow Heath, Dymock, Kempley

West Malvern, Colwall, Bosbury, Castle Frome, Stretton Grandison, Tarrington, Stoke Lacy, Bredenbury, Edwyn Ralph, Collington, Stoke Bliss, Kyre Magna, Clifton upon Teme, Shelsley Walsh, Sapey Common, Stanford Bridge, Great Witley

Pontrilas, Ewyas Harold, Abbey Dore, Kilpeck, Much Dewchurch, Kingstone, Allensmore, Callow, Much Birch, Hoarwithy, King's Caple, Brampton Abbotts, Upton Bishop, Gorsley

M50 · B4214 · B4204 · B4203 · B4220 · B4214 · B4224 · B4348 · B4347 · B4349 · B4352 · B4362 · B4361 · B4360 · B4529 · B4110 · B4530 · B4385 · B4368 · B4364 · B4365 · B4117 · B4363 · B4199 · B4201 · B4202

60 · 61 · 50 · 35 · 36

Teme · Arrow · Lugg · Wye · Frome · Leadon · Golden Valley

Worcestershire
Kidderminster
Stourbridge
HALESOWEN
Bromsgrove
Redditch
Droitwich Spa
Worcester
Great Malvern
Malvern Link
West Malvern
Ledbury
Tewkesbury
Pershore
Evesham
Bewdley
Stourport on Severn
Bromyard
Upton upon Severn
Bishop's Cleeve
Winchcombe
Catshill
Aston Fields
Longbridge
Wyre Forest
Abberley Hill
MALVERN HILLS
VALE
SO
Kinver
Hagley
Blakedown
Chaddesley Corbett
Hartlebury
Ombersley
Fernhill Heath
Claines
Hallow
Broadwas
Leigh
Powick
Kempsey
Callow End
Hanley Swan
Welland
Colwall
Bredon
Eckington
Defford
Fladbury
Cropthorne
Inkberrow
Feckenham
Hanbury
Wychbold
Bretforton
Ashchurch
Deerhurst
Apperley
Corse
Staunton
Pendock
Eldersfield
Kemerton
Beckford
Ashton under Hill
Dumbleton
Gotherington
Woodmancote
Cleeve Hill
Greet
Hailes
Tenbury
Stanford Bridge
Great Witley
Shelsley Beauchamp
Clifton upon Teme
Martley
Knightwick
Suckley
Cradley
Mathon
Colwall Stone
Wellington Heath
Eastnor
Much Marcle
Dymock
Kempley
Bosbury
Castle Frome
Bishops Frome
Whitbourne
Stoke Bliss
Hanley Child
Edvin Loach
Tedstone Delamere
Stanford on Teme
Sapey Common
Stockton on Teme
Pensax
Lindridge
Eardiston
Newnham Bridge
Clows Top
Bayton
Mamble
Far Forest
Callow Hill
Rock
Astley
Dunley
Areley Kings
Wilden
Stone
Shenstone
Elmley Lovett
Cutnall Green
Crossway Green
Hampton Lovett
Salwarpe
Hindlip
Martin Hussingtree
Oddingley
Tibberton
Crowle
Himbleton
Huddington
Upton Snodsbury
Flyford Flavell
Abbots Morton
Rous Lench
Church Lench
Atch Lench
Harvington
Norton
Lenchwick
Throckmorton
Pinvin
Peopleton
Drakes Broughton
Wadborough
Stoulton
Spetchley
Whittington
White Ladies Aston
Bishampton
Abberton
Naunton Beauchamp
Severn Stoke
Kinnersley
Earl's Croome
Baughton
Pirton
Besford
Birlingham
Little Comberton
Great Comberton
Elmley Castle
Netherton
Bricklehampton
Kersoe
Hinton on the Green
Sedgeberrow
Wormington
Overbury
Conderton
Kinsham
Teddington
Alstone
Oxenton
Dixton
Twyning
Shuthonger
Ripple
Queenhill
Longdon
Birts Street
Castlemorton
Rye Street
Welland
Sledge Green
Bushley
Forthampton
Chaceley
Tirley
Hasfield
Ashleworth
Coombe Hill
Hardwicke
Tredington
Fiddington
Walton Cardiff
Stoke Orchard
Elmstone Hardwicke
Redmarley D'Abitot
Bromsberrow Hth.
Preston
Donnington
Ryton
Pixley
Aylton
Putley
Trumpet
Munsley
Staplow
Coddington
Canon Frome
Fromes Hill
Evesbatch
Stanford Bishop
Munderfield Row
Acton Beauchamp
Linley Green
Alfrick
Alfrick Pound
Lulsley
Horsham
Berrow Green
Shoulton
Wichenford
Holt Heath
Grimley
Sinton Green
Hawford
Moseley
Harpley
Sweet Green
High Lane
Edwyn Ralph
Bromyard Downs
Tedstone Wafer
ELGAR'S BIRTHPLACE
CROOME PARK
WITLEY COURT
HARTLEBURY / WORCESTERSHIRE COUNTY MUSEUM
HANBURY HALL
AVONCROFT MUS OF HISTORIC BUILDINGS
HARVINGTON HALL
SEVERN VALLEY RAILWAY
WEST MIDLAND SAFARI PARK
BODENHAM ARBORETUM & EARTH CENTRE
THREE COUNTIES SHOWGROUND
EASTNOR
HELLENS MANOR
ST MARY'S CHURCH
ODDA'S CHAPEL
SUDELEY CASTLE & GARDENS
BELAS KNAP LONG BARROW
STRENSHAM SERVICES (Northbound Only)
STRENSHAM SERVICES (Southbound Only)
M5
M50
A449
A44
A38
A456
A4440
A422
A417
A46
A4103
0 1 2 3 4 5 6 miles
0 1 2 3 4 5 6 7 8 9 10 km

Warwick

Major towns and places:

Coventry, Royal Leamington Spa, Warwick, Kenilworth, Solihull, Shirley, Olton, Dorridge, Stratford-upon-Avon, Alcester, Studley, Henley-in-Arden, Southam, Banbury, Broadway, Moreton-in-Marsh, Shipston-on-Stour, Chipping Norton, Stow-on-the-Wold

A-roads and places:

Acock's Green, Sheldon, Butler's End, Meriden, Hawkes End, Allesley, Walsgrave on Sowe, Stretton under Fosse, Elmdon, Bickenhill, Hampton in Arden, Eastern Green, Coundon, Spon End, Wyken, King's Heath, Moseley, Sparkhill, Elmdon Heath, Four Oaks, Berkswell, Whoberley, Earlsdon, Pinley, Binley, Binley Woods, Bretford, Brinklow

Hall Green, Copt Heath, Barston, Balsall Common, Catchems Corner, Tile Hill, Stivichall, Willenhall, Brandon, King's Newnham, Church Lawford

Monkspath, Knowle, Balsall, Fen End, Burton Green, Baginton, Ryton-on-Dunsmore, Ryton Organic Gardens, Easenhall

Bentley Heath, Temple Balsall, Meer End, Crackley, Stoneleigh, Bubbenhall, Stretton-on-Dunsmore

Dorridge, Chadwick End, Honiley, Beausale, Ashow, Weston under Wetherley, Princethorpe, Frankton, Draycote, Birdingbury

Hockley Heath, Packwood House, Baddesley Clinton, Kingswood, Wroxall, Kenilworth, Old Milverton, Cubbington, Hunningham, Lillington, Leamington Hastings, Marton

Lapworth, Tanworth-in-Arden, Kemps Green, Rowington, Haseley, Hatton Country World, Milverton, Offchurch, Long Itchington, Bascote, Stockton

Portway, Wood End, Oldborrow, Lowsonford, Shrewley, Hatton, Budbrooke, Hampton on the Hill, St Mary's, Warwick, Radford Semele, Whitnash, Ufton, Southam

Earlswood, Beoley, Holt End, Gorcott Hill, Ullenhall, Henley-in-Arden, Preston Bagot, Claverdon, Langley, Edstone, Norton Lindsey, Wolverton, Longbridge, Sherbourne, Barford, Bishop's Tachbrook, Harbury, Chesterton, Cross Green, Bishop's Itchington, Ladbroke, Marston Doles, Priors Hardwick

Ipsley, Mappleborough Green, Morton Bagot, Wootton Wawen, Shelfield, Great Alne, Bearley, Snitterfield, Wasperton, Newbold Pacey, Ashorne, Moreton Morrell, Lighthorne, Gaydon, Knightcote, Northend, Burton Dassett

Studley, Coughton, King's Coughton, Alcester, Haselor, Walcote, Billesley, Aston Cantlow, Wilmcote, Bishopton, Stratford-upon-Avon, Alveston, Charlecote, Wellesbourne, Walton, Combrook, Kineton, Temple Herdewyke, Avon Dassett, Farnborough, Claydon

New End, Cookhill, Alcester, Overley Green, Exhall, Temple Grafton, Ardens Grafton, Binton, Shottery, Anne Hathaway's Cottage, Shakespeare's Birthplace, Tiddington, Charlecote, Loxley, Wellesbourne Watermill, Compton Verney, Chadshunt, Little Kineton, Radway, Warmington, Ratley, Shotteswell

Arrow, Weethley Gate, Wixford, Dunnington, Broom, Luddington, Welford-on-Avon, Clifford Chambers, Shire Horse Centre, Atherstone on Stour, Preston on Stour, Alderminster, Ettington, Pillerton Hersey, Pillerton Priors, Butlers Marston, Oxhill, Lower Tysoe, Whatcote, Upper Tysoe, Middle Tysoe, Alkerton, Hornton, Horley, Hanwell

Salford Priors, Bidford-on-Avon, Barton, Marlcliff, Dorsington, Long Marston, Wimpstone, Lower Quinton, Newbold on Stour, Armscote, Halford, Idlicote, Tredington, Honington Hall, Winderton, Epwell, Shutford, North Newington, Wroxton, Balscote, Drayton, Neithrop

Harvington, Cleeve Prior, Abbots Salford, Offenham, South Littleton, North Littleton, Middle Littleton, Pebworth, Upper Quinton, Admington, Ilmington, Blackwell, Honington, Shipston-on-Stour, Barchester, Upper Brailes, Lower Brailes, Sutton under Brailes, Sibford Gower, Sibford Ferris, Swalcliffe, Tadmarton, Broughton, Bodicote

Aldington, Honeybourne, Bretforton, Mickleton, Broad Marston, Broad Campden, Chipping Campden, Hidcote Manor Garden, Hidcote Boyce, Charingworth, Willington, Tidmington, Burmington, Cherington, Stourton, Sibford Ferris, Swalcliffe, Milcombe, Bloxham, West Adderbury, Adderbury

Childswickham, Wickhamford, Badsey, Willersley, Saintbury, Weston-Sub-Edge, Aston Subedge, Ebrington, Darlingscott, Paxford, Stretton-on-Fosse, Todenham, Little Wolford, Great Wolford, Whichford, Ascott, Hook Norton, Wigginton, South Newington, Milton, Barford St John, Barford St Michael, Hempton

Broadway, Buckland, Laverton, Snowshill, Stanton, Blockley, Batsford, Draycott, Aston Magna, Lower Lemington, Moreton-in-Marsh, Bourton on the Hill, Barton on the Heath, Long Compton, Great Rollright, Little Rollright, Hook Norton, Swerford, Nether Worton, Over Worton

Stanway, Didbrook, Cutsdean, Ford, Farmcote, Temple Guiting, Condicute, Longborough, Donnington, Sezincote, Evenlode, Chastleton, Broadwell, Adlestrop, Cornwell, Salford, Over Norton, Chipping Norton, Little Tew, Great Tew, Heythrop, Ledwell, Sandford St Martin, Westcott Barton

Stow-on-the-Wold, Lower Swell, Upper Swell, Kineton, Oddington, Daylesford, Chastleton, Rollright Stones, Wellington Aviation Museum

Motorways: M6, M42, M40, M45

Grid references: A, B, C, D, E, F, G (vertical); numbered 1-9 (horizontal)

Junction numbers: 62, 63, 52, 16, 15, 14, 13, 12, 37, 38

Points of interest: Cadbury World, Sarehole Mill, Forge Mill Needle Mus, Arrow Valley, Ragley Hall, Coughton Court, Mary Arden's House, Kiftsgate Court Garden, Hidcote Manor Garden, Cotswold Country Cycles, Snowshill Manor, Broadway Tower, Snowshill Lavender, Gloucestershire Warwickshire Steam Railway, Stanway House, Hailes Abbey, Cotswold Farm Park, Manor Farm Craft Centre, Umberslade Farm, Packwood House, Kenilworth Castle, Warwick Castle, Jephson Gardens, St Mary's, Stoneleigh National Agricultural Centre, Lunt Roman Fort, Ryton Pools, Ryton Organic Gardens, Coombe Abbey, Midland Air Mus, Nat Motorcycle Mus, Transport Mus, Heritage Motor Centre, Chesterton Windmill, Upton House, Broughton Castle, Swalcliffe Barn, Hook Norton Brewery Visitors Centre, Wellesbourne Watermill, Compton Verney, Shakespeare's Birthplace, Anne Hathaway's Cottage, Shire Horse Centre, Domestic Fowl Trust, The Fleece Inn, Hatton Country World, Nickelodeon, Warwick Services, Warwick Castle

N O R T H A

Coventry

Rugby

Daventry

Southam

Banbury

Middleton Cheney

Brackley

Buckingham

Towcester

Silverstone

Whittlewood Forest

Naseby Field

Sulby Reservoir

Stanford Res.

Welford

Husbands Bosworth

Great Oxenden

Clipston

Kelmarsh

Naseby

Haselbech

Maidwell

Cottesbrooke

Creaton

Hollowell

Ravensthorpe

Teeton

Brixworth

Spratton

Guilsborough

Coton

West Haddon

East Haddon

Holdenby

Brington

Great Brington

Little Brington

Brockhall

Nobottle

New Duston

Duston

Dallington

Queen's Park

Harlestone

Harpole

Flore

Upton

Far Cotton

Kislingbury

Nether Heyford

Upper Heyford

Weedon Bec

Church Stowe

Upper Stowe

Bugbrooke

Rothersthorpe

Gayton

Pattishall

Eastcote

Milton Malsor

Blisworth

Astcote

Tiffield

Caldecote

Shutlanger

Stoke Bruerne

Gayton

Litchborough

Grimscote

Cold Higham

Duncote

Adstone

Blakesley

Woodend

Greens Norton

Bradden

Slapton

Abthorpe

Wappenham

Weston

Weedon Lois

Moreton Pinkney

Canons Ashby

Eydon

Woodford Halse

Maidford

Everdon

Preston Capes

Badby

Newnham

Dodford

Fawsley

Charwelton

Hellidon

Priors Marston

Priors Hardwick

Wormleighton

Upper Boddington

Lower Boddington

Byfield

Hinton

Boddington Reservoir

Claydon

Farnborough

Mollington

Chipping Warden

Wardington

Upper Wardington

Williamscott

Chacombe

Marston St Lawrence

Greatworth

Thenford

Helmdon

Sulgrave

Thorpe Mandeville

Culworth

Sulgrave Manor

Crowfield

Radstone

Syresham

Whitfield

Biddlesden

Turweston

Westbury

Water Stratford

Mixbury

Finmere

Tingewick

Gawcott

Thornborough

Radclive

Buckingham

Maids Moreton

Chackmore

Buffler's Holt

Akeley

Dadford

Lillingstone Dayrell

Lillingstone Lovell

Wicken

Leckhampstead

Stowe School and Gardens

Whittlebury

Paulerspury

Pury End

Silverstone

Alderton

Stoke Bruerne

Stoke Park Pavilions

Over Worton

Great Tew

Nether Worton

North Aston

Middle Aston

Steeple Aston

Fritwell

Somerton

Upper Heyford

Ardley

Fewcott

Stoke Lyne

Hethe

Hardwick

Cottisford

Newton Purcell

Fringford

Hardwick

Preston Bissett

Barton Hartshorn

Chetwode

Hillesden

Addington

Steeple Claydon

East Claydon

Twyford

Padbury

Adstock

Hogshaw

Deddington

Clifton

Aynho

Souldern

Barford St John

Barford St Michael

Hempton

Wigginton

South Newington

Bloxham

Milton

Bodicote

East Adderbury

West Adderbury

King's Sutton

Charlton

Newbottle

Astrop

Upper Astrop

Farthinghoe

Warkworth

Overthorpe

Grimsbury

Neithrop

Drayton

Hanwell

Wroxton

Balscote

Horley

Hornton

Shotteswell

Shenington

Alkerton

Epwell

Sibford Gower

Sibford Ferris

Swalcliffe

Tadmarton

Broughton

Shutford

North Newington

Easington

Bourton

Great Bourton

Cropredy

Mollington

Warmington

Avon Dassett

Farnborough

Fenny Compton

Burton Dassett

Northend

Knightcote

Temple Herdewyke

Gaydon

Lighthorne

Chesterton

Harbury

Bishop's Itchington

Ladbroke

Marston Doles

Napton on the Hill

Chapel Green

Staverton

Lower Shuckburgh

Flecknoe

Nethercote

Braunston

Welton

Ashby St Ledgers

Watford

Long Buckby

Crick

West Haddon

Winwick

Lilbourne

Clifton upon Dunsmore

Hillmorton

Barby

Kilsby

Kilsby

Clay Coton

Yelvertoft

Cold Ashby

Thornby

Cottesbrooke

Willoughby

Grandborough

Broadwell

Sawbridge

Woolscott

Birdingbury

Kites Hardwick

Leamington Hastings

Marton

Frankton

Draycote

Thurlaston

Bourton on Dunsmore

Dunchurch

Stretton-on-Dunsmore

Princethorpe

Wappenbury

Eathorpe

Hunningham

Offchurch

Long Itchington

Bascote

Stockton

Southam

Ufton

Cubbington

Weston under Wetherley

Church Lawford

Long Lawford

New Bilton

Bilton

Newbold on Avon

Newton

Catthorpe

Swinford

Stanford on Avon

Cotesbach

Walcote

North Kilworth

South Kilworth

Welford

Misterton

Shawell

Catthorpe

Gibbet Hill

Churchover

Harborough Magna

Easenhall

Pailton

Monks Kirby

Withybrook

Shilton

Barnacle

Aristy

Cross in Hand

Brinklow

Coombe Abbey

Brandon

Wolston

Ryton-on-Dunsmore

Ryton Organic Gardens

Bubbenhall

Baginton

Willenhall

Binley Woods

Binley

Pinley

Bretford

King's Newnham

Church Lawford

Little Heath

Foleshill

Walsgrave on Sowe

Wyken

Great Heath

Tollbar End

Brandon

Wolston

Frankton

Draycote Water

Cubbington

Leamington Hastings

Warwick Services

Chesterton Windmill

Cross Green

SCALE

| 0 | 1 | 2 | 3 | 4 | 5 | 6 miles |
| 0 | 1 | 2 | 3 | 4 | 5 | 6 | 7 | 8 | 9 | 10km |

M6 · M45 · M1 · M40 · M42 · M45

A426 · A428 · A45 · A14 · A5 · A361 · A422 · A43 · A421 · A423 · A425 · A4303 · A4304 · A508 · A5199 · A4600 · A427 · A46 · A423 · A4071 · A452

Grand Union Canal

Oxford Canal

Grand Union Canal

Cherwell

River Avon

Nene

Great Ouse

Sor Brook

Map

Braybrooke Desborough RUSHTON TRIANGULAR LODGE Rushton Newton Geddington ELEANOR CROSS Sudborough HERBS FERMYN WOODS Wadenhoe Barnwell All Saints Luddington in the Brook Great Gidding Little Gidding

Arthingworth A6 A576 Rothwell Weekley Warkton BOUGHTON HOUSE Grafton Underwood Lowick Islip Thorpe Waterville 65 Clopton Winwick HAMERTON ZOO PARK Hamerton Coppingford

Harrington Orton Loddington Thorpe Malsor Kettering Barton Seagrave Cranford St Andrew Cranford St John Twywell Thrapston Titchmarsh Bythorn Brington Molesworth Old Weston Buckworth

Draughton Great Cransley WICKSTEED PARK A43 A14 Woodford Denford A14 Keyston Leighton Bromswold Barham Wool

Lamport LAMPORT HALL Old Mawsley Broughton Pytchley Isham Burton Latimer Great Addington Little Addington Ringstead Keyston 17 Catworth Spaldwick Easton

Scaldwell Walgrave Orlinbury B574 Little Harrowden Great Harrowden Finedon A45 Raunds Stanwick STANWICK LAKES Hargrave Covington Stow Longa 19 20

Hannington Holcot Hardwick A510 Irthlingborough Stanwick Chelveston Caldecott Shelton Lower Dean Upper Dean Kimbolton West Perry East P

BRIXWORTH Pitsford Reservoir Pitsford A43 Sywell SYWELL Mears Ashby A509 HERITAGE CENTRE Little Irchester Higham Ferrers CHICHELE COLLEGE Warmonds Hill Yeldon Melchbourne Pertenhall Swineshead 54 Dillington Staughton Green Staughton Highway B645

Moulton Overstone Sywell Reservoir Wilby IRCHESTER Rushden Newton Bromswold Knotting Riseley Brook End Keysoe Great Staughton Little Staughton Hail Weston

Boughton A5076 Ecton Great Billing New Barton Great Doddington Irchester NARROW GAUGE RAILWAY MUS Little Wymington Farndish Podington Knotting Green Keysoe Row Duloe

Kingsthorpe Kingsley Park Weston Favell Little Billing A45 Strixton Wollaston Wymington Souldrop BUSHMEAD PRIORY Staploe

Northampton Little Houghton Cogenhoe Grendon Hinwick SANTA POD Sharnbrook Bletsoe Thurleigh Rootham's Green Colmworth

Hardingstone Brafield-on-the-Green Castle Ashby CASTLE ASHBY Easton Maudit Bozeat Odell Felmersham HARROLD-ODELL Radwell Milton Ernest GLENN MILLER MUSEUM BODYFLIGHT Clapham Salph End Renhold Green End Great Barford Blunham A421

Wootton Collingtree B526 Denton Yardley Hastings Harrold Chellington Carlton Pavenham Oakley STEVINGTON WINDMILL Bromham BROMHAM MILL Bedford BEDFORD MUSEUM Goldington Willington Roxton

A508 Roade Hackleton Horton Lavendon West End Stevington Turvey A428 Bromham BEDFORD PRIORY Fenlake A603 Moggerhanger MOGGERHANGER PARK Thorncote Green Northill Cald

Courteenhall Salcey Forest Eakley Lanes Warrington Cold Brayfield Newton Blossomville Stagsden Box End Great Denham Queen's Park Biddenham Cardington Ickwell Green SHUTTLEWORTH COLL THE SWISS

Hartwell Ashton Stoke Goldington Weston Underwood Ravenstone Olney EMBERTON Clifton Reynes Emberton Milton Keynes Filgrave Hardmead Astwood Kempston ELSTOW MOOT HALL Harrowden Shortstown BIRD OF PREY CENTRE Old Warden

Grafton Regis Hanslope Tathall End Gayhurst Tyringham Sherington CHICHELEY HALL North Crawley Bourne End Wootton Kempston Hardwick Wilstead Haynes Southill

Yardley Gobion Potterspury Castlethorpe Haversham M1 Lathbury Newport Pagnell Broad Green Lower Shelton Upper Shelton MARSTON VALE MILLENNIUM Marston Moretaine Stewartby 54

Cosgrove Old Stratford New Bradwell NEWPORT PAGNELL SERVICES Great Linford Willen GULLIVER'S LAND Cranfield Moulsoe Salford Houghton Conquest HOW CONQUEST HOUSE HOUGHTON HOUSE Haynes Church End

Stony Stratford Passenham Calverton Wolverton MILTON KEYNES NATIONAL HOCKEY Bradwell Milton Keynes ST LAWRENCE'S Lidlington Millbrook Ampthill Maulden Clophill Beadlow Shefford Clifton HOO H MAZE

Upper Weald Beachampton Loughton Shenley Church End Shenley Brook End Whaddon Woughton on the Green Milton Keynes Village Simpson Wavendon Walton Aspley Guise Ridgmont Brogborough Steppingley Denel End DE GREY MAUSOLEUM Flitton Upper Gravenhurst Meppershall WREST PARK HOUSE

Thornton Nash Tattenhoe Bletchley BLETCHLEY PARK Fenny Stratford Woburn Sands Aspley Heath Husborne Crawley WILD ANIMAL KINGDOM Eversholt Flitwick Greenfield Silsoe Pulloxhill Higham Gobion Shillington STONDON TRANSPORT MUS

Singleborough Great Horwood Little Horwood Newton Longville Far Bletchley Bow Brickhill WOBURN ABBEY Woburn Church End Tingrith M1 Westoning Barton-le-Clay Hexton KNOCKING HOE Apsley End Pirton

Winslow WINSLOW HALL Mursley Swanbourne Drayton Parslow Stoke Hammond Great Brickhill Little Brickhill KINGS WOOD STOCKGROVE PARK Battlesden Toddington TODDINGTON SERVICES Harlington Sharpenhoe SUNDON HILLS BARTON HILLS Streatley Lilley Great Offley

Soulbury Heath and Reach Leighton Buzzard Hockliffe Chalton Upper Sundon Lower Sundon GALLEY HILL

39 64 65 54 40

Cambridge

Major towns: Bedford, Huntingdon, St Neots, St Ives, Biggleswade, Sandy, Letchworth, Hitchin, Baldock, Royston, Cambourne, Buntingford, Clophill, Flitwick, Kimbolton, Godmanchester, Brampton

Roads and junctions: A1, A14, A141, A421, A428, A505, A507, A600, A603, A1198, A1303, A1307, A10, M11, A6, A142, A1123, A1096, A1050, A1072, B660, B661, B645, B1040, B1042, B1043, B1046, B1090, B1100, B1368, B1381, B656, B658, B668, B530

Places (north to south, west to east):

Luddington in the Brook, Thurning, Wigsthorpe, Sawtry, Great Gidding, Little Gidding, Steeple Gidding, Hamerton, Winwick, Clopton, Upwood, Upwood Meadows, Wistow, Great Raveley, Little Raveley, Bury, Warboys, Pidley Fen, Chapel Head, Horseley Fen, Langwood Fen, Ferry Hill, Mepal, Sutton

Upton, Alconbury Weston, Alconbury, Buckworth, Barham, Little Stukeley, Great Stukeley, Abbots Ripton, King's Ripton, Broughton, Old Hurst, Woodhurst, Somersham, Colne, Bluntisham, Earith, Aldreth, Hill Row Doles, Chatteris Fen, Great Ouse

Molesworth, Brington, Leighton Bromswold, Woolley, Catworth, Spaldwick, Easton, Stow Longa, Ellington, Brampton, Huntingdon, Hartford, Sapley, Wyton, Houghton, Houghton Mill, St Ives, Holywell, Needingworth, Over, Willingham, Smithey, Rampton, Cottenham

Covington, Tilbrook, Kimbolton, Stonely, West Perry, East Perry, Grafham, Grafham Water, Buckden, Buckden Towers, Offord Cluny, Offord Darcy, Hilton, Papworth St Agnes, Fenstanton, Fen Drayton, Swavesey, Boxworth End, Longstanton, Westwick, Oakington, Histon, Impington, Girton

Lower Dean, Upper Dean, Swineshead, Pertenhall, Keysoe, Little Staughton, Great Staughton, Staughton Green, Staughton Highway, Southoe, Diddington, Great Paxton, Little Paxton, Toseland, Graveley, Yelling, Papworth Everard, Elsworth, Knapwell, Conington, Boxworth, Lolworth, Bar Hill, Dry Drayton, Madingley, Coton, Newnham

Keysoe Row, Bolnhurst, Thurleigh, Rootham's Green, Colmworth, Duloe, Staploe, St Neots, Eaton Socon, Eynesbury, Croxton, Eltisley, Caxton, Cambourne, Highfields, Hardwick, Toft, Comberton, Barton, Grantchester, Botanic Garden

Wilden, Ravensden, Renhold, Salph End, Green End, Roxton, Chawston, Colesden, Tempsford, Wyboston, Little Barford, Abbotsley, Great Gransden, Little Gransden, Waresley, Gamlingay, Bourn, Caldecote, Kingston, Great Eversden, Little Eversden, Harlton, Haslingfield, Hauxton, Harston

Bedford, Bedford Museum, Goldington, Cardington, Cople, Willington, Great Barford, Blunham, Girtford, Sandy, Beeston, Potton, Hatley St George, East Hatley, Longstowe, Arrington, Orwell, Barrington, Shepreth, Foxton, Newton, Thriplow

Kempston, Elstow, Wilstead, Haynes, Harrowden, Shortstown, Moggerhanger, Hatch, Thorncote Green, Northill, Ickwell Green, Cotton End, Old Warden, Biggleswade, Dunton, Cockayne Hatley, Wrestlingworth, Tadlow, Croydon, New Wimpole, Wendy, Whaddon, Chiswick End, Meldreth, Melbourn, Fowlmere

Wilshamstead, Haynes Church End, Shefford, Clophill, Beadlow, Clifton, Henlow, Upper Caldecote, Sutton, Eyeworth, Guilden Morden, Abington Pigotts, Bassingbourn, Kneesworth, Litlington, Steeple Morden, Royston, Barley, Barkway, Reed, Sandon, Buckland

Ampthill, Maulden, Clophill, Campton, Meppershall, Stotfold, Astwick, Edworth, Langford, Broom, Southill, Stanford, Shillington, Arlesey, Radwell, Norton, Therfield, Kelshall, Reed, Buckland, Chipping, Anstey, Meesden, Brent Pelham

Flitton, Silsoe, Greenfield, Pulloxhill, Westoning, Higham Gobion, Apsley End, Pirton, Holwell, Lower Stondon, Upper Stondon, Shillington, Ickleford, Willian, Letchworth, Baldock, Weston, Rushden, Sandon, Wallington, Clothall, Bygrave, Slip End, Roe Green, Mill End, Throcking, Wyddial, Hare Street, Buntingford

Sundon, Streatley, Barton-le-Clay, Hexton, Pegsdon, Knocking Hoe, Hitchin, Walsworth, Great Wymondley, Little Wymondley, Graveley, Ippollytts, Hall's Green, Cottered, Ardeley, Aspenden, Westmill, Furneaux Pelham, Hay Street, Gravesend

Points of interest: Hamerton Zoo Park, Monks Wood, Cromwell Museum, Hinchingbrooke, Buckden Towers, Wood Green Animal Shelter, Galley Hill, Cambridge Services, The Busway Guided Bus, Wimpole Hall and Home Farm, Shepreth Wildlife Park, Rupert Brooke Museum, Bushmead Priory, Bird of Prey Centre, Shuttleworth Collection, The Swiss Garden, Moggerhanger Park, Hoo Hill Maze, Wrest Park House, De Grey Mausoleum, Stondon Transport Museum, Baldock Services, Royston & District Museum, Cromer Windmill, Houghton House, Bedford Museum, Sundon Hills, Barton Hills, Galley Hill

Scale
0 1 2 3 4 5 6 miles
0 1 2 3 4 5 6 7 8 9 10 km

Woody Hill • Downham • Chettisham • West Fen • A10 • Shippea Hill Sta. • Lakenheath 8 • A1065 • Wangford Warren • B1106 • High Lodge Forest Centre • Park • 9 • Thetford Warren

Coveney • Prickwillow • B1382 • Great Ouse • Kenny Hill • A1112 • 67 • A1066 • Thetford Heath

Witcham • Ely • Queen Adelaide • 14 • B1104 • Lark • Beck Row • A1101 • Holywell Row • Eriswell • A11 • Elveden • EAST OF ENGLAND TANK MUSEUM

Wentworth • g • e • Witchford • Middle Fen • Great Fen • Mildenhall Fen • West Row • Worlington • Mildenhall • A1101 • Icklingham • B1112 • The King's Forest • B1106

North Hill • Haddenham • A10 • Little Thetford • Stuntney • Broad Hill • Isleham Fen • Thistley Green • West Row • Barton Mills • Freckenham • A11 • Tuddenham • Cavenham Heath • WEST STOW • West Stow • Ingham

Wilburton • B1049 • A142 • Soham Cotes • WINDMILL • Isleham • PRIORY CHURCH • Worlington • A1101 • Herringswell • Cavenham • Lackford • Culford • A134

Stretham • Barway • Soham • Soham Mere • DOWN FIELD WINDMILL • B1123 • Fordham • Chippenham • Red Lodge • Flempton • Hengrave • HENGRAVE HALL • Fornham All Saints • 56 • Fornham St

Chittering • Wicken • WICKEN CORN WINDMILL • A142 • CHIPPENHAM FEN • Snailwell • Kennett • B1085 • Risby • A14 • Westley • CATHEDRAL AND ABBEY RUINS • Bury St Edmunds

CAP DYKE • Upware • WICKEN FEN • New River • Landwade • B1102 • Exning • A14 • 38 • Kentford • 39 • 40 • A14 • 41 • 42 • 43

FARMLAND MUS & DENNY ABBEY • A10 • River Bank • Adventures Fen • Burwell • B1103 • 37 • A142 • B1506 • Moulton • PACKHORSE BRIDGE • Higham • Little Saxham • Great Saxham • ICKWORTH HOUSE • Horringer

Reach • Swaffham Prior • Newmarket Heath • Newmarket • NATIONAL HORSERACING MUSEUM • Gazeley • Barrow • A143 • Chevington

Waterbeach • Lode • Commercial End • LODE MILL • ANGLESEY ABBEY • Swaffham Bulbeck • NATIONAL STUD • Cheveley • Ashley • Dalham • Denham • Hargrave • Depden Green • Chedburgh • Hawstead • Whepstead

Landbeach • Milton • P&R • 33 • Horningsea • Stow cum Quy • Bottisham • 36 • A1303 • 70 • Saxon Street • Woodditton • Ousden • Lidgate • Depden • Rede • Brockley Green

Kings Hedges • 34 • MUS OF TECHNOLOGY • Fen Ditton • B1102 • Little Wilbraham • A1304 • Stetchworth • Ditton Green • Kirtling • Thorns • Wickhambrook • Clopton Green • Hawkedon • Hartest

CAMBRIDGE • 30 • 35 • A14 • A1303 • Teversham • Great Wilbraham • Dullingham • 119 • Kirtling Green • Cowlinge • Wickham Street • Denston • Stansfield • Boxted • Shimpling

FITZWILLIAM MUS • Cambridge • Romsey Town • Six Mile Bottom • Westley Waterless • Burrough Green • Great Bradley • Stradishall • Stansfield

Cambridge • A1134 • Cherry Hinton • Fulbourn • A11 • Brinkley • Weston Colville • Carlton • Little Bradley • Denston • 18 • Hartest • Shimpling

Trumpington • P&R • B1307 • WANDLEBURY • Weston Green • Carlton Green • Great Bradley • Little Thurlow • Barnardiston • Hundon • 104 • Glemsford • High Stre...

Great Shelford • Stapleford • Granta • Babraham • Balsham • West Wratting • Great Wratting • Little Thurlow • Poslingford • Cavendish • SUE RYDER FOUNDATION MUS • Pentlow • A1092

Little Shelford • 95 • Little Abington • Hildersham • West Wickham • Great Wratting • Withersfield • Kedington • Chilton Street • Clare • CLARE CASTLE • Foxearth • A1065 • B1064

Sawston • FOURWENTWAYS SERVICES • Great Abington • Streetly End • Horseheath • Little Wratting • Boyton End • Stoke by Clare • 11 • CLARE ANCIENT HOUSE • 56 • Borley

Whittlesford • A505 • Pampisford • Linton • A1307 • LINTON ZOO • Bartlow • Haverhill • Wixoe • Baythorne End • A1017 • Ashen • Ovington • Belchamp St Paul • 85 • Belchamp Otten • Borley

Duxford • IMPERIAL WAR MUSEUM DUXFORD • DUXFORD CHAPEL • Hinxton • Ickleton • Stump Cross • 9 • Hadstock • Shudy Camps • 112 • Castle Camps • Sturmer • Stoke by Clare • Ridgewell • Tilbury Juxta Clare • Little Yeldham • Belchamp Walter • Ballingdon • Bulmer

Strethall • Elmdon • M11 • B1383 • B1052 • Great Chesterford • Little Chesterford • Little Walden • Church End • Helions Bumpstead • 126 • Birdbrook • Steeple Bumpstead • A1017 • Stambourne • Bulmer Tye • Henny

B1039 • Bridge Green • Littlebury • Saffron Walden • Sewards End • Radwinter • Hempstead • Cornish Hall End • Gainsford End • Toppesfield • Great Yeldham • COLNE VALLEY RAILWAY • HEDINGHAM CASTLE • Castle Hedingham • Wickham St Paul • Gestingthorpe • B1058 • A131

Littlebury Green • AUDLEY END HOUSE & GDNS • B1053 • Wimbish • Tye Green • Wimbish Green • Great Sampford • Little Sampford • Howe Street • Finchingfield • 92 • Morris Green • Sible Hedingham • Great Maplestead • Little Maplestead • Alphams...

Duddenhoe End • 118 • Wendens Ambo • B1054 • Howlett End • Great Sampford • Little Sampford • Wethersfield • Highstreet Green • Castle Hedingham • Great Maplestead • Pebma...

Arkesden • Newport • Debden • Debden Cross • B1051 • Pant • Little Bardfield • Great Bardfield • Blackmore End • A1124 • 15 • A1017 • Halstead • Colne

Clavering • Wicken Bonhunt • Rickling • PRIORS HALL BARN • Widdington • MOLE HALL WILDLIFE PARK • Thaxted • B1057 • Wethersfield • Beazley End • A131 • Gosfield • Greens...

Starling's Green • Quendon • 41 • ST MARY'S CHURCH • Hamperden End • Cutlers Green • Lindsell • Great Bardfield • Shalford • 42 • Church End • High Garre... • Earls Colne

Stocking Pelham • Berden • B1038 • Ugley • Henham • GLENDALE FORGE • Monk Street • B1057 • Bardfield Saling • 74 • Shalford Green • Cocking Churchstreet • 9

East End • Farnham Green • HOUSE ON THE HILL TOY MUS • Elsenham • Broxted • Duton Hill • Great Easton • Jasper's Green • Greens Gd

Wangford Warren
Thetford Warren
Thetford
ANCIENT HOUSE MUS
Brettenham
Shadwell
Rushford
Gasthorpe
Garboldisham
North Lopham
South Lopham
Fersfield
Shelfanger
Bressingham
Roydon
Diss
Mill Green
Walcot Green
Lakenheath Warren
Elveden
EAST OF ENGLAND TANK MUSEUM
Barnham
Euston
EUSTON HALL
Knettishall
KNETTISHALL HEATH
Coney Weston
Hopton
Market Weston
Blo' Norton
THELNETHAM WINDMILL
Thelnetham
BRESSINGHAM STEAM MUSEUM AND GARDENS
Redgrave
Magpie Green
Palgrave
Wortham
Stuston
Hinderclay
Thrandeston
Brome
Fakenham Magna
Barningham
Sapiston
Honington
Hepworth
Botesdale
Rickinghall
Burgate
Langton Green
Yaxley
Mellis
Eye
The King's Forest
Icklingham
CAVENHAM HEATH
Tuddenham
WEST STOW
West Stow
Lackford
Culford
Ingham
Ampton
Great Livermere
Troston
Ixworth Thorpe
Bardwell
Stanton
Upthorpe
Walsham le Willows
Wattisfield
Cranmer Green
Allwood Green
Gislingham
Thornham Parva
Thornham Magna
Braiseworth
Cavenham
Flempton
Hengrave
HENGRAVE HALL
Fornham All Saints
Fornham St Martin
Timworth Green
Conyers Green
Ixworth
ABBEY (REM)
Langham
Four Ashes
Crownland
Badwell Ash
Stowlangtoft
Hunston
Long Thurlow
Westhorpe
Wickham Street
Finningham
Wickham Skeith
Stoke Ash
Thorndon
Wyverstone
Wyverstone Street
Bacton
Cotton
Thwaite
Brockford Street
Wetheringsett
Great Ashfield
Stanton Street
Pakenham
Great Barton
Earl's Green
Ford's Green
Risby
Higham
Little Saxham
Westley
Bury St Edmunds
CATHEDRAL AND ABBEY RUINS
Thurston
Norton
Bacton Green
Elmswell
Canham's Green
Mendlesham
Blacksmith's Green
Barrow
Great Saxham
Blackthorpe
Tostock
Beyton
Haughley Park
Ward Green
Gipping
Mendlesham Green
Wetherup Street
Denham
Horringer
ICKWORTH HOUSE
Rushbrooke
Rougham
Hessett
Woolpit
Wetherden
HAUGHLEY PARK
Haughley
Saxham Street
Middlewood Green
Mickfield
Hargrave
Sicklesmere
Rougham Green
Drinkstone
WOOLPIT BYGONES MUSEUM
Drinkstone Green
Thorney Green
Stowupland
Little Stonham
Chevington
Little Welnetham
Bradfield St George
Rattlesden
Harleston
Forward Green
Stonham Aspal
Hawstead
Whepstead
Great Welnetham
Bradfield St Clare
Buxhall Fen Street
MUSEUM OF EAST ANGLIAN LIFE
Stowmarket
Earl Stonham
Creeting Bottoms
Depden Green
REDE HALL
Bradfield Combust
BRADFIELD WOODS
Gedding
Poystreet Green
Buxhall
Great Finborough
Combs
Combs Ford
Gipping
Creeting St Mary
Crowfield
Chedburgh
Depden
Felsham
Hightown Green
High Street Green
Moats Tye
BEACON HILL SERVICES
Thorns
Rede
Hoggard's Green
Cross Green
Great Green
Battisford
Needham Market
Coddenham
Wickhambrook
Clopton Green
Brockley Green
Lawshall
Cockfield
Thorpe Green
Little Finborough
Wickham Street
Hawkedon
Brettenham
Battisford Tye
NEEDHAM LAKE
Denston
Stansfield
Thorpe Morieux
Charles Tye
Ringshall
Barking
Stradishall
Hartest
Shimpling Street
Cross Green
WATTISHAM AIRFIELD MUSEUM
Barking Tye
Baylham
Boxted
Shimpling
Alpheton
Hitcham
Wattisham
Ringshall Stocks
Willisham Tye
Barham
Great Blakenham
Claydon
Stanstead
Lavenham
GUILDHALL
Preston St Mary
Kettlebaston
Great Bricett
Nedging Tye
Offton
Little Blakenham
Hundon
Poslingford
Glemsford
KENTWELL HALL
Bridge Street
Bildeston
Naughton
Somersham
Akenham
High Street
Monks Eleigh
Chelsworth
Brent Eleigh
Flowton
Chilton Street
Cavendish
SUE RYDER FOUNDATION MUS
Long Melford
MELFORD HALL
Semer
Ash Street
Elmsett
Whatfield
Bramford
Whitton
Westbourne
Clare
Pentlow
Milden
Sproughton
CLARE CASTLE
CLARE ANCIENT HOUSE
Foxearth
Acton
Little Waldingfield
Lindsey
ST JAMES'S CHAPEL
Aldham
Burstall
Great Waldingfield
Kersey
WOLVES WOOD RSPB RESERVE
Hintlesham
Chantry
Borley
Mill Green
Hadleigh
Chattisham
Ashen
Ovington
Edwardstone
Copdock
Belchamp Otten
Sudbury
Groton
Ridgewell
Tilbury Juxta Clare
Belchamp Walter
Ballingdon
Great Cornard
Newton
Boxford
Layham
Coles Green
Mace Green
Belstead
Little Yeldham
Bulmer
GAINSBOROUGH'S HO
Stone Street
Calais Street
Whitestreet Green
Raydon
Great Wenham
Capel St Mary
Bulmer Tye
Gestingthorpe
Middleton
Little Cornard
Assington
Great Yeldham
Henny Street
Polstead
Shelley
Holton St Mary
Audley End
Great Henny
Twinstead
Harrow Street
Stoke-by-Nayland
Bentley
Tattingstone
COLNE VALLEY RAILWAY
HEDINGHAM CASTLE
Wickham St Paul
Twinstead Green
Lamarsh
Honey Tye
DEDHAM VALE
Higham
The Heath
Alton Water Res
Highstreet Green
Castle Hedingham
Great Maplestead
Alphamstone
Bures Green
Thorington Street
Stratford St Mary
East Bergholt
EAST BERGHOLT PLACE
Sible Hedingham
Little Maplestead
Bures
Nayland
Boxted
Dedham
BRIDGE COTTAGE
Brantham
STOUR VALLEY
Upper Street
Cattawade
Pebmarsh
Stour
Little Horkesley
Boxted Cross
SIR ALFRED MUNNINGS ART MUSEUM
MISTLEY TOWERS
Mount Bures
Boxted Heath
Dedham Heath
Lawford
Mistley
Bradfield
Halstead
Colne Engaine
Wormingford
Langham
Manningtree
Blackmore End
Great Horkesley
Gosfield
Wakes Colne
EAST ANGLIAN RAILWAY MUSEUM
WESTON HOMES COMMUNITY STADIUM
Horkesley Heath
Ardleigh
Bradfield Heath
Beazley End
Chappel
Fordham
Mile End
Little Bromley
Horsleycross Street
West Bergholt
Horsley Cross
Colne
Fox Street
Great Bromley
Bocking Churchstreet
Fordstreet
Eight Ash Green
HIGHWOODS
Colchester
Tendring Green
Little Bentley
A11
A1066
A134
A143
A14
A140
A1101
A1088
A1092
A131
A1124
A12
A137
A120
A1071
A1141
A1214
B1106
B1112
B1111
B1113
B1077
B1117
B1115
B1063
B1066
B1064
B1065
B1058
B1068
B1070
B1087
B1029
B1035
B1080
B1508
Bury St Edmunds
Thetford
Diss
Eye
Stowmarket
Sudbury
Hadleigh
Colchester
0 1 2 3 4 5 6 miles
0 1 2 3 4 5 6 7 8 9 10 km

A140 · A143 · A14 · A12 · A1120 · A1094 · A1152 · A1156 · A1214

HARLESTON · **Halesworth** · **Southwold** · **Framlingham** · **Saxmundham** · **Leiston** · **Aldeburgh** · **Wickham Market** · **Woodbridge** · **Ipswich** · **Walton** · **FELIXSTOWE** · **HARWICH** · **Dovercourt**

Shimpling · Rushall · Garlic Street · Wortwell · St Michael South Elmham · Ilketshall St Lawrence · Redisham · Sotterley · Benacre · BENACRE · Covehithe

Dickleburgh · Redenhall · Mendham · St Margaret South Elmham · All Saints South Elmham · Stone Street · Cox Common · West End · Wrentham

Thelveton · Needham · Withersdale Street · Rumburgh · Spexhall · Brampton · Stoven · Clay Common · Frostenden · South Cove

Thorpe Abbotts · Brockdish · Metfield · St James South Elmham · Wissett · Broadway · Westhall · Wangford · Cove Bottom

Scole · Oakley · Hoxne · Syleham · Fressingfield · Wingfield Old College · Little Whittingham Green · Linstead Parva · Chediston · Holton · Blyford · Reydon Smear · Reydon · SOUTHWOLD MUSEUM

100TH BOMB GROUP MEMORIAL MUS · BILLINGFORD WINDMILL

Brome Street · Cross Street · Wingfield · Chippenhall Green · Silverley's Green · Cratfield · Cookley · Wenhaston · Blackheath · Thorington · Blythburgh · HEN REEDBED NATURE RESERVE · Walberswick

Cranley · Denham Street · Heckfield Green · Denham · Battlesea Green · Pixey Green · Swan Green · Banyard's Green · Huntingfield · Walpole · Bramfield · SUFFOLK COAST · Dunwich

Redlingfield · Athelington · Wilby · Wootten Green · Russel's Green · Laxfield · Heveningham · Sibton Green · DUNWICH UNDERWATER EXPLORATION EXHIBITION

Occold · Southolt · Fingal Street · Stanway Green · Brundish · Worlingworth · Ubbeston Green · High Street · Darsham · WESTLETON HEATH · Dunwich Forest · Westleton

Rishangles · Bedingfield · Tannington · Brundish Street · Crown Corner · Owl's Green · Badingham · Peasenhall · Sibton · Yoxford · Middleton Moor · MINSMERE RSPB NATURE RESERVE

Debenham · Bedfield · Monk Soham · Saxtead · Brabling Green · Dennington · Bruisyard · Rotten End · Hemp Green · North Green · Middleton · Theberton · Eastbridge

Ashfield · Kenton · Maypole Green · Earl Soham · SAXTEAD GREEN POST MILL · Saxtead Green · Cransford · Rendham · Curlew Green · Kelsale · LEISTON ABBEY

Winston · Winston Green · Peats Corner · Lampardbrook · Cole's Green · Great Glemham · Sweffling · Carlton · Knodishall · Sizewell

Pettaugh · Framsden · Cretingham · Kettleburgh · Brandeston · Parham · Hacheston · Stratford St Andrew · Benhall Street · Sternfield · Benhall Green · Coldfair Green · Aldringham · Thorpeness

HELMINGHAM HALL GARDENS · Helmingham · Monewden · Easton · Marlesford · Farnham · Gromford · Friston · NORTH WARREN RSPB NATURE RESERVE

Gosbeck · Ashbocking · Charsfield · EASTON FARM PARK · Letheringham · AKENFIELD · Little Glemham · SNAPE MALTINGS · Snape · Iken · High Street

Otley · Clopton Corner · Dallinghoo · Debach · Lower Hacheston · Campsey Ash · Blaxhall · Aldeburgh

Hemingstone · Swilland · Clopton · Bredfield · Pettistree · Rendlesham · Tunstall · Tunstall Forest · Sudbourne · Chillesford

Henley · Witnesham · Grundisburgh · Hasketon · Ufford · Eyke · Butley · Bromeswell · Melton · ORFORD CASTLE · Orford · Orford Ness

Tuddenham St Martin · Culpho · Boot Street · Great Bealings · Maidensgrave · Rendlesham Forest · Capel St Andrew · Butley High Corner · ORFORDNESS-HAVERGATE

Westerfield · Playford · Little Bealings · SUTTON HOO · Martlesham · Sutton · Boyton

Rushmere St Andrew · CHRISTCHURCH MANSION · Kesgrave · Martlesham Heath · Waldringfield Heath · Duck Corner · Stores Corner

Rose Hill · MARTLESHAM HEATH CONTROL TOWER · Brightwell · Waldringfield · Shottisham · Hollesley · HOLLESLEY BAY

Stoke · Maidenhall · Warren Heath · Bucklesham · Newbourne · Hemley · Alderton · Shingle Street

Gainsborough · Wherstead · Nacton · ORWELL · Kirton · Falkenham · Bawdsey

Freston · Woolverstone · Levington · Pin Mill · Thorpe Common · Trimley St Martin · Felixstowe Ferry

Holbrook · Chelmondiston · Trimley Lower Street · Trimley St Mary · Old Felixstowe

Lower Holbrook · Shotley · Walton · TRIMLEY MARSHES NATURE RESERVE · CHARLES MANNING'S AMUSEMENT PARK

Stutton · Harkstead · Shop Corner · Shotley Gate · HARWICH REDOUBT FORT

Wrabness · Ramsey · Parkeston · Upper Dovercourt · Dovercourt

A120 · Little Oakley · Wix · Great Oakley · Stones Green

ESBJERG 18:00 · HOEK VAN HOLLAND 6:15

TM · A12

1   2 5   2   3   4   5

A

TREMADOG BAY
BAE TREMADOG

Morfa
Harlech

Eisingrug

Glyn-
cywarch

623
MOEL
YSGYFARNOGOD

MOEL
LLYFRANT

A470

Bronaber

Mynydd
Bach

Mynydd
Bryn-llech

Buarthmeini

Harlech

B4573

Llanfair
LLANFAIR
SLATE CAVERNS

Pen-sarn

Llandanwg

Pen-y-pont

Pentre Gwynfryn

SNOWDONIA

RHINOG

720
RHINOG FAWR

Bed-y-
coedwr

RHAEADR
MAWDDACH

Pont
Aber-Geirw

Cwm-
hesgen

B

754
Y LLETHR

NATIONAL

COED Y BRENIN
VISITOR CENTRE

12   Coed y Brenin
Forest

Capel Hermon

734
RHOBELL
FAWR

Pont Fronwydd

Afon Wnion

Llanbedr

MORFA
DYFFRYN

Coed Ystumgwern

Morfa
Dyffryn

11

PARK

DIFFWYS
750

GANLLWYD

COED
GANLLWYD

Llanfachreth

ALLT Y
BENGLOG

A494

Llanenddwyn

Dyffryn Ardudwy

Cors-y-Gedol

SH

Blaen-y-cwm

Rhydymain

Llanddwywe

Tal-y-bont

71

cau

71

Plas-canol

PEN-Y-
BRYN

Llanelltyd

CYMER
ABBEY

Bont Newydd

Llanaber

Caerdeon

Bontddu

PENMAENPOOL CENTRE

B4416

Brithdir

Cutiau

TOLL

9

Penmaenpool

A470

Y Gribin

Abergwynant

Dolgellau

Barmouth
(Abermaw)

A496

Afon Mawddach

A493

Rhydwen

KINGS

670
WAUN-OER

Afon Cerist

A470

C

RNLI LIFEBOAT MUSEUM

BARMOUTH BAY   The Bar

FAIRBOURNE & BARMOUTH
STEAM RAILWAY

BAE BERMO

Fairbourne

Arthog

Ynysgyfflog

PARC

MEIRION
MILL

Friog

893 CADAIR
IDRIS

Mynydd
Ceiswyn

Mynydd
Dolgoed

20

CADER
IDRIS

CENEDLAETHOL

Minffordd

Dyfi Forest

Llwyngwril

Afon Dysynni

Tal-y-llyn

A487

Corris
Uchaf

Aberllefenni

Aberangell

A470

Llanfihangel-
y-pennant

KING ARTHUR'S
LABYRINTH &
CRAFT CENTRE

ERYRI

Cwm- Llinau

D

Llangelynin

A493

CASTELL Y BERE

Corris

CORRIS RAILWAY
AND MUSEUM

Dol-fôr

Rhoslefain

Llanegryn

Peniarth

Abergynolwyn

B4405

Esgairgeiliog

Cemmaes

Llanfendigaid

309

Plas Llwyngwern

CENTRE FOR
ALTERNATIVE
TECHNOLOGY

B4404

Llanwrin

Tonfanau

633
TARRENHENDRE

Pantperthog

Cemmaes
Road

Bryncrug

Pandy

VALLEY DYFI

Pen-y-bont

A489

Abercegir

Commins
Coch

Rhyd-yr-onen
TALYLLYN RAILWAY

SENEDD-
DY-OWAIN
GLYNDWR

Machynlleth

Darowen

Tywyn

Caethle

Cwrt

Pennal A493

DOVEY
DYFI

Penegoes

FELIN CREWI
WATER MILL

Tal-y-wern

30

Forge

Melinbyrhedyn

Derwenlas

468
MOELFRE

15

279

Aberdovey

A493

Glaspwll

Pant-glâs

582

Aberhosan

E

Aberdovey Bar
Bae Aberdyfi

DYFI

Dovey
Dyfi

YNYS HIR
RESERVE

Glandyfi

Eglwys Fach
DYFI FURNACE

A487

Glaslyn

Ynyslas

Fochno

18

SN

Source of
R. Severn
Blaen Hafren

Llancynfelyn

B4353

Tre'r-ddôl

Nant-y-Moch
Reservoir

BORTH

Tre-Taliesin

521
MOEL-Y-LLYN

Borth

Upper Borth

Tal-y-bont

Dôl-y-Bont

PLYNLIMON
PUMLUMON
FAWR

741

752

Source of
R. Wye
Blaen Gwy

Llandre

Pen-y-garn

Bont-goch

610
PEN Y GARN

F

ARTS CENTRE

NATIONAL
LIBRARY
CLIFF RAILWAY

B4572

Clarach

Bow
Street

Salem

506

Penrhyn-coch

Pen-bont
Rhydybeddau

13

148

Plas Gogerddan

Aberystwyth

P&R

A4159

Capel Dewi

Dollwen

LLYWERNOG SILVER
LEAD MINE

Dyffryn
Castell

Comins
Coch

Capel
Bangor

Goginan

Trefechan

CASTLE

Llanbadarn Fawr

A44

Cwmbrwyno

Ponterwyd

28

46

Penparcau

Glanrafon

VALE OF RHEIDOL
RAILWAY

Afon Rheidol

RHEIDOL HYDRO
ELECTRIC STAT.

47

564

Rhydyfelin

Moriah

Capel Seion

Aberffrwd

Ystumtuen

Ysbytycynfyn

A487

Southgate

Gors

Pisgah

COED
RHEIDOL

Devil's
Bridge

610
PEN Y GARN

Llanfarian

New Cross

6

A4120

3

Mynydd
Bach

4

Trisant

5

Blaenplwyf

A485

Llanfihangel-
y-Creuddyn

Blaenycwm

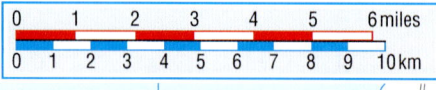

A B C (grid rows)
D E F G

5 6 7 8 9

Powys

SJ
SO

Parc
Rhos-y-gwaliau
Pennant
Tregeiriog
Llechrydau
Llanarmon Dyffryn Ceiriog
Rhiwlas
Cefn Canol
Llawnt
Rhydycroesau
Aber-Hirnant
Blaen-y-Cwm
Tyn-y-fedwen
Tyn-y-ffridd
Llangadwaladr
Moel Sych (827)
Moel Sych
Dolhendre
Llangower
Bala Lake Railway
Pont Cwm Pydew
Tai-bach (534)
Moelfre
Llansilin
Tyn-y-coed
Ola's Dyke Path
Llwybr Clawdd Offa
72 Aberhirnant Forest
Pistyll Rhaeadr
Tan-y-pistyll
Llanuwchllyn
72
Pont-Rhyd-sarn
Talardd
Foel y Geifr (626)
Pencraig (666)
Llangynog
Cefn Coch (607)
Llanrhaeadr-ym-Mochnant
B4580
Pen-y-bont
Porth-y-waen
Llanfechain
Llansantffraid-ym-Mechain
Llanymynech
Y Berwyn
Alltforgan
Pennant Melangell
Penybontfawr
Penygarnedd
B4396
Llangedwyn
B4396
Afon Tanat
Rhos-y-brithdir (389)
Llanyblodwel
Cwm Cynllwyd
Ty-nant
Hirnant
Lake Vyrnwy
Ty-uchaf
Blaen-y-cwm (540)
Abernaint
Bwlchyddar
B4391
Aber-Rhiwlech
Pont y Pennant
B4393
Llanwddyn
Abertridwr
Llanfyllin
Tycrwyn
Bwlch-y-cibau
Waen Fach
Deuddwr
Arddleen
Cywarch (513)
Hen Gerrig
Ddôl-Cownwy
Llanfihangel-yn-Ngwynfa
Main
Sarnau
Bryn Sion
Aber Cowarch
Llanymawddwy
Dyfnant Forest
A490
Afon Vyrnwy
60
Trefnanney
Geufford
Wern
Aran Fawddwy (907)
TIR RHIWIOG (545)
Pont-Llogel
Meifod
Trefeirig
Pentrebeirdd
Dinas-Mawddwy
Minllyn
Cwm-Cewydd
Moel y Llyn
Mynydd y Gadfa
Afon Vyrnwy (Afon Efyrnwy)
Dolanog
Pontrobert
Maesgwyn-Isaf
Pool Quay
Guilsfield
Mallwyd
A458 Wern
Foel
Llangadfan (330)
Glascoed
Groes-lwyd
Welshpool (Y Trallwng)
POWYSLAND
Buttin
Ffridd Goch (523)
Pen Coed
GLYNDWR'S WAY
Llanerfyl
Heniarth
A495
B4385
Cyfronydd
WELSHPOOL & LLANFAIR LIGHT RAILWAY
POWIS CASTLE
Hope
Mynydd y Cemaes
Clegyrnant
Dolwen
Four Crosses
Melin-y-grug
Melin-y-ddôl
Llanfair Caereinion
A458 10
Castle Caereinion
Leighton
B4388
Pentre-Celyn
Neinthirion
Cwmderwen
Sychtyn
Mynydd Waun Fawr
Bryn-penarth (364)
Llwynderw
Fron
MID-WALES
Waun
Tafolwern
Llanbrynmair (440)
Pandy
Llanllugan
Llanwyddelan
B4390
Pant-y-ffridd
Manafon
Berriew
A483
Kingswood
Stockton
Llan
Dolfach
A470
Talerddig
Rhyd
Adfa
New Mills
B4389
Garthmyl
Fron
B4386
Bont-Dolgadfan (13)
Brooks
B4385
Pennant
Carno (458)
Tregynon
Bettws Cedewain (13)
Green Lane
Montgomery (Trefaldwyn)
OFFA'S DYKE PATH
LLWYBR CLAWD OFFA
Dylife
Clatter (398)
Llanwnog
Bwlch-y-ffridd (265)
DOLFORWYN CASTLE
Abermûle
Llandyssil
Pentreheyling
60
Staylittle
Llawr-y-glyn
Gleiniant
B4569
Caersws
A489
Milford
Llanllwchaiarn
Llenmerewig
Hodley
Sarn
GLYNDWR'S WAY
Llyn Clywedog
Trefeglwys
Newtown (Y Drenewydd)
Kerry
Glanmule
City
A489
Hafren Forest
Tan Hinon
Old Hall
Glan-y-nant
FAN HILL (482)
Van
Oakley Park (307)
Little London
Llandinam
Mochdre
Dolfor
SO
Pant Mawr
Llanidloes
Glynbrochan
Cwmbelan
Newchapel
Pentre
CILFAESTY HILL (528)
Anchor
Clun Forest
Hall of the Forest
BLACK MT (448)
Newcastle
Llanifyny
A44
Llangurig
A470
Tylwch
47
A470 6
Nantgwyn
B4518
Glyndwr's Way (584)
Llaithddu
David's Well
48
Llanbadarn Fynydd
Beguildy
Dutlas
Llanfair Waterdine
Pant-y-dwr
RED LION HILL (493)
Rhydmoelddu
Black Mountain
GLYNDWR'S WAY
BEACON (547)
Bettws-y-crwyn
Quabbs
Felindre
B4355
B4368
G

Llechrydau
Selattyn
Hengoed
Gobowen
Perthy
Tetchill
Balmer Heath
Lyneal
Northwood
Waterloo
Quina Brook
Prees
Llanarmon Dyffryn Ceiriog
Rhiwlas
Pant-glas
Hindford
Welsh Frankton
Lee
Colemere
Wolverley
Newtown
Edstaston
Llangadwaladr
Cefn Canol
Llawnt
Old Oswestry Hill Fort
Whittington Castle
Whittington
Lower Frankton
Hordley
English Frankton
Kenwick
Horton
Lowe
Babbinswood
Oswestry
Offa's Dyke Path
Llansilin
Moelfre
Tyn-y-coed
Middleton
Wootton
Lower Hordley
Rednal
Stanwardine in the Wood
Cockshutt
Loppington
Wem
Tilley
Aston
Noneley
Lee Brockhurst
Trefonen
Morda
Queen's Head
Haughton
Bagley
Petton
Ball
Grimpo
Weston Lullingfields
Burlton
Preston Brockhurst
Llangedwyn
Nantmawr
Maesbury
Maesbury Marsh
West Felton
Westoncommon
Wykey
Afon Tanat
Pen-y-bont
Porth-y-waen
Morton
Woolston
Eardiston
Stanwardine in the Fields
Marton
Myddle
Alderton
Clive
Rhos-y-brithdir
Llanyblodwel
Pant
Llynclys
Crickheath
Osbaston
Shotatton
Yorton
Grinshill
Bwlchyddar
Cambrian Heritage Railway
Maesbrook
Knockin
Brownhill
Baschurch
Harmer Hill
Llansantffraid-ym-Mechain
Llanfechain
Llanymynech
Kinnerley
Dovaston
Ruyton-XI-Towns
Prescott
Merrington
Llanfyllin
Kynaston
Hopton
Little Ness
Walford
Walford Heath
Preston Gubbals
Hadnall
Kinton
Nesscliffe
Yeaton
Bomere Heath
Astley
Llandysilio
Crosslanes
Great Ness
Leaton
Bwlch-y-cibau
Waen Fach
Four Crosses
Melverley Green
Wilcott
Felton Butler
Grafton
Albrighton
Bings Heath
Deuddwr
Llandrinio
Pentre
Forton Heath
Fitz
Mytton
Battlefield
Main
Sarnau
Arddleen
Melverley
Ensdon
Forton
Montford Bridge
Harlescott
Haughmond Abbey
Afon Vyrnwy (Afon Efyrnwy)
Trefnanney
Geuffordd
Criggion
Coedway
Shrawardine
Bicton
Ditherington
Meifod
Pentrebeirdd
Wern
Crewgreen
Alberbury
Montford
Ford
Coton Hill
Uffington
Shelton
Shrewsbury
Maesgwyn-Isaf
Middletown
Wollaston
Copthorne
Porthill
Glyndŵr's Way
Pool Quay
Groes-lwyd
Trewern
Cardeston
Rowton
Shoot Hill
Hortonlane
Meole Brace
Preston
Guilsfield
Halfway House
Wattlesborough Heath
Yockleton
Nox
Cruckton
Emstrey
Attingham Park
Cloddiau
Welshpool (Y Trallwng)
Nelly Andrews Green
Vennington
Westbury
Stoney Stretton
Edge
Cruckmeole
Hanwood
Atcham
Cyfronydd
Buttington
Powysland
Farley
Hinton
Lea
Annscroft
Bayston Hill
Welshpool & Llanfair Light Railway
Powis Castle
Hope
SJ
Aston Rogers
Westley
Asterley
Plealey
Great Lyth
Lyth Hill
Cross Houses
Castle Caereinion
Offa's Dyke Path
Rowley
Longden
Berrington
Bridge
Leighton
Worthen
Minsterley
Pontesbury
Condover
Cantlop
Binweston
Brockton
Oaks
Stapleton
Llwynderw
Mid-Wales
Fron
Trelystan
Betton
Leigh
Wrentnall
Ploxgreen
Habberley
Great Ryton
Pitchford
Golding
Pant-y-ffridd
Marton
Snailbeach
Church Pulverbatch
Dorrington
Acton Pigott
Kingswood
Meadowtown
Bentlawnt
Hope
Pulverbatch
Berriew
Forden
Stockton
Crowsnest
Frodesley
Acton Burnell
Longnor
Langley Chapel and Gatehouse
Rorrington
Severn (Hafren)
Wotherton
Mitchell's Fold Stone Circle
Gravels
Garthmyl
Middleton
Black Marsh
Stiperstones
Ruckley
Pennerley
Picklescott
Woolstaston
Leebotwood
Church Preen
Chirbury
The Marsh
Shelve
Fron
Priest Weston
The Bog
Ratlinghope
Enchmarsh
Plaish
Green Lane
Montgomery (Trefaldwyn)
Corndon Hill
Bridges
All Stretton
Cardington
Gretton
Llandyssil
Coldyeld
Bridges Long Mynd
Abermule
Roundton Hill
Hyssington
Church Stretton
Longville in the Dale
Churchstoke
SO
East Wall
Wall Bank
Llwybr Clawdd Offa
West Onny
East Onny
The Long Mynd
Llanmerewig
Pentreheyling
Linley
Norbury
Wentnor
Hope Bowdler
Wall under Heywood
Rushbury
Wilderhope Manor
Hodley
Pentre
Snead
Owlbury
More
Little Stretton
Tickerton
Sarn
Glanmule
Lydham
Asterton
Minton
Acton Scott
Hatton
Eaton
Broadstone
Kerry
City
Myndtown
Marshbrook
Working Farm
Bishop's Castle
House on Crutches
Lea
Eaton
Whittingslow
Wenlock Edge
Harton
Middlehope
Ape Dale
Mainstone
Choulton
Eyton
Plowden
Woolston
Alcaston
Munslow
Colebatch
Horderley
Upper Affcot
Wistanstow
Aston Munslow
Corve
Clun Forest
Lydbury North
Edgton
Strefford
Westhope
Diddlebury
Corfton
Boulden
Cefn Einion
Brockton
Acton
Cheny Longville
Lower Dinchope
Anchor
Bryn
Lower Down
Walcot
Newington
Peaton
Hall of the Forest
Hopesay
Kempton
Sibdon Carwood
Halford
Seifton
Great Sutton
Whitcott Keysett
Aston on Clun
Craven Arms
Culmington
Black Mt
Newcastle
Bicton
Little Brampton
Stokesay
Stokesay Castle
Norton
Hayton's Bent
Hopton Cangeford
Felindre
Bettws-y-crwyn
Quabbs
Clunton
Broome
Vernolds Common
Llwyn
Clun
Purslow
Clunbury
Onibury
Beguildy
Churchbank
Redlake
Brandhill
The Wernlas Collection
Twitchen
Stanton Lacy
Hobarris
Hopton Castle
Abcott
Clungunford
Wootton
Shelderton
Hoptonheath
Bromfield
Ludlow
Middleton
Henley
New Invention
Chapel Lawn
Bedstone
Marlow
Beacon
Upper
0 1 2 3 4 5 6 miles
0 1 2 3 4 5 6 7 8 9 10 km

Telford and Wrekin

Shropshire

Stone • Little Stoke • Walton • Yarnfield • Norton Bridge • Eccleshall • Chebsey • Great Bridgeford • Seighford • Ranton • Derrington • Doxey • **Stafford** • Forebridge • Holmcroft • Coppenhall • Moss Pit

Market Drayton • Hales • Fairoak • Wetwood • Croxton • Croxtonbank • Bishop's Offley • Pershall • Adbaston • Knighton • Shebdon • Woodseaves • High Offley • Norbury • Lawnhead • Knightley • Long Compton • Gnosall • Gnosall Heath • Haughton • Whitecross • Coton • Allimore Green • Bradley • Dunston • Acton Trussell • Bednall

Darliston • Bletchley • Fauls • The Four Alls • Sutton • Woodseaves • Chipnall • Cheswardine • Soudley • Lockleywood • Hinstock • Mill Green • Knighton

Prees Heath • Lostford • Wollerton • Wollerton Old Hall • Stoke Heath • Wistanswick • Great Bridgeford

Prees Lower Heath • Weston • Wixhill • Moston • Hopton • Marchamley • Hodnet • Stoke on Tern • Peplow • Ellerton

High Hatton • Radmoor • Ollerton • Child's Ercall • Sambrook • Pickstock • Sutton • Puleston • Forton • Newport • Chetwynd Aston • Moreton • Orslow • Great Chatwell • Brineton • Marston • Mitton • Congreve • Penkridge • Levedale • Longridge • Whiston • Wheaton Aston • Stretton

Shawbury • Muckleton • Ercall Heath • Edgebolton • Great Wytheford • Rowton • Waters Upton • Crudgington • Tibberton • Edgmond Marsh • Edgmond • Coton • Gnosall Heath • Apeton • Church Eaton • High Onn • Blymhill • Mottey Meadows • Brewood • Kiddemore Green • Belvide Res. • Horsebrook • Hatherton • Coven • Standeford • Shareshill • Featherstone

Moreton Corbet • Ellerdine Heath • Eaton on Tern • Great Bolas • Cherrington • Meese • Adeney • Longford • Church Aston • Brockton • Lilleshall • Weston Heath • Tong Norton • Weston under Lizard • Bishops Wood • Boscobel House & The Royal Oak • Chillington Hall • Codsall Wood • Oaken • Codsall • Fordhouses

Telford and Wrekin

Poynton Green • High Ercall • Roden • Rodington • Walcot • Withington • Upton Magna • Sleapford • Eyton upon the Weald Moors • Preston upon the Weald Moors • Hoo Farm Animals Kingdom • Muxton • Lilleshall Abbey • Heath Hill • Lilyhurst • Weston Heath • White Ladies Priory • Tong • Albrighton • David Austin Roses • Ryton • Boningale • Oaken • Oxley • Tettenhall • Wolverhampton • Bushbury

Wellington • Hadley • Ketley • Ketley Bank • Arleston • Oakengates • Priorslee • Crackleybank • Telford Services • Shifnal • Haughton • The Wyke • RAF Museum • Cosford • Tong • Bishops Wood

Wroxeter Roman City • Wroxeter • Donnington • Eaton Constantine • Longwood • The Wrekin • Little Wenlock • Horsehay • Horsehay Steam Trust • **Dawley** • Stirchley • **Telford** • Telford Wonderland • Haughton • Brockton • Grindle • Ryton • Beckbury • Burnhill Green • Pattingham • Perton • Wightwick Manor • Lower Penn • Penn • Blakenhall • Bradmore

Shropshire

Cound • Cressage • Sheinton • Homer • Harley • Kenley • Leighton • Buildwas • Buildwas Abbey • Mus. of Iron • Mus. of the Gorge • Ironbridge • Benthall Hall • Benthall • Wyke • Broseley • Much Wenlock • Coalbrookdale • Rosehill Ho. • Little Dawley • Madeley • Tollhouse • Coalport • Jackfield Tile Mus. • Halesfield • Kemberton • Sutton Maddock • Norton • Stockton • Stableford • Badger • Ackleton • Rudge • Chesterton • Shipley • Seisdon • Trysull • Wombourne • Heathton • Swindon • Himley • Himley Hall • Gornalwood • Sedgley • Tipton • Dudley

Stretton Westwood • Hughley • Presthope • Bourton • Easthope • Brockton • Weston • Shipton • Stanton Long • Holdgate • Tugford • Abdon • Brown Clee Hill • Upper Heath • Clee St Margaret • Stoke St Milborough • Cleedownton

Acton Round • Haughton • Nordley • Worfield • Hilton • Hopstone • Claverley • Roughton • Farmcote • Halfpenny Green • Wolverhampton Halfpenny Green • Highgate Common • Wall Heath • Kingswinford • Bromley • Brierley Hill • Wordsley • Amblecote • Quarry Bank • Lye • Cradley Heath • Wollescote

Morville Hall • Morville • Cliff Railway • Tasley • Morville Heath • **Bridgnorth** • Oldbury • Watermill • Danesford • Quatford • Eardington • Bobbington • Six Ashes • Four Ashes • Enville • Stourton • Kinver • Kingsford • Blakeshall • Potter's Cross • Caunsall • **Stourbridge** • Pedmore • Hagley • West Hagley • **HALESOWEN** • Hasbury

Aston Eyre • Monkhopton • Aston Botterell • Chorley • Stottesdon • Billingsley • Sidbury • Hampton • Hampton Loade • Alveley • Highley • Woodhill • Birdsgreen • Romsley • Rays Farm Country Matters • Severn Valley • Shatterford • Upper Arley • Cookley • Wolverley • Franche • **Kiddandminster**

Middleton Priors • Ditton Priors • Neenton • Cleobury North • Middleton Scriven • Sutton • Glazeley • Chelmarsh • Quatt • Tuckhill • Dudmaston

Holdgate • Tugford • Loughton • Wheathill • Cleeton St Mary • Foxwood • Doddington • Catherton • Cleobury Mortimer

Bitterley • Silvington • Farlow • Oreton • Kinlet • Pound Green • Low Habberley • Trimpley • Button Oak • Wyre Forest • Wribbenhall • Blakebrook • Bewdley • Severn Valley Railway

Stafford
West Midlands
Stone
Uttoxeter
Eccleshall
Stafford
Weston
Abbots Bromley
Gnosall
Newport
Cannock Chase
Rugeley
Penkridge
Hednesford
Heath Hayes
Cannock
Burntwood
Lichfield
Shifnal
Brewood
Cheslyn Hay
Brownhills
Albrighton
Codsall
Tettenhall
Wolverhampton
Wednesfield
Willenhall
Walsall
Bilston
Darlaston
Aldridge
Streetly
Sutton Coldfield
Great Barr
Kingstanding
Sedgley
Coseley
Wednesbury
Wombourne
Tipton
West Bromwich
Dudley
Oldbury
Rowley Regis
Smethwick
Handsworth
Kingswinford
Brierley Hill
Wordsley
Stourbridge
Halesowen
Birmingham
Harborne
Edgbaston
Kinver
Solihull
Shirley
Longbridge
Erdington
Castle Bromwich
Olton
Northfield
Bournville
Hagley
Clent
Chatcull
Fairoak
Croxton
Sugnall
Bishop's Offley
Adbaston
Knighton
High Offley
Woodseaves
Norbury
Weston Jones
Sutton
Puleston
Forton
Aqualate Mere
Chetwynd Aston
Lilleshall
Orslow
Great Chatwell
Heath Hill
Lilyhurst
Weston Heath
Sheriffhales
Blymhill
Brineton
Weston under Lizard
Tong
Tong Norton
Boningale
Beckbury
Ryton
Grindle
Badger
Ackleton
Stableford
Worfield
Rudge
Chesterton
Shipley
Hilton
Hopstone
Roughton
Farmcote
Quatford
Quatt
Tuckhill
Alveley
Birdsgreen
Romsley
Kingsford
Shatterford
Upper Arley
Kidderminster
Cookley
Blakedown
Churchill
Broome
Belbroughton
Drayton
Walton
Millmeece
Slindon
Yarnfield
Norton Bridge
Chebsey
Great Bridgeford
Wootton
Ellenhall
Seighford
Ranton
Haughton
Coton Clanford
Derrington
Allimore Green
Church Eaton
High Onn
Marston
Wheaton Aston
Mitton
Bradley
Dunston
Acton Trussell
Bednall
Levedale
Longridge
Whiston
Congreve
Lapley
Stretton
Gailey
Hatherton
Huntington
Standeford
Shareshill
Coven
Featherstone
Essington
Oaken
Pattingham
Perton
Trescott
Lower Penn
Penn
Trysull
Seisdon
Swindon
Himley
Wall Heath
Bobbington
Six Ashes
Four Ashes
Enville
Stourton
Potter's Cross
Whittington
Blakeshall
Caunsall
Dayhills
Garshall Green
Little Stoke
Aston-By-Stone
Milwich
Coton Hill
Fradswell
Sandon
Burston
Yarlet
Whitgreave
Marston
Salt
Gayton
Hopton
Ingestre
Tixall
Weeping Cross
Milford
Walton on the Hill
Brocton
Great Haywood
Little Haywood
Colwich
Stowe-by-Chartley
Drointon
Hixon
Newton
Admaston
Gratwich
Field
Bramshall
Grindley
Kingstone
Blount's Green
Doveridge
Marchington
Marchington Woodlands
Newborough
Hoar Cross
Colton
Blithbury
Hill Ridware
Hamstall Ridware
Yoxall
Morrey
Woodlane
Hadley End
Handsacre
Armitage
King's Bromley
Rileyhill
Longdon
Upper Longdon
Longdon Green
Cannock Wood
Gentleshaw
Farewell
Chorley
Elmhurst
Streethay
Hammerwich
Chasetown
Norton Canes
Wall
Shenstone
Stonnall
Little Hay
Weeford
Muckley Corner
Pelsall
Walsall Wood
Shelfield
Rushall
Leighswood
Clayhanger
Little Wyrley
Great Wyrley
Churchbridge
Bridgtown
Landywood
Bloxwich
Short Heath
New Invention
Wood Hayes
Bushbury
Fordhouses
Oxley
Moseley
Ettingshall
Bradmore
Bradley
Moxley
Hill Top
Great Bridge
Churchfield
Hamstead
Upper Witton
New Oscott
Walmley
Wylde Green
Four Oaks
Mere Green
Roughley
Hill
Watford Gap
Little Aston
Hardwick
Perry Barr
Gravelly Hill
Tyburn
Sandwell
Winson Green
Aston
Ward End
Yardley
Bearwood
Chad Valley
Balsall Heath
Sparkhill
Acock's Green
Moseley
King's Heath
Springfield
Hall Green
Selly Oak
Bartley Green
Woodgate
Illey
Frankley
Quinton
Blackheath
Old Hill
Cradley Heath
Quarry Bank
Wollescote
Lye
Hasbury
Pedmore
Netherton
Tividale
Dudley Port
Gornalwood
Upper Gornal
Amblecote
Romsley
Rubery
Hollywood
Drakes Cross
Whitlock's End
Monkspath
King's Norton
Hopwood
Wildmoor
Bell End
Holy Cross
Staffordshire and Worcestershire Canal
Shropshire Union Canal
Belvide Res.
Blithfield Res.
Trent
M6
M54
M5
M6 Toll
A5
A34
A38
A41
A449
A51
A518
A513
A456
A458
A442
A454
A4041
A452
A461
A491
A441
A435
A45
SJ
SO
0 1 2 3 4 5 6 miles
0 1 2 3 4 5 6 7 8 9 10 km

Mickleover
Littleover
Osmaston
Borrowash
Breaston
Dalbury
Oaks Green
Church Broughton
Sutton on the Hill
Burnaston
Normanton
Elvaston
Draycott
Long Eaton
Sawley
Thrumpton
Gotham
Sudbury
Foston
Etwall
Alvaston
Thulston
Shardlow
Cavendish Bridge
Scropton
Hatton
Findern
Chellaston
Stenson
Aston-on-Trent
Ratcliffe on Soar
Draycott in the Clay
Tutbury
Marston on-Dove
Egginton
Willington
Twyford
Barrow upon Trent
Swarkestone
Weston-on-Trent
Hemington
Lockington
New Kingston
Kingston on Soar
West Leake
East Leake
Hanbury
Rolleston on-Dove
Repton
Ingleby
Stanton by Bridge
King's Newton
Castle Donington
Kegworth
Hanbury Woodend
Anslow Gate
Anslow
Stretton
Milton
Donington Park
East Midlands
Needwood Forest
Needwood
Horninglow
Newton Solney
Melbourne
Isley Walton
Diseworth
Long Whatton
Sutton Bonington
Newchurch
Rangemore
Shobnall
Burton upon Trent
Winshill
Bretby
Foremark Res.
Ticknall
Calke
Staunton Harold Res.
Breedon on the Hill
Tonge
Normanton on Soar
Hathern
Tatenhill
Stapenhill
Upper Midway
Lower Midway
Hartshorne
Calke Abbey
Worthington
Belton
Stanford on Soar
Branston
Newhall
Swadlincote
Church Gresley
Woodville
Smisby
Lount
Osgathorpe
Shepshed
Thorpe Acre
Loughborough
Dunstall
Woodhouses
Barton-under-Needwood
Walton-on-Trent
Castle Gresley
Blackfordby
Newbold
Coleorton
Thringstone
Shelthorpe
Woodthorpe
Caldwell
Linton
Mount Pleasant
Norris Hill
Ashby-de-la-Zouch
Swannington
Whitwick
Quorndon
Orgreave
Alrewas
Rosliston
Moira
Coalville
Charnwood Forest
Woodhouse
Woodhouse Eaves
Fradley
Coton in the Elms
Overseal
Donisthorpe
Packington
Ravenstone
Greenhill
Croxall
Edingale
Lullington
Netherseal
Oakthorpe
Measham
Normanton le Heath
Bardon
Hugglescote
Copt Oak
Swithland
Elford
Harlaston
Haunton
Chilcote
Clifton Campville
Appleby Magna
Swepstone
Heather
Ibstock
Ellistown
Stanton under Bardon
Markfield
Cropston
Whittington
Thorpe Constantine
No Man's Heath
Appleby Parva
Snarestone
Newton Burgoland
Battram
Bagworth
Field Head
Newtown Linford
Anstey
Hademore
Norton-Juxta-Twycross
Odstone
Nailstone
Thornton
Groby
Wigginton
Seckington
Newton Regis
Shackerstone
Ratby
Glenfield
Hopwas
Leyfields
Tamworth
Shuttington
Austrey
Twycross
Congerstone
Barton in the Beans
Barlestone
Botcheston
Alvecote
Bilstone
Carlton
Newtown Unthank
Kirby Muxloe
Amington
Warton
Orton-on-the-Hill
Market Bosworth
Newbold Verdon
Desford
Leicester Forest East
Braunstone Town
Hints
Glascote
Wellsborough
Bonehill
Fazeley
Polesworth
St Helena
Sheepy Magna
Sheepy Parva
Cadeby
Peckleton
Drayton Bassett
Wilnecote
Birchmoor
Grendon
Sibson
Kirkby Mallory
Dosthill
Dordon
Shenton
Sutton Cheney
Enderby
Middleton
Grendon Common
Ratcliffe Culey
Upton
Thurlaston
Narborough
Wood End
Baddesley Ensor
Atherstone
Witherley
Dadlington
Stapleton
Earl Shilton
Huncote
Bodymoor Heath
Kingsbury
Baxterley
Mancetter
Fenny Drayton
Higham on the Hill
Stoke Golding
Barwell
Elmesthorpe
Littlethorpe
Hurley
Bentley
Croft
Wishaw
Ridge Lane
Oldbury
Hinckley
Stoney Stanton
Cosby
Sutton in the Elms
Over Green
Lea Marston
Marston
Hartshill
Nether Whitacre
Camp Hill
Weddington
Sketchley
Sapcote
Curdworth
Whiteacre Heath
Church End
Galley Common
Chapel End
Burbage
Aston Flamville
Primethorpe
Broughton Astley
Minworth
Water Orton
Furnace End
Over Whitacre
Ansley
Stockingford
Nuneaton
Sharnford
Shustoke
Church End
Old Arley
Chilvers Coton
Attleborough
Burton Hastings
Frolesworth
Dunton Bassett
Coleshill
Astley
Whitestone
Smockington
Claybrooke Magna
Leire
New Arley
Griff
Collycroft
Bramcote
Claybrooke Parva
Ashby Parva
Kitt's Green
Maxstoke
Fillongley
Bedworth
Copston Magna
Wibtoft
Ullesthorpe
Tile Cross
Marston Green
Corley Ash
Bedworth Heath
Bulkington
Wolvey
Sheldon
Chapel Green
Corley
Corley Moor
Ash Green
Neal's Green
Hawkesbury
Barnacle
Withybrook
Bitteswell
Willey
Lutterworth
Butler's End
Keresley
Longford
Shilton
Cross in Hand
Elmdon
Bickenhill
Elmdon Heath
Meriden
Hawkes End
Little Heath
Foleshill
Ansty
Monks Kirby
Cotesbach
Coundon
Walsgrave on Sowe
Pailton
Churchover
Allesley
Spon End
Wyken
Stretton under Fosse
Gibbet Hill
Hampton in Arden
Eastern Green
Great Heath
Coventry
Brinklow
Harborough Magna
Four Oaks
Eastcote
Berkswell
Whoberley
Binley
Binley Woods
King's Newnham
Newbold on Avon
Newton
Catthorpe
Copt Heath
Barston
Tile Hill
Earlsdon
Pinley
Bretford
Church Lawford
Long Lawford
Knowle
Balsall Common
Stivichall
Willenhall
Brandon
Clifton upon Dunsmore
Bentley Heath
Temple Balsall
Catchems Corner
Tollbar End
Wolston
SK
SP
The National Forest
Tamworth Services
Corley Services
Leicester Forest East Services
Leicester Services
Donington Park Services
Shardlow Services
Birmingham International
NEC
National Memorial Arboretum
Drayton Manor
Twycross
Bosworth Battlefield Heritage Centre & Country Park
Mallory Park
Snibston Discovery Park
The Manor House
Heart of the National Forest
Ferrers Centre for Arts & Crafts
Bradgate Park & Swithland Wood
Charnwood Lodge
Beacon Hill
Broombriggs Farm
Tropical Bird Gardens
Burbage Common & Woods
Coombe Abbey
Arbury Hall
Hoar Park Craft Village
Kingsbury Water Park
Hartshill Hayes
Ash End House Children's Farm
Broomey Croft Children's Farm
Nat Motorcycle Mus
Transport Mus
Forest of Arden
Grand Prix Racing Cars
Donington Park
Melbourne Hall
Bass Mus
The Old Rectory Museum
Charnwood Museum
The Bell Foundry Museum
Great Central Rly (Nott'm)
Great Central Railway
Battlefield Line
Market Bosworth
Shackerstone
M1
M6
M6 Toll
M42
M69
A50
A38
A42
A444
A5
A47
A46
A45
A446
A452
A4600
A427
A428
A4303
A426
A6
A453
A511
A512
A516
A5111
A563
A51
A453
A447

Leicestershire

Towns and cities: Long Eaton, Clifton, Ruddington, Loughborough, Shepshed, Whitwick, Melton Mowbray, Waltham on the Wolds, Leicester, Leicester City, Oadby, Wigston, Birstall, Thurmaston, Earl Shilton, Lutterworth, Market Harborough, Desborough, Rothwell, Barrow upon Soar, Sileby, Mountsorrel, Anstey, Syston

Places: Sawley, Thrumpton, Ratcliffe on Soar, Castle Donington, Kegworth, Lockington, Kingston on Soar, West Leake, East Leake, Costock, New Kingston, Sutton Bonington, Normanton on Soar, Hathern, Stanford on Soar, Cotes, Burton on the Wolds, Walton on the Wolds, Wymeswold, Willoughby-on-the-Wolds, Rempstone, Bunny, Bradmore, Keyworth, Stanton-on-the-Wolds, Plumtree, Tollerton, Normanton-on-the-Wolds, Owthorpe, Colston Bassett, Kinoulton, Hickling, Upper Broughton, Nether Broughton, Long Clawson, Hose, Eastwell, Eaton, Branston, Croxton Kerrial, Knipton, Belvoir, Woolsthorpe by Belvoir, Harston, Stathern, Plungar, Barkestone-le-Vale, Langar

Whissendine, Langham, Barleythorpe, Oakham, Braunston-in-Rutland, Brooke, Ridlington, Belton in Rutland, Wardley, Allexton, Loddington, Skeffington, East Norton, Tugby, Billesdon, Halstead, Tilton on the Hill, Cold Newton, Lowesby, Owston, Knossington, Somerby, Burrough on the Hill, Pickwell, Cold Overton, Great Dalby, Little Dalby, Gaddesby, Ashby Folville, Thorpe Satchville, Barsby, Twyford, Marefield, Hungarton, Keyham, Scraptoft, Bushby, Houghton on the Hill, Thurnby, Evington, Stoughton, Gaulby, King's Norton, Rolleston, East Langton, West Langton, Thorpe Langton, Church Langton, Tur Langton, Kibworth Harcourt, Kibworth Beauchamp, Smeeton Westerby, Saddington, Mowsley, Gumley, Laughton, Foxton, Lubenham, Theddingworth, Marston Trussell, East Farndon, Great Oxendon, Braybrooke, Arthingworth, Harrington, Kelmarsh, Naseby

Shepshed, Charnwood Forest, Charnwood Lodge, Greenhill, Bardon, Copt Oak, Markfield, Newtown Linford, Bradgate Park & Swithland Wood, Groby, Ratby, Botcheston, Kirby Muxloe, Leicester Forest East, Braunstone Town, Glenfield, New Humberstone, Beeby, Barkby, Queniborough, East Goscote, Rearsby, Ratcliffe on the Wreake, Rotherby, Hoby, Thrussington, Seagrave, Ragdale, Shoby, Six Hills, Grimston, Saxelbye, Kirby Bellars, Frisby on the Wreake, Asfordby, Asfordby Hill, Holwell, Scalford, Chadwell, Wycomb, Goadby Marwood, Stonesby, Garthorpe, Freeby, Saxby, Wyfordby, Stapleford, Burton Lazars, Great Dalby

Thornton, Newtown Unthank, Desford, Peckleton, Kirkby Mallory, Stapleton, Barwell, Elmesthorpe, Huncote, Croft, Stoney Stanton, Sapcote, Sutton in the Elms, Cosby, Littlethorpe, Narborough, Enderby, Whetstone, Blaby, South Wigston, Newton Harcourt, Great Glen, Burton Overy, Carlton Curlieu, Illston on the Hill, Noseley, Goadby, Shangton, Glooston, Cranoe, Stonton Wyville, Welham, Slawston, Medbourne, Bringhurst, Drayton, Great Easton, Cottingham, Middleton, Ashley, Weston by Welland, Sutton Bassett, Great Bowden, Little Bowden, Dingley, Brampton Ash, Stoke Albany, Wilbarston, East Carlton, Pipewell, Rushton

Burbage, Aston Flamville, Sharnford, Frolesworth, Claybrooke Magna, Claybrooke Parva, Ullesthorpe, Bitteswell, Willey, Withybrook, Monks Kirby, Pailton, Copston Magna, Wibtoft, Ashby Parva, Leire, Dunton Bassett, Ashby Magna, Broughton Astley, Primethorpe, Peatling Magna, Peatling Parva, Arnesby, Willoughby Waterleys, Shearsby, Bruntingthorpe, Gilmorton, Kimcote, Walton, Swinford, Stanford on Avon, North Kilworth, South Kilworth, Husbands Bosworth, Sibbertoft, Welford, Sulby Reservoir, Naseby Field, Clipston, Haselbech, Maidwell, Cold Ashby, Coton, Thornby, Draughton, Rushton Triangular Lodge, Orton, Loddington, Thorpe Malsor, Great Cransley, Mawsley, Churchover, Gibbet Hill, Shawell, Cotesbach, Misterton, North Kilworth, Walcote

Roads: M1, M69, M6, A42, A453, A606, A607, A46, A6, A50, A47, A563, A426, A4303, A4304, A5199, A508, A14, A428, A427, A6, A512, A6006, B676, B591, B582, B581, B4114, B4669, B664, B6047, A5, A43

Leicester, National Space Science Centre, Leicester Forest East Services, Leicester Services, Donington Park Services, East Midlands (airport)

Scale: 0 1 2 3 4 5 6 miles / 0 1 2 3 4 5 6 7 8 9 10km

Denton, Harlaxton, Harlaxton Manor, Little Ponton, Old Somerby, Ropsley, Sapperton, Folkingham, Billingborough, South Ing, Quadring, Gosberton

Great Ponton, Hungerton, Wyville, Stroxton, Saltby, Skillington, Stoke Rochford, Easton, Woolsthorpe, Woolsthorpe Manor, Colsterworth, Twyford, Stainby, North Witham, Gunby, Burton-le-Coggles, Bassingthorpe, Bitchfield, Birkholme, Swayfield, Corby Glen, Hawthorpe, Irnham, Kirkby Underwood, Keisby, Bulby, Stainfield, Hanthorpe, Haconby, Morton, Humby, Hanby, Laughton, Aslackby, Dowsby, Pointon, Millthorpe, Dunsby, Birthorpe, Rippingale, Graby, Dyke, Gosberton Clough, Risegate, Surfleet, Northgate, Pinchbeck Bars, Pinchbeck, Pinchbeck West, Crossgate

Grantham South Services, Sproxton, Buckminster, Sewstern, Stainby, North Witham, South Witham, Wymondham, Edmondthorpe, Teigh, Market Overton, Barrow, Ashwell, Cottesmore, Greetham, Stretton, Clipsham, Pickworth, Careby, Castle Bytham, Little Bytham, Swinstead, Scottlethorpe, Creeton, Grimsthorpe, Grimsthorpe Castle, Edenham, Elsthorpe, Cawthorpe, Bourne, Twenty, Tongue End, Pode Hole, Spalding, Little London, Clay Lake

Rutland, Rutland Railway Mus, Oakham, Burley, Egleton, Whitwell, Upper Hambleton, Empingham, Rutland Water, Normanton, Edith Weston, North Luffenham, Ketton, Tinwell, Tickencote, Great Casterton, Little Casterton, Ryhall, Belmesthorpe, Barholm, Towngate, Market Deeping, Deeping St James, Deeping Gate, Frognall, Crowland, Northborough, Peakirk, Newborough, Bedford Level (North), Eye Green, Deeping Fen, Deeping St Nicholas

Barnsdale Gardens, Falconry Centre, Manton, Lyndon, Wing, Preston, Ayston, Brooke, Glaston, Bisbrooke, Uppingham, Morcott, Barrowden, Tixover, Duddington, Collyweston, Wittering, Thornhaugh, Wansford, Stibbington, Sutton, Ailsworth, Castor, Upton, Marholm, Walton, Dogsthorpe, Newark, Werrington, Gunthorpe, Glinton, Helpston, Etton, Maxey, Tallington, West Deeping, Uffington, Northfields, Stamford, Burghley, Pilsgate, Barnack, Ufford, Bainton, Southorpe, Barnack Hills and Holes

Stoke Dry, Lyddington, Seaton, Harringworth, Wakerley, King's Cliffe, Yarwell, Nassington, Apethorpe, Woodnewton, Fotheringhay, Elton, Elton Hall, Castle Site, Warmington, Tansor, Cotterstock, Glapthorn, Oundle, Ashton, Polebrook, Lutton, Haddon, Morborne, Caldecote, Stilton, Denton, Folksworth, Norman Cross, Yaxley, Farcet, Whittlesey, King's Delph, Farcet Fen, Whittlesey Mere, Holme Fen, Holme, Conington

Corby, Great Weldon, Little Weldon, Stanion, Brigstock, Sudborough, Geddington, Newton, Weekley, Warkton, Boughton House, Grafton Underwood, Lowick, Aldwincle, Achurch, Wadenhoe, Pilton, Stoke Doyle, Barnwell, Barnwell St Andrew, Barnwell All Saints, Thurning, Luddington in the Brook, Clopton, Winwick, Hemington, Great Gidding, Little Gidding, Steeple Gidding, Coppingford, Sawtry, Glatton, Upton, Alconbury Weston, Buckworth, Brington, Bythorn, Molesworth, Old Weston

Kettering, Barton Seagrave, Cranford St Andrew, Cranford St John, Twywell, Islip, Thrapston, Woodford, Denford, Titchmarsh, Thorpe Waterville, Wigsthorpe, Wickstead Park, Ramsey Heights, Church End, Wood Walton, Upwood Meadows, Woodwalton Fen, Monks Wood, Great Raveley, Little Raveley, Wennington, Abbots Ripton, Little Stukeley

Kirby Hall, Deene, Deene Park, Deenethorpe, Bulwick, Blatherwycke, Laxton, Southwick, Southwick Hall, Chesterton, Water Newton, Alwalton, Orton Waterville, Orton Longueville, Stanground, Peterborough, Fengate, Flag Fen Bronze Age Excavations, Old Fletton, Crown Lakes, Longthorpe, Longthorpe Tower, Ferry Meadows, Nene Valley Railway, Railworld, Sibson, Sacrewell Farm & Country Centre, Castor Hanglands, Bedford Purlieus

A1, A15, A16, A47, A43, A427, A605, A606, A607, A6003, A6121, A151, A1139, A1(M), A14

B1174, B1176, B1177, B1180, B1397, B1443, B660, B661, B662, B668, B670, B672, B676, B1090, B1091, B1040, B1043, B1166, B1180, B1356, B1397, B1525

A

B

C

D

E

F

1 2 3 4 5

Bicker Haven
Quadring
Westhorpe
Gosberton
79
Gosberton Clough
Risegate
Northgate
Pinchbeck Bars
Pinchbeck
Pinchbeck West
Crossgate
Spalding
Pode Hole
Little London
Twenty
Tongue End
Deeping Fen
65
Hop Pole
Market Deeping
Deeping St James
Deeping Gate
Northborough
Peakirk
Glinton
Newborough
Werrington
Gunthorpe
Walton
Dogsthorpe
Eye
Eye Green
Thorney
Newark
A47
Peterborough
Fengate
Old Fletton
Orton Longueville
Stanground
Whittlesey
Farcet
Longthorpe
Orton Waterville
A1139
65
Yaxley
Norman Cross
Stilton
Denton
Glatton
Sawtry
little Gidding
Coppingford
Upton
Alconbury

Surfleet Seas End
Surfleet
Moulton Seas End
Halesgate
Weston
Moulton
Whaplode
Low Fulney
Clay Lake
Weston Hills
Austendike
Cowbit
Moulton Chapel
Moulton Eaugate
Deeping St Nicholas
Brotherhouse Bar
Shepeau Stow
Whaplode Drove
Dowsdale
Crowland
North Fen
Nene Terrace
Morris Fen
Bedford Level (North)
Thorney Toll
Stone Bridge Corner
North Side
Coates
Eastrea
Inham's End
Turves
King's Delph
Farcet Fen
Whittlesey Mere
Pondersbridge
Middle Moor
Ramsey Mereside
Holme
Conington
Holme Fen
Ramsey Heights
Ramsey St Mary's
Ramsey Forty Foot
Ramsey Hollow
Ramsey
Bury
Upwood
Church End
Wood Walton
Wistow
Great Raveley
Little Raveley
Warboys
Fenton
Pidley
Somersham
Old Hurst
Woodhurst
Colne
Bluntisham

Fosdyke
A17
Holbeach St Marks
Saracen's Head
Holbeach Hurn
Holbeach Bank
Holbeach Clough
Holbeach
Fleet Hargate
Gedney Dyke
Gedney
Fleet
Gedney Broadgate
Sutton Crosses
Holbeach St Johns
Holbeach St Matthew
Gedney Marsh
HOLBEACH MARSH
Lutton
Long Sutton
Little London
Chapelgate
Sutton St James
Sutton St Edmund
Gorefield
Leverington
Tydd St Mary
Tydd Gote
Tydd St Giles
Newton
Fitton End
Tydd St Giles Fen
Church End
Throckenholt
Parson Drove
Rogue's Alley
Guyhirn Gull
Guyhirn
Ring's End
Murrow
Tholomas Drove
Wisbech St Mary
Walsoken
Wisbech
New Walsoken
Elm
A47
Waldersey
Coldham
Laddus Fens
Chainbridge
Eldernell
West Fen
Westry
Norwoodside
March
Town End
Binnimoor Fen
Euximoor Fen
Euximoor Drove
Ranson Moor
Wimblington
Flood's Ferry
Doddington
Benwick
White Fen
BEDFORD LEVEL (MIDDLE)
Chatteris
Wimblington Fen
Purls Fen
Horseway
Welches Dam
A141
Langwood Fen
Ferry Hill
Horseley Fen
Chapel Head
Pidley Fen
Chatteris Fen
Sutton
Wentworth
Hill Row
North Hill
Haddenham
Witchford

THE WASH
Daws
79
Gedney Drove End
Guy's Head
Sutton Bridge
A17
Walpole Cross Keys
Orange Row
Walpole St Andrew
Hay Green
Walpole St Peter
Walpole Marsh
A1101
Ingleborough
West Walton
West Walton Highway
St John's Highway
St John
Walpole Terrington
Highway
Marshland St John's Fen End
Marshland St James
Emneth Hungate
Holly End
Emneth
A1101
Friday Bridge
Outwell
Stow
A1122
Upwell
Three Holes
South District
Upwell
Upwell Fen
Christchurch
Lakesend
Tipsend
Welney
Gold Hill
Manea
Pymoor
Little Downham
Wardy Hill
Coveney
West Fen
Chettisham
Ely
A10
Little Thetford
Terrington
Lynn Channel

Cambridge

Scale:
0 1 2 3 4 5 6 miles
0 1 2 3 4 5 6 7 8 9 10 km

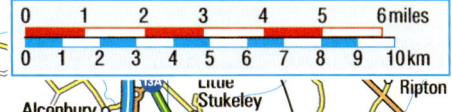

Norfolk

TF

TL

King's Lynn
Fakenham
Dersingham
Downham Market
Swaffham
Watton
Thetford
Brandon
Lakenheath
Littleport
Clenchwarton
Terrington St Clement

Snettisham Park
Snettisham Nature Reserve
Shepherd's Port
Ingoldisthorpe
Great Bircham
Newton
Barmer
Syderstone
Blenheim Park
Sculthorpe
Snoring
East Barsham
West Barsham
Bircham Mill
Bircham Tofts
Bagthorpe
Wicken Green Village
Shernborne
Anmer
Houghton Hall
West Rudham
Coxford
Tatterford
Shereford
Hempton
Dunton
Little Ryburgh
Fakenham
Penshurst Reserve

Wolferton
Sandringham
Sandringham
West Newton
Flitcham
New Houghton
Harpley
East Rudham
Helhoughton
West Raynham
East Raynham
Colkirk
Oxwick
Hamrow
Horningtoft

North Wootton
Castle Rising
Castle Rising
Roydon
Gongham
Congham Hall Herb Garden
Grimston
Little Massingham
Great Massingham
Weasenham St Peter
South Raynham
Whissonsett
Brisley
Tittleshall

South Wootton
Gaywood
Maritime Exhibition
Guildhall
Roydon Common
Pott Row
Massingham Heath
Weasenham All Saints
Extreeme Adventure
Wellingham
Rough
Stanfield
East Bilney

West Lynn
Hardwick
Fairstead
Leziate
Ashwicken
Gayton
Gayton Thorpe
West Lexham
East Lexham
Litcham
Mileham
Bittering
Norfolk Rural Life Museum
Gressenhall

Tilney High End
Tilney All Saints
Fair Green
Tower End
East Walton
West Acre
Castle Acre
Castle Acre Priory
Newton
Great Dunham
Drury Square
Crane's Corner
Beeston
Longham
Sparrow Green

Saddle Bow
West Winch
Middleton
North Runcton
East Winch
West Bilney
Pentney
South Acre
Little Dunham
Great Fransham
Great Dunham
Wendling

Tilney St Lawrence
Wiggenhall St Germans
Setchey
Blackborough End
Narborough
Great Palgrave
Sporle
A47
Little Fransham
Scarning

Wiggenhall St Mary the Virgin
Watlington
Tottenhill Row
Wormegay
Marham
Swaffham
Necton
West End
Bradenham
Daffy Green

Wiggenhall St Mary Magdalen
Runcton Holme
Shouldham
Beachamwell Warren
North Pickenham
Holme Hale
Crowshill
Ship Lane

Marshland Fen
South Runcton
Shouldham Thorpe
Fincham
Beachamwell
Shingham
A1065
South Pickenham
Ashill
Saham Hills
Ovington
Carbrooke

Stowbridge
Stow Bardolph
Barton Bendish
Cockley Cley
Iceni Village and Museums
Saham Toney
Caudlespring

West Head
Wimbotsham
Broomhill
Crimplesham
Stradsett
Eastmoor
Gooderstone Water Gardens
Gooderstone
Great Cressingham
Watton
Griston

Downham Market
Bexwell
Boughton
Oxborough
Hilborough
Little Cressingham
Merton
Northacre
Caston
Stow

Bardolph Fen
Barroway Drove
Denver
Wereham
Oxburgh Hall, Garden & Estate
Bodney
The Arms
Thompson

Nordelph
West Dereham
Whittington
Foulden
Little Cressingham

Fordham
Wretton
Stoke Ferry
Northwold
Ickburgh
Great Hockham

Hilgay
Brookville
Cranwich
Lynford Arboretum and Lakes
Wretham

Ten Mile Bank
Southery
Methwold Hythe
Methwold
Mundford
West Tofts
Peddars Way & Norfolk Coast Path

Hilgay Fen
Southery Fens
Methwold Fens
Queen's Ground
THETFORD
BRECKLAND

Apes Hall
Brandon Creek
Feltwell
Weeting Castle
Grimes Graves
Great Hockham

Mare Fen
Brandon Bank
Feltwell Fens
Hockwold cum Wilton
Weeting
Weeting Heath
FOREST
Croxton
A11

Burnt Fen
Hockwold Fens
Brandon
Santon Downham
Thetford Warren Lodge
Bridgham

Littleport
BEDFORD LEVEL (SOUTH)
Brandon Park
High Lodge Forest Centre
PARK
Thetford Warren
Thetford
Brettenham

Shippea Hill Sta.
Ancient House Mus.
A1066
Shadwell

Prickwillow
Wangford Warren
Thetford Warren
Rushford

Queen Adelaide
Kenny Hill
Lakenheath Warren
Elveden
Barnham
Euston
Knettishall

Middle Fen
Stuntney
Great Fen
Broad Hill
Mildenhall Fen
Eriswell
Holywell Row
East of England Tank Museum
Euston Hall
Barningham
Knettishall Heath
Coney Weston

Beck Row
West Row
Thistley Green
Isleham Fen
Windmill
Broad Hill

Fakenham
Briston
Aylsham
Reepham
Dereham
Drayton
Earlham
Cringleford
Lakenham
Wymondham
Watton
Attleborough
Thetford
Diss
Harleston

PENSTHORPE NATURE RESERVE & GARDENS
FAKENHAM
MANNINGTON GARDENS
WOLTERON PARK
BLICKLING HALL
FOXLEY WOOD
ANIMAL ARK
DINOSAUR ADVENTURE PARK
NORFOLK RURAL LIFE MUSEUM
MID-NORFOLK RAILWAY
BRADENHAM HALL GDNS & ARBORETUM
PEDDARS WAY & NORFOLK COAST PATH
SAINSBURY CENTRE FOR VISUAL ARTS
NORWICH INTERNATIONAL
TROPICAL BUTTERFLY WORLD
INDUSTRIAL STEAM MUSEUM
OLD BUCKENHAM MILL
SNETTERTON
BANHAM ZOO
BRESSINGHAM STEAM MUSEUM AND GARDENS
THELNETHAM WINDMILL
REDGRAVE & LOPHAM FEN
BILLINGFORD WINDMILL
100TH BOMB GROUP MEMORIAL MUS
WINGFIELD OLD COLLEGE
STRAW MUSEUM
ALBY CRAFTS
EXTREME ADVENTURE
THETFORD WARREN LODGE
ANCIENT HOUSE MUS
EAST OF ENGLAND TANK MUSE

Blenheim Park · Wicken Green Village · Sculthorpe · West Barsham · East Barsham · Great Snoring · Little Snoring · Thursford · Gunthorpe · Briningham · Plumstead · Matlaske · Aldborough · Alby Hill · Wickmere · Erpingham · Colby · Suffield

Dunton · Shereford · Hempton · Kettlestone · Fulmodestone · Barney · Swanton Novers · Melton Constable · Edgefield Street · Little Barningham · Calthorpe · Itteringham · Saxthorpe · Corpusty

Coxford · Tatterford · Toftrees · Little Ryburgh · Stibbard · Hindolveston · Wood Norton · Guestwick · Norton Corner · Thurning · Heydon · Oulton · Silvergate · Blickling · Ingworth · Banningham · Dunkirk · Marsham · Burgh next Aylsham · Tuttington

West Rayn Bam · East Raynham · South Raynham · Oxwick · Hamrow · Horningtoft · Gateley · Broom Green · Bintree · Twyford · Foulsham · Guestwick Green · Wood Dalling · Salle · Southgate · Cawston · Eastgate · The Heath · Buxton · Lamas

Whissonsett · Tittleshall · Stanfield · Brisley · North Elmham · Billingford · Bawdeswell · Sparham · Foxley · Whitwell Street · Brandiston · Booton · Hevingham · Stratton Strawless

West Lexham · East Lexham · Litcham · Mileham · Bittering · East Bilney · Worthing · Beetley · Swanton Morley · Hoe · Elsing · Lyng · Lenwade · Alderford · Upgate · Swannington · Felthorpe · Horsford · Waterloo · Hainford

Great Dunham · Little Dunham · Beeston · Longham · Gressenhall · Sparrow Green · Crane's Corner · Etling Green · North Tuddenham · Primrose Green · Weston Longville · Ringland · Attlebridge · Morton · Taverham · Thorpe Marriot · Hellesdon · New Hainford · Newton St Faith · Frettenham · Spixworth · Horsham St Faith

Necton · West End · Bradenham · Scarning · Toftwood · Daffy Green · Clint Green · Mattishall Burgh · Mattishall · East Tuddenham · Honingham · Hockering · Weston Green · Costessey · New Costessey · Upper Hellesdon · Old Catton · Catton

Sporle · Wendling · Little Fransham · Great Fransham · Shipdham · Westfield · Yaxham · Whinburgh · Welborne · Colton · Easton · Marlingford · Bowthorpe · Bawburgh · Keswick · Eaton

Holme Hale · Ashill · Saham Hills · Ovington · Carbrooke · Woodrising · Letton Green · Cranworth · Reymerston · Southburgh · Garveston · Thuxton · Runhall · Brandon Parva · Barford · Hethersett · Great Melton · Little Melton · High Green · Ketteringham

North Pickenham · South Pickenham · Saham Toney · Caudlesprings · Caston · Griston · Merton · Thompson · Stow Bedon · Rockland St Peter · Northacre · Shropham · Great Hockham · Wretham · Larling · Quidenham · Kenninghall

Little Cressingham · Great Cressingham · The Arms · Rockland All Saints · Little Ellingham · Great Ellingham · Besthorpe · Deopham · Deopham Green · Scoulton · Hingham · Hackford · Wicklewood · Hardingham · Danemoor Green · Kimberley · Crownthorpe · Morley St Botolph · Suton · Silfield · Wreningham · Ashwellthorpe · Spooner Row · Hapton · Fundenhall · Flordon · Swainsthorpe · Mulbarton · Swardeston · East Carleton · Dunston · Stoke Holy Cross · Caistor St Edmund · Bracon Ash · Newton Flotman · Saxlingham Thorpe · Saxlingham Nethergate · Saxlingham Green · Tasburgh · Hempnall

West Tofts · Lower Stow Bedon · Shropham · Puddledock · Wilby · Eccles Road · Old Buckenham · New Buckenham · Carleton Rode · Bunwell · Forncett End · Forncett St Mary · Forncett St Peter · Tacolneston · Fundenhall Street · Pristow Green · Sneath Common · Tibenham · Wacton · Aslacton · Great Moulton · Hargate · Tivetshall St Margaret · Tivetshall St Mary · Pulham Market · Pulham St Mary · Starston

Croxton · Bridgham · East Harling · Hunt's Corner · Banham · Kenninghall Heath · Dam Green · Winfarthing · Gissing · Burston · Shimpling · Dickleburgh · Rushall · Needham · Weybread · Brockdish

Brettenham · Shadwell · Rushford · Gasthorpe · Knettishall · Garboldisham · North Lopham · South Lopham · Fersfield · Shelfanger · Blo' Norton · Bressingham · Roydon · Walcot Green · Thelveton · Thorpe Abbotts · Syleham · Wingfield

Euston · Conery · Hopton · Market Weston · Thelnetham · Redgrave · Hinderclay · Wortham · Magpie Green · Palgrave · Stuston · Brome · Oakley · Hoxne · Cross Street

A148 · A1065 · A1067 · A47 · A1075 · A1066 · A1065 · A11 · A134 · A140 · A143 · A1074 · A11 · A140

MAP SCALE
0 ————— 6 miles
0 ————— 10km

BRECKLAND

NORFOLK

A B C D E F G

5 6 7 8 9

Bradfield Knapton Bacton
Antingham Broomholm Keswick Walcott
Swafield Edingthorpe
North Walsham Edingthorpe Green Witton Bridge Happisburgh
Felmingham Spa Ridlington Whimpwell Green
Common Crostwight Happisburgh Eccles on Sea
Common
81 Honing EAST RUSTON OLD VICARAGE GARDENS Lessingham Hempstead
Westwick Bengate Ingham Sea Palling
Worstead East Corner WAXHAM GREAT BARN Waxham
Skeyton Ruston Stalham Ingham
Swanton Sco B1159 Dilham Stalham Waxham
Abbott Ruston Smallburgh MUSEUM OF THE BROADS Green **NORFOLK**
Little Tunstead Barton Turf Sutton Hickling **COAST**
Hautbois Pennygate Wood Hickling
Coltishall ANT BROADS AND MARSHES Street Catfield Green Horsey
Horstead Neatishead Barton Hickling Heath HORSEY WINDMILL WINTERTON
Belaugh Ashmanhaugh RA BOAT TRIP Broad Irstead Sharp Hickling Broad Horsey DUNES
Hoveton Threehammer Street MARTHAM East Somerton
HILLSIDE ANIMAL SANCTUARY Common Potter BROAD West Somerton Winterton-on-Sea
Wroxham Upper Lower Street Heigham Somerton
Crostwick Street Ludham Thurne Martham
Horning LUDHAM MARSHES Bastwick **Hemsby** Newport
Rackheath Woodbastwick BURE MARSHES Repps Rollesby Ormesby Scratby
New Salhouse Ranworth FAIRHAVEN WOODLAND & WATER GARDEN Clippesby St Michael California
P&R Rackheath Panxworth Billockby Filby Ormesby Caister-on-Sea
Sprowston Little South Walsham Burgh St St Margaret CAISTER ROMAN TOWN
Thorpe End Plumstead Upton Margaret West YARMOUTH
NORWICH Hemblington THE CANDLEMAKER WORKSHOP Thrigby Caister
Thorpe St Andrew Great Blofield Acle Runham West Great Yarmouth
Plumstead Heath Stokesby End GREAT YARMOUTH GREAT DENES
Postwick Blofield **A47** Damgate Runham **Great Yarmouth**
Trowse Newton Brundall Lingwood Beighton THE Cobholm SEA LIFE
Kirby Surlingham Moulton Tunstall Halvergate Island GREAT YARMOUTH
Bedon Bramerton St Mary BROADS Burgh Southtown ELIZABETHAN HOUSE
Arminghall Rockland St Mary Strumpshaw South MARSHES Castle NELSON/TOLHOUSE MUSEUMS
Framingham Hassingham Burlingham Wickhampton BERNEY ARMS Bradwell Gorleston-
Pigot MID-YARE Southwood Freethorpe WINDMILL on-Sea
Framingham Earl Hellington Cantley Limpenhoe Belton
Poringland Yelverton Ashby St Mary PETTITTS ANIMAL Hopton on Sea
Howe Bergh Claxton ADVENTURE PARK REDWINGS
Apton Langley Reedham HORSE SANCTUARY
Shotesham Thurton Street Hardley ST OLAVES Fritton Somerleyton
Stubb's Green Chedgrave Street Ferry PRIORY Lound
Brooke Lower The Dell SOMERLEYTON Corton
Sisland Thurlton Dell HALL Blundeston PLEASUREWOOD HILLS
Seething Loddon Thurlton Thorpe Herringfleet LEISURE PARK
Road Green Mundham Hales Somerleyton LOWESTOFT AND EAST SUFFOLK
Woodton Stubbs HALES HALL BARN & GARDENS Haddiscoe Oulton MARITIME MUSEUM
Kirstead Green Green Raveningham Maypole Green Normanstone
Hedenham Thwaite RAVENINGHAM Toft Monks Oulton HERITAGE/VISITOR
St Mary GARDENS Wheatacre Broad CENTRE
Topcroft Cobbler's Kirby Stockton Burgh LOWESTOFT **Lowestoft**
Topcroft Green Cane Aldeby St Peter MUSEUM
Street Ellingham Kirby Row Kirkley
Ditchingham Broome Geldeston Gillingham CARLTON MARSHES Pakefield
Great Green Bungay Shipmeadow Waveney NATURE RESERVE Carlton
Denton Earsham Mettingham Worlingham North Colville
NORFOLK AND SUFFOLK AVIATION MUSEUM Barsham Cove Barnby Gisleham
Alburgh Flixton Ringsfield Mutford
Homersfield Ilketshall Ringsfield Hulver Rushmere Kessingland
St Cross St Margaret St Andrew Corner Street AFRICA Kessingland
Wortwell South Elmham Ilketshall Ellough ALIVE Beach
Redenhall St Michael St Lawrence Henstead Benacre
Mendham South Elmham Redisham Sotterley
St Margaret All Saints Shadingfield West End BENACRE
South Elmham South Elmham Stone Street Wrentham
Withersdale Street SOUTH ELMHAM HALL Cox Common
Metfield St James Mill Stoven Clay Covehithe
South Elmham Rumburgh Common Brampton Common Frostenden South Cove
57 Spexhall Westhall Wangford Cove Bottom
Linstead Broadway REYDON SMEAR
Fressingfield Parva Cheddiston Holton Blyford HEN REEDBED Reydon
Little Whittingham Halesworth Blyford NATURE RESERVE SOUTHWOLD MUSEUM
Green Wenhaston **Southwold**
Chippenhall Green Silverley's Green

A

B

C

D

E

F

1 1 2 2 3

Malltraeth Bay
Bae Malltraeth
Newborough
Forest
MODEL VILLAGE
4
Llanddwyn I.
Ynys Llanddwyn
5
SEIONT II MARITIME MUSEUM
CASTLE & REGIMENTAL MUS.
The Bar
Abermenai Pt.
Trwyn Abermenai

CAERNARFON
AIR MUSEUM
CAERNARFON
Morfa Dinlle
Dinas Dinlle
Llandwrog
GLYNLLIFON

C A E R N A R F O N
B A Y
B A E
C A E R N A R F O N

Pontllyfni

Aberdesach
WELSH LIFE
Clynnog-fawr
82
Tainlon
Capel Uchaf

Gyrn-goch
Bryn-yr-eryr
509 BWLCH MAWR
522 GYRN DDU
Trefor
564 YR EIFL
Llanaelhaearn
Pen-sarn
B4417
6
Llithfaen
B4417
Llwyndyrys
Pencaenewydd
Llangybi
Carreg Ddu
Porth Dinllaen
Pistyll
Fron
7
Llanarmon
Morfa Nefyn
Nefyn
Rhos-fawr
Y Ffôr
Chwilog
Porth Ysgadan
Edern
LLEYN HISTORICAL MARITIME MUSEUM
Tan-y-graig
Boduan
A497
Llannor
PENARTH FAWR MEDIEVAL HOUSE
Glanrhyd
B4417
CORS GEIRCH
BODVEL HALL ADVENTURE PARK
Efailnewydd
Abererch
HAVEN
Rhos-y-llan
Tudweiliog
Dinas
Rhyd-y-clafdy
Denio
Pwllheli
Porth Golmon
14
Garnfadryn
A4413
Penrhos
Carreg yr Imbill
Bryn-mawr
Llaniestyn
A4415
South Beach
Pen-y-graig
Sarn Meyllteyrn
Rhedyn
B4413
7
Llanbedrog
Penrhyn Mawr
Llangwnnadl
Botwnnog
Nanhoron
Trwyn Llanbedrog
Ty-hen
Pen-y-groeslon
Bryncroes
Mynytho
Methlem
Llandegwning
St Tudwal's Road
Angorfa St Tudwal
Rhydlios
304 MYNYDD RHIW
PLAS-YN-RHIW
Llawrdref
Bellaf
Llangian
A499
Abersoch
Capel Carmel
Rhoshirwaun
B4413
Rhiw
191
Llanengan
St Tudwal's Island East
Ynys St Tudual Dwyrain
Uwchmynydd
Aberdaron
Llanfaelrhys
Sarn Bach
Bwlchtocyn
Marchroes
St Tudwal's Island West
Ynys St Tudwal Gorllewin
Bodermid
Porth Neigwl or Hell's Mouth
Cilan Uchaf
Pen-y-cil
Bardsey Sound
Swnt Enlli
Trwyn Cilan
167
Bardsey Island
Ynys Enlli
YNYS ENLLI

P E N R H Y N L L Ŷ N
S H
L L Ŷ N
L L Ŷ N

0 1 2 3 4 5 6 miles
0 1 2 3 4 5 6 7 8 9 10 km

Map — Snowdonia / Gwynedd region

Grid references (top): 5, 6, 7, 8, 9 — **(sides):** A, B, C, D, E, F, G

Towns and places

Caernarfon, Waterloo Port, Llanrug, Pont-rug, Cwm-y-glo, Penisarwaun, Deiniolen, Dinorwic, Clwt-y-bont, Brynrefail, Llanberis, Llanberis Lake Railway, Nant Peris, Pen-y-Pass, Pass of Llanberis

Betws-Garmon, Waunfawr, Caeathro, Croesywaun, Bontnewydd, Saron, Llanfaglan, Glan-rhyd, Llanwnda, Efrwd, Groeslon, Rhostryfan, Rhosgadfan, Penyffridd, Fron, Carmel, Cilgwyn, Penygroes, Talysarn, Tan-yr-allt, Nebo, Llanllyfni, Nasareth, Pant-glas, Upper Clynnog, Cenin, Glan-Dwyfach, Llecheiddior, Bryncir, Garndolbenmaen, Dolbenmaen, Golan, Prenteg, Penmorfa, Tremadog, Pentrefelin, Criccieth, Llanystumdwy, Rhoslan

Snowdon Ranger, Rhyd-Ddu, Ffridd-Uchaf, Beddgelert, Nantmor, Croesor, Llanfihangel-y-pennant, Tyddyn-mawr, Moel-ddu, Garreg, Rhyd, Tan-lan, Llanfrothen, Penrhyndeudraeth, Minffordd, Portmeirion, Portmadog, Borth-y-Gest, Morfa Bychan

Pass of Aberglaslyn, Nantgwynant, Pen-y-Gwryd Hotel, Capel Curig, Pont Cyfyng, Betws-y-Coed, Swallow Falls, Capel Garmon, Nebo, Penmachno, Cwm Penmachno, Rhiwbryfdir, Blaenau Ffestiniog, Tanygrisiau, Bethania, Congl-y-wal, Llan Ffestiniog, Rhyd-y-sarn, Pont Newydd, Maentwrog, Gellilydan, Trawsfynydd, Bronaber

Dolwyddelan, Pentre-bont, Garnedd, Gwydir Forest, Padog, Ysbyty Ifan, Penmachno

Harlech, Llanfair, Llandanwg, Pen-sarn, Pentre-Gwynfryn, Llanbedr, Coed Ystumgwern, Llanddwywe, Dyffryn Ardudwy, Llanenddwyn, Cors-y-Gedol, Tal-y-bont, Plas-canol, Llanaber, Cutiau, Barmouth (Abermaw), Arthog, Ynysgyfflog, Fairbourne, Friog, Llangelynin, Llwyngwril, Rhoslefain, Llanegryn

Dolgellau, Penmaenpool, Bontddu, Penmaenpool Centre, Caerdeon, Rhydwen, Abergwynant, Bont Newydd, Brithdir, Pen-y-bryn, Llanelltyd, Cymer Abbey, Ganllwyd, Llanfachreth, Nannau, Blaen-y-cwm, Rhydymain, Llanfachreth

Coed y Brenin, Coed y Brenin Visitor Centre, Bed-y-coedwr, Capel Hermon, Rhobell Fawr, Cwm-hesgen, Pont Aber-Geirw, Pont-Rhyd-sarn, Buarthmeini, Dolhendre, Pont Fronwydd

Corris, Aberllefenni, Corris Uchaf, Tal-y-llyn, Minffordd, Cader Idris, Cadair Idris, Dinas-Mawddwy, Mallwyd, Cwm-Cewydd, Llanfihangel-y-pennant, Abergynolwyn

Mountains / heights (m)

Carnedd Llywelyn 1064, Carnedd Dafydd 1044, Glyder Fawr 999, Snowdon / Yr Wyddfa 1085, Moel Siabod 872, Carnedd Moel Siabod, Moel Penamnen 623, Moelwyn Mawr 770, Moel Hebog 782, 726, 734, 552, 747, Arenig Fach 689, Arenig Fawr 854, Moel Llyfrant 750, Moel Ysgyfarnogod 623, 556 Graig Wen, Rhinog Fawr 720, Rhinog, Y Llethr 754, Diffwys 750, 734, Aran Fawddwy 90?, Waun-oer 670, Cader Idris 893

Water features

Marchlyn Mawr Res., Llyn Padarn, Llyn Peris, Llyn Idwal, Llyn Llydaw, Llyn Gwynant, Llyn Dinas, Llyn Cwellyn, Llyn Ogwen, Llyn Cowlyd, Llyn Crafnant, Llyn Conwy, Llyn Arenig fawr, Llyn Trawsfynydd, Afon Dwyfor, Afon Glaslyn, Afon Eden, Afon Mawddach, Afon Dysynni, Afon Dyfi, Afon Cerist, Afon Wnion, Tremadog Bay / Bae Tremadog, Barmouth Bay / Bae Bermo, Traeth Bach, Morfa Harlech, Morfa Dyffryn

Parks / forests

SNOWDONIA NATIONAL PARK, Beddgelert Forest, Gwydyr Forest Park, Coed y Brenin Forest, Dyfi Forest, Migneint, Mynydd Dolgoed, Mynydd Ceiswyn, Mynydd Bryn-llech

Roads

A487, A4085, A4086, A5, A498, A4085, A496, A470, A494, A4212, A493, A4406, A4407, A4391, A497, B4418, B4411, B4573, B4405, B4113

Attractions / points of interest

Segontium Fort, Welsh Highland Railway, Inigo Jones Tudor Slateworks, Power of Wales, Bryn-Bras Castle, Dolbadarn, Padarn, Slate Museum, Snowdon Mountain Railway, Snowdon Summit Visitor Centre (Hafod Eryri), Idwal Cottage, Conwy Valley Railway Museum, Conwy Falls, Rhaeadr Conwy, Penmachno Woollen Mill, Ty Mawr Wybrnant, Llechwedd Slate Caverns, Ffestiniog Power Station, Ffestiniog Rly, Trawsfynydd Nuclear Power Station, Rhaeadr Mawddach, Sygun Copper Mine, Welsh Highland Rly, Brynkir Woollen Mill, Maritime Museum, Pottery, The Ropeworks, Lloyd George Memorial Museum, Llanfair Slate Caverns, Morfa Dyffryn, Rhaeadr Mawddach, Cymer Abbey, Kings, RNLI Lifeboat Museum, Fairbourne & Barmouth Steam Railway, King Arthur's Labyrinth & Craft Centre, Castell y Bere, Corris Railway and Museum, Meirion Mill

Woollen Mill, Fairy Glen, Burial Chamber, Cwm Idwal

Llandudno
Great Orme Copper Mines
Alice in Wonderland
Penrhynside
Penrhyn Bay
Craig-y-don
Rhos-on-Sea
Llandrillo-yn-Rhos
Conwy Sands
Traeth Conwy
Llanrhos
Deganwy
Butterfly Jungle
Llandudno Junction (Cyffordd Llandudno)
Colwyn Bay (Bae Colwyn)
Welsh Mountain Zoo
Mochdre
Old Colwyn
Abergele Roads
Angorfa Abergele
Llanddulas
Llysfaen
Abergele
Pensarn
Towyn
Kinmel Bay
Rhyl (Y Rhyl)
Seaquarium
Y-Ffrith
Gronant
Gwespyr
Prestatyn
Gwaenysgor
Ffynnongroyw
Picton
Meliden
Llanasa
Offa's Dyke Path
Llwybr Clawdd Offa
Axton
Trelawnyd
Dyserth
Rhuddlan
Cwm
Whitford
Pant-y-Wacco
Conwy
Gyffin
Dolwyd
Aberconwy House/Plas Mawr
Glan Conwy
Bryn-y-maen
Llanelian-yn-Rhos
Rhyd-y-foel
Dolwen
St George
Bodelwyddan
Rhuallt
Henryd
Felin Isaf Water Mill
Pentrefelin
Dawn
Betws-yn-Rhos
Glascoed
Groesffordd Marli
St Asaph (Llanelwy)
St Asaph Cathedral
Waen
Goleugoed
Tremeirchion
Pen-y-cefn
Caerwys
Afon-wen Craft and Antique Centre
Rowen
Tal-y-cafn
Bodnant
Graig
Ty'n-y-groes
Pontwgan
Hafod-lom
Moelfre Uchaf
Moelfre Isaf
Llanfair Talhaiarn
Llannefydd
Bont-newydd
Plas-yn-Cefn
Trefnant
Vale of Clwyd
Dyffryn Clwyd
Bodfari
Afon-wen
Eglwysbach
Tal-y-Bont
Pentre'r Felin
Gell
Cefn-coch
Pentre Isaf
Bryn-nantllech
Cefn Berain
Green
Castell
Dolgarrog
Coed Dolgarrog
Vale of Conwy
Dyffryn Conwy
Llangernyw
Bryn Rhyd-yr-Arian
Henllan
Denbigh (Dinbych)
Fron
Castle & Town Walls
Llangwyfan
Bryn-glas
Hendre-ddu
Llansannan
Waen
Llandyrnog
Woollen Mill
Trefriw
Tan-lan
Llanddoged
Pandy Tudur
Tŷ'n-felin-isaf
Tan-y-fron
Clwt-grugoer
Groes
Llanrhaeadr
Llangynhafal
Moel Famau
Tai
Pentre-tafarn-y-fedw
Llanrwst
Bylchau
Waen
Nantglyn
Peniel
Prion
Pentre Llanrhaeadr
Llanynys
Gellifor
Gwydyr Uchaf
Gwydyr Forest
Melin-y-coed
Gwytherin
Saron
Rhewl
Hirwaen
Cornel
Gwydyr Uchaf Chapel
Bryn Trillyn
Gorsedd Bran
Meifod
Llanbedr-Dyffryn-Clwyd
Craft Centre
Ruthin (Rhuthun)
Forest Park
Ty-draw
Cyffylliog
Llanfwrog
Bontuchel
Swallow Falls
Betws-y-Coed
Conwy Valley Railway Museum
Moel Seisiog
Llyn Aled
Llyn Alwen
Mynydd Hiraethog
Tai-Ucha
Conwy
Denbighshire (Sir Ddinbych)
Nebo
Capel Garmon
Burial Chamber
Brenig Res.
Nant Uchaf
Efenechtyd
Pwll-glas
Llanfair-Dyffryn-Clwyd
Mynydd Cribau
Fairy Glen
Alwen Reservoir
Hafod Elwy Moor
Llyn Brenig Visitor Centre
Nilig
Pennant
Clocaenog
Clawdd-newydd
Conwy Falls
Rhaeadr Conwy
Penmachno Woollen Mill
Ty Mawr Wybrnant
Glan-Conwy
Hafod-Dinbych
Mwdwl-eithin
Clocaenog Forest
Pentre-celyn
Gwydyr Forest
Penmachno
Pentrefoelas
Pentre-llyn-cymmer
Padog
Rhydlydan
Glasfryn
Cefn-brith
Derwen
Rhyd-y-meudwy
Llanfihangel Glyn Myfyr
Llanelidan
Snowdonia National Park
Ysbyty Ifan
Cerrigydrudion
Melin-y-Wig
Bryn Saith Marchog
Cwm Penmachno
Carrog
Garn Prys
Afon Ceirw
Ffynnon Wen
Betws Gwerfil Goch
Gwyddelwern
Bryneglwys
Llyn Conwy
Ty Mawr Cwm
Ty-nant
Pen-y-gop
Llangwm
Dinmael
Maerdy
Morfydd
Carnedd y Filiast
Tai-mawr
Glan-yr-afon
Druid
Corwen
Llangollen Steam Railway
Carrog
Llidiart-y-parc
Glyndyfrdwy
Pont yr Afon-Gam
Migneint
Foel Goch
Wenallt
Glassblobbery
Cynwyd Forest
Arenig Fach
Ciltalgarth
Glan-yr-afon
Cynwyd
Llyn Celyn
Sarnau
Bethel
Moel Fferna
Llyn Arenig fawr
Frongoch
Cefn-ddwysarn
Berwyn
Lldiardau
Rhyd-uchaf
Rhiwlas
Llandderfel
Llandrillo
Cwm Prysor
Parc Cenedlaethol Eryri
Arenig Fawr
Bala (Y Bala)
Llanfor
Pale
Cefn Coch
Pentre
Bryn Du
Moel Llyfnant
Llanycil
Rhos-y-gwaliau
Parc
Pennant
Llyn Tegid or Bala Lake
Aber-Hirnant
Buarthmeini
Mynydd Bryn-llech
Blaen-y-Cwm
Mynydd Bach
Dolhendre
Llangower
Bala Lake Rly
Pont Cwm Pydew
Aberhirnant Forest
Moel Sych
Tyn-y-fedwen
Tyn-y-ffridd
Gwynedd
Llanuwchllyn
Pistyll Rhaeadr
Tyn-y-pistyll
Cwm-hesgen
Pont-Rhyd-y-fen
Bed-y-coedwr
Rhaeadr Mawddach
Talardd
Ty-nant
Foel y Geifr
Cwm Cynllwyd
Pennant Melangell
Pencraig
Llangynog
Cefn Coch
Llanrhaeadr-ym-Mochnant
Capel Hermon
SH
0 1 2 3 4 5 6 miles
0 1 2 3 4 5 6 7 8 9 10 km

Halton
Cheshire
West and Chester
Flintshire (Sir Y Fflint)
Wrexham (Wrecsam)
Chester
Wrexham (Wrecsam)
Ellesmere Port
Queensferry
Mold
Llangollen
Oswestry
Whitchurch
Runcorn
Garston
Speke
Liverpool Airport
Holywell (Treffynnon)
Flint (Y Fflint)
Connah's Quay
Shotton
Hawarden (Penarlâg)
Buckley (Bwcle)
Hope (Yr Hôb)
Caergwrle
Gresford
Rhosllanerchrugog
Ruabon (Rhiwabon)
Chirk (Y Waun)
Ellesmere
Overton (Owrtyn)
Malpas
Farndon
Holt
Frodsham
Helsby
Neston
Heswall
Willaston
Tarvin
Kelsall
Wem
River Dee Afon Dyfrdwy
Mersey
Dee
DELAMERE FOREST PARK
Shropshire Union Canal
Llangollen Canal
M53
M56
A55
A483
A5
A41
A49
A534
A495
A51
A54
A5117
A550
A539
85
86
74
60
SJ

A Halton

1 · 2 · 3 · 4 · 5

Runcorn
A557
Weston
86
Sutton Weaver
Frodsham
Newtown
Overton · Fivecrosses
M56
Helsby
Ince Banks
Hapsford · Alvanley
Dunham-on-the-Hill
Manley · Birch Hill · Commonside
Mouldsworth · Norley
Kingsley · Crowton
Acton Bridge
Little Leigh
Daresbury · Hatton · Norton · Preston on the Hill · Dutton
Stretton · Lower Stretton
Lower Whitley · Higher Whitley
Comberbach · Great Budworth
Anderton · Barnton · Marston
Northwich · Wincham
Higher Wincham
Arley Hall · Arley · Mere · New Mills
Knutsford · Over Knutsford · Ollerton
M6 · A556 · Knutsford Services
Plumley · Smithy Green
WILMSLOW · Davenport Green
Alderley Edge · Nether Alderley
Marthall · Over Peover · Peover Heath
Chelford · Monks Heath
Jodrell Bank Visitor Centre

B Chester · Cheshire Forest

Weaverham · Hartford · Davenham
Cuddington · Sandiway
Delamere · Oakmere
Kelsall · Kelsall Hill · Oscroft · Willington Corner
Ashton · Mouldsworth
Duddon · Clotton · Tarvin
73
Tarporley · Rhuddall Heath
Utkinton · Eaton · Little Budworth
Oulton Park · Rushton
Winsford · Wharton · Over
Church Hill · School Green
Middlewich · Holmes Chapel
Sandbach · Elworth
Sandbach Services
Cranage · Twemlow Green
Brereton Green · Brereton Heath
West Heath · Astbury
A54 · A533 · A530 · A534

C West and Chester

Tattenhall · Beeston · Beeston Castle
Bunbury · Bunbury Heath
Spurstow · Haughton Moss
Bickerton · Cholmondeley Castle Gdns
Wardle · Barbridge
Aston juxta Mondrum · Worleston
Woolstanwood
Crewe · Haslington
Alsager · Kidsgrove
Talke · Radway Green
Church Lawton · Scholar Green
Mount Pleasant
A500 · A534 · A51

D Malpas · Broxton · Bickerton
Duckington · No Man's Heath
Bickley Moss · Wrenbury
Norbury · Marbury
Nantwich · Wistaston · Willaston
Shavington · Weston · Hough
Stapeley Water Gardens
Wybunbury · Hatherton · Hunsterson
Blakenhall · Wrinehill
Madeley Heath · Keele
Newcastle-under-Lyme
A41 · A49 · A529 · A51 · A531

E Whitchurch · Grindley Brook
Brooklands · Chemistry
Waymills · Redbrook
Ash Magna · Alkington
Bronington · Tilstock
Fenn's, Whixall and Bettisfield Mosses
Bettisfield · Wem Moss
Prees · Prees Heath
Audlem · Buerton · Coxbank
Adderley · Woore · Ireland's Cross
Knighton · Bearstone · Blackbrook
Mucklestone · Loggerheads
Market Drayton · Betton · Hales
Madeley · Keele Services
A525 · A53 · A5182 · A51

Wem · Loppington
Hawkstone Park
Hodnet · Marchamley
Wistanswick · Stoke on Tern
Eccleshall
A49 · A53 · A41

Scale:
0 1 2 3 4 5 6 miles
0 1 2 3 4 5 6 7 8 9 10 km

Kitt's Moss
Handforth
Poynton
Midway
Hope Green
Wood Lanes
Newtown
Mills
Furness Vale
Bridgemont
Buxworth
Chinley
Chinley Head
Chapel Milton
Malcoff
CHESTNUT CENTRE OTTER, OWL & WILDLIFE PARK
Whaley Bridge
Whitehough
Slackhall
Chapel-en-le-Frith
Sparrowpit
Perryfoot
Booth
BLUE JOHN CAVERN
PEAK CAVERN
SPEEDWELL CAVERN
MAM TOR
TREAK CLIFF CAVERN
Hope
Castleton
PEVERIL CASTLE
Aston
Thornhill
Bamford
Brough
Bradwell
HATHERSAGE
Hathersage
Upper Padley
Nether Padley
Grindleford
Froggatt
EYAM HALL
Eyam
Abney
Great Hucklow
Little Hucklow
BRETTON
Bretton
Grindlow
Foolow
Coplow Dale
Peak Forest
Dove Holes
Combs
Horwich End
Taxal
Fernilee
Fernilee Res.
Lower Crossings
Peak Dale
Upper End
Buxton
Fairfield
BUXTON MUS & ART GALLERY
Burbage
GRIN LOW
POOLE'S CAVERN
Cowdale
King Sterndale
Harpur Hill
Canholes
Tunstead
Wormhill
Wheston
Tideswell
Hargatewall
Miller's Dale
Litton
DERBYSHIRE DALES
Wardlow
Cressbrook
Little Longstone
Great Longstone
Hassop
Rowland
Stoney Middleton
Calver
Curbar
Baslow
Burnt Heath
RAVENSTOR
Blackwell
Taddington
Chelmorton
Ashford in the Water
Pilsley
Edensor
Bakewell
HADDON HALL
PEAK VILLAGE
Rowsley
CAUDWELL'S MILL
Sheldon
Flagg
Sterndale Moor
Earl Sterndale
Monyash
Over Haddon
Youlgrave
Alport
Stanton in Peak
Bradford
NINE LADIES STONE CIRCLE
Churchtown
Darley Bridge
Birchover
Elton
Winster
Middleton
ARBOR LOW HENGE
Parsley Hay
THE PENNINE BRIDLEWAY
Hurdlow
PEAK DISTRICT NATIONAL PARK
Dean Row
Hough
Mottram St Andrew
Prestbury
Whiteley Green
Pott Shrigley
Bollington
Bollington Cross
Kettleshume
Rainow
NETHER ALDERLEY MILL
Tytherington
Broken Cross
WEST PARK
Hurdsfield
Walker Barn
SHINING TOR
Henbury
SILK MUS & HERITAGE CENTRE
Macclesfield
PARADISE MILL
TEGG'S NOSE
Gurnett
Langley
Macclesfield Forest
Sutton Lane Ends
SHUTLINGSLOE
Lower Pexhill
Warren
Gawsworth
GAWSWORTH HALL
Oakgrove
Haddon
Wildboarclough
Highlane
Marton
Rodeheath
North Rode
Allgreave
Flash
Axe Edge
Brand Side
Hollinsclough
Glutton Bridge
Longnor
Crowdicote
Wincle
Danebridge
GRADBACH
Bosley
Eaton
Key Green
Buglawton
Congleton
Lower Heath
Timbersbrook
Rushton Spencer
Heaton
Hightown
Mossley
Whitemore
Ryecroft Gate
Newtown
Meerbrook
Upper Hulme
Fawfieldhead
Pilsbury
Brund
Sheen
SHEEN
Hartington
HARTINGTON HALL
Hulme End
Heathcote
Biggin
BIGGIN DALE
Newhaven
Pikehall
Poolfold
BIDDULPH GRANGE
Rudyard Res.
Tittesworth Res.
Marsh Green
Gillow Heath
MOW COP CASTLE
Mow Cop
Biddulph
Biddulph Moor
Rudyard
Poolend
Ball Haye Green
BRINDLEY MILL AND MUSEUM
Horton
Upper Elkstone
Lower Elkstone
Thorncliffe
Warslow
Knypersley
Blackwood Hill
Leek
Dunwood
LADDEREDGE
GREENWAY BANK
Newchapel
Brindley Ford
Brown Edge
Endon Bank
Endon
Horse Bridge
Longsdon
Lowe Hill
Bradnop
Butterton
Grindonmoor Gate
Onecote
Ford
Grindon
Wetton
Alstonefield
ALSTONEFIELD
Hope
Milldale
Alsop en le Dale
Parwich
Ballidon
Aldwark
Longcliffe
Brassington
Bradbourne
Carsington
Tissington
Dove Dale
Manifold
DOVEDALE
Ilam
ILAM HALL
Thorpe
Fenny Bentley
Kniveton
Hognaston
Carsington Res.
Goldenhill
Chell Heath
Sandyford
Norton-in-the-Moors
Tunstall
Bradeley
FORD GREEN HALL
Stanley
DEEP HAYES
FLINT MILL
Cheddleton
CHEDDLETON RAILWAY CENTRE
Leekbrook
Bottom House
Baddeley Green
Bagnall
Basford Green
CHURNET VALLEY RLY
Ipstones
BLACKBROOK
New Street
Winkhill
Waterfall
Waterhouses
Calton
Cauldon
Blore
Swinscoe
Mapleton
Ashbourne
Atlow
Hulland
Bradley
Burslem
Stoke-on-Trent
Milton
Wetley Rocks
CONSALL HALL GDNS
Consall
KINGSLEY BIRD & FALCONRY CENT
Foxt
Froghall
Whiston
Cotton
Weaver Hills
Stanton
Wootton
Mayfield
Church Mayfield
Clifton
Osmaston
Wolstanton
Abbey Hulton
Bucknall
Werrington
Cellarhead
Hanley
POTTERIES MUS. & ART GAL
Blakeley Lane
Kingsley
Kingsley Holt
Oakamoor
Ramshorn
Farley
Ellastone
ALTON TOWERS
Alton
Snelston
Wyaston
Shirley
Ednaston
Fenton
PARK HALL
Boothen
Trent Vale
Longton
GLADSTONE POTTERY
Weston Coyney
Dilhorne
Cheadle
Caverswall
DIMMINGSDALE
Threapwood
Dresden
Hanford
Trentham
Lightwood
Meir
Blythe Bridge
FOXFIELD STEAM RAILWAY
Forsbrook
Freehay
Mobberley
Gallows Green
Bradley in the Moors
Quixhill
Denstone
Norbury
Roston
Darley Moor
Yeaveley
Rodsley
Hollington
Rocester
Cubley Common
Great Cubley
BENTLEY FIELDS OPEN FARM
Alkmonton
Hollington Grove
TRENTHAM
Rough Close
WEDGWOOD VISITOR CENTRE & MUSEUM
Meir Heath
Draycott in the Moors
Greatgate
CROXDEN ABBEY
Croxden
Cresswell
Upper Tean
Lower Tean
Hollington
Checkley
Tittensor
Barlaston
Knenhall
Fulford
Fole
Combridge
Marston Montgomery
Waldley
Thurvaston
Longford
Longfordlane
Moddershall
Upper Leigh
Beamhurst
Crakemarsh
Somersal Herbert
Boylestone
Swynnerton
Oulton
Meaford
Cotwalton
Middleton Green
Lower Leigh
Church Leigh
Withington
Stramshall
HERITAGE CENTRE
Hilderstone
Stone
Walton
Dayhills
Garshall Green
Dods Leigh
Field
Bramshall
Uttoxeter
Doveridge
UTTOXETER
Oaks Green
Dalbury
Sutton on the Hill
Church Broughton
Trusley
Little Stoke
Yarnfield
STAFFORD SERVICES
Milwich
Coton
Coton Hill
Fradswell
Gratwich
Blount's Green
Sudbury
SUDBURY HALL
Foston
Scropton
Hatton
Hilton
Norton Bridge
Aston-By-Stone
Burston
Sandon
Marchington
Yarlet
Chebsey
IZAAK WALTON COTTAGE MUSEUM
Whitgreave
Great Bridgeford
Marston
Salt
Gayton
Grindley
CHARTLEY MOSS
Stowe-by-Chartley
Drointon
Weston
Kingstone
Gorsty Hill
Marchington Woodlands
Draycott in the Clay
TUTBURY
Tutbury
Hanbury
Hanbury Woodend
Anslow
Rolleston-on-Dove
Egginton
Stretton
Hopton
Newton
Newborough
Staffordshire
East Cheshire

Derby

Derby City

Chesterfield

ECKINGTON

Dronfield

Staveley

Bolsover

MANSFIELD WOODHOUSE

Mansfield

SUTTON IN ASHFIELD

KIRKBY IN ASHFIELD

Shirebrook

Matlock

Bakewell

Ashbourne

Ashford in the Water

ALFRETON

Pinxton

Somercotes

RIPLEY

HEANOR

Eastwood

Kimberley

ILKESTON

HUCKNALL

Annesley Woodhouse

LONG EATON

BEESTON

Stapleford

Sandiacre

Belper

Duffield

Mickleover

Willington

Repton

Castle Donington

Kegworth

Woodsetts, in Lindrick, Sutton, Hayton, Wheatley, le Steeple, Knaith, Norma'by Stow, by S, N

Wigthorpe, Gateford, West Retford, Babworth, Ranby, Scofton, Ordsall, RETFORD, BASSETLAW MUSEUM, Welham, North Leverton with Habblesthorpe, Littleborough, Marton, Gate Burton, Stow, Cammeringham, Thorpe in the Fallows, Brattle

Worksop, Manton, A57, A620, B6079, B6420, Grove, Eaton, Headon, Woodbeck, Treswell, South Leverton, Coates, Cottam, Sturton by Stow, Brampton, Torksey, Ingleby, North Carlton, South Carlton, Aisthorpe, Scampton

Shireoaks, Rhodesia, Kilton, Darfoulds, Clumber Park, Hardwick Village, A614, West Drayton, Elkesley, Bothamsall, Haughton, Gamston, Markham Moor, Markham Moor Services, Upton, Askham, East Drayton, Laneham, Church Laneham, Fenton, Saxilby, Kettlethorpe, Odder, Burton, MUSEUM OF LINCOLNSHIRE LIFE

Creswell Crags Museum, Great Lake, Norton, Carburton, Perlethorpe, Bevercotes, West Markham, Milton, East Markham, Tuxford, WALKS OF LIFE, Normanton on Trent, Weston, High Marnham, Low Marnham, Grassthorpe, North Clifton, South Clifton, Spalford, Wigsley, Harby, Doddington, DODDINGTON HALL, Thorney, Skellingthorpe, Broadholme, A156, A57, TOLL

Cuckney, A60, Meden Vale, Church Warsop, Budby, Sherwood Forest, Hamlyn Lodge Cottage Industry, Kirton, New Ollerton, Egmanton, Laxton, Moorhouse, Sutton on Trent, Girton, North Scarle, Eagle Moor, Eagle Barnsdale, Eagle, Swinderby, Whisby, Birchwood, Boultham, A46, New Boultham, Bracebridge, North Hykeham, LINCOLNSHIRE ROAD TRANSPORT MUSEUM

Market Warsop, Edwinstowe, SHERWOOD FOREST VISITORS CENTRE, Ollerton, Boughton, Wellow, BETH SHALOM HOLOCAUST CENTRE, Ompton, Kneesall, Ossington, Norwell Woodhouse, Carlton on Trent, Besthorpe, South Scarle, Morton, Thorpe on the Hill, South Hykeham, Haddington, Auborn, Harms

Lidgett, SHERWOOD FOREST FARM PARK, Old Clipstone, RUFFORD, Kersall, Eakring, Maplebeck, Norwell, THE VINA COOKE MUS OF DOLLS & BYGONE CHILDHOOD, Cromwell, Collingham, Thurlby, Bassingham, Norton Disney, Stapleford, Carlton le Moorland

Clipstone, SHERWOOD PINES FOREST PARK, Bilsthorpe, Bilsthorpe Moor, A614, Winkburn, Caunton, Knapthorpe, Bathley, North Muskham, Langford, Brough, Swinderby

Forest Town, Rainworth, A617, WONDERLAND PLEASURE PARK, White Post, WHITE POST FARM CENTRE, A617, Kirklington, Farnsfield, Hockerton, Little Carlton, South Muskham, Winthorpe, NEWARK AIR MUSEUM, Coddington, Brant Broughton, Welbourn

Blidworth, Ravenshead, Haywood Oaks, Edingley, Halam, Normanton, Southwell, SOUTHWELL MINSTER, THE WORKHOUSE, Upton, Averham, Kelham, Newark-on-Trent, Balderton, Beckingham, Barnby in the Willows, A17, Leadenham, MANOR STABLES CRAFT WORKSHOPS

Calverton, Oxton, Epperstone, Thurgarton, Bleasby, Morton, Rolleston, Easthorpe, Farndon, Fiskerton, Staythorpe, Hawton, Fenton, Claypole, Caythorpe, Frieston, Brandon, Hough-on-the-Hill, Carlton Scroop, West Willoughby

Bestwood, LONGDALE RURAL CRAFT CENTRE, PAPPLEWICK PUMPING STATION, BURNT STUMP, Woodborough, A6097, Gonalston, Hoveringham, East Stoke, Thorpe, Elston, Syerston, Cotham, Sibthorpe, Shelton, Long Bennington, Dry Doddington, Staunton in the Vale, Westborough, Houghton, Gelston, Honington

ARNOLD, Lambley, Lowdham, Caythorpe, Kneeton, Bulcote, Burton Joyce, Gedling, East Bridgford, Flintham, Hawksworth, Flawborough, Kilvington, Alverton, Normanton, Allington, Marston, Foston, MARSTON, Barkston, Belton, BELTON HOUSE

Mapperley Park, Carlton, Porchester, Colwick, Stoke Bardolph, Shelford, Newton, Car Colston, Scarrington, Screveton, Thoroton, Orston, Aslockton, GRANTHAM NORTH SERVICES, BOUNDARY MILLS, Syston, Barkston

Nottingham, P&R, THE TALES OF ROBIN HOOD, GREEN'S MILL & SCIENCE CEN, Radcliffe on Trent, Saxondale, Bingham, Whatton, Bottesford, Sedgebrook, A52, Great Gonerby, GRANTHAM MUS

WEST BRIDGFORD, Wilford, NOTTINGHAM, HOLME PIERREPONT, Upper Saxondale, A52, Harlequin, Elton, Easthorpe, Sutton, Granby, Muston, MUSTON MEADOWS, Redmile, Stenwith, Barrowby, Earlsfield, Grantham, Cold Harbour

Clifton, RUSHCLIFFE, Edwalton, A52, Cotgrave, Tollerton, Owthorpe, Cropwell Butler, Cropwell Bishop, Tithby, Colston Bassett, Langar, NATURESCAPE WILD FLOWER FARM, Barnstone, VALE OF BELVOIR, Barkestone-le-Vale, Plungar, Belvoir, BELVOIR CASTLE, Woolsthorpe by Belvoir, Denton, HARLAXTON MANOR, Harlaxton

Ruddington, FRAMEWORK KNITTERS MUS, Normanton-on-the-Wolds, Plumtree, Keyworth, Bradmore, GREAT CENTRAL RLY (NOTT'M), Stanton-on-the-Wolds, Kinoulton, Colston Bassett, Harby, Stathern, Harston, Knipton, Stroxton, Great Ponton, Little Ponton, Old Somerby

East Leake, Costock, Wysall, Widmerpool, Willoughby-on-the-Wolds, Hickling, Hose, Long Clawson, Goadby Marwood, Eaton, Croxton Kerrial, Eastwell, Wyville, Stoke Rochford, Skillington, Woolsthorpe, Bassing

Bunny, Upper Broughton, WALTHAM, Saltby

A1500
Normanby by Stow
Ingham
Hackthorn
Cold Hanworth
Friesthorpe
Lissington
East Orrington
West Willingham
South Willingham
Donington on Bain
Biscathorpe

A
Stow
Cammeringham
Thorpe in the Fallows
Prattleby
90
DAMBUSTERS INN & HERITAGE CENTRE
Welton
A46
Snarford
Welton Hill
Wickenby
Holton cum Beckering
91
East Barkwith
West Barkwith
Market Stainton
Benniworth

Sturton by Stow
Brampton
Aisthorpe
Scampton
Snelland
Fulnetby
Rand
Rand Farm Park
Panton
Sotby
Ranby

Torksey
Bransby
Broxholme
North Carlton
Scothern
Dunholme
Stainton by Langworth
Bullington
WOODSIDE FALCONRY AND CONSERVATION CENTRE
Langworth
Wragby
Langton by Wragby
Hatton
Great Sturton

B
Fenton
A156
Kettlethorpe
Saxilby
Odder
South Carlton
Riseholme
Nettleham
Reepham
A158
Low Barlings
Apley
Kingthorpe
Baumber
Hemingby
Minting

Newton on Trent
Broadholme
Skellingthorpe
Burton
MUSEUM OF LINCOLNSHIRE LIFE
ERMINE
ELLIS MILL
St Giles
Bunker's Hill
North Greetwell
Cherry Willingham
Stainfield
Young Wood
Gautby
Wispington
Edlington
A158

Thorney
Clifton
Harby
Wigsley
Spalford
DODDINGTON HALL
Doddington
Birchwood
A46
Boultham
New Boultham
Lincoln
CATH
Washingborough
Branston Booths
B1190
Bardney
BARDNEY LIMEWOODS
Bucknall
Horsington
Thornton
Old Woodhall
Thimbleby
Langton
B1190

77
LINCOLNSHIRE ROAD TRANSPORT MUSEUM
HARTSHOLME
Bracebridge
Canwick
Heighington
Branston
Potterhanworth Booths
Southrey
Stixwould
Reeds Beck
Woodhall Spa
COTTAGE MUSEUM
Roughton Moor
Roughton
Haltham

C
Eagle Moor
Eagle
WHISBY NATURAL WORLD
Whisby
North Hykeham
A15
Bracebridge Heath
Bracebridge Low Fields
Potterhanworth
Nocton
Dunston
Wasps Nest
Sots Hole
Kirkstead
Kirkby on Bain
Toft Hill

North Scarle
Eagle Barnsdale
Thorpe on the Hill
South Hykeham
Waddington
Coleby
Metheringham
Martin Dales
Dalderby

South Scarle
Swinderby
Morton
Haddington
Harmston
Boothby Graffoe
Blankney
METHERINGHAM AIRFIELD VISITOR CENTRE
Martin
TIMBERLAND ART & DESIGN
TATTERSHALL COLLEGE
Tattershall Thorpe
Coningsby
BATTLE OF BR MEMORIAL FL

Collingham
A46
Thurlby
Bassingham
Auborn
Navenby
B1202
Scopwick
Kirkby Green
Thorpe Tilney
Timberland
Walcott
Tattershall
Tattershall Bridge
COLLEGIATE CHURCH OF THE HOLY TRINITY
Hawthorn Hill

D
Brough
Stapleford
Carlton le Moorland
Wellingore
Welbourn
Ashby de la Launde
Bloxholm
Digby
Dorrington
North Kyme
BILLINGHAY COTTAGE
Billinghay
Dogdyke
Scrub Hill
New York

NEWARK AIR MUSEUM
Coddington
Beckingham
Brant Broughton
A17
Leadenham
Cranwell
A15
Ruskington
Anwick
A153
South Kyme
South Kyme Fen
Chapel Hill
Haven Bank
Wildn

Barnby in the Willows
Stragglethorpe
Fenton
Fulbeck
MANOR STABLES CRAFT WORKSHOPS
BUBBLE CAR MUSEUM
B1429
B1209
Leasingham
Evedon
Ewerby
Ewerby Thorpe
Amber Hill
HOLLAND FEN

E
Claypole
Stubton
Caythorpe
Brandon
Frieston
Normanton
North Rauceby
CRANWELL AVIATION HERITAGE CENTRE
South Rauceby
Holdingham
COGGLESFORD WATERMILL
Kirkby la Thorpe
Howell
Howto

Dry Doddington
Hough on the Hill
Gelston
Carlton Scroop
West Willoughby
Sudbrook
Ancaster
Quarrington
Silk Willoughby
Sleaford
A17
Asgarby
Burton Pedwardine
East Heckington
Swineshead Bridge

A1
Long Bennington
Hougham
Westborough
Marston
MARSTON HALL
77
Foston
Honington
Wilsford
Heckington
HECKINGTON WINDMILL
THE PEAROOM CENTRE
Great Hale
Little Hale
Swineshead

Allington
Sedgebrook
A52
Barrowby
BOUNDARY MILES
GRANTHAM NORTH SERVICES
Great Gonerby
BELTON HOUSE
Barkston
Belton
Syston
Kelby
Culverthorpe
Swarby
Scredington
Helpringham
Aswarby
Osbournby
Drayton
Bicker
A17
A52

F
Woolsthorpe by Belvoir
Denton
HARLAXTON MANOR
Harlaxton
Earlsfield
Grantham
GRANTHAM MUSEUM
Manthorpe
Welby
Londonthorpe
Cold Harbour
A52
Haceby
Braceby
Newton
Sapperton
Pickworth
Threekingham
Stow
Swaton
Spanby
Dembleby
Horbling
Billingborough
Bridge End
Donington
Church End
Quadring
Northorpe
A17
A52

Hungerton
Stroxton
Little Ponton
Great Ponton
65
Ropsley
Boothby Pagnell
Old Somerby
Humby
Hanby
Folkingham
Laughton
Birthorpe
Pointon
Dowsby
Gosberton Clough
Gosberton
Westhorpe

Croxton Kerrial
Saltby
Skillington
WOOLSTHORPE MANOR
Woolsthorpe
Bitchfield
Ingoldsby
Lenton
Aslackby
Millthorpe
Graby
65
Rippingale
Northgate
Pinchbeck

Kirkby Underwood
Hawthorpe
Irnham
Bulby
Keisby
Dunsby
B1397
Dowsby

0 1 2 3 4 5 6 miles
0 1 2 3 4 5 6 7 8 9 10km

5 6 7 8 9 5 6 9

Raithby
Vithcall
Little Ca 6 thorpe
North Reston 13
South Reston
Gayton le Marsh
Strubby
Trusthorpe
8

Tathwell
Haugham
151
Muckton
Withern
A157
Thorpe
Sutton on Sea
Sandilands

Cadwell Park
Maidenwell
Burwell
91
11
Tothill
Authorpe
Woodthorpe
Maltby le Marsh
Beesby
Hannah
Markby
Asserby
Huttoft

Stenigot
Cawkwell
Goulceby
13
Scamblesby
Farforth
Ruckland
White Pit
Swaby
Aby
Saleby
Claythorpe Water Mill and Wildfowl Gardens

Woody's Top
Belleau
Alford Windmill
Alford Manor House
Anderby
On Your Marques

Oxcombe
Ketsby
South Thoresby
Rigsby
Alford
Bilsby
Mumby
Authorpe Row

Belchford
Tetford
Brinkhill
Driby
Haugh
Well
Farlesthorpe
Chapel St Leonards

Fulletby
Salmonby
Somersby
Sutterby
Ulceby
Cumberworth
Helsey
Hogsthorpe

West Ashby
127
Bag Enderby
Harrington
Langton
Claxby
Bonthorpe
Willoughby
Sloothby

High Toynton
Greetham
10
Aswardby
Skendleby
Welton le Marsh
Hardy's Animal Farm
Addlethorpe
Ingoldmells

Horncastle
Hagworthingham
Sausthorpe
Partney
Scremby
Candlesby
Orby
Orby Marsh
Winthorpe
Seathorne
Fantasy Island Children's Playdrome & The Millennium Rollercoaster
Funcoast World

Scrafield
Snipe Dales
Lusby
Mavis Enderby
Raithby
Spilsby
Ashby by Partney
Gunby Hall
Bratoft
Burgh le Marsh
Natureland Seal Sanctuary

Mareham on the Hill
Scrivelsby
Hameringham
Asgarby
Old Bolingbroke
Hundleby
Northcote Heavy Horse Centre
Great Steeping
Irby in the Marsh
Burgh le Marsh Windmill
Church Farm Mus
Skegness
The Lifeboat Station

Wood Enderby
Oslinc Ostrich Farm
Moorby
Miningsby
Bolingbroke
West Keal
East Keal
Toynton All Saints
Halton Holegate
Firsby

Mareham le Fen
Revesby
Lincolnshire Aviation Heritage Centre
Keal Cotes
Toynton St Peter
Toynton Fen Side
Little Steeping
Thorpe Culvert
Thorpe St Peter
Croft
A52
Seacroft
Croft Marsh

East Kirkby
Revesby Bridge
Stickford
Thorpe Fendykes
Wainfleet All Saints
Magdalen Museum
Wainfleet St Mary
Gibraltar Point

New Bolingbroke
Fen Side
Wainfleet Bank
Wainfleet Tofts

Tumby Woodside
Stickney
Midville
New Leake
Friskney Eaudike

Medlam
East Fen
Eastville
Friskney
Wainfleet Sand

Sandy Bank
Carrington
Lade Bank
Wrangle Bank
Friskney Tofts

Bunker's Hill
Northlands
20

Hundle Houses
ore Fen
West Fen
Leake Commonside

Gipsey Bridge
Sibsey Trader Mill
Sibsey
Old Leake
Wrangle Lowgate
Friskney Flats

Langrick
Frithville
Wrangle
Hurn's End

Fishtoft Drove
Anton's Gowt
Hill Dyke
Boston Long Hedges
Leverton Outgate
Leverton Highgate
Boston Deeps

Brothertoft
Frith Bank
Cowbridge
Leverton
Benington
Leverton Lucasgate
Lynn Deeps

Boston West
Boston
Guildhall
Haltoft End
Butterwick
Freiston

Chain Bridge
A1121
Skirbeck
Skirbeck Quarter
Fishtoft
TF

Kirton Holme
Wyberton
Scrane End
The Wash
80
Hunstan
Sea Life Sanctuary

Fenhouses
Frampton West End
Kirton End
Frampton
Heach

Kirton
Sandholme
Skeldyke

Asperton
Wigtoft
Sutterton
Seadyke
Bucklegate

Algarkirk
Lynn Channel

Fosdyke
Holbeach St Matthew

Ricker Haven
Holbeach St Marks
Snettisham Nature Reserve
Sheph Por

Surfleet Seas End
Surfleet
A17
Holbeach St Marks
Dawsmere
Dersingham

A16
66
Holbeach Marsh
Gedney Marsh
Gedney Drove End
The Wash
66
Wolferton

Baytree Owl Centre
Moulton Seas End
Saracen's Head
Holbeach Bank
Holbeach Clough
Gedney Dyke
Lutton
Guy's

1
2
3
4
5
A
B
C
D
E
F
TF
NATURELAND SEAL SANCTUARY
THE LIFEBOAT STATION
Skegness
Seacroft
Croft Marsh
GIBRALTAR POINT
Wainfleet Sand
79
LYNN DEEPS
NORFOLK COAST
BRANCASTER ROADS
Brancaster Bay
SCOLT HEAD ISLAND
Holkham Bay
HOLME DUNES
HOLME BIRD OBSERVATORY
Holme next the Sea
Titchwell
Brancaster Staithe
Burnham Deepdale
Brancaster
Thornham
Burnham Norton
Burnham Overy Staithe
Burnham Overy Town
Burnham Market
Burnham Westgate
Burnham Thorpe
PEDDARS WAY & NORFOLK COAST PATH
HOLKHAM
WELLS-NEXT-THE-SEA
Wells-next-the-Sea
Holkham
HOLKHAM HALL
Warham
WELLS AND WALSINGHAM RAILWAY
Wighton
New Holkham
CREAKE ABBEY
North Creake
Copy's Green
Great Walsingham
Little Walsingham
SHIREHALL MUS
Old Hunstanton
Hunstanton
SEA LIFE SANCTUARY
Ringstead
HUNSTANTON
Heacham
NORFOLK LAVENDER
Summerfield
Docking
Sedgeford
Stanhoe
South Creake
SOUTH CREAKE MAIZE MAZE
Waterden
North Barsham
Houghton St Giles
West Barsham
Great Snoring
East Barsham
Snettisham
SNETTISHAM PARK
Fring
Bircham Newton
Great Bircham
Barmer
Syderstone
Ingoldisthorpe
SNETTISHAM NATURE RESERVE
Shepherd's Port
Shernborne
BIRCHAM MILL
Bircham Tofts
Bagthorpe
Blenheim Park
Wicken Green Village
Sculthorpe
Dersingham
Anmer
PEDDARS WAY
Tattersett
Dunton
Shereford
Fakenham
FAKENHAM
67
DERSINGHAM BOG
Wolferton
SANDRINGHAM
Sandringham
HOUGHTON HALL
West Rudham
Coxford
Tatterford
Hempton
East Rudham
West Newton
New Houghton
Toftrees
Flitcham
Harpley
Helhoughton
Colkirk
Castle Rising
Hillington
Little Massingham
West Raynham
East Raynham
Oxwick
Terrington Marsh
Ongar Hill
North Wootton
CASTLE RISING
Congham
CONGHAM HALL HERB GARDEN
Great Massingham
South Raynham
Hamrow
South Wootton
Roydon
ROYDON COMMON
Weasenham St Peter
Whissonsett
Horningtoft
King's Lynn
MARITIME EXHIBITION
Grimston
Pott Row
Massingham Heath
Weasenham All Saints
Wellingham
EXTREEME ADVENTURE
Tittleshall
Clenchwarton
GUILDHALL
Gaywood
Stanfield
Terrington St Clement
West Lynn
Fairstead
Gayton
Rougham
Hardwick
Leziate
Ashwicken
Mileham
Tilney All Saints
Tilney High End
Fair Green
Tower End
Gayton Thorpe
West Lexham
Litcham
Bittering
Middleton
East Walton
East Lexham
Terrington St John
Saddle Bow
West Winch
North Runcton
East Winch
West Bilney
Pentney
Castle Acre
CASTLE ACRE PRIORY
West Acre
Newton
Beeston
Longham
Tilney St Lawrence
Wiggenhall St Germans
Wiggenhall St Mary the Virgin
Setchey
Blackborough End
South Acre
Great Dunham
Drury Square
Sparrow Green
Crane's Corner
Tottenhill Row
Narborough
Little Dunham
Great Fransham
Wendling
Wiggenhall St Mary Magdalen
Watlington
Tottenhill
Wormegay
Great Palgrave
Sporle
Little Fransham
BRADENHAM HALL GDNS & ARBORETUM
Runcton Holme
Shouldham
Marham
Swaffham
Necton
West End
Bradenham
Beachamwell Warren
PEDDARS WAY & NORFOLK COAST PATH
North Pickenham
Holme Hale
Fincham
Barton Bendish
Crowshill
West Head
Bardolph
Marsh
A149
A148
A1065
A47
A10
A134
A1122
A1078
B1153
B1155
B1454
B1355
B1105
B1440
B1439
B1145
B1146
0 1 2 3 4 5 6 miles
0 1 2 3 4 5 6 7 8 9 10 km

5   6   7   8   9

A

B

C

TG

Blakeney Point

BLAKENEY
GUILDHALL
CLEY MILL
Cley next the Sea
PEDDARS WAY AND NORFOLK COAST PATH
MUCKLEBURGH COLLECTION
NORTH NORFOLK RAILWAY
PRIORY MAZE & GARDENS
Sheringham
NORFOLK SHIRE HORSE CENTRE
CROMER MUSEUM
Morston
Salthouse
Weybourne
West Runton
Cromer
Stiffkey
Blakeney
Wiveton
Newgate
Kelling
16
SHERINGHAM PARK
SHERINGHAM
Beeston Regis
East Runton
Cockthorpe
Langham
A149
Upper Sheringham
A1082
Overstrand
Westgate
Glandford
High Kelling
Bodham
A148
East Beckham
Aylmerton
Felbrigg
Northrepps
Sidestrand
Binham
B1156
Saxlingham
Letheringsett
Holt
PICTURECRAFT GALLERY
West Beckham
Gresham
FELBRIGG HALL
Crossdale Street
Frogshail
Trimingham
WAYSIDE CROSS
THE TEXTILE CENTRE
Field Dalling
LETHERINGSETT WATERMILL
HOLT
BACONSTHORPE CASTLE
89
Sustead
Roughton
Lower Street
Thorpe Market
Trunch
Paston
Mundesley
STOW WINDMILL
Lower Green
Bale
Sharrington
Hempstead
Baconsthorpe
Bessingham
Hanworth
Thurgarton
Alby Hill
B1436
B1145
B1159
Knapton
Bacton
Keswick
Broomholm
Hindringham
60
Thornage
Hunworth
Edgefield
Plumstead
Matlaske
Aldborough
Wickmere
ALBY CRAFTS
Erpingham
A140
ALBY GARDENS
Suffield
Bradfield
Swafield
Edingthorpe
THURSFORD COLLECTION
Gunthorpe
Stody
Briningham
13
B1354
Edgefield Street
Little Barningham
Calthorpe
Colby
STRAW MUSEUM
Antingham
North Walsham
Edingthorpe Green
Witton Bridge
Ridlington
Crostwight
Happis
Thursford
Little Snoring
A148
Barney
Swanton Novers
Melton Constable
Briston
101
Corpusty
Saxthorpe
MANNINGTON GARDENS
WOLTERTON PARK
Itteringham
Ingworth
Banningham
Felmingham
Spa Common
EAST RUSTON OLD VICARAGE GARDEN
Honing
East Ruston
Kettlestone
Fulmodestone
60
B1354
B1149
PENSTHORPE NATURE RESERVE & GARDENS
Little Ryburgh
Stibbard
B1110
Hindolveston
Thurning
Oulton
Silvergate
BLICKLING HALL
Blickling
Dunkirk
Tuttington
Westwick
Bengate
Worstead
A149
Dilham
Wallburgh
MUSE THE B
Great Ryburgh
A1067
Wood Norton
Guestwick
Norton Corner
Wood Dalling
Heydon
Oulton Street
Aylsham
Burgh next Aylsham
Skeyton
Swanton Abbott
Sloley
B1150
Pennygate
Guist
Gateley
Twyford
Guestwick Green
Salle
Southgate
Fengate
Marsham
Brampton
BURE VALLEY RAILWAY
Scottow
Lamas
Buxton
Little Hautbois
Sco Ruston
69
Tunstead
WROXHAM BARNS
RA BOAT TRIP
ANT BROADS AND MARSHES
Neatishead
Barto
Broom Green
Bintree
FOXLEY WOOD
Reepham
Booton
Cawston
Little London
Eastgate
Brandiston
The Heath
12
Hevingham
Stratton Strawless
B1354
Coltishall
Threehamm
Common
Brisley
North Elmham
Foxley
B1145
Whitwell Street
Haveringland
Buxton
Waterloo
stead
68
Belaugh
Hoveton
Horning
Lower S
East Bilney
Worthing
Sparham
68
Bawdeswell
ANIMAL ARK
Alderford
Swannington
Upgate
New Hainford
Hainford
HILLSIDE ANIMAL SANCTUARY
Wroxham
Upper Street
MUSE THE B
Beetley
B1147
26
Mill Street
A1067
Lenwade
DINOSAUR ADVENTURE PARK
Morton
Felthorpe
Newton St Faith
Frettenham
Crostwick
8
Wroxham Broad
BURE MARSHES
Woodbastwick
Rar
NORFOLK RURAL LIFE MUSEUM
Gressenhall
Swanton Morley
Hoe
Lyng
Elsing
Primrose Green
Weston Longville
Attlebridge
Horsford
Thorpe Marriot
Horsham St Faith
Spixworth
Rackheath
A140
Salhouse
B1140
Panxworth
Dereham
A47
Hockering
Weston Green
Ringland
Taverham
Drayton
Hellesdon
NORWICH INTERNATIONAL
P&R
Old Catton
New Rackheath
Little Plumstead
Hembling
Scarning
Toftwood
MID-NORFOLK RAILWAY
North Tuddenham
Honingham
New Costessey
Costessey
Mile Cross
Upper Hellesdon
P&R
Sprowston
Thorpe End
Thorpe St Andrew
Great Plumstead
Blofield Heath
Burl
Daffy Green
Westfield
Mattishall Burgh
Clint Green
Mattishall
East Tuddenham
Easton
A1074
Bowthorpe
P&R
Earlham
THE FORUM
30
40
NEW Catton
CATHEDRAL
NORWICH
WHITLINGHAM
Thorpe St Andrew
Brundall
Blofield
Yaxham
Welborne
Colton
Marlingford
Bawburgh
SAINSBURY CENTRE FOR VISUAL ARTS
Colney
Cringleford
Eaton
Lakenham
A47
Postwick
Surlingl
Shipdham
5
Letton Green
Whinburgh
63
Runhall
Brandon Parva
Barford
B1108
Great Melton
Little Melton
Bowse Newton
Kirby Bedon
Great
9
A1075
Reymerston
Thuxton
Barnham Broom
Wramplingham
High Green
B1135
Danemoor
f

O

E

F

K

G

COAST

NORFOLK

1   2   2   2   3   4   5

A

40

B

The Skerries
Ynysoedd y
Moelrhoniaid

Wilfa
Head
Pen Wilfa   Cemaes
Bay
Bae Cemaes
Cemlyn Bay
Bae Cemlyn   Porthllechog
Bull Bay
Porth
Llechog   Amlwch
Port
WYLFA POWER STATION
AND OBSERVATION TOWER   Burwen   Point Lynas
Trwyn
Eilian

Carmel Head
Pen Carmel   Tregele   Llanbadrig   Cemaes   Amlwch   Llaneilian
Rhosbeirio   Bodewryd   Pengorffwysfa
Llanfairynghornwy   17   Llanfechell   Rhosgoch   Penysarn
Bodewryd   Nebo   Dulas
Llanfflewyn   Llanbabo   Llanddeusant   Rhosybol   City
Dulas   Brynrefail
Rhydwyn   Llanrhyddlad   Carreglefn   Rhosybol
Tyn-y-pwll   Ty-mawr   Moelfre
Church Bay
Porth Swtan   I s l e   o f   Gwredog   Dulas Bay
Bae Dulas
Llanfaethlu   LLYNON
WINDMILL   8   Llandyfrydog   Llanallgo
HOLYHEAD BAY
BAE CAERGYBI   Llanfwrog   A n g l e s e y   Elim   Llanerchymedd   Bachau   Mynydd
Bodafon   Maenaddwyn   Tynygongl   Marianglas
DUBLIN 1:49
DUN LAOGHAIRE 1:59   Llantrisant   Carmel   Capel Coch   Hebron   Benllech
DUBLIN 3:15   Llanfachraeth   (S i r   Y n y s   M ô n)   Pen-llyn   B5112   CORS
ERDDREINIOG   Brynteg   Red Wr
Traeth
North Stack   BREAKWATER   Llanynghenedl   Llechcynfarwy   Glan
Gors   Llanbedrgoch   Cors Goch   Red
Wharf Bay
HOLYHEAD MOUNTAIN   220   Llaingoch   Holyhead
(Caergybi)   Bodedern   Trefor   Tregaian   Rhosmeirch   Llanddyfnan   Tan-y-graig
South Stack   Goferydd   Kingsland   Valley   Bryngwran   Llangwyllog   Llynfaes   B5110   Pentraeth
ELLINS TOWER RSPB RESERVE
PENRHOS FEILW
STANDING STONES   ANGLESEY   A55   Gwalchmai   Bodffordd   Heneglwys   ORIEL
YNYS MÔN   Llangefni   THE STONE
SCIENCE   Peny-garnedd
Penrhosfeilw   Newlands
Park   6   Llanfihangel
yn Nhowyn   A5   Rhosmeirch   A5114   CORS
BODEILIO   PILI PALAS
Trearddur
Glan-traeth   Caergeiliog   Llanfaelog   Llanfairyneubwll   Llandddaniel
Fab   Talwrn   Rhoscefnhir
Penrhyn Mawr   Four Mile
Bridge   B4545   Capel-gwyn   Ddrydwy   Pencarnisiog   Cerrigceinwen   A55   Penmynydd
Holy Island
Ynys Gybi   Cymyran
Bay
Bae Cymyran   Bryn Du   Soar   Llangristiolus   JAMES
PRINGLE
WEAVERS
SH   Rhoscolyn   Rhosneigr   HENBLAS COUNTRY
PARK   Pentre
Berw   Gaerwen   Llanfairpwll-
gwyngyll   (Porthaeth
Capel Mawr   Bethel   Trefdraeth   B4419   PLAS
NEWYDD   9
Llangwyfan-isaf   Llangadwaladr   B4421   Llangaffo   PLAS COCH
GARDEN ZOO   Capel-y-
graig   GREENV
CENTRE
Aberffraw   Hermon   Malltraeth   20   Brynsiencyn   SEA ZOO   Y Felinheli   Seion
Bodorgan   NEWBOROUGH WARREN
AND YNYS LLANDDWYN   Newborough   Dwyran   FOEL
FARM PARK   Llanddeiniolen   BRYN/BRA
CASTI
Malltraeth Bay
Bae Malltraeth   Pen-lon   MODEL
VILLAGE
BIRD
WORLD   A487   Waterloo
Port   Llanrug
Newborough
Forest   SEIONT II MARITIME MUSEUM
CASTLE &
REGIMENTAL MUS   Pont-rug   Segontium Fort
Llanddwyn I.
Ynys Llanddwyn   The Bar   Caernarfon   Caeathro   Cwm-y-glo
Abermenai
Pt.
Trwyn
Abermenai   WELSH
HIGHLAND
RAILWAY   2   Ceunant
C A E R N A R F O N   Llanfaglan   INIGO JONES TUDOR
SLATEWORKS   Groeslon
CAERNARFON
AIR MUSEUM   Saron   Bontnewydd   Croesywaun   Waunfaw
Morfa Dinlle   Glan-rhyd   Rhostryfan
Dinas Dinlle   Llanwnda   Penyffridd   Rhosgadfan   A4085   Betws-Garmon
B A Y   Ffrwd   Groeslon
Llandwrog   Fron   Llyn
Cw
B A E   GLYNLLIFON   A487   Carmel
14   A499   Penygroes   Cilgwyn   Nantlle   B4418
C A E R N A R F O N   Pontllyfni   WELSH LIFE   Talysarn   Tan-yr-allt
Aberdesach   Tainlon   Llanllyfni
35   Clynnog-fawr   Nebo   734
70   Gyrn-goch   Capel U   71   19   Nasareth
Bryn-yr-eryr   509
BWLCH
MAWR   4

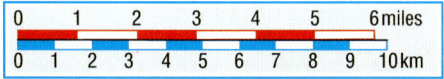
3   23   522
GYRN DDU   3   Trefor   Dafarn Faig   5
Pant-glas   Afon Dwyfor

A

B

C

5 6 7 8 9

Great Ormes Head
Pen-y-Gogarth
TRAMWAY
GREAT ORME
TOLL
GREAT ORME
COPPER MINES
Llandudno
ALICE IN WONDERLAND
207
Penrhynside
ORIEL MOSTYN
Penrhyn Bay
Craig-y-don
Puffin Island
Ynys Seiriol
Mariandyrys
Caim
CONWY BAY
BAE CONWY
Conwy
Sands
Traeth Conwy
Llanrhos
Rhos-on-Sea
Glan-yr-afon
Penmon
BUTTERFLY
JUNGLE
Deganwy
Llandrillo
yn-Rhos
COLWYN BAY
(BAE COLWYN)
Abergele Roads
Angorfa
Abergele
Llanddona
Llangoed
A470
Tywyn
Llandudno
Junction
(Cyffordd
Llandudno)
20
Bryn-y-
maen
23
A55
Penmaenmawr
Dwygyfylchi
18A
17
WELSH MOUNTAIN
ZOO
Mochdre
22
Old
Colwyn
Pensa
Llanfaes
Llansadwrn
B5109
7
Conwy
18
19
Llanddulas
24
Llysfaen
Abergele
Beaumaris
16
CONWY
Gyffin
ABERCONWY
HOUSE/PLAS
MAWR
Dolwyd
B5383
Llanelian-yn-
Rhos
Dolwen
Rhyd-y-foel
St Ge
A545
15A
Capelulo
Penmaenan
Glan Conwy
Lavan Sands
Traeth Lafan
14
FELIN ISAF
WATER MILL
Pentrefelin
MOELFRE
ISAF
Llandegfan
Garth
Llanfairfechan
Henryd
396
Llanfair
Talhaiarn
MOELFRE
UCHAF
TEGFRYN
Hirael
13
Nant-y-pandy
610
TAL-Y-
FAN
Dawn
Betws-yn-
Rhos
PENRHYN
BANGOR
Bangor
Abergwyngregyn
A55
Hafod-lom
Bryn-
nantllech
Crymlyn
ROWEN
Rowen
Graig
A5
Llandegai
Talsy-bont
SH
Ty'n-y-groes
Pontwgan
Eglwysbach
Pentre'r
Felin
Coed
Mawr
Glan
Adda
10
Minffordd
COEDYDD
ABER
Aber Falls
Rhaeadr Aber
Tal-y-caf
Bodnant
Gell
Cefn-coch
Pentre Isaf
A5442
11
12
Llanllechid
COED
GORSWEN
Llanbedr-y-cennin
389
Glasinfryn
BANGOR
SERVICES
COCHWILLAN OLD HALL
Rachub
Tal-y-Bont
Langernyw
Bryn-
yr-A
Pentir
A4244
Bethesda
S N O W D O N I A
Bryn-glas
A548
B5382
Llansannan
B4409
Tregarth
Gerlan
N A T I O N A L
942
FOEL FRAS
16
Hendre-ddu
8
Sling
Braichmelyn
P A R K
Dolgarrog
Bryn-glas
Rhiwlas
Aber Dulyn
COED
DOLGARROG
Llanddoged
Pandy
Tudur
Tŷ'r-felin-isaf
Penisarwaun
Ty'n-y-maes
1064
CARNEDD
LLYWELYN
Llyn
Eigiau
Tan-
lan
A470
Llanfair
Deiniolen
Marchlyn
Mawr Res.
WOOLLEN MILL
Trefriw
Pentre-tafarn-
y-fedw
B5113
Clwt-y-bont
16
1044
CARNEDD
DAFYDD
Tai
Gwydyr
Uchaf
Gwythyrin
Brynrefail
Llyn
Cowlyd
Llanrwst
Llyn Padarn
Dinorwic
Pont
Pen-y-benglog
Pont Rhyd-goch
Llyn
Crafnant
Melin-
y-coed
LLANBERIS LAKE
RAILWAY
PADARN
IDWAL
COTTAGE
Cornel
Llanberis
SLATE MUS
Afon Ogwen
CWM GLAS
CRAFNANT
G w y d y r
Ty-draw
BRYN TRILLYN
496
DOLBADARN
CWM
IDWAL
F O R E S T
GWDYR UCHAF
CHAPEL
C o n w y
14
Nant Peris
999
GLYDER
FAWR
Capel Curig
CAPEL
CURIG
6
P A R K
468
MOEL SEISIOG
Llyn Aled
A543
Llyn
Peris
PARC
Pass of
Llanberis
A4086
Pont
Cyfyng
SWALLOW
FALLS
CONWY VALLEY
RAILWAY MUSEUM
Nebo
Llyn
Alwen
Mynydd
Hiraethog
532
SNOWDON
RANGER
1085
SNOWDON
SUMMIT
VISITOR CENTRE
(HAFOD ERYRI)
PEN-Y-
PASS
Pen-y-Gwryd
Hotel
BETWS-Y-COED
Betws-y-Coed
Capel
Garmon
BURIAL
CHAMBER
HAFOD
ELWY MOOR
SNOWDON
MOUNTAIN
RAILWAY
SNOWDON
YR WYDDFA
Mynydd Cribau
Fairy Glen
Hafod-Dinbych
Alwen
Reservoir
Rhyd-Ddu
YR WYDDFA
872
CARNEDD
MOEL SIABOD
Pont-y-pant
C E N E D L A E T H O L
Llyn
Llydaw
Conwy Falls
Rhaeadr Conwy
Glan-
Conwy
Mwdwl-
eithin
Ffridd-Uchaf
747
Dolwyddelan
Pentre-bont
PENMACHNO
WOOLLEN MILL
Pentrefoelas
Cefn-brith
Bethania
DOLWYDDELAN
TY MAWR
WYBRNANT
A5
E R Y R I
Garnedd
Gwydyr Forest
A498
BRYN
GWYNANT
Penmachno
Padog
Rhydlydan
Glasfryn
A470
Bethania
Nantgwynant
71
A4086
Llyn
Dinas
623
MOEL
PENAMNEN
72
Cwm
B4407
Beddgelert
Forest
SYGUN COPPER MINE
Carrog
Ysbyty
Ifan
539
GARN PRYS
Cerrigydrudion
782
MOEL HEBOG
Pass of
Aberglaslyn
Beddgelert
WELSH
HIGHLAND RLY
LLECHWEDD SLATE
CAVERNS
Cwm
Penmac no
Llyn
Conwy
A5
Ty
Mawr Cwm
A498
Nantmor
Rhiwbryfdir
Blaenau
Ffestiniog
YNNON WEN

5 6 7 8 9

A   B   C   D   E   F   G

POINT OF AYRE

NX

SC

Rue Pt.   The Ayres

Glentruan   Cranstal
The Lhen   Dhowin   Bride
A10   A19   B2   B6   A17   A16
Jurby Head   MANX CROSSES   JURBY SOUTH   Jurby East   Sandygate   **Andreas**   MANX CROSSES   Regaby   A10
Ballasalla   Jurby West   B3   A9   B7
The Cronk   A14   A17   St Judes   Dhoor   A13   B14
Ballaugh   CURRAGHS WILDLIFE PARK   Sulby   GROVE MUSEUM   **Ramsey**   *RAMSEY BAY*
Orrisdale   9   T.T. Course   A3   Churchtown   Port e Vullen
Rhencullen   30   Ravensdale   Glen Auldyn   MANX ELECTRIC RAILWAY   A15   Maughold
Kirk Michael   A14   Sulby   A18   T.T. Course   Dreemskerry   *Maughold Head*
MANX CROSSES   565   NORTH BARRULE   MANX CROSSES   Ballajora
Ballaleigh   CELTIC CRAFT CENTRE   SNAEFELL   Corrany   Cornaa
Barregarrow   B10   621   Glen Mona   9
Druidale   14   Dhoon
MURRAYS MOTORCYCLE MUSEUM   544   Agneash   LAXEY WHEEL AND MINES
MANX TRANSPORT MUSEUM   Knocksharry   A4   A3   SNAEFELL MOUNTAIN RAILWAY   **Laxey**   *Bulgham Bay*
St Patrick's I.   Cronk-y-Voddy   T.T. Course   487   COLDEN   Ballaquine   LAXEY WOOLLEN MILLS
PEEL   HOUSE OF MANANNAN   **Peel**   A20   Res.   BALLAHEANNAGH GARDENS   Old Laxey
Contrary Head   KIPPER MUSEUM   A1   A18   Creg-ny-Baa   *Laxey Head*
TYNWALD CRAFT CENTRE   TYNWALD HILL   **M a n**   B22   Fairy Cottage   *Laxey Bay*
Patrick   A30   St John's   Greeba   Baldwin   B21   Ballacannel   Baldrine
Glenmaye   333   Lower Foxdale   Crosby   B12   B20   *Clay Head*
Dalby Pt.   Glen Vine   A1   Strang   MANX CROSSES
Dalby   Foxdale   A24   B35   Union Mills   A22   A21   **Onchan**   GROUDLE GLEN RAILWAY
Niarbyl   483   SOUTH BARRULE   B36   Braaid   B32   Spring Valley   Tromode   ONCHAN PLEASURE PARK
Niarbyl Bay   Eairy   A3   B37   222   Cooil   A5   **Douglas**   *Douglas Bay*
Close Clark   A26   St Mark's   Ellenbrook   *Douglas Head*
Ballamodha   B30   Newtown   A6   CAMERA OBSCURA
Lingague   Ronague   B41   B40   Grenaby   A3   Ballaveare   A25   *Little Ness*
Surby   B44   Colby   Ballabeg   ISLE OF MAN STEAM RAILWAY   *Santon Head*
Fleshwick Bay   RUSHEN ABBEY   A25   *Port Greenaugh*
Bradda   A1   **Castletown**   Ballasalla
Bradda Head   RAILWAY MUS   **Port Erin**   Four Roads   A5   BILLOWN   ISLE OF MAN   Derbyhaven
The Howe   Cregneash   A31   Port St Mary   CASTLE RUSHEN   NAUTICAL MUS   OLD HOUSE OF KEYS   *St Michael's I.*
128   CREGNEASH VILLAGE FOLK MUSEUM   SCARLETT VISITOR CENTRE
Calf of Man   *Spanish Head*   *Scarlett Point*   *Dreswick Pt.*
Chicken Rock

I s l e   o f   M a n

HEYSHAM 3:30
HEYSHAM 2:00 (TT race period only)
LIVERPOOL 2:30 (March-Nov)
LIVERPOOL 4:15 (Winter only)
BELFAST 2:55
DUBLIN 2:55 } (April-Sept)

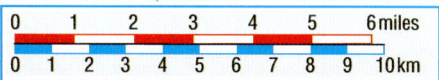

0 1 2 3 4 5 6 miles
0 1 2 3 4 5 6 7 8 9 10km

Grid columns: 1 2 3 4 5
Grid rows: A B C D E F G

IRISH SEA

SD
SJ

LIVERPOOL BAY

Ferry times:
BELFAST 8:00
DOUGLAS 4:15 (Winter only)
DUBLIN 7:00
DOUGLAS 2:30 (March–Nov)

Crosby Channel
Mockbeggar Wharf
West Hoyle Bank
Hilbre I.
Welsh Channel
River Dee / Afon Dyfrdwy
West Hoyle Bank

Place names (row A):
South Shore, BLACKPOOL PLEASURE BEACH, Squires Gate, BLACKPOOL INTERNATIONAL, TOY AND TEDDY BEAR MUSEUM, Hawes Side, Mereside, Common Edge, Westby, Moss Side, St Annes, ROYAL LYTHAM & ST ANNES, LYTHAM HALL, Lytham St Anne's, Ansdell, Lytham, Fairhaven, Salters Bank, Little Plumpton, Great Plumpton, Wesham, Kirkham, Dowbridge, Wrea Green, Newton, Scales, Warton, Freckleton

Row B:
Banks Sands, Great Bank, RIBBLE MARSHES, Hesketh Bank, Becconsall, Hundred-End, Tarleton

Row C:
Horse Bank, ECO VISITOR CENTRE, Southport, SOUTHPORT MODEL RAILWAY VILLAGE, P&R, Marshside, Churchtown, Crossens, Banks, Mere Brow, Holmeswood, Birkdale, Blowick, Brown Edge, MARTIN MERE WILDFOWL AND WETLAND CENTRE, Rufford, Hillside, Scarisbrick, Snape Green, Bescar, New Lane, Burscough Bridge, ROYAL BIRKDALE, Shirdley Hill, Pinfold, Burscough, Ainsdale-on-Sea, Ainsdale, Woodvale, Halsall, Barton, Haskayne, ORMSKIRK, Westhead

Row D:
Formby Hills, AINSDALE SAND DUNES, Freshfield, Formby, Little Altcar, CABIN HILL, Formby Pt., Hightown, Downholland Cross, Great Altcar, Ince Blundell, Lydiate, Aughton Park, Stanley Gate, Aughton, Royal Oak, Bickerstaffe, Maghull, Lunt, Barrow Nook, Little Crosby, Thornton, Sefton, Netherton, Melling Mount, M58, M57, Kirkby, Southdene

Row E:
Waterloo, Seaforth, Great Crosby, Aintree, AINTREE, LITHERLAND, Orrell, Fazakerley, Knowsley, Bootle, New Brighton, NEW PALACE, Kirkdale, Walton, Norris Green, Croxteth, Mockbeggar Wharf, Liscard, Egremont, WALKER GALL, Anfield, West Derby, Longview, Wallasey, Leasowe, Seacombe, Everton, LIVERPOOL, Knotty Ash, Roby, Huyto, Meols, Moreton, Poulton, Bidston, MARITIME MUS, Edge Hill, Wavertree, Childwall, Netherley

Row F:
HOYLAKE, Upton, Claughton, TATE, ALBERT DOCK, Toxteth, Mossley Hill, A562, Gateacre, West Kirby, Greasby, Grange, Woodchurch, Frankby, Birkenhead, Tranmere, Rock Ferry, Dingle, SUDLEY, Aigburth, Woolton, MENDIPS, ARROWE, Point of Ayr / Yr Parlwr Du, Talacre, Gwespyr, Caldy, Irby, Thingwall, Prenton, New Ferry, SUNLIGHT VISION MUS, Grassendale, Garston, Speke, Gronant, Thurstaston, Pensby, Barnston, Storeton, Port Sunlight, LADY LEVER ART GALLERY, Prestatyn, Gwaenysgor, Picton, Brimstage, WIRRAL, Bromborough, LIVERPOOL JOHN LENNON, SPEKE HALL, Liverpool Airport, Llanasa, OFFA'S DYKE PATH / LLWYBR CLAWDD OFFA, Mostyn Quay, Dawpool Bank, Heswall, Thornton Hough, EASTHAM, Eastham Ferry, Axton, Trelogan, Mostyn, Gayton, Raby, Eastham, Trelawnyd

Row G:
Greenfield, GREENFIELD VALLEY HERITAGE PARK, Holywell Bank, Gayton Sands, Neston, Little Neston, Ness, Parkgate, Hinderton, Willaston, Childer Thornton, Little Sutton, Hooton, RIVACRE, ELLESMERE PORT, BOAT MUSEUM, Ince Banks, Whitby, Overpool, Elton, Great, Holywell, A55, A550, A5151, A548

Motorway/junction numbers: M55, M58, M57, M53, A565, A570, A59, A580, A41, A552, A553, A540, A548, A55, A550

Scale:
0 1 2 3 4 5 6 miles
0 1 2 3 4 5 6 7 8 9 10 km

Preston
Fulwood
Ribbleton
Penwortham
Freckleton
Lytham
Kirkham
Wrea Green
Blackburn
Darwen
Blackburn with Darwen
Leyland
Chorley
Lancashire
Burscough
Ormskirk
Skelmersdale
Wigan
Standish
Horwich
Bolton
Westhoughton
Hindley
Atherton
Tyldesley
Leigh
Ashton-in-Makerfield
Golborne
St Helens
Newton-le-Willows
Warrington
Lymm
Merseyside
Liverpool
Kirkby
Maghull
Huyton
Prescot
Widnes
Runcorn
Halton
Speke
Garston
Liverpool Airport
Frodsham
Banks Sands
Ribble
Anglezarke Moor
Chat Moss
Manchester Ship Canal
M6
M55
M61
M62
M65
M57
M58
M56
0 1 2 3 4 5 6 miles
0 1 2 3 4 5 6 7 8 9 10 km

A671 Read · Pamham · A646 · Walshaw Dean Res. · Wadsworth Moor · Denholme · Allerton · A

M65 · Rose Grove · Burnley Syke · 10 · Burnley · Worsthorne · Widdop Res. · Heptonstall Moor · Queensbury · Buttershaw · Wibsey

ACCRINGTON · A56 · Clow Bridge · Holme Chapel · Hebden Bridge · Halifax · BRIGHOUSE

waldtwistle · Forest of Rossendale · Todmorden · Mytholmroyd · A646 · Sowerby Bridge · Elland

Haslingden · RAWTENSTALL · Bacup · Whitworth · A58 · Huddersfield

Ramsbottom · Littleborough · Hollingworth Lake · M62 · Slaithwaite · Marsden · Meltham · HOLMFIRTH

Bury · HEYWOOD · A58 · Rochdale · Milnrow · Shaw · ROYTON

Radcliffe · Whitefield · Middleton · Chadderton · Oldham · Greenfield · Saddleworth Moor

PRESTWICH · M60 · A62 · Oldham · Mossley · STALYBRIDGE

MANCHESTER · SALFORD · Eccles · Droylsden · Dukinfield · Hadfield

Trafford Park · Stretford · A57 · Denton · Hyde · M67 · GLOSSOP · HOPE FOREST

URMSTON · SALE · M60 · Gee Cross · Charlesworth

Stockport · Cheadle · Marple · Marple Bridge

GATLEY · HAZEL GROVE · Hayfield · KINDER SCOUT

Altrincham · Bramhall · High Lane · Disley · New Mills

Manchester Airport · Handforth · Poynton · Whaley Bridge · Chapel-en-le-Frith

WILMSLOW · A538 · Bollington · 75 · Peak Forest

Knutsford · Alderley Edge · Prestbury · Bollington Cross

Bradford
LEEDS
GARFORTH
PUDSEY
Queensbury
Halifax
BRIGHOUSE
Cleckheaton
BATLEY
MORLEY
Rothwell
Middleton
CASTLEFORD
Sowerby Bridge
Elland
Heckmondwike
Dewsbury
OSSETT
Normanton
Wakefield
Pontefract
Featherstone
Mirfield
Horbury
Huddersfield
Slaithwaite
Marsden
Meltham
HOLMFIRTH
Denby Dale
Skelmanthorpe
Clayton West
Darton
Royston
Hemsworth
South Kirkby
Cudworth
Barnsley
Darfield
Wombwell
Hoyland
Wath upon Dearne
Swinton
Rawmarsh
Penistone
Stocksbridge
Chapeltown
Worsbrough
Dodworth
Wharncliffe Wood
Grenoside
Ecclesfield
Sheffield
Handsworth
Woodhouse
ECKINGTON
Dronfield
Hathersage
Bradfield Moors
Broomhead Moor
Midhope Moors
Howden Moors
PEAK DISTRICT NATIONAL PARK
HOPE FOREST
HIGH PEAK
West Yorkshire
South Yorkshire
GLOSSOP
Charlestown
Hayfield
Chinley
Chapel-en-le-Frith
Castleton
Bamford
Hope
Edale
Tideswell
Eyam
Grindleford
Crowden
Holme
Wessenden Moor
Reservoirs
M1
M62
M606
M621
0 1 2 3 4 5 6 miles
0 1 2 3 4 5 6 7 8 9 10 km

Sherburn in Elmet
Selby
Osgodby
Menthorpe
Breighton
Spaldington
Selby Abbey
Lund
South Duffield
Cliffe
Thorpe Willoughby
Hambleton
Brayton
Monk Fryston
South Milford
Newthorpe
Steeton Hall Gateway
Ledsham
Lumby
Hillam
Fairburn
Burton Salmon
Brotherton
New Fryston
Birkin
Yorkshire Garden World
West Haddlesey
Chapel Haddlesey
Gateforth
Burn
Selby Canal
Aire
Temple Hirst
Hirst Courtney
Camblesforth
Barlow
Long Drax
Drax
Barmby on the Marsh
Hemingbrough
East Common
Wressle
Brind
North Howden
Newsholme
Howden
Howden Minster
Asselby
Knedlington
Boothferry
Ouse
Derwent
Kilpin
Kilpin Pike
Skelton
Laxton
Saltmarshe
Yokefleet
Blacktoft
Ousefleet
Blacktoft RSPB
Whitgift
Reedness
Little Reedness
Swinefleet
Adlingfleet
Goole
Old Goole
Hook
Airmyn
Newland
Rawcliffe
Rawcliffe Bridge
The Yorkshire Waterways Museum
Dutch River
Goole Fields
Goole Moors
Fockerby
Garthorpe
Burton Stather
Burton upon Stather
Luddington
Amcotts
Ealand
Crowle
Keadby
Gunness
Burringham
Althorpe
Derrythorpe
Foulness
Portington
Hive
Caville
Eastrington
Sandholme
Gilberdyke
Staddlethorpe
Balkholme
Ferrybridge
Knottingley
Kellingley
Beal
Kellington
Sutton
Eggborough
Hensall
Carlton
Snaith
Gowdall
East Cowick
West Cowick
High Eggborough
Whitley
Great Heck
Balne
Pollington
Southfield Reservoir
Aire and Calder Navigation
Went
Womersley
Cridling Stubbs
Chequerfield
Darrington
East Hardwick
Wentbridge
Low Ackworth
Thorpe Audlin
Badsworth
Ferrybridge Services
Little Smeaton
Walden Stubbs
Kirk Smeaton
Barnsdale Bar Services
Norton
Campsall
Askern
Instoneville
Sutton
Haywood
Burghwallis
Owston
Thorpe in Balne
Braithwaite
Sykehouse
Fenwick
Moss
Pincheon Green
Fosterhouses
Fishlake
Far Bank
Kirk Bramwith
Stainforth
Hatfield
Doncaster North Services
Moorends
Humberhead Peatlands
Thorne Waste or Moors
Thorne
Canal Side
Wike Well End
Stainforth & Keadby Canal
Hatfield Chase
Woodhouse
Sandtoft
The Trolleybus Museum at Sandtoft
Westgate
Grey Green
Belton
Church Town
Beltoft
East Butterwick
West Butterwick
Isle of Axholme
Epworth
Old Rectory
Epworth Turbary
Wroot
Hatfield Moors
Hatfield Woodhouse
West End
Dunsville
Dunscroft
Barnby Dun
Kirk Sandall
Edenthorpe
Armthorpe
Upton
North Elmsall
South Elmsall
Skelbrooke
Moorthorpe
Hampole
Skellow
Carcroft
Adwick le Street
Almholme
Toll Bar
Woodlands
Highfields
Arksey
Bentley
Scawsby
Hooton Pagnell
Clayton
Brodsworth
Brodsworth Hall
Thurnscoe
Thurnscoe East
Hickleton
Marr
Goldthorpe
Bolton upon Dearne
Barnburgh
Melton Wood
Cusworth
Cusworth Hall Museum
Newton
Sprotbrough
Harlington
Adwick upon Dearne
High Melton
Mexborough
Cadeby
Warmsworth
Balby
Hyde Park
Doncaster
Museum & Art Gallery
Wheatley
Intake
Nutwell
Doncaster Racecourse
Cantley
Bessacarr
Lakeside Village
Aeroventure
Branton
Auckley
Lidget
Blaxton
Finningley
Westwoodside
Haxey
Upperthorpe
Craiseland
Owston Ferry
Low Burnham
Kelfield
Susworth
Scotter
East Lound
East Ferry
Wildsworth
Laughton Forest
Laughton
Robin Hood Airport Doncaster Sheffield
Idle
Old Denaby
Denaby Main
Conisbrough
Conisbrough Ivanhoe
New Edlington
Loversall
Rossington
New Rossington
Old Edlington
Kilnhurst
Hooton Roberts
Thrybergh
Ravenfield
Clifton
Wadworth
St Leger Horse Park
Micklebring
Braithwell
Stainton
Dalton
Bramley
Wickersley
Hellaby
Maltby
Tickhill
Spital Hill
Harworth
Bircotes
Bawtry
Austerfield
Misson
Newington
Misterton
West Stockwith
East Stockwith
Walkerith
Morton
Gainsborough
Gainsborough Old Hall
Walkeringham
Gringley on the Hill
Beckingham
Blyton
Everton
Scaftworth
Scrooby
Hooton Levitt
Carr
Stone
Roche Abbey
Styrrup
Thurcroft
Brampton en le Morthen
Laughton en le Morthen
Firbeck
Oldcotes
Serlby
Mattersey Thorpe
Mattersey
Cuckoo Hill
Wiseton
Clayworth
Saundby
Bole
Lea
Blyth
Blyth Services
Ranskill
Torworth
Langold
Letwell
Gildingwells
Dinnington
Ulley
Aughton
Aston
Laughton Common
North Anston
South Anston
Woodsetts
Carlton in Lindrick
Lound
Wetlands Animal Park
Barnby Moor
Sutton
Hayton
North Wheatley
South Wheatley
Sturton le Steeple
Knaith Park
Knaith
Gate Burton
Swallownest
Todwick
Kiveton Park
Wales
Rother Valley
Killamarsh
Norwood
Thorpe Salvin
Harthill
Woodall Services
Wigthorpe
Gateford
Shireoaks
Netherthorpe
Scofton
Ranby
West Retford
Babworth
Retford
Bassetlaw Museum
Clarborough
Welham
North Leverton with Habblesthorpe
North Leverton Windmill
Littleborough
Marton
South Leverton
Coates
Sturton
Brampton
Torksey
Cottam
Treswell
Sundown Adventureland
Rampton
Ordsall
Grove
Eaton
Headon
Upton
Gamston
Woodbeck
Stokeham
Church Laneham
Laneham
Laughterton
Fenton
Kilton
Manton
Worksop
Rhodesia
Darfoulds
Spinkhill
Barlborough
Mastin Moor
Clowne
Whitwell
Hodthorpe
Clumber Park
Rotherham

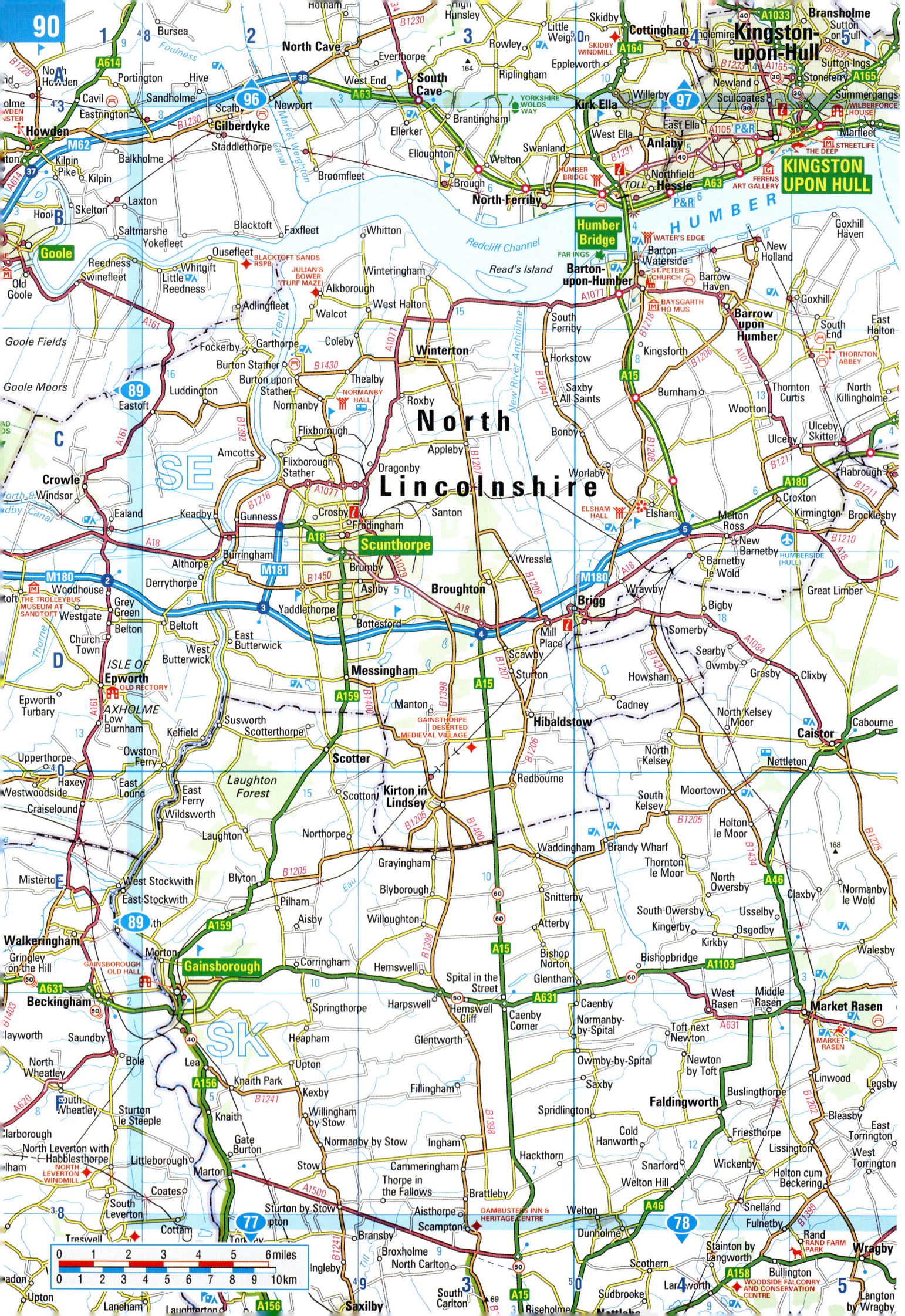

KINGSTON UPON HULL

North Lincolnshire

Goole · Howden · Scunthorpe · Brigg · Gainsborough · Caistor · Market Rasen · Epworth

Kingston-upon-Hull · Cottingham · Willerby · Kirk Ella · East Ella · Anlaby · Hessle · Northfield · Sculcoates · Newland · Summergangs · Sutton Ings · Stoneferry · Marfleet · Bransholme

Humber Bridge · Barton-upon-Humber · Barrow upon Humber · Barrow Haven · Barton Waterside · New Holland · Goxhill · Goxhill Haven · East Halton · South End · Thornton Abbey · Ulceby · Ulceby Skitter · Habrough · Croxton · Kirmington · Brocklesby · Wootton · Thornton Curtis · North Killingholme · Burnham · Kingsforth

North Cave · South Cave · West End · Everthorpe · Rowley · Riplingham · Epplewich · Weedley · Brantingham · Ellerker · Broomfleet · Welton · Brough · North Ferriby · Swanland · West Ella · Willerby · Skidby

Howden · Kilpin · Kilpin Pike · Laxton · Hook · Skelton · Saltmarshe · Yokefleet · Blacktoft · Faxfleet · Whitton · Winteringham · Alkborough · West Halton · Walcot · Coleby · Whitgift · Ousefleet · Reedness · Swinefleet · Adlingfleet · Garthorpe · Fockerby · Luddington · Amcotts · Eastoft · Crowle · Ealand · Keadby · Gunness · Burringham

Scunthorpe · Frodingham · Crosby · Brumby · Ashby · Bottesford · Yaddlethorpe · Messingham · Holme · Burton · Derrythorpe · Althorpe · Belton · Epworth · Haxey · Owston Ferry · Kelfield · Susworth · Scotterthorpe · Scotter · Scotton

Burton upon Stather · Burton Stather · Flixborough · Flixborough Stather · Normanby · Thealby · Roxby · Winterton · Appleby · Dragonby · Santon · Wressle · Broughton · Scawby · Sturton · Mill Place · Brigg · Wrawby · Bigby · Somerby · Searby · Owmby · Grasby · Clixby · Caistor · Nettleton · Cabourne · Howsham · Cadney · Hibaldstow · Redbourne · Waddingham · Snitterby · Atterby · Bishop Norton · Glentham

Worlaby · Bonby · Saxby All Saints · Horkstow · South Ferriby · New Barnetby · Barnetby le Wold · Melton Ross · Elsham · Great Limber · Grasby · North Kelsey · North Kelsey Moor · South Kelsey · Moortown · Holton le Moor · Thornton le Moor · North Owersby · South Owersby · Usselby · Osgodby · Kingerby · Kirkby · Bishopbridge · Walesby · Claxby · Normanby le Wold · Tealby

Isle of Axholme · Low Burnham · Upperthorpe · Westwoodside · Craiselound · Misterton · West Stockwith · East Stockwith · Blyton · Pilham · Aisby · Willoughton · Grayingham · Blyborough · Corringham · Hemswell · Harpswell · Spital in the Street · Hemswell Cliff · Glentworth · Caenby · Caenby Corner · Normanby-by-Spital · Owmby-by-Spital · Saxby · Spridlington · Cold Hanworth · Snarford · Friesthorpe · Wickenby · Lissington · Holton cum Beckering · Faldingworth · Buslingthorpe · Linwood · Legsby · East Torrington · West Torrington · Bleasby · Market Rasen · Middle Rasen · West Rasen · Toft next Newton · Newton by Toft

Walkeringham · Gringley on the Hill · Beckingham · Saundby · Bole · Lea · Morton · Gainsborough · Knaith · Knaith Park · Kexby · Upton · Heapham · Springthorpe · Willingham by Stow · Normanby by Stow · Stow · Sturton by Stow · Ingham · Cammeringham · Thorpe in the Fallows · Brattleby · Aisthorpe · Scampton · Dunholme

North Wheatley · South Wheatley · Sturton le Steeple · Littleborough · Gate Burton · Marton · Coates · Treswell · Cottam · Torksey · Saxilby · South Carlton · North Carlton · Broxholme · Ingleby · Bransby · Brampton

Goole · Gainsborough Old Hall · The Trolleybus Museum at Sandtoft · The Deep · Ferens Art Gallery · Streetlife · Wilberforce House · Water's Edge · St Peter's Church · Baysgarth Ho Mus · Normanby Hall · Elsham Hall · Humberside (Hull) Airport · Market Rasen Racecourse · Woodside Falconry and Conservation Centre · Dambusters Inn & Heritage Centre · Gainsthorpe Deserted Medieval Village · Julian's Bower (Turf Maze) · Blacktoft Sands RSPB · North Leverton Windmill · Skidby Windmill · Epworth Old Rectory

Roads: M62 · M180 · M181 · A614 · A63 · A164 · A165 · A1033 · A1079 · A1105 · A1077 · A15 · A18 · A159 · A156 · A161 · A1103 · A46 · A631 · A1084 · A620 · A156

Scale:
0 1 2 3 4 5 6 miles
0 1 2 3 4 5 6 7 8 9 10 km

5 6 7 8 9
A B C D E F G

Thirtleby Sproatley Humbleton Fitling
Ganstead
Bilton Lelley Elstronwick Hilston
Preston Owstwick Tunstall
West End Burton Pidsea North End Roos
Salt End A1033
Hedon Waxholme
Haven Side Rimswell Owthorne Withernsea
Paull Burstwick Halsham East End Hollym
FORT PAULL Thorngumbald Camerton Keyingham Holmpton
Ryehill Ottringham Out Newton
Little Humber Winestead A1033
Thorney Crofts Patrington Welwick Weeton
Cherry Cob Sands TA Skeffling Easington
Sunk Island
Kilnsea

South Killingholme A160 Immingham SPURN
MUSEUM SPURN HEAD
Stallingborough A180 MOUTH OF THE HUMBER
Keelby Healing Pyewipe Grimsby ROTTERDAM 10:25 ZEEBRUGGE 10:25
Riby Cross Roads West Marsh CLEETHORPES
Riby Great Coates Old Clee
Aylesby FISHING HERITAGE CENTRE
Laceby Nunsthorpe Scartho CLEETHORPES COAST LIGHT RAILWAY
Bradley A46 PLEASURE ISLAND THEME PARK
North East A1098 CLEETHORPES
Irby upon Humber Humberston
Lincolnshire A16 Waltham New Waltham
Swallow A18 Barnoldby le Beck WALTHAM WINDMILL Holton le Clay
Beelsby Brigsley Tetney Lock
Cuxwold Hatcliffe Ashby cum Fenby Waithe Tetney North Cotes
Rothwell East Ravendale Grainsby Donna Nook
Croxby Marshchapel
Thoresway Thorganby Wold Newton Eskham Wragholme Grainthorpe
Swinhope North Thoresby Fulstow North Somercotes DONNA NOOK
Brookenby LINCOLNSHIRE WOLDS RLY Conisholme Skidbrooke North End
Binbrook Ludborough Covenham St Bartholomew South Somercotes Saltfleet
Stainton le Vale Covenham St Mary
Kirmond le Mire Utterby Yarburgh Skidbrooke
Tealby North Ormsby ALVINGHAM MILL Saltfleetby St Clements
North Willingham Fotherby Alvingham North Cockerington Saltfleetby St Peter SALTFLEETBY THEDDLETHORPE
Great Tows Little Grimsby RUSHMOOR Saltfleetby All Saints
Sixhills Ludford Kelstern North Elkington South Cockerington Theddlethorpe St Helen
Hainton A157 South Elkington Keddington Grimoldby B1200 Theddlethorpe All Saints
Burgh on Bain Welton le Wold Louth Manby SEAL SANCTUARY & NATURE CENTRE
Grimblethorpe ST JAMES Stewton Meers Bridge
South Willingham Gayton le Wold Little Carlton Great Carlton Mablethorpe
Biscathorpe Hallington Legbourne Trusthorpe
East Barkwith Donington on Bain Raithby Little Cawthorpe South Reston Gayton le Marsh Strubby Thorpe
West Barkwith Withcall North Reston Withern Maltby le Marsh Sutton on Sea
Benniworth Tathwell Haugham Muckton Tothill A157 Sandilands
Panton CADWELL PARK Authorpe Woodthorpe Beesby
Market Stainton Stenigot Maidenwell Burwell CLAYTHORPE WATER AND WILDFOWL GARDENS Hannah
Ranby Cawkwell WOODY'S TOP Belleau Saleby Markby
Goulceby Scamblesby Farforth Ruckland Aby Asserby
Hatton Oxcombe White Pit Swaby ALFORD WINDMILL Bilsby Huttoft
Great Sturton Belchford Ketsby South Thoresby ALFORD MANOR HOUSE Alford
Rigsby A1111

LINCOLNSHIRE WOLDS TF

Grid references: 1 2 3 4 5

A
Green, The Hill, Whicham, Kirkby-in-Furness, Beck Side, Gawthwaite, Bridge, Backbarrow, Witherslack, Mill Side, Crooklands, Leasgill, HALL, Penny Bridge, Broughton Beck, Greenodd, Haverthwaite, Ayside, High Newton, Town End, Heversham, Railway, ARTCRYSTAL, Low Newton, Meathop, Milnthorpe, A590, Arrad Foot, Mansriggs, A590, ROUDSEA WOOD AND MOSSES, Field Broughton, Lindale, Storth, Beetham, HERON CORN MILL, Farleton
Millom, Soutergate, LAUREL & HARDY MUS, ULVERSTON, CARTMEL PRIORY, Cartmel, CARTMEL PRIORY, ARNSIDE, Arnside, B5282, Holme, MILLOM FOLK MUSEUM, Haverigg, A595

B
Askam in Furness, Pennington, Ireleth, Lindal in Furness, Swarthmoor, Great Urswick, Bardsea, Little Urswick, HOLKER HALL, Holker, Allithwaite, Grange-over-Sands, GAIT BARROWS, LAKELAND WILDLIFE OASIS, Yealand Redmayne, Yealand Conyers, Burton-in-Kendal, BURTON-IN-KENDAL (Northbound only), Priest Hutton
SANDSCALE HAWS, NORTH WALNEY, BARROW (WALNEY ISLAND), Dalton-in-Furness, DALTON CASTLE, Stainton with Adgarley, Scales, SOUTH LAKES WILD ANIMAL PARK, Hawcoat, BOW BRIDGE, Newton, FURNESS ABBEY, GLEASTON WATERMILL, Baycliff, Cark, CONISHEAD PRIORY & MANJUSHRI KADAMPA MEDITATION CENTRE, Cartmel Sands, Ravenstown, Flookburgh, Kents Bank, ARNSIDE AND SILVERDALE, Silverdale, Warton, LEIGHTON HALL, Borwick, Capernwray, OLD RECTORY, Millhead
Barrow-in-Furness, Ormsgill, Newbarns, Dendron, Gleaston, Aldingham, LAKELAND RIDING CENTRE, Humphrey Head Pt., Warton Sands, Carnforth

C
North Scale, Vickerstown, THE DOCK MUSEUM, CUSTOM HO., Barrow Island, Leece, Roosebeck, Newbiggin, Yarlside, MORECAMBE BAY, Bolton-le-Sands, Over-Kellet, Nether Kellet, Eaton Green, Aughton
Biggar, Hest Bank, Bolton Town End, Halton, Caton, Caton Brook
Roa Island, Rampside, Foulney Island, Morecambe, Slyne, Bare, Skerton, A5105, A6
South End, Piel Island, Sandylands, Torrisholme, MARITIME MUS
Isle of Walney, South Channel, White Lund, Lancaster, CITY
South End Point, Heysham, PRIORY CHURCH, Aldcliffe, ASHTON MEMORIAL, LEISURE PARK, Clou...

D
DOUGLAS 3:30, Heaton, Scotforth, Quernmore
DOUGLAS 2:00 (TT race period only), A683, Middleton, Overton, M6, 6
Glasson, Conder Green, Galgate, Smith Green, Ortner
Sunderland Pt., Shoulder of Lune, Lune, Thurnham, Dolphinholme, W...
LARNE 8:00, Cockerham Sands, Cockerham, Forton, LANCASTER (FORTON) SERV, Street
Braides, Hollins Lane, Scorton

E
Knott End-on-Sea, Dam Side, Pilling Lane, Pilling, Stake Pool, Winmarleigh, Cabus, Oakenclough, Calder Vale
Fleetwood, Rossall Point, Preesall, Eagland Hill, Garstang, GARSTANG DISCOVERY CENTRE
FREEPORT FLEETWOOD, Stalmine, Staynall, Nateby, Bowgreave, Churchtown, Catterall, Claughton
SD, Cleveleys, MARSH MILL IN WYRE, WYRE ESTUARY, Trunnah, Hambleton, Out Rawcliffe, Moss Edge, Ratten Row, Inglewhite
Anchorsholme, Thornton, Little Eccleston, TOLL, St Michael's on Wyre, Bilsborrow
Norbreck, Skippool, Carleton, Little Singleton, Great Eccleston, Elswick, Myerscough

F
Bispham, Warbreck, Poulton-le-Fylde, Singleton, Crossmoor, Cuddy Hill, M6
BLACKPOOL, North Shore, Layton, Normoss, Thistleton, Inskip, Roseacre, Barton
Queenstown, Staining, A585, Esprick, Catforth, Woodplumpton, Broughton, CHINGLE HALL
Blackpool, ZOO PARK, LANCASTER, Corner Row, Wharles, 1, 32
BLACKPOOL TOWER, SEA LIFE CENTRE, LOUIS TUSSAUD'S WAXWORKS, Great Marton, Weeton, Lower Bartle, Higher Bartle
South Shore, Hawes Side, Mereside, Common Edge, Little Plumpton, Great Plumpton, Wesham, Treales, Cottam, Ingol, Fulwood
BLACKPOOL PLEASURE BEACH, Westby, Kirkham, Lea Town, Cadley
BLACKPOOL INTERNATIONAL, Squires Gate, Moss Side, Dowbridge, Sharoe Green
TOY AND TEDDY BEAR MUSEUM, Higher Ballam, Newton, Scales, Preston, P&R
St Annes, ROYAL LYTHAM & ST ANNES, Wrea Green, Clifton, Bottom of Hutton, Higher Penwortham
Lytham St Anne's, Fairhaven, Ansdell, LYTHAM HALL, Lytham, Freckleton, Warton, Middleforth Green
Salters Bank, A584, Ribble, Longton, Hutton, Lostock

Ferry/sea references:
MORECAMBE BAY

Scale bar:
0 1 2 3 4 5 6 miles
0 1 2 3 4 5 6 7 8 9 10 km

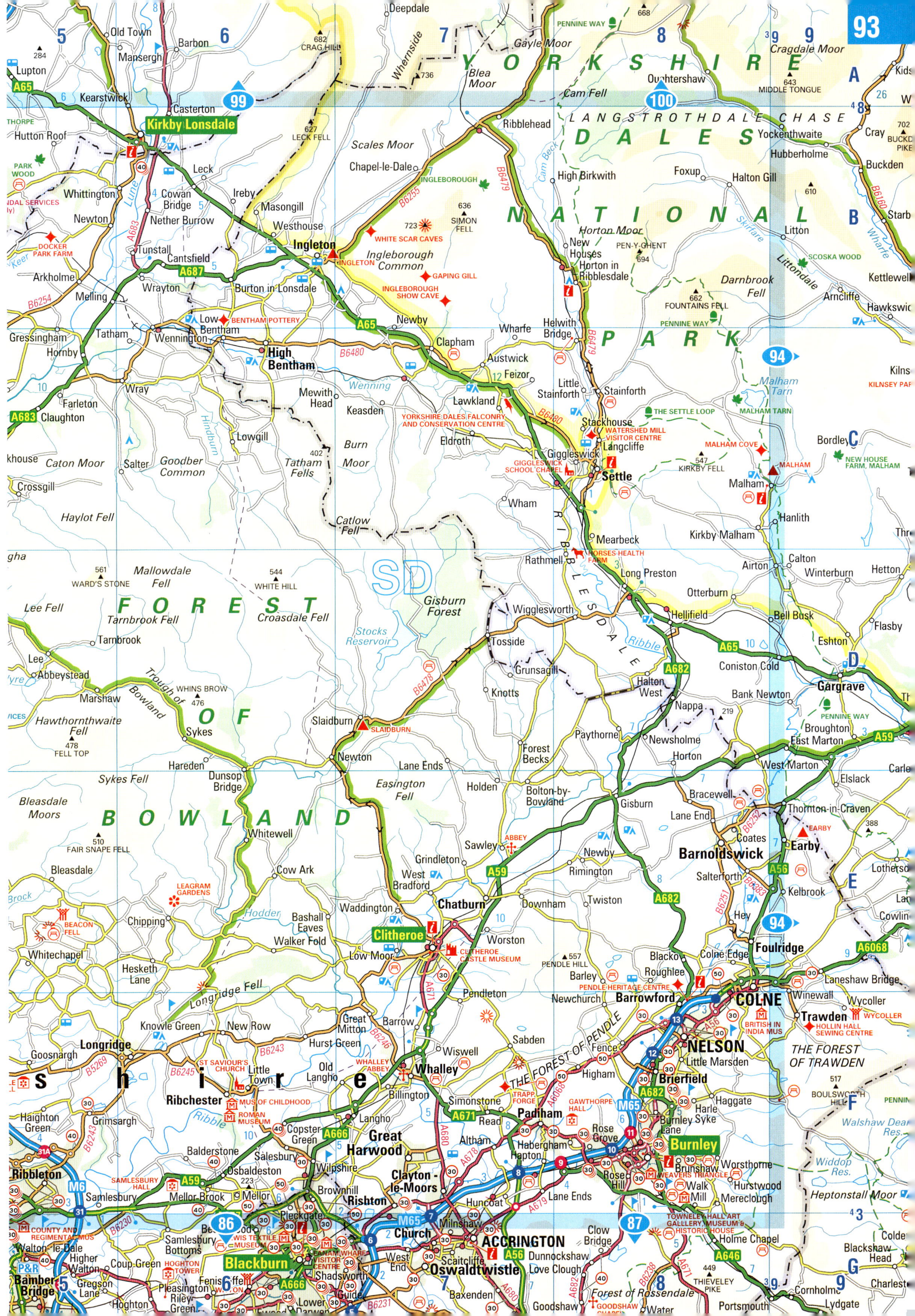
YORKSHIRE DALES NATIONAL PARK
FOREST OF BOWLAND
LANGSTROTHDALE CHASE
RIBBLESDALE
THE FOREST OF PENDLE
THE FOREST OF TRAWDEN
SD
99
100
94
86
87
Kirkby Lonsdale
Old Town
Barbon
Mansergh
Casterton
Kearstwick
Lupton
Hutton Roof
Whittington
Newton
Cowan Bridge
Nether Burrow
Leck
Ireby
Masongill
Westhouse
Ingleton
Tunstall
Cantsfield
Burton in Lonsdale
Arkholme
Melling
Wrayton
Low Bentham
High Bentham
Wennington
Tatham
Gressingham
Hornby
Wray
Farleton
Claughton
Caton Moor
Salter
Goodber Common
Lowgill
Crossgill
Haylot Fell
Mewith Head
Keasden
Burn Moor
Tatham Fells
Catlow Fell
Deepdale
Whernside
Crag Hill
Blea Moor
Gayle Moor
Scales Moor
Chapel-le-Dale
Ingleborough
Simon Fell
White Scar Caves
Ingleborough Common
Gaping Gill
Ingleborough Show Cave
Ribblehead
Newby
Clapham
Austwick
Feizor
Wharfe
Lawkland
Eldroth
Yorkshire Dales Falconry and Conservation Centre
Pennine Way
Cam Fell
Oughtershaw
Cragdale Moor
Middle Tongue
Yockenthwaite
Hubberholme
Buckden
Cray
High Birkwith
Foxup
Halton Gill
Horton Moor
Pen-y-ghent
New Houses
Horton in Ribblesdale
Litton
Scoska Wood
Darnbrook Fell
Littondale
Arncliffe
Kettlewell
Fountains Fell
Helwith Bridge
Little Stainforth
Stainforth
Stackhouse
Watershed Mill Visitor Centre
Langcliffe
Giggleswick
Giggleswick School Chapel
Settle
The Settle Loop
Malham Tarn
Malham Cove
Kirkby Fell
Malham
New House Farm, Malham
Bordley
Wham
Hanlith
Kirkby Malham
Mearbeck
Rathmell
Horses Health Farm
Long Preston
Airton
Calton
Winterburn
Hetton
Otterburn
Hellifield
Bell Busk
Flasby
Eshton
Coniston Cold
Gargrave
Bank Newton
Wigglesworth
Tosside
Grunsagill
Knotts
Gisburn Forest
Stocks Reservoir
Halton West
Nappa
Paythorne
Newsholme
Horton
Broughton
East Marton
West Marton
Ward's Stone
Mallowdale Fell
White Hill
Lee Fell
Tarnbrook Fell
Croasdale Fell
Tarnbrook
Lee
Abbeystead
Marshaw
Trough of Bowland
Whins Brow
Hawthornthwaite Fell
Fell Top
Sykes
Slaidburn
Newton
Hareden
Dunsop Bridge
Sykes Fell
Bleasdale Moors
Fair Snape Fell
Lane Ends
Easington Fell
Holden
Forest Becks
Bolton-by-Bowland
Gisburn
Bracewell
Lane End
Thornton-in-Craven
Elslack
Earby
Coates
Barnoldswick
Salterforth
Kelbrook
Whitewell
Sawley
Abbey
Grindleton
West Bradford
Newby
Rimington
Bleasdale
Cow Ark
Leagram Gardens
Beacon Fell
Chipping
Bashall Eaves
Waddington
Chatburn
Downham
Twiston
Walker Fold
Clitheroe
Clitheroe Castle Museum
Worston
Low Moor
Pendle Hill
Barley
Pendle Heritage Centre
Blacko
Roughlee
Hey
Foulridge
Colne Edge
Laneshaw Bridge
Whitechapel
Hesketh Lane
Longridge Fell
Pendleton
Newchurch
Barrowford
Colne
British in India Mus
Winewall
Wycoller
Trawden
Hollin Hall Sewing Centre
Knowle Green
New Row
Great Mitton
Barrow
Hurst Green
Wiswell
Sabden
Fence
Nelson
Little Marsden
Goosnargh
Longridge
St Saviour's Church
Little Town
Whalley Abbey
Old Langho
Whalley
Higham
Brierfield
Boulsworth Hill
Ribchester
Mus of Childhood
Roman Museum
Billington
Simonstone
Trapp Forge
Padiham
Gawthorpe Hall
Harle Syke
Haggate
Burnley
Walshaw Dean Res.
Haighton Green
Grimsargh
Langho
Copster Green
Great Harwood
Read
Altham
Habergham
Hapton
Rose Grove
Worsthorne
Widdop Res.
Ribbleton
Balderstone
Salesbury
Osbaldeston
Wilpshire
Clayton-le-Moors
Rishton
Lane Ends
Rose Hill
Weavers Triangle
Brunshaw
Walk Mill
Hurstwood
Mereclough
Heptonstall Moor
Samlesbury Hall
Samlesbury
Mellor Brook
Mellor
Brownhill
Huncoat
Towneley Hall Art Gallery, Museum & Historic House
Holme Chapel
County and Regimental Mus
Samlesbury Bottoms
Pleckgate
Blackburn
Church
Milnshaw
Accrington
Clow Bridge
Dunnockshaw
Love Clough
Walton-le-Dale
Higher Walton
Coup Green
Hoghton Tower
Oswaldtwistle
West End
Scaitcliffe
Bamber Bridge
Gregson Lane
Hoghton
Pleasington
Riley Green
Shadsworth
Guide
Lower Darwen
Baxenden
Goodshaw
Forest of Rossendale
Thieveley Pike
Cornholme
Portsmouth
Lydgate
Blackshaw Head
Charlestown
Kilnsey Park
Hawkswick
Kildwick
Lothersdale
Cowling
Lancashire
A65
A683
A687
A682
A59
A56
A6068
A671
A666
A646
A680
A678
A679
A56
M65
M6
B6480
B6479
B6255
B6478
B6254
B6243
B6245
B6246
B6251
B6252
B6383
B6230
B6231
B6228
B6160
Lune
Wenning
Hindburn
Ribble
Hodder
Wharfe
Skirfare
Cam Beck
Brock
Keer

YORKSHIRE
DALES
NATIONAL
PARK
North
NIDDERDALE
SD
SE
Masham
Pateley Bridge
Grassington
Skipton
Keighley
Bingley
Bradford
Shipley
Burnley
NELSON
COLNE
Barnoldswick
Earby
Ilkley
Otley
Addingham
Silsden
Gargrave
Kettlewell
Buckden
Malham
Settle
Hebden Bridge
Queensbury
PUDSEY
Horsforth
Yeadon
Guiseley
Baildon
Haworth
Oxenhope
Foulridge
Trawden
Hellifield
KEIGHLEY MOOR
THE FOREST OF TRAWDEN
RUMBALDS MOOR
miles
km

Grid references: A B C D E F G — columns 5 6 7 8 9

Helmsley
Thirsk
Sowerby
Ripon
Boroughbridge
Easingwold
Knaresborough
Harrogate
Spofforth
Wetherby
York
Copmanthorpe
Bishopthorpe
Boston Spa
Bramham
Tadcaster
LEEDS
GARFORTH
Selby
Sherburn in Elmet
MORLEY
Middleton
Rothwell
CASTLEFORD

Major roads: A1, A1(M), A61, A168, A19, A59, A64, A658, A661, A660, A6120, A58, A63, A1237, A1079, A19, M1, M62, M621, A653, A6110

Place names (selection): Snape, Carthorpe, Pickhill, South Kilvington, Cold Kirby, Sproxton, Nunnington, Hovingham, Coulton, Scackleton, Dalby, West Lilling, Sheriff Hutton, Strensall, Towthorpe, Haxby, Earswick, Huntington, Clifton, Heworth, Osbaldwick, Murton, Heslington, Fulford, Naburn, Escrick, Skipwith, Riccall, Wistow, Barlby, Selby Abbey, Osgodby

Kirklington, Nosterfield, Thornborough, Sutton Howgrave, Middleton Quernham, Baldersby, Catton, Topcliffe, Asenby, Rainton, Dishforth, Cundall, Norton-le-Clay, Brafferton, Helperby, Raskelf, Crayke, Stillington, Farlington, Whenby, Brandsby, Stearsby, Skewsby, Yearsley, Coxwold, Ampleforth, Oswaldkirk, Gilling East, Cawton

Ripon Cathedral, Studley Royal, Fountains Abbey, Newby Hall, Aldborough Roman Town, Beningbrough Hall, Sutton Park, York Minster, Jorvik Viking Centre, National Railway Museum, Castle Museum, York Designer Outlet, Harewood House, Bramham Park, Lotherton Hall, Temple Newsam House, Thwaite Mills Industrial Museum, Middleton Railway, Selby Toll

Knaresborough Castle & Courthouse Museum, Mother Shipton's Cave, Plumpton Rocks, RHS Garden Harlow Carr, Mercer Art Gallery, Lightwater Valley, Norton Conyers, Marmion Tower, St Mary's Church, Ripley Castle

Rivers: Ure, Swale, Nidd, Ouse, Wharfe, Aire

A170 Nawton
Helmsley
Rye Dale
DUNCOMBE PARK
Duncombe Park
Pickering
PICKERING CASTLE
Ellerburn
Thornton-le-Dale
A170 Wilton
Ebberston
B1415
Snainton
Brompton

Great Edstone
Marton
Normanby
Costa Beck
FLAMINGO LAND
Allerston
B1258
Yedingham
East Heslerton

Wass
Ampleforth
BYLAND ABBEY
Coxwold
Sproxton
Harome
Nunnington
NUNNINGTON HALL
West Ness
East Ness
Salton
Little Barugh
Kirby Misperton
High Marishes
Low Marishes
Scampston
SCAMPSTON HALL
West Knapton
East Knapton
A64
West Heslerton

HOWARDIAN HILLS
Yearsley
Oswaldkirk
B1257
Stonegrave
South Holme
Butterwick
Great Habton
Ryton
EDEN CAMP MODERN HISTORY THEME MUSEUM
Broughton
Rillington
WOLDS WAY LAVENDER
Thorpe Bassett
Wintringham

Brandsby
Coulton
Hovingham
HOVINGHAM HALL
Wath
Slingsby
Fryton
Barton-le-Street
Appleton-le-Street
Swinton
Amotherby
Malton
Old Malton
Norton-on-Derwent
Scagglethorpe
Settrington
Place Newton

Scackleton
Stearsby
Dalby
Skewsby
Terrington
Ganthorpe
Coneysthorpe
Whitewall Corner
High Hutton
Low Hutton
North Grimston
Duggleby
Kirby Grindalythe
East Lutton
West Lutton

Crayke
Whenby
Farlington
Bulmer
Welburn
CASTLE HOWARD
YORKSHIRE LAVENDER
Firby
Langton
Kennythorpe
Birdsall
Wharram le Street
Sledmere
SLEDMERE HOUSE

Stillington
Sheriff Hutton
Whitwell-on-the-Hill
Thornton-le-Clay
Kirkham
KIRKHAM PRIORY
Westow
Burythorpe
Leavening
WHARRAM PERCY MEDIEVAL VILLAGE
Fimber

Huby
Sutton-on-the-Forest
SUTTON PARK
West Lilling
Foston
Crambe
Barton-le-Willows
Howsham
Harton
Leppington
Acklam
Thixendale

Shipton
Wigginton
Strensall
Flaxton
Bossall
Claxton
Scrayingham
Kirby Underdale
Painsthorpe
Fridaythorpe
Wetwang

A19
Skelton
Haxby
A1237
Earswick
Towthorpe
Huntington
Moor End
Stockton on the Forest
Gate Helmsley
Upper Helmsley
Buttercrambe
Skirpenbeck
Bugthorpe
A166
Great Givendale
Huggate
THE
North Dalton

Overton
Poppleton
West Huntington
New Earswick
Warthill
Holtby
Low Catton
Stamford Bridge
1066
Full Sutton
Bishop Wilton
246
Yorkshire Wolds Way

York
YORK MINSTER
JORVIK VIKING CENTRE
Osbaldwick
Murton
Dunnington
YORKSHIRE MUSEUM OF FARMING
High Catton
Youlthorpe
Gowthorpe
Fangfoss
Meltonby
Millington
Warter
Middleton-on-the-Wolds

Acomb
NATIONAL RAILWAY MUSEUM
CASTLE MUS
Heworth
Grimston
Kexby
Wilberfoss
Bolton
Yapham
Kilnwick Percy
Pocklington
STEWART'S BURNBY HALL GARDENS & MUSEUM
Nunburnholme

Woodthorpe
Holgate
Nunthorpe
Heslington
A1079
Newton upon Derwent
Barmby Moor
Hayton
Londesborough
Everingham

Bishopthorpe
YORK DESIGNER OUTLET
Crockey Hill
YORKSHIRE AIR MUSEUM
Elvington
Sutton upon Derwent
Thornton
Allerthorpe
Burnby
Thorpe le Street
Shiptonthorpe
Market Weighton
Goodmanham

Copmanthorpe
Acaster Malbis
Naburn
Wheldrake
Storwood
Melbourne
Bielby
Seaton Ross
Everingham
Harswell
A614
Sancton

Colton
Appleton Roebuck
Deighton
Escrick
LOWER DERWENT VALLEY
East Cottingwith
Thorganby
A19
Water End
Holme-on-Spalding-Moor
North Cliffe
North Newbald

Holme Green
Stillingfleet
Skipwith
North Duffield
Aughton
Ellerton
Laytham
Harlthorpe
Foggathorpe
Moor End
Sand Hole
Rascal Moor
South Cliffe
Hotham
South Newbald

Ryther
Kelfield
B1222
Bubwith
A163
Highfield
Gribthorpe
Willitoft
Spaldington
Bursea

Cawood
Wistow
Barlby
SELBY ABBEY
Selby
Osgodby
Menthorpe
Gunby
Breighton
North Cave
Everthorpe

Thorpe Willoughby
Brayton
South Duffield
Lund
Cliffe
Wressle
North Howden
Portington
Hive
Sandholme
West End
South Cave

Hemingbrough
Newsholme
Cavil
Eastrington
Gilberdyke
Newport
B1230
Ellerker
Brantingham

A63
Howden
HOWDEN MINSTER
Barmby on the Marsh
Asselby
Knedlington
Kilpin
Kilpin Pike
M62
Balkholme
Broomfleet
Brough

YORKSHIRE GARDEN WORLD
Drax
Boothferry
Laxton

0 1 2 3 4 5 6 miles
0 1 2 3 4 5 6 7 8 9 10km

A170 Buscel
Irton
Eastfield
Seamer
Yons Nab
CLEVELAND WAY
Ruston
Wykeham
A64
B1261
B126
Cayton
A165
A1039
Filey Brigg
Lebberston
Gristhorpe
A1039
Filey
Flixton
103
Folkton
Muston
FILEY BAY
Willerby
Staxton
A1039
Filey Bay
Primrose Valley
Sherburn
Ganton
YORKSHIRE WOLDS WAY
Hunmanby Moor
Hunmanby
Reighton Sands
Potter Brompton
Fordon
Reighton
Reighton Gap
Foxholes
Wold Newton
Speeton
B1229
Buckton
Bempton
Butterwick
Burton Fleming
Weaverthorpe
Grindale
A165
FLAMBOROUGH HEAD
Helperthorpe
Octon
Thwing
Flamborough
B1255
B1259
Octon Cross Roads
B1253
Boynton
PRIORY
SEWERBY HALL AND GARDENS
Sewerby
BONDVILLE MODEL VILLAGE
Rudston
BAYLE MUSEUM
Bridlington
Langtoft
Bessingby
West Hill
OLD PENNY MEMORIES
Cottam
Carnaby
Hilderthorpe
Kilham
Haisthorpe
A614
Thornholme
BURTON AGNES HALL
BURTON AGNES MANOR HOUSE
BRIDLINGTON BAY
Ruston Parva
Harpham
Burton Agnes
PARK ROSE BIRD OF PREY CENTRE
Garton-on-the-Wolds
Lowthorpe
Fraisthorpe
A166
Nafferton
Gransmoor
Elmswell
Little Driffield
Driffield
Great Kelk
Barmston
B1248
Kelleythorpe
Lissett
Gembling
A165
Ulrome
Tibthorpe
Kirkburn
Southburn
Wansford
Skerne
Foston on the Wolds
16
SKIPSEA CASTLE
Hutton
Brigham
CRUCKLEY ANIMAL FARM
B1249
Skipsea
Bainton
Hutton Cranswick
Church End
Beeford
Skipsea Brough
Kilnwick
Watton
Rotsea
North Frodingham
B1242
Lund
Lockington
Beswick
Hempholme
Dunnington
Thorpe
Burshill
Bewholme
Atwick
Holme on the Wolds
Baswick Steer
Brandesburton
North Cliff
South Dalton
Aike
Leven
Seaton
Hornsea
Scorborough
Arram
Leven Canal
Catwick
HORNSEA MUSEUM
Etton
Leconfield
Hull
Sigglesthorne
FREEPORT HORNSEA
Hornsea Bridge
Gardham
Eske
Routh
Little Hatfield
Goxhill
Rolston
Cherry Burton
Tickton
A1035
Rise
Great Hatfield
Mappleton
Long Riston
Arnold
Withernwick
Great Cowden
Molescroft
BEVERLEY
Beverley
Weel
Meaux
Skirlaugh
New Ellerby
Marton
West Newton
Aldbrough
A1079
A1035
BEVERLEY FRIARY
MINSTER
Woodmansey
Wawne
Old Ellerby
BURTON CONSTABLE HALL
Flinton
East Newton
Bishop Burton
Walkington
Thearne
Swine
Coniston
Thirtleby
Sproatley
Garton
Grimston
Bentley
Dunswell
Ganstead
Humbleton
Fitling
Hilston
High Hunsley
A164
A1033
Bransholme
Sutton on Hull
B1238
B1240
Little Weighton
SKIDBY WINDMILL
Inglemire
Kingston-upon-Hull
Bilton
Lelley
Elstronwick
Owstwick
Tunstall
Rowley
Cottingham
Sutton Ings
B1239
Burton Pidsea
Roos
North End
Riplingham
Eppleworth
Newland
Sculcoates
Stoneferry
Preston
B1362
Welton
YORKSHIRE WOLDS WAY
Kirk Ella
Willerby
A165
Summergangs
WILBERFORCE HOUSE
West End
Salt End
Hedon
Waxholme
90
West Ella
Anlaby
A1105
THE DEEP
STREETLIFE
Marfleet
A1033
Haven Side
Rimswell
Owthorne
Withernsea
North Ferriby
Hessle
HUMBER BRIDGE
TOLL
FERENS ART GALLERY
KINGSTON UPON HULL
91
Paull
FORT
Thorngumbald
Camerton
Halsham
Keyingham

1   **2**   **3**   **4**

A

B

C

D

E

F

NX

SC

NY

SD

St Bees Head

Workington

Whitehaven

Keswick

Cockermouth

Distington

Egremont

Cleator Moor

Frizington

Seascale

Ravenglass

Broughton in Furness

Millom

Ulverston

Askam in Furness

Flimby

Seaton

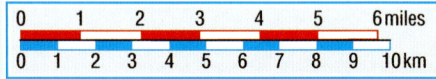

0 1 2 3 4 5 6 miles
0 1 2 3 4 5 6 7 8 9 10km

Penrith
Windermere
Kendal
Kirkby Lonsdale
Appleby-in-Westmorland
Ambleside
Bowness-on-Windermere
Sedbergh
Grange-over-Sands
Milnthorpe
Staveley
Coniston
Hawkshead
Arnside
Shap
Tebay
Orton
Glenridding
Patterdale
Pooley Bridge
Grasmere
Rydal
Troutbeck
Mungrisdale
Greystoke
Eamont Bridge
Clifton
Askham
Lowther
Hackthorpe
Bampton
Bampton Grange
Haweswater Reservoir
Kentmere
Long Sleddale
Sadgill
Shap Fells
Ralfland Forest
Kirkstone Pass
Ullswater
Helvellyn
Thirlmere
Keswick
Threlkeld
Matterdale End
Dockray
Dowthwaitehead
Wythburn
Brothers Water
Hartsop
Bridgend
Great Strickland
Little Strickland
Morland
Newby
King's Meaburn
Crosby Ravensworth
Maulds Meaburn
Great Asby
Raisbeck
Gaisgill
Kelleth
Bowderdale
Weasdale
Langdale Fell
Ravenstonedale Common
Howgill Fell
Brant Fell
The Calf
Cautley
Millthorp
Dent
Gawthrop
Killington
Middleton
Old Town
Barbon
Mansergh
Kearstwick
Casterton
Lupton
Farleton
Holme
Burton-in-Kendal
Hutton Roof
Clawthorpe
Whittington
Leck
Cowan Bridge
Ireby
Beetham
Storth
Yealand Redmayne
Heversham
Leasgill
Hincaster
Levens
Sampool Bridge
Crooklands
Endmoor
Gatebeck
Stainton
Sedgwick
Natland
Oxenholme
Old Hutton
Barrows Green
Burneside
Garth Row
Patton Bridge
Grayrigg
Lambrigg Fell
Lowgill
Beck Foot
Meal Bank
Watchgate
Garnett Bridge
Bowston
Ings
Crook
Underbarrow
Crosthwaite
Gregg Hall
Brigsteer
Row
The Howe
Cotes
Winster
Storrs
Far Sawrey
Near Sawrey
Grizedale
Satterthwaite
Force Mills
Rusland
Finsthwaite
Lakeside
Newby Bridge
Backbarrow
Haverthwaite
Ayside
High Newton
Low Newton
Witherslack
Lindale
Meathop
Field Broughton
Cartmel
Allithwaite
Holker
Cark
Kents Bank
Flookburgh
Penny Bridge
Greenodd
Arrad Foot
Bouth
Colton
Spark Bridge
Oxen Park
Grizedale Forest Park
Furness Fells
Bowmanstead
Skelwith Bridge
Elterwater
Little Langdale
Clappersgate
Waterhead
Chapel Stile
Low Wray
High Wray
Outgate
Colthouse
Troutbeck Bridge
Elfhowe
Lowbridge House
Forest Hall
Borrowdale
Bretherdale Head
Greenholme
Oddendale
Keld
Rosgill
Helton
Whale
Tirril
Sockbridge
Stainton
Dacre
Hutton
Penruddock
Motherby
Berrier
Troutbeck
Scales
Stanah
Fisher Place
Grisedale Tarn
Angle Tarn
Martindale Common
Dale Head
Bampton Common
Howtown
Sandwick
Knotts
Watermillock
Longthwaite
Wreay
Newbiggin
Carleton
Fair Hill
Catterlen
Laithes
Great Blencow
Newton Reigny
Little Blencow
Johnby
Hutton Roof
Moseдale
Langwathby
Edenhall
Culgaith
Ousby
Skirwith
Kirkland
Blencarn
Milburn
Newbiggin
Temple Sowerby
Knock
Lowmoor Row
Kirkby Thore
Dufton
Long Marton
Brampton
Bolton
Crackenthorpe
Colby
Burrells
Hoff
Drybeck
Cliburn
Melkinthorpe
Sleagill
Reagill
M6
A6
A66
A591
A592
A590
A685
A684
A65
A683
Lakeland Climbing Centre
Holehird Gardens
Dove Cottage and Wordsworth Museum
Rydal Mount
Brougham Castle
Mayburgh Henge
Castlerigg Stone Circle
Sizergh
Levens Hall
Lakeside and Haverthwaite Railway
Stott Park Bobbin Mill
Aquarium of the Lakes
Holker Hall
Conishead Priory & Manjushri Kadampa Meditation Centre
Killington Services (Southbound Only)
Tebay Services
Burton-in-Kendal Services
Farfield Mill Arts & Heritage Centre
Eden Valley Railway
Shap Abbey
Aira Force
Lakeland Bird of Prey Centre
Wetheriggs Country Pottery
Acorn Bank
Dalemain
Rheged
Beckstones Art Gallery
Windermere Steamboats & Mus.
The World of Beatrix Potter
Beatrix Potter Gallery
Hawkshead Courthouse
Brockhole - Nat Pk Visitor Centre
Townend
Windermere Submarine
Whitbarrow
Kendal
K Village Heritage Cen
Lakeland Wildlife Oasis
Heron Corn Mill
Great Asby Scar
Smardale
Clawthorpe Fell
Roudsea Wood and Mosses
Rusland Moss
Tarn Moss
Cliburn Moss
Saddleback or Blencathra
868
949
Helvellyn
802
828 High Street
774 Harter Fell
Loadpot Hill 671
609 Calf Top
682 Crag Hill
627 Leck Fell
NY
SD
108
109
100
92
93
Lake District National Park
Cumbria

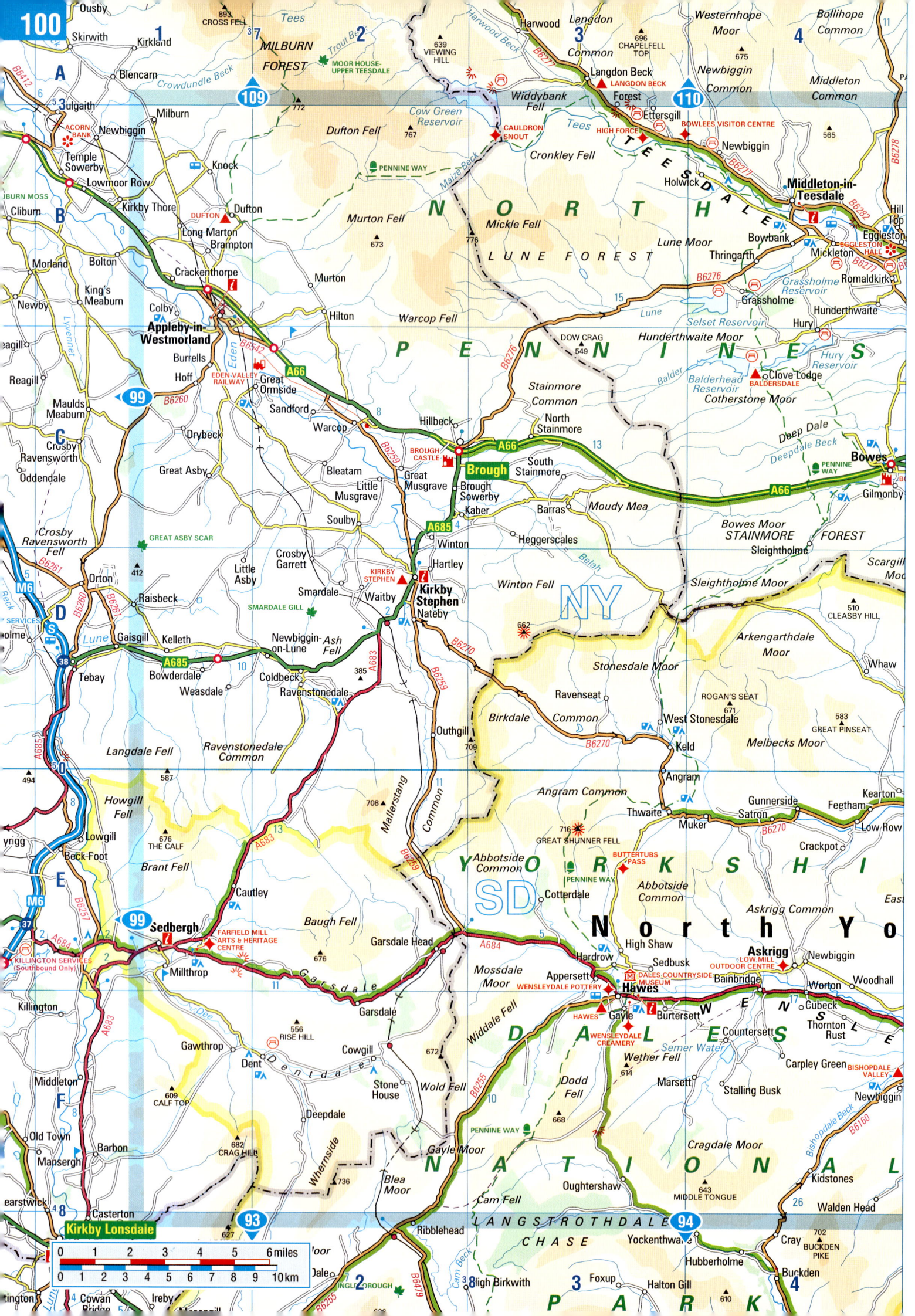

A B C D E F

1 2 3 4

Ousby
Skirwith
Kirkland
CROSS FELL 893
Tees
MILBURN FOREST
Trout Bk
Harwood Beck
Harwood
Langdon
Westernhope Moor
Bollihope Common

Blencarn
Newbiggin
Crowdundle Beck
MOOR HOUSE-UPPER TEESDALE
VIEWING HILL 639
Langdon Common
CHAPELFELL TOP 696
Newbiggin Common
Middleton Common

ACORN BANK
Temple Sowerby
Knock
Dufton Fell
Cow Green Reservoir 767
PENNINE WAY
Widdybank Fell
CAULDRON SNOUT
Langdon Beck
Forest
Ettersgill
HIGH FORCE
BOWLEES VISITOR CENTRE
Newbiggin 565
675

Lowmoor Row
Kirkby Thore
DUFTON
Dufton
Long Marton
Brampton
Murton Fell
Mickle Fell 776
673
Cronkley Fell
TEESDALE
Holwick
Middleton-in-Teesdale
Bowbank
Thringarth
EGGLESTON HALL
Mickleton
Hill Top

Cliburn
Morland
Bolton
King's Meaburn
Crackenthorpe
Colby
Murton
Hilton
LUNE FOREST
Lune Moor
Warcop Fell
Lune
Selset Reservoir
Grassholme Reservoir
Grassholme
Romaldkirk
Hunderthwaite
Hury

Newby
Reagill
Appleby-in-Westmorland
Burrells
Hoff
EDEN VALLEY RAILWAY
Great Ormside
Sandford
PENNINES
DOW CRAG 549
Hunderthwaite Moor
Balderhead Reservoir
BALDERSDALE
Clove Lodge
Cotherstone Moor
Hury Reservoir
Balder

Maulds Meaburn
Crosby Ravensworth
Oddendale
Great Asby
Drybeck
Warcop
Hillbeck
BROUGH CASTLE
Brough
Stainmore Common
North Stainmore
South Stainmore
Barras
Moudy Mea
Deep Dale
Deepdale Beck
Bowes
Gilmonby

GREAT ASBY SCAR
Little Asby
Bleatarn
Little Musgrave
Great Musgrave
Brough Sowerby
Kaber
Heggerscales
Bowes Moor
STAINMORE FOREST
Sleightholme

Crosby Ravensworth Fell
Orton
412
Raisbeck
Crosby Garrett
Smardale
KIRKBY STEPHEN
Kirkby Stephen
Nateby
Hartley
Winton
Winton Fell
NY
Sleightholme Moor
CLEASBY HILL 510
Scargill Moor

SMARDALE GILL
Waitby
Belah
662

Kelleth
Newbiggin-on-Lune
Ash Fell
Gaisgill
A685
Bowderdale
Coldbeck
385
Ravenstonedale
Arkengarthdale Moor
Whaw

Tebay
Weasdale
Outhgill
709
Ravenseat
ROGAN'S SEAT 671
GREAT PINSEAT 583
West Stonesdale
Keld

Langdale Fell
Ravenstonedale Common
Birkdale Common
Melbecks Moor

494
587
Howgill Fell
676 THE CALF
Brant Fell
708
Mallerstang Common
Angram Common
Angram
Thwaite
Muker
Gunnerside
Satron
Kearton
Feetham
Low Row
Crackpot

Lowgill
Beck Foot
Cautley
GREAT SHUNNER FELL 716
BUTTERTUBS PASS
PENNINE WAY
Abbotside Common
Askrigg Common

Abbotside Common
Y SD
Cotterdale
North Yorks

Sedbergh
FARFIELD MILL ARTS & HERITAGE CENTRE
Baugh Fell
676
Garsdale Head
Mossdale Moor
Hardrow
Sedbusk
High Shaw
DALES COUNTRYSIDE MUSEUM
Bainbridge
Askrigg
LOW MILL OUTDOOR CENTRE
Newbiggin
Worton
Woodhall

Millthrop
Garsdale
WENSLEYDALE POTTERY
Appersett
Hawes
Gayle
Burtersett
Countersett
Cubeck
Thornton Rust

Killington
Dee
Gawthrop
Dent
RISE HILL 556
Cowgill
Stone House
672
Widdale Fell
HAWES
WENSLEYDALE CREAMERY
Semer Water
WETHER FELL 614
Marsett
Stalling Busk
Carpley Green
BISHOPDALE VALLEY
Newbiggin

Middleton
Dentdale
CALF TOP 609
Deepdale
Dodd Fell 668
Cragdale Moor
Bishopdale Beck

Old Town
Barbon
Mansergh
682 CRAG HILL
Whernside
736
Blea Moor
Wold Fell
PENNINE WAY
Gayle Moor
NATIONAL

Casterton
627
Blea Moor
Cam Fell
LANGSTROTHDALE CHASE
Oughtershaw
MIDDLE TONGUE 643
Kidstones
Walden Head
26

Kirkby Lonsdale
Ribblehead
Yockenthwaite
Cray
BUCKDEN PIKE 702
Buckden

Cowan Bridge
Ireby
Masongill
Ingleton
Clapham
Sleigh Birkwith
Foxup
Halton Gill
610
Hubberholme
PARK

99 M6 M5
109 110
93 94

0 1 2 3 4 5 6 miles
0 1 2 3 4 5 6 7 8 9 10km

Spennymoor · Ferryhill · Trimdon · Fishburn · Byers Green · Middlestone Moor · Kirk Merrington · Rushyford · Chilton · Bishop Middleham · Butterwick

Newfield · High Grange · Binchester Blocks · Westerton · Mainsford · Ferryhill Station · Sedgefield · Hardwick Hall

Fir Tree · Howden-le-Wear · Hunwick · Witton-le-Wear · Binchester Fort · Auckland Castle · Coundon · Leasingthorne · Shilton Lane · A689 · A167

Bedburn · Hamsterley · Toronto · Witton Park · Escomb · Bishop Auckland · Coundon Grange · Eldon · Old Eldon · Mordon · Bradbury · Wynyar Village

Redford · Hamsterley Forest · Low Etherley · High Etherley · Toft Hill · St Helen's · St Helen Auckland · Shildon · Middridge · Newton Aycliffe · Foxton · Stillington · Thorpe Larche

Pikeston Fell · Woodland · Morley · West Auckland · Bildershaw · Royal Oak · Redworth · Aycliffe · Heighington · Great Stainton · Whitton · Redmarshall · Carlton

Woodland Fell · Butterknowle · High Lands · Evenwood · Cockfield · Bolam · Houghton le-Side · Walworth Gate · Brafferton · Coatham Mundeville · Bishopton · Little Stainton

Burnt Houses · Raby Castle · Wackerfield · Hilton · Ingleton · Killerby · Denton · Walworth · Beaumont Hill · Barmpton · Great Burdon · Sadberge · Elton · Longnewton

Kinninvie · Staindrop · Cleatlam · Little Newsham · Langton · Headlam · Summerhouse · Harrowgate Hill · Great Burdon

Cotherstone · Stainton · Winston · Whorlton · Piercebridge · Roman Bridge · High Coniscliffe · Darlington · Middleton St George · Eggscliffe

Barnard Castle · The Bowes Museum · Startforth · Boldron · Egglestone Abbey · Rokeby Park · Greta Bridge · Ovington · Caldwell · Eppleby · Forcett · Carlton · Manfield · Low Coniscliffe · Haughton Le Skerne · Durham Tees Valley · Aislaby

Westwick · Hutton Magna · Lane Head · Stanwick Iron Age Fortifications · Stanwick-St John · Aldbrough St John · Cleasby · Stapleton · Blackwell · Middleton One Row · Low Worsall

Brignall · Scargill · West Layton · Newsham · East Layton · Melsonby · Newton Morrell · Barton · Croft-on-Tees · Hurworth Place · Dalton-on-Tees · Neasham · Low Dinsdale · Girsby · Pictor

The Stang Forest · Dalton · Ravensworth · Gayles · Kirby Hill · Hartforth · Whashton · Gilling West · Barton Park Services · Middleton Tyas · Scotch Corner Services · Scotch Corner · Moulton · North Cowton · Atley Hill · East Cowton · Birkby · Hornby · Appleton Wiske · West Rounton

Langthwaite · Arkle Town · Hurst · Washfold · Skelton · Richmond · Richmond Castle · Easby · Easby Abbey · Skeeby · Uckerby · Scorton · Great Smeaton · Deighton · Welbury

Healaugh · Reeth · Fremington · Grinton · Swaledale Museum · Grinton Lodge · Marrick · Hudswell · Colburn · Brompton-on-Swale · Catterick · Catterick Bridge · Bolton-on-Swale · Whitwell · Streetlam · Danby Wiske · Lovesome Hill · East Harl

Swale Dale · Stainton · Marske · Downholme · Hipswell · Walkerville · Catterick · Catterick Garrison · Scotton · Tunstall · East Appleton · Great Langton · Kirkby Fleetham · Great Fencote · Thrintoft · Morton-on-Swale · Brompton · Winton

Reserve · Redmire Moor · Barden · East Hauxwell · Arrathorne · Hackforth · Little Fencote · Ainderby Steeple · Scruton · Northallerton · Romanby · Kirby Sigston

Yorkshire · Castle Bolton · Bolton Castle · Redmire · Preston-under-Scar · Bellerby · Garriston · Constable Burton · Patrick Brompton · Little Crakehall · Langthorne · Leeming · Morton-on-Swale · Warlaby

Carperby · Wensley · Leyburn · Swineside Ceramics · Great Crakehall · Crakehall Water Mill · Leeming Bar · Gatenby · Ainderby Quernhow · North Otterington · Thornton le-Bean

Aysgarth Falls · Swinithwaite · Harmby · Finghall · The Wensleydale Railway · Newton-le-Willows · Bedale · Aiskew · Londonderry · Sowber Gate · Newby Wiske · Thornton-le-Moor · South Otterington

Aysgarth · Thoralby · West Witton · White Rose Candles · Middleham · Spennithorne · Cowling · Burrill · Exelby · Maunby · Thornton-le-Street

Penhill · West Burton · Agglethorpe · Middleham Castle · Thornton Steward · Jervaulx Abbey · Thirn · Thornton Watlass · Firby · Theakston · Burneston · Snape · Thorp Perrow Arboretum · Kirby Wiske · Ne Esham

Melmerby · Carlton · Caldbergh · East Witton · Ellingstring · Low Ellington · Well · Carthorpe · Sion Hill Hall & Birds of Prey Centre · Maunby · South Kilv

Carlton Moor · Gammersgill · West Scrafton · Colsterdale · High Ellington · Low Burton · Kirklington · Pickhill · Holme · Sandhutton · Thirsk

Horsehouse · Coverdale · Healey · Fearby · Uredale Glass · Masham · Theakston Brewery · Nosterfield · Sinderby · Ainderby Quernhow · Howe · Carlton Miniott

Braidley · Hindlethwaite Moor · Colsterdale Moor · Leighton · Warthermarske · Swinton · Binsoe · Thornborough · Aerial Extreme · Pickhill · Baldersby

Woodale · Great Haw · Masham Moor · Leighton Res · Ilton · West Tanfield · Marmion Tower · North Stainley · Lightwater Village · Middleton Quernhow · Catton · Baldersby St James

Little Whernside · Scar House Res · Roundhill Res · Grewelthorpe · Mickley · North Stainley · Norton Conyers · Wath · Howgrave · Topcliffe · Asenby

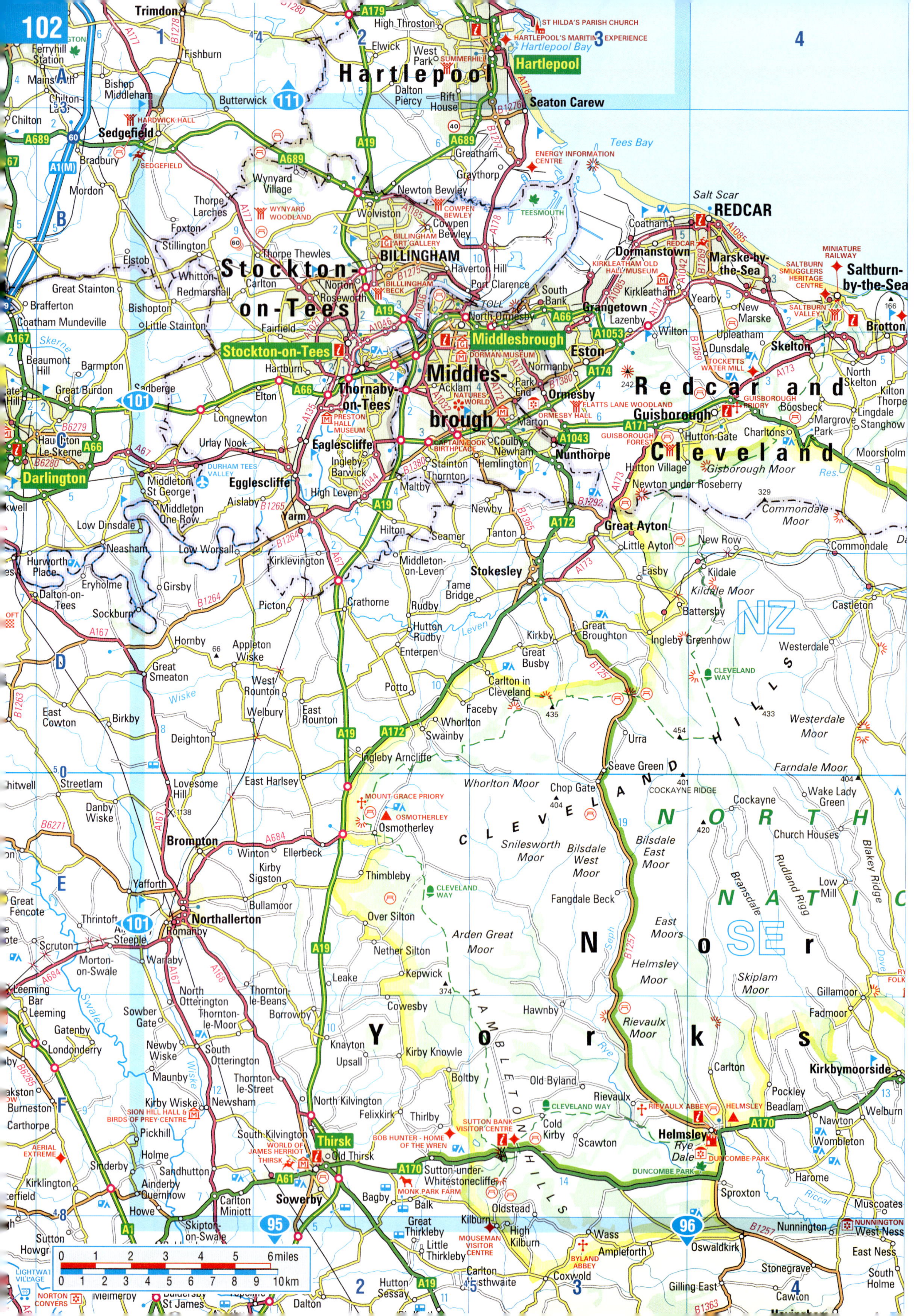

Trimdon

High Throston

A179

Elwick West Park

Hartlepool's Maritime Experience
Hartlepool Bay
ST HILDA'S PARISH CHURCH

Hartlepool

Ferryhill Station
Mainsforth
Chilton Lane
Chilton

Bishop Middleham

Fishburn

Butterwick

111

Summerhill

Dalton Piercy

Rift House

Seaton Carew

Bradbury
Mordon
A1(M)
67
A689
60

HARDWICK HALL
Sedgefield

Hardwick Hall

SEDGEFIELD

Bishopton

A19

A689

Greatham

Graythorp

ENERGY INFORMATION CENTRE

Tees Bay

Wynyard Village

Thorpe Larches

Foxton

Wolviston

Newton Bewley

Cowpen Bewley

Teesmouth

Salt Scar

REDCAR

WYNYARD WOODLAND

Thorpe Thewles

A177

A167
9

Great Stainton
Brafferton
Coatham Mundeville

Elstob
Stillington

Whitton
Redmarshall

Carlton
Roseworth

Norton

BILLINGHAM
BILLINGHAM ART GALLERY
BILLINGHAM BECK

COWPEN BEWLEY

Coatham

Kirkleatham
KIRKLEATHAM OLD HALL MUSEUM

Dormanstown

Marske-by-the-Sea

New Marske

SALTBURN SMUGGLERS HERITAGE CENTRE

MINIATURE RAILWAY

Saltburn-by-the-Sea

Great Burdon

Beaumont Hill
Barmpton

Bishopton
Little Stainton
Fairfield

Haverton Hill
North Ormesby

Port Clarence
TOLL
South Bank

Grangetown
Lazenby

Wilton

Upleatham
Dunsdale

Yearby

SALTBURN VALLEY
166

Brotton

Stockton-on-Tees

Darlington

DURHAM TEES VALLEY

Middleton St George

Middleton One Row

Middlesbrough
DORMAN MUSEUM

Middles-brough

Eston

Normanby

A174

242

Skelton

North Skelton

A173

Kilton Thorpe
Lingdale
Stanghow

Boosbeck

Margrove Park

Moorsholm

Redcar and

Cleveland

Haughton Le Skerne
A66

Hurworth Place
Eryholme

Neasham

Low Dinsdale

Middleton St George

Egglescliffe

Eaglescliffe

Ingleby Barwick

Stainton
Thornton

High Leven

Maltby

Newby

Hemlington
Coulby Newham

Nunthorpe

GUISBOROUGH FOREST

GISBOROUGH PRIORY

Guisborough

Hutton Gate

Hutton Village

Gisborough Moor

Newton under Roseberry

Commondale Moor
329

Dalton-on-Tees
Sockburn

Girsby

Picton

Low Worsall

Kirklevington

Yarm

Hilton

Seamer

Tanton

Middleton-on-Leven

Great Ayton

Little Ayton
New Row

Easby

Kildale

Kildale Moor

Commondale

Great Smeaton

Hornby

Appleton Wiske
66

West Rounton

East Rounton
Welbury

Deighton

Crathorne

Rudby

Hutton Rudby
Enterpen

Potto

Stokesley

Tame Bridge

Kirkby

Great Broughton

Battersby

Ingleby Greenhow

Westerdale

Castleton

NZ

Westerdale Moor
433

East Cowton

Birkby

Great Busby

Carlton in Cleveland
435

Wharlton

Urra
454

Seave Green

Farndale Moor
404

Streetlam

Danby Wiske
B6271

Lovesome Hill
1138

East Harlsey

Ingleby Arncliffe

Whorlton Moor

Chop Gate
404

COCKAYNE RIDGE
401

Cockayne

Wake Lady Green

Whitwell

Brompton

A684

Winton
Ellerbeck

MOUNT GRACE PRIORY

Osmotherley

Snilesworth Moor

Bilsdale West Moor

Bilsdale East Moor

420

Church Houses

NORTH

Yafforth

Kirby Sigston

Thimbleby

Fangdale Beck

Rudland Rigg

Low Mill

Blakey Ridge

Bullamoor

CLEVELAND WAY

Over Silton

East Moors

Helmsley Moor

Northallerton
101
Romanby

Nether Silton

Arden Great Moor

Skiplam Moor

Gillamoor

Fadmoor

Warlaby

Kepwick

Leake
374

Hawnby

Rievaulx Moor

Thrintoft

Morton-on-Swale

Cowesby

Scruton

North Otterington
Thornton-le-Beans
Thornton-le-Moor

Borrowby

Knayton

Kirby Knowle

Old Byland

Rievaulx

Carlton

Kirkbymoorside

Leeming Bar
Gatenby

Newby Wiske

Upsall

Boltby

KIRKBYMOORSIDE

Pockley
Beadlam

Welburn

Londonderry

Maunby

South Otterington

Thornton-le-Street
Newsham

Felixkirk

Thirlby

Cold Kirby

Rievaulx
CLEVELAND WAY

RIEVAULX ABBEY

Helmsley

Rye Dale

DUNCOMBE PARK

A170

Nawton
Wombleton

Burneston

Pickhill

Sowber Gate

Kirby Wiske

South Kilvington

North Kilvington

Sutton Bank Visitor Centre

BOB HUNTER - HOME OF THE WREN

Scawton

DUNCOMBE PARK

Harome

Muscoates

AERIAL EXTREME

Kirklington
Sinderby

Holme
Sandhutton

Thirsk
WORLD OF JAMES HERRIOT THIRSK

Old Thirsk

Sutton-under-Whitestonecliffe

HAMBLETON HILLS
14

Sproxton

LIGHTWATER VILLAGE

NORTON CONYERS

St James

Ainderby Quernhow
Howe

Sowerby
A61

MONK PARK FARM

Bagby

Balk

Kilburn

High Kilburn

Little Thirkleby

Great Thirkleby

MOUSEMAN VISITOR CENTRE

Oldstead

BYLAND ABBEY

Wass

Ampleforth

Oswaldkirk

Stonegrave

West Ness

East Ness

South Holme

Skipton-on-Swale

95

96

B1257

Nunnington
NUNNINGTON

Sutton Howgrave

Melmerby
St James

Carlton Miniott

Hutton Sessay

Coxwald

Gilling East

Cawton

0 1 2 3 4 5 6 miles
0 1 2 3 4 5 6 7 8 9 10km

5 6 7 8

A

B

C

D

E

F

G

CHRIS BIRKBECK INTERNATIONAL RALLY SCHOOL
Skinningrove
Carlin How
Boulby
Loftus A174
Staithes
Easington
Port Mulgrave
Hinderwell
Runswick Bay
Liverton
Roxby
Newton Mulgrave
Kettleness
Runswick Bay
Scaling
B1366
Ellerby
Mickleby
Goldsborough
A174
Lythe
East Barnby
Sandsend
THE DRACULA EXPERIENCE
SUTCLIFFE GALLERY
Sandsend Wyke
West Barnby
East Row
Whitby
Saltwick Bay
B1266
Ugthorpe
Dunsley
Newholm
WHITBY ABBEY
WHITBY
Scaling Dam Res.
Scaling Low Moor
Lealholm Moor
A171
Ruswarp
CAPTAIN COOK MEMORIAL MUSEUM
THE MOORS CENTRE
Danby
Stonegate
B1410
Stainsacre
High Hawsker
Ainthorpe
Houlsyke
Lealholm
Aislaby
Sleights
Briggswath
Sneaton
Ness Pt.
CLEVELAND WAY
Low Garth
Street
Glaisdale
Ugglebarnby
Sneatonthorpe
Raw
Robin Hood's Bay
OLD COASTGUARD STATION
Egton
MUSEUM OF VICTORIAN SCIENCE
Grosmont
Littlebeck
Fylingthorpe
BOGGLE HOLE
Glaisdale
Egton Bridge
GROSMONT GALLERY
Esk Valley
Robin Hood's Bay
Glaisdale Moor
Egton High Moor
Beck Hole
Old Peak
Goathland
A171
Ravenscar
Rosedale Moor
Flask Inn
Fylingdales Moor
Staintondale
YORK MOORS
Thorgill
WHEELDALE MOOR ROMAN ROAD
Wheeldale Moor
Goathland Moor
Saltergate
Harwood Dale Forest
SE
STAINTONDALE SHIRE HORSE FARM
CLEVELAND WAY
Rosedale Abbey
PICKERING MOOR
Pickering Forest
Langdale Forest
Harwood Dale
Cloughton Newlands
Cloughton Wyke
ROSEDALE
Cropton
Hartoft End
Stape
Broxa Forest
Cloughton
TA
Spaunton Moor
Forest
PARK
MOORLAND EXPERIENCE
TOLL
Broxa
Silpho
A171
Burniston
Cromer Pt.
Lastingham
Levisham
Langdale End
Hackness
Suffield
Scalby
Scalby Ness Rocks
SEA LIFE CENTRE
KINDERLAND
Hutton-le-Hole
Newton-on-Rawcliffe
LOCKTON
Lockton
Staindale Forest
Wrench Green
Everley
Barrowcliff
Newby
North Bay
Appleton-le-Moors
Cropton
NORTH RIDING FOREST PARK
Trouts Dale
Wykeham Forest
Scarborough
SCARBOROUGH CASTLE
ROTUNDA MUSEUM
Keldholme
Sinnington
Aislaby
NORTH YORKSHIRE MOORS RAILWAY
Low Dalby
Scarborough
South Bay
Kirkby Mills
Middleton
ST PETER AND ST PAUL CHURCH
DALBY FOREST VISITOR CENTRE
Dalby Forest
Sawdon
Hutton Buscel
West Ayton
East Ayton
Falsgrave
P&R
THE HONEY FARM
P&R
Cayton Bay
Great Edstone
Marton
Pickering
PICKERING CASTLE
Ellerburn
WORDSWORTH GALLERY
Ruston
A170
Seamer
Irton
Osgodby
Eastfield
Yons Nab
CLEVELAND WAY
Normanby
Thornton-le-Dale
Wilton
Allerston
Ebberston
Snainton
B1415
Wykeham
Brompton
A64
Cayton
Lebberston
A165
Little Barugh
FLAMINGO LAND
96
A169
High Marishes
Yedingham
B1258
East Heslerton
Sherburn
THE CARRS
Staxton
97
Flixton
Folkton
Muston
Salton
Great Barugh
Kirby Misperton
Low Marishes
West Knapton
East Knapton
Ganton
Potter Brompton
YORKSHIRE WOLDS WAY
A1039
Butterwick
Brawby
Little Habton
Great Habton
Ryton
Scampston
West Heslerton
A64
Fordon
Hunmanby

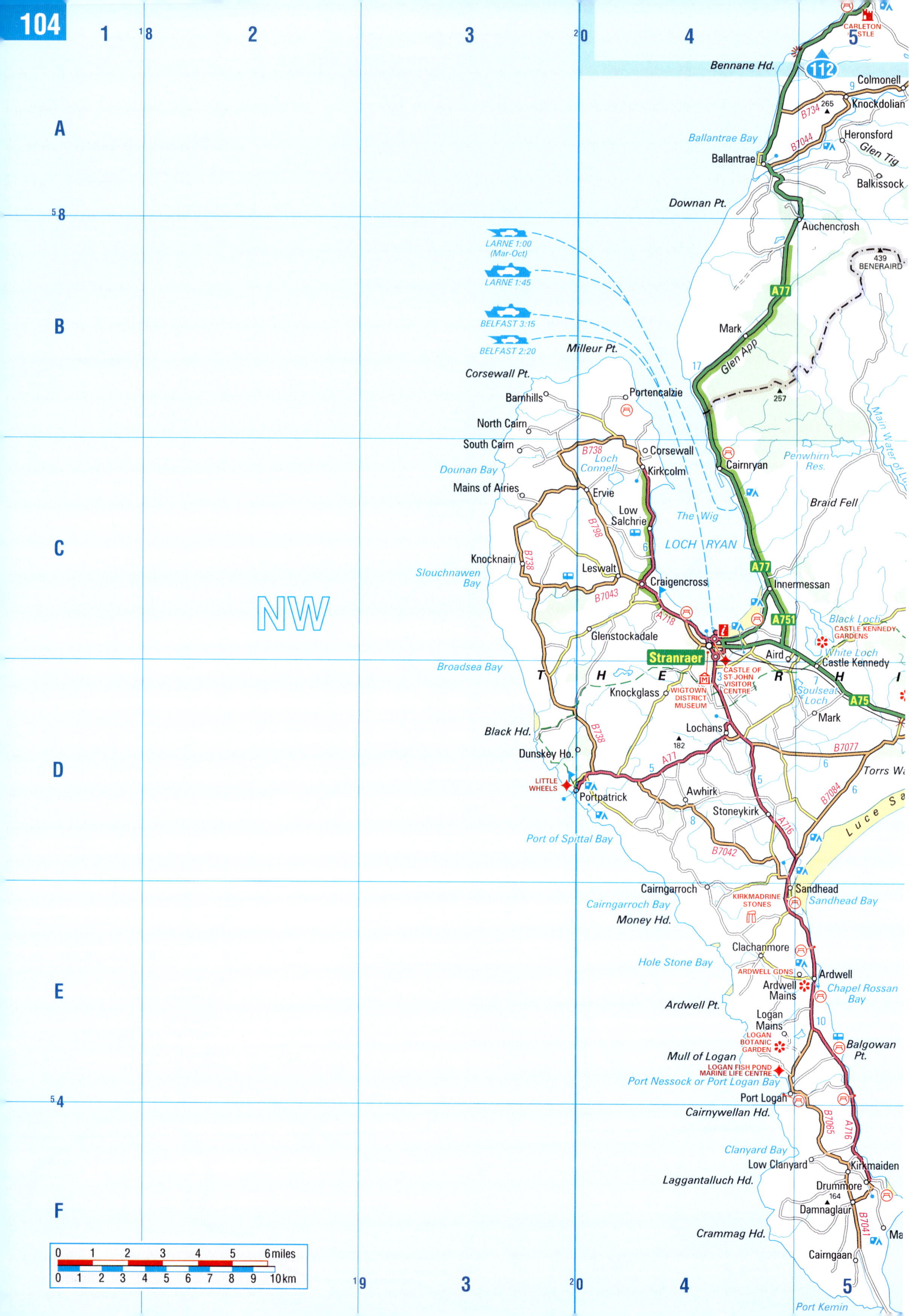
1
2
3
4
5
A
B
C
D
E
F
NW
Bennane Hd.
112
Colmonell
Knockdolian
CARLETON CASTLE
B734
265
Ballantrae Bay
Ballantrae
B7044
Heronsford
Glen Tig
Balkissock
Downan Pt.
Auchencrosh
439 BENERAIRD
LARNE 1:00 (Mar-Oct)
LARNE 1:45
BELFAST 3:15
BELFAST 2:20
Milleur Pt.
Corsewall Pt.
A77
Mark
Glen App
257
Barnhills
Portencalzie
North Cairn
South Cairn
Corsewall
B738
Loch Connell
Kirkcolm
Cairnryan
Penwhirn Res.
Dounan Bay
Mains of Airies
Ervie
Low Salchrie
B798
The Wig
Braid Fell
LOCH RYAN
Knocknain
B738
Leswalt
Slouchnawen Bay
Craigencross
Innermessan
B7043
A718
A751
Black Loch
CASTLE KENNEDY GARDENS
Glenstockadale
Stranraer
Aird
White Loch
Castle Kennedy
Broadsea Bay
T H E R H I
CASTLE OF ST JOHN VISITOR CENTRE
WIGTOWN DISTRICT MUSEUM
Knockglass
Soulseat Loch
A75
Mark
Black Hd.
Lochans
182
B738
B7077
Dunskey Ho.
A77
Torrs W
LITTLE WHEELS
Portpatrick
Awhirk
B7084
Luce Sa
Stoneykirk
A716
Port of Spittal Bay
B7042
Cairngarroch
Sandhead
KIRKMADRINE STONES
Sandhead Bay
Cairngarroch Bay
Money Hd.
Clachanmore
Hole Stone Bay
ARDWELL GDNS
Ardwell
Ardwell Mains
Chapel Rossan Bay
Ardwell Pt.
Logan Mains
LOGAN BOTANIC GARDEN
Balgowan Pt.
Mull of Logan
LOGAN FISH POND MARINE LIFE CENTRE
Port Nessock or Port Logan Bay
Port Logan
Cairnywellan Hd.
B7065
A716
Clanyard Bay
Low Clanyard
Kirkmaiden
Laggantalluch Hd.
Drummore
164
Damnaglaur
B7041
Crammag Hd.
Ma
Cairngaan
Port Kemin
0 1 2 3 4 5 6 miles
0 1 2 3 4 5 6 7 8 9 10 km

Pinmore Mains
260
5 6 7 8 9
Poundland
B734
Pinwherry
Bellamore
335 PINDONNAN
GALLOWAY
Corserine 814
25
Loch Harrow
Forrest Lodge
A
Ballochmorrie
Black Clauchrie
Cree
Loch Moan
MULLWHARCHAR 692
RHINNS OF KELLS
Loch Dungeon
746
Water of Tig
Duisk
Barrhill
Laggan
Eldrick
FOREST
Palgowan
843 MERRICK
Loch Enoch
Loch Neldricken
SILVER FLOWE
Loch Valley
Drumb

Arecleoch Forest
112
A714
9
Glentrool Forest
Glen Trool Lodge
BRUCE'S STONE
Trool 1307
112
Clatteringshaws Forest
5
8

Chirmorrie
B7027
Drumlamford Loch
Dornal
Bargrennan
Glentrool Village
GLENTROOL VISITOR CENTRE
Glen
Loch Trool
PARK
Loch Dee
Loch Grannoch
Clatteringshaws Loch
3

Miltonise
Craig Airie Fell
287
Loch Dornal
Loch Maberry
Clachaneasy
Dumfries
Loch Middle
Kirroughtree Forest
716 LAMACHAN HILL
CLA WIL
B

LAGGANGAIRN STANDING STONES
Polbae
Loch Derry
Knowe
and
353
106
18
Loch Grannoch
FELL

244
Artfield Fell
Carseriggan
Penninghame Forest
Challoch
A714
B7027
Minnigaff
Creebridge
A712
Palnure Burn
CAIRNSMORE OF FLEET
711
CAINSMORE OF FLEET
Galloway

New Luce
SOUTHERN UPLAND WAY
Drumphail 205
Black Loch
Loch Heron
Loch Ronald
213
Shennanton
Benfield
MINNIGAFF
Newton Stewart
Penkiln Burn
Clints of Dromore
C
Auchmantle
A75
B7052
Kirkcowan
123
A714
Palnure
Cree
9

Whitecairn
N S
Carscreugh
Craiglaw Mains
Dernaglar Loch
High Mindork
131
Baltersan
Causeway End
Carsegowan
6
GEM ROCK MUSEUM
Creetown
Glen

GLENWHAN GARDENS
GLENLUCE ABBEY
Glenluce
CASTLE OF-PARK
Dunragit
A47
3
Knock Moss
Fell Loch
Spittal
Torhousemuir
Carsegowan
TORHOUSE STONE CIRCLE
B733
Wigtown Sands
Wigtown
SCOTLAND'S BOOK TOWN
A75
CARSLUITH CASTLE
Carsluith
456 CAIRNHARROW
CAIRNHOLY CAIRNS
7
D

Milton
A747
7
Auchenmalg
Whitefield Loch
Castle Loch
Mochrum Loch
T H E
B7052
Culmazie
B7005
Bladnoch
A714
VISITOR CENTRE
Braehead
Kirkinner
B733
Baldoon Sands
Ravenshall Pt.
Ringdoo Pt.
Fleet Bay

Stairhaven
Auchenmalg Bay
Culshabbin
Alticry
B7005
197
Loch Head
Barrachan
M A C H A R S
11
B7005
B7052
B7085
Whauphill
A746
B7004
106
Stairhaven

CHAPEL FINIAN
Elrig
Mochrum
MOTE OF DRUCHTAG
75
B7085
Sorbie
B7052
Garlieston
Eggerness Pt.

Milton Pt.
A747
6
Airyhassen
Drumtroddan
Drummoddie
DRUMTRODDAN STONES
11
A746
B7004
GALLOWAY HOUSE GARDENS
B7063
Cults
E

Port William
B7085
B7021
Monreith Mains
Moor of Ravenstone
Bishopton
A746
Whithorn
Port Allen
CRUGGLETON CHURCH AND CASTLE

Barsalloch Pt.
BARSALLOCH FORT
Monreith
MONREITH ANIMAL WORLD, SHORE CENTRE AND MUSEUM
Monreith Bay
PRIORY AND MUSEUM
WHITHORN TRUST DISCOVERY CENTRE
A747
9
A746
Portyerrock Bay
Cairn Hd.
5
4

L U C E   B A Y
Glasserton
A746
4
146 FELL OF CARLETON
B7004
ST NINIAN'S CHAPEL
St Ninian's Chapel
Isle of Whithorn

Cailliness Pt.
ryport
ST NINIAN'S CAVE
Port Castle Bay
Cutcloy
F

5 6 7 8 9
MULL OF GALLOWAY
BURROW HEAD

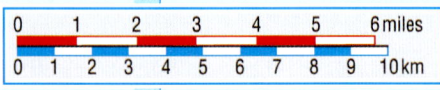

Loch Dungeon
Millquarter
Sundaywell
Milton
Loch Urr
417
373
SILVER FLOWE
746
Drumbuie
St John's Town of Dairy
Bogue
A702
Corriedoo Forest
Loch Valley
Garroch
113
B7075
Blackcraig
113
Clatteringshaws Forest
Glenlee
Balmaclellan
A712
Knocklearn
Gibbshill
Glenkiln
Loch Dee
Glatteringshaws Loch
381
New Galloway
A712
BLOWPLAIN OPEN FARM
398
Glen
HAN HILL
A762
Ironmacannie
Craig
317
Corsock
14
Merkland
Brooklands
A712
CLATTERINGSHAWS FOREST WILDLIFE CENTRE
RAIDERS ROAD FOREST DRIVE
Bennan Forest
Cairn Edward Hill
Drumrash
Loch Ken
Dumfries and
Auchenreoch Loch
Crocketford or Ninemile Bar
Milton
353
WILD GOAT PARK
18
Loch Grannoch
470
FELL OF FLEET
Mossdale
Parton
13
Galloway
Kirkpatrick Durham
A762
Stroan Loch
A713
Loch Ken
Crossmichael
8
Springholm
A712
Palnure
Cree
CAINSMORE OF FLEET
711
105
CAIRNSMORE OF FLEET
Fleet Forest
Loch Skerrow
14
Woodhall Loch
Craig
Old Bridge of Urr
Townhead of Greenlaw
Clarebrand
Haugh of Urr
Palnure Burn
A712
Clints of Dromore
Lochenbreck Loch
Laurieston
B795
MOTE OF URR
A713
B794
A711
B795
san
Big Water of Fleet
Loch Whinyeon
Laurieston Forest
A762
Loch Glentoo
THREAVE CASTLE
Castle Douglas
OLD BUITTLE TOWER
182
Barhill
Dalbeattie
way
GEM ROCK MUSEUM
B796
366 BENGRAY
Glengap Forest
Loch Mannoch
Loch Bargatton
KELTON MAINS OPEN FARM
THREAVE GARDENS
Carlingwark Loch
A745
Creetown
343
Glengap
Bridge of Dee
Rhonehouse or Kelton Hill
A75
B736
Dalb
Wigtown Sands
Glen
456 CAIRNHARROW
Ringford
A75
Gelston
B727
Barnbarroch
Wigtown
A75
MILL ON THE FLEET
Gatehouse of Fleet
Valleyfield
A711
9
Airieland
391 BENGAIRN
ORCHARDTON TOWER
Carsluith
CARSLUITH CASTLE
Anwoth
CARDONESS CASTLE
B727
FLEET
B721
Twynholm
GALLOWAY HYDRO VISITOR CENTRE
Kippford or Scaur
CAIRNHOLY CAIRNS
Girthon
VALLEY
Barharrow
A755
6
Tongland
BROUGHTON HOUSE AND GARDEN
MOTE OF MARK
EAST
Ravenshall Pt.
Sandgreen
MACLELLAN'S CASTLE
B727
Whinnieliggate
ROUGH ISLAND
STEWARTRY
Baldoon Sands
Ringdoo Pt.
Fleet Bay
Knockbrex
STEWARTRY MUSEUM
Kirkcudbright
Kirkcarswell
Auchencairn
COAST
Islands of Fleet
Borgue
89
St Mary's Island
Mutehill
135
Rascarrel
Balcary Pt.
Sorbie
B7004
Garlieston
Kirkandrews
B721
A711
Dundrennan
Orroland
Rascarrel Bay
Eggerness Pt.
WIGTOWN BAY
Borness
Kirkcudbright Bay
Townhead
Netherlaw
DUNDRENNAN ABBEY
GALLOWAY HOUSE GARDENS
105
Ross
Balmae
108
Abbey Hd.
Port Mary
Cults
CRUGGLETON CHURCH AND CASTLE
Borness Pt.
Little Ross
Whithorn
Port Allen
Portyerrock Bay
Cairn Hd.
NX
ST NINIAN'S CHAPEL
Isle of Whithorn
Cutcloy

0 1 2 3 4 5 6 miles
0 1 2 3 4 5 6 7 8 9 10 km

Dunscore
ELLISLAND FARM
Duncow
Applegarthtown
A74(M)
B723
5
6
7 Lochmaben
Marjoriebanks
17
8
9
P
A

Galaberry
Amisfield
Kirkton
A701
Tinwald
LOCHMABEN CASTLE
Castle Loch
Lockerbie
Bankshill
319

B729
A76
Newtonairds
240
Holywood
114
Newbridge
Locharbriggs
A709
Heck
114
B7068
Burnswark
287
Burnswark

Drumpark
Irongray
Heathhall
The Grove
DUMFRIES AND GALLOWAY AVIATION MUS
Hightae
18
BURNSWARK HILLFORT
Waterbeck

Shawhead
Terregles Banks
LINCLUDEN COLLEGE
Torthorwald
A709
Birkshaw Forest
Castlemilk
B7076
B7068
Middlebie
KIRKCO CHURC
Sp

Lincluden
OLD BRIDGE HOUSE MUS
Greystone
Collin
Kettleholm
Middleshaw
19
Ecclefechan
THOMAS CARLYLE'S BIRTHPLACE
19
BIRRENS FO
Eaglesfield
B

Dumfries
Maxwelltown
RAMMERSCALES HOUSE
249
Dalton
Middlebie
Creca
B722
Newt

A711
Cargenbridge
DUMFRIES MUSEUM & CAMERA OBSCURA
BURNS HOUSE
ROBERT BURNS CENTRE
Racks
Greenlea
A75
Carrutherstown
Hoddom Mains
B725
Kirtlebridge
20
A74(M)

Brae
Lochfoot
9
Islesteps
Kingholm Quay
Cleughbrae
Mouswald
B724
Hoddomcross
Brydekirk
Holle

Lochrutton Loch
Loch Arthur
Mabie Forest
Mabie
Kirkconnell
B725
Bankend
Lochar Moss
Lochar Water
A75
B7020
Charlesfield
108
B6357

Beeswing
Lochaber Loch
KIRKONNELL FLOW
Glencaple
Clarencefield
RUTHWELL CROSS
B725
B721
Annan
A75

DRUMCOLTRAN TOWER
SHAMBELLIE HOUSE COSTUME MUSEUM
New Abbey
SWEETHEART ABBEY
Shearington
Blackshaw
Ruthwell
DUNCAN SAVINGS BANK MUSEUM
Cummertrees
B724
Welldale
Dornock
Eastriggs

Kirkgunzeon
NEW ABBEY POW
NEW ABBEY CORN MILL
Bowhouse
CAERLAVEROCK CASTLE
Eastpark
Powfoot
Shawhill
Brov

N I T H
Overton
WILDFOWL AND WETLAND CENTRE
CAERLAVEROCK
Blackshaw Bank
C

383 LONG FELL
Loch Kindar
E S T U A R Y
Bowness-on-Solway
Port Carlisle
Glasson
Drumburgh

569 CRIFFEL
Drumburn
Bowness Common
Cardurnock
Anthon
DRUMBURGH MOSS
Whitrigg

B793
Carsethorn
Kirkbean
S O L W A Y   F I R T H   C O A S T
Wedholme Flow
Kirkbride
Fingl
FINGL

Drumstinchall
Caulkerbush
Prestonmill
ARBIGLAND GARDENS
Skinburness
23
SOUTH SOLWAY MOSSES
Oulton

Sandyhills
Colvend
JOHN PAUL JONES COTTAGE MUSEUM
Mainsriddle
Southerness
Silloth
Greenrow
Calvo
Seaville
Kingside Hill
Abbey Town
Newton Arlosh
Kelsick
Lessonhall
Waverbridge
Wigton
D

Rockcliffe
13
Portling
Southerness Pt.
Blitterlees
Highlaws
B5302
Dundraw
Waverbridge

Castlehill Pt.
Mersehead Sands
Beckfoot
Pelutho
Causewayhead
Newtown
Blencogo
Bromfield
B5302
13
Waverton
Waterside
E
A595

NX
Dubmill Pt.
Mawbray
Holme St Cuthbert
Langrigg
Bolton Low Houses

Edderside
New Cowper
Westnewton
108
Bolton Low Houses

Allonby
NY
Allonby Bay
Hayton
Aspatria
A596
B5299
Mealsgate
Boltongate
Sandal

Prospect
Oughterside
Blennerhasset
Torpenhow
Whitrigg
Ireby
Uldale

Crosscanonby
Allerby
Crosby-Villa
Parsonby
Threapland
Plumbland
Bothel
High Ireby
447 BINSEY
Over Water

Crosby
Bullgill
Gilcrux
B5301
Sunderland
931 SKIDD

MARYPORT MARITIME MUSEUM
Maryport
Dearham
Tallentire
Blindcrake
A595
Bewaldeth
Orthw

Flimby
Broughton Moor
Standingstone
Dovenby
Bridekirk
A594
Derwent
B5291
Bassenthwaite

Siddick
Camerton
Great Broughton
Little Broughton
Papcastle
WORDSWORTH HO
Embleton
BASSENTHWAITE LAKE

98
Seaton
Great Clifton
Brigham
Cockermouth
CASTLEGATE HO
COCKERMO
G

Workington
North Side
Bridgefoot
Greysouthen
A66
SANDYBECK MEADOW
WYTHOP MILL
Wythop Mill
MIREHOUSE

Westfield
Stainburn
Little Clifton
Eaglesfield
A595
A596
Mossbay
Winscales
Deanscales
Low Lorton
Thornthwaite Forest
A66

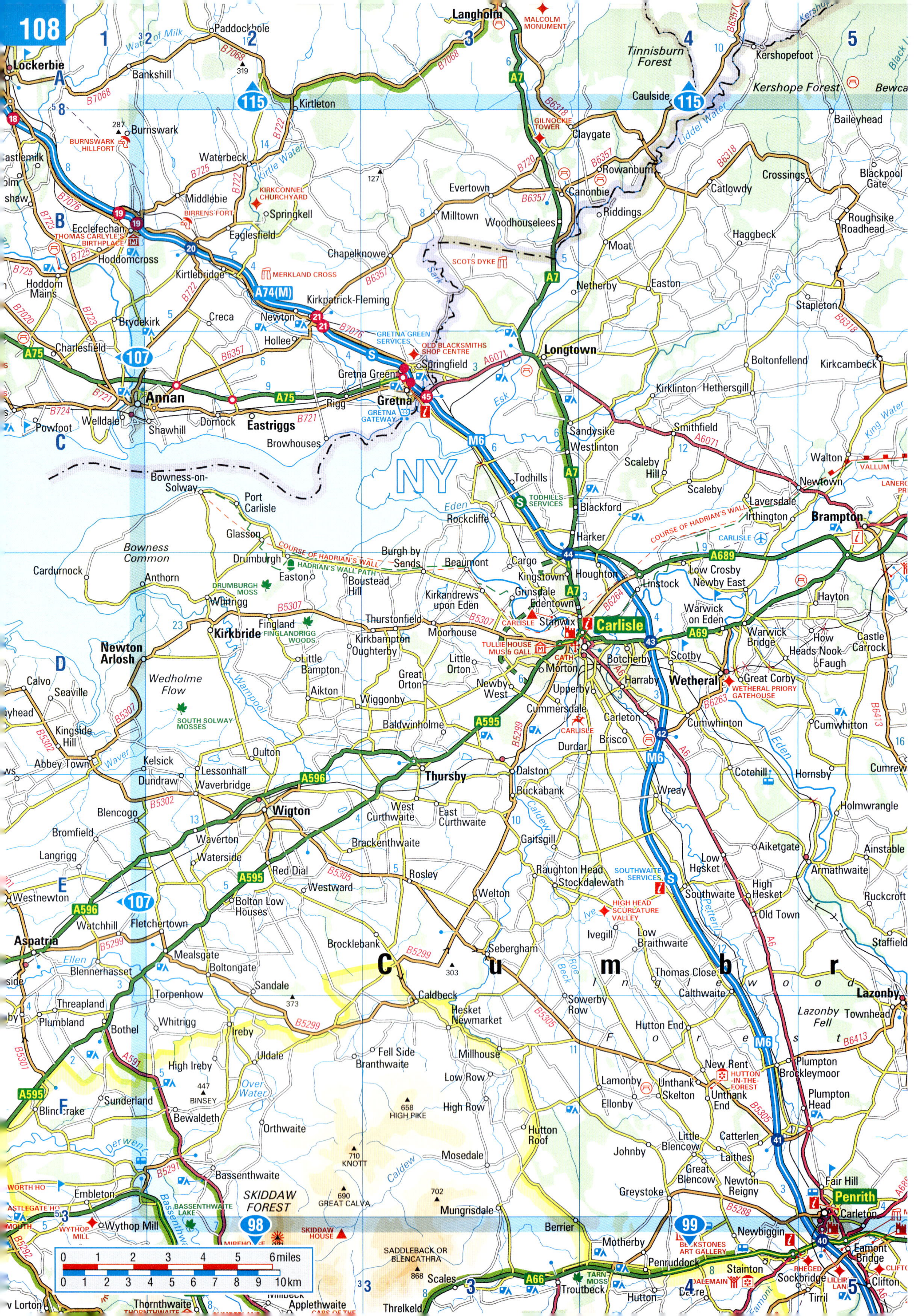
Lockerbie
Paddockhole
Water of Milk
Bankshill
Langholm
MALCOLM MONUMENT
Tinnisburn Forest
Kershopefoot
Kershope Forest
Bewcastle
Kirtleton
Burnswark
BURNSWARK HILLFORT
Caulside
Baileyhead
GILNOCKIE TOWER
Claygate
Waterbeck
Kirtle Water
KIRKCONNEL CHURCHYARD
Rowanburn
Canonbie
Riddings
Crossings
Blackpool Gate
Catlowdy
Liddel Water
Middlebie
BIRRENS FORT
Springkell
Evertown
Milltown
Woodhouselees
Roughsike
Roadhead
Ecclefechan
THOMAS CARLYLE'S BIRTHPLACE
Eaglesfield
Hoddomcross
Chapelknowe
Moat
Haggbeck
SCOTS DYKE
Hoddom Mains
Kirtlebridge
MERKLAND CROSS
Netherby
Easton
Kirkpatrick-Fleming
Stapleton
Brydekirk
Creca
Newton
A74(M)
Charlesfield
Hollee
GRETNA GREEN SERVICES
OLD BLACKSMITHS SHOP CENTRE
Longtown
Boltonfellend
Kirkcambeck
Springfield
Gretna Green
Annan
A75
Eastriggs
Dornock
Rigg
Gretna
GRETNA GATEWAY
Kirklinton
Hethersgill
Powfoot
Welldale
Shawhill
Browhouses
Esk
Sandysike
Westlinton
Smithfield
King Water
Walton
VALLUM
NY
Bowness-on-Solway
Port Carlisle
Todhills
TODHILLS SERVICES
Scaleby Hill
Scaleby
Newtown
Blackford
Eden
Rockcliffe
COURSE OF HADRIAN'S WALL
Laversdale
Irthington
Brampton
CARLISLE
Glasson
Bowness Common
Harker
Drumburgh
HADRIAN'S WALL PATH
Burgh by Sands
Beaumont
Cargo
Houghton
Linstock
Low Crosby
Newby East
A689
Hayton
Cardurnock
Anthorn
Easton
Boustead Hill
DRUMBURGH MOSS
Whitrigg
Kingstown
Grinsdale
Kirkandrews upon Eden
Edentown
Warwick on Eden
Stanwix
Carlisle
Fingland
FINGLANDRIGG WOODS
Kirkbride
Thurstonfield
Kirkbampton
Oughterby
Moorhouse
TULLIE HOUSE MUS & GALL
CATH
Botcherby
Scotby
Warwick Bridge
How
Heads Nook
Castle Carrock
Faugh
Newton Arlosh
Little Bampton
Little Orton
Great Orton
Newby West
Morton
Harraby
Wetheral
Great Corby
WETHERAL PRIORY GATEHOUSE
Calvo
Seaville
Wedholme Flow
Wampool
Aikton
Wiggonby
Upperby
SOUTH SOLWAY MOSSES
Kingside Hill
Baldwinholme
A595
Cummersdale
Carleton
Cumwhinton
Cumwhitton
CARLISLE
Brisco
Abbey Town
Waver
Oulton
Durdar
Kelsick
Lessonhall
Dundraw
Waverbridge
A596
Thursby
Dalston
Cotehill
Hornsby
Cumrew
Wreay
M6
Blencogo
Wigton
West Curthwaite
East Curthwaite
Buckabank
Caldew
Holmwrangle
Bromfield
Waverton
Brackenthwaite
Gaitsgill
Aiketgate
Ainstable
Langrigg
Waterside
Red Dial
Westward
Rosley
Raughton Head
Stockdalewath
SOUTHWAITE SERVICES
Low Hesket
High Hesket
Armathwaite
Westnewton
Bolton Low Houses
Welton
Southwaite
HIGH HEAD SCULPTURE VALLEY
Old Town
Ruckcroft
Watchhill
Fletchertown
Ivegill
Low Braithwaite
Staffield
Aspatria
Brocklebank
Sebergham
Mealsgate
Ellen
Blennerhasset
Boltongate
Cumbria
Inglewood Forest
Thomas Close
Calthwaite
Lazonby
Lazonby Fell
Townhead
Sandale
Caldbeck
Hesket Newmarket
Sowerby Row
Torpenhow
Threapland
Plumbland
Whitrigg
Bothel
Ireby
Hutton End
Uldale
Fell Side
Branthwaite
Millhouse
New Rent
HUTTON-IN-THE-FOREST
Plumpton
Brockleymoor
High Ireby
BINSEY
Low Row
Lamonby
Unthank
Skelton
Unthank End
Plumpton Head
Sunderland
Blindcrake
Over Water
HIGH PIKE
High Row
Ellonby
Bewaldeth
Orthwaite
Hutton Roof
Little Blencow
Catterlen
Derwent
KNOTT
Mosedale
Johnby
Great Blencow
Laithes
Fair Hill
Bassenthwaite
Newton Reigny
Embleton
GREAT CALVA
SKIDDAW FOREST
Mungrisdale
Greystoke
Penrith
Carleton
BASSENTHWAITE LAKE
Bassenthwaite
WYTHOP MILL
Wythop Mill
SKIDDAW HOUSE
Berrier
Newbiggin
BLAKESTONES ART GALLERY
Motherby
Eamont Bridge
SADDLEBACK OR BLENCATHRA
Penruddock
Stainton
Sockbridge
RHEGED
DALEMAIN
Scales
TARN MOSS
Troutbeck
Hutton
Dacre
Tirril
Clifton
Lorton
Thornthwaite
Applethwaite
Threlkeld
Millbeck
0 1 2 3 4 5 6 miles
0 1 2 3 4 5 6 7 8 9 10 km

Ridsdale
Bower
Hesleyside
Bellingham
Redesmouth
Swethope Loughs

116

Hopehouse
518 SIGHTY CRAG
490
KIELDER MIRES
312
116
Blacka Burn
Birtley
A68
Colt Crag Reservoir

Whitelyne Common
The Flatt
Paddaburn Moor
Churnsike Lodge
424 WHITE PRESTON
325
Whygate
Stonehaugh
Warks Burn
Wark
Park End
Simonburn
B6320
North Tyne
Great Swinburne
Gunnerton
Barrasford
A6079
B

Bewcastle
Spadeadam Forest
Butterburn
Black Fell
W a r k
F o r e s t
NORTHUMBERLAND
NATIONAL PARK
Haughton Common
Haughton Castle
Humshaugh
Chollerton
Colwe

Spadeadam Farm
Irthing
Wiley Sike
Thirlwall Common
Whiteside
Greenlee Lough
Broomlee Lough
PENNINE WAY
Simonburn
COURSE OF HADRIAN'S WALL
HADRIAN'S WALL PATH
Walwick
Chesters Roman Fort
Low Brunton
BRUNTON TURRET
Hill Head
Wall

West Hall
Gilsland Spa
BIRDOSWALD ROMAN FORT
HADRIAN'S WALL PATH
HOUSESTEADS ROMAN FORT VISITOR CENTRE
ROMAN ARMY MUSEUM
HADRIAN'S
GRINDON
345
VALLUM
18
Newbrough
110
A69
Warden
Fourstones
Acomb
TYNE GRE

Banks
Lanercost
Low Row
B6318 BIRDOSWALD
HADRIAN'S WALL PATH
Upper Denton
Gilsland
Greenhead
VALLUM
WALL
Henshaw
ONCE BREWED
CHESTERHOLM MUSEUM (VINDOLANDA)
Bardon Mill
Chesterwood
Chesterwood
B6319
6
110
MOOTHALL
Low Gate
Haydon Bridge
BORDER HISTORY MUS
HEXHAM
Hexham
ABBEY
C

Milton
A69
Haltwhistle
A69
Melkridge
Redburn
Plenmeller
South Tyne
Haydon Bridge
Langley
B6305
B6306

Denton Fell
Rowfoot
Plenmellar Common
B6295
Dye House
Dalton
Whitley Chapel

Hallbankgate
Tindale
Midgeholme
Lambley
Stonehouse
Bearsbridge
Whitfield
West Allen
Catton
B6303
Slaley Forest
D

TALKIN TARN
Farlam
Talkin
Tindale Fells
Forest Head
Halton Lea Gate
19
MAIDEN WAY
Eals
NY
Whitfield Moor
525
Ninebanks
Allendale Town
East Allen
15
Sinderhope
Hexhamshire Common
Broadwell House
Blanchland Moor
Devil's Water

621 COLD FELL
King's Forest of Geltsdale
Glendue Fell
South Tyne
Knarsdale
Slaggyford
14
NINEBANKS
Ninebanks
Allendale Common
489
Spartylea
Hunstanworth
478 NOOKTON FELL
Blanchland

482
Geltsdale Middle
Newbiggin
591
Ayle
574
Carrshield
614
Dirt Pot
Allenheads
540 BOLT'S LAW
E

Croglin
Scale Houses
656
602 WATCH HILL
SOUTH TYNEDALE RAILWAY
Blagill
GOSSIPGATE GALLERY
B6294
Nenthall
Nenthead
Coalcleugh
Middlehope Moor
ROOKHOPE NURSERIES
Rookhope

Renwick
Haresceugh
261
i
a
Raise
Bayles
Alston
ALSTON
Middle Fell
Nenthead
10
A689
NENTHEAD MINES HERITAGE CENTRE
NORTH OF ENGLAND LEAD MINING MUSEUM
Lanehead
N O R T H
Cowshill
673
604
W E A R D A L E
110
Eastg

High Bankhill
14
Unthank
GILDERDALE FOREST
Leadgate
B6277
A686
Garrigill
Wearhead
Ireshopeburn
St John's Chapel
10
Westgate
A689

Newbiggin
Gamblesby
Melmerby
710 MELMERBY FELL
MAIDEN WAY
Black Burn
Alston Moor
PENNINE WAY
746 BURNHOPE SEAT
Burnhope Reservoir
Daddry Shield
Ireshope Moor
Langdon Common
696 CHAPELFELL TOP
675 Newbiggin Common
Westernhope Moor

Glassonby
Winskill
Langwathby
Great Salkeld
Little Salkeld
Hunsonby
Ousby
Kirkland
Blencarn
893 CROSS FELL
Tees
685 ROUND HILL
22
Harwood
Ireshope Moor
Langdon Beck Forest
Ettersgill

Edenhall
B6412
Eden
Skirwith
Crowdundle Beck
MILBURN FOREST
Trout Beck
MOOR HOUSE-UPPER TEESDALE
639 VIEWING HILL
Widdybank Fell
Langdon Beck
LANGDON BECK
Newbiggin
BOWLES VISITOR CENTRE

MAYBURGH HENGE
BROUGHAM CASTLE
A66
99
Milburn
Newbigg
772
Dufton Fell
767
Cow Green Reservoir
100
CAULDRON SNOUT
HIGH FORCE
Cronkley Fell
A689
G

ACORN BANK
Temple Sowerby
Lowmoor Row
5
Newbigg
6
Knock
PENNINE WAY
Maize Beck
7
Holwick
8
Middleton-in-Teesdale

Northumberland

Ridsdale · Redesmouth · Birtley · Wark · Parl End · Simonburn · Haughton Castle · Humshaugh · Chollerton · Colwell · Great Swinburne · Gunnerton · Barrasford · Chollerford · Low Brunton · Walwick · Fourstones · Newbrough · Warden · Low Gate · Acomb · Sandhoe · Aydon · Newton Hall · Newton · Ovingham · Wylam · West Wylam · Clara Vale · Crawcrook · Ryton

Sweethope Loughs · Colt Crag Reservoir · Hallington Reservoir · Kirkharle · Kirkheaton · Great Bavington · Little Bavington · Thockrington · Hallington · Ryal · Ingoe · Fenwick · Heugh · Black Heddon · Matfen · Stamfordham · Ouston · Eachwick · Medburn · Dalton · Harlow Hill · Horsley · Heddon-on-the-Wall · North Walbottle

Wallington · Bolam Lake · Bolam · Capheaton · Harnham · Meldon · Molesden · Whalton · Belsay · Belsay Hall · Higham Dykes · West Newham · Milbourne · Ogle · Shilvington · Tranwell · Stannington · Ponteland · Prestwick · Darras Hall · High Callerton · Black Callerton · Woolsington · Kenton Bankfoot

Kirkley Hall · Berwick Hill · Northumberland Cheese Farm · Brenkley · Dinnington · Brunswick Village · Hazlerigg · Newcastle International · Westerhope · Gosforth · Kenton

Clifton · Bedlington · Nedderton · Plessey Woods · Saltwick · Seaton Burn · Blyth

NEWCASTLE UPON TYNE · Scotswood · Newburn · Throckley · Walbottle · Blaydon · Dunston · Whickham · Swalwell · Winlaton · Greenside · Coalburns · Barlow · High Spen · Highfield · Sunniside · Street Gate · Marley Hill · Kibblesworth

Course of Hadrian's Wall · Hadrian's Wall Path · Chesters Roman Fort · Wall · Hill Head · Moothall · Tyne Green · **Corbridge** · **Hexham** · Dilston · Riding Mill · Broomhaugh · Stocksfield · Painshawfield · Prudhoe · Mickley Square · High Mickley · Branch End · Cherryburn · Stephenson's Birthplace · Wylam Railway Mus · George Stephenson's

Border History Mus · Dilston Physic Gdn · Broomley · New Ridley · Hedley on the Hill · Chopwell · Blackhall Mill · Hamsterley · Rowlands Gill · Byermoor · Tantobie · Beamish · Urpeth

Dye House · Dalton · Slaley · Healey · Whitley Chapel · Highland Cattle Centre · St Andrew's Church · Kiln Pit Hill · Whittonstall · Newlands · Ebchester · High Westwood · Medomsley · Dipton · Tanfield · Tanfield Lea · Tanfield Railway · **STANLEY** · Catchgate · West Pelton · Grange Villa · The Middles · Craghead

Slaley Forest · Blanchland Moor · Derwent Res · Pow Hill · Edmundbyers · Muggleswick · Carterway Heads · Bridgehill · **Consett** · Shotley Bridge · Leadgate · Templetown · Iveston · Delves · Knitsley · Annfield Plain · Maiden Law · Burnhope · Lanchester

Hexhamshire Common · Broadwell House · Allendale Town · Allendale Common · Sinderhope · Spartylea · Hunstanworth · Blanchland · Castleside · Allensford · Muggleswick Common · Horsleyhope · East Butsfield · Satley · Cornsay · Cornsay Colliery · Esh · Quebec · Bearpark · Broom House Farm · Sacriston · Witton Gilbert

NY · **NZ** · Bolt's Law · Waskerley · Dirt Pot · Allenheads · Rookhope · Rookhope Nurseries · Stanhope Common · Collier Law · Wolsingham Park Moor · High Stoop · Tow Law · Sunniside · Cornsay · Hall Hill Farm · Diggerland · Langley Park · Ushaw Moor · Broompark · Esh Winning · New Brancepeth · Brandon · Brancepeth

North Pennines

Middlehope Moor · Lanehead · Cowshill · Wearhead · Ireshopeburn · St John's Chapel · Daddry Shield · Westgate · Eastgate · Stanhope · Frosterley · Wolsingham · Crawleyside · Weardale Railway · Durham Dales Centre · Thornley · Billy Row · Crook · Helmington Row · Oakenshaw · Page Bank · Willington

Langdon Common · Chapelfell Top · Langdon Beck · Forest · Ettersgill · Westernhope Moor · Newbiggin Common · Bollihope Common · Middleton Common · Pikeston Fell · Hill End · Bedburn · Hamsterley Forest · Fir Tree · Howden-le-Wear · Hunwick · High Grange · Witton-le-Wear · Binchester · Escomb

Weardale · **Durham** · Pawlaw Pike · Redford · Hamsterley · Howle · Woodland · Butterknowle · West Auckland · St Helen's Auckland · **Bishop Auckland** · Shildon · Coundon · Eldon

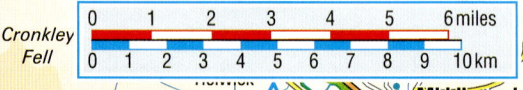

Cronkley Fell · High Force · Bowlees Visitor Centre · **Middleton-in-Teesdale** · Tees

Scale: 0 · 1 · 2 · 3 · 4 · 5 · 6 miles · 0 · 1 · 2 · 3 · 4 · 5 · 6 · 7 · 8 · 9 · 10km

5 6 7 8 9

A

B

C

D

E

F

G

BLYTH

West Sleekburn
Cambois
East Sleekburn
Cowpen
Bebside
New Delaval
Newsham
Seaton Sluice
Seaton Delaval Hall
Hartley
ST MARY'S LIGHTHOUSE
St Mary's or Bait I.
Holywell
New Hartley
Seaton
Delaval
Seghill
Earsdon
WHITLEY BAY
Monkseaton
Shiremoor
Marden
Cullercoats
BLUE REEF AQUARIUM
TYNEMOUTH CASTLE & PRIORY
Tynemouth
ARBEIA ROMAN FORT AND MUSEUM
North Shields
STEPHENSON RAILWAY MUSEUM
THE RISING SUN
Willington
South Shields
SOUTH SHIELDS MUSEUM
WALLSEND
Heaton
Tyne Tunnel TOLL
BEDE'S WORLD
ST PAUL'S MONASTERY
THE LEAS AND MARSDEN ROCK
Westoe
Marsden Bay
Jarrow
SEGEDUNUM FORT
Walker
Harton
Marsden
Gateshead
INTERNATIONAL STADIUM
NEWCASTLE KEEP
Byker
Hebburn
Hedworth
Whiteleas Cleadon
SOUTER LIGHTHOUSE
Whitburn Colliery
Boldon Colliery
Felling
Carr Hill
Pelaw
Boldon
Whitburn
Low Fell
W e a r
Downhill
Hylton Castle
Southwick
Fulwell
Roker
Wrekenton
Usworth
FULWELL WINDMILL
Monkwearmouth
NATIONAL GLASS CENTRE
ST PETER'S CHURCH
SUNDERLAND MINSTER
Castletown
STATION MUS
South Hylton
Pallion
High Barnes
WASHINGTON
Lambton
Pennywell
Sunderland
Hendon
WASHINGTON SERVICES
THE WILDFOWL & WETLANDS TRUST
PENSHAW MON
Fatfield
East Herrington
New Silksworth
NZ
Birtley
Ouston
Barley Mow
Rickleton
Penshaw
Shiney Row
Bournmoor
New Herrington
Doxford Park
Tunstall
Ryhope
RYHOPE ENGINES MUS
THE ANKERS HOUSE
Newbottle
Fence Houses
Burdon
Chester Moor
Great Lumley
Colliery Row
Seaton
Northlea
SEAHAM
A167
A1(M)
HOUGHTON-LE-SPRING
East Rainton
West Lea
West Rainton
Hetton-le-Hole
Dalton-le-Dale
Kimblesworth
FINCHALE PRIORY
Leamside
Murton
Cold Hesledon
Pity Me
Low Moorsley
DALTON PARK
Easington Lane
Hawthorn
Framwellgate Moor
Pittington
South Hetton
Beacon Pt.
DURHAM LIGHT INFANTRY MUS
Carville
Easington Colliery
Sherburn
Sherburn Hill
Haswell
Haswell Plough
Easington
Littletown
DURHAM CITY
DURHAM CATH
DURHAM UNIV ORIENTAL MUS
Shincliffe
Shadforth
Ludworth
Shotton Colliery
Horden
Old Cassop
Thornley
PETERLEE
Shotton
CASTLE EDEN DENE
Blackhall Colliery
Wheatley Hill
Blackhall Rocks
Bowburn
Old Cassop
Quarrington
CASSOP VALE
Castle Eden
High Hesleden
DURHAM COAST
Croxdale
Sunderland Bridge
DURHAM SERVICES
Quarrington Hill
Wingate
Hesleden
Deaf Hill
Station Town
Hart Station
Kelloe
Hutton Henry
Sheraton
Hart
Coxhoe
Trimdon Colliery
Tudhoe
Cornforth
Trimdon Grange
Trimdon
High Throston
ST HILDA'S PARISH CHURCH
Spennymoor
HARTLEPOOL'S MARITIME EXPERIENCE
Hartlepool Bay
Ferryhill
THRISLINGTON
Fishburn
Elwick
West Park
SUMMERHILL
Kirk Merrington
Ferryhill Station
Middlestone
Mainsforth
Hartlepool
Bishop Middleham
Seaton Carew
Leasingthorne
Chilton Lane
Dalton Piercy
Rift House
Chilton
Butterwick
Rushyford
A689
Sedgefield
Tees Bay
NEWTON AYCLIFFE
Bradbury
SEDGEFIELD
A19
A689
Greatham
ENERGY INFORMATION CENTRE
Middridge
Mordon
Graythorp
Wynyard Village
Newton Bewley
Thorpe
WYNYARD
COWPEN
Salt Scar

AMSTERDAM 15:30

117
101
102

1 2 2

A

Sornhill

Crossroads

B731 DUNDONALD CASTLE A77 Craigie

Barassie B730 Bogend

North Bay Muirhead A759 Loans Symington A76 B744

Troon A78 Hansel Millburn Auchmillan

South Bay Village A719 Bachelor's Mossgiel

ROYAL TROON A749 50 70 Club Burn's House Water

118 118 Museum Mauchline

Lady Isle A759 70 Tarbolton M

Monkton A77 B739 12 Ayr Gorge Failford

LARNE 1:50 A77 B742 Woodlands Haugh

(March-Oct) GLASGOW PRESTWICK INTERNATIONAL Mossblown Stair

Prestwick A79 St B743 Crosshill

Woodfield 30 Quivox Annbank Trabboch Ochiltree

B

Newton on Ayr B743 Whitletts B744

Wallacetown 30 B742 Coylton Coalhall

Ayr AYR Belston Joppa Hillhead Drongan

Seafield Belmont Masonhill A70 B7046

BURNS COTTAGE MACLAURIN GALLERY Martnaham Barbieston B7046

Heads of Ayr & ROZELLE HOUSE Loch Sinclairston

HEADS OF AYR FARM PARK Doonfoot 60 Hayhill

C A719 Laigh Glengall TAM O'SHANTER Littlemill

Alloway EXPERIENCE B742 Hollybush Rankinston

Fisherton BURNS NATIONAL HERITAGE PARK A713 13

Dunure 287 A77 B7034 Minishant Dalrymple Water of Coyle

ELECTRIC BRAE Culroy B7024 429 NS

Culzean Bay B7023 B7045 196 KILMEIN HILL

270 Whitefaulds Maybole Kirkmichael Polnessan Patna Burnfoot

CULZEAN CASTLE 60 COLLEGIATE CHURCH Waterside BENBEOCH

CULZEAN 77 60 7 Aitkenhead Loch Spallander DOON VALLEY 464 Burnton

Maidenhead Bay A719 CROSSRAGUEL ABBEY Reservoir HERITAGE MUSEUM SCOTTISH INDUSTRIAL

Maidens Kirkoswald B7045 Crosshill RAILWAY CENTRE

TURNBERRY SOUTER JOHNNIE'S COTTAGE 4 A713

Turnberry Bay 252 BLAIRQUHAN 11 B741 Dalmellington

Turnberry Brest Rocks 60 Ruglen B741 Straiton Bogton Loch CATHCARTSON

D 60 Townhead B7023 361 Bellsbank VISITOR CENTRE

Dipple Wallacetown South 425 CAMPE HILL

5 Burnhead B741 11 Dailly BIG HILL OF GLENMOUNT 453

Old Dailly BARGANY GARDENS Ayrshire 382 10

6 0 60 Penkill Tairlaw Forest Loch Finlas LOCH DOON

Girvan B734 Houdston Linfern Loch Bradan Lamloch

Glendoune Penwhapple Loch Loch Doon CASTLE

Woodland Bay Res. Dalwyne 472 Craigmalloch

E 60 355 MULL OF MILJOAN Loch Riecawr

A77 Pinminnoch Tormitchell South Balloch K

Kennedy's Pass 60 C A Barr R R I C Loch

297 Auchensoul Changue Macaterick

12 GREY HILL A714 Pinmore Forest CARRICK FOREST 695 MEAUL

Lendalfoot Straid Currarie Merkland Stinchar B734 565 768

CARLETON CASTLE 260 Pinmore Mains CRAIGENREOCH NX

Poundland 335 843 CORSERINE

Colmonell B734 Pinwherry PINDONNAN MERRICK 814

104 Bellamore G A L L O W A Y MULLWHARCHAR RHINNS OF KELLS

F Knoc olian Ballochmorrie Black Loch 716

Heronsford Clauchrie Cree Moan Loch Enoch Loch Harrow

Glen Tig Water of Tig Dusk Palgowan Loch Neldricken 746

Balkissock Barrhill F O R E S T Loch Valley SILVER FLOWE Loch

265 Laggan Eldrick BRUCE'S Harrow

A714 9 Glentrool STONE 1307

hencrosh Arecleoch Forest 105 Forest Glen Trool Trool Loch Trool 105 Loch Dee

8 Glentrool Lodge Clatt

B7027 Drumlamford Village GLENTROOL P A R K

Loch VISITOR CENTRE

Dornal Bargrennan Loch Dornal LAMACHAN HILL Glat

0 1 2 3 4 5 6 miles

0 1 2 3 4 5 6 7 8 9 10km

Glengavel Reservoir

Avon

522 NUTBERRY HILL

River Wethan

Soulburn

Braehead

Happendon

CAIRN LODGE (HAPPENDON) SERVICES

8

12

Uddington

Glarf Water

5 6 7 2 9

434 WEDDER HILL

119

466 MIDDLEFIELD LAW

B743

Netherwood

A70

Glenbuck

Douglas West

ST ES

Dc

119

M74

Robert

DUNC

Roberton Law

A

3

Catrine

SORN CASTLE

Sorn

Smallburn

Muirkirk

Kames

Hareshaw Hill 465

Glespin

12

Douglas Water

392 AUCHENSAUGH HILL

Middle Muir

Crawfordjohn

Glentaggart

B7078

i S

13

B

Airds Moss

Ayr

B743

Cronberry

593 CAIRN TABLE

Duneaton Water

B740

DRAKE LAW 483

494 RAKE LAW

B797

E a s t

B705

Back Rogerton

Lugar

497 WARDLAW HILL

Glenmuir

Glenmuirshaw

LOWTHER

553 WELLGRAIN DOD

B7040

Elv

B7036

Auchinleck

Holmhead

Logan

Craigens

Dalblair

Glenmuir Water

478 MOUNT STUART

114

Elvan Water

A y r s h i r e

BAIRD INSTITUTE MUS.

KEIR HARDIE STATUE

Cumnock

Netherthird

Fingland

Leadhills

LEADHILLS & WANLOCKHEAD RLY

C

Skares

DOON VALLEY RARE BREEDS CENTRE

A76

Pathhead

Mansfield

509 KIRKLAND HILL

Kirkland

MUSEUM OF LEAD MINING

WANLOCKHEAD BEAM ENGINE

Wanlockhead

LOTUS LODGE

732 GREEN LOWTHER

Connel Park Bankglen

New Cumnock

Nith

10

Kirkconnel

B740

485 CONRIG HILL

725 LOWTHER HILL

Burnside

Dalleagles

THE KNIPE 575

Kelloholm

Kello Water

Crawick

Sanquhar

Mennock Pass

18

Potrail Water

Afton Water

10

B741

700 BLACKCRAIG HILL

Euchan Water

TOLBOOTH MUSEUM

SANQUHAR POST OFFICE

Mennock

B797

13

449 CAIRN HILL

SOUTHERN UPLAND WAY

H

I

L

L

S

569 ENOCH HILL

Afton Reservoir

NS

478

A76

Durisdeermill

691

BALLENCLE

DURISDEER PARISH CH.

D

Scar Water

554 CAIRNKINNA HILL

Enterkinfoot

Durisdeer

Enoch

A702

6 0

Carsphairn Forest

D u m f r i e s

DRUMLANRIG CASTLE

Holestane

443 MORTON CASTLE

797 CAIRNSMORE OF CARSPHAIRN

Corlae

a n d

Auchenbrack

Carronbridge

Gatelawbridge

Brockloch

A713

580 BENBRACK

Benbuie

G a l l o w a y

NX

500

Shinnel Water

Scar Water

Auchenbainzie

Burnhead

Thornhill

E

Garryhorn

Carsphairn

B729

CAIRN AVEL

Bardennoch

Water of Ken

Dundeugh Forest

SOUTHERN UPLAND WAY

Dalwhat Water

Penpont

Tynron

372

8

Keir Mill

114

Closeburn

Castlemaddy

Knowehead

KENDOON

Glenhoul

Black Water

Craigdarroch

JAMES PATERSON MUSEUM

Moniaive

Kirkland

A702

357

Park

A76

G L E N K E N S

Dundeugh

Kendoon

Carsfad Loch

Glencrosh

MAXWELTON HOUSE

Straith

Wallaceton

Dalmacallan Forest

Glenmidge

Auldgirth

Forrest Lodge

Kendoon Loch

B7000

385 WETHER HILL

Castlefairn

Holmhead

12

Lochurr

432 BOGRIE HILL

Loch Urr

Nith

13

ELLIS FARM

Loch Dungeon

Earlstoun Loch

Millquarter

417

Lochinvar

Sundaywell

Milton

Dunscore

B729

240

F

Drumbuie

St John's Town of Dalry

Bogue

A702

Corriedoo Forest

373

Newtonairds

ringshaws Forest

381

Garroch

A762

2

Blackcraig

Knocklearn

Drumpark

Irongray

5 8

Glenlee

106

A712

B

A762

New Galloway

A712

Balmaclellan

Gibbshill

106

Glenkiln Res.

Terregles

G

Loch

CLATTERINGSHAWS FOREST WILDLIFE CENTRE

BLOWPLAIN N FARM

Ironmacannie

317

Corsock

14 7

Glenkiln

Glen

398

Shawhead

8

9

Newbr

5 6 7

S
Happendon
Uddington
12
11
Synnington
Coulter
3
Drumelzier
Rachan Mill
4
5

West
A
ST BRIDES
Douglas
A70
406
Wiston
Newton
Lamington
B7055
2
B7078
Clyde Water
A702
0
1
PYKESTONE HILL
737
Langhaugh
A

Roberton Law
M74
120
DUNGAVEL HILL
569
8
Culter Water
543
BLAKEHOPE HEAD
11
120
Stanhope

AUCHENSAUGH HILL
392
B7078
Roberton
Cowgill Upper Reservoir
CULTER FELL
748
Crookhaugh
510
Hearthstane
637
817
DOLLAR LAW
696
BLACK LAW

Middle Muir
B7078
3
i
S
ABINGTON SERVICES
Culter Waterhead Reservoir
GLENWHAPPEN RIG
688
Tweedsmuir
840
BROAD LAW

Glentaggart
B
Crawfordjohn
13
Abington
TEWSGILL HILL
Camps Water
Camps Reservoir
Glenbreck
Meggethead
Megget Reservoir

B740
DRAKE LAW
Kirkton
Crawford
Talla Reservoir
Talla Linnfoots
LOCHCRAIG HEAD
800

neaton Water
483
5
14
550
553
CRAIGMAID
690
Fruid Reservoir
Loch Skeen
882
WHITE COOMB
Birkhill
21

14
RAKE LAW
494
553
WELLGRAIN DOD
B7040
Elvanfoot
15
546
CLYDE LAW
Source of River Tweed
GREY MARE'S TAIL WATERFALLS
677

113
Elvan Water
Leadhills
March
Watermeetings
14
DEVIL'S BEEF TUB
808
HART FELL
753
SADDLE YOKE

C
MUSEUM OF LEAD MINING
LEADHILLS & WANLOCKHEAD RLY
A702
Nether Howecleuch
Ericstane
Capplegill

WANLOCKHEAD BEAM ENGINE
Wanlockhead
LOTUS LODGE
GREEN LOWTHER
732
B719
Granton
Howslack
Roundstonefoot
CAPEL FELL
692
ETTRICK PEN

ONRIG HILL
485
725
LOWTHER HILL
SOUTHERN UPLAND WAY
SOUTHERN UPLAND WAY
A74(M)
A701
Moffat
MUSEUM
Moffat Water
678
Dumcrieff
688
LOCH FELL

Mennock
Mennock Pass
18
Daer Reservoir
NS
NT
Coatsgate
15
ANNAN
BLACK

A76
13
449
CAIRN HILL
Potrail Water
691
BALLENCLEUCH LAW
Easter Earshaig
Beattock
Dumcrieff

D
Enterkinfoot
Durisdeermill
DURISDEER PARISH CHURCH
Durisdeer
407
Kinnelhead
Eskdale

6
0
Enoch
668
GANA HILL
QUEENSBERRY
512
Laverhay
484

Holestane
443
MORTON CASTLE
Locherben
399
Lochwood
Waterhead
Sandyford

DRUMLANRIG CASTLE
Carronbridge
NX
NY
Newton
Black Es Reservoir

E
Auchenbainzie
Burnhead
Gatelawbridge
Forest of Ae
St Ann's
16
S
ANNANDALE WATER SERVICES

Pe ont
Thornhill
113
Loch Ettrick
Johnstonebridge
Dinwoodie Mains
Boreland

8
Keir Mill
Closeburn
353
Chapelhill
B7020
14

A702
357
Park
Blackacre
Courance
Dumfries and

MAXWELTON HOUSE
B729
A76
Ae Village
Water of Ae
18
Templand
Sibbaldbie
Corrie Common

F
Straith
Wallaceton
Glenmidge
Auldgirth
Dalswinton
Shieldhill
Millhousebridge
A74(M)
A B723

Dalmacallan Forest
Dunscore
13
Dalswinton
Auchencairn
Duncow
A701
Applegarthtown
Marjoriebanks

Sundaywell
Milton
240
ELLISLAND FARM
Gallaberry
Lochmaben
17
Lockerbie
Bankshill

398
Drumpark
Newtonairds
Holywood
Kirkton
Tinwald
LOCHMABEN CASTLE
B7068
287
BURNSWARK HILLFORT
Burnswark

G
Glen
Irongray
107
Heathhall
The Grove
Locharbriggs
Castle Loch
Heck
18
107

LINCLUDEN COLLEGE
Dumfries
DUMFRIES AND GALLOWAY AVIATION MUS
Torthorwald
Hightae
Birkshaw Forest
Castlemilk

Shawhead
Maxwelltown
OLD BRIDGE HOUSE MUS
Collin
RAMMERSCALES HOUSE
3
Kettleholm
Middleshaw
4

0 1 2 3 4 5 6 miles
0 1 2 3 4 5 6 7 8 9 10 km

Scottish Borders

Galloway

Traquair Forest
Caddonfoot
ABBOTSFORD
Darnick
Newstead
A6091
Boleside
Melrose
PRIORWOOD GDNS
TRIMONTIUM EXHIBITION
Dyburgh
Kirkhouse
576
Minch Moor
Yair Hill Forest
B7060
B6359
Eildon Hills
Newtown St. Boswells
ABBEY
B6404
MERTOUN GDN
St. Boswells
743 DUN RIG
Blake Muir
121
504
Broadmeadows
BROADMEADOWS
Ovenscloss
A707
Lindean
323
WHITLAW MOSSES
121
B6398
Bow
60
A68
Maxton
Yarrow
13
Yarrow Water
501
Bowhill
SELKIRK GLASS
Selkirk
9
A699
B6453
B6359
Longnewton
60
A68
543
FASTHEUGH HILL
BOWHILL HOUSE & COUNTRY PARK
B7039
Philiphaugh
HALLIWELL'S HOUSE MUSEUM
SIR WALTER SCOTT'S COURTROOM
Midlem
B6400
Bloomfield
Ancrum
Mountbenger
A708
Yarrow Feus
Sundhope
Ettrickbridge
B7009
Kirkhope
15
B7009
Clerklands
Lilliesleaf
Greenhouse
Chesters
A698
Dryhope Tower
589
THE WISS
Cappercleuch
St. Mary's Loch
676
Dryhope
Crosslee
Newburgh
B7009
Ettrick Forest
A7
11
Woll
Ashkirk
276
Belses
Minto
Newton
MARY QUEEN SCOTS HO
JEDBURGH ABBEY
Lanton
BLACK KNOWE HEAD
550
Gilmanscleuch
CAVER'S HILL
369
Akermoor Loch
Hassendean
E
B6405
Horsleyhill
338
Hundale
Ramsey Knowe
Tushielaw
471
Redfordgreen
Shaws Under Loch
Todrig
Hellmoor Loch
Ale Water
333
SMASHA HILL
Clariław
Appletreehall
Denholm
12
Bedrule
116
B6357
Bai
Wardlaw
590
Borthwickshiels
Burnfoot
A698
Cauldmill
424
RUBERS LAW
Ettrickhill
Ettrick
JAMES HOGG MONUMENT
Ramseycleuch
498
Buccleuch
Roberton
B711
Wilton
MUSEUM AND SCOTT GALLERY
Hawick
Kirkton
Ashybank
Hallrule
Glenkerry
Borthwickbrae
Burnfoot
Branxholm Park
DRUMLANRIG'S TOWER
A6088
Hobkirk
Bonchester Bridge
390
REDCLEUCH EDGE
Borthwick Water
Branxholme
301
Chesters
KNOWE
Craik Forest
Craik
Newmill
9
Cleuch Head
393
Southdean
Nether Dalgliesh
B709
488
Howpasley
RIDDELL MONUMENT
Broadhaugh
Northhouse
Dodburn
Allan Water
CRAGBANK WOOD
417
PIKE HILL
Teviothead
THE PIKE
462
Priesthaugh
Wauchope
Forest
D
Davington
477
A7
Castleweary
532
CALDCLEUCH HEAD
608
599
514
FANNA HILL
Singdean
KAGYU SAMYE LING TIBETAN CENTRE
White Esk
Eskdalemuir
emuir Forest
16
602
PEEL FELL
WISP HILL
599
TUDHOPE HILL
21
Deadwater
Jamestown
Gorrenberry
HERMITAGE CASTLE
Saughtree
529
Hermitage
446
19
Eskdalemuir
492
NY
499
PIKE FELL
Newlands
B6357
Larriston
Kielder
KIELDER
116
Castle O'er Forest
B709
Castle O'er
Georgefield
568
ROAN FELL
Steele Road
Larriston Fells
329
KIE VIS
13
Bentpath
Ewes
Arkleton
Dinlabyre
ESKDALE
Old Castleton
Galloway
331
ART FELL
450
CALKIN RIG
Potholm
A7
446
BLACK EDGE
JANET ARMSTRONG HOUSE
Newcastleton
Newcastleton or Copshaw Holm
Forest
514
GLENDHU HILL
KIELDER BIRDS OF PREY
Paddockhole
CRAIGCLEUCH CASTLE COLLECTION
Langholm
MALCOLM MONUMENT
B709
18
B7068
319
Kershopefoot
Kershope Forest
Bewcastle Fells
518
SIGHTY CRAG
Kirtleton
108
GILNOCKIE TOWER
Claygate
Tinnisburn Forest
LIDDESDALE
10
Caulside
Liddel Water
Baileyhead
Whitelyne Common
108
Waterbeck
B722
14
127
Evertown
B7068
B720
Rowanburn
B6357
Canonbie
Catlowdy
Crossings
Blackpool Gate
The Flatt
424
WHITE PRES ON
KIRKCONNEL CHURCHYARD
B725
B722
5
6
Everton
7
8
G
9

Newstead
SMAILHOLM TOWER
FLOORS CASTLE
Kelso
KELSO ABBEY
Maxw
Downham
Howtel
B6352
PRIORWOOD GDNS
TRIMONTIUM EXHIBITION
Dryburgh
Somersyde
Clintmains
Manorhill
Trows
ROXBURGH CASTLE
Windywalls
B6396
Mindrum
A6091
Eildon Hills
DRYBURGH ABBEY
Newtown St. Boswells
St. Boswells
Maxton
Roxburgh
Heiton
B6352
Blakelaw
Lempitlaw
Pawston
Kilham
B6351

Bowden
B6398
WHITLAW MOSS
A699
ford
122
Hoselaw
Glen
267
Westnewton
Kirknewton

Longnewton
Muirhouselaw
Kalemouth
WATERLOO MONUMENT
Frogden
Crookhouse
Linton
B6401
Town Yetholm
282
Kirk Yetholm
KIRK YETHOLM
Hethpool
537

Lilliesleaf
Belses
B6400
Bloomfield
Ancrum
HARESTANES COUNTRYSIDE VISITOR CENTRE
Crailing
TEVIOT WATER GARDENS
Eckford
Morebattle
Cliftoncote
HOWNAM LAW
449
PENNINE WAY
THE SCHIL
601
MOUNTHOOLEY

Greenhouse
Chesters
A698
Bonjedward
Crailinghall
Cessford
Whitton
Hownam Mains
Mowhaugh
Sourhope
AUCHOPE CAIRN
726
815
THE CHEVIOT

Hassendean
Minto
276
Lanton
Newton
MARY QUEEN OF SCOTS HOUSE
Jedburgh
JEDBURGH ABBEY
Crailinghall
Oxnam
Hownam
Craik Moor
456
Nether Hindhope
Beefstand Hill
561
PENNINE WAY
Windy Gyle
619
NORTH

Horsleyhill
B6405
Clariclaw
Denholm
115
Bedrule
Hundalee
Howden
JEDBURGH CASTLE JAIL & MUSEUM
338
FERNIEHIRST CASTLE
Swinside Hall
335
Chatto
WODEN LAW
423
507
BROWNHART LAW
Usway Burn
Kidland Forest
Barrowburn
NATIONA

Appletreehall
Ashybank
Burnfoot
Bairnkine
NT
Mossburnford
Falla
Leithope Forest
Shillmoor
501
Alwinton
Linshiels

Culdmill
Hawick
DRUMLANRIG'S TOWER
Kirkton
Hallrule
Mervinslaw
Camptown
JEDFOREST DEER & FARM PARK
Hungry Law
501
527
CRIGDON HILL
377
412
WATTY BELL'S CAIRN
355

Bonchester Bridge
Hobkirk
Chesters
Cleuch Head
Southdean
418
579
THE C
Catcleugh
Byrness
Featherwood
STREET

Langburnshiels
B6357
CRAGBANK WOOD
393
Wauchope Forest
553
WHITELEE MOOR
499
KNOX KNOWE
Catcleugh Reservoir
BYRNESS
Redesdale Forest
Byrness
13
Sills

Fanna Hill
514
Singdean
KIELDERHEAD
Kielderhead Moor
602
PEEL FELL
551
WOOL MEATH
TOLL
Redesdale Camp
Rochester
A68
Horsley
BRIGANTIUM
274
Otterburn Camp

Hermitage
446
Larriston
Newlands
B6357
Steele Road
Larriston Fells
Saughtree
Deadwater
Kielder Burn
Emblehope Moor
513
Blackburn Common
Blackhope Fell
PENNINE WAY
Elishaw
1388
Otterburn
378
PADON HILL

Dinlabyre
329
115
Kielder
TOLL
KIELDER CASTLE VISITOR CENTRE
Wainhope Moor
KIELDER
Northu
Troughend Common

Old Castleton
KIELDER FOREST PARK
Forest
BLACK MIDDENS BASTLE HOUSE
Shipley Shiels
Gatehouse
Hareshaw Head
B6320

Newcastleton
Forest
KIELDER WATER BIRDS OF PREY CENTRE
KIELDER WATER
Falstone
Greenhaugh
326
West Woodburn
East Woodburn

GLENDHU HILL
514
TOWER KNOWE VISITOR CENTRE
The Eals
Lanehead
Charlton
BELLINGHAM
Bellingham
Ridsdale
A68

NY
Bower
Hesleyside
Chirdon Burn
Redesmouth

Bewcastle Fells
518
SIGHTY CRAG
490
Hopehouse
312
15
Baileyhead
White Lyne
Whiteline Common
Paddaburn
109
KIELDER MIRES
Wark
Forest
Stonehaugh
Whygate
109
B6320
Birtley

0 1 2 3 4 5 6 miles
0 1 2 3 4 5 6 7 8 9 10km

NORTHUMBERLAND COAST

Milfield · Fenton · Nesbit · North Hazelrigg · Belford · Easington · Waren Mill · Glororum · Burton
Doddington · South Hazelrigg · East Hort · Spindleston · Mousen · Bradford · Elford · North Sunderland · Seahouses
Lanton · Coupland · West Horton · Warenton · Bellshill · Adderstone · Lucker · Newham Hall · Swinhoe · Beadnell
Akeld · Humbleton · Weetwood Hall · Chatton · Greendikes · Warenford · Newham · Fleetham · Benthall · Beadnell Bay
Wooler · Haugh Head · Chillingham · WILD CATTLE OF CHILLINGHAM · Newstead · Chathill · High Newton-by-the-Sea · Low Newton-by-the-Sea
Earle · Middleton Hall · Newtown · Lilburn Tower · East Lilburn · Hepburn · Rosebrough · Ellingham · Preston · Brunton · Embleton Bay
North Middleton · Ilderton · Roseden · Old Bewick · Harehope · West Ditchburn · South Charlton · Christon Bank · Dunstan Steads · Castle Point · DUNSTANBURGH CASTLE
South Middleton · Langleeford · Roddam · Wooperton · New Bewick · Eglingham · Beanley · Rock · Dunstan · Craster
Greensidehill · Brandon · Powburn · Titlington · Shipley · HULNE PRIORY · Rennington · Littlemill · Howick · Howick Haven
INGRAM NATIONAL PARK CENTRE · Ingram · Branton · Glanton · Shawdon Hall · ALNWICK ABBEY · Denwick · Littlehoughton · Longhoughton · Boulmer Haven
Prendwick · Great Ryle · Glanton Pike · Bolton · Abberwick · ALNWICK · Hawkhill · Lesbury · Boulmer
Alnham · Little Ryle · Whittingham · Broome Park · Lemmington Hall · Bilton · Alnmouth
Scrainwood · Yetlington · Thrunton · EDLINGHAM CASTLE · Shilbottle · High Buston · Alnmouth Bay
Biddlestone · Netherton · Callaly · Thrunton Wood · Edlingham · Low Buston · A1068 · Birling
Burradon · Lorbottle Hall · Newton-on-the-Moor · Eastfield Hall · Warkworth
Harbottle · High Trewhitt · Lorbottle · Cartington · Hazon · Gloster Hill · Amble · Coquet I.
Sharperton · Warton · Snitter · SHIRLAW PIKE · Swarland Estate · Brainshaugh · Guyzance · North Togston · Hauxley
Lady's Well · Holystone · Flotterton · Rothbury · CRAGSIDE HOUSE · Swarland · Acklington · Togston · Radcliffe
Caistron · Hepple · Thropton · Newtown · Whitton · NATIONAL PARK VISITOR CENTRE · Longframlington · LONGFRAMLINGTON GARDENS · Felton · Broomhill · South Broomhill · DRURIDGE BAY
Great Tosson · TOSSON HILL · BRINKBURN PRIORY · Low Hesleyhurst · Weldon · West Thirston · East Thirston · Red Row · Druridge Bay
NY · NZ · Harwood Forest · Forestburn Gate · Wingates · Eshott · Helm · West Chevington · A1068
Elsdon · Fontburn Res. · Nunnykirk · Longhorsley · Causey Park Bridge · Stobswood · Widdrington · The Scars
Raylees · Ewesley · Netherwitton · Fenrother · Tritlington · Widdrington Station · Cresswell · Ellington · Lynemouth
Rothley Shield East · Stanton · Ulgham · Linton · THE SANCTUARY WILDLIFE CENTRE · COLLIERY MUSEUM · Woodhorn · Beacon Pt.
Longwitton · HERTERTON HOUSE GARDEN · Rothley · Pigdon · Hebron · Longhirst · QUEEN ELIZABETH II · Ashington · Newbiggin-by-the-Sea
Knowesgate · Cambo · Scots Gap · Hartburn · Throphill · Mitford · NORTHUMBRIA CRAFT CENTRE · Bothal · Pegswood · WANSBECK · Hirst · North Seaton
Kirkwhelpington · Middleton · High Angerton · Meldon · Molesden · Morpeth · Stakeford · Cambois
Kirkharle · WALLINGTON · Bolam · BOLAM LAKE · Tranwell · Clifton · Guide Post · Choppington · Hepscott · Scotland Gate · West Sleekburn · Blyth
Sweethope Loughs · Capheaton · Harnham · Whalton · Shilvington · Saltwick · Bedlington · Bedlington Station · Cowpen · East Sleekburn · Bebside · Newsham
Great Bavington · Thockrington · Little Bavington · Belsay · BELSAY HALL · Ogle · Stannington · PLESSEY WOODS · Nedderton · New Delaval · Seaton Delaval
Colt Crag Reservoir · Kirkheaton · West Newham · Higham Dykes · Berwick Hill · KIRKLEY HALL · NORTHUMBERLAND CHEESE FARM · Shankhouse · Nelson Village · Cramlington · Southfield · Seaton
Hallington Reservoir · Hallington · Black Heddon · Ogle · NORTHUMBERLAND CHEESE FARM · Cramlington

A697 · A1 · A696 · A192 · A197 · A196 · A189 · A193 · A1068

West Dunbartonshire
Inverclyde
Renfrewshire
East Renfrewshire
North Ayrshire
Cunninghame
Firth of Clyde
Clyde-Muirshiel Regional Park
Helensburgh
Craigendoran
Rhu
Rosneath
Clynder
Kilcreggan
Cove
Cove Bay
Portkil
Rosneath Pt.
Strone Pt.
Kilmun
Blairmore
Strone
Ardnadam
Sandbank
Holy Loch
Hunter's Quay
Kirn
Dunoon
Cloch Pt.
Bullwood
Lunderston Bay
Innellan
Toward
Wemyss Bay
Upper Skelmorlie
Skelmorlie
Meigle
Routenburn
Largs
Largs Bay
Tomont End
Great Cumbrae Island
Downcraig Ferry
Millport
Fairlie
The Tan
Fairlie Roads
Portencross
Farland Hd.
Thirdpart
Seamill
West Kilbride
Horse Isle
Ardrossan
Saltcoats
Stevenston
Kilwinning
Irvine
Irvine Bay
Fullarton
Dreghorn
Springside
Girdle Toll
Perceton
Bensli
Torranyard
Cunninghamhead
Kilmaurs
Knockentiber
Crosshouse
Knockinlaw
Onthank
Kilmarnock
Grange
Riccarton
Crookedholm
Hurlford
Galston
Newmilns
Greenholm
Sornhill
Crossroads
Shortlees
Earlston
Gatehead
Dundonald
Drybridge
Barassie
Muirhead
Troon
South Bay
Loans
Symington
Bogend
Craigie
Hansel Village
Monkton
Prestwick
Tarbolton
Mossgiel
Mauchline
Catrine
Auchmillan
Lady Isle
Gourock
Ashton
Greenock
Greenock West
Midton
Levan
Larkfield
Braeside
Ravenscraig
Strone
Central
Port Glasgow
Devol
Mid Auchinlech
Woodhall
Bardrainney
Langbank
Inverkip
Shielhill
Garvock
Loch Thom
Gryfe Resrs.
Kilmacolm
Strathgryfe
Quarrier's Village
Bridge of Weir
Houston
Crosslee
Craigends
Brookfield
Ranfurly
Linwood
Johnstone
Kilbarchan
Millarston
Elderslie
Millikenpark
Paisley
Charleston
Glenburn
Foxbar
Howwood
Lochwinnoch
Castle Semple
Barr Loch
Kilbirnie Loch
Kilbirnie
Beith
Glengarnock
Longbar
Gateside
Barrmill
Greenhills
The Den
Drakemyre
Dalry
Highfield
Blairland
Giffordland
Auchentiber
Dalgarven
Burnhouse
Dunlop
Lugton
Halket
Fullwood
Gabroc Hill
Uplawmoor
Neilston
Barrhead
Gateside
Nitshill
Waterside
Thornliebank
Auchenback
Newton Mearns
Netherplace
Kingsford
Stewarton
Laighmuir
Waterside
Fenwick
Laigh Fenwick
Moscow
Flow Moss
Wallace Muir
Long Loch
Loch Libo
Rowbank Reservoir
Muirhead Reservoir
Camphill Reservoir
Knockendon Reservoir
Rye Water
Garnock
Lugton Water
Annick Water
Ladyland Moor
Mistylaw Muir
Queenside Muir
Waterhead Moor
Duchal Moor
Noddsdale Water
Calder
441 Creuch Hill
522 Hill of Stake
484 Irish Law
387 Kaim Hill
259
210
Alexandria
Geilston
Cardross
Colgrain
Balloch
Jamestown
Bonhill
Renton
Townend
Dumbarton
Castlehill
Brucehill
Milton
Bowling
Old Kilpatrick
Duntocher
Bishopton
Rossland
Erskine
Erskine Bridge
Clydebank
Dalmuir
Inchinnan
Renfrew
Yoker
Scotstoun
Whiteinch
Hillington
Cardonald
Pollok
Bearsden
Drumchapel
Knightswood
Dumbarton Muir
Kilpatrick Hills
401 Duncolm
Auchencarroch
Craighat
Stockiemuir
Dumgoyne
Blairquhosh
Blane Water
Bannachra Muir
Scottish Maritime Museum
Dundonald Castle
Dean Castle
Loudon Castle Park
Eglinton
Kilmarnock Services
Hunterston Power Station Visitor Centre
Museum of the Cumbraes
Christian Heritage Museum
Vikingar!
Kelburn Country Centre
Blackshaw Farm Park
North Ayrshire Museum
Ayrshire Museum of Country Life & Costume
Muirshiel
Weaver's Cottage
Glennifer Braes
Nature Reserve Visitor Cen
Finlaystone House & Gardens
Newark Castle
HM Customs & Excise Museum & Exhibition
McLean Mus & Art Gall
Highland Mary's Statue
Linn Botanic Gardens
Kilmun Arboretum
Nat Pk Gateway Centre
Loch Lomond
Balloch Castle
Dumbarton Castle
Dick Institute
Bachelor's Club
Burns House Museum
Glasgow Prestwick International
Rothesay 0:35
Brodick 0:55
Larne 1:50 (March-Oct)
0 1 2 3 4 5 6 miles
0 1 2 3 4 5 6 7 8 9 10 km

CAMPSIE FELLS
Carron Valley Forest
Carron Valley Res.
Kilsyth Hills
Muirmill
Carron Bridge
Dunipace
DENNY
Stenhousemuir
GRANGEMOUTH
Larbert
Fankerton
Stoneywood
Head of Muir
Bonnybridge
Dennyloanhead
FALKIRK
Laurieston
Polmont
Brightons
Redding
Reddingmuirhead
Glen Village
High Bonnybridge
Greenhill
Longcroft
Banknock
Banton
Kilsyth
COLZIUM HOUSE
ANTONINE WALL
Castlecary
Cumbernauld Village
Dullatur
Croy
Balloch
Abronhill
CUMBERNAULD
Falkirk
Shieldhill
California
Maddiston
Jawcraig
Standburn
Slamannan
Avonbridge
Westfield
Crossburn
Binniehill
Limerigg
Longriggend
Blanefield
Netherton
Strathblane
Clachan of Campsie
East Lennoxtown
Dunbartonshire
Balgrochan
Milton of Campsie
Queenzieburn
Twechar
Mugdock
Blairskaith
Birdston
Milngavie
Torrance
KIRKINTILLOCH
Waterside
Westfield
Condorrat
Luggiebank
Bardowie
Cadder
Jellyhill
Lenzie
Kessington
Moodiesburn
Bridgend
Mollinsburn
Bishopbriggs
Lumloch
Auchinloch
Chryston
Muirhead
Riggend
Greengairs
Wattston
Lambhill
Balornock
Marnock
Glenboig
North
Stand
Caldercruix
Hillend Res.
Black Loch
Armadale
Windyknowe
Bathville
Mayfield
Westrigg
Blackridge
Forrestfield
Glasgow
Maryhill
Springburn
Stepps
Garnkirk
Gartcosh
Glenmavis
Plains
Kelvinside
Partick
Garthamlock
Easterhouse
Gartsherrie
Thrashbush
COATBRIDGE
AIRDRIE
Craigneuk
Gartness
Chapelhall
Roughrigg Res.
Forrestburn Res.
Harthill
Whitburn
Eastfield
West Benhar
Longridge
Govan
GLASGOW
Riddrie
Old Monkland
Coatdyke
Shettleston
Baillieston
Calderbank
Salsburgh
Kirk of Shotts
Hirst
Pollokshields
Bridgeton
Dalmarnock
Fullarton
Birkenshaw
Viewpark
Newhouse
Lanarkshire
Fauldhouse
Govanhill
Cathcart
Rutherglen
Carmyle
Newton
Uddingston
Mossend
Holytown
Hareshaw
Shotts
Dykehead
Stane
Greenburn
Burnside
Castlemilk
Cambuslang
Flemington
Bothwell
Bellshill
Newarthill
Hartwood
Giffnock
New Stevenston
Forgewood
Cleland
Allanton
Sheddens
Carmunnock
Stonefield
Blantyre
Nerston
High Blantyre
MOTHERWELL
Bonkle
Coltness
Newmains
Clarkston
Busby
Burnbank
Craigneuk
Knowetop
Morningside
Wilson
Climpy
College Milton
Calderwood
Udston
HAMILTON
Fernlegair
WISHAW
Bogside
Kingshill Plantation
Waterfoot
Thorntonhall
Peel Park
East Kilbride
Cadzow
Waterloo
314 HARE HILL
Forth
Hairmyres
The Murray
Saint Leonards
Meikle Earnock
Overtown
Law
Newlandsmuir
Kelvin
Whitehills
Eaglesham
Quarter
Larkhall
Carluke
Yieldshields
Roadmeetings
Braehead
Limekilnburn
Millheugh
Dalserf
Auldhouse
Shawtonhill
Shawton
Chapelton
Stutherhill
Ashgill
Rosebank
Kilncadzow
Dunwan Dam
Heads
Braidwood
Udstonhead
Glassford
Stonehouse
Netherburn
Crossford
Carnduff
376 CORSE HILL
Cartland
Carstairs
West End
Hazelbank
Nemphlar
Draffan
Ravenstruther
Strathaven
Auchenheath
Kirkfieldbank
Lanark
Pettinain
Whitelaw
Sandford
Blackwood
Kirkmuirhill
New Lanark
Hyndford Bridge
Caldermill
Avon Water
Boghead
Dillarburn
Gilmourton
Stobieside
South
Lesmahagow
Hawksland
Drumclog
Kype Muir
Brocketsbrae
New Trows
Auchlochan
Sandilands
Harleyholm
Darvel
Broken Cross Muir
Douglas Water
Rough Moss
Lanarkshire
Rigside
MILL RIG 335
Glengavel Reservoir
Coalburn
Braehead
Happendon
TINTO HILLS
569 TINTO
NUTBERRY HILL
River Wethan
Uddington
434 WEDDER HILL
Douglas West
Douglas
Wiston
Newton
466 MIDDLEFIELD LAW
Glenbuck
465 HARESHAW HILL
Netherwood
Glespin
Roberton Law
Roberton
Smallburn
Muirkirk
Kames
Sorn
392 AUCHENSAUGH HILL
Middle Muir
M80
M876
M9
M73
M8
M74
A80
A8
A725
A71
A70
126
127
120
113

Antonshill
Stenhousemuir
Skinflats
MUSEUM
GRANGEMOUTH
Larbert
Carron
Carronshore
Bainsford
Bonness
Grangepans
Carriden
Muirhouses
CHARLESTOWN WORKSHOPS
Charlestown
Limekilns
Rosyth
Hill
ST BRIDGET'S CHURCH
Dalgety Bay
ST COLM'S ABBEY
Inchcolm
Inverkeithing
Torry Bay

FALKIRK WHEELS
BO'NESS AND KINNEIL RAILWAY
Bo'ness
BIRKHILL CLAY MINE
Blackness
St. Margaret's Hope
BLACKNESS CASTLE
North Queensferry
Forth Road Bridge
FORTH BRIDGES MUSEUM
World of Golf
Inchmickery
Inverkeithing Bay
P&R
FIR
FALKIRK
Laurieston
ROUGH CASTLE
Redding
Glen Village
Reddingmuirhead
Polmont
Brightons
Whitecross
Groufoot
Mannerston
HOUSE OF THE BINNS
Newton
Dalmeny
Cramond
MAID OF THE FORTH CRUISES
Drum Sands
DALMENY HOUSE
Granton
ROYAL BOTANIC GARDEN
Cramond I.

Falkirk
Glen Village
Shieldhill
Maddiston
California
Standburn
Linlithgow
LINLITHGOW PALACE
Philpstoun
Old Philpstoun
Bridgend
Threemiletown
Winchburgh
Kirkliston
Turnhouse
EDINBURGH ZOO
Barnton
Drylaw
Davidson's Mains
Lauriston Castle

West
Lothian
Binniehill
Limerigg
Slamannan
Crossburn
Avonbridge
Westfield
TORPHICHEN PRECEPTORY
Torphichen
MURAVONSIDE
Standburn
BEECRAIGS
Ecclesmachan
Broxburn
Uphall
Newbridge
Burnside
Ratho Station
Ratho
EDINBURGH CANAL CENTRE
Bonnington
Wilkieston
Gogar
Corstorphine
Morningside
Gorgie
Murrayfield

BLAWHORN MOSS
Westrigg
Bathville
Mayfield
Whiteside
Armadale
Windyknowe
Bathgate
BENNIE MUSEUM
Wester Dechmont
Dechmont
Boghall
Deans
Pumpherston
Uphall Station
ALMONDELL AND CALDER WOOD
LIVINGSTON
Mid Calder
East Calder
Kirknewton
Burnwynd
Juniper Green
Currie
Balerno
Edinburgh
Colinton
Fairmilehead

Blackridge
Harthill
HARTHILL SERVICES
Polkemmet
Blackburn
Seafield
Livingston Village
ALMOND VALLEY HERITAGE CENTRE
LIVINGSTON DESIGNER OUTLET
Oakbank
Bellsquarry
Kirknewton
MALLEENY GARDEN
HILLEND SKI CENTRE
BONALY
Woodhouselee
Easter Howgate

Eastfield
West Benhar
Harthill
Whitburn
East Whitburn
Croftmalloch
FREEPORT WESTWOOD
Polbeth
West Calder
Mallenny Mills
PENTLAND HILLS
Threipmuir Reservoir
SCALD LAW

Kirk of Shotts
Hirst
Fauldhouse
Longridge
Stoneyburn
Bents
Addiewell
Loganlea
Breich
Harperrig Reservoir
REGIONAL PARK
Silverburn
Penicuik
Kirkhill

Shotts
Dykehead
Stane
HERITAGE CENTRE
Greenburn
Woodmuir Plantation
Cobbinshaw Reservoir
Crosswood Reservoir
EAST CAIRN HILL
WEST CAIRN HILL
Nine Mile Burn
Howgate

Allanton
Kingshill Plantation
Wilsontown
Woolfords Cottages
Tarbrax
WHITE CRAIG
Baddinsgill Reservoir
BYREHOPE MOUNT
Carlops

Morningside
Climpy
Rootpark
Auchengray
Forth
HARE HILL
West Water Reservoir
BLEAK LAW
West Linton
Cowdenburn
Whim Farm
Leadburn

Carluke
Yieldshields
Roadmeetings
Kilncadzow
Braehead
BRAEHEAD MOSS
NS
NT
MENDICK HILL
Waterheads

Braidwood
Cartland
CLYDE VALLEY WOODLANDS
Carstairs
West End
Kaimend
Dunsyre
Newbigging
Walston
Dolphinton
BLACK MOUNT
Melbourne
Halmyre Mains
WETHER LAW
Damside
Romannobridge
Eddleston

Nemphlar
Lanark
Ravenstruther
Carstairs Junction
Elsrickle
Kirkurd
Blyth Bridge
Drochil
BLACK MELDON
WHITE MELDON

Kirkfieldbank
New Lanark
NEW LANARK WORLD HERITAGE VILLAGE
Hyndford Bridge
Pettinain
Libberton
Whitecastle
Shieldhill
Candy Mill
Kirkurd
LYNE ROMAN CAMP
NEIDPATH CASTLE

Hawksland
Sandilands
CARMICHAEL VISITOR CENTRE
Harleyholm
Covington
Quothquan
Thankerton
Biggar
GLADSTONE COURT
COVENANTER'S HOUSE
GASWORKS MUSEUM
Broughton
BROUGHTON HEIGHTS
Hallyne
Stobo
Kirkton Manor

Braidwood
Douglas Water
Symington
Wolfclyde
Causewayend
JOHN BUCHAN CENTRE
UPPER TWEEDDALE
Dreva Forest
DAWYCK BOTANIC GARDEN
Castlehill

Broken Cross Muir
Roberton
TINTO HILLS
TINTO
Wiston
Newton
Lamington
Coulter
Rachan Mill
Drumelzier
Bellspool

Happendon
Uddington
Douglas
DUNGAVEL HILL
Cowgill Upper Reservoir
CULTER FELL
BLAKEHOPE HEAD
Stanhope
PYKESTONE HILL
Langhaugh
STOB LAW

Crookhaugh
Hearthstane
DOLLAR LAW
BLACK LAW

FORTH OF FORTH

Inchkeith

Gullane Bay
MUIRFIELD
Dirleton
Aberdour
Youghall

Gullane
West Fenton
Fenton Barns
Kingston
Whitekirk

Aberlady Bay
Aberlady
MYRETON MOTOR MUSEUM
Drem
THE CHESTERS FORT
MUSEUM OF FLIGHT
Tyne Mouth
JOHN MUIR
Craigielaw
Gosford Bay
GOSFORD HOUSE
Spittal
SETON COLLEGIATE CHURCH
Ballencrieff
Athelstaneford
East Fortune
Peffer Burn
Tyninghame
Belhaven
West Barns

Black Rocks
HMY BRITANNIA
Newhaven
Leith
EDINBURGH
Portobello
Joppa
Cockenzie and Port Seton
Longniddry
Huntington
Elvingston
HOPETOUN MON
JANE WELSH CARLYLE MUSEUM
ST MARY'S COLLEGIATE CH
HAILES CASTLE
East Linton
PRESTON MILL & PHANTASSIE DOOCOT
Traprain
Pitcox
Stenton
Halls

ZEEBRUGGE 17:30
128
129
140

Prestonpans
MUSSELBURGH INDUSTRIAL HERITAGE MUSEUM
Fisherrow Sands
Musselburgh
1745
Tranent
Gladsmuir
Macmerry
Penston
Haddington
LENNOXLOVE
Luggate Burn

PALACE OF HOLYROOD HOUSE
Duddingston
NAT MUS OF SCOTLAND
Newhailes
INVERESK LODGE GDNS
Wallyford
Inveresk
Elphinstone
New Winton
New Town
Samuelston
Bolton
Papple
Garvald
Dunbar Common

East Lothian

Craigmillar
CRAIGMILLAR CASTLE
EDINBURGH SERVICES
Whitecraig
Ormiston
Crossgatehall
Cousland
Pencaitland
East Saltoun
West Saltoun
Gifford
Danskine
Carfrae

Royal Observatory
Liberton
Danderhall
Gilmerton
DALKEITH PARK
Dalkeith
Newbattle
Easthouses
Mayfield
GLENKINCHIE DISTILLERY
Peastonbank
Gilchriston
Long Newton
Quarryford
Longyester
LAMMERMUIR HILLS
Spartleton Edge

Straiton
BUTTERFLY FARM
Loanhead
Bilston
Polton
Eskbank
Newbattle
Pathhead
Peaston
Humbie
Stobshiel
Blegbie
LAMMER LAW 527
Hopes Reservoir
MEIKLE SAYS LAW 535
Whiteadder Reservoir

ROSSLYN CHAPEL
ROSLIN GLEN
Roslin
Bonnyrigg and Lasswade
Rosewell
MINING MUSEUM
VOGRIE
Newtongrange
Newlandrig
Crichton
Fala Dam
Fala
Blegbie

Auchendinny
Gorebridge
ARNISTON HOUSE
Arniston
CRICHTON CASTLE
North Middleton
Tynehead
HUNT LAW 495
HOG'S LAW
Dye Water

West Lothian

Carrington
Temple
Middleton
Fala Moor
Gilston
415
Hillhouse
Kirktonhill
448 HOG'S LAW
Addinston
Watch Water Reservoir

Rosebery Reservoir
Falahill
468
Oxton
381 COLLIE LAW
389
Wedderlie

TORFICHEN HILL 460
Carcant
Heriot
NT
Fountainhall
Blythe
Thornydykes
Whiteburn
Westruther
Houndslow

MOORFOOT HILLS
651 BLACKHOPE SCAR
Dewar
516
Torquhan
THIRLSTANE CASTLE
Lauder
Thirlestane
Boon

625
Scottish Borders

WHITEHOPE LAW 602 621
Killochyett
Stow 423
Nether Blainslie
Legerwood
GREEN KNOWE TOWER
Gordon

WINDLESTRAW LAW 659
Bow
Caitha Bowland
SOUTHERN UPLAND WAY
122
Fans
MELLERSTAIN HOUSE

TWEED
Glentress Forest
538 BLACK LAW
Colquhar
508 GREAT LAW
324
Langshaw
West Morriston

Peebles
TWEEDDALE MUS & GALL
Glentress
Kings Muir
KAILZIE GARDENS
Kirkburn
549
502
Blackhaugh
372
Buckholm
Galashiels
PETER ANDERSON WOOLLEN MILL
Earlston
EILDON AND LEADERFOOT
Redpath
Brotherstone

Cardrona
ST RONAN'S WELL INTERPRETATIVE CENTRE
Walkerburn
ROBERT SMAIL'S PRINTING WORKS
Clovenfords
OLD GALA HOUSE
Gattonside
ABBEY
MELROSE
Newstead
SMAILHOLM TOWER

Cardrona Forest
459
Innerleithen
TRAQUAIR HOUSE
FOREST
Elibank and Traquair Forest
276
Abbotsford
Boleside
Darnick
PRIORWOOD GDNS
Melrose
TRIMONTIUM EXHIBITION
Dryburgh
ABBEY
MERTOUN GDNS

Glen Ho
Kirkhouse
576
Minch Moor
373
Yair Hill Forest
PARK
Ovenscloss
Lindean
422
Eildon Hills
Newtown
St Boswells
Bowden
Clintmains
Manorhill

743 IN RIG
Blake Muir
Broadmeadows
BROADMEADOWS
SELKIRK GLASS
WHITLAW MOSSES
323
115

115
Yarrow
504
Bowhill
SIR WALTER SCOTT'S COURTROOM
Selkirk
Longnewton
Midlem
Maxton
Muirhouselaw

SOUTHERN UPLAND WAY
543
501
FASTHEUGH HILL
BOWHILL HOUSE & COUNTRY PARK
Philiphaugh
HALLIWELL'S HOUSE MUSEUM
Midlem
Belses
WEST MONTROSE

DRYHOPE TOWER
Yarrow
A708
A7
A68

1
2
3
4
5
A
B
C
D
E
F
Auldhame
Scoughall
Kingston
Whitekirk
St. Baldred's Cradle
Tyne Mouth
129
JOHN MUIR BIRTHPLACE
Dunbar
East Fortune
Tyninghame
JOHN MUIR
Belhaven
West Barns
Preston
East Linton
Peffer Burn
PRESTON MILL & PHANTASSIE DOOCOT
Broxburn
Barns Ness
East Barns
Skateraw
Meikle Pinkerton
Spott
Biel Water
Pitcox
Traprain
HAILES CASTLE
Luggate Burn
Stenton
Halls
Dry Burn
Innerwick
Thorntonloch
COCKLAW HILL 319
DUNGLASS COLLEGIATE CHURCH
Reed Pt.
Cove
Cockburnspath
Papple
Garvald
Oldhamstocks
Siccar Pt.
Wheat Stack
FAST CASTLE
ST ABB'S HEAD
St. Abb's Head
KITTIWAKE GALLERY
Dunbar Common
397 BRANSLY HILL
Carfrae
Ecclaw
Lumsdaine
Coldingham Moor
Northfield
St Abbs
Coldingham Bay
St. Abb's Haven
Danskine
121
391 HEART LAW
SOUTHERN UPLAND WAY
Grantshouse
Huxton
Coldingham
COLDINGHAM PRIORY
Quarryford
Longyester
LAMMERMUIR HILLS
Spartleton Edge
Bothwell Water
Monynut Water
Nether Monynut
Ale Water
Eyemouth
Houndwood
Whiteadder Reservoir
Eye Water
Cairncross
535 MEIKLE SAYS LAW
Hopes Reservoir
379 CRANSHAWS HILL
Cranshaws
Whiteadder Water
Abbey St. Bathans
Reston
AYTON CASTLE
Auchencrow
Ayton
Ellemford
EDINSHALL BROCH
LAMMERMUIR
Prenderguest
495 HUNT LAW
Dye Water
Lintlaw
Preston
Chirnside
Longformacus
Chirnsidebridge
Edrom
Foulden
Clappers
FOULDEN TITHE BARN
Watch Water Reservoir
NT
JIM CLARK ROOM
Whiteadder Water
448 HOG'S LAW
398 DIRRINGTON GREAT LAW
Buxley
MANDERSTON
Allanton
Duns
Hutton
Clockmill
Cheeklaw
CRUMSTANE FARM PARK
Blackadder West
Paxton
PAXTON HOUSE
Scottish Borders
Wedderlie
Choicelee
Gavinton
UNION SUSPENSION BRIDGE
Loanend
Fishwick
389
Westruther
Polwarth
Sinclair's Hill
Whitsome
Blyth
Thornydykes
Halliburton
Fogo
Bogend
Horndean
Horncliffe
Thornton Park
Whiteburn
Sisterpath
Fogorig
Leet Water
Ladykirk
NORHAM CASTLE
Thirlestane
Houndslow
Swinton
SWINTON KIRK
Norham
MERSE
Swintonmill
Boon
Eden Water
Blackadder Water
Greenlaw
Simprim
Shoreswood
Grindon
Legerwood
Huntlywood
272
GREEN KNOWE TOWER
Gordon
Middlethird
Easter Howlaws
Lambden
Leitholm
Felkington
Shellacres
West Morriston
Fans
Falsidehill
Hume
HUME CASTLE
Eccles
Orange Lane
Castle Heaton
Duddo
245
223
Lennel
Coldstream
HIRSEL
THE HIRSEL
Cornhill-on-Tweed
HEATHERSLAW LIGHT RAILWAY
ERROL
Etal
Earlston
MELLERSTAIN HOUSE
Stichill
Birgham
Carham
Wark
East Learmouth
West Learmouth
Crookham
Branxton
Ford
281
Nenthorn
Ednam
Tweed
Smailholm
Hadden
Pressen
EILDON AND LEADERFOOT
Redpath
Brotherstone
Kerchesters
Sprouston
Holefield
Downham
Howtel
Flodden
ABBEY
MELROSE
Newstead
SMAILHOLM TOWER
FLOORS CASTLE
KELSO
Kelso
KELSO ABBEY
MUS
Windywalls
Mindrum
Milfield
Melrose
PRIORWOOD GDNS
Bemersyde
Clintmains
Dryburgh
ABBEY
Manorhill
Trows
ROXBURGH CASTLE
Maxwellheugh
Lempitlaw
Pawston
Kilham
267
Glen
TRIMONTIUM EXHIBITION
Eildon Hills
Newtown St. Boswells
MERTOUN GDNS
Hoselaw
Lanton
St. Boswells
Rutherford
Roxburgh
Blakelaw
Bowden
Maxton
Heiton
Shotton
Westnewton
Coupland
116
269
Kirknewton
Frogden
KIRK YETHOLM
Town Yetholm
Kirk Yetholm
Hethpool
282
537
Kalemouth
TEVIOT WATER GARDENS
Kale Water
Crookhouse
Linton
Eckford
Nisbet
Belses
Bowmont Water
College Burn
0 1 2 3 4 5 6 miles
0 1 2 3 4 5 6 7 8 9 10 km
A1
A68
A697
A6105
A6089
A6112
A1107
A199
A198
A6091
A699
A698
B6370
B6355
B6438
B6437
B6365
B6456
B6460
B6461
B6470
B6364
B6397
B6404
B6398
B6356
B6360
B6350
B6396
B6352
B6351
B6353
B6354
B6401
B6436
B6359
B1377
B1347
B1407

5   6   7   8   9

A B C D E F G

EYEMOUTH MUSEUM

Burnmouth

Lamberton Beach

Lamberton

Highfields

Berwick-upon-Tweed

BARRACKS MUSEUM & RAMPARTS

East Ord

Tweedmouth

TOWER HOUSE POTTERY

Spittal

Prior Park

Redshin Cove

Murton

Thornton

Scremerston

West Allerdean

Shoresdean

Cheswick

Goswick

Ancroft

North Low

Haggerston

Berrington

South Low

Beal

NU

NORTHUMBERLAND COAST

Bowsden

Barmoor Castle

Barmoor Lane End

West Kyloe

Lowick

East Kyloe

Kyloe Hills

Buckton

LINDISFARNE

Causeway Holy Island Sands

Fenham

Holy Island

Emmanuel Hd.

Holy Island (Lindisfarne)

LINDISFARNE CASTLE

Castle Pt.

HERITAGE CENTRE

LINDISFARNE PRIORY

Guile Pt.

Farne Islands

Staple Sound

FARNE ISLANDS

Inner Sound

ST CUTHBERTS WAY

Fenwick

HUT SMITHY WOOD WORKSHOP

HERSLAW MILL

LADY WATERFORD HALL

Holburn

Detchant

Elwick

Ross

Budle Bay

BAMBURGH CASTLE

Bamburgh

Kimmerston

Hetton Steads

Middleton

Budle

Easington

Waren Mill

Nesbit

North Hazelrigg

Belford

Spindlestone

Glororum

Burton

Fenton Town

Doddington

South Hazelrigg

Mousen

Bradford

Elford

Sunderland

North Sunderland

Seahouses

Newtown

West Horton

East Horton

Warenton

Bellshill

Adderstone

Lucker

Newham Hall

Beadnell Bay

Akeld

Weetwood Hall

Chatton

Greendikes

Warenford

Newham

Swinhoe

Beadnell

Benthall

Wooler

Humbleton

Haugh Head

CHILLINGHAM CASTLE

Chillingham

WILD CATTLE OF CHILLINGHAM

Rosebrough

Newstead

Chathill

Ellingham

High Newton-by-the-Sea

Earle

Middleton Hall

North Low / Burnmouth Bay

117

NORTHUMBERLAND

Kilundine
Claggan
Larachbeg
KINLOCHALINE CASTLE
ARDTORNISH GARDENS
Achranich
Loch Tearnait
Rannoch
437 BEINN A' CHAISIL
Loch nan Clach
Glensanda
Shuna I.
Appin House
Portnacroish
Fiunary
Savary
Loch Aline
Lochaline
SOUND OF MULL
GLAIS BHEINN 479
AN SLEAGHACH 513
Eignaig
Port Ramsay
Port Appin
Appin
Aros Mains
Rubha Mor
Clachan
LYNN OF
Eriska
North Shian
Salen
Pennygown
Fishnish Bay
ARDTORNISH CASTLE
Ardtornish Pt.
Lismore
South Shian
Killbeg
Corrynachenchy
Inninmore Bay
Garbh Shlios
Camas Gorm
Achnacroish
LYNN OF LORN
SCOTTISH SEA LIFE SANCTUARY
chronan
412
Forsa
Garmony
147
Scallastle Bay
Rubha an Ridire
Bernera I.
Achinduin
130
Baravullin
Ferlochan
Knock
ISLAND OF MULL
Scallastle
Java
Craignure Bay
Kilcheran
LORN
Kiel Crofts
Benderloch
BENDERLOCH
Loch Bà
Craignure
MULL AND WEST HIGHLAND NARROW GAUGE RAILWAY
Eilean Dubh
Ledaig
Achnaba
591 BEINN CHRAIG
766 DUN DA GHAOITHE
Duart Bay
Duart Pt.
0:50
Ardmucknish Bay
A828
Glen Cannel
TOROSAY CASTLE & GARDEN
DUART CASTLE
Eilean Musdile
Eilean Mor
North Connel
Black Crofts
761 BEINN TALAIDH
DUNSTAFFNAGE CASTLE
Connel
FALLS OF LORA
Lochdon
0:45
Dunbeg
704 CORRA-BHEINN
Glen More
Lussa
CASTLEBAY 4:50
COLL 2:40
TIREE 3:20
LOCHBOISDALE 5:20
Ganavan
Loch Don
Dunollie
OBAN/OBAN LODGE
MCCAIG'S TOWER
Black Lochs
Coladoir
A849
Strathcoil
Grass Pt.
OBAN VISITOR CENTRE
OBAN DISTILLERY
Altnacraig
OBAN RARE BREEDS FARM PARK
Oban
Kerrera
Loch Airdeglais
Loch Spelve
248
Balliemore
Glenamachrie
383
BEN BUIE 717
698 CREACH BEINN
Ardmore
Glen
Loch Fuaron
Croggan
Rubha nan Sailthean
Bach I.
Loch Nell
Kinlochspelve
Gallanach
Barran
Lochbuie
Barachandroman
Rubha Seanach
Sound of Kerrera
Kilbride
Kilmore
503 BEINN NA CROISE
Loch Uisg
Am Buth
Loch Feochan
Glen Feochan
Kilbride
GLENFEOCHAN HOUSE GARDENS
Loch Buie
405 DRUIM FADA
A816
Carsaig
Laggan Deer Forest
NM
Kilninver
368 A'CHRUACH
Musdale
Carsaig Bay
Rubha Dubh
LORD LOVAT'S CAVE
CLACHAN BRIDGE
B844
Barochreal
Glen Euchar
Bragleenmore
Insh I.
Loch Scamadale
515 BEINN CHAPULL
Frank Lockwood's Island
Sound of Insh
Clachan-Seil
Clachan
Seil
438 CARN DEARG
Easdale
AN CALA GARDENS
Easdale
EASDALE ISLAND FOLK MUSEUM
Braes of Lorn
Balvicar
Blaran
B8003
267 CRUACH RAREY
Loch Tralaig
Drissaig
Lochavich
FIRTH OF LORN
Dubh-fheith
Seil Sound
Kilmun
Cuan
Ferry
Melfort
Cullipool
94
Torsa
Kilchoan
Ardanstur
Kilmelford
Loch Avich
Garbh Eileach
Garvellachs
Luing
Loch Melfort
Glenmore
SCARBA, LUNGA AND THE GARVELLACHS
Eilean Dubh Mor
Achafolla
ARDUAINE GARDEN
Arduaine
Kames
Lagalochan
491 CARN DUCHARA
Eileach an Naoimh
Sound of Luing
365
Inverliever Forest
Garraron
Barbreck
Liever
Kilmaha
Toberonochy
Shuna Sound
COLONSAY 2:20
Lunga
Shuna
Craobh Haven
Barravullin
Lunga
350 CRUACH AN EACHLAICH
Arichamish
Shuna Pt.
B840
CRUACH SCARBA 449
Scarba
Rubha Aird Luing
Kintraw
Torran
144
Ardfern
A816
Ford
Finchairn
Ederline
FINCHAIRN CASTLE
B8002
227 CREAG MHÒR
458 CRUACH FHIONN
Gulf of Corryvreckan
Eilean Righ
CARNASSARIE CASTLE
Loch Craignish
Aird
Loch Gaineamhach
Rèisa an t-Sruith
319
Kinuachdrachd
Kilmartin
GLEBE CAIRN
KILMARTIN HOUSE TRUST
Craignish Pt.
Island Macaskin
Glengarrisdale Bay
296 CRUACH NA SEILCHEIG
Kinuachdrachd Harbour
KILMARTIN SCULPTURED STONES
RI CRUIN CAIRN
Slockavullin
Gleann Airigh
NR
Poltalloch
Loch Crinan
231 DUN DUBH
Glendebadel Bay
144
145
365 BEN GARRISDALE
Crinan
CUP AND RING MARKS
Killmahumaig
B8025
Add
MOINE MHOR
DUNADD FORT
Kilmichael Glassary
Loch Glashan
Bridgend
Bellanoch
B841
Mòine Mhòr
CAIRNBAAN CUP & RING MARKS
A83
Asknish
Lussa
265
ROCK MARKINGS
0 1 2 3 4 5 6 miles
0 1 2 3 4 5 6 7 8 9 10 km

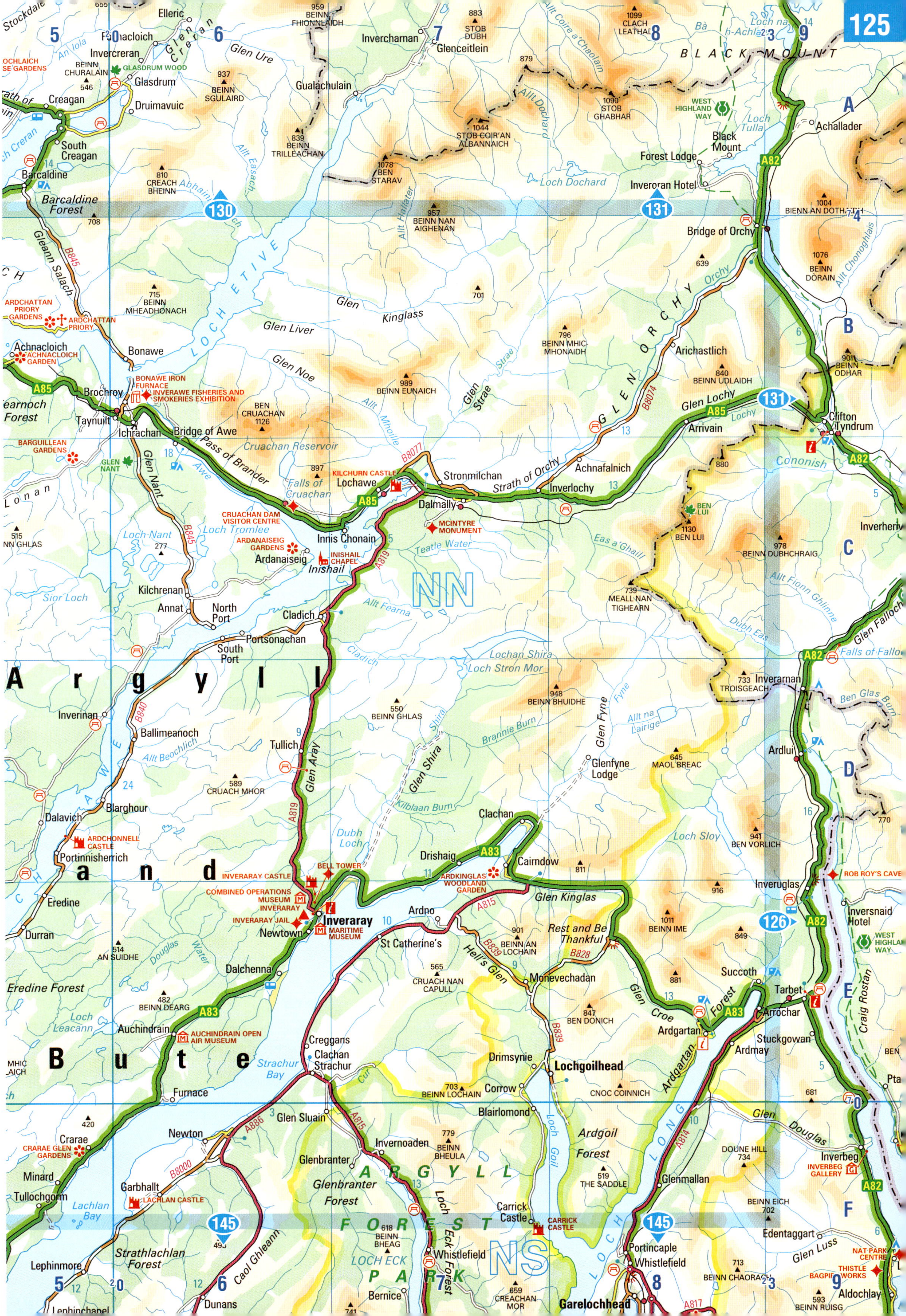

Stockdale
Elleric
BEINN FHIONNLAIDH 959
Invercharnan
STOB DUBH 883
Glenceitlein
Allt Coire a Chaplain
CLACH LEATHAD 1099
Bà
Loch na h-Achlaise
A
BLACK MOUNT
Achallader

naicloich
Invercreran
Glen Ure
Glasdrum Wood
GLASDRUM WOOD
Glasdrum 937
BEINN SGULAIRD
Gualachulain
STOB GHABHAR 1090
WEST HIGHLAND WAY
Black Mount 1078
Loch Tulla

OCHLAICH SE GARDENS
546
Creagan
Druimavuic
BEINN TRILLEACHAN 839
STOB COIR'AN ALBANNAICH 1044
879
Forest Lodge
A82

rath of Creran
708
130
Barcaldine
14
South Creagan
Barcaldine Forest
810 CREACH BHEINN
Abhainn ch
Inveroran Hotel
131
BIENN AN DOTHA 1004
B

BEN STARAV 1078
Loch Dochard
Bridge of Orchy
639

Gleann Salach B845
715 BEINN MHEADHONACH
Glen Liver
Glen Kinglass
957 BEINN NAN AIGHENAN
Orchy
1076 BEINN DORAIN
Allt Chonoghlais

ARDCHATTAN PRIORY GARDENS
ARDCHATTAN PRIORY
Bonawe
Glen Noe
701
796 BEINN MHIC-MHONAIDH
GLEN LOCHY
Arichastlich
B

Achnacloich
ACHNACLOICH GARDEN
Brochroy
BONAWE IRON FURNACE
INVERAWE FISHERIES AND SMOKERIES EXHIBITION
BEN CRUACHAN 1126
989 BEINN EUNAICH
Glen Strae
Allt Strae
B8074
840 BEINN UDLAIDH
Glen Lochy
Lochy
A85
131

A85
Taynuilt
Ichrachan
Bridge of Awe
Pass of Brander
Cruachan Reservoir
B8077
Arrivain
880
Clifton
Tyndrum
A82

earnoch Forest
BARGUILLEAN GARDENS
GLEN NANT
Glen Nant
18
Loch Tromlee
897
KILCHURN CASTLE
Stronmilchan
Strath of Orchy
Achnafalnich
13
BEN LUI
Cononish
C

515 NN GHLAS
Loch Nant
277
B845
Falls of Cruachan
CRUACHAN DAM VISITOR CENTRE
Lochawe
A85
Dalmally
Inverlochy
13
1130 BEN LUI
Inverheri

ARDANASEIG GARDENS
Ardanaiseig
INISHAIL CHAPEL
Inishail
MCINTYRE MONUMENT
Teatle Water
NN
739 MEALL NAN TIGHEARN
978 BEINN DUBHCHRAIG
Allt Fionn Ghlinne
Glen Falloch

Lonan
Kilchrenan
Annat
North Port
Cladich
B819
Allt Fearna
Lochan Shira
Loch Stron Mor
Dubh Eas
A82
Falls of Fallo

Sior Loch
Portsonachan
South Port
Cladich
550 BEINN GHLAS
Loch Shira
948 BEINN BHUIDHE
733 Inverarnan
TROISGEACH

A
Inverinan
Ballimeanoch
Allt Beochlich
AWE B840
Tullich
9
Glen Aray
Brannie Burn
Glen Fyne
Allt na Lairige
Ben Glas Burn
Ardlui
D

r
g
y
l
l
589 CRUACH MHOR
645 MAOL BREAC
D

24
Dalavich
Blarghour
A819
Glenfyne Lodge
Glen Shira
Kilblaan Burn
Clachan
Loch Sloy
941 BEN VORLICH
770

ARDCHONNELL CASTLE
Portinnisherrich
a
n
d
Dubh Loch
Drishaig
A83
Cairndow
811
916
Inveruglas
126
A82
ROB ROY'S CAVE

Eredine
ARDKINGLAS WOODLAND GARDEN
BELL TOWER
INVERARAY CASTLE
Ardno
Glen Kinglas
A815
901 BEINN AN LOCHAIN
1011 BEINN IME
849
Inversnaid Hotel
WEST HIGHLAND WAY

Durran
514 AN SUIDHE
Douglas Water
COMBINED OPERATIONS MUSEUM INVERARAY
INVERARAY JAIL
Inveraray
MARITIME MUSEUM
Newtown
10
St Catherine's
Rest and Be Thankful
B828
1011 BEINN IME
881
Succoth
Tarbet
E

B
u
t
e
Dalchenna
565 CRUACH NAN CAPULL
Hell's Glen
Monevechadan
847 BEN DONICH
Glen Croe
13
Ardgartan Forest
A83
Arrochar
Stuckgown
Ardmay

482 BEINN DEARG
A83
AUCHINDRAIN OPEN AIR MUSEUM
Auchindrain
Eredine Forest
Loch Leacann
Creggans
Clachan Strachur
Drimsynie
Lochgoilhead
Glen Croe
Ardgartan
Craig Rostan
BEN

MHIC AICH
Furnace
Strachur Bay
Curr
703 BEINN LOCHAIN
Corrow
CNOC COINNICH
Ardgoil Forest
681
7 0
Pta

420
Crarae
Newton
A886
Glen Sluain
A815
Blairlomond
Loch Goil
779 BEINN BHEULA
Glen Douglas
Inverbeg
A82

CRARAE GLEN GARDENS
B8000
Garbhallt
Invernoaden
ARGYLL
519 THE SADDLE
DOUNE HILL 734
INVERBEG GALLERY

Minard
Tullochgorm
LACHLAN CASTLE
Glenbranter
Glenbranter Forest
FOREST
Glenmallan
BEINN EICH 702

Lachlan Bay
145
618 BEINN BHREAG
Carrick Castle
CARRICK CASTLE
NS
BEINN CHAORACH 713
Edentaggart
NAT PARK CENTRE
THISTLE WORKS
BAGPIP

Lephinmore
Strathlachlan Forest
493
Caol Gleann
PARK
Whistlefield
Portincaple
Whistlefield
145
Glen Luss
Aldochla

5
Lephinchapel
12
Dunans
6
Bernice
7
Garelochhead
8
A817
659 CREACHAN MOR
3
593 BEINN RUISG
9

LOCH LOMOND AND THE TROSSACHS NATIONAL PARK

QUEEN ELIZABETH FOREST PARK

Stirling

West Dunbartonshire

East Dunbartonshire

BEINN UDLAIDH
Glen Lochy
A85
Arrivain
Lochy
BEN LUI
1130
BEINN DUBHCHRAIG
MEALL NAN TIGHEARN
Fyne
Dubh Eas
Allt na Lairige

BEINN ODHAR
901
BEINN CHALLUM
1025
Clifton
Tyndr
131
Cononish
Strath Fillan
A82
Inverhenve
WEST HIGHLAND WAY
Crianlarich
A82
Glen Falloch
Falls of Falloch
733 Inverarnan
TROISGEACH
125
Ardlui
645 MAOL BREAC
941 BEN VORLICH
Loch Sloy
1011 BEINN IME
916
849
881
Succoth
Glen Croe
A83
Arrochar
Ardgartan
Ardgartan Forest
Ardmay
Stuckgowan
Glenmallan
BEINN EICH 702
Edentaggart
Glen Luss
713
BEINN CHAORACH
593 BEINN RUISG
Garelochhead
STRONE HOUSE GARDENS
Glen Fruin
Shandon
Duchlage
Blairglas
GLENARN GARDEN
THE HILL HOUSE
Rhu
Rosneath
Kilcreggan
Portkil
Gourock
Greenock West
Greenock
Midton
MCLEAN MUS & ART GALL
Cardross

BEINN CHEATHAICH 937
Allt Riblrain
GLEN DOCHART
Lochdochart House
Benmore
Portnellan
1174 BEN MORE
1165 STOB BINNEIN
Loch Iubhair
Loch Dochart
CRIANLARICH
Braes of Balquhidder
Monachylemore
Craigruie
940 BEINN A'CHROIN
Inverlochlarig
865 STOB A'CHOIN
687 BEINN BHREAC
820 BENVANE
771
770
Strath Gartney
Stronachlachar
LOCH KATRINE
Loch Arklet
Inversnaid Hotel
WEST HIGHLAND WAY
598
Frenich
Loch Ard Forest
Loch Chon
B829
LOCH LOMOND
LOCH KATRINE
Kinlochard
Altskeith
B829
Loch Ard
DUCHRAY Water
Rowardennan
ROWARDENNAN LODGE
596 BEINN UIRD
577 BEINN BHREAC
Rowardennan Forest
Kelly Water
461
Milarrochy
NAT. PARK CENTRE
Inchfad
Balmaha
Milton of Buchanan
Garadhban Forest
Inchcailloch
Inchmurrin
LOCH LOMOND
ROWAN GALLERY
B837
Drymen
Gartocharn
Croftamie
Balloch
BALLOCH CASTLE
Jamestown
ALEXANDRIA
Bonhill
Renton
West Dunbartonshire
Dumbarton Muir
401 DUNCOLM
KILPATRICK HILLS
DUMBARTON

Killin
BREADALBANE FOLKLORE CENTRE
Achmore
FALLS OF DOCHART
Finlarig
MOIRLANICH LONGHOUSE
Boreland
Dochart
A827
Auchlyne
Ardchyle
Ledcharrie
Glen Ogle
A85
Lochearnhead
EDINAMPLE FALLS
Edinample
Ardvorlich
852
985 BEN VORLICH
A84
Balquhidder
ROB ROY'S GRAVE
Auchtubh
Loch Voil
Ballimore
Loch Doine
Calair Burn
Strathyre Forest
Strathyre
811 BEINN EACH
Ardchullarie More
Loch Lubnaig
879 BEN LEDI
Anie
Pass of Leny
Leny Ho.
ROB ROY VISITOR C
FALLS OF LENY
Kilmahog
Bochastle
Callander
Coilantogle
Brig o'Turk
A821
Loch Achray
THE TROSSACHS
Loch Venachar
The Trossachs
TROSSACHS PIER COMPLEX
SS SIR WALTER SCOTT
Trossachs Hotel
BEN VENUE 727
Duncraggan
Lendrick Lodge
Loch Drunkie
Achray Forest
Menteith Hills
Loch Rusky
Torrie
D. MARSHALL LODGE VISITOR CENTRE
Milton
SCOTTISH WOOL CENTRE
TROSSACHS DISCOVERY CENTRE
Aberfoyle
Kirkton
Port of Menteith
INCHMAHOME PRIORY
Ruskie
A873
DUNAVERIG FARMLIFE CENTRE
Malling
Lake of Menteith
Cobleland
Gartmore
Dalmary
Dykehead
FLANDERS MOSS
Flanders Moss
Flanders Moss
Arnprior
Cauldhame
A811
Buchlyvie
Buchlyvie Muir
Kippen
Muir
B835
Moor Park
Balfron Station
Balfron
Harvieston
Boquhan
Gartness
Spittal
Killearn
Ballikinrain
Fintry
Fintry Hills
CULCREUCH CASTLE
Craighat
Dumgoyne
GLENGOYNE DISTILLERY
Blairquhosh
EARL'S SEAT 578
CAMPSIE FELL
Blairglas
Strathblane
Blanefield
Netherton
Clachan of Campsie
East Dunbartonshire
Balgrochan
Lennoxtown
Mugdock

0 1 2 3 4 5 6 miles
0 1 2 3 4 5 6 7 8 9 10 km

118
119
131
132
125
145

Perth and Kinross
Clackmannanshire
Falkirk
NN
NS
GLEN ALMOND
STRATHEARN
STRATHALLAN
CREAG UCHDAG
BEN CHONZIE
MEALL NAN CAORAICH
MEALL TARSUINN
Loch Lednock Reservoir
Loch Turret Reservoir
Invergeldie
Funtullich
Newton
Logiealmond Lodge
Logiealmond
Harrietfield
Chapelhill
Buchanty
Methven
Almondbank
Lochty
Keillour
Braegrum
Tibbermore
St Fillans
LOCH EARN
Ardtrostan
Dunira
RIVER EARN
MELVILLE MONUMENT
Comrie
COMRIE CROFT
Ochtertyre
Lawers
Quoig
FALLS OF TURRET
Monzie
Monzie Castle
Hosh
Gilmerton
Fowlis Wester
STANDING STONES
Keillour Forest
Pow Water
Tullybannocher
EARTHQUAKE HOUSE
Ross
Dalginross
Lochlane
GLENTURRET DISTILLERY
Crieff
Madderty
Findo Gask
Clathy
St David's
Dupplin Castle
Kirkton
Forteviot
AUCHINGARRICH WILDLIFE & HIGHLAND CATTLE CENTRE
CRIEFF VISITORS' CENTRE
The Balloch
STUART CRYSTAL VISITOR CENTRE
Forest of Glenartney
Water of Ruchill
Culloch
Torlum Wood
DRUMMOND CASTLE GARDENS
OLD CHURCH & TOWER
Muthill
INNERPEFFRAY LIBRARY
Kinkell Bridge
Dalchruin
Glen Artney
Tigh-na-Blair
Ochtermuthill
Machany Water
Auchnashelloch
BEN CLACH
Langside
Aberuthven
Tullibardine
Dunning
TULLIBARDINE CHAPEL
Auchterarder
Milton
HERITAGE CENTRE
Glenlichorn
Garrick
Knaik
UAMH BHEAG
BLACKHALL ROMAN CAMPS
ARDOCH ROMAN CAMP
Gleneagles Hotel
GLENEAGLES
Braco
Blackford
Gleneagles House
Common of Dunning
Middle Rigg
Bullie Burn
Muckle Burn
Greenloaning
TULLIBARDINE DISTILLERY
Braes of Ogilvie
Glen Eagles
STEEL'S KNOWE
INNERDOUNY HILL
Braes of Doune
Allan Water
Glendevon Resvrs.
Glen Devon
Glendevon
Burnfoot
Castle Hill Reservoir
Carnbo
South Queich
Drumvaich
Burn of Cambus
Kinbuck
Ashfield
Balhaldie
Sheriff Muir
Doune
Deanston
CATHEDRAL
Dunblane
Pisgah
LEIGHTON LIBRARY
BLAIRDENON HILL
BEN CLEUCH
Pool o' Muckhart
Yetts o' Muckhart
Drum
Crook of Devon
Thornhill
Blair Drummond
Easter Row
BLAIR DRUMMOND SAFARI PARK
Sunnylaw
KING'S SEAT HILL
CASTLE CAMPBELL
DOLLAR GLEN
Rumbling Bridge
RUMBLING BRIDGE GORGE
Blairdrummond Moss
Bridge of Allan
Blairlogie
Menstrie
MILL TRAIL VISITOR CENTRE
Tillicoultry
Dollar
Powmill
Alva
STERLING MILLS
Devonside
Blairingone
Drip Moss
Causewayhead
NATIONAL WALLACE MONUMENT
Tullibody
Fishcross
Coalsnaughton
GARTMORN DAM
Hill End
Kippen
Glentirranmuir
Gargunnock
STIRLING CASTLE
OLD TOWN JAIL
Raploch
Cambuskenneth
ABBEY
Cambus
Branshill
Sauchie
Forest Mill
Balgonar
KNOCK HILL
CARLEATHERAN
SMITH ART GALL & MUSEUM
Stirling
Torbrex
ALLOA
ALLOA TOWER
Touch Hills
Cambusbarron
Fallin
Keilarsbrae
Saline
Gargunnock Hills
St Ninians
Throsk
Clackmannan
Kennet
Kilbagie
South Alloa
Cowstrandburn
Bannockburn
BANNOCKBURN HERITAGE CENTRE
Earlsburn Reservoirs
Cowie
Dunmore
THE PINEAPPLE
Devilla Forest
Blairhall
Comrie
Oakley
Carnock
Gowkhall
Craigend
STIRLING SERVICES
Kincardine
CULROSS ABBEY
High Valleyfield
Loch Walton
Loch Coulter
Plean
PLEAN
Airth
CULROSS PALACE
Culross
Low Torry
Torryburn
Cairneyhill
Easter Cringate
Letham
Kincardine Bridge
Torry Bay
CHARLESTOWN WORKSHOPS
Charlestown
Carron
Muirmill
Torwood
Antonshill
Skinflats
MUSEUM
Carron Valley Forest
Carron Bridge
Carron Valley Res.
Dunipace
DENNY
Fankerton
Stoneywood
Larbert
Stenhousemuir
Carron
Carronshore
GRANGEMOUTH
Grangepans
BO'NESS AND KINNEIL RAILWAY
Carriden
TOMTAIN
Head of Muir
Bainsford
FALKIRK WHEEL
Bo'ness
Muirhouses
Kilsyth Hills
Bonnybridge
Dennyloanhead
FALKIRK
Laurieston
BIRKHILL CLAY MINE
Blackness
Manner
COLZIUM HOUSE
Banton
Longcroft
High Bonnybridge
ROUGH CASTLE
Redding
Grougfoot
Kilsyth
Banknock
Greenhill
Glen Village
CALLENDAR HOUSE
Reddingmuirhead
Polmont
Brightons
Whitecross
Linlithgow
Milton of Campsie
Queenzieburn
Dullatur
ANTONINE WALL
Castlecary
Linlithgow Bridge
PALACE
Philpstoun
Croy
Cumbernauld Village
Abronhill
Twechar
Jawcraig
Shieldhill
California
Maddiston
Loan
Bridgend

Perth and Kinross
FIFE
NO
NT
FIRTH OF TAY
FIRTH OF FORTH
BRAES OF THE CARSE
CARSE OF GOWRIE
Perth
Scone
Stanley
Luncarty
Methven
Almondbank
Huntingtower
Tibbermore
Bridge of Earn
Aberargie
Abernethy
Newburgh
Auchtermuchty
Falkland
Ladybank
Glenrothes
Leslie
Markinch
Kirkcaldy
Kinross
Milnathort
Kelty
Lochgelly
Cowdenbeath
Lochore
Ballingry
Cardenden
Dunfermline
Rosyth
Inverkeithing
North Queensferry
Queensferry
Burntisland
Kinghorn
Aberdour
Dalgety Bay
Dollar
Rumbling Bridge
Yetts o' Muckhart
Pool o' Muckhart
Auchterarder
Dunning
Forteviot
Aberdalgie
Glenfarg
Invergowrie
Errol
St Madoes
Glencarse
Kinfauns
Dundee
Grangemouth
Bo'ness
Culross
Kincardine
Oakley
Saline
High Valleyfield
Low Torry
Torryburn
Crossford
Cairneyhill
Charlestown
Limekilns
Inchcolm
Inchkeith
Inchmickery
Cramond I.
Dalmeny
Leith
Newhaven
Granton
EDINBURGH
Forth Road Bridge
Loch Leven
Lomond Hills Regional Park
Lochore Meadows
Common of Dunning
Cleish Hills
Glen Devon
Burnfoot
Glendevon
Castle Hill Reservoir
Pitmedden Forest
Kinfauns Forest
Keillour Forest
Devilla Forest
Gleneagles House
St Serf's Island
Loch Glow
Loch Fitty
Loch Ore
Loch Gelly
M90
A9
A85
A91
A92
A90
A977
A823
A985
A921
A909
133
134
127
120
121
0 1 2 3 4 5 6 miles
0 1 2 3 4 5 6 7 8 9 10 km

5 6 7 8 9

A

B

C

D

E

F

G

Birkhill
Downfield
Fintry
Baldovie
Mains of Ardestie
Carnoustie
Dundee
Lochee
Douglas & Angus
Craigie
West Ferry
Monifieth
Barnhill
Barry Links
CARNOUSTIE

VERDANT WORKS
MUS AND ART GALL
Stannergate
Broughty
BROUGHTY CASTLE MUSEUM
Buddon Ness
135

134
FRIGATE UNICORN

Dundee
DISCOVERY POINT
Tayport
Scotscraig
TENTSMUIR

Newport-on-Tay
A92
Woodhaven
Tay Rail Bridge
Wormit
Tentsmuir Forest

Kirkton
Bottomcraig
Balmerino
Gauldry
Pickletillem

Kilmany
Lucklawhill
Rhynd
Carrick
Leuchars
LEUCHARS NORMAN CHURCH

Rathillet
Logie
Balmullo

Guardbridge
EDEN ESTUARY CENTRE
Eden Mouth

Kilmaron Castle
Dairsie or Osnaburgh
Kincaple
ST ANDREWS BAY

Cupar
Strathkinness
Newpark
ST ANDREWS
BRITISH GOLF MUS
St Andrews
ST ANDREWS AQUARIUM
CATH & ST RULE'S TOWER
Brownhills
Buddo Ness

Cupar Muir
Kemback
Blebocraigs
Balone
ST ANDREWS BOTANIC GARDEN
Boarhills
Babbet Ness

HILL OF TARVIT MANSIONHOUSE
Pitscottie
CRAIGTOUN
Denhead
Prior Muir
Stravithie
Kingsbarns
Cambo Ness
Carr Brigs

SCOTSTARVIT TOWER
Bridgend
Ceres
Baldinnie
FIFE FOLK MUSEUM
Dunino
CAMBO GARDENS
Tullybothy Craigs
Craighead

Craigrothie
Woodside
Peat Inn
Radernie
Kingsmuir
Lochty
Balcomie
Fife Ness

Montrave
Lathones
Largoward
Carnbee
SCOTLAND'S SECRET BUNKER
CRAIL TOLBOOTH
Crail
CRAIL MUSEUM AND HERITAGE CENTRE

PRAYTIS FARM PARK
Wester Newburn
SCOTLAND'S LARDER
Pitcorthie
Pitkierie
West Ness

Kirkton of Largo
Drumeldrie
Colinsburgh
Arncroach
KELLIE CASTLE AND GARDEN
Kilrenny
FIFE COASTAL PATH

Bonnybank
Lundin Links
ROBINSON CRUSOE STATUE
Lower Largo
Balchrystie
Abercrombie
Kilconquhar
Pittenweem
Anstruther Wester
Anstruther Easter
SCOTTISH FISHERIES MUSEUM

Kennoway
Scoonie
SILVERBURN ESTATE
Ardross
ST FILLAN'S CAVE
ST MONAN'S WINDMILL
St Monans

LETHAM GLEN
Leven
Earlsferry
Elie
ST MONAN'S CHURCH

Methil
MUSEUM
Innerleven
Ruddons Pt.
Chapel Ness
Sauchar Pt.
Isle of May

Buckhaven
FIFE COASTAL PATH
Largo Bay
Isle of May

NO

NT

FORTH

Fidra
Craigleith
Bass Rock

Eyebroughy
North Berwick
SCOTTISH SEABIRD CENTRE MUSEUM

DIRLETON CASTLE & GARDENS
MUIRFIELD
Dirleton
TANTALLON CASTLE
Auldhame
Gullane Bay

Gullane
Scoughall

West Fenton
Kingston
Whitekirk
St. Baldred's Cradle

Aberlady Bay
Fenton Barns
Tyne Mouth

Aberlady
MYRETON MOTOR MUSEUM
Drem
East Fortune
Tyninghame
JOHN MUIR BIRTHPLACE
Dunbar

121
Craigielaw
THE CHESTERS FORT
MUSEUM OF FLIGHT
Preston
122
JOHN MUIR
Belhaven
West Barns

GOSFORD HOUSE
Ballencrieff
Athelstaneford
East Linton
PRESTON MILL & PHANTASSIE DOOCOT
Broxburn
Barns Ness

Cockenzie and Port Seton
SETON COLLEGIATE CHURCH
Spittal
HOPETOUN MON
JANE WELSH CARLYLE MUSEUM
HAILES
Biel Water
Spott
Meikle
East Barns
Skateraw

Longniddry
Gosford Bay
A1

Loch Beoraid
Polnish
Lochailort
Ranochan
A830
796 SGURR AN UTHA
Glen Finnan
Glen Dubh Lighe
Wauchan
Gleann Suileag
Druim
Fada
Ardnish
Inverailort
Loch Eilt
147
STATION MUSEUM
GLENFINNAN MONUMENT
Glenfinnan
136
Laggan
Loch Ailort
Alisary
Callop
Kinlocheil
Fassfern
Drumsallie
A830
TREASURES OF THE EARTH
Roshven
869 DRUIM FIACLACH
882 ROIS-BHEINN
882 BEINN ODHAR BHEAG
LOCH EIL
A861
South Garvan
Duisky
Blaich
Corpach
Achaphubuil
Camusnagaul
Trislaig
Glen Garvan
666 BEINN GAIRE
755 MEALL NAN CREAG LEAC
Kinlochmoidart
MOIDART
Gaskan
Scamodale
Loch Moidart
Ardmolich
Brunery
Gorstanvorran
SGOR AN TARMACHAIN 756
Cona
Cona Glen
770 STOB COIRE A'CHEARCAILL
Stronchreggan
Ach'an Todhair
Drumarbin
A82
LOCH SHIEL
Glen Hurich
Dalnabreck
Dalelia
786 BEINN MHEADHOIN
Conaglen House
Blarmachfoldach
CLAISH MOSS
Polloch
Glenhurich
Loch Doilet
888 SGURR DHOMHNUILL
Scaddle
Aryhoulan
Inverscaddle Bay
Coruanan Lodge
Ardshealach
Kinlochan
Glen Scaddle
SUNART
Ardgour
SGURR NA H-EANCHAINNE 730
616 BEINN NA GUCAIG
845 BEINN RESIPOL
ARIUNDLE CENTRE
ARIUNDLE OAKWOOD
Resipole
Glen Gour
Ardgour
Glenrigh Forest
Corran Narrows
Ariundle
Scotstown
Strontian
701
Clovullin
Inchree
LOCH SUNART
A861
Anaheilt
Sallachan
Corran
Keppanach
Onich
Ardnastang
Strontian
885 GARBH BHEINN
Sallachan Pt.
615
GLENCRIPESDALE
Glen Tarbert
A82
North Ballachulish
Camuschoirk
Tarbert
Inversanda Bay
Inversanda
HIGHLAND MYSTERYWORLD
Liddesdale
LOCH LINNHE
South Ballachulish
Glencoe
516 MEALL AN DAMHAIN
NM
583 CREACH BHEINN
A828
Kentallen
Ballachulish
B8043
Glenduror Forest
582 BEINN NAM BEATHRACH
Lochuisge
765 FUAR BHEINN
Kilmalieu
Duror
947
571
Loch Uisge
Rubha Mor
Beinn a'Bheithir
Glen an Fhiodh
A884
Cuil Bay
Gleann Dubh
B8043
Eilean Balnagowan
Keil
Glen Duror
Beach
Kingairloch
Camasnacroise
Salachan Glen
Loch Arienas
Loch a'Choire
879 FRAOCHAIDH
Acharn
739 BEINN MHEADHOIN
Gleann Geal
KINGAIRLOCH
Shuna I.
Appin House
655
Elleric
959 BEINN FHIONNLA
Claggan
147
Glen Stockdale
A828
Glen Creran
ARDTORNISH GARDENS
Loch Teàrnait
437 BEINN A' CHAISIL
Portnacroish
Fasnacloich
Invercreran
Glen Ure
Achranich
Rannoch
KINLOCHLAICH HOUSE GARDENS
An Iola
BEINN CHURALAIN 546
GLASDRUM WOOD
Glasdrum
Loch Aline
Glensanda
Loch nan Clach
Appin
Strath of Appin
Creagan
937 BEINN SGULAIRD
Port Ramsay
Port Appin
Druimavuic
LYNN OF LORN
GLAIS BHEINN 479
AN SLEAGHACH 513
Clachan
Eriska
North Shian
Loch Creran
839 BEINN TRILLEACHAN
ARDTORNISH CASTLE
Eignaig
South Shian
South Creagan
Lismore
B8045
SCOTTISH SEA LIFE SANCTUARY
Barcaldine
810 CREACH BHEINN
Innimore Bay
Garbh Shlios
Camas Gorm
Achnacroish
Barcaldine Forest
Allt Easach
Abhainn Dalach
LORN
Scallastle Bay
Rubha an Ridire
Bernera I.
124
Achinduin
Baravullin
Ferlochan
125
Kilcheran
Eilean Dubh
LYNN OF LORN
Kiel Crofts
Benderloch
BENDERLOCH
Gleann Salach
LOCH ETIVE
Java
Craignure Bay
Ledaig
B845
Craignure
MULL AND WEST HIGHLAND NARROW GAUGE RAILWAY
Ardmucknish Bay
Achnaba
715 BEINN MHEADHONACH
0:50
A828
ARDCHATTAN PRIORY GARDENS
ARDCHATTAN PRIORY
Duart Bay
Duart Pt.
TOROSAY CASTLE & GARDEN
DUART CASTLE
Eilean Musdile
Eilean Mor
North Connel
Black Crofts
FALLS OF LORA
Glen Liver
Connel
DUNSTAFFNAGE CASTLE
Achnacloich
ACHNACLOICH GARDEN
Bonawe
Lochdon
0:45
Dunbeg
Glen Noe
CASTLEBAY 4:50
COLL 2:20
TIREE 3:20
LOCHBOISDALE 5:20
Ganavan
A85
Brochroy
BONAWE IRON FURNACE
INVERAWE FISHERIES AND SMOKERIES EXHIBITION
Black Lochs
Fearnoch Forest
A849
Loch Don
Dunollie
OBAN/OBAN LODGE
MCCAIG'S TOWER
Taynuilt
Ichrachan
Bridge of Awe
BEN CRUACHAN 1126
Grass Pt.
OBAN VISITOR CENTRE
OBAN DISTILLERY
Pass of Brander
Altnacraig
OBAN RARE BREEDS FARM PARK
BARGUILLEAN GARDENS
Cruachan Res.
Kerrera
Oban
GLEN NANT
Glen Nant
Awe
897
Loch Spelve
COLONSAY 2:20
383
Glenamachrie
Glen Lonan
Falls of Cruachan
0 1 2 3 4 5 6 miles
0 1 2 3 4 5 6 7 8 9 10 km
Gallanach
Loch Nell
Barran
515
RUACHAN DAM VISITOR CENTRE
Loch-Nant
Loch Tromlee
A
B
C
D
E
F
1
2
3
4

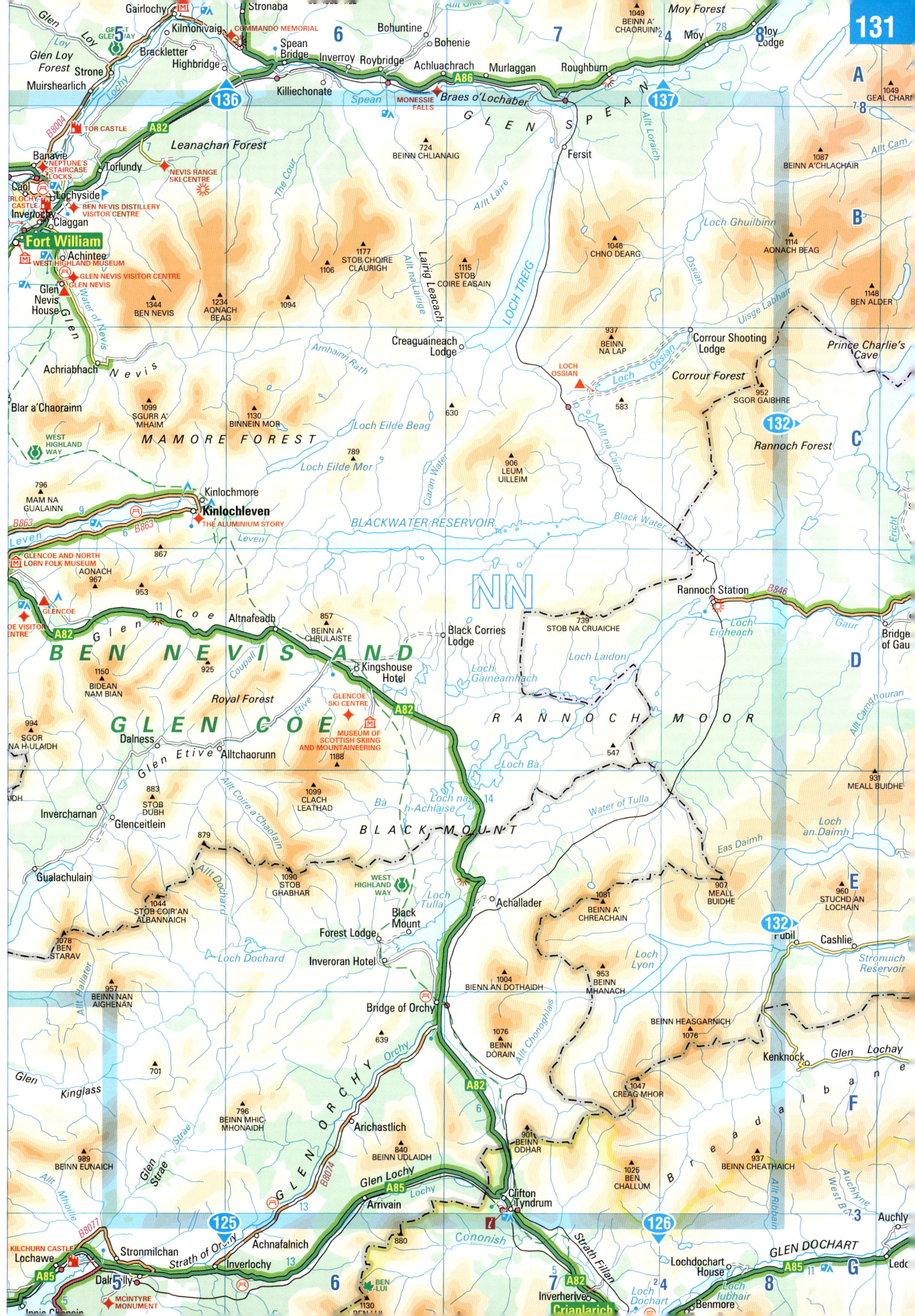

Glen Loy

Gairlochy
Stronaba
Moy Forest
Loy
GF GLEN
5 T TAY
Kilmonivaig
COMMANDO MEMORIAL
6
Bohuntine
7
1049 BEINN A' CHAORUINN
Moy
28
8 loy Lodge
Brackletter
Spean Bridge
Inverroy
Roybridge
Bohenie
Highbridge
Achluachrach
Murlaggan
Roughburn

Glen Loy Forest
Strone
Muirshearlich
Highbridge
Killiechonate
A86
Braes o'Lochaber
1049 GEAL CHARN
7-8

Lochy
136
Spean
MONESSIE FALLS
GLEN SPEAN
137
A

Tor Castle
A82
Leanachan Forest
724 BEINN CHLIANAIG
Fersit
1087 BEINN A'CHLACHAIR
Allt Cam

Banavie
NEPTUNE'S STAIRCASE LOCKS
Torlundy
NEVIS RANGE SKI CENTRE
The Cour
Allt Laire
Allt Loraich

Caol
Lochyside
BEN NEVIS DISTILLERY VISITOR CENTRE
1177 STOB CHOIRE CLAURIGH
1115 STOB COIRE EASAIN
1046 CHNO DEARG
Loch Ghuilbinn
1114 AONACH BEAG
B

Inverlochy
Claggan
1106
Loch Treig
Ossian

Fort William
Achintee
WEST HIGHLAND MUSEUM
GLEN NEVIS VISITOR CENTRE
GLEN NEVIS
Laing Leacach
Allt na Lairige
1148 BEN ALDER

Glen Nevis House
1344 BEN NEVIS
1234 AONACH BEAG
1094
Creaguaineach Lodge
937 BEINN NA LAP
Corrour Shooting Lodge
Uisge Labhair
Prince Charlie's Cave

Achriabhach
Nevis
Amhainn Rath
LOCH OSSIAN
Loch Ossian
Corrour Forest

Blar a'Chaorainn
1099 SGURR A' MHAIM
1130 BINNEIN MOR
630
583
952 SGOR GAIBHRE
C

WEST HIGHLAND WAY
MAMORE FOREST
Loch Eilde Beag
906 LEUM UILLEIM
132
Rannoch Forest

796 MAM NA GUALAINN
Kinlochmore
Loch Eilde Mor
789
Ciaran Water
BLACKWATER RESERVOIR
Black Water

B863
Kinlochleven
THE ALUMINIUM STORY
Leven
NN

GLENCOE AND NORTH LORN FOLK MUSEUM
867
Rannoch Station
B846

AONACH 967
953
Altnafeadh
857 BEINN A' CHRULAISTE
Black Corries Lodge
739 STOB NA CRUAICHE
Loch Eigheach
Bridge of Gau

GLENCOE
A82
Glen Coe
925
Coupall
Kingshouse Hotel
Loch Gaineamhach
Loch Laidon
D

BEN NEVIS AND
1150 BIDEAN NAM BIAN
Royal Forest
GLENCOE SKI CENTRE
MUSEUM OF SCOTTISH SKIING AND MOUNTAINEERING
1188
RANNOCH MOOR

GLEN COE
Dalness
Glen Etive
Alltchaorunn
Etive
547
931 MEALL BUIDHE

994 SGOR NA H-ULAIDH
883 STOB DUBH
1099 CLACH LEATHAD
Loch Ba
Loch an Daimh

Invercharnan
Glenceitlein
Allt Coire a Chaolain
Ba
BLACK MOUNT
14
Water of Tulla

879
Allt Dochard
Loch na h-Achlaise
E

Gualachulain
1090 STOB GHABHAR
WEST HIGHLAND WAY
Loch Tulla
1081
907 MEALL BUIDHE
960 STUCHD AN LOCHAIN

1044 STOB COIR'AN ALBANNAICH
Black Mount
Achallader
BEINN A' CHREACHAIN
132
Pubil
Cashlie
Stronuich Reservoir

1078 BEN STARAV
Forest Lodge
Inveroran Hotel
Loch Dochard
Loch Lyon

957 BEINN NAN AIGHENAN
Allt Hallater
1004 BIENN AN DOTHAIDH
953 BEINN MHANACH
Glen Lochay

Glen Kinglass
Bridge of Orchy
639
1076 BEINN DORAIN
Allt Chonoghais
BEINN HEASGARNICH
1076
Kenknock
F

701
GLEN ORCHY
Orchy
1047 CREAG MHOR
Glen Lochay

989 BEINN EUNAICH
796 BEINN MHIC MHONAIDH
Arichastlich
901 BEINN ODHAR
1025 BEN CHALLUM
937 BEINN CHEATHAICH

Glen Strae
B8074
840 BEINN UDLAIDH
Glen Lochy
West B
Auchlyne

125
Achnafalnich
A85
Clifton Tyndrum
126
Inverherive
Glen Lochay
3

KILCHURN CASTLE
Stronmilchan
Inverlochy
13
880
Cononish
Lochdochart House
GLEN DOCHART
A85

Lochawe
A85
Dalmally
6
BEN LUI
7
A82
24
Loch Dochart
Benmore
G

MCINTYRE MONUMENT
1130
Crianlarich
Inverherive
Strath Fillan

Moy 28
Moy Lodge
Lochan na h-Earba
Pattack
674 BEINN EILDE
911
A9
Gaick Forest
Loch Bhrodainn
Allt Gharbh Ghaig

Ardverikie Forest
1049 GEAL CHARN
137
Loch Pattack
Ben Alder Lodge
Loch Ericht Forest
774 CREAGAN MOR
941 CARN'NA-CAIM
138
Loch an Duin

Allt Loraich
Allt Cam
917
Cama Choire
Sronphadruig Lodge
Dail-na-Mine Forest
816 SRON A'CHLEIRICH
Allt Glas Choire

1087 BEINN A'CHLACHAIR
Ben Alder Forest
936 A'BHUIDHEANACH BHEAG
Allt a'Chireachain

B
Loch Ghuilbinn
Allt a'Chaoil-rèidhe
934
803 THE SOW OF ATHOLL
Dalnacardoch Forest
Allt a'Mhuilinn
FOREST
NATH

1114 AONACH BEAG
BEINN UDLAMAIN
Dalnaspidal Lodge
17
Dalnacardoch Lodge

Loch a' Bhealaich Bheithe
1148 BEN ALDER
Corrievarkie Lodge
Dalnaspidal Forest
775 MEALL NA LEITREACH
Loch Garry
A9

Ossian
Uisge Labhair
Loch Con
GLEN GARRY
Garry

Corrour Shooting Lodge
Prince Charlie's Cave
Allt na Glaise
Loch Errochty
Dalchalloch
B847
CJ

Corrour Forest
855
Talla Bheith Forest
612
Trinafour
GLEN ERROCHTY
Errochty Water
10

952 SGOR GAIBHRE
131
Allt Ghlas
612
891 BEINN A'CHUALLAICH
B846
Tummel Forest
477 Tummel Bridge
B8019

Rannoch Forest
515 SRON BHEAG
841 BEINN MHOLACH
Aulich Burn
Killichonan Burn
B846 Tummel

k Water
Ericht
Craiganor Lodge
B846
Kinloch Rannoch
Dunalastair Water
Foss

G
Bridge of Ericht
Killichonan
19
LOCH RANNOCH
Carie
Inverhadden
Loch Kinardochy
B846

Rannoch Station
B846
Gaur
Bridge of Gaur
Finnart
Black Wood of Rannoch
Dunalastair
1083 SCHIEHALLION
Kaltney Burn

Loch Eigheach
Camghouran
Rannoch
Dall Burn
Allt na Bogair
Innerhadden Burn
TAY FOR
Allt Mor

D
Loch
Forest
1042 CARN MAIRG
GLENGOULANDIE DEER PARK
13

LOCH RANNOCH AND
GLEN LYON
745 MEALL A'MHUIC
1029 CARN GORM
Keltneyburn

931 MEALL BUIDHE
Invervar
ST FILLAN'S CHURCH & FORTINGALL YEW

Loch an Daimh
GLEN LYON GALLERY
Camusvrachan
Lyon
Fortingall
Taymouth Castle

907 MEALL BUIDHE
960 STUCHD AN LOCHAIN
Innerwick
Bridge of Balgie
A827
Kenmore

131
Gallin
780
1118
SCOTTISH CRANN

Pubil
Cashlie
Allt Conait
Allt Ball a'Mhuilinn
Fearnan
Remony
Acharn

Loch Lyon
Stronuich Reservoir
Glen Lyon
Allt Gleann Da-Eig
1214 BEN LAWERS
Falls of Acharn

Eas Daimh
MEALL NAN TARMACHAN
Loch na Lairige
BEN LAWERS
Lawers
716 BEINN BHREAC
Quaich

Beinn Heasgarnich
1076
1043
BEN LAWERS VISITOR CENTRE
Carie
Ardtalnaig
888
Gleann a'Chilleine

Kenknock
Glen Lochay
Lochay
Milton Morenish
Morenish
Ardeonaig
Finglen Burn

1047 G MHOR
FALLS OF LOCHAY AND FISH LIFT
Boreland
MOIRLANICH LONGHOUSE
Finlarig
25
LOCH TAY

937 BEINN CHEATHAICH
Killin
BREADALBANE FOLKLORE CENTRE
Achmore
637
879 CREAG UCHDAG
Loch Lednock Reservoir

25 EN LLUM
Allt Ribbain
West Burn
Auchlyne Burn
Dochart
FALLS OF DOCHART
Loch Lednock Reservoir
931 BEN CHONZIE

Loch Iubhair
Auchlyne
126
Ardchyle
A85
Glen Ogle
Invergeldie Burn
Glen Lednock
Invergeldie

0 1 2 3 4 5 6 miles
0 1 2 3 4 5 6 7 8 9 10km

Loch Iut
Benmore
672 SRON MHOR
127
Glen Lochnock
untullich

994 CARN EALAR
1006 AN SGARSOCH
Baddoch
834
A
920 CARN BHAC
1019 CARN AN TUIRC
958 TOLMO
788 UCHD A'CHLARSAIR

138
Tarf Water
139
1048 BEINN IUTHARN MHOR
Loch Vrotachan
GLENSHEE SKI CENTRE
1068 GLAS MAOL

M O U N T A I N S

MO
1008 BEINN DEARG
879 BRAIGH SRON GHORM
Loch nan Eun
930 THE CAIRNWELL
Devil's Elbow
Caenlochan Forest

M Glen Bruar
Bruar Lodge
Glen Diridh Tilt
BEN GULABIN 806
808 MONAMEANACH
Isla
FINAL HILL

OF ATHOLL
899
Forest Lodge
Loch Loch
1051 GLAS TULAICHEAN
Glenlochsie
Auchavan

OLL
1120 BEINN A'GHLO
Glen
Spittal of Glenshee
DUCHRAY HILL 702
740 BADENDII HILL

Falls of the Bruar
BLAIR CASTLE
CLAN DONNACHAIDH MUSEUM
975 CARN LIATH
903 BEN VUIRICH
Gleann Fearnach
801 BEN EARB
794 MEALL UAINE
134
Dalnaglar Castle
Meikle Forter
808
Folda

Pitagowan B8079
Calvine
Struan
Blair-Atholl
Old Bridge of Tilt
Lude House
BLAIR ATHOLL MILL
Ballentoul
BLAIR ATHOLL DISTILLERY
TULACH HILL
Dalnavaid
Tarvie
19
Straloch
Enochdhu
Kirkmichael
B950
Cray
744 MOUNT BLAIR
Brewlan Bridge

470
Aldclune
1689
ATHOLL COUNTRY COLLECTION
Killiecrankie
KILLIECRANKIE VISITOR CENTRE
12
841 BEN VRACKIE
A924
Glen Brerachan
641 CREAG DHUBH
STRATHARDLE
Ashintully Castle
B991
520 CAIRN GIBBS

LOCH
Tressait
13
Queen's View
Bonskeid House
B8019
A9
PITLOCHRY
Loch Broom
KNOCK OF BALMYLE 444
Blacklunans
13
Forest of Alyth

TUMMEL
Queen's View Centre
Falls of Tummel
LINN OF TUMMEL
Moulin
Pitlochry
EDRADOUR DISTILLERY
Loch Faskally
Milton of Edradour
BLAIR ATHOLL DISTILLERY VISITOR CENTRE
534 MEALL REAMHAR
Ballintuim
A924
Netherton
Tullym

TUMMEL
Balmore
HYDRO-ELECTRIC VISITOR CENTRE
SCOTTISH PLANT COLLECTORS GARDEN
THEATRE FESTIVAL
NO
561 CREAG NAM MIAL
Blackcraig Forest
Bridge of Cally

NN
780 FARRAGON HILL
Loch Derculich
CHILDHOOD HERITAGE MUSEUM
Milton of Dalcapon
Loch Ordie
Forest of Clunie
A93

EST PARK
Strathtay
Ballechin
Grandtully
Tulliemet
Loch Benachally
Cochrage Muir

Edradynate
CLUNY HOUSE GARDENS
Little Ballinluig
ST MARY'S CHURCH
Balnaguard
Logierait
Ballinluig
Kindallachan
Riemore
Lornty Burn
Middleton
308
Westfields of Rattray

CASTLE MENZIES
Camserney
Weem
ABERFELDY DISTILLERY & DEWAR'S WORLD OF WHISKY
Balmacneil
Kincraigie
Guay
Dowally
509 DEUCHARY HILL
Riechip
Lornty
A926
Rattray

Dull
WADE'S BRIDGE
Aberfeldy
532
Loch Skiach
Butterstone
13
Forneth
Achalader
A923
BLAIRGOWRIE
Kinloch
Rosemount

FALLS OF MONESS
BOLFRACKS GARDEN
Loch Kennard
Craigvinean Forest
RIVER TAY
SCOTTISH HORSE REGIMENTAL MUSEUM
LOCH OF LOWES NATURE RESERVE
Concraigie
Loch of Clunie
A923
B947
Muirton of Ballo
Rosemount

566 OG CENTRE
Loch Hoil
690 MEALL DEARG
Scotston
THE HERMITAGE
WATERFALL
Dunkeld
Inver
Little Dunkeld
Birnam
Snaigow House
Kirkton of Lethendy
134

Garrow
Glen Cochill
Ballinlick
Trochry
404
Spittalfield
Delvine
A984

P e r t h
Cablea
Strathbraan
Obney Hills
Caputh
Gellyburn
Murthly
Ardoch
Meikleour
BEECH HEDGE
Isla
Woodside
Burrelton

805 MEALL NAM FUARAN
Amulree
Upper Obney
Muir of Thorn
B9099
Kinclaven
Cargill
Whitefie
A94

a n d
Corrymuckloch
A822
Little Glenshee
Waterloo
12
Bankfoot
Aimtully
Woodside
Saucher
Coll

K i n
623 MEALL NAN CAORAICH
LIQUEUR CENTRE
Tullybelton
West Tofts
13
A923
Wolfhill
Kinrossie
Kirkton Collace
Bar

Newton
14
Logiealmond Lodge
Logiealmond
Stanley
West Tofts
A9
Downhill
Newmin
St Martins
B8953
Balbeggie

648 MEALL TARSUINN
127
Harrietfield
Chapelhill
Moneydie
128
Redgorton
PERTH
A94
14

Loch Turret Reservoir
Buchanty
B8063
B8063
Pitcairngreen
CAITHNESS GLASS
SCONE PALACE
288

5
Glen Turret
6
A822
7
Keillour
Almondbank
Hunting
PERTH MART VISITOR CENTRE
Scone
G
8 R

Baddoch
Glen Callater
Loch Callater
Dubh Loch
Glas-allt Shiel
Spittal of Glenmuick
Loch Muick
Glen Mark
Water of Mark
Burn of Branny
Water of Tarf
1012 CAIRN BANNOCH
998 BROAD CAIRN
939 AN SOCACH
1019 CARN AN TUIRC
958 TOLMOUNT
Invermark Lodge
Auchronie
696 AWEE
Glen Lee
Loch Lee
Inchgrundle
Tarfside
Cairncross
Water of Unich
832 LAIR OF ALDARARIE
Clunie Water
Loch Vrotachan
GLENSHEE SKI CENTRE
933 THE CAIRNWELL
Devil's Elbow
1068 GLAS MAOL
Caenlochan Forest
Glen Doll
Glendoll Lodge
Glendoll Forest
Braedownie
CORRIE FEE
MUCKLE CAIRN 826
Loch Brandy
Glen Effock
CRUYS 741
Water of Saughs
691 WEST KNOCK
BEN GULABIN 806
Isla
905 FINALTY HILL
947 DRIESH
Clova
758
778 WHITE HILL
Hunthill Lodge
808 MONAMEANACH
Wheen
Spittal of Glenshee
Auchavan
Loch Beanie
Angus
Kilburn
Rottal
756 FINBRACKS
Glenprosen Lodge
Glen Prosen
Glen Shee
794 MEALL UAINE
702 DUCHRAY HILL
740 BADENDUN HILL
NO
Balnaboth
PROSEN
Glenprosen Village
512
Clachnabrain
545 AULD DARKNEY
Dalnaglar Castle
Meikle Forter
Folda
Glenisla Forest
611
Glenmoy
Auchnacree
Cray
744 MOUNT BLAIR
Backwater Res.
Glenhead Farm
Easter Lednathie
South Esk
Glen Clova
Glenogil
Ashintully Castle
Brewlands Bridge
Freuchies
Glenquiech
Ogil
Fern
Kirkmichael
Blacklunans
Kirkton of Glenisla
Bellaty
668 CAT LAW
CAPTAIN SCOTT & DR WILSON CAIRN
Horniehaugh
Dykehead
Newmill of Inshewan
Noran
520 CAIRN GIBBS
497 CREIGH HILL
Balintore
Pearsie
Cortachy
Memus
Tannadice
Dykends
Balloch
Inverquharity
Murthill
Finavon
Forest of Alyth
KNOCK OF BALMYLE 444
Black Water
409 MILE HILL
Shielhill
Oathlaw
Loch of Lintrathen
PEEL FARM TRAIL
Kirkton of Kingoldrum
Northmuir
Bintuim
BALDUFF HILL 425
Bridgend of Lintrathen
LOCH OF KINNORDY NATURE RESERVE
Kinnordy
Kirriemuir
BARRIE'S BIRTHPLACE
Carse Gray
Ardle
REEKIE LINN WATERFALL
Bridge of Craigisla
Auchrannie
Westmuir
GATEWAY TO THE GLENS MUS
Mosside
Blackcraig Forest
Netherton
Tullymurdoch
Kirkton of Airlie
Mains of Ballindarg
Lunanhead
RESTENNETH PRIORY
Bridge of Cally
Bamff
Craigton
Padanaram
Forfar
FORFAR LOCH
THE MEFFAN GALL & MUS
Cochrage Muir
Shanzie
Drumgley
Ruthven
Ruthven House
EASSIE SCULPTURED STONE
Leys of Cossans
ST ORLAND'S STONE
Dean Water
Kingsmuir
Lornty Burn
Tullyfergus
Alyth
New Alyth
Westfields of Rattray
GLAMIS CASTLE
Caldhame
Lownie Moor
Middleton
308
Douglastown
Lornty
Balhary
Castleton
Glamis
Thornton
Kirkton
Charleston
ANGUS FOLK MUSEUM
Blairgowrie
Achalader
Kinloch
Rattray
Leitfie
MEIGLE MUSEUM
Balkeerie
Eassie
Foffarty
Inverarity
Loch of Clunie
Loch of Drumellie
River Ericht
Kinloch
Meigle
Kirkinch
Gateside
Whigstreet
Clunie
Craigie
Muirton
Ardblair
Rosemount
Milton
Kirkton of Lethendy
Lunan Burn
Arthurstone
Wester Denoon
ARK HILL 340
Gallowfauld
Spittalfield
Ardler
New-bigging
Nether Handwick
Newtyle
Delvine
Keillor
Coupar Angus
259
Caputh
Meikleour
BEECH HEDGE
Kinclaven
Tay
Kettins
Markethill
Hallyburton House
Long Loch
Coldstream
Murthly
Ardoch
Campmuir
Bonnyton
Kirkton of Auchterhouse
Balkemback
Tealing
Newbigging
Monikie
Woodside
Burrelton
Leys
Lundie
Auchterhouse
Leoch
Kirkton
Inveraldie
East March
Wellbank
Cargill
Pitcur
Muir of Pert
Bucklerheads
Newbigging
Sidlaw Hills
Burnside of Duntrune
Kellas
Drumsturdy
Whitefield
Dronley
Bridgefoot
Muirhead
Birkhill
CLATTO
Littleton
Fintry
SOUTHERRAIN ARDESTIE
West Tofts
Stanley
Saucher
KING'S SEAT 377
Fowlis
CAMPERDOWN AND TEMPLETON WOODS
Downfield
Douglas & Angus
Baldovie
Wolfhill
Collace
Liff
Dundee
Guildtown
Kinrossie
Kirkton of Collace
Denhead of Gray
VERDANT WORKS
Craigie
West Ferry
Monifieth
Abernyte
Braes of the Carse
Knapp
Benvie
Lochee
MILLS OBSERVATORY
MUS AND ART GALL
BROUGHTY CASTLE
Barnhill
Newmiln
St Martins
Bandirran
Rossie Priory
Invergowrie
Stannergate
FRIGATE UNICORN
Broughty Ferry
BROUGHTY CASTLE MUSEUM
Dowrhill
Balbeggie
Ballindean
Longforgan
Kingoodie
DUNDEE
DISCOVERY POINT
Tay Bridge
Tayport
Luncarty
PERTH
Kinnaird
Inchture
Castle Huntly
UNIVERSITY BOTANIC GARDENS
Newport-on-Tay
Scotscraig
TENTSMUIR
PERTH MART VISITOR CENTRE
Woodhaven
Tay Rail Bridge
Wormit
Tentsmuir
Scone
288
Kilspindie
Grange
0 1 2 3 4 5 6 miles
0 1 2 3 4 5 6 7 8 9 10 km

Burn of Tennet
MOUNT BATTOCK
778
Glen Dye
5
6
7
Tannachie
Carmont
Nev Mill
8
A92
Thornyhive Bay
A

140
Cairn o' Mount
Drumtochty Forest
464 525 MELUNCART
Mains of Dellavaird
BURNS FAMILY MEMORIALS
141
Drumlithie
Fiddes
Barras
70
Mill of Uras
Crawton
10

THE RETREAT GLEN ESK FOLK MUS
Milden Lodge
Glenfarquhar Lodge
Drumtochty Castle
Glenbervie
Mondynes
70
Pitforthie
Roadside of Catterline
FOWLSHEUGH NATURE RESERVE
Crawton Bay
Catterline
Braidon Bay
Todhead Point

Strath Finella
Clatterin Bridge
Glensaugh
Auchenblae
Monboddo House
14
B967
Parkneuk
Arbuthnott
Roadside of Kinneff
Kinneff
B

Auchmull
Mains of Balnakettle
FASQUE HOUSE
Thainston
East Cairnbeg
Brownmuir
Fordoun
70
GRASSIC GIBBON CENTRE
ARBUTHNOTT HOUSE GARDENS
ARBUTHNOTT CHURCH
Mains of Allardice
Little John's Haven

678 HILL OF WIRREN
FETTERCAIRN DISTILLERY VISITOR CENTRE
Fettercairn
Howe of the Mearns
Scotston
70
B9120
Inverbervie
Bervie Bay

Witton
Dalbog
Gannochy
Inch of Arnhall
Edzell
Meikle Strath
Sauchieburn
Bent
Laurencekirk
A90
Garvock
Tulloch
DAMSIDE GARDEN HERBS & ARBORETUM
Gourdon

EDZELL CASTLE AND GARDENS
Bridgend
Balfield
Dunlappie
B966
Luthermuir
Luther Water
50
Dykelands
Garvock Hill
Redford
Benholm
MILL OF BENHOLM

Tillyarblet
440
North Water Bridge
70
B974
North Esk
Marykirk
Ecclesgreig
Johnshaven
13

BROWN CATERTHUN
WHITE CATERTHUN
Inchbare
70
Pert
Craigo
Logie Pert
Logie
Lochside
Morphie
St Cyrus
Milton Ness

Kirkton of Menmuir
Tigerton
Newtonmill
70
Muirton of Ballochy
Hillside
ST CYRUS
Pathhead

Mains of Balhall
Lochty
Belliehill
Little Brechin
Keithock
Trinity
Kirkhill
A92
C

Careston Castle
BRECHIN CASTLE CENTRE
A935
Brechin
PICTAVIA
CATHEDRAL ROUND TOWER
HOUSE OF DUN
Dun
A935
CALEDONIAN RAILWAY
Montrose Basin
Montrose
MUSEUM AND ART GALLERY
Scurdie Ness
WILLIAM LAMB MEMORIAL STUDIO

Netherton
Mains of Melgund
Aldbar Castle
Middle Drums
A933
Kinnaird Castle
Bridge of Dun
Barnhead
MONTROSE BASIN VISITOR CENTRE
Inchbraoch
Ferryden
Kirkton of Craig

ABERLEMNO SCULPTURED STONES
Aberlemno
B9134
Pitkennedy
Montreathmont Forest
Farnell
Bonnyton
Carcary
Maryton
Dunninald
Long Craig
Fishtown of Usan
D

252
Turin
Rescobie
B9113
Dubton
Bolshan
Rossie Moor
Westerton
Boddin Pt.
NO

Reswallie
Balgavies
Milldens
Glasterlaw
Kinnell
Braehead of Lunan
Lunan
LUNAN BAY

Burnside
A932
Guthrie
Redcastle

Dunnichen
Letham
Pitmuies
HOUSE OF PITMUIES GARDEN
Friockheim
Boysack
Chapelton
Inverkeilor
Lang Craig
Ethie Mains

Craichie
Idvies
Leysmill
Lunan Water
B965
Cauldcots
Red Head
Ethie Castle
E

Tulloes
Mosston
Colliston
Letham Grange
Drunkendub
Meg's Craig

Kirkbuddo
B9128
Greystone
Redford
St Vigeans
Marywell
Auchmithie

Hayhillock
B9127
Carmyllie
Denhead of Arbilot
ST VIGEANS MUSEUM
Hayshead
Cliffburn
The Deil's Heid

CROMBIE
B961
Arbirlot
ARBROATH ABBEY
Arbroath
SIGNAL TOWER MUSEUM

Kirkton of Monikie
Craigton
CARLUNGIE SOUTERRAIN
Balmirmer
Elliot
A92
F

BARRY MILL
Muirdrum
Panbride
East Haven

Mains of Ardestie
Barry
A930
Salmond's Muir
Carnoustie
CARNOUSTIE

Barry Links
Buddon Ness
129
Buddon Ness
G

5
6
7
8
8

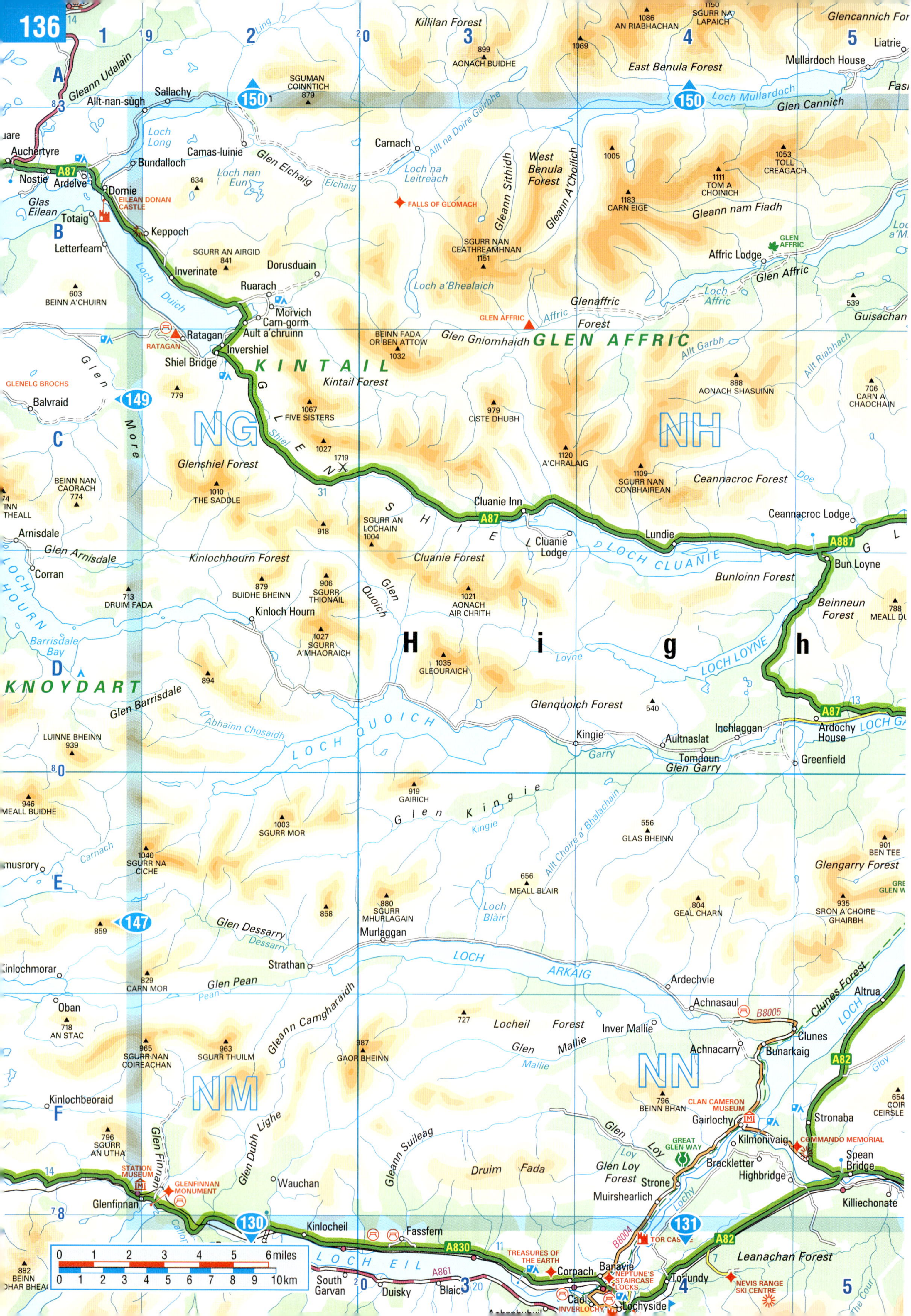

Gleann Udalain
Allt-nan-sugh
Sallachy
SGUMAN COINNTICH 879
Killilan Forest
899 AONACH BUIDHE
1086 AN RIABHACHAN
SGURR NA LAPAICH
Glencannich For
Liatrie
Mullardoch House
Fash

150

East Benula Forest
150
Loch Mullardoch
Glen Cannich

uare
Auchertyre
Nostie
Ardelve
A87
Bundalloch
Camas-luinie
Carnach
Loch na Leitreach
Allt na Doire Gairbhe

West Benula Forest
1005
1069
1111 TOM A CHOINICH
1053 TOLL CREAGACH

Dornie
EILEAN DONAN CASTLE
Glen Elchaig
Elchaig
Loch nan Eun
634

FALLS OF GLOMACH
Gleann Sithidh
Gleann A'Choilich
1183 CARN EIGE

GLEN AFFRIC

Gleann nam Fiadh

Totaig
B
Letterfearn
Keppoch
SGURR AN AIRGID 841
Dorusduain
Inverinate
Ruarach

SGURR NAN CEATHREAMHNAN 1151
Loch a'Bhealaich
Glenaffric
GLEN AFFRIC
Affric

888 AONACH SHASUINN

GLEN AFFRIC
Affric Lodge
Glen Affric
Loch Affric
539
Guisachan

Glas Eilean

Morvich
Carn-gorm
Ault a'chruinn
Invershiel
BEINN FADA OR BEN ATTOW 1032
Glen Gniomhaidh
Forest
GLEN AFFRIC
Allt Garbh
Allt Riabhach

Glen More
Ratagan
RATAGAN
Shiel Bridge

KINTAIL
779
Kintail Forest

GLE
NG

149

GLENELG BROCHS
Balvraid

NX
1067 FIVE SISTERS
1027
1719
31

979 CISTE DHUBH

706 CARN A CHAOCHAIN

NH

1120 A'CHRALAIG

BEINN NAN CAORACH 774
INN THEALL

Glenshiel Forest
1010 THE SADDLE

918
SGURR AN LOCHAIN 1004

SHIE
L

Cluanie Inn
A87

1109 SGURR NAN CONBHAIREAN

Ceannacroc Forest
Doe

Ceannacroc Lodge

Arnisdale
Glen Arnisdale
Corran

Kinlochhourn Forest
Cluanie Forest
Cluanie Lodge
Cluanie Lodge

Lundie
LOCH CLUANIE

A887
Bun Loyne
GL

LOCH HOURN

713 DRUIM FADA

879 BUIDHE BHEINN
906 SGURR THIONAIL
Kinloch Hourn

Glen Quoich

1021 AONACH AIR CHRITH

Bunloinn Forest
Beinneun Forest
788 MEALL DU

Barrisdale Bay
1027 SGURR A'MHAORAICH

H i g h

Loyne

g

h

KNOYDART
894
Glen Barrisdale
Abhainn Chosaidh

1035 GLEOURAICH
LOCH QUOICH
Garry

Glenquoich Forest
540

LOCH LOYNE

A87
13
Ardochy House
LOCH GA

LUINNE BHEINN 939
8

Kingie
Aultnaslat
Inchlaggan

Tomdoun
Greenfield
Glen Garry

MEALL BUIDHE 946
919 GAIRICH
Glen Kingie
Kingie

Allt Choire a' Bhalachain

GLAS BHEINN 556

901 BEN TEE

musrory
1003 SGURR MOR
1040 SGURR NA CICHE

656 MEALL BLAIR

804 GEAL CHARN

935 SRON A'CHOIRE GHAIRBH

Glengarry Forest
GRE GLEN W

147
859

Glen Dessarry
Dessarry
858
880 SGURR MHURLAGAIN
Murlaggan

Loch Blair

Clunes Forest
LOCH

Altrua

Kinlochmorar
829 CARN MOR
Strathan
Glen Pean
Pean

LOCH ARKAIG

Ardechvie
Achnasaul
B8005

Clunes
Bunarkaig
A82

Oban
718 AN STAC

Gleann Camgharaidh
727
Locheil Forest
Inver Mallie

Glen Mallie
Mallie

NN
Achnacarry
CLAN CAMERON MUSEUM

882 DHAR BHEA

965 SGURR NAN COIREACHAN
963 SGURR THUILM
987 GAOR BHEINN

796 BEINN BHAN

Gairlochy
GREAT GLEN WAY
Kilmonivaig

654 COIR CEIRSLE

NM
Kinlochbeoraid
796 SGURR AN UTHA
STATION MUSEUM
GLENFINNAN MONUMENT
Glen Finnan

Druim Fada

Glen Loy Forest
Muirshearlich
Strone
Stronaba
COMMANDO MEMORIAL
Spean Bridge
Brackletter
Highbridge

Glenfinnan
130
Wauchan
Kinlocheil
Fassfern
131
TOR CASTLE

A82
Killiechonate

14
7
8
Glen Dubh Lighe
Gleann Suileag
Glen Loy
Lochy
Leanachan Forest
7
5

0 1 2 3 4 5 6 miles
0 1 2 3 4 5 6 7 8 9 10km

A830
11
TREASURES OF THE EARTH
Corpach
Banavie
NEPTUNE'S STAIRCASE LOCKS
NEVIS RANGE SKI CENTRE

South Garvan
Duisky
Blaic
A861
LOCH EIL
Caol
INVERLOCHY
Lochyside
the Cour

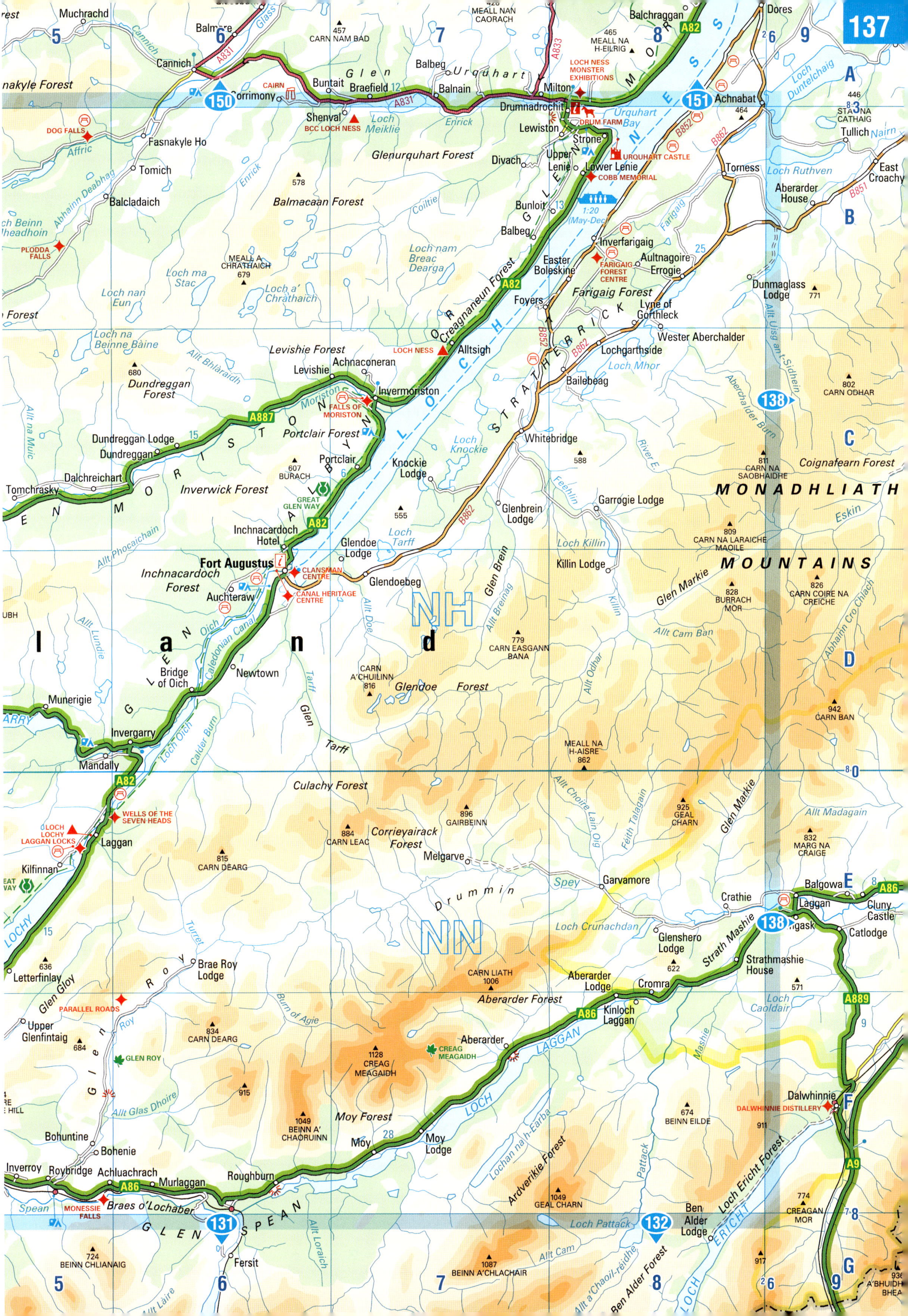

A82 Balchraggan · Dores
Muchrachd · Balmore · MEALL NAN CAOACH · MEALL NA H-EILRIG 465 · 8
Cannich · 457 CARN NAM BAD · 7 · Balbeg · Urquhart · LOCH NESS MONSTER EXHIBITIONS · Milton · 9
Glass · A831 · A823
150 orrimony · Buntait · Braefield 12 · Balnain · Drumnadrochit · 151 Achnabat · STRA NA CATHAIG 446
CAIRN · Glen · Urquhart · Lewiston · DRUM FARM
Shenval · Loch Meiklie · Enrick · Strone · URQUHART CASTLE · Tullich · Nairn
BCC LOCH NESS · Upper Lenie · Achmony · East Croachy
DOG FALLS · Fasnakyle Ho · Divach · Lower Lenie · COBB MEMORIAL · Aberarder House · B851
Affric · Tomich · Glenurquhart Forest · Bunloit 13 · 1:20 (May-Dec) · Torness · Loch Ruthven
Balcladaich · Balmacaan Forest · 578 · Balbeg · Easter Boleskine · Inverfarigaig · Aultnagoire Errogie 25 · Dunmaglass Lodge 771
PLODDA FALLS · MEALL A' CHRATHAICH 679 · Loch nam Breac Dearga · Foyers · FARIGAIG FOREST CENTRE · Lyne of Gorthleck
Loch ma Stac · Loch a' Chrathaich · Farigaig Forest · Wester Aberchalder
Loch nan Eun · Loch na Beinne Bàine · Creagnaneun Forest · Lochgarthside · 802 CARN ODHAR · C
Levishie Forest · LOCH NESS · Alltsigh · 138 · Bailebeag · CARN NA SAOBHAIDHE 811 · Coignafearn Forest
Dundreggan Forest 680 · Levishie · Achnaconeran · Whitebridge · MONADHLIATH
Allt Bhlàraidh · Invermoriston · Loch Knockie · 588 · River E. · CARN NA LARAICHE MAOILE 809
A887 · FALLS OF MORISTON · Knockie Lodge · Glenbrein Lodge · Garrogie Lodge · MOUNTAINS
Dundreggan Lodge 15 · Portclair Forest · 555 · Feehlin · BURRACH MOR 828 · CARN COIRE NA CREICHE 826
Dundreggan · 607 BURACH · Portclair 6 · Loch Tarff · Loch Killin · Glen Markie · Eskin
Tomchrasky · Dalchreichart · Inverwick Forest · GREAT GLEN WAY · Glendoe Lodge · Killin Lodge · CARN BAN 942
Inchnacardoch Hotel · A82 · Glendoebeg · Glen Brein · Allt Cam Ban · Abhainn Cro Chlach
Fort Augustus · CLANSMAN CENTRE · NH · Glen Markie · D
Inchnacardoch Forest · Auchteraw · CANAL HERITAGE CENTRE · CARN A'CHUILINN 816 · CARN EASGANN BANA 779 · Allt Odhar · MEALL NA H-AISRE 862 · CARN BAN 942
Bridge of Oich · Newtown · Caledonian Canal · Glen Tarff · Glendoe Forest · GEAL CHARN 925
Munerigie · Loch Oich · Allt Madagain
Invergarry · Calder Burn · Culachy Forest · GAIRBEINN 896 · Glen Markie · MARG NA CRAIGE 832
Mandally · A82 · Glen · Tarff · CARN LEAC 884 · Corrieyairack Forest · Spey · Garvamore · Crathie · Balgowan · A86 · E
WELLS OF THE SEVEN HEADS · Melgarve · Loch Crunachdan · Glenshero Lodge · Laggan · Cluny Castle · Catlodge
Loch Lochy LAGGAN LOCKS · Laggan · CARN DEARG 815 · Drummin · ngask
Kilfinnan · NN · CARN LIATH 1006 · Aberarder Lodge · Cromra · Strathmashie House · 571 · Loch Caoldair · A889
Letterfinlay · Glen Gloy 636 · Brae Roy Lodge · Aberarder Forest · A86 · Kinloch Laggan · Mashie
PARALLEL ROADS · CARN DEARG 834 · CREAG MEAGAIDH 1128 · CREAG MEAGAIDH · Aberarder · LOCH LAGGAN · Dalwhinnie · F
Upper Glenfintaig 684 · GLEN ROY · 915 · Moy Forest · Moy · Moy Lodge · BEINN EILDE 674 · DALWHINNIE DISTILLERY · 911
Bohuntine · BEINN A' CHAORUINN 1049 · 28 · Lochan na h-Earba · Ardverikie Forest · Loch Ericht · 774 CREAGAN MOR
Inverroy · Roybridge · Achluachrach · Murlaggan · Roughburn · GEAL CHARN 1049 · Ben Alder Lodge · A9
MONESSIE FALLS · Braes o'Lochaber · GLEN SPEAN · 131 · Loch Pattack · 132 · Ben Alder Forest · LOCH ERICHT · 917 · G
BEINN CHLIANAIG 724 · Fersit · BEINN A'CHLACHAIR 1087 · Allt Cam · Ben Alder Forest · A'BHUIDH BHEA

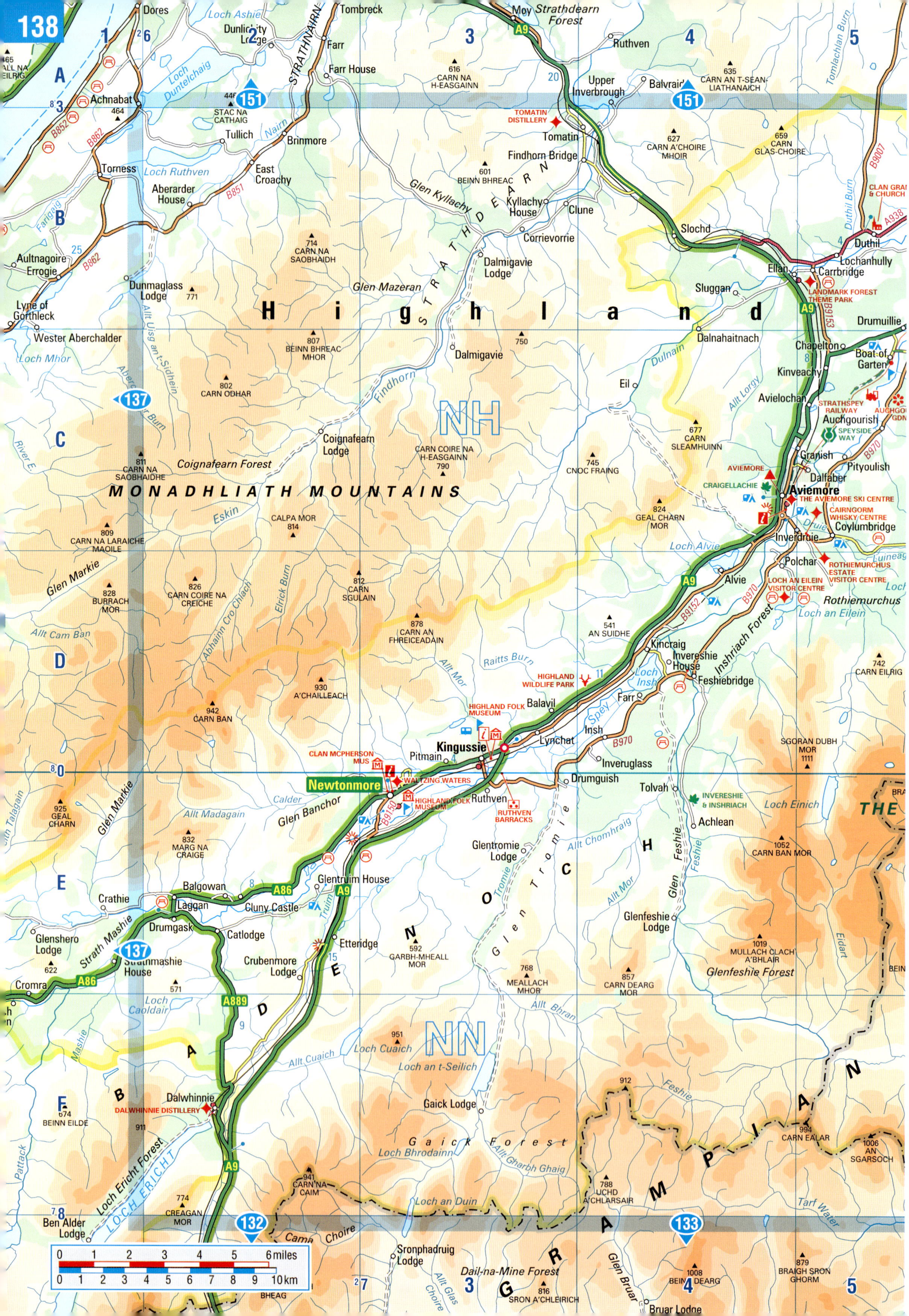

1 6 2 3 4 5

Dores
Loch Ashie
Tombreck
Moy
Strathdearn Forest
A9
Ruthven

A
Loch Duntelchaig
Dunlichity Lodge
Farr
Farr House
CARN NA H-EASGAINN 616
Upper Inverbrough
Balvraid 635
CARN AN T-SEAN-LIATHANAICH
151
Tomlachlan Burn

Achnabat 464
Stac na Cathaig
151
TOMATIN DISTILLERY
Tomatin
CARN A'CHOIRE MHOIR 627
CARN GLAS-CHOIRE 659
B9007

B852
Tullich
Nairn
Brinmore
Findhorn Bridge
CLAN GRANT & CHURCH
A938

B
B862
Torness
Loch Ruthven
East Croachy
Glen Kyllachy
BEINN BHREAC 601
Kyllachy House
Clune
Slochd
Duthil
Lochanhully
Carrbridge

Aberarder House
Corrievorrie
LANDMARK FOREST THEME PARK
Ellan
B9153

Aultnagoire
Errogie
B851
CARN NA SAOBHAIDH 714
Dalmigavie Lodge
Sluggan
A9
Drumuillie

Lyne of Gorthleck
Dunmaglass Lodge 771
Glen Mazeran
Dalnahaitnach
Chapelton
Boat-of-Garten

Wester Aberchalder
H i g h l a n d
BEINN BHREAC MHOR 807
Dalmigavie
750
Dulnain
Eil
Allt Lorgy
Kinveachy
Avielochan
STRATHSPEY RAILWAY
AUCHGO GDN

137
Loch Mhor
CARN ODHAR 802
Coignafearn Lodge
NH
CARN COIRE NA H-EASGAINN 790
CNOC FRAING 745
CARN SLEAMHUINN 677
Auchgourish
SPEYSIDE WAY
Granish
Pityoulish
B970

C
River E
CARN NA SAOBHAIDHE 811
Coignafearn Forest
AVIEMORE
CRAIGELLACHIE
Aviemore
THE AVIEMORE SKI CENTRE
CAIRNGORM WHISKY CENTRE
Coylumbridge

M O N A D H L I A T H   M O U N T A I N S
CARN NA LARAICHE MAOILE 809
Eskin
CALPA MOR 814
GEAL CHARN MOR 824
Loch Alvie
Inverdruie
Druie

Glen Markie
BURRACH MOR 828
CARN COIRE NA CREICHE 826
CARN SGULAIN 812
AN SUIDHE 541
A9
Alvie
B9152
B9170
ROTHIEMURCHUS ESTATE VISITOR CENTRE
Polchar
LOCH AN EILEIN VISITOR CENTRE
Rothiemurchus
Loch an Eilein

D
Allt Cam Ban
CARN AN FHREICEADAIN 878
Raitts Burn
HIGHLAND WILDLIFE PARK
Kincraig
Invereshie House
Farr
Feshiebridge
Inshriach Forest
CARN EILRIG 742
Loch Insh

A'CHAILLEACH 930
Allt Mor
Balavil
HIGHLAND FOLK MUSEUM
Insh
B970
SGORAN DUBH MOR 1111

CARN BAN 942
CLAN MCPHERSON MUS
Kingussie
Pitmain
Lynchat
Inverglass
Inveruglass

E
925 GEAL CHARN
Glen Markie
Allt Madagain
Calder
Newtonmore
WALTZING WATERS
HIGHLAND FOLK MUSEUM
Ruthven
RUTHVEN BARRACKS
Drumguish
Tolvah
INVERESHIE & INSHRIACH
Loch Einich
THE

MARG NA CRAIGE 832
Glen Banchor
Glentromie Lodge
Glen Tromie
Glen Feshie
Achlean
CARN BAN MOR 1052

Crathie
Balgowan
A86
Glentruim House
A9
GARBH-MHEALL MOR 592
Allt Mor
Glenfeshie Lodge

Laggan
Cluny Castle
Truim
Etteridge
MEALLACH MHOR 768
CARN DEARG MOR 857
MULLACH CLACH A'BHLAIR 1019
Glenfeshie Forest

Glenshero Lodge
Drumgask
Catlodge
Crubenmore Lodge
Eidart

137
Cromra
A86
Strath Mashie
Strathmashie House
571
A889
Loch Caoldair
D
BEIN

F
Loch Cuaich 951
NN
Feshie 912

Ben Alder Lodge
B
Mashie
Dalwhinnie
DALWHINNIE DISTILLERY
911
BEINN EILDE 674
A9
Loch Ericht
Loch an t-Seilich
Gaick Lodge
G a i c k   F o r e s t
Loch Bhrodainn
Allt Gharbh Ghaig
CARN EALAR 994
AN SGARSOCH 1006

Loch Ericht Forest
CREAGAN MOR 774
132
Camo Choire
BHEAG
Sronphadruig Lodge
CARN 'NA CAIM 941
Loch an Duin
788 UCHD A'CHLARSAIR
133
AN DEARG 1008
BRAIGH SRON GHORM 879

Dail-na-Mine Forest
Glen Bruar
Bruar Lodge
816 SRON A'CHLEIRICH
G
R A M P I A N

0 1 2 3 4 5 6 miles
0 1 2 3 4 5 6 7 8 9 10 km

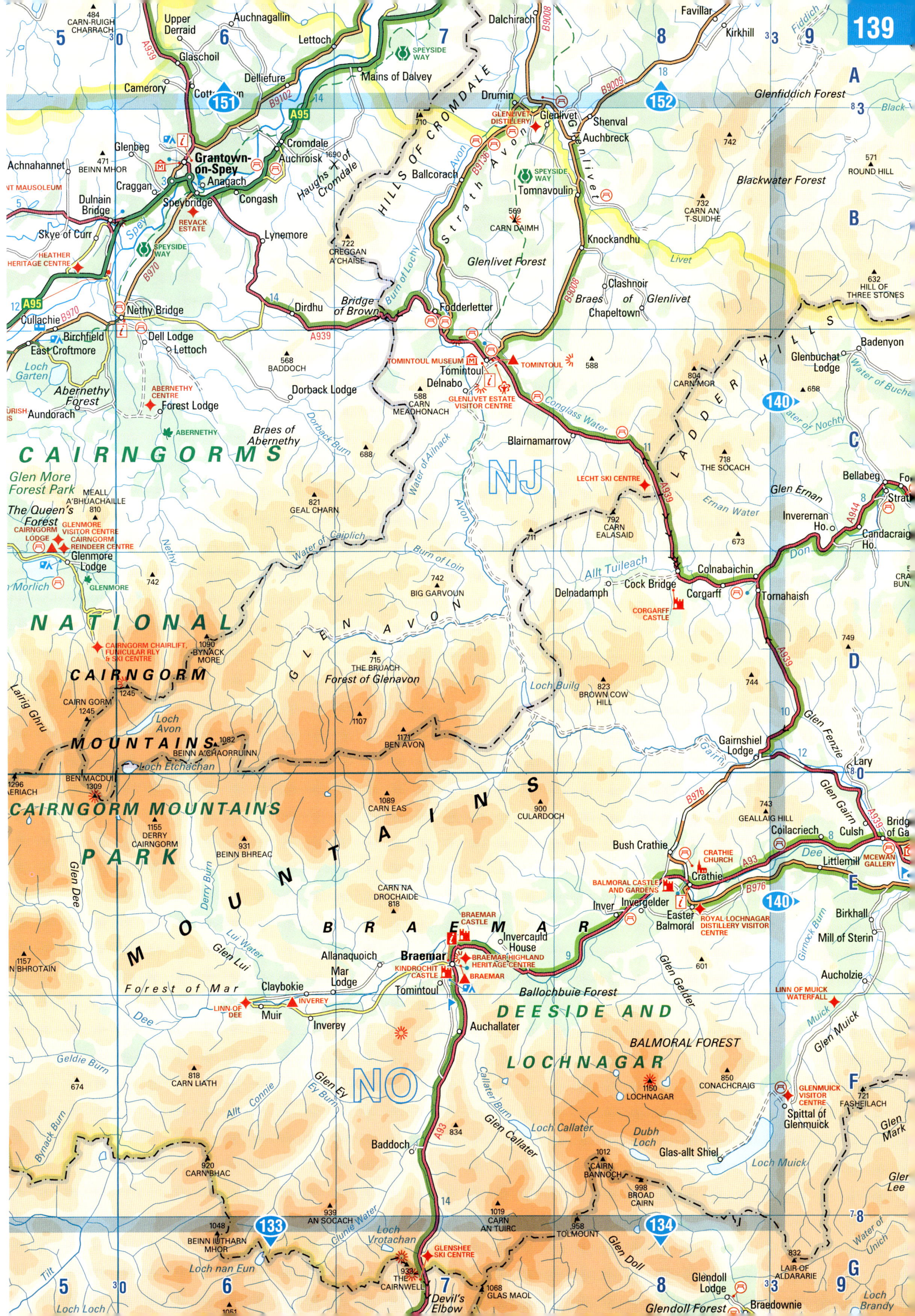

CAIRNGORMS NATIONAL PARK
CAIRNGORM MOUNTAINS
MOUNTAINS
BRAEMAR
DEESIDE AND LOCHNAGAR
HILLS OF CROMDALE
LADDER HILLS
GLEN AVON
NJ
NO
Grantown-on-Spey
Upper Derraid
Auchnagallin
Glaschoil
Lettoch
Dellefure
Mains of Dalvey
Camerory
Cottown
Dalchirach
Favillar
Kirkhill
Glenfiddich Forest
Drumin
Glenlivet
Shenval
Auchbreck
GLENLIVET DISTILLERY
SPEYSIDE WAY
Cromdale
Auchroisk
Haughs of Cromdale
Glenbeg
Achnahannet
BEINN MHOR
Craggan
Anagach
Congash
Speybridge
REVACK ESTATE
Dulnain Bridge
Skye of Curr
HEATHER HERITAGE CENTRE
Lynemore
Ballcorach
Strath Avon
Tomnavoulin
CARN DAIMH
Blackwater Forest
CARN AN T-SUIDHE
ROUND HILL
Knockandhu
Glenlivet Forest
CREGGAN A'CHAISE
Burn of Lochy
Clashnoir
Braes of Glenlivet
Chapeltown
HILL OF THREE STONES
Livet
Cullachie
Nethy Bridge
Dirdhu
Bridge of Brown
Fodderletter
Birchfield
East Croftmore
Dell Lodge
Lettoch
Loch Garten
Abernethy Forest
Aundorach
ABERNETHY CENTRE
Forest Lodge
ABERNETHY
BADDOCH
Dorback Lodge
TOMINTOUL MUSEUM
Tomintoul
TOMINTOUL
Delnabo
CARN MEADHONACH
GLENLIVET ESTATE VISITOR CENTRE
Conglass Water
Glenbuchat Lodge
Badenyon
CARN MOR
Water of Buchat
Water of Nochty
Braes of Abernethy
Dorback Burn
Water of Ailnack
Blairnamarrow
LECHT SKI CENTRE
THE SOCACH
Bellabeg
Glen Ernan
Ernan Water
Inverernan Ho.
Candacraig Ho.
Strathdon
Glen More Forest Park
MEALL A'BHUACHAILLE
The Queen's Forest
CAIRNGORM LODGE
GLENMORE VISITOR CENTRE
CAIRNGORM REINDEER CENTRE
Glenmore Lodge
Loch Morlich
GLENMORE
GEAL CHARN
Water of Caiplich
CARN EALASAID
Burn of Loin
BIG GARVOUN
Allt Tuileach
Cock Bridge
Delnadamph
Colnabaichin
Corgarff
Tornahaish
CORGARFF CASTLE
Don
Nethy
CAIRNGORM CHAIRLIFT, FUNICULAR RLY & SKI CENTRE
BYNACK MORE
THE BRUACH
Forest of Glenavon
Loch Builg
BROWN COW HILL
Lairig Ghru
CAIRN GORM
Loch Avon
BEINN A'CHAORRUINN
BEN AVON
Loch Etchachan
BEN MACDUI
Gairnshiel Lodge
Glen Fenzie
Lary
Gairn
Glen Gairn
CARN EAS
CULARDOCH
GEALLAIG HILL
Coilacriech
Culsh
Bridge of Gairn
DERRY CAIRNGORM
BEINN BHREAC
Bush Crathie
CRATHIE CHURCH
Crathie
Littlemill
MCEWAN GALLERY
Dee
Glen Dee
Derry Burn
CARN NA DROCHAIDE
BALMORAL CASTLE AND GARDENS
Inver
Invergelder
Easter Balmoral
ROYAL LOCHNAGAR DISTILLERY VISITOR CENTRE
Birkhall
Mill of Sterin
BRAEMAR CASTLE
Invercauld House
BRAEMAR HIGHLAND HERITAGE CENTRE
Braemar
KINDROCHIT CASTLE
BRAEMAR
Allanaquoich
Mar Lodge
Glen Lui
Lui Water
BHROTAIN
Forest of Mar
Claybokie
Tomintoul
LINN OF DEE
INVEREY
Muir
Inverey
Ballochbuie Forest
Glen Gelder
Aucholzie
LINN OF MUICK WATERFALL
Auchallater
Glen Muick
Muick
BALMORAL FOREST
Geldie Burn
CARN LIATH
Glen Ey
Ey Burn
Allt Connie
Callater Burn
Glen Callater
LOCHNAGAR
CONACHCRAIG
GLENMUICK VISITOR CENTRE
Spittal of Glenmuick
FASHEILACH
Glen Mark
Bynack Burn
Baddoch
Loch Callater
Dubh Loch
Glas-allt Shiel
Loch Muick
CARN BHAC
CAIRN BANNOCH
BROAD CAIRN
Glen Lee
AN SOCACH
CARN AN TUIRC
TOLMOUNT
BEINN IUTHARN MHOR
Clunie Water
Loch Vrotachan
GLENSHEE SKI CENTRE
Glen Doll
LAIR OF ALDARARIE
Water of Unich
Loch nan Eun
THE CAIRNWELL
Devil's Elbow
GLAS MAOL
Glendoll Lodge
Braedownie
Glendoll Forest
Loch Brandy
Loch Loch
Tilt
Fiddich
Black Water
A939
A95
A93
A944
B9102
B9136
B9008
B9009
B970
B976
151
152
140
133
134

B9009
Fiddich
Glen Fiddich
Ballochford
Tomnaven
525
Coynachie
Kirkney Water
Culdrain
Blackburn
Glens of Foundland
A96
467
HILL OF
FOUNDLAND
Colpy
Largie
Wrangham

A
742
Clashindarroch Forest
Kirkney
Gartly
Clashindarroch
Cults
Clashindarroch Forest
KNOCKANDY
Oldtown
Ardlair
B9002
Insch
B992

Glenfiddich Forest
152
Black Water
Bridgend
Inverharroch
Milton of Lesmore
Milton of Noth
Kennethmont
B9002
152
Aulton
B992

Blackwater Forest
Auchmair
505
Cabrach
Belhinnie
Milton of Noth
Rhynie
Cottown
Clatt
Duncanstone
Kirkton
The Shevock

571
ROUND HILL
Aldunie
Wheedlemont
Craig Castle
A97
Coldwells
Croft
Whitehaugh Forest
Muckletown
Glenton

732
BARN AN SUIDHE
B9002 ST MARY'S CHURCH
721 THE BUCK
Clova
Lumsden
CORREEN HILLS
Tullynessle
Keig
Castle Forbes

Livet
632
HILL OF THREE STONES
Badenyon
Mossat
518 LORD ARTHUR'S CAIRN
Bridge of Alford
Montgarrie
HAUGHTON
GRAMPIAN TRANSPORT MUS
Gateside

Chapeltown
LADDER HILLS
804 CARN MOR
Glenbuchat Lodge
Water of Buchat
Rinmore
Kildrummy
Don
A97
A944
ALFORD VALLEY RAILWAY
Alford
HERITAGE CENTRE
Whitehouse

139
658
Belnacraig
KILDRUMMY CASTLE & GARDEN
Milltown of Kildrummy
532
Auchintoul
A980
Kirkton of Tough
14

718 THE SOCACH
Kirkton of Glenbuchat
9
Glenkindie
Towie
Milltown of Towie
Sinnahard
Hillockhead
Asloun
Ley
Muir of Fowlis
Little Lynturk
Tillyfourie

Glen Ernan
Bellabeg
Forbestown
Heugh-head
Boultenstone
A97
Milton of Cushnie
Leochel-Cushnie
Bridgend
Tillyfour
Corrennie Forest

Inverernan Ho.
Ernan Water
Strathdon
Candacraig Ho.
Tornashean Forest
CRAIGIEVAR CASTLE
Kintocher
Corrennie Moor

Don
Colnabaichin
531 CRAIG OF BUNZEACH
Hillockhead
619
B9119
494 BENAQUHALLIE

Cock Bridge
Corgarff
Tornahaish
Deskry Water
Easter Davoch
Migvie
Douneside
Craskins 476
CULSH SOUTERRAIN
Lumphanan
21
A980
Findrack Ho.
Drumlasie

CORGARFF CASTLE
749
Coynach
B9119
Tarland
Milton of Auchinhove
PEEL RING OF LUMPHANAN
Tornaveen
B993

D
744
871 MORVEN
Logie Coldstone
CROMAR
Coull
Auchlossan
Torphins

A939
10
Glen Fenzie
Milton of Logie
Glendavan Ho.
Ordie
TOMNAVERIE STONE CIRCLE
SLUG OF DESS FALLS
Mid Beltie

Gairnshiel Lodge
Lary
604
MUIR OF DINNET
299 SCAR HILL
B9094
Milton of Campfield

Gairn
12
0
743 GEALLAIG HILL
Glen Gairn
BURN O VAT
A97
Loch Davan
Loch Kinord
11
Aboyne
Kincardine O'Neil
B993
Tillydrine
13

B976
Coilacriech
Culsh
Milton of Tullich
A93
Muir of Dinnet
Dinnet
B976
Birsemore
Backhill of Trustach
A93

Bush Crathie
CRATHIE CHURCH
A93
Bridge of Gairn
Glascorrie
Ballater
Glen Tanar House
BRAELOINE INTERPRETIVE CENTRE
Birse
Marywell
Burn of Cattie

CASTLE GARDENS
Crathie
Littlemill
MCEWAN GALLERY
Dee
Tom's Cairn
Tillygarmond

Ergelder
Easter Balmoral
ROYAL LOCHNAGAR DISTILLERY CENTRE
139
B976
Birkhall
Mill of Sterin
House of Glenmuick
529
Finzean
Percie
Water of Feugh

Glen Gelder
601
Aucholzie
LINN OF MUICK WATERFALL
Glen Tanar
Water of Tanar
GLEN TANAR
525 CARNFERG
Forest of Birse
Ballochan
310

BALMORAL FOREST
850 CONACHCRAIG
GLENMUICK VISITOR CENTRE
Spittal of Glenmuick
CLACHAN YELL 526
727 COCK CAIRN
742 HILL OF CAT
617
MOUNT SHADE 507

F
1150 LOCHNAGAR
721 FASHEILACH
Glen Muick
939 MOUNT KEEN
NO
Burn of Branny
Water of Tarf
Burn of Tennet
778 MOUNT BATTOCK
Glendye Lodge

Dubh Loch
Glas-allt Shiel
Glen Mark
Water of Mark
Glen Dye

998 ROAD CAIRN
Loch Muick
Glen Lee
696 MONAWEE
Invermark Lodge
Auchronie
Cairncross
Tarfside
THE RETREAT - GLEN ESK FOLK MUS
135
Cairn o' Mount

134
Water of Unich
Inchgrundle
Loch Lee
GLENS
Glen Effock
North Esk

0 1 2 3 4 5 6 miles
0 1 2 3 4 5 6 7 8 9 10km

B922 B900 Folla St Katherine's Chapel HADDO Ythanbank Hilton Mains of Birness
Kirkton of Culsalmond 5 Rothmaise Newseat 6 ross of Jackston St Katherine's 7 Wedderlairs Earlsford HOUSE AND GARDENS Inverebrie Broomfield Neth Leas 9
Cairnhill Tocher Meikle Wartle Jackstown Balgove Tulloch B9170 Raxton MEDIEVAL TOMB West Kinharrachie Ythsie Esslemont Ellon Artrochie Auchmacoy Kirktown of
Bonnyton Mounie 12 Meldrum TOLQUHON CASTLE Tarves A920 Ythan A948 VISITOR CENTRE Slains Colliestan
Newton Ho. Old Rayne LOANHEAD STONE CIRCLE Castle Ho. Auquharthies Craigdam Pitmedden A920 6 Kirkton of Logie Buchan Waterside St Catherine's Dub
Pitmachie Durno Daviot Fingask Cairnbrogie PITMEDDEN GARDENS Pitmedden Udny Green Tipperty Meikle Tarty FORVIE Hackley Hd. or Forvie Ness
Ardoyne Westhall Mounie Castle Barra Castle Mill of Kingoodie Hattoncrook Pettymuick Cultercullen B9000 Newburgh Sands of Forvie
ARCHAEOLINK PREHISTORY PARK Oyne Kirkton of Oyne Whiteford Pitcaple Harlaw Ho. Oldmeldrum Whiterashes B9000 Udny Station Minnes Rashiereive Foveran A975 Drums Newburgh Bar
BENNACHIE 528 Chapel of Garioch A96 Kirkton of Bourtie Hillbrae Affleck Tillygreig Tillycorthie Delfrigs
518 Pittodrie BATTLE OF HARLAW MEMORIAL Balhalgardy BRANDSBUTT STONE Burgh Muir Nether Crimond Ardo Ho. Middlemuir
237 INVERURIE MUSEUM Inverurie Tillykerrie Stroloch B999 Craigie Causeyend Whitecairns
ARIOCH Upper Woodend Bograxie Burnhervie Manar Ho. Port Elphinstone Kinmuck Middleton Newmachar Kinmundy Belhelvie BALMEDIE Balmedie
Rorandle Pitfichie Blairdaff Aquhythie Balbithan Ho. Cairnpark Drumligair B977 8
Pitfichie Forest Grantlodge Dalmadilly Clovenstone Balbithan Wester Fintray Hatton of Fintray Kinmundy Whitecairns Potterton Blackdog
Pitmunie MONYMUSK ARTS CENTRE Kemnay B994 Cottown Kintore OLD CHURCH Overton Parkhill Ho. Mundurno
Todlachie Monymusk Craigearn Leylodge B977 Blackburn A96 Dyce Stoneywood Denmore
B993 Ordhead Sauchen Achath Lyne of Skene Skene Ho. Haughs of Clinterty Bankhead Hayton Bridge of Don
Milton of Corsindae Old Kinnernie Corsindae Dunecht Kirkton of Skene East Auchronie Bucksburn Woodside BRIG O'BALGOWNIE CRUICKSHANK BOTANIC GARDEN
Comers Midmar STONE CIRCLE Tillybirloch Marionburgh Echt Garlogie Northfield Mastrick ST MACHAR'S CATHEDRAL Old Aberdeen
B9119 274 CASTLE FRASER Loch of Skene Westhill Kingswells A944 KING'S COLLEGE VISITOR CENTRE
Midmar Forest South Kirkton Cairnie Elrick P&R Aberdeen SATROSPHERE MARISCHAL MUSEUM
433 HILL OF FARE Landerberry Redhill Blacktop GORDON HIGHLANDERS MUSEUM Mannofield Ferryhill Torry Girdle Ness
Burn of Corrichie B9125 West Cullery Benthoul Easter Ord Contlaw Bieldside Ruthrieston DAVID WELCH WINTER GARDENS Kincorth Nigg Bay Greg Ness
Hardgate Craigton Milton of Murtle Milltimber Cults Garthdee Nigg
Brathens Hirn DRUM CASTLE Mains of Drum Kirkton of Maryculter Banchory Devenick Charlestown Cove Bay
Bridge of Canny East Mains Upper Lochton The Neuk Drumoak A93 Dee B9077 Auchlunies Hare Ness
BANCHORY MUSEUM Woodside of Arbeadie CRATHES CASTLE AND GARDENS Muirske Marywell Findon Ness
Arbeadie Deebank Banchory ROYAL DEESIDE RLY Crathes Kirkton of Durris Woodlands Denside Upper Burnhaugh Cammachmore Hillside Findon
khall Forest Auchattie Bridge of Feugh Crossroads Borrowfield Netherley Cookney Portlethen Downies Cammachmore Bay
Belts of Collonach Strachan Durris Forest CAIRN MON EARN Lochton Unton Cottage RAEDYKES ROMAN CAMP Bridge of Muchalls Muchalls Newtonhill
Bridge of Dye 534 KERLOCH Garrol Hill 376 MONGOUR Mergie Rickarton NO Garron Pt.
Garrol Hill Cowie Water Cowie Garron Pt.
Drumtochty Forest 464 Mains of Dellavaird Glenfarquhar Lodge Tannachie New Mill Carmont Kirktown of Fetteresso Tewel Stonehaven TOLBOOTH MUSEUM Castle Haven DUNNOTTAR CASTLE Thornyhive Bay
Drumtochty Castle Glenbervie Drumlithie Fiddes Barras Mill of Uras Crawton
Strath Finella 135 boddo Huse Mondynes Pitforthie Roadside of Catterline Catterline Crawton Bay
Clatterin Bridge Glensaugh Auchenblae Brownmuir Fordoun B967 Parkneuk Arbuthnott Roadside of Kinneff Braidon Bay Todhead Point
B966 5 6 7 8 0 9

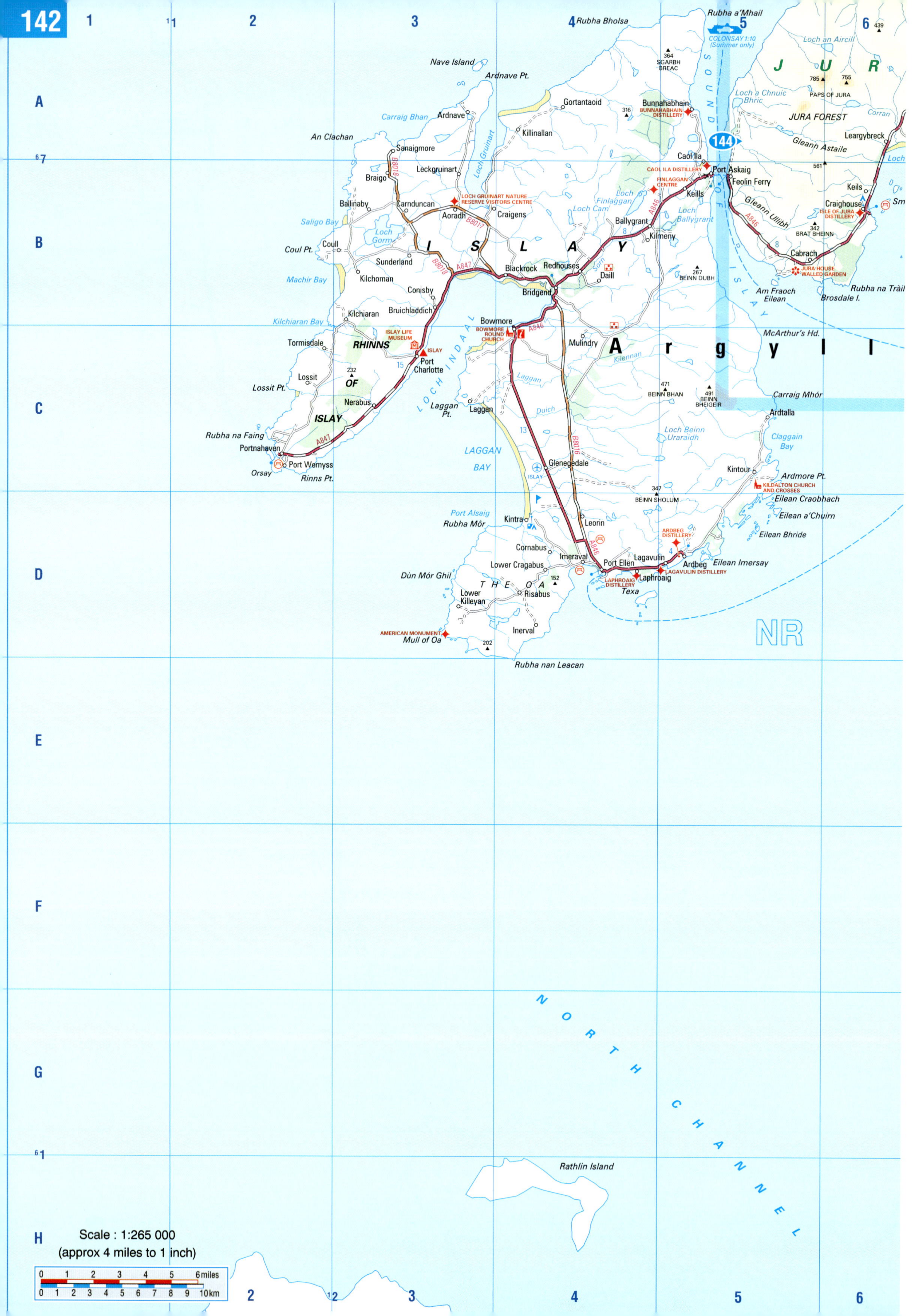

1 | 1 | 2 | 3 | 4 | 5 | 6

Rubha a'Mhail

COLONSAY 1:10
(Summer only)

Rubha Bholsa

Loch an Aircill

439

J U R

785 | 755

PAPS OF JURA

JURA FOREST

Loch a Chnuic Bhric

Corran

Nave Island

Ardnave Pt.

Gortantaoid

316

Bunnahabhain

BUNNAHABHAIN
DISTILLERY

561

Gleann Astaile

Leargybreck

Loch

A

An Clachan

Carraig Bhan | Ardnave

Killinallan

Caol Ila

Keills

144

Sanaigmore

CAOL ILA DISTILLERY

Port Askaig

Feolin Ferry

Keills

Braigo

B8018

Leckgruinart

Loch Finlaggan

FINLAGGAN
CENTRE

Gleann Ullibh

A846

Craighouse

ISLE OF JURA
DISTILLERY

Sm

Ballinaby

Carnduncan

LOCH GRUINART NATURE
RESERVE VISITORS CENTRE

Aoradh

B8017

Craigens

Ballygrant

Loch Cam

Kilmeny

342

BRAT BHEINN

Cabrach

B

Coull

Coul Pt.

Sunderland

A847

B8018

A847

Blackrock

Redhouses

Daill

Sorn

267

BEINN DUBH

JURA HOUSE
WALLED GARDEN

Am Fraoch
Eilean

Rubha na Tràil

Brosdale I.

Saligo Bay

Loch
Gorm

Kilchoman

Conisby

Bridgend

Machir Bay

Kilchiaran

Bruichladdich

Kilchiaran Bay

Bowmore

BOWMORE
ROUND
CHURCH

A846

Mulindry

McArthur's Hd.

C

Tormisdale

ISLAY LIFE
MUSEUM

RHINNS

232

M

ISLAY

Port
Charlotte

I S L A Y

A r g y l l

Lossit

Lossit Pt.

OF

Nerabus

15

LOCHINDAAL

Laggan
Pt.

Laggan

Kilennan

471

BEINN BHAN

491

BEINN
BHEIGEIR

Carraig Mhòr

Ardtalla

ISLAY

Duich

Loch Beinn
Uraraidh

Claggain
Bay

Rubha na Faing

A847

ISLAY

Portnahaven

13

B8016

Kintour

Ardmore Pt.

Orsay

Port Wemyss

LAGGAN

BAY

ISLAY

Glenegedale

347

BEINN SHOLUM

KILDALTON CHURCH
AND CROSSES

Eilean Craobhach

Rinns Pt.

Port Alsaig

Rubha Mòr

Kintra

Leorin

Eilean a'Chuirn

Eilean Bhride

D

Dùn Mór Ghil

T H E   O A

Cornabus

Imeraval

A846

Port Ellen

Lagavulin

Ardbeg

ARDBEG
DISTILLERY

Eilean Imersay

Lower Cragabus

152

Risabus

Laphroaig

LAGAVULIN DISTILLERY

Texa

Lower
Killeyan

Inerval

LAPHROAIG
DISTILLERY

NR

AMERICAN MONUMENT

Mull of Oa

202

Rubha nan Leacan

E

F

N O R T H

G

Rathlin Island

C H A N N E L

61

H

Scale : 1:265 000
(approx 4 miles to 1 inch)

0 1 2 3 4 5 6 miles
0 1 2 3 4 5 6 7 8 9 10km

1 | 2 | 3 | 4 | 5 | 6

Column headers
6 7 8 9 10 11

Row labels
A B C D E F G H

Loch Lesgamaill
Lagg
Loch ha
Island of Danna
CASTLE SWEEN
Lochead
Kilfinan
Kilfinan Bay
Drum
BEINN BHREAC 454
BEINN BHREAC 506
KYLES OF BUTE
LOCH STRIVEN
Inv

An Dùnan
Knockrome
Lowlandman's Bay
na Mile
Eilean Mòr
ST COLUMBA'S CAVE
Achahoish
Ellary
Clachbreck
Erines
Melldalloch
Port Driseach
Tighnabruaich
Ardentraive
Colintraive
Algaltraig
ISLAND
Kames B.
Windy Hill 278
Port Lamont

St CORMAC'S CHAPEL
Kilmory
Baile Boidheach
Ormsary
STOB ODHAR 562
Barmore I.
Auchalick Bay
Ardmarnock Bay
Auchenlochan
Kames
Millhouse
Blair's Ferry
Ardlamont Ho.
St Colmac
ROTHESAY CASTLE
Port B
A844
Kilmory Bay
Pt. of Knap
Druimdrishaig
Loch nan Torran 305
Loch Chaorain
Loch Caolisport
Barfad 329
Tarbert
West Tarbert
East Loch Tarbert 0:25
Glenan Bay
Asgog Loch
Portavadie
Asgog Bay
Kilbride Bay
Ardlamont Pt.
Straad
ROTHESAY
Rothes.
Ettrick Bay

Miller's Bay
Cretshengan
CRUACH LAGAIN 264
Coulaghailtro
Kilberry
Kilberry Hd.
SCULPTURED STONES
Corranbuie
Torinturk
Rhu
DUN
Kennacraig
Redhouse
CNOC A'BHAILESHIOS 422
Rubha Leathan
Inchmarnock
Ardscalpsie Pt.
Loch Fad
Scalpsie
Loch Quien
A845

Carse Ho.
Dunmore
Ardpatrick
Kilchamaig
Whitehouse
Gartnagrenach
Glenreasdell Mains
Skipness
SKIPNESS CASTLE
Skipness Pt.
254
Scalpsie Bay
Stravanan Bay

Ardpatrick Ho.
Portachoillan
Ardpatrick Pt.
Eilean Traighe
Ronachan Pt.
Clachan
CRUACH NAM FIADH 269
Claonaig
Skipness Bay
Claonaig Bay
SOUND OF BUTE
157

Loch Stornoway
Loch Ciaran
Balochroy
Loch Garasdale
Crossaig Glen
Crossaig
Cock of Arran
LOCHRANZA CASTLE
Lochranza
Millstone Pt.
144
145

Gigha Island
Tarbert
East Tarbert Bay
West Tarbert Bay
Druimyeon More
Rhunahaorine
CRUACH MHIC GOUGAN 248
Cour Bay
Cour
Loch Ranza
Catacol Bay
Catacol
LOCHRANZA ISLE OF ARRAN DISTILLERY
444
NORTH

Eilean Garbh
Ardminish
ACHAMORE GARDENS
Ardminish Bay
Tayinloan
CNOC NAN CRAOBH 322
Killean
CRUACH MHIC-AN T-SAOIR 364
Grogport
BEINN BHREAC 241
Whitefarland
Thundergay
MEALL NAN DAMH 570
CIR MHOR 798
Loch Tanna
BEINN TARSUINN 825
GOAT FELL 874
14
North Sannox
NORTH SANNOX FARM PARK
Sannox
Sannox Bay
Corrie
NS

Gigafum Island
Cara Island
Beacharr
Muasdale
CRUACH NAN GABHAR 364
Brackley
Pirnmill
Imachar
BEINN BHARRAIN 721
573
ISLE
OF
ARRAN
Glen Sannox
859

Glenacardoch Pt.
Belloch
Amod
BEINN BHREAC 426
Bridgend
Torrisdale-Square
Carradale
Port Righ
Dougarie
Glen Iorsa
Glen Rosa
BRODICK CASTLE
BRODICK
ARRAN AROMATICS VISITOR CENTRE
ARDROSSAN 0:55
Brodick Bay

Glenbarr
CLAN MACALISTER CENTRE
Barr Water
Carradale Pt.
Carradale Bay
Auchagallon
228
Glenloig
A'CHRUACH 512
ISLE OF ARRAN HERITAGE MUSEUM
Brodick
Strathwhillan
Clauchlands Pt.

Cleongart
Bellochantuy
Bellochantuy Bay
BEINN AN TUIRC 454
Saddell Glen
SADDELL ABBEY
Saddell
A'CHRUACH 341
Saddell Bay
Tormore
MACHRIE MOOR STANDING STONES
Glencloy
Blairbeg
Margnaheglish
Lamlash Bay
Holy Island
314

Killocraw
Lussa Loch
SGREADAN HILL 397
Ugadale
KING'S CAVE
BALMICHAEL VISITOR CENTRE
Balmichael
503
Lamlash
Cordon

Tangy Loch
Skeroblingarry
Black Bay
Ardnacross Bay
Drumadoon Pt.
Torbeg
Shiskine
TIGHVEIN 458
Auchencairn
Knockenkelly
Kingscross Pt.
Kingscross

Westport
Kilchenzie
Glenlussa Water
Peninver
Blackwaterfoot
Drumadoon Bay
KILPATRICK DUN
Kilpatrick
Glenree
North Kiscadale
South Kiscadale
Whiting Bay
Largymore

West Darlochan
Kilmichael
Low Smerby
Brown Hd.
CARN BAN
Corriecravie
Sliddery Water
GLENASHDALE FALLS
Largybeg
Dippin

Machrihanish Bay
Campbeltown
CAMPBELTOWN HERITAGE CENTRE
Campbeltown Loch
Sliddery
Lagg
Kilmory
Bennan
SOUTH BANK FARM PARK
Bennan Hd.
Levencorroch
Dippin Head
Kildonan

Machrihanish
Trodigal
Stewarton
Kilkerran
Kildalloig
DAVAAR ISLAND CAVE PAINTING
Island Davaar
TORRYLINN CAIRN
Sound of Pladda
Pladda

Drumlemble
Knocknaha
BEINN GHUILEAN 352
Achinhoan Hd.

Earadale Pt.
THE SLATE 385
CNOC MOY 446
Woodbank
Feochaig
Johnston's Pt.
Sheep I.

Rubh'a' Mharaiche
Glen Breackerie
CNOC ODHAR 277
Keprigan
Carskiey
428
North Carrine
Macharioch
Polliwilline Bay

MULL OF KINTYRE
Rubha Chlachan
Strone Glen
Southend
Cove Pt.
Brunerican Bay
Port Mean
123
Sanda Island

ARDMEANACH

Killiemore House
Aird of Kinloch
STAFFA 0:45 (April-Oct)
Eilean Annraidh
Rubha nan Cearc
Kilfinichen Bay
BEN BUIE 717
Loch Airdeglais
Loch Spelve
248
Ardmore
Bach I.
MACLEAN'S CROSS
Iona
THE BURG
LOCH SCRIDAIN
Pennycross
Loch Fuaron
CREACH BEINN 698
Croggan
Rubha nan Sailthean
Rubha Seanach

IONA ABBEY AND CATHEDRAL
IONA HERITAGE CENTRE
ST COLUMBA EXHIBITION & WELCOME CENTRE
Kintra
Torrans
BEINN NA CROISE 503
Lochbuie
Kinlochspelve
Barachandroman

Iona
Fionnphort
Aridhglas
Eorabus
Lee
Carsaig
A849
Loch Buie
Laggan Deer Forest
DRUIM FADA 405
Insh I.
Clachan-Seil
Seil
CLACHAN BRIDGE

Baile Mor
Fidden
Tiraghoil
Bunessan
376
Loch Assapol
CRUACHAN MIN
376
Carsaig Bay
Rubha Dubh
LORD LOVAT'S CAVE
Frank Lockwood's Island
Easdale
AN CALA GARDENS
Clachan

ROSS OF MULL
BROLASS
Easdale
EASDALE ISLAND FOLK MUSEUM
Balvicar

Erraid
Ardalanish
Uisken
Scoor
Malcolm's Pt.
CARSAIG ARCHES
Dubh-fheith
Cuan
Torsa
Kilchoan

Eilean a'Chalmain
Ardchiavaig
125
Rubha nam Braithrean
Cullipool
94
Luing
Achafolla

Rubh Ardalanish
146
Garbh Eileach
Garvellachs
SCARBA, Eilean Dubh Mor
Arduaine
ARDUAINE GARDEN

Torran Rocks
NM
Eileach an Naoimh
LUNGA AND THE GARVELLACHS
Lunga
Toberonochy
Craobh Haven
Shuna

FIRTH OF LORN
OBAN 2:20
124
CRUACH SCARBA 449
Lunga
Shuna Pt.
Shuna

Rubha Aird Luing

Scarba
Gulf of Corryvreckan
Aird
Rèisa an t-Sruith
Island Macaskin

Rubh'a'Geadha
Balnahard
Kinuachdrach
Craignish Pt.

Kiloran Bay
Glengarrisdale Bay
Kinuachdrach Harbour
KILI SCULPTURED S RI

KILORAN GARDENS
Kiloran
296 CRUACH NA SEILCHEIG
Kilchattan
Scalasaig
Glendebadel Bay
124
Loch Crinan

COLONSAY
BEN GARRISDALE 365
Crinan
Killmahumaig
Bellanoch

Garvard
Rubha Dubh
Loch Staosnaig
Corpach Bay
267
Gallachoille
KNAPD

Dubh Eilean
PRIORY
Oronsay
467 BEINN BHREAC
Lealt
Carsaig
Tayvallich
Achanamara

Eilean nan Ron
Shian Bay
453 RAINBERG MOR
Gleann Aoistail
Ardlussa
Ardlussa Bay
Inverlussa
Lussagiven
Kilmichael of Inverlussa

Loch Righ Mor
318
Barrahormid
TAYNISH
Taynish
466 CRUACH LUSACH

Rubh'an t-Sàilein
Tarbert
KEILLS CHAPEL
Keillmore
New Ulva
Dunrostan

Rubha Lang-aoinidh
Loch Tarbert
Island of Danna
CASTLE SWEEN
Lochead

Rubha a'Mhail
439
Lagg
ST COLUMBA'S CAVE
241
Achahoish

Rubha Bholsa
Loch an Aircill
Loch Lesgamaill
Eilean Môr
ST CORMAC'S CHAPEL
CHAPEL
Kilmory
Ellary
Clachbreck
Baile Boidheach

Nave Island
Ardnave Pt.
364 SGARBH BREAC
JURA
785
755
PAPS OF JURA
An Dùnan
Kilmory Bay
Pt. of Knap
Ormsary

Ardnave
Gortantaoid
Loch a Chnuic Bhric
JURA FOREST
Corran
Knockrome
Lowlandman's Bay
Druimdrishaig

Killinallan
316
Bunnahabhain
BUNNAHABHAIN DISTILLERY
Gleann Astaile
Leargybreck
Miller's Bay
Cretshengan
305
Loch nan Torran

Leckgruinart
LOCH GRUINART NATURE RESERVE VISITORS CENTRE
Caol Ila
CAOL ILA DISTILLERY
FINLAGGAN CENTRE
561
Keils
Small Isles
CRUACH LAGAIN 264
Coulaghailtro

Aoradh
Craigens
Port Askaig
Feolin Ferry
Craighouse
ISLE OF JURA DISTILLERY
Kilberry Hd.
SCULPTURED STONES
Kilberry

ISLAY
Ballygrant
Keills
Loch na Mile
342 BRAT BHEINN
Kilberry Hd.

Blackrock
Redhouses
Kilmeny
142
Cabrach
NR
Ardpatrick

Bridgend
Daill
JURA HOUSE WALLED GARDEN
Coulaghailtro
DUN

Bowmore
BOWMORE ROUND CHURCH
Mulindry
Kilennan
267 BEINN DUBH
Am Fraoch Eilean
Brosdale I.
Ardpatrick Ho.
Eilean Traighe
Portachoillan

Port Charlotte
Laggan
Laggan Pt.
471 BEINN BHAN
491 BEINN BHEIGEIR
Carraig Mhor
Ardtalla
McArthur's Hd.
2:05
Ardpatrick Pt.
Ronachan Pt.
A83
Clachan

Scale 1:265 000
(approx 4 miles to 1 inch)
Claggain Bay
PORT ELLEN 2:20
Eilean Garbh
West Tarbert Bay
143
Loch Ciaran
Balochroy

ISLAY
Port Charlotte
Kilnaughton
Ardmore Pt.
Kintra
Gigha Island
Tarbert
East Tarbert Bay
Loch Garasdale

0 1 2 3 4 5 6 miles
0 1 2 3 4 5 6 7 8 9 10km

Kerrera
Balliemore
Oban
Glenamachrie
Glen Lonan
Pass of Brander
Falls of Cruachan
Kilchurn Castle
Lochawe
Cruachan Dam Visitor Centre
Loch Tromlee
Dalmally
Strath of Orchy
Achnafalnich
Inverlochy
Ben Lui

ARGYLL and BUTE

Gallanach
Kilbride
Kilmore
Barran
Beinn Ghlas
Loch Nell
Cladich
North Port
South Port
Portsonachan
Loch Awe

Inveraray
Newtown
Inveraray Castle
Combined Operations Museum Inveraray
Inveraray Jail
Maritime Museum

LOCH LOMOND AND THE TROSSACHS NATIONAL PARK

Lochgilphead
Ardrishaig
Tarbert
West Tarbert
Corranbuie

Dunoon
Sandbank
Kirn
Innellan
Wemyss Bay
Skelmorlie

Rothesay
Port Bannatyne
ISLAND OF BUTE
Kyles of Bute

Greenock
PORT GLASGOW
Gourock
Helensburgh
Garelochhead
Rhu
Rosneath
Kilcreggan

INVERCLYDE

Largs
Fairlie
Millport
Great Cumbrae Island
Little Cumbrae Island

SOUND OF BUTE
Cock of Arran
Lochranza

CLYDE MUIRSHIEL REGIONAL PARK

Kilbirnie
Beith
Lochwinnoch

143

NF
NL
Canna
A'Chill
Garrisdale Pt.
Canna Harbour
Sanday
Sound of Canna
Guirdil Bay
Rubha Shamhnan Insir
Kilmory
Kilmory Glen
Kinloch Glen
Rubha na Roinne
MALLAIG 2:30
Kinloch
Loch Scresort
KINLOCH CASTLE
Rubha Port na Caranean
RÙM
ORVAL
ASKIVAL
AINSHVAL
Harris
Glen Harris
Schooner Pt.
A'Bhrideanach
Rubha Sgorr an t-Snidhe
Rubha nam Meirleach
Oigh-sgeir
THE SMALL ISLES
SOUND OF RÙM
Bay of Laig
Cleadale
Rubha an Fhasaidh
Eigg
AN SGURR
Kildonnan
Galmisdale
SOUND OF EIGG
Eilean nan Each
Muck
Port Mor
Bhatarsaigh (Vatersay)
Uidh
Bagh Bhatarsaigh
Bhatarsaigh
Caolas Shanndraigh
Flodaigh (Floddaigh)
Sanndraigh (Sandray)
Lingeigh (Lingay)
Greanamul
Caolas Phabaigh
Theisgeir (Heiskers)
Pabaidh (Pabbay)
Caolas Mhiui Laigh
Miùgh Laigh (Mingulay)
Bearnaraigh (Berneray)
Caolas Bhearnaraigh
Barra Hd.
Sanna Point
Sanna
Sanna Bay
Portuairk
Achnaha
Point of Ardnamurchan
ARDNAMURCHAN LIGHTHOUSE
Achosnich
Ormsaigmore
Ormsaigbeg
Kilchoan
Kilchoan Bay
An Acairseid
Cairns of Coll
Eilean Mor
Rubha Mor
Bousd
Sorisdale
Cliad Bay
Arnabost
Gallanach
Grishipoll
Ballyhaugh
Hogh Bay
Loch Cliad
COLL
OBAN 2:40
Arinagour
Totronald
Acha
Feall Bay
Arileod
Breachacha Castle
Friesland
Eilean Ornsay
Loch Eatharna
Calgary Pt.
Gunna
Crossapol Bay
Soa
Loch Breachacha
TIREE
Vaul Bay
Salum
Caolas
Vaul
Rubha Dubh
Ruaig
Balephetrish Bay
Hough Skerries
Balevullin
Kenovay
Gott Bay
R. Chraiginis
Kilkenneth
Moss
Scarinish
Middleton
Heylipol
Crossapol
Heanish
Port Mor
Loch a'Phuill
Barrapol
Hynish Bay
Rubha Traigh an Duin
Balemartine
Rinn Thorbhais
Balephuil
Mannal
Balephuil Bay
Hynish
Port Snoig
Ardmore Bay
Ardmore Pt.
Bloody Bay
Quinish Pt.
Glengorm Castle
MULL MUSEUM
Rubha an Aird
Caliach Pt.
Sunipol
Mornish
Quinish
Mishnish
Penmore Mill
MULL LITTLE THEATRE
Dervaig
Achnadrish
Calgary
Calgary Bay
THE OLD BYRE HERITAGE CENTRE
Treshnish Pt.
Ensay
CARN MOR
Haunn
Lettermore
Rubh a'Chaoil
Burg
Kilninian
Achnacraig
Achleck
Fanmore
Treshnish Isles
Fladda
LOCH TUATH
Ballygown
EAS FORS WATERFALL
BEINN NA DRISE
Eilean Dioghlum
Lunga
Gometra
Laggan Bay
Lagganulva
Beamus
Oskamull
Ulva
Ulva House
Killiemor
Bac Mor
LOCH NA KEAL
Sound of Ulva
Eorsa
Little Colonsay
Staffa
STAFFA
FINGAL'S CAVE
INCH KENNETH CHAPEL
Inch Kenneth
ISLE OF
Derryguaig
Balnahard
MACKINNON'S CAVE
Erisgeir
Glen Seilisdeir
BEINN NA SREINE
ARDMEANACH
Killiemore House
Kilfinichen Bay
THE BURG
(April-Oct) 0:45
MACLEAN'S CROSS
Eilean Annraidh
IONA ABBEY AND CATHEDRAL
Rubha nan Cearc
IONA HERITAGE CENTRE
Iona
Baile Mor
ST COLUMBA EXHIBITION & WELCOME CENTRE
Kintra
Aridhglas
Loch na Lathaich
LOCH SCRIDAIN
Torrans
Stac an Aoineidh
Fionnphort
Eorabus
Fidden
Tiraghoil
Bunessan
Lee
CRUACHAN MIN
Loch Assapol
Erraid
Soa I.
ROSS OF MULL
Ardalanish
Uisken
Scoor
Ardchiavaig
Malcolm's Pt.
Rubha nam Braithrean
Eilean a'Chalmain
Rubh Ardalanish
Torran Rocks
148
149
144
miles
km

Scale : 1:332 000
(approx 5 miles to 1 inch)

NG   NH

KNOYDART

Mallaig

MORAR, MOIDART AND ARDNAMURCHAN

Highland

LOCH SHIEL

MOIDART

SUNART

ARDNAMURCHAN

Glenfinnan

Fort William

BEN NEVIS

NM   NN

Tobermory

MORVERN

LOCH LINNHE

Ballachulish

Glencoe

ISLAND OF MULL

LYNN OF LORN

Argyll

Lismore

Oban

Kerrera

Bute

Seil

Easdale

Western Isles

UIBHIST A TUATH (NORTH UIST)

BEINN NA FAOGHLA (BENBECULA)

UIBHIST A DEAS (SOUTH UIST)

EILEAN BHARRAIGH (BARRA)

Bhatarsaigh (Vatersay)

Na h-eileanan Monach (Heisker or Monach Islands)

Haskeir I.
Haskeir Eagach

Sound of Spuir
Spuir
Eilean Bhearnaraigh (Berneray)
Boreray
Borgh
Baile
Ruisigearraidh
St Clement's Church
Roghadal
Ensay
Carminish Is.
Killegray
Langay
Valay
Valay Renish Pt.
Boirseam
Lingreabhagh
Ben Fionnsbhagh
Lingarabay I.

CAOLAS NA HEARADH

Aird a'Mhòrain
Veilish Pt.
Valay
Valay Strand
Oronsay
Port nan Long
Torogay
Baile Mhic Phail
Griminish Pt.
Scolpaig
SCOLPAIG TOWER
Manish Pt.
Baile Mhartainn
Hosta
Taigh a Ghearraidh
Hogha Gearraidh
Baile Raghaill
Baile Mor
Paibeil
Greinetobht
Malaclet
Solas
Trumaisgearraidh
Loch nan Geireann
Sursay
Tahay
Groay
Gilsay
Lingay
Scaravay
Opsay
Hermetray
Groatay
Loch Amhlasraigh
Lochportain
TARBERT 1:40
LOCHMADDY 1:45

Aird an Rùnair
Causamul
Rubha Port Scolpaig
Ceann a'Bhaigh
Cladach knockline
Cladach Chireboist
Cladach Chireboist
MARRIVAL
Loch Scadabhagh
Loch nam Madadh (Lochmaddy)
Weaver's Pt.
UIG 1:45
Rubha nam Plèac
Madadh Gruamach
Waternish Point

AN CAOLAS MHONACH
Kirkibost Island
Teanna Mhachair
Samhla
Vorogay
Clachan na Luib
Loch Hunra
Loch Euphoirt
Saighdinis
Rubha Mhic Gille-mhicheil
An t-Aigeach
SOUTH LEE
BARPA LANGASS CAIRN
EAVAL
Ben Geary
Geary
Trumpan Church
Knockbreck
Ard Beag
Ardmore Pt.
Halistra
Gillen
Hallin
Stein

Baile Sear (Baleshare)
Cairinis
TRINITY TEMPLE
Bail Iochdrach
Baile Glas
Griomasaigh (Grimsay)
Floddaybeg
Floddaymore
Ronay
Dunvegan Head
Isay
Mingay
Claigan

Baile a Mhanaich
Uachdar
Scotbheinn
Flodaigh
Flodday
Rubha na Rodagrich
Maragay Mor
Oisigearry

Gramsdal
Baile nan Cailleach
COMMUNITY MUSEUM
Griminis
Torlum
Lionaclet
Maaey Riabhach
Loch Uisgebhagh

Gualan
Creagh Ghoraidh
Hornish Pt.
Ardivachar Pt.
Aird a Mhachair
Iochdar
Clachan
Rubha Cam nan Gall
Fuidhaigh (Wiay)

Loch Bi
Loch a Charnain
Steisay
Gasay
Sandabhaig
Geirinis
OUR LADY OF THE ISLES STATUE
Luirsay Dubh

Stadhlaigearraidh
Dreumasdal
HOWMORE
Tobha Mor
LOCH DRUIDIBEG
Loch Druidibeg
Loch Sgioport
Ornish I.
Loch Sgioport
Mol a Tuath

Verran I.
Sniseabhal
Staoinebrig
Rubha'Aird-mhicheil
HECLA
BEINN MHOR
Rubha Rossel
Rubha Bhilidh
Rubha Hellisdale
NF

Ormiclate Castle
Bornais
Rubha Ardvule
Loch Cill Donnain
Calvay
KILDONAN MUSEUM
Cill Donnain
Unasary
Gearraidh Bhailteas
FLORA MACDONALD'S BIRTHPLACE
Minngearraidh
Taobh a Thuath Loch Aineort
Rubha Bolum
Loch Aineort
Macleod's Maidens
Idrigill P

Aisgernis
STULAVAL
Loch Stulabhal
Stuley

Dalabrog
Crois Dughaill
Cille Pheadair
Baghasdal
Taobha Tuath Loch Baghasdail
Loch Baghasdail (Lochboisdale)
Ceann a Deas Loch Baghasdail
Calvay
Rubha na Creige Mòire
Rubha Meall na Hoe

Gearraidh na Monadh
Smercleit
Pol a Charra
Cille Bhrighde
South Glendale
Taobh a Chaolais
Ludag
Rubha na h-Ordaig
Sgeir a'Mhill

Lingeigh (Lingay)
Haun
Am Baile
Bun a'Mhuillin
Coilleag
Eiriosgaigh (Eriskay)
Calvay
Hartamul

Fiaraigh (Fiaray)
Scurrival Pt.
Fuideigh (Fuday)
Stack Is.
CASTLEBAY 1:30
OBAN 5:20

Eolaigearraidh
CILLE BHARRA
Orosay
Traigh Mhor
Hellisay
Gighay
Canna

Greian Head
Cliaid
Cuidhir
BEN CLIAD
Aird Mhor
Aird Mhidhinis
Bruernis
Fuiay
Garrisdale Pt.
A'Chill

Borve Pt.
Allathasdal
Baile na Creige
Borgh
Buaile nam Bodach
Bruernish Pt.
Bagh Shiarabhagh

EILEAN BHARRAIGH (BARRA)
CRAIGSTON MUSEUM
Tangasdal
HEAVAL
Earsairidh
LOCHBOISDALE 1:30
BARRA HERITAGE CENTRE
Bagh a Chaisteil (Castlebay)
KISIMUL CASTLE
Breibhig
Rubha Mor

Bhatarsaigh (Vatersay)
Uidh
Bhatarsaigh
Muldoanich
OBAN 4:50

Flodaigh (Flodday)
Sanndraigh (Sandray)
Lingeigh (Lingay)
Greanamul
Pabaigh

Scale : 1:332 000
(approx 5 miles to 1 inch)

0   1   2   3   4   5   6miles
0 1 2 3 4 5 6 7 8 9 10km

ISLAND OF SKYE

TROTTERNISH

THE CUILLIN HILLS

CUILLIN HILLS

ISLAND OF RAASAY

WESTER ROSS

KNOYDART

THE SMALL ISLES

RÙM

SOUND OF RÙM

SOUND OF SLEAT

INNER SOUND

SOUND OF RAASAY

LOCH SNIZORT

NG

Uig
Portree
Gairloch
Broadford
Kyle of Lochalsh
Kyleakin
Mallaig
Armadale Castle
Sligachan Hotel
Torridon
Plockton
Lochcarron
Applecross
Shieldaig
Poolewe
Talladale
Elgol

A87 A855 A863 A896 A830 A82

155   150   146   147   136

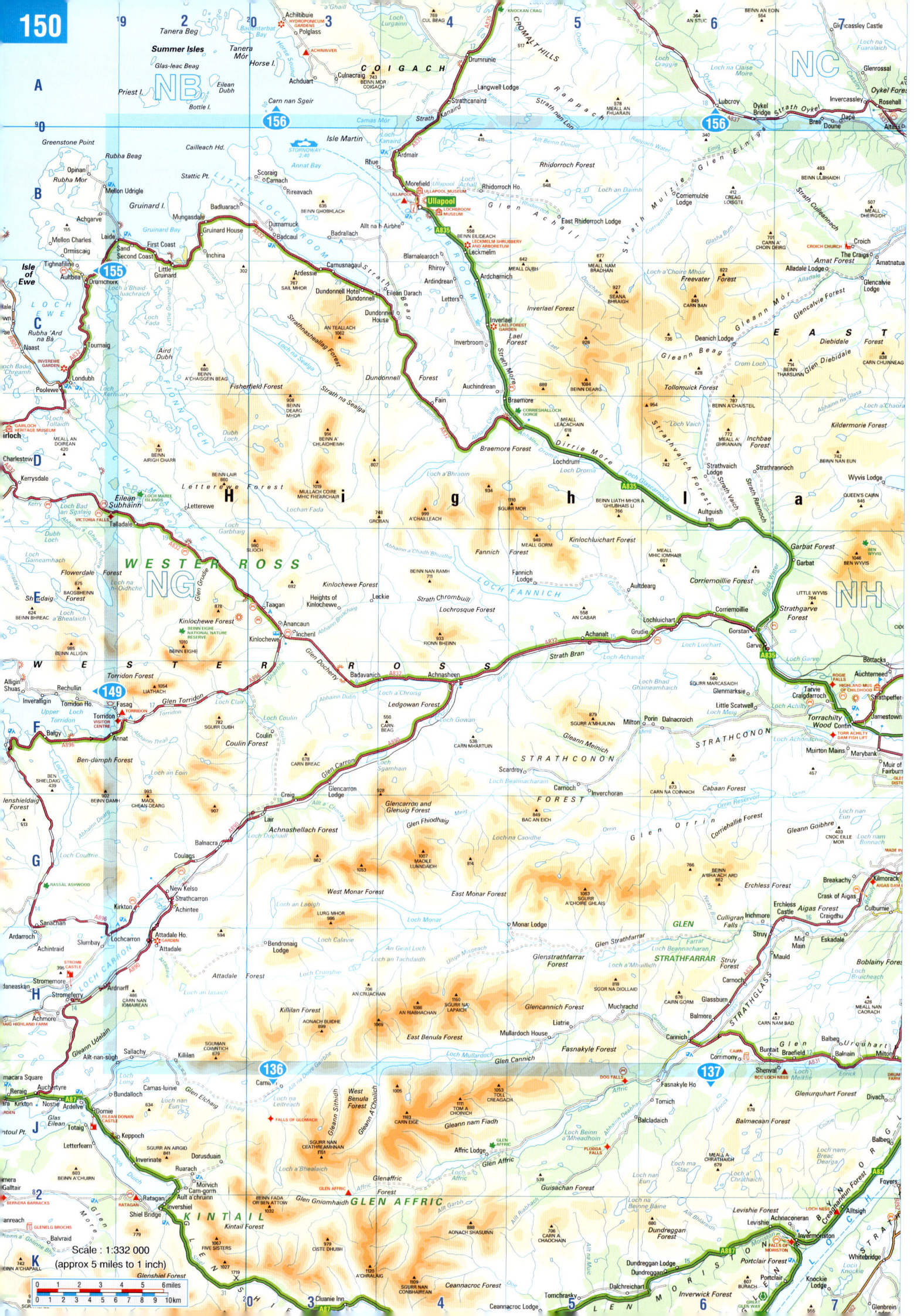

NB NC NH NG

Summer Isles

COIGACH CROMALT HILLS

Ullapool ULLAPOOL MUSEUM LOCHBROOM MUSEUM

Isle of Ewe

WESTER ROSS

HIGHLAND

LOCH FANNICH

STRATHCONON FOREST

GLEN STRATHFARRAR

KINTAIL GLEN AFFRIC

Scale : 1 : 332 000
(approx 5 miles to 1 inch)

0 1 2 3 4 5 6 miles
0 1 2 3 4 5 6 7 8 9 10km

ND
NJ
157
152
138
139
Inverness
Dingwall
Alness
Invergordon
Tain
Dornoch
Golspie
Brora
Bonar Bridge
Cromarty
Fortrose
Nairn
Forres
Burghead
Grantown-on-Spey
Aviemore
Beauly
Muir of Ord
Conon Bridge
Balintore
Portmahomack
Tarbat Ness
Dornoch Firth
Cromarty Firth
Moray Firth
Beauly Firth
Black Isle
Ross
Moray
Cairngorms National Park
Monadhliath Mountains
Strathdearn
Strathspey
Hills of Cromdale
Culloden Forest
Cawdor
Fort George
Whiteness Head
Culbin Forest
The Aird
Drumnadrochit
Loch Ness
Strathcarron
Dornoch Sands
Whiteness Sands
Morangie Forest
Carrbridge
Boat of Garten
Nethy Bridge
Tomatin
Slochd
Dulnain Bridge
Abernethy Forest
Glen More Forest Park
Findhorn
Kinloss
Dallas
Burghead Bay
Nigg Bay
Munlochy Bay
Shin Forest
Strath Fleet
Strath Rory
Glen Mazeran
Strathnairn
Culbokie
Avoch
Rosemarkie
Lairg

1   2   3   4   5

A

Covesea Skerries
Halliman Skerries
Branderburgh
Stotfield
Lossiemouth
Covesea
Hopeman
Gordonstoun
BURGHEAD MUSEUM
Burghead
Cummingston
Duffus
Roseisle
Roseisle Forest

B

Lower Hempriggs
Newton
Quarrywood
Coltfield
Alves
Miltonhill
Mains of Burgie
PLUSCARDEN ABBEY
DUFFUS CASTLE
PALACE OF SPYNIE
Loch Spynie
Spynie
Bishopmill
Leuchars Ho.
Lochhill
Elgin
OLD MILLS
MORAY MOTOR MUSEUM
ELGIN MUSEUM CATHEDRAL
CASHMERE VISITOR CENTRE
New Elgin
Lhanbryde
Lochs Crofts
Urquhart
SPEY BAY
Kingston
Spey Bay
TUGNET ICE HOUSE
DOLPHIN CENTRE
Garmouth
Porttanachy
Nether Dallachy
Upper Dallachy
Portgordon
Buckie
Buckpool
Rathven
Portessie
Gordonsburgh
Findochty
Portknockie
THE BUCKIE DRIFTER
Cullen Bay
Logie Hd.
Cullen
Lintmill
Sandend Bay
Redhythe Pt.
Sandend
Portsoy
Seatown
JOINER'S WORKSHOP
Easter Whyntie
FINDLATER CASTLE

C

Briach
Branchill
Dallas
Dallas Forest
Kellas
Glenlatterach
Moray
Craigroy
MILL BUIE
CAIRN UISH
Auchinroath
Newlands
BAXTERS HIGHLAND VILLAGE
SPEYSIDE WAY
Fochabers
FOCHABERS FOLK MUSEUM
Dipple
Ordiequish
Inchberry
Forgie
Wood of Ordiequish
Speymouth Forest
Shiel Muir
MILLSTONE HILL
Broadrashes
Deerhill
Aultmore
Newmill
ST. GREGORY'S CHAPEL
Clochan
Broadley
Nether Dallachy
Craibstone
Little Toux
Newmills of Boyne
Oldtown of Ord
Cornhill
Gordonstown
Old Crombie
Marnoch
Aberchirder
Finnygaud
Knowes of Elrick
Kirktown of Deskford
DESKFORD CHURCH
Ardiecow
Berryhillock
Mains of Edingight
Edingight Ho.
KNOCK HILL
Crannoch
Sillyearn
Knock
Bracobb
Davoch of Grange
Drumnagorrach
Farmtown
Knauchland
Mains of Mayen
Hillbrae

D

CARN NA CAILLICHE
Elchies Forest
Whiteacen
Dandaleith
LADYCROFT AGRICULTURAL MUSEUM
Archiestown
Ringorm
Craigellachie
CARDHU DISTILLERY
Upper Knockando
Cardow
Knockando
Carron
Daugh of Kinermony
SPEYSIDE COOPERAGE VISITOR CENTRE
Charlestown of Aberlour
Milltown of Edinville
Dufftown
BALVENIE CASTLE
GLENFIDDICH DISTILLERY
Milltown of Auchindoun
Maggieknockater
Drummuir
Drummuir Castle
Kininvie Ho.
Midtown of Buchromb
Daugh of Cairnborrow
Cairnborrow
Torry
THE BIN
THE BIN FOREST
Daugh of Cairnborrow
Haugh of Glass
Towiemore
Edintore
Little Pitlurg
Coachford
Glen of Coachford
Ruthven
Cairnie
Corse of Kinnoir
Yonder Bognie
Bogniebrae
FOURMAN HILL
GLENDRONACH DISTILLERY
Keith
STRATHISLA DISTILLERY
KEITH AND DUFFTOWN RLY
Rosarie Forest
BEN AIGAN
Mulben
NJ
Coynachie
Ruthven
Milltown of Rothiemay
Lessendrum
Drumblade
Corse
Huntly
HUNTLY CASTLE
NORDIC SKI CENTRE
BRANDER MUSEUM
Brideswell
Slioch
Thomastown
Denend

E

Lettoch
Mains of Delvey
Advie
Dalchirach
Bridge of Avon
Favillar
Kirkhill
BEN RINNES
Marypark
Bellehiglash
GLENFARCLAS DISTILLERY
CRAGGANMORE DISTILLERY
SPEYSIDE WAY
Glen Rinnes
MEIKLE CONVAL
Kirktown of Mortlach
AUCHINDOUN CASTLE
THE SCALP
Ballochford
Tomnaven
Bridgend
Inverharroch
Glenfiddich Forest
Black Water
Clashindarroch
Clashindarroch Forest
Kirkney
STRATHBOGIE
Bailiesward
Bridgend
Succoth
Tillathrowie
Kirkstile
Shanquhar
Coynachie
Culdrain
Blackburn
Gartly
Cults
KNOCKANDY HILL
LEITH HALL
Largie
HILL OF FOUDLAND
Glens of Foudland
Bainshole

F

CREGGAN A'CHAISE
Glenlivet Forest
GLENLIVET DISTILLERY
Glenlivet
Shenval
139
Auchbreck
Tomnavoulin
CARN DAIMH
Knockandhu
Clashnoir
Braes of Glenlivet
Chapeltown
Blackwater Forest
ROUND HILL
CARN AN T-SUIDHE
Aldunie
HILL OF THREE STONES
THE BUCK
Clova
SCOTTISH SCULPTURE WORKSHOP
Milton of Lesmore
140
Kennethmont
Milton of Noth
Oldtown
Ardlair
Auchmair
Cabrach
Belhinnie
Rhynie
Cottown
Clatt
Duncanstone
Wheedlemont
CRAIG CASTLE
Knockespock Ho.
Leslie
CORREEN HILLS
Whitehaugh Forest
Muckletown
Aberd
Tullynessle

G

BADDOCH
Dorback Lodge
CARN MEADHONACH
TOMINTOUL MUSEUM
Tomintoul
Delnabo
GLENLIVET ESTATE VISITOR CENTRE
CARN MOR
Glenbuchat Lodge
Blairnamarrow
Badenyon
Glenbuchat Lodge
Rinmore
Belnacraig
Kirkton of Glenbuchat
LADDER HILLS
Water of Buchat
Mossat
LORD ARTHUR'S CAIRN
KILDRUMMY CASTLE & GARDEN
Miltown of Kildrummy
Kildrummy
Auchintoul
Bridge of Alford
Montgarrie
Haughton
ALFORD VALLEY RAILWAY
GRAMPIAN TRANSPORT MUS.
Alford
HERITAGE CENTRE
Gateside
Whitehouse
Keig
Castle Forbes
Tullynessle

H

GEAL CHARN
CAIRNGORMS
CARN EALASAID
LECHT SKI CENTRE
BIG GARVOUN
CARN MOR
Delnadamph
CORGARFF CASTLE
Cock Bridge
Corgarff
Tornahaish
Colnabaichin
NATIONAL
PARK
Glen Ernan
Inverernan Ho.
Candacraig Ho.
Strathdon
Bellabeg
Forbestown
Towie
Milton of Towie
Heughhead
Boultenstone
Tornashean Forest
Sinnahard
Glenkindie
Hillockhead
Ley
Muir of Fowlis
Little Lynturk
Kirkton of Tough
Bridgend
Leochel Cushnie
CRAIGIEVAR CASTLE
Milton of Cushnie
Corrennie Moor
Tillyfour
CROMAR
Coynach
Logie Coldstone
Craskins
Milton of Auchinhove
Findrack Ho.
Lumphanan
PEEL RING OF LUMPHANAN
CULSH SOUTERRAIN
Migvie
Tarland
TOMNAVERIE STONE CIRCLE
Easter Davoch
Douneside
Coull
Gairnshiel
GLEN FENZIE
Glendavan Ho.
Ordie
Torphins

Scale : 1:265 000
(approx 4 miles to 1 inch)

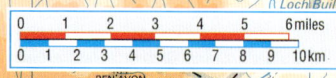

0 1 2 3 4 5 6 miles
0 1 2 3 4 5 6 7 8 9 10km

A B C D E F G H

6 7 8 9 10 11

Major places: Fraserburgh, Peterhead, Aberdeen, Banff, Macduff, Rosehearty, Turriff, New Pitsligo, New Deer, Mintlaw, Ellon, Inverurie, Oldmeldrum, Newmachar, Dyce, Westhill, Cruden Bay, Boddam, Crimond, Insch, Kemnay, Kintore, Bridge of Don.

Other labels include: Sandhaven, Inverallochy, St Combs, Cairnbulg, Strichen, Maud, Old Deer, Stuartfield, Longside, Buchanhaven, Newburgh, Foveran, Balmedie, Blackdog, Pitmedden, Tarves, Methlick, Fyvie, Rothienorman, Auchnagatt, Hatton, Cruden Bay, Port Erroll, Boddam, Stirling Ness.

FORMARTINE · BUCHAN · GARIOCH · Aberdeenshire · Aberdeen City

Kinnaird Head, Fraserburgh Bay, Rattray Head, Loch of Strathbeg, Bay of Cruden, Sands of Forvie, Newburgh Bar, Girdle Ness, Nigg Bay.

(Detailed road map of northeast Aberdeenshire, Scotland, with numerous place names, roads A90, A96, A947, A950, A952, A98, and others.)

1 2 3 4 5 6 7

A

B

NA

C

Na h-Eileanan Flannach

Siabost bho Thuath
SHAWBOST NORSE MILL
Siabost bho Dheas
Bàgh Dhail Beag
GEARRANNAN BLACKHOUSE VILLAGE
GARENIN
Dail Beag
Dail Mòr
Na Gearrannan
Borghastan
Carlabhagh
Pairc Shiaboist
Campay
Loch Chàrlabhaigh
DUN CARLOWAY BROCH
Dun Charlabhaigh
Carlabhagh
Floday
Little Bernera
Harsgeir
IRON AGE HOUSE
Tobson
Crothair
Loch a' Tuath
An Galan Uigeach
AN CAOLAS
Pabay Mòr
Tolastadh a Chaolais
BERNERA
BRAEACLEIT
Aird Uig
Bhaltos
Vacsay
Breacleit
Great Bernera
Cliobh
205
Vuia Mòr
Circebost
Keava
Timsgearraidh
Miabhig
Barraglom
Eilean Kearstay
Breascleit
Cradhlastadh
Uigen
Riof
Tobhtarol
CALLANISH VISITOR CENTRE
Ard More Mangersta
Eadar Dha Fhadhail
Floday
Vuia Beag
Crulabhig
Calanais
CALLANISH STANDING STONES
Gearraidh na h-Aibhne
Càrnais
Cairisiadar
Linsiadar
Mangurstadh
SUAINAVAL 429
Geisiadar
256
Aird Fenish
Einacleite
Loch Rog
Loch Tungabhat
Loch Smuaisabhal
Aird Brenish
Islibhig
574 MEALISVAL
Loch Grunabhat
Giosla
Loch Fuaroil
Loch Airigh na h-Airde
Breanais
Loch Chaolartan
Loch Cro Criosdaig
Loch Morsgail
Mealasta Island
Caolas an Eilera
397 BEINN MHEADHONACH
Loch Coirgerod
Loch Strandabhat
Loch Beinnseabhal
Morsgail Forest
Ceann Tarabhaigh
A859
Aird an Troim
Kearstay
Loch Tealasabhaigh
Reasort
Aird a Bhruaich
308
Bràighe Mòr
Scarp
F
Gaisgeir
SOUTH LEWIS,
STULAVAL
Aird a' Mhulaidh
Seaforth I.
679 TIRGA MOR
659 ULLAVAL
572 BEINN MHOR
Huisinis
499
Hushinish Pt.
UISGNAVAL MORE 729
Gobhaig
Forest of Harris
HARRIS AND
17
Horsanish
Abhainn Suidhe
CEANN A TUATH NA HEARADH
CLISHAM 799
Taransay Glorigs
Soay Beag
Cliasmol
Maraig
Soay Mòr
Bun Abhainn Eadarra
449
Camus an t-suithean
OLD WHALING STATION
809
NORTH UST
G
Tarasaigh (Taransay)
436
Aird Asaig
RHENIGIDALE
BEN LUSKENTYRE
Isay
'Lochan Lacasdail
Reinigeadal
Loch Trollamarig
Paible
Losgaintir
Tairbeart (Tarbert)
Carragraich
Caolas Scalpaigh
Rubha Sgeirigin
South Harris Forest
467
Urgha
Carnach
Rudha Crago
Caolas Tharasaigh
Loch Ceann Dibig
Miabhag
Sgeotasaigh
Eilean Scalpa (Scalp)
LUSKENTYRE BEACH
Loch an Tairbeart
Scalpay
Seilebost
A859
Drinisiadar
Toe Head
Borve Lodge
Kennaclay
Plocropol Pt.
Coppay
Buirgh
Greosabhagh
Aird Mhighe
Leac a Li
Plocrapol
NA HEARADH (HARRIS)
Scadabhagh
CHAIPAVAL 365
Sgarasta Mhòr
386
Liceasto
Geocrab
Rubha Bhocaig
Shillay
Rubha'an Teampuill
398 BLEAVAL
Caolas Stocinis
Little Shillay
Loch Langabhat
Beacrabhaic
Sound of Shillay
Flepideabhagh
Stockinish I.
Brenish Pt.
Taobh Tuath
SEALLAM!
Aird Mhighe
Manais
196
Loch Steiseabhat
UIG 1:40
Pabaidh (Pabbay)
SEALLAM!
Boirseam
Quinish
An t-Ob (Leverburgh)
Fionnsbhagh
Lingreabhagh
J
NF
Ensay
Carminish Is.
ROINEBHAL 459
Lingarabay I.
Ensay
Cuidhtinis
Haskeir I.
Killegray
Cairminis Srannda
ST CLEMENT'S CHURCH
Langay
Valley Renish Pt.
Haskeir Eagach
Eilean Bhearnaraigh (Berneray)
Ruisigearraidh
BERNERAY
Roghadal
Gilsay
Borgh
Baile
Langay
Lingay
Boreray
Caolas Bhearnaraigh
Groay
Scaravay
Aird a'Mhòrain
Torogay
Sursay
Vallay
Veilish Pt.
Lingay
Opsay
Scolpaig
Griminish Pt.
Port nan Long
Baile Mhic Phail
Tahay
CAOLAS NA HEARADH

Scale : 1:332 000
(approx 5 miles to 1 inch)
0 1 2 3 4 5 6 miles
0 1 2 3 4 5 6 7 8 9 10km
A865
Scolpaig
Vallay Strand
Solas
Grèinetobht
Trumaisgearraidh

St. Kilda

NA

ST KILDA
Boreray
CNOC GLAS 376
Soay
Loch a' Ghlinne
CONACHAIR 370
MULLACH BI 358
ST KILDA
St Kilda or Hirta (Hiort)
Bàgh a' Bhaile
Dun
NF

West ern

W e s t e r n

I s l e s

8 9 10 11 12 13

RUBHA ROBHANAIS
(BUTT OF LEWIS)

Cunndal
Eòropaidh
CHURCH OF ST MOULAG
Coig Peighinnean
HARBOUR VIEW GALLERY
Lional
Port Nis
Cross Sands
Suainebost
Cros
Tàbost
Aird Dhail
Dail bhó Dheas
Dail bho Thuath
Sgiogarstaigh

A

Gabhsann bho Thuath
Gabhsann bho Dheas
Mealabost Bhuirgh
Bail Àrd Bhuirgh
Coig Peighinnean Bhuirgh
Siàdar
Siàdar Iarach
Rubha Leathann
Siàdar Uarach
Aird Barvas
Baile an Truiseil
TRUSHAL STONE

Cellar Head

Glen Cross

248
MUIRNEAG

Loch
Langabhat

Loch Mòr
Shanndatihat

B

Abhainn Ghearadha

Bail Ur Tholastaidh
Tolastadh bho Thuath

Labost
Bragar
Arnol
Brú
BLACK HOUSE MUSEUM
Barabhas Iarach
Barabhas Uarach
Barabhas

Tolsta Head

Loch
Urghag
WBOST MUSEUM

Loch
Breibhat

Gleann Mòr Barvas

Gleann Bhruthadail

Loch
Sgeireach
Mòr

Gleann Tholàstaidh
Port Bun
a'Ghlinne

C

156

Grais
Creag Fhraoch

Gras

Loch Scarabhat Mhòr

292
BEINN MHOLACH

Griais
Bac
Col

Lacasdal

Loch Mòr an
Stairr

Vatisker Pt.
Col Uarach
Coll Sands
Breibhig

Loch
nan Stearnag

Grianan
An Gleann Ur
Newmarket
Aird Thunga
Tunga
Sròn Ruadh

Port Nan Giùran
Broad Bay
OR
LOCH A TUATH
Port Mholair
Aird
Cnoc
Amhlaigh
Rubha an t-Siumpain

NB

D

Loch Urabhal

Lacasdal
LEWIS LODM
CENTRE
Sanndabhaig
AN LANNTAIR GALLERY
MUSEUM NAN EILEAN
Stornoway
Mealabost
Garrabost
Sulaisiadar
Seisiadar
Eye
PENINSULA

223
Loch a'
Ghainmhich

Tolm
An Cnoc
Pabail Uarach
Pabail Iarach
Bàgh Phabail

ST COLUMBA'S
Aiglnis
Suardail

Acha Mòr
Arnish Moor
Holm I.
A'Chearc

Loch
Orasaigh
Grìomsidar
Ben Casgro
ULLAPOOL
2:40

Liurbost
Ranais
Raerinish Pt.

E

Loch Tobhta
Bridein

Soval Lodge
Crosbost

Loch
Trealabhal

Barkin Is.
Tabhaidh Mhor
Eilean Chaluim
Chille
Cromor
Eilean Orasaidh
Baile
Ailein
Ceos
Gearraidh Bhaird
Eilean Thoraidh

Sildinis
Cearsiadar
Cabharstadh
Marbhig
Tabost
KERSHADER
Calbost

F

Ceann
Shiphoirt
Taobh a' Ghlinne
Grabhair
Loch Odhairn
Kebock Head

Loch Sgibacleit

Loch Shanndabhat

PARK
OR
PAIRC
Orasaigh
Elsgean
Leumrabhagh

470
CRIONAIG

Loch Shell or Loch Sealg
Srianach
Eilean Iubhard

Mol Truisg

156
G

Glas-leac
Beag

Gob Rubh'Uisenis
Rubha Bhrollum
Priest I.

Rubha
a'Bhaird

CAOLAS NAN EILEAN

Garbh
Eilean
Greenstone Point
Rubha Beag

Na h-Eileanan Mòra
(Shiant Islands)
Eilean Mhuire
Eilean an Tighe
Opinan
Rubha Mor
Mellon Udrigle
Gruinard I.

H

Sròn a' Gheodha
Dhuibh
Eilean
Furadh Mór
Achgarve
Gruinard Bay

Camas
Mór
Rubha Reidh
155
Laide
First Coast

Mellon Charles
Ormiscaig
Sand
Second Coast

Cove
Isle
of
Ewe
Tighnafiline
Aultbea
Drumchork
150
Little
Gruinard

igh
ay)

NG

Melvaig
Aultgrishan
Inverasdale
Midtown
Brae
Rubha 'Ard
na Bà
Aird
Dubh

296
AN CUAIDH

LOCH
EWE

Loch
Squod

Tournaig
Loch
Fada

Peterburn
Naast
INVEREWE
GARDEN

FIONN
LOCH

Seana
Chamas
Loch Bad
a'Chreamh

Port Erradale
North
Erradale
Rubha Bàn
Big Sand
149
Poolewe
Londubh

J

Loch
Kernsary

149
Fladda-chùan
Eilean Troddday
Long Island
Strath
CARN DEARG
Loch
Tollaidh
Gairloch
GAIRLOCH
HERITAGE MUSEUM

Rubha Hunish
Rubha na h-Aiseig
Smithstown
MEALL AN
DOIREAN
420

791
BEINN
AIRGH CHARR

DUNTULM
CASTLE
Bagh Shasdun
Charlestown

Port
Henderson
LOCH GAIRLOCH

8 9 10 11 12 13

19 2 3 4 5 6 7

A

⁹8

B

CAPE WRATH
Faraid Head

Kearvaig
Geodha Ruadh na Fola
371 SGRIBHIS-BHEINN
Inshore
Whiten
Bay of Keisgaig
Loch Keisgaig
Balnakeil Bay
DURNESS VISITOR CENTRE
SMOO CAVE
Eilean Hoan
BALNAKEIL CHURCH
Balnakeil
Durness
Geodh'a' Bhrideoin
Geodha Ruadh
457 FASHVEN
Achiemore
BALNAKEIL CRAFT VILLAGE
Sangomore
DURNESS
Leirinmore
Am Balg
Keoldale
Loch Airigh na Beinne

C
◄155
423 BEINN DEARG
332 GHLAS BHEINN
Sangobeg
Eilean Clùimhrig
Rubh'an Fhir Léithe
Sarsgrum
Rispond
Strath Shinary
485 CREAG RIABHACH
422 MEALL MEADHONACH
Loch na Gainimh
Sheigra
Balchrick
Portnancon
Heilam
Hope
Droman
Oldshore Beg
Eilean Choraidh
Lochside
Eilean Roin Mor
Oldshoremore
521 FARRMHEALL
Eriboll
230

D
Kinlochbervie
Gualin Ho.
Badcall
772 BEINN SPIONNAIDH
Achriesgill
Polla
800 CRANSTACKIE
Achlyness
Strath Dionard
Ardmore Pt.
Ceathramh Garbh
Rhiconich
na Claise Carnaich
521 AN LEAN-CHARN
30
Rubha Ruadh
Ardmore
GANU MOR 908
Foinaven
Loch Dionard
Fanagmore
Tarbet
NORTH-WEST SUTHERLAND
927
FEINNE-BHEINN MOR 465
BEN HOPE
Handa Island
Loch a' Garbh-bhaid Mòr
Foindle
Laxford Bridge
Loch an Easain Uaine
Loch Crocach

E
NB
Scourie Bay
787 ARKLE
Gobernuisgach Lodge
Scourie More
Scourie
777
Rubh'Aird an t-Sionnaich
Gorm Loch
Lochstack Lodge
Alltnacaillich
DUN DORNAIGIL BROCH
Glen Golly
Upper Badcall
Lower Badcall
719 BEN STACK
Strath Stack
Eil. a'Bhreitheimh
Badcall Bay
859 BEINN AUSKAIRD 386
LOCH A'MHUILINN
Rubha a'Mhucard
Loch Crocach
Achfary
332
Loch More
759
Meall Mór
Calbha Mór
REAY FOREST
Lochmore Lodge
Calbha Beg
Duartmore Forest
Loch an Leathaid Bhuain
Aultanrynie

F
Point of Stoer
R. nan Còsan
Oldany Island
Eddrachillis Bay
Loch a'Chairn Bhain
Kylestrome
547
Kinloch
34
Cìrean Geàrrdail
Eilean Chrona
Culkein Drumbeg
Kylesku
Glendhu
873 BEN HEE
Loch a'Ghorm-choire
Cluas Deas
Culkein
Oldany
Nedd
Unapool
Glendhu Forest
Gleann Dubh
566
Achnacarnin
Clashnessie Bay
Drumbeg
Newton
530
Clashmore
Clashnessie
Gleann Leireag
BEINN AIRD DA LOCH
792 BEINN LEOID
Loch Merkland
Balchladich
Rienachait
Stoer
Loch Poll
Glen Coul
Loch Dubh a'Chuail
Merkland Lodge
Rubh'a' Mhill Dheirg
Bay of Stoer
Clachtoil
Loch an Leothaid
808 QUINAG
776
Loch an Eircill
404
312 CNOC ALASKIE
R. Leumair
Achmelvich Bay
Lochassynt Lodge
EAS COUL AULIN WATERFALL
BEINN UIDHE 740
Corrykinloch
Flag Plantation

G
◄155
Rhicarn
HIGH
Little Assynt
Skiag Bridge
Gorm Loch Mor
512 MAOVALLY
Overscaig Hotel
Achmelvich
ACHMELVICH BEACH
ASSYNT VISITOR CENTRE
Inver
Bracloch
ARDVRECK CASTLE
998 BEN MORE ASSYNT
LOCH
Flag Bridge
Rubha Rodha
Baddidarach
Lochinver
Glencanisp Lodge
Inchnadamph
Loch Feith nan Leothaid
540
715 MEALLAN AONACH
Soyea I.
Loch Inver
Glencanisp Forest
Inchnadamph Forest
546 BREABAG
391
Kirkaig Pt.
Badnaban
Strathan
INCHNADAMPH
A'Chleit
Loch Kirkaig
Inverkirkaig
ASSYNT-
SUILVEN
Stronchrubie
Duchally
Strath an Lòin

H
Rubha Coigeach
Rubha na Breige
Glencanisp Forest
731
Falls
Fionn Loch
Loch na Gainimh
846 CANISP
COIGACH
Benmore Forest
BEINN SGEIREACH 476
Camas Eilean Ghlais
Rubh Mòr
Eilean Mór
ENARD BAY
Rubh'a' Choin
Inverpolly Lodge
Ledmore
Reiff
Brae of Achnahaird
Cam Loch
Loch Veyatie
Loch Ailsh
BEINN AN EOIN 554
Altandhu
Aird of Coigach
Loch Sionascaig
Ledbeg
Benmore Lodge
Eilean Mullagrach
Inverpolly Forest
Altnacealgach Hotel
364 AN STUC
Isle Ristol
Polbain
613
CUL MOR
849 STAC POLLAIDH
Loch Urigill
Glencassley Castle
Glas-leac Mór
Drumrunie Forest
Knockan
Loch na Fuaralaich

J
Achiltibuie
HYDROPONICUM GARDENS
Bacentarbat Bay
Polglass
Loch Lurgainn
769 CUL BEAG
HIGHLAND & RARE BREEDS FARM
Elphin
Knockan
KNOCKAN CRAG
Loch Craggie
Summer Isles
Tanera Beg
Tanera Mór
Horse I.
Achduart
Culnacraig
743 BEINN MOR COIGACH
COIGACH
Drumrunie
CROMALT HILLS
517
Langwell Lodge
Loch Craggie
Loch Craggie
Lubcroy
Invercassley
Glenrossal
Glas-leac Beag
Priest I.
Eilean Dubh
Carn nan Sgeir
Strath Kanaird
Strathcanaird
Strath nan Lon
Rappach
MEALL AN FHUARAIN
Oykel Bridge
Strath Oykel
Rosehall
Bottle I.
Camas Mór

⁹0
Greenstone Point
Rubha Beag
Cailleach Hd.
◄150
Isle Martin
416
◄150
Brae
Doune
Altass

K
NG
Opinan
Stattic Pt.
STORNOWAY 2:40
Rhue
Ardmair
Rhidorroch Forest
Glen Einig
493 BEINN ULBHAICH
Scoraig
Carnach
Annat Bay
Morefield
ULLAPOOL MUSEUM
Rhidorroch Ho.
648
507 MEALL DHEIRGIDH
Scale 1:332 000
(approx 5 miles to 1 inch)
Rireavach
Ullapool
LOCHBROOM MUSEUM
Loch Achall
Loch an Daimh
Corriemulzie Lodge
CREAG LOISGTE
0 1 2 3 4 5 6miles
Badluarach
Dùrnamuck
A835
East Rhidorroch Lodge
Glen Achall
Glasha Burn
701 CARN A'
0 1 2 3 4 5 6 7 8 9 10km
Mellon Charles
Gruinard House
Badcaul
Allt na h-Airbhe
LECKMELM SHRUBBERY
Corriemulzie
Croich

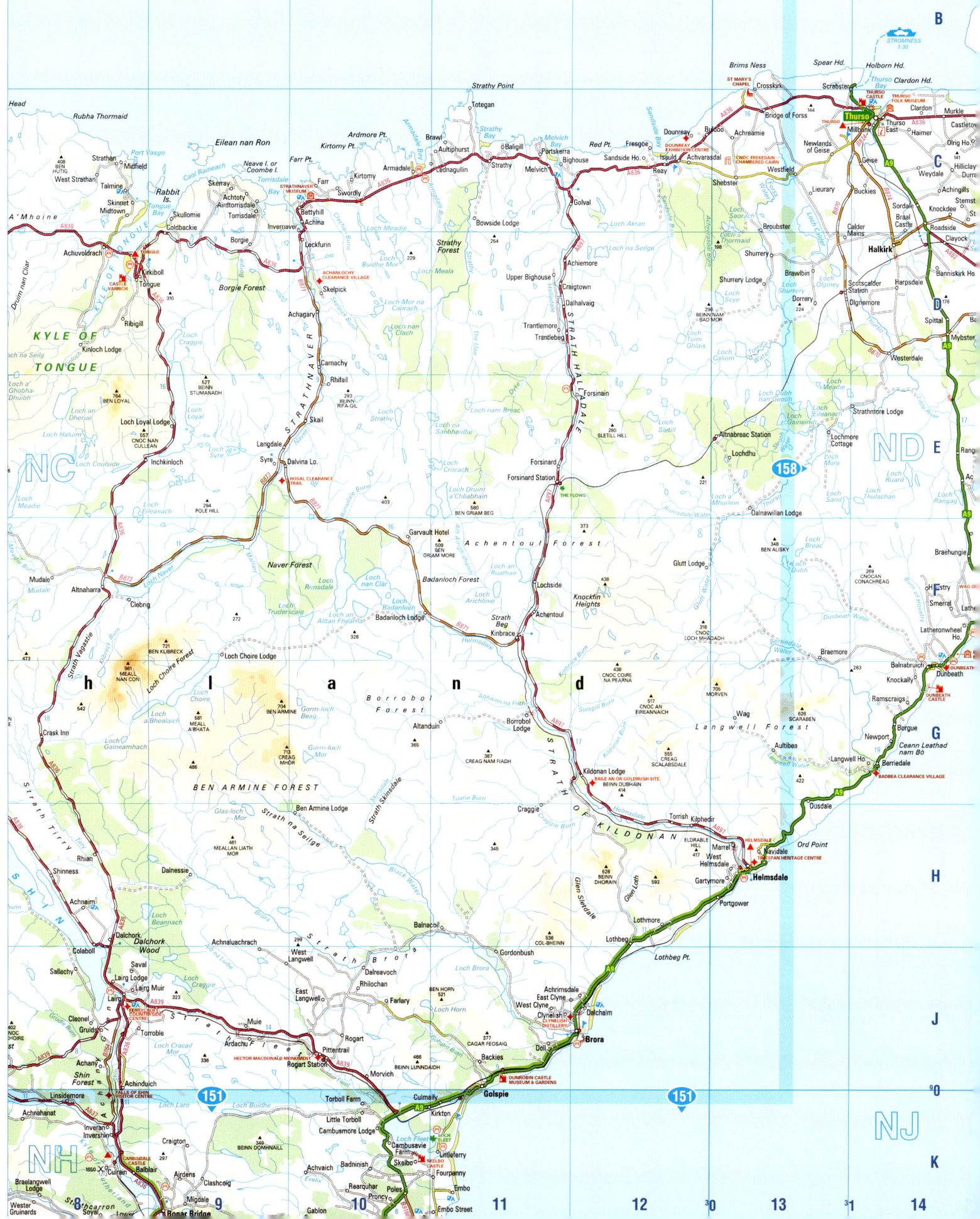

8 9 10 11 12 13

A

B

STROMNESS 1:30

Brims Ness Spear Hd. Holborn Hd.
ST MARY'S CHAPEL Crosskirk Clardon Hd. Thurso
Bay Scrabster
Head Clardon Murkle
Rubha Thormaid Strathy Point THURSO CASTLE Castleton
Eilean nan Ron Ardmore Pt. Totegan Red Pt. Dounreay Bridge of Forss THURSO FOLK MUSEUM Thurso Olrig Ho.
Neave I. or Coombe I. Kirtomy Pt. Brawl Strathy Bay Fresgoe Buldoo Achreamie Thurso East Haimer
Farr Pt. Aultiphurst Baligill Melvich Bay Sandside Ho. Newlands of Geise Geise
Rabbit Is. Skerray Torrisdale Bay Kirtomy Armadale Portskerra Isauld Achvarasdal Westfield Weydale Hilliclay Durran
Achtoty Farr Strathy Melvich Reay CNOC FREKEDAIN CHAMBERED CAIRN Shebster Achingills Sordale
Skinnet Midtown Airdtorrisdale Swordly Golval Shurrery Braal Castle Roadside
Coldbackie Torrisdale Bettyhill Achina Bowside Lodge Shurrery Lodge Brawlbin Scotscalder Station Harpsdale Halkirk Clayock
Achuvoldrach Invernaver Leckfurin Strathy Forest Achiemore Loch na Seilge Dorrery Olgrinmore Banniskirk Sta.
KYLE OF TONGUE Tongue Kirkiboll Borgie Upper Bighouse Craigtown Shurrery Spittal Mybster
CASTLE VARRICH Ribigill Achagary Dalhalvaig Westerdale
Kinloch Lodge Borgie Forest Skelpick Trantlemore BEINN NAM BAD MOR Strathmore Lodge
BEN LOYAL Achany Trantlebeg Lochmore Cottage
Loch Loyal Lodge Carnachy Forsinain Altnabreac Station Loch More
Loch Loyal Rhifail Lochdhu
NC CNOC NAN CULLEAN Skail Forsinard 158 ND
Inchkinloch Langdale Forsinard Station
Syre Dalvina Lo. THE FLOWS Dalnawillan Lodge
ROSAL CLEARANCE TRAIL Ben Griam Beg Lochluichart
Mudale Garvault Hotel Achentoul Forest Glutt Lodge Knocan Conachreag
Altnaharra Ben Griam More Loch an Ruathair Braehungie
Clebrig Naver Forest Badanloch Forest Lochside Ben Alisky Smerral
Crask Inn BEN KLIBRECK Loch Choire Lodge Badanloch Lodge Achentoul Morven Balnabruich Dunbeath
MEALL NAN CON Strath Beg Kinbrace CNOC LOCH MHADAIDH DUNBEATH CASTLE
h i g h l a n d Borrobol Forest Altanduin Ben Armine CNOC AN EIREANNAICH Scaraben Knockally Ramscraigs
BEN ARMINE FOREST Ben Armine Lodge Borrobol Lodge STRATH OF KILDONAN CREAG SCALABSDALE Langwell Forest Newport Borgue
Craggie Wag Aultibea Langwell Ho. Berriedale
Crask Glas-loch Mor Creag Nam Fiadh Kildonan Lodge BEINN DUBHAIN BADBEA CLEARANCE VILLAGE
Rhian MEALLAN LIATH MOR BAILE AN OR GOLDRUSH SITE Torrish Kilphedir Ousdale
Shinness Dalnessie Ben Armine Lodge Craggie West Helmsdale Marrel Ord Point
Achnairn Achnaluachrach ELDRABLE HILL HELMSDALE Navidale TIMESPAN HERITAGE CENTRE
Colaboll DALCHORK WOOD West Langwell Balnacoil BEINN DHORAIN Helmsdale
Saval Dalreavoch Gordonbush Gartymore Portgower
Lairg Lodge East Langwell Rhilochan BEINN LUNNDAIDH Lothmore Lothbeg Pt.
Lairg Muie Rogart Farlary BEN HORN Achrimsdale Lothbeg
Claonel Torroble HECTOR MACDONALD MONUMENT Pittentrail Loch Horn East Clyne Lothbeg
Gruids Achinduich Rogart Station Morvich CAGAR FEOSAIG West Clyne CLYNELISH DISTILLERY Dalchalm
Achany Shin Forest Muie Backies Doll Brora
Linsidemore FALLS OF SHIN VISITOR CENTRE 151 Culmaily DUNROBIN CASTLE MUSEUM & GARDENS 151 NJ
Achnahanat Torboll Farm Golspie
Inveran CARBISDALE CASTLE Little Torboll Kirkton
Invershin Cambusmore Lodge Cambusavie Farm Littleferry
Braelangwell Lodge Craigton BEINN DOMHNAILL Skelbo SKELBO CASTLE Embo
Wester Gruinards Airdens Badninish Fourpenny Embo Street
St Gaolton Clashcoig Rearquhar Poles Gablon
Bonar Bridge Migdale Proncy

A838 A836 A897 A9 A99

KYLE OF TONGUE

NC ND NH NJ

Map — Caithness / North Highland Coast

Grid references: columns 1–7; rows A–K

Islands and headlands (north)

HOY — Rysa Little, Calf of Flotta, Roan Hd., Hunda, Holm Sound, Rose Ness, Northtown, **Burray**, Burray Ness, Grimness, Grim Ness, Newark Bay, Papley, Aikers, SOUTH RONALDSAY, Lythes, Wind Wick, Halcro Hd., Linklater, Cleat, Burwick, Old Hd., Liddel, Brough Ness

Lyness, SCAPA FLOW VISITOR CENTRE, Rinnigill, Bow, Pan Hope, Flotta, Uppertown, St. Margaret's Hope, Herston, Herston Hd., Widewall, Sandwick, Suckquoy, Quindry

Sneuk Hd., Little Ayre, Crockness, Wyng, Hackness, MARTELLO TOWERS, Longhope, Melsetter, Hurliness, Brims, SOUTH WALLS, Tor Ness, Brims Ness, Cantick Hd., Swona, Dundas Ho.

Heldale Water, Little Rack Wick, Hoglinns Water

TOMB OF THE EAGLES AND BRONZE AGE HOUSE

FOSSIL AND VINTAGE CENTRE, Echnaloch Bay, Holm Sound

Pentland Firth

PENTLAND FIRTH, Muckle Skerry, Pentland Skerries, Langaton Point, Nethertown, Red Head, **Island of Stroma**, Mell Head, Uppertown, Boars of Duncansby

159

Mainland (Caithness)

DUNNET HEAD, Briga Hd., Brough, Hunspow, Dunnet Bay, Scarfskerry Pt., Scarfskerry, Ham, Rattar, Men of Mey, St John's Pt., East Mey, CASTLE OF MEY, Mey, Gills Bay, Gills, Kirkstyle, Canisby, JOHN O'GROATS, John o' Groats, DUNCANSBY HEAD, Stacks of Duncansby

The Thirl, Holborn Hd., Clardon Hd., ST JOHN'S CHAPEL, Corsback, Barrock, Brabster, Skirza, Skirza Head, Freswick, Freswick Bay, Ness Head

STROMNESS, Scrabster, THURSO CASTLE, **Thurso**, THURSO FOLK MUSEUM, Millbank, Thurso East, Haimer, Castletown, Castlehill, Greenland, Loch Heilen, Lochend, Reaster, Slickly, Alterwall, Tofts, BUCHOLLY CASTLE, NORTHLANDS VIKING CENTRE, Auckengill, Nybster, Brough Head, Keiss, KEISS CASTLE, Mireland, Keiss

Brims Ness, Spear Hd., ST MARY'S CHAPEL, Crosskirk, Dounreay, DOUNREAY EXHIBITION CENTRE, Bridge of Forss, Buldoo, Achreamie, CNOC FREKEDAIN CHAMBERED CAIRN, Newlands of Geise, Clardon, Murkle, Castletown, FLAGSTONE INTERPRETATIVE TRAIL, NATURAL HISTORY DISPLAY, Dunnet

Freegoe, Isauld, Iside Ho., Reay, Achvarasdal, Shebster, Westfield, Geise, Weydale, Hilliclay, Durran, Orlig Ho., Tain, Bowermadden, Reaster, LYTH ARTS CENTRE, Lyth, Sortat, Barrock Ho., Howe

Loch Saorach, Loch Thormaid, Broubster, Lieurary, Buckies, Sordale, Braal Castle, Knockdee, Stemster, Halcro, Hastigrow, Kirk, Myrelandhorn, Killimster

NC, ND

Shurrery, Brawlbin, Shurrery Lodge, Dorrery, Calder Mains, Scotscalder Station, Harpsdale, Banniskirk Ho., Clayock, Gillock, North Watten, SINCLAIR'S BAY, Reiss, CASTLE GIRNIGOE, CASTLE SINCLAIR, Noss Head

Halkirk, Olgrinmore, Roadside, Loch Scarmclate, Loch Watten, Mains of Watten, Watten, Winless, Ackergill, Staxigoe, Papigoe, WICK HERITAGE CENTRE, Sealky Head

Loch Scye, BEINN NAM BAD MOR, Spittal, Backlass, Mybster, Loch of Toftingall, Bilbster, Strath, **Wick**, Broadhaven

Loch Tuim Ghlais, Loch Calum, Westerdale, Acharole, Burn of Acharole, Strath, Strkoke Ho., Milton, Old Wick, CASTLE OF OLD WICK, Newton, Whiterow, South Hd., Gote O'Tram

H i g h l a n d, Loch Meadie, Strathmore Lodge, Loch Eileanach, Altnabreac Station, Lochmore Cottage, Badlipster, HEMPRIGGS HOUSE, Loch of Hempriggs, Helman Hd.

157, Loch Dubh nan Geodh, Loch Gaineimh, Loch More, Rangag, GREY CAIRNS OF CAMSTER, HILL OF OLICLETT, Gansclet, Thrumster, Sarclet, Sarclet Hd.

Lochdhu, Loch Ruard, Loch Thulachan, Loch Sand, Achavanich, Camster, Ulbster, CAIRN OF GET, Whaligoe, A882

Dalnawillan Lodge, Loch a Mhuilinn, Rumsdale Water, STEMSTER HILL, Roster, Mid Clyth, Bruan, HILL O' MANY STANES, Upper Lybster, LYBSTER ART GALLERY, West Clyth

Glutt Lodge, BEN ALISKY, Crofts of Benachielt, Braehungie, RUMSTER FOREST, Houstry, Swiney, **Lybster**, WAG OF FORSE, Forse Ho., Forse

CNOCAN CONACHREAG, Smerral, Latheron, Latheronwheel, Latheronwheel Ho., CLAN GUNN HERITAGE CENTRE

CNOC LOCH MHADADH, Braemore, Dunbeath Water, Knockally, Balnabruich, LAIDHAY CROFT MUSEUM, DUNBEATH HERITAGE CENTRE, Dunbeath, DUNBEATH CASTLE, Dunbeath Bay

CNOC COIRE NA PEARNA, MORVEN, Wag, CNOC AN EIREANNAICH, SCARABEN, Langwell Forest, Newport, Borgue, Ceann Leathad nam Bò, Ramscraigs

Glut Lodge, CREAG SCALABSDALE, Aultibea, Langwell Ho., Berriedale, Langwell Water, BADBEA CLEARANCE VILLAGE

BEINN DUBHAIN, OR GOLDRUSH SITE, Torrish, Kilphedir, Ousdale, Ord Point

ELDRABLE HILL, Marrel, West Helmsdale, Navidale, TIMESPAN HERITAGE CENTRE, HELMSDALE

Glen Loth, Lothmore, Gartymore, **Helmsdale**, Portgower, Lothbeg Pt.

Scale

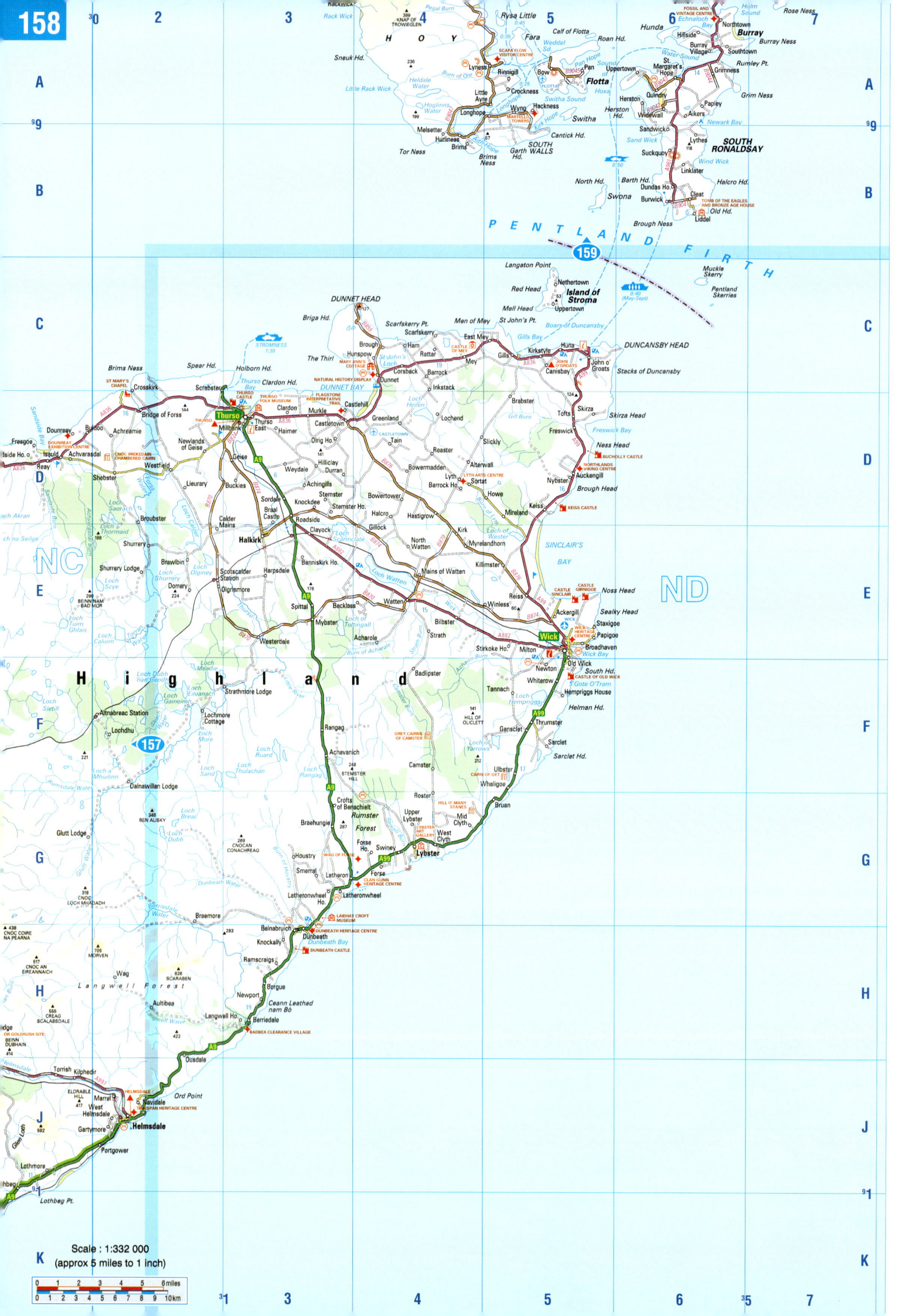

Scale : 1:332 000
(approx 5 miles to 1 inch)

0 1 2 3 4 5 6 miles
0 1 2 3 4 5 6 7 8 9 10km

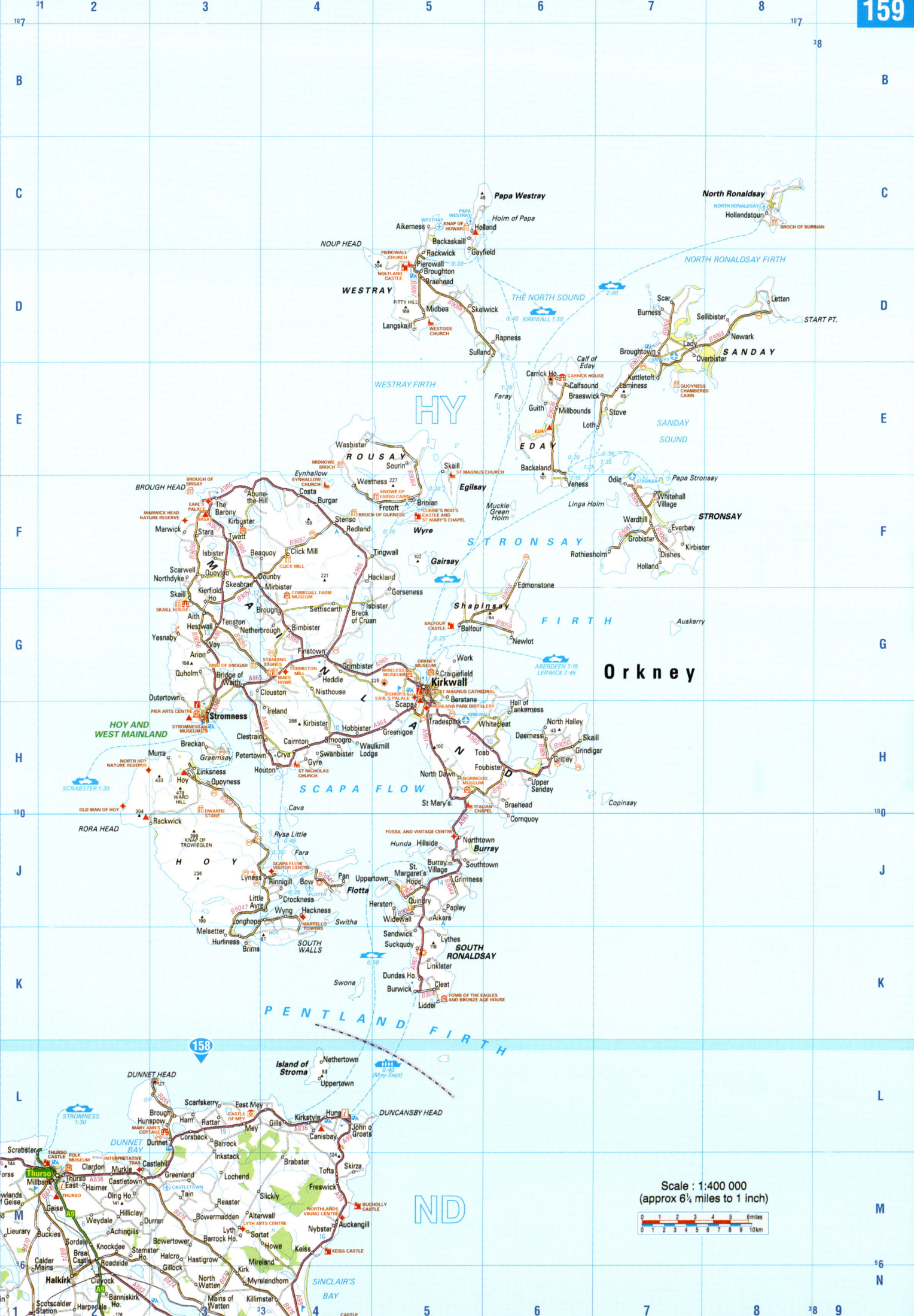

Orkney

ND · **HY**

Major islands and areas
WESTRAY · Papa Westray · North Ronaldsay · SANDAY · ROUSAY · EDAY · STRONSAY · Papa Stronsay · SHAPINSAY · HOY · SOUTH WALLS · SOUTH RONALDSAY · BURRAY · Flotta · MAINLAND

Waters
THE NORTH SOUND · NORTH RONALDSAY FIRTH · WESTRAY FIRTH · SANDAY SOUND · STRONSAY FIRTH · FIRTH · SCAPA FLOW · PENTLAND FIRTH · SINCLAIR'S BAY · DUNNET BAY

Selected place names

Papa Westray / Westray area: Aikerness, Backaskaill, Holland, Rackwick, Gayfield, Pierowall, Broughton, Braehead, Noetland Castle, Midbea, Skelwick, Langskaill, Westside Church, Sulland, Rapness, Holm of Papa, Knap of Howar, Pierowall Church, Fitty Hill, Noup Head

North Ronaldsay: Hollandstoun, Broch of Burrian

Sanday: Scar, Burness, Sellibister, Lettan, Newark, Lady, Overbister, Broughtown, Kettletoft, Lamiless, Quoyness Chambered Cairn, Start Pt.

Eday: Carrick Ho., Calfsound, Braeswick, Guith, Millbounds, Stove, Loth, Backaland, Veness, Calf of Eday, Faray

Stronsay: Whitehall Village, Wardhill, Grobister, Everbay, Kirbister, Dishes, Holland, Rothiesholm, Odie, Edmonstone

Rousay / Egilsay / Wyre: Wasbister, Sourin, Westness, Frotoft, Brinian, Skaill, St Magnus Church, Midhowe Broch, Eynhallow Church, Knowe of Yarso Cairn, Cubbie Roo's Castle and St Mary's Chapel

Mainland (west): Brough of Birsay, The Barony, Kirbuster, Costa, Burgar, Abune-the-Hill, Marwick, Stara, Twatt, Isbister, Scarwell, Northdyke, Skaill, Kierfield Ho., Aith, Hestwall, Yesnaby, Arion, Quholm, Outertown, Click Mill, Beaquoy, Skeabrae, Dounby, Mirbister, Redland, Stenso, Tingwall, Hackland, Gorseness, Finstown, Grimbister, Heddle, Nisthouse, Bridge of Waith, Bimbister, Netherbrough, Settiscarth, Breck of Cruan, Isbister, Clouston, Ireland, Kirbister, Clestrain, Cairston, Smoogro, Swanbister, Waulkmill Lodge, Gyre, Crya, Houton, Petertown, Standing Stones, Ring of Brogar, Maes Howe, Voy

Stromness: Stromness, Pier Arts Centre, Stromness Museum

Kirkwall: Kirkwall, Orkney Museum, St Magnus Cathedral, Bishop's & Earl's Palace, Scapa, Berstane, Craigiefield, Wireless Museum, Highland Park Distillery, Tradespark, Work, Hall of Tankerness, Greenigoe, Hobbister, Whitecleat, North Halley, Deerness, Norwood Museum, Skaill, Gritley, Grindigar, Toab, Foubister, Upper Sanday, North Dawn, St Mary's, Italian Chapel, Braehead, Cornquoy

Shapinsay: Balfour, Balfour Castle, Newlot

Hoy / South Walls / Flotta: Hoy, Quoyness, Linksness, Rackwick, Old Man of Hoy, Rora Head, Dwarfie Stane, Ward Hill, Knap of Trowieglen, Lyness, Rinnigill, Bow, North Hoy Nature Reserve, Scapa Flow Visitor Centre, Little Ayre, Longhope, Melsetter, Hurliness, Brims, Graemsay, Breckan, Murra, Cava, Fara, Rysa Little, Flotta, Pan, Crockness, Hackness, Wyng, Martello Towers, Swatha

Burray / South Ronaldsay: Burray Village, Southtown, Northtown, Hillside, Hunda, Grimness, St Margaret's Hope, Herston, Widewall, Quindry, Papley, Aikers, Sandwick, Suckquoy, Lythes, Linklater, Dundas Ho., Burwick, Cleat, Liddel, Tomb of the Eagles and Bronze Age House, Fossil and Vintage Centre

Caithness mainland (ND): Dunnet Head, Scarfskerry, Brough, Harn, Rattar, East Mey, Castle of Mey, Gills, Kirkstyle, Huna, John o' Groats, Canisbay, Duncansby Head, Island of Stroma, Nethertown, Uppertown, Hunspow, Mary Ann's Cottage, Corsback, Barrock, Mey, Inkstack, Brabster, Skirza, Freswick, Bucholly Castle, Auckengill, Keiss, Keiss Castle, Northlands Viking Centre, Nybster, Lyth Arts Centre, Sortat, Howe, Thurso, Thurso Castle, Folk Museum, Scrabster, Murkle, Castletown, Castlehill, Clardon, Greenland, Lochend, Slickly, Reaster, Alterwall, Bowermadden, Bowertower, Barrock Ho., Stemster, Hastigrow, Mireland, Myrelandhorn, Kirk, North Watten, Gillock, Halcro, Roadside, Knockdee, Sordale, Braal Castle, Halkirk, Calder Mains, Bannskirk Ho., Lieurary, Buckies, Geise, Weydale, Durran, Hilliclay, Achingills, Olrig Ho., Haimer, Tain, Millbank, Thurso East, Forss, Lowlands, Olgrinmore, Harpsdale, Scotscalder Station, Mains of Watten, Killimster, Castle Sinclair, Castle Girnigoe

Scale : 1:400 000 (approx 6¼ miles to 1 inch)

0 1 2 3 4 5 6 miles
0 1 2 3 4 5 6 7 8 9 10km

HO

HP

Shetland

HT

HU

Fair Isle

UNST

YELL

FETLAR

WHALSAY

FOULA

ST. MAGNUS BAY

SHETLAND

COLGRAVE SOUND

YELL SOUND

Esha Ness
Fitful Head
Sumburgh Head
Sandness Hill
Ronas Hill
Royl Field
Vord Hill
Saxa Vord

Lerwick
Scalloway
Sumburgh
Brae
Voe
Walls
Sandness
Aith
Bixter
Tingwall
Gott
Cunningsburgh
Bigton
Maywick
Sandwick
Levenwick
Hoswick
Channerwick
Boddam
Exnaboe
Toab
Scatness
Grutness
Quendale
Hillwell
Ringasta
Noss
Longfield
Skelberry
Scousburgh
Bremirehoull
Mail
Leebotten
Stove
Cumlewick
Northpunds
Southpunds
Ireland
Bigton

Gluss
Hamnavoe
Burravoe
Brough
Mossbank
Laxobigging
Graven
Voxter
Collafirth
Lunna
Vidlin
Laxo
Swining
Gardie
Symbister
Nisthouse
Isbister
Huxter
Clate
Skaw
Marrister
Brough

Sullom Voe Oil Terminal

Belmont
Gutcher
Colvister
Sellafirth
North Sandwick
Cunnister
Basta
Camb
Mid Yell
West Yell
Setter
Ulsta
Hamnavoe
Burravoe
Copister
Houlland
Old Haa

Haroldswick
Norwick
Baltasound
Buness
Baliasta
Westing
Caldback
Clivocast
Uyeasound
Muness
Muness Castle
Ramnageo

Hermaness Visitor Centre
Unst Heritage Centre
Keen of Hamer
Unst Boat Haven

Brough Lodge
Houbie
Tresta
Aith
Funzie
Fetlar Interpretative Centre

Hascosay

Gloup
Cullivoe
Stonganess
Greenbank
Underhoull
Lund
Grimister
Windhouse
Harkland
West Sandwick
Aywick
Otterswick
Swarister
Gossabrough

North Roe
South-haa
Isbister
North Collafirth
Ollaberry
Eastwick
Bardister
Burraland
Nibon
Mangaster
Haggrister
Trondavoe
Islesburgh
Busta
Burravoe
Roesound
Wethersta
Hillside
Gonfirth
Voe
Little-ayre

Hamnavoe
Scarff
Braehoulland
Burnside
Hillswick
Ure
Stenness
Tangwick
Urafirth
Heylor
Housetter
Voe
North Gluss
Sullom

Tangwick Haa Museum

Papa Stour
Papa Little
Vementry

Melby
Sandness
Garth
Engamoor
Brindister
Noonsbrough
Clousta
West Burrafirth
Unifirth
Twatt
Houlland
Aith
Braewick
East Burrafirth
Setter
Bridge of Walls
Dale of Walls
Mid Walls
Annifirth
Burraland
Browland
Walls
Gruting
Stanydale
Semblister
Effirth
Tresta
Sound
Bixter
Westerfield
Heglibister
Huxter
Girlsta
Hellister
Wadbister
Catfirth
Skellister
Brough
Freester
Eswick
Gletness
Breiwick
Laxfirth

Shetland Textile Working Museum

Temple

Garderhouse
Sandsound
Sand
Leeans
Culswick
Easter Skeld
Wester Skeld
Reawick
South Whiteness
White Ness
Westerwick
Silwick
Veensgarth
Gremista
Heogan
Gunnista
Setter
Brough
Isle of Noss
Noss
Grindiscol
Kirkabister

Tingwall Agricultural Mus

Fort Charlotte
Shetland Museum
Clickimin

Holmsgarth
Port Arthur
Cutts
Uppersound
Uradale
Wick
Gulberwick
Brindister
Wester Quarff
Easter Quarff
Fladdabister
Aithsetter
Gord
Greenmow
Hamnavoe
West Burra
Grunasound
Papil
Houss
Okraquoy

Cave of the Bard
Croft Trail
Mousa Broch

Maywick
Hoswick
Channerwick
Sandwick

Stoneybreck
Fair Isle
Fair Isle Lodge & Bird Observatory
George Waterston Museum

Foula
Harrier
Ham
Hametoun
The Sneug

Croft House Museum
Quendale Mill
Jarlshof
Ness of Burgi

A970
A971
A968
B9071
B9075
B9076
B9077
B9078
B9079
B9081
B9082
B9083
B9084
B9086
B9087
B9088
B9122
A966

Foula 2:15
Scalloway 3:30 (Summer only)
Walls 2:15
Foula 3:30 (Summer only)
Aberdeen 12:00 Kirkwall 5:30
Fair Isle 4:30 (Summer only)
Sumburgh 2:40 Lerwick 4:30 (Summer only)
Fair Isle 2:40

Scale : 1:400 000
(approx 6¼ miles to 1 inch)

0 1 2 3 4 5 6 miles
0 1 2 3 4 5 6 7 8 9 10km

BRISTOL
AVONMOUTH
FILTON
KINGSWOOD
Frampton End
Coalpit Heath
Mayshill
Ram Hill
Henfield
Watley's End
Winterbourne
Winterbourne Down
Kendleshire
Pye Corner
Whiteshill
Bromley Heath
Downend
Mangotsfield
Shortwood
Siston
Webb's Heath
Goose Green
Siston Common
Warmley
Bridge Yate
North Common
Bitton
Cadbury Heath
Oldland
Longwell Green
Soundwell
Hillfields
Fishponds
Frenchay
Broomhill
Stoke Gifford
Harry Stoke
Great Stoke
Little Stoke
Broad Mead
Stapleton
Eastville
Lockleaze
Clay Hill
Speedwell
St. George
Crew's Hole
Conham
Hanham
Hanham Green
St. Anne's Park
Broom Hill
Brislington
Stockwood
Flowers Hill
Arno's Vale
Knowle
Hengrove
Filwood Park
Lower Knowle
Windmill Hill
Novers Park
Hartcliffe
Bedminster Down
Headley Park
Highridge
Bedminster
Ashton Vale
Bower Ashton
Long Ashton
Barrow Wood
Horfield
Ashley Down
Montpelier
Bishopston
Golden Hill
Henleaze
Redland
Cotham
Westbury Park
Southmead
Brentry
Eastfield
Cribbs Causeway
Catbrain
Compton Greenfield
Berwick
Hallen
Henbury
Westbury on Trym
Stoke Bishop
Sneyd Park
Sea Mills
Clifton
Hotwells
Avon Gorge
Leigh Woods
Abbots Leigh
Lawrence Weston
Shirehampton
Ham Green
Pill
Easton-in-Gordano
Portbury
Lower Failand
Failand
Tyntesfield
Tyntesfield Plantation
Ashton Hill Plantation
Cambridge Batch
Flax Bourton
Avonmouth Docks
The Royal Portbury Dock
River Avon
River Frome
M4
M5
M32
M49
A4
A38
A37
A4174
A4018
A420
A431
A432
A403
A369
A370
AVON RING ROAD
BRISTOL (FILTON)
BRISTOL PARKWAY
BLAISE CASTLE
BLAISE CASTLE HOUSE
BRISTOL ZOO GARDENS
CLIFTON SUSPENSION BRIDGE
CABOT TOWER
ASHTON COURT ESTATE
ROMAN VILLA
GORDANO SERVICES
AVON VALLEY RAILWAY
MEMORIAL STADIUM (BRISTOL ROVERS F.C. BRISTOL R.U.F.C.)
COUNTY CRICKET GD
ASHTON GATE (BRISTOL CITY F.C.)
BRITISH EMPIRE & COMMONWEALTH MUSEUM
ARNOLFINI GALLERY
BRISTOL TEMPLE MEADS
2 miles
3 km
0
1
2
3
17
18
36

The Black Country

WOLVERHAMPTON
WALSALL
WILLENHALL
BILSTON
DARLASTON
WEDNESBURY
COSELEY
SEDGLEY
TIPTON
WEST BROMWICH
DUDLEY
Upper Gornal
Gornalwood
Pensnett
Netherton
BRIERLEY HILL
AMBLECOTE
Lye
Cradley
OLDBURY
ROWLEY REGIS
Old Hill
Blackheath
Langley Green
SMETHWICK
Sandwell
HALESOWEN
Pedmore
Hagley
Woodgate
World's End
Weoley Castle
Shenley Fields

Oakham
Lyndon
Newton
Hurst Green
Warley Woods
Wychbury Hill
Hagley Wood
Uffmoor Wood
Twiland Wood

WEST PARK
Town Hall
ST GEORGES
THE ROYAL P&R
PRIESTFIELD P&R
BILSTON CENTRAL
THE CRESCENT
LOXDALE
BRADLEY LANE
WEDNESBURY PARKWAY
WEDNESBURY GREAT WESTERN ST
TAME BRIDGE PARKWAY
BESCOT STADIUM
SANDWELL VALLEY COUNTRY PARK
WOODGATE VALLEY COUNTRY PARK
BAGGERIDGE COUNTRY PARK
Nature Centre
BLACK COUNTRY MUSEUM
DUDLEY ZOO & CASTLE
MERRY HILL CENTRE
DUDLEY ST GUNS VILLAGE
THE PUBLIC SITE
WEST BROMWICH CENTRAL
THE HAWTHORNS
SMETHWICK ROLFE STREET
LANGLEY GREEN
STOURBRIDGE TOWN
STOURBRIDGE JUNCTION
CRADLEY HEATH
ROWLEY REGIS
HALESOWEN ABBEY (REMS)
BIRCHILLS CANAL MUSEUM
ARBORETUM
FRANKLEY SERVICES
Bartley Resr

Roads: A454, A449, A4123, A41, A463, A457, A459, A461, A4036, A4100, A456, A458, A491, A4101, A4037, A4033, A4168, A4148, A34, A454, A462, A4038, A461, A41, A4031, M6, M5, A4041, A4149, A4182, A4034, A4030, A4136, A4040, A4123

WOLVERHAMPTON ROAD
WILLENHALL ROAD
WALSALL ROAD
BIRMINGHAM ROAD
DUDLEY ROAD
HAGLEY ROAD
HALESOWEN ROAD
STOURBRIDGE ROAD
MANOR WAY
THE EXPRESSWAY
ALL SAINTS WAY
KELVIN WAY
TRINITY WAY
RING ROAD
PLECK ROAD
BROADWAY
BROADWAY NORTH
BROADWAY WEST

Birmingham approaches

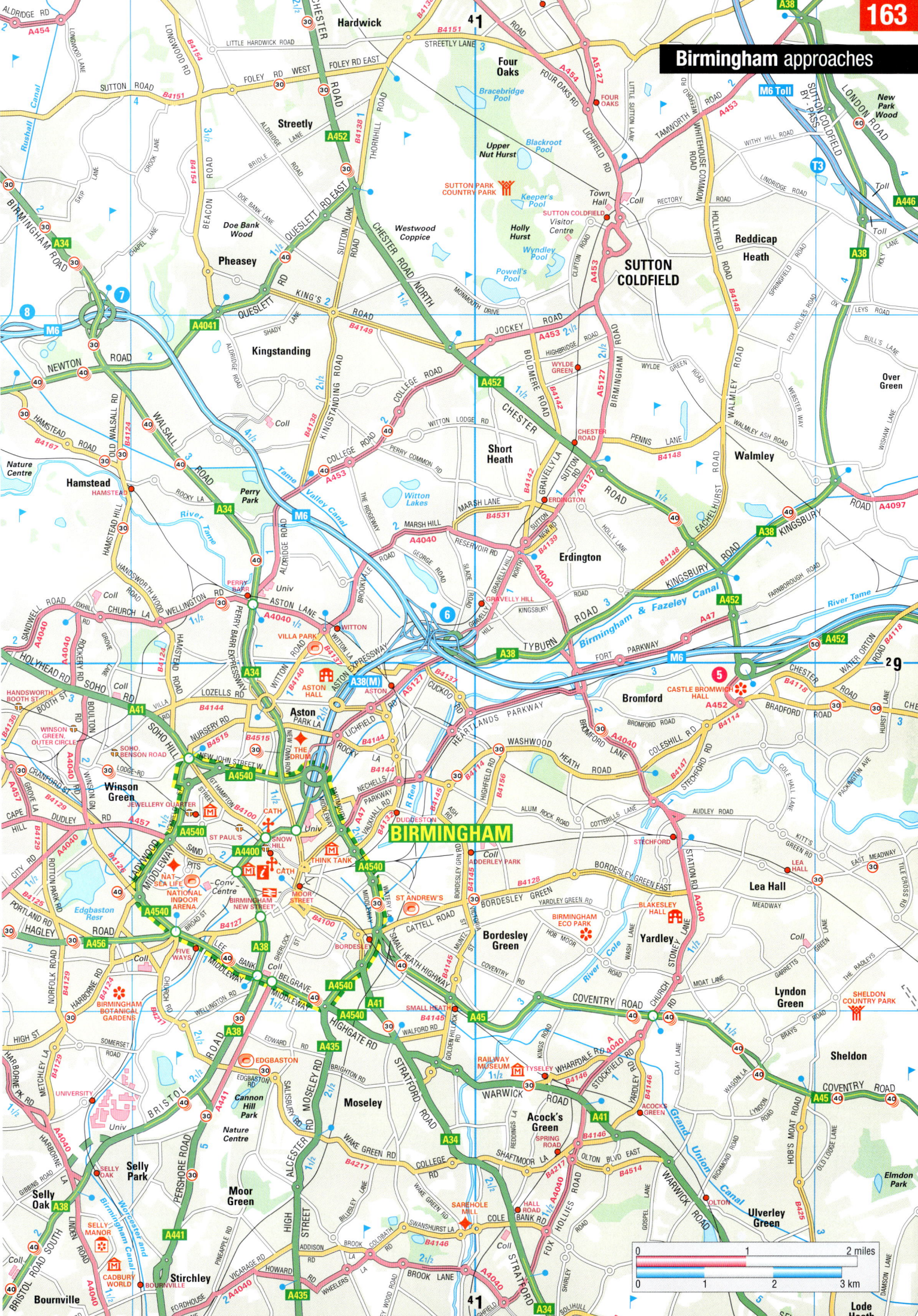

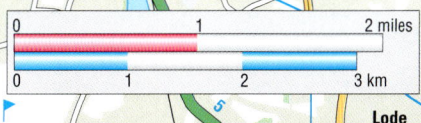

Hardwick
Four Oaks
Bracebridge Pool
Upper Nut Hurst
Blackroot Pool
SUTTON PARK COUNTRY PARK
Keeper's Pool
Town Hall
SUTTON COLDFIELD Visitor Centre
Holly Hurst
Wyndley Pool
Powell's Pool
SUTTON COLDFIELD
Reddicap Heath
New Park Wood
M6 Toll
Streetly
Westwood Coppice
Doe Bank Wood
Pheasey
Kingstanding
Over Green
Short Heath
Witton Lakes
Walmley
Nature Centre
Hamstead
Perry Park
Erdington
River Tame
Tame Valley Canal
Birmingham & Fazeley Canal
Bromford
CASTLE BROMWICH HALL
VILLA PARK
ASTON HALL
Aston
Winson Green
JEWELLERY QUARTER
ST PAUL'S
SNOW HILL
THE DRUM
THINK TANK
NAT. SEA LIFE
NATIONAL INDOOR ARENA
BIRMINGHAM NEW STREET
MOOR STREET
ST ANDREW'S
Edgbaston Resr
FIVE WAYS
Bordesley Green
BIRMINGHAM ECO PARK
BLAKESLEY HALL
Yardley
Lea Hall
Lyndon Green
SHELDON COUNTRY PARK
Sheldon
BIRMINGHAM BOTANICAL GARDENS
EDGBASTON
Cannon Hill Park
Nature Centre
Moseley
RAILWAY MUSEUM
TYSELEY
Acock's Green
Grand Union Canal
Elmdon Park
Selly Park
Selly Oak
SELLY MANOR
Moor Green
SAREHOLE MILL
Ulverley Green
CADBURY WORLD
Bournville
Stirchley
Worcester and Birmingham Canal
Lode Heath
0 1 2 miles
0 1 2 3 km

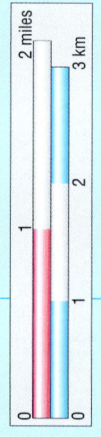

St Mellons (Llaneirwg)
Peterstone Wentlooge (Llanbedr Gwynllŵg)
Marshfield
Castleton
Blacktown
Michaelston-y-Fedw
Park Wood
Began
Trowbridge
Newton
Rumney (Rhymni)
Pwll-Mawr
Llanrumney
Pentwyn
Llanedeyrn
Cefn Mably Woods
Cardiff Gate Services
Llwyncelyn
Coed Coesau-Whips
Lisvane (Llys Faen)
Cyncoed
Tremorfa
Splott
Roath
CARDIFF (CAERDYDD)
Wales Millennium Centre
National Assembly
Cardiff Bay Visitor Centre
Cardiff Bay Barrage
Cardiff Bay
Butetown
Techniquest
Bute E Dock
Llanishen Reservoir
The Lake
Roath Park
Cathays
National Museum Cardiff
Heath
Maindy
Thornhill
Llanishen
Birchgrove
Gabalfa
Cardiff Castle
Millennium Stadium
Cardiff Arms
Cardiff Central
Cardiff City
Salmead
Riverside
Grangetown
The Warren
Watford
Caerphilly Common
Coed-y-Wenallt
Rhiwbina
Whitchurch
Llandaff North
Llandaff (Llandaf)
Llandaff Cathedral
Canton
Pontcanna
Ninian Park
Leckwith
Michaelston-le-Pit
Nantgarw
Glan-y-llyn
Taff's Well (Ffynnon-Taf)
Castell Coch
Tongwynlais
Radyr
Morganstown
Pentyrch
Garth Wood
Forest Farm
Fairwater
Ely (Tre-lai)
Caerau
Michaelston-super-Ely
Culverhouse Cross
Wenvoe (Gwenfô)
Wallston
Twyn-yr-odyn
Downs
Church Village
St Fagans (Sain Ffagan)
St Fagans National History Museum
St Brides-super-Ely (Llansanffraid-ar-Elái)
St George's
St Nicholas (Sain Nicolas)
Inkinswood Burial Chamber
St Lythans
Cardiff West Services
Taff vale
Coed y Gedrys
Grath Hill
Soar

M4 · A48 · A470 · A469 · A4232 · A4234 · A4119 · A4161 · A4232 · A48(M)

EDINBURGH
Musselburgh
Fisherrow Sands
Inveresk
Dalkeith
Old Craighall
Stoneybank
Portobello
Joppa
Leith
Middle Craigs
Eastern Craigs
Craigentinny
Northfield
Bingham
Niddrie
Danderhall
Easter Millerhill
Gilmerton
Moredun
The Inch
Holyrood Park
Arthur's Seat
Duddingston Loch
Dunsapie Loch
Prestonfield
Calton Hill
Meadow Park
Newhaven
Port of Leith
Ocean Terminal Centre
HMY BRITANNIA
Granton Harbour
Wardie
Granton
Drylaw
Craigleith
Blackhall
Murrayfield
Corstophine
Merchiston
Churchill
Nether Liberton
Liberton
Alnwickhill
Braid Hills
Muirhouse
Loanhead
Comiston
Craiglockhart
Colinton
Bonaly
Longstone
Torphin
Baberton
Clermiston
Cramond
Cramond Island
Drum Sands
South Gyle
Cammo
Cramond Bridge
Craigiehall
Hermiston
Currie
EDINBURGH AIRPORT
DALMENY HOUSE
LAURISTON CASTLE
EDINBURGH ZOO
ROYAL BOTANIC GARDEN
ROYAL OBSERVATORY
CRAIGMILLAR CASTLE
PALACE OF HOLYROOD HOUSE
Scottish Parliament
NATIONAL MUSEUM OF SCOTLAND
SCOTTISH NATIONAL GALLERY OF MODERN ART
MURRAYFIELD
TYNECASTLE
HILLEND SKI CENTRE
HILLEND COUNTRY PARK
BONALY COUNTRY PARK
EDINBURGH BUTTERFLY & INSECT WORLD
DALKEITH PARK
INVERESK LODGE GARDENS
MALLENY GARDEN
WATER OF LEITH VISITOR CENTRE
EDINBURGH SERVICES
DREGHORN SERVICES
THE CITY OF EDINBURGH BY-PASS

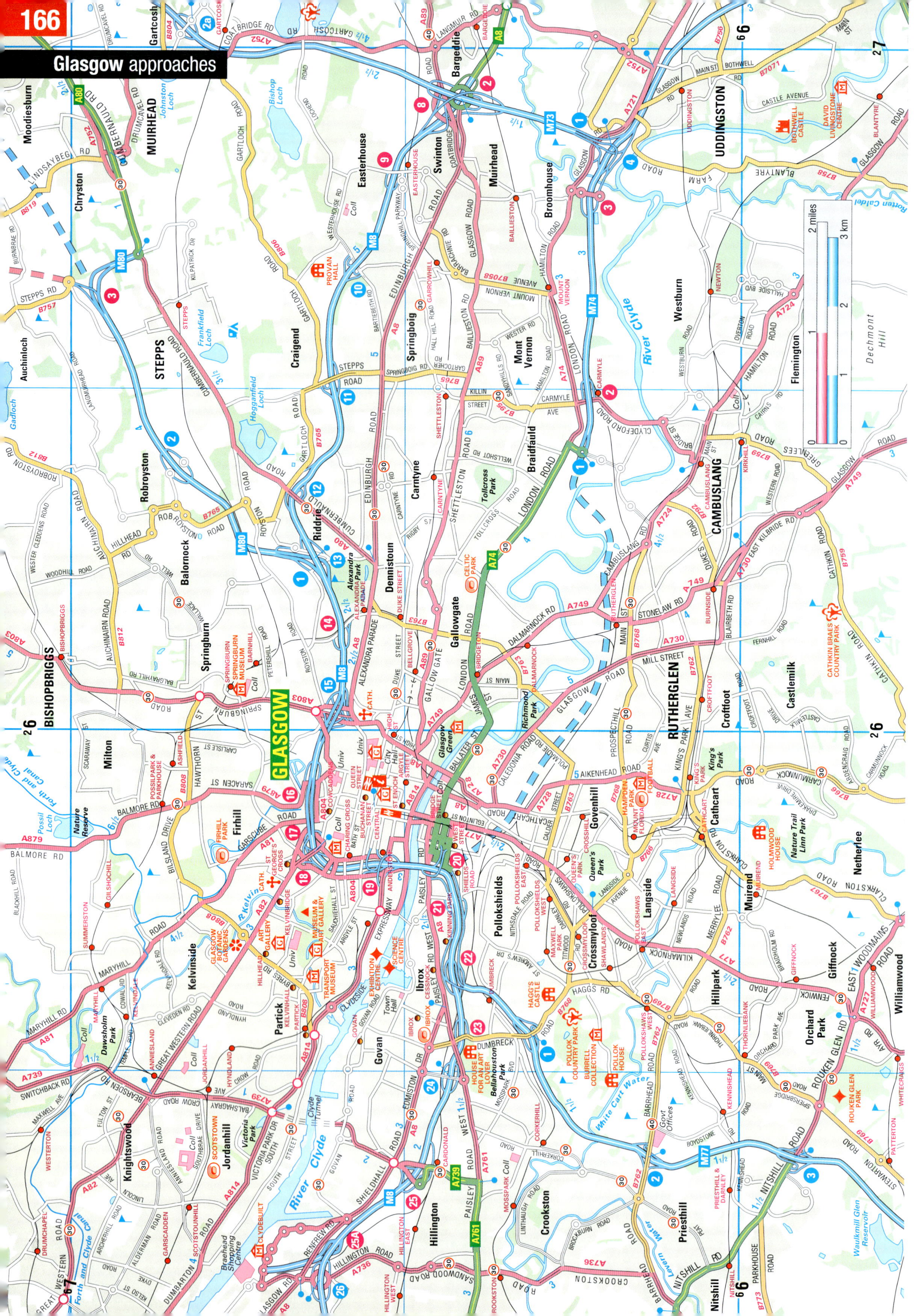
GLASGOW
Bishopbriggs
Milton
Springburn
Balornock
Robroyston
Stepps
Muirhead
Chryston
Moodiesburn
Gartcosh
Auchinloch
Craigend
Easterhouse
Swinton
Bargeddie
Muirhead
Broomhouse
Mount Vernon
Springboig
Carntyne
Braidfauld
Riddrie
Dennistoun
Gallowgate
Uddingston
Westburn
Flemington
Cambuslang
Rutherglen
Croftfoot
Castlemilk
King's Park
Cathcart
Netherlee
Muirend
Giffnock
Williamwood
Orchard Park
Hillpark
Langside
Govanhill
Crossmyloof
Pollokshields
Ibrox
Govan
Partick
Kelvinside
Firhill
Maryhill
Knightswood
Jordanhill
Hillington
Crookston
Priesthill
Nitshill
River Clyde
White Cart Water
Forth and Clyde Canal
Dechmont Hill
2 miles
3 km

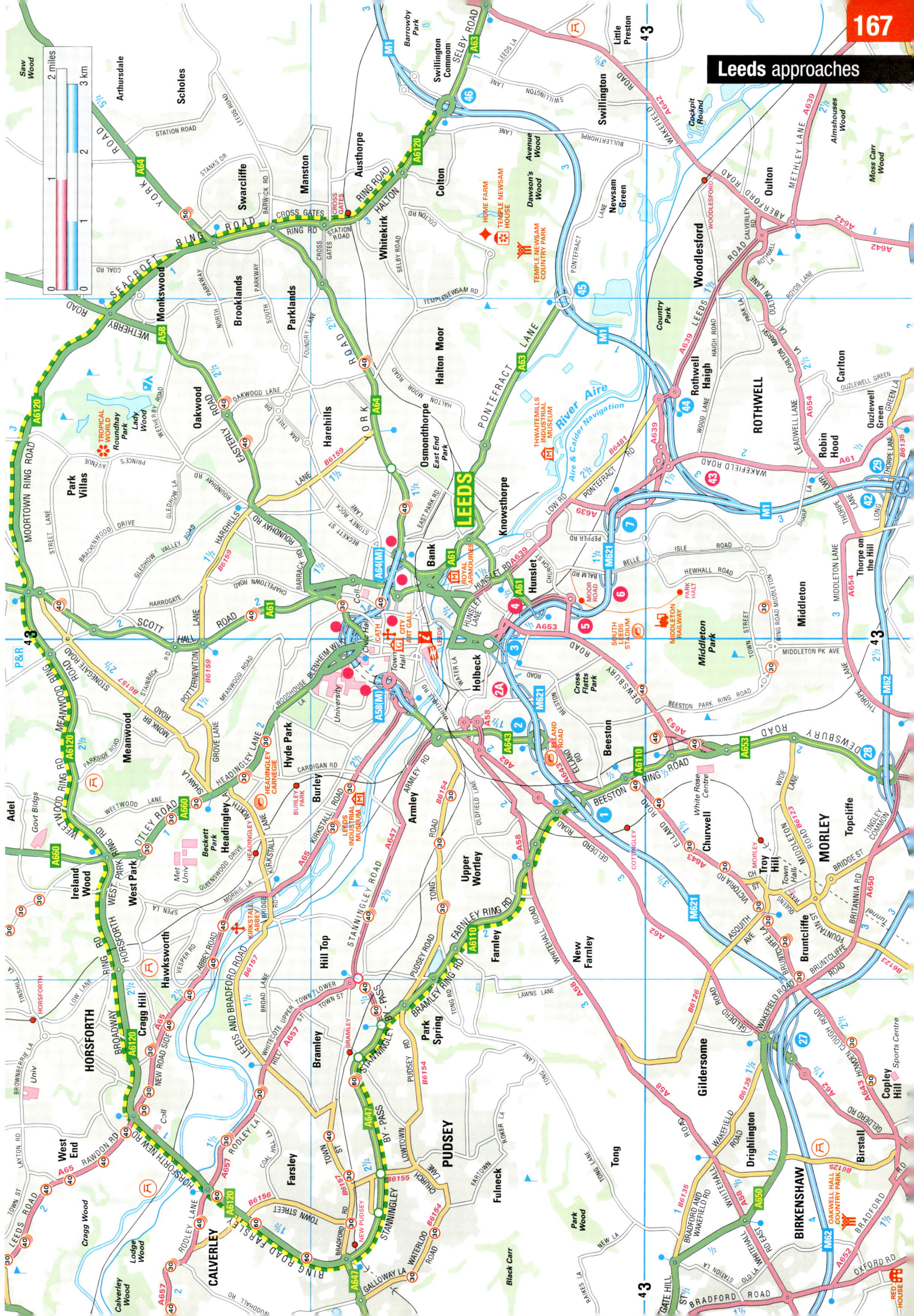

Places: Saw Wood, Arthursdale, Scholes, Station Road, Swarcliffe, Manston, Austhorpe, Colton, Monkswood, Brooklands, Parklands, Swillington Common, Little Preston, Swillington, Barrowby Park, Oulton, Moss Carr Wood, Almshouses Wood, Woodlesford, Carlton, Oakwood, Harehills, Osmondthorpe, Whitekirk, Halton, Halton Moor, Temple Newsam House, Home Farm, Avenue Wood, Dawson's Wood, Newsam Green, Woodlesford, Cockpit Round, Park Villas, Leeds, Knowsthorpe, Hunslet, Thwaitemills Industrial Museum, Rothwell Haigh, Robin Hood, Ouzlewell Green, ROTHWELL, Adel, Meanwood, Ireland Wood, West Park, West End, Hawksworth, Headingley, Hyde Park, Burley, Armley, Bank, Holbeck, Beeston, Churwell, Middleton, Thorpe on the Hill, Middleton Park, Cross Flatts Park, South Leeds Stadium, Middleton Railway, Troy Hill, White Rose Centre, MORLEY, Topcliffe, Gildersome, HORSFORTH, Cragg Hill, Calverley, Farsley, Bramley, Hill Top, Upper Wortley, New Farnley, Farnley, Park Spring, Stanningley, New Pudsey, PUDSEY, Fulneck, Tong, Park Wood, Black Carr, Bruntcliffe, Drighlington, Birstall, Copley Hill, BIRKENSHAW, Oakwell Hall Country Park, Red House

Roads: A64, A58, A6120, A63, A639, A642, A654, A61, A653, A62, A643, A65, A660, A657, A647, A6110, A650, M1, M621, M62, B6159, B6157, B6155, B6156, B6154, B6157, B6126, B6123, B6135, B6481

Points of interest: TROPICAL WORLD, Roundhay Park, Lady Wood, ROYAL ARMOURIES, LEEDS INDUSTRIAL MUSEUM, KIRKSTALL ABBEY, HEADINGLEY CARNEGIE, Beckett Park, Burley Park, TEMPLE NEWSAM COUNTRY PARK, AIRE & CALDER NAVIGATION, River Aire, MOOR ROAD, PARK HALT

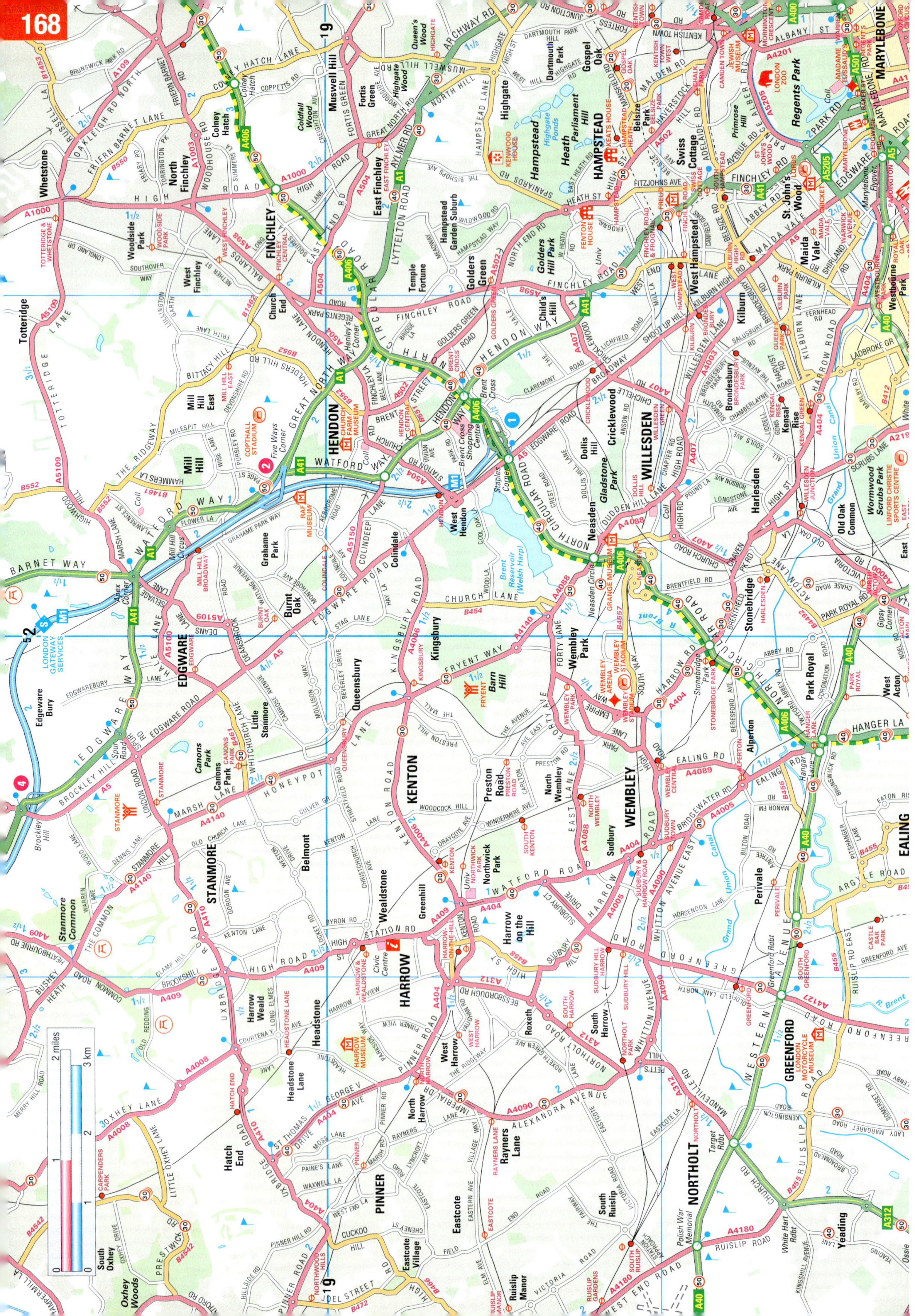
Whetstone
Totteridge
North Finchley
FINCHLEY
Muswell Hill
Highgate
Hampstead Heath
HAMPSTEAD
Swiss Cottage
Regents Park
MARYLEBONE
St. John's Wood
Maida Vale
Kilburn
West Hampstead
Golders Green
Hampstead Garden Suburb
East Finchley
Temple Fortune
Church End
HENDON
Mill Hill
Cricklewood
WILLESDEN
Harlesden
Neasden
Kingsbury
Queensbury
EDGWARE
Edgware Bury
STANMORE
Stanmore Common
Burnt Oak
Colindale
KENTON
WEMBLEY
Wembley Park
Sudbury
Alperton
Stonebridge
Park Royal
Perivale
EALING
GREENFORD
Northolt
NORTHOLT
HARROW
Harrow on the Hill
Harrow Weald
Headstone
Wealdstone
Belmont
South Harrow
West Harrow
North Harrow
Rayners Lane
PINNER
Hatch End
Eastcote
Eastcote Village
Ruislip Manor
South Ruislip
Yeading
Oxhey Woods
South Oxhey
Roxeth
Northwick Park
Preston Road
North Wembley
Barn Hill
Canons Park
Little Stanmore
Dollis Hill
Gladstone Park
Brondesbury
Kensal Rise
Queen's Park
Old Oak Common
Wormwood Scrubs Park
Westbourne Park
West Acton
Hanger La
Brent Reservoir (Welsh Harp)
Brent Cross Shopping Centre
LONDON GATEWAY SERVICES
WEMBLEY STADIUM
WEMBLEY ARENA
RAF MUSEUM
LONDON ZOO
MADAME TUSSAUD'S
KENWOOD HOUSE
KEATS HOUSE
FREUD MUSEUM
LORDS CRICKET GROUND
HARROW MUSEUM
CHURCH FARM MUSEUM
COPTHALL STADIUM
GRANGE MUSEUM
LONDON MOTORCYCLE MUSEUM
NORTH CIRCULAR ROAD
EDGWARE ROAD
WATFORD WAY
BARNET WAY
A1
A41
A406
A5
A40
A404
A409
A4140
A312
A4090
M1
0 1 2 miles
0 1 2 3 km

PADDINGTON
Bayswater
Hyde Park
Kensington Gardens
Knightsbridge
CHELSEA
Pimlico
BATTERSEA
Battersea Park
Clapham Common
Balham
Upper Tooting
Tooting
Collier's Wood
Holland Park
Notting Hill
Earl's Court
Parsons Green
FULHAM
Hurlingham Park
WANDSWORTH
Wandsworth Common
Earlsfield
Southfields
West Hill
Wimbledon Park
WIMBLEDON
MERTON
MORDEN
Morden Hall Park
HAMMERSMITH
Shepherd's Bush
River Thames
BARNES
PUTNEY
Putney Heath
Roehampton
Wimbledon Common
Crooked Billet
Raynes Park
Bushey Mead
Putney Vale
Kingston Vale
Coombe
NEW MALDEN
Acton
ACTON
Bedford Park
CHISWICK
Mortlake
East Sheen
North Sheen
Richmond Park
Gunnersbury Park
Kew
RICHMOND
Richmond Hill
Petersham
KINGSTON UPON THAMES
Norbiton
West Ealing
HANWELL
Northfields
BRENTFORD
Syon Park
Old Deer Park
St Margarets
Ham
TEDDINGTON
Hampton Wick
Hampton Court Park
Drayton Green
Osterley Park
Norwood Green
HESTON
HOUNSLOW
ISLEWORTH
Woodlands
Whitton
TWICKENHAM
Bushy Park
Hampton
Dormer's Wells
SOUTHALL
North Hyde
Hounslow West
Hounslow Heath
Hanworth Park
HANWORTH
FELTHAM
SUNBURY
Hayes Town
Cranford
River Crane
River Brent
Grand Union Canal
Roads in Richmond Park open in daylight hours only

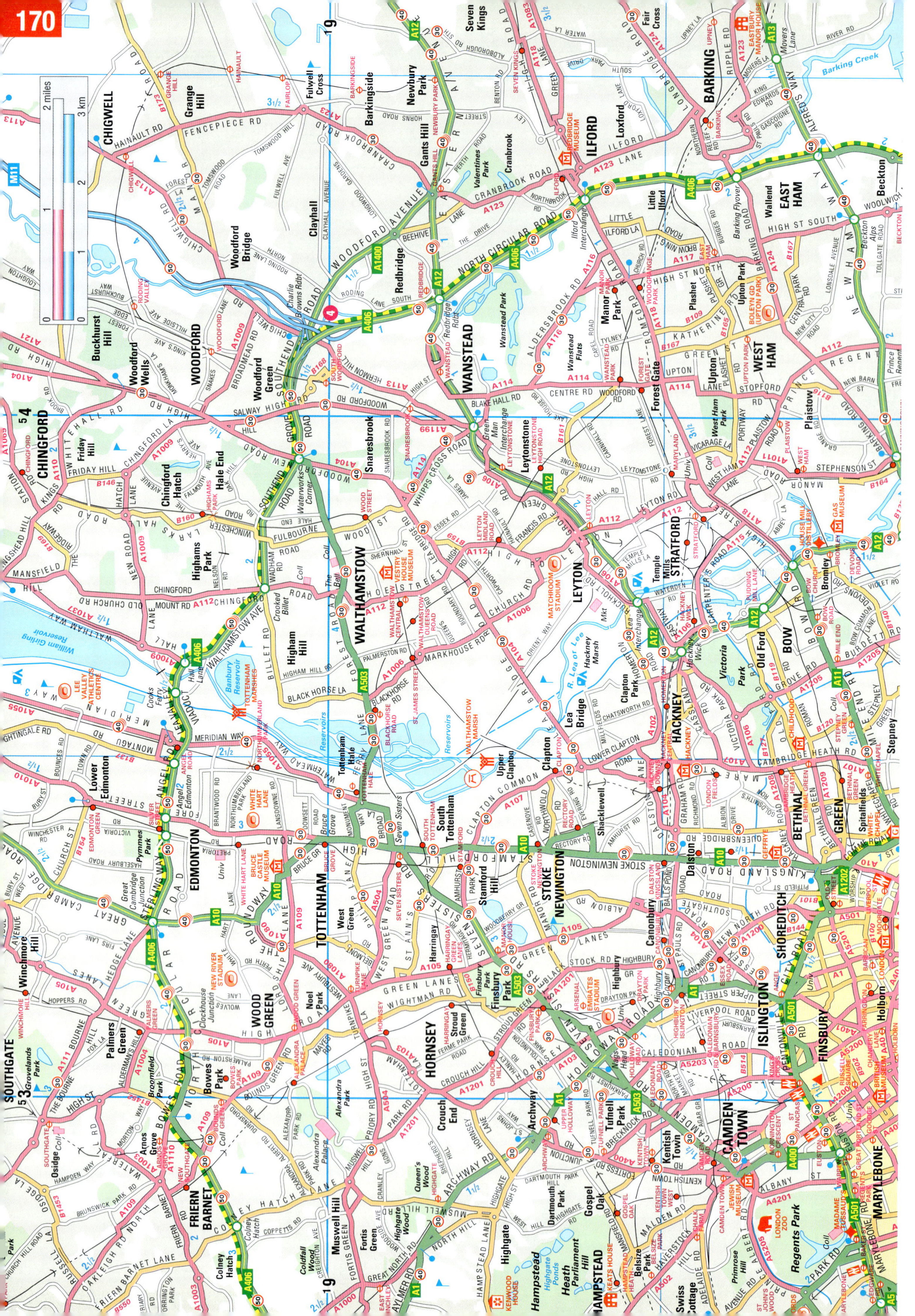

CHIGWELL
Grange Hill
Barkingside
Newbury Park
Seven Kings
ILFORD
BARKING
Gants Hill
Cranbrook
Valentines Park
Clayhall
Woodford Bridge
Redbridge
Buckhurst Hill
Woodford Wells
WOODFORD
Woodford Green
WANSTEAD
Wanstead Park
Manor Park
Little Ilford
Plashet
Upton Park
EAST HAM
Wallend
Beckton
WEST HAM
Upton
Forest Gate
Plaistow
CHINGFORD
Friday Hill
Chingford Hatch
Hale End
Highams Park
Snaresbrook
Leytonstone
STRATFORD
Temple Mills
LEYTON
WALTHAMSTOW
Higham Hill
Crooked Billet
BOW
Old Ford
Bromley
Victoria Park
HACKNEY
Hackney Wick
Clapton Park
Lea Bridge
Clapton
Upper Clapton
Shacklewell
Stepney
BETHNAL GREEN
Spitalfields
Dalston
SHOREDITCH
STOKE NEWINGTON
Stamford Hill
South Tottenham
Seven Sisters
TOTTENHAM
West Green
Lower Edmonton
EDMONTON
Pymmes Park
Canonbury
Highbury
ISLINGTON
FINSBURY
Holborn
HORNSEY
Harringay
Finsbury Park
Stroud Green
Crouch End
Archway
Tufnell Park
Kentish Town
CAMDEN TOWN
MARYLEBONE
Regents Park
Primrose Hill
Belsize Park
HAMPSTEAD
Gospel Oak
Dartmouth Park
Highgate
Muswell Hill
Fortis Green
Alexandra Palace
WOOD GREEN
Noel Park
Bowes Park
FRIERN BARNET
Colney Hatch
Arnos Grove
Palmers Green
Winchmore Hill
SOUTHGATE
Osidge
Swiss Cottage

River Thames

North Woolwich · Silvertown · Custom House · Canning Town · Plumstead · Shooters Hill · Oxleas Wood · Falconwood · New Eltham · Longlands · CHISLEHURST · Sidcup · Bickley · BROMLEY

WOOLWICH · Woolwich Ferry · Charlton · Kidbrooke · ELTHAM · Eltham Common · Mottingham · Grove Park · Sundridge Park · Widmore · Shortlands

Blackwall · POPLAR · ISLE OF DOGS · Millwall · Canary Wharf · GREENWICH · North Greenwich · BLACKHEATH · Lee · Hither Green · LEWISHAM · CATFORD · Downham · Beckenham Place Park · BECKENHAM · Eden Park · Wickham · Hayes

Limehouse · Wapping · Rotherhithe · DEPTFORD · New Cross · Brockley · Ladywell · Bellingham · PENGE · Elmers End

Aldgate · BERMONDSEY · Nunhead · Peckham · Honor Oak · Forest Hill · SYDENHAM · CRYSTAL PALACE · Anerley · South Norwood

LAMBETH · Kennington · CAMBERWELL · East Dulwich · Dulwich · West Dulwich · West Norwood · STREATHAM · Streatham Common · Norbury

Mayfair · Pimlico · CHELSEA · BATTERSEA · CLAPHAM · BRIXTON · Stockwell · Tulse Hill · Balham · Tooting · Tooting Bec · MITCHAM · Collier's Wood · Upper Tooting · Hyde Park

CROSBY

Great Crosby

Melling

AINTREE

Kirkby Park

Westvale

KIRKBY

LITHERLAND

Waterloo

Aintree Race Course

Fazakerley

Croxteth

Seaforth

BOOTLE

Ferries to Belfast, Douglas & Dublin

Walton

West Derby

Croxteth Country Park

Stockbridge Village

NEW BRIGHTON

New Brighton

NEW PALACE

WALLASEY

Kirkdale

Stanley Park

Anfield

Goodison Park

Newsham Park

Broad Green

Prescot

Liscard

Poulton

Univ

Univ

Wavertree Technology Park

MARITIME MUSEUM

Wavertree Park

Edge Hill

Wavertree

Childwall

BIRKENHEAD NORTH

BIRKENHEAD

Birkenhead Park

TATE GALLERY

Town Hall

Edge Hill

Picton Road

LIVERPOOL

Toxteth

Oxton

Tranmere

Green Lane

Rock Ferry

Brunswick

Sefton Park

Dingle

AIGBURTH

Aigburth

West Allerton

Allerton

Otterspool

BEBINGTON

Port Sunlight

Spital

LADY LEVER ART GALLERY

Brimstage

Bromborough

GARSTON

SPEKE HALL

LIVERPOOL JOHN LENNON AIRPORT

Eastham Ferry

EASTHAM COUNTRY PARK

0   1   2 miles

0   1   2   3 km

River Mersey

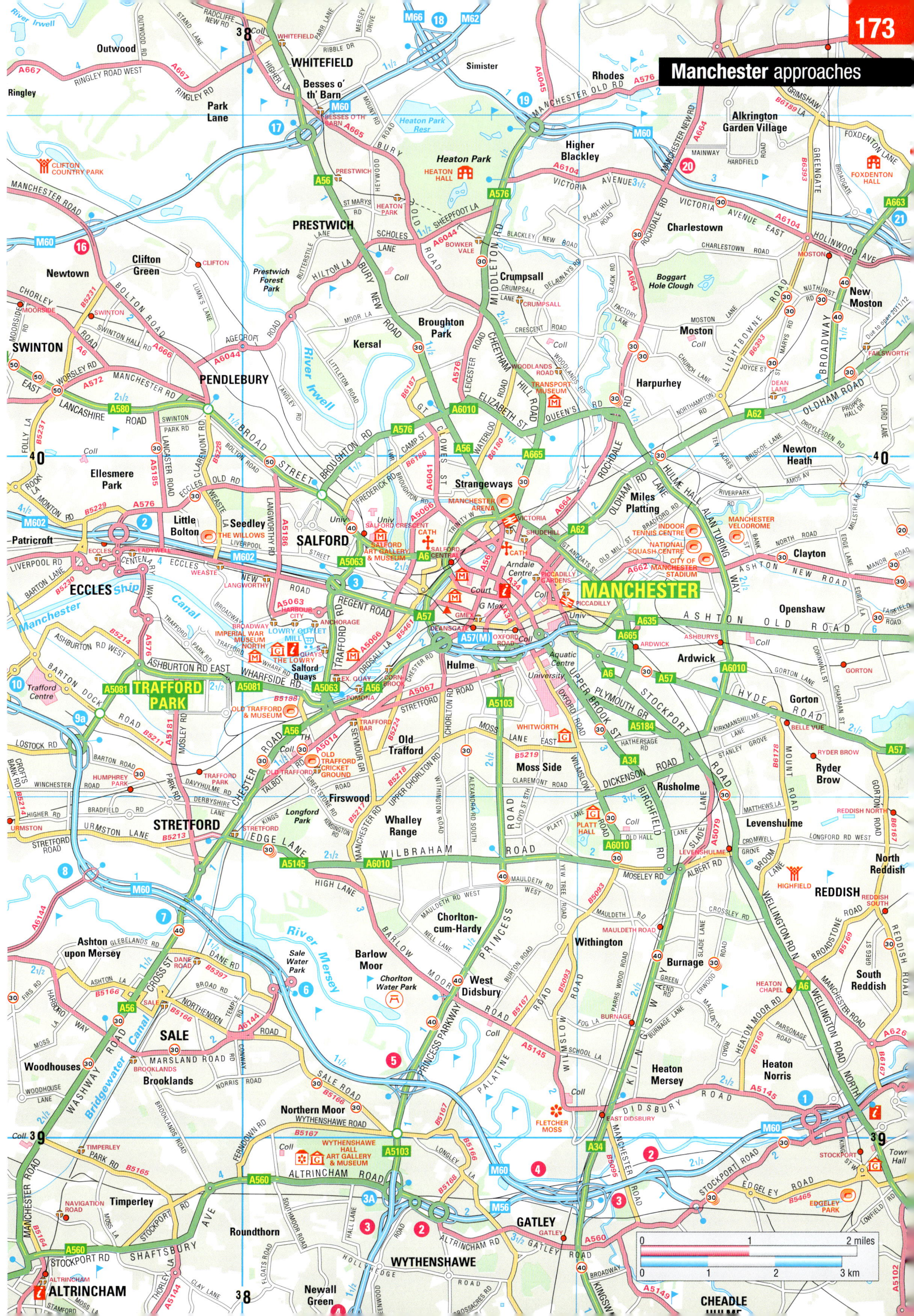
MANCHESTER
SALFORD
TRAFFORD PARK
WHITEFIELD
PRESTWICH
SWINTON
PENDLEBURY
ECCLES
STRETFORD
SALE
ALTRINCHAM
WYTHENSHAWE
GATLEY
CHEADLE
REDDISH
Outwood
Ringley
Besses o' th' Barn
Simister
Rhodes
Alkrington Garden Village
Higher Blackley
Park Lane
Heaton Park
Heaton Park Resr
Newtown
Clifton Green
Prestwich Forest Park
Kersal
Broughton Park
Crumpsall
Charlestown
Boggart Hole Clough
New Moston
Moston
Harpurhey
Ellesmere Park
Little Bolton
Seedley
Patricroft
Strangeways
Miles Platting
Newton Heath
Clayton
Openshaw
Ardwick
Hulme
Old Trafford
Moss Side
Gorton
Rusholme
Ryder Brow
Levenshulme
North Reddish
Firswood
Longford Park
Whalley Range
Chorlton-cum-Hardy
Withington
Burnage
South Reddish
Ashton upon Mersey
Barlow Moor
West Didsbury
Sale Water Park
Chorlton Water Park
Heaton Mersey
Heaton Norris
Woodhouses
Brooklands
Northern Moor
Timperley
Roundthorn
Newall Green
Trafford Centre
Salford Quays
River Irwell
River Mersey
Manchester Ship Canal
Bridgewater Canal
Fletcher Moss
Aquatic Centre
University
Arndale Centre
M60
M602
M62
M66
M56
A57(M)
A56
A6
A34
A62
A635
A665
A6010
A5103
A560
A5145
A576
A580
A664
A663
A6104
1 2 miles
1 2 3 km

Newcastle approaches

NEWCASTLE UPON TYNE

GATESHEAD

WASHINGTON

Brunswick Village, Wide Open, Hazlerigg, Newcastle International Airport, Woolsington, Kingston Park, Fawdon, Gosforth, Blakelaw, Fenham, Benwell, Scotswood, Elswick, Dunston, Metro Centre, Metroland, Sunniside, Kibblesworth, Camperdown, Killingworth, Killingworth Centre, Backworth, Shiremoor, Boundary Mill Newcastle, Northumberland Park, Longbenton, Benton, Four Lane Ends, West Jesmond, Jesmond, Heaton, Byker, Walker, Wallsend, Segedunum Roman Fort, Willington, Howdon, Tyne Tunnel, Jarrow, Hebburn, Fellgate, Wardley, Felling, Heworth, Pelaw, Bensham, Lobley Hill, Whickham, Wrekenton, Lyndhurst, Chowdene, Angel of the North, Birtley, Ouston, Urpeth, Beamish Open Air Museum, Causey Arch, Tanfield Railway, Andrews House, Springwell, Bowes Railway, Usworth, Washington, Washington Old Hall, Biddick, Lampton, Fatfield, Washington Birtley Services

Military Vehicle Museum, Civic Centre, Haymarket, Monument, Manors, Central, Discovery, Baltic Centre, The Sage, Gateshead International Stadium, Shipley Art Gallery, Stephenson Railway Museum, Rising Sun Country Park, Gosforth Wood, Gosforth Lake

River Tyne

A1, A19, A167, A184, A186, A187, A188, A189, A191, A193, A194, A195, A696, A692, A695, A1056, A1058, A1114, A1231, A1290, A6127, A6076

0 1 2 miles
0 1 2 3 km

Aberystwyth

A487 MACHYNLLETH • A44 RHAYADER

Bangor

A5 BETWS-Y-COED, A55 CONWY

Aberdeen

A96 INVERNESS • A956 PETERHEAD (A90) • A944 ALFORD • A93 BRAEMAR • A956 DUNDEE (A90)

Ayr

A719 KILMARNOCK (A77) • A70 CUMNOCK • A79 KILMARNOCK (A77) • A713 DALMELLINGTON • A719 TURNBERRY • A79, A77

Ashford

A292 FOLKESTONE (M20) • A28 CANTERBURY • A20 CHARING • A2042 RYE (A2070, A259)

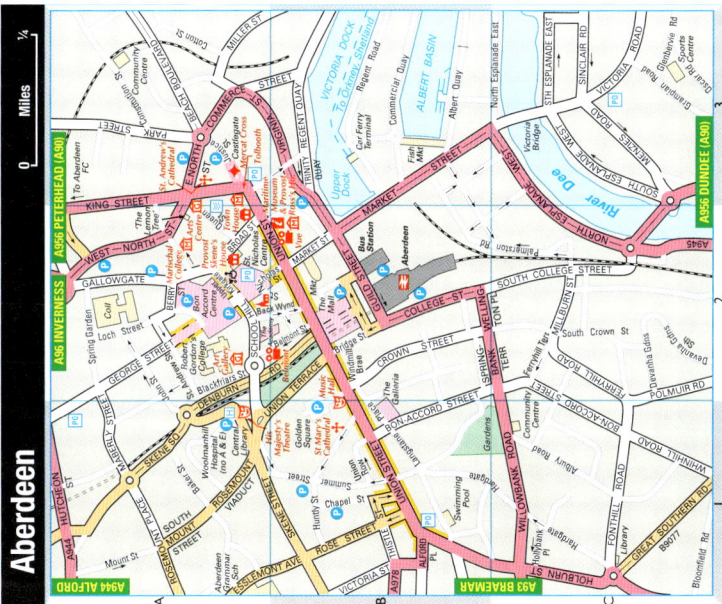

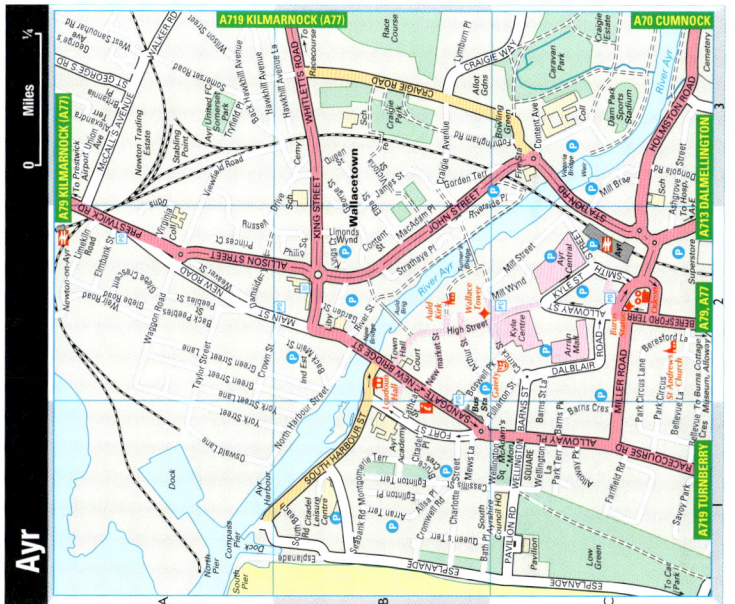

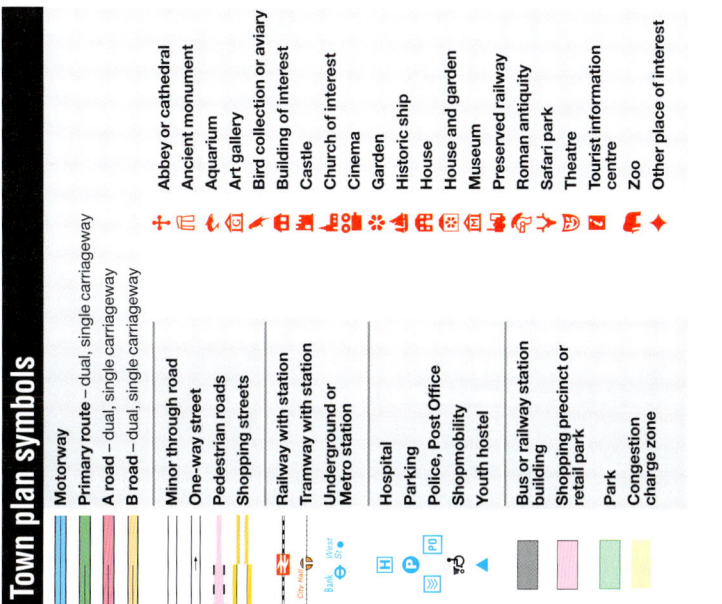

Town plan symbols

- Motorway
- Primary route – dual, single carriageway
- A road – dual, single carriageway
- B road – dual, single carriageway
- Minor through road
- One-way street
- Pedestrian roads
- Shopping streets
- Railway with station
- Tramway with station
- Underground or Metro station
- Hospital
- Parking
- Police, Post Office
- Shopmobility
- Youth hostel
- Bus or railway station building
- Shopping precinct or retail park
- Park
- Congestion charge zone

- Abbey or cathedral
- Ancient monument
- Aquarium
- Art gallery
- Bird collection or aviary
- Building of interest
- Castle
- Church of interest
- Cinema
- Garden
- Historic ship
- House
- House and garden
- Museum
- Preserved railway
- Roman antiquity
- Safari park
- Theatre
- Tourist information centre
- Zoo
- Other place of interest

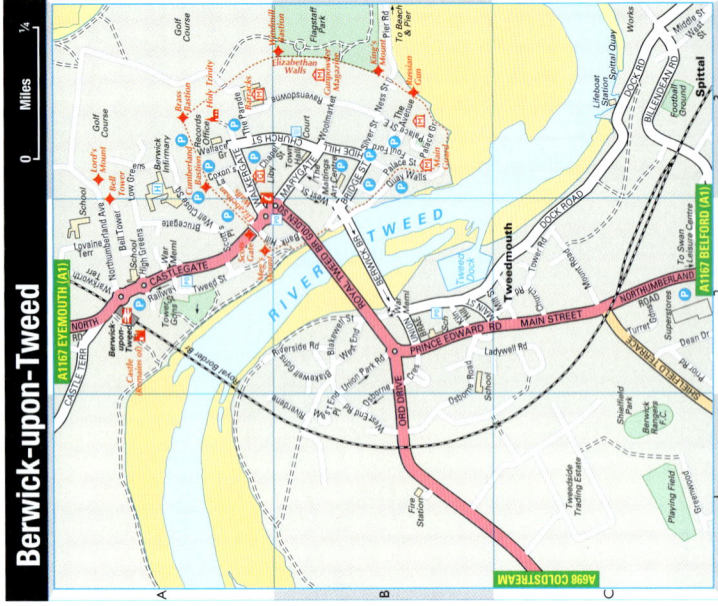

Berwick-upon-Tweed

Blackpool

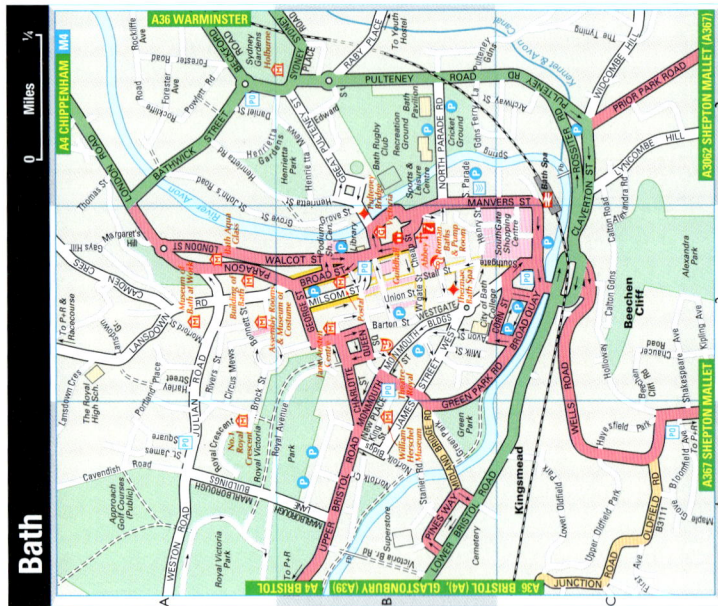

Bath

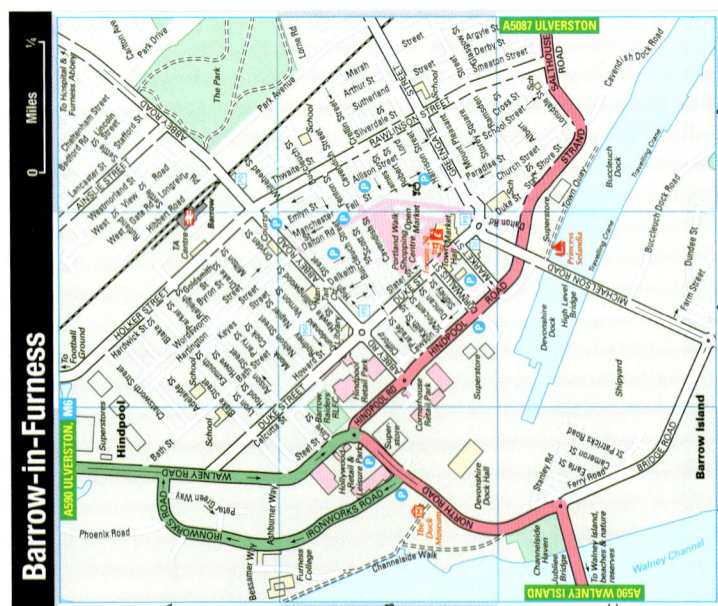

Barrow-in-Furness

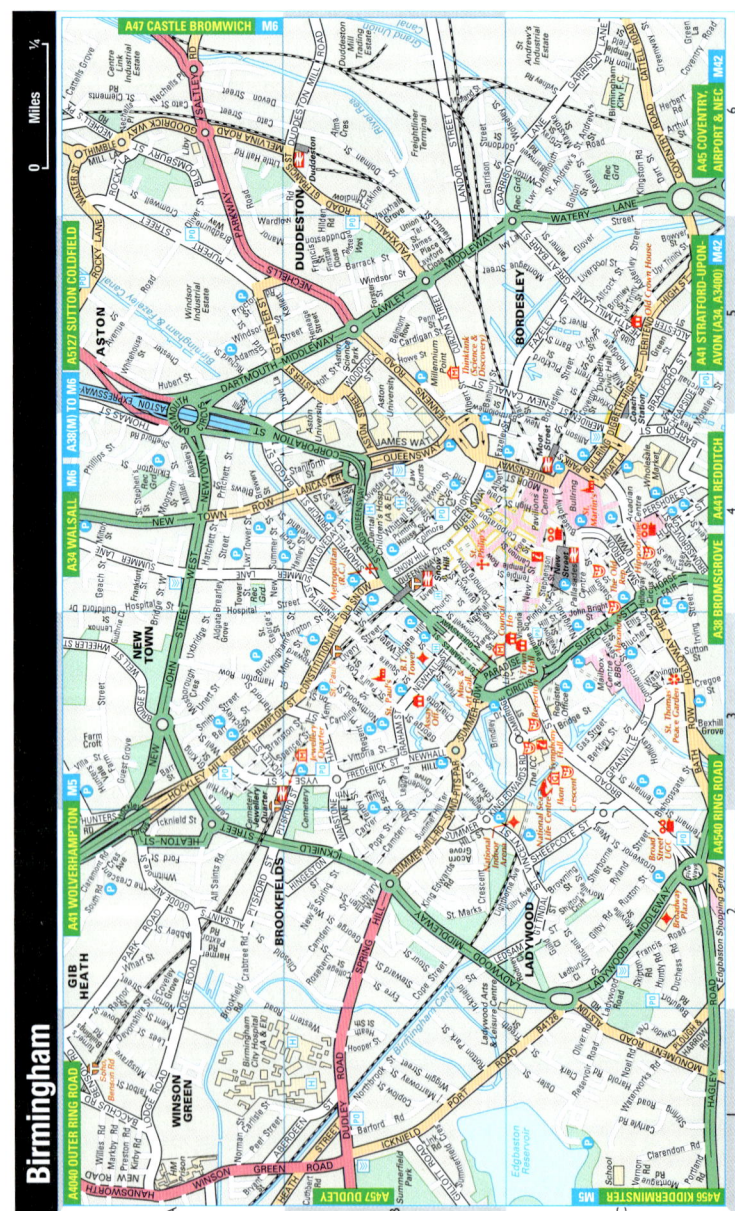

Birmingham

Brighton

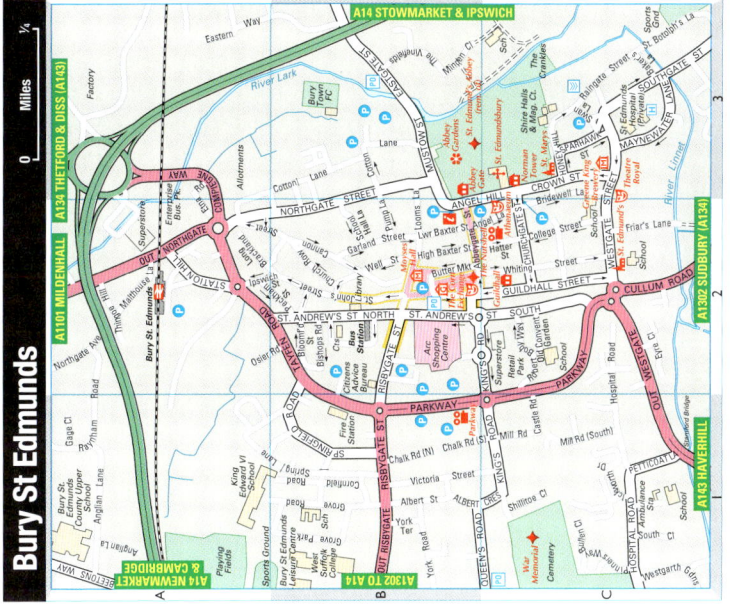

Bury St Edmunds

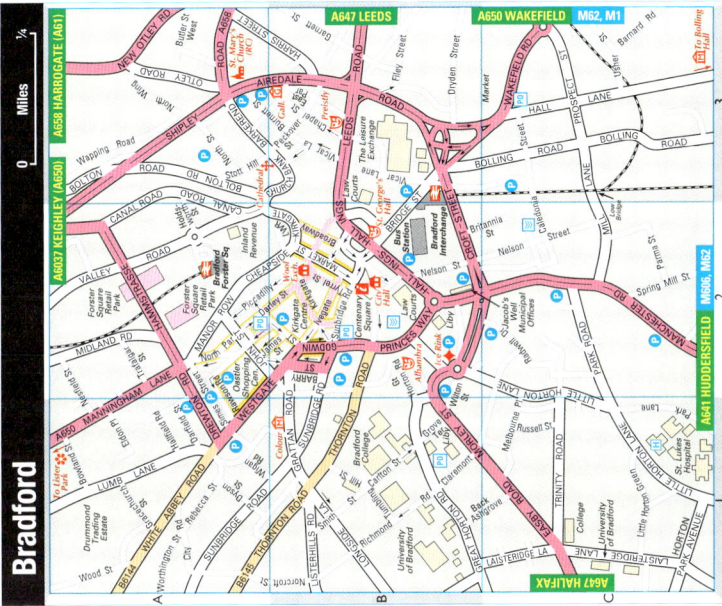

Bradford

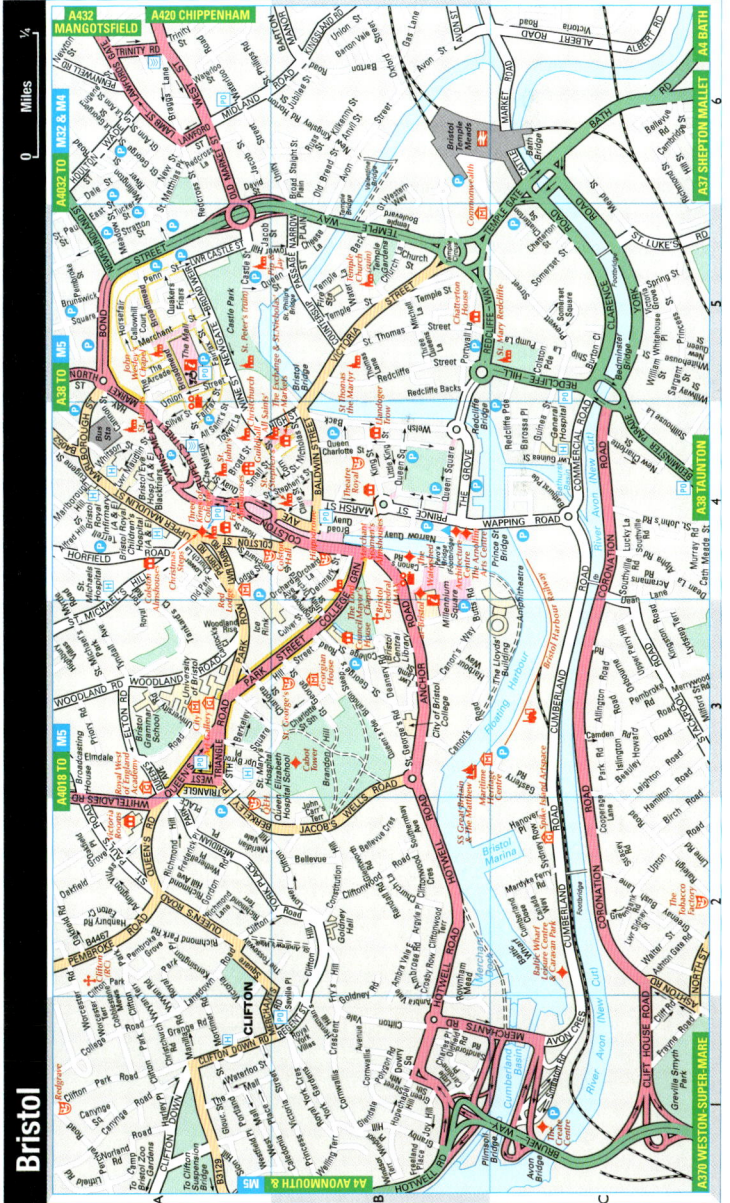

Bristol

Bournemouth

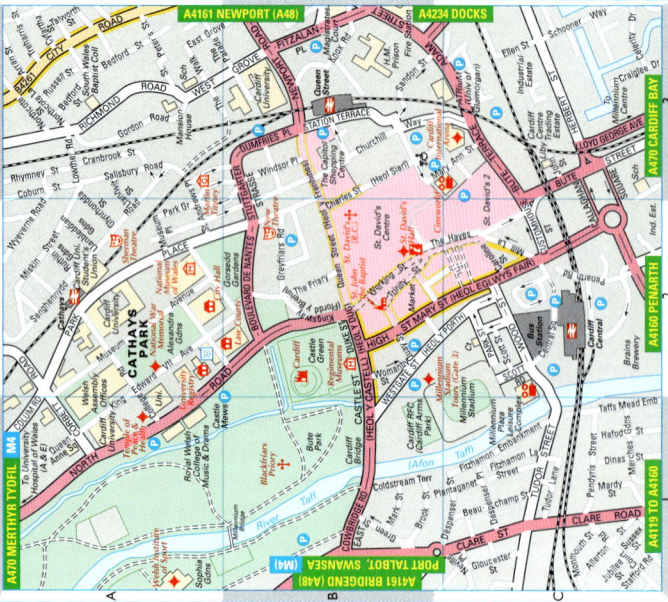

Cardiff / Caerdydd

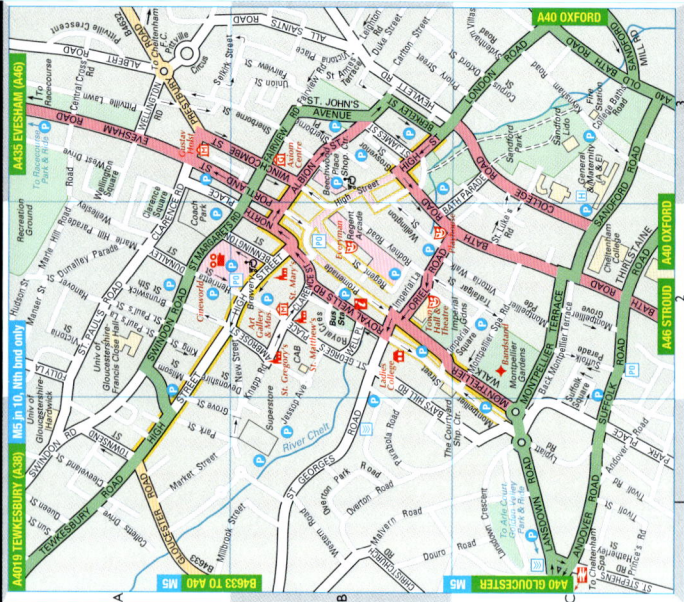

Cheltenham

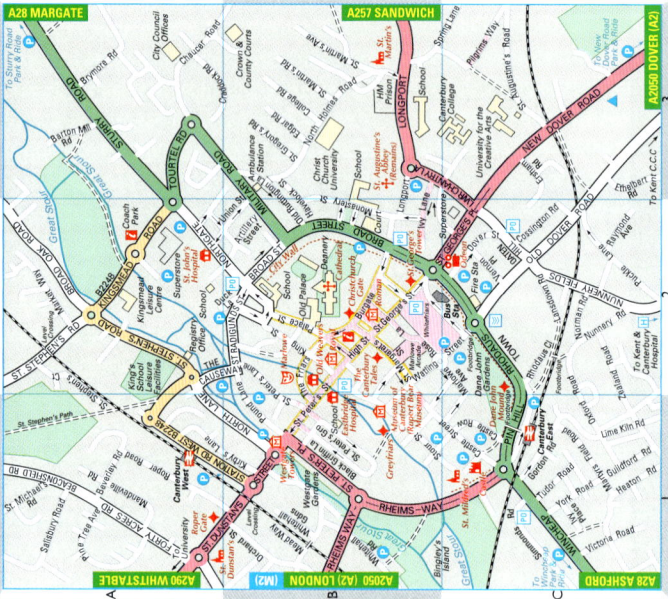

Canterbury

Chelmsford

Cambridge

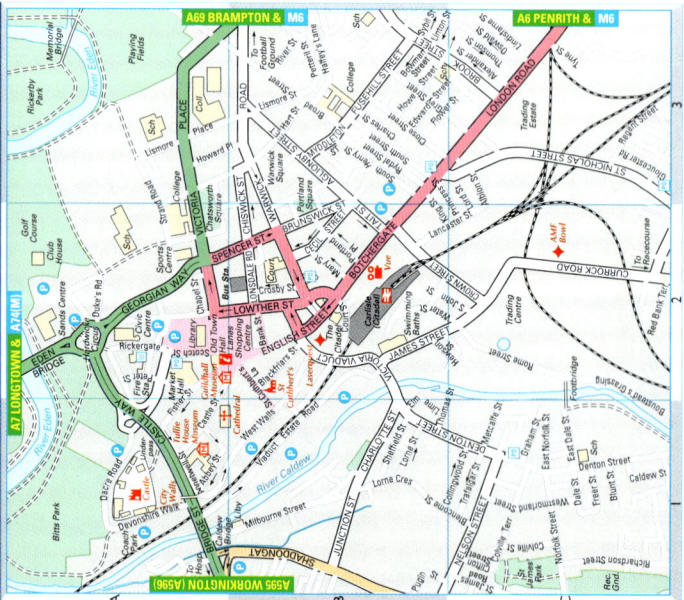

Carlisle

Chester page 73 • **Chichester** page 16 • **Colchester** page 43 • **Coventry** page 51 • **Derby** page 76 • **Dorchester** page 12

179

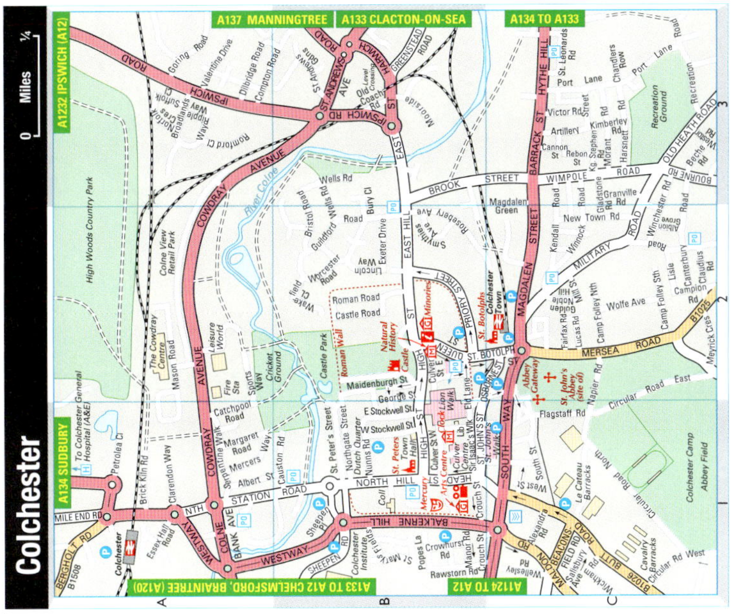

Colchester

Dorchester

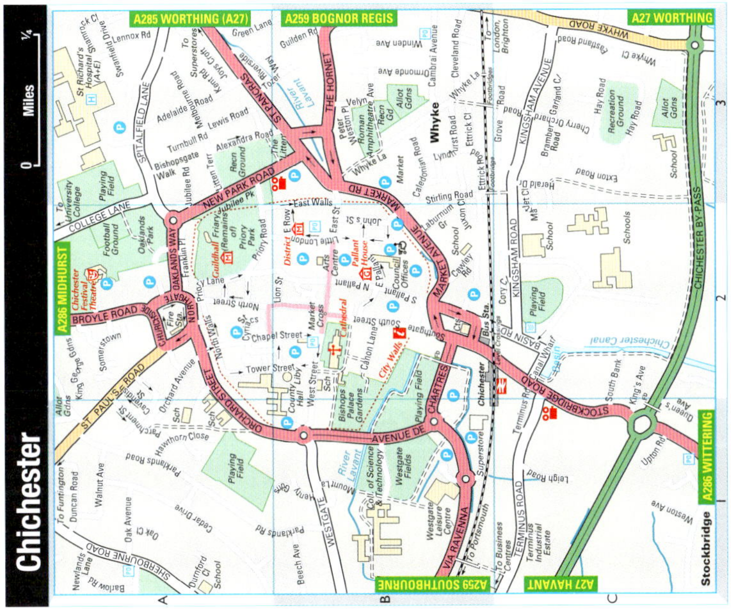

Chichester

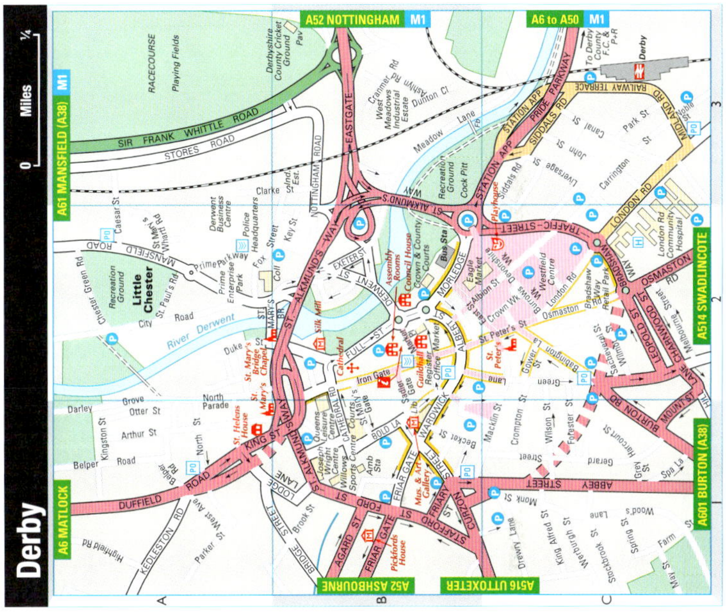

Derby

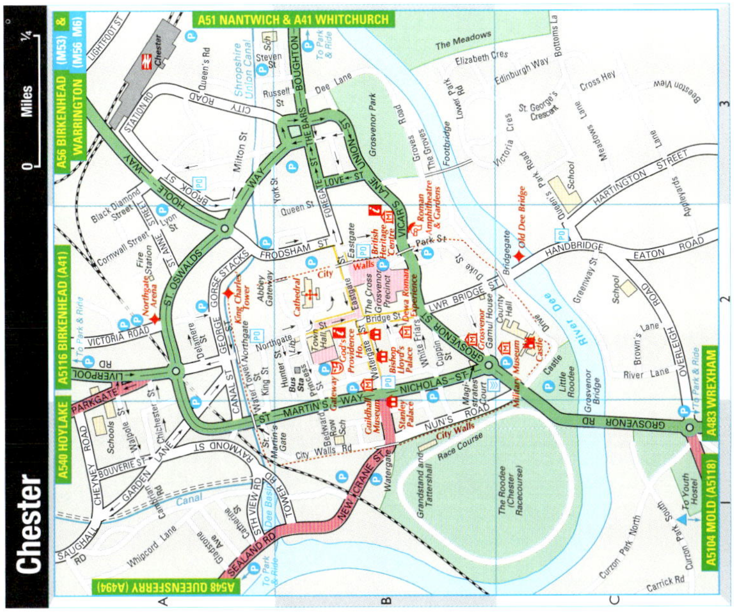

Chester

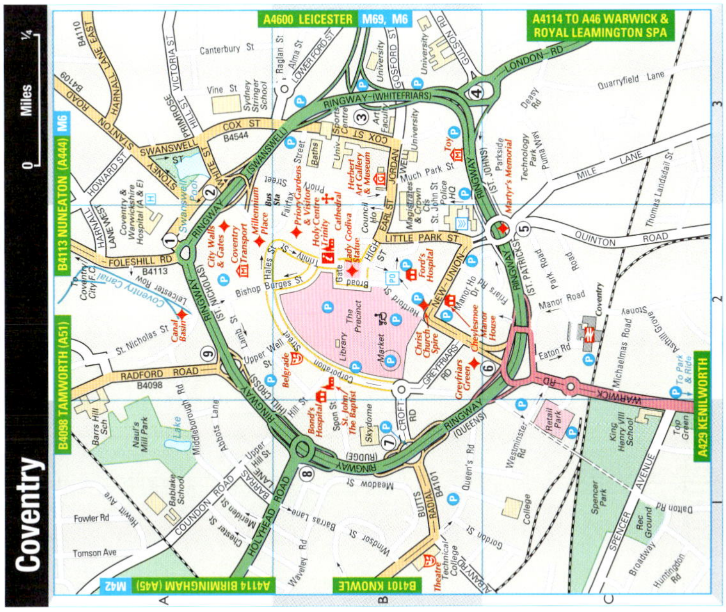

Coventry

Durham
A690 SUNDERLAND A1 (M)
A177 STOCKTON A1 (M)
A691 CONSETT
A167 DARLINGTON A1 (M)
A177 TO A167
A690 WILLINGTON
A167 NEWCASTLE A1 (M)
Miles

Exeter
B3212
B3183 HONITON (A30), TAUNTON (M5)
A3015 EXMOUTH (A376)
B3183 TIVERTON (A396)
A377 BARNSTAPLE
B3212 OKEHAMPTON (A30)
A377 PLYMOUTH (A38)
Miles

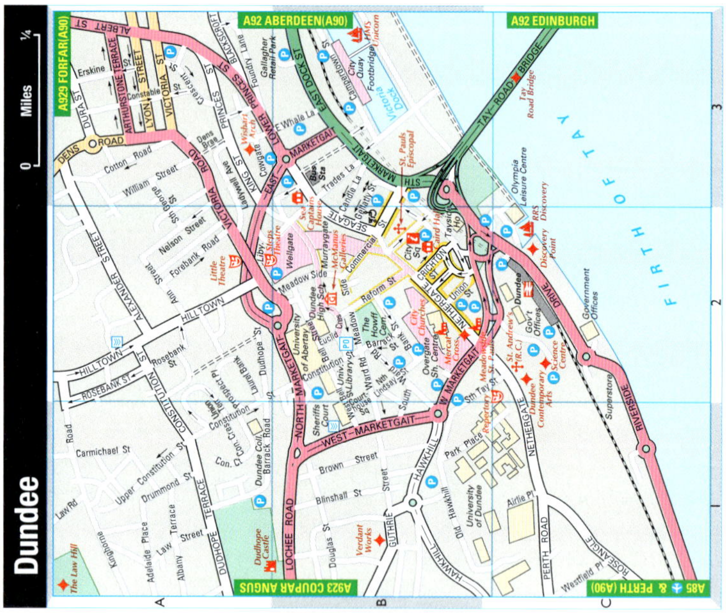
Dundee
A92 ABERDEEN(A90)
A92 EDINBURGH
A929 FORFAR(A90)
A923 COUPAR ANGUS
A85 & PERTH (A90)
FIRTH OF TAY
Miles

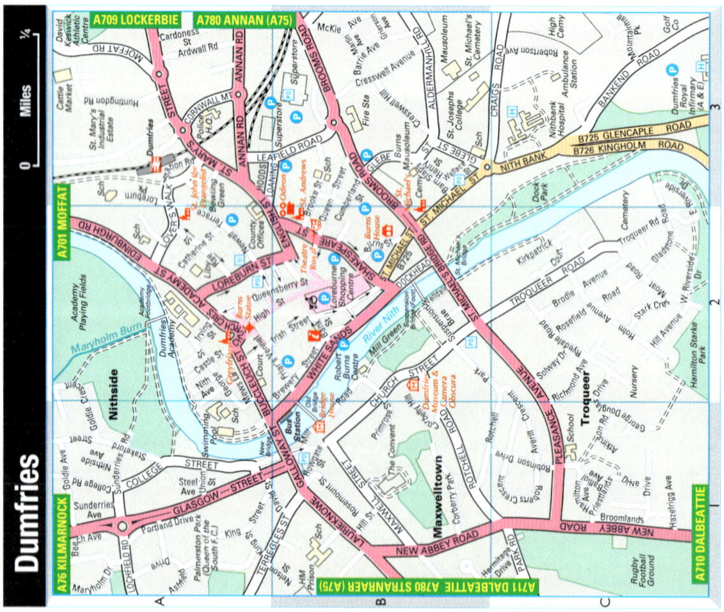
Dumfries
A709 LOCKERBIE
A780 ANNAN (A75)
A701 MOFFAT
A76 KILMARNOCK
A711 DALBEATTIE A780 STRANRAER (A75)
A710 DALBEATTIE
Miles

Edinburgh
A1 BERWICK-UPON-TWEED
A900 LEITH
A7 GALASHIELS & JEDBURGH (A68)
A90 FORTH ROAD BRIDGE & PERTH (M90)
A8 GLASGOW (M8) & STIRLING (M9)
A71 KILMARNOCK
A702 CARLISLE & M74
TO A7
Miles

Glasgow

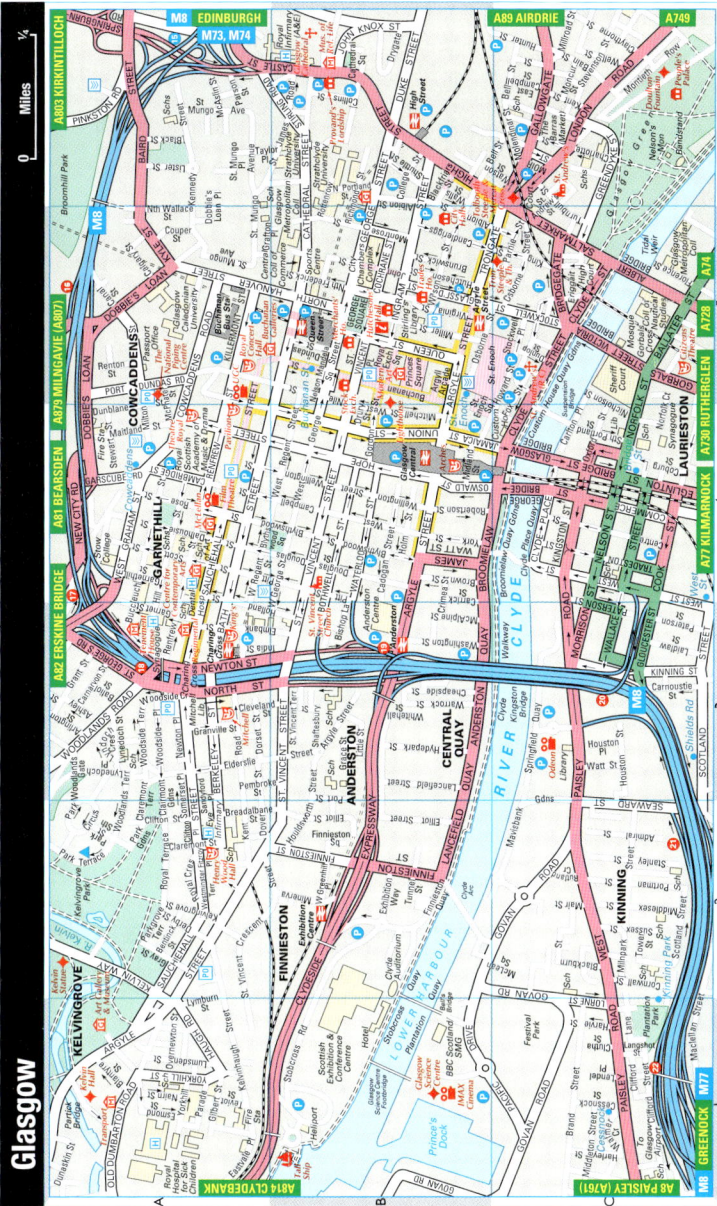

Hanley (Stoke-on-Trent)

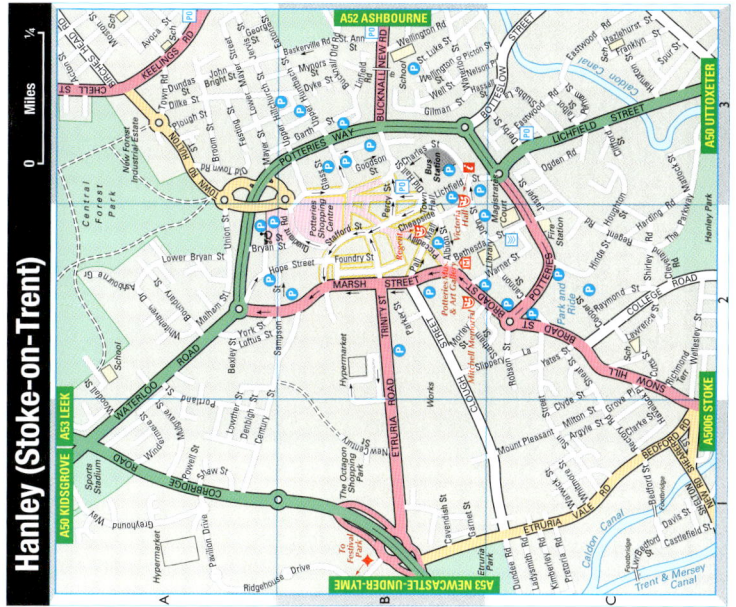

Grimsby

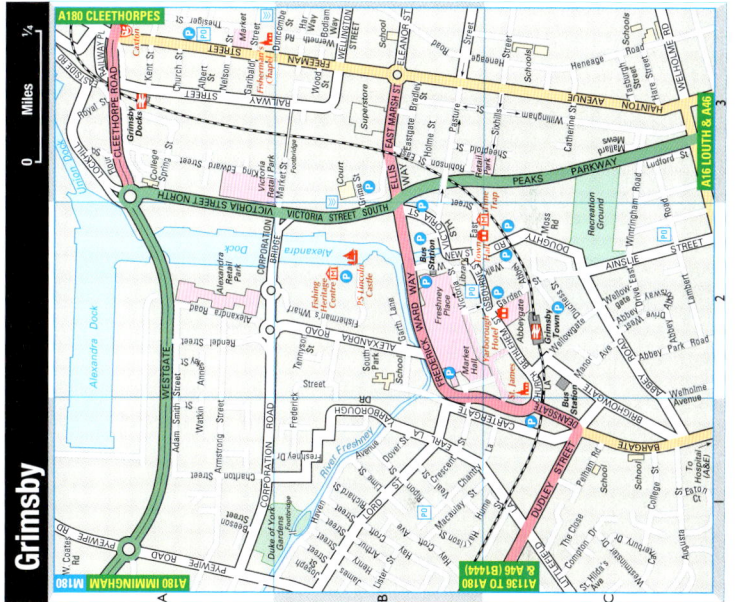

Fort William

Gloucester

Hull

Kendal

Holyhead / Caergybi

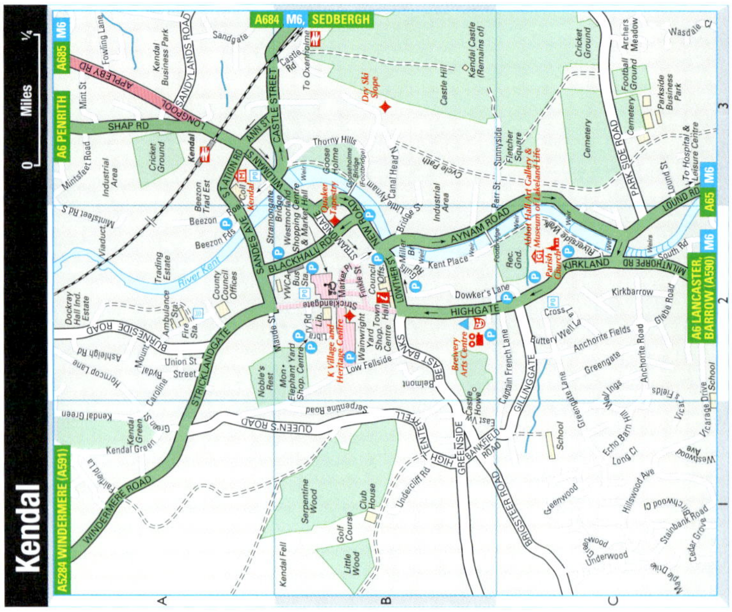

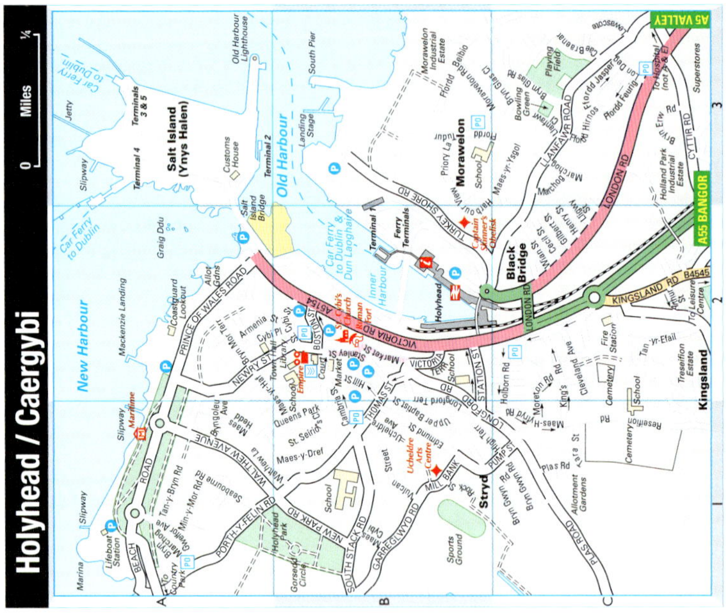

Ipswich

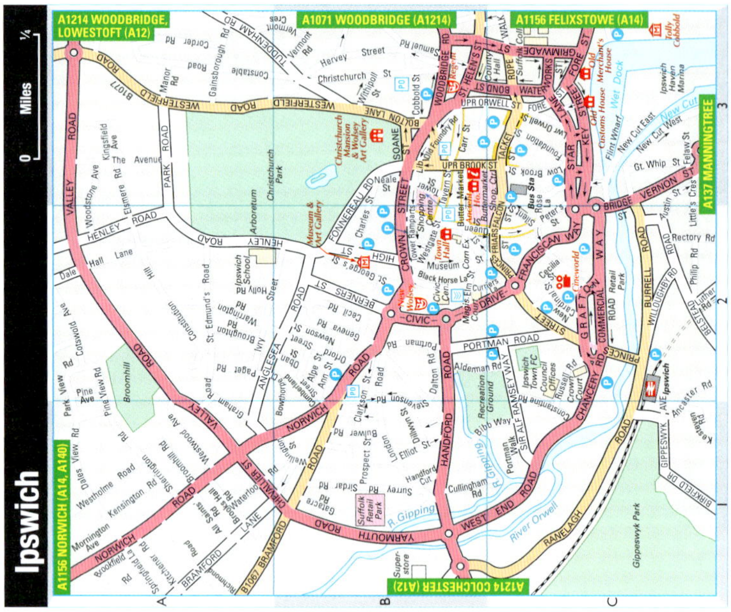

Harrogate

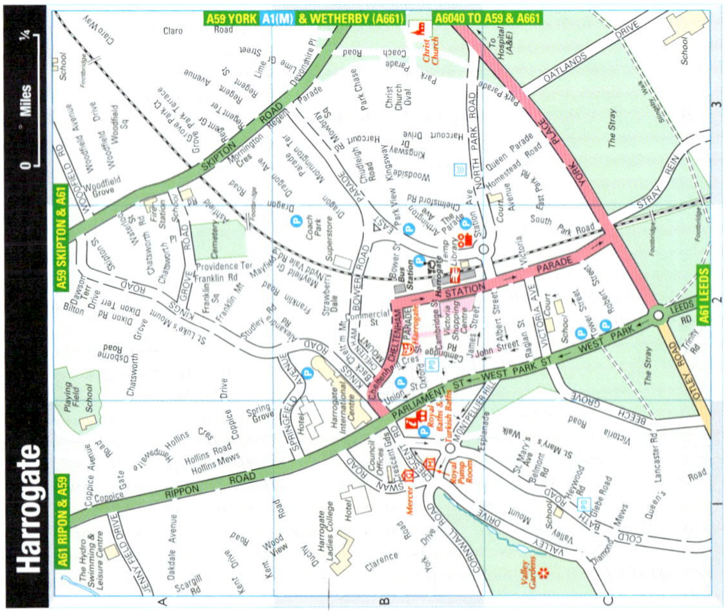

Inverness

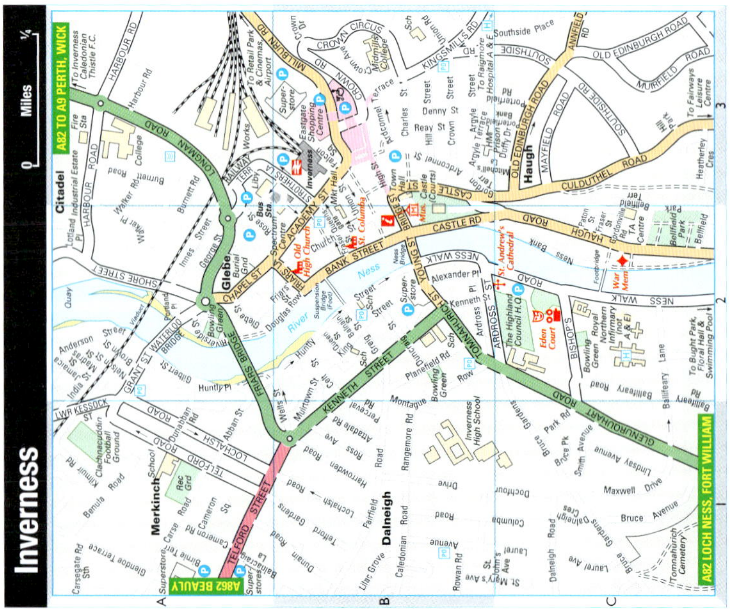

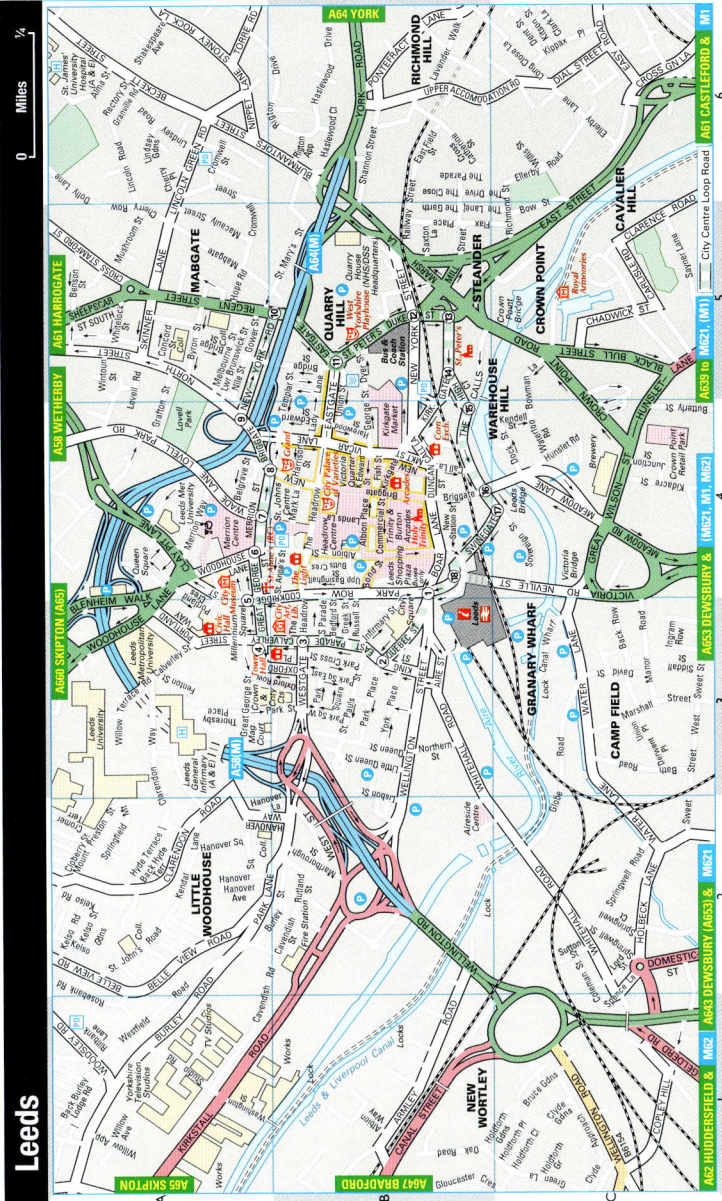

Leeds

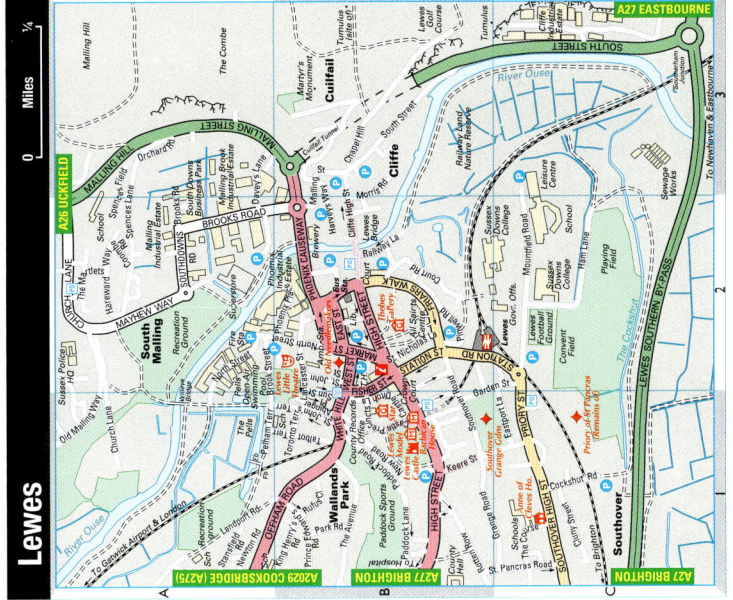

Lewes

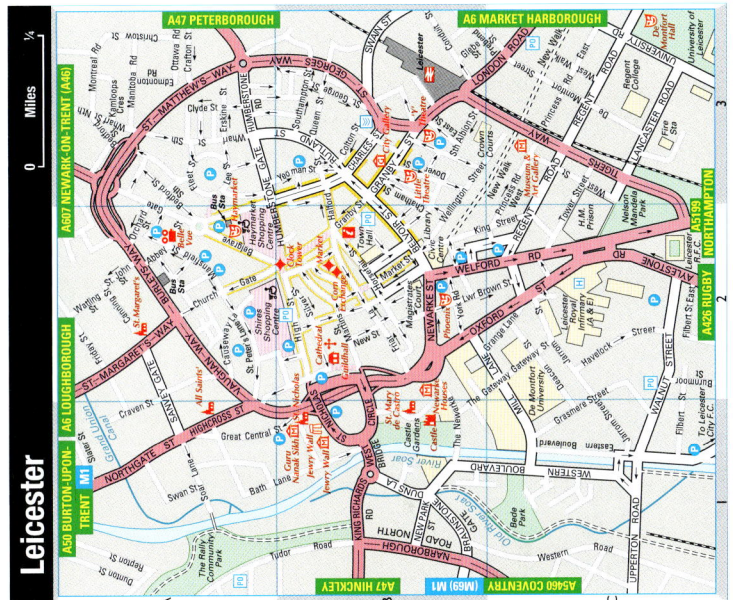

Leicester

King's Lynn

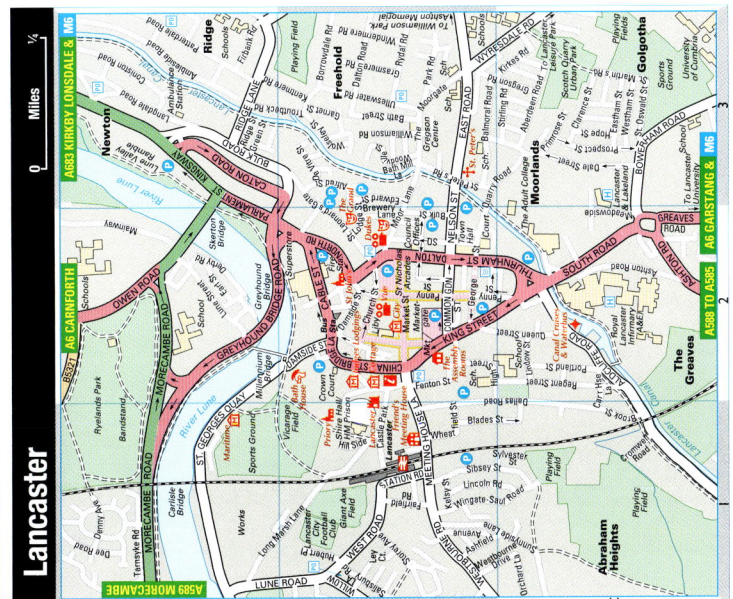

Lancaster

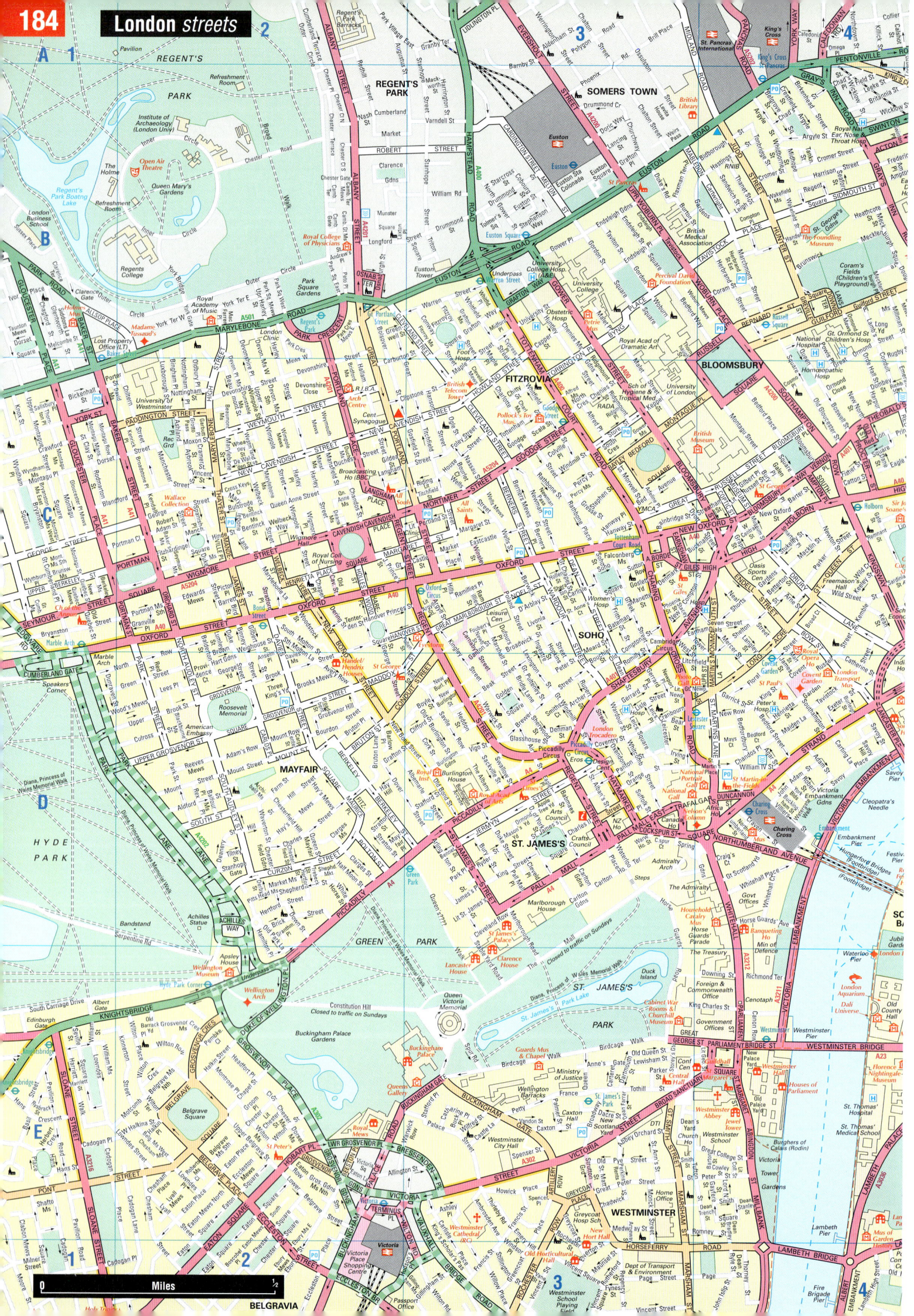

A 1   2   3   4

REGENT'S PARK

SOMERS TOWN

King's Cross

REGENT'S PARK

B

FITZROVIA

BLOOMSBURY

C

SOHO

MAYFAIR

D

HYDE PARK

ST. JAMES'S

GREEN PARK

E

ST. JAMES'S PARK

WESTMINSTER

Buckingham Palace

BELGRAVIA

0   Miles   ½

1   2   3   4

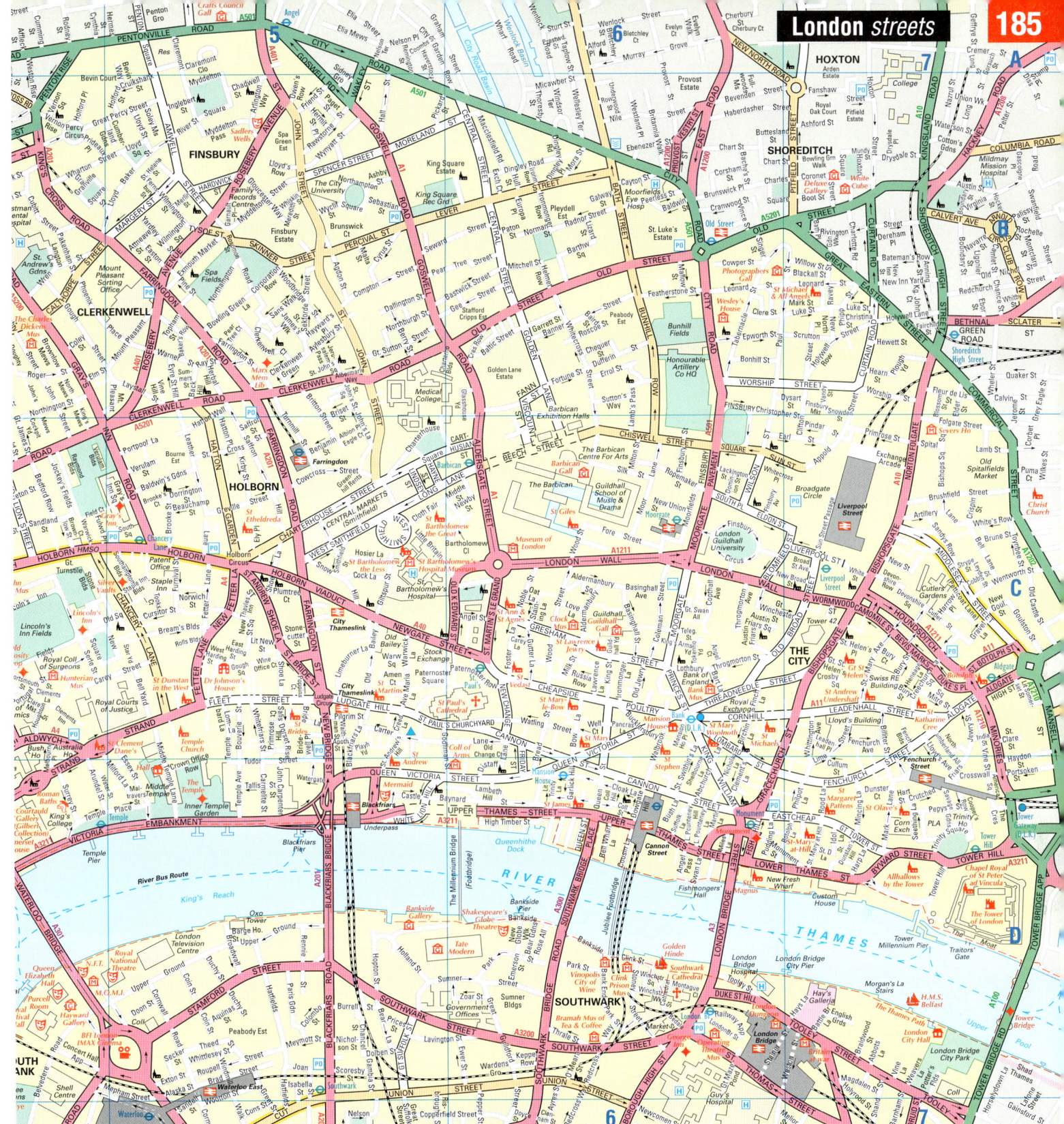

London Docklands

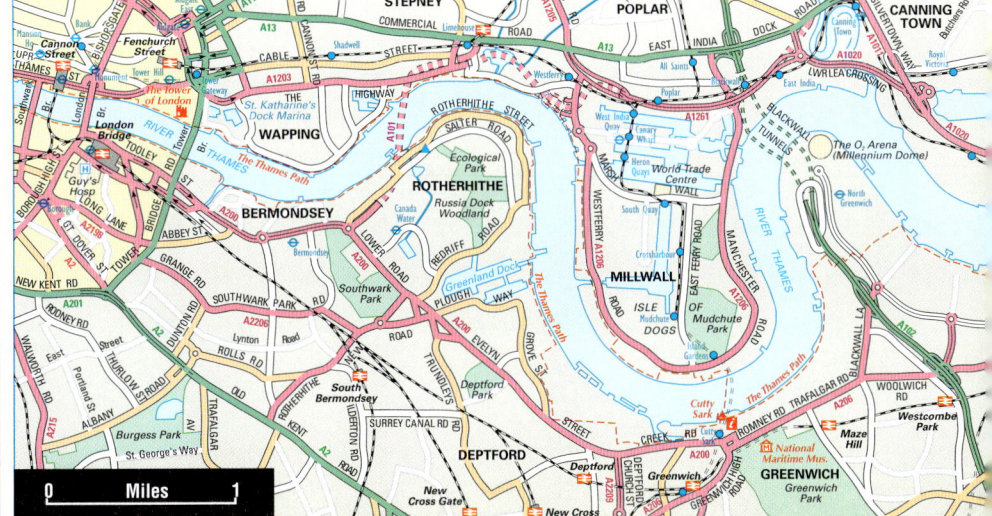

Congestion Charging Zone

Uncharged Roads

0   Miles   1

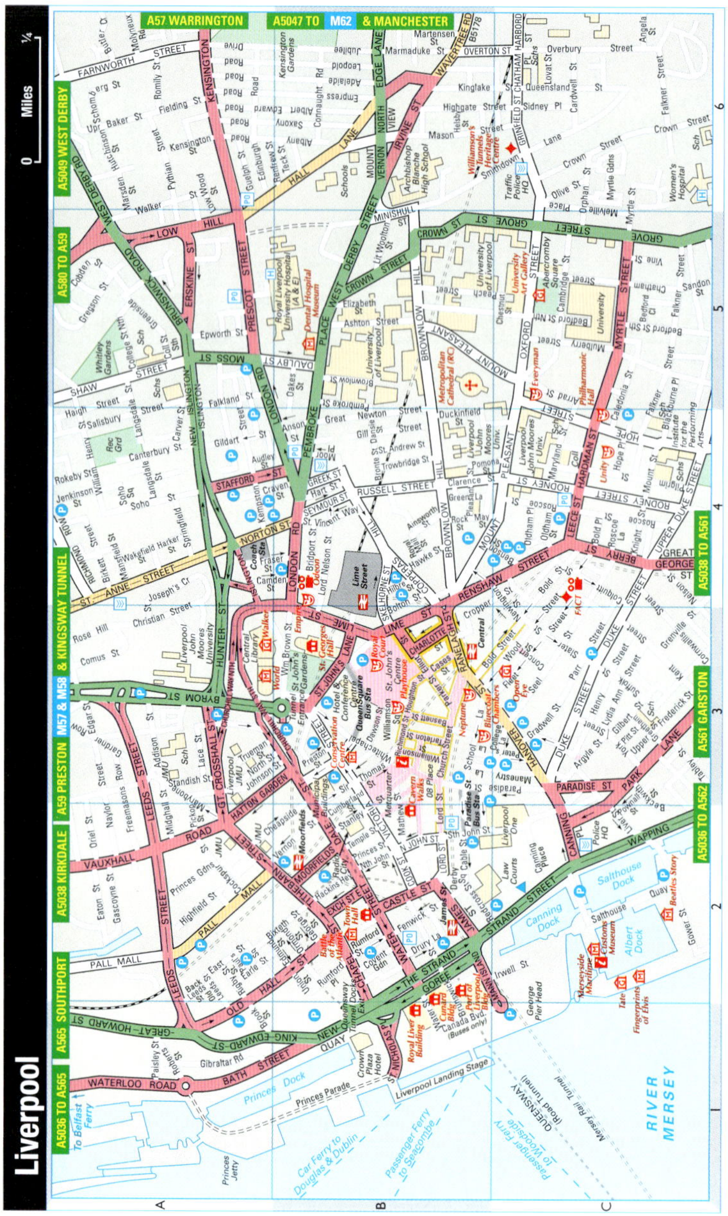
Liverpool
A57 WARRINGTON
A5047 TO M62 & MANCHESTER
A5049 WEST DERBY
A580 TO A59
M57 & M58 & KINGSWAY TUNNEL
A59 PRESTON
A5038 KIRKDALE
A565 SOUTHPORT
A5036 TO A565
A5038 TO A561
A561 GARSTON
A5036 TO A562
RIVER MERSEY
Miles

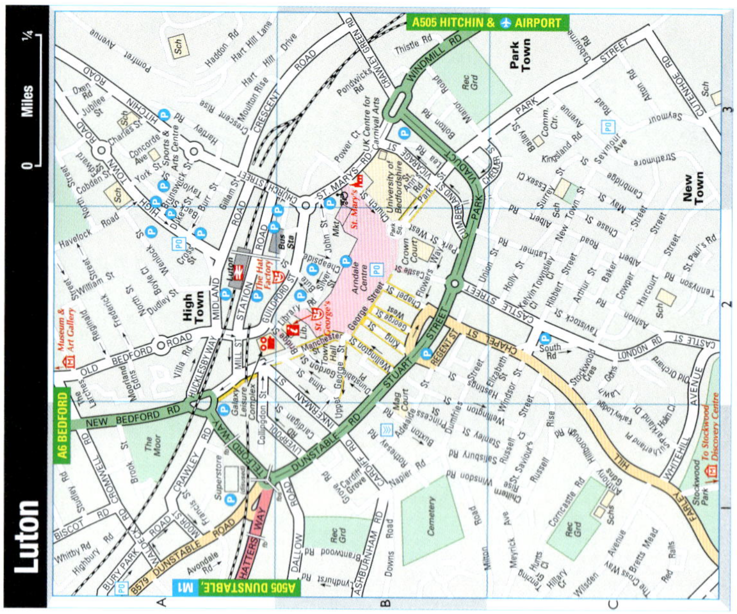
Luton
A505 HITCHIN & AIRPORT
A6 BEDFORD
A505 DUNSTABLE M1
Miles

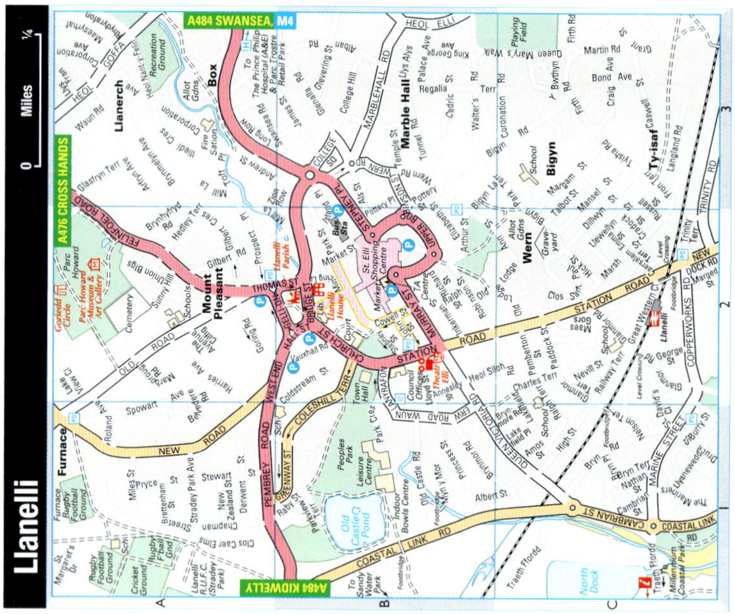
Llanelli
A484 SWANSEA, M4
A476 CROSS HANDS
A484 KIDWELLY
Miles

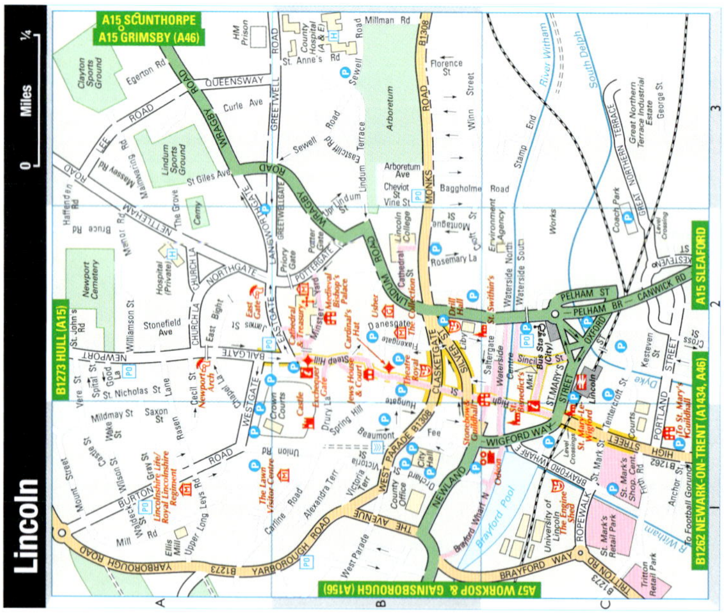
Lincoln
A15 SCUNTHORPE
A15 GRIMSBY (A46)
B1273 HULL (A15)
A15 SLEAFORD
B1262 NEWARK-ON-TRENT (A1434, A46)
A57 WORKSOP & GAINSBOROUGH (A156)
Miles

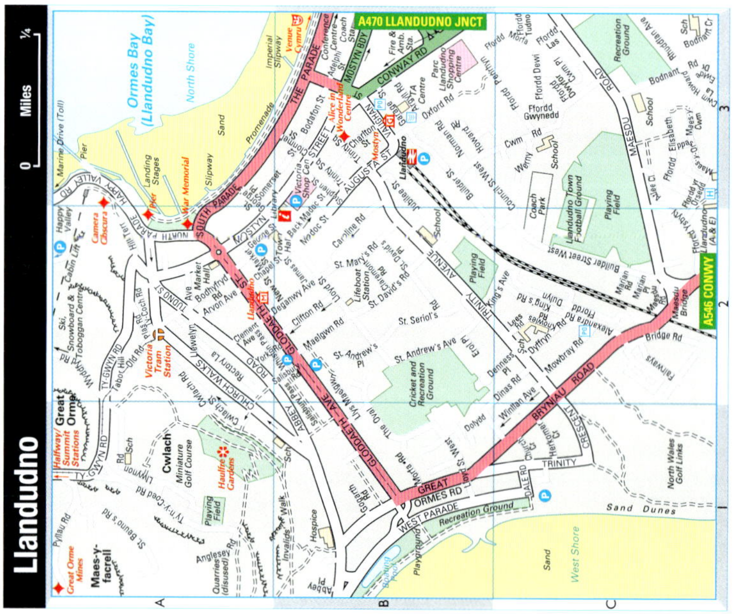
Llandudno
A470 LLANDUDNO JNCT
A546 CONWY
Ormes Bay (Llandudno Bay)
Miles

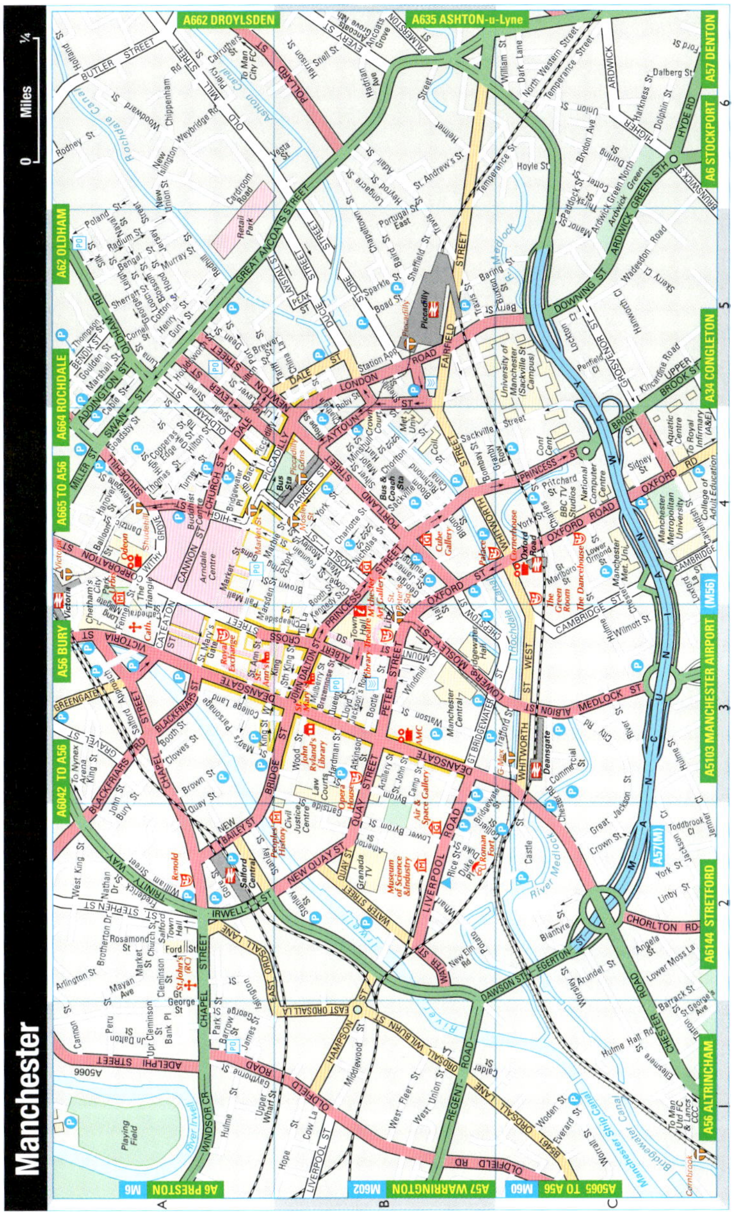

Manchester

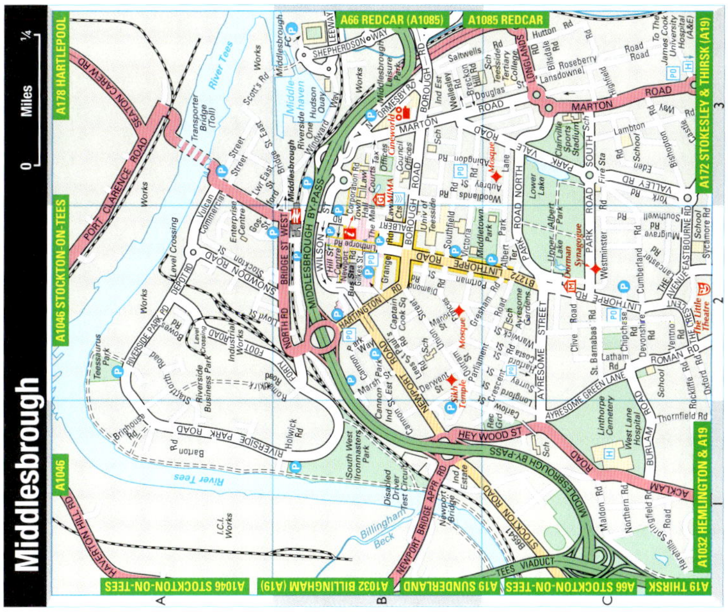

Middlesbrough

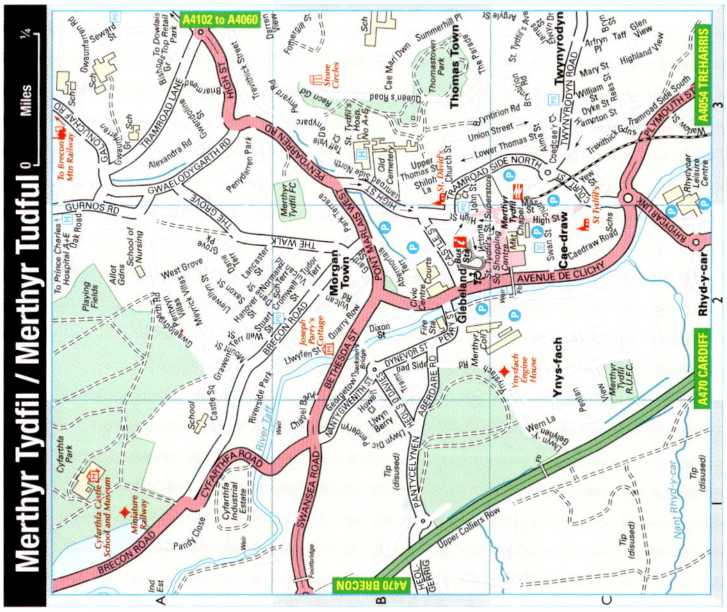

Merthyr Tydfil / Merthyr Tudful

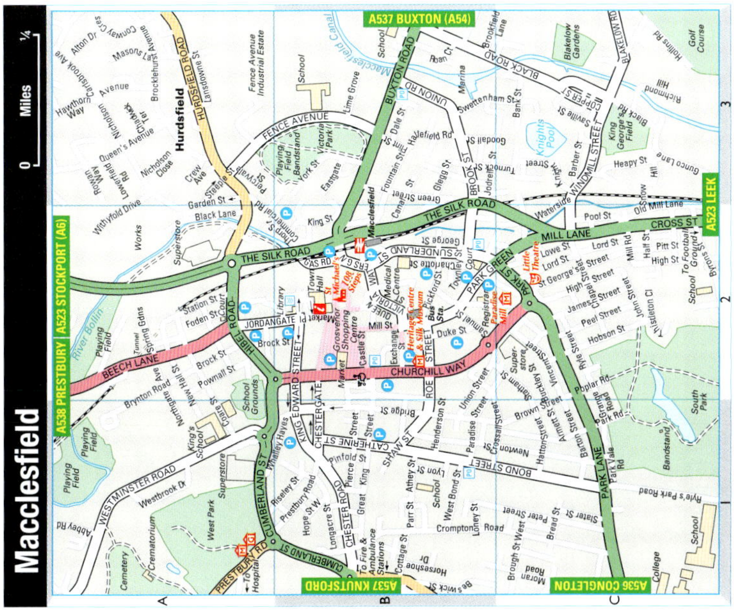

Macclesfield

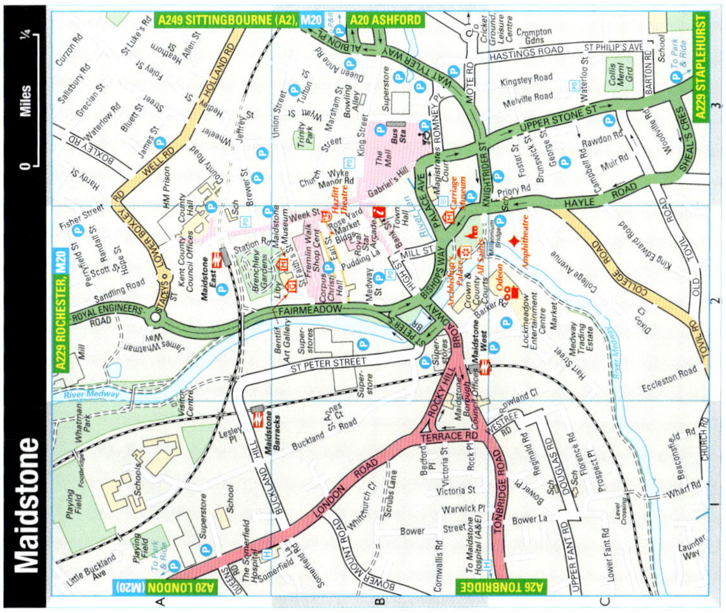

Maidstone

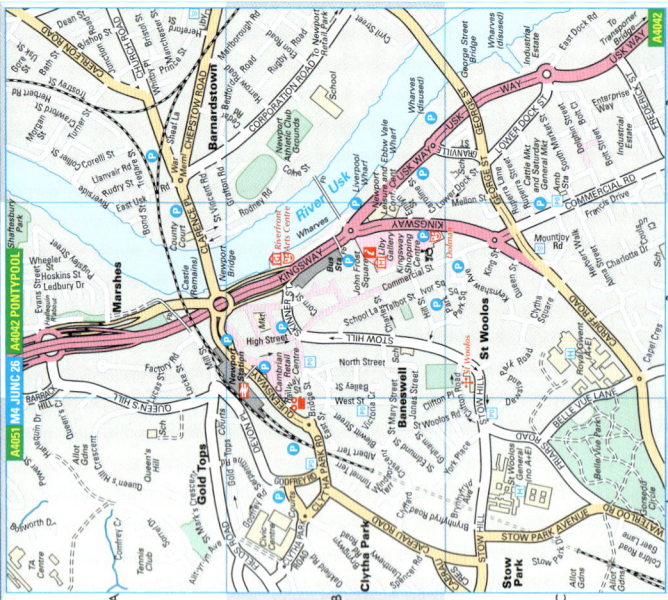

Newport / Casnewydd

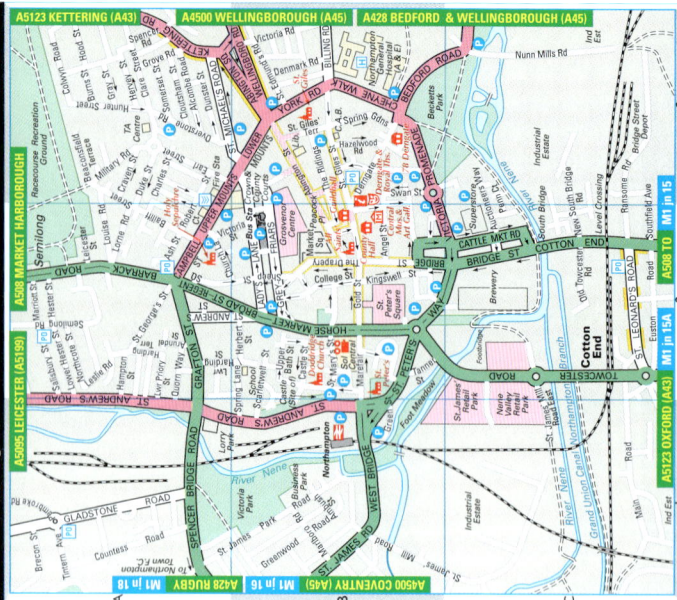

Northampton

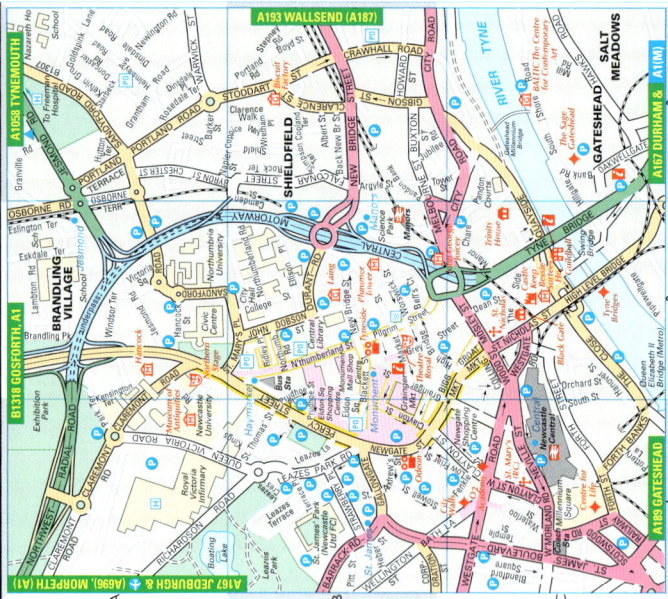

Newcastle upon Tyne

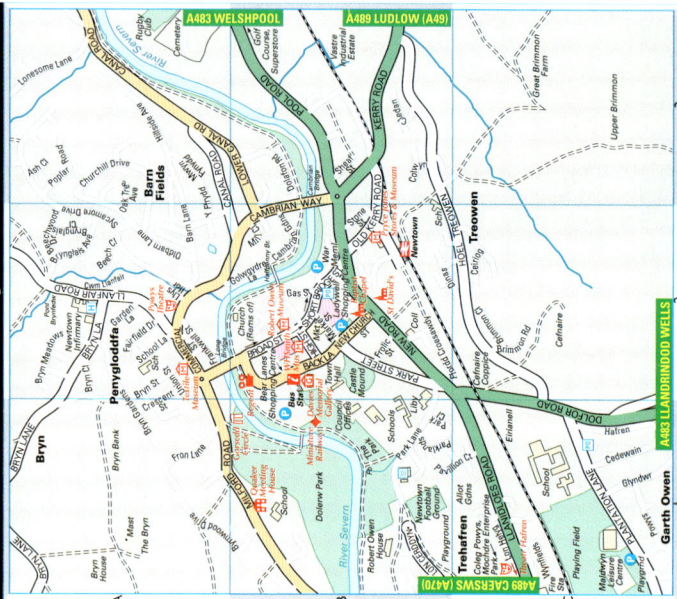

Newtown / Y Drenewydd

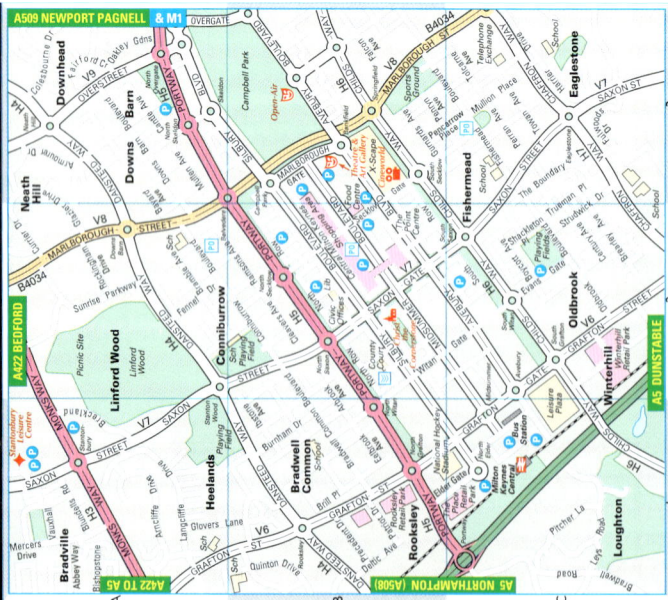

Milton Keynes

Newquay

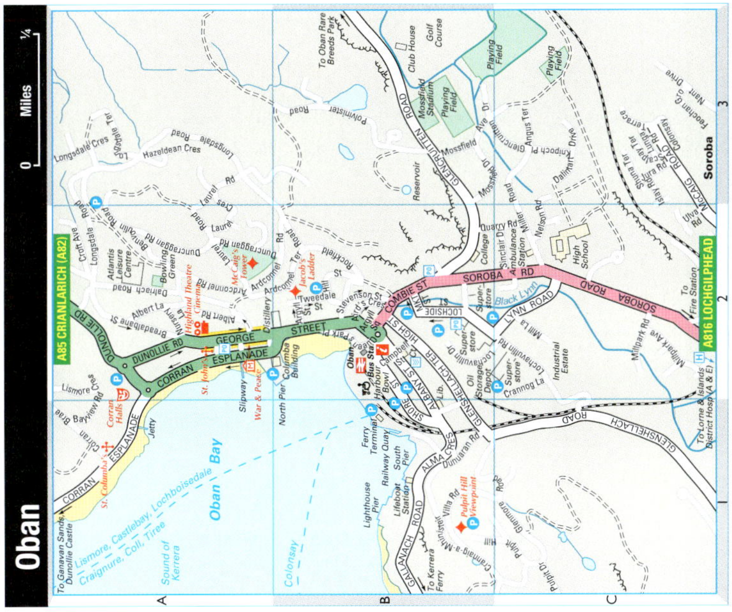
Oban
Miles
A85 CRIANLARICH (A82)
A816 LOCHGILPHEAD
Oban Bay
Soroba

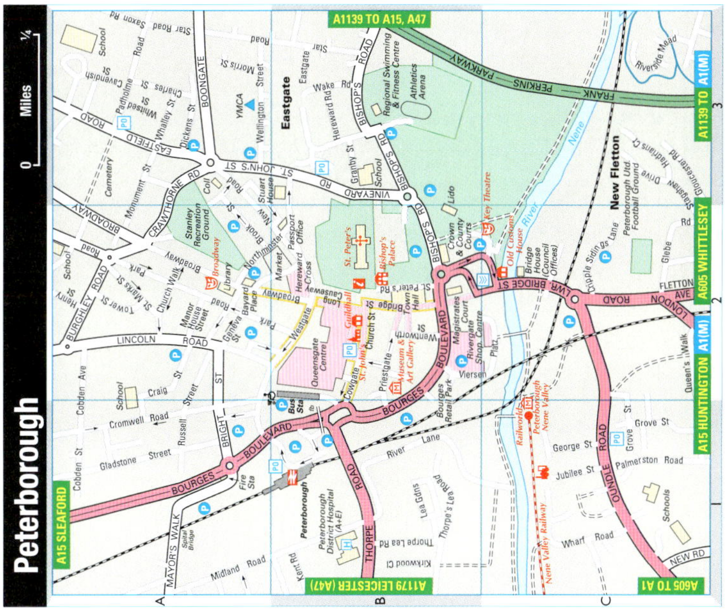
Peterborough
Miles
A1139 TO A15, A47
A15 SLEAFORD
A1179 LEICESTER (A47)
A605 TO A1
A15 HUNTINGTON A1(M)
A605 WHITTLESEY
A1139 TO A1(M)
Eastgate
New Fletton

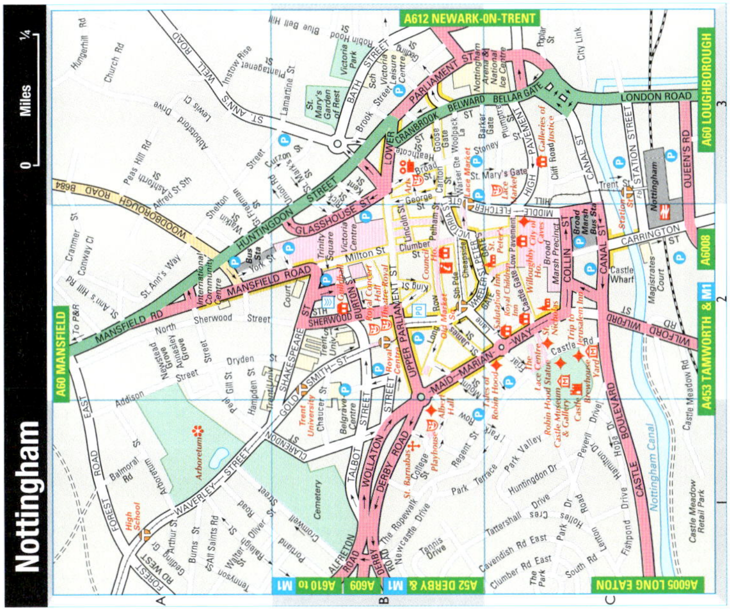
Nottingham
Miles
A60 MANSFIELD
A612 NEWARK-ON-TRENT
A60 LOUGHBOROUGH
A453 TAMWORTH & M1
A6005 LONG EATON
A52 DERBY & M1
A609
A610 to M1

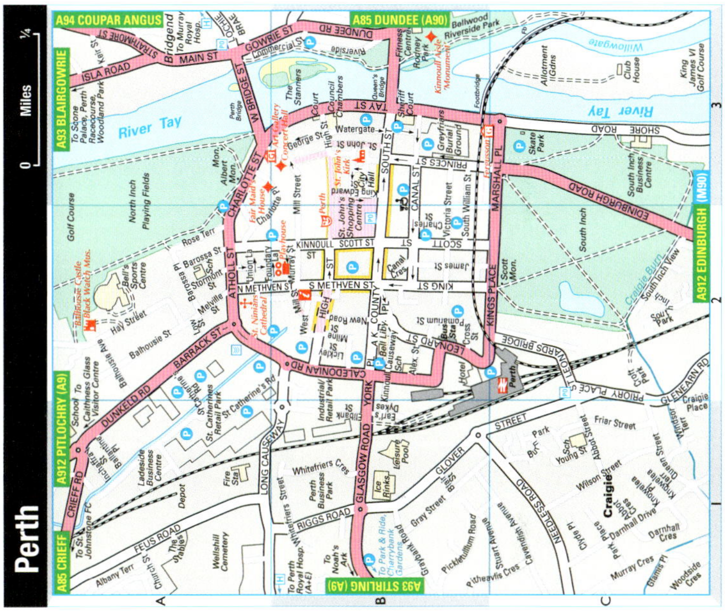
Perth
Miles
A94 COUPAR ANGUS
A85 DUNDEE (A90)
A93 BLAIRGOWRIE
A912 PITLOCHRY (A9)
A85 CRIEFF
A93 STIRLING (A9)
A912 EDINBURGH (M90)
River Tay
Craigie

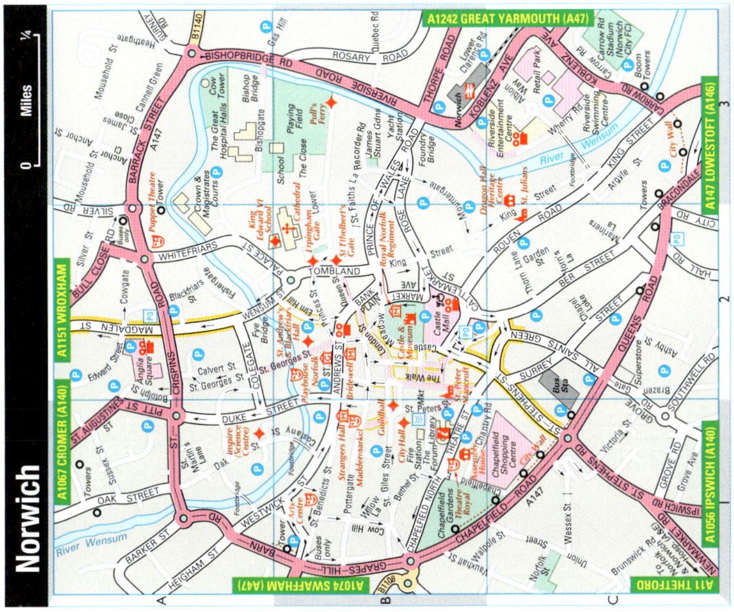
Norwich
Miles
A1242 GREAT YARMOUTH (A47)
A1151 WROXHAM
A1067 CROMER (A140)
A1074 SWAFFHAM (A47)
A11 THETFORD
A1056 IPSWICH (A140)
A147 LOWESTOFT (A146)
River Wensum

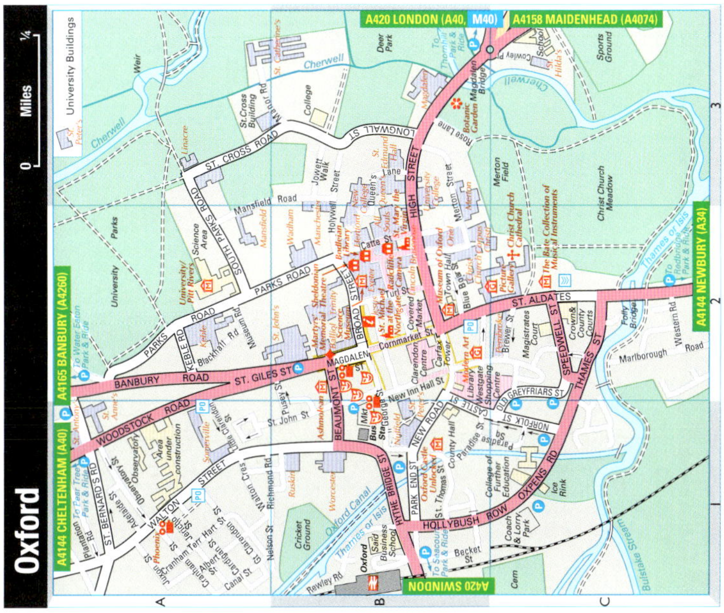
Oxford
Miles
A420 LONDON (A40, M40)
A4158 MAIDENHEAD (A4074)
A4165 BANBURY (A4260)
A4144 CHELTENHAM (A40)
A420 SWINDON
A4144 NEWBURY (A34)
Cherwell

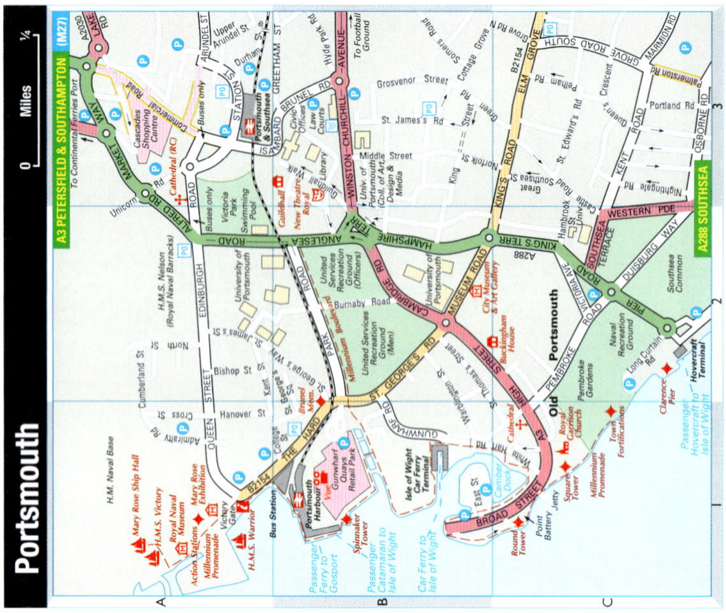
Portsmouth
Miles
A3 PETERSFIELD & SOUTHAMPTON (M27)
A288 SOUTHSEA

St Andrews
Miles
St Andrews Bay
A91 CUPAR
A917 CRAIL
A915 KIRKCALDY

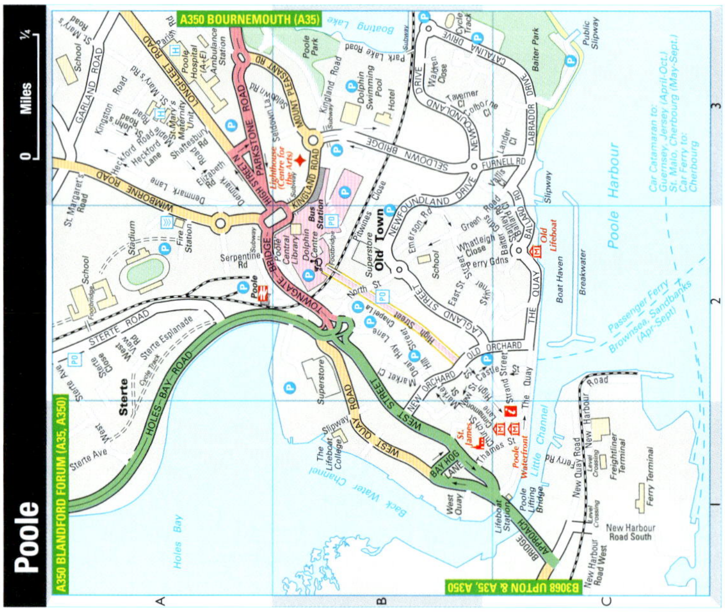
Poole
Miles
A350 BLANDFORD FORUM (A35, A350)
A350 BOURNEMOUTH (A35)
B3068 UPTON & A35, A350
Poole Harbour

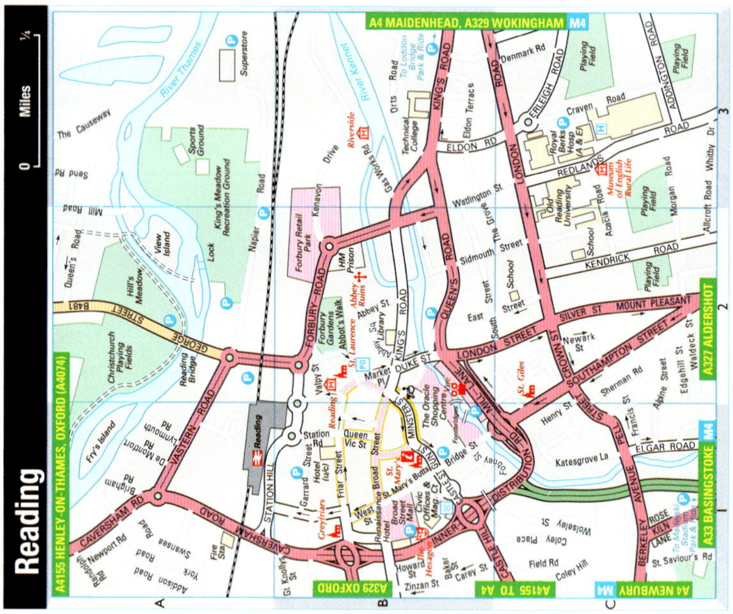
Reading
Miles
A4155 HENLEY-ON-THAMES, OXFORD (A4074)
A4 MAIDENHEAD, A329 WOKINGHAM M4
A327 ALDERSHOT
A33 BASINGSTOKE M4
A4 NEWBURY M4
A4155 TO A4
A329 OXFORD

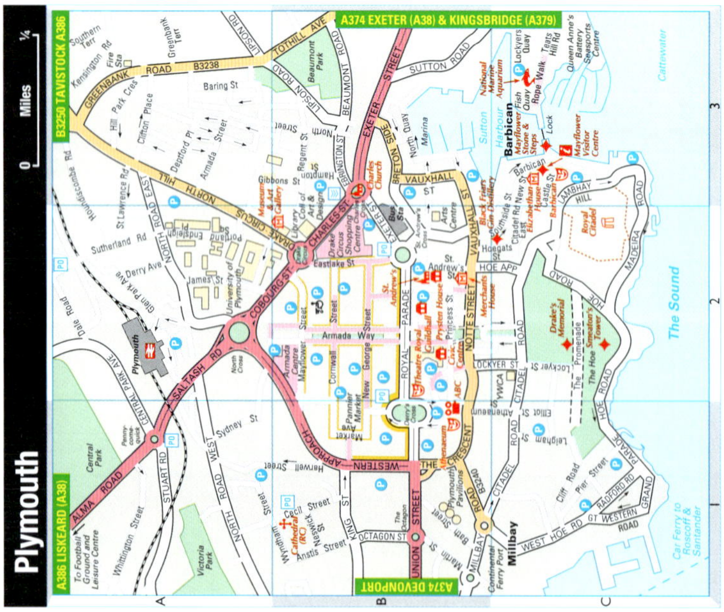
Plymouth
Miles
A386 LISKEARD (A38)
B3250 TAVISTOCK A386
A374 EXETER (A38) & KINGSBRIDGE (A379)
A374 DEVONPORT
The Sound

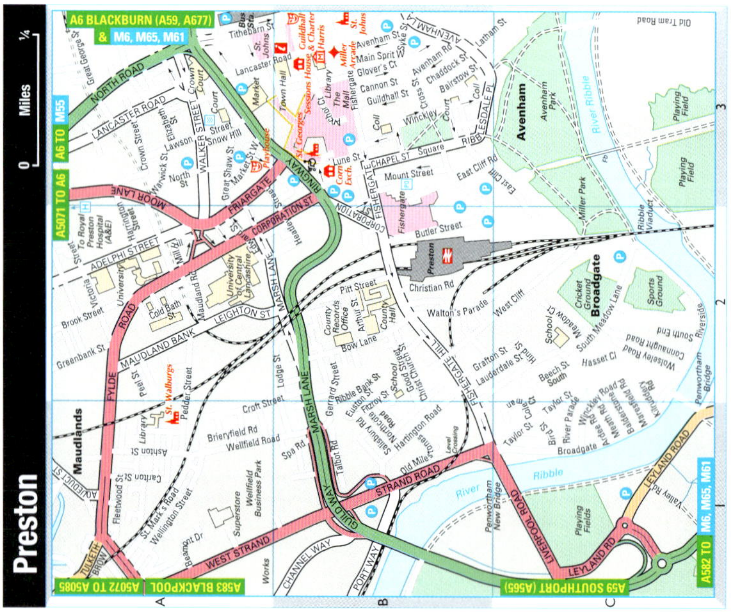
Preston
Miles
A6 BLACKBURN (A59, A677) & M6, M65, M61
A5071 TO A6
A6 TO M55
A583 BLACKPOOL
A5072 TO A5085
A59 SOUTHPORT (A565)
A582 TO M6, M65, M61

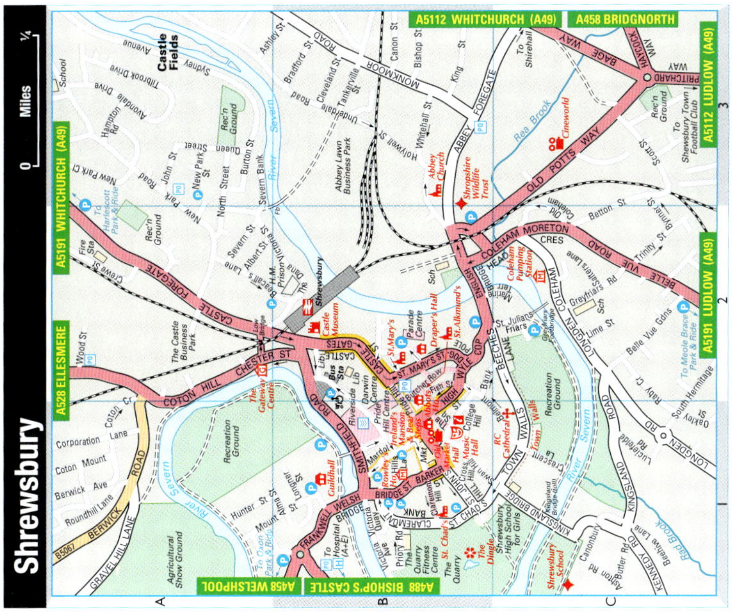
Shrewsbury

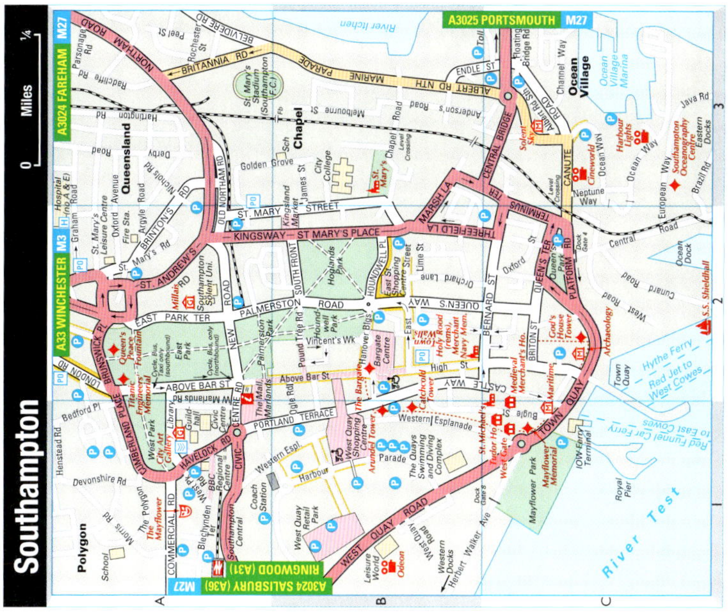
Southampton

Scarborough

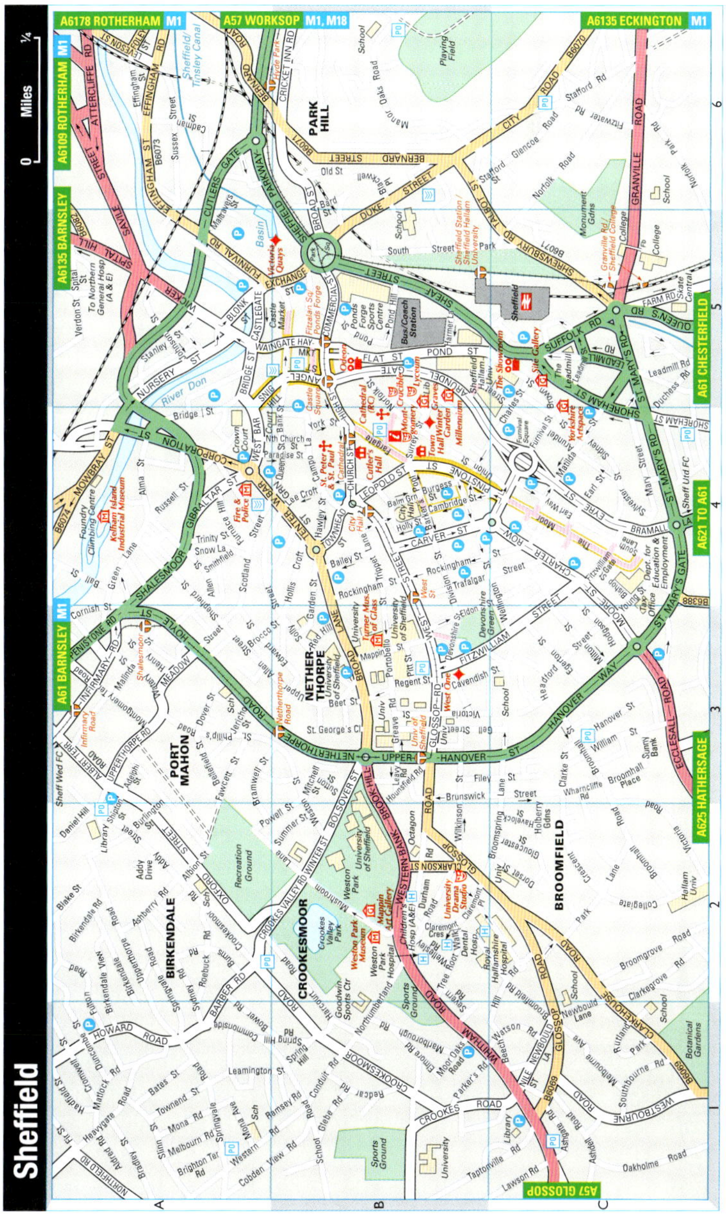
Sheffield

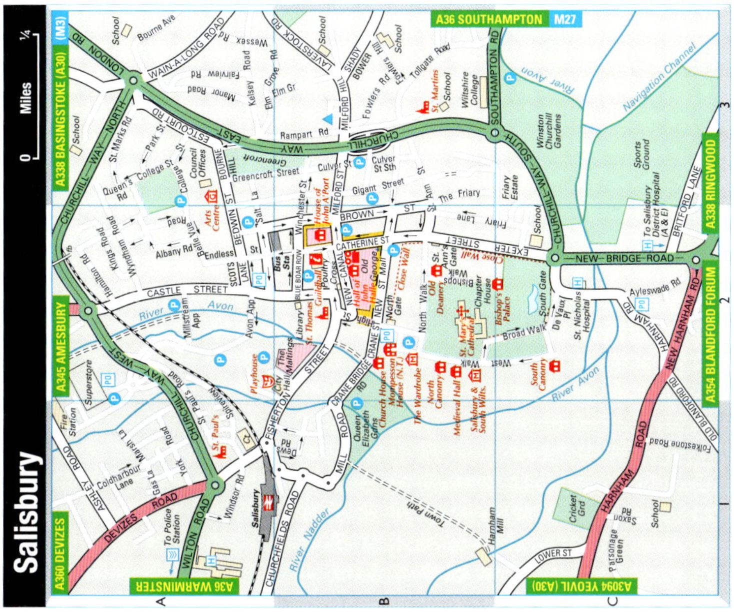
Salisbury

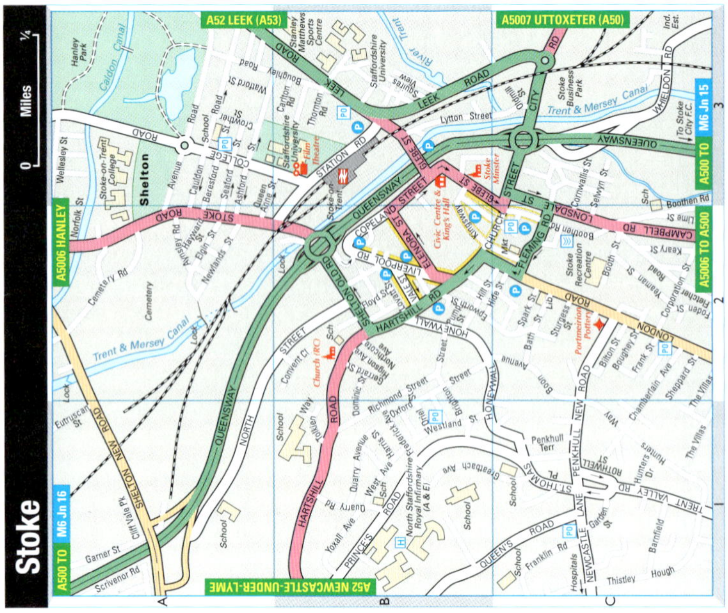

Stoke

Swansea / Abertawe

Stirling

Sunderland

Southend-on-Sea

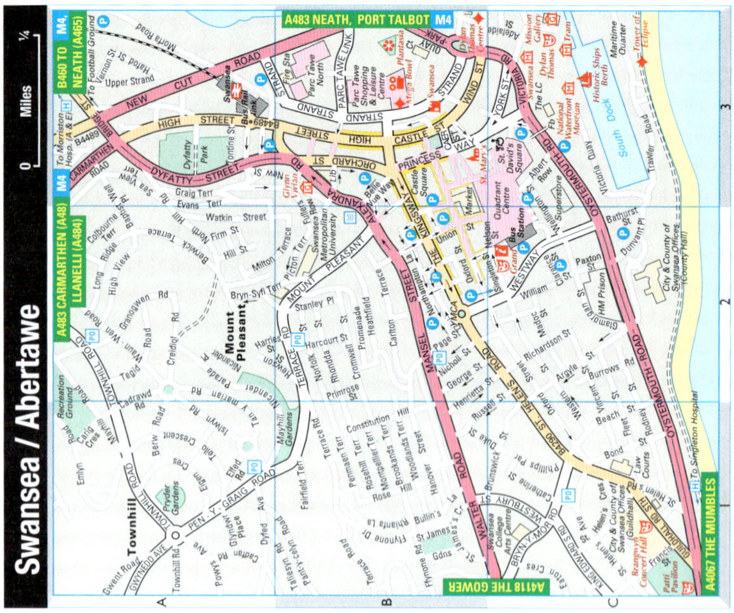

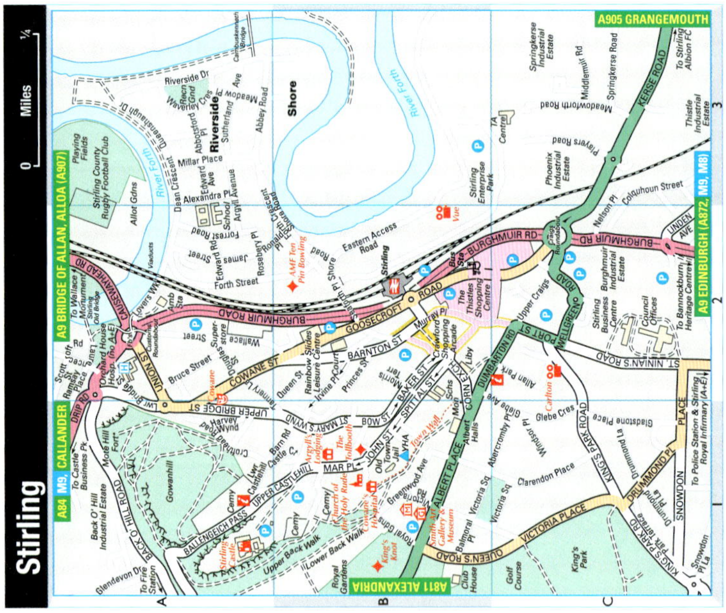

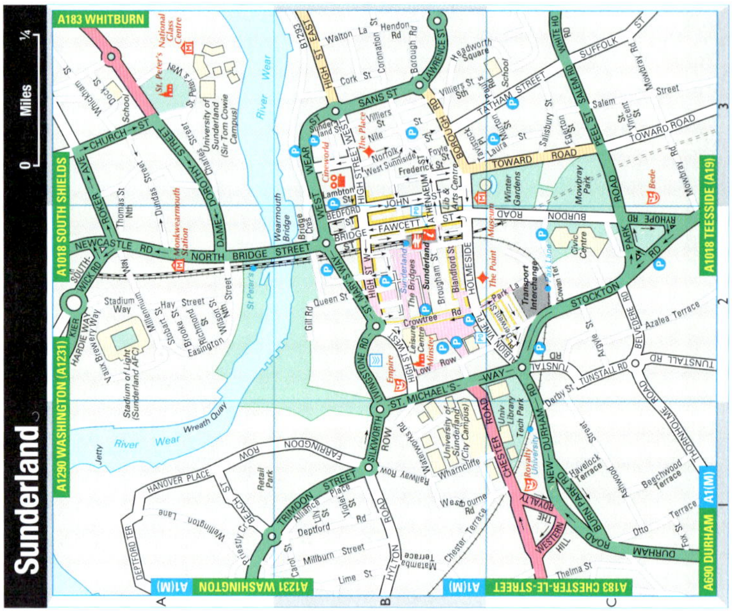

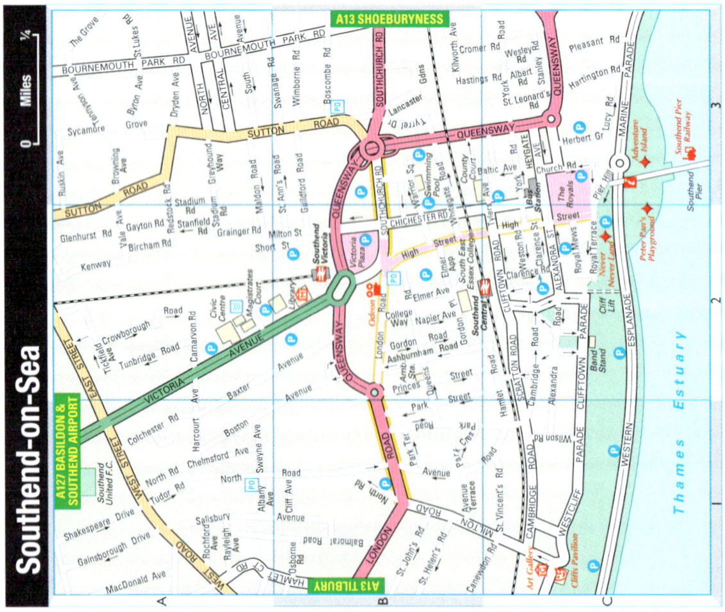

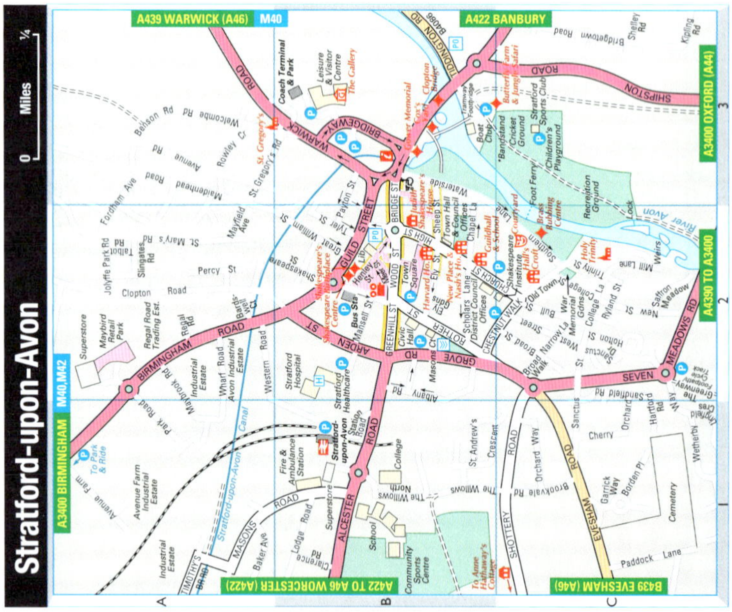

Stratford-upon-Avon

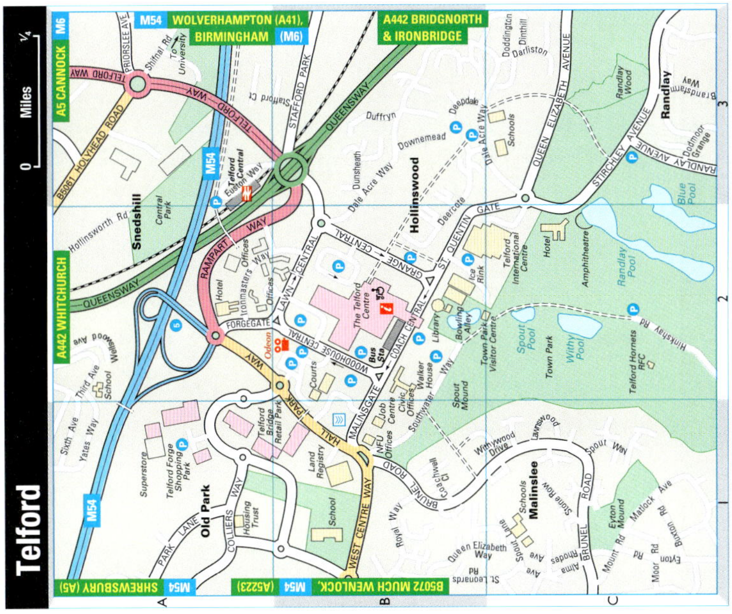
Telford
Miles
A5 CANNOCK
M54 WOLVERHAMPTON (A41), BIRMINGHAM (M6)
A442 BRIDGNORTH & IRONBRIDGE
A442 WHITCHURCH
M54 SHREWSBURY (A5)
M54 (A5223)
B5072 MUCH WENLOCK

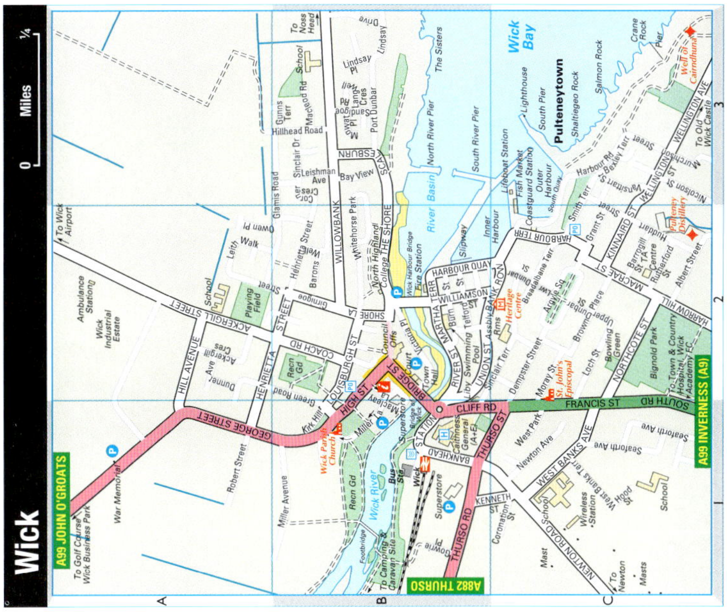
Wick
Miles
A99 JOHN O'GROATS
A882 THURSO
A99 INVERNESS (A9)

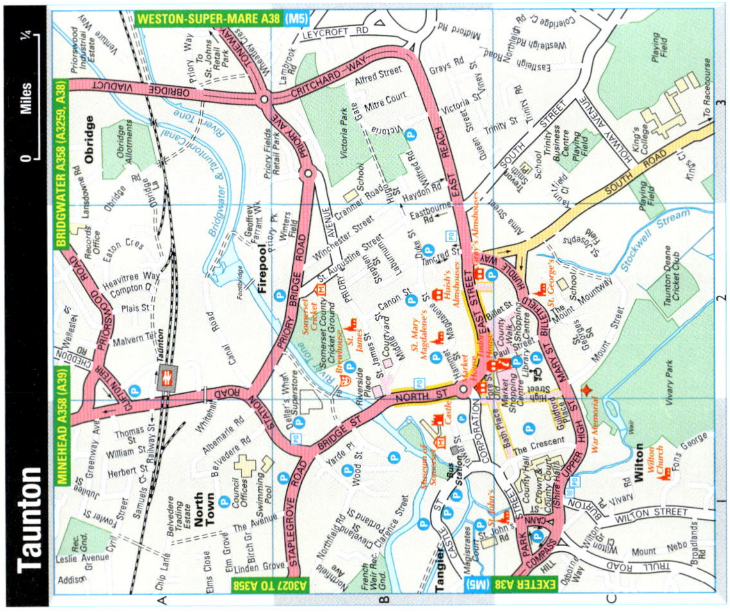
Taunton
Miles
WESTON-SUPER-MARE A38 (M5)
BRIDGWATER A358 (A3259, A38)
MINEHEAD A358 (A39)
A3027 TO A358
EXETER A38 (M5)

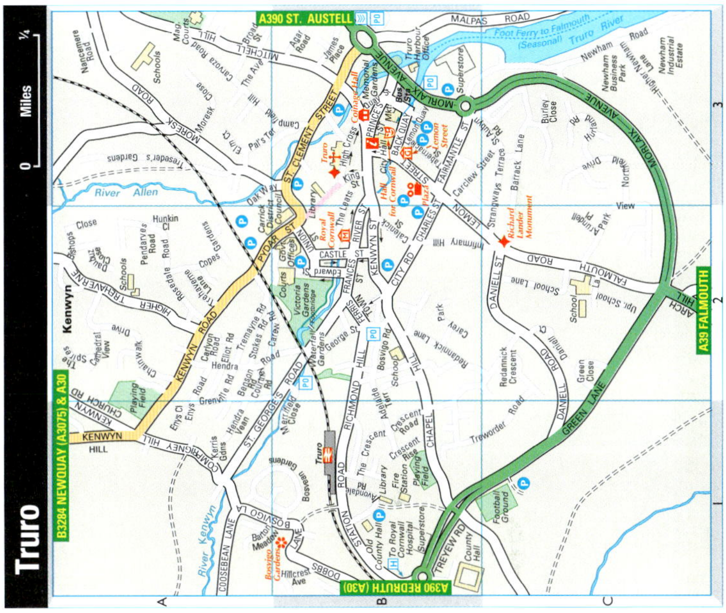
Truro
Miles
A390 ST. AUSTELL
A39 FALMOUTH
B3284 NEWQUAY (A3075) & A30
A390 REDRUTH (A30)

Swindon
Miles
A4311 CIRENCESTER (A419)
A4313 TO A4259
A4259 OXFORD (A4312, A420) MARLBOROUGH (A419, A346)
A4361 DEVIZES
B4289 TO B4006
A4289 BRISTOL (A3102, M4)
BRISTOL (M4)

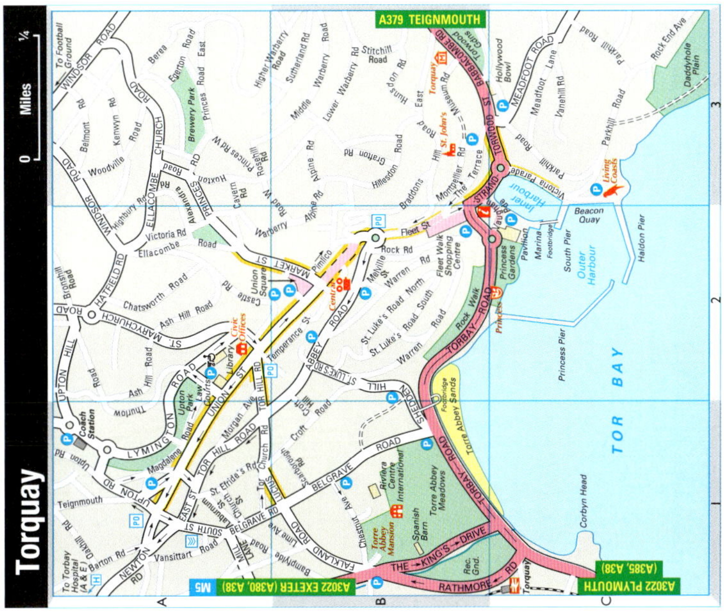
Torquay
Miles
A379 TEIGNMOUTH
A3022 PLYMOUTH (A385, A38)
A3022 EXETER (A380, A38) M5
TOR BAY

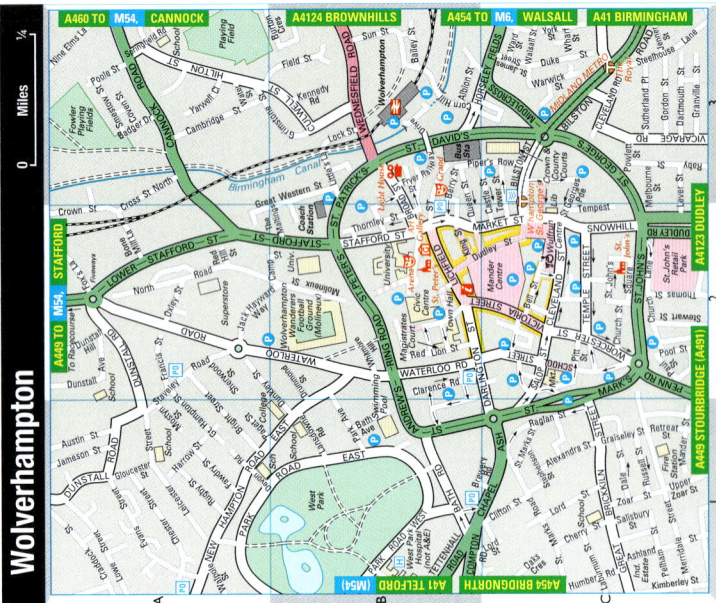

Wolverhampton

York

Windsor

Wrexham / Wrecsam

Winchester

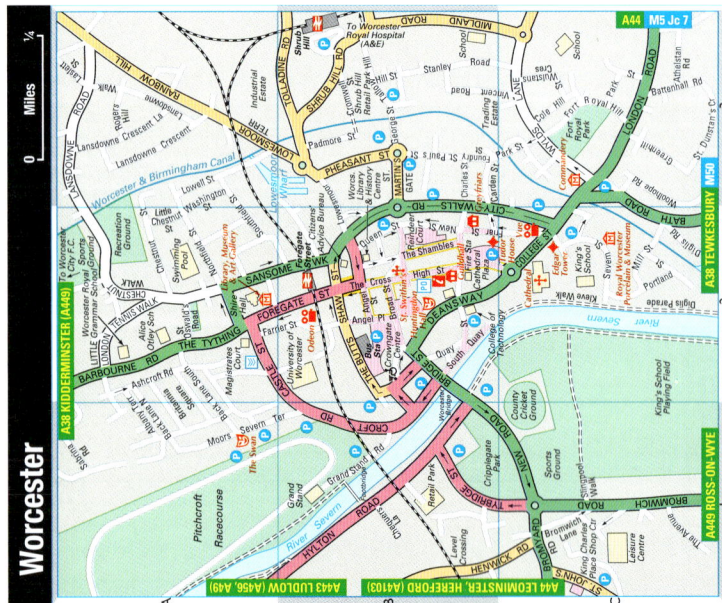

Worcester

Aberdeen • Aberystwyth • Ashford • Ayr • Bangor • Barrow-in-Furness • Bath • Berwick-upon-Tweed • Birmingham
195

Town plan indexes

Aberdeen 175

Aberdeen B2
Aberdeen Grammar School A1
Academy, The B2
Albert Basin B3
Albert Quay B3
Albury Rd C1
Alford Pl B1
Art Gallery A2
Arts Centre A2
Back Wynd A2
Baker St A1
Beach Blvd A3
Belmont B2
Belmont St B2
Berry St A2
Blackfriars St A2
Bloomfield Rd C1
Bon Accord Centre A2
Bon-Accord St B1/C1
Bridge St B2
Broad St A2
Bus Station B2
Car Ferry Terminal B3
Castlegate A3
Central Library A1
Chapel St B1
College A2
College St B2
Commerce St A3
Commercial Quay B3
Community Centre A3/C1
Constitution St A3
Cotton St A3
Crown St B2
Denburn Rd A2
Devanha Gdns C2
Devanha Gdns South C2
East North St A3
Esslemont Ave A1
Ferryhill Rd C2
Ferryhill Terr C2
Fish Market B3
Fonthill Rd C1
Galleria, The B1
Gallowgate A2
George St A2
Glenbervie Rd C3
Golden Sq B1
Grampian Rd C3
Great Southern Rd C1
Guild St B2
Hardgate B1/C1
His Majesty's Theatre A1
Holburn St C1
Hollybank Pl C1
Huntly St B1
Hutcheon St A1
Information Ctr B2
John St A2
Justice St A3
King St A2
Langstane Pl B1
Lemon Tree, The A2
Library C1
Loch St A2
Maberly St A1
Marischal College A2
Maritime Museum & Provost Ross's House B2
Market St B2/B3
Menzies Rd C3
Mercat Cross A3
Millburn St C2
Miller St A3
Market B2
Mount St A1
Music Hall B1
North Esp East C3
North Esp West C2
Oscar Rd C3
Palmerston Rd C2
Park St A3
Police Station A2
Polmuir Rd C2
Post Office A1/A2/A3/B1/C3
Provost Skene's House A2
Queen St A2
Regent Quay B3
Regent Road B3
Robert Gordon's College A2
Rose St B1
Rosemount Pl A1
Rosemount Viaduct A1
St Andrew St A2
St Andrew's Cathedral A3
St Mary's Cathedral B1
St Nicholas Centre A2
St Nicholas St A2
School Hill A2
Sinclair Rd C3
Skene Sq A1
Skene St B1
South College St C2
South Crown St C2
South Esp East C3
South Esp West C3
South Mount St A1
Sports Centre C3
Spring Garden A2
Springbank Terr C2
Summer St B1
Swimming Pool B1
The Mall B1
Thistle St B1
Tolbooth A3
Town House A2
Trinity Quay B3
Union Row B1
Union St B1/B2
Upper Dock B3
Upper Kirkgate A2
Victoria Bridge C3
Victoria Dock B3
Victoria Rd C3
Victoria St B2
Virginia St A3
Vue B2
Wellington Pl B2
West North St A2
Whinhill Rd C1
Willowbank Rd C1
Windmill Brae B2
Woolmanhill Hospital A1

Aberystwyth 175

Aberystwyth Holiday Village C2
Aberystwyth RFC C3
Aberystwyth Station B2
Aberystwyth Town Football Ground B2
Alexandra Rd B2
Ambulance Station C3
Baker St B1
Banadl Rd B2
Bandstand A1
Bath St A2
Boat Landing Stage A1
Boulevard de Saint-Brieuc C3
Bridge St B1
Bronglais Hospital B3
Bryn-y-Mor Rd A2
Buarth Rd B2
Bus Station B2
Cae Ceredig C3
Cae Melyn A2
Cae'r-Gog B3
Cambrian St B2
Caradoc Rd B3
Caravan Site C2
Castle (Remains of) B1
Castle St B1
Cemetery B3
Ceredigion Museum A1
Chalybeate St B1
Cliff Terr A2
Club House A2
Commodore A1
County Court A2
Crown Buildings B2
Dan-y-Coed A3
Dinas Terr C1
Eastgate B1
Edge-hill Rd B2
Elm Tree Ave B2
Elysian Gr A2
Felin-y-Mor Rd C1
Fifth Ave C2
Fire Station C1
Glanrafon Terr B1
Glyndwr Rd B2
Golf Course A3
Gray's Inn Rd B1
Great Darkgate St B1
Greenfield St B2
Heol-y-Bryn A2
High St B1
Infirmary Rd A2
Information Ctr B1
Iorwerth Ave B3
King St B1
Lauraplace B1
Library B1
Lifeboat Station C1
Llanbadarn Rd B3
Loveden Rd A2
Magistrates Court A1
Marina C1
Marine Terr A1
Market B1
Mill St B1
Moor La B2
National Library of Wales B3
New Promenade B1
New St B1
North Beach A1
North Parade B2
North Rd A2
Northgate St B2
Parc Natur Penglais A3
Parc-y-Llyn Retail Park C3
Park & Ride B2
Park Ave B2
Pavillion B1
Pendinas C1
Penglais Rd B3
Penrheidol C2
Pen-y-Craig A2
Pen-yr-angor C1
Pier St B1
Plas Ave B3
Plas Helyg C2
Plascrug Ave B2/C3
Plascrug Leisure Centre C3
Police Station C2
Poplar Row B2
Portland Rd B2
Portland St A2
Post Office B1/B3
Powell St B1
Prospect St B1
Quay Rd B1
Queen St B1
Queen's Ave A2
Queen's Rd A2
Rheidol Retail Park B2
Riverside Terr B1
St Davids Rd B3
St Michael's B1
School of Art B2
Seaview Pl B1
South Beach B1
South Rd B1
Sports Ground B2
Spring Gdns C1
Stanley Terr B2
Swimming Pool & Leisure Centre C3
Superstore B2/C3
Tanybwlch Beach C1
Tennis Courts B3
Terrace Rd B1
The Bar C1
Town Hall A2
Trefechan Bridge B1
Trefechan Rd C2
Trefor Rd A2
Trinity Rd B2
University Campus B3
University of Wales (Aberystwyth) B1
Vale of Rheidol Railway C3
Vaynor St B2
Victoria Terr A1
Viewpoint A2
Viewpoint A3
War Memorial B1
Wharf Quay C1
Y Lanfa C1
Ystwyth Retail Park B2

Ashford 175

Albert Rd A1
Alfred Rd C3
Apsley St A1
Ashford A1
Ashford Borough Museum A1
Ashford International Station B2
Bank St A1
Barrowhill Gdns A1
Beaver Industrial Estate C1
Beaver Rd C1
Beazley Ct C3
Birling Rd B3
Blue Line La A1
Bond Rd C1
Bowens Field B1
Bulleid Pl C2
Cade Rd C1
Chart Rd A1
Chichester Cl B1
Christchurch Rd B1
Chunnel Industrial Estate B1
Church Rd A1
Civic Centre A2
County Square Shopping Centre A1
Court A1
Court A1
Croft Rd A3
Cudworth Rd C3
Curtis Rd C3
Dering Rd A3
Dover Pl B2
Drum La A1
East Hill A2
East St A1
Eastmead Ave B2
Edinburgh Rd A1
Elwick Rd A1
Essella Pk B3
Essella Rd B3
Fire Sta A3
Forge La A1
Francis Rd C1
George St B1
Godfrey Walk B1
Godinton Rd A1
Gordon Cl A3
Hardinge Rd A2
Henwood A3
Henwood Business Centre A3
Henwood Industrial Estate A3
High St A2
Hythe Rd A3
Information Ctr A1
Jemmett Rd B1
Kent Ave A1
Library A1
Linden Rd B3
Lower Denmark Rd C1
Mabledon Ave B3
Mace Ind Est A2
Mace La A2
Maunsell Pl C3
McArthur Glen Designer Outlet C2
Memorial Gdns A2
Mill Ct A2
Miller Cl A2
Mortimer Cl C1
New St A1
Newtown Green C3
Newtown Rd B2/C3
Norman Rd C1
North St A2
Norwood Gdns A1
Norwood St A1
Old Railway Works Industrial Estate C3
Orion Way C3
Park Mall Shopping Centre A1
Park Pl A1
Park St A1/A2
Pemberton Rd A3
Police Station A1
Post Office A1/A3
Providence St C2
Queen St A1
Queens Rd A2
Regents Pl A1
Riversdale Rd C2
Romney Marsh Rd B2
St John's La A2
Somerset Rd A2
South Stour Ave B2
Star Rd A3
Station Rd B2
Stirling Rd C2
Stour Centre, The B2
Sussex Ave A1
Tannery La A2
Technical College B2
Torrington Rd C2
Trumper Bridge B1
Tufton Rd A3
Tufton St A1
Vicarage La A2
Victoria Cres B1
Victoria Park B1
Victoria Rd B1
Wallis Rd A3
Wellesley Rd A2
West St A1
Whitfeld Rd C1
William Rd C1
World War I Tank A1

Ayr 175

Ailsa Pl B1
Alexandra Terr A3
Allison St B2
Alloway Pk C1
Alloway Pl C1
Alloway St C2
Arran Mall C2
Arran Terr B1
Arthur St B2
Ashgrove St C2
Auld Brig B2
Auld Kirk B2
Ayr C2
Ayr Academy B1
Ayr Central Shopping Centre C2
Ayr Harbour A1
Ayr United FC A3
Back Hawkhill Ave A3
Back Main St B2
Back Peebles St A2
Barns Cres C1
Barns Pk C1
Barns St C1
Barns Street La C1
Bath Pl B1
Bellevue Cres C1
Bellevue La C1
Beresford La C2
Beresford Terr C2
Boswell Pk B2
Britannia Pl A3
Bruce Cres B1
Burns Statue C2
Bus Sta B1
Carrick St C2
Cassillis St B1
Cathcart St B1
Charlotte St B1
Citadel Leisure Ctr B1
Citadel Pl B1
Compass Pier A1
Content Ave C3
Content St B2
Craigie Ave B3
Craigie Rd B3
Craigie Way B3
Cromwell Rd B1
Crown St A2
Dalblair Rd C2
Dam Park Sports Stadium C3
Damside A2
Dongola Rd C3
Eglinton Pl B1
Eglinton Terr B1
Elba St B2
Elmbank St A2
Esplanade B1
Farifield Rd C1
Fort St B1
Fothringham Rd C3
Fullarton St C1
Gaiety C2
Garden St B2
George St B2
George's Ave A3
Glebe Cres A2
Glebe Rd A2
Gorden Terr B3
Green St A2
Green Street La A2
Hawkhill Ave A3
Hawkhill Avenue La B3
High St B2
Holmston Rd C3
Information Ctr B1
James St B3
John St B2
King St B2
Kings Ct B2
Kyle Centre C2
Kyle St C2
Library B2
Limekiln Rd A2
Limonds Wynd B2
Loudoun Hall B2
Lymburn Pl B3
Macadam Pl B2
Main St B2
Mcadam's Monument C1
Mccall's Ave A3
Mews La B1
Mill Brae C3
Mill St C2
Mill Wynd C2
Miller Rd C1
Montgomerie Terr B1
New Bridge B2
New Bridge St B2
New Rd A2
Newmarket St B2
Newton-on-Ayr Station A2
North Harbour St B1
North Pier A1
Odeon C2
Oswald La A1
Park Circus C1
Park Circus La C1
Park Terr C1
Pavilion Rd C1
Peebles St A2
Philip Sq B2
Police Station B2
Post Office A2/B2
Prestwick Rd B1
Princes Ct A2
Queen St B3
Queen's Terr B1
Racecourse Rd C1
River St B2
Riverside Pl B2
Russell Dr A2
St Andrews Church C2
St George's Rd A3
Sandgate B1
Savoy Park C1
Seabank Rd B2
Smith St C2
Somerset Rd A3
South Beach Rd B1
South Harbour St B1
South Pier A1
Station Rd C2
Strathaye Pl B2
Taylor St A2
Town Hall B2
Tryfield Pl A3
Turner's Bridge B2
Union Ave A3
Victoria Bridge C3
Victoria St B3
Viewfield Rd A3
Virginia Gdns A2
Waggon Rd A2
Walker Rd A3
Wallace Tower B2
Weaver St A2
Weir Rd A2
Wellington La C1
Wellington Sq C1
West Sanouhar Rd A3
Whitletts Rd B3
Wilson St A3
York St A1
York Street La B1

Bangor 175

Abbey Rd C2
Albert St B1
Ambrose St A3
Ambulance Station A3
Arfon Sports Hall C1
Ashley Rd B3
Bangor City Football Ground C2
Bangor Mountain B3
Bangor Station C1
Bangor University B2
Beach Rd A3
Belmont St C3
Bishop's Mill Rd C3
Boat Yard A3
Brick St B3
Buckley Rd B2
Bus Station B3
Caellepa B2
Caernarfon Rd C1
Cathedral B2
Cemetery C1
Clarence St C1
Clock B3
College B2/C2
College La B2
College Rd B2
Convent La C1
Council Offices B2
Craig y Don Rd B2
Dean St B3
Deiniol Rd B2
Deiniol Shopping Centre B2
Deiniol St B2
Edge Hill A3
Euston Rd C1
Fairview Rd A3
Farrar Rd C2
Ffordd Cynfal C1
Ffordd Elfed C3
Ffordd Islwyn A3
Ffordd y Castell C3
Ffriddoedd Rd B1
Field St B1
Fountain St A3
Friars Ave B3
Friars Rd B3
Friary (Site of) B3
Gardd Deman C1
Garth Hill A3
Garth Point A3
Garth Rd A3
Glanrafon B2
Glanrafon Hill B2
Glynne Rd B3
Golf Course B3
Golf Course C3
Gorad Rd B1
Gorsedd Circle A2
Gwern Las C3
Heol Dewi C1
High St B3/C2
Hill St B1
Holyhead Rd B1
Hwfa Rd B1
Information Ctr B2
James St B3
Library B2
Llys Emrys A3
Lon Ogwen C1
Lon-Pobty C2
Lon-y-Felin C3
Lon-y-Glyder C1
Love La B2
Lower Penrallt Rd B2
Lower St B2
Maes-y-Dref B3
Maeshyfryd A3
Meirion La A2
Meirion Rd A2
Menai Ave B1
Menai College C1
Menai Shopping Centre B2
Min-y-Ddol C3
Minafon B2
Mount St B3
Museum and Art Gallery B2
Orme Rd A3
Parc Victoria B1
Penchwintan Rd C1
Penlon Gr B3
Penrhyn Ave C3
Pier A3
Police Station B2
Post Office B2/B3/C1/C3
Prince's Rd B2
Queen's Ave C3
Sackville Rd B2
St Paul's St B2
Seion Rd A3
Seiriol Rd A3
Siliwen Rd A2
Snowdon View B1
Sports Ground B1
Station Rd C1
Strand St B3
Swimming Pool and Leisure Centre A3
Tan-y-Coed C3
Tegid Rd B3
Temple Rd B2
The Crescent B2
Theatr Gwynedd B2
Totton Rd A3
Town Hall B2
Treflan B2
Trem Elidir C1
Upper Garth Rd A3
Victoria Ave B1
Victoria Dr B1
Victoria St B1
Vron St B2
Well St B3
West End C1
William St B3
York Pl B3

Barrow-in-Furness 176

Abbey Rd A3/B2
Adelaide St A2
Ainslie St A3
Albert St C3
Allison St B3
Anson St A2
Argyle St B3
Arthur St B3
Ashburner Way A1
Barrow Raiders RLFC B1
Barrow Station A2
Bath St A1/B2
Bedford Rd A3
Bessamer Way A1
Blake St A1/A2
Bridge Rd C1
Buccleuch Dock C3
Buccleuch Dock Rd C2/C3
Buccleuch St B2/B3
Byron St A2
Calcutta St A1
Cameron St C1
Carlton Ave A3
Cavendish Dock Rd C3
Cavendish St B2/B3
Channelside Walk B1
Channelside Haven C1
Chatsworth St A2
Cheltenham St A3
Church St C3
Clifford St B2
Clive St B1
Collingwood St B2
Cook St A2
Cornerhouse Retail Park B2
Cornwallis St B2
Courts A2
Crellin St B3
Cross St C3
Dalkeith St B2
Dalton Rd B2/C2
Derby St B3
Devonshire Dock C2
Devonshire Dock Hall B1
Dock Museum, The B1
Drake St A2
Dryden St A2
Duke St A1/B2/C3
Duncan St B2
Dundee St C2
Dundonald St B2
Earle St C1
Emlyn St B2
Exmouth St A2
Farm St C2
Fell St B3
Fenton St B3
Ferry Rd C1
Forum 28 B2
Furness College B1
Glasgow St B3
Goldsmith St A2
Greengate St B3
Hardwick St A2
Harrison St B3
Hartington St A2
Hawke St B2
Hibbert Rd A2
High Level Bridge C2
High St B2
Hindpool Retail Park B2
Hindpool Rd B2
Holker St A2
Hollywood Retail & Leisure Park B1
Hood St A2
Howard St B2
Howe St B2
Information Ctr B2
Ironworks Rd A1/B1
James St B3
Jubliee Bridge C1
Keith St B2
Keyes St A2
Lancaster St A3
Lawson St B2
Library B2
Lincoln St A3
Longreins Rd A3
Lonsdale St C3
Lord St B3
Lorne Rd B3
Lyon St A2
Manchester St B2
Market B2
Market St B2
Marsh St B3
Michaelson Rd C2
Milton St A2
Monk St B2
Mount Pleasant B3
Nan Tait Centre B2
Napier St B2
Nelson St B2
North Rd B1
Open Market B2
Parade St B2
Paradise St B3
Park Ave A3
Park Dr A3
Parker St A2
Parry St A2
Peter Green Way A1
Phoenix Rd A1
Police Station B2
Portland Walk Shopping Centre B2
Post Office A3/B2
Princess Selandia C2
Raleigh St A2
Ramsden St B3
Rawlinson St B3
Robert St B3
Rodney St B2
Rutland St A2
St Patricks Rd C1
Salthouse Rd C3
School St B2
Scott St B2
Settle St A3
Shore St C3
Sidney St B2
Silverdale St B3
Slater St B2
Smeaton St B3
Stafford St A3
Stanley Rd A1
Stark St C3
Steel St B1
Storey Sq B3
Strand C3
Superstore A1/B1/C3
Sutherland St B3
TA Centre A2
The Park A3
Thwaite St B3
Town Hall B2
Town Quay C3
Vernon St B2
Vincent St B2
Walney Rd A1
West Gate Rd A2
West View Rd A3
Westmorland St A3
Whitehead St A3
Wordsworth St A2

Bath 176

Alexandra Park C2
Alexandra Rd C2
Approach Golf Courses (Public) A1
Archway St C3
Assembly Rooms and Museum of Costume A2
Avon St B2
Barton St B2
Bath Abbey B2
Bath City College B2
Bath Pavilion B3
Bath Rugby Club B3
Bath Spa Station C3
Bathwick St A3
Beckford Road A3
Beechen Cliff Rd C2
Bennett St A2
Bloomfield Ave C1
Broad Quay C2
Broad St B2
Brock St A1
Building of Bath Museum A2
Bus Station C2
Calton Gdns C2
Calton Rd C2
Camden Cr A2
Cavendish Rd A1
Cemetery B1
Charlotte St B2
Chaucer Rd C2
Cheap St B2
Circus Mews A2
Claverton St C2
Corn St C2
Cricket Ground B3
Daniel St A3
Edward St B3
Ferry La B3
First Ave C1
Forester Ave A3
Forester Rd A3
Gays Hill A2
George St B2
Great Pulteney St B3
Green Park B1
Green Park Rd B2
Grove St B2
Guildhall B2
Harley St A2
Hayesfield Park C1
Henrietta Gdns A3
Henrietta Mews B3
Henrietta Park B3
Henrietta Rd A3
Henrietta St B3
Henry St B2
Holburne Museum B3
Holloway C2
Information Ctr B2
James St West B1/B2
Jane Austen Centre B2
Julian Rd A1
Junction Rd C1
Kipling Ave C2
Lansdown Cr A1
Lansdown Gr A2
Lansdown Rd A2
Library B2
London Rd A3
London St A2
Lower Bristol Rd B1
Lower Oldfield Park C1
Lyncombe Hill C3
Manvers St B3
Maple Gr C1
Margaret's Hill A2
Marlborough Buildings A1
Marlborough La B1
Midland Bridge Rd B1
Milk St B2
Milsom St B2
Monmouth St B2
Morford St A2
Museum of Bath at Work A2
New King St B1
No. 1 Royal Crescent A1
Norfolk Bldgs B1
Norfolk Cr B1
North Parade Rd B3
Oldfield Rd C1
Paragon A2
Pines Way B1
Podium Shopping Centre B2
Police Station B3
Portland Pl A2
Post Office A1/A3/B2/C1/C2
Postal Museum B2
Powlett Rd A3
Prior Park Rd C3
Pulteney Bridge B2
Pulteney Gdns B3
Pulteney Rd B3/C3
Queen Sq B2
Raby Pl B3
Recreation Ground B3
Rivers St A2
Rockliffe Ave A3
Rockliffe Rd A3
Roman Baths & Pump Room B2
Rossiter Rd C3
Royal Ave A1
Royal Cr A1
Royal High School, The A2
Royal Victoria Park A1
St James Sq A1
St John's Rd A3
Shakespeare Ave C2
Southgate C2
South Pde B3
Sports & Leisure Centre B3
Spring Gdns C3
Stall St B2
Stanier Rd B1
Superstore B1
Sydney Gdns A3
Sydney Pl B3
Sydney Rd B3
Theatre Royal B2
Thermae Bath Spa B2
The Tyning C3
Thomas St A3
Union St B2
Upper Bristol Rd B1
Upper Oldfield Park C1
Victoria Art Gallery B2
Victoria Bridge Rd B1
Walcot St B2
Wells Rd C1
Westgate Buildings B2
Westgate St B2
Weston Rd A1
Widcombe Hill C3
William Herschel Museum B1

Berwick-upon-Tweed 176

Bank Hill B2
Barracks A3
Bell Tower A3
Bell Tower Pl A2
Berwick Br B2
Berwick Infirmary A3
Berwick Rangers F.C. C1
Berwick-upon-Tweed A2
Billendean Rd C3
Blakewell Gdns B2
Blakewell St B2
Brass Bastion A3
Bridge St B3
Brucegate St A2
Castle (Remains of) A2
Castle Terr A2
Castlegate A2
Chapel St A3
Church Rd C2
Church St B3
Court B3
Coxon's La B3
Cumberland Bastion A3
Dean Dr C2
Dock Rd C2/C3
Elizabethan Walls A2/B3
Fire Station B1
Flagstaff Park B3
Football Ground C3
Foul Ford B3
Gallery A3
Golden Sq B2
Golf Course A3
Greenwood C1
Gunpowder Magazine B3
Hide Hill B3
High Greens A2
Holy Trinity A3
Information Ctr A2
Kiln Hill B2
King's Mount B3
Ladywell Rd C2
Library A3
Lifeboat Station C3
Lord's Mount A3
Lovaine Terr A2
Low Greens A3
Main Guard B3
Main St B2/C2
Maltings Art Centre, The B3
Marygate B3
Meg's Mount A2
Middle St C3
Mill St C2
Mount Rd C2
Museum B3
Ness St B3
North Rd A2
Northumberland Ave A2
Northumberland Rd C2
Ord Dr B1
Osborne Cr B2
Osborne Rd B1
Palace Gr B3
Palace St B3
Palace St East B3
Pier Rd B3
Playing Field C1
Police Station B3
Post Office A2/B2/B2
Prince Edward Rd B2
Prior Rd C2
Quay Walls B3
Railway St A2
Ravensdowne B3
Records Office A3
Riverdene B1
Riverside Rd B2
Royal Border Br A2
Royal Tweed Br B2
Russian Gun B3
Scots Gate A2
Scott's Pl A2
Shielfield Park C1
Shielfield Terr C2
Silver St B3
Spittal Quay C3
Superstores C2
The Avenue B3
The Parade A3
Tower Gdns A2
Tower Rd C2
Town Hall B3
Turret Gdns C2
Tweed Dock B2
Tweed St A2
Tweedside Trading Estate C1
Union Brae B2
Union Park Rd B2
Walkergate A3
Wallace Gr A3
War Memorial A2
War Memorial B2
Warkworth Terr A2
Well Close Sq A2
West End B2
West End Pl B1
West End Rd B1
West St B3
West St C3
Windmill Bastion B3
Woolmarket B3
Works C3

Birmingham 176

Abbey St A2
Aberdeen St A1
Acorn Gr B2
Adams St A5
Adderley St C5
Albert St B4/B5
Albion St B2
Alcester St C5
Aldgate Gr A3
Alexandra Theatre C3
All Saint's St A2
All Saints Rd A2

Broad Quay B4
Broad St A4
Broad Weir A5
Broadcasting House A3
Broadmead A5
Brunel Way C1
Brunswick Sq A5
Burton Cl C5
Bus Station A4
Butts Rd B3
Cabot Tower ✦ B3
Caledonia Pl B1
Callowhill Ct A5
Cambridge St C6
Camden Rd C3
Camp Rd A1
Canada Way C2
Cannon St A4
Canon's Rd B3/B4
Canon's Way B3
Cantock's Cl A3
Canynge Rd A1
Canynge Sq A1
Castle Park A5
Castle St A5
Catherine Meade St C4
Cattle Market Rd C6
Charles Pl B1
Charlotte St B3
Charlotte St South B3
Chatterton House B5
Chatterton Sq C5
Chatterton St C5
Cheese La B5
Christchurch A4
Christchurch Rd A1
Christmas Steps ✦ A4
Church La B2/B5
Church St B5
City Museum A3
City of Bristol College B3
Clare St B4
Clarence Rd C5
Cliff Rd C1
Clift House Rd C1
Clifton Cathedral (RC) ✝ A2
Clifton Down A1
Clifton Down Rd A1
Clifton Hill B2
Clifton Park A1/A2
Clifton Park Rd A1
Clifton Rd A2
Cliftonwood Cr B2
Cliftonwood Rd B2
Cliftonwood Terr B2
Clifton Vale B1
Cobblestone Mews A1
College Green B3
College Rd A1
College St B3
Colston Almshouses A4
Colston Ave B4
Colston Hall B4
Colston Parade C5
Colston St A4
Commercial Rd C4
Commonwealth Museum B5
Constitution Hill B2
Cooperage La C2
Corn St B4
Cornwallis Ave B1
Cornwallis Cr B1
Coronation Rd C2/C4
Council House B3
Counterslip B5
Courts A4
Create Centre, The ✦ C1
Crosby Row B2
Culver St B3
Cumberland Basin C1
Cumberland Cl C2
Cumberland Rd C2/C3
Dale St A6
David St A6
Dean La C4
Deanery Rd B3
Denmark St B4
Dowry Sq B1
East St A5
Eaton Cr A2
Elmdale Rd A3
Elton Rd A3
Eugene St A4/A6
Exchange, The and St Nicholas' Mkts B4
Fairfax St A4
Fire Station B5
Floating Harbour C3
Foster Almshouses A4
Frayne Rd C1
Frederick Pl A2
Freeland Pl B1
Frogmore St B3
Fry's Hill B2
Gas La B6
Gasferry Rd C3
General Hospital C4
Georgian House B3
Glendale B1
Glentworth Rd B2
Gloucester St A1
Goldney Hall B2
Goldney Rd B1
Gordon Rd A2
Granby Hill B1
Grange Rd A1
Great Ann St A6
Great George St A6/B3
Great George Rd B3
Great Western Way B6
Green St North B1
Green St South B1
Greenay Bush La C2
Greenbank Rd C2
Greville Smyth Park C1
Guildhall A4
Guinea St C4
Hamilton Rd C3
Hanbury Rd A2
Hanover Pl C2
Harbour Way B3
Harley Pl A1
Haymarket A5
Hensman's Hill B1
High St B4
Highbury Villas A3
Hill St B3
Hill St C6
Hippodrome B4
Hopechapel Hill B1
Horfield Rd A4
Horton St B6
Host St A4
Hotwell Rd B1/B2
Houlton St A6
Howard Rd C3
Ice Rink B4
IMAX Cinema B4
Information Ctr B4
Islington Rd C3
Jacob St A5/A6
Jacob's Wells Rd B2
John Carr's Terr B2
John Wesley's Chapel A5
Joy Hill B1
Jubilee St B6
Kensington Pl A2
Kilkenny St B6
King St B4
Kingsland Rd B6
Kingston Rd C3
Lamb St A6
Lansdown Rd A2
Lawford St A6
Lawfords Gate A6
Leighton Rd C3
Lewins Mead A4
Lime Rd C2
Little Ann St A6
Little Caroline Pl B1
Little George St A6
Little King St B4
Litfield Rd A1
Llandoger Trow B4
Lloyds' Building, The C3
Lodge St A4
Lord Mayor's Chapel, The B4
Lower Castle St A5
Lower Church La A4
Lower Clifton Hill B2
Lower Guinea St C4
Lower Lamb St B3
Lower Maudlin St A4
Lower Park Rd A4
Lower Sidney St C2
Lucky La C4
Lydstep Terr C3
Mall (Galleries Shopping Centre), The A5
Manilla Rd A1
Mardyke Ferry Rd C2
Maritime Heritage Centre B3
Marlborough Hill A4
Marlborough St A4
Marsh St B4
Mead St C5
Meadow St A5
Merchant Dock B2
Merchant Seamen's Almshouses B4
Merchant St A5
Merchants Rd A1
Merchants Rd C1
Meridian Pl A2
Meridian Vale A2
Merrywood Rd C3
Midland Rd A6
Milford St C3
Millennium Sq B3
Mitchell La B5
Mortimer Rd A1
Murray Rd C4
Myrtle Rd A3
Narrow Plain B5
Narrow Quay B4
Nelson St A4
New Charlotte St C4
New Kingsley Rd B6
New Queen St C5
New St A6
Newfoundland St A5
Newgate A5
Newton St A6
Norland Rd A1
North St C2
Oakfield Gr A2
Oakfield Pl A2
Oakfield Rd A2
Old Bread St B6
Old Market St A6
Old Park Hill A4
Oldfield Rd B1
Orchard Ave B4
Orchard La B4
Orchard St B4
Osbourne Rd C3
Oxford St B6
Park Pl A2
Park Rd C3
Park Row A3
Park St A3
Passage St B5
Pembroke Gr A2
Pembroke Rd A2
Pembroke Rd C3
Pembroke St A5
Penn St A5
Pennywell Rd A6
Percival Rd A1
Pero's Bridge B4
Perry Rd A4
Pip & Jay A5
Plimsoll Bridge B1
Police Sta A4/A6
Polygon Rd B1
Portland St A1
Portwall La B5
Post Office A1/A3/A4/A5/A6/B1/B4/C4/C5
Prewett St C5
Prince St B4
Prince St Bridge C4
Princess St C5
Princess Victoria St B1
Priory Rd A3
Pump La C5
Queen Charlotte St B4
Quakers Friars A5
Quay St A4
Queen Elizabeth Hospital School B2
Queen Sq B4
Queen St A5
Queen's Ave A3
Queen's Parade B3
Queen's Rd A2/A3
Raleigh Rd C2
Randall Rd B2
Redcliffe Backs B5
Redcliffe Bridge B4
Redcliffe Hill C5
Redcliffe Parade C4
Redcliffe St B5
Redcliffe Way B5
Redcross La A6
Redcross St A6
Redgrave Theatre A1
Red Lodge A4
Regent St B1
Richmond Hill A2
Richmond Hill Ave A2
Richmond La A2
Richmond Park Rd A2
Richmond St C6
Richmond Terr A2
River St A6
Rownham Mead B2
Royal Fort Rd A3
Royal Park A2
Royal West of England Academy A3
Royal York Cr B1
Royal York Villas B1
Rupert St A4
Russ St B6
St Andrew's Walk B2
St George's B3
St George's Rd B3
St James A4
St John's A4
St John's Rd C4
St Luke's Rd C5
St Mary Redcliffe C5
St Mary's Hospital A3
St Matthias Park A6
St Michael's Hill A3
St Michael's Hospital A4
St Michael's Park A3
St Nicholas St B4
St Paul St A5
St Paul's Rd A2
St Peter's (ruin) A5
St Philip's Bridge B5
St Philips Rd A6
St Stephen's B4
St Stephen's St B4
St Thomas St B5
St Thomas the Martyr B5
Sandford Rd B1
Sargent St C5
Saville Pl B1
Ship La C5
Silver St A4
Sion Hill A1
Small St A4
Smeaton Rd C1
Somerset Sq C5
Somerset St C5
Southernhay Ave B2
Southville Rd C4
Spike Island Artspace C2
Spring St C5
SS Great Britain and The Matthew B2
Stackpool Rd C3
Staight St B6
Stillhouse La C4
Stracey Rd C2
Stratton St A5
Sydney Row C2
Tankard's Cl A3
Temple Back B5
Temple Boulevard B5
Temple Bridge B5
Temple Church B5
Temple Circus B5
Temple Gate C5
Temple St B5
Temple Way B5
Terrell St A4
The Arcade A5
The Fosseway A2
The Grove B4
The Horsefair A5
The Mall A1
Theatre Royal B4
Thomas La B5
Three Kings of Cologne A4
Three Queens La B5
Tobacco Factory, The C2
Tower Hill B5
Tower La A4
Trenchard St A4
Triangle South A3
Triangle West A3
Trinity Rd A6
Trinity St A6
Tucker St A5
Tyndall Ave A3
Union St A5
Union St B6
Unity St A6
Unity St B3
University of Bristol A3
University Rd A3
Upper Maudlin St A4
Upper Perry Hill C3
Upper Byron Pl A3
Upton Rd C2
Valentine Bridge B6
Victoria Gr C5
Victoria Rd C6
Victoria Rooms A2
Victoria Sq A2
Victoria St B5
Vyvyan Rd A1
Vyvyan Terr A1
Wade St A6
Walter St C2
Wapping Rd C4
Water La B5
Waterloo Rd A6
Waterloo St A1
Waterloo St A6
Watershed, The ✦ B4
Welling Terr B1
Wellington Rd A6
Welsh Back B4
West Mall A1
West St A6
Westfield Pl A1
Wetherell Pl A2
Whitehouse Pl C5
Whitehouse St C5
Whiteladies Rd A2
Whitson St A4
William St C5
Willway St C5
Windsor Pl B1
Windsor Terr B1
Wine St A4
Woodland Rise A3
Woodland Rd A3
Worcester Rd A1
Worcester Terr A1
YHA B4
York Gdns B1
York Pl A2
York Rd C5

Bury St Edmunds 177

Abbey Gardens B3
Abbey Gate B3
Abbeygate St B2
Albert Cr B1
Albert St B1
Ambulance Sta C1
Angel Hill B2
Angel La B2
Anglian Lane A1
Arc Shopping Centre B2
Athenaeum C2
Baker's La C3
Beetons Way A1
Bishops Rd B2
Bloomfield St B2
Bridewell La C2
Bullen Cl C1
Bury St Edmunds A2
Bury St Edmunds County Upper School A1
Bury St Edmunds Leisure Centre B1
Bury Town FC B3
Bus Station B2
Butter Mkt B2
Cannon St B2
Castle Rd C1
Cemetery C1
Chalk Rd (N) B1
Chalk Rd (S) B1
Church Row B2
Churchgate St C2
Citizens Advice Bureau B2
College St C2
Compiegne Way A3
Corn Exchange, The B2
Cornfield Rd B1
Cotton Lane B3
Courts B2
Covent Garden C2
Crown St C3
Cullum Rd C2
Eastern Way A3
Eastgate St B3
Enterprise Business Park A2
Etna Rd A2
Eyre Cl C2
Fire Station B1
Friar's Lane C2
Gage Cl A1
Garland St B2
Greene King Brewery C3
Grove Park B1
Grove Rd B1
Guildhall C2
Guildhall St C2
Hatter St C2
High Baxter St B2
Honey Hill C2
Hospital Rd C1/C2
Ickworth Dr C1
Information Ctr B2
Ipswich St A2
King Edward VI School A1
King's Rd C1/B2
Library B2
Long Brackland A2
Looms La B2
Lwr Baxter St B2
Malthouse La A2
Manor House C3
Maynewater La C3
Mill Rd C1
Mill Rd (South) C1
Minden Close B3
Moyses Hall B2
Mustow St B3
Norman Tower C3
Northgate Ave A2
Northgate St B2
Nutshell, The B2
Osier Rd A2
Out Northgate A2
Out Risbygate B1
Out Westgate C2
Parkway B1/C2
Parkway B1
Peckham St B2
Petticoat La C1
Phoenix Day Hospital C1
Pinners Way C1
Police Station C3
Post Office B2/B3
Pump La B2
Queen's Rd B1
Raingate St C3
Raynham Rd A1
Retail Park C1
Risbygate St B1/B2
Robert Boby Way C2
St Andrew's St North B2
St Andrew's St South B2
St Botolph's La C3
St Edmunds Hospital (private) C3
St Edmund's C2
St Edmund's Abbey (Remains) ✦ B3
St Edmundsbury ✝ C3
St John's St B2
St Marys C3
School Hall La B2
Shillitoe Cl C1
Shire Halls & Magistrates Ct C3
South Cl C3
Southgate St C3
Sparhawk St C3
Spring Lane B1
Springfield Rd B1
Station Hill A2
Swan La C3
Tayfen Rd B2
The Vinefields B3
Theatre Royal C3
Thingoe Hill A2
Victoria St B1
War Memorial ✦ C1
Well St B2
West Suffolk College B1
Westgarth Gdns C1
Westgate St C2
Whiting St C2
York Rd B1
York Terr B1

Cambridge 178

Abbey Rd A3
ADC A2
Anglia Ruskin University B3
Archaeology & Anthropology B2
Art Gallery A1
Arts Picture House B2
Arts Theatre B1
Auckland Rd A3
Bateman St C2
BBC C3
Benet St B1
Bradmore St B3
Bridge St A1
Broad St B3
Brookside C2
Brunswick Terr A3
Burleigh St B3
Bus Station B2
Butt Green A2
Cambridge Contemporary Art Gallery B1
Castle Mound A1
Castle St A1
Chesterton La A1
Christ's (Coll) B2
Christ's Pieces B2
City Rd B3
Clare (Coll) B1
Clarendon St B2
Coe Fen C2
Coronation St C2
Corpus Christi (Coll) B1
Council Offices C3
Cross St C3
Crusoe Bridge C1
Darwin (Coll) C1
Devonshire Rd C3
Downing (Coll) C2
Downing St B2
Earl St B2
East Rd B3
Eden St B3
Elizabeth Way A3
Elm St B2
Emery St B3
Emmanuel (Coll) B2
Emmanuel Rd B2
Emmanuel St B2
Fair St A3
Fenners Physical Education Centre C3
Fire Station B3
Fitzroy St A3
Fitzwilliam Museum C2
Fitzwilliam St C2
Folk Museum A1
Glisson Rd C3
Gonville & Caius (Coll) B1
Gonville Place C2
Grafton Centre A3
Grand Arcade B2
Gresham Rd C3
Green St B1
Guest Rd B3
Guildhall B2
Harvey Rd C3
Hills Rd C3
Hobson St B2
Hughes Hall (Coll) B3
Information Ctr B2
James St A3
Jesus (Coll) A2
Jesus Green A2
Jesus La A2
Jesus Terr B3
John St B3
Kelsey Kerridge Sports Centre B3
King St A2
King's (Coll) B1
King's College Chapel B1
King's Parade B1
Lammas Land Recreation Ground C1
Lensfield Rd C2
Little St Mary's La B1
Lyndewod Rd C3
Magdalene (Coll) A1
Magdalene St A1
Maid's Causeway A3
Malcolm St A2
Market Hill B1
Market St B1
Mathematical Bridge B1
Mawson Rd C3
Midsummer Common A3
Mill La B1
Mill Rd B3
Mill St C3
Napier St A3
New Square A2
Newmarket Rd A3
Newnham Rd C1
Norfolk St B3
Northampton St A1
Norwich St C2
Orchard St B2
Panton St C2
Paradise Nature Reserve C1
Paradise St B3
Park Parade A1
Park St A2
Park Terr B2
Parker St B2
Parker's Piece B2
Parkside B3
Parkside Pools B3
Parsonage St A3
Pemberton Terr C2
Pembroke (Coll) B2
Pembroke St B1
Perowne St B3
Peterhouse (Coll) C1
Petty Cury B2
Police Station B3
Post Office A1/A3/B2/B3/C1/C2/C3
Queens' (Coll) B1
Queen's La B1
Queen's Rd B1
Regent St B2
Regent Terr B2
Ridley Hall (Coll) C1
Riverside A3
Round Church, The A1
Russell St C2
St Andrew's St B2
St Benet's B1
St Catharine's (Coll) B1
St Eligius St C2
St John's (Coll) A1
St Mary's B1
St Paul's Rd C3
Saxon St C2
Scott Polar Institute & Museum C2
Sedgwick Museum B2
Sheep's Green C1
Shire Hall A1
Sidgwick Ave C1
Sidney St A2
Sidney Sussex (Coll) A2
Silver St B1
Station Rd C3
Tenison Ave C3
Tenison Rd C3
Tennis Court Rd B2
The Backs B1
The Fen Causeway C1
Thompson's La A1
Trinity (Coll) A1
Trinity Hall (Coll) B1
Trinity St B1
Trumpington Rd C2
Trumpington St B1
Union Rd C2
University Botanic Gardens C2
Victoria Ave A2
Victoria St B2
Warkworth St B3
Warkworth Terr B3
Wesley House (Coll) A2
West Rd B1
Westcott House (Coll) A2
Westminster (Coll) A1
Whipple B2
Willis Rd B3
Willow Walk A2
Zoology B2

Canterbury 178

Artillery St B2
Barton Mill Rd A3
Beaconsfield Rd A1
Beverley Rd A1
Bingley's Island B1
Black Griffin La B1
Broad Oak Rd A2
Broad St B2
Brymore Rd A3
Burgate B2
Bus Station C2
Canterbury College C3
Canterbury East C1
Canterbury Tales, The ✦ B2
Canterbury West A1
Castle C1
Castle Row C1
Castle St C1
Cathedral ✝ B2
Chaucer Rd A3
Christ Church University B3
Christchurch Gate ✦ B2
City Council Offices A3
City Wall B2
Coach Park A2
College Rd B3
Cossington Rd C2
Court B2
Craddock Rd A3
Crown & County Courts B3
Dane John Gdns C2
Dane John Mound ✦ C1
Deanery B2
Dover St C2
Duck La B2
Eastbridge Hospital B1
Edgar Rd B3
Ersham Rd C3
Ethelbert Rd C3
Fire Station C2
Forty Acres Rd A1
Gordon Rd C1
Greyfriars ✦ B1
Guildford Rd C1
Havelock St B2
Heaton Rd C1
High St B2
HM Prison B3
Information Ctr A2/B2
Ivy La B2
Ivy Pl C1
King St B2
King's School B2/B3
King's School Leisure Facilities A2
Kingsmead Leisure Centre A2
Kingsmead Rd A2
Kirby's La B1
Lansdown Rd C2
Lime Kiln Rd C1
Longport B3
Lower Chantry La C3
Mandeville Rd A1
Market Way A2
Marlowe Arcade B2
Marlowe Ave C2
Marlowe Theatre B2
Martyrs Field Rd C1
Mead Way B1
Military Rd B2
Monastery St B2
Museum of Canterbury (Rupert Bear Museum) B1
New Dover Rd C3
Norman Rd C2
North Holmes Rd B3
North La B1
Northgate A2
Nunnery Fields C2
Nunnery Rd C2
Oaten Hill C2
Odeon Cinema C2
Old Dover Rd C2
Old Palace B2
Old Ruttington La B2
Old Weavers B2
Orchard St B1
Oxford Rd C1
Palace St B2
Pilgrims Way C3
Pin Hill C1
Pine Tree Ave A1
Police Station C2
Post Office B2/C1/C2
Pound La B1
Puckle La C2
Raymond Ave C2
Registry Office A2
Rheims Way B1
Rhodaus Cl C2
Rhodaus Town C2
Roman Museum B2
Roper Gateway A1
Roper Rd A1
Rose La B2
Royal Museum B2
St Augustine's Abbey (remains) ✝ B3
St Augustine's Rd C3
St Dunstan's A1
St Dunstan's St A1
St George's Pl C2
St George's St B2
St George's Tower ✦ B2
St Gregory's Rd B3
St John's Hospital A2
St Margaret's St B2
St Martin's B3
St Martin's Ave B3
St Martin's Rd B3
St Michael's Rd A1
St Mildred's C1
St Peter's Gr B1
St Peter's La B2
St Peter's Pl B1
St Peter's St B1
St Radigunds St B2
St Stephen's Ct A1
St Stephen's Path A1
St Stephen's Rd A2
Salisbury Rd A1
Simmonds Rd C1
Spring La C3
Station Rd West B1
Stour St B1
Sturry Rd A3
The Causeway A2
The Friars B2
Tourtel Rd A3
Tudor Rd C1
Union St B2
University for the Creative Arts C3
Vernon Pl C2
Victoria Rd C1
Watling St B2
Westgate Gdns B1
Westgate Towers B1
Whitefriars B2
Whitehall Gdns B1
Whitehall Rd B1
Wincheap C1
York Rd C1
Zealand Rd C2

Cardiff *Caerdydd* 178

Adam St B3
Alexandra Gdns A2
Allerton St C1
Arran St A3
ATRiuM (Univ. of Glamorgan) C3
Beauchamp St C1
Bedford St A3
Blackfriars Priory ✝ B1
Boulevard De Nantes B2
Brains Brewery C2
Brook St B1
Bus Station C2
Bute Park B1
Bute St C2
Bute Terr C3
Callaghan Sq C2/C3
Capitol Shopping Centre, The B3
Cardiff Bridge B1
Cardiff Castle B2
Cardiff Central Station C2
Cardiff Centre Trading Estate C3
Cardiff International Arena ✦ C3
Cardiff Rugby Football Ground B1
Cardiff University A1/A2/B3
Cardiff University Student's Union A2
Caroline St C2
Castle Green B2
Castle Mews A1
Castle St (Heol y Castell) B1
Cathays Station A2
Celerity Drive C3
Central Sq C2
Charles St (Heol Siarl) B3
Churchill Way B3
City Hall A2
City Rd A3
Clare Rd C1
Clare St C1
Coburn St A3
Coldstream Terr B1
College Rd A1
Colum Rd A1
Court C2
Court Rd C1
Craiglee Drive C3
Cranbrook St A3
Customhouse St C2
Cyfartha St A3
Despenser Place C1
Despenser St C1
Dinas St C1
Duke St (Heol y Dug) B2
Dumfries Place B3
East Grove A3
Ellen St C3
Fire Station B3
Fitzalan Place B3
Fitzhamon Embankment C1
Fitzhamon La C1
Gloucester St C1
Glynrhondda St A2
Gordon Rd A3
Gorsedd Gdns B2
Green St B1
Greyfriars Rd B2
HM Prison B3
Hafod St C1
Herbert St C3
High St B2
Industrial Estate C3
John St C3
Jubilee St C1
King Edward VII Ave A1
Kingsway (Ffordd y Brenin) B2
Knox Rd B3
Law Courts B2
Library C3
Llanbleddian Gdns A2
Llantwit St A2
Lloyd George Ave C3
Lower Cathedral Rd B1
Lowther Rd A3
Magistrates Court B3
Mansion House A3
Mardy St C1
Mark St B1
Market B2
Mary Ann St C3
Merches Gdns C1
Mill La C2
Millennium Bridge B1
Millennium Plaza Leisure Complex C1
Millennium Stadium C1
Millennium Stadium Tours (Gate 3) ✦ B2
Miskin St A2
Monmouth St C1
Museum Ave A2
Museum Place A2
National Museum of Wales A2
National War Memorial ✦ A2
Neville Place C1
New Theatre B2
Newport Rd B3
Northcote La A3
Northcote St A3
Park Grove A4
Park Place A2
Park St C2
Penarth Rd C2
Pendyris St C1
Plantaganet St C1
Quay St B2
Queen Anne Sq A1
Queen St (Heol y Frenhines) B2
Queen St Station B3
Regimental Museums B2
Rhymney St A3
Richmond Rd A3
Royal Welsh College of Music and Drama A1
Russell St A3
Ruthin Gdns A2
St Andrews Place A2
St David's ✝ B2
St David's 2 C2
St David's Centre B2
St David's Hall ✦ B2
St John The Baptist B2
St Mary St (Heol Eglwys Fair) B2
St Peter's St A3
Salisbury Rd A3
Sandon St B3
Schooner Way C3
Scott Rd C2
Scott St C2
Senghennydd Rd A2
Sherman Theatre A2
Sophia Gardens A1
South Wales Baptist College A3
Stafford Rd C1
Station Terr B3
Stuttgarter Strasse B2
Sussex St C1
Taffs Mead Embankment C1
Talworth St A3
Temple of Peace & Health ✦ A1
The Friary B2
The Hayes B2
The Parade A3
The Walk A3
Treharris St A3
Trinity St B2
Tudor La C1
Tudor St C1
Welsh Assembly Offices A1
Welsh Institute of Sport ✦ A1
West Grove A3
Westgate St (Heol y Porth) B2
Windsor Place B3
Womanby St B2
Wood St C2
Working St B2
Wyeverne Rd A2

Carlisle 178

Abbey St A1
Aglionby St B3
Albion St C3
Alexander St C3
AMF Bowl ✦ C2
Annetwell St A1
Bank St B2
Bitts Park A1
Blackfriars St B2
Blencome St C1
Blunt St C1
Botchergate B2
Boustead's Grassing C2
Bowman St B3
Broad St B3
Bridge St A1
Brook St C3
Brunswick St B2
Bus Station B2
Caldew Bridge A1
Caldew St C1
Carlisle (Citadel) Station B2
Castle A1
Castle St A1
Castle Way A1
Cathedral ✝ A1
Cecil St B2
Chapel St A2
Charles St B3
Charlotte St B1
Chatsworth Square A2
Chiswick St B2
Citadel, The B2
City Walls A1
Civic Centre A2
Clifton St C1
Close St B3
Collingwood St C1
Colville St C1
Colville Terr C1
Court B2
Court St B2
Crosby St B2
Crown St C2
Currock Rd C2

Dacre Rd A1
Dale St C1
Denton St C1
Devonshire Walk A1
Duke's Rd A2
East Dale St C1
East Norfolk St C1
Eden Bridge A2
Edward St B3
Elm St B1
English St B2
Fire Station A2
Fisher St A1
Flower St B3
Freer St C1
Fusehill St B3
Georgian Way A2
Gloucester Rd C3
Golf Course A2
Graham St C1
Grey St B3
Guildhall Mus A2
Halfey's La B3
Hardwicke Circus A2
Hart St B3
Hewson St C2
Howard Pl A3
Howe St B3
Information Ctr A2
James St B2
Junction St B1
King St B2
Lancaster St B2
Lanes Shopping Centre B2
Laserquest B2
Library A2/B1
Lime St B1
Lindisfarne St C3
Linton St B3
Lismore Pl A3
Lismore St B3
London Rd C3
Lonsdale Rd B2
Lord St C3
Lorne Cres B1
Lorne St B1
Lowther St B2
Market Hall A2
Mary St B2
Memorial Bridge A3
Metcalfe St C1
Milbourne St B1
Myddleton St B3
Nelson St C1
Norfolk St C1
Old Town Hall A2
Oswald St C3
Peter St A2
Petteril St B3
Police Station A2
Portland Pl B2
Portland Sq B2
Post Office A2/B2/B3/C1/C3
Princess St C2
Pugin St B1
Red Bank Terr C2
Regent St C3
Richardson St C1
Rickerby Park A3
Rickergate A2
River St B3
Rome St C2
Rydal St B3
St Cuthbert's B2
St Cuthbert's La B2
St James' Park C1
St James' Rd C1
St Nicholas St C3
Sands Centre A2
Scotch St A2
Shaddongate B1
Sheffield St B1
South Henry St B3
South John St C2
South St B3
Spencer St B2
Sports Centre A2
Strand Rd A2
Swimming Baths B2
Sybil St B3
Tait St B2
Thomas St B1
Thomson St C3
Trafalgar St C1
Tullie House Museum A1
Tyne St C3
Viaduct Estate Rd B1
Victoria Pl A2
Victoria Viaduct B2
Vue B2
Warwick Rd B2
Warwick Sq B3
Water St B2
West Walls B1
Westmorland St C1

Chelmsford 178

Ambulance Station B1
Anchor St C1
Anglia Polytechnic University A2
Arbour La A3
Baddow Rd B2/C3
Baker St C1
Barrack Sq B2
Bellmead B2
Bishop Hall La A2
Bishop Rd A2
Bond St B2
Boswells Dr B3
Boudicca Mews C2
Bouverie Rd C2
Bradford St C1
Braemar Ave C1
Brook St A2
Broomfield Rd A1
Burns Cres C2
Bus Station B2
Can Bridge Way B2
Cedar Ave A1
Cedar Ave West A1
Cemetery A1
Cemetery A2
Cemetery C1
Central Park B1
Chelmsford ✝ B2
Chelmsford ⇌ A1
Chichester Dr A3
Chinery Cl A3
Cinema B2
Civic Centre A1
College C1
Cottage Pl A2
County Hall B2
Coval Ave B1
Coval La B1
Coval Wells B1
Cricket Ground B2
Crown Court B2
Duke St B2
Elm Rd C1
Elms Dr A1
Essex Record Office, The B3
Fairfield Rd B1
Falcons Mead B1
George St C2
Glebe Rd A1
Godfrey's Mews C2
Goldlay Ave C3
Goldlay Rd C2
Grove Rd C2
HM Prison A3
Hall St C2
Hamlet Rd C2
Hart St C1
Henry Rd A2
High Bridge Rd B2
High Chelmer Shopping Centre B2
High St B2
Hill Cres B3
Hill Rd Sth B3
Hill Rd B3
Hillview Rd A3
Hoffmans Way A2
Hospital B2
Information Ctr B2
Lady La C2
Langdale Gdns C3
Legg St B2
Library A1
Library B2
Library C1
Lionfield Terr A3
Lower Anchor St C1
Lynmouth Ave C2
Lynmouth Gdns C3
Magistrates Court B2
Maltese Rd A1
Manor Rd C2
Marconi Rd A2
Market B2
Market Rd B2
Marlborough Rd C1
Meadows Shopping Centre, The B2
Meadowside A3
Mews Ct C2
Mildmay Rd C2
Moulsham Dr C2
Moulsham Mill C3
Moulsham St C1/C2
Navigation Rd B3
New London Rd B2/C1
New St A2/B2
New Writtle St C1
Nursery Rd C2
Orchard St C2
Park Rd B1
Parker Rd C2
Parklands Dr A3
Parkway A1/B1/B2
Police Station A2
Post Office A3/B2/C2
Primrose Hill A1
Prykes Dr B1
Queen St C1
Queen's Rd B3
Railway St A1
Rainsford Rd A1
Ransomes Way A2
Rectory La A2
Regina Rd A2
Riverside Leisure Centre B2
Rosebery Rd C2
Rothesay Ave C1
St John's Rd C2
Sandringham Pl B3
Seymour St B1
Shrublands Cl B3
Southborough Rd C1
Springfield Basin B3
Springfield Rd A3/B2/B3
Stapleford Cl C1
Swiss Ave A1
Telford Pl A3
The Meades B1
Tindal St B2
Townfield St A1
Trinity Rd B3
University B1
Upper Bridge Rd C1
Upper Roman Rd C2
Van Dieman's Rd C3
Viaduct Rd B1
Vicarage Rd C1
Victoria Rd A2
Victoria Rd South B2
Vincents Rd C2
Waterloo La B2
Weight Rd B3
Westfield Ave A1
Wharf Rd B3
Writtle Rd C1
YMCA A2
York Rd C1

Cheltenham 178

Albert Rd A3
Albion St B3
All Saints Rd B3
Ambrose St B2
Andover Rd C1
Art Gallery & Museum B2
Axiom Centre B3
Back Montpellier Terr C2
Bandstand C2
Bath Pde B2
Bath Rd C2
Bays Hill Rd C1
Beechwood Place Shopping Centre B3
Bennington St B2
Berkeley St B3
Brewery A2
Brunswick St South A2
Bus Station B2
CAB B2
Carlton St B3
Central Cross Road A3
Cheltenham College C2
Cheltenham FC A3
Cheltenham General (A & E) C3
Christchurch Rd B1
Cineworld A2
Clarence Rd A2
Clarence Sq A2
Clarence St B2
Cleeveland St A1
Coach Park A2
College Baths Road C3
College Rd C2
Colletts Dr A1
Corpus St C3
Devonshire St A2
Douro Rd B1
Duke St B3
Dunalley Pde A2
Dunalley St A2
Everyman B2
Evesham Rd A3
Fairview Rd B3
Fairview St A3
Fire Station C3
Folly La A2
Gloucester Rd A1
Grosvenor St B3
Grove St A1
Gustav Holst A3
Hanover St A2
Hatherley St C1
Henrietta St A2
Hewlett Rd B3
High St B2/B3
Hudson St A2
Imperial Gdns C2
Imperial La B2
Imperial Sq C2
Information Ctr B2
Keynsham Rd C3
King St A2
Knapp Rd B2
Ladies College B2
Lansdown Cr C1
Lansdown Rd C1
Leighton Rd B3
London Rd C3
Lypiatt Rd C1
Malvern Rd B1
Manser St A2
Market St A1
Marle Hill Pde A2
Marle Hill Rd A2
Millbrook St A1
Milsom St A2
Montpellier Gdns C2
Montpellier Gr C2
Montpellier Pde C2
Montpellier Spa Rd C2
Montpellier St C1
Montpellier Terr C2
Montpellier Walk C2
New St B2
North Pl B2
Old Bath Rd C3
Oriel Rd B2
Overton Park Rd B1
Overton Rd B1
Oxford St C3
Parabola Rd B1
Park Pl C1
Park St A1
Pittville Circus A3
Pittville Cr A3
Pittville Lawn A3
Playhouse B2
Police Station B1/C1
Portland St B3
Post Office B2/C2
Prestbury Rd A3
Prince's Rd C1
Priory St B3
Promenade B2
Queen St A1
Recreation Ground A2
Regent Arcade B2
Regent St B2
Rodney Rd B2
Royal Cr B2
Royal Wells Rd B2
St George's Pl B2
St Georges Rd B1
St Gregory's B2
St James St B3
St John's Ave B3
St Luke's Rd C2
St Margarets Rd A2
St Mary's B2
St Matthew's B2
St Paul's La A2
St Paul's Rd A2
St Paul's St A2
St Stephen's Rd C1
Sandford Lido C3
Sandford Mill Road C3
Sandford Park C3
Sandford Rd C2
Selkirk St A3
Sherborne Pl B3
Sherborne St B3
Suffolk Pde C2
Suffolk Rd C1
Suffolk Sq C1
Sun St A1
Swindon Rd B2
Sydenham Villas Rd C3
Tewkesbury Rd A1
The Courtyard B1
Thirlstaine Rd C2
Tivoli Rd C1
Tivoli St C1
Town Hall & Theatre B2
Townsend St A1
Trafalgar St C2
Union St B3
University of Gloucestershire (Francis Close Hall) A2
University of Gloucestershire (Hardwick) A1
Victoria Pl B3
Victoria St A2
Vittoria Walk C2
Wel Pl B2
Wellesley Rd A2
Wellington Rd A3
Wellington Sq A3
Wellington St B2
West Drive A3
Western Rd B1
Winchcombe St B3

Chester 179

Abbey Gateway A2
Appleyards La C3
Bedward Row B1
Beeston View C3
Bishop Lloyd's Palace B2
Black Diamond St A2
Bottoms La C3
Boughton B3
Bouverie St A1
Bridge St B2
Bridgegate C2
British Heritage Centre B2
Brook St A3
Brown's La C2
Bus Station B2
Cambrian Rd A1
Canal St A2
Carrick Rd C1
Castle B2
Castle Dr C2
Cathedral ✝ B2
Catherine St A1
Chester ⇌ A3
Cheyney Rd A1
Chichester St A1
City Rd A3
City Walls B1/B2
City Walls Rd B1
Cornwall St A2
County Hall C2
Cross Hey C3
Cuppin St B2
Curzon Park North C1
Curzon Park South C1
Dee Basin A1
Dee La B3
Delamere St A2
Dewa Roman Experience B2
Duke St B2
Eastgate B2
Eastgate St B2
Eaton Rd C2
Edinburgh Way C3
Elizabeth Cr B3
Fire Station A2
Foregate St B2
Frodsham St B2
Gamul House B2
Garden La A1
Gateway Theatre B2
George St A2
Gladstone Ave A1
God's Providence House B2
Gorse Stacks A2
Greenway St C2
Grosvenor Bridge C1
Grosvenor Museum B2
Grosvenor Park B3
Grosvenor Precinct B2
Grosvenor Rd C1
Grosvenor St B2
Groves Rd B3
Guildhall Museum B1
Handbridge C2
Hartington St C3
Hoole Way A2
Hunter St B2
Information Ctr B2
King Charles' Tower A2
King St A2
Library B2
Lightfoot St A3
Little Roodee C2
Liverpool Rd A2
Love St B3
Lower Bridge St B2
Lower Park Rd B3
Lyon St A2
Magistrates Court B2
Meadows La C3
Military Museum C2
Milton St A3
New Crane St B1
Nicholas St B2
Northgate A2
Northgate Arena A2
Northgate St A2
Nun's Rd B1
Old Dee Bridge C2
Overleigh Rd C2
Park St B2
Police Station B2
Post Office A2/A3/B2/C2
Princess St B2
Queen St B2
Queen's Park Rd C3
Queen's Rd A3
Race Course B1
Raymond St A1
River La C2
Roman Amphitheatre & Gardens B2
Roodee, The (Chester Racecourse) B1
Russell St A3
St Anne St A2
St George's Cr C3
St Martin's Gate A1
St Martin's Way B1
St Oswalds Way A2
Saughall Rd A1
Sealand Rd A1
South View Rd A1
Stanley Palace B1
Station Rd A3
Steven St A3
The Bars B3
The Cross B2
The Groves B3
The Meadows B3
Tower Rd B1
Town Hall B2
Union St B3
Vicar's La B2
Victoria Cr C3
Victoria Rd A2
Walpole St A1
Water Tower St A1
Watergate B1
Watergate St B2
Whipcord La A1
White Friars B2
York St B3

Chichester 179

Adelaide Rd A3
Alexandra Rd A3
Arts Centre B2
Ave de Chartres B1/B2
Barlow Rd A1
Basin Rd C2
Beech Ave B1
Bishops Palace Gardens B2
Bishopsgate Walk A3
Bramber Rd C3
Broyle Rd A2
Bus Station B2
Caledonian Rd B3
Cambrai Ave B3
Canal Wharf C2
Canon La B2
Cathedral ✝ B2
Cavendish St A1
Cawley Rd B2
Cedar Dr A1
Chapel St A2
Cherry Orchard Rd C3
Chichester By-Pass C2/C3
Chichester Festival A2
Chichester ⇌ B2
Churchside A2
Cinema B3/C1
City Walls B2
Cleveland Rd B3
College La A2
Coll. Of Science & Technology B1
Cory Cl C2
Council Offices B2
County Hall B2
Courts B2
District B2
Duncan Rd A1
Durnford Cl A1
East Pallant B2
East Row B2
East St B2
East Walls B3
Eastland Rd C3
Ettrick Cl B3
Ettrick Rd B3
Exton Rd C3
Fire Station A2
Football Ground A2
Franklin Pl A2
Friary (Rems. of) A2
Garland Cl C3
Green La A3
Grove Rd C3
Guilden Rd B3
Guildhall A2
Hawthorn Cl A1
Hay Rd C3
Henty Gdns B1
Herald Dr C3
Information Ctr B2
John's St B2
Joys Croft A3
Jubilee Pk A3
Jubilee Rd A3
Juxon Cl B1
Kent Rd A3
King George Gdns A2
King's Ave C2
Kingsham Ave C3
Kingsham Rd C2
Laburnum Gr B2
Leigh Rd C1
Lennox Rd A3
Lewis Rd A3
Library B2
Lion St B2
Litten Terr A3
Little London B2
Lyndhurst Rd B3
Market B3
Market Ave B2
Market Cross B2
Market Rd B3
Martlet Cl C2
Melbourne Rd A3
Mount La B1
New Park Rd A3
Newlands La A1
North Pallant B2
North St A2
North Walls A2
Northgate A2
Oak Ave A1
Oak Cl A1
Oaklands Park A2
Oaklands Way A2
Orchard Ave A1
Orchard St A1
Ormonde Ave B3
Pallant House B2
Parchment St A1
Parklands Rd A1/B1
Peter Weston Pl B3
Police Station C2
Post Office A1/B2/B3
Priory La A2
Priory Park A2
Priory Rd A2
Queen's Ave C1
Riverside A3
Roman Amphitheatre B3
St Cyriacs A2
St Pancras A3
St Paul's Rd A2
St Richard's Hospital (A + E) A3
Shamrock Cl A3
Sherbourne Rd A1
Somerstown A2
South Bank C2
South Pallant B2
South St B2
Southgate B2
Spitalfield La A3
Stirling Rd B3
Stockbridge Rd C1/C2
Swanfield Dr A3
Terminus Industrial Estate C1
Terminus Rd C1
The Hornet B3
The Litten A3
Tower St A2
Tozer Way A3
Turnbull Rd A3
Upton Rd C1
Velyn Ave B3
Via Ravenna B1
Walnut Ave A1
West St B2
Westgate B1
Westgate Fields B1
Westgate Leisure Centre B1
Weston Ave C1
Whyke Cl C3
Whyke La B3
Whyke Rd C3
Winden Ave B3

Colchester 179

Abbey Gateway ✝ C2
Albert St A1
Albion Grove C2
Alexandra Rd C1
Artillery St C3
Arts Centre B1
Balkerne Hill B1
Barrack St C3
Beaconsfield Rd C1
Beche Rd C3
Bergholt Rd A1
Bourne Rd C3
Brick Kiln Rd A1
Bristol Rd B2
Broadlands Way A3
Brook St B3
Bury Cl B2
Butt Rd C1
Camp Folley North C2
Camp Folley South C2
Campion Rd C2
Cannon St C3
Canterbury Rd C2
Castle B2
Castle Park B2
Castle Rd B2
Catchpool Rd A1
Causton Rd B1
Cavalry Barracks C1
Chandlers Row C3
Circular Rd East C2
Circular Rd North C1
Circular Rd West C1
Clarendon Way A1
Claudius Rd C2
Clock B1
Colchester Camp Abbey Field C1
Colchester Institute B1
Colchester ⇌ A1
Colchester Town ⇌ C2
Colne Bank Ave A1
Colne View Retail Park A2
Compton Rd A3
Cowdray Ave A1/A2
Cowdray Centre, The A2
Crouch St B1
Crowhurst Rd B1
Culver Centre B1
Culver St East B2
Culver St West B1
Dilbridge Rd A3
East Hill B2
East St B3
East Stockwell St B1
Eld La B1
Essex Hall Rd A1
Exeter Dr B2
Fairfax Rd C2
Fire Station A2
Flagstaff Rd C1
George St B2
Gladstone Rd C2
Golden Noble Hill C2
Goring Rd A3
Granville Rd C3
Greenstead Rd B3
Guildford Rd B2
Harsnett Rd C3
Harwich Rd B3
Head St B1
High St B1/B2
High Woods Country Park A2
Hythe Hill C3
Information Ctr B2
Ipswich Rd A3
Kendall Rd C3
Kimberley Rd C3
King Stephen Rd C3
Le Cateau Barracks C1
Leisure World A2
Library B1
Lincoln Way B2
Lion Walk Shopping Centre B1
Lisle Rd C2
Lucas Rd C2
Magdalen Green C3
Magdalen St C2
Maidenburgh St B2
Maldon Rd C1
Manor Rd B1
Margaret Rd A1
Mason Rd A2
Mercers Way A1
Mersea Rd C2
Meyrick Cr C2
Mile End Rd A1
Military Rd C2
Mill St C2
Minories B2
Moorside B3
Morant Rd C3
Napier Rd C2
Natural History B2
New Town Rd C2
Norfolk Cr A3
North Hill B1
North Station Rd A1
Northgate St B1
Nunns Rd B1
Odeon B1
Old Coach Rd B3
Old Heath Rd C3
Osborne St B2
Petrolea Cl A1
Police Station C1
Popes La B1
Port La C3
Post Office A1/B1/B2/C2/C3
Priory St B2
Queen St B2
Rawstorn Rd B1
Rebon St C3
Recreation Rd C3
Ripple Way A3
Roman Rd B2
Roman Wall B2
Romford Cl A3
Rosebery Ave B2
St Andrews Ave B3
St Andrews Gdns B3
St Botolph St B2
St Botolphs B2
St John's Abbey (site of) ✝ C2
St John's St B1
St John's Walk Shopping Centre B1
St Leonards Rd C3
St Marys Fields B1
St Peters B1
St Peter's St B1
Salisbury Ave C1
Serpentine Walk A1
Sheepen Pl B1
Sheepen Rd B1
Sir Isaac's Walk B1
Smythies Ave B2
South St C1
South Way C1
Sports Way A2
Suffolk Cl A3
Town Hall B1
Valentine Dr A3
Victor Rd C3
Wakefield Cl B2
Wellesley Rd C1
Wells Rd B2/B3
West St C1
West Stockwell St B1
Weston Rd C3
Westway A1
Wickham Rd C1
Wimpole Rd C3
Winchester Rd C2
Winnock Rd C2
Wolfe Ave C2
Worcester Rd B2

Coventry 179

Abbots La A1
Albany Rd B1
Alma St B3
Art Faculty B3
Asthill Grove C2
Bablake School A1
Barras La A1/B1
Barrs Hill School A1
Belgrade B2
Bishop Burges St A2
Bond's Hospital B1
Broad Gate B2
Broadway C1
Bus Station A3
Butts Radial B1
Canal Basin A2
Canterbury St A3
Cathedral ✝ B3
Chester St A1
Cheylesmore Manor House B2
Christ Church Spire B2
City Walls & Gates A2
Corporation St B2
Council House B2
Coundon Rd A1
Coventry & Warwickshire Hospital (A&E) A2
Coventry Station ⇌ C2
Coventry Transport Museum A2
Cox St A3
Croft Rd B1
Dalton Rd C1
Deasy Rd C3
Earl St B2
Eaton Rd C2
Fairfax St B2
Foleshill Rd A2
Ford's Hospital B2
Fowler Rd A1
Friars Rd C2
Gordon St C1
Gosford St B3
Greyfriars Green B2
Greyfriars Rd B2
Gulson Rd B3
Hales St A2
Harnall Lane East A3
Harnall Lane West A2
Herbert Art Gallery & Museum B3
Hertford St B2
Hewitt Ave A1
High St B2
Hill St B1
Holy Trinity B2
Holyhead Rd A1
Howard St A3
Huntingdon Rd C1
Information Ctr B2
Jordan Well B3
King Henry VIII School C1
Lady Godiva Statue B2
Lamb St A2
Leicester Row A2
Library B2
Little Park St B2
London Rd C3
Lower Ford St B3
Magistrates & Crown Courts B2
Manor House Drive B2
Manor Rd C2
Market B2
Martyr's Memorial C2
Meadow St B1
Meriden St A1
Michaelmas Rd C2
Middleborough Rd A1
Mile La C3
Millennium Place A2
Much Park St B3
Naul's Mill Park A1
New Union B2
Park Rd C2
Parkside C3
Police HQ B2
Post Office B2
Primrose Hill St A3
Priory Gardens & Visitor Centre B2
Priory St B3
Puma Way C3
Quarryfield La C3
Queen's Rd B1
Quinton Rd C2
Radford Rd A2
Raglan St B3
Retail Park C1
Ringway (Hill Cross) A1
Ringway (Queens) B1
Ringway (Rudge) B1
Ringway (St Johns) B3
Ringway (St Nicholas) A2
Ringway (St Patricks) C2
Ringway (Swanswell) A2
Ringway (Whitefriars) B3
St John St B2
St John The Baptist B2
St Nicholas St A2
Skydome B1
Spencer Ave C1
Spencer Park C1
Spon St B1
Sports Centre B3
Stoney Rd C2
Stoney Stanton Rd A3
Swanswell Pool A3
Sydney Stringer School A3
Technical College B1
Technology Park C3
The Precinct B2
Theatre B1
Thomas Landsdail St C2
Tomson Ave A1
Top Green C1
Toy Museum B3
Trinity St B2
University B3
Upper Hill St A1
Upper Well St A2
Victoria St A3
Vine St A3
Warwick Rd C2
Waveley Rd B1
Westminster Rd C1
White St A3
Windsor St B1

Derby 179

Abbey St C1
Agard St B1
Albert St B2
Albion St B2
Ambulance Station B1
Arthur St A1
Ashlyn Rd B3
Assembly Rooms B2
Babington La C2
Becket St B1
Belper Rd A1
Bold La B1
Bradshaw Way C2
Bradshaw Way Retail Park C2
Bridge St B1
Brook St B1
Burrows Walk C2
Burton Rd C1
Bus Station B2
Caesar St A2
Canal St C3
Carrington St C3
Cathedral ✝ B2
Cathedral Rd B1
Charnwood St C2
Chester Green Rd A2
City Rd A2
Clarke St A3
Cock Pitt B3
Council House B2
Courts B1
Cranmer Rd B3
Crompton St C1
Crown & County Courts B2
Crown Walk C2
Curzon St B1
Darley Grove A1
Derby ⇌ C3
Derbyshire County Cricket Ground B3
Derwent Business Centre A2
Derwent St B2
Devonshire Walk C2
Drewry La C1
Duffield Rd A1
Duke St A2
Dunton Cl B3
Eagle Market C2
Eastgate B3
East St B2
Exeter St B2
Farm St C1
Ford St B1
Forester St C1
Fox St A2
Friar Gate B1
Friary St B1
Full St B2
Gerard St C1
Gower St C2
Green La C2
Grey St C1
Guildhall B2
Harcourt St C1
Highfield Rd A1
Hill La C2
Information Ctr B2
Iron Gate B2
John St C3
Joseph Wright Centre B1
Kedleston Rd A1
Key St B2
King Alfred St C1
King St A1
Kingston St A1
Leopold St C2
Library B1
Liversage St C3
Lodge La B1
London Rd C2
London Rd Community Hospital C2
Macklin St C1
Mansfield Rd A2
Market B2
Market Pl B2
May St C1
Meadow La B3
Melbourne St C2
Midland Rd C3
Monk St C1
Morledge B2
Mount St C1
Museum and Art Gallery B1
Noble St C3
North Parade A1
North St A1
Nottingham Rd B3
Osmaston Rd C2
Otter St A1
Park St C3
Parker St A1
Pickfords House B1
Playhouse C2
Police HQ A2
Police Station B2
Post Office A1/A2/B1/B2/C2/C3
Prime Enterprise Park A2
Prime Parkway A2
Queens Leisure Centre B1
Racecourse A3
Railway Terr C3
Register Office B2
Sacheverel St C2
Sadler Gate B1
St Alkmund's Way B1/B2
St Helens House A1
St Mary's A1
St Mary's Bridge A2

Spicer Rd B3
Sports Centre A3
Summerland St A3
Swimming Pool B3
Sydney Rd C1
Tan La C2
The Quay C2
Thornton Hill A2
Topsham Rd C3
Tucker's Hall 🏛 B1
Tudor St B1
Velwell Rd A1
Verney St A3
Water La C1/C2
Weirfield Rd C2
Well St A3
West Ave A2
West Grove Rd C3
Western Way A3/B1/B2
Wonford Rd B3/C3
York Rd A2

Fort William 181

Abrach Rd A3
Achintore Rd C1
Alma Rd B2
Am Breun Chamas A2
Ambulance Station A3
An Aird A2
Argyll Rd C1
Argyll Terr C1
Bank St B2
Belford Hospital 🏥 B2
Belford Rd B2/B3
Black Parks A3
Braemore Pl C2
Bruce Pl C2
Bus Station B2
Camanachd Cr A3/B2
Cameron Rd C1
Cameron Sq B1
Carmichael Way A2
Claggan Rd B3
Connochie Rd C1
Cow Hill C3
Creag Dhubh A2
Croft Rd B3
Douglas Pl B2
Dudley Rd B2
Dumbarton Rd C1
Earl of Inverness Rd A3
Fassifern Rd B1
Fort William ⇌ B2
Fort William (Remains) ✦ B2
Glasdrum Rd C1
Glen Nevis Pl B3
Gordon Sq B1
Grange Rd C1
Heather Croft Rd C1
Henderson Row C2
High St B1
Highland Visitor Centre B3
Hill Rd B2
Hospital Belhaven Annexe B3
Information Ctr ℹ A3
Inverlochy Ct A3
Kennedy Rd B2/C2
Library B2
Linnhe Rd B1
Lochaber College A2
Lochaber Leisure Centre B3
Lochiel Rd A3
Lochy Rd A3
Lundavra Cres C1
Lundavra Rd C1
Lundy Rd A3
Mamore Cr B2
Mary St B2
Middle St B1
Montrose Ave A3
Moray Pl C1
Morven Pl C2
Moss Rd B2
Nairn Cres C1
Nevis Bridge B3
Nevis Rd A3
Nevis Sports Centre A2
Nevis Terr B2
North Rd B3
Obelisk B2
Ocean Frontier Underwater Centre A2
Parade Rd B2
Police Station ◘ A3/C1
Post Office ✉ A3/B2
Ross Pl C1
St Andrews ⛪ B2
Shaw Pl B2
Station Brae B1
Studio 🎦 B1
Treig Rd A3
Union Rd C1
Victoria Rd B2
Wades Rd A3
West Highland 🏛 B2
Young Pl B2

Glasgow 181

Admiral St C2
Albert Bridge C5
Albion St B5
Anderston ⇌ B3
Anderston Centre B3
Anderston Quay B3
Arches 🎭 B4
Argyle St A1/A2/B3/B4/B5
Argyle Street ⇌ B5
Argyll Arcade B5
Arlington St A3
Art Gallery and Museum 🏛 A1
Arts Centre 🏛 B3
Ashley St A3
Bain St C6
Baird St A6
Baliol St A3
Ballater St C5
Barras, The (Market) C6
Bath St A3
BBC Scotland/SMG B1
Bell St C6
Bell's Bridge B1
Bentinck St A2
Berkeley St A3
Bishop La B3
Black St A6
Blackburn St C2
Blackfriars St B6
Blantyre St A1
Blythswood Sq A4
Blythswood St B4
Bothwell St B4
Brand St C1
Breadalbane St A2
Bridge St C4
Bridge St (Metro Station) C4
Bridgegate C5
Briggait C5
Broomhill Park A6
Broomielaw B4
Broomielaw Quay Gdns B3
Brown St B4
Brunswick St B5
Buccleuch St A3
Buchanan Bus Station A5
Buchanan Galleries 🏛 A5
Buchanan St B5
Buchanan St (Metro Station) B5
Cadogan St B4
Caledonian University A5
Calgary St A5
Cambridge St A4
Canal St A5
Candleriggs B5
Carlton Pl C4
Carnarvon St A3
Carnoustie St C3
Carrick St B4
Castle St B6
Cathedral Sq B6
Cathedral St B5
Central College of Commerce B5
Centre for Contemporary Arts 🏛 A4
Centre St C4
Cessnock (Metro Station) C1
Cessnock St C1
Charing Cross ⇌ A3
Charlotte St C6
Cheapside St B3
Citizens' Theatre 🎭 C5
City Chambers Complex B5
City Halls 🏛 B5
Clairmont Gdns A2
Claremont St A2
Claremont Terr A2
Claythorne St C6
Cleveland St A3
Clifford La C1
Clifford St C1
Clifton Pl A2
Clifton St A2
Clutha St C1
Clyde Arc B2
Clyde Auditorium B2
Clyde Pl C4
Clyde Place Quay C4
Clyde St C5
Clyde Walkway C3
Clydeside Expressway B2
Coburg St C4
Cochrane St B5
College of Nautical Studies C5
College St B6
Collins St B6
Commerce St C4
Cook St C4
Cornwall St C2
Couper St A5
Cowcaddens A4
Cowcaddens (Metro Station) A4
Cowcaddens Rd A4
Crimea St B3
Custom House 🏛 C4
Custom House Quay Gdns C4
Dalhousie St A4
Dental Hospital 🏥 A4
Derby St A2
Dobbie's Loan A4/A5
Dobbie's Loan Pl A5
Dorset St A3
Douglas St B4
Doulton Fountain ✦ C6
Dover St A2
Drury St B4
Drygate B6
Duke St B6
Dunaskin St A1
Dunblane St A4
Dundas St B5
Dunlop St C5
East Campbell St C6
Eastvale Pl A1
Eglinton St C4
Elderslie St A3
Elliot St B2
Elmbank St A3
Esmond St A1
Exhibition Centre ⇌ B2
Exhibition Way B2
Eye Infirmary 🏥 A2
Festival Park C1
Film Theatre 🎦 A4
Finnieston Quay B2
Finnieston Sq B2
Finnieston St B2
Fitzroy Pl A2
Florence St C5
Fox St C5
Gallowgate C6
Garnet St A3
Garnethill St A4
Garscube Rd A4
George Sq B5
George St B5
George V Bridge C4
Gilbert St A1
Glasgow Bridge C4
Glasgow Cathedral ✝ B6
Glasgow Central ⇌ B4
Glasgow Green C6
Glasgow Metropolitan College B5/C5
Glasgow Science Centre ✦ B1
Glasgow Science Centre Footbridge B1
Glassford St B5
Glebe St A6
Gloucester St C3
Gorbals Cross C5
Gorbals St C5
Gordon St B4
Govan Rd B1/C1/C2
Grace St B3
Grafton Pl A5
Grant St A3
Granville St A3
Gray St A2
Greendyke St C6
Harley St C1
Harvie St C1
Haugh Rd A1
Heliport B1
Henry Wood Hall 🎭 A2
High Court C5
High St B6
High Street ⇌ B6
Hill St A3
Holland St A3
Holm St B4
Hope St A5
Houldsworth St B2
Houston Pl C3
Houston St C3
Howard St C5
Hunter St C6
Hutcheson St B5
Hutchesons Hall 🏛 B5
Hydepark St B3
Imax Cinema 🎦 B1
India St A3
Information Ctr ℹ B5
Ingram St B5
Jamaica St B4
James Watt St B4
John Knox St B6
John St B5
Kelvin Hall ✦ A1
Kelvin Statue ✦ A2
Kelvin Way A2
Kelvingrove Park A2
Kelvingrove St A2
Kelvinhaugh St A1
Kennedy St A6
Kent Rd A2
Killermont St A5
King St B5
King's 🎭 A3
Kingston Bridge C3
Kingston St C4
Kinning Park (Metro Station) C2
Kinning St C3
Kyle St A5
Laidlaw St C3
Lancefield Quay B2
Lancefield St B3
Langshot St C1
Lendel Pl C1
Lighthouse ✦ B4
Lister St A6
Little St B3
London Rd C6
Lorne St C1
Lower Harbour B1
Lumsden St A1
Lymburn St A1
Lyndoch Cr A3
Lynedoch Pl A3
Lynedoch St A3
Maclellan St C1
Mair St C2
Maitland St A4
Mavisbank Gdns C2
Mcalpine St B3
Mcaslin St A6
McLean Sq C2
McLellan Gallery 🏛 A4
McPhater St A4
Merchants' House 🏛 B5
Middlesex St C2
Middleton St C1
Midland St B4
Miller St B5
Millroad St C6
Milnpark St C2
Milton St A4
Minerva St B2
Mitchell Library A3
Mitchell St West B4
Mitchell Theatre 🎭 A3
Modern Art Gallery 🏛 B5
Moir St C6
Molendinar St C6
Moncur St C6
Montieth Row C6
Montrose St B5
Morrison St C3
Mosque C5
Museum of Religious Life 🏛 B6
Nairn St A1
Nelson Mandela Sq B5
Nelson St C4
Nelson's Monument C6
New City Rd A4
Newton St A3
Newton Pl A3
Nicholson St C4
Nile St B5
Norfolk Court C4
Norfolk St C4
North Frederick St B5
North Hanover St B5
North Portland St B6
North St A3
North Wallace St A5
Odeon 🎦 C3
Old Dumbarton Rd A1
Osborne St B5/C5
Oswald St B4
Overnewton St A1
Oxford St C4
Pacific Dr B1
Paisley Rd C3
Paisley Rd West C1
Park Circus A2
Park Gdns A2
Park St South A2
Park Terr A2
Parkgrove Terr A2
Parnie St C5
Parson St A6
Partick Bridge A1
Passport Office A5
Paterson St C3
Pavilion Theatre 🎭 A4
Pembroke St A3
People's Palace 🏛 C6
Pinkston Rd A6
Piping Centre, The National ✦ A5
Pitt St A4/B4
Plantation Park C1
Plantation Quay B1
Police Station ◘ A4/A6/B5
Port Dundas Rd A5
Port St B2
Portman St C2
Prince's Dock B1
Princes Sq B5
Provand's Lordship 🏛 B6
Queen St B5
Queen Street ⇌ B5
Regimental Mus 🏛 A3
Renfrew St A3/A4
Renton St A5
Richmond St B5
Robertson St B4
Rose St A4
Rottenrow B5
Royal Concert Hall 🎭 A5
Royal Cr A2
Royal Exchange Sq B5
Royal Hospital For Sick Children 🏥 A1
Royal Infirmary 🏥 B6
Royal Scottish Academy of Music & Drama A4
Royal Terr A2
Rutland Cr C2
St Kent St C6
St Andrew's (R.C.) ✝ C5
St Andrew's ⛪ C6
St Andrew's St C5
St Enoch (Metro Station) B5
St Enoch Shopping Centre B5
St Enoch Sq B4
St George's Rd A3
St James Rd B6
St Mungo Ave A5/A6
St Mungo Pl A6
St Vincent Cr A2
St Vincent Pl B5
St Vincent St B3/B4
St Vincent Street Church ⛪ B4
St Vincent Terr B3
Saltmarket C5
Sandyford Pl A3
Sauchiehall St A2/A4
School of Art A4
Scotland St C2/C3
Scott St A4
Scottish Exhibition & Conference Centre B1
Seaward St C2
Shaftesbury St B3
Sheriff Court C5
Shields Rd (Metro Station) C3
Shuttle St B6
Somerset Pl A2
South Portland St C4
Springburn Rd A6
Springfield Quay C3
Stanley St C2
Stevenson St C6
Stewart St A4
Stirling Rd B6
Stirling's Library B5
Stobcross Quay B1
Stobcross Rd B1
Stock Exchange 🏛 B5
Stockwell Pl C5
Stockwell St B5
Stow College A4
Strathclyde University B6
Sussex St C2
Synagogues A3/C4
Tall Ship ⛵ B1
Taylor Pl A6
Tenement House 🏛 A3
Teviot St A1
Theatre Royal 🎭 A4
Tolbooth Steeple & Mercat Cross ✦ C6
Tower St C2
Trades House 🏛 B5
Tradeston St C4
Transport Mus 🏛 A1
Tron Steeple & Theatre 🎭 C5
Trongate B5
Tunnel St B2
Turnbull St C5
UGC 🎦 A5
Union St B4
Victoria Bridge C5
Virginia St B5
West Greenhill Pl B2
West Regent St A4
Wallace St C3
Walls St B6
Walmer Cr C1
Warrock St B3
Washington St B3
Waterloo St B4
Watson St B6
Watt St C3
Wellington St B4
West Campbell St B4
West George St B4
West Graham St A4
West Regent St B4
West St C4
West St (Metro Station) C4
Westminster Terr A2
Whitehall St B3
Wilson St B5
Woodlands Gate A3
Woodlands Rd A3
Woodlands Terr A2
Woodside Cr A3
Woodside Pl A3
Woodside Terr A3
York St B4
Yorkhill Pde A1
Yorkhill St A1

Gloucester 181

Albion St C1
Alexandra Rd B3
Alfred St C3
All Saints Rd C2
Alvin St B2
Arthur St C2
Baker St C1
Barton St C2
Blackfriars ✝ B1
Blenheim Rd C2
Bristol Rd C1
Brunswick Rd C2
Bruton Way B2
Bus Station B2
Cattle Market A1
City Council Offices B1
City Museum, Art Gallery and Library 🏛 B2
Clarence St B2
College of Art C2
Commercial Rd B1
Cromwell St C2
Deans Way A2
Denmark Rd A3
Derby Rd C3
Docks ✦ C1
Eastgate St B2
Edwy Pde A2
Estcourt Cl A3
Estcourt Rd A3
Falkner St C2
Folk Museum 🏛 B1
GL1 Leisure Centre C2
Gloucester Cathedral ✝ B1
Gloucester Station ⇌ B2
Gloucestershire Royal Hospital (A & E) 🏥 B3
Goodyere St C2
Gouda Way A1
Great Western Rd B3
Guildhall 🏛 B2
Heathville Rd A3
Henry Rd B3
Henry St B2
High Orchard St C1
Hinton Rd A2
India Rd C3
Information Ctr ℹ B1
Jersey Rd C3
King's 🎭 C2
King's Sq B2
Kingsholm Rd A2
Kingsholm Rugby Football Ground A2
Lansdown Rd A3
Library C2
Llanthony Rd C1
London Rd B3
Longsmith St B1
Malvern Rd A3
Market Pde B2
Merchants Rd C1
Mercia Rd A1
Metz Way C3
Midland Rd C2
Millbrook St C3
Market B2
Montpellier C1
Napier St C3
National Waterways 🏛 C1
Nettleton Rd C2
New Inn 🏛 B2
New Olympus 🎭 C3
North Rd A3
Northgate St B2
Oxford Rd A2
Oxford St B2
Park & Ride Gloucester A1
Park Rd C2
Park St B2
Parliament St C1
Pitt St B1
Police Station ◘ B1
Post Office ✉ B2
Quay St B1
Recreation Gd A1/A2
Regent St C2
Robert Raikes House 🏛 B1
Royal Oak Rd B1
Russell St B2
Ryecroft St C2
St Aldate St B2
St Ann Way C1
St Catherine St A2
St Mark St A2
St Mary De Crypt ⛪ B1
St Mary De Lode ⛪ B1
St Nicholas's ⛪ B1
St Oswald's Rd A1
St Oswald's Trading Estate A1
St Peter's ⛪ B2
Seabroke Rd A3
Sebert St A2
Severn Rd C1
Sherborne St B2
Shire Hall 🏛 B1
Sidney St C3
Soldiers of Gloucestershire 🏛 B1
Southgate St B1/C1
Spa Field C1
Spa Rd C1
Sports Ground A2/B2
Station Rd B2
Stratton Rd C3
Stroud Rd C1
Superstore A1
Swan Rd A2
Technical College C1
The Mall B1
The Park C2
The Quay B1
Trier Way C1/C2
Union St A2
Vauxhall Rd C3
Victoria St C2
Wellington St C2
Westgate St B1
Widden St C2
Worcester St B2

Grimsby 181

Abbey Drive East C2
Abbey Drive West C2
Abbey Park Rd C2
Abbey Rd C2
Abbey Walk C2
Abbeygate Shopping Centre C2
Abbotsway C2
Adam Smith St A1/A2
Ainslie St C2
Albert St A3
Alexandra Dock A2/B2
Alexandra Retail Park A2
Alexandra Rd A2/B2
Annesley St A2
Armstrong St A1
Arthur St B1
Augusta St C1
Bargate C1
Beeson St A1
Bethlehem St C2
Bodiam Way B3
Bradley St B3
Brighowgate C1/C2
Bus Station B2/C2
Canterbury Dr C1
Cartergate B1/C1
Catherine St C3
Caxton 🎭 A3
Chantry La B1
Charlton St A1
Church La C2
Church St A3
Cleethorpe Rd A3
College C2
College St C1
Compton Dr C1
Corporation Bridge A2
Corporation Rd A1
Court B3
Crescent St B1
Deansgate C1
Doughty Rd C2
Dover St B1
Duchess St C2
Dudley St C1
Duke of York Gardens B1
Duncombe St B3
Earl La B1
East Marsh St B3
East St B2
Eastgate B3
Eastside Rd A3
Eaton Ct C1
Eleanor St B3
Ellis Way B3
Fisherman's Chapel ⛪ A3
Fisherman's Wharf B2
Fishing Heritage Centre 🏛 B2
Flour Sq A3
Frederick St B1
Frederick Ward Way B2
Freeman St A3/B3
Freshney Dr B1
Freshney Pl B2
Garden St C2
Garibaldi St A3
Garth La B2
Grime St B3
Grimsby Docks Station ⇌ A3
Grimsby Town Station ⇌ C2
Hainton Ave C3
Har Way B3
Hare St C3
Harrison St B1
Haven Ave B1
Hay Croft Ave B1
Hay Croft St B1
Heneage Rd B3/C3
Henry St B1
Holme St B3
Hume St C1
James St B1
Joseph St B1
Kent St A3
King Edward St A3
Lambert Rd C2
Library B2
Lime St B1
Lister St B1
Littlefield La C1
Lockhill A3
Lord St B1
Ludford St C3
Macaulay St B1
Mallard Mews C3
Manor Ave C2
Market A3
Market Hall B2
Market St B3
Moss Rd C2
Nelson St A3
New St B2
Osbourne St B2
Pasture St B3
Peaks Parkway C3
Pelham Rd C1
Police Station ◘ A3
Post Office ✉ B1/B2/C2
PS Lincoln Castle ⛴ B2
Pyewipe Rd A1
Railway Pl A3
Railway St A3
Recreation Ground C2
Rendel St A2
Retail Park B3
Richard St B1
Ripon St B1
Robinson St East B3
Royal St A3
St Hilda's Ave C1
St James ⛪ C2
Sheepfold St B3/C3
Sixhills St C3
South Park B2
Spring St A3
Superstore B3
Tasburgh St C3
Tennyson St B2
The Close C1
Thesiger St A3
Time Trap 🏛 C2
Town Hall 🏛 B2
Veal St B1
Victoria Retail Park A3
Victoria St North A2
Victoria St South B2
Victoria St West B2
Watkin St A1
Welholme Ave C2
Welholme Rd C3
Wellington St B3
Wellowgate C2
Werneth Rd B3
West Coates Rd A1
Westgate A2
Westminster Dr C1
Willingham St C3
Wintringham Rd C2
Wood St B3
Yarborough Dr B1
Yarborough Hotel 🏛 C2

Hanley 181

Acton St A3
Albion St B2
Argyle St C1
Ashbourne Gr A2
Avoca St A3
Baskerville Rd B3
Bedford Rd C1
Bedford St C1
Bethesda St B2
Bexley St A2
Birches Head Rd A3
Botteslow St C3
Boundary St A2
Broad St C2
Broom St A3
Bryan St A2
Bucknall New Rd B3
Bucknall Old Rd B3
Bus Station B3
Cannon St C2
Castlefield St C1
Cavendish St B1
Central Forest Pk A2
Charles St B3
Cheapside B2
Chell St A3
Clarke St C1
Cleveland Rd C2
Clifford St C3
Clough St B2
Clyde St C1
College Rd C2
Cooper St C2
Corbridge Rd A1
Cutts St C2
Davis St C1
Denbigh St A1
Derby St C3
Dilke St A3
Dundas St A3
Dundee Rd C1
Dyke St B3
Eastwood Rd C3
Eaton St A3
Etruria Park B1
Etruria Rd B1
Etruria Vale Rd C1
Festing St A3
Fire Station C2
Foundry St B2
Franklyn St C3
Garnet St B1
Garth St B3
George St A3
Gilman St B3
Glass St B3
Goodson St B3
Greyhound Way A1
Grove Pl C1
Hampton St C3
Hanley Park C2
Harding Rd C2
Hassall St B3
Havelock Pl C1
Hazlehurst St C3
Hinde St C2
Hope St B2
Houghton St C2
Hulton St A3
Hypermarket A1/B2
Information Ctr ℹ B3
Jasper St C2
Jervis St A3
John Bright St A3
John St B2
Keelings Rd A3
Kimberley Rd C1
Ladysmith Rd C1
Lawrence St C2
Leek Rd C3
Library C2
Lichfield St C3
Linfield Rd B3
Loftus St A2
Lower Bedford St C1
Lower Bryan St A2
Lower Mayer St A3
Lowther St A1
Magistrates Court C2
Malham St A2
Marsh St B2
Matlock St C3
Mayer St A3
Milton St C1
Mitchell Memorial Theatre 🎭 B2
Morley St B2
Moston St A3
Mount Pleasant C1
Mulgrave St A1
Mynors St B3
Nelson Pl B3
New Century St B1
New Forest Industrial Estate A3
Octagon, The Shopping Park B1
Ogden Rd C3
Old Hall St B3
Old Town Rd A3
Pall Mall B2
Palmerston St C3
Park and Ride C2
Parker St B2
Pavilion Dr A1
Pelham St C3
Percy St B2
Piccadilly B2
Picton St B3
Plough St A3
Police Station ◘ C2
Portland St A1
Post Office ✉ A3/B3/C3
Potteries Museum & Art Gallery 🏛 B2
Potteries Shopping Centre B2
Potteries Way C2
Powell St A1
Pretoria Rd C1
Quadrant Rd B2
Ranelagh St C2
Raymond St C2
Rectory Rd C1
Regent Rd C2
Regent Theatre 🎭 B2
Richmond Terr C2
Ridgehouse Dr A1
Robson St C2
St Ann St B3
St Luke St B3
Sampson St B2
Shaw St A1
Sheaf St C2
Shearer St C1
Shelton New Rd C1
Shirley Rd C2
Slippery La B2
Snow Hill C2
Sports Stadium A1
Spur St C3
Stafford St B2
Statham St B2
Stubbs La C3
Sun St C1
Talbot St C3
The Parkway C2
Town Hall B2
Town Rd A3
Trinity St B2
Union St A2
Upper Hillchurch St A3
Upper Huntbach St B3
Victoria Hall Theatre 🎭 B3
Warner St C2
Warwick St C1
Waterloo Rd A1
Waterloo St B3
Well St B3
Wellesley St C2
Wellington Rd B3
Wellington St B3
Whitehaven Dr A2
Whitmore St C1
Windermere St A1
Woodall St A1
Yates St C2
York St A2

Harrogate 182

Albert St C2
Alexandra Rd B2
Arthington Ave B2
Ashfield Rd A2
Back Cheltenham Mount B2
Beech Grove C1
Belmont Rd C1
Bilton Dr A2
Bower Rd B2
Bower St B2
Bus Station B2
Cambridge Rd B2
Cambridge St B2
Cemetery A2
Chatsworth Pl A2
Chatsworth Grove A2
Chatsworth Rd A2
Chelmsford Rd B3
Cheltenham Cr B2
Cheltenham Mt B2
Cheltenham Pde B2
Christ Church ⛪ B3
Christ Church Oval B3
Chudleigh Rd B3
Clarence Dr B1
Claro Rd A3
Claro Way A3
Coach Park B2
Coach Rd B3
Cold Bath Rd C1
Commercial St B2
Coppice Ave A1
Coppice Dr A1
Coppice Gate A1
Cornwall Rd B1
Council Offices B1
Court C3
Crescent Gdns B1
Crescent Rd B1
Dawson Terr A2
Devonshire Pl B3
Diamond Mews C1
Dixon Rd A2
Dixon Terr A2
Dragon Ave B3
Dragon Parade B2
Dragon Rd B2
Duchy Rd B1
East Parade B2
East Park Rd C3
Esplanade B1
Fire Station A2
Franklin Mount A2
Franklin Rd B2
Franklin Square A2
Glebe Rd C1
Grove Park Ct A3
Grove Park Terr A3
Grove Rd A2
Hampswaite Rd A1
Harcourt Dr B3
Harcourt Rd B3
Harrogate ⇌ B2
Harrogate International Centre B1
Harrogate Ladies College B1
Harrogate Theatre 🎭 B2
Heywood Rd C1
Hollins Cr A1
Hollins Mews A1
Hollins Rd A1
Homestead Rd C3
Hydro Leisure Centre, The A1
Information Ctr ℹ B1
James St B2
Jenny Field Dr A1
John St B2
Kent Dr A1
Kent Rd A1
Kings Rd A2
Kingsway B3
Kingsway Dr B3
Lancaster Rd C1
Leeds Rd C2
Lime Grove B3
Lime St A3
Mayfield Grove B2
Mayfield Pl A2
Mercer 🏛 B1
Montpellier Hill B1
Mornington Cr A3
Mornington Terr B3
Mowbray Sq B3
North Park Rd B3
Nydd Vale Rd B2
Oakdale Ave A1
Oatlands Dr C3
Odeon 🎦 B2
Osborne Rd A2
Otley Rd C2
Oxford St B2
Park Chase B3
Park Parade B3
Park View B2
Parliament St B1
Police Station ◘ B3
Post Office ✉ B2/C1
Providence Terr A2
Queen Parade C3
Queen's Rd C1
Raglan St C2
Regent Ave A3
Regent Grove A3
Regent Parade A3
Regent St A3
Regent Terr A3
Rippon Rd A1
Robert St C2
Royal Baths and Turkish Baths 🏛 B1
Royal Pump Room 🏛 B1
St Luke's Mount A2
St Mary's Ave C1
St Mary's Walk C1
Scargill Rd A1
Skipton Rd A3
Skipton St A2
Slingsby Walk C3
South Park Rd C2
Spring Grove A1

Springfield Ave B1
Station Ave B2
Station Parade B2
Strawberry Dale B2
Stray Rein C3
Studley Rd A2
Superstore B2
Swan Rd B1
The Parade B2
The Stray C2/C3
Tower St C2
Trinity Rd C2
Union St B2
Valley Dr C1
Valley Gardens C1
Valley Mount C1
Victoria Ave C2
Victoria Rd C1
Victoria Shopping Centre B2
Waterloo St A2
West Park C2
West Park St C2
Wood View A1
Woodfield Ave A3
Woodfield Dr A3
Woodfield Grove A3
Woodfield Rd A3
Woodfield Square A3
Woodside B3
York Pl C3
York Rd B1

Holyhead *Caergybi* 182

Armenia St A2
Arthur St C2
Beach Rd A1
Boston St B2
Bowling Green C3
Bryn Erw Rd C3
Bryn Glas Cl C3
Bryn Glas Rd C3
Bryn Gwyn Rd C1
Bryn Marchog A1
Bryn Mor Terr A2
Bryngoleu Ave A1
Cae Braenar C3
Cambria St B1
Captain Skinner's Obelisk B2
Cecil St C2
Cemetery C1/C2
Cleveland Ave C2
Coastguard Lookout A2
Court B2
Customs House A3
Cybi Pl A2
Cyttir Rd C3
Edmund St B1
Empire B2
Ferry Terminals B2
Ffordd Beibio B3
Ffordd Feurig C3
Ffordd Hirnos C3
Ffordd Jasper C3
Ffordd Tudur B3
Fire Station C2
Garreglwyd Rd B1
Gilbert St C2
Gorsedd Circle B1
Gwelfor Ave A1
Harbour View B3
Henry St C2
High Terr C1
Hill St B2
Holborn Rd C2
Holland Park Industrial Estate C3
Holyhead Park B1
Holyhead Station B2
Information Ctr B2
King's Rd C2
Kingsland Rd C2
Lewascote C3
Library B2
Lifeboat Station A1
Llanfawr Cl C3
Llanfawr Rd C3
Lligwy St C2
Lon Deg C3
London Rd C3
Longford Rd B1
Longford Terr B1
Maes Cybi B1
Maes Hedd A1
Maes-Hyfryd Rd C1
Maes-y-Dref B1
Maes-y-Haf A2/B1
Maes-yr-Ysgol C3
Marchog C3
Marina A1
Maritime Museum A1
Market B2
Market St B2
Mill Bank B1
Min-y-Mor Rd A1
Morawelon Industrial Estate B3
Morawelon Rd B3
Moreton Rd C1
New Park Rd B1
Newry St A2
Old Harbour Lighthouse A3
Plas Rd C1
Police Station B2
Porth-y-Felin Rd A1
Post Office A1/B1/B2/B3/C2/C3
Prince of Wales Rd A2
Priory La B3
Pump St C1
Queens Park B1
Reseifion Rd C1
Rock St B1
Roman Fort B2
St Cybi St B2
St Cybi's Church B2
St Seiriol's Cl B1
Salt Island Bridge A2
Seabourne Rd A1
South Stack Rd B1
Sports Ground B1
Stanley St B2
Station St B2
Tan-y-Bryn Rd A1
Tan-yr-Efail C2
Tara St C1
Thomas St B1
Town Hall A2
Treseifion Estate C2
Turkey Shore Rd B2
Ucheldre Arts Centre B1
Ucheldre Ave B1
Upper Baptist St B1
Victoria Rd B2
Victoria Terr B2
Vulcan St B1
Walthew Ave A1
Walthew La A1
Wian St C2

Hull 182

Adelaide St C1
Albert Dock C1
Albion St B2
Alfred Gelder St B2
Anlaby Rd B1
Beverley Rd A1
Blanket Row C2
Bond St B2
Bridlington Ave A2
Brook St B1
Brunswick Ave A1
Bus Station B1
Camilla Cl C3
Canning St B1
Cannon St A2
Cannon's C1
Caroline St A2
Carr La B2
Castle St C2
Central Library B1
Charles St A2
Citadel Way B3
City Hall B2
Clarence St B3
Cleveland St A3
Clifton St A1
Collier St B1
Colonial St B1
Court B2
Deep, The C3
Dock Office Row B3
Dock St B2
Drypool Bridge B3
Egton St A3
English St C1
Ferens Gallery B2
Ferensway B1
Francis St A2
Francis St West A2
Freehold St A1
Freetown Way A2
Garrison Rd B3
George St B2
Gibson St A2
Great Thornton St B1
Great Union St A3
Green La A2
Grey St A1
Grimston St B2
Grosvenor St A1
Guildhall B2
Guildhall Rd B2
Hands-on History B2
Harley St A1
Hessle Rd C1
High St B3
Holy Trinity B2
Hull & East Riding Museum B3
Hull Arena C1
Hull College B3
Hull (Paragon) Station B1
Hull Truck Theatre B1
Humber Dock Marina C2
Humber Dock St C2
Humber St C2
Hyperion St A3
Information Ctr B2
Jameson St B1
Jarratt St B2
Jenning St A3
King Billy Statue C2
King Edward St B2
King St A2
Kingston Retail Park C1
Kingston St C2
Library Theatre B1
Liddell St A1
Lime St A3
Lister St C1
Lockwood St A2
Maister House B3
Maritime Museum B2
Market B2
Market Place B2
Minerva Pier C2
Mulgrave St A3
Myton Bridge C3
Myton St B1
Nelson St C2
New Cleveland St A3
New George St A2
New Theatre A2
Norfolk St A1
North Bridge A3
North St B1
Odeon C1
Old Harbour C3
Osborne St B1
Paragon St B2
Park St B1
Percy St A2
Pier St C2
Police Station B1
Post Office A1/B1/B2
Porter St C1
Portland St B1
Posterngate B2
Prince's Quay B2
Prospect Centre B1
Prospect St B1
Queen's Gdns B2
Railway Dock Marina C2
Railway St C2
Reform St A2
Retail Park B1
Riverside Quay C2
Roper St B2
St James St C1
St Luke's St B1
St Mark St A3
St Mary the Virgin B3
Scott St A2
South Bridge Rd B3
Spring Bank A1
Spring St B1
Spurn Lightship C2
Spyvee St A3
Streetlife Transport Museum B3
Sykes St A2
Tidal Surge Barrier C3
Tower St B3
Trinity House B2
University B2
Vane St A1
Victoria Pier C3
Waterhouse La B2
Waterloo St A1
Waverley St C1
Wellington St C2
Wellington St West C2
West St B1
Whitefriargate B2
Wilberforce Dr B2
Wilberforce House B3
Wilberforce Monument B3
William St C1
Wincolmlee A3
Witham A3
Wright St A1

Inverness 182

Abban St A1
Academy St B2
Alexander Pl B2
Anderson St A2
Annfield Rd C3
Ardconnel St B3
Ardconnel Terr B3
Ardross Pl B2
Ardross St B2
Argyle St B3
Argyle Terr B3
Attadale Rd B1
Ballifeary La C2
Ballifeary Rd C1/C2
Balnacraig La A1
Balnain St B2
Bank St B2
Bellfield Park C2
Bellfield Terr C3
Benula Rd A1
Birnie Terr A1
Bishop's Rd C2
Bowling Green A2/B2/C2
Bridge St B2
Brown St A2
Bruce Ave C1
Bruce Gdns C1
Bruce Pk C1
Burial Ground A2
Burnett Rd A3
Bus Station B3
Caledonian Rd B1
Cameron Rd A1
Cameron Sq A1
Carse Rd A1
Carsegate Rd Sth A1
Castle (Courts) B3
Castle Rd B2
Castle St B3
Celt St B2
Chapel St A2
Charles St B3
Church St B2
Clachnacuddin Football Ground A1
College A3
Columba Rd B1/C1
Crown Ave B3
Crown Circus B3
Crown Dr B3
Crown Rd B3
Crown St B3
Culduthel Rd C3
Dalneigh Cres C1
Dalneigh Rd C1
Denny St B3
Dochfour Dr B1/C1
Douglas Row B2
Duffy Dr C3
Dunabban Rd A1
Dunain Rd B1
Duncraig St B2
Eastgate Shopping Centre B3
Eden Court C2
Fairfield Rd B1
Falcon Sq B3
Fire Station A3
Fraser St B2
Fraser St C2
Friars' Bridge A2
Friars' La B2
Friars' St A2
George St A2
Gilbert St A2
Glebe St A2
Glendoe Terr A1
Glenurquhart Rd C1
Gordon Terr B3
Gordonville Rd C2
Grant St A2
Greig St B2
HM Prison B3
Harbour Rd A3
Harrowden Rd B1
Haugh Rd C2
Heatherley Cres C3
High St B3
Highland Council HQ, The C2
Hill Park C3
Hill St B3
Huntly Pl A2
Huntly St B2
India St A2
Industrial Estate A3
Information Ctr B2
Inverness B3
Inverness High School B1
Jamaica St A2
Kenneth St B2
Kilmuir Rd A1
King St B2
Kingsmills Rd B3
Laurel Ave B1/C1
Library A3
Lilac Gr B1
Lindsay Ave C1
Lochalsh Rd A1/B1
Longman Rd A3
Lotland Pl A2
Lower Kessock St A1
Madras St A2
Market Hall B3
Maxwell Dr C1
Mayfield Rd C3
Midmills College B3
Millburn Rd B3
Mitchell's La C3
Montague Row B2
Muirfield Rd C3
Muirtown St B1
Museum B2
Nelson St A2
Ness Bank C2
Ness Bridge B2
Ness Walk B2/C2
Old Edinburgh Rd C3
Old High Church B2
Park Rd C1
Paton St C2
Perceval Rd B1
Planefield Rd B2
Police Station A3
Porterfield Bank C3
Porterfield Rd C3
Portland Pl A2
Post Office A2/B1/B2/B3
Queen St B2
Queensgate B2
Railway Terr A3
Rangemore Rd B1
Reay St B3
Riverside St A2
Rose St A2
Ross Ave B1
Rowan Rd B1
Royal Northern Infirmary C2
St Andrew's Cathedral C2
St Columba B2
St John's Ave C1
St Mary's Ave C1
Shore St A2
Smith Ave C1
Southside Pl C3
Southside Rd C3
Spectrum Centre B2
Strothers La B3
Superstore B2
TA Centre C2
Telford Gdns B1
Telford Rd A1
Telford St A1
Tomnahurich Cemetery C1
Tomnahurich St B2
Town Hall B3
Union Rd B3
Union St B3
Walker Pl A2
Walker Rd A3
War Memorial C2
Waterloo Bridge A2
Wells St B1
Young St B2

Ipswich 182

Alderman Rd B2
All Saints' Rd A1
Alpe St B2
Ancaster Rd C1
Ancient House B3
Anglesea Rd B2
Ann St B2
Arboretum A2
Austin St C2
Belstead Rd C2
Berners St B2
Bibb Way B1
Birkfield Dr C1
Black Horse La B2
Bolton La B3
Bond St C3
Bowthorpe Cl B2
Bramford La A1
Bramford Rd A1
Bridge St C2
Brookfield Rd A1
Brooks Hall Rd A1
Broomhill A2
Broomhill Rd A1
Broughton Rd A2
Bulwer Rd B1
Burrell Rd C2
Butter Market B2
Butter Market Centre B3
Carr St B3
Cecil Rd B2
Cecilia St C2
Chancery Rd C2
Charles St B2
Chevallier St A1
Christchurch Mansion & Wolsey Art Gallery B3
Christchurch Park A3
Christchurch St B3
Cineworld C2
Civic Centre B2
Civic Dr B2
Clarkson St B1
Cobbold St B3
Commercial Rd C2
Constable Rd A3
Constantine Rd C1
Constitution Hill A2
Corder Rd A3
Corn Exchange B2
Cotswold Ave A2
Council Offices C2
County Hall B3
Crown Court C2
Crown St B2
Cullingham Rd B1
Cumberland St B2
Curriers La B2
Dale Hall La A2
Dales View Rd A1
Dalton Rd B2
Dillwyn St B1
Elliot St B1
Elm St B2
Elsmere Rd A3
Falcon St C2
Felaw St C3
Flint Wharf C3
Fonnereau Rd B2
Fore St C3
Foundation St C3
Franciscan Way C2
Friars St C2
Gainsborough Rd A3
Gatacre Rd B1
Geneva Rd B2
Gippeswyk Ave C1
Gippeswyk Park C1
Grafton Way C2
Graham Rd A1
Grimwade St C3
Great Whip St C3
Handford Cut B1
Handford Rd B1
Henley Rd A2
Hervey St B3
High St B2
Holly Rd A2
Information Ctr B3
Ipswich Haven Marina C3
Ipswich School A2
Ipswich Station C2
Ipswich Town FC (Portman Road) C2
Ivry St A2
Kensington Rd A1
Kesteven Rd C1
Key St C3
Kingsfield Ave A3
Kitchener Rd A1
Magistrates Court B2
Little's Cr C2
London Rd B1
Low Brook St C3
Lower Orwell St C3
Luther Rd C2
Manor Rd A3
Mornington Ave A1
Museum & Art Gallery B2
Museum St B2
Neale St B3
New Cardinal St C2
New Cut East C3
New Cut West C3
New Wolsey B2
Newson St B2
Norwich Rd A1/B1
Oban St B2
Old Customs House C3
Old Foundry Rd B3
Old Merchant's House C3
Orford St B2
Paget Rd A2
Park Rd A3
Park View Rd A2
Peter's St C2
Philip Rd C2
Pine Ave A2
Pine View Rd A2
Police Station B2
Portman Rd B2
Portman Walk C1
Post Office B2/B3
Princes St C2
Prospect St B1
Queen St B2
Ranelagh Rd C1
Recreation Ground B1
Rectory Rd C2
Regent Theatre B3
Retail Park C1
Richmond Rd A1
Rope Walk C3
Rose La C2
Russell Rd C2
St Edmund's Rd A2
St George's St B2
St Helen's St B3
Samuel Rd B3
Sherrington Rd A1
Silent St C2
Sir Alf Ramsey Way C1
Sirdar Rd B1
Soane St B3
Springfield La A1
Star La C3
Stevenson Rd B1
Suffolk College C3
Suffolk Retail Park B1
Superstore B1
Surrey Rd B1
Tacket St C3
Tavern St B3
The Avenue A3
Tolly Cobbold Museum C3
Tower Ramparts B2
Tower Ramparts Shopping Centre B2
Tower St B3
Town Hall B2
Tuddenham Rd A3
Upper Brook St B3
Upper Orwell St B3
Valley Rd A2
Vermont Cr B3
Vermont Rd B3
Vernon St C3
Warrington Rd A2
Waterloo Rd A1
Waterworks St C3
Wellington St B1
West End Rd B1
Westerfield Rd A3
Westgate St B2
Westholme Rd A1
Westwood Ave A1
Willoughby Rd C2
Withipoll St B3
Woodbridge Rd B3
Woodstone Ave A3
Yarmouth Rd B1

Kendal 182

Abbot Hall Art Gallery and Museum of Lakeland Life C2
Ambulance Station A2
Anchorite Fields C2
Anchorite Rd C2
Ann St A3
Appleby Rd A3
Archers Meadow C3
Ashleigh Rd A2
Aynam Rd B2
Bankfield Rd B1
Beast Banks B2
Beezon Fields A2
Beezon Rd A2
Beezon Trad Est A3
Belmont B2
Birchwood Cl C1
Blackhall Rd B2
Brewery Arts Centre B2
Bridge St B2
Brigsteer Rd C1
Burneside Rd A2
Bus Station B2
Buttery Well La C2
Canal Head North B3
Captain French La C2
Caroline St A2
Castle Hill B3
Castle Howe B2
Castle Rd B3
Castle St A3/B3
Cedar Gr C1
Council Offices B2
County Council Offices A2
Cricket Ground A3
Cricket Ground C3
Cross La C2
Dockray Hall Ind Estate A2
Dowker's La B2
Dry Ski Slope B3
East View B1
Echo Barn Hill C1
Elephant Yard Shopping Centre B2
Fairfield La A1
Finkle St B2
Fire Station A2
Fletcher Square C3
Football Ground C3
Fowling La A3
Gillinggate C2
Glebe Rd C2
Golf Course B1
Goose Holme B3
Gooseholme Bridge B3
Green St A1
Greengate C2
Greengate La C1/C2
Greenside B1
Greenwood C1
Gulfs Rd B2
High Tenterfell B1
Highgate B2
Hillswood Ave C1
Horncop La A2
Information Ctr B2
K Village and Heritage Centre C2
Kendal Business Park A3
Kendal Castle (Remains Of) B3
Kendal Fell B1
Kendal Green A1
Kendal A3
Kendal Station A3
Kent Pl B2
Kirkbarrow C2
Kirkland C2
Library B2
Library Rd B2
Little Aynam B3
Little Wood B1
Long Cl C1
Longpool A3
Lound Rd C3
Lound St C3
Low Fellside B2
Lowther St B2
Maple Dr C1
Market Pl B2
Maude St B2
Miller Bridge B2
Milnthorpe Rd C2
Mint St A3
Mintsfeet Rd A3
Mintsfeet Rd South A2
New Rd B2
Noble's Rest B2
Parish Church C2
Park Side Rd C3
Parkside Business Park C3
Parr St B3
Police Station A2
Post Office A3/B2/C2
Quaker Tapestry B2
Queen's Rd B1
Riverside Walk C2
Rydal Mount A2
Sandes Ave A2
Sandgate A3
Sandylands Rd A3
Serpentine Rd B1
Serpentine Wood B1
Shap Rd A3
South Rd C2
Stainbank Rd C1
Station Rd A3
Stramongate B2
Stramongate Bridge B2
Stricklandgate A2/B2
Sunnyside C3
Thorny Hills B3
Town Hall B2
Undercliff Rd B1
Underwood C1
Union St A2
Vicar's Fields C2
Vicarage Dr C1/C2
Wainwright Yard Shopping Centre B2
Wasdale Cl C3
Well Ings C2
Westmorland Shopping Centre & Market Hall B2
Westwood Ave C1
Wildman St A3
Windermere Rd A1
YHA B2
YWCA B2

King's Lynn 183

Albert St A2
Albion St B2
All Saints B2
All Saints St B2
Austin Fields A2
Austin St A2
Avenue Rd B3
Bank Side B1
Beech Rd C2
Birch Tree Cl B2
Birchwood St A2
Blackfriars Rd B2
Blackfriars St B2
Boal St B1
Bridge St B2
Broad St B2
Broad Walk B3
Burkitt St A2
Bus Station A2
Carmelite Terr C2
Chapel St A2
Chase Ave C3
Checker St C2
Church St B2
Clough La B2
Coburg St B2
College of West Anglia A3
Columbia Way A3
Corn Exchange A1
County Court Rd B2
Cresswell St A2
Custom House A1
Eastgate St A2
Edma St A2
Exton's Rd C3
Ferry La B1
Ferry St A1
Framingham's Almshouses B2
Friars St C2
Friars Walk C2
Gaywood Rd A3
George St A2
Gladstone Rd C2
Goodwin's Rd C3
Green Quay B1
Greyfriars' Tower B2
Guanock Terr C2
Guildhall A1
Hansa Rd C3
Hardwick Rd C2
Hextable Rd A2
High St B1
Holcombe Ave C3
Hospital Walk C2
Information Ctr B1
John Kennedy Rd A2
Kettlewell Lane A2
King George V Ave B3
King's Lynn Art Centre A1
King's Lynn FC B3
King's Lynn Station B2
King St B1
Library B2
Littleport St A2
Loke Rd A2
London Rd B2
Lynn Museum B2
Majestic B2
Magistrates Court B1
Market La A1
Millfleet B2
Milton Ave A3
Nar Valley Walk C2
Nelson St B1
New Conduit St B2
Norfolk St A2
North Lynn Discovery Centre A3
North St A2
Oldsunway B2
Ouse Ave C1
Page Stair Lane A1
Park Ave B3
Police Station B2
Portland Pl C1
Portland St B2
Post Office A3/C2
Purfleet B1
Queen St B1
Raby Ave A3
Railway Rd A2
Red Mount Chapel B3
Regent Way B2
River Walk A1
Robert St C2
Saddlebow Rd C2
St Ann's St A1
St James' Rd B2
St James' Swimming Pool B2
St James St B2
St John's Walk B3
St Margaret's B1
St Nicholas A2
St Nicholas St A1
St Peter's Rd B1
Sir Lewis St A2
Smith Ave A3
South Everard St C2
South Gate C2
South Quay B1
South St B2
Southgate St C2
Stonegate St B2
Surrey St A1
Sydney St C3
Tennyson Ave B3
Tennyson Rd B3
Tower St B2
Town Hall B1
Town House and Tales of The Old Gaol House B1
Town Wall (Remains) B3
True's Yard Museum A2
Valingers Rd C2
Vancouver Ave C2
Waterloo St B2
Wellesley St B2
White Friars Rd C2
Windsor Rd C2
Winfarthing St C2
Wyatt St A2
York Rd C3

Lancaster 183

Aberdeen Rd C3
Adult College, The C3
Aldcliffe Rd C2
Alfred St B3
Ambleside Rd A3
Ambulance Sta A3
Ashfield Ave B1
Ashton Rd C2
Assembly Rooms, The B2
Balmoral Rd B3
Bath House B2
Bath Mill La B3
Bath St B3
Blades St B1
Borrowdale Rd B3
Bowerham Rd C3
Brewery La B2
Bridge La B2
Brook St C1
Bulk Rd A3
Bulk St B2
Bus Station B2
Cable St B2
Canal Cruises & Waterbus C2
Carlisle Bridge A1
Carr House La C2
Castle B1
Castle Park B1
Caton Rd A3
China St B2
Church St B2
City Museum B2
Clarence St C3
Common Gdn St B2
Coniston Rd A3
Cottage Museum B2
Council Offices B2
Court B2
Cromwell Rd C2
Crown Court B1
Dale St C3
Dallas Rd B1/C1
Dalton Rd B3
Dalton Sq B2
Damside St B2
De Vitre St B3
Dee Rd A1
Denny Ave A1
Derby Rd A2
Dukes B2
Earl St A2
East Rd B3
Eastham St C3
Edward St B3
Fairfield Rd B1
Fenton St B2
Firbank Rd A3
Fire Station B2
Friend's Meeting House B1
Garnet St B3
George St B2
Giant Axe Field B1
Grand, The B2
Grasmere Rd B3
Greaves Rd C2
Green St A3
Gregson Centre, The B3
Gregson Rd C3
Greyhound Bridge A2
Greyhound Bridge Rd A2
High St B2
Hill Side B1
Hope St C3
Hubert Pl B1
Information Ctr B2
Judges Lodgings B2
Kelsy St B1
Kentmere Rd B3
King St B2
Kingsway A3
Kirkes Rd C3
Lancaster and Lakeland C3
Lancaster City Football Club B1
Lancaster Station B1
Langdale Rd A3
Ley Ct B1
Library B2
Lincoln Rd B1
Lindow St C2
Lodge St B2
Long Marsh La B1
Lune Rd A1
Lune St A2
Lune Valley Ramble A3
Mainway A2
Maritime Museum A1
Market St B2
Marketgate Shopping Centre B2
Meadowside C2
Meeting House La B1
Millennium Bridge A2
Moor La B2
Moorgate B3
Morecambe Rd A1/A2
Nelson St B2
North Rd B2
Orchard La C1
Owen Rd A2
Park Rd B3
Parliament St A3
Patterdale Rd A3
Penny St B2
Police Station B2
Portland St C2
Post Office A3/B1/B2/B3/C3
Primrose St C3
Priory B1
Prospect St C3
Quarry Rd B3
Queen St C2
Regent St C2
Ridge La A3
Ridge St A3
Royal Lancaster Infirmary (A&E) C2
Rydal Rd B3
Ryelands Park A1
St Georges Quay A1
St John's B2
St Leonard's Gate B2
St Martin's Rd C3
St Nicholas Arcades Shopping Centre B2
St Oswald St C3
St Peter's B3
St Peter's Rd B3
Salisbury Rd B1
Scotch Quarry Urban Park C3
Shire Hall/HM Prison B1
Sibsey St B1
Skerton Bridge A2
South Rd C2
Station Rd B1
Stirling Rd C3
Storey Ave B1
Sunnyside La C1
Sylvester St C1
Tarnsyke Rd A1
Thurnham St C2
Town Hall B2
Troutbeck Rd B3
Ulleswater Rd B3
University of Cumbria C3
Vicarage Field B1
Vue B2
West Rd B1
Westbourne Dr C1
Westbourne Rd B1
Westham St C3
Wheatfield St B1
Williamson Rd B3
Willow La B1
Windermere Rd B3
Wingate-Saul Rd B1
Wolseley St B3
Woodville St B3
Wyresdale Rd C3

Leeds 183

Aire St B3
Aireside Centre B2
Albion Pl B4
Albion St B4
Albion Way B1
Alma St A6
Arcades B4
Armley Rd B1
Back Burley Lodge Rd A1
Back Hyde Terr A2
Back Row C3
Bath Rd C3

The Barbican Centre for Arts C6
The Cut E5
The Mall E3
Theobald's Rd C4
Thorney St F4
Threadneedle St C6
Throgmorton St C6
Tonbridge St B4
Tooley St D7
Torrington Pl B3
Tothill St E3
Tottenham Court Rd B3
Tottenham Court Rd C3
Tottenham St C3
Tower Bridge D7
Tower Bridge App D7
Tower Bridge Rd E7
Tower Hill D7
Tower of London, The D7
Toynbee St C7
Trafalgar Square D3
Trinity Sq D7
Trocadero Centre D3
Tudor St D5
Turnmill St C5
Ufford St E5
Union St D5
University College Hospital B3
University of London C3
University of Westminster C2
University St B3
Upper Belgrave St E2
Upper Berkeley St C1
Upper Brook St D2
Upper Grosvenor St D2
Upper Ground D5
Upper Montague St C1
Upper St A5
Upper St Martin's La D4
Upper Thames St D6
Upper Wimpole St C2
Upper Woburn Pl B3
Vere St C2
Vernon Pl C4
Vestry St B6
Victoria E2
Victoria Embankment D4
Victoria Place Shopping Centre F2
Victoria St E3
Villiers St D4
Vincent Sq F3
Vinopolis City of Wine D6
Virginia Rd B7
Wakley St B5
Walbrook C6
Wallace Collection C2
Wardour St C3/D3
Warner St B5
Warren St B3
Warren St B3
Waterloo E4
Waterloo Bridge D4
Waterloo East D5
Waterloo Rd E5
Watling St C6
Webber St E5
Welbeck St C2
Wellington Arch E2
Wellington Mus E2
Wells St C3
Wenlock Rd A6
Wenlock St A6
Wentworth St C7
Werrington St A3
West Smithfield C5
West Sq E5
Westminster E4
Westminster Abbey E4
Westminster Bridge E4
Westminster Bridge Rd E5
Westminster Cathedral (RC) E3
Westminster City Hall E3
Westminster Hall E4
Weymouth St C2
Wharf Rd A6
Wharfdale Rd A4
Wharton St B4
Whitcomb St D3
White Cube B7
White Lion Hill D5
White Lion St A5
Whitecross St B6
Whitefriars St C5
Whitehall D4
Whitehall Pl D4
Wigmore Hall C2
Wigmore St C2
William IV St D4
Wilmington Sq B5
Wilson St C6
Wilton Cres E2
Wimpole St C2
Windmill Walk D5
Woburn Pl B4
Woburn Sq B3
Women's Hosp C3
Wood St C6
Woodbridge St B5
Wootton St D5
Wormwood St C7
Worship St B6
Wren St B4
Wynford Rd A4
Wynyatt St B5
York Rd E4
York St C1
York Terrace East B2
York Terrace West B2
York Way A4

Luton 186

Adelaide St B1
Albert Rd C2
Alma St B2
Alton Rd C3
Anthony Gdns C1
Arndale Centre B2
Arthur St C2
Ashburnham Rd B1
Ashton Rd C2
Avondale Rd A1
Back St A2
Bailey St C3
Baker St C2
Biscot Rd A1
Bolton Rd B3
Boyle Cl A2
Brantwood Rd B1
Bretts Mead C1
Bridge St B2
Brook St A1
Brunswick St A3
Burr St A3
Bury Park Rd A1
Bus Station B2
Bute St B2
Buxton Rd B2
Cambridge St C3
Cardiff Grove B1
Cardiff Rd B1
Cardigan St A2
Castle St B2/C2
Chapel St C2
Charles St A3
Chase St C2
Cheapside B2
Chequer St C3
Chiltern Rise C1
Church St B2/B3
Cinema A2
Cobden St A3
Collingdon St A1
Community Centre C3
Concorde Ave A3
Corncastle Rd C1
Cowper St C2
Crawley Green Rd B3
Crawley Rd A1
Crescent Rise A3
Crescent Rd A3
Cromwell Rd A1
Cross St A2
Crown Court B2
Cumberland St B2
Cutenhoe Rd C3
Dallow Rd B1
Downs Rd B1
Dudley St A2
Duke St A2
Dumfries St B1
Dunstable Place B2
Dunstable Rd A1/B1
Edward St A3
Elizabeth St C2
Essex Cl C3
Farley Hill C1
Farley Lodge C1
Flowers Way B2
Francis St A1
Frederick St A2
Galaxy Leisure Complex A2
George St B2
George St West B2
Gillam St A3
Gordon St B2
Grove Rd B1
Guildford St A2
Haddon Rd A3
Harcourt St C2
Hart Hill Drive A3
Hart Hill Lane A3
Hartley Rd A3
Hastings St B2
Hat Factory, The B2
Hatters Way A1
Havelock Rd A2
Hibbert St C2
High Town Rd A3
Highbury Rd A1
Hightown Community Sports & Arts Centre A3
Hillary Cres C1
Hillborough Rd C1
Hitchin Rd A3
Holly St C2
Holm C1
Hucklesby Way A2
Hunts Cl C1
Information Ctr B2
Inkerman St A2
John St B2
Jubilee St A3
Kelvin Cl C2
King St B2
Kingsland Rd C3
Latimer Rd C2
Lawn Gdns C2
Lea Rd B3
Library B2
Library Rd B2
Liverpool Rd B1
London Rd C2
Luton Station A2
Lyndhurst Rd B1
Magistrates Court B2
Manchester St B2
Manor Rd B3
May St C3
Meyrick Ave C1
Midland Rd A2
Mill St A2
Milton Rd B1
Moor St A1
Moor, The A1
Moorland Gdns A2
Moulton Rise A3
Museum and Art Gallery A2
Napier Rd B1
New Bedford Rd A1
New Town St C2
North St A3
Old Bedford Rd A2
Old Orchard C2
Osbourne Rd C3
Oxen Rd A3
Park Sq B2
Park St B3/C3
Park St West B2
Park Viaduct B3
Parkland Drive C1
Police Station B1
Pomfret Ave A3
Pondwicks Rd B3
Post Office A1/A2/B2/C3
Power Court B3
Princess St B1
Red Rails C1
Regent St B2
Reginald St A2
Rothesay Rd B1
Russell Rise C1
Russell St C1
St Ann's Rd B3
St George's B2
St Mary's B3
St Marys Rd B3
St Paul's Rd C2
St Saviour's Cres C1
Salisbury Rd B1
Seymour Ave C3
Seymour Rd C3
Silver St B2
South Rd C2
Stanley St B1
Station Rd A2
Stockwood Cres C2
Stockwood Park C1
Strathmore Ave C2
Stuart St B2
Studley Rd A1
Surrey St C3
Sutherland Place C1
Tavistock St C2
Taylor St A3
Telford Way A1
Tennyson Rd C2
Tenzing Grove C1
The Cross Way C1
The Larches A2
Thistle Rd B3
Town Hall B2
Townsley Cl C2
UK Centre for Carnival Arts B3
Union St B2
University of Bedfordshire B3
Upper George St B2
Vicarage St B3
Villa Rd A2
Waldeck Rd A1
Wellington St B1/B2
Wenlock St A2
Whitby Rd A1
Whitehill Ave C1
William St A2
Wilsden Ave C1
Windmill Rd B3
Windsor St C2
Winsdon Rd B1
York St A3

Macclesfield 187

108 Steps B2
Abbey Rd A1
Alton Dr A3
Armett St C1
Athey St B1
Bank St C3
Barber St C3
Barton St C1
Beech La A2
Beswick St B1
Black La A2
Black Rd C3
Blakelow Gardens C3
Blakelow Rd C3
Bond St B1/C1
Bread St C1
Bridge St B1
Brock St A2
Brocklehurst Ave A3
Brook St B3
Brookfield La B3
Brough St West C1
Brown St C1
Brynton Rd A2
Buckley St C2
Bus Station B2
Buxton Rd B3
Byrons St C2
Canal St B3
Carlsbrook Ave A3
Castle St B2
Catherine St B1
Cemetery A1
Chadwick Terr A3
Chapel St C2
Charlotte St B2
Chester Rd B1
Chestergate B1
Churchill Way B2
Coare St A1
Commercial Rd B2
Conway Cres A3
Copper St C3
Cottage St B1
Court B2
Court B2
Crematorium A1
Crew Ave A3
Crompton Rd B1/C1
Cross St C2
Crossall St C1
Cumberland St A1/B1
Dale St B3
Duke St B2
Eastgate B3
Exchange St B2
Fence Ave B3
Fence Avenue Industrial Estate A3
Flint St B3
Foden St A2
Fountain St B3
Garden St A3
Gas Rd B2
George St B2
Glegg St B3
Golf Course C3
Goodall St B3
Grange Rd C1
Great King St B1
Green St B3
Grosvenor Shopping Centre B2
Gunco La C3
Half St C2
Hallefield Rd B3
Hatton St C1
Hawthorn Way A3
Heapy St C3
Henderson St B1
Heritage Centre & Silk Museum B2
Hibel Rd A2
High St C2
Hobson St C2
Hollins Rd C3
Hope St West C1
Horseshoe Dr B1
Hurdsfield Rd A3
Information Ctr B2
James St C2
Jodrell St B3
John St C2
Jordangate A2
King Edward St B2
King George's Field C3
King St B2
King's School A1
Knight Pool C3
Knight St C3
Lansdowne St A3
Library B2
Lime Gr B3
Little Theatre C2
Loney St B1
Longacre St B1
Lord St C2
Lowe St C2
Lowerfield Rd A3
Lyon St B1
Macclesfield Station B2
Marina B3
Market B2
Market Pl B2
Masons La A3
Mill La C2
Mill Rd C2
Mill St B2
Moran Rd C1
New Hall St A2
Newton St C1
Nicholson Ave A3
Nicholson Cl A3
Northgate Ave A2
Old Mill La C2
Paradise Mill C2
Paradise St B1
Park Green B2
Park La C1
Park Rd C1
Park St C2
Park Vale Rd C1
Parr St B1
Peel St C2
Percyvale St A3
Peter St C1
Pickford St B2
Pierce St B1
Pinfold St B1
Pitt St C2
Police Station B2
Pool St C2
Poplar Rd C2
Post Office B1/B2/B3
Pownall St A2
Prestbury Rd A1/B1
Queen Victoria St B2
Queen's Ave A3
Registrar B2
Richmond Hill C3
Riseley St B1
Roan Ct B3
Roe St B2
Rowan Way A3
Ryle St C2
Ryle's Park Rd C1
St George's St C2
St Michael's B2
Samuel St B2
Saville St C3
Shaw St B1
Slater St C1
Snow Hill C3
South Park C1
Spring Gdns A2
Statham St C2
Station St A2
Steeple St A3
Sunderland St B2
Superstore A1/A2/C2
Swettenham St B3
The Silk Rd A2/B2
Thistleton Cl C2
Thorp St B2
Town Hall B2
Townley St B2
Turnock St C3
Union Rd B3
Union St B2
Victoria Park B3
Vincent St C2
Waters Green B2
Waterside C2
West Bond St B1
West Park A1
Westbrook Dr A1
Westminster Rd A1
Whalley Hayes B1
Windmill St C3
Withyfold Dr A2
York St B3

Maidstone 187

Albion Pl B3
All Saints B2
Allen St A3
Amphitheatre C2
Archbishop's Palace B2
Bank St B2
Barker Rd C2
Barton Rd C3
Beaconsfield Rd C1
Bedford Pl B1
Bentlif Art Gallery B2
Bishops Way B2
Bluett St A3
Bower La C1
Bower Mount Rd B1
Bower Pl C1
Bower St B1
Bowling Alley B3
Boxley Rd A3
Brenchley Gardens A2
Brewer St A3
Broadway B2
Brunswick St C3
Buckland Hill A1
Buckland Rd B1
Bus Station B3
Campbell Rd C3
Carriage Museum B2
Church Rd C1
Church St B3
Cinema C2
College Ave C2
College Rd C2
Collis Memorial Garden C3
Cornwallis Rd B1
Corpus Christi Hall B2
County Hall A2
County Rd A3
Crompton Gdns C3
Crown & County Courts B2
Curzon Rd A3
Dixon Cl C2
Douglas Rd C1
Earl St B2
Eccleston Rd C2
Fairmeadow B2
Fisher St A2
Florence Rd C1
Foley St A3
Foster St C3
Fremlin Walk Shopping Centre B2
Gabriel's Hill B3
George St C3
Grecian St A3
Hardy St A3
Hart St C2
Hastings Rd C3
Hayle Rd C3
Hazlitt Theatre B2
Heathorn St A3
Hedley St A3
High St B2
HM Prison A3
Holland Rd A3
Hope St A2
Information Ctr B2
James St A3
James Whatman Way A2
Jeffrey St A3
Kent County Council Offices A2
King Edward Rd C2
King St B3
Kingsley Rd C3
Knightrider St B3
Launder Way C1
Lesley Pl A1
Library B2
Little Buckland Ave A1
Lockmeadow Leisure Complex C2
London Rd B1
Lower Boxley Rd A2
Lower Fant Rd C1
Magistrates Court B3
Maidstone Barracks Station A1
Maidstone Borough Council Offices B1
Maidstone East Station A2
Maidstone Museum B2
Maidstone West Station B2
Market C2
Market Buildings B2
Marsham St B3
Medway St B2
Medway Trading Estate C2
Melville Rd C3
Mill St B2
Millennium Bridge C2
Mote Rd B3
Muir Rd C3
Old Tovil Rd C2
Palace Ave B3
Perryfield St A2
Police Station B3
Post Office A2/B2/B3/C3
Priory Rd C3
Prospect Pl C1
Pudding La B2
Queen Anne Rd B3
Queens Rd A1
Randall St A2
Rawdon Rd C3
Reginald Rd C1
Rock Pl B1
Rocky Hill B1
Romney Pl B3
Rose Yard B2
Rowland Cl C1
Royal Engineers' Rd A2
Royal Star Arcade B2
St Annes Ct B1
St Faith's St B2
St Luke's Rd A3
St Peter St B2
St Peter's Br B2
St Philip's Ave C3
Salisbury Rd A3
Sandling Rd A2
Scott St A2
Scrubs La B1
Sheal's Cres C3
Somerfield La B1
Somerfield Rd B1
Staceys St A2
Station Rd A2
Superstore A1/B2/B3
Terrace Rd B1
The Mall B3
The Somerfield Hospital A1
Tonbridge Rd C1
Tovil Rd C2
Town Hall B2
Trinity Park B3
Tufton St B3
Union St B3
Upper Fant Rd C1
Upper Stone St C3
Victoria St B1
Visitor Centre A1
Warwick Pl B1
Wat Tyler Way B3
Waterloo St C3
Waterlow Rd A3
Week St B2
Well Rd A3
Westree Rd C1
Wharf Rd C1
Whatman Park A1
Wheeler St A3
Whitchurch Cl B1
Woodville Rd C3
Wyatt St B3
Wyke Manor Rd B3

Manchester 187

Adair St B6
Addington St A5
Adelphi St A1
Air & Space Gallery B2
Albert Sq B3
Albion St C3
AMC Great Northern B3
Ancoats Gr B6
Ancoats Gr North B6
Angela St C2
Aquatic Centre C4
Ardwick Green C5
Ardwick Green North C5
Ardwick Green South C5
Arlington St A2
Arndale Centre A4
Artillery St B3
Arundel St C2
Atherton St B2
Atkinson St B3
Aytoun St B4
Back Piccadilly A4
Baird St B5
Balloon St A4
Bank Pl A1
Baring St B5
Barrack St C1
Barrow St A1
BBC TV Studios C4
Bengal St A5
Berry St C5
Blackfriars Rd A3
Blackfriars St A3
Blantyre St C2
Bloom St B4
Blossom St A5
Boad St B5
Bombay St B4
Booth St A3
Booth St B4
Bootle St B3
Brazennose St B3
Brewer St A5
Bridge St A3
Bridgewater Hall B3
Bridgewater Pl A4
Bridgewater St B2
Brook St C4
Brotherton Dr A2
Brown St A3
Brown St B4
Brunswick St C6
Brydon Ave C6
Buddhist Centre A4
Bury St A2
Bus & Coach Station B4
Bus Station B4
Butler St A6
Buxton St C5
Byrom St B3
Cable St A5
Calder St B1
Cambridge St C3/C4
Camp St B3
Canal St B4
Cannon St A4
Cannon St A1
Cardroom Rd A6
Carruthers St A6
Castle St C2
Cateaton St A3
Cathedral A3
Cathedral St A3
Cavendish St C4
Chapel St A1/A3
Chapeltown St B5
Charles St C4
Charlotte St B4
Chatham St B4
Cheapside A3
Chepstow St B3
Chester Rd C1/C2
Chester St C4
Chetham's (Dept Store) A3
China La B5
Chippenham Rd A6
Chorlton Rd C2
Chorlton St B4
Church St A2
Church St A4
City Park A4
City Rd C3
Civil Justice Centre B2
Cleminson St A2
Clowes St A3
College Land A3
College of Adult Education C4
Collier St B2
Commercial St C3
Conference Centre C4
Cooper St B4
Copperas St A4
Cornbrook (Metro Station) C1
Cornell St A5
Cornerhouse C4
Corporation St A4
Cotter St C6
Cotton St A5
Cow La B1
Cross St B3
Crown Court B4
Crown St C2
Cube Gallery B4
Dalberg St C6
Dale St A4/B5
Dancehouse, The C4
Dantzic St A4
Dark La C6
Dawson St C2
Dean St A5
Deansgate A3/B3
Deansgate Station C3
Dolphin St C6
Downing St C5
Ducie St B5
Duke Pl B2
Duke St B2
Durling St C6
East Ordsall La A2/B1
Edge St A4
Egerton St C2
Ellesmere St C1
Everard St C1
Every St B6
Fairfield St B5
Faulkner St B4
Fennel St A3
Ford St A2
Ford St C6
Fountain St B4
Frederick St A2
Gartside St B2
Gaythorne St A1
George Leigh St A5
George St A1
George St B4
G-Mex (Metro Station) C3
Goadsby St A4
Gore St A2
Goulden St A5
Granada TV Studios B2
Granby Row B4
Gravel St A3
Great Ancoats St A5
Great Bridgewater St B3
Great George St A1
Great Jackson St C2
Great Marlborough St C4
Greengate A3
Green Room, The C4
Grosvenor St C5
Gun St A5
Hadrian Ave B6
Hall St B3
Hampson St B1
Hanover St A4
Hanworth Cl C5
Hardman St B3
Harkness St C6
Harrison St B6
Hart St B4
Helmet St B6
Henry St A5
Heyrod St B6
High St A4
Higher Ardwick C6
Hilton St A4/A5
Holland St A6
Hood St A5
Hope St B1
Hope St B4
Houldsworth St A5
Hoyle St C6
Hulme Hall Rd C1
Hulme St A1
Hulme St C3
Hyde Rd C6
Information Ctr B3
Irwell St A2
Islington St A2
Jackson Cr C2
Jackson's Row B3
James St A1
Jenner Cl C2
Jersey St A5
John Dalton St A1
John Dalton St B3
John Ryland's Library B3
John St A2
Kennedy St B3
Kincardine Rd C5
King St A3
King St West A3
Law Courts B3
Laystall St B5
Lever St A5
Library B3
Library Theatre B3
Linby St C2
Little Lever St A4
Liverpool Rd B2
Liverpool St B1
Lloyd St B3
Lockton Cl C5
London Rd B5
Long Millgate A3
Longacre St B6
Loom St A5
Lower Byrom St B2
Lower Mosley St B3
Lower Moss La C2
Lower Ormond St C4
Loxford La C4
Luna St A5
Major St B4
Manchester Art Gallery B4
Manchester Central B3
Manchester Metropolitan University B4/C4
Mancunian Way C3
Manor St C5
Marble St A4
Market St A2
Market St A4
Market St (Metro Station) A4
Marsden St A3
Marshall St A5
Mayan Ave A2
Medlock St C3
Middlewood St B1
Miller St A4
Minshull St B4
Mosley St A4
Mosley St (Metro Station) B4
Mount St B3
Mulberry St B3
Murray St A5
Museum of Science & Technology B2
Nathan Dr A2
National Computer Centre C4
Naval St A5
New Bailey St A2
New Elm Rd B2
New Islington A6
New Quay St B2
New Union St A6
Newgate St A4
Newton St A5
Nicholas St B4
North Western St C6
Oak St A4
Odeon B4
Old Mill St A6
Oldfield Rd A1/C1
Oldham Rd A5
Oldham St A4
Opera House B3
Ordsall La C1
Oxford Rd C4
Oxford Rd C4
Oxford St B4
Paddock St C6
Palace Theatre B4
Pall Mall A3
Palmerston St B6
Park St A1
Parker St B4
Peak St B5
Penfield Cl C5
Peoples' History Museum B2
Peru St A1
Peter St B3
Piccadilly A4
Piccadilly (Metro Station) B5
Piccadilly Gdns (Metro Station) B4
Piccadilly Station B5
Piercy St A6
Poland St A5
Police Station B3/B5
Pollard St B6
Port St A5
Portland St B4
Portugal St East B5
Post Office A1/A4/A5/B3
Potato Wharf B2
Princess St B3/C4
Pritchard St C4
Quay St A2
Quay St B2
Queen St B3
Radium St A5
Redhill St A5
Regent Rd B1
Renold Theatre A2
Retail Park A5
Rice St B2
Richmond St B4
River St C3
Roby St B5
Rodney St A6
Roman Fort B2
Rosamond St A2
Royal Exchange A3
Sackville St B4
St Andrew's St B6
St Ann St A3
St Ann's A3
St George's Ave C1
St James St B4
St John St B3
St John's Cathedral (RC) A2
St Mary's B3
St Mary's Gate A3
St Mary's Parsonage A3
St Peter's Sq (Metro Station) B3
St Stephen St A2
Salford Approach A3
Salford Central A2
Sheffield St B5
Shepley St B5
Sherratt St A5
Shudehill A4
Shudehill (Metro Station) A4
Sidney St C4
Silk St A5
Silver St B4
Skerry Cl C5
Snell St B6
South King St B3
Sparkle St B5
Spear St A4
Spring Gdns A4
Stanley St A2/B2
Station Approach B5
Store St B5
Swan St A4
Tariff St B5
Tatton St C1
Temperance St B6/C6
The Triangle A4
Thirsk St C6
Thomas St A4
Thompson St A5
Tib La B3
Tib St A4
Town Hall (Manchester) B3
Town Hall (Salford) A2
Trafford St C3
Travis St B5
Trinity Way A2
Turner St A4
Union St C6
University of Manchester (Sackville Street Campus) C5
Upper Brook St C5
Upper Cleminson St A1
Upper Wharf St A1
Urbis Museum A4
Vesta St B6
Victoria (Metro Station) A4
Victoria Station A4
Victoria St A3
Wadesdon Rd C5
Water St B2
Watson St B3
West Fleet St B1
West King St A2
West Mosley St B4
West Union St B1
Weybridge Rd A6
Whitworth St B4
Whitworth St West C3
Wilburn St B1
William St A2
William St C6
Wilmott St C3
Windmill St B3
Windsor Cr A1
Withy Gr A4
Woden St C1
Wood St B3
Woodward St A6
Worrall St C1
Worsley St C2
York St B4
York St C2
York St C4

Merthyr Tydfil
Merthyr Tudful 187

Aberdare Rd B2
Abermorlais Terr B2
Alexandra Rd A3
Alma St C3
Arfryn Pl C3
Argyle St C3
Avenue De Clichy C2
Bethesda St B2
Bishops Gr A3
Brecon Rd A1/B2
Briarmead A3
Bryn St C3
Bryntirion Rd B3/C3
Bus Station B2
Caedraw Rd C2
Cae Mari Dwn B3
Castle Sq A1
Castle St B2
Chapel C2
Chapel Bank B1
Church St B3
Civic Centre B2
Coedcae'r Ct C3
Court B3
Courts B2
Court St C3
Cromwell St B2
Cyfarthfa Castle School and Museum A1
Cyfarthfa Industrial Estate A1
Cyfarthfa Park A1
Cyfarthfa Rd A1
Dane St A2
Dane Terr A2
Danyparc B3
Darren View A3
Dixon St B2
Dyke St C3
Dynevor St B2

Elwyn Dr C3
Fire Station B2
Fothergill St B1
Galonuchaf Rd A3
Garth St B2
Georgetown B2
Grawen Terr A2
Grove Pk A2
Gurnos Rd A2
Gwaelodygarth Rd A2/A3
Gwaunfarren Gr A3
Gwaunfarren Rd A3
Gwendoline St A3
Hampton St C3
Hanover St A2
Heol S O Davies B1
Heol-Gerrig B1
Highland View C3
High St A3/B2/B3/C2
Howell Cl B1
Information Ctr B2
Jackson's Bridge B2
James St C3
John St B3
Joseph Parry's Cottage B2
Lancaster St A2
Llewellyn St A2
Llwyfen St B2
Llwyn Berry B1
Llwyn Dic Penderyn B1
Llwyn-y-Gelynen C1
Lower Thomas St B3
Market C2
Mary St C3
Masonic St C2
Merthyr College B2
Merthyr Tydfil FC B3
Merthyr Tydfil RUFC C2
Merthyr Tydfil Station C3
Meyrick Villas A2
Miniature Railway A1
Mount St A2
Nantygwenith St B1
Norman Terr B2
Oak Rd A2
Old Cemetery B3
Pandy Cl A1
Pantycelynen B1
Park Terr B2
Penlan View C2
Penry St B2
Pentwyn Villas A2
Penyard Rd B3
Penydarren Park A3
Penydarren Rd B3
Plymouth St C3
Police Station C2
Pont Marlais West B2
Post Office A3/B2/C3
Quarry Row B2
Queen's Rd B3
Rees St C3
Rhydycar Leisure Centre C3
Rhydycar Link C2
Riverside Park A1
St David's B2
St Tydfil's C2
St Tydfil's Ave C3
St Tydfil's Hospital (No A+E) B3
St Tydfil's Square Shopping Centre C2
Saxon St A2
School of Nursing A2
Seward St A3
Shiloh La B3
Stone Circles B3
Stuart St A2
Summerhill Pl B3
Superstore B3
Swan St C2
Swansea Rd B1
Taff Glen View C3
Taff Vale Ct B3
The Grove A2
The Parade B3
The Walk B2
Thomastown Park B3
Tramroad La A3
Tramroad Side B2
Tramroad Side North B3
Tramroad Side South C3
Trevithick Gdns C3
Trevithick St A3
Tudor Terr B2
Twynyrodyn Rd C3
Union St B3
Upper Colliers Row B1
Upper Thomas St B3
Victoria St B2
Vulcan Rd B2
Warlow St C3
Well St A2
Wern La C1
West Gr A2
William St C3
Yew St C3
Ynysfach Engine House C2
Ynysfach Rd C2

Middlesbrough 187

Abingdon Rd C3
Acklam Rd C1
Albert Park C2
Albert Rd B2
Albert Terr C2
Aubrey St C3
Ayresome Gdns C2
Ayresome Green La C1
Ayresome St C2
Barton Rd A1
Bilsdale Rd C3
Bishopton Rd C3
Borough Rd B2/B3
Bowes Rd A2
Breckon Hill Rd B3
Bridge St East B3
Bridge St West B2
Brighouse Rd A1
Burlam Rd C1
Bus Station B2
Cannon Park B1
Cannon Park Way B2
Cannon St B1
Captain Cook Sq B2
Carlow St C1
Castle Way C3
Chipchase Rd C2
Cineworld B3
Clairville Sports Stadium C3
Cleveland Centre B2
Clive Rd C2
Commercial St A2
Corporation Rd B2
Costa St C2
Council Offices B3
Crescent Rd C2
Cumberland Rd C2
Depot Rd A2
Derwent St B2
Devonshire Rd C2
Diamond Rd B2
Disabled Driver Test Circuit B1
Dorman Museum C2
Douglas St B3
Eastbourne Rd C2
Eden Rd C3
Enterprise Centre A2
Forty Foot Rd A2
Gilkes St B2
Gosford St A2
Grange Rd B2
Gresham Rd B2
Harehills Rd C1
Harford St C2
Hartington Rd B2
Haverton Hill Rd A1
Hey Wood St B1
Highfield Rd C3
Hill St Centre B2
Holwick Rd B1
Hudson Quay C3
Hutton Rd C3
I.C.I. Works A1
Information Ctr B2
Lambton Rd C3
Lancaster Rd C2
Lansdowne Rd C3
Latham Rd C2
Law Courts B2/B3
Lees Rd B2
Leeway B3
Linthorpe Cemetery C1
Linthorpe Rd B2
Little Theatre, The C2
Lloyd St B2
Longford St C2
Longlands Rd C3
Lower East St A3
Lower Lake C3
Maldon Rd C1
Manor St B2
Marsh St B2
Marton Rd B3
Middlehaven B3
Middlesbrough By-Pass B2/C1
Middlesbrough F.C. B3
Middlesbrough Leisure Park B3
Middlesbrough Station B2
Middletown Park C2
MIMA B3
Mosque B2
Mosque C3
Mulgrave Rd C2
North Ormesby Rd B3
Newport Bridge B1
Newport Bridge Approach Rd B1
Newport Rd B2
North Rd B2
Northern Rd C1
Outram St B2
Oxford Rd C2
Park La C2
Park Rd North C2
Park Rd South C2
Park Vale Rd C3
Parliament Rd B1
Police Station A3
Port Clarence Rd A3
Portman St B2
Post Office B3/C1/C2/C3
Princes Rd B2
Riverside Business Park A2
Riverside Park Rd A1
Rockliffe Rd C2
Romaldkirk Rd B1
Roman Rd C2
Roseberry Rd C3
St Barnabas' Rd C2
St Paul's Rd B2
Saltwells Rd B3
Scott's Rd A3
Seaton Carew Rd A3
Shepherdson Way B3
Sikh Temple B2
Snowdon Rd A2
South West Ironmasters Park B1
Southfield Rd B2
Southwell Rd C2
Springfield Rd C1
Startforth Rd A2
Stockton Rd C1
Stockton St A2
Surrey St C2
Sycamore Rd C2
Synagogue C2
Tax Offices B3
Tees Viaduct C1
Teessaurus Park A2
Teesside Tertiary College C3
The Avenue C2
The Crescent C2
Thornfield Rd C1
Town Hall B2
Transporter Bridge (Toll) A3
Union St B2
University of Teesside B2
Upper Lake C2
Valley Rd C3
Ventnor Rd C2
Victoria Rd B2
Vulcan St A2
Warwick St C2
Wellesley Rd B3
West Lane Hospital C1
Westminster Rd C2
Wilson St B2
Windward Way B3
Woodlands Rd B2
York Rd C3

Milton Keynes 188

Abbey Way A1
Arbrook Ave B1
Armourer Dr A3
Arncliffe Dr A1
Avebury (r'about) C2
Avebury Blvd C2
Bankfield (r'about) B3
Bayard Ave A2
Belvedere (r'about) A2
Bishopstone A1
Blundells Rd A1
Boycott Ave C2
Bradwell Common Blvd B1
Bradwell Rd C1
Bramble Ave A2
Brearley Ave C2
Breckland A1
Brill Place B1
Burnham Dr B1
Bus Station C1
Campbell Park (r'about) B3
Cantle Ave A3
Central Milton Keynes Shopping Area B2
Century Ave C2
Chaffron Way C3
Childs Way C1
Christ the Cornerstone B2
Cineworld B2
Civic Offices B2
Cleavers Ave B2
Colesbourne Dr A3
Conniburrow Blvd B2
County Court B2
Currier Dr A2
Dansteed Way A2/A3/B1
Deltic Ave B1
Downs Barn (r'about) A2
Downs Barn Blvd A3
Eaglestone (r'about) C3
Eelbrook Ave B1
Elder Gate B1
Evans Gate C2
Fairford Cr A3
Falcon Ave B3
Fennel Dr A2
Fishermead Blvd C3
Food Centre B3
Fulwoods Dr C3
Glazier Dr A2
Glovers La A1
Grafton Gate C1
Grafton St A1/C2
Gurnards Ave B3
Harrier Dr C3
Ibstone Ave B1
Langcliffe Dr A1
Leisure Plaza C1
Leys Rd C1
Library B2
Linford Wood A2
Marlborough Gate B3
Marlborough St A2/B3
Mercers Dr A1
Midsummer (r'about) C2
Midsummer Blvd B2
Milton Keynes Central C1
Monks Way A1
Mullen Ave A3
Mullion Pl C3
National Hockey Stadium B1
Neath Hill (r'about) A3
North Elder (r'about) C1
North Grafton (r'about) B1
North Overgate (r'about) A3
North Row B2
North Saxon (r'about) B2
North Secklow (r'about) B2
North Skeldon (r'about) A3
North Witan (r'about) B1
Oakley Gdns A3
Oldbrook Blvd C2
Open-Air Theatre B3
Overgate A3
Overstreet A3
Patriot Dr B1
Pencarrow Pl B3
Penryn Ave B3
Perran Ave C3
Pitcher La C1
Place Retail Park, The C1
Point Centre, The B2
Police Station B2
Portway (r'about) B2
Post Office A2/B2/C3
Precedent Dr B1
Quinton Dr B1
Ramsons Ave B2
Rockingham Dr A2
Rooksley (r'about) B1
Rooksley Retail Park C1
Saxon Gate B2
Saxon St A1/C3
Secklow Gate B2
Shackleton Pl C2
Silbury Blvd B2
Skeldon (r'about) A3
South Grafton (r'about) C2
South Row C2
South Saxon (r'about) C2
South Secklow (r'about) B3
South Witan (r'about) C2
Springfield (r'about) B3
Stanton Wood (r'about) A1
Stantonbury (r'about) A1
Stantonbury Leisure Centre A1
Strudwick Dr C2
Sunrise Parkway A2
Telephone Exchange C3
The Boundary C3
Theatre and Art Gallery B3
Tolcarne Ave C3
Towan Ave C3
Trueman Pl C2
Vauxhall A1
Winterhill Retail Park C2
Witan Gate B2
X-Scape B3

Newcastle upon Tyne 188

Albert St B3
Argyle St B3
Back New Bridge St B3
BALTIC The Centre for Contemporary Art C3
Bank Rd C3
Barker St A3
Barrack Rd B1
Bath La B1
Bell's Court B2
Bessie Surtees House C2
Bigg Market C2
Biscuit Factory B3
Black Gate C2
Blackett St B2
Blandford Sq C1
Boating Lake A1
Boyd St B3
Brandling Park A2
Bus Station B2
Buxton St B3
Byron St A3
Camden St B2
Castle Keep C2
Central (metro station) C1
Central Library B2
Central Motorway B2
Chester St A3
City Hall B2
City Rd B3/C3
City Walls C1
Civic Centre A2
Claremont Rd A1
Clarence St B3
Clarence Walk B3
Clayton St C1/B1
Clayton St West C1
Coach Station C1
College St B2
Collingwood St C2
Copland Terr B3
Coppice Way B3
Corporation St B1
Courts C3
Crawhall Rd B3
Dean St C2
Dinsdale Pl A3
Dinsdale Rd A3
Doncaster Rd A3
Durant Rd B2
Eldon Sq B1
Eldon Sq Shopping Centre B2
Ellison Pl B2
Eskdale Terr A2
Eslington Terr A2
Exhibition Park A1
Falconar St B3
Fenkle St C1
Forth Banks C1
Forth St C1
Gallowgate B1
Gateshead Millennium Bridge C3
Gibson St B3
Goldspink La A3
Grainger Market B2
Grainger St B2
Grantham Rd A3
Granville Rd A3
Grey St B2
Groat Market C2
Guildhall C2
Hancock Mus A2
Hancock St A2
Hanover St C2
Hawks Rd C3
Haymarket (metro station) B2
Heber St B1
Helmsley Rd A3
High Bridge C2
High Level Bridge C2
Hillgate C3
Howard St B3
Hutton Terr A3
Information Ctr B2
Jesmond (metro station) A2
Jesmond Rd A2/A3
John Dobson St B2
John George Joicey Museum C2
Jubilee Rd B3
Kelvin Gr A3
Kensington Terr A2
Laing Gallery B2
Lambton Rd A2
Leazes Cr B1
Leazes La B1
Leazes Park B1
Leazes Park Rd B1
Leazes Terr B1
Low Friar St C1
Manor Chare C2
Manors (metro station) B2
Manors Station B2
Market St B2
Melbourne St B2
Mill Rd C3
Millennium Sq C1
Monument (metro station) B2
Monument Mall Shopping Centre B2
Morpeth St A2
Mosley St C2
Napier St A3
Nazareth House A3
New Bridge St B2/B3
Newcastle Central Station C1
Newcastle University A1
Newgate Shopping Centre C1
Newgate St B1
Newington Rd A3
Northern Stage Theatre A2
Northumberland Rd B2
Northumberland St B2
Northumbria University A2
Northwest Radial Rd A1
Oakwellgate C3
Odeon B1
Orchard St C2
Osborne Rd A2
Osborne Terr A3
Pandon C3
Pandon Bank B3
Park Terr A1
Percy St B1
Pilgrim St B2
Pipewellgate C2
Pitt St B1
Plummer Tower A2
Police Station B2
Portland Rd A3/B3
Portland Terr A3
Post Office A3/B1/B2/B3
Pottery La C1
Prudhoe Pl B1
Prudhoe St B1
Quayside C2
Queen Elizabeth II Bridge C2
Queen Victoria Rd A1
Richardson Rd A1
Ridley Pl B2
Rock Terr B3
Rosedale Terr A3
Royal Victoria Infirmary A1
Sage Gateshead, The C3
St Andrew's St B1
St James (metro station) B1
St James' Blvd C1
St James' Park (Newcastle Utd FC) B1
St Mary's (RC) C1
St Mary's Place B2
St Nicholas C2
St Nicholas St C2
St Thomas' St B1
Sandyford Rd A2/A3
Science Park B2
Shield St B3
Shieldfield B3
Simpson Terr B3
South Shore Rd C3
South St C1
Starbeck Ave A3
Stepney Rd B3
Stoddart St B3
Stowell St B1
Strawberry Pl B1
Swing Bridge C2
Temple St C1
Terrace Pl B1
The Close C2
The Side C2
Theatre Royal B2
Tower St B3
Trinity House C2
Tyne Bridge C2
Tyne Bridges C2
Tyneside B2
Victoria Sq A2
Warwick St A3
Waterloo St C1
Wellington St B1
Westgate Rd C1/C2
Windsor Terr A2
Worswick St B2
Wretham Pl B3

Newport Casnewydd 188

Albert Terr B1
Allt-yr-Yn Ave A1
Alma St C2
Ambulance Station C3
Bailey St B2
Barrack Hill A2
Bath St A3
Bedford Rd B3
Belle Vue La C1
Belle Vue Park C1
Bishop St A3
Blewitt St B1
Bolt Cl C3
Bolt St C3
Bond St A2
Bosworth Dr A1
Bridge St B1
Bristol St A3
Bryngwyn Rd B1
Brynhyfryd Ave C1
Brynhyfryd Rd C1
Bus Station B2
Caerau Cres C1
Caerau Rd B1
Caerleon Rd A3
Cambrian Retail Centre B2
Capel Cres C2
Cardiff Rd C2
Caroline St B3
Castle (Remains) A2
Cattle Market and Saturday General Market C3
Cedar Rd B3
Charles St B2
Charlotte Dr C2
Chepstow Rd A3
Church Rd A3
City Cinema B1
Civic Centre B1
Clarence Pl A2
Clifton Pl B1
Clifton Rd C1
Clyffard Cres B1
Clytha Park Rd B1
Clytha Sq C2
Coldra Rd C1
Collier St A3
Colne St B3
Comfrey Cl A1
Commercial Rd C3
Commercial St B2
Corelli St A3
Corn St B2
Corporation Rd B3
Coulson Cl C2
County Court A2
Courts A1
Courts B1
Crawford St A3
Cyril St B3
Dean St A3
Devon Pl B1
Dewsland Park Rd C2
Dolman B2
Dolphin St C3
East Dock Rd C3
East St B1
East Usk Rd A3
Ebbw Vale Wharf B3
Emlyn St B2
Enterprise Way C3
Eton Rd B3
Evans St A2
Factory Rd A2
Fields Rd B1
Francis Dr C2
Frederick St C3
Friars Rd C1
Gaer La C1
George St C3
George Street Bridge C3
Godfrey Rd B1
Gold Tops B1
Gore St A3
Gorsedd Circle C1
Grafton Rd A3
Graham St B1
Granville St C3
Harlequin Dr A1
Harrow Rd B3
Herbert Rd A3
Herbert Walk C2
Hereford St A3
High St B2
Hill St B2
Hoskins St A2
Information Ctr B2
Ivor Sq B2
John Frost Sq B2
Jones St B1
Junction Rd A3
Keynshaw Ave C2
King St C2
Kingsway B2
Kingsway Shopping Centre B2
Ledbury Dr A2
Library A3
Library, Museum & Art Gallery B2
Liverpool Wharf B3
Llanthewy Rd B1
Llanvair Rd A3
Locke St A2
Lower Dock St C3
Lucas St A2
Manchester St A3
Market B2
Marlborough Rd B3
Mellon St C3
Mill St A2
Morgan St A3
Mountjoy Rd C2
Newport Athletic Club Grounds B3
Newport Bridge A2
Newport Leisure and Conference Ctr B2
Newport Station B2
North St B2
Oakfield Rd B1
Park Sq C2
Police Station A3/C2
Post Office B1/B2/C1/C3
Power St A1
Prince St A3
Pugsley St A2
Queen St C2
Queen's Cl A1
Queen's Hill A1
Queen's Hill Cres A1
Queensway B2
Railway St B2
Riverfront Arts Centre B2
Riverside A3
Rodney Rd B2
Royal Gwent (A+E) C2
Rudry St A3
Rugby Rd B3
Ruperra La C3
Ruperra St C3
St Edmund St B1
St Mark's Cres A1
St Mary St B1
St Vincent Rd A3
St Woolos C2
St Woolos General (no A+E) C1
St Woolos Rd B1
School La B2
Serpentine Rd B1
Shaftesbury Park A2
Sheaf La A3
Skinner St B2
Sorrel Dr A1
South Market St C3
Spencer Rd B1
Stow Hill B2/C1/C2
Stow Park Ave C1
Stow Park Dr C1
TA Centre A1
Talbot St B2
Tennis Club A1
Tregare St A3
Trostrey St A3
Tunnel Terr B1
Turner St A3
Usk St A3
Usk Way B3/C3
Victoria Cr B1
War Memorial A3
Waterloo Rd C1
West St B1
Wharves B2
Wheeler St A2
Whitby Pl A3
Windsor Terr B1
York Pl C1

Newquay 188

Agar Rd B2
Alma Pl B1
Ambulance Station B2
Anthony Rd C1
Atlantic Hotel A1
Bank St B1
Barrowfields A3
Bay View Terr B2
Beachfield Ave B1
Beach Rd B1
Beacon Rd A1
Belmont Pl A1
Berry Rd B2
Blue Reef Aquarium B1
Boating Lake C2
Bus Station B1
Chapel Hill B1
Chester Rd A3
Cheviot Rd C1/C2
Chichester Cres C2
Chynance Dr C1
Chyverton Cl C1
Cliff Rd B2
Coach Park B2
Colvreath Rd A3
Council Offices B1
Crantock St B1
Criggar Rocks A3
Dale Cl C3
Dale Rd C3
Dane Rd A1
East St B2
Edgcumbe Ave B3
Edgcumbe Gdns B3
Eliot Gdns B3
Elm Cl C3
Ennor's Rd B1
Fernhill Rd B1
Fire Station B1
Fore St B1
Gannel Rd C2
Golf Driving Range B3
Gover La B1
Great Western Beach A2
Grosvenor Ave B2
Harbour A1
Hawkins Rd C2
Headleigh Rd B2
Hilgrove Rd A3/B3
Holywell Rd B3
Hope Terr B1
Huer's House, The A1
Information Ctr B1
Island Cres B2
Jubilee St B1
Kew Cl C3
Killacourt Cove A2
King Edward Cres A1
Lanhenvor Ave B2
Library B1
Lifeboat Station A1
Linden Ave C2
Listry Rd C2
Lusty Glaze Beach A3
Lusty Glaze Rd A3
Manor Rd B1
Marcus Hill B2
Mayfield Rd B2
Meadowside C3
Mellanvrane La C2
Michell Ave B2
Miniature Golf Course C3
Miniature Railway B3
Mount Wise B1
Mowhay Cl C3
Narrowcliff A3
Newquay B2
Newquay Hospital (no A&E) B2
Newquay Town Football Ground B1
Newquay Zoo B3
North Pier A1
North Quay Hill A1
Oakleigh Terr B2
Pargolla Rd B2
Pendragon Cres C3
Pengannel Cl C1
Penina Ave C3
Police Station & Courts B2
Post Office B1/B2
Quarry Park Rd B3
Rawley La C2
Reeds Way B1
Robartes Rd B2
St Anne's Rd A3
St Aubyn Cres B3
St George's Rd B1
St John's Rd B1
St Mary's Rd B1
St Michael's B1
St Michael's Rd B1
St Thomas' Rd B2
Seymour Ave B2
South Pier A1
South Quay Hill A1
Sweet Briar Cres C3
Sydney Rd A1
The Crescent B1
Tolcarne Beach A2
Tolcarne Point A2
Tolcarne Rd B2
Tor Rd B2
Towan Beach A1
Towan Blystra Rd B3
Tower Rd A1
Trebarwith Cres B2
Tredour Rd C2
Treforda Rd C3
Tregoss Rd B3
Tregunnel Hill B1/C1
Tregunnel Saltings C1
Trelawney Rd B2
Treloggan La C3
Treloggan Rd C3
Trembath Cres C1
Trenance Ave B2
Trenance Gardens B2
Trenance La C2
Trenance Leisure Park B3
Trenance Rd B2
Trenarth Rd B2
Treninnick Hill C3
Tretherras Rd B3
Trethewey Way C1
Trevemper Rd C2
Tunnels Through Time B1
Ulalia Rd B3
Vivian Cl B2
Waterworld B3
Whitegate Rd B3
Wych Hazel Way C3

Newtown Y Drenewydd 188

Ash Cl A3
Back La B2
Baptist Chapel B2
Barn La A2
Bear Lanes Shopping Centre B2
Beech Cl A2
Beechwood Dr A2
Brimmon Cl C2
Brimmon Rd C2
Broad St B2
Bryn Bank A1
Bryn Cl A1
Bryn Gdns A1
Bryn House A1
Bryn La A1/A2
Bryn Meadows A2
Bryn St A1
Brynglais Ave A2
Brynglais Cl A2
Bus Station B2
Byrnwood Dr A1
Cambrian Bridge B3
Cambrian Gdns B2
Cambrian Way B2
Canal Rd A3
Castle Mound B2
Cedewain C1
Cefnaire C2
Cefnaire Coppice C2
Ceiriog A2
Cemetery A3
Church (Remains of) B2
Churchill Dr A3
Cledan B3
Colwyn B3
Commercial St A2
Council Offices B1
Crescent St A2
Cwm Llanfair A2
Davies Memorial Gallery B2
Dinas B3
Dolafon Rd B3
Dolerw Park B1
Dolfor Rd C1
Eirianell C1
Fairfield Dr A2
Ffordd Croesawdy B2
Fire Station C1
Frankwell St A2
Frolic St B2
Fron La A1
Garden La A2
Gas St B2
Glyndwr C1
Golwgydre La B2
Gorsedd Circle B1
Great Brimmon Farm C3
Hafren C1
Halfpenny Bridge B2
High St B2
Hillside Ave A3
Hoel Treowen C2
Information Ctr B2
Kerry Rd B3
Ladywell Shopping Centre B2
Library B2
Llanfair Rd A2
Llanidloes Rd C1
Llys Ifor A2
Lon Cerddyn B1
Lonesome La A3
Long Bridge A2
Lon Helyg C1
Lower Canal Rd B3
Maldwyn Leisure Centre C1
Market B2
Market St B2
Milford Rd B1
Mill Cl B2
Miniature Railway B1
Mwyn Fynydd A3
New Church St B2
New Rd B2
Newtown Football Ground B1
Newtown Infirmary A2
Newtown Station B2
Oak Tree Ave A3
Old Kerry Rd B2
Oldbarn La A2
Park Cl B1
Parklands B1
Park La B1
Park St B2
Pavillion Ct C1
Plantation La C1
Police Station B1
Pont Brynfedw A2
Pool Rd B3
Poplar Rd A3
Post Office B2/C1
Powys C1
Powys Theatre A2
Pryce Jones Stores & Museum B2
Quaker Meeting House B1
Regent B2
Robert Owen House B1
Robert Owen Museum B2
Rugby Club A3
St David's B2
School La B2
Sheaf St B3
Short Bridge St B2
Stone St B2
Sycamore Dr A2
Textile Museum A2
The Bryn A1
The Park B1
Town Hall B1
Union St A2
Upper Brimmon C3
Vastre Industrial Estate B3
War Memorial B2
WH Smith Museum B2
Wynfields C1
Y Ffrydd A2

Northampton 188

78 Derngate B3
Abington Sq B3
Abington St B3
Alcombe St A3
All Saints' B2
Ambush St B1
Angel St B2
Arundel St A2
Ash St A2
Auctioneers Way C2
Bailiff St A2
Barrack Rd A2
Beaconsfield Terr A3
Becketts Park C3
Bedford Rd B3
Billing Rd B3
Brecon St A1
Brewery C2
Bridge St C2
Bridge St Depot C3
Broad St B2
Burns St A3
Bus Station B2
Campbell St A2
Castle (Site of) B2
Castle St B2
Cattle Market Rd C2
Central Museum & Art Gallery B2
Charles St A3
Cheyne Walk B3
Church La A2
Clare St A3
Cloutsham St A3
College St B2
Colwyn Rd A3
Cotton End C2
Countess Rd A1
County Hall B2
Court A2
Craven St A3
Crown and County Courts B3

Denmark Rd B3
Dergate B3
Derngate & Royal Theatres B3
Doddridge Church B2
Duke St A3
Dunster St A3
Earl St A3
Euston Rd C2
Fire Station A3
Foot Meadow B2
Gladstone Rd A1
Gold St B2
Grafton St A2
Gray St A3
Green St B1
Greenwood Rd B1
Greyfriars B2
Grosvenor Centre B2
Grove Rd A3
Guildhall B2
Hampton St A2
Harding Terr A2
Hazelwood Rd B3
Herbert St B2
Hervey St A3
Hester St A2
Holy Sepulchre A2
Hood St A3
Horse Market B2
Hunter St A3
Information Ctr B1
Kettering Rd A3
Kingswell St B2
Lady's La B2
Leicester St A2
Leslie Rd A2
Library B3
Lorne Rd A2
Lorry Park A1
Louise Rd A2
Lower Harding St A2
Lower Hester St A2
Lower Mounts B3
Lower Priory St A2
Main Rd C1
Marefair B2
Market Sq B2
Marlboro Rd B1
Marriott St A2
Military Rd A3
Nene Valley Retail Park C1
New South Bridge Rd C2
Northampton General Hospital (A & E) B3
Northampton Station B1
Northcote St A2
Nunn Mills Rd C3
Old Towcester Rd C2
Overstone Rd A3
Peacock Pl B2
Pembroke Rd A1
Penn Court C2
Police Station B3
Post Office A1/A2/B3/C2
Quorn Way A2
Ransome Rd C3
Regent Sq A2
Robert St A2
St Andrew's Rd B1
St Andrew's St A2
St Edmund's Rd B3
St George's St A2
St Giles B3
St Giles St B3
St Giles' Terr B3
St James' Mill Rd B1
St James' Mill Rd East C1
St James Park Rd B1
St James Retail Park C1
St James Rd B1
St Leonard's Rd C2
St Mary's St B2
St Michael's Rd A3
St Peter's B2
St Peter's Square Shopping Precinct B2
St Peter's Way B2
Salisbury St A2
Scarletwell St B2
Semilong Rd A2
Sheep St B2
Sol Central (Leisure Centre) B2
Somerset St A3
South Bridge C2
Southfield Ave C2
Spencer Bridge Rd A1
Spencer Rd A3
Spring Gdns B3
Spring La B2
Swan St B3
TA Centre A3
Tanner St B2
The Drapery B2
The Ridings B3
Tintern Ave A1
Towcester Rd C2
Upper Bath St B2
Upper Mounts A2
Victoria Park A1
Victoria Promenade B2
Victoria Rd B3
Victoria St A2
Wellingborough Rd B3
West Bridge B1
York Rd B3

Norwich 189

Albion Way C3
All Saints Green C2
Anchor Cl A3
Anchor St A3
Anglia Sq A2
Argyle St C3
Arts Centre B1
Ashby St C2
Assembly House B1
Bank Plain B2
Barker St A1
Barn Rd A1
Barrack St A3
Ber St C2
Bethel St B1
Bishop Bridge A3
Bishopbridge Rd A3
Bishopgate A3
Blackfriars St A2
Botolph St A2
Bracondale C3
Brazen Gate C2
Bridewell B2
Brunswick Rd C1
Bull Close Rd A2
Bus Station C2
Calvert St A2
Cannell Green A3
Carrow Rd C3
Castle Mall B2
Castle Meadow B2
Castle and Museum B2
Cathedral B2
Cattlemarket St B2
Chantry Rd C1
Chapel Loke C2
Chapelfield East B1
Chapelfield Gdns B1
Chapelfield North B1
Chapelfield Rd B1
Chapelfield Shopping Centre C1
City Hall B1
City Rd C2
City Wall C1/C3
Colegate A2
Coslany St B1
Cow Hill B1
Cow Tower A3
Cowgate A2
Crown & Magistrates Courts A2
Dragon Hall Heritage Centre C3
Duke St A1
Edward St A2
Elm Hill B2
Erpingham Gate B2
Fire Station B1
Fishergate A2
Foundry Bridge B3
Fye Bridge A2
Garden St C2
Gas Hill B3
Grapes Hill B1
Great Hospital Halls, The A3
Grove Ave C1
Grove Rd C1
Guildhall B1
Gurney Rd A3
Hall Rd C2
Heathgate A3
Heigham St A1
Horn's La C2
Information Ctr B1
Inspire (Science Centre) A1
Ipswich Rd C1
James Stuart Gdns B3
King Edward VI School B2
King St B2
King St C3
Koblenz Ave C3
Library B1
London St B2
Lower Clarence Rd B3
Lower Cl B3
Maddermarket B1
Magdalen St A2
Mariners La C2
Market B2
Market Ave B2
Mountergate B3
Mousehold St A3
Newmarket Rd C1
Norfolk Gallery B2
Norfolk St C1
Norwich City FC C3
Norwich Station B3
Oak St A1
Palace St A2
Pitt St A1
Playhouse B2
Post Office A2/B2/C2
Pottergate B1
Prince of Wales Rd B2
Princes St B2
Pull's Ferry B3
Puppet Theatre A2
Quebec Rd B3
Queen St B2
Queens Rd C2
Recorder Rd B3
Retail Park C3
Riverside Entertainment Centre C3
Riverside Swimming Centre C3
Riverside Rd B3
Rosary Rd B3
Rose La B2
Rouen Rd C2
Royal Norfolk Regiment Museum B2
St Andrew's & Blackfriars Hall B2
St Andrews St B2
St Augustines St A1
St Benedicts St B1
St Ethelbert's Gate B2
St Faiths La B3
St Georges St A2
St Giles St B1
St James Cl A3
St Julians C2
St Martin's La A1
St Peter Mancroft B2
St Peters St B1
St Stephens Rd C1
St Stephens St C1
Silver Rd A2
Silver St A2
Southwell Rd C2
Strangers Hall B1
Superstore C2
Surrey St C2
Sussex St A1
The Close B3
The Forum B1
The Walk B2
Theatre Royal B1
Theatre St B1
Thorn La C2
Thorpe Rd B3
Tombland B2
Union St C1
Vauxhall St B1
Victoria St C1
Walpole St B1
Wensum St A2
Wessex St C1
Westwick St A1
Wherry Rd C3
Whitefriars A2
Willow La B1
Yacht Station B3

Nottingham 189

Abbotsford Dr A3
Addison St A1
Albert Hall B1
Alfred St South A3
Alfreton Rd B1
All Saints Rd A1
Annesley Gr A2
Arboretum A1
Arboretum St A1
Arthur St A1
Arts Theatre B3
Ashforth St A3
Balmoral Rd A1
Barker Gate B3
Bath St B3
Belgrave Centre B1
Bellar Gate B3
Belward St B3
Blue Bell Hill Rd B3
Brewhouse Yard C2
Broad Marsh Bus Station C2
Broad Marsh Precinct C2
Broad St B3
Brook St B3
Burns St A1
Burton St B2
Bus Station A2
Canal St C2
Carlton St B3
Carrington St C2
Castle Blvd C1
Castle C2
Castle Gate C2
Castle Meadow Retail Park C1
Castle Meadow Rd C1
Castle Museum & Gallery C2
Castle Rd C2
Castle Wharf C2
Cavendish Rd East C1
Cemetery B1
Chaucer St B1
Cheapside B2
Church Rd A3
City Link C3
City of Caves C2
Clarendon St B1
Cliff Rd C3
Clumber Rd East C1
Clumber St B2
College St B1
Collin St C2
Conway Cl A2
Council House B2
Court B2
Cranbrook St B3
Cranmer St A2
Cromwell St B1
Curzon St B3
Derby Rd B1
Dryden St A2
Fishpond Dr C1
Fletcher Gate B3
Forest Rd East A1
Forest Rd West A1
Friar La C2
Galleries of Justice C3
Gedling Gr A1
Gedling St B3
George St B3
Gill St A2
Glasshouse St B2
Goldsmith St B2
Goose Gate B3
Great Freeman St A2
Guildhall B2
Hamilton Dr C1
Hampden St A1
Heathcote St B3
High Pavement C3
High School (tram stop) A1
Holles Cr C1
Hope Dr C1
Hungerhill Rd A3
Huntingdon Dr C1
Huntingdon St A2
Information Ctr B2
Instow Rise A3
International Community Centre A2
Kent St B3
King St B2
Lace Centre, The C2
Lace Market (tram stop) B3
Lace Market Theatre C3
Lamartine St B3
Lenton Rd C1
Lewis Cl A3
Lincoln St B2
London Rd C3
Long Row B2
Low Pavement C2
Lower Parliament St B3
Magistrates Court C2
Maid Marian Way B2
Mansfield Rd A2/B2
Middle Hill C2
Milton St B2
Mount St B2
National Ice Centre C3
Newcastle Dr B1
Newstead Gr A2
North Sherwood St A2
Nottingham Arena C3
Nottingham Station C3
Old Market Square (tram stop) B2
Oliver St A1
Park Dr C1
Park Row C1
Park Terr B1
Park Valley C1
Peas Hill Rd A3
Peel St A1
Pelham St B2
Peveril Dr C1
Plantagenet St A3
Playhouse Theatre B1
Plumptre St C3
Police Station B2
Poplar St C3
Portland Rd B1
Post Office B2
Queen's Rd C3
Raleigh St A1
Regent St B1
Rick St B3
Robin Hood Statue C2
Robin Hood St B3
Royal Centre (tram stop) B2
Royal Children Inn C2
Royal Concert Hall B2
St Ann's Hill Rd A2
St Ann's Way A2
St Ann's Well Rd A3
St Barnabas B1
St James' St B2
St Mark's St B3
St Mary's Garden of Rest B3
St Mary's Gate B3
St Nicholas C2
St Peter's C2
St Peter's Gate B2
Salutation Inn C2
Shakespeare St B2
Shelton St A2
South Pde B2
South Rd C1
South Sherwood St B2
Station St C3
Station Street (tram stop) C3
Stoney St B3
Talbot St B1
Tales of Robin Hood C2
Tattershall Dr C1
Tennis Dr B1
Tennyson St A1
The Park C1
The Ropewalk B1
Theatre Royal B2
Trent St C3
Trent University A2/B2
Trent University (tram stop) B2
Trinity Square Shopping Centre B2
Trip to Jerusalem Inn C2
Union Rd B3
Upper Parliament St B2
Victoria Centre B2
Victoria Leisure Centre B3
Victoria Park B3
Victoria St B2
Walter St A1
Warser Gate B3
Watkin St A2
Waverley St A1
Wheeler Gate B2
Wilford Rd C2
Wilford St C2
Willoughby House C2
Wollaton St B1
Woodborough Rd A2
Woolpack La B3
York St A2

Oban 189

Aird's Cres B2
Albany St B2
Albert La A2
Albert Rd A2
Alma Cres B1
Ambulance Station C2
Angus Terr C3
Ardconnel Rd A2
Ardconnel Terr B2
Argyll Sq B2
Argyll St B2
Atlantis Leisure Centre A2
Bayview Rd A1
Benvoulin Rd A2
Bowling Green A2
Breadalbane St A2
Bus Station B2
Campbell St B2
College B2
Colonsay Terr C3
Columba Building B2
Combie St B2
Corran Brae A1
Corran Esplanade A1/A2
Corran Halls A2
Court B2
Crannaig-a-Mhinisteir B1
Crannog La C2
Croft Ave A2
Dalintart Dr C3
Dalriach Rd A2
Drummore Rd C2
Duncraggan Rd A2
Dunollie Rd A2
Dunuaran Rd B1
Feochan Gr C3
Ferry Terminal B1
Gallanach Rd B1
George St A2
Glencruitten Dr C3
Glencruitten Rd B3
Glenmore Rd C1
Glenshellach Rd C1
Glenshellach Terr B2
Harbour Bowl B2
Hazeldean Cres A3
High St B2
Highland Theatre Cinema A2
Hill St B2
Industrial Estate C2
Information Ctr B2
Islay Rd C3
Jacob's Ladder B2
Jura Rd C3
Knipoch Pl C3
Laurel Cres A2
Laurel Rd A2/A3
Library B1
Lifeboat Station B1
Lighthouse Pier B1
Lismore Cres A2
Lochavullin Dr B2
Lochavullin Rd C2
Lochside St B2
Longsdale Cres A3
Longsdale Rd A2/A3
Longsdale Terr A3
Lunga Rd C3
Lynn Rd C2
Market St B2
McCaig Rd C3
McCaig's Tower A2
Mill La C2
Miller Rd C2
Millpark Ave C2
Millpark Rd C2
Mossfield Ave B3
Mossfield Dr B3
Mossfield Stadium B3
Nant Dr C3
Nelson Rd C2
North Pier B2
Nursery La A2
Oban B2
Police Station B2
Polvinister Rd B3
Post Office A2/B2
Pulpit Dr C1
Pulpit Hill C1
Pulpit Hill Viewpoint B1
Quarry Rd C2
Queen's Park Pl B2
Railway Quay B2
Rockfield Rd B2
St Columba's A1
St John's A2
Scalpay Terr C3
Shore St B1
Shuna Terr C3
Sinclair Dr C2
Soroba Rd B2/C2
South Pier B2
Stevenson St B2
Tweedale St B2
Ulva Rd C2
Villa Rd B1
War & Peace A2

Oxford 189

Adelaide St A1
Albert St A1
All Souls (Coll) B2
Ashmolean Museum B2
Balliol (Coll) B2
Banbury Rd A2
Bate Collection of Musical Instruments C2
Beaumont St B1
Becket St B1
Blackhall Rd A2
Blue Boar St B2
Bodleian Library B2
Botanic Garden B3
Brasenose (Coll) B2
Brewer St C2
Broad St B2
Burton-Taylor Theatre B2
Bus Station B1
Canal St A1
Cardigan St A1
Carfax Tower B2
Castle B1
Castle St B1
Catte St B2
Cemetery C1
Christ Church (Coll) B2
Christ Church Cathedral C2
Christ Church Meadow C2
Clarendon Centre B2
Coach & Lorry Park C1
College B3
College of Further Education C1
Cornmarket St B2
Corpus Christi (Coll) B2
County Hall B1
Covered Market B2
Cowley Pl C3
Cranham St A1
Cranham Terr A1
Cricket Ground B1
Crown & County Courts C2
Deer Park B3
Exeter (Coll) B2
Folly Bridge C2
George St B1
Great Clarendon St A1
Hart St A1
Hertford (Coll) B2
High St B3
Hollybush Row B1
Holywell St B2
Hythe Bridge St B1
Ice Rink C1
Information Ctr B2
Jericho St A1
Jesus (Coll) B2
Jowett Walk B3
Juxon St A1
Keble (Coll) A2
Keble Rd A2
Library B2
Linacre (Coll) A3
Lincoln (Coll) B2
Little Clarendon St A1
Longwall St B3
Magdalen (Coll) B3
Magdalen Bridge B3
Magdalen St B2
Magistrate's Court C2
Manchester (Coll) B2
Manor Rd B3
Mansfield (Coll) A2
Mansfield Rd A3
Market B1
Marlborough Rd C2
Martyrs' Memorial B2
Merton Field B3
Merton (Coll) B3
Merton St B2
Museum of Modern Art B2
Museum of Oxford B2
Museum Rd A2
New College (Coll) B3
New Inn Hall St B2
New Rd B1
New Theatre B2
Norfolk St C1
Nuffield (Coll) B1
Observatory A1
Observatory St A1
Odeon B1/B2
Old Fire Station B1
Old Greyfriars St C2
Oriel (Coll) B2
Oxford Station B1
Oxford Story, The B2
Oxford University Research Centres A1
Oxpens Rd C1
Paradise Sq C1
Paradise St B1
Park End St B1
Parks Rd A2/B2
Pembroke (Coll) C2
Phoenix A1
Picture Gallery C2
Plantation Rd A1
Playhouse B2
Police Station C2
Post Office A1/B2
Pusey St B1
Queen's La B3
Queen's (Coll) B3
Radcliffe Camera B2
Rewley Rd B1
Richmond Rd A1
Rose La B3
Ruskin (Coll) B1
Saïd Business School B1
St Aldates C2
St Anne's (Coll) A1
St Antony's (Coll) A1
St Bernard's Rd A1
St Catherine's (Coll) B3
St Cross Building A3
St Cross Rd A3
St Edmund Hall (Coll) B3
St Giles St A2
St Hilda's (Coll) C3
St John St B2
St John's (Coll) B2
St Mary the Virgin B2
St Michael at the Northgate B2
St Peter's (Coll) B1
St Thomas St B1
Science Area A2
Science Museum B2
Sheldonian Theatre B2
Somerville (Coll) A1
South Parks Rd A2
Speedwell St C2
Sports Ground C3
Thames St C2
Town Hall B2
Trinity (Coll) B2
Turl St B2
University College (Coll) B3
University Museum and Pitt Rivers Museum A2
University Parks A2
Wadham (Coll) B2
Walton Cr A1
Walton St A1
Western Rd C2
Westgate Shopping Centre B2
Woodstock Rd A1
Worcester (Coll) B1

Perth 189

A K Bell Library B2
Abbot Cres C1
Abbot St C1
Albany Terr A1
Albert Monument A3
Alexandra St B2
Art Gallery B3
Atholl St A2
Balhousie Ave A2
Balhousie Castle Black Watch Museum A2
Balhousie St A2
Ballantine Pl A1
Barossa Pl A2
Barossa St A2
Barrack St A2
Bell's Sports Centre A2
Bellwood B3
Blair St B1
Burn Park C1
Bus Station B2
Caledonian Rd B2
Canal Cres B2
Canal St B3
Cavendish Ave C1
Charles St B2
Charlotte Pl A2
Charlotte St A3
Church St A1
City Hall B3
Club House C3
Clyde Pl C1
Commercial St A3
Concert Hall B3
Council Chambers B3
County Pl B2
Court B3
Craigie Pl C2
Crieff Rd A1
Croft Park C2
Cross St B2
Darnhall Cres C1
Darnhall Dr C1
Dundee Rd B3
Dunkeld Rd A1
Earl's Dykes B1
Edinburgh Rd C3
Elibank St B1
Fair Maid's House A3
Fergusson B3
Feus Rd A1
Fire Station A1
Fitness Centre B3
Foundary La A2
Friar St C2
George St B3
Glamis Pl C1
Glasgow Rd B1
Glenearn Rd C2
Glover St B1/C1
Golf Course A2
Gowrie St A3
Gray St B1
Graybank Rd B1
Greyfriars Burial Ground B3
Hay St A2
High St B2/B3
Hotel B2
Ice Rinks B1
Inchaffray St A1
Industrial/Retail Park B1
Information Ctr B2
Isla Rd A3
James St B2
Keir St A3
King Edward St B3
King James VI Golf Course C3
King St B2
Kings Pl C2
Kinnoull Causeway B2
Kinnoull Aisle 'Monument' B3
Kinnoull St B2
Knowelea Pl C1
Knowelea Terr C1
Ladeside Business Centre A1
Leisure Pool B1
Leonard St B2
Lickley St B2
Lochie Brae A3
Long Causeway A1
Low St A2
Main St A3
Marshall Pl C3
Melville St A2
Mill St B3
Milne St B2
Murray Cres C1
Murray St B2
Needless Rd C1
New Rd B2
North Inch A3
North Methven St A2
Park Pl C1
Perth B2
Perth Bridge A3
Perth Business Park B1
Perth Station C2
Pickletulllum Rd B1
Pitheavlis Cres C1
Playhouse B2
Police Station B2
Pomarium St B2
Post Office A3/B2/C2
Princes St B3
Priory Pl C2
Queen St C1
Queen's Bridge B3
Riggs Rd B1
Riverside B3
Riverside Park B3
Rodney Park B3
Rose Terr A2
St Catherines Retail Park A1
St Catherine's Rd A1/A2
St John St B3
St John's Kirk B3
St John's Shopping Centre B2
St Leonards Bridge C2
St Ninians Cathedral A2
Scott Monument C2
Scott St B2
Sheriff Court B3
Shore Rd C3
Skate Park C3
South Inch C2
South Inch Business Centre C3
South Inch Park C2
South Inch View C2
South Methven St B2
South St B3
South William St B2
Stormont St A2
Strathmore St A3
Stuart Ave C1
Tay St B3
The Stables A1
The Stanners B3
Union La A2
Victoria St B2
Watergate B3
Wellshill Cemetery A1
West Bridge St A3
West Mill St B2
Whitefriers Cres B1
Whitefriers St B1
Wilson St C1
Windsor Terr C1
Woodside Cres C1
York Pl B2
Young St C1

Peterborough 189

Athletics Arena B3
Bishop's Palace B2
Bishop's Rd B2/B3
Boongate A3
Bourges Boulevard A1
Bourges Retail Park B1/B2
Bridge House (Council Offices) C2
Bridge St B2
Bright St A1
Broadway A2
Broadway A2
Brook St A2
Burghley Rd A2
Bus Station B2
Cavendish St A3
Charles St A3
Church St B2
Church Walk A2
Cobden Ave A1
Cobden St A1
Cowgate B2
Craig St A2
Crawthorne Rd A2
Cripple Sidings La C2
Cromwell Rd A1
Dickens St A3
Eastfield Rd A3
Eastgate B3
Fire Station A1
Fletton Ave C2
Frank Perkins Parkway C3
Geneva St A2
George St C2
Gladstone St A1
Glebe Rd C2
Gloucester Rd C3
Granby St B3
Grove St C1
Guildhall B2
Hadrians Ct C3
Henry St A2
Hereward Cross (shopping) B2
Hereward Rd B3
Information Ctr B2
Jubilee St C1
Key Theatre C2
Kent Rd B1
Kirkwood Cl B1
Lea Gdns B1
Library A2
Lincoln Rd A2
London Rd C2
Long Causeway B2
Lower Bridge St C2
Magistrates Court B2
Manor House St A2
Mayor's Walk A1
Midland Rd A1
Monument St A2
Morris St A3
Museum & Art Gallery B2
Nene Valley Railway C1
New Rd A2
New Rd C1
Northminster A2
Old Customs House C2
Oundle Rd C1
Padholme Rd A3
Palmerston Rd C1
Park Rd A2
Passport Office B2
Peterborough District Hospital (A+E) B1
Peterborough Station B1
Peterborough Nene Valley C1
Peterborough United FC C2
Police Station B2
Post Office A3/B1/B2/B3/C1
Priestgate B2
Queen's Walk C2
Queensgate Centre B2
Railworld C1
Regional Swimming & Fitness Centre B3
River La B1
Rivergate Shopping Centre B2
Riverside Mead C3
Russell St A1
St John's B2
St John's St A3
St Marks St A2
St Peter's B2
St Peter's Rd B2
Saxon Rd A3
Spital Bridge A1
Stagshaw Dr C3
Star Rd B3
Thorpe Lea Rd B1
Thorpe Rd B1
Thorpe's Lea Rd B1
Tower St A2
Town Hall B2
Viersen Platz B2
Vineyard Rd B3
Wake Rd B3
Wellington St A3
Wentworth St B2
Westgate B2
Whalley St A3
Wharf Rd C1
Whitsed St A3
YMCA A3

Plymouth 190

ABC B2
Alma Rd A1
Anstis St B1
Armada Centre B2
Armada St A3
Armada Way B2
Arts Centre B2
Athenaeum B1
Athenaeum St C1
Barbican C3
Barbican C3
Baring St A3
Bath St B1
Beaumont Park B3
Beaumont Rd B3
Black Friars Gin Distillery C2
Breton Side B3
Bus Station B2
Castle St C3
Cathedral (RC) B1
Cecil St B1
Central Park A1
Central Park Ave A2
Charles Church B3
Charles Cross (r'about) B3
Charles St B2
Citadel Rd C2
Citadel Rd East C2
Civic Centre B2
Cliff Rd C1
Clifton Pl A3
Cobourg St A2
College of Art and Design B2
Continental Ferry Port B1
Cornwall St B2
Dale Rd A2
Deptford Pl A3
Derry Ave A2
Derry's Cross (r'about) B1
Drake Circus B2
Drake Circus Shopping Centre B2
Drake's Memorial C2
Eastlake St B2
Ebrington St B3
Elizabethan House C3
Elliot St C1
Endsleigh Pl A2
Exeter St B3
Fire Station A3
Fish Quay C3
Gibbons St A3
Glen Park Ave A2
Grand Pde C1
Great Western Rd C1
Greenbank Rd A3
Greenbank Terr A3
Guildhall B2
Hampton St B3
Harwell St B1
Hill Park Cr A3
Hoe Approach B2
Hoe Rd C2
Hoegate St C2
Houndiscombe Rd A2
Information Ctr C3
James St A2
Kensington Rd A3
King St B1
Lambhay Hill C3
Leigham St C1
Library B2
Lipson Rd A3/B3
Lockyer St C2
Lockyers Quay C3
Madeira Rd C2
Marina B3
Market Ave B1
Martin St B1

Mayflower Stone & Steps ✦ C3
Mayflower St B2
Mayflower Visitor Centre ✦ C3
Merchants House B2
Millbay Rd B1
Museum and Art Gallery B2
National Marine Aquarium C3
Neswick St B1
New George St B2
New St C3
North Cross (r'about) A2
North Hill A3
North Quay B2
North Rd East A2
North Rd West A1
North St B3
Notte St B2
Octagon St B1
Pannier Market B1
Pennycomequick (r'about) A1
Pier St C1
Plymouth Pavilions B1
Plymouth Station A2
Police Station B3
Portland Sq A2
Post Office A1/B1/B2
Princess St B2
Prysten House B2
Queen Anne's Battery Seasports Centre C3
Radford Rd C1
Regent St B3
Rope Walk C3
Royal Citadel C2
Royal Pde B2
St Andrew's B2
St Andrew's Cross (r'about) B2
St Andrew's St B2
St Lawrence Rd A2
Saltash Rd A2
Smeaton's Tower ✦ C2
Southern Terr A3
Southside St C2
Stuart Rd A1
Sutherland Rd A2
Sutton Rd B3
Sydney St A1
Teats Hill Rd C3
The Crescent B1
The Hoe C2
The Octagon (r'about) B1
The Promenade C2
Theatre Royal B2
Tothill Ave B3
Union St B1
University of Plymouth A2
Vauxhall St B2/3
Victoria Park A1
West Hoe Rd C1
Western Approach B1
Whittington St A1
Wyndham St B1
YMCA B2
YWCA C2

Poole 190

Ambulance Station A3
Baiater Gdns C2
Baiter Park C3
Ballard Cl C2
Ballard Rd C2
Bay Hog La B1
Bridge Approach C1
Bus Station B2
Castle St B2
Catalina Dr B3
Chapel La B2
Church St B1
Cinnamon La B1
Colborne Cl B3
Dear Hay La B2
Denmark La A3
Denmark Rd A3
East St B2
Elizabeth Rd A3
Emerson Rd B2
Ferry Rd C1
Ferry Terminal C1
Fire Station A2
Freightliner Terminal C1
Furnell Rd B3
Garland Rd A3
Green Rd B2
Heckford La A3
Heckford Rd A3
High St B2
High St North A3
Hill St B2
Holes Bay Rd A1
Hospital (A + E) A3
Information Ctr C2
Kingland Rd B3
Kingston Rd A3
Labrador Dr C3
Lagland St B2
Lander Cl C3
Lighthouse - Poole Centre for the Arts ✦ B3
Longfleet Rd A3
Maple Rd A3
Market Cl B2
Market St B2
Mount Pleasant Rd B3
New Harbour Rd C1
New Harbour Rd South C1
New Harbour Rd West C1
New Orchard B1
New Quay Rd C1
New St B2
Newfoundland Dr B2
North St B2
Old Lifeboat C2
Old Orchard B2
Parish Rd A3
Park Lake Rd B3
Parkstone Rd A3
Perry Gdns B2
Pitwines Cl B2
Police Station A2
Poole Central Library B2
Poole Lifting Bridge C1
Poole Park B2
Poole Station A2
Poole Waterfront Museum C1
Post Office A2/B2
St John's Rd A3
St Margaret's Rd A2
St Mary's Maternity Unit A3
St Mary's Rd A3
Seldown Bridge B3
Seldown La B3
Seldown Rd B3
Serpentine Rd A2
Shaftesbury Rd A3
Skinner St B2
Slipway B1
Stanley Rd C2
Sterte Ave A2
Sterte Ave West A1
Sterte Cl A2
Sterte Esplanade A2
Sterte Rd A2
Strand St C2
Swimming Pool B3
Taverner Cl B3
Thames St B1
The Lifeboat College B2
The Quay C2
Towngate Bridge B2
Vallis Cl C3
Waldren Cl B3
West Quay B1
West Quay Rd B1
West St B1
West View Rd A2
Whatleigh Cl B2
Wimborne Rd A3

Portsmouth 190

Action Stations ✦ C1
Admiralty Rd A1
Alfred Rd A2
Anglesea Rd A2
Arundel St B3
Bishop St A2
Broad St C1
Buckingham House C2
Burnaby Rd B2
Bus Station B1
Camber Dock C1
Cambridge Rd B2
Car Ferry to Isle of Wight B1
Cascades Shopping Centre A3
Castle Rd C3
Cathedral † C1
Cathedral (RC) † A3
City Museum & Art Gallery B2
Civic Offices B3
Clarence Pier C2
College St B1
Commercial Rd A3
Cottage Gr B3
Cross St A1
Cumberland St A2
Duisburg Way C2
Durham St A3
East St B1
Edinburgh Rd A2
Elm Gr C3
Great Southsea St C3
Green Rd B3
Greetham St B3
Grosvenor St B3
Grove Rd North C3
Grove Rd South C3
Guildhall B3
Guildhall Walk B3
Gunwharf Quays Retail Park B1
Gunwharf Rd B1
Hambrook St C2
Hampshire Terr B2
Hanover St A1
High St C2
HM Naval Base A1
HMS Nelson (Royal Naval Barracks) A2
HMS Victory A1
HMS Warrior A1
Hovercraft Terminal C2
Hyde Park Rd B3
Information Ctr A1/B3
Isambard Brunel Rd B3
Isle of Wight Car Ferry Terminal B1
Kent Rd C3
Kent St A2
King St B3
King's Rd C3
King's Terr C2
Lake Rd A3
Law Courts B3
Library B3
Long Curtain Rd C2
Market Way A3
Marmion Rd C3
Mary Rose Exhibition A1
Mary Rose Ship Hall A1
Middle St B3
Millennium Blvd B2
Millennium Promenade A1/C1
Museum Rd B2
Naval Recreation Ground C2
Nightingale Rd C3
Norfolk St B3
North St A2
Osborne Rd C3
Park Rd B2
Passenger Catamaran to Isle of Wight B1
Passenger Ferry to Gosport B1
Pelham Rd C3
Pembroke Gdns C2
Pier Rd C2
Point Battery C1
Police Station B3
Portsmouth and Southsea A3
Portsmouth Harbour B1
Post Office A2/A3/B1/B3/C3
Queen St A1
Queen's Cr C3
Round Tower ✦ C1
Royal Garrison Church C1
Royal Naval Museum A1
St Edward's Rd C3
St George's Rd B2
St George's Sq B1
St George's Way B2
St James's Rd B3
St James's St A2
St Thomas's St B2
Somers Rd B3
Southsea Common C2
Southsea Terr C2
Spinnaker Tower ✦ B1
Square Tower ✦ C1
Station St A3
Swimming Pool A2
The Hard B1
Town Fortifications ✦ C1
Unicorn Rd A2
United Services Recreation Ground B2
University of Portsmouth A2/B2
University of Portsmouth – College of Art, Design and Media B3
Upper Arundel St A3
Victoria Ave C2
Victoria Park A2
Victory Gate A1
Vue B1
Warblington St B1
Western Pde C2
White Hart Rd C1
Winston Churchill Ave B3

Preston 190

Adelphi St A2
Anchor Ct B3
Aqueduct St A1
Ardee Rd C1
Arthur St B2
Ashton St A1
Avenham La B3
Avenham Park C3
Avenham Rd B3
Avenham St B3
Bairstow St B3
Balderstone Rd C1
Beamont Dr A1
Beech St South C2
Bird St C1
Bow La B2
Brierfield Rd A1
Broadgate C1
Brook St A2
Bus Station A3
Butler St B2
Cannon St B3
Carlton St A1
Chaddock St B3
Channel Way B1
Chapel St B3
Christ Church St B2
Christian Rd B2
Cold Bath St A2
Coleman Ct C1
Connaught Rd C2
Corn Exchange B3
Corporation St A2/B2
County Hall B2
County Records Office B2
Court A3
Court B3
Cricket Ground C2
Croft St A1
Cross St B3
Crown Court A3
Crown St A3
East Cliff C3
East Cliff Rd B3
Edward St A2
Elizabeth St A3
Euston St B1
Fishergate B2/B3
Fishergate Hill B2
Fishergate Shopping Centre B2
Fitzroy St B1
Fleetwood St A1
Friargate A3
Fylde Rd A1/A2
Gerrard St B2
Glover's Ct B3
Good St B2
Grafton St B2
Great George St A3
Great Shaw St A3
Greenbank St A2
Guild Way B1
Guildhall and Charter B3
Guildhall St B3
Harrington St A2
Harris Museum B3
Hartington Rd B1
Hasset Cl C2
Heatley St B2
Hind St C2
Information Ctr B3
Kilruddery Rd C1
Lancaster Rd A3/B3
Latham St B3
Lauderdale St C2
Lawson St A3
Leighton St A2
Leyland Rd C1
Library A1
Library B3
Liverpool Rd C1
Lodge St B2
Lune St B3
Main Sprit West B3
Maresfield Rd C1
Market St West A3
Marsh La B1/B2
Maudland Bank A2
Maudland Rd A2
Meadow Ct C2
Meath Rd C1
Mill Hill A2
Miller Arcade ✦ B3
Miller Park C3
Moor La A3
Mount St B3
North Rd A3
North St A3
Northcote Rd B1
Old Milestones B1
Old Tram Rd C3
Pedder St A1/A2
Peel St A2
Penwortham Bridge C2
Penwortham New Bridge C1
Pitt St B2
Playhouse A3
Police Station A3
Port Way B1
Post Office B3
Preston Station B2
Ribble Bank St B2
Ribble Viaduct C2
Ribblesdale Pl B3
Ringway B3
River Parade C1
Riverside C2
St Georges B3
St Georges Shopping Centre B3
St Johns B3
St Johns Shopping Centre A3
St Mark's Rd A1
St Walburges A1
Salisbury Rd B1
Sessions House B3
Snow Hill A3
South End C2
South Meadow La C2
Spa Rd B1
Sports Ground C2
Strand Rd B1
Syke St B3
Talbot Rd B1
Taylor St C1
Tithebarn St A3
Town Hall B3
Tulketh Brow A1
University of Central Lancashire A2
Valley Rd C1
Victoria St A2
Walker St A3
Walton's Parade B2
Warwick St A3
Wellfield Business Park A1
Wellfield Rd A1
Wellington St A1
West Cliff C2
West Strand A1
Winckley Rd C1
Winckley Square B3
Wolseley Rd C2

Reading 190

Abbey Ruins † B2
Abbey Sq B2
Abbey St B2
Abbot's Walk B2
Acacia Rd C2
Addington Rd C3
Addison Rd A1
Allcroft Rd C3
Alpine St C2
Baker St B1
Berkeley Ave C1
Bridge St B1
Brigham Rd A1
Broad St B1
Broad Street Mall B1
Carey St B1
Castle Hill C1
Castle St B1
Caversham Rd A1
Christchurch Playing Fields A2
Civic Offices and Magistrate's Court B1
Coley Hill C1
Coley Pl C1
Craven Rd C3
Crown St C2
De Montfort Rd A1
Denmark Rd C3
Duke St B2
East St B2
Edgehill St C2
Eldon Rd B3
Eldon Terr B3
Elgar Rd C1
Erleigh Rd C3
Field Rd C1
Fire Station A1
Fobney St B1
Forbury Gdns B2
Forbury Retail Park B2
Forbury Rd B2
Francis St C1
Friar St B1
Garrard St B1
Gas Works Rd B3
George St A2
Great Knollys St B1
Greyfriars B1
Gun St B1
Henry St C1
Hexagon Theatre, The B1
Hill's Meadow A2
HM Prison B2
Howard St B1
Information Ctr B1
Inner Distribution Rd B1
Katesgrove La C1
Kenavon Dr B2
Kendrick Rd C2
King's Meadow Rec Ground A2
King's Rd B2
Library B2
London Rd C3
London St B2
Lynmouth Rd A1
Market Pl B2
Mill La B2
Mill Rd A2
Minster St B1
Morgan Rd C3
Mount Pleasant C2
Museum of English Rural Life C3
Napier Rd A2
Newark St C2
Newport Rd A1
Old Reading University C3
Oracle Shopping Centre, The B1
Orts Rd B3
Pell St C1
Queen Victoria St B1
Queen's Rd A2
Queen's Rd B2
Police Station B1
Post Office B2
Randolph Rd A1
Reading Bridge A2
Reading Station A1
Redlands Rd C3
Renaissance Hotel B1
Riverside Museum B3
Rose Kiln La C1
Royal Berks Hospital (A & E) C3
St Giles C2
St Laurence B2
St Mary's B1
St Mary's Butts B1
St Saviour's Rd C1
Send Rd A3
Sherman Rd C2
Sidmouth St B2
Silver St C2
South St B2
Southampton St C2
Station Hill A1
Station Rd B1
Superstore A3
Swansea Rd A1
Technical College B3
The Causeway A3
The Grove B2
Valpy St B2
Vastern Rd A1
Vue B2
Waldeck St C2
Watlington St B3
West St B1
Whitby Dr C3
Wolseley St C1
York Rd A1
Zinzan St B1

St Andrews 190

Abbey St B2
Abbey Walk B3
Abbotsford Cres A1
Albany Pk C3
Allan Robertson Dr C2
Ambulance Station C1
Anstruther Rd C3
Argyle St B1
Argyll Business Park C1
Auld Burn Rd B2
Bassaguard Industrial Estate B1
Bell St B2
Blackfriars Chapel (Ruins) B2
Boase Ave B2
Braid Cres C3
Brewster Pl C3
Bridge St B1
British Golf Museum A1
Broomfaulds Ave C1
Bruce Embankment A1
Bruce St C2
Bus Station A1
Byre B2
Canongate C1
Cathedral and Priory (Ruins) † B3
Cemetery B3
Chamberlain St C1
Church St B2
Churchill Cres C2
City Rd A1
Claybraes C1
Cockshaugh Public Park B1
Cosmos Community Centre B3
Council Office A2
Crawford Gdns C1
Doubledykes Rd B1
Drumcarrow Rd C1
East Sands B3
East Scores A3
Fire Station C1
Forrest St C1
Fraser Ave C1
Freddie Tait St C2
Gateway Centre A1
Glebe Rd B2
Golf Pl A1
Grange Rd C3
Greenside Pl B2
Greyfriars Gdns A2
Hamilton Ave C2
Hepburn Gdns B1
Horseleys Park C1
Information Ctr B2
Irvine Cres C3
James Robb Ave C1
James St B1
John Knox Rd C1
Kennedy Gdns B1
Kilrymont Cl C3
Kilrymont Pl C3
Kilrymont Rd C3
Kinburn Park B1
Kinkell Terr C3
Kinnesburn Rd B2
Ladebraes Walk B2
Lady Buchan's Cave A3
Lamberton Pl C1
Lamond Dr C2
Langlands Rd B2
Largo Rd C1
Learmonth Pl C1
Library B2
Links Clubhouse A1
Links, The A1
Livingstone Cres B2
Long Rocks A2
Madras College B2
Market St A2
Martyr's Monument A1
Memorial Hospital (No A + E) B3
Murray Pk A2
Murray Pl A2
Nelson St B2
New Course, The A1
New Picture House A2
North Castle St A3
North St A2
Old Course, The A1
Old Station Rd A1
Pends, The B3
Pilmour Links A1
Pipeland Rd B2/C2
Police Station A2
Post Office B2
Preservation Trust B2
Priestden Pk C3
Priestden Pl C3
Priestden Rd C3
Queen's Gdns B2
Queen's Terr B2
Roundhill Rd C2
Royal & Ancient Golf Club A1
St Andrews B1
St Andrews Aquarium A2
St Andrews Botanic Gardens B1
St Andrews Castle (Ruins) & Visitor Centre A2
St Mary St B3
St Mary's College B2
St Nicholas St C3
St Rules Tower B3
St Salvator's College A2
Sandyhill Cres C2
Sandyhill Rd C2
Scooniehill Rd C2
Shields Ave C3
Shoolbraids C2
Sloan St B1
South St B2
Spottiswoode Gdns C1
Station Rd A1
Swilken Bridge A1
The Scores A2
The Shore B3
Tom Morris Dr C2
Tom Stewart La C1
Town Hall B2
Union St A2
University Chapel A2
University Library A2
University of St Andrews A1
Viaduct Walk B1
War Memorial A3
Wardlaw Gdns B1
Warrack St C3
Watson Ave B2
West Port B2
West Sands A1
Westview B2
Windmill Rd A1
Winram Pl C1
Wishart Gdns C2
Woodburn Pk B3
Woodburn Pl B3
Woodburn Terr B3
Younger Hall A2

Salisbury 191

Albany Rd A2
Arts Centre A3
Ashley Rd A1
Avon Approach A2
Ayleswade Rd C2
Bedwin St A2
Belle Vue A2
Bishop's Palace C2
Bishops Walk B2
Blue Boar Row B2
Bourne Ave A3
Bourne Hill A3
Britford La C2
Broad Walk C2
Brown St B2
Bus Station B2
Castle St A2
Catherine St B2
Chapter House B2
Church House B2
Churchfields Rd B1
Churchill Way East B3
Churchill Way North A3
Churchill Way South C2
Churchill Way West A1
City Hall B2
Close Wall B2
Coldharbour La A1
College St A3
Council Offices A3
Court A1
Crane Bridge Rd B2
Crane St B2
Cricket Ground C1
Culver St South B3
De Vaux Pl C2
Devizes Rd A1
Dews Rd B1
Elm Grove B3
Elm Grove Rd A3
Endless St A2
Estcourt Rd A3
Exeter St C2
Fairview Rd A3
Fire Station A1
Fisherton St A1
Folkestone Rd C1
Fowlers Hill B3
Fowlers Rd B3
Friary Estate C3
Friary La B2
Gas La A1
Gigant St B3
Greencroft B3
Greencroft St A3
Guildhall B2
Hall of John Halle B2
Hamilton Rd A2
Harnham Mill B1
Harnham Rd C1/C2
High St B2
Hospital A1
House of John A'Port B2
Information Ctr B2
Kelsey Rd A3
King's Rd A2
Laverstock Rd B3
Library B2
London Rd A3
Lower St C1
Maltings, The B2
Manor Rd A3
Marsh La A1
Medieval Hall B2
Milford Hill B3
Milford St B3
Mill Rd B1
Millstream Approach A2
Mompesson House (NT) B2
New Bridge Rd C2
New Canal B2
New Harnham Rd C2
New St B2
North Canonry B2
North Gate B2
North Walk B2
Old George Hall B2
Old Blandford Rd C1
Old Deanery B2
Park St A3
Parsonage Green C1
Playhouse Theatre A2
Post Office A2/B2/C2
Poultry Cross B2
Queen Elizabeth Gdns B1
Queen's Rd A3
Rampart Rd B3
St Ann's Gate B2
St Ann St B3
St Marks Rd A3
St Martins B3
St Mary's Cathedral † B2
St Nicholas Hospital C2
St Paul's A1
St Paul's Rd A1
St Thomas B2
Salisbury & South Wiltshire Mus B2
Salisbury General Hospital (A & E) C2
Salisbury Station A1
Salt La A3
Saxon Rd C1
Scots La A2
Shady Bower B3
South Canonry C2
South Gate C2
Southampton Rd B2
Spire View A1
Sports Ground C3
The Friary B3
Tollgate Rd B3
Town Path B1
Wain-a-Long Rd A3
Wardrobe, The B2
Wessex Rd A3
West Walk C2
Wilton Rd A1
Wiltshire College B3
Winchester St B3
Windsor Rd A1
Winston Churchill Gdns C3
Wyndham Rd A2
YHA B3
York Rd A1

Scarborough 191

Aberdeen Walk B2
Albert Rd A2
Albion Rd C2
Alexandra Bowling Hall A1
Alexandra Gardens A1
Auborough St B2
Belle Vue St C1
Belmont Rd C2
Brunswick Shopping Centre B2
Castle Dykes B3
Castlegate B3
Castle Holms A3
Castle Hill A3
Castle Rd B2
Castle Walls A3
Cemetery B1
Central Lift ✦ C2
Clarence Gardens A2
Coach Park B1
Columbus Ravine A1
Court B1
Cricket Ground A1
Cross St B2
Crown Terr C2
Dean Rd B1
Devonshire Dr A1
East Harbour B3
East Pier B3
Eastborough B2
Elmville Ave B1
Esplanade C2
Falconers Rd B2
Falsgrave Rd C1
Fire Station B2
Foreshore Rd B2
Friargate B2
Futurist Theatre B2
Gladstone Rd B1
Gladstone St B1
Hoxton Rd B1
Information Ctr B2/B3
King St B2
Londesborough Rd C1
Longwestgate B3
Marine Dr A3
Miniature Railway A1
Nelson St B1
Newborough B2
Nicolas St B2
North Marine Rd A1
North St B2
Northway B1
Old Harbour B3
Peasholm Park A1
Peasholm Rd A1
Plaza A1
Police Station B1
Post Office B2/C1
Princess St B3
Prospect Rd B1
Queen St B2
Queen's Parade A2
Queen's Tower (Remains) A3
Ramshill Rd C2
Roman Signal Station A3
Roscoe St C1
Rotunda Museum C2
Royal Albert Dr A2
St Martin-on-the-Hill C2
St Martin's Ave C2
St Mary's B3
St Nicholas' Lift ✦ B2
St Thomas St B2
Sandside B3
Scarborough Art Gallery and Crescent Art Studio C2
Scarborough Castle A3
Scarborough C1
Somerset Terr C2
South Cliff Lift ✦ C2
Spa, The ✦ C2
Spa Theatre, The C2
Stephen Joseph Theatre B1
Tennyson Ave B1
The Crescent C2
Tollergate B2
Town Hall B2
Trafalgar Rd B1
Trafalgar Square A1
Trafalgar St West B1
Valley Bridge Parade C2
Valley Rd C1
Vernon Rd C2
Victoria Park Mount A1
Victoria Rd B1
West Pier B3
Westborough C1
Westover Rd C1
Westwood C1
Woodall Ave A1
York Pl B2
Yorkshire Coast College (Westwood Campus) C1

Sheffield 191

Addy Dr A2
Addy St A2
Adelphi St A3
Albert Terrace Rd A3
Albion St A2
Aldred Rd A1
Allen St A4
Alma St A4
Angel St B5
Arundel Gate B5
Arundel St C4
Ashberry Rd A2
Ashdell Rd C1
Ashgate Rd C1
Athletics Centre B2
Attercliffe Rd A6
Bailey St B4
Ball St A4
Balm Green B4
Bank St B4
Barber Rd A2
Bard St B5
Barker's Pool B4
Bates St A1
Beech Hill Rd C1
Beet St B3
Bellefield St A3
Bernard Rd A6
Bernard St B6
Birkendale A2
Birkendale Rd A2
Birkendale View A1
Bishop St C4
Blackwell Pl B6
Blake St A2
Blonk St A5
Bolsover St B2
Botanical Gdns C1
Bower Rd A1
Bradley St A1
Bramall La C4
Bramwell St A3
Bridge St A4/A5
Brighton Terrace Rd A1
Broad La B3
Broad St B6
Brocco St A3
Brook Hill B3
Broomfield Rd C1
Broomgrove Rd C2
Broomhall Pl C3
Broomhall Rd C2
Broomhall St C3
Broomspring La C2
Brown St C5
Brunswick St B3
Burgess St B4
Burlington St A2
Burns Rd A2
Bus/Coach Station B5
Cadman St A6
Cambridge St B4
Campo La B4
Carver St B4
Castle Market B5
Castle Square (tram station) B5
Castlegate A5
Cathedral (RC) † B4
Cathedral (tram station) B4
Cavendish St B3
Charles St C4
Charter Row C4
Children's Hospital (A&E) B2
Church St B4
City Hall B4
City Hall (tram station) B4
City Rd C6
Claremont Cr B2
Claremont Pl B2
Clarke St C3
Clarkegrove Rd C2
Clarkehouse Rd C1
Clarkson St B2
Cobden View Rd A1
Collegiate Cr C2
Commercial St B5
Commonside A1
Conduit Rd B1
Cornish St A3
Corporation St A4
Court B4
Cricket Inn Rd B6
Cromwell St A1
Crookes Rd B1
Crookes Valley Park B2
Crookes Valley Rd B2
Crookesmoor Rd A2
Crown Court A4
Crucible Theatre B5
Cutlers Gate A6
Cutler's Hall B4
Daniel Hill A2
Dental Hospital B2
Dept for Education & Employment C4
Devonshire Green B3
Devonshire St B3
Division St B4
Dorset St C2
Dover St A3
Duchess Rd C5
Duke St B5
Duncombe St A1
Durham Rd B2
Earl St C4
Earl Way C4
Ecclesall Rd C3
Edward St B3
Effingham Rd A6
Effingham St A6
Egerton St C3
Eldon St B3
Elmore Rd B1
Exchange St B5
Eyre St C4
Fargate B4
Farm Rd C5
Fawcett St A3
Filey St B3

208 Shrewsbury • Southampton • Southend • Stirling • Stoke • Stratford-upon-Avon

Fire and Police Museum A4
Fir St A1
Fitzalan Sq/Ponds Forge (tram station) B5
Fitzwater Rd C6
Fitzwilliam Gate C4
Fitzwilliam St B3
Flat St B5
Foley St A6
Foundry Climbing Centre A4
Fulton Rd A1
Furnace Hill A4
Furnival Rd A5
Furnival Sq C4
Furnival St C4
Garden St B3
Gell St B3
Gibraltar St A4
Glebe Rd B1
Glencoe Rd C6
Glossop Rd B2/B3/C1
Gloucester St C2
Granville Rd C6
Granville Rd/ Sheffield College (tram station) C5
Graves Gallery B5
Greave Rd B3
Green La A4
Hadfield St A1
Hanover St C3
Hanover Way C3
Harcourt Rd B1
Harmer La B5
Havelock St C2
Hawley St B4
Haymarket B5
Headford St C3
Heavygate Rd A1
Henry St A3
High St B4
Hodgson St C3
Holberry Gdns C2
Hollis Croft B4
Holly St B4
Hounsfield Rd B3
Howard Rd A1
Hoyle St A3
Hyde Park (tram station) A6
Infirmary Rd A3
Infirmary Rd (tram station) A3
Information Ctr B4
Jericho St A3
Johnson St A5
Kelham Island Industrial Museum A4
Lawson Rd C1
Leadmill Rd C5
Leadmill St C5
Leadmill, The C5
Leamington St A1
Leavy Rd B3
Lee Croft B4
Leopold St B4
Leveson St A6
Library A2
Library B5
Library C1
Lyceum Theatre B5
Malinda St A3
Maltravers St A5
Manor Oaks Rd B6
Mappin Art Gallery B2
Mappin St B3
Marlborough Rd B1
Mary St C4
Matilda St C4
Matlock Rd A1
Meadow St A3
Melbourn Rd A1
Melbourne Ave C1
Millennium Galleries B5
Milton St C3
Mitchell St B3
Mona Ave A1
Mona Rd A1
Montgomery Terrace Rd A3
Montgomery Theatre B4
Monument Gdns C6
Moor Oaks Rd B1
Moore St C3
Mowbray St A4
Mushroom La B2
Netherthorpe Rd B3
Netherthorpe Rd (tram station) B3
Newbould La C1
Nile St C1
Norfolk Park Rd C6
Norfolk Rd C6
Norfolk St B4
North Church St B4
Northfield Rd A1
Northumberland Rd B1
Nursery St A5
Oakholme Rd C1
Octagon B2
Odeon B5
Old St B6
Oxford St A2
Paradise St B4
Park La C2
Park Sq B5
Parker's Rd B1
Pearson Building (Univ) C2
Penistone Rd A3
Pinstone St B4
Pitt St B3
Police Station A4/B5
Pond Hill B5
Pond St B5
Ponds Forge Sports Centre B5
Portobello St B3
Post Office A1/A2/B3/B4/B5/B6/C1/C3/C4/C6
Powell St A2
Queen St B4
Queen's Rd C5
Ramsey Rd B1
Red Hill B3
Redcar Rd B1
Regent St B3
Rockingham St B4
Roebuck Rd A2
Royal Hallamshire Hospital C2
Russell St A4
Rutland Park C1
St George's Cl B3
St Mary's Gate C3
St Mary's Rd C4/C5
St Peter & St Paul Cathedral B4
St Philip's Rd A3
Savile St A5
School Rd B1
Scotland St A4
Severn Rd B1
Shalesmoor A4
Shalesmoor (tram station) A3
Sheaf St B5
Sheffield Hallam University B5
Sheffield Ice Sports Centre – Skate Central C5
Sheffield Parkway A6
Sheffield Station C5
Sheffield Station/ Sheffield Hallam University (tram station) B5
Sheffield University B2
Shepherd St A3
Shipton St A2
Shoreham St C4
Showroom, The C5
Shrewsbury Rd C5
Sidney St C4
Site Gallery C5
Slinn St A1
Smithfield A4
Snig Hill A5
Snow La A4
Solly St B3
Southbourne Rd C1
South La C4
South Street Park B5
Spital Hill A5
Spital St A5
Spring Hill B1
Spring Hill Rd B1
Springvale Rd A1
Stafford Rd C6
Stafford St B6
Stanley St A5
Suffolk Rd C5
Summer St B2
Sunny Bank C3
Surrey St B4
Sussex St A6
Sutton St B3
Sydney Rd A2
Sylvester St C4
Talbot St B5
Taptonville Rd B1
Tax Office C4
Tenter St B4
The Moor C4
Town Hall B4
Townend St A1
Townhead St B4
Trafalgar St B4
Tree Root Walk B2
Trinity St A4
Trippet La B4
Turner Museum of Glass B3
Union St B4
University Drama Studio B2
University of Sheffield (tram station) B3
Upper Allen St A3
Upper Hanover St B3
Upperthorpe Rd A2/A3
Verdon St A5
Victoria Quays B5
Victoria Rd C2
Victoria St B3
Waingate B5
Watery St A3
Watson Rd C1
Wellesley Rd B2
Wellington St C3
West Bar A4
West Bar Green A4
West One B3
West St B3
West St (tram station) B4
Westbourne Rd C1
Western Bank B2
Western Rd A1
Weston Park B2
Weston Park Hospital B2
Weston Park Museum B2
Weston St B2
Wharncliffe Rd C3
Whitham Rd B1
Wicker A5
Wilkinson St B2
William St C3
Winter Garden B4
Winter St B2
York St B4
Yorkshire Artspace C5
Young St C4

Shrewsbury 191

Abbey Church B3
Abbey Foregate B3
Abbey Lawn Business Park B3
Abbots House B2
Agricultural Show Gd A1
Albert St A2
Alma St B1
Ashley St A3
Ashton Rd C1
Avondale Dr A3
Bage Way C3
Barker St B1
Beacall's La A2
Beeches La C2
Beehive La C1
Belle Vue Gdns C2
Belle Vue Rd C2
Belmont Bank C1
Berwick Ave A1
Berwick Rd A1
Betton St C2
Bishop St B3
Bradford St B3
Bridge St B1
Bus Station B2
Butcher Row B2
Burton St A3
Butler Rd C1
Bynner St C2
Canon St B3
Canonbury C1
Castle Business Park, The A2
Castle Foregate A2
Castle Gates B2
Castle Museum B2
Castle St B2
Cathedral (RC) C1
Chester St A2
Cineworld C3
Claremont Bank B1
Claremont Hill B1
Cleveland St B3
Coleham Head B2
Coleham Pumping Station C2
College Hill B1
Corporation La A1
Coton Cres A1
Coton Hill A2
Coton Mount A1
Crescent La C1
Crewe St A2
Cross Hill B1
Darwin Centre B2
Dingle, The B1
Dogpole B2
Draper's Hall B2
English Bridge B2
Fish St B2
Frankwell B1
Gateway Centre, The A2
Gravel Hill La A1
Greyfriars Rd C2
Guildhall B1
Hampton Rd A3
Haycock Way C3
HM Prison B2
High St B1
Hills La B1
Holywell St B3
Hunter St A1
Information Ctr B1
Ireland's Mansion & Bear Steps B1
John St A3
Kennedy Rd C1
King St B3
Kingsland Bridge C1
Kingsland Bridge (toll) C1
Kingsland Rd C1
Library B2
Lime St C2
Longden Coleham C2
Longden Rd C1
Longner St B1
Luciefelde Rd C1
Mardol B1
Market B1
Marine Terr C2
Monkmoor Rd B3
Moreton Cr C2
Mount St A1
Music Hall B1
New Park Cl A3
New Park Rd A2
New Park St A3
North St A2
Oakley St C1
Old Coleham C2
Old Market Hall B1
Old Potts Way C3
Parade Centre B2
Police Station B1
Post Office A2/B1/B2/B3
Pride Hill B1
Pride Hill Centre B1
Priory Rd B1
Pritchard Way C3
Queen St A3
Raby Cr C2
Rad Brook C1
Rea Brook C3
Riverside B1
Roundhill La A1
Rowley's House B1
St Alkmund's B2
St Chad's B1
St Chad's Terr B1
St John's Hill B1
St Julians Friars C2
St Mary's B2
St Mary's St B2
Salters La C2
Scott St C3
Severn Bank A3
Severn St A2
Shrewsbury B2
Shrewsbury High School for Girls C1
Shrewsbury School C1
Shropshire Wildlife Trust B3
Smithfield Rd B1
South Hermitage C1
Swan Hill B1
Sydney Ave A3
Tankerville St B3
The Dana B2
The Quarry B1
The Square B1
Tilbrook Dr A3
Town Walls C1
Trinity St C2
Underdale Rd B3
Victoria Ave B1
Victoria Quay B1
Victoria St B2
Welsh Bridge B1
Whitehall St B3
Wood St A2
Wyle Cop B2

Southampton 191

Above Bar St A2
Albert Rd North B3
Albert Rd South C3
Anderson's Rd B3
Archaeology Museum C2
Argyle Rd A2
Arundel Tower B1
Bargate, The B2
Bargate Centre B2
BBC Regional Centre A1
Bedford Pl A1
Belvidere Rd A3
Bernard St C2
Blechynden Terr A1
Brazil Rd C3
Brinton's Rd A2
Britannia Rd A3
Briton St C2
Brunswick Pl A2
Bugle St C1
Canute Rd C3
Castle Way C2
Catchcold Tower B1
Central Bridge C3
Central Rd C2
Channel Way C3
Chapel Rd B3
Cineworld C3
City Art Gallery A1
City College B3
Civic Centre A1
Civic Centre Rd A1
Coach Station B1
Commercial Rd A1
Cumberland Pl A1
Cunard Rd C2
Derby Rd A3
Devonshire Rd A1
Dock Gate 4 C2
Dock Gate 8 B1
East Park A2
East Park Terr A2
East St B2
East St Shopping Centre B2
Endle St B3
European Way C2
Fire Station A2
Floating Bridge Rd C3
God's House Tower C2
Golden Gr A3
Graham Rd A2
Guildhall A1
Hanover Bldgs B2
Harbour Lights C3
Harbour Pde B1
Hartington Rd A3
Havelock Rd A1
Henstead Rd A1
Herbert Walker Ave B1
High St B2
Hoglands Park B2
Holy Rood (Rems), Merchant Navy Memorial B2
Houndwell Park B2
Houndwell Pl B2
Hythe Ferry C2
Information Ctr A1
Isle of Wight Ferry Terminal C1
James St B3
Java Rd C2
Kingsland Market B2
Kingsway A2
Leisure World B1
Library A1
Lime St B2
London Rd A2
Marine Pde B3
Maritime C1
Marsh La B2
Mayflower Memorial C1
Mayflower Park C1
Mayflower Theatre, The A1
Medieval Merchant's House C1
Melbourne St B3
Millais A2
Morris Rd A1
Neptune Way C3
New Rd A2
Nichols Rd A3
Northam Rd A3
Ocean Dock C2
Ocean Village Marina C3
Ocean Way C3
Odeon B1
Ogle Rd B1
Old Northam Rd A2
Orchard La B2
Oxford Ave A2
Oxford St C2
Palmerston Park A2
Palmerston Rd A2
Parsonage Rd A3
Peel St A3
Platform Rd C2
Police Station A1
Portland Terr B1
Post Office A2/A3/B2
Pound Tree Rd B2
Quays Swimming and Diving Complex, The B1
Queen's Park C2
Queen's Peace Fountain A2
Queen's Terr C2
Queen's Way B2
Radcliffe Rd A3
Rochester St A3
Royal Pier C1
St Andrew's Rd A2
St Mary St A2
St Mary's B3
St Mary's Leisure Centre A2
St Mary's Pl B2
St Mary's Rd A2
St Mary's Stadium (Southampton FC) A3
St Michael's C1
Solent Sky C3
South Front B2
Southampton Central Station A1
Southampton Solent University A2
Southampton Oceanography Centre C3
SS Shieldhall C2
Terminus Terr C2
The Mall, Marlands A1
The Polygon A1
Threefield La B2
Titanic Engineers' Memorial A2
Town Quay C1
Town Walls B2
Tudor House C1
Vincent's Walk B2
West Gate C1
West Marlands Rd A1
West Park A1
West Park Rd A1
West Quay Rd B1
West Quay Retail Park B1
West Quay Shopping Centre B1
West Rd C2
Western Esplanade B1

Southend-on-Sea 192

Adventure Island C3
Albany Ave A1
Albert Rd C3
Alexandra Rd C2
Alexandra St C2
Art Gallery C1
Ashburnham Rd B2
Ave Rd B1
Avenue Terr B1
Balmoral Rd B1
Baltic Ave B3
Baxter Ave A2/B2
Bircham Rd A2
Boscombe Rd B3
Boston Ave A1/B2
Bournemouth Park Rd A3
Browning Ave A3
Bus Station C3
Byron Ave A3
Cambridge Rd C1/C2
Canewdon Rd B1
Carnarvon Rd A2
Central Ave A3
Chelmsford Ave A1
Chichester Rd B2
Church Rd C3
Civic Centre A2
Clarence Rd C2
Clarence St C2
Cliff Ave B1
Cliffs Pavilion C1
Clifftown Parade C2
Clifftown Rd C2
Colchester Rd A1
College Way B2
County Court B3
Cromer Rd B3
Crowborough Rd A2
Dryden Ave A3
East St A2
Elmer App B2
Elmer Ave B2
Gainsborough Dr A1
Gayton Rd A2
Glenhurst Rd A2
Gordon Pl B2
Gordon Rd B2
Grainger Rd A2
Greyhound Way A3
Guildford Rd B3
Hamlet Ct Rd B1
Hamlet Rd C1
Harcourt Ave A1
Hartington Rd C3
Hastings Rd B3
Herbert Gr C3
Heygate Ave C3
High St B2/C2
Information Ctr C3
Kenway A2
Kilworth Ave B3
Lancaster Gdns B3
Library B2
London Rd B1
Lucy Rd C3
MacDonald Ave A1
Magistrates Court A2
Maldon Rd A2
Marine Parade C3
Milton Rd B1
Milton St B2
Napier Ave B2
Never Never Land C2
North Ave A3
North Rd A1/B1
Odeon B2
Osborne Rd B1
Park Cres B1
Park Rd B1
Park St B1
Park Terr B1
Peter Pan's Playground C2
Pier Hill C3
Pleasant Rd C3
Police Station A2
Post Office B2/B3
Princes St B2
Queens Rd B2
Queensway B2/B3/C3
Rayleigh Ave A1
Redstock Rd A2
Rochford Ave A1
Royal Mews C2
Royal Terr C2
Royals Shopping Precinct, The C3
Ruskin Ave A3
St Ann's Rd B3
St Helen's Rd B1
St John's Rd B1
St Leonard's Rd C3
St Lukes Rd A3
St Vincent's Rd C1
Salisbury Ave A1/B1
Scratton Rd C2
Shakespeare Dr A1
Short St A2
South Ave A3
Southchurch Rd B3
South East Essex College B2
Southend Central B2
Southend Pier Railway C3
Southend United FC A1
Southend Victoria B2
Stadium Rd A2
Stanfield Rd A2
Stanley Rd C3
Sutton Rd A3/B3
Swanage Rd B3
Sweyne Ave A1
Swimming Pool B3
Sycamore Gr A3
Tennyson Ave A3
The Grove A3
Tickfield Ave A2
Tudor Rd A1
Tunbridge Rd A2
Tylers Ave B3
Tyrrel Dr B3
Vale Ave A2
Victoria Ave A2
Victoria Plaza Shopping Precinct B2
Warrior Sq B3
Wesley Rd C3
West Rd A1
West St A1
Westcliff Parade C1
Western Esplanade C1
Weston Rd C2
Whitegate Rd B3
Wilson Rd C1
Wimborne Rd B3
York Rd C3

Stirling 192

Abbey Rd A3
Abbotsford Pl A3
Abercromby Pl C1
Albert Halls B1
Albert Pl B1
Alexandra Pl A3
Allan Park C2
Ambulance Station A2
AMF Ten Pin Bowling B2
Argyll Ave A3
Argyll's Lodging B1
Back O' Hill Industrial Estate A1
Back O' Hill Rd A1
Baker St B2
Ballengeich Pass A1
Balmoral Pl B1
Barn Rd B1
Barnton St B2
Bow St B1
Bruce St A2
Burghmuir Industrial Estate C2
Burghmuir Rd A2/B2/C2
Bus Station B2
Cambuskenneth Bridge A3
Carlton C2
Castle Ct B1
Causewayhead Rd A2
Cemetery A1
Church of the Holy Rude B1
Clarendon Pl C1
Club House B1
Colquhoun St C3
Corn Exchange B2
Council Offices C2
Court B2
Cowane A2
Cowane St A2
Cowane's Hospital B1
Crawford Shopping Arcade B2
Crofthead Rd A1
Dean Cres A3
Douglas St A2
Drip Rd A1
Drummond La C1
Drummond Pl C1
Drummond Pl La C1
Dumbarton Rd C2
Eastern Access Rd B2
Edward Ave A3
Edward Rd A2
Forrest Rd A2
Fort A1
Forth Cres B2
Forth St A2
Gladstone Pl C1
Glebe Ave C1
Glebe Cres C1
Glendevon Dr A1
Golf Course C1
Goosecroft Rd B2
Gowanhill A1
Greenwood Ave B1
Harvey Wynd A1
Information Ctr A1/C2
Irvine Pl B2
James St A2
John St B1
Kerse Rd C3
King's Knot B1
King's Park C1
King's Park Rd C1
Laurencecroft Rd A2
Leisure Pool B2
Library B2
Linden Ave C2
Lovers Wk A2
Lower Back Walk B1
Lower Bridge St A2
Lower Castlehill A1
Mar Pl B1
Meadow Pl A3
Meadowforth Rd C3
Middlemuir Rd C3
Millar Pl A3
Morris Terr B2
Mote Hill A1
Murray Pl B2
Nelson Pl C2
Old Town Jail B1
Orchard House Hospital (No A+E) A2
Park Terr C1
Phoenix Industrial Estate C3
Players Rd C3
Port St C2
Princes St B2
Queen St B2
Queen's Rd B1
Queenshaugh Dr A3
Rainbow Slides B2
Ramsay Pl A2
Riverside Dr A3
Ronald Pl A1
Rosebery Pl A2
Royal Gardens B1
Royal Gdns B1
St Mary's Wynd B1
St Ninian's Rd C2
Scott St A2
Seaforth Pl B2
Shore Rd B2
Smith Art Gallery & Museum B1
Snowdon Pl C1
Snowdon Pl La C1
Spittal St B2
Springkerse Industrial Estate C3
Springkerse Rd C3
Stirling Business Centre C2
Stirling Castle A1
Stirling County Rugby Football Club A3
Stirling Enterprise Park B3
Stirling Old Bridge A2
Stirling Station B2
Superstore A2
Sutherland Ave A3
TA Centre C3
Tannery La A2
Thistle Industrial Estate C3
Thistles Shopping Centre, The B2
Tolbooth, The B1
Town Wall B1
Union St A2
Upper Back Walk B1
Upper Bridge St A1
Upper Castlehill B1
Upper Craigs C2
Victoria Pl C1
Victoria Rd B1
Victoria Sq B1/C1
Vue B2
Wallace St A2
Waverley Cres A3
Wellgreen Rd C2
Windsor Pl C1
YHA B1

Stoke-on-Trent 192

Ashford St A3
Avenue Rd A3
Aynsley Rd A2
Barnfield C1
Bath St C2
Beresford St A3
Bilton St C2
Boon Ave C2
Booth St C2
Boothen Rd C2/C3
Boughey St C2
Boughey Rd B3
Brighton St B1
Campbell Rd C2
Carlton Rd B3
Cauldon Rd A3
Cemetery A2
Cemetery Rd A2
Chamberlain Ave C1
Church (RC) B2
Church St C2
City Rd C3
Civic Centre and King's Hall B2
Cliff Vale Pk A1
College Rd A3
Convent Cl B2
Copeland St B2
Cornwallis St C3
Corporation St C2
Crowther St A3
Dominic St B1
Elenora St B2
Elgin St B2
Epworth St A3
Etruscan St A1
Film Theatre B3
Fleming Rd C2
Fletcher Rd C2
Floyd St B2
Foden St C2
Frank St C2
Franklin Rd C1
Frederick Ave B1
Garden St C1
Garner St A1
Gerrard St B2
Glebe St B3
Greatbach Ave B1
Hanley Park A3
Harris St B1
Hartshill Rd B1
Hayward St A2
Hide St B2
Higson Ave B2
Hill St B2
Honeywall B2
Hunters Dr C1
Hunters Way C1
Keary St C2
Kingsway B2
Leek Rd B3
Library C2
Lime St C2
Liverpool Rd B2
London Rd C2
Lonsdale St C2
Lovatt St B2
Lytton St B3
Market C2
Newcastle La C1
Newlands St A2
Norfolk St A2
North St A1/B2
North Staffordshire Royal Infirmary (A&E) B1
Northcote Ave B2
Oldmill St C3
Oriel St B1
Oxford St B1
Penkhull New Rd C1
Penkhull St C1
Police Station C2
Portmeirion Pottery C2
Post Office A3/B1/B3/C1/C2
Prince's Rd B1
Pump St B2
Quarry Ave B1
Quarry Rd B1
Queen Anne St A3
Queen's Rd C1
Queensway A1/B2/C3
Richmond St B1
Rothwell St C1
St Peter's B3
St Thomas Pl C1
Scrivenor Rd A1
Seaford St A3
Selwyn St C3
Shelton New Rd A1
Shelton Old Rd B2
Sheppard St C2
Spark St C2
Spencer Rd B3
Spode St C2
Squires View B3
Staffordshire Univ B3
Stanley Matthews Sports Centre B3
Station Rd B3
Stoke Business Park C3
Stoke Recreation Centre C2
Stoke Rd A2
Stoke-on-Trent College A3
Stoke-on-Trent Station B3
Sturgess St C2
The Villas C1
Thistley Hough C1
Thornton Rd B3
Tolkien Way B1
Trent Valley Rd C1
Vale St B2
Watford St A3
Wellesley St A3
West Ave B1
Westland St B1
Yeaman St C2
Yoxall Ave B1

Stratford-upon-Avon 192

Albany Rd B1
Alcester Rd B1
Ambulance Station B1
Arden St B2
Avenue Farm A1
Avenue Farm Industrial Estate A1
Avenue Rd A3
Avon Industrial Estate A2
Baker Ave A1
Bandstand C3
Benson Rd A3
Birmingham Rd A2
Boat Club B3
Borden Pl C1
Brass Rubbing Centre C2
Bridge St B2
Bridgetown Rd C3
Bridgeway B3
Broad St C2
Broad Walk C2
Brookvale Rd C1
Bull St C2
Butterfly Farm and Jungle Safari C3
Cemetery C1
Chapel La B2
Cherry Orchard C1
Chestnut Walk B2
Children's Playground C3
Church St C2
Civic Hall B2
Clarence Rd B1
Clopton Bridge B3
Clopton Rd A2
Coach Terminal and Park B3
College B1
College La C2
College St C2
Community Sports Centre B1
Council Offices (District) B2
Courtyard C2
Cox's Yard B3
Cricket Ground C3
Ely Gdns B2
Ely St B2
Evesham Rd C1
Fire Station B1
Foot Ferry C3
Fordham Ave A2
Gallery, The B3
Garrick Way C1
Gower Memorial B3
Great William St B2
Greenhill St B2
Grove Rd B2
Guild St B2
Guildhall & School B2
Hall's Croft C2
Hartford Rd C1
Harvard House B2
Henley St B2
High St B2
Holton St C2
Holy Trinity C2
Information Ctr B3
Jolyffe Park Rd A2
Judith Shakespeare's House B2
Kipling Rd C3
Leisure & Visitor Centre B3
Library B2
Lodge Rd B1
Maidenhead Rd A3
Mansell St B2
Masons Court B2
Masons Rd A1
Maybird Retail Park A2
Maybrook Rd A1
Mayfield Ave A2
Meer St B2
Mill La C2
Moat House Hotel B3
Narrow La C2
New Place & Nash's House B2
New St C2
Old Town C2
Orchard Way C1
Paddock La C1
Park Rd A1
Payton St B2
Percy St A2
Police Station B2
Post Office B2/B3
Recreation Ground C2
Regal Road A2
Regal Road Trading Estate A2
Rother St B2
Rowley Cr A3
Ryland St C2
Saffron Meadow C2
St Andrew's Cr B1
St Gregory's A3
St Gregory's Rd A3
St Mary's Rd A2
Sanctus Dr C2
Sanctus St C1
Sandfield Rd C2
Scholars La B2
Seven Meadows Rd C2
Shakespeare Centre B2
Shakespeare Institute C2
Shakespeare St B2
Shakespeare's Birthplace B2
Sheep St B2
Shelley Rd C3
Shipston Rd C3
Shottery Rd C1
Slingates Rd A2
Southern La C2
Station Rd B1
Stratford Healthcare B2

Sunderland • Swansea • Swindon • Taunton • Telford • Torquay • Truro • Wick 209

Stratford Hospital B2
Stratford Sports Club B1
Stratford-upon-Avon Station B1
Talbot Rd A2
The Greenway C2
The Willows B1
The Willows North B1
Tiddington Rd B3
Timothy's Bridge Rd A1
Town Hall & Council Offices B2
Town Sq B2
Tramway Bridge B3
Trinity St C2
Tyler St B2
War Memorial Gdns B3
Warwick Rd B3
Waterside B3
Welcombe Rd A3
West St C2
Western Rd A2
Wharf Rd A2
Wood St B2

Sunderland 192

Albion Pl C2
Alliance Pl B1
Argyle St C2
Ashwood St C1
Athenaeum St B2
Azalea Terr C2
Beach St A1
Bede Theatre C3
Bedford St B2
Beechwood Terr C1
Belvedere Rd C2
Blandford St B2
Borough Rd B3
Bridge Cr B2
Bridge St B2
Brooke St A2
Brougham St B2
Burdon Rd C2
Burn Park C1
Burn Park Rd C1
Burn Park Tech Park C1
Carol St B1
Charles St A3
Chester Rd C1
Chester Terr B1
Church St A3
Cineworld B3
Civic Centre C2
Cork St B3
Coronation St B3
Cowan Terr C2
Crowtree Rd B2
Dame Dorothy St A2
Deptford Rd B1
Deptford Terr A1
Derby St C2
Derwent St C2
Dock St A3
Dundas St A2
Durham Rd C1
Easington St A2
Egerton St C3
Empire Theatre B2
Farringdon Row B1
Fawcett St B2
Fox St C1
Foyle St B3
Frederick St B3
Gill Rd B2
Hanover Pl A1
Havelock Terr C1
Hay St A2
Headworth Sq B3
Hendon Rd B3
High St East B3
High St West B2/B3
Holmeside B2
Hylton Rd B1
Information Ctr B2
John St B3
Kier Hardie Way A2
Lambton St B3
Laura St C3
Lawrence St B3
Leisure Centre B2
Library & Arts Centre B3
Lily St B1
Lime St B1
Livingstone Rd B2
Low Row B2
Matamba Terr B1
Millburn St B1
Millennium Way A2
Minster B2
Monkwearmouth Station Museum A2
Mowbray Park C3
Mowbray Rd C3
Murton St C3
Museum B3
National Glass Centre ✦ A3
New Durham Rd C1
Newcastle Rd A2
Nile St B3
Norfolk St B3
North Bridge St A2
Otto Terr C1
Park La C2
Park Lane (metro station) C2
Park Rd C2
Paul's Rd B3
Peel St C3
Police Station B2
Post Office B2
Priestly Cr A1
Queen St B2
Railway Row B1
Retail Park B1
Richmond St A2
Roker Ave A2
Royalty Theatre C1
Ryhope Rd C2
St Mary's Way B2
St Michael's Way B2
St Peter's A3
St Peter's (metro station) A2
St Peter's Way A3
St Vincent St C3
Salem Rd C3
Salem St C3
Salisbury St C3
Sans St B3
Silkworth Row B1
Southwick Rd A2
Stadium of Light (Sunderland AFC) A2
Stadium Way A2
Stobart St A2
Stockton Rd C2
Suffolk St C3
Sunderland (metro station) B2
Sunderland Station B2
Sunderland St B3
Tatham St C3
Tavistock Pl B3
The Bridges B2
The Place B3
The Royalty C1
Thelma St C1
Thomas St North A2
Thornholme Rd C1
Toward Rd C3
Transport Interchange C2
Trimdon St Way B1
Tunstall Rd C2
University (metro station) C1
University Library C1
University of Sunderland (City Campus) B1
University of Sunderland (Sir Tom Cowie Campus) A3
Vaux Brewery Way A2
Villiers St B3
Villiers St South B3
Vine Pl C2
Violet St B1
Walton La B3
Waterworks Rd B1
Wearmouth Bridge B2
Wellington La A1
West Sunniside B3
West Wear St B3
Westbourne Rd B1
Western Hill C1
Wharncliffe B1
Whickham St A3
White House Rd C3
Wilson St North A2
Winter Gdns C3
Wreath Quay A1

Swansea *Abertawe* 192

Adelaide St C3
Albert Row C3
Alexandra Rd B3
Argyle St C1
Baptist Well Pl A2
Beach St C1
Belle Vue Way B3
Berw Rd A1
Berwick Terr A2
Bond St C1
Brangwyn Concert Hall C1
Bridge St A3
Brookands Terr B1
Brunswick St C1
Bryn-Syfi Terr A2
Bryn-y-Mor Rd C1
Bullins La B1
Burrows Rd C1
Bus/Rail link A3
Bus Station C2
Cadfan Rd A1
Cadrawd Rd A1
Caer St B3
Carig Cr A1
Carlton Terr B2
Carmarthen Rd A3
Castle Square B3
Castle St B3
Catherine St C1
City & County of Swansea Offices (County Hall) C2
City & County of Swansea Offices (Guildhall) C1
Clarence St C2
Colbourne Terr A2
Constitution Hill B1
Court B3
Creidiol Rd A2
Cromwell St B2
Duke St B1
Dunvant Pl C2
Dyfatty Park A3
Dyfatty St A3
Dyfed Ave A1
Dylan Thomas Ctr ✦ B3
Dylan Thomas Theatre C3
Eaton Cr C1
Eigen Cr A1
Elfed Rd A1
Emlyn Rd A1
Evans Terr A3
Fairfield Terr B1
Ffynone Dr B1
Ffynone Rd B1
Fire Station B3
Firm St A2
Fleet St C1
Francis St C1
Fullers Row B2
George St B2
Glamorgan St C2
Glyndwr Pl A1
Glynn Vivian B3
Graig Terr A3
Grand Theatre C2
Granogwen Rd A2
Guildhall Rd South C1
Gwent Rd A1
Gwynedd Ave A1
Hafod St A3
Hanover St B1
Harcourt St B2
Harries St A2
Heathfield B2
Henrietta St B2
Hewson St B2
High St A3/B3
High View A2
Hill St A2
Historic Ships Berth C3
HM Prison C2
Information Ctr C2
Islwyn Rd A1
King Edward's Rd C1
Law Courts C1
Library B3
Long Ridge A2
Madoc St C2
Mansel St B2
Maritime Quarter C3
Market B3
Mayhill Gdns B1
Mayhill Rd A1
Mega Bowl ✦ B3
Milton Terr A2
Mission Gallery C3
Montpellier Terr B1
Morfa Rd A3
Mount Pleasant B2
National Waterfront Museum C3
Nelson St C2
New Cut Rd A3
New St A3
Nicander Pde A2
Nicander Pl A2
Nicholl St B2
Norfolk St B2
North Hill Rd A2
Northampton La B2
Orchard St B3
Oxford St B2
Oystermouth Rd C1
Page St B2
Pant-y-Celyn Rd B1
Parc Tawe Link B3
Parc Tawe North B3
Parc Tawe Shopping & Leisure Centre B3
Patti Pavilion C1
Paxton St C2
Penmaen Terr B1
Pen-y-Graig Rd A1
Phillips Pde C1
Picton Terr B2
Plantasia B3
Police Station B2
Post Office A1/A2/B2/C1
Powys Ave A1
Primrose St B2
Princess Way B3
Promenade B2
Pryder Gdns A1
Quadrant Centre C2
Quay Park B3
Rhianfa La B1
Rhondda St B2
Richardson St C2
Rodney St C1
Rose Hill B1
Rosehill Terr B1
Russell St B1
St David's Sq C3
St Helen's Ave C1
St Helen's Cr C1
St Helen's Rd C1
St James Gdns B1
St James's Cr B1
St Mary's B3
Sea View Terr A3
Singleton St C2
South Dock C3
Stanley Pl B2
Strand B3
Swansea Castle B3
Swansea College Arts Centre C1
Swansea Metropolitan University B2
Swansea Museum C3
Swansea Station A3
Taliesyn Rd B1
Tan y Marian Rd A1
Tegid Rd A2
Teilo Cr A1
Terrace Rd B1/B2
The Kingsway B2
The LC C3
Tontine St A3
Tower of Eclipse ✦ C3
Townhill Rd A1
Tram Museum C3
Trawler Rd C3
Union St B2
Upper Strand A3
Vernon St A3
Victoria Quay C3
Victoria Rd B3
Vincent St C1
Walter Rd B1
Watkin St A2
Waun-Wen Rd A2
Wellington St C2
Westbury St C1
Western St C1
Westway C2
William St C2
Wind St B3
Woodlands Terr B1
YMCA B2
York St C3

Swindon 193

Albert St C3
Albion St C1
Alfred St A2
Alvescot Rd C3
Art Gallery & Museum C3
Ashford Rd C1
Aylesbury St A2
Bath Rd C2
Bathampton St B1
Bathurst Rd B3
Beatrice St A2
Beckhampton St B3
Bowood Rd C1
Bristol St B1
Broad St A3
Brunel Arcade B2
Brunel Plaza B2
Brunswick St C2
Bus Station B2
Cambria Bridge Rd B1
Cambria Place B1
Canal Walk B2
Carfax St B2
Carr St B1
Cemetery C1/C3
Chandler Cl C3
Chapel C1
Chester St B1
Christ Church C3
Church Place B1
Cirencester Way A3
Clarence St B2
Clifton St C1
Cockleberry Rdbt A2
Colbourne Rdbt A3
Colbourne St A3
College St B2
Commercial Rd B2
Corporation St A2
Council Offices B3
County Rd A3
Courts B2
Cricket Ground A3
Cricklade Street C3
Crombey St B1/C2
Cross St C2
Curtis St B1
Deacon St C1
Designer Outlet (Great Western) B1
Dixon St C2
Dover St C2
Dowling St C2
Drove Rd C3
Dryden St C1
Durham St C3
East St B1
Eastcott Hill C2
Eastcott Rd C2
Edgeware Rd B2
Edmund St C2
Elmina Rd A3
Emlyn Square B1
Euclid St B3
Exeter St B1
Fairview C1
Faringdon Rd B1
Farnsby St B1
Fire Station C3
Fleet St B2
Fleming Way B2/B3
Florence St A2
Gladstone St A3
Gooch St A2
Graham St A3
Great Western Way A1/A2
Groundwell Rd B3
Hawksworth Way A1
Haydon St A2
Henry St B2
Hillside Ave C1
Holbrook Way B2
Hunt St C3
Hydro B1
Hythe Rd C2
Information Ctr B2
Joseph St C1
Kent Rd C2
King William St C2
Kingshill Rd C1
Lansdown Rd C2
Leicester St B3
Library B2
Lincoln St B3
Little London C3
London St B1
Magic Rdbt B3
Maidstone Rd C2
Manchester Rd A3
Maxwell St B1
Milford St B2
Milton Rd B1
Morse St C2
National Monuments Record Centre B1
Newcastle St B3
Newcombe Drive A1
Newcombe Trading Estate A1
Newhall St C2
North St C2
North Star Ave A1
North Star Rdbt A1
Northampton St B3
Oasis Leisure Centre A1
Ocotal Way A3
Okus Rd C1
Old Town C3
Oxford St B1
Park Lane B1
Park Lane Rdbt B1
Pembroke St C2
Plymouth St B3
Polaris House A2
Polaris Way A2
Police Station B2
Ponting St A2
Post Office B1/B2/C1/C3
Poulton St A3
Princes St B2
Prospect Hill C2
Prospect Place C2
Queen St B2
Queen's Park C3
Radnor St C1
Read St C1
Reading St B1
Regent St B2
Retail Park A2/A3/B3
Rosebery St A3
St Mark's B1
Salisbury St A3
Savernake St C2
Shelley St C1
Sheppard St B1
South St C2
Southampton St B3
Spring Gardens B3
Stafford Street C2
Stanier St C2
Station Road A2
Steam B1
Swindon College A2
Swindon Rd C2
Swindon Station A2
Swindon Town Football Club A3
T A Centre B1
Tennyson St B1
The Lawn C3
The Nurseries C1
The Parade B2
The Park B1
Theobald St B1
Town Hall B2
Transfer Bridges Rdbt A3
Union St C2
Upham Rd C3
Victoria Rd C3
Walcot Rd B3
War Memorial ✦ B2
Wells St B3
Western St C2
Westmorland Rd B3
Whalebridge Rdbt B2
Whitehead St C1
Whitehouse Rd A2
William St C1
Wood St C3
Wyvern Theatre & Arts Centre B2
York Rd B3

Taunton 193

Addison Gr A1
Albemarle Rd A1
Alfred St B3
Alma St C2
Bath Pl C1
Belvedere Rd A1
Billet St B2
Billetfield C2
Birch Gr A1
Brewhouse Theatre B2
Bridge St B1
Bridgwater and Taunton Canal A2
Broadlands Rd C1
Burton Pl C1
Bus Station B1
Canal Rd A2
Cann St C1
Canon St B2
Castle B1
Castle St B1
Cheddon Rd A2
Chip Lane A1
Clarence St B1
Cleveland St B1
Clifton Terr A2
Coleridge Cres C3
Compass Hill C1
Compton Cl A2
Corporation St B1
Council Offices A1
County Walk Shopping Centre C2
Courtyard B2
Cranmer Rd B2
Critchard Way B3
Cyril St A1
Deller's Wharf B1
Duke St B2
East Reach B3
East St B3
Eastbourne Rd B2
Eastleigh Rd C3
Eaton Cres A2
Elm Gr A1
Elms Cl A1
Fons George C1
Fore St B2
Fowler St A1
French Weir Recreation Grd B1
Geoffrey Farrant Wk A2
Gray's Almshouses B2
Grays Rd B3
Greenway Ave A1
Guildford Pl C1
Hammet St B2
Haydon Rd B3
Heavitree Way A2
Herbert St A2
High St C2
Holway Ave C3
Hugo St B3
Huish's Almshouses B2
Hurdle Way C2
Information Ctr C2
Jubilee St A1
King's College C3
Kings Cl C3
Laburnum St B2
Lambrook Rd B3
Lansdowne Rd A3
Leslie Ave A1
Leycroft Rd B3
Library C2
Linden Gr A1
Magdalene St B2
Magistrates Court B1
Malvern Terr A2
Market House B2
Mary St C2
Middle St B2
Midford Rd B3
Mitre Court B3
Mount Nebo C1
Mount St C2
Mountway C2
Museum of Somerset B1
North St B2
Northfield Ave B1
Northfield Rd B1
Northleigh Rd C3
Obridge Allotments A3
Obridge Lane A3
Obridge Rd A3
Obridge Viaduct A3
Old Market Shopping Centre C2
Osborne Way C1
Park St C1
Paul St C2
Plais St A2
Playing Field C3
Police Station C1
Portland St B1
Post Office B1/B2/C1
Priorswood Industrial Estate A3
Priorswood Rd A2
Priory Ave B2
Priory Bridge Rd B2
Priory Fields Retail Park A3
Priory Park A2
Priory Way A3
Queen St B3
Railway St A1
Records Office A2
Recreation Grd A1
Riverside Place B2
St Augustine St B2
St George's C2
St Georges Sq C2
St James B2
St James St B2
St John's C1
St John's Rd B1
St Josephs Field C2
St Mary Magdalene's B2
Samuels Ct A1
Shire Hall and Law Courts C1
Somerset County Cricket Ground B2
Somerset County Hall C1
Somerset Cricket B2
South Rd C3
South St C3
Staplegrove Rd B1
Station Rd A1
Stephen St B2
Swimming Pool A1
Tancred St B2
Tauntfield Cl C3
Taunton Dean Cricket Club C2
Taunton Station A2
The Avenue A1
The Crescent C1
The Mount C2
Thomas St A1
Toneway A3
Tower St B1
Trevor Smith Pl C3
Trinity Business Centre C3
Trinity Rd C3
Trinity St B3
Trull Rd C1
Tudor House B2
Upper High St C1
Venture Way A3
Victoria Gate B3
Victoria Park B3
Victoria St B3
Viney St B3
Vivary Park C2
Vivary Rd C1
War Memorial ✦ C1
Wellesley St A2
Wheatley Cres A3
Whitehall A1
Wilfred Rd B3
William St A1
Wilton Church C1
Wilton Cl C1
Wilton Gr C1
Wilton St C1
Winchester St B2
Winters Field B2
Wood St B1
Yarde Pl B1

Telford 193

Alma Ave C1
Amphitheatre C2
Bowling Alley B2
Brandsfarm Way C3
Brunel Rd B1
Bus Station B2
Buxton Rd C1
Central Park A2
Civic Offices B2
Coach Central B2
Coachwell Cl B1
Colliers Way A1
Courts B2
Dale Acre Way B3
Darliston C3
Deepdale B3
Deercote B2
Dinthill C3
Doddington C3
Dodmoor Grange C3
Downemead B3
Duffryn B3
Dunsheath B3
Euston Way A3
Eyton Mound C1
Eyton Rd C1
Forgegate A2
Grange Central B2
Hall Park Way B1
Hinkshay Rd C2
Hollinsworth Rd A2
Holyhead Rd A3
Housing Trust A1
Ice Rink B2
Information Ctr B2
Ironmasters Way A2
Job Centre B1
Land Registry B1
Lawn Central B2
Lawnswood C1
Library B2
Malinsgate B1
Matlock Ave C1
Moor Rd C1
Mount Rd C1
NFU Offices B1
Odeon B2
Park Lane A1
Police Station B1
Priorslee Ave A3
Queen Elizabeth Ave C3
Queen Elizabeth Way B1
Queensway A2/B3
Rampart Way A2
Randlay Ave C3
Randlay Wood C3
Rhodes Ave C1
Royal Way B1
St Leonards Rd B1
St Quentin Gate B2
Shifnal Rd A3
Sixth Ave A1
Southwater Way B1
Spout Lane C1
Spout Mound B1
Spout Way C1
Stafford Court B3
Stafford Park B3
Stirchley Ave C3
Stone Row C1
Telford Bridge Retail Park A1
Telford Central Station A3
Telford Centre, The B2
Telford Forge Retail Park A1
Telford Hornets RFC C2
Telford International Centre C2
Telford Way A3
Third Ave A2
Town Park C2
Town Park Visitor Centre B2
Walker House B2
Wellswood Ave A2
West Centre Way B1
Withywood Drive C1
Woodhouse Central B2
Yates Way A1

Torquay 193

Abbey Rd B2
Alexandra Rd A2
Alpine Rd B3
Ash Hill Rd A2
Babbacombe Rd B3
Bampfylde Rd B1
Barton Rd A1
Beacon Quay C2
Belgrave Rd A1/B1
Belmont Rd A3
Berea Rd A3
Braddons Hill Rd East B3
Brewery Park A3
Bronshill Rd A2
Castle Rd A2
Cavern Rd A3
Central B2
Chatsworth Rd A2
Chestnut Ave B1
Church St A1
Civic Offices A2
Coach Station A1
Corbyn Head C1
Croft Hill B1
Croft Rd B1
Daddyhole Plain C3
East St A1
Egerton Rd A3
Ellacombe Church Rd A3
Ellacombe Rd A2
Falkland Rd B1
Fleet St B2
Fleet Walk Shopping Centre B2
Grafton Rd B3
Haldon Pier C2
Hatfield Rd A2
Highbury Rd A2
Higher Warberry Rd A3
Hillesdon Rd B3
Hollywood Bowl C3
Hoxton Rd A3
Hunsdon Rd B3
Information Ctr B2
Inner Harbour C3
Kenwyn Rd A3
Laburnum St A1
Law Courts A2
Library A2
Lime Ave B1
Living Coasts C3
Lower Warberry Rd B3
Lucius St B1
Lymington Rd A1
Magdalene Rd A1
Marina C2
Market St B2
Meadfoot Lane C3
Meadfoot Rd C3
Melville St B2
Middle Warberry Rd B3
Mill Lane A1
Montpellier Rd B3
Morgan Ave A1
Museum Rd B3
Newton Rd A1
Oakhill Rd A1
Outer Harbour C2
Parkhill Rd C3
Pavilion C2
Pimlico B2
Police Station A1
Post Office A1/B2
Princes Rd A3
Princes Rd East A3
Princes Rd West A3
Princess Gdns C2
Princess Pier C2
Princess Theatre C2
Rathmore Rd B1
Recreation Grd B1
Riviera Centre International B1
Rock End Ave C3
Rock Rd B2
Rock Walk B2
Rosehill Rd A3
St Efride's Rd A1
St John's B3
St Luke's Rd B2
St Luke's Rd North B2
St Luke's Rd South B2
St Marychurch Rd A2
Scarborough Rd B1
Shedden Hill B2
South Pier C2
South St A1
Spanish Barn B1
Stitchill Rd B3
Strand B3
Sutherland Rd B3
Teignmouth Rd A1
Temperance St B2
The King's Drive B1
The Terrace B3
Thurlow Rd A1
Tor Bay B1
Tor Church Rd A1
Tor Hill Rd A1
Torbay Rd B2
Torquay Museum B3
Torquay Station C1
Torre Abbey Mansion B1
Torre Abbey Meadows B1
Torre Abbey Sands B1
Torwood Gdns B3
Torwood St C3
Union Square A2
Union St A1
Upton Hill A2
Upton Park A1
Upton Rd A1
Vanehill Rd C3
Vansittart Rd A1
Vaughan Parade C2
Victoria Parade C3
Victoria Rd A2
Warberry Rd West B2
Warren Rd B2
Windsor Rd A2/A3
Woodville Rd A3

Truro 193

Adelaide Ter B1
Agar Rd B3
Arch Hill C2
Arundell Pl C2
Avondale Rd B1
Back Quay B3
Barrack La C3
Barton Meadow A1
Benson Rd A2
Bishops Cl A2
Bosvean Gdns B1
Bosvigo Gardens B1
Bosvigo La A1
Bosvigo Rd B2
Broad St A3
Burley Cl C3
Bus Station B3
Calenick St B2
Campfield Hill B3
Carclew St B3
Carew Rd A2
Carey Park B2
Carlyon Rd A2
Carvoza Rd A3
Castle St B2
Cathedral View A2
Chainwalk Dr A2
Chapel Hill B1
Charles St B2
City Hall B3
City Rd B2
Coinage Hall B3
Comprigney Hill A1
Coosebean La A1
Copes Gdns A2
County Hall B1
Courtney Rd A2
Crescent Rd B1
Crescent Rise B1
Daniell Court C2
Daniell Rd C2
Daniell St C2
Daubuz Cl A2
Dobbs La B1
Edward St B2
Eliot Rd A2
Elm Court A3
Enys Cl A1
Enys Rd A1
Fairmantle St B3
Falmouth Rd C2
Ferris Town B2
Fire Station B1
Frances St B2
George St B2
Green Cl C2
Green La C1
Grenville Rd A2
Hall For Cornwall B3
Hendra Rd A2
Hendra Vean A1
High Cross B3
Higher Newham La C3
Higher Trehaverne A2
Hillcrest Ave B1
Hospital B2
Hunkin Cl A2
Hurland Rd C3
Infirmary Hill B2
James Pl B3
Kenwyn Church Rd A1
Kenwyn Hill A1
Kenwyn Rd A2
Kenwyn St B2
Kerris Gdns A1
King St B3
Lemon Quay B3
Lemon Street Gallery B3
Library B1/B3
Malpas Rd B3
Market B3
Memorial Gdns B3
Merrifield Close B1
Mitchell Hill A3
Moresk Cl A3
Moresk Rd A3
Morlaix Ave C3
Nancemere Rd A3
Newham Business Park C3
Newham Industrial Estate C3
Newham Rd C3
Northfield Dr C3
Oak Way A3
Old County Hall B1
Pal's Terr A3
Park View C2
Pendarves Rd A2
Plaza Cinema B3
Police Station B3
Post Office B2/B3
Prince's St B3
Pydar St A2
Quay St B3
Redannick Cres C2
Redannick La B2
Richard Lander Monument ✦ C2
Richmond Hill B1
River St B2
Rosedale Rd A2
Royal Cornwall Museum B2
St Aubyn Rd C3
St Clement St B3
St George's Rd A1
School La C2
Station Rd B1
Stokes Rd A2
Strangways Terr C3
Tabernacle St B3
The Avenue A3
The Crescent B1
The Leats B2
The Spires A2
Trehaverne La A2
Tremayne Rd A2
Treseder's Gdns A3
Treworder Rd B1
Treyew Rd B1
Truro Cathedral B3
Truro Harbour Office B3
Truro Station B3
Union St B2
Upper School La C2
Victoria Gdns B2
Waterfall Gdns B2

Wick 193

Ackergill Cres A2
Ackergill St A2
Albert St C2
Ambulance Station C2
Argyle Sq C2
Assembly Rooms C2
Bank Row C2
Bankhead B1
Barons Well B2
Barrogill St C2
Bay View B3
Bexley Terr C3
Bignold Park C2
Bowling Green C2
Breadalbane Terr C2
Bridge of Wick B1
Bridge St B2
Brown Pl C2
Burn St B2
Bus Station B1
Caithness General Hospital (A+E) B1
Cliff Rd B1
Coach Rd B2
Coastguard Station C3
Corner Cres B3
Coronation St C1
Council Offices B2
Court B2
Crane Rock C3
Dempster St C2
Dunnet Ave A2

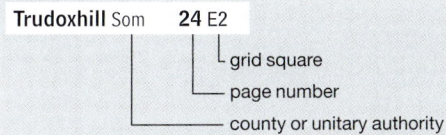

Index to road maps of Britain

Abbreviations used in the index

Aberdeen	**Aberdeen City**
Aberds	**Aberdeenshire**
Ald	**Alderney**
Anglesey	**Isle of Anglesey**
Angus	**Angus**
Argyll	**Argyll and Bute**
Bath	**Bath and North East Somerset**
Bedford	**Bedford**
Bl Gwent	**Blaenau Gwent**
Blackburn	**Blackburn with Darwen**
Blackpool	**Blackpool**
Bmouth	**Bournemouth**
Borders	**Scottish Borders**
Brack	**Bracknell**
Bridgend	**Bridgend**
Brighton	**City of Brighton and Hove**
Bristol	**City and County of Bristol**
Bucks	**Buckinghamshire**
C Beds	**Central Bedfordshire**
Caerph	**Caerphilly**
Cambs	**Cambridgeshire**
Cardiff	**Cardiff**
Carms	**Carmarthenshire**
Ceredig	**Ceredigion**
Ches E	**Cheshire East**
Ches W	**Cheshire West and Chester**
Clack	**Clackmannanshire**
Conwy	**Conwy**
Corn	**Cornwall**
Cumb	**Cumbria**
Darl	**Darlington**
Denb	**Denbighshire**
Derby	**City of Derby**
Derbys	**Derbyshire**
Devon	**Devon**
Dorset	**Dorset**
Dumfries	**Dumfries and Galloway**
Dundee	**Dundee City**
Durham	**Durham**
E Ayrs	**East Ayrshire**
E Dunb	**East Dunbartonshire**
E Loth	**East Lothian**
E Renf	**East Renfrewshire**
E Sus	**East Sussex**
E Yorks	**East Riding of Yorkshire**
Edin	**City of Edinburgh**
Essex	**Essex**
Falk	**Falkirk**
Fife	**Fife**
Flint	**Flintshire**
Glasgow	**City of Glasgow**
Glos	**Gloucestershire**
Gtr Man	**Greater Manchester**
Guern	**Guernsey**
Gwyn	**Gwynedd**
Halton	**Halton**
Hants	**Hampshire**
Hereford	**Herefordshire**
Herts	**Hertfordshire**
Highld	**Highland**
Hrtlpl	**Hartlepool**
Hull	**Hull**
IoM	**Isle of Man**
IoW	**Isle of Wight**
Invclyd	**Inverclyde**
Jersey	**Jersey**
Kent	**Kent**
Lancs	**Lancashire**
Leicester	**City of Leicester**
Leics	**Leicestershire**
Lincs	**Lincolnshire**
London	**Greater London**
Luton	**Luton**
M Keynes	**Milton Keynes**
M Tydf	**Merthyr Tydfil**
Mbro	**Middlesbrough**
Medway	**Medway**
Mers	**Merseyside**
Midloth	**Midlothian**
Mon	**Monmouthshire**
Moray	**Moray**
N Ayrs	**North Ayrshire**
N Lincs	**North Lincolnshire**
N Lanark	**North Lanarkshire**
N Som	**North Somerset**
N Yorks	**North Yorkshire**
NE Lincs	**North East Lincolnshire**
Neath	**Neath Port Talbot**
Newport	**City and County of Newport**
Norf	**Norfolk**
Northants	**Northamptonshire**
Northumb	**Northumberland**
Nottingham	**City of Nottingham**
Notts	**Nottinghamshire**
Orkney	**Orkney**
Oxon	**Oxfordshire**
Pboro	**Peterborough**
Pembs	**Pembrokeshire**
Perth	**Perth and Kinross**
Plym	**Plymouth**
Poole	**Poole**
Powys	**Powys**
Ptsmth	**Portsmouth**
Reading	**Reading**
Redcar	**Redcar and Cleveland**
Renfs	**Renfrewshire**
Rhondda	**Rhondda Cynon Taff**
Rutland	**Rutland**
S Ayrs	**South Ayrshire**
S Glos	**South Gloucestershire**
S Lanark	**South Lanarkshire**
S Yorks	**South Yorkshire**
Scilly	**Scilly**
Shetland	**Shetland**
Shrops	**Shropshire**
Slough	**Slough**
Som	**Somerset**
Soton	**Southampton**
Staffs	**Staffordshire**
Southend	**Southend-on-Sea**
Stirling	**Stirling**
Stockton	**Stockton-on-Tees**
Stoke	**Stoke-on-Trent**
Suff	**Suffolk**
Sur	**Surrey**
Swansea	**Swansea**
Swindon	**Swindon**
T&W	**Tyne and Wear**
Telford	**Telford and Wrekin**
Thurrock	**Thurrock**
Torbay	**Torbay**
Torf	**Torfaen**
V Glam	**The Vale of Glamorgan**
W Berks	**West Berkshire**
W Dunb	**West Dunbartonshire**
W Isles	**Western Isles**
W Loth	**West Lothian**
W Mid	**West Midlands**
W Sus	**West Sussex**
W Yorks	**West Yorkshire**
Warks	**Warwickshire**
Warr	**Warrington**
Wilts	**Wiltshire**
Windsor	**Windsor and Maidenhead**
Wokingham	**Wokingham**
Worcs	**Worcestershire**
Wrex	**Wrexham**
York	**City of York**

How to use the index

Example

Trudoxhill Som **24** E2

- grid square
- page number
- county or unitary authority

A

Ab Kettleby Leics 64 B4
Ab Lench Worcs 50 D5
Abbas Combe Som 12 B5
Abberley Worcs 50 C2
Abberton Essex 43 C6
Abberton Worcs 50 D4
Abberwick Northumb 117 C7
Abbess Roding Essex 42 C1
Abbey Devon 11 C6
Abbey-cwm-hir Powys 48 B2
Abbey Dore Hereford 49 F5
Abbey Field Essex 43 B5
Abbey Hulton Stoke 75 E6
Abbey St Bathans Borders 122 C3
Abbey Town Cumb 107 D8
Abbey Village Lancs 86 B4
Abbey Wood London 29 B5
Abbeydale S Yorks 88 F4
Abbeystead Lancs 93 D5
Abbots Bickington Devon 9 C5
Abbots Bromley Staffs 62 B4
Abbots Langley Herts 40 D3
Abbots Leigh N Som 23 B7
Abbots Morton Worcs 50 D5
Abbots Ripton Cambs 54 B3
Abbots Salford Warks 51 D5
Abbotsbury Dorset 12 F3
Abbotsham Devon 9 B6
Abbotskerswell Devon 7 C6
Abbotsley Cambs 54 D3
Abbotswood Hants 14 B4
Abbotts Ann Hants 25 E8
Abcott Shrops 49 B5
Abdon Shrops 61 F5
Aber Ceredig 46 E3
Aber-Arad Carms 46 F2
Aber-banc Ceredig 46 E2
Aber Cowarch Gwyn 59 C5
Aber-Giâr Carms 46 E4
Aber-gwynfi Neath 34 E2
Aber-Hirnant Gwyn 72 F3
Aber-nant Rhondda 34 D4
Aber-Rhiwlech Gwyn 59 B6
Aber-Village Powys 35 B5
Aberaeron Ceredig 46 C3
Aberaman Rhondda 34 D4
Aberangell Gwyn 58 C5
Aberarder Highld 137 F7
Aberarder House Highld 138 B2
Aberarder Lodge Highld 137 F8
Aberargie Perth 128 C3
Aberarth Ceredig 46 C3
Aberavon Neath 33 E8
Aberbeeg Bl Gwent 35 D6
Abercanaid M Tydf 34 D4
Abercarn Caerph 35 E6
Abercastle Pembs 44 B3
Abercegir Powys 58 D5
Aberchirder Aberds 152 C6
Abercraf Powys 34 C2
Abercrombie Fife 129 D7
Abercych Pembs 45 E4
Abercynafon Powys 34 C4
Abercynon Rhondda 34 E4
Aberdalgie Perth 128 B2
Aberdâr = Aberdare Rhondda 34 D3
Aberdare = Aberdâr Rhondda 34 D3
Aberdaron Gwyn 70 E2
Aberdaugleddau = Milford Haven Pembs 44 E4
Aberdeen Aberdeen 141 D8
Aberdesach Gwyn 82 F4
Aberdour Fife 128 F3
Aberdovey Gwyn 58 E3
Aberdulais Neath 34 D1
Aberedw Powys 48 E2
Abereiddy Pembs 44 B2
Abererch Gwyn 70 D4
Aberfan M Tydf 34 D4
Aberfeldy Perth 133 E5
Aberffraw Anglesey 82 E3
Aberffrwd Ceredig 47 B5
Aberford W Yorks 95 F7
Aberfoyle Stirling 126 D4
Abergavenny = Y Fenni Mon 35 C6
Abergele Conwy 72 B3
Abergorlech Carms 46 F4
Abergwaun = Fishguard Pembs 44 B4
Abergwesyn Powys 47 D7
Abergwili Carms 33 B5
Abergwynant Gwyn 58 C3
Abergwyngregyn Gwyn 83 D6
Abergynolwyn Gwyn 58 D3
Aberhonddu = Brecon Powys 34 B4
Aberhosan Powys 58 E5
Aberkenfig Bridgend 34 F2
Aberlady E Loth 129 F6
Aberlemno Angus 135 D5
Aberllefenni Gwyn 58 D4
Abermagwr Ceredig 47 B5
Abermaw = Barmouth Gwyn 58 C3
Abermeurig Ceredig 46 D4
Abermule Powys 59 E8
Abernaint Powys 59 B8
Abernant Carms 32 B4
Abernethy Perth 128 C3
Abernyte Perth 134 F2
Aberpennar = Mountain Ash Rhondda 34 E4
Aberporth Ceredig 45 D4
Abersoch Gwyn 70 E4
Abersychan Torf 35 D6
Abertawe = Swansea Swansea 33 E7
Aberteifi = Cardigan Ceredig 45 E3
Aberthin V Glam 22 B2
Abertillery = Abertyleri Bl Gwent 35 D6
Abertridwr Caerph 35 F5
Abertridwr Powys 59 C7
Abertyleri = Abertillery Bl Gwent 35 D6
Abertysswg Caerph 35 D5
Aberuthven Perth 127 C8
Aberyscir Powys 34 B3
Aberystwyth Ceredig 58 F2
Abhainn Suidhe W Isles 154 G5
Abingdon Oxon 38 E4
Abinger Common Sur 28 E2
Abinger Hammer Sur 27 E8
Abington S Lanark 114 B2
Abington Pigotts Cambs 54 E4
Ablington Glos 37 D8
Ablington Wilts 25 E6
Abney Derbys 75 B8
Aboyne Aberds 140 E4
Abram Gtr Man 86 D4
Abriachan Highld 151 H8
Abridge Essex 41 E7
Abronhill N Lanark 119 B7
Abson S Glos 24 B2
Abthorpe Northants 52 E4
Abune-the-Hill Orkney 159 F3
Aby Lincs 79 B7
Acaster Malbis York 95 E8
Acaster Selby N Yorks 95 E8
Accrington Lancs 87 B5
Acha Argyll 146 F4
Acha Mor W Isles 155 E8
Achabraid Argyll 145 E7
Achachork Highld 149 D9
Achafolla Argyll 124 D3
Achagary Highld 157 D10
Achahoish Argyll 144 F6
Achalader Perth 133 E8
Achallader Argyll 131 E7
Ach'an Todhair Highld 130 B4
Achanalt Highld 150 E5
Achanamara Argyll 144 E6
Achandunie Highld 151 D9
Achany Highld 157 J8
Achaphubuil Highld 130 B4
Acharacle Highld 147 E9
Acharn Highld 147 F10
Acharn Perth 132 E4
Acharole Highld 158 E4
Achath Aberds 141 C6
Achavanich Highld 158 F3
Achavraat Highld 151 G12
Achddu Carms 33 D5
Achduart Highld 156 J3
Achentoul Highld 157 F11
Achfary Highld 156 F5
Achgarve Highld 155 H13
Achiemore Highld 156 C6
Achiemore Highld 157 D11
A'Chill Highld 148 H7
Achiltibuie Highld 156 J3
Achina Highld 157 C10
Achinduich Highld 157 J8
Achinduin Argyll 124 B4
Achingills Highld 158 D3
Achintee Highld 131 B5
Achintee Highld 150 G2
Achintraid Highld 149 E13
Achlean Highld 138 E4
Achleck Argyll 146 G7
Achluachrach Highld 137 F5
Achlyness Highld 156 D5
Achmelvich Highld 156 G3
Achmore Highld 149 E13
Achmore Stirling 132 F2
Achnaba Argyll 124 B5
Achnaba Argyll 145 E8
Achnabat Highld 151 H8
Achnacarnin Highld 156 F3
Achnacarry Highld 136 F4
Achnacloich Argyll 125 B5
Achnacloich Highld 149 H10
Achnaconeran Highld 137 C7
Achnacraig Argyll 146 G7
Achnacroish Argyll 130 E2
Achnadrish Argyll 146 F7
Achnafalnich Argyll 125 C8
Achnagarron Highld 151 E9
Achnaha Highld 146 E7
Achnahanat Highld 151 B8
Achnahannet Highld 139 B5
Achnairn Highld 157 H8
Achnaluachrach Highld 157 J9
Achnasaul Highld 136 F4
Achnasheen Highld 150 F4
Achosnich Highld 146 E7
Achranich Highld 147 G10
Achreamie Highld 157 C13
Achriabhach Highld 131 C5
Achriesgill Highld 156 D5
Achrimsdale Highld 157 J12
Achtoty Highld 157 C9
Achurch Northants 65 F7
Achuvoldrach Highld 157 D8
Achvaich Highld 151 B10
Achvarasdal Highld 157 C12
Ackergill Highld 158 E5
Acklam Mbro 102 C2
Acklam N Yorks 96 C3
Ackleton Shrops 61 E7
Acklington Northumb 117 D8
Ackton W Yorks 88 B5
Ackworth Moor Top W Yorks 88 C5
Acle Norf 69 C7
Acock's Green W Mid 62 F5
Acol Kent 31 C7
Acomb Northumb 110 C2
Acomb York 95 D8
Aconbury Hereford 49 F7
Acre Lancs 87 B5
Acre Street W Sus 15 E8
Acrefair Wrex 73 E6
Acton Ches E 74 D3
Acton Dorset 13 G7
Acton London 41 F5
Acton Shrops 60 F3
Acton Suff 56 E2
Acton Wrex 73 D7
Acton Beauchamp Hereford 49 D8
Acton Bridge Ches W 74 B2
Acton Burnell Shrops 60 D5
Acton Green Hereford 49 D8
Acton Pigott Shrops 60 D5
Acton Round Shrops 61 E6
Acton Scott Shrops 60 F4
Acton Trussell Staffs 62 C3
Acton Turville S Glos 37 F5
Adbaston Staffs 61 B7
Adber Dorset 12 B3
Adderley Shrops 74 E3
Adderstone Northumb 123 F7
Addiewell W Loth 120 C2
Addingham W Yorks 94 E3
Addington Bucks 39 B7
Addington Kent 29 D7
Addington London 28 C4
Addinston Borders 121 D8
Addiscombe London 28 C4
Addlestone Sur 27 C8
Addlethorpe Lincs 79 C8
Adel W Yorks 95 F5
Adeney Telford 61 C7
Adfa Powys 59 D7
Adforton Hereford 49 B6
Adisham Kent 31 D6
Adlestrop Glos 38 B2
Adlingfleet E Yorks 90 B2
Adlington Lancs 86 C4
Admaston Staffs 62 B4
Admaston Telford 61 C6
Admington Warks 51 E7
Adstock Bucks 52 F5
Adstone Northants 52 D3
Adversane W Sus 16 B4
Advie Highld 152 E1
Adwalton W Yorks 88 B3
Adwell Oxon 39 E6
Adwick le Street S Yorks 89 D6
Adwick upon Dearne S Yorks 89 D5
Adziel Aberds 153 C9
Ae Village Dumfries 114 F2
Affleck Aberds 141 B7
Affpuddle Dorset 13 E6
Affric Lodge Highld 136 B4
Afon-wen Flint 72 B5
Afton IoW 14 F4
Agglethorpe N Yorks 101 F5
Agneash IoM 84 D4
Aigburth Mers 85 F4
Aiginis W Isles 155 D9
Aike E Yorks 97 E6
Aikerness Orkney 159 C5
Aikers Orkney 159 J5
Aiketgate Cumb 108 E4
Aikton Cumb 108 D2
Ailey Hereford 48 E5
Ailstone Warks 51 D7
Ailsworth Pboro 65 E8
Ainderby Quernhow N Yorks 102 F1
Ainderby Steeple N Yorks 101 E8
Aingers Green Essex 43 B7
Ainsdale Mers 85 C4
Ainsdale-on-Sea Mers 85 C4
Ainstable Cumb 108 E5
Ainsworth Gtr Man 87 C5
Ainthorpe N Yorks 103 D5
Aintree Mers 85 E4
Aird Argyll 124 E3
Aird Dumfries 104 C4
Aird Highld 149 A12
Aird W Isles 155 D10
Aird a Mhachair W Isles 148 D2
Aird a' Mhulaidh W Isles 154 F6
Aird Asaig W Isles 154 G6
Aird Dhail W Isles 155 A9
Aird Mhidhinis W Isles 148 H2
Aird Mhighe W Isles 154 H6
Aird Mhighe W Isles 154 J5
Aird Mhor W Isles 148 H2
Aird of Sleat Highld 149 H10
Aird Thunga W Isles 155 D9
Aird Uig W Isles 154 D5
Airdens Highld 151 B9
Airdrie N Lanark 119 C7
Airdtorrisdale Highld 157 C9
Airidh a Bhruaich W Isles 154 F7
Airieland Dumfries 106 D4
Airmyn E Yorks 89 B8
Airntully Perth 133 F7
Airor Highld 149 H12
Airth Falk 127 F7
Airton N Yorks 94 D2
Airyhassen Dumfries 105 E7
Aisby Lincs 78 F3
Aisby Lincs 90 E2
Aisgernis W Isles 148 F2
Aiskew N Yorks 101 F7
Aislaby N Yorks 103 D6
Aislaby N Yorks 103 F5
Aislaby Stockton 102 C2
Aisthorpe Lincs 78 A2
Aith Orkney 159 G3
Aith Shetland 160 D8
Aith Shetland 160 H5
Aithsetter Shetland 160 K6
Aitkenhead S Ayrs 112 D3
Aitnoch Highld 151 H12
Akeld Northumb 117 B5
Akeley Bucks 52 F5
Akenham Suff 56 E5
Albaston Corn 6 B2
Alberbury Shrops 60 C3
Albourne W Sus 17 C6
Albrighton Shrops 60 C4
Albrighton Shrops 62 D2
Alburgh Norf 69 F5
Albury Herts 41 B7
Albury Sur 27 E8
Albury End Herts 41 B7
Alby Hill Norf 81 D7
Alcaig Highld 151 F8
Alcaston Shrops 60 F4
Alcester Warks 51 D5
Alciston E Sus 18 E2
Alcombe Som 21 E8
Alcombe Wilts 24 C3
Alconbury Cambs 54 B2
Alconbury Weston Cambs 54 B2
Aldbar Castle Angus 135 D5
Aldborough N Yorks 95 C7
Aldborough Norf 81 D7
Aldbourne Wilts 25 B7
Aldbrough E Yorks 97 F8
Aldbrough St John N Yorks 101 C7
Aldbury Herts 40 C2
Aldcliffe Lancs 92 C4
Aldclune Perth 133 C6
Aldeburgh Suff 57 D8
Aldeby Norf 69 E7
Aldenham Herts 40 E4
Alderbury Wilts 14 B2
Aldercar Derbys 76 E4
Alderford Norf 68 C4
Alderholt Dorset 14 C2
Alderley Glos 36 E4
Alderley Edge Ches E 74 B5
Aldermaston W Berks 26 C3
Aldermaston Wharf W Berks 26 C4
Alderminster Warks 51 E7
Alder's End Hereford 49 E8
Aldersey Green Ches W 73 D8
Aldershot Hants 27 D6
Alderton Glos 50 F5
Alderton Northants 52 E5
Alderton Shrops 60 B4
Alderton Suff 57 E7
Alderton Wilts 37 F5
Alderwasley Derbys 76 D3
Aldfield N Yorks 95 C5
Aldford Ches W 73 D8
Aldham Essex 43 B5
Aldham Suff 56 E4
Aldie Highld 151 C10
Aldingbourne W Sus 16 D3
Aldingham Cumb 92 B2
Aldington Kent 19 B7
Aldington Worcs 51 E5
Aldington Frith Kent 19 B7
Aldochlay Argyll 126 E2
Aldreth Cambs 54 B5
Aldridge W Mid 62 D4
Aldringham Suff 57 C8
Aldsworth Glos 38 C1
Aldunie Moray 140 B2
Aldwark Derbys 76 D2
Aldwark N Yorks 95 C7
Aldwick W Sus 16 E3
Aldwincle Northants 65 F7
Aldworth W Berks 26 B3
Alexandria W Dunb 118 B3
Alfardisworthy Devon 8 C4
Alfington Devon 11 E6
Alfold Sur 27 F8
Alfold Bars W Sus 27 F8
Alfold Crossways Sur 27 F8
Alford Aberds 140 C4
Alford Lincs 79 B7
Alford Som 23 F8
Alfreton Derbys 76 D4
Alfrick Worcs 50 D2
Alfrick Pound Worcs 50 D2
Alfriston E Sus 18 E2
Algaltraig Argyll 145 F9
Algarkirk Lincs 79 F5
Alhampton Som 23 F8
Aline Lodge W Isles 154 F6
Alisary Highld 147 D10
Alkborough N Lincs 90 B2
Alkerton Oxon 51 E8
Alkham Kent 31 E6
Alkington Shrops 74 F2
Alkmonton Derbys 75 F8
All Cannings Wilts 25 C5
All Saints South Elmham Suff 69 F6
All Stretton Shrops 60 E4
Alladale Lodge Highld 150 C7
Allaleigh Devon 7 D6
Allanaquoich Aberds 139 E7
Allangrange Mains Highld 151 F9
Allanton Borders 122 D4
Allanton N Lanark 119 D8
Allathasdal W Isles 148 H1
Allendale Town Northumb 109 D8
Allenheads Northumb 109 E8
Allens Green Herts 41 C7
Allensford Durham 110 D3
Allensmore Hereford 49 F6
Allenton Derby 76 F3
Aller Som 12 B2
Allerby Cumb 107 F7
Allerford Som 21 E8
Allerston N Yorks 103 F6
Allerthorpe E Yorks 96 E3
Allerton Mers 86 F2
Allerton W Yorks 94 F4
Allerton Bywater W Yorks 88 B5
Allerton Mauleverer N Yorks 95 D7
Allesley W Mid 63 F7
Allestree Derby 76 F3
Allet Corn 3 B6
Allexton Leics 64 D5
Allgreave Ches E 75 C6
Allhallows Medway 30 B2
Allhallows-on-Sea Medway 30 B2
Alligin Shuas Highld 149 C13
Allimore Green Staffs 62 C2
Allington Lincs 77 E8
Allington Wilts 25 C5
Allington Wilts 25 F7
Allithwaite Cumb 92 B3
Alloa Clack 127 E7
Allonby Cumb 107 E7
Alloway S Ayrs 112 C3
Allt Carms 33 D6
Allt na h-Airbhe Highld 150 B4
Allt-nan-sùgh Highld 136 B2
Alltchaorunn Highld 131 D5
Alltforgan Powys 59 B6
Alltmawr Powys 48 E2
Alltnacaillich Highld 156 E7
Alltsigh Highld 137 C7
Alltwalis Carms 46 F3
Alltwen Neath 33 D8
Alltyblaca Ceredig 46 E4
Allwood Green Suff 56 B4
Almeley Hereford 48 D5
Almer Dorset 13 E7
Almholme S Yorks 89 D6
Almington Staffs 74 F4
Alminstone Cross Devon 8 B5
Almondbank Perth 128 B2
Almondbury W Yorks 88 C2
Almondsbury S Glos 36 F3
Alne N Yorks 95 C7
Alness Highld 151 E9
Alnham Northumb 117 C5
Alnmouth Northumb 117 C8
Alnwick Northumb 117 C7
Alperton London 40 F4
Alphamstone Essex 56 F2
Alpheton Suff 56 D2
Alphington Devon 10 E4
Alport Derbys 76 C2
Alpraham Ches E 74 D2
Alresford Essex 43 B6
Alrewas Staffs 63 C5
Alsager Ches E 74 D4
Alsagers Bank Staffs 74 E5
Alsop en le Dale Derbys 75 D8
Alston Cumb 109 E7
Alston Devon 11 D8
Alstone Glos 50 F4
Alstonefield Staffs 75 D8
Alswear Devon 10 B2
Altandhu Highld 156 H2
Altanduin Highld 157 G11
Altarnun Corn 8 F4
Altass Highld 156 J7
Alterwall Highld 158 D4
Altham Lancs 93 F7
Althorne Essex 43 E5
Althorpe N Lincs 90 D2
Alticry Dumfries 105 D6
Altnabreac Station Highld 157 E13
Altnacealgach Hotel Highld 156 H5
Altnacraig Argyll 124 C4
Altnafeadh Highld 131 D6
Altnaharra Highld 157 F8
Altofts W Yorks 88 B4
Alton Derbys 76 C3
Alton Hants 26 F5
Alton Staffs 75 E7
Alton Pancras Dorset 12 D5
Alton Priors Wilts 25 C6
Altrincham Gtr Man 87 F5
Altrua Highld 136 F5
Altskeith Stirling 126 D3
Altyre Ho. Moray 151 F13
Alva Clack 127 E7
Alvanley Ches W 73 B8
Alvaston Derby 76 F3
Alvechurch Worcs 50 B5
Alvecote Warks 63 D6
Alvediston Wilts 13 B7
Alveley Shrops 61 F7
Alverdiscott Devon 9 B7
Alverstoke Hants 15 E7
Alverstone IoW 15 F6
Alverton Notts 77 E7
Alves Moray 152 B1
Alvescot Oxon 38 D2
Alveston S Glos 36 F3
Alveston Warks 51 D7
Alvie Highld 138 D4
Alvingham Lincs 91 E7
Alvington Glos 36 D3
Alwalton Cambs 65 E8
Alweston Dorset 12 C4
Alwinton Northumb 116 D5
Alwoodley W Yorks 95 E5
Alyth Perth 134 E2
Am Baile W Isles 148 G2
Am Buth Argyll 124 C4
Amatnatua Highld 150 B7
Amber Hill Lincs 78 E5
Ambergate Derbys 76 D3
Amberley Glos 37 D5
Amberley W Sus 16 C4
Amble Northumb 117 D8
Amblecote W Mid 62 F2
Ambler Thorn W Yorks 87 B8
Ambleside Cumb 99 D5
Ambleston Pembs 44 C5
Ambrosden Oxon 39 C6
Amcotts N Lincs 90 C2
Amersham Bucks 40 E2
Amesbury Wilts 25 E6
Amington Staffs 63 D6
Amisfield Dumfries 114 F2
Amlwch Anglesey 82 B4
Amlwch Port Anglesey 82 B4
Ammanford = Rhydaman Carms 33 C7
Amod Argyll 143 E8
Amotherby N Yorks 96 B3
Ampfield Hants 14 B5
Ampleforth N Yorks 95 B8
Ampney Crucis Glos 37 D7
Ampney St Mary Glos 37 D7
Ampney St Peter Glos 37 D7
Amport Hants 25 E7
Ampthill C Beds 53 F8
Ampton Suff 56 B2
Amroth Pembs 32 D2
Amulree Perth 133 F5
An Caol Highld 149 C11
An Cnoc W Isles 155 D9
An Gleann Ur W Isles 155 D9
An t-Ob = Leverburgh W Isles 154 J5
Anagach Highld 139 B6
Anaheilt Highld 130 C2
Anancaun Highld 150 E3
Ancaster Lincs 78 E2
Anchor Shrops 59 F8
Anchorsholme Blackpool 92 E3
Ancroft Northumb 123 E5
Ancrum Borders 116 B2
Anderby Lincs 79 B8
Anderson Dorset 13 E6
Anderton Ches W 74 B3
Andover Hants 25 E8
Andover Down Hants 25 E8
Andoversford Glos 37 C7
Andreas IoM 84 C4
Anfield Mers 85 E4
Angersleigh Som 11 C6
Angle Pembs 44 E3
Angmering W Sus 16 D4
Angram N Yorks 95 E8
Angram N Yorks 100 E3
Anie Stirling 126 C4
Ankerville Highld 151 D11
Anlaby E Yorks 90 B4
Anmer Norf 80 E3
Anna Valley Hants 25 E8
Annan Dumfries 107 C8
Annat Argyll 125 C6
Annat Highld 149 C13
Annbank S Ayrs 112 B4
Annesley Notts 76 D5
Annesley Woodhouse Notts 76 D4
Annfield Plain Durham 110 D4
Annifirth Shetland 160 J3
Annitsford T&W 111 B5
Annscroft Shrops 60 D4
Ansdell Lancs 85 B4
Ansford Som 23 F8
Ansley Warks 63 E6
Anslow Staffs 63 B6
Anslow Gate Staffs 63 B5
Anstey Herts 54 F5
Anstey Leics 64 D2
Anstruther Easter Fife 129 D7
Anstruther Wester Fife 129 D7
Ansty Hants 26 E5
Ansty W Sus 17 B6
Ansty Warks 63 F7

Baulking Oxon 38 E3
Baumber Lincs 78 B5
Baunton Glos 37 D7
Baverstock Wilts 24 F5
Bawburgh Norf 68 D4
Bawdeswell Norf 81 E6
Bawdrip Som 22 F5
Bawdsey Suff 57 E7
Bawtry S Yorks 89 E7
Baxenden Lancs 87 B5
Baxterley Warks 63 E6
Baybridge Hants 15 B6
Baycliff Cumb 92 B2
Baydon Wilts 25 B7
Bayford Herts 41 D6
Bayford Som 12 B5
Bayles Cumb 109 E7
Baylham Suff 56 D5
Baynard's Green Oxon 39 B5
Bayston Hill Shrops 60 D4
Baythorn End Essex 55 E8
Bayton Worcs 49 B8
Beach Highld 130 D1
Beachampton Bucks 53 F5
Beachamwell Norf 67 D7
Beachans Moray 151 G13
Beacharr Argyll 143 D7
Beachborough Kent 19 B8
Beachley Glos 36 E2
Beacon Devon 11 D6
Beacon End Essex 43 B5
Beacon Hill Sur 27 F6
Beacon's Bottom Bucks 39 E7
Beaconsfield Bucks 40 F2
Beacrabhaic W Isles 154 H6
Beadlam N Yorks 102 F4
Beadlow C Beds 54 F2
Beadnell Northumb 117 B8
Beaford Devon 9 C7
Beal N Yorks 89 B6
Beal Northumb 123 E6
Beamhurst Staffs 75 F7
Beaminster Dorset 12 D2
Beamish Durham 110 D5
Beamsley N Yorks 94 D3
Bean Kent 29 B6
Beanacre Wilts 24 C4
Beanley Northumb 117 C6
Beaquoy Orkney 159 F4
Bear Cross Bmouth 13 E8
Beardwood Blackburn 86 B4
Beare Green Sur 28 E2
Bearley Warks 51 C6
Bearnus Argyll 146 G6
Bearpark Durham 110 E5
Bearsbridge Northumb 109 D7
Bearsden E Dunb 118 B5
Bearsted Kent 29 D8
Bearstone Shrops 74 F4
Bearwood Hereford 49 D5
Bearwood Poole 13 E8
Bearwood W Mid 62 F4
Beattock Dumfries 114 D3
Beauchamp Roding Essex 42 C1
Beauchief S Yorks 88 F4
Beaufort Bl Gwent 35 C5
Beaufort Castle Highld 151 G8
Beaulieu Hants 14 D4
Beauly Highld 151 G8
Beaumaris Anglesey 83 D6
Beaumont Cumb 108 D3
Beaumont Essex 43 B7
Beaumont Hill Darl 101 C7
Beausale Warks 51 B7
Beauworth Hants 15 B6
Beaworthy Devon 9 E6
Beazley End Essex 42 B3
Bebington Mers 85 F4
Bebside Northumb 117 F8
Beccles Suff 69 E7
Becconsall Lancs 86 B2
Beck Foot Cumb 99 E8
Beck Hole N Yorks 103 D6
Beck Row Suff 55 B7
Beck Side Cumb 98 F4
Beckbury Shrops 61 D7
Beckenham London 28 C4
Beckermet Cumb 98 D2
Beckfoot Cumb 98 D3
Beckfoot Cumb 107 E7
Beckford Worcs 50 F4
Beckhampton Wilts 25 C5
Beckingham Lincs 77 D8
Beckingham Notts 89 F8
Beckington Som 24 D3
Beckley E Sus 19 C5
Beckley Hants 14 E3
Beckley Oxon 39 C5
Beckton London 41 F7
Beckwithshaw N Yorks 95 D5
Becontree London 41 F7
Bed-y-coedwr Gwyn 71 E8
Bedale N Yorks 101 F7
Bedburn Durham 110 F4
Bedchester Dorset 13 C6
Beddau Rhondda 34 F4
Beddgelert Gwyn 71 C6
Beddingham E Sus 17 D8
Beddington London 28 C4
Bedfield Suff 57 C6
Bedford Bedford 53 D8
Bedham W Sus 16 B4
Bedhampton Hants 15 D8
Bedingfield Suff 57 C5
Bedlam N Yorks 95 C5
Bedlington Northumb 117 F8
Bedlington Station Northumb 117 F8
Bedlinog M Tydf 34 D4
Bedminster Bristol 23 B7
Bedmond Herts 40 D3
Bednall Staffs 62 C3
Bedrule Borders 116 C2
Bedstone Shrops 49 B5
Bedwas Caerph 35 F5
Bedworth Warks 63 F7
Bedworth Heath Warks 63 F7
Beeby Leics 64 D3
Beech Hants 26 F4
Beech Staffs 75 F5
Beech Hill Gtr Man 86 D3
Beech Hill W Berks 26 C4
Beechingstoke Wilts 25 D5
Beedon W Berks 26 B2
Beeford E Yorks 97 D7
Beeley Derbys 76 C2
Beelsby NE Lincs 91 D6
Beenham W Berks 26 C3
Beeny Corn 8 E3
Beer Devon 11 F7
Beer Hackett Dorset 12 C3
Beercrocombe Som 11 B8
Beesands Devon 7 E6
Beesby Lincs 91 F8
Beeson Devon 7 E6
Beeston C Beds 54 E2
Beeston Ches W 74 D2
Beeston Norf 68 C2
Beeston Notts 76 F5
Beeston W Yorks 95 F5
Beeston Regis Norf 81 C7
Beeswing Dumfries 107 C5
Beetham Cumb 92 B4
Beetley Norf 68 C2
Begbroke Oxon 38 C4
Begelly Pembs 32 D2
Beggar's Bush Powys 48 C4
Beguildy Powys 48 B3
Beighton Norf 69 D6
Beighton S Yorks 88 F5
Beighton Hill Derbys 76 D2
Beith N Ayrs 118 D3
Bekesbourne Kent 31 D5
Belaugh Norf 69 C5
Belbroughton Worcs 50 B4
Belchamp Otten Essex 56 E2
Belchamp St Paul Essex 55 E8
Belchamp Walter Essex 56 E2
Belchford Lincs 79 B5
Belford Northumb 123 F7
Belhaven E Loth 122 B2
Belhelvie Aberds 141 C8
Belhinnie Aberds 140 B3
Bell Bar Herts 41 D5
Bell Busk N Yorks 94 D2
Bell End Worcs 50 B4
Bell o'th'Hill Ches W 74 E2
Bellabeg Aberds 140 C2
Bellamore S Ayrs 112 F2
Bellanoch Argyll 144 D6
Bellaty Angus 134 D2
Belleau Lincs 79 B7
Bellehiglash Moray 152 E1
Bellerby N Yorks 101 E6
Bellever Devon 6 B4
Belliehill Angus 135 C5
Bellingdon Bucks 40 D2
Bellingham Northumb 116 F4
Belloch Argyll 143 E7
Bellochantuy Argyll 143 E7
Bells Yew Green E Sus 18 B3
Bellsbank E Ayrs 112 D4
Bellshill N Lanark 119 C7
Bellshill Northumb 123 F7
Bellspool Borders 120 F4
Bellsquarry W Loth 120 C3
Belmaduthy Highld 151 F9
Belmesthorpe Rutland 65 C7
Belmont Blackburn 86 C4
Belmont London 28 C3
Belmont S Ayrs 112 B3
Belmont Shetland 160 C7
Belnacraig Aberds 140 C2
Belowda Corn 4 C4
Belper Derbys 76 E3
Belper Lane End Derbys 76 E3
Belsay Northumb 110 B4
Belses Borders 115 B8
Belsford Devon 7 D5
Belstead Suff 56 E5
Belston S Ayrs 112 B3
Belstone Devon 9 E8
Belthorn Blackburn 86 B5
Beltinge Kent 31 C5
Beltoft N Lincs 90 D2
Belton Leics 63 B8
Belton Lincs 78 F2
Belton N Lincs 89 D8
Belton Norf 69 D7
Belton in Rutland Rutland 64 D5
Beltring Kent 29 E7
Belts of Collonach Aberds 141 E5
Belvedere London 29 B5
Belvoir Leics 77 F8
Bembridge IoW 15 F7
Bemersyde Borders 121 F8
Bemerton Wilts 25 F6
Bempton E Yorks 97 B7
Ben Alder Lodge Highld 132 B2
Ben Armine Lodge Highld 157 H10
Ben Casgro W Isles 155 E9
Benacre Suff 69 F8
Benbuie Dumfries 113 E7
Benderloch Argyll 124 B5
Bendronaig Lodge Highld 150 H3
Benenden Kent 18 B5
Benfield Dumfries 105 C7
Bengate Norf 69 B6
Bengeworth Worcs 50 E5
Benhall Green Suff 57 C7
Benhall Street Suff 57 C7
Benholm Aberds 135 C8
Beningbrough N Yorks 95 D8
Benington Herts 41 B5
Benington Lincs 79 E6
Benllech Anglesey 82 C5
Benmore Argyll 145 E10
Benmore Stirling 126 B3
Benmore Lodge Highld 156 H6
Bennacott Corn 8 E4
Bennan N Ayrs 143 F10
Benniworth Lincs 91 F6
Benover Kent 29 E8
Bensham T&W 110 C5
Benslie N Ayrs 118 E3
Benson Oxon 39 E6
Bent Aberds 135 B6
Bent Gate Lancs 87 B5
Benthall Northumb 117 B8
Benthall Shrops 61 D6
Bentham Glos 37 C6
Benthoul Aberdeen 141 D7
Bentlawnt Shrops 60 D3
Bentley E Yorks 97 F6
Bentley Hants 27 E5
Bentley S Yorks 89 D6
Bentley Suff 56 F5
Bentley Warks 63 E6
Bentley Worcs 50 C4
Bentley Heath W Mid 51 B6
Benton Devon 21 F5
Bentpath Dumfries 115 E6
Bents W Loth 120 C2
Bentworth Hants 26 E4
Benvie Dundee 134 F3
Benwick Cambs 66 E3
Beoley Worcs 51 C5
Beoraidbeg Highld 147 B9
Bepton W Sus 16 C2
Berden Essex 41 B7
Bere Alston Devon 6 C2
Bere Ferrers Devon 6 C2
Bere Regis Dorset 13 E6
Berepper Corn 3 D5
Bergh Apton Norf 69 D6
Berinsfield Oxon 39 E5
Berkeley Glos 36 E3
Berkhamsted Herts 40 D2
Berkley Som 24 E3
Berkswell W Mid 51 B7
Bermondsey London 28 B4
Bernera Highld 149 F13
Bernice Argyll 145 D10
Bernisdale Highld 149 C9
Berrick Salome Oxon 39 E6
Berriedale Highld 158 H3
Berrier Cumb 99 B5
Berriew Powys 59 D8
Berrington Northumb 123 E6
Berrington Shrops 60 D5
Berrow Som 22 D5
Berrow Green Worcs 50 D2
Berry Down Cross Devon 20 E4
Berry Hill Glos 36 C2
Berry Hill Pembs 45 E2
Berry Pomeroy Devon 7 C6
Berryhillock Moray 152 B5
Berrynarbor Devon 20 E4
Bersham Wrex 73 E7
Berstane Orkney 159 G5
Berwick E Sus 18 E2
Berwick Bassett Wilts 25 B5
Berwick Hill Northumb 110 B4
Berwick St James Wilts 25 F5
Berwick St John Wilts 13 B7
Berwick St Leonard Wilts 24 F4
Berwick-upon-Tweed Northumb 123 D5
Bescar Lancs 85 C4
Besford Worcs 50 E4
Bessacarr S Yorks 89 D7
Bessels Leigh Oxon 38 D4
Bessingby E Yorks 97 C7
Bessingham Norf 81 D7
Bestbeech Hill E Sus 18 B3
Besthorpe Norf 68 E3
Besthorpe Notts 77 C8
Bestwood Nottingham 77 E5
Bestwood Village Notts 77 E5
Beswick E Yorks 97 E6
Betchworth Sur 28 E3
Bethania Ceredig 46 C4
Bethania Gwyn 71 C8
Bethania Gwyn 83 F6
Bethel Anglesey 82 D3
Bethel Gwyn 72 F3
Bethel Gwyn 82 E5
Bethersden Kent 30 E3
Bethesda Gwyn 83 E6
Bethesda Pembs 32 C1
Bethlehem Carms 33 B7
Bethnal Green London 41 F6
Betley Staffs 74 E4
Betsham Kent 29 B7
Betteshanger Kent 31 D7
Bettiscombe Dorset 11 E8
Bettisfield Wrex 73 F8
Betton Shrops 60 D3
Betton Shrops 74 F3
Bettws Bridgend 34 F3
Bettws Mon 35 C6
Bettws Newport 35 E6
Bettws Cedewain Powys 59 E8
Bettws Gwerfil Goch Denb 72 E4
Bettws Ifan Ceredig 46 E2
Bettws Newydd Mon 35 D7
Bettws-y-crwyn Shrops 60 F2
Bettyhill Highld 157 C10
Betws Carms 33 C7
Betws Bledrws Ceredig 46 D4
Betws-Garmon Gwyn 82 F5
Betws-y-Coed Conwy 83 F7
Betws-yn-Rhos Conwy 72 B3
Beulah Ceredig 45 E4
Beulah Powys 47 D8
Bevendean Brighton 17 D7
Bevercotes Notts 77 B6
Beverley E Yorks 97 F6
Beverston Glos 37 E5
Bevington Glos 36 E3
Bewaldeth Cumb 108 F2
Bewcastle Cumb 109 B5
Bewdley Worcs 50 B2
Bewerley N Yorks 94 C4
Bewholme E Yorks 97 D7
Bexhill E Sus 18 E4
Bexley London 29 B5
Bexleyheath London 29 B5
Bexwell Norf 67 D6
Beyton Suff 56 C3
Bhaltos W Isles 154 D5
Bhatarsaigh W Isles 148 J1
Bibury Glos 37 D8
Bicester Oxon 39 B5
Bickenhall Som 11 C7
Bickenhill W Mid 63 F5
Bicker Lincs 78 F5
Bickershaw Gtr Man 86 D4
Bickerstaffe Lancs 86 D2
Bickerton Ches E 74 D2
Bickerton N Yorks 95 D7
Bickington Devon 7 B5
Bickington Devon 20 F4
Bickleigh Devon 6 C3
Bickleigh Devon 10 D4
Bickleton Devon 20 F4
Bickley London 28 C5
Bickley Moss Ches W 74 E2
Bicknacre Essex 42 D3
Bicknoller Som 22 F3
Bicknor Kent 30 D2
Bickton Hants 14 C2
Bicton Shrops 60 C4
Bicton Shrops 60 F2
Bidborough Kent 29 E6
Biddenden Kent 19 B5
Biddenham Bedford 53 E8
Biddestone Wilts 24 B3
Biddisham Som 23 D5
Biddlesden Bucks 52 E4
Biddlestone Northumb 117 D5
Biddulph Staffs 75 D5
Biddulph Moor Staffs 75 D6
Bideford Devon 9 B6
Bidford-on-Avon Warks 51 D6
Bidston Mers 85 E3
Bielby E Yorks 96 E3
Bieldside Aberdeen 141 D7
Bierley IoW 15 G6
Bierley W Yorks 94 F4
Bierton Bucks 39 C8
Big Sand Highld 149 A12
Bigbury Devon 6 E4
Bigbury on Sea Devon 6 E4
Bigby Lincs 90 D4
Biggar Cumb 92 C1
Biggar S Lanark 120 F3
Biggin Derbys 75 D8
Biggin Derbys 76 E2
Biggin N Yorks 95 F8
Biggin Hill London 28 D5
Biggings Shetland 160 G3
Biggleswade C Beds 54 E2
Bighouse Highld 157 C11
Bighton Hants 26 F4
Bignor W Sus 16 C3
Bigton Shetland 160 L5
Bilberry Corn 4 C5
Bilborough Nottingham 76 E5
Bilbrook Som 22 E2
Bilbrough N Yorks 95 E8
Bilbster Highld 158 E4
Bildershaw Durham 101 B7
Bildeston Suff 56 E3
Billericay Essex 42 E2
Billesdon Leics 64 D4
Billesley Warks 51 D6
Billingborough Lincs 78 F4
Billinge Mers 86 D3
Billingford Norf 81 E6
Billingham Stockton 102 B2
Billinghay Lincs 78 D4
Billingley S Yorks 88 D5
Billingshurst W Sus 16 B4
Billingsley Shrops 61 F7
Billington C Beds 40 B2
Billington Lancs 93 F7
Billockby Norf 69 C7
Billy Row Durham 110 F4
Bilsborrow Lancs 92 F5
Bilsby Lincs 79 B7
Bilsham W Sus 16 D3
Bilsington Kent 19 B7
Bilson Green Glos 36 C3
Bilsthorpe Notts 77 C6
Bilsthorpe Moor Notts 77 D6
Bilston Midloth 121 C5
Bilston W Mid 62 E3
Bilstone Leics 63 D7
Bilting Kent 30 E4
Bilton E Yorks 97 F7
Bilton Northumb 117 C8
Bilton Warks 52 B2
Bilton in Ainsty N Yorks 95 E7
Bimbister Orkney 159 G4
Binbrook Lincs 91 E6
Binchester Blocks Durham 110 F5
Bincombe Dorset 12 F4
Bindal Highld 151 C12
Binegar Som 23 E8
Binfield Brack 27 B6
Binfield Heath Oxon 26 B5
Bingfield Northumb 110 B2
Bingham Notts 77 F7
Bingley W Yorks 94 F4
Bings Heath Shrops 60 C5
Binham Norf 81 D5
Binley Hants 26 D2
Binley W Mid 51 B8
Binley Woods Warks 51 B8
Binniehill Falk 119 B8
Binsoe N Yorks 94 B5
Binstead IoW 15 E6
Binsted Hants 27 E5
Binton Warks 51 D6
Bintree Norf 81 E6
Binweston Shrops 60 D3
Birch Essex 43 C5
Birch Gtr Man 87 D6
Birch Green Essex 43 C5
Birch Heath Ches W 74 C2
Birch Hill Ches W 74 B2
Birch Vale Derbys 87 F8
Bircham Newton Norf 80 D3
Bircham Tofts Norf 80 D3
Birchanger Essex 41 B8
Birchencliffe W Yorks 88 C2
Bircher Hereford 49 C6
Birchgrove Cardiff 22 B3
Birchgrove Swansea 33 E8
Birchington Kent 31 C6
Birchmoor Warks 63 D6
Birchover Derbys 76 C2
Birchwood Lincs 78 C2
Birchwood Warr 86 E4
Bircotes Notts 89 E7
Birdbrook Essex 55 E8
Birdforth N Yorks 95 B7
Birdham W Sus 16 E2
Birdholme Derbys 76 C3
Birdingbury Warks 52 C2
Birdlip Glos 37 C6
Birds Edge W Yorks 88 D3
Birdsall N Yorks 96 C4
Birdsgreen Shrops 61 F7
Birdsmoor Gate Dorset 11 D8
Birdston E Dunb 119 B6
Birdwell S Yorks 88 D4
Birdwood Glos 36 C4
Birgham Borders 122 F3
Birkby N Yorks 101 D8
Birkdale Mers 85 C4
Birkenhead Mers 85 F4
Birkenhills Aberds 153 D7
Birkenshaw N Lanark 119 C6
Birkenshaw W Yorks 88 B3
Birkhall Aberds 140 E2
Birkhill Angus 134 F3
Birkhill Borders 114 C5
Birkholme Lincs 65 B6
Birkin N Yorks 89 B6
Birley Hereford 49 D6
Birling Kent 29 C7
Birling Northumb 117 D8
Birling Gap E Sus 18 F2
Birlingham Worcs 50 E4
Birmingham W Mid 62 F4
Birnam Perth 133 E7
Birse Aberds 140 E4
Birsemore Aberds 140 E4
Birstall Leics 64 D2
Birstall W Yorks 88 B3
Birstwith N Yorks 94 D5
Birthorpe Lincs 78 F4
Birtley Hereford 49 C5
Birtley Northumb 109 B8
Birtley T&W 111 D5
Birts Street Worcs 50 F2
Bisbrooke Rutland 65 E5
Biscathorpe Lincs 91 F6
Biscot Luton 40 B3
Bish Mill Devon 10 B2
Bisham Windsor 39 F8
Bishampton Worcs 50 D4
Bishop Auckland Durham 101 B7
Bishop Burton E Yorks 97 F5
Bishop Middleham Durham 111 F6
Bishop Monkton N Yorks 95 C6
Bishop Norton Lincs 90 E3
Bishop Sutton Bath 23 D7
Bishop Thornton N Yorks 95 C5
Bishop Wilton E Yorks 96 D3
Bishopbridge Lincs 90 E4
Bishopbriggs E Dunb 119 C6
Bishopmill Moray 152 B2
Bishops Cannings Wilts 24 C5
Bishop's Castle Shrops 60 F3
Bishop's Caundle Dorset 12 C4
Bishop's Cleeve Glos 37 B6
Bishops Frome Hereford 49 E8
Bishop's Green Essex 42 C2
Bishop's Hull Som 11 B7
Bishop's Itchington Warks 51 D8
Bishops Lydeard Som 11 B6
Bishops Nympton Devon 10 B2
Bishop's Offley Staffs 61 B7
Bishop's Stortford Herts 41 B7
Bishop's Sutton Hants 26 F4
Bishop's Tachbrook Warks 51 C8
Bishops Tawton Devon 20 F4
Bishop's Waltham Hants 15 C6
Bishop's Wood Staffs 62 D2
Bishopsbourne Kent 31 D5
Bishopsteignton Devon 7 B7
Bishopstoke Hants 15 C5
Bishopston Swansea 33 F6
Bishopstone Bucks 39 C8
Bishopstone E Sus 17 D8
Bishopstone Hereford 49 E6
Bishopstone Swindon 38 F2
Bishopstone Wilts 13 B8
Bishopstrow Wilts 24 E3
Bishopswood Som 11 C7
Bishopsworth Bristol 23 C7
Bishopthorpe York 95 E8
Bishopton Darl 102 B1
Bishopton Dumfries 105 E8
Bishopton N Yorks 95 B6
Bishopton Renfs 118 B4
Bishopton Warks 51 D6
Bishton Newport 35 F7
Bisley Glos 37 D6
Bisley Sur 27 D7
Bispham Blackpool 92 E3
Bispham Green Lancs 86 C2
Bissoe Corn 3 B6
Bisterne Close Hants 14 D3
Bitchfield Lincs 65 B6
Bittadon Devon 20 E4
Bittaford Devon 6 D4
Bittering Norf 68 C2
Bitterley Shrops 49 B7
Bitterne Soton 15 C5
Bitteswell Leics 64 F2
Bitton S Glos 23 C8
Bix Oxon 39 F7
Bixter Shetland 160 H5
Blaby Leics 64 E2
Black Bourton Oxon 38 D2
Black Callerton T&W 110 C4
Black Clauchrie S Ayrs 112 F2
Black Corries Lodge Highld 131 D6
Black Crofts Argyll 124 B5
Black Dog Devon 10 D3
Black Heddon Northumb 110 B3
Black Lane Gtr Man 87 D5
Black Marsh Shrops 60 E3
Black Mount Argyll 131 E6
Black Notley Essex 42 B3
Black Pill Swansea 33 E7
Black Tar Pembs 44 E4
Black Torrington Devon 9 D6
Blackacre Dumfries 114 E3
Blackadder West Borders 122 D4
Blackawton Devon 7 D6
Blackborough Devon 11 D5
Blackborough End Norf 67 C6
Blackboys E Sus 18 C2
Blackbrook Derbys 76 E3
Blackbrook Mers 86 E3
Blackbrook Staffs 74 F4
Blackburn Aberds 141 C7
Blackburn Aberds 152 E5
Blackburn Blackburn 86 B4
Blackburn W Loth 120 C2
Blackcraig Dumfries 113 F7
Blackden Heath Ches E 74 B4
Blackdog Aberds 141 C8
Blackfell T&W 111 D5
Blackfield Hants 14 D5
Blackford Cumb 108 C3
Blackford Perth 127 D7
Blackford Som 12 B4
Blackford Som 23 E6
Blackfordby Leics 63 C7
Blackgang IoW 15 G5
Blackhall Colliery Durham 111 F7
Blackhall Mill T&W 110 D4
Blackhall Rocks Durham 111 F7
Blackham E Sus 29 F5
Blackhaugh Borders 121 F7
Blackheath Essex 43 B6
Blackheath Suff 57 B8
Blackheath Sur 27 E8
Blackheath W Mid 62 F3
Blackhill Aberds 153 C10
Blackhill Aberds 153 D10
Blackhill Highld 149 C8
Blackhills Highld 151 F12
Blackhills Moray 152 C2
Blackhorse S Glos 23 B8
Blackland Wilts 24 C5
Blacklaw Aberds 153 C6
Blackley Gtr Man 87 D6
Blacklunans Perth 134 C1
Blackmill Bridgend 34 F3
Blackmoor Hants 27 F5
Blackmoor Gate Devon 21 E5
Blackmore Essex 42 D2
Blackmore End Essex 55 F8
Blackmore End Herts 40 C4
Blackness Falk 120 B3
Blacknest Hants 27 E5
Blacko Lancs 93 E8
Blackpool Blackpool 92 F3
Blackpool Devon 7 E6
Blackpool Pembs 32 C1
Blackpool Gate Cumb 108 B5
Blackridge W Loth 119 C8
Blackrock Argyll 142 B4
Blackrock Mon 35 C6
Blackrod Gtr Man 86 C4
Blackshaw Dumfries 107 C7
Blackshaw Head W Yorks 87 B7
Blacksmith's Green Suff 56 C5
Blackstone W Sus 17 C6
Blackthorn Oxon 39 C6
Blackthorpe Suff 56 C3
Blacktoft E Yorks 90 B2
Blacktop Aberdeen 141 D7
Blacktown Newport 35 F6
Blackwall Tunnel London 41 F6
Blackwater Corn 3 B6
Blackwater Hants 27 D6
Blackwater IoW 15 F6
Blackwaterfoot N Ayrs 143 F9
Blackwell Darl 101 C7
Blackwell Derbys 75 B8
Blackwell Derbys 76 D4
Blackwell W Sus 28 F4
Blackwell Warks 51 E7
Blackwell Worcs 50 B4
Blackwood = Coed Duon Caerph 35 E5
Blackwood S Lanark 119 E7
Blackwood Hill Staffs 75 D6
Blacon Ches W 73 C7
Bladnoch Dumfries 105 D8
Bladon Oxon 38 C4
Blaen-gwynfi Neath 34 E2
Blaen-waun Carms 32 B3
Blaen-y-coed Carms 32 B4
Blaen-y-Cwm Denb 72 F4
Blaen-y-cwm Gwyn 71 E8
Blaen-y-cwm Powys 59 B7
Blaenannerch Ceredig 45 E4
Blaenau Ffestiniog Gwyn 71 C8
Blaenavon Torf 35 D6
Blaencelyn Ceredig 46 D2
Blaendyryn Powys 47 F8
Blaenffos Pembs 45 F3
Blaengarw Bridgend 34 E3
Blaengwrach Neath 34 D2
Blaenpennal Ceredig 46 C5
Blaenplwyf Ceredig 46 B4
Blaenporth Ceredig 45 E4
Blaenrhondda Rhondda 34 D3
Blaenycwm Ceredig 47 B7
Blagdon N Som 23 D7
Blagdon Torbay 7 C6
Blagdon Hill Som 11 C7
Blagill Cumb 109 E7
Blaguegate Lancs 86 D2
Blaich Highld 130 B4
Blain Highld 147 E9
Blaina Bl Gwent 35 D6
Blair Atholl Perth 133 C5
Blair Drummond Stirling 127 E6
Blairbeg N Ayrs 143 E11
Blairdaff Aberds 141 C5
Blairglas Argyll 126 F2
Blairgowrie Perth 134 E1
Blairhall Fife 128 F2
Blairingone Perth 127 E8
Blairland N Ayrs 118 E3
Blairlogie Stirling 127 E7
Blairlomond Argyll 125 F7
Blairmore Argyll 145 E10
Blairnamarrow Moray 139 C8
Blairquhosh Stirling 126 F4
Blair's Ferry Argyll 145 G8
Blairskaith E Dunb 119 B5
Blaisdon Glos 36 C4
Blakebrook Worcs 50 B3
Blakedown Worcs 50 B3
Blakelaw Borders 122 F3
Blakeley Staffs 62 E2
Blakeley Lane Staffs 75 E6
Blakemere Hereford 49 E5
Blakeney Glos 36 D3
Blakeney Norf 81 C6
Blakenhall Ches E 74 E4
Blakenhall W Mid 62 E3
Blakeshall Worcs 62 F2
Blakesley Northants 52 D4
Blanchland Northumb 110 D2
Bland Hill N Yorks 94 D5
Blandford Forum Dorset 13 D6
Blandford St Mary Dorset 13 D6
Blanefield Stirling 119 B5
Blankney Lincs 78 C3
Blantyre S Lanark 119 D6
Blar a'Chaorainn Highld 131 C5
Blaran Argyll 124 D4
Blarghour Argyll 125 D5
Blarmachfoldach Highld 130 C4
Blarnalearoch Highld 150 B4
Blashford Hants 14 D2
Blaston Leics 64 E5
Blatherwycke Northants 65 E6
Blawith Cumb 98 F4
Blaxhall Suff 57 D7
Blaxton S Yorks 89 D7
Blaydon T&W 110 C4
Bleadon N Som 22 D5
Bleak Hey Nook Gtr Man 87 D8
Blean Kent 30 C5
Bleasby Lincs 90 F5
Bleasby Notts 77 E7
Bleasdale Lancs 93 E5
Bleatarn Cumb 100 C2
Blebocraigs Fife 129 C6
Bleddfa Powys 48 C4
Bledington Glos 38 B2
Bledlow Bucks 39 D7
Bledlow Ridge Bucks 39 E7
Blegbie E Loth 121 C7
Blencarn Cumb 109 F6
Blencogo Cumb 107 E8
Blendworth Hants 15 C8
Blenheim Park Norf 80 D4
Blennerhasset Cumb 107 E8
Blervie Castle Moray 151 F13
Bletchingdon Oxon 39 C5
Bletchingley Sur 28 D4
Bletchley M Keynes 53 F6
Bletchley Shrops 74 F3
Bletherston Pembs 32 B1
Bletsoe Bedford 53 D8
Blewbury Oxon 39 F5
Blickling Norf 81 E7
Blidworth Notts 77 D5
Blindburn Northumb 116 C4
Blindcrake Cumb 107 F8
Blindley Heath Sur 28 E4
Blisland Corn 5 B6
Bliss Gate Worcs 50 B2
Blissford Hants 14 C2
Blisworth Northants 52 D5
Blithbury Staffs 62 B4
Blitterlees Cumb 107 D8
Blockley Glos 51 F6
Blofield Norf 69 D6
Blofield Heath Norf 69 C6
Blo' Norton Norf 56 B4
Bloomfield Borders 115 B8
Blore Staffs 75 E8
Blount's Green Staffs 75 F7
Blowick Mers 85 C4
Bloxham Oxon 52 F2
Bloxholm Lincs 78 D3
Bloxwich W Mid 62 D3
Bloxworth Dorset 13 E6
Blubberhouses N Yorks 94 D4
Blue Anchor Som 22 E2
Blue Anchor Swansea 33 E6
Blue Row Essex 43 C6
Blundeston Suff 69 E8
Blunham C Beds 54 D2
Blunsdon St Andrew Swindon 37 F8
Bluntington Worcs 50 B3
Bluntisham Cambs 54 B4
Blunts Corn 5 C8
Blyborough Lincs 90 E3
Blyford Suff 57 B8
Blymhill Staffs 62 C2
Blyth Northumb 117 F9
Blyth Notts 89 F7
Blyth Bridge Borders 120 E4
Blythburgh Suff 57 B8
Blythe Borders 121 E8
Blythe Bridge Staffs 75 E6
Blyton Lincs 90 E2
Boarhills Fife 129 C7
Boarhunt Hants 15 D7
Boars Head Gtr Man 86 D3
Boars Hill Oxon 38 D4
Boarshead E Sus 18 B2
Boarstall Bucks 39 C6
Boasley Cross Devon 9 E6
Boat of Garten Highld 138 C5
Boath Highld 151 D8
Bobbing Kent 30 C2
Bobbington Staffs 62 E2
Bobbingworth Essex 41 D8
Bocaddon Corn 5 D6
Bochastle Stirling 126 D5
Bocking Essex 42 B3
Bocking Churchstreet Essex 42 B3
Boddam Aberds 153 D11
Boddam Shetland 160 M5
Boddington Glos 37 B5
Bodedern Anglesey 82 C3
Bodelwyddan Denb 72 B4
Bodenham Hereford 49 D7
Bodenham Wilts 14 B2
Bodenham Moor Hereford 49 D7
Bodermid Gwyn 70 E2
Bodewryd Anglesey 82 B3
Bodfari Denb 72 B4
Bodffordd Anglesey 82 D4
Bodham Norf 81 C7
Bodiam E Sus 18 C4
Bodicote Oxon 52 F2
Bodieve Corn 4 B4
Bodinnick Corn 5 D6
Bodle Street Green E Sus 18 D3
Bodmin Corn 5 C5
Bodney Norf 67 E8
Bodorgan Anglesey 82 E3
Bodsham Kent 30 E5
Boduan Gwyn 70 D4
Bodymoor Heath Warks 63 E5
Bogallan Highld 151 F9
Bogbrae Aberds 153 E10
Bogend Borders 122 E3
Bogend S Ayrs 118 F3
Boghall W Loth 120 C2
Boghead S Lanark 119 E7
Bogmoor Moray 152 B3
Bogniebrae Aberds 152 D5
Bognor Regis W Sus 16 E3
Bograxie Aberds 141 C6
Bogside N Lanark 119 D8
Bogton Aberds 153 C6
Bogue Dumfries 113 F6
Bohenie Highld 137 F5
Bohortha Corn 3 C7
Bohuntine Highld 137 F5
Boirseam W Isles 154 J5
Bojewyan Corn 2 C2
Bolam Durham 101 B6
Bolam Northumb 117 F6
Bolberry Devon 6 F4
Bold Heath Mers 86 F3
Boldon T&W 111 C6
Boldon Colliery T&W 111 C6
Boldre Hants 14 E4
Boldron Durham 101 C5
Bole Notts 89 F8
Bolehill Derbys 76 D2
Boleside Borders 121 F7
Bolham Devon 10 C4
Bolham Water Devon 11 C6
Bolingey Corn 4 D2
Bollington Ches E 75 B6
Bollington Cross Ches E 75 B6
Bolney W Sus 17 B6
Bolnhurst Bedford 53 D8
Bolshan Angus 135 D6
Bolsover Derbys 76 B4
Bolsterstone S Yorks 88 E3
Bolstone Hereford 49 F7
Boltby N Yorks 102 F2
Bolter End Bucks 39 E7
Bolton Cumb 99 B8
Bolton E Loth 121 B8
Bolton E Yorks 96 D3
Bolton Gtr Man 86 D5
Bolton Northumb 117 C7
Bolton Abbey N Yorks 94 D3
Bolton Bridge N Yorks 94 D3
Bolton-by-Bowland Lancs 93 E7
Bolton-le-Sands Lancs 92 C4
Bolton Low Houses Cumb 108 E2
Bolton-on-Swale N Yorks 101 E7
Bolton Percy N Yorks 95 E8
Bolton Town End Lancs 92 C4
Bolton upon Dearne S Yorks 89 D5
Boltonfellend Cumb 108 C4
Boltongate Cumb 108 E2
Bolventor Corn 5 B6
Bomere Heath Shrops 60 C4
Bon-y-maen Swansea 33 E7
Bonar Bridge Highld 151 B9
Bonawe Argyll 125 B6
Bonby N Lincs 90 C4
Boncath Pembs 45 F4
Bonchester Bridge Borders 115 C8
Bonchurch IoW 15 G6
Bondleigh Devon 9 D8
Bonehill Devon 6 B5
Bonehill Staffs 63 D5
Bo'ness Falk 127 F8
Bonhill W Dunb 118 B3
Boningale Shrops 62 D2
Bonjedward Borders 116 B2
Bonkle N Lanark 119 D8
Bonnavoulin Highld 147 F8
Bonnington Edin 120 C4
Bonnington Kent 19 B7
Bonnybank Fife 129 D5
Bonnybridge Falk 127 F7
Bonnykelly Aberds 153 C8
Bonnyrigg and Lasswade Midloth 121 C6
Bonnyton Aberds 153 E6
Bonnyton Angus 134 F3
Bonnyton Angus 135 D6
Bonsall Derbys 76 D2
Bonskeid House Perth 133 C5
Bont Mon 35 C7
Bont-Dolgadfan Powys 59 D5
Bont-goch Ceredig 58 F3
Bont-newydd Conwy 72 B4
Bont Newydd Gwyn 71 C8
Bont Newydd Gwyn 71 E8
Bontddu Gwyn 58 C3
Bonthorpe Lincs 79 B7
Bontnewydd Ceredig 46 C5
Bontnewydd Gwyn 82 F4
Bontuchel Denb 72 D4
Bonvilston V Glam 22 B2
Booker Bucks 39 E8
Boon Borders 121 E8
Boosbeck Redcar 102 C4
Boot Cumb 98 D3
Boot Street Suff 57 E6
Booth W Yorks 87 B8
Booth Wood W Yorks 87 C8
Boothby Graffoe Lincs 78 D2
Boothby Pagnell Lincs 78 F2
Boothen Stoke 75 E5
Boothferry E Yorks 89 B8
Boothville Northants 53 C5
Bootle Cumb 98 F3
Bootle Mers 85 E4
Booton Norf 81 E7
Boquhan Stirling 126 F4
Boraston Shrops 49 B8
Borden Kent 30 C2
Borden W Sus 16 B2
Bordley N Yorks 94 C2
Bordon Hants 27 F6
Bordon Camp Hants 27 F5
Boreham Essex 42 D3
Boreham Wilts 24 E3
Boreham Street E Sus 18 D3
Borehamwood Herts 40 E4
Boreland Dumfries 114 E4
Boreland Stirling 132 F2
Borgh W Isles 148 H1
Borgh W Isles 154 J4
Borghastan W Isles 154 C7
Borgie Highld 157 D9
Borgue Dumfries 106 E3
Borgue Highld 158 H3
Borley Essex 56 E2
Bornais W Isles 148 F2
Bornesketaig Highld 149 A8
Borness Dumfries 106 E3
Borough Green Kent 29 D7
Boroughbridge N Yorks 95 C6
Borras Head Wrex 73 D7
Borreraig Highld 148 C6
Borrobol Lodge Highld 157 G11
Borrowash Derbys 76 F4
Borrowby N Yorks 102 F2
Borrowdale Cumb 98 C4
Borrowfield Aberds 141 E7
Borth Ceredig 58 E3
Borth-y-Gest Gwyn 71 D6
Borthwickbrae Borders 115 C7
Borthwickshiels Borders 115 C7
Borve Highld 149 D9
Borve Lodge W Isles 154 H5
Borwick Lancs 92 B5
Bosavern Corn 2 C2
Bosbury Hereford 49 E8
Boscastle Corn 8 E3
Boscombe Bmouth 14 E2
Boscombe Wilts 25 F7
Boscoppa Corn 4 D5
Bosham W Sus 16 D2
Bosherston Pembs 44 F4
Boskenna Corn 2 D3
Bosley Ches E 75 C6
Bossall N Yorks 96 C3
Bossiney Corn 8 F2
Bossingham Kent 31 E5
Bossington Som 21 E7
Bostock Green Ches W 74 C3
Boston Lincs 79 E6
Boston Long Hedges Lincs 79 E6
Boston Spa W Yorks 95 E7
Boston West Lincs 79 E5
Boswinger Corn 3 B8
Botallack Corn 2 C2
Botany Bay London 41 E5
Botcherby Cumb 108 D4
Botcheston Leics 63 D8
Botesdale Suff 56 B4
Bothal Northumb 117 F8
Bothamsall Notts 77 B6
Bothel Cumb 107 F8
Bothenhampton Dorset 12 E2
Bothwell S Lanark 119 D7
Botley Bucks 40 D2
Botley Hants 15 C6
Botley Oxon 38 D4
Botolph Claydon Bucks 39 B7
Botolphs W Sus 17 D5
Bottacks Highld 150 E7
Bottesford Leics 77 F8
Bottesford N Lincs 90 D2
Bottisham Cambs 55 C6
Bottlesford Wilts 25 D6
Bottom Boat W Yorks 88 B4
Bottom House Staffs 75 D7
Bottom o'th'Moor Gtr Man 86 C4
Bottom of Hutton Lancs 86 B2
Bottomcraig Fife 129 B5
Botusfleming Corn 6 C2
Botwnnog Gwyn 70 D3
Bough Beech Kent 29 E5
Boughrood Powys 48 F3
Boughspring Glos 36 E2
Boughton Norf 67 D6
Boughton Northants 53 C5
Boughton Notts 77 C6
Boughton Aluph Kent 30 E4
Boughton Lees Kent 30 E4
Boughton Malherbe Kent 30 E2
Boughton Monchelsea Kent 29 D8
Boughton Street Kent 30 D4
Boulby Redcar 103 C5
Boulden Shrops 60 F5
Boulmer Northumb 117 C8
Boulston Pembs 44 D4
Boultenstone Aberds 140 C3
Boultham Lincs 78 C2
Bourn Cambs 54 D4
Bourne Lincs 65 B7
Bourne End Bucks 40 F1
Bourne End C Beds 53 E7
Bourne End Herts 40 D3
Bournemouth Bmouth 13 E8
Bournes Green Glos 37 D6
Bournes Green Southend 43 F5
Bournheath Worcs 50 B4
Bournmoor Durham 111 D6
Bournville W Mid 62 F4
Bourton Dorset 24 F2
Bourton N Som 23 C5
Bourton Oxon 38 F2
Bourton Shrops 61 E5
Bourton on Dunsmore Warks 52 B2
Bourton on the Hill Glos 51 F6
Bourton-on-the-Water Glos 38 B1
Bousd Argyll 146 E5
Boustead Hill Cumb 108 D2
Bouth Cumb 99 F5
Bouthwaite N Yorks 94 B4
Boveney Bucks 27 B7
Boverton V Glam 21 C8
Bovey Tracey Devon 7 B6
Bovingdon Herts 40 D3
Bovingdon Green Bucks 39 F8
Bovingdon Green Herts 40 D3
Bovinger Essex 41 D8
Bovington Camp Dorset 13 F6
Bow Borders 121 E7
Bow Devon 10 D2
Bow Orkney 159 J4
Bow Brickhill M Keynes 53 F7
Bow of Fife Fife 128 C5
Bow Street Ceredig 58 F3
Bowbank Durham 100 B4
Bowburn Durham 111 F6
Bowcombe IoW 15 F5
Bowd Devon 11 E6
Bowden Borders 121 F8
Bowden Devon 7 E6
Bowden Hill Wilts 24 C4
Bowderdale Cumb 100 D1
Bowdon Gtr Man 87 F5
Bower Northumb 116 F3
Bower Hinton Som 12 C2
Bowerchalke Wilts 13 B8
Bowerhill Wilts 24 C4
Bowermadden Highld 158 D4
Bowers Gifford Essex 42 F3
Bowershall Fife 128 E2
Bowertower Highld 158 D4
Bowes Durham 100 C4
Bowgreave Lancs 92 E4
Bowgreen Gtr Man 87 F5
Bowhill Borders 115 B7
Bowhouse Dumfries 107 C7
Bowland Bridge Cumb 99 F6
Bowley Hereford 49 D7
Bowlhead Green Sur 27 F7
Bowling W Dunb 118 B4
Bowling W Yorks 94 F4
Bowling Bank Wrex 73 E7
Bowling Green Worcs 50 D3
Bowmanstead Cumb 99 E5
Bowmore Argyll 142 C4
Bowness-on-Solway Cumb 108 C2
Bowness-on-Windermere Cumb 99 E6
Bowsden Northumb 123 E5
Bowside Lodge Highld 157 C11
Bowston Cumb 99 E6
Bowthorpe Norf 68 D4
Box Glos 37 D5
Box Wilts 24 C3
Box End Bedford 53 E8
Boxbush Glos 36 C4
Boxford Suff 56 E3
Boxford W Berks 26 B2
Boxgrove W Sus 16 D3
Boxley Kent 29 D8
Boxmoor Herts 40 D3
Boxted Essex 56 F4
Boxted Suff 56 D2
Boxted Cross Essex 56 F4
Boxted Heath Essex 56 F4
Boxworth Cambs 54 C4
Boxworth End Cambs 54 C4
Boyden Gate Kent 31 C6
Boylestone Derbys 75 F8
Boyndie Aberds 153 B6
Boynton E Yorks 97 C7
Boysack Angus 135 E6
Boyton Corn 8 E5
Boyton Suff 57 E7
Boyton Wilts 24 F4
Boyton Cross Essex 42 D2
Boyton End Suff 55 E8
Bozeat Northants 53 D7

Bux – Chu 215

Buxton Norf 81 E8
Buxworth Derbys 87 F8
Bwcle = Buckley Flint 73 C6
Bwlch Powys 35 B5
Bwlch-Llan Ceredig 46 D4
Bwlch-y-cibau Powys 59 C8
Bwlch-y-fadfa Ceredig 46 E3
Bwlch-y-ffridd Powys 59 E7
Bwlch-y-sarnau Powys 48 B2
Bwlchgwyn Wrex 73 D6
Bwlchnewydd Carms 32 B4
Bwlchtocyn Gwyn 70 E4
Bwlchyddar Powys 59 B8
Bwlchygroes Pembs 45 F4
Byermoor T&W 110 D4
Byers Green Durham 110 F5
Byfield Northants 52 D3
Byfleet Sur 27 C8
Byford Hereford 49 E5
Bygrave Herts 54 F3
Byker T&W 111 C5
Bylchau Conwy 72 C3
Byley Ches W 74 C4
Bynea Carms 33 E6
Byrness Northumb 116 D3
Bythorn Cambs 53 B8
Byton Hereford 49 C5
Byworth W Sus 16 B3

C

Cabharstadh W Isles 155 E8
Cablea Perth 133 F6
Cabourne Lincs 90 D5
Cabrach Argyll 144 G3
Cabrach Moray 140 B2
Cabrich Highld 151 G8
Cabus Lancs 92 E4
Cackle Street E Sus 17 B8
Cadbury Devon 10 D4
Cadbury Barton Devon 9 C8
Cadder E Dunb 119 B6
Caddington C Beds 40 C3
Caddonfoot Borders 121 F7
Cade Street E Sus 18 C3
Cadeby Leics 63 D8
Cadeby S Yorks 89 D6
Cadeleigh Devon 10 D4
Cadgwith Corn 3 E6
Cadham Fife 128 D4
Cadishead Gtr Man 86 E5
Cadle Swansea 33 E7
Cadley Lancs 92 F5
Cadley Wilts 25 C7
Cadley Wilts 25 D7
Cadmore End Bucks 39 E7
Cadnam Hants 14 C3
Cadney N Lincs 90 D4
Cadole Flint 73 C6
Cadoxton V Glam 22 C3
Cadoxton-Juxta-Neath Neath 34 E1
Cadshaw Blackburn 86 C5
Cadzow S Lanark 119 D7
Caeathro Gwyn 82 E4
Caehopkin Powys 34 C2
Caenby Lincs 90 F4
Caenby Corner Lincs 90 F3
Caér-bryn Carms 33 C6
Caer Llan Mon 36 D1
Caerau Bridgend 34 E2
Caerau Cardiff 22 B3
Caerdeon Gwyn 58 C3
Caerdydd = Cardiff Cardiff 22 B3
Caerfarchell Pembs 44 C2
Caerffili = Caerphilly Caerph 35 F5
Caerfyrddin = Carmarthen Carms 33 B5
Caergeiliog Anglesey 82 D3
Caergwrle Flint 73 D7
Caergybi = Holyhead Anglesey 82 C2
Caerleon = Caerllion Newport 35 E7
Caerllion = Caerleon Newport 35 E7
Caernarfon Gwyn 82 E4
Caerphilly = Caerffili Caerph 35 F5
Caersws Powys 59 E7
Caerwedros Ceredig 46 D2
Caerwent Mon 36 E1
Caerwych Gwyn 71 D7
Caerwys Flint 72 B5
Caethle Gwyn 58 E3
Caim Anglesey 83 C6
Caio Carms 47 F5
Cairinis W Isles 148 B3
Cairisiadar W Isles 154 D5
Cairminis W Isles 154 J5
Cairnbaan Argyll 145 D7
Cairnbanno Ho. Aberds 153 D8
Cairnborrow Aberds 152 D4
Cairnbrogie Aberds 141 B7
Cairnbulg Castle Aberds 153 B10
Cairncross Angus 134 B4
Cairncross Borders 122 C4
Cairndow Argyll 125 D7
Cairness Aberds 153 B10
Cairneyhill Fife 128 F2
Cairnfield Ho. Moray 152 B4
Cairngaan Dumfries 104 F5
Cairngarroch Dumfries 104 E4
Cairnhill Aberds 153 E6
Cairnie Aberds 141 D7
Cairnie Aberds 152 D4
Cairnorrie Aberds 153 D8
Cairnpark Aberds 141 C7
Cairnryan Dumfries 104 C4
Cairnton Orkney 159 H4
Caister-on-Sea Norf 69 C8
Caistor Lincs 90 D5
Caistor St Edmund Norf 68 D5
Caistron Northumb 117 D5
Caitha Bowland Borders 121 E7
Calais Street Suff 56 F3
Calanais W Isles 154 D7
Calbost W Isles 155 F9
Calbourne IoW 14 F5
Calceby Lincs 79 B6
Calcot Row W Berks 26 B4
Calcott Kent 31 C5
Caldback Shetland 160 C8
Caldbeck Cumb 108 F3
Caldbergh N Yorks 101 F5
Caldecote Cambs 54 D4
Caldecote Cambs 65 F8
Caldecote Herts 54 F3
Caldecote Northants 52 D4
Caldecott Northants 53 C7
Caldecott Oxon 38 E4
Caldecott Rutland 65 E5
Calder Bridge Cumb 98 D2
Calder Hall Cumb 98 D2
Calder Mains Highld 158 E2
Calder Vale Lancs 92 E5
Calderbank N Lanark 119 C7
Calderbrook Gtr Man 87 C7
Caldercruix N Lanark 119 C8
Caldermill S Lanark 119 E6
Calderwood S Lanark 119 D6
Caldhame Angus 134 E4
Caldicot Mon 36 F1
Caldwell Derbys 63 C6
Caldwell N Yorks 101 C6
Caldy Mers 85 F3
Caledrhydiau Ceredig 46 D3
Calfsound Orkney 159 E6
Calgary Argyll 146 F6
Califer Moray 151 F13
California Falk 120 B2
California Norf 69 C8
Calke Derbys 63 B7
Callakille Highld 149 C11
Callaly Northumb 117 D6
Callander Stirling 126 D5
Callaughton Shrops 61 E6
Callestick Corn 4 D2
Calligarry Highld 149 H11
Callington Corn 5 C8
Callow Hereford 49 F6
Callow End Worcs 50 E3
Callow Hill Wilts 37 F7
Callow Hill Worcs 50 B2
Callows Grave Worcs 49 C7
Calmore Hants 14 C4
Calmsden Glos 37 D7
Calne Wilts 24 B5
Calow Derbys 76 B4
Calshot Hants 15 D5
Calstock Corn 6 C2
Calstone Wellington Wilts 24 C5
Calthorpe Norf 81 D7
Calthwaite Cumb 108 E4
Calton N Yorks 94 D2
Calton Staffs 75 D8
Calveley Ches E 74 D2
Calver Derbys 76 B2
Calver Hill Hereford 49 E5
Calverhall Shrops 74 F3
Calverleigh Devon 10 C4
Calverley W Yorks 94 F5
Calvert Bucks 39 B6
Calverton M Keynes 53 F5
Calverton Notts 77 E6
Calvine Perth 133 C5
Calvo Cumb 107 D8
Cam Glos 36 E4
Camas-luinie Highld 136 B2
Camasnacroise Highld 130 D2
Camastianavaig Highld 149 E10
Camasunary Highld 149 G10
Camault Muir Highld 151 G8
Camb Shetland 160 D7
Camber E Sus 19 D6
Camberley Sur 27 C6
Camberwell London 28 B4
Camblesforth N Yorks 89 B7
Cambo Northumb 117 F6
Cambois Northumb 117 F9
Camborne Corn 3 B5
Cambourne Cambs 54 D4
Cambridge Cambs 55 D5
Cambridge Glos 36 D4
Cambridge Town Southend 43 F5
Cambus Clack 127 E7
Cambusavie Farm Highld 151 B10
Cambusbarron Stirling 127 E6
Cambuskenneth Stirling 127 E7
Cambuslang S Lanark 119 C6
Cambusmore Lodge Highld 151 B10
Camden London 41 F5
Camelford Corn 8 F3
Camelsdale Sur 27 F6
Camerory Highld 151 H13
Camer's Green Worcs 50 F2
Camerton Bath 23 D8
Camerton Cumb 107 F7
Camerton E Yorks 91 B6
Camghouran Perth 132 D2
Cammachmore Aberds 141 E8
Cammeringham Lincs 90 F3
Camore Highld 151 B10
Camp Hill Warks 63 E7
Campbeltown Argyll 143 F8
Camperdown T&W 111 B5
Campmuir Perth 134 F2
Campsall S Yorks 89 C6
Campsey Ash Suff 57 D7
Campton C Beds 54 F2
Camptown Borders 116 C2
Camrose Pembs 44 C4
Camserney Perth 133 E5
Camster Highld 158 F4
Camuschoirk Highld 130 C1
Camuscross Highld 149 G11
Camusnagaul Highld 130 B4
Camusnagaul Highld 150 C3
Camusrory Highld 147 B11
Camusteel Highld 149 D12
Camusterrach Highld 149 D12
Camusvrachan Perth 132 E3
Canada Hants 14 C3
Canadia E Sus 18 D4
Canal Side S Yorks 89 C7
Candacraig Ho. Aberds 140 C2
Candlesby Lincs 79 C7
Candy Mill S Lanark 120 E3
Cane End Oxon 26 B4
Canewdon Essex 42 E4
Canford Bottom Dorset 13 D8
Canford Cliffs Poole 13 F8
Canford Magna Poole 13 E8
Canham's Green Suff 56 C4
Canholes Derbys 75 B7
Canisbay Highld 158 C5
Cann Dorset 13 B6
Cann Common Dorset 13 B6
Cannard's Grave Som 23 E8
Cannich Highld 150 H6
Cannington Som 22 F4
Cannock Staffs 62 D3
Cannock Wood Staffs 62 C4
Canon Bridge Hereford 49 E6
Canon Frome Hereford 49 E8
Canon Pyon Hereford 49 E6
Canonbie Dumfries 108 B3
Canons Ashby Northants 52 D3
Canonstown Corn 2 C4
Canterbury Kent 30 D5
Cantley Norf 69 D6
Cantley S Yorks 89 D7
Cantlop Shrops 60 D5
Canton Cardiff 22 B3
Cantraybruich Highld 151 G10
Cantraydoune Highld 151 G10
Cantraywood Highld 151 G10
Cantsfield Lancs 93 B6
Canvey Island Essex 42 F3
Canwick Lincs 78 C2
Canworthy Water Corn 8 E4
Caol Highld 131 B5
Caol Ila Argyll 142 A5
Caolas Argyll 146 G3
Caolas Scalpaigh W Isles 154 H7
Caolas Stocinis W Isles 154 H6
Capel Sur 28 E2
Capel Bangor Ceredig 58 F3
Capel Betws Lleucu Ceredig 46 D5
Capel Carmel Gwyn 70 E2
Capel Coch Anglesey 82 C4
Capel Curig Conwy 83 F7
Capel Cynon Ceredig 46 E2
Capel Dewi Carms 33 B5
Capel Dewi Ceredig 46 E3
Capel Dewi Ceredig 58 F3
Capel Garmon Conwy 83 F8
Capel-gwyn Anglesey 82 D3
Capel Gwyn Carms 33 B5
Capel Gwynfe Carms 33 B8
Capel Hendre Carms 33 C6
Capel Hermon Gwyn 71 E8
Capel Isaac Carms 33 B6
Capel Iwan Carms 45 F4
Capel le Ferne Kent 31 F6
Capel Llanilltern Cardiff 34 F4
Capel Mawr Anglesey 82 D4
Capel St Andrew Suff 57 E7
Capel St Mary Suff 56 F4
Capel Seion Ceredig 46 B5
Capel Tygwydd Ceredig 45 E4
Capel Uchaf Gwyn 70 C5
Capel-y-graig Gwyn 82 E5
Capelulo Conwy 83 D7
Capenhurst Ches W 73 B7
Capernwray Lancs 92 B5
Capheaton Northumb 117 F6
Cappercleuch Borders 115 B5
Capplegill Dumfries 114 D4
Capton Devon 7 D6
Caputh Perth 133 F7
Car Colston Notts 77 E7
Carbis Bay Corn 2 C4
Carbost Highld 149 D9
Carbost Highld 149 E8
Carbrook S Yorks 88 F4
Carbrooke Norf 68 D2
Carburton Notts 77 B6
Carcant Borders 121 D6
Carcary Angus 135 D6
Carclaze Corn 4 D5
Carcroft S Yorks 89 C6
Cardenden Fife 128 E4
Cardeston Shrops 60 C3
Cardiff = Caerdydd Cardiff 22 B3
Cardigan = Aberteifi Ceredig 45 E3
Cardington Bedford 53 E8
Cardington Shrops 60 E5
Cardinham Corn 5 C6
Cardonald Glasgow 118 C5
Cardow Moray 152 D1
Cardrona Borders 121 F6
Cardross Argyll 118 B3
Cardurnock Cumb 107 D8
Careby Lincs 65 C7
Careston Castle Angus 135 D5
Carew Pembs 32 D1
Carew Cheriton Pembs 32 D1
Carew Newton Pembs 32 D1
Carey Hereford 49 F7
Carfrae E Loth 121 C8
Cargenbridge Dumfries 107 B6
Cargill Perth 134 F1
Cargo Cumb 108 D3
Cargreen Corn 6 C2
Carham Northumb 122 F4
Carhampton Som 22 E2
Carharrack Corn 3 B6
Carie Perth 132 D3
Carie Perth 132 F3
Carines Corn 4 D2
Carisbrooke IoW 15 F5
Cark Cumb 92 B3
Carlabhagh W Isles 154 C7
Carland Cross Corn 4 D3
Carlby Lincs 65 C7
Carlecotes S Yorks 88 D2
Carlesmoor N Yorks 94 B4
Carleton Cumb 99 B7
Carleton Cumb 108 D4
Carleton Lancs 92 F3
Carleton N Yorks 94 E2
Carleton Forehoe Norf 68 D3
Carleton Rode Norf 68 E4
Carlin How Redcar 103 C5
Carlingcott Bath 23 D8
Carlisle Cumb 108 D4
Carlops Borders 120 D4
Carlton Bedford 53 D7
Carlton Cambs 55 D7
Carlton Leics 63 D7
Carlton N Yorks 89 B7
Carlton N Yorks 101 C6
Carlton N Yorks 101 F5
Carlton N Yorks 102 F4
Carlton Notts 77 E6
Carlton S Yorks 88 C4
Carlton Stockton 102 B1
Carlton Suff 57 C7
Carlton W Yorks 88 B4
Carlton Colville Suff 69 F8
Carlton Curlieu Leics 64 E3
Carlton Husthwaite N Yorks 95 B7
Carlton in Cleveland N Yorks 102 D3
Carlton in Lindrick Notts 89 F6
Carlton le Moorland Lincs 78 D2
Carlton Miniott N Yorks 102 F1
Carlton on Trent Notts 77 C7
Carlton Scroop Lincs 78 E2
Carluke S Lanark 119 D8
Carmarthen = Caerfyrddin Carms 33 B5
Carmel Anglesey 82 C3
Carmel Carms 33 C6
Carmel Flint 73 B5
Carmel Guern 16
Carmel Gwyn 82 F4
Carmont Aberds 141 F7
Carmunnock Glasgow 119 D6
Carmyle Glasgow 119 C6
Carmyllie Angus 135 E5
Carn-gorm Highld 136 B2
Carnaby E Yorks 97 C7
Carnach Highld 136 B3
Carnach Highld 150 B3
Carnach W Isles 154 H7
Carnachy Highld 157 D10
Càrnais W Isles 154 D5
Carnbee Fife 129 D7
Carnbo Perth 128 D2
Carnbrea Corn 3 B5
Carnduff S Lanark 119 E6
Carnduncan Argyll 142 B3
Carne Corn 3 C8
Carnforth Lancs 92 B4
Carnhedryn Pembs 44 C3
Carnhell Green Corn 2 C5
Carnkie Corn 3 C5
Carnkie Corn 3 C6
Carno Powys 59 E6
Carnoch Highld 150 F5
Carnoch Highld 150 H6
Carnock Fife 128 F2
Carnon Downs Corn 3 B6
Carnousie Aberds 153 C6
Carnoustie Angus 135 F5
Carnwath S Lanark 120 E2
Carnyorth Corn 2 C2
Carperby N Yorks 101 F5
Carpley Green N Yorks 100 F4
Carr S Yorks 89 E6
Carr Hill T&W 111 C5
Carradale Argyll 143 E9
Carragraich W Isles 154 H6
Carrbridge Highld 138 B5
Carrefour Selous Jersey 17
Carreg-wen Pembs 45 E4
Carreglefn Anglesey 82 C3
Carrick Argyll 145 E8
Carrick Fife 129 B6
Carrick Castle Argyll 145 D10
Carrick Ho. Orkney 159 E6
Carriden Falk 128 F2
Carrington Gtr Man 86 E5
Carrington Lincs 79 D6
Carrington Midloth 121 C6
Carrog Conwy 71 C8
Carrog Denb 72 E5
Carron Falk 127 F7
Carron Moray 152 D2
Carron Bridge Stirling 127 F6
Carronbridge Dumfries 113 E8
Carronshore Falk 127 F7
Carrshield Northumb 109 E8
Carrutherstown Dumfries 107 B8
Carrville Durham 111 E6
Carsaig Argyll 144 E6
Carsaig Argyll 147 J8
Carscreugh Dumfries 105 D6
Carse Gray Angus 134 D4
Carse Ho. Argyll 144 G6
Carsegowan Dumfries 105 D8
Carseriggan Dumfries 105 C7
Carsethorn Dumfries 107 D6
Carshalton London 28 C3
Carsington Derbys 76 D2
Carskiey Argyll 143 H7
Carsluith Dumfries 105 D8
Carsphairn Dumfries 113 E5
Carstairs S Lanark 120 E2
Carstairs Junction S Lanark 120 E2
Carswell Marsh Oxon 38 E3
Carter's Clay Hants 14 B4
Carterton Oxon 38 D2
Carterway Heads Northumb 110 D3
Carthew Corn 4 D5
Carthorpe N Yorks 101 F8
Cartington Northumb 117 D6
Cartland S Lanark 119 E8
Cartmel Cumb 92 B3
Cartmel Fell Cumb 99 F6
Carway Carms 33 D5
Cary Fitzpaine Som 12 B3
Cas-gwent = Chepstow Mon 36 E2
Cascob Powys 48 C4
Cashlie Perth 132 E1
Cashmoor Dorset 13 C7
Casnewydd = Newport Newport 35 F7
Cassey Compton Glos 37 C7
Cassington Oxon 38 C4
Cassop Durham 111 F6
Castell Denb 72 C5
Castell-Howell Ceredig 46 E3
Castell-Nedd = Neath Neath 33 E8
Castell Newydd Emlyn = Newcastle Emlyn Carms 46 E2
Castell-y-bwch Torf 35 E6
Castellau Rhondda 34 F4
Casterton Cumb 93 B6
Castle Acre Norf 67 C8
Castle Ashby Northants 53 D6
Castle Bolton N Yorks 101 E5
Castle Bromwich W Mid 62 F5
Castle Bytham Lincs 65 C6
Castle Caereinion Powys 59 D8
Castle Camps Cambs 55 E7
Castle Carrock Cumb 108 D5
Castle Cary Som 23 F8
Castle Combe Wilts 24 B3
Castle Donington Leics 63 B8
Castle Douglas Dumfries 106 C4
Castle Eaton Swindon 37 E8
Castle Eden Durham 111 F7
Castle Forbes Aberds 140 C5
Castle Frome Hereford 49 E8
Castle Green Sur 27 C7
Castle Gresley Derbys 63 C6
Castle Heaton Northumb 122 E5
Castle Hedingham Essex 55 F8
Castle Hill Kent 29 E7
Castle Huntly Perth 128 B5
Castle Kennedy Dumfries 104 D5
Castle O'er Dumfries 115 E5
Castle Pulverbatch Shrops 60 D4
Castle Rising Norf 67 B6
Castle Stuart Highld 151 G10
Castlebay = Bagh a Chaisteil W Isles 148 J1
Castlebythe Pembs 32 B1
Castlecary N Lanark 119 B7
Castlecraig Highld 151 E11
Castlefairn Dumfries 113 F7
Castleford W Yorks 88 B5
Castlehill Borders 120 F5
Castlehill Highld 158 D3
Castlehill W Dunb 118 B3
Castlemaddy Dumfries 113 F5
Castlemartin Pembs 44 F4
Castlemilk Dumfries 107 B8
Castlemilk Glasgow 119 D6
Castlemorris Pembs 44 B4
Castlemorton Worcs 50 F2
Castleside Durham 110 E3
Castlethorpe M Keynes 53 E6
Castleton Angus 134 E3
Castleton Argyll 145 E7
Castleton Derbys 88 F2
Castleton Gtr Man 87 C6
Castleton N Yorks 102 D4
Castleton Newport 35 F6
Castletown Ches W 73 D8
Castletown Highld 151 G10
Castletown Highld 158 D3
Castletown IoM 84 F2
Castletown T&W 111 D6
Castleweary Borders 115 D7
Castley N Yorks 95 E5
Caston Norf 68 E2
Castor Pboro 65 E8
Catacol N Ayrs 143 D10
Catbrain S Glos 36 F2
Catbrook Mon 36 D2
Catchall Corn 2 D3
Catchems Corner W Mid 51 B7
Catchgate Durham 110 D4
Catcleugh Northumb 116 D3
Catcliffe S Yorks 88 F5
Catcott Som 23 F5
Caterham Sur 28 D4
Catfield Norf 69 B6
Catfirth Shetland 160 H6
Catford London 28 B4
Catforth Lancs 92 F4
Cathays Cardiff 22 B3
Cathcart Glasgow 119 C5
Cathedine Powys 35 B5
Catherington Hants 15 C7
Catherton Shrops 49 B8
Catlodge Highld 138 E2
Catlowdy Cumb 108 B4
Catmore W Berks 38 F4
Caton Lancs 92 C5
Caton Green Lancs 92 C5
Catrine E Ayrs 113 B5
Cat's Ash Newport 35 E7
Catsfield E Sus 18 D4
Catshill Worcs 50 B4
Cattal N Yorks 95 D7
Cattawade Suff 56 F5
Catterall Lancs 92 E4
Catterick N Yorks 101 E7
Catterick Bridge N Yorks 101 E7
Catterick Garrison N Yorks 101 E6
Catterlen Cumb 108 F4
Catterline Aberds 135 B8
Catterton N Yorks 95 E8
Catthorpe Leics 52 B3
Cattistock Dorset 12 E3
Catton N Yorks 95 B6
Catton Northumb 109 D8
Catwick E Yorks 97 E7
Catworth Cambs 53 B8
Caudlesprings Norf 68 D2
Caulcott Oxon 39 B5
Cauldcots Angus 135 E6
Cauldhame Stirling 126 E5
Cauldmill Borders 115 C8
Cauldon Staffs 75 E7
Caulkerbush Dumfries 107 D6
Caulside Dumfries 115 F7
Caunsall Worcs 62 F2
Caunton Notts 77 D7
Causeway End Dumfries 105 C8
Causeway Foot W Yorks 94 F3
Causeway-head Stirling 127 E6
Causewayend S Lanark 120 F3
Causewayhead Cumb 107 D8
Causey Park Bridge Northumb 117 E7
Causeyend Aberds 141 C8
Cautley Cumb 100 E1
Cavendish Suff 56 E2
Cavendish Bridge Leics 63 B8
Cavenham Suff 55 C8
Caversfield Oxon 39 B5
Caversham Reading 26 B5
Caverswall Staffs 75 E6
Cavil E Yorks 96 F3
Cawdor Highld 151 F11
Cawkwell Lincs 79 B5
Cawood N Yorks 95 F8
Cawsand Corn 6 D2
Cawston Norf 81 E7
Cawthorne S Yorks 88 D3
Cawthorpe Lincs 65 B7
Cawton N Yorks 96 B2
Caxton Cambs 54 D4
Caynham Shrops 49 B7
Caythorpe Lincs 78 E2
Caythorpe Notts 77 E6
Cayton N Yorks 103 F8
Ceann a Bhaigh W Isles 148 B2
Ceann a Deas Loch Baghasdail W Isles 148 G2
Ceann Shiphoirt W Isles 155 F7
Ceann Tarabhaigh W Isles 154 F7
Ceannacroc Lodge Highld 136 C5
Cearsiadair W Isles 155 E8
Cefn Berain Conwy 72 C3
Cefn-brith Conwy 72 D3
Cefn Canol Powys 73 F6
Cefn-coch Conwy 83 E8
Cefn Coch Powys 59 B8
Cefn-coed-y-cymmer M Tydf 34 D4
Cefn Cribbwr Bridgend 34 F2
Cefn Cross Bridgend 34 F2
Cefn-ddwysarn Gwyn 72 F3
Cefn Einion Shrops 60 F2
Cefn-gorwydd Powys 47 E8
Cefn-mawr Wrex 73 E6
Cefn-y-bedd Flint 73 D7
Cefn-y-pant Carms 32 B2
Cefneithin Carms 33 C6
Cei-bach Ceredig 46 D3
Ceinewydd = New Quay Ceredig 46 D2
Ceint Anglesey 82 D4
Cellan Ceredig 46 E5
Cellarhead Staffs 75 E6
Cemaes Anglesey 82 B3
Cemmaes Powys 58 D5
Cemmaes Road Powys 58 D5
Cenarth Carms 45 E4
Cenin Gwyn 71 C5
Central Invclyd 118 B2
Ceos W Isles 155 E8
Ceres Fife 129 C6
Cerne Abbas Dorset 12 D4
Cerney Wick Glos 37 E7
Cerrigceinwen Anglesey 82 D4
Cerrigydrudion Conwy 72 E3
Cessford Borders 116 B3
Ceunant Gwyn 82 E5
Chaceley Glos 50 F3
Chacewater Corn 3 B6
Chackmore Bucks 52 F4
Chacombe Northants 52 E2
Chad Valley W Mid 62 F4
Chadderton Gtr Man 87 D7
Chadderton Fold Gtr Man 87 D6
Chaddesden Derby 76 F3
Chaddesley Corbett Worcs 50 B3
Chaddleworth W Berks 26 B2
Chadlington Oxon 38 B3
Chadshunt Warks 51 D8
Chadwell Leics 64 B4
Chadwell St Mary Thurrock 29 B7
Chadwick End W Mid 51 B7
Chadwick Green Mers 86 E3
Chaffcombe Som 11 C8
Chagford Devon 10 F2
Chailey E Sus 17 C7
Chain Bridge Lincs 79 E6
Chainbridge Cambs 66 D4
Chainhurst Kent 29 E8
Chalbury Dorset 13 D8
Chalbury Common Dorset 13 D8
Chaldon Sur 28 D4
Chaldon Herring Dorset 13 F5
Chale IoW 15 G5
Chale Green IoW 15 G5
Chalfont Common Bucks 40 E3
Chalfont St Giles Bucks 40 E2
Chalfont St Peter Bucks 40 E3
Chalford Glos 37 D5
Chalgrove Oxon 39 E6
Chalk Kent 29 B7
Challacombe Devon 21 E5
Challoch Dumfries 105 C7
Challock Kent 30 D4
Chalton C Beds 40 B3
Chalton Hants 15 C8
Chalvington E Sus 18 E2
Chancery Ceredig 46 B4
Chandler's Ford Hants 14 B5
Channel Tunnel Kent 19 B8
Channerwick Shetland 160 L6
Chantry Som 24 E2
Chantry Suff 56 E5
Chapel Fife 128 E4
Chapel Allerton Som 23 D6
Chapel Allerton W Yorks 95 F6
Chapel Amble Corn 4 B4
Chapel Brampton Northants 52 C5
Chapel Chorlton Staffs 74 F5
Chapel-en-le-Frith Derbys 87 F8
Chapel End Warks 63 E7
Chapel Green Warks 52 C2
Chapel Green Warks 63 F6
Chapel Haddlesey N Yorks 89 B6
Chapel Head Cambs 66 F3
Chapel Hill Aberds 153 E10
Chapel Hill Lincs 78 D5
Chapel Hill Mon 36 E2
Chapel Hill N Yorks 95 E6
Chapel Lawn Shrops 48 B5
Chapel-le-Dale N Yorks 93 B7
Chapel Milton Derbys 87 F8
Chapel of Garioch Aberds 141 B6
Chapel Row W Berks 26 C3
Chapel St Leonards Lincs 79 B8
Chapel Stile Cumb 99 D5
Chapelgate Lincs 66 B4
Chapelhall N Lanark 119 C7
Chapelhill Dumfries 114 E3
Chapelhill Highld 151 D11
Chapelhill N Ayrs 118 E2
Chapelhill Perth 128 B4
Chapelhill Perth 133 F7
Chapelknowe Dumfries 108 B3
Chapelton Angus 135 E6
Chapelton Devon 9 B7
Chapelton Highld 138 C5
Chapelton S Lanark 119 E6
Chapeltown Blackburn 86 C5
Chapeltown Moray 139 B8
Chapeltown S Yorks 88 E4
Chapmans Well Devon 9 E5
Chapmanslade Wilts 24 E3
Chapmore End Herts 41 C6
Chappel Essex 42 B4
Chard Som 11 D8
Chardstock Devon 11 D8
Charfield S Glos 36 E4
Charford Worcs 50 C4
Charing Kent 30 E3
Charing Cross Dorset 14 C2
Charing Heath Kent 30 E3
Charingworth Glos 51 F7
Charlbury Oxon 38 C3
Charlcombe Bath 24 C2
Charlecote Warks 51 D7
Charles Devon 21 F5
Charles Tye Suff 56 D4
Charlesfield Dumfries 107 C8
Charleston Angus 134 E3
Charleston Renfs 118 C4
Charlestown Aberdeen 141 D8
Charlestown Corn 4 D5
Charlestown Derbys 87 E8
Charlestown Dorset 12 G4
Charlestown Fife 128 F2
Charlestown Gtr Man 87 D6
Charlestown Highld 149 A13
Charlestown Highld 151 G9
Charlestown W Yorks 87 B7
Charlestown of Aberlour Moray 152 D2
Charlesworth Derbys 87 E8
Charleton Devon 7 E5
Charlton Hants 25 E8
Charlton Herts 40 B4
Charlton London 28 B5
Charlton Northants 52 F3
Charlton Northumb 116 F4
Charlton Som 23 D8
Charlton Telford 61 C5
Charlton W Sus 16 C2
Charlton Wilts 13 B7
Charlton Wilts 25 D6
Charlton Wilts 37 F6
Charlton Worcs 50 E5
Charlton Abbots Glos 37 B7
Charlton Adam Som 12 B3
Charlton-All-Saints Wilts 14 B2
Charlton Down Dorset 12 E4
Charlton Horethorne Som 12 B4
Charlton Kings Glos 37 B6
Charlton Mackerell Som 12 B3
Charlton Marshall Dorset 13 D6
Charlton Musgrove Som 12 B5
Charlton on Otmoor Oxon 39 C5
Charltons Redcar 102 C4
Charlwood Sur 28 E3
Charlynch Som 22 F4
Charminster Dorset 12 E4
Charmouth Dorset 11 E8
Charndon Bucks 39 B6
Charney Bassett Oxon 38 E3
Charnock Richard Lancs 86 C3
Charsfield Suff 57 D6
Chart Corner Kent 29 D8
Chart Sutton Kent 30 E2
Charter Alley Hants 26 D3
Charterhouse Som 23 D6
Charterville Allotments Oxon 38 C3
Chartham Kent 30 D5
Chartham Hatch Kent 30 D5
Chartridge Bucks 40 D2
Charvil Wokingham 27 B5
Charwelton Northants 52 D3
Chasetown Staffs 62 D4
Chastleton Oxon 38 B2
Chasty Devon 8 D5
Chatburn Lancs 93 E7
Chatcull Staffs 74 F4
Chatham Medway 29 C8
Chathill Northumb 117 B7
Chattenden Medway 29 B8
Chatteris Cambs 66 F3
Chattisham Suff 56 E4
Chatto Borders 116 C3
Chatton Northumb 117 B6
Chawleigh Devon 10 C2
Chawley Oxon 38 D4
Chawston Bedford 54 D2
Chawton Hants 26 F5
Cheadle Gtr Man 87 F6
Cheadle Staffs 75 E7
Cheadle Heath Gtr Man 87 F6
Cheadle Hulme Gtr Man 87 F6
Cheam London 28 C3
Cheapside Sur 27 D8
Chearsley Bucks 39 C7
Chebsey Staffs 62 B2
Checkendon Oxon 39 F6
Checkley Ches E 74 E4
Checkley Hereford 49 F7
Checkley Staffs 75 F7
Chedburgh Suff 55 D8
Cheddar Som 23 D6
Cheddington Bucks 40 C2
Cheddleton Staffs 75 D6
Cheddon Fitzpaine Som 11 B7
Chedglow Wilts 37 E6
Chedgrave Norf 69 E6
Chedington Dorset 12 D2
Chediston Suff 57 B7
Chedworth Glos 37 C7
Chedzoy Som 22 F5
Cheeklaw Borders 122 D3
Cheeseman's Green Kent 19 B7
Cheglinch Devon 20 E4
Cheldon Devon 10 C2
Chelford Ches E 74 B5
Chell Heath Stoke 75 D5
Chellaston Derby 76 F3
Chellington Bedford 53 D7
Chelmarsh Shrops 61 F7
Chelmer Village Essex 42 D3
Chelmondiston Suff 57 F6
Chelmorton Derbys 75 C8
Chelmsford Essex 42 D3
Chelsea London 28 B3
Chelsfield London 29 C5
Chelsworth Suff 56 E3
Cheltenham Glos 37 B6
Chelveston Northants 53 C7
Chelvey N Som 23 C6
Chelwood Bath 23 C8
Chelwood Common E Sus 17 B8
Chelwood Gate E Sus 17 B8
Chelworth Wilts 37 E6
Chelworth Green Wilts 37 E7
Chemistry Shrops 74 E2
Chenies Bucks 40 E3
Cheny Longville Shrops 60 F4
Chepstow = Cas-gwent Mon 36 E2
Chequerfield W Yorks 89 B5
Cherhill Wilts 24 B5
Cherington Glos 37 E6
Cherington Warks 51 F7
Cheriton Devon 21 E6
Cheriton Hants 15 B6
Cheriton Kent 19 B8
Cheriton Swansea 33 E5
Cheriton Bishop Devon 10 E2
Cheriton Fitzpaine Devon 10 D3
Cheriton or Stackpole Elidor Pembs 44 F4
Cherrington Telford 61 B6
Cherry Burton E Yorks 97 E5
Cherry Hinton Cambs 55 D5
Cherry Orchard Worcs 50 D3
Cherry Willingham Lincs 78 B3
Cherrybank Perth 128 B3
Chertsey Sur 27 C8
Cheselbourne Dorset 13 E5
Chesham Bucks 40 D2
Chesham Bois Bucks 40 E2
Cheshunt Herts 41 D6
Cheslyn Hay Staffs 62 D3
Chessington London 28 C2
Chester Ches W 73 C8
Chester-Le-Street Durham 111 D5
Chester Moor Durham 111 E5
Chesterblade Som 23 E8
Chesterfield Derbys 76 B3
Chesters Borders 116 B2
Chesters Borders 116 C2
Chesterton Cambs 55 C5
Chesterton Cambs 65 E8
Chesterton Glos 37 D7
Chesterton Oxon 39 B5
Chesterton Shrops 61 E7
Chesterton Staffs 74 E5
Chesterton Warks 51 D8
Chesterwood Northumb 109 C8
Chestfield Kent 30 C5
Cheston Devon 6 D4
Cheswardine Shrops 61 B7
Cheswick Northumb 123 E6
Chetnole Dorset 12 D4
Chettiscombe Devon 10 C4
Chettisham Cambs 66 F5
Chettle Dorset 13 C7
Chetton Shrops 61 E6
Chetwode Bucks 39 B6
Chetwynd Aston Telford 61 C7
Cheveley Cambs 55 C7
Chevening Kent 29 D5
Chevington Suff 55 D8
Chevithorne Devon 10 C4
Chew Magna Bath 23 C7
Chew Stoke Bath 23 C7
Chewton Keynsham Bath 23 C8
Chewton Mendip Som 23 D7
Chicheley M Keynes 53 E7
Chichester W Sus 16 D2
Chickerell Dorset 12 F4
Chicklade Wilts 24 F4
Chicksgrove Wilts 24 F4
Chidden Hants 15 C7
Chiddingfold Sur 27 F7
Chiddingly E Sus 18 D2
Chiddingstone Kent 29 E5
Chiddingstone Causeway Kent 29 E6
Chiddingstone Hoath Kent 29 E5
Chideock Dorset 12 E2
Chidham W Sus 15 D8
Chidswell W Yorks 88 B3
Chieveley W Berks 26 B2
Chignall Smealy Essex 42 C2
Chignall St James Essex 42 D2
Chigwell Essex 41 E7
Chigwell Row Essex 41 E7
Chilbolton Hants 25 F8
Chilcomb Hants 15 B6
Chilcombe Dorset 12 E3
Chilcompton Som 23 D8
Chilcote Leics 63 C6
Child Okeford Dorset 13 C6
Childer Thornton Ches W 73 B7
Childrey Oxon 38 F3
Child's Ercall Shrops 61 B6
Childswickham Worcs 51 F5
Childwall Mers 86 F2
Childwick Green Herts 40 C4
Chilfrome Dorset 12 E3
Chilgrove W Sus 16 C2
Chilham Kent 30 D4
Chilhampton Wilts 25 F5
Chilla Devon 9 D6
Chillaton Devon 9 F6
Chillenden Kent 31 D6
Chillerton IoW 15 F5
Chillesford Suff 57 D7
Chillingham Northumb 117 B6
Chillington Devon 7 E5
Chillington Som 11 C8
Chilmark Wilts 24 F4
Chilson Oxon 38 C3
Chilsworthy Corn 6 B2
Chilsworthy Devon 8 D5
Chilthorne Domer Som 12 C3
Chiltington E Sus 17 C7
Chilton Bucks 39 C6
Chilton Durham 101 B7
Chilton Oxon 38 F4
Chilton Cantelo Som 12 B3
Chilton Foliat Wilts 25 B8
Chilton Lane Durham 111 F6
Chilton Polden Som 23 F5
Chilton Street Suff 55 E8
Chilton Trinity Som 22 F4
Chilvers Coton Warks 63 E7
Chilwell Notts 76 F5
Chilworth Hants 14 C5
Chilworth Sur 27 E8
Chimney Oxon 38 D3
Chineham Hants 26 D4
Chingford London 41 E6
Chinley Derbys 87 F8
Chinley Head Derbys 87 F8
Chinnor Oxon 39 D7
Chipnall Shrops 74 F4
Chippenhall Green Suff 57 B6
Chippenham Cambs 55 C7
Chippenham Wilts 24 B4
Chipperfield Herts 40 D3
Chipping Herts 54 F4
Chipping Lancs 93 E6
Chipping Campden Glos 51 F6
Chipping Hill Essex 42 C4
Chipping Norton Oxon 38 B3
Chipping Ongar Essex 42 D1
Chipping Sodbury S Glos 36 F4
Chipping Warden Northants 52 E2
Chipstable Som 10 B5
Chipstead Kent 29 D5
Chipstead Sur 28 D3
Chirbury Shrops 60 E2
Chirk = Y Waun Wrex 73 F6
Chirk Bank Shrops 73 F6
Chirmorrie S Ayrs 105 B6
Chirnside Borders 122 D4
Chirnsidebridge Borders 122 D4
Chirton Wilts 25 D5
Chisbury Wilts 25 C7
Chiselborough Som 12 C2
Chiseldon Swindon 25 B6
Chiserley W Yorks 87 B8
Chislehampton Oxon 39 E5
Chislehurst London 28 B5
Chislet Kent 31 C6
Chiswell Green Herts 40 D4
Chiswick London 28 B3
Chiswick End Cambs 54 E4
Chisworth Derbys 87 E7
Chithurst W Sus 16 B2
Chittering Cambs 55 B5
Chitterne Wilts 24 E4
Chittlehamholt Devon 9 B8
Chittlehampton Devon 9 B8
Chittoe Wilts 24 C4
Chivenor Devon 20 F4
Chobham Sur 27 C7
Choicelee Borders 122 D3
Cholderton Wilts 25 E7
Cholesbury Bucks 40 D2
Chollerford Northumb 110 B2
Chollerton Northumb 110 B2
Cholmondeston Ches E 74 C3
Cholsey Oxon 39 F5
Cholstrey Hereford 49 D6
Chop Gate N Yorks 102 E3
Choppington Northumb 117 F8
Chopwell T&W 110 D4
Chorley Ches E 74 D2
Chorley Lancs 86 C3
Chorley Shrops 61 F6
Chorley Staffs 62 C4
Chorleywood Herts 40 E3
Chorlton cum Hardy Gtr Man 87 E6
Chorlton Lane Ches W 73 E8
Choulton Shrops 60 F3
Chowdene T&W 111 D5
Chowley Ches W 73 D8
Chrishall Essex 54 F5
Christchurch Cambs 66 E4
Christchurch Dorset 14 E2
Christchurch Glos 36 C2
Christchurch Newport 35 F7
Christian Malford Wilts 24 B4
Christleton Ches W 73 C8
Christmas Common Oxon 39 E7
Christon N Som 23 D5
Christon Bank Northumb 117 B8
Christow Devon 10 F3
Chryston N Lanark 119 B6
Chudleigh Devon 7 B6
Chudleigh Knighton Devon 7 B6
Chulmleigh Devon 9 C8
Chunal Derbys 87 E8
Church Lancs 86 B5
Church Aston Telford 61 C7
Church Brampton Northants 52 C5
Church Broughton Derbys 76 F2
Church Crookham Hants 27 D6
Church Eaton Staffs 62 C2
Church End C Beds 40 B2
Church End C Beds 53 F7
Church End C Beds 53 F8
Church End Cambs 66 D3
Church End Cambs 66 F2
Church End E Yorks 97 D6
Church End Essex 42 B3
Church End Essex 55 E6
Church End Hants 26 D4
Church End Lincs 78 F5
Church End Warks 63 E6
Church End Warks 63 E6
Church End Wilts 24 B5
Church Enstone Oxon 38 B3
Church Fenton N Yorks 95 F8
Church Green Devon 11 E6
Church Green Norf 68 E3
Church Gresley Derbys 63 C6
Church Hanborough Oxon 38 C4
Church Hill Ches W 74 C3
Church Houses N Yorks 102 E4
Church Knowle Dorset 13 F7
Church Laneham Notts 77 B8
Church Langton Leics 64 E4
Church Lawford Warks 52 B2
Church Lawton Ches E 74 D5
Church Leigh Staffs 75 F7
Church Lench Worcs 50 D5
Church Mayfield Staffs 75 E8
Church Minshull Ches E 74 C3
Church Norton W Sus 16 E2
Church Preen Shrops 60 E5
Church Pulverbatch Shrops 60 D4
Church Stoke Powys 60 E2
Church Stowe Northants 52 D4
Church Street Kent 29 B8
Church Stretton Shrops 60 E4
Church Town N Lincs 89 D8
Church Town Sur 28 D4
Church Village Rhondda 34 F4
Church Warsop Notts 77 C5
Churcham Glos 36 C4
Churchbank Shrops 48 B4
Churchbridge Staffs 62 D3
Churchdown Glos 37 C5
Churchend Essex 42 B2
Churchend Essex 43 E6
Churchend S Glos 36 E4
Churchfield W Mid 62 E4
Churchgate Street Essex 41 C7
Churchill Devon 11 D8
Churchill Devon 20 E4
Churchill N Som 23 D6
Churchill Oxon 38 B2
Churchill Worcs 50 B3
Churchill Worcs 50 D4
Churchinford Som 11 C7
Churchover Warks 64 F2
Churchstanton Som 11 C6
Churchstow Devon 6 E5
Churchtown Derbys 76 C2
Churchtown IoM 84 C4
Churchtown Lancs 92 E4

Golden Hill Hants 14 E3
Golden Pot Hants 26 E5
Golden Valley Glos 37 B6
Goldenhill Stoke 75 D5
Golders Green London 41 F5
Goldhanger Essex 43 D5
Golding Shrops 60 D5
Goldington Bedford 53 D8
Goldsborough N Yorks 95 D6
Goldsborough N Yorks 103 C6
Goldsithney Corn 2 C4
Goldsworthy Devon 9 B5
Goldthorpe S Yorks 89 D5
Gollanfield Highld 151 F11
Golspie Highld 157 J11
Golval Highld 157 C11
Gomeldon Wilts 25 F6
Gomersal W Yorks 88 B3
Gomshall Sur 27 E8
Gonalston Notts 77 E6
Gonfirth Shetland 160 G5
Good Easter Essex 42 C2
Gooderstone Norf 67 D7
Goodleigh Devon 20 F5
Goodmanham E Yorks 96 E4
Goodnestone Kent 30 C4
Goodnestone Kent 31 D6
Goodrich Hereford 36 C2
Goodrington Torbay 7 D6
Goodshaw Lancs 87 B6
Goodwick = Wdig Pembs 44 B4
Goodworth Clatford Hants 25 E8
Goole E Yorks 89 B8
Goonbell Corn 3 B6
Goonhavern Corn 4 D2
Goose Eye W Yorks 94 E3
Goose Green Gtr Man 86 D3
Goose Green Norf 68 F4
Goose Green W Sus 16 C5
Gooseham Corn 8 C4
Goosey Oxon 38 E3
Goosnargh Lancs 93 F5
Goostrey Ches E 74 B4
Gorcott Hill Warks 51 C5
Gord Shetland 160 L6
Gordon Borders 122 E2
Gordonbush Highld 157 J11
Gordonsburgh Moray 152 B4
Gordonstoun Moray 152 B1
Gordonstown Aberds 152 C5
Gordonstown Aberds 153 E7
Gore Kent 31 D7
Gore Cross Wilts 24 D5
Gore Pit Essex 42 C4
Gorebridge Midloth 121 C6
Gorefield Cambs 66 C4
Gorey Jersey 17
Gorgie Edin 120 B5
Goring Oxon 39 F6
Goring-by-Sea W Sus 16 D5
Goring Heath Oxon 26 B4
Gorleston-on-Sea Norf 69 D8
Gornalwood W Mid 62 E3
Gorrachie Aberds 153 C7
Gorran Churchtown Corn 3 B8
Gorran Haven Corn 3 B9
Gorrenberry Borders 115 E7
Gors Ceredig 46 B5
Gorse Hill Swindon 38 F1
Gorsedd Flint 73 B5
Gorseinon Swansea 33 E6
Gorseness Orkney 159 G5
Gorsgoch Ceredig 46 D3
Gorslas Carms 33 C6
Gorsley Glos 36 B3
Gorstan Highld 150 E6
Gorstanvorran Highld 130 B2
Gorsteyhill Staffs 74 D4
Gorsty Hill Staffs 62 B5
Gortantaoid Argyll 142 A4
Gorton Gtr Man 87 E6
Gosbeck Suff 57 D5
Gosberton Lincs 78 F5
Gosberton Clough Lincs 65 B8
Gosfield Essex 42 B3
Gosford Hereford 49 C7
Gosforth Cumb 98 D2
Gosforth T&W 110 C5
Gosmore Herts 40 B4
Gosport Hants 15 E7
Gossabrough Shetland 160 E7
Gossington Glos 36 D4
Goswick Northumb 123 E6
Gotham Notts 76 F5
Gotherington Glos 37 B6
Gott Shetland 160 J6
Goudhurst Kent 18 B4
Goulceby Lincs 79 B5
Gourdas Aberds 153 D7
Gourdon Aberds 135 B8
Gourock Invclyd 118 B2
Govan Glasgow 119 C5
Govanhill Glasgow 119 C5
Goveton Devon 7 E5
Govilon Mon 35 C6
Gowanhill Aberds 153 B10
Gowdall E Yorks 89 B7
Gowerton Swansea 33 E6
Gowkhall Fife 128 F2
Gowthorpe E Yorks 96 D3
Goxhill E Yorks 97 E7
Goxhill N Lincs 90 B5
Goxhill Haven N Lincs 90 B5
Goybre Neath 34 F1
Grabhair W Isles 155 F8
Graby Lincs 65 B7
Grade Corn 3 E6
Graffham W Sus 16 C3
Grafham Cambs 54 C2
Grafham Sur 27 E8
Grafton Hereford 49 F6
Grafton N Yorks 95 C7
Grafton Oxon 38 D2
Grafton Shrops 60 C4
Grafton Worcs 49 C7
Grafton Flyford Worcs 50 D4
Grafton Regis Northants 53 E5
Grafton Underwood Northants 65 F6
Grafty Green Kent 30 E2
Graianrhyd Denb 73 D6
Graig Conwy 83 D8
Graig Denb 72 B4
Graig-fechan Denb 72 D5
Grain Medway 30 B2
Grainsby Lincs 91 E6
Grainthorpe Lincs 91 E7
Grampound Corn 3 B8
Grampound Road Corn 4 D4
Gramsdal W Isles 148 C3
Granborough Bucks 39 B7
Granby Notts 77 F7
Grandborough Warks 52 C2
Grandtully Perth 133 D6
Grange Cumb 98 C4
Grange E Ayrs 118 F4
Grange Medway 29 C8
Grange Mers 85 F3
Grange Perth 128 B4
Grange Crossroads Moray 152 C4
Grange Hall Moray 151 E13
Grange Hill Essex 41 E7
Grange Moor W Yorks 88 C3
Grange of Lindores Fife 128 C4
Grange-over-Sands Cumb 92 B4
Grange Villa Durham 110 D5
Grangemill Derbys 76 D2
Grangemouth Falk 127 F8
Grangepans Falk 128 F2
Grangetown Cardiff 22 B3
Grangetown Redcar 102 B3
Granish Highld 138 C5
Gransmoor E Yorks 97 D7
Granston Pembs 44 B3
Grantchester Cambs 54 D5
Grantham Lincs 78 F2
Grantley N Yorks 94 C5
Grantlodge Aberds 141 C6
Granton Dumfries 114 D3
Granton Edin 120 B5
Grantown-on-Spey Highld 139 B6
Grantshouse Borders 122 C4
Grappenhall Warr 86 F4
Grasby Lincs 90 D4
Grasmere Cumb 99 D5
Grasscroft Gtr Man 87 D7
Grassendale Mers 85 F4
Grassholme Durham 100 B4
Grassington N Yorks 94 C3
Grassmoor Derbys 76 C4
Grassthorpe Notts 77 C7
Grateley Hants 25 E7
Gratwich Staffs 75 F7
Graveley Cambs 54 C3
Graveley Herts 41 B5
Gravelly Hill W Mid 62 E5
Gravels Shrops 60 D3
Graven Shetland 160 F6
Graveney Kent 30 C4
Gravesend Herts 41 B7
Gravesend Kent 29 B7
Grayingham Lincs 90 E3
Grayrigg Cumb 99 E7
Grays Thurrock 29 B7
Grayshott Hants 27 F6
Grayswood Sur 27 F7
Graythorp Hrtlpl 102 B3
Grazeley Wokingham 26 C4
Greasbrough S Yorks 88 E5
Greasby Mers 85 F3
Great Abington Cambs 55 E6
Great Addington Northants 53 B7
Great Alne Warks 51 D6
Great Altcar Lancs 85 D4
Great Amwell Herts 41 C6
Great Asby Cumb 100 C1
Great Ashfield Suff 56 C3
Great Ayton N Yorks 102 C3
Great Baddow Essex 42 D3
Great Bardfield Essex 55 F7
Great Barford Bedford 54 D2
Great Barr W Mid 62 E4
Great Barrington Glos 38 C2
Great Barrow Ches W 73 C8
Great Barton Suff 56 C2
Great Barugh N Yorks 96 B3
Great Bavington Northumb 117 F5
Great Bealings Suff 57 E6
Great Bedwyn Wilts 25 C7
Great Bentley Essex 43 B7
Great Billing Northants 53 C6
Great Bircham Norf 80 D3
Great Blakenham Suff 56 D5
Great Blencow Cumb 108 F4
Great Bolas Telford 61 B6
Great Bookham Sur 28 D2
Great Bourton Oxon 52 E2
Great Bowden Leics 64 F4
Great Bradley Suff 55 D7
Great Braxted Essex 42 C4
Great Bricett Suff 56 D4
Great Brickhill Bucks 53 F7
Great Bridge W Mid 62 E3
Great Bridgeford Staffs 62 B2
Great Brington Northants 52 C4
Great Bromley Essex 43 B6
Great Broughton Cumb 107 F7
Great Broughton N Yorks 102 D3
Great Budworth Ches W 74 B3
Great Burdon Darl 101 C8
Great Burgh Sur 28 D3
Great Burstead Essex 42 E2
Great Busby N Yorks 102 D3
Great Canfield Essex 42 C1
Great Carlton Lincs 91 F8
Great Casterton Rutland 65 D7
Great Chart Kent 30 E3
Great Chatwell Staffs 61 C7
Great Chesterford Essex 55 E6
Great Cheverell Wilts 24 D4
Great Chishill Cambs 54 F5
Great Clacton Essex 43 C7
Great Cliff W Yorks 88 C4
Great Clifton Cumb 98 B2
Great Coates NE Lincs 91 D6
Great Comberton Worcs 50 E4
Great Corby Cumb 108 D4
Great Cornard Suff 56 E2
Great Cowden E Yorks 97 E8
Great Coxwell Oxon 38 E2
Great Crakehall N Yorks 101 E7
Great Cransley Northants 53 B6
Great Cressingham Norf 67 D8
Great Crosby Mers 85 E4
Great Cubley Derbys 75 F8
Great Dalby Leics 64 C4
Great Denham Bedford 53 E8
Great Doddington Northants 53 C6
Great Dunham Norf 67 C8
Great Dunmow Essex 42 B2
Great Durnford Wilts 25 F6
Great Easton Essex 42 B2
Great Easton Leics 64 E5
Great Eccleston Lancs 92 E4
Great Edstone N Yorks 103 F5
Great Ellingham Norf 68 E3
Great Elm Som 24 E2
Great Eversden Cambs 54 D4
Great Fencote N Yorks 101 E7
Great Finborough Suff 56 D4
Great Fransham Norf 67 C8
Great Gaddesden Herts 40 C3
Great Gidding Cambs 65 F8
Great Givendale E Yorks 96 D4
Great Glemham Suff 57 C7
Great Glen Leics 64 E3
Great Gonerby Lincs 77 F8
Great Gransden Cambs 54 D3
Great Green Norf 69 F5
Great Green Suff 56 D3
Great Habton N Yorks 96 B3
Great Hale Lincs 78 E4
Great Hallingbury Essex 41 C8
Great Hampden Bucks 39 D8
Great Harrowden Northants 53 B6
Great Harwood Lancs 93 F7
Great Haseley Oxon 39 D6
Great Hatfield E Yorks 97 E7
Great Haywood Staffs 62 B4
Great Heath W Mid 63 F7
Great Heck N Yorks 89 B6
Great Henny Essex 56 F2
Great Hinton Wilts 24 D4
Great Hockham Norf 68 E2
Great Holland Essex 43 C8
Great Horkesley Essex 56 F3
Great Hormead Herts 41 B6
Great Horton W Yorks 94 F4
Great Horwood Bucks 53 F5
Great Houghton Northants 53 D5
Great Houghton S Yorks 88 D5
Great Hucklow Derbys 75 B8
Great Kelk E Yorks 97 D7
Great Kimble Bucks 39 D8
Great Kingshill Bucks 40 E1
Great Langton N Yorks 101 E7
Great Leighs Essex 42 C3
Great Lever Gtr Man 86 D5
Great Limber Lincs 90 D5
Great Linford M Keynes 53 E6
Great Livermere Suff 56 B2
Great Longstone Derbys 76 B2
Great Lumley Durham 111 E5
Great Lyth Shrops 60 D4
Great Malvern Worcs 50 E2
Great Maplestead Essex 56 F2
Great Marton Blackpool 92 F3
Great Massingham Norf 80 E3
Great Melton Norf 68 D4
Great Milton Oxon 39 D6
Great Missenden Bucks 40 D1
Great Mitton Lancs 93 F7
Great Mongeham Kent 31 D7
Great Moulton Norf 68 E4
Great Munden Herts 41 B6
Great Musgrave Cumb 100 C2
Great Ness Shrops 60 C3
Great Notley Essex 42 B3
Great Oakley Essex 43 B7
Great Oakley Northants 65 F5
Great Offley Herts 40 B4
Great Ormside Cumb 100 C2
Great Orton Cumb 108 D3
Great Ouseburn N Yorks 95 C7
Great Oxendon Northants 64 F4
Great Oxney Green Essex 42 D2
Great Palgrave Norf 67 C8
Great Parndon Essex 41 D7
Great Paxton Cambs 54 C3
Great Plumpton Lancs 92 F3
Great Plumstead Norf 69 C6
Great Ponton Lincs 78 F2
Great Preston W Yorks 88 B5
Great Raveley Cambs 66 F2
Great Rissington Glos 38 C1
Great Rollright Oxon 51 F8
Great Ryburgh Norf 81 E5
Great Ryle Northumb 117 C6
Great Ryton Shrops 60 D4
Great Saling Essex 42 B3
Great Salkeld Cumb 109 F5
Great Sampford Essex 55 F7
Great Sankey Warr 86 F3
Great Saxham Suff 55 C8
Great Shefford W Berks 25 B8
Great Shelford Cambs 55 D5
Great Smeaton N Yorks 101 D8
Great Snoring Norf 80 D5
Great Somerford Wilts 37 F6
Great Stainton Darl 101 B8
Great Stambridge Essex 42 E4
Great Staughton Cambs 54 C2
Great Steeping Lincs 79 C7
Great Stonar Kent 31 D7
Great Strickland Cumb 99 B7
Great Stukeley Cambs 54 B3
Great Sturton Lincs 78 B5
Great Sutton Ches W 73 B7
Great Sutton Shrops 60 F5
Great Swinburne Northumb 110 B2
Great Tew Oxon 38 B3
Great Tey Essex 42 B4
Great Thurkleby N Yorks 95 B7
Great Thurlow Suff 55 D7
Great Torrington Devon 9 C6
Great Tosson Northumb 117 D6
Great Totham Essex 42 C4
Great Totham Essex 42 C4
Great Tows Lincs 91 E6
Great Urswick Cumb 92 B2
Great Wakering Essex 43 F5
Great Waldingfield Suff 56 E3
Great Walsingham Norf 80 D5
Great Waltham Essex 42 C2
Great Warley Essex 42 E1
Great Washbourne Glos 50 F4
Great Weldon Northants 65 F6
Great Welnetham Suff 56 D2
Great Wenham Suff 56 F4
Great Whittington Northumb 110 B3
Great Wigborough Essex 43 C5
Great Wilbraham Cambs 55 D6
Great Wishford Wilts 25 F5
Great Witcombe Glos 37 C6
Great Witley Worcs 50 C2
Great Wolford Warks 51 F7
Great Wratting Suff 55 E7
Great Wymondley Herts 41 B5
Great Wyrley Staffs 62 D3
Great Wytheford Shrops 61 C5
Great Yarmouth Norf 69 D8
Great Yeldham Essex 55 F8
Greater Doward Hereford 36 C2
Greatford Lincs 65 C7
Greatgate Staffs 75 E7
Greatham Hants 27 F5
Greatham Hrtlpl 102 B2
Greatham W Sus 16 C4
Greatstone on Sea Kent 19 C7
Greatworth Northants 52 E3
Greave Lancs 87 B6
Greeba IoM 84 D3
Green Denb 72 C4
Green End Bedford 54 D2
Green Hammerton N Yorks 95 D7
Green Lane Powys 59 E8
Green Ore Som 23 D7
Green St Green London 29 C5
Green Street Herts 40 E4
Greenbank Shetland 160 C7
Greenburn W Loth 120 C2
Greendikes Northumb 117 B6
Greenfield C Beds 53 F8
Greenfield Flint 73 B5
Greenfield Gtr Man 87 D7
Greenfield Highld 136 D5
Greenfield Oxon 39 E7
Greenford London 40 F4
Greengairs N Lanark 119 B7
Greenham W Berks 26 C2
Greenhaugh Northumb 116 F3
Greenhead Northumb 109 C6
Greenhill Falk 119 B8
Greenhill Kent 31 C5
Greenhill Leics 63 C8
Greenhill London 40 F4
Greenhills N Ayrs 118 D3
Greenhithe Kent 29 B6
Greenholm E Ayrs 118 F5
Greenholme Cumb 99 D7
Greenhouse Borders 115 B8
Greenhow Hill N Yorks 94 C4
Greenigoe Orkney 159 H5
Greenland Highld 158 D4
Greenlands Bucks 39 F7
Greenlaw Aberds 153 C6
Greenlaw Borders 122 E3
Greenlea Dumfries 107 B7
Greenloaning Perth 127 D7
Greenmount Gtr Man 87 C5
Greenmow Shetland 160 L6
Greenock Invclyd 118 B2
Greenock West Invclyd 118 B2
Greenodd Cumb 99 F5
Greenrow Cumb 107 D8
Greens Norton Northants 52 E4
Greenside T&W 110 C4
Greensidehill Northumb 117 C5
Greenstead Green Essex 42 B4
Greensted Essex 41 D8
Greenwich London 28 B4
Greet Glos 50 F5
Greete Shrops 49 B7
Greetham Lincs 79 B6
Greetham Rutland 65 C6
Greetland W Yorks 87 B8
Gregg Hall Cumb 99 E6
Gregson Lane Lancs 86 B3
Greinetobht W Isles 148 A3
Greinton Som 23 F6
Gremista Shetland 160 J6
Grenaby IoM 84 E2
Grendon Northants 53 C6
Grendon Warks 63 D6
Grendon Common Warks 63 E6
Grendon Green Hereford 49 D7
Grendon Underwood Bucks 39 B6
Grenofen Devon 6 B2
Grenoside S Yorks 88 E4
Greosabhagh W Isles 154 H6
Gresford Wrex 73 D7
Gresham Norf 81 D7
Greshornish Highld 149 C8
Gressenhall Norf 68 C2
Gressingham Lancs 93 C5
Gresty Green Ches E 74 D4
Greta Bridge Durham 101 C5
Gretna Dumfries 108 C3
Gretna Green Dumfries 108 C3
Gretton Glos 50 F5
Gretton Northants 65 E5
Gretton Shrops 60 E5
Grewelthorpe N Yorks 94 B5
Grey Green N Lincs 89 D8
Greygarth N Yorks 94 B4
Greynor Carms 33 D6
Greysouthen Cumb 98 B2
Greystoke Cumb 108 F4
Greystone Angus 135 E5
Greystone Dumfries 107 B6
Greywell Hants 26 D5
Griais W Isles 155 C9
Grianan W Isles 155 D9
Gribthorpe E Yorks 96 F3
Gridley Corner Devon 9 E5
Griff Warks 63 F7
Griffithstown Torf 35 E6
Grimbister Orkney 159 G4
Grimblethorpe Lincs 91 F6
Grimeford Village Lancs 86 C4
Grimethorpe S Yorks 88 D5
Griminis W Isles 148 C2
Grimister Shetland 160 D6
Grimley Worcs 50 C3
Grimness Orkney 159 J5
Grimoldby Lincs 91 F7
Grimpo Shrops 60 B3
Grimsargh Lancs 93 F5
Grimsbury Oxon 52 E2
Grimsby NE Lincs 91 C6
Grimscote Northants 52 D4
Grimscott Corn 8 D4
Grimsthorpe Lincs 65 B7
Grimston E Yorks 97 F8
Grimston Leics 64 B3
Grimston Norf 80 E3
Grimston York 96 D2
Grimstone Dorset 12 E4
Grinacombe Moor Devon 9 E6
Grindale E Yorks 97 B7
Grindigar Orkney 159 H6
Grindiscol Shetland 160 K6
Grindle Shrops 61 D7
Grindleford Derbys 76 B2
Grindleton Lancs 93 E7
Grindley Staffs 62 B4
Grindley Brook Shrops 74 E2
Grindlow Derbys 75 B8
Grindon Northumb 122 E5
Grindon Staffs 75 D7
Grindonmoor Gate Staffs 75 D7
Gringley on the Hill Notts 89 E8
Grinsdale Cumb 108 D3
Grinshill Shrops 60 B5
Grinton N Yorks 101 E5
Griomsidar W Isles 155 E8
Grishipoll Argyll 146 F4
Grisling Common E Sus 17 B8
Gristhorpe N Yorks 103 F8
Griston Norf 68 E2
Gritley Orkney 159 H6
Grittenham Wilts 37 F7
Grittleton Wilts 37 F5
Grizebeck Cumb 98 F4
Grizedale Cumb 99 E5
Grobister Orkney 159 F7
Groby Leics 64 D2
Groes Conwy 72 C4
Groes Neath 34 F1
Groes-faen Rhondda 34 F4
Groes-lwyd Powys 60 C2
Groesffordd Marli Denb 72 B4
Groeslon Gwyn 82 E5
Groeslon Gwyn 82 F4
Grogport Argyll 143 D9
Gromford Suff 57 D7
Gronant Flint 72 A4
Groombridge E Sus 18 B2
Grosmont Mon 35 B8
Grosmont N Yorks 103 D6
Groton Suff 56 E3
Grougfoot Falk 120 B3
Grouville Jersey 17
Grove Dorset 12 G5
Grove Kent 31 C6
Grove Notts 77 B7
Grove Oxon 38 E4
Grove Park London 28 B5
Grove Vale W Mid 62 E4
Grovesend Swansea 33 D6
Grudie Highld 150 E6
Gruids Highld 157 J8
Gruinard House Highld 150 B2
Grula Highld 149 F8
Gruline Argyll 147 G8
Grunasound Shetland 160 K5
Grundisburgh Suff 57 D6
Grunsagill Lancs 93 D7
Gruting Shetland 160 J4
Grutness Shetland 160 N6
Gualachulain Highld 131 E5
Gualin Ho. Highld 156 D6
Guardbridge Fife 129 C6
Guarlford Worcs 50 E3
Guay Perth 133 E7
Guestling Green E Sus 19 D5
Guestling Thorn E Sus 18 D5
Guestwick Norf 81 E6
Guestwick Green Norf 81 E6
Guide Blackburn 86 B5
Guide Post Northumb 117 F8
Guilden Morden Cambs 54 E3
Guilden Sutton Ches W 73 C8
Guildford Sur 27 E7
Guildtown Perth 133 F8
Guilsborough Northants 52 B4
Guilsfield Powys 60 C2
Guilton Kent 31 D6
Guineaford Devon 20 F4
Guisborough Redcar 102 C4
Guiseley W Yorks 94 E4
Guist Norf 81 E5
Guith Orkney 159 E6
Guiting Power Glos 37 B7
Gulberwick Shetland 160 K6
Gullane E Loth 129 F6
Gulval Corn 2 C3
Gulworthy Devon 6 B2
Gumfreston Pembs 32 D2
Gumley Leics 64 E3
Gummow's Shop Corn 4 D3
Gun Hill E Sus 18 D2
Gunby E Yorks 96 F3
Gunby Lincs 65 B6
Gundleton Hants 26 F4
Gunn Devon 20 F5
Gunnerside N Yorks 100 E4
Gunnerton Northumb 110 B2
Gunness N Lincs 90 C2
Gunnislake Corn 6 B2
Gunnista Shetland 160 J7
Gunthorpe Norf 81 D6
Gunthorpe Notts 77 E6
Gunthorpe Pboro 65 D8
Gunville IoW 15 F5
Gunwalloe Corn 3 D5
Gurnard IoW 15 E5
Gurnett Ches E 75 B6
Gurney Slade Som 23 E8
Gurnos Powys 34 D1
Gussage All Saints Dorset 13 C8
Gussage St Michael Dorset 13 C7
Guston Kent 31 E7
Gutcher Shetland 160 D7
Guthrie Angus 135 D5
Guyhirn Cambs 66 D3
Guyhirn Gull Cambs 66 D3
Guy's Head Lincs 66 B4
Guy's Marsh Dorset 13 B6
Guyzance Northumb 117 D8
Gwaenysgor Flint 72 A4
Gwalchmai Anglesey 82 D3
Gwaun-Cae-Gurwen Neath 33 C8
Gwaun-Leision Neath 33 C8
Gwbert Ceredig 45 E3
Gweek Corn 3 D6
Gwehelog Mon 35 D7
Gwenddwr Powys 48 E2
Gwennap Corn 3 C6
Gwenter Corn 3 E6
Gwernaffield Flint 73 C6
Gwernesney Mon 35 D8
Gwernogle Carms 46 F4
Gwernymynydd Flint 73 C6
Gwersyllt Wrex 73 D7
Gwespyr Flint 85 F2
Gwithian Corn 2 B4
Gwredog Anglesey 82 C4
Gwyddelwern Denb 72 E4
Gwyddgrug Carms 46 F3
Gwydyr Uchaf Conwy 83 E7
Gwynfryn Wrex 73 D6
Gwystre Powys 48 C2
Gwytherin Conwy 83 E8
Gyfelia Wrex 73 E7
Gyffin Conwy 83 D7
Gyre Orkney 159 H4
Gyrn-goch Gwyn 70 C5

H

Habberley Shrops 60 D3
Habergham Lancs 93 F8
Habrough NE Lincs 90 C5
Haceby Lincs 78 F3
Hacheston Suff 57 D7
Hackbridge London 28 C3
Hackenthorpe S Yorks 88 F5
Hackford Norf 68 D3
Hackforth N Yorks 101 E7
Hackland Orkney 159 F4
Hackleton Northants 53 D6
Hackness N Yorks 103 E7
Hackness Orkney 159 J4
Hackney London 41 F6
Hackthorn Lincs 90 F3
Hackthorpe Cumb 99 B7
Haconby Lincs 65 B8
Hacton London 41 F8
Hadden Borders 122 F3
Haddenham Bucks 39 D7
Haddenham Cambs 55 B5
Haddington E Loth 121 B8
Haddington Lincs 78 C2
Haddiscoe Norf 69 E7
Haddon Cambs 65 E8
Haddon Ches E 75 C6
Hade Edge W Yorks 88 D2
Hademore Staffs 63 D5
Hadfield Derbys 87 E8
Hadham Cross Herts 41 C7
Hadham Ford Herts 41 B7
Hadleigh Essex 42 F4
Hadleigh Suff 56 E4
Hadley Telford 61 C6
Hadley End Staffs 62 B5
Hadlow Kent 29 E7
Hadlow Down E Sus 18 C2
Hadnall Shrops 60 C5
Hadstock Essex 55 E6
Hady Derbys 76 B3
Hadzor Worcs 50 C4
Haffenden Quarter Kent 30 E2
Hafod-Dinbych Conwy 83 F8
Hafod-Iom Conwy 83 D8
Haggate Lancs 93 F8
Haggbeck Cumb 108 B4
Haggerston Northumb 123 E6
Haggrister Shetland 160 F5
Hagley Hereford 49 E7
Hagley Worcs 62 F3
Hagworthingham Lincs 79 C6
Haigh Gtr Man 86 D4
Haigh S Yorks 88 C3
Haigh Moor W Yorks 88 B3
Haighton Green Lancs 93 F5
Hail Weston Cambs 54 C2
Haile Cumb 98 D2
Hailes Glos 50 F5
Hailey Herts 41 C6
Hailey Oxon 38 C3
Hailsham E Sus 18 E2
Haimer Highld 158 D3
Hainault London 41 E7
Hainford Norf 68 C5
Hainton Lincs 91 F5
Hairmyres S Lanark 119 D6
Haisthorpe E Yorks 97 C7
Hakin Pembs 44 E3
Halam Notts 77 D6
Halbeath Fife 128 F3
Halberton Devon 10 C5
Halcro Highld 158 D4
Hale Gtr Man 87 F5
Hale Halton 86 F2
Hale Hants 14 C2
Hale Bank Halton 86 F2
Hale Street Kent 29 E7
Halebarns Gtr Man 87 F5
Hales Norf 69 E6
Hales Staffs 74 F4
Hales Place Kent 30 D5
Halesfield Telford 61 D7
Halesgate Lincs 66 B3
Halesowen W Mid 62 F3
Halesworth Suff 57 B7
Halewood Mers 86 F2
Halford Shrops 60 F4
Halford Warks 51 E7
Halfpenny Furze Carms 32 C3
Halfpenny Green Staffs 62 E2
Halfway Carms 46 F5
Halfway Carms 47 F7
Halfway W Berks 26 C2
Halfway Bridge W Sus 16 B3
Halfway House Shrops 60 C3
Halfway Houses Kent 30 B3
Halifax W Yorks 87 B8
Halket E Ayrs 118 D4
Halkirk Highld 158 E3
Halkyn Flint 73 B6
Hall Dunnerdale Cumb 98 E4
Hall Green W Mid 62 F5
Hall Green W Yorks 88 C4
Hall Grove Herts 41 C5
Hall of Tankerness Orkney 159 H6
Hall of the Forest Shrops 60 F2
Halland E Sus 18 D2
Hallaton Leics 64 E4
Hallatrow Bath 23 D8
Hallbankgate Cumb 109 D5
Hallen S Glos 36 F2
Halliburton Borders 122 E2
Hallin Highld 148 C7
Halling Medway 29 C8
Hallington Lincs 91 F7
Hallington Northumb 110 B2
Halliwell Gtr Man 86 C5
Halloughton Notts 77 D6
Hallow Worcs 50 D3
Hallrule Borders 115 C8
Halls E Loth 122 B2
Hall's Green Herts 41 B5
Hallsands Devon 7 F6
Hallthwaites Cumb 98 F3
Hallworthy Corn 8 F3
Hallyburton House Perth 134 F2
Hallyne Borders 120 E4
Halmer End Staffs 74 E4
Halmore Glos 36 D3
Halmyre Mains Borders 120 E4
Halnaker W Sus 16 D3
Halsall Lancs 85 C4
Halse Northants 52 E3
Halse Som 11 B6
Halsetown Corn 2 C4
Halsham E Yorks 91 B6
Halsinger Devon 20 F4
Halstead Essex 56 F2
Halstead Kent 29 C5
Halstead Leics 64 D4
Halstock Dorset 12 D3
Haltham Lincs 78 C5
Haltoft End Lincs 79 E6
Halton Bucks 40 C1
Halton Halton 86 F3
Halton Lancs 92 C5
Halton Northumb 110 C2
Halton W Yorks 95 F6
Halton Wrex 73 F7
Halton East N Yorks 94 D3
Halton Gill N Yorks 93 B8
Halton Holegate Lincs 79 C7
Halton Lea Gate Northumb 109 D6
Halton West N Yorks 93 D8
Haltwhistle Northumb 109 C7
Halvergate Norf 69 D7
Halwell Devon 7 D5
Halwill Devon 9 E6
Halwill Junction Devon 9 D6
Ham Devon 11 D7
Ham Glos 36 E3
Ham Highld 158 C4
Ham Kent 31 D7
Ham London 28 B2
Ham Shetland 160 K1
Ham Wilts 25 C8
Ham Common Dorset 13 B6
Ham Green Hereford 50 E2
Ham Green Kent 19 C5
Ham Green Kent 30 C2
Ham Green N Som 23 B7
Ham Green Worcs 50 C5
Ham Street Som 23 F7
Hamble-le-Rice Hants 15 D5
Hambleden Bucks 39 F7
Hambledon Hants 15 C7
Hambledon Sur 27 F7
Hambleton Lancs 92 E3
Hambleton N Yorks 95 F8
Hambridge Som 11 B8
Hambrook S Glos 23 B8
Hambrook W Sus 15 D8
Hameringham Lincs 79 C6
Hamerton Cambs 54 B2
Hametoun Shetland 160 K1
Hamilton S Lanark 119 D7
Hammer W Sus 27 F6
Hammerpot W Sus 16 D4
Hammersmith London 28 B3
Hammerwich Staffs 62 D4
Hammerwood E Sus 28 F5
Hammond Street Herts 41 D6
Hammoon Dorset 13 C6
Hamnavoe Shetland 160 E4
Hamnavoe Shetland 160 E6
Hamnavoe Shetland 160 F6
Hamnavoe Shetland 160 K5
Hampden Park E Sus 18 E3
Hamperden End Essex 55 F6
Hampnett Glos 37 C7
Hampole S Yorks 89 C6
Hampreston Dorset 13 E8
Hampstead London 41 F5
Hampstead Norreys W Berks 26 B3
Hampsthwaite N Yorks 95 D5
Hampton London 28 C2
Hampton Shrops 61 F7
Hampton Worcs 50 E5
Hampton Bishop Hereford 49 F7
Hampton Heath Ches W 73 E8
Hampton in Arden W Mid 63 F6
Hampton Loade Shrops 61 F7
Hampton Lovett Worcs 50 C3
Hampton Lucy Warks 51 D7
Hampton on the Hill Warks 51 C7
Hampton Poyle Oxon 39 C5
Hamrow Norf 80 E5
Hamsey E Sus 17 C8
Hamsey Green London 28 D4
Hamstall Ridware Staffs 62 C5
Hamstead IoW 14 E5
Hamstead W Mid 62 E4
Hamstead Marshall W Berks 26 C2
Hamsterley Durham 110 D4
Hamsterley Durham 110 F4
Hamstreet Kent 19 B7
Hamworthy Poole 13 E7
Hanbury Staffs 63 B5
Hanbury Worcs 50 C4
Hanbury Woodend Staffs 63 B5
Hanby Lincs 78 F3
Hanchurch Staffs 74 E5
Handbridge Ches W 73 C8
Handcross W Sus 17 B6
Handforth Ches E 87 F6
Handley Ches W 73 D8
Handsacre Staffs 62 C4
Handsworth S Yorks 88 F5
Handsworth W Mid 62 E4
Handy Cross Devon 9 B6
Hanford Stoke 75 E5
Hanging Langford Wilts 24 F5
Hangleton W Sus 16 D4
Hanham S Glos 23 B8
Hankelow Ches E 74 E3
Hankerton Wilts 37 E6
Hankham E Sus 18 E3
Hanley Stoke 75 E5
Hanley Castle Worcs 50 E3
Hanley Child Worcs 49 C8
Hanley Swan Worcs 50 E3
Hanley William Worcs 49 C8
Hanlith N Yorks 94 C2
Hanmer Wrex 73 F8
Hannah Lincs 79 B8
Hannington Hants 26 D3
Hannington Northants 53 B6
Hannington Swindon 38 E1
Hannington Wick Swindon 38 E1
Hansel Village S Ayrs 118 F3
Hanslope M Keynes 53 E6
Hanthorpe Lincs 65 B7
Hanwell London 40 F4
Hanwell Oxon 52 E2
Hanwood Shrops 60 D4
Hanworth London 28 B2
Hanworth Norf 81 D7
Happendon S Lanark 119 F8
Happisburgh Norf 69 A6
Happisburgh Common Norf 69 B6
Hapsford Ches W 73 B8
Hapton Lancs 93 F7
Hapton Norf 68 E4
Harberton Devon 7 D5
Harbertonford Devon 7 D5
Harbledown Kent 30 D5
Harborne W Mid 62 F4
Harborough Magna Warks 52 B2
Harbottle Northumb 117 D5
Harbury Warks 51 D8
Harby Leics 77 F7
Harby Notts 77 B8
Harcombe Devon 11 E6
Harden W Mid 62 D4
Harden W Yorks 94 F3
Hardenhuish Wilts 24 B4
Hardgate Aberds 141 D6
Hardham W Sus 16 C4
Hardingham Norf 68 D3
Hardingstone Northants 53 D5
Hardington Som 24 D2
Hardington Mandeville Som 12 C3
Hardington Marsh Som 12 D3
Hardley Hants 14 D5
Hardley Street Norf 69 D6
Hardmead M Keynes 53 E7
Hardrow N Yorks 100 E3
Hardstoft Derbys 76 C4
Hardway Hants 15 D7
Hardway Som 24 F2
Hardwick Bucks 39 C8
Hardwick Cambs 54 D4
Hardwick Norf 67 C6
Hardwick Norf 68 F5
Hardwick Northants 53 C6
Hardwick Notts 77 B6
Hardwick Oxon 38 D3
Hardwick Oxon 39 B5
Hardwick W Mid 62 E4
Hardwicke Glos 36 C4
Hardwicke Glos 37 B6
Hardwicke Hereford 48 E4
Hardy's Green Essex 43 B5
Hare Green Essex 43 B6
Hare Hatch Wokingham 27 B6
Hare Street Herts 41 B6
Hareby Lincs 79 C6
Hareden Lancs 93 D6
Harefield London 40 E3
Harehills W Yorks 95 F6
Harehope Northumb 117 B6
Harescough Cumb 109 E6
Harescombe Glos 37 C5
Haresfield Glos 37 C5
Hareshaw N Lanark 119 C8
Hareshaw Head Northumb 116 F4
Harewood W Yorks 95 E6
Harewood End Hereford 36 B2
Harford Carms 46 E5
Harford Devon 6 D4
Hargate Norf 68 E4
Hargatewall Derbys 75 B8
Hargrave Ches W 73 C8
Hargrave Northants 53 B8
Hargrave Suff 55 D8
Harker Cumb 108 C3
Harkland Shetland 160 E6
Harkstead Suff 57 F5
Harlaston Staffs 63 C6
Harlaw Ho. Aberds 141 B6
Harlaxton Lincs 77 F8
Harle Syke Lancs 93 F8
Harlech Gwyn 71 D6
Harlequin Notts 77 F6
Harlescott Shrops 60 C5
Harlesden London 41 F5
Harleston Devon 7 E5
Harleston Norf 68 F5
Harleston Suff 56 D4
Harlestone Northants 52 C5
Harley S Yorks 88 E4
Harley Shrops 61 D5
Harleyholm S Lanark 120 F2
Harlington C Beds 53 F8
Harlington London 27 B8
Harlington S Yorks 89 D5
Harlosh Highld 149 D7
Harlow Essex 41 C7
Harlow Hill N Yorks 95 D5
Harlow Hill Northumb 110 C3
Harlthorpe E Yorks 96 F3
Harlton Cambs 54 D4
Harman's Cross Dorset 13 F7
Harmby N Yorks 101 F6
Harmer Green Herts 41 C5
Harmer Hill Shrops 60 B4
Harmondsworth London 27 B8
Harmston Lincs 78 C2
Harnham Northumb 110 B3
Harnhill Glos 37 D7
Harold Hill London 41 E8
Harold Wood London 41 E8
Haroldston West Pembs 44 D3
Haroldswick Shetland 160 B8
Harome N Yorks 102 F4
Harpenden Herts 40 C4
Harpford Devon 11 E5
Harpham E Yorks 97 C6
Harpley Norf 80 E3
Harpley Worcs 49 C8
Harpole Northants 52 C4
Harpsdale Highld 158 E3
Harpsden Oxon 39 F7
Harpswell Lincs 90 F3
Harpur Hill Derbys 75 B7
Harpurhey Gtr Man 87 D6
Harraby Cumb 108 D4
Harrapool Highld 149 F11
Harrier Shetland 160 J1
Harrietfield Perth 127 B8
Harrietsham Kent 30 D2
Harrington Cumb 98 B1
Harrington Lincs 79 B6
Harrington Northants 64 F4
Harringworth Northants 65 E6
Harris Highld 146 B6
Harrogate N Yorks 95 D6
Harrold Bedford 53 D7
Harrow London 40 F4
Harrow on the Hill London 40 F4
Harrow Street Suff 56 F3
Harrow Weald London 40 E4
Harrowbarrow Corn 5 C8
Harrowden Bedford 53 E8
Harrowgate Hill Darl 101 C7
Harston Cambs 54 D5
Harston Leics 77 F8
Harswell E Yorks 96 E4
Hart Hrtlpl 111 F7
Hart Common Gtr Man 86 D4
Hart Hill Luton 40 B4
Hart Station Hrtlpl 111 F7
Hartburn Northumb 117 F6
Hartburn Stockton 102 C2
Hartest Suff 56 D2
Hartfield E Sus 29 F5
Hartford Cambs 54 B3
Hartford Ches W 74 B3
Hartford End Essex 42 C2
Hartfordbridge Hants 27 D5
Hartforth N Yorks 101 D6
Harthill Ches W 74 D2
Harthill N Lanark 120 C2
Harthill S Yorks 89 F5
Hartington Derbys 75 C8
Hartland Devon 8 B4
Hartlebury Worcs 50 B3
Hartlepool Hrtlpl 111 F8
Hartley Cumb 100 D2
Hartley Kent 18 B4
Hartley Kent 29 C7
Hartley Northumb 111 B6
Hartley Westpall Hants 26 D4
Hartley Wintney Hants 27 D5
Hartlip Kent 30 C2
Hartoft End N Yorks 103 E5
Harton N Yorks 96 C3
Harton Shrops 60 F4
Harton T&W 111 C6
Hartpury Glos 36 B4
Hartshead W Yorks 88 B2
Hartshill Warks 63 E7
Hartshorne Derbys 63 B7
Hartsop Cumb 99 C6
Hartwell Northants 53 D5
Hartwood N Lanark 119 D8
Harvieston Stirling 126 F4
Harvington Worcs 51 E5
Harvington Cross Worcs 51 E5
Harwell Oxon 38 F4
Harwich Essex 57 F6
Harwood Durham 109 F8
Harwood Gtr Man 86 C5
Harwood Dale N Yorks 103 E7
Harworth Notts 89 E7
Hasbury W Mid 62 F3
Hascombe Sur 27 E7
Haselbech Northants 52 B5
Haselbury Plucknett Som 12 C2
Haseley Warks 51 C7
Haselor Warks 51 D6
Hasfield Glos 37 B5
Hasguard Pembs 44 E3
Haskayne Lancs 85 D4
Hasketon Suff 57 D6
Hasland Derbys 76 C3
Haslemere Sur 27 F7
Haslingden Lancs 87 B5
Haslingfield Cambs 54 D5
Haslington Ches E 74 D4
Hassall Ches E 74 D4
Hassall Green Ches E 74 D4
Hassell Street Kent 30 E4
Hassendean Borders 115 B8
Hassingham Norf 69 D6
Hassocks W Sus 17 C6
Hassop Derbys 76 B2
Hastigrow Highld 158 D4
Hastingleigh Kent 30 E4
Hastings E Sus 18 E5
Hastingwood Essex 41 D7
Hastoe Herts 40 D2
Haswell Durham 111 E6
Haswell Plough Durham 111 E6
Hatch C Beds 54 E2
Hatch Hants 26 D4
Hatch Wilts 13 B7
Hatch Beauchamp Som 11 B8
Hatch End London 40 E4
Hatch Green Som 11 C8
Hatchet Gate Hants 14 D4
Hatching Green Herts 40 C4
Hatchmere Ches W 74 B2
Hatcliffe NE Lincs 91 D6
Hatfield Hereford 49 D7
Hatfield Herts 41 D5
Hatfield S Yorks 89 D7
Hatfield Worcs 50 D3
Hatfield Broad Oak Essex 41 C8
Hatfield Garden Village Herts 41 D5
Hatfield Heath Essex 41 C8
Hatfield Hyde Herts 41 C5
Hatfield Peverel Essex 42 C3
Hatfield Woodhouse S Yorks 89 D7
Hatford Oxon 38 E3
Hatherden Hants 25 D8
Hatherleigh Devon 9 D7
Hathern Leics 63 B8
Hatherop Glos 38 D1
Hathersage Derbys 88 F3
Hathershaw Gtr Man 87 D7

Hatherton Ches E 74 E3
Hatherton Staffs 62 C3
Hatley St George Cambs 54 D3
Hatt Corn 5 C8
Hattingley Hants 26 F4
Hatton Aberds 153 E10
Hatton Derbys 63 B6
Hatton Lincs 78 B4
Hatton Shrops 60 E4
Hatton Warks 51 C7
Hatton Warr 86 F3
Hatton Castle Aberds 153 D7
Hatton Heath Ches W 73 C8
Hatton of Fintray Aberds 141 C7
Hattoncrook Aberds 141 B7
Haugh E Ayrs 112 B4
Haugh Gtr Man 87 C7
Haugh Lincs 79 B7
Haugh Head Northumb 117 B6
Haugh of Glass Moray 152 E4
Haugh of Urr Dumfries 106 C5
Haugham Lincs 91 F7
Haughley Suff 56 C4
Haughley Green Suff 56 C4
Haughs of Clinterty Aberdeen 141 C7
Haughton Notts 77 B6
Haughton Shrops 60 B3
Haughton Shrops 61 C5
Haughton Shrops 61 D7
Haughton Shrops 61 E6
Haughton Staffs 62 B2
Haughton Castle Northumb 110 B2
Haughton Green Gtr Man 87 E7
Haughton Moss Ches E 74 D2
Haultwick Herts 41 B6
Haunn Argyll 146 G6
Haunn W Isles 148 G2
Haunton Staffs 63 C6
Hauxley Northumb 117 D8
Hauxton Cambs 54 D5
Havant Hants 15 D8
Haven Hereford 49 D6
Haven Bank Lincs 78 D5
Haven Side E Yorks 91 B5
Havenstreet IoW 15 E6
Havercroft W Yorks 88 C4
Haverfordwest = Hwlffordd Pembs 44 D4
Haverhill Suff 55 E7
Haverigg Cumb 92 B1
Havering-atte-Bower London 41 E8
Haveringland Norf 81 E7
Haversham M Keynes 53 E6
Haverthwaite Cumb 99 F5
Haverton Hill Stockton 102 B2
Hawarden = Penarlâg Flint 73 C7
Hawcoat Cumb 92 B2
Hawen Ceredig 46 E2
Hawes N Yorks 100 F3
Hawes' Green Norf 68 E5
Hawes Side Blackpool 92 F3
Hawford Worcs 50 C3
Hawick Borders 115 C8
Hawk Green Gtr Man 87 F7
Hawkchurch Devon 11 D8
Hawkedon Suff 55 D8
Hawkenbury Kent 18 B2
Hawkenbury Kent 30 E2
Hawkeridge Wilts 24 D3
Hawkerland Devon 11 F5
Hawkes End W Mid 63 F7
Hawkesbury S Glos 36 F4
Hawkesbury Warks 63 F7
Hawkesbury Upton S Glos 36 F4
Hawkhill Northumb 117 C8
Hawkhurst Kent 18 B4
Hawkinge Kent 31 F6
Hawkley Hants 15 B8
Hawkridge Som 21 F7
Hawkshead Cumb 99 E5
Hawkshead Hill Cumb 99 E5
Hawksland S Lanark 119 F8
Hawkswick N Yorks 94 B2
Hawksworth Notts 77 E7
Hawksworth W Yorks 94 E4
Hawksworth W Yorks 95 F5
Hawkwell Essex 42 E4
Hawley Hants 27 D6
Hawley Kent 29 B6
Hawling Glos 37 B7
Hawnby N Yorks 102 F3
Haworth W Yorks 94 F3
Hawstead Suff 56 D2
Hawthorn Durham 111 E7
Hawthorn Rhondda 35 F5
Hawthorn Wilts 24 C3
Hawthorn Hill Brack 27 B6
Hawthorn Hill Lincs 78 D5
Hawthorpe Lincs 65 B7
Hawton Notts 77 D7
Haxby York 96 D2
Haxey N Lincs 89 D8
Hay Green Norf 66 C5
Hay-on-Wye = Y Gelli Gandryll Powys 48 E4
Hay Street Herts 41 B6
Haydock Mers 86 E3
Haydon Dorset 12 C4
Haydon Bridge Northumb 109 C8
Haydon Wick Swindon 37 F8
Haye Corn 5 C8
Hayes London 28 C5
Hayes London 40 F4
Hayfield Derbys 87 F8
Hayfield Fife 128 E4
Hayhill E Ayrs 112 C4
Hayhillock Angus 135 E5
Hayle Corn 2 C4
Haynes C Beds 53 E8
Haynes Church End C Beds 53 E8
Hayscastle Pembs 44 C3
Hayscastle Cross Pembs 44 C4
Hayshead Angus 135 E6
Hayton Aberdeen 141 D8
Hayton Cumb 107 E8
Hayton Cumb 108 D5
Hayton E Yorks 96 E4
Hayton Notts 89 F8
Hayton's Bent Shrops 60 F5
Haytor Vale Devon 7 B5
Haywards Heath W Sus 17 B7
Haywood S Yorks 89 C6
Haywood Oaks Notts 77 D6
Hazel Grove Gtr Man 87 F7
Hazel Street Kent 18 B3
Hazelbank S Lanark 119 E8
Hazelbury Bryan Dorset 12 D5
Hazeley Hants 26 D5
Hazelhurst Gtr Man 87 D7
Hazelslade Staffs 62 C4
Hazelton Glos 37 C7
Hazelton Walls Fife 128 B5
Hazelwood Derbys 76 E3
Hazlemere Bucks 40 E1
Hazlerigg T&W 110 B5
Hazlewood N Yorks 94 D3
Hazon Northumb 117 D7
Heacham Norf 80 D2
Head of Muir Falk 127 F7
Headbourne Worthy Hants 26 F2
Headbrook Hereford 48 D5
Headcorn Kent 30 E2
Headingley W Yorks 95 F5
Headington Oxon 39 D5
Headlam Durham 101 C6
Headless Cross Worcs 50 C5
Headley Hants 26 C3
Headley Hants 27 F6
Headley Sur 28 D3
Headon Notts 77 B7
Heads S Lanark 119 E7
Heads Nook Cumb 108 D4
Heage Derbys 76 D3
Healaugh N Yorks 95 E7
Healaugh N Yorks 101 E5
Heald Green Gtr Man 87 F6
Heale Devon 20 E5
Heale Som 23 E8
Healey Gtr Man 87 C6
Healey N Yorks 101 F6
Healey Northumb 110 D3
Healing NE Lincs 91 C6
Heamoor Corn 2 C3
Heanish Argyll 146 G3
Heanor Derbys 76 E4
Heanton Punchardon Devon 20 F4
Heapham Lincs 90 F8
Hearthstane Borders 114 B4
Heasley Mill Devon 21 F6
Heast Highld 149 G11
Heath Cardiff 22 B3
Heath Derbys 76 C4
Heath and Reach C Beds 40 B2
Heath End Hants 26 C3
Heath End Sur 27 E6
Heath End Warks 51 C7
Heath Hayes Staffs 62 C4
Heath Hill Shrops 61 C7
Heath House Som 23 E6
Heath Town W Mid 62 E3
Heathcote Derbys 75 C8
Heather Leics 63 C7
Heatherfield Highld 149 D9
Heathfield Devon 7 B6
Heathfield E Sus 18 C2
Heathfield Som 11 B6
Heathhall Dumfries 107 B6
Heathrow Airport London 27 B8
Heathstock Devon 11 D7
Heathton Shrops 62 E2
Heatley Warr 86 F5
Heaton Lancs 92 C4
Heaton Staffs 75 C6
Heaton T&W 111 C5
Heaton W Yorks 94 F4
Heaton Moor Gtr Man 87 E6
Heaverham Kent 29 D6
Heaviley Gtr Man 87 F7
Heavitree Devon 10 E4
Hebburn T&W 111 C6
Hebden N Yorks 94 C3
Hebden Bridge W Yorks 87 B7
Hebron Anglesey 82 C4
Hebron Carms 32 B2
Hebron Northumb 117 F7
Heck Dumfries 114 F3
Heckfield Hants 26 C5
Heckfield Green Suff 57 B5
Heckfordbridge Essex 43 B5
Heckington Lincs 78 E4
Heckmondwike W Yorks 88 B3
Heddington Wilts 24 C4
Heddle Orkney 159 G4
Heddon-on-the-Wall Northumb 110 C4
Hedenham Norf 69 E6
Hedge End Hants 15 C5
Hedgerley Bucks 40 F2
Hedging Som 11 B8
Hedley on the Hill Northumb 110 D3
Hednesford Staffs 62 C4
Hedon E Yorks 91 B5
Hedsor Bucks 40 F2
Hedworth T&W 111 C6
Hegdon Hill Hereford 49 D7
Heggerscales Cumb 100 C3
Heglibister Shetland 160 H5
Heighington Darl 101 B7
Heighington Lincs 78 C3
Heights of Brae Highld 151 E8
Heights of Kinlochewe Highld 150 E3
Heilam Highld 156 C7
Heiton Borders 122 F3
Hele Devon 10 D4
Hele Devon 20 E4
Helensburgh Argyll 145 E11
Helford Corn 3 D6
Helford Passage Corn 3 D6
Helhoughton Norf 80 E4
Helions Bumpstead Essex 55 E7
Hellaby S Yorks 89 E6
Helland Corn 5 B5
Hellesdon Norf 68 C5
Hellidon Northants 52 D3
Hellifield N Yorks 93 D8
Hellingly E Sus 18 D2
Hellington Norf 69 D6
Hellister Shetland 160 J5
Helm Northumb 117 E7
Helmdon Northants 52 E3
Helmingham Suff 57 D5
Helmington Row Durham 110 F4
Helmsdale Highld 157 H13
Helmshore Lancs 87 B5
Helmsley N Yorks 102 F4
Helperby N Yorks 95 C7
Helperthorpe N Yorks 97 B5
Helpringham Lincs 78 E4
Helpston Pboro 65 D8
Helsby Ches W 73 B8
Helsey Lincs 79 B8
Helston Corn 3 D5
Helstone Corn 8 F2
Helton Cumb 99 B7
Helwith Bridge N Yorks 93 C8
Hemblington Norf 69 C6
Hemel Hempstead Herts 40 D3
Hemingbrough N Yorks 96 F2
Hemingby Lincs 78 B5
Hemingford Abbots Cambs 54 B3
Hemingford Grey Cambs 54 B3
Hemingstone Suff 57 D5
Hemington Leics 63 B8
Hemington Northants 65 F7
Hemington Som 24 D2
Hemley Suff 57 E6
Hemlington Mbro 102 C3
Hemp Green Suff 57 C7
Hempholme E Yorks 97 D6
Hempnall Norf 68 E5
Hempnall Green Norf 68 E5
Hempriggs House Highld 158 F5
Hempstead Essex 55 F7
Hempstead Medway 29 C8
Hempstead Norf 69 B7
Hempstead Norf 81 D7
Hempsted Glos 37 C5
Hempton Norf 80 E5
Hempton Oxon 52 F2
Hemsby Norf 69 C7
Hemswell Lincs 90 E3
Hemswell Cliff Lincs 90 F3
Hemsworth W Yorks 88 C5
Hemyock Devon 11 C6
Hen-feddau fawr Pembs 45 F4
Henbury Bristol 23 B7
Henbury Ches E 75 B5
Hendon London 41 F5
Hendon T&W 111 D7
Hendre Flint 73 C5
Hendre-ddu Conwy 83 E8
Hendreforgan Rhondda 34 F3
Hendy Carms 33 D6
Heneglwys Anglesey 82 D4
Henfield W Sus 17 C6
Henford Devon 9 E5
Henghurst Kent 19 B6
Hengoed Caerph 35 E5
Hengoed Powys 48 D4
Hengoed Shrops 73 F6
Hengrave Suff 56 C2
Henham Essex 41 B8
Heniarth Powys 59 D8
Henlade Som 11 B7
Henley Shrops 49 B7
Henley Som 23 F6
Henley Suff 57 D5
Henley W Sus 16 B2
Henley-in-Arden Warks 51 C6
Henley-on-Thames Oxon 39 F7
Henley's Down E Sus 18 D4
Henllan Ceredig 46 E2
Henllan Denb 72 C4
Henllan Amgoed Carms 32 B2
Henllys Torf 35 E6
Henlow C Beds 54 F2
Hennock Devon 10 F3
Henny Street Essex 56 F2
Henryd Conwy 83 D7
Henry's Moat Pembs 32 B1
Hensall N Yorks 89 B6
Henshaw Northumb 109 C7
Hensingham Cumb 98 C1
Henstead Suff 69 F7
Henstridge Som 12 C5
Henstridge Ash Som 12 B5
Henstridge Marsh Som 12 B5
Henton Oxon 39 D7
Henton Som 23 E6
Henwood Corn 5 B7
Heogan Shetland 160 J6
Heol-las Swansea 33 E7
Heol Senni Powys 34 B3
Heol-y-Cyw Bridgend 34 F3
Hepburn Northumb 117 B6
Hepple Northumb 117 D5
Hepscott Northumb 117 F8
Heptonstall W Yorks 87 B7
Hepworth Suff 56 B3
Hepworth W Yorks 88 D2
Herbrandston Pembs 44 E3
Hereford Hereford 49 E7
Heriot Borders 121 D6
Hermiston Edin 120 B4
Hermitage Borders 115 E8
Hermitage Dorset 12 D4
Hermitage W Berks 26 B3
Hermitage W Sus 15 D8
Hermon Anglesey 82 E3
Hermon Carms 33 B7
Hermon Carms 46 F2
Hermon Pembs 45 F4
Herne Kent 31 C5
Herne Bay Kent 31 C5
Herner Devon 9 B7
Hernhill Kent 30 C4
Herodsfoot Corn 5 C7
Herongate Essex 42 E2
Heronsford S Ayrs 104 A5
Herriard Hants 26 E4
Herringfleet Suff 69 E7
Herringswell Suff 55 B8
Hersden Kent 31 C6
Hersham Corn 8 D4
Hersham Sur 28 C2
Herstmonceux E Sus 18 D3
Herston Orkney 159 J5
Hertford Herts 41 C6
Hertford Heath Herts 41 C6
Hertingfordbury Herts 41 C6
Hesket Newmarket Cumb 108 F3
Hesketh Bank Lancs 86 B2
Hesketh Lane Lancs 93 E6
Heskin Green Lancs 86 C3
Hesleden Durham 111 F7
Hesleyside Northumb 116 F4
Heslington York 96 D2
Hessay York 95 D8
Hessenford Corn 5 D8
Hessett Suff 56 C3
Hessle E Yorks 90 B4
Hest Bank Lancs 92 C4
Heston London 28 B2
Hestwall Orkney 159 G3
Heswall Mers 85 F3
Hethe Oxon 39 B5
Hethersett Norf 68 D4
Hethersgill Cumb 108 C4
Hethpool Northumb 116 B4
Hett Durham 111 F5
Hetton N Yorks 94 D2
Hetton-le-Hole T&W 111 E6
Hetton Steads Northumb 123 F6
Heugh Northumb 110 B3
Heugh-head Aberds 140 C2
Heveningham Suff 57 B7
Hever Kent 29 E5
Heversham Cumb 99 F6
Hevingham Norf 81 E7
Hewas Water Corn 3 B8
Hewelsfield Glos 36 D2
Hewish N Som 23 C6
Hewish Som 12 D2
Heworth York 96 D2
Hexham Northumb 110 C2
Hextable Kent 29 B6
Hexton Herts 54 F2
Hexworthy Devon 6 B4
Hey Lancs 93 E8
Heybridge Essex 42 D4
Heybridge Essex 42 E2
Heybridge Basin Essex 42 D4
Heybrook Bay Devon 6 E3
Heydon Cambs 54 E5
Heydon Norf 81 E7
Heydour Lincs 78 F3
Heylipol Argyll 146 G2
Heylor Shetland 160 E4
Heysham Lancs 92 C4
Heyshott W Sus 16 C2
Heyside Gtr Man 87 D7
Heytesbury Wilts 24 E4
Heythrop Oxon 38 B3
Heywood Gtr Man 87 C6
Heywood Wilts 24 D3
Hibaldstow N Lincs 90 D3
Hickleton S Yorks 89 D5
Hickling Norf 69 B7
Hickling Notts 64 B3
Hickling Green Norf 69 B7
Hickling Heath Norf 69 B7
Hickstead W Sus 17 B6
Hidcote Boyce Glos 51 E6
High Ackworth W Yorks 88 C5
High Angerton Northumb 117 F6
High Bankhill Cumb 109 E5
High Barnes T&W 111 D6
High Beach Essex 41 E7
High Bentham N Yorks 93 C6
High Bickington Devon 9 B8
High Birkwith N Yorks 93 B7
High Blantyre S Lanark 119 D6
High Bonnybridge Falk 119 B8
High Bradfield S Yorks 88 E3
High Bray Devon 21 F5
High Brooms Kent 29 E6
High Bullen Devon 9 B7
High Buston Northumb 117 D8
High Callerton Northumb 110 B4
High Catton E Yorks 96 D3
High Cogges Oxon 38 D3
High Coniscliffe Darl 101 C7
High Cross Hants 15 B8
High Cross Herts 41 C6
High Easter Essex 42 C2
High Eggborough N Yorks 89 B6
High Ellington N Yorks 101 F6
High Ercall Telford 61 C5
High Etherley Durham 101 B6
High Garrett Essex 42 B3
High Grange Durham 110 F4
High Green Norf 68 D4
High Green S Yorks 88 E4
High Green Worcs 50 E3
High Halden Kent 19 B5
High Halstow Medway 29 B8
High Ham Som 23 F6
High Harrington Cumb 98 B2
High Hatton Shrops 61 B6
High Hawsker N Yorks 103 D7
High Hesket Cumb 108 E4
High Hesleden Durham 111 F7
High Hoyland S Yorks 88 C3
High Hunsley E Yorks 97 F5
High Hurstwood E Sus 17 B8
High Hutton N Yorks 96 C3
High Ireby Cumb 108 F2
High Kelling Norf 81 C7
High Kilburn N Yorks 95 B8
High Lands Durham 101 B6
High Lane Gtr Man 87 F7
High Lane Worcs 49 C8
High Laver Essex 41 D8
High Legh Ches E 86 F5
High Leven Stockton 102 C2
High Littleton Bath 23 D8
High Lorton Cumb 98 B3
High Marishes N Yorks 96 B4
High Marnham Notts 77 B8
High Melton S Yorks 89 D6
High Mickley Northumb 110 C3
High Mindork Dumfries 105 D7
High Newton Cumb 99 F6
High Newton-by-the-Sea Northumb 117 B8
High Nibthwaite Cumb 98 F4
High Offley Staffs 61 B7
High Ongar Essex 42 D1
High Onn Staffs 62 C2
High Roding Essex 42 C2
High Row Cumb 108 F3
High Salvington W Sus 16 D5
High Sellafield Cumb 98 D2
High Shaw N Yorks 100 E3
High Spen T&W 110 D4
High Stoop Durham 110 E4
High Street Corn 4 D4
High Street Kent 18 B4
High Street Suff 56 E2
High Street Suff 57 B8
High Street Suff 57 D8
High Street Green Suff 56 D4
High Throston Hrtlpl 111 F7
High Toynton Lincs 79 C5
High Trewhitt Northumb 117 D6
High Valleyfield Fife 128 F2
High Westwood Durham 110 D4
High Wray Cumb 99 E5
High Wych Herts 41 C7
High Wycombe Bucks 40 E1
Higham Derbys 76 D3
Higham Kent 29 B8
Higham Lancs 93 F8
Higham Suff 55 C8
Higham Suff 56 F4
Higham Dykes Northumb 110 B4
Higham Ferrers Northants 53 C7
Higham Gobion C Beds 54 F2
Higham on the Hill Leics 63 E7
Higham Wood Kent 29 E6
Highampton Devon 9 D6
Highbridge Highld 136 F4
Highbridge Som 22 E5
Highbrook W Sus 28 F4
Highburton W Yorks 88 C2
Highbury Som 23 E8
Highclere Hants 26 C2
Highcliffe Dorset 14 E3
Higher Ansty Dorset 13 D5
Higher Ashton Devon 10 F3
Higher Ballam Lancs 92 F3
Higher Bartle Lancs 92 F5
Higher Boscaswell Corn 2 C2
Higher Burwardsley Ches W 74 D2
Higher Clovelly Devon 8 B5
Higher End Gtr Man 86 D3
Higher Kinnerton Flint 73 C7
Higher Penwortham Lancs 86 B3
Higher Town Scilly 2 E4
Higher Walreddon Devon 6 B2
Higher Walton Lancs 86 B3
Higher Walton Warr 86 F3
Higher Wheelton Lancs 86 B4
Higher Whitley Ches W 86 F4
Higher Wincham Ches W 74 B3
Higher Wych Ches W 73 E8
Highfield E Yorks 96 F3
Highfield Gtr Man 86 D5
Highfield N Ayrs 118 D3
Highfield Oxon 39 B5
Highfield S Yorks 88 F4
Highfield T&W 110 D4
Highfields Cambs 54 D4
Highfields Northumb 123 D5
Highgate London 41 F5
Highlane Ches E 75 C5
Highlane Derbys 88 F5
Highlaws Cumb 107 E8
Highleadon Glos 36 B4
Highleigh W Sus 16 E2
Highley Shrops 61 F7
Highmoor Cross Oxon 39 F7
Highmoor Hill Mon 36 F1
Highnam Glos 36 C4
Highnam Green Glos 36 B4
Highsted Kent 30 C3
Highstreet Green Essex 55 F8
Hightae Dumfries 107 B7
Hightown Ches E 75 C5
Hightown Mers 85 D4
Hightown Green Suff 56 D3
Highway Wilts 24 B5
Highweek Devon 7 B6
Highworth Swindon 38 E2
Hilborough Norf 67 D8
Hilcote Derbys 76 D4
Hilcott Wilts 25 D6
Hilden Park Kent 29 E6
Hildenborough Kent 29 E6
Hildersham Cambs 55 E6
Hilderstone Staffs 75 F6
Hilderthorpe E Yorks 97 C7
Hilfield Dorset 12 D4
Hilgay Norf 67 E6
Hill Pembs 32 D2
Hill S Glos 36 E3
Hill W Mid 62 E5
Hill Brow W Sus 15 B8
Hill Dale Lancs 86 C2
Hill Dyke Lincs 79 E6
Hill End Durham 110 F3
Hill End Fife 128 E2
Hill End N Yorks 94 D3
Hill Head Hants 15 D6
Hill Head Northumb 110 C2
Hill Mountain Pembs 44 E4
Hill of Beath Fife 128 E3
Hill of Fearn Highld 151 D11
Hill of Mountblairy Aberds 153 C6
Hill Ridware Staffs 62 C4
Hill Top Durham 100 B4
Hill Top Hants 14 D5
Hill Top W Mid 62 E3
Hill Top W Yorks 88 C4
Hill View Dorset 13 E7
Hillam N Yorks 89 B6
Hillbeck Cumb 100 C2
Hillborough Kent 31 C6
Hillbrae Aberds 141 B6
Hillbrae Aberds 152 D6
Hillbutts Dorset 13 D7
Hillclifflane Derbys 76 E2
Hillcommon Som 11 B6
Hillend Fife 128 F3
Hillerton Devon 10 E2
Hillesden Bucks 39 B6
Hillesley Glos 36 F4
Hillfarance Som 11 B6
Hillhead Aberds 152 E5
Hillhead Devon 7 D7
Hillhead S Ayrs 112 C4
Hillhead of Auchentumb Aberds 153 C9
Hillhead of Cocklaw Aberds 153 D10
Hillhouse Borders 121 D8
Hilliclay Highld 158 D3
Hillingdon London 40 F3
Hillington Glasgow 118 C5
Hillington Norf 80 E3
Hillmorton Warks 52 B3
Hillockhead Aberds 140 C3
Hillockhead Aberds 140 D2
Hillside Aberds 141 E8
Hillside Angus 135 C7
Hillside Mers 85 C4
Hillside Orkney 159 J5
Hillside Shetland 160 G6
Hillswick Shetland 160 F4
Hillway IoW 15 F7
Hillwell Shetland 160 M5
Hilmarton Wilts 24 B5
Hilperton Wilts 24 D3
Hilsea Ptsmth 15 D7
Hilston E Yorks 97 F8
Hilton Aberds 153 E9
Hilton Cambs 54 C3
Hilton Cumb 100 B2
Hilton Derbys 76 F2
Hilton Dorset 13 D5
Hilton Durham 101 B6
Hilton Highld 151 C10
Hilton Shrops 61 E7
Hilton Stockton 102 C2
Hilton of Cadboll Highld 151 D11
Himbleton Worcs 50 D4
Himley Staffs 62 E2
Hincaster Cumb 99 F7
Hinckley Leics 63 E8
Hinderclay Suff 56 B4
Hinderton Ches W 73 B7
Hinderwell N Yorks 103 C5
Hindford Shrops 73 F7
Hindhead Sur 27 F6
Hindley Gtr Man 86 D4
Hindley Green Gtr Man 86 D4
Hindlip Worcs 50 D3
Hindolveston Norf 81 E6
Hindon Wilts 24 F4
Hindringham Norf 81 D5
Hingham Norf 68 D3
Hinstock Shrops 61 B6
Hintlesham Suff 56 E4
Hinton Hants 14 E3
Hinton Hereford 48 F5
Hinton Northants 52 D3
Hinton S Glos 24 B2
Hinton Shrops 60 D4
Hinton Ampner Hants 15 B6
Hinton Blewett Bath 23 D7
Hinton Charterhouse Bath 24 D2
Hinton-in-the-Hedges Northants 52 F3
Hinton Martell Dorset 13 D8
Hinton on the Green Worcs 50 E5
Hinton Parva Swindon 38 F2
Hinton St George Som 12 C2
Hinton St Mary Dorset 13 C5
Hinton Waldrist Oxon 38 E3
Hints Shrops 49 B8
Hints Staffs 63 D5
Hinwick Bedford 53 C7
Hinxhill Kent 30 E4
Hinxton Cambs 55 E5
Hinxworth Herts 54 E3
Hipperholme W Yorks 88 B2
Hipswell N Yorks 101 E6
Hirael Gwyn 83 D5
Hiraeth Carms 32 B2
Hirn Aberds 141 D6
Hirnant Powys 59 B7
Hirst N Lanark 119 C8
Hirst Northumb 117 F8
Hirst Courtney N Yorks 89 B7
Hirwaen Denb 72 C5
Hirwaun Rhondda 34 D3
Hiscott Devon 9 B7
Histon Cambs 54 C5
Hitcham Suff 56 D3
Hitchin Herts 40 B4
Hither Green London 28 B4
Hittisleigh Devon 10 E2
Hive E Yorks 96 F4
Hixon Staffs 62 B4
Hoaden Kent 31 D6
Hoaldalbert Mon 35 B7
Hoar Cross Staffs 62 B5
Hoarwithy Hereford 36 B2
Hoath Kent 31 C6
Hobarris Shrops 48 B5
Hobbister Orkney 159 H4
Hobkirk Borders 115 C8
Hobson Durham 110 D4
Hoby Leics 64 C3
Hockering Norf 68 C3
Hockerton Notts 77 D7
Hockley Essex 42 E4
Hockley Heath W Mid 51 B6
Hockliffe C Beds 40 B2
Hockwold cum Wilton Norf 67 F7
Hockworthy Devon 10 C5
Hoddesdon Herts 41 D6
Hoddlesden Blackburn 86 B5
Hoddom Mains Dumfries 107 B8
Hoddomcross Dumfries 107 B8
Hodgeston Pembs 32 E1
Hodley Powys 59 E8
Hodnet Shrops 61 B6
Hodthorpe Derbys 76 B5
Hoe Hants 15 C6
Hoe Norf 68 C2
Hoe Gate Hants 15 C7
Hoff Cumb 100 C1
Hog Patch Sur 27 E6
Hoggard's Green Suff 56 D2
Hoggeston Bucks 39 B8
Hogha Gearraidh W Isles 148 A2
Hoghton Lancs 86 B4
Hognaston Derbys 76 D2
Hogsthorpe Lincs 79 B8
Holbeach Lincs 66 B3
Holbeach Bank Lincs 66 B3
Holbeach Clough Lincs 66 B3
Holbeach Drove Lincs 66 C3
Holbeach Hurn Lincs 66 B3
Holbeach St Johns Lincs 66 C3
Holbeach St Marks Lincs 79 F6
Holbeach St Matthew Lincs 79 F7
Holbeck Notts 76 B5
Holbeck W Yorks 95 F5
Holbeck Woodhouse Notts 76 B5
Holberrow Green Worcs 50 D5
Holbeton Devon 6 D4
Holborn London 41 F6
Holbrook Derbys 76 E3
Holbrook S Yorks 88 F5
Holbrook Suff 57 F5
Holburn Northumb 123 F6
Holbury Hants 14 D5
Holcombe Devon 7 B7
Holcombe Som 23 E8
Holcombe Rogus Devon 11 C5
Holcot Northants 53 C5
Holden Lancs 93 E7
Holdenby Northants 52 C4
Holdenhurst Bmouth 14 E2
Holdgate Shrops 61 F5
Holdingham Lincs 78 E3
Holditch Dorset 11 D8
Hole-in-the-Wall Hereford 36 B3
Holefield Borders 122 F4
Holehouses Ches E 74 B4
Holemoor Devon 9 D6
Holestane Dumfries 113 E8
Holford Som 22 E3
Holgate York 95 D8
Holker Cumb 92 B3
Holkham Norf 80 C4
Hollacombe Devon 9 D5
Holland Orkney 159 C5
Holland Orkney 159 F7
Holland Fen Lincs 78 E5
Holland-on-Sea Essex 43 C8
Hollandstoun Orkney 159 C8
Hollee Dumfries 108 C2
Hollesley Suff 57 E7
Hollicombe Torbay 7 C6
Hollingbourne Kent 30 D2
Hollington Derbys 76 F2
Hollington E Sus 18 D4
Hollington Staffs 75 F7
Hollington Grove Derbys 76 F2
Hollingworth Gtr Man 87 E8
Hollins Gtr Man 87 D6
Hollins Green Warr 86 E4
Hollins Lane Lancs 92 D4
Hollinsclough Staffs 75 C7
Hollinwood Gtr Man 87 D7
Hollinwood Shrops 74 F2
Hollocombe Devon 9 C8
Hollow Meadows S Yorks 88 F3
Holloway Derbys 76 D3
Hollowell Northants 52 B4
Holly End Norf 66 D4
Holly Green Worcs 50 E3
Hollybush Caerph 35 D5
Hollybush E Ayrs 112 C3
Hollybush Worcs 50 F2
Hollym E Yorks 91 B7
Hollywood Worcs 51 B5
Holmbridge W Yorks 88 D2
Holmbury St Mary Sur 28 E2
Holmbush Corn 4 D5
Holmcroft Staffs 62 B3
Holme Cambs 65 F8
Holme Cumb 92 B5
Holme N Yorks 102 F1
Holme Notts 77 D8
Holme W Yorks 88 D2
Holme Chapel Lancs 87 B6
Holme Green N Yorks 95 E8
Holme Hale Norf 67 D8
Holme Lacy Hereford 49 F7
Holme Marsh Hereford 48 D5
Holme next the Sea Norf 80 C3
Holme-on-Spalding-Moor E Yorks 96 F4
Holme on the Wolds E Yorks 97 E5
Holme Pierrepont Notts 77 F6
Holme St Cuthbert Cumb 107 E8
Holme Wood W Yorks 94 F4
Holmer Hereford 49 E7
Holmer Green Bucks 40 E2
Holmes Chapel Ches E 74 C4
Holmesfield Derbys 76 B3
Holmeswood Lancs 86 C2
Holmewood Derbys 76 C4
Holmfirth W Yorks 88 D2
Holmhead Dumfries 113 F7
Holmhead E Ayrs 113 B5
Holmisdale Highld 148 D6
Holmpton E Yorks 91 B7
Holmrook Cumb 98 E2
Holmsgarth Shetland 160 J6
Holmwrangle Cumb 108 E5
Holne Devon 6 C5
Holnest Dorset 12 D4
Holsworthy Devon 8 D5
Holsworthy Beacon Devon 9 D5
Holt Dorset 13 D8
Holt Norf 81 D6
Holt Wilts 24 C3
Holt Worcs 50 C3
Holt Wrex 73 D8
Holt End Hants 26 F4
Holt End Worcs 51 C5
Holt Fleet Worcs 50 C3
Holt Heath Worcs 50 C3
Holt Park W Yorks 95 E5
Holtby York 96 D2
Holton Oxon 39 D6
Holton Som 12 B4
Holton Suff 57 B7
Holton cum Beckering Lincs 90 F5
Holton Heath Dorset 13 E7
Holton le Clay Lincs 91 D6
Holton le Moor Lincs 90 E4
Holton St Mary Suff 56 F4
Holwell Dorset 12 C5
Holwell Herts 54 F2
Holwell Leics 64 B4
Holwell Oxon 38 D2
Holwick Durham 100 B4
Holworth Dorset 13 F5
Holy Cross Worcs 50 B4
Holy Island Northumb 123 E7
Holybourne Hants 26 E5
Holyhead = Caergybi Anglesey 82 C2
Holymoorside Derbys 76 C3
Holyport Windsor 27 B6
Holystone Northumb 117 D5
Holytown N Lanark 119 C7
Holywell Cambs 54 B4
Holywell Corn 4 D2
Holywell Dorset 12 D3
Holywell E Sus 18 F2
Holywell = Treffynnon Flint 73 B5
Holywell Northumb 111 B6
Holywell Green W Yorks 87 C8
Holywell Lake Som 11 B6
Holywell Row Suff 55 B8
Holywood Dumfries 114 F2
Hom Green Hereford 36 B2
Homer Shrops 61 D6
Homersfield Suff 69 F5
Homington Wilts 14 B2
Honey Hill Kent 30 C5
Honey Street Wilts 25 C6
Honey Tye Suff 56 F3
Honeyborough Pembs 44 E4
Honeybourne Worcs 51 E6
Honeychurch Devon 9 D8
Honiley Warks 51 B7
Honing Norf 69 B6
Honingham Norf 68 C4
Honington Lincs 78 E2
Honington Suff 56 B3
Honington Warks 51 E7
Honiton Devon 11 D6
Honley W Yorks 88 C2
Hoo Green Ches E 86 F5
Hoo St Werburgh Medway 29 B8
Hood Green S Yorks 88 D4
Hooe E Sus 18 E3
Hooe Plym 6 D3
Hooe Common E Sus 18 D3
Hook E Yorks 89 B8
Hook Hants 26 D5
Hook London 28 C2
Hook Pembs 44 D4
Hook Wilts 37 F7
Hook Green Kent 18 B3
Hook Green Kent 29 C7
Hook Norton Oxon 51 F8
Hooke Dorset 12 E3
Hookgate Staffs 74 F4
Hookway Devon 10 E3
Hookwood Sur 28 E3
Hoole Ches W 73 C8
Hooley Sur 28 D3
Hoop Mon 36 D2
Hooton Ches W 73 B7
Hooton Levitt S Yorks 89 E6
Hooton Pagnell S Yorks 89 D5
Hooton Roberts S Yorks 89 E5
Hop Pole Lincs 65 C8
Hope Derbys 88 F2
Hope Devon 6 F4
Hope Highld 156 B7
Hope Powys 60 D2
Hope Shrops 60 D3
Hope Staffs 75 D8
Hope = Yr Hôb Flint 73 D7
Hope Bagot Shrops 49 B7
Hope Bowdler Shrops 60 E4
Hope End Green Essex 42 B1
Hope Green Ches E 87 F7
Hope Mansell Hereford 36 C3
Hope under Dinmore Hereford 49 D7
Hopeman Moray 152 B1
Hope's Green Essex 42 F3
Hopesay Shrops 60 F3
Hopley's Green Hereford 48 D5
Hopperton N Yorks 95 D7
Hopstone Shrops 61 E7
Hopton Shrops 60 B3
Hopton Shrops 61 B5
Hopton Staffs 62 B3
Hopton Suff 56 B3
Hopton Cangeford Shrops 60 F5
Hopton Castle Shrops 49 B5
Hopton on Sea Norf 69 D8
Hopton Wafers Shrops 49 B8
Hoptonheath Shrops 49 B5
Hopwas Staffs 63 D5
Hopwood Gtr Man 87 D6
Hopwood Worcs 50 B5
Horam E Sus 18 D2
Horbling Lincs 78 F4
Horbury W Yorks 88 C3
Horcott Glos 38 D1
Horden Durham 111 E7
Horderley Shrops 60 F4
Hordle Hants 14 E3
Hordley Shrops 73 F7
Horeb Carms 33 B6
Horeb Carms 33 D5
Horeb Ceredig 46 E2
Horfield Bristol 23 B8
Horham Suff 57 B6
Horkesley Heath Essex 43 B5
Horkstow N Lincs 90 C3
Horley Oxon 52 E2
Horley Sur 28 E3
Hornblotton Green Som 23 F7
Hornby Lancs 93 C5
Hornby N Yorks 101 E7
Hornby N Yorks 102 D1
Horncastle Lincs 79 C5
Hornchurch London 41 F8
Horncliffe Northumb 122 E5
Horndean Borders 122 E4
Horndean Hants 15 C8
Horndon Devon 6 B3
Horndon on the Hill Thurrock 42 F2
Horne Sur 28 E4
Horniehaugh Angus 134 C4
Horning Norf 69 C6
Horninghold Leics 64 E5
Horninglow Staffs 63 B6
Horningsea Cambs 55 C5
Horningsham Wilts 24 E3
Horningtoft Norf 80 E5
Horns Corner Kent 18 C4
Horns Cross Devon 9 B5
Horns Cross E Sus 18 C5
Hornsby Cumb 108 D5
Hornsea E Yorks 97 E8
Hornsea Bridge E Yorks 97 E8
Hornsey London 41 F6
Hornton Oxon 51 E8
Horrabridge Devon 6 C3
Horringer Suff 56 C2
Horringford IoW 15 F6
Horse Bridge Staffs 75 D6
Horsebridge Devon 6 B2
Horsebridge Hants 25 F8
Horsebrook Staffs 62 C2
Horsehay Telford 61 D6
Horseheath Cambs 55 E7
Horsehouse N Yorks 101 F5
Horsell Sur 27 D7
Horseman's Green Wrex 73 E8
Horseway Cambs 66 F4
Horsey Norf 69 B7
Horsford Norf 68 C4
Horsforth W Yorks 94 F5
Horsham W Sus 28 F2
Horsham Worcs 50 D2
Horsham St Faith Norf 68 C5
Horsington Lincs 78 C4
Horsington Som 12 B5
Horsley Derbys 76 E3
Horsley Glos 37 E5
Horsley Northumb 110 C3
Horsley Northumb 116 E4
Horsley Cross Essex 43 B7
Horsley Woodhouse Derbys 76 E3
Horsleycross Street Essex 43 B7
Horsleyhill Borders 115 C8
Horsleyhope Durham 110 E3
Horsmonden Kent 29 E7
Horspath Oxon 39 D5
Horstead Norf 69 C5
Horsted Keynes W Sus 17 B7
Horton Bucks 40 C2
Horton Dorset 13 D8
Horton Lancs 93 D8
Horton Northants 53 D6
Horton S Glos 36 F4
Horton Shrops 60 B4
Horton Som 11 C8
Horton Staffs 75 D6
Horton Swansea 33 F5
Horton Wilts 25 C5
Horton Windsor 27 B8
Horton-cum-Studley Oxon 39 C5
Horton Green Ches W 73 E8
Horton Heath Hants 15 C5
Horton in Ribblesdale N Yorks 93 B8
Horton Kirby Kent 29 C6
Hortonlane Shrops 60 C4
Horwich Gtr Man 86 C4
Horwich End Derbys 87 F8
Horwood Devon 9 B7
Hose Leics 64 B4
Hoselaw Borders 122 F4
Hoses Cumb 98 E4
Hosh Perth 127 B7
Hosta W Isles 148 A2
Hoswick Shetland 160 L6
Hotham E Yorks 96 F4
Hothfield Kent 30 E3
Hoton Leics 64 B2
Houbie Shetland 160 D8
Houdston S Ayrs 112 E1
Hough Ches E 74 D4
Hough Ches E 75 B5
Hough Green Halton 86 F2
Hough-on-the-Hill Lincs 78 E2
Hougham Lincs 77 E8
Houghton Cambs 54 B3
Houghton Cumb 108 D4
Houghton Hants 25 F8
Houghton Pembs 44 E4
Houghton W Sus 16 C4
Houghton Conquest C Beds 53 E8
Houghton Green E Sus 19 C6
Houghton Green Warr 86 E4
Houghton-le-Side Darl 101 B7
Houghton-Le-Spring T&W 111 E6
Houghton on the Hill Leics 64 D3
Houghton Regis C Beds 40 B3
Houghton St Giles Norf 80 D5
Houlland Shetland 160 F7
Houlland Shetland 160 H5
Houlsyke N Yorks 103 D5
Hound Hants 15 D5
Hound Green Hants 26 D5
Houndslow Borders 122 E2
Houndwood Borders 122 C4
Hounslow London 28 B2
Hounslow Green Essex 42 C2
Housay Shetland 160 F8
House of Daviot Highld 151 G10
House of Glenmuick Aberds 140 E2
Housetter Shetland 160 E5
Houss Shetland 160 K5
Houston Renfs 118 C4
Houstry Highld 158 G3
Houton Orkney 159 H4
Hove Brighton 17 D6
Hoveringham Notts 77 E6
Hoveton Norf 69 C6
Hovingham N Yorks 96 B2
How Cumb 108 D5
How Caple Hereford 49 F8
How End C Beds 53 E8
How Green Kent 29 E5
Howbrook S Yorks 88 E4
Howden Borders 116 B2
Howden E Yorks 89 B8
Howden-le-Wear Durham 110 F4
Howe Highld 158 D5
Howe N Yorks 101 F8
Howe Norf 69 D5
Howe Bridge Gtr Man 86 D4
Howe Green Essex 42 D3
Howe of Teuchar Aberds 153 D7
Howe Street Essex 42 C2
Howe Street Essex 55 F7
Howell Lincs 78 E4
Howey Powys 48 D2
Howgate Midloth 120 D5
Howick Northumb 117 C8
Howle Durham 101 B5
Howle Telford 61 B6
Howlett End Essex 55 F6
Howley Som 11 D7
Hownam Borders 116 C3
Hownam Mains Borders 116 B3
Howpasley Borders 115 D6
Howsham N Lincs 90 D4
Howsham N Yorks 96 C3
Howslack Dumfries 114 D3
Howtel Northumb 122 F4
Howton Hereford 35 B8
Howtown Cumb 99 C6
Howwood Renfs 118 C3
Hoxne Suff 57 B5
Hoy Orkney 159 H3
Hoylake Mers 85 F3
Hoyland S Yorks 88 D4
Hoylandswaine S Yorks 88 D3
Hubberholme N Yorks 94 B2
Hubbert's Bridge Lincs 79 E5
Huby N Yorks 95 C8
Huby N Yorks 95 E5
Hucclecote Glos 37 C5
Hucking Kent 30 D2
Hucknall Notts 76 E5
Huddersfield W Yorks 88 C2
Huddington Worcs 50 D4
Hudswell N Yorks 101 D6
Huggate E Yorks 96 D4
Hugglescote Leics 63 C8
Hugh Town Scilly 2 E4
Hughenden Valley Bucks 40 E1
Hughley Shrops 61 E5
Huish Devon 9 C7
Huish Wilts 25 C6
Huish Champflower Som 11 B5
Huish Episcopi Som 12 B2
Huisinis W Isles 154 F4
Hulcott Bucks 40 C1
Hulland Derbys 76 E2
Hulland Ward Derbys 76 E2
Hullavington Wilts 37 F5
Hullbridge Essex 42 E4
Hulme Gtr Man 87 E6

Hulme End Staffs 75 D8
Hulme Walfield Ches E 74 C5
Hulver Street Suff 69 F7
Hulverstone IoW 14 F4
Humber Hereford 49 D7
Humber Bridge N Lincs 90 B4
Humberston NE Lincs 91 D7
Humbie E Loth 121 C7
Humbleton E Yorks 97 F8
Humbleton Northumb 117 B5
Humby Lincs 78 F3
Hume Borders 122 E3
Humshaugh Northumb 110 B2
Huna Highld 158 C5
Huncoat Lancs 93 F7
Huncote Leics 64 E2
Hundalee Borders 116 C2
Hunderthwaite Durham 100 B4
Hundle Houses Lincs 79 D5
Hundleby Lincs 79 C6
Hundleton Pembs 44 E4
Hundon Suff 55 E8
Hundred Acres Hants 15 C6
Hundred End Lancs 86 B2
Hundred House Powys 48 D3
Hungarton Leics 64 D3
Hungerford Hants 14 C2
Hungerford W Berks 25 C8
Hungerford Newtown W Berks 25 B8
Hungerton Lincs 65 B5
Hungladder Highld 149 A8
Hunmanby N Yorks 97 B6
Hunmanby Moor N Yorks 97 B7
Hunningham Warks 51 C8
Hunny Hill IoW 15 F5
Hunsdon Herts 41 C7
Hunsingore N Yorks 95 D7
Hunslet W Yorks 95 F6
Hunsonby Cumb 109 F5
Hunspow Highld 158 C4
Hunstanton Norf 80 C2
Hunstanworth Durham 110 E2
Hunsterson Ches E 74 E3
Hunston Suff 56 C3
Hunston W Sus 16 D2
Hunstrete Bath 23 C8
Hunt End Worcs 50 C5
Hunter's Quay Argyll 145 F10
Hunthill Lodge Angus 134 B4
Hunting-tower Perth 128 B2
Huntingdon Cambs 54 B3
Huntingfield Suff 57 B7
Huntingford Dorset 24 F3
Huntington E Loth 121 B7
Huntington Hereford 48 D4
Huntington Staffs 62 C3
Huntington York 96 D2
Huntley Glos 36 C4
Huntly Aberds 152 E5
Huntlywood Borders 122 E2
Hunton Kent 29 E8
Hunton N Yorks 101 E6
Hunt's Corner Norf 68 F3
Hunt's Cross Mers 86 F2
Huntsham Devon 10 B5
Huntspill Som 22 E5
Huntworth Som 22 F5
Hunwick Durham 110 F4
Hunworth Norf 81 D6
Hurdsfield Ches E 75 B6
Hurley Warks 63 E6
Hurley Windsor 39 F8
Hurlford E Ayrs 118 F4
Hurliness Orkney 159 K3
Hurn Dorset 14 E2
Hurn's End Lincs 79 E7
Hursley Hants 14 B5
Hurst N Yorks 101 D5
Hurst Som 12 C2
Hurst Wokingham 27 B5
Hurst Green E Sus 18 C4
Hurst Green Lancs 93 F6
Hurst Wickham W Sus 17 C6
Hurstbourne Priors Hants 26 E2
Hurstbourne Tarrant Hants 25 D8
Hurstpierpoint W Sus 17 C6
Hurstwood Lancs 93 F8
Hurtmore Sur 27 E7
Hurworth Place Darl 101 D7
Hury Durham 100 C4
Husabost Highld 148 C7
Husbands Bosworth Leics 64 F3
Husborne Crawley C Beds 53 F7
Husthwaite N Yorks 95 B8
Hutchwns Bridgend 21 B7
Huthwaite Notts 76 D4
Huttoft Lincs 79 B8
Hutton Borders 122 D5
Hutton Cumb 99 B6
Hutton E Yorks 97 D6
Hutton Essex 42 E2
Hutton Lancs 86 B2
Hutton N Som 22 D5
Hutton Buscel N Yorks 103 F7
Hutton Conyers N Yorks 95 B6
Hutton Cranswick E Yorks 97 D6
Hutton End Cumb 108 F4
Hutton Gate Redcar 102 C3
Hutton Henry Durham 111 F7
Hutton-le-Hole N Yorks 103 E5
Hutton Magna Durham 101 C6
Hutton Roof Cumb 93 B5
Hutton Roof Cumb 108 F3
Hutton Rudby N Yorks 102 D2
Hutton Sessay N Yorks 95 B7
Hutton Village Redcar 102 C3
Hutton Wandesley N Yorks 95 D8
Huxley Ches W 74 C2
Huxter Shetland 160 G7
Huxter Shetland 160 H5
Huxton Borders 122 C4
Huyton Mers 86 E2
Hwlffordd = Haverfordwest Pembs 44 D4
Hycemoor Cumb 98 F2
Hyde Glos 37 D5
Hyde Gtr Man 87 E7
Hyde Hants 14 C2
Hyde Heath Bucks 40 D2
Hyde Park S Yorks 89 D6
Hydestile Sur 27 E7
Hylton Castle T&W 111 D6
Hyndford Bridge S Lanark 120 E2
Hynish Argyll 146 H2
Hyssington Powys 60 E3
Hythe Hants 14 D5
Hythe Kent 19 B8
Hythe End Windsor 27 B8
Hythie Aberds 153 C10

I

Ibberton Dorset 13 D5
Ible Derbys 76 D2
Ibsley Hants 14 D2
Ibstock Leics 63 C8
Ibstone Bucks 39 E7
Ibthorpe Hants 25 D8
Ibworth Hants 26 D3
Ichrachan Argyll 125 B6
Ickburgh Norf 67 E8
Ickenham London 40 F3
Ickford Bucks 39 D6
Ickham Kent 31 D6
Ickleford Herts 54 F2
Icklesham E Sus 19 D5
Ickleton Cambs 55 E5
Icklingham Suff 55 B8
Ickwell Green C Beds 54 E2
Icomb Glos 38 B2
Idbury Oxon 38 C2
Iddesleigh Devon 9 D7
Ide Devon 10 E3
Ide Hill Kent 29 D5
Ideford Devon 7 B6
Iden E Sus 19 C6
Iden Green Kent 18 B4
Iden Green Kent 18 B5
Idle W Yorks 94 F4
Idlicote Warks 51 E7
Idmiston Wilts 25 F6
Idole Carms 33 C5
Idridgehay Derbys 76 E2
Idrigill Highld 149 B8
Idstone Oxon 38 F2
Idvies Angus 135 E5
Iffley Oxon 39 D5
Ifield W Sus 28 F3
Ifold W Sus 27 F8
Iford E Sus 17 D8
Ifton Heath Shrops 73 F7
Ightfield Shrops 74 F2
Ightham Kent 29 D6
Iken Suff 57 D8
Ilam Staffs 75 D8
Ilchester Som 12 B3
Ilderton Northumb 117 B6
Ilford London 41 F7
Ilfracombe Devon 20 E4
Ilkeston Derbys 76 E4
Ilketshall St Andrew Suff 69 F6
Ilketshall St Lawrence Suff 69 F6
Ilketshall St Margaret Suff 69 F6
Ilkley W Yorks 94 E4
Illey W Mid 62 F3
Illingworth W Yorks 87 B8
Illogan Corn 3 B5
Illston on the Hill Leics 64 E4
Ilmer Bucks 39 D7
Ilmington Warks 51 E7
Ilminster Som 11 C8
Ilsington Devon 7 B5
Ilston Swansea 33 E6
Ilton N Yorks 94 B4
Ilton Som 11 C8
Imachar N Ayrs 143 D9
Imeraval Argyll 142 D4
Immingham NE Lincs 91 C5
Impington Cambs 54 C5
Ince Ches W 73 B8
Ince Blundell Mers 85 D4
Ince in Makerfield Gtr Man 86 D3
Inch of Arnhall Aberds 135 B6
Inchbare Angus 135 C6
Inchberry Moray 152 C3
Inchbraoch Angus 135 D7
Incheril Highld 150 E3
Inchgrundle Angus 134 B4
Inchina Highld 150 B2
Inchinnan Renfs 118 C4
Inchkinloch Highld 157 E8
Inchlaggan Highld 136 D4
Inchlumpie Highld 151 D8
Inchmore Highld 150 G6
Inchnacardoch Hotel Highld 137 C6
Inchnadamph Highld 156 G5
Inchree Highld 130 C4
Inchture Perth 128 B4
Inchyra Perth 128 B3
Indian Queens Corn 4 D4
Inerval Argyll 142 D4
Ingatestone Essex 42 E2
Ingbirchworth S Yorks 88 D3
Ingestre Staffs 62 B3
Ingham Lincs 90 F3
Ingham Norf 69 B6
Ingham Suff 56 B2
Ingham Corner Norf 69 B6
Ingleborough Norf 66 C4
Ingleby Derbys 63 B7
Ingleby Lincs 77 B8
Ingleby Arncliffe N Yorks 102 D2
Ingleby Barwick Stockton 102 C2
Ingleby Greenhow N Yorks 102 D3
Inglemire Hull 97 F6
Inglesbatch Bath 24 C2
Inglesham Swindon 38 E2
Ingleton Durham 101 B6
Ingleton N Yorks 93 B6
Inglewhite Lancs 92 E5
Ingliston Edin 120 B4
Ingoe Northumb 110 B3
Ingol Lancs 92 F5
Ingoldisthorpe Norf 80 D2
Ingoldmells Lincs 79 C8
Ingoldsby Lincs 78 F3
Ingon Warks 51 D7
Ingram Northumb 117 C6
Ingrow W Yorks 94 F3
Ings Cumb 99 E6
Ingst S Glos 36 F2
Ingworth Norf 81 E7
Inham's End Cambs 66 E2
Inkberrow Worcs 50 D5
Inkpen W Berks 25 C8
Inkstack Highld 158 C4
Inn Cumb 99 D6
Innellan Argyll 145 F10
Innerleithen Borders 121 F6
Innerleven Fife 129 D5
Innermessan Dumfries 104 C4
Innerwick E Loth 122 B3
Innerwick Perth 132 E2
Innis Chonain Argyll 125 C7
Insch Aberds 140 B5
Insh Highld 138 D4
Inshore Highld 156 C6
Inskip Lancs 92 F4
Instoneville S Yorks 89 C6
Instow Devon 20 F3
Intake S Yorks 89 D6
Inver Aberds 139 E8
Inver Highld 151 C11
Inver Perth 133 E7
Inver Mallie Highld 136 F4
Inverailort Highld 147 C10
Inveraldie Angus 134 F4
Inveralligin Highld 149 C13
Inverallochy Aberds 153 B10
Inveran Highld 151 B8
Inveraray Argyll 125 E6
Inverarish Highld 149 E10
Inverarity Angus 134 E4
Inverarnan Stirling 126 C2
Inverasdale Highld 155 J13
Inverbeg Argyll 126 E2
Inverbervie Aberds 135 B8
Inverboyndie Aberds 153 B6
Inverbroom Highld 150 C4
Invercassley Highld 156 J7
Invercauld House Aberds 139 E7
Inverchaolain Argyll 145 F9
Invercharnan Highld 131 E5
Inverchoran Highld 150 F5
Invercreran Argyll 130 E4
Inverdruie Highld 138 C5
Inverebrie Aberds 153 E9
Invereck Argyll 145 E10
Inverernan Ho. Aberds 140 C2
Invereshie House Highld 138 D4
Inveresk E Loth 121 B6
Inverey Aberds 139 F6
Inverfarigaig Highld 137 B8
Invergarry Highld 137 D6
Invergelder Aberds 139 E8
Invergeldie Perth 127 B6
Invergordon Highld 151 E10
Invergowrie Perth 134 F3
Inverguseran Highld 149 H12
Inverhadden Perth 132 D3
Inverharroch Moray 152 E3
Inverherive Stirling 126 B2
Inverie Highld 147 B10
Inverinan Argyll 125 D5
Inverinate Highld 136 B2
Inverkeilor Angus 135 E6
Inverkeithing Fife 128 F3
Inverkeithny Aberds 153 D6
Inverkip Invclyd 118 B2
Inverkirkaig Highld 156 H3
Inverlael Highld 150 C4
Inverlochlarig Stirling 126 C3
Inverlochy Argyll 125 C7
Inverlochy Highld 131 B5
Inverlussa Argyll 144 E5
Invermark Lodge Angus 140 F3
Invermoidart Highld 147 D9
Invermoriston Highld 137 C7
Invernaver Highld 157 C10
Inverneill Argyll 145 E7
Inverness Highld 151 G9
Invernettie Aberds 153 D11
Invernoaden Argyll 125 F7
Inveroran Hotel Argyll 131 E6
Inverpolly Lodge Highld 156 H3
Inverquharity Angus 134 D4
Inverquhomery Aberds 153 D10
Inverroy Highld 137 F5
Inversanda Highld 130 D3
Invershiel Highld 136 C2
Invershin Highld 151 B8
Inversnaid Hotel Stirling 126 D2
Inverugie Aberds 153 D11
Inveruglas Argyll 126 D2
Inveruglass Highld 138 D4
Inverurie Aberds 141 B6
Invervar Perth 132 E3
Inverythan Aberds 153 D7
Inwardleigh Devon 9 E7
Inworth Essex 42 C4
Iochdar W Isles 148 D2
Iping W Sus 16 B2
Ipplepen Devon 7 C6
Ipsden Oxon 39 F6
Ipsley Worcs 51 C5
Ipstones Staffs 75 D7
Ipswich Suff 57 E5
Irby Mers 85 F3
Irby in the Marsh Lincs 79 C7
Irby upon Humber NE Lincs 91 D5
Irchester Northants 53 C7
Ireby Cumb 108 F2
Ireby Lancs 93 B6
Ireland Orkney 159 H4
Ireland Shetland 160 L5
Ireland's Cross Shrops 74 E4
Ireleth Cumb 92 B2
Ireshopeburn Durham 109 F8
Irlam Gtr Man 86 E5
Irnham Lincs 65 B7
Iron Acton S Glos 36 F3
Iron Cross Warks 51 D5
Ironbridge Telford 61 D6
Irongray Dumfries 107 B6
Ironmacannie Dumfries 106 B3
Ironside Aberds 153 C8
Ironville Derbys 76 D4
Irstead Norf 69 B6
Irthington Cumb 108 C4
Irthlingborough Northants 53 B7
Irton N Yorks 103 F8
Irvine N Ayrs 118 F3
Isauld Highld 157 C12
Isbister Orkney 159 F3
Isbister Orkney 159 G4
Isbister Shetland 160 D5
Isbister Shetland 160 G7
Isfield E Sus 17 C8
Isham Northants 53 B6
Isle Abbotts Som 11 B8
Isle Brewers Som 11 B8
Isle of Whithorn Dumfries 105 F8
Isleham Cambs 55 B7
Isleornsay Highld 149 G12
Islesburgh Shetland 160 G5
Islesteps Dumfries 107 B6
Isleworth London 28 B2
Isley Walton Leics 63 B8
Islibhig W Isles 154 E4
Islington London 41 F6
Islip Northants 53 B7
Islip Oxon 39 C5
Istead Rise Kent 29 C7
Isycoed Wrex 73 D8
Itchen Soton 14 C5
Itchen Abbas Hants 26 F3
Itchen Stoke Hants 26 F3
Itchingfield W Sus 16 B5
Itchington S Glos 36 F3
Itteringham Norf 81 D7
Itton Devon 9 E8
Itton Common Mon 36 E1
Ivegill Cumb 108 E4
Iver Bucks 40 F3
Iver Heath Bucks 40 F3
Iveston Durham 110 D4
Ivinghoe Bucks 40 C2
Ivinghoe Aston Bucks 40 C2
Ivington Hereford 49 D6
Ivington Green Hereford 49 D6
Ivy Chimneys Essex 41 D7
Ivy Cross Dorset 13 B6
Ivy Hatch Kent 29 D6
Ivybridge Devon 6 D4
Ivychurch Kent 19 C7
Iwade Kent 30 C3
Iwerne Courtney or Shroton Dorset 13 C6
Iwerne Minster Dorset 13 C6
Ixworth Suff 56 B3
Ixworth Thorpe Suff 56 B3

J

Jack Hill N Yorks 94 D5
Jack in the Green Devon 10 E5
Jacksdale Notts 76 D4
Jackstown Aberds 153 E7
Jacobstow Corn 8 E3
Jacobstowe Devon 9 D7
Jameston Pembs 32 E1
Jamestown Dumfries 115 E6
Jamestown Highld 150 F7
Jamestown W Dunb 126 F2
Jarrow T&W 111 C6
Jarvis Brook E Sus 18 C2
Jasper's Green Essex 42 B3
Java Argyll 124 B3
Jawcraig Falk 119 B8
Jaywick Essex 43 C7
Jealott's Hill Brack 27 B6
Jedburgh Borders 116 B2
Jeffreyston Pembs 32 D1
Jellyhill E Dunb 119 B6
Jemimaville Highld 151 E10
Jersey Farm Herts 40 D4
Jesmond T&W 111 C5
Jevington E Sus 18 E2
Jockey End Herts 40 C3
John o'Groats Highld 158 C5
Johnby Cumb 108 F4
John's Cross E Sus 18 C4
Johnshaven Aberds 135 C7
Johnston Pembs 44 D4
Johnstone Renfs 118 C4
Johnstonebridge Dumfries 114 E3
Johnstown Carms 33 C5
Johnstown Wrex 73 E7
Joppa Edin 121 B6
Joppa S Ayrs 112 C4
Jordans Bucks 40 E2
Jordanthorpe S Yorks 88 F4
Jump S Yorks 88 D4
Jumpers Green Dorset 14 E2
Juniper Green Edin 120 C4
Jurby East IoM 84 C3
Jurby West IoM 84 C3

K

Kaber Cumb 100 C2
Kaimend S Lanark 120 E2
Kaimes Edin 121 C5
Kalemouth Borders 116 B3
Kames Argyll 124 D4
Kames Argyll 145 F8
Kames E Ayrs 113 B6
Kea Corn 3 B7
Keadby N Lincs 90 C2
Keal Cotes Lincs 79 C6
Kearsley Gtr Man 87 D5
Kearstwick Cumb 99 F8
Kearton N Yorks 100 E4
Kearvaig Highld 156 B5
Keasden N Yorks 93 C7
Keckwick Halton 86 F3
Keddington Lincs 91 F7
Kedington Suff 55 E8
Kedleston Derbys 76 E3
Keelby Lincs 91 C5
Keele Staffs 74 E5
Keeley Green Bedford 53 E8
Keeston Pembs 44 D4
Keevil Wilts 24 D4
Kegworth Leics 63 B8
Kehelland Corn 2 B5
Keig Aberds 140 C5
Keighley W Yorks 94 E3
Keil Highld 130 D3
Keilarsbrae Clack 127 E7
Keilhill Aberds 153 C7
Keillmore Argyll 144 E5
Keillor Perth 134 E2
Keillour Perth 127 B8
Keills Argyll 142 B5
Keils Argyll 144 G4
Keinton Mandeville Som 23 F7
Keir Mill Dumfries 113 E8
Keisby Lincs 65 B7
Keiss Highld 158 D5
Keith Moray 152 C4
Keith Inch Aberds 153 D11
Keithock Angus 135 C6
Kelbrook Lancs 94 E2
Kelby Lincs 78 E3
Keld Cumb 99 C7
Keld N Yorks 100 D3
Keldholme N Yorks 103 F5
Kelfield N Lincs 90 D2
Kelfield N Yorks 95 F8
Kelham Notts 77 D7
Kellan Argyll 147 G8
Kellas Angus 134 F4
Kellas Moray 152 C1
Kellaton Devon 7 F6
Kelleth Cumb 100 D1
Kelleythorpe E Yorks 97 D5
Kelling Norf 81 C6
Kellingley N Yorks 89 B6
Kellington N Yorks 89 B6
Kelloe Durham 111 F6
Kelloholm Dumfries 113 C7
Kelly Devon 9 F5
Kelly Bray Corn 5 B8
Kelmarsh Northants 52 B5
Kelmscot Oxon 38 E2
Kelsale Suff 57 C7
Kelsall Ches W 74 C2
Kelsall Hill Ches W 74 C2
Kelshall Herts 54 F4
Kelsick Cumb 107 D8
Kelso Borders 122 F3
Kelstedge Derbys 76 C3
Kelstern Lincs 91 E6
Kelston Bath 24 C2
Keltneyburn Perth 132 E4
Kelton Dumfries 107 B6
Kelty Fife 128 E3
Kelvedon Essex 42 C4
Kelvedon Hatch Essex 42 E1
Kelvin S Lanark 119 D6
Kelvinside Glasgow 119 C5
Kelynack Corn 2 C2
Kemback Fife 129 C6
Kemberton Shrops 61 D7
Kemble Glos 37 E6
Kemerton Worcs 50 F4
Kemeys Commander Mon 35 D7
Kemnay Aberds 141 C6
Kemp Town Brighton 17 D7
Kempley Glos 36 B3
Kemps Green Warks 51 B6
Kempsey Worcs 50 E3
Kempsford Glos 38 E1
Kempshott Hants 26 D4
Kempston Bedford 53 E8
Kempston Hardwick Bedford 53 E8
Kempton Shrops 60 F3
Kemsing Kent 29 D6
Kemsley Kent 30 C3
Kenardington Kent 19 B6
Kenchester Hereford 49 E6
Kencot Oxon 38 D2
Kendal Cumb 99 E7
Kendoon Dumfries 113 F6
Kendray S Yorks 88 D4
Kenfig Bridgend 34 F2
Kenfig Hill Bridgend 34 F2
Kenilworth Warks 51 B7
Kenknock Stirling 132 F1
Kenley London 28 D4
Kenley Shrops 61 D5
Kenmore Highld 149 C12
Kenmore Perth 132 E4
Kenn Devon 10 F4
Kenn N Som 23 C6
Kennacley W Isles 154 H6
Kennacraig Argyll 145 G7
Kennerleigh Devon 10 D3
Kennet Clack 127 E8
Kennethmont Aberds 140 B4
Kennett Cambs 55 C7
Kennford Devon 10 F4
Kenninghall Norf 68 F3
Kenninghall Heath Norf 68 F3
Kennington Kent 30 E4
Kennington Oxon 39 D5
Kennoway Fife 129 D5
Kenny Hill Suff 55 B7
Kennythorpe N Yorks 96 C3
Kenovay Argyll 146 G2
Kensaleyre Highld 149 C9
Kensington London 28 B3
Kensworth C Beds 40 C3
Kensworth Common C Beds 40 C3
Kent's Oak Hants 14 B4
Kent Street E Sus 18 D4
Kent Street Kent 29 D7
Kent Street W Sus 17 B6
Kentallen Highld 130 D4
Kentchurch Hereford 35 B8
Kentford Suff 55 C8
Kentisbeare Devon 11 D5
Kentisbury Devon 20 E5
Kentisbury Ford Devon 20 E5
Kentmere Cumb 99 D6
Kenton Devon 10 F4
Kenton Suff 57 C5
Kenton T&W 110 C5
Kenton Bankfoot T&W 110 C5
Kentra Highld 147 E9
Kents Bank Cumb 92 B3
Kent's Green Glos 36 B4
Kenwick Shrops 73 F8
Kenwyn Corn 3 B7
Keoldale Highld 156 C6
Keppanach Highld 130 C4
Keppoch Highld 136 B2
Keprigan Argyll 143 G7
Kepwick N Yorks 102 E2
Kerchesters Borders 122 F3
Keresley W Mid 63 F7
Kernborough Devon 7 E5
Kerne Bridge Hereford 36 C2
Kerris Corn 2 D3
Kerry Powys 59 F8
Kerrycroy Argyll 145 G10
Kerry's Gate Hereford 49 F5
Kerrysdale Highld 149 A13
Kersall Notts 77 C7
Kersey Suff 56 E4
Kershopefoot Cumb 115 F7
Kersoe Worcs 50 F4
Kerswell Devon 11 D5
Kerswell Green Worcs 50 E3
Kesgrave Suff 57 E6
Kessingland Suff 69 F8
Kessingland Beach Suff 69 F8
Kessington E Dunb 119 B5
Kestle Corn 3 B8
Kestle Mill Corn 4 D3
Keston London 28 C5
Keswick Cumb 98 B4
Keswick Norf 68 D5
Keswick Norf 81 D9
Ketley Telford 61 C6
Ketley Bank Telford 61 C6
Ketsby Lincs 79 B6
Kettering Northants 53 B6
Ketteringham Norf 68 D4
Kettins Perth 134 F2
Kettlebaston Suff 56 D3
Kettlebridge Fife 128 D5
Kettleburgh Suff 57 C6
Kettlehill Fife 128 D5
Kettleholm Dumfries 107 B8
Kettleness N Yorks 103 C6
Kettleshume Ches E 75 B6
Kettlesing Bottom N Yorks 94 D5
Kettlesing Head N Yorks 94 D5
Kettlestone Norf 81 D5
Kettlethorpe Lincs 77 B8
Kettletoft Orkney 159 E7
Kettlewell N Yorks 94 B2
Ketton Rutland 65 D6
Kew London 28 B2
Kew Br. London 28 B2
Kewstoke N Som 22 C5
Kexbrough S Yorks 88 D4
Kexby Lincs 90 F2
Kexby York 96 D3
Key Green Ches E 75 C5
Keyham Leics 64 D3
Keyhaven Hants 14 E4
Keyingham E Yorks 91 B6
Keymer W Sus 17 C7
Keynsham Bath 23 C8
Keysoe Bedford 53 C8
Keysoe Row Bedford 53 C8
Keyston Cambs 53 B8
Keyworth Notts 77 F6
Kibblesworth T&W 110 D5
Kibworth Beauchamp Leics 64 E3
Kibworth Harcourt Leics 64 E3
Kidbrooke London 28 B5
Kiddemore Green Staffs 62 D2
Kidderminster Worcs 50 B3
Kiddington Oxon 38 B4
Kidlington Oxon 38 C4
Kidmore End Oxon 26 B4
Kidsgrove Staffs 74 D5
Kidstones N Yorks 100 F4
Kidwelly = Cydweli Carms 33 D5
Kiel Crofts Argyll 124 B5
Kielder Northumb 116 E2
Kierfiold Ho Orkney 159 G3
Kilbagie Fife 127 F8
Kilbarchan Renfs 118 C4
Kilbeg Highld 149 H11
Kilberry Argyll 144 G6
Kilbirnie N Ayrs 118 D3
Kilbride Argyll 124 C4
Kilbride Argyll 124 C5
Kilbride Highld 149 F10
Kilburn Angus 134 C3
Kilburn Derbys 76 E3
Kilburn London 41 F5
Kilburn N Yorks 95 B8
Kilby Leics 64 E3
Kilchamaig Argyll 145 G7
Kilchattan Argyll 144 D2
Kilchattan Bay Argyll 145 H10
Kilchenzie Argyll 143 F7
Kilcheran Argyll 124 B4
Kilchiaran Argyll 142 B3
Kilchoan Argyll 124 D3
Kilchoan Highld 146 E7
Kilchoman Argyll 142 B3
Kilchrenan Argyll 125 C6
Kilconquhar Fife 129 D6
Kilcot Glos 36 B3
Kilcoy Highld 151 F8
Kilcreggan Argyll 145 E11
Kildale N Yorks 102 D4
Kildalloig Argyll 143 G8
Kildary Highld 151 D10
Kildermorie Lodge Highld 151 D8
Kildonan N Ayrs 143 F11
Kildonan Lodge Highld 157 G12
Kildonnan Highld 146 C7
Kildrummy Aberds 140 C3
Kildwick N Yorks 94 E3
Kilfinan Argyll 145 F8
Kilfinnan Highld 137 E5
Kilgetty Pembs 32 D2
Kilgwrrwg Common Mon 36 E1
Kilham E Yorks 97 C6
Kilham Northumb 122 F4
Kilkenneth Argyll 146 G2
Kilkerran Argyll 143 G8
Kilkhampton Corn 9 E6
Killamarsh Derbys 89 F5
Killay Swansea 33 E7
Killbeg Argyll 147 G9
Killean Argyll 143 D7
Killearn Stirling 126 F4
Killen Highld 151 F9
Killerby Darl 101 C6
Killichonan Perth 132 D2
Killiechonate Highld 136 F5
Killiechronan Argyll 147 G8
Killiecrankie Perth 133 C6
Killiemor Argyll 146 H7
Killiemore House Argyll 146 J7
Killilan Highld 150 H2
Killimster Highld 158 E5
Killin Stirling 132 F2
Killin Lodge Highld 137 D8
Killinallan Argyll 142 A4
Killinghall N Yorks 95 D5
Killington Cumb 99 F8
Killingworth T&W 111 B5
Killmahumaig Argyll 144 D6
Killochyett Borders 121 E7
Killocraw Argyll 143 E7
Killundine Highld 147 G8
Kilmacolm Invclyd 118 C3
Kilmaha Argyll 124 E5
Kilmahog Stirling 126 D5
Kilmalieu Highld 130 D2
Kilmaluag Highld 149 A9
Kilmany Fife 129 B5
Kilmarie Highld 149 G10
Kilmarnock E Ayrs 118 F4
Kilmaron Castle Fife 129 C5
Kilmartin Argyll 124 F4
Kilmaurs E Ayrs 118 E4
Kilmelford Argyll 124 D4
Kilmeny Argyll 142 B4
Kilmersdon Som 23 D8
Kilmeston Hants 15 B6
Kilmichael Argyll 143 F7
Kilmichael Glassary Argyll 145 D7
Kilmichael of Inverlussa Argyll 144 E6
Kilmington Devon 11 E7
Kilmington Wilts 24 F2
Kilmonivaig Highld 136 F4
Kilmorack Highld 150 G7
Kilmore Argyll 124 C4
Kilmore Highld 149 H11
Kilmory Argyll 144 F6
Kilmory Highld 147 D8
Kilmory Highld 149 H8
Kilmory N Ayrs 143 F10
Kilmuir Highld 148 D7
Kilmuir Highld 149 A8
Kilmuir Highld 151 D10
Kilmuir Highld 151 G9
Kilmun Argyll 124 D5
Kilmun Argyll 145 E10
Kiln Pit Hill Northumb 110 D3
Kilncadzow S Lanark 119 E8
Kilndown Kent 18 B4
Kilnhurst S Yorks 89 E5
Kilninian Argyll 146 G6
Kilninver Argyll 124 C4
Kilnsea E Yorks 91 C8
Kilnsey N Yorks 94 C2
Kilnwick E Yorks 97 E5
Kilnwick Percy E Yorks 96 D4
Kiloran Argyll 144 D2
Kilpatrick N Ayrs 143 F10
Kilpeck Hereford 49 F6
Kilphedir Highld 157 H12
Kilpin E Yorks 89 B8
Kilpin Pike E Yorks 89 B8
Kilrenny Fife 129 D7
Kilsby Northants 52 B3
Kilspindie Perth 128 B4
Kilsyth N Lanark 119 B7
Kiltarlity Highld 151 G8
Kilton Notts 77 B5
Kilton Som 22 E3
Kilton Thorpe Redcar 102 C4
Kilvaxter Highld 149 B8
Kilve Som 22 E3
Kilvington Notts 77 E7
Kilwinning N Ayrs 118 E3
Kimber worth S Yorks 88 E5
Kimberley Norf 68 D3
Kimberley Notts 76 E5
Kimble Wick Bucks 39 D8
Kimblesworth Durham 111 E5
Kimbolton Cambs 53 C8
Kimbolton Hereford 49 C7
Kimcote Leics 64 F2
Kimmeridge Dorset 13 G7
Kimmerston Northumb 123 F5
Kimpton Hants 25 E7
Kimpton Herts 40 C4
Kinbrace Highld 157 F11
Kinbuck Stirling 127 D6
Kincaple Fife 129 C6
Kincardine Fife 127 F8
Kincardine Highld 151 C9
Kincardine Bridge Falk 127 F8
Kincardine O'Neil Aberds 140 E4
Kinclaven Perth 134 F1
Kincorth Aberdeen 141 D8
Kincorth Ho. Moray 151 E13
Kincraig Highld 138 D4
Kincraigie Perth 133 E6
Kindallachan Perth 133 E6
Kineton Glos 37 B7
Kineton Warks 51 D8
Kinfauns Perth 128 B3
King Edward Aberds 153 C7
King Sterndale Derbys 75 B7
Kingairloch Highld 130 D2
Kingarth Argyll 145 H9
Kingcoed Mon 35 D8
Kingerby Lincs 90 E4
Kingham Oxon 38 B2
Kingholm Quay Dumfries 107 B6
Kinghorn Fife 128 F4
Kingie Highld 136 D4
Kinglassie Fife 128 E4
Kingoodie Perth 128 B5
King's Acre Hereford 49 E6
King's Bromley Staffs 62 C5
King's Caple Hereford 36 B2
King's Cliffe Northants 65 E7
King's Coughton Warks 51 D5
King's Heath W Mid 62 F4
Kings Hedges Cambs 55 C5
Kings Langley Herts 40 D3
King's Hill Kent 29 D7
King's Lynn Norf 67 B6
King's Meaburn Cumb 99 B8
King's Mills Wrex 73 E7
Kings Muir Borders 121 F5
King's Newnham Warks 52 B2
King's Newton Derbys 63 B7
King's Norton Leics 64 D3
King's Norton W Mid 51 B5
King's Nympton Devon 9 C8
King's Pyon Hereford 49 D6
King's Ripton Cambs 54 B3
King's Somborne Hants 25 F8
King's Stag Dorset 12 C5
King's Stanley Glos 37 D5
King's Sutton Northants 52 F2
King's Thorn Hereford 49 F7
King's Walden Herts 40 B4
Kings Worthy Hants 26 F2
Kingsand Corn 6 D2
Kingsbarns Fife 129 C7
Kingsbridge Devon 6 E5
Kingsbridge Som 21 F8
Kingsburgh Highld 149 C8
Kingsbury London 41 F5
Kingsbury Warks 63 E6
Kingsbury Episcopi Som 12 B2
Kingsclere Hants 26 D3
Kingscote Glos 37 E5
Kingscott Devon 9 C7
Kingscross N Ayrs 143 F11
Kingsdon Som 12 B3
Kingsdown Kent 31 E7
Kingseat Fife 128 E3
Kingsey Bucks 39 D7
Kingsfold W Sus 28 F2
Kingsford E Ayrs 118 E4
Kingsford Worcs 62 F2
Kingsforth N Lincs 90 C4
Kingsgate Kent 31 B7
Kingsheanton Devon 20 F4
Kingshouse Hotel Highld 131 D6
Kingside Hill Cumb 107 D8
Kingskerswell Devon 7 C6
Kingskettle Fife 128 D5
Kingsland Anglesey 82 C2
Kingsland Hereford 49 C6
Kingsley Ches W 74 B2
Kingsley Hants 27 F5
Kingsley Staffs 75 E7
Kingsley Green W Sus 27 F6
Kingsley Holt Staffs 75 E7
Kingsley Park Northants 53 C5
Kingsmuir Angus 134 E4
Kingsmuir Fife 129 D7
Kingsnorth Kent 19 B7
Kingstanding W Mid 62 E4
Kingsteignton Devon 7 B6
Kingsthorpe Northants 53 C5
Kingston Cambs 54 D4
Kingston Devon 6 E4
Kingston Dorset 13 D5
Kingston Dorset 13 G7
Kingston E Loth 129 F7
Kingston Hants 14 D2
Kingston IoW 15 F5
Kingston Kent 31 D5
Kingston Moray 152 B3
Kingston Bagpuize Oxon 38 E4
Kingston Blount Oxon 39 E7
Kingston by Sea W Sus 17 D6
Kingston Deverill Wilts 24 F3
Kingston Gorse W Sus 16 D4
Kingston Lisle Oxon 38 F3
Kingston Maurward Dorset 12 E5
Kingston near Lewes E Sus 17 D7
Kingston on Soar Notts 64 B2
Kingston Russell Dorset 12 E3
Kingston Seymour N Som 23 C6
Kingston St Mary Som 11 B7
Kingston Upon Hull Hull 90 B4
Kingston upon Thames London 28 C2
Kingston Vale London 28 B3
Kingstone Hereford 49 F6
Kingstone Som 11 C8
Kingstone Staffs 62 B4
Kingstown Cumb 108 D3
Kingswear Devon 7 D6
Kingswells Aberdeen 141 D7
Kingswinford W Mid 62 F2
Kingswood Bucks 39 C6
Kingswood Glos 36 E4
Kingswood Hereford 48 D4
Kingswood Kent 30 D2
Kingswood Powys 60 D2
Kingswood S Glos 23 B8
Kingswood Sur 28 D3
Kingswood Warks 51 B6
Kingthorpe Lincs 78 B4
Kington Hereford 48 D4
Kington Worcs 50 D4
Kington Langley Wilts 24 B4
Kington Magna Dorset 13 B5
Kington St Michael Wilts 24 B4
Kingussie Highld 138 D3
Kingweston Som 23 F7
Kininvie Ho. Moray 152 D3
Kinkell Bridge Perth 127 C8
Kinknockie Aberds 153 D10
Kinlet Shrops 61 F7
Kinloch Fife 128 C4
Kinloch Highld 146 B6
Kinloch Highld 149 G11
Kinloch Highld 156 F6
Kinloch Perth 133 E8
Kinloch Perth 134 E2
Kinloch Hourn Highld 136 D2
Kinloch Laggan Highld 137 F8
Kinloch Lodge Highld 157 D8
Kinloch Rannoch Perth 132 D3
Kinlochan Highld 130 C2
Kinlochard Stirling 126 D3
Kinlochbeoraid Highld 147 C11
Kinlochbervie Highld 156 D5
Kinlocheil Highld 130 B3
Kinlochewe Highld 150 E3
Kinlochleven Highld 131 C5
Kinlochmoidart Highld 147 D10
Kinlochmorar Highld 147 B11
Kinlochmore Highld 131 C5
Kinlochspelve Argyll 124 C2
Kinloid Highld 147 C9
Kinloss Moray 151 E13
Kinmel Bay Conwy 72 A3
Kinmuck Aberds 141 C7
Kinmundy Aberds 141 C7
Kinnadie Aberds 153 D9
Kinnaird Perth 128 B4
Kinnaird Castle Angus 135 D6
Kinneff Aberds 135 B8
Kinnelhead Dumfries 114 D3
Kinnell Angus 135 D6
Kinnerley Shrops 60 B3
Kinnersley Hereford 48 E5
Kinnersley Worcs 50 E3
Kinnerton Powys 48 C4
Kinnesswood Perth 128 D3
Kinninvie Durham 101 B5
Kinnordy Angus 134 D3
Kinoulton Notts 77 F6
Kinross Perth 128 D3
Kinrossie Perth 134 F1
Kinsbourne Green Herts 40 C4
Kinsey Heath Ches E 74 E3
Kinsham Hereford 49 C5
Kinsham Worcs 50 F4
Kinsley W Yorks 88 C5
Kinson Bmouth 13 E8
Kintbury W Berks 25 C8
Kintessack Moray 151 E12
Kintillo Perth 128 C3
Kintocher Aberds 140 D4
Kinton Hereford 49 B6
Kinton Shrops 60 C3
Kintore Aberds 141 C6
Kintour Argyll 142 C5
Kintra Argyll 142 D4
Kintra Argyll 146 J6
Kintraw Argyll 124 E4
Kinuachdrachd Argyll 124 F3
Kinveachy Highld 138 C5
Kinver Staffs 62 F2
Kippax W Yorks 95 F7
Kippen Stirling 127 E5
Kippford or Scaur Dumfries 106 D5
Kirbister Orkney 159 F7
Kirbister Orkney 159 H4
Kirbuster Orkney 159 F3
Kirby Bedon Norf 69 D5
Kirby Bellars Leics 64 C4
Kirby Cane Norf 69 E6
Kirby Cross Essex 43 B8
Kirby Grindalythe N Yorks 96 C5
Kirby Hill N Yorks 95 C6
Kirby Hill N Yorks 101 D6
Kirby Knowle N Yorks 102 F2
Kirby-le-Soken Essex 43 B8
Kirby Misperton N Yorks 96 B3
Kirby Muxloe Leics 64 D2
Kirby Row Norf 69 E6
Kirby Sigston N Yorks 102 E2
Kirby Underdale E Yorks 96 D4
Kirby Wiske N Yorks 102 F1
Kirdford W Sus 16 B4
Kirk Highld 158 E4
Kirk Bramwith S Yorks 89 C7
Kirk Deighton N Yorks 95 D6
Kirk Ella E Yorks 90 B4
Kirk Hallam Derbys 76 E4
Kirk Hammerton N Yorks 95 D7
Kirk Ireton Derbys 76 D2
Kirk Langley Derbys 76 F2
Kirk Merrington Durham 111 F5
Kirk Michael IoM 84 C3
Kirk of Shotts N Lanark 119 C8
Kirk Sandall S Yorks 89 D7
Kirk Smeaton N Yorks 89 C6
Kirk Yetholm Borders 116 B4
Kirkabister Shetland 160 K6
Kirkandrews Dumfries 106 E3
Kirkandrews upon Eden Cumb 108 D3
Kirkbampton Cumb 108 D3
Kirkbean Dumfries 107 D6
Kirkbride Cumb 108 D2
Kirkbuddo Angus 135 E5
Kirkburn Borders 121 F5
Kirkburn E Yorks 97 D5
Kirkburton W Yorks 88 C2
Kirkby Lincs 90 E4
Kirkby Mers 86 E2
Kirkby N Yorks 102 D3
Kirkby Fleetham N Yorks 101 E7
Kirkby Green Lincs 78 D3
Kirkby In Ashfield Notts 76 D5
Kirkby-in-Furness Cumb 98 F4
Kirkby la Thorpe Lincs 78 E3
Kirkby Lonsdale Cumb 93 B6
Kirkby Malham N Yorks 93 C8
Kirkby Mallory Leics 63 D8
Kirkby Malzeard N Yorks 94 B5
Kirkby Mills N Yorks 103 F5
Kirkby on Bain Lincs 78 C5
Kirkby Overflow N Yorks 95 E6
Kirkby Stephen Cumb 100 D2
Kirkby Thore Cumb 99 B8
Kirkby Underwood Lincs 65 B7
Kirkby Wharfe N Yorks 95 E8
Kirkbymoorside N Yorks 102 F4
Kirkcaldy Fife 128 E4
Kirkcambeck Cumb 108 C5
Kirkcarswell Dumfries 106 E4
Kirkcolm Dumfries 104 C4
Kirkconnel Dumfries 113 C7
Kirkconnell Dumfries 107 C6
Kirkcowan Dumfries 105 C7
Kirkcudbright Dumfries 106 D3
Kirkdale Mers 85 E4
Kirkfieldbank S Lanark 119 E8
Kirkgunzeon Dumfries 107 C5
Kirkham Lancs 92 F4
Kirkham N Yorks 96 C3
Kirkhamgate W Yorks 88 B3
Kirkharle Northumb 117 F6
Kirkheaton Northumb 110 B3
Kirkheaton W Yorks 88 C2
Kirkhill Angus 135 C6
Kirkhill Highld 151 G8
Kirkhill Midloth 120 C5
Kirkhill Moray 152 E2
Kirkhope Borders 115 B6
Kirkhouse Borders 121 F6
Kirkiboll Highld 157 D8
Kirkibost Highld 149 G10
Kirkinch Angus 134 E3
Kirkinner Dumfries 105 D8
Kirkintilloch E Dunb 119 B6
Kirkland Cumb 98 C2
Kirkland Cumb 109 F6
Kirkland Dumfries 113 C7
Kirkland Dumfries 113 E8
Kirkleatham Redcar 102 B3
Kirklevington Stockton 102 D2
Kirkley Suff 69 E8
Kirklington N Yorks 101 F8
Kirklington Notts 77 D6
Kirklinton Cumb 108 C4
Kirkliston Edin 120 B4
Kirkmaiden Dumfries 104 F5
Kirkmichael Perth 133 D7
Kirkmichael S Ayrs 112 D3
Kirkmuirhill S Lanark 119 E7
Kirknewton Northumb 122 F5
Kirknewton W Loth 120 C4
Kirkney Aberds 152 E5
Kirkoswald Cumb 109 E5
Kirkoswald S Ayrs 112 D2
Kirkpatrick Durham Dumfries 106 B4
Kirkpatrick-Fleming Dumfries 108 B2
Kirksanton Cumb 98 F3
Kirkstall W Yorks 95 F5
Kirkstead Lincs 78 C4
Kirkstile Aberds 152 E5
Kirkstyle Highld 158 C5
Kirkton Aberds 140 B5
Kirkton Aberds 153 D6
Kirkton Angus 134 E4
Kirkton Angus 134 F4
Kirkton Borders 115 C8
Kirkton Dumfries 114 F2
Kirkton Fife 129 B5
Kirkton Highld 149 F13
Kirkton Highld 150 G2
Kirkton Highld 151 B10
Kirkton Highld 151 F10
Kirkton Perth 127 C8
Kirkton S Lanark 114 B2
Kirkton Stirling 126 D4
Kirkton Manor Borders 120 F5
Kirkton of Airlie Angus 134 D3

Kirkton of Auchterhouse Angus 134 F3
Kirkton of Auchterless Aberds 153 D7
Kirkton of Barevan Highld 151 G11
Kirkton of Bourtie Aberds 141 B7
Kirkton of Collace Perth 134 F1
Kirkton of Craig Angus 135 D7
Kirkton of Culsalmond Aberds 153 E6
Kirkton of Durris Aberds 141 E6
Kirkton of Glenbuchat Aberds 140 C2
Kirkton of Glenisla Angus 134 C2
Kirkton of Kingoldrum Angus 134 D3
Kirkton of Largo Fife 129 D6
Kirkton of Lethendy Perth 133 E8
Kirkton of Logie Buchan Aberds 141 B8
Kirkton of Maryculter Aberds 141 E7
Kirkton of Menmuir Angus 135 C5
Kirkton of Monikie Angus 135 F5
Kirkton of Oyne Aberds 141 B5
Kirkton of Rayne Aberds 153 F6
Kirkton of Skene Aberds 141 D7
Kirkton of Tough Aberds 140 C5
Kirktonhill Borders 121 D7
Kirktown Aberds 153 C10
Kirktown of Alvah Aberds 153 B6
Kirktown of Deskford Moray 152 B5
Kirktown of Fetteresso Aberds 141 F7
Kirktown of Mortlach Moray 152 E3
Kirktown of Slains Aberds 141 B9
Kirkurd Borders 120 E4
Kirkwall Orkney 159 G5
Kirkwhelpington Northumb 117 F5
Kirmington N Lincs 90 C5
Kirmond le Mire Lincs 91 E5
Kirn Argyll 145 F10
Kirriemuir Angus 134 D3
Kirstead Green Norf 69 E5
Kirtlebridge Dumfries 108 B2
Kirtleton Dumfries 115 F5
Kirtling Cambs 55 D7
Kirtling Green Cambs 55 D7
Kirtlington Oxon 38 C4
Kirtomy Highld 157 C10
Kirton Lincs 79 F6
Kirton Notts 77 C6
Kirton Suff 57 F6
Kirton End Lincs 79 E5
Kirton Holme Lincs 79 E5
Kirton in Lindsey N Lincs 90 E3
Kislingbury Northants 52 D4
Kites Hardwick Warks 52 C2
Kittisford Som 11 B5
Kittle Swansea 33 F6
Kitt's Green W Mid 63 F5
Kitt's Moss Gtr Man 87 F6
Kittybrewster Aberdeen 141 D8
Kitwood Hants 26 F4
Kivernoll Hereford 49 F6
Kiveton Park S Yorks 89 F5
Knaith Lincs 90 F2
Knaith Park Lincs 90 F2
Knap Corner Dorset 13 B6
Knaphill Sur 27 D7
Knapp Perth 134 F2
Knapp Som 11 B8
Knapthorpe Notts 77 D7
Knapton Norf 81 D9
Knapton York 95 D8
Knapton Green Hereford 49 D6
Knapwell Cambs 54 C4
Knaresborough N Yorks 95 D6
Knarsdale Northumb 109 D6
Knauchland Moray 152 C5
Knaven Aberds 153 D8
Knayton N Yorks 102 F2
Knebworth Herts 41 B5
Knedlington E Yorks 89 B8
Kneesall Notts 77 C7
Kneesworth Cambs 54 E4
Kneeton Notts 77 E7
Knelston Swansea 33 F5
Knenhall Staffs 75 F6
Knettishall Suff 68 F2
Knightacott Devon 21 F5
Knightcote Warks 51 D8
Knightley Dale Staffs 62 B2
Knighton Devon 6 E3
Knighton Leicester 64 D2
Knighton = Tref-Y-Clawdd Powys 48 B4
Knighton Staffs 61 B7
Knighton Staffs 74 E4
Knightswood Glasgow 118 C5
Knightwick Worcs 50 D2
Knill Hereford 48 C4
Knipton Leics 77 F8
Knitsley Durham 110 E4
Kniveton Derbys 76 D2
Knock Argyll 147 H8
Knock Cumb 100 B1
Knock Moray 152 C5
Knockally Highld 158 H3
Knockan Highld 156 H5
Knockandhu Moray 139 B8
Knockando Moray 152 D1
Knockando Ho. Moray 152 D2
Knockbain Highld 151 F9
Knockbreck Highld 148 B7
Knockbrex Dumfries 106 E2
Knockdee Highld 158 D3
Knockdolian S Ayrs 104 A5
Knockenkelly N Ayrs 143 F11
Knockentiber E Ayrs 118 F3
Knockespock Ho. Aberds 140 B4
Knockfarrel Highld 151 F8
Knockglass Dumfries 104 D4
Knockholt Kent 29 D5
Knockholt Pound Kent 29 D5
Knockie Lodge Highld 137 C7
Knockin Shrops 60 B3
Knockinlaw E Ayrs 118 F4
Knocklearn Dumfries 106 B4
Knocknaha Argyll 143 G7
Knocknain Dumfries 104 C3
Knockrome Argyll 144 F4
Knocksharry IoM 84 D2
Knodishall Suff 57 C8
Knolls Green Ches E 74 B5
Knolton Wrex 73 F7
Knolton Bryn Wrex 73 F7
Knook Wilts 24 E4
Knossington Leics 64 D5
Knott End-on-Sea Lancs 92 E3
Knotting Bedford 53 C8
Knotting Green Bedford 53 C8
Knottingley W Yorks 89 B6
Knotts Cumb 99 B6
Knotts Lancs 93 D7
Knotty Ash Mers 86 E2
Knotty Green Bucks 40 E2
Knowbury Shrops 49 B7
Knowe Dumfries 105 B7
Knowehead Dumfries 113 E6
Knowes of Elrick Aberds 152 C6
Knowesgate Northumb 117 F5
Knoweton N Lanark 119 D7
Knowhead Aberds 153 C9
Knowl Hill Windsor 27 B6
Knowle Bristol 23 B8
Knowle Devon 10 D2
Knowle Devon 11 F5
Knowle Devon 20 F3
Knowle Shrops 49 B7
Knowle W Mid 51 B6
Knowle Green Lancs 93 F6
Knowle Park W Yorks 94 E3
Knowlton Dorset 13 C8
Knowlton Kent 31 D6
Knowsley Mers 86 E2
Knowstone Devon 10 B3
Knox Bridge Kent 29 E8
Knucklas Powys 48 B4
Knuston Northants 53 C7
Knutsford Ches E 74 B4
Knutton Staffs 74 E5
Knypersley Staffs 75 D5
Kuggar Corn 3 E6
Kyle of Lochalsh Highld 149 F12
Kyleakin Highld 149 F12
Kylerhea Highld 149 F12
Kylesknoydart Highld 147 B11
Kylesku Highld 156 F5
Kylesmorar Highld 147 B11
Kylestrome Highld 156 F5
Kyllachy House Highld 138 B3
Kynaston Shrops 60 B3
Kynnersley Telford 61 C6
Kyre Magna Worcs 49 C8

L

La Fontenelle Guern 16
La Planque Guern 16
Labost W Isles 155 C7
Lacasaidh W Isles 155 E8
Lacasdal W Isles 155 D9
Laceby NE Lincs 91 D6
Lacey Green Bucks 39 E8
Lach Dennis Ches W 74 B4
Lackford Suff 55 B8
Lacock Wilts 24 C4
Ladbroke Warks 52 D2
Laddingford Kent 29 E7
Lade Bank Lincs 79 D6
Ladock Corn 4 D3
Lady Orkney 159 D7
Ladybank Fife 128 C5
Ladykirk Borders 122 E4
Ladysford Aberds 153 B9
Laga Highld 147 E9
Lagalochan Argyll 124 D4
Lagavulin Argyll 142 D5
Lagg Argyll 144 F4
Lagg N Ayrs 143 F10
Laggan Argyll 142 C3
Laggan Highld 137 E5
Laggan Highld 138 E2
Laggan Highld 147 D10
Laggan S Ayrs 112 F2
Lagganulva Argyll 146 G7
Laide Highld 155 H13
Laigh Fenwick E Ayrs 118 E4
Laigh Glengall S Ayrs 112 C3
Laighmuir E Ayrs 118 E4
Laindon Essex 42 F2
Lair Highld 150 G3
Lairg Highld 157 J8
Lairg Lodge Highld 157 J8
Lairg Muir Highld 157 J8
Lairgmore Highld 151 H8
Laisterdyke W Yorks 94 F4
Laithes Cumb 108 F4
Lake IoW 15 F6
Lake Wilts 25 F6
Lakenham Norf 68 D5
Lakenheath Suff 67 F7
Lakesend Norf 66 E5
Lakeside Cumb 99 F5
Laleham Sur 27 C8
Laleston Bridgend 21 B7
Lamarsh Essex 56 F2
Lamas Norf 81 E8
Lambden Borders 122 E3
Lamberhurst Kent 18 B3
Lamberhurst Quarter Kent 18 B3
Lamberton Borders 123 D5
Lambeth London 28 B4
Lambhill Glasgow 119 C5
Lambley Northumb 109 D6
Lambley Notts 77 E6
Lamborough Hill Oxon 38 D4
Lambourn W Berks 25 B8
Lambourne End Essex 41 E7
Lambs Green W Sus 28 F3
Lambston Pembs 44 D4
Lambton T&W 111 D5
Lamerton Devon 6 B2
Lamesley T&W 111 D5
Laminess Orkney 159 E7
Lamington Highld 151 D10
Lamington S Lanark 120 F2
Lamlash N Ayrs 143 E11
Lamloch Dumfries 112 E5
Lamonby Cumb 108 F4
Lamorna Corn 2 D3
Lamorran Corn 3 B7
Lampardbrook Suff 57 C6
Lampeter = Llanbedr Pont Steffan Ceredig 46 E4
Lampeter Velfrey Pembs 32 C2
Lamphey Pembs 32 D1
Lamplugh Cumb 98 B2
Lamport Northants 53 B5
Lamyatt Som 23 F8
Lana Devon 8 E5
Lanark S Lanark 119 E8
Lancaster Lancs 92 C4
Lanchester Durham 110 E4
Lancing W Sus 17 D5
Landbeach Cambs 55 C5
Landcross Devon 9 B6
Landerberry Aberds 141 D6
Landford Wilts 14 C3
Landford Manor Wilts 14 B3
Landimore Swansea 33 E5
Landkey Devon 20 F4
Landore Swansea 33 E7
Landrake Corn 5 C8
Landscove Devon 7 C5
Landshipping Pembs 32 C1
Landshipping Quay Pembs 32 C1
Landulph Corn 6 C2
Landwade Suff 55 C7
Lane Corn 4 C3
Lane End Bucks 39 E8
Lane End Cumb 98 E3
Lane End Dorset 13 E6
Lane End Hants 15 B6
Lane End IoW 15 F7
Lane End Lancs 93 E8
Lane Ends Lancs 93 D7
Lane Ends Lancs 93 F7
Lane Ends N Yorks 94 E2
Lane Head Derbys 75 B8
Lane Head Durham 101 C6
Lane Head Gtr Man 86 E4
Lane Head W Yorks 88 D2
Lane Side Lancs 87 B5
Laneast Corn 8 F4
Laneham Notts 77 B8
Lanehead Durham 109 E8
Lanehead Northumb 116 F3
Lanercost Cumb 109 C5
Laneshaw Bridge Lancs 94 E2
Lanfach Caerph 35 E6
Langar Notts 77 F7
Langbank Renfs 118 B3
Langbar N Yorks 94 D3
Langburnshiels Borders 115 D8
Langcliffe N Yorks 93 C8
Langdale Highld 157 E9
Langdale End N Yorks 103 E7
Langdon Corn 8 F5
Langdon Beck Durham 109 F8
Langdon Hills Essex 42 F2
Langdyke Fife 128 D5
Langenhoe Essex 43 C6
Langford C Beds 54 E2
Langford Devon 10 D5
Langford Essex 42 D4
Langford Notts 77 D8
Langford Oxon 38 D2
Langford Budville Som 11 B6
Langham Essex 56 F4
Langham Norf 81 C6
Langham Rutland 64 C5
Langham Suff 56 C3
Langhaugh Borders 120 F5
Langho Lancs 93 F7
Langholm Dumfries 115 F6
Langleeford Northumb 117 B5
Langley Ches E 75 B6
Langley Hants 14 D5
Langley Herts 41 B5
Langley Kent 30 D2
Langley Northumb 109 C8
Langley Slough 27 B8
Langley W Sus 16 B2
Langley Warks 51 C6
Langley Burrell Wilts 24 B4
Langley Common Derbys 76 F2
Langley Heath Kent 30 D2
Langley Lower Green Essex 54 F5
Langley Marsh Som 11 B5
Langley Park Durham 110 E5
Langley Street Norf 69 D6
Langley Upper Green Essex 54 F5
Langney E Sus 18 E3
Langold Notts 89 F6
Langore Corn 8 F5
Langport Som 12 B2
Langrick Lincs 79 E5
Langridge Bath 24 C2
Langridge Ford Devon 9 B7
Langrigg Cumb 107 E8
Langrish Hants 15 B8
Langsett S Yorks 88 D3
Langshaw Borders 121 F8
Langside Perth 127 C6
Langskaill Orkney 159 D5
Langstone Hants 15 D8
Langstone Newport 35 E7
Langthorne N Yorks 101 E7
Langthorpe N Yorks 95 C6
Langthwaite N Yorks 101 D5
Langtoft E Yorks 97 C6
Langtoft Lincs 65 C8
Langton Durham 101 C6
Langton Lincs 78 C5
Langton Lincs 79 B6
Langton N Yorks 96 C3
Langton by Wragby Lincs 78 B4
Langton Green Kent 18 B2
Langton Green Suff 56 B5
Langton Herring Dorset 12 F4
Langton Matravers Dorset 13 G8
Langtree Devon 9 C6
Langwathby Cumb 109 F5
Langwell Ho. Highld 158 H3
Langwell Lodge Highld 156 J4
Langwith Derbys 76 C5
Langwith Junction Derbys 76 C5
Langworth Lincs 78 B3
Lanivet Corn 4 C5
Lanlivery Corn 5 D5
Lanner Corn 3 C6
Lanreath Corn 5 D6
Lansallos Corn 5 D6
Lansdown Glos 37 B6
Lanteglos Highway Corn 5 D6
Lanton Borders 116 B2
Lanton Northumb 122 F5
Lapford Devon 10 D2
Laphroaig Argyll 142 D4
Lapley Staffs 62 C2
Lapworth Warks 51 B6
Larachbeg Highld 147 G9
Larbert Falk 127 F7
Larden Green Ches E 74 D2
Largie Aberds 152 E6
Largiemore Argyll 145 E8
Largoward Fife 129 D6
Largs N Ayrs 118 D2
Largybeg N Ayrs 143 F11
Largymore N Ayrs 143 F11
Larkfield Invclyd 118 B2
Larkhall S Lanark 119 D7
Larkhill Wilts 25 E6
Larling Norf 68 F2
Larriston Borders 115 E8
Lartington Durham 101 C5
Lary Aberds 140 D2
Lasham Hants 26 E4
Lashenden Kent 30 E2
Lassington Glos 36 B4
Lassodie Fife 128 E3
Lastingham N Yorks 103 E5
Latcham Som 23 E6
Latchford Herts 41 B6
Latchford Warr 86 F4
Latchingdon Essex 42 D4
Latchley Corn 6 B2
Lately Common Warr 86 E4
Lathbury M Keynes 53 E6
Latheron Highld 158 G3
Latheronwheel Highld 158 G3
Latheronwheel Ho. Highld 158 G3
Lathones Fife 129 D6
Latimer Bucks 40 E3
Latteridge S Glos 36 F3
Lattiford Som 12 B4
Latton Wilts 37 E7
Latton Bush Essex 41 D7
Lauchintilly Aberds 141 C6
Lauder Borders 121 E8
Laugharne Carms 32 C4
Laughterton Lincs 77 B8
Laughton E Sus 18 D2
Laughton Leics 64 F3
Laughton Lincs 78 F3
Laughton Lincs 90 E2
Laughton Common S Yorks 89 F6
Laughton en le Morthen S Yorks 89 F6
Launcells Corn 8 D4
Launceston Corn 8 F5
Launton Oxon 39 B6
Laurencekirk Aberds 135 B7
Laurieston Dumfries 106 C3
Laurieston Falk 120 B2
Lavendon M Keynes 53 D7
Lavenham Suff 56 E3
Laverhay Dumfries 114 E4
Laversdale Cumb 108 C4
Laverstock Wilts 25 F6
Laverstoke Hants 26 E2
Laverton Glos 51 F5
Laverton N Yorks 94 B5
Laverton Som 24 D2
Lavister Wrex 73 D7
Law S Lanark 119 D8
Lawers Perth 127 B6
Lawers Perth 132 F3
Lawford Essex 56 F4
Lawhitton Corn 9 F5
Lawkland N Yorks 93 C7
Lawley Telford 61 D6
Lawnhead Staffs 62 B2
Lawrenny Pembs 32 D1
Lawshall Suff 56 D2
Lawton Hereford 49 D6
Laxey IoM 84 D4
Laxfield Suff 57 B6
Laxfirth Shetland 160 H6
Laxfirth Shetland 160 J6
Laxford Bridge Highld 156 E5
Laxo Shetland 160 G6
Laxobigging Shetland 160 F6
Laxton E Yorks 89 B8
Laxton Northants 65 E6
Laxton Notts 77 C7
Laycock W Yorks 94 E3
Layer Breton Essex 43 C5
Layer de la Haye Essex 43 C5
Layer Marney Essex 43 C5
Layham Suff 56 E4
Laylands Green W Berks 25 C8
Laytham E Yorks 96 F3
Layton Blackpool 92 F3
Lazenby Redcar 102 B3
Lazonby Cumb 108 F5
Le Planel Guern 16
Le Skerne Haughton Darl 101 C8
Le Villocq Guern 16
Lea Derbys 76 D3
Lea Hereford 36 B3
Lea Lincs 90 F2
Lea Shrops 60 D4
Lea Shrops 60 F3
Lea Wilts 37 F6
Lea Marston Warks 63 E6
Lea Town Lancs 92 F4
Leabrooks Derbys 76 D4
Leac a Li W Isles 154 H6
Leachkin Highld 151 G9
Leadburn Midloth 120 D5
Leaden Roding Essex 42 C1
Leadenham Lincs 78 D2
Leadgate Cumb 109 E7
Leadgate Durham 110 D4
Leadgate T&W 110 D4
Leadhills S Lanark 113 C8
Leafield Oxon 38 C3
Leagrave Luton 40 B3
Leake N Yorks 102 E2
Leake Commonside Lincs 79 D6
Lealholm N Yorks 103 D5
Lealt Argyll 144 D5
Lealt Highld 149 B10
Leamington Hastings Warks 52 C2
Leamonsley Staffs 62 D5
Leamside Durham 111 E6
Leanaig Highld 151 F8
Leargybreck Argyll 144 F4
Leasgill Cumb 99 F6
Leasingham Lincs 78 E3
Leasingthorne Durham 101 B7
Leasowe Mers 85 E3
Leatherhead Sur 28 D2
Leatherhead Common Sur 28 D2
Leathley N Yorks 94 E5
Leaton Shrops 60 C4
Leaveland Kent 30 D4
Leavening N Yorks 96 C3
Leaves Green London 28 C5
Leazes Durham 110 D4
Lebberston N Yorks 103 F8
Lechlade-on-Thames Glos 38 E2
Leck Lancs 93 B6
Leckford Hants 25 F8
Leckfurin Highld 157 D10
Leckgruinart Argyll 142 B3
Leckhampstead Bucks 52 F5
Leckhampstead W Berks 26 B2
Leckhampstead Thicket W Berks 26 B2
Leckhampton Glos 37 C6
Leckie Highld 150 E3
Leckmelm Highld 150 B4
Leckwith V Glam 22 B3
Leconfield E Yorks 97 E6
Ledaig Argyll 124 B5
Ledburn Bucks 40 B2
Ledbury Hereford 50 F2
Ledcharrie Stirling 126 B4
Ledgemoor Hereford 49 D6
Ledicot Hereford 49 C6
Ledmore Highld 156 H5
Lednagullin Highld 157 C10
Ledsham Ches W 73 B7
Ledsham W Yorks 89 B5
Ledston W Yorks 88 B5
Ledston Luck W Yorks 95 F7
Ledwell Oxon 38 B4
Lee Argyll 146 J7
Lee Devon 20 E3
Lee Hants 14 C4
Lee Lancs 93 D5
Lee Shrops 73 F8
Lee Brockhurst Shrops 60 B5
Lee Clump Bucks 40 D2
Lee Mill Devon 6 D4
Lee Moor Devon 6 C3
Lee-on-the-Solent Hants 15 D6
Leeans Shetland 160 J5
Leebotten Shetland 160 L6
Leebotwood Shrops 60 E4
Leece Cumb 92 C2
Leechpool Pembs 44 D4
Leeds Kent 30 D2
Leeds W Yorks 95 F5
Leedstown Corn 2 C5
Leek Staffs 75 D6
Leek Wootton Warks 51 C7
Leekbrook Staffs 75 D6
Leeming N Yorks 101 F7
Leeming Bar N Yorks 101 E7
Lees Derbys 76 F2
Lees Gtr Man 87 D7
Lees W Yorks 94 F3
Leeswood Flint 73 C6
Legbourne Lincs 91 F7
Legerwood Borders 121 E8
Legsby Lincs 90 F5
Leicester Leicester 64 D2
Leicester Forest East Leics 64 D2
Leigh Dorset 12 D4
Leigh Glos 37 B5
Leigh Gtr Man 86 D4
Leigh Kent 29 E6
Leigh Shrops 60 D3
Leigh Sur 28 E3
Leigh Wilts 37 E7
Leigh Worcs 50 D2
Leigh Beck Essex 42 F4
Leigh Common Som 12 B5
Leigh Delamere Wilts 24 B3
Leigh Green Kent 19 B6
Leigh on Sea Southend 42 F4
Leigh Park Hants 15 D8
Leigh Sinton Worcs 50 D2
Leigh upon Mendip Som 23 E8
Leigh Woods N Som 23 B7
Leighswood W Mid 62 D4
Leighterton Glos 37 E5
Leighton N Yorks 94 B4
Leighton Powys 60 D2
Leighton Shrops 61 D6
Leighton Som 24 E2
Leighton Bromswold Cambs 54 B2
Leighton Buzzard C Beds 40 B2
Leinthall Earls Hereford 49 C6
Leinthall Starkes Hereford 49 C6
Leintwardine Hereford 49 B6
Leire Leics 64 E2
Leirinmore Highld 156 C7
Leiston Suff 57 C8
Leitfie Perth 134 E2
Leith Edin 121 B5
Leitholm Borders 122 E3
Lelant Corn 2 C4
Lelley E Yorks 97 F8
Lem Hill Worcs 50 B2
Lemmington Hall Northumb 117 C7
Lempitlaw Borders 122 F3
Lenchwick Worcs 50 E5
Lendalfoot S Ayrs 112 F1
Lendrick Lodge Stirling 126 D4
Lenham Kent 30 D2
Lenham Heath Kent 30 E3
Lennel Borders 122 E4
Lennoxtown E Dunb 119 B6
Lenton Lincs 78 F3
Lenton Nottingham 77 F5
Lentran Highld 151 G8
Lenwade Norf 68 C3
Leny Ho. Stirling 126 D5
Lenzie E Dunb 119 B6
Leoch Angus 134 F3
Leochel-Cushnie Aberds 140 C4
Leominster Hereford 49 D6
Leonard Stanley Glos 37 D5
Leorin Argyll 142 D4
Lepe Hants 15 E5
Lephin Highld 148 D6
Lephinchapel Argyll 145 D8
Lephinmore Argyll 145 D8
Leppington N Yorks 96 C3
Lepton W Yorks 88 C3
Lerryn Corn 5 D6
Lerwick Shetland 160 J6
Lesbury Northumb 117 C8
Leslie Aberds 140 B4
Leslie Fife 128 D4
Lesmahagow S Lanark 119 F8
Lesnewth Corn 8 E3
Lessendrum Aberds 152 D5
Lessingham Norf 69 B6
Lessonhall Cumb 108 D2
Leswalt Dumfries 104 C4
Letchmore Heath Herts 40 E4
Letchworth Herts 54 F3
Letcombe Bassett Oxon 38 F3
Letcombe Regis Oxon 38 F3
Letham Angus 135 E5
Letham Falk 127 F7
Letham Fife 128 C5
Letham Perth 128 B2
Letham Grange Angus 135 E6
Lethenty Aberds 153 D8
Letheringham Suff 57 D6
Letheringsett Norf 81 D6
Lettaford Devon 10 F2
Lettan Orkney 159 D8
Letterewe Highld 150 D2
Letterfearn Highld 149 F13
Letterfinlay Highld 137 E5
Lettermorar Highld 147 C10
Lettermore Argyll 146 G7
Letters Highld 150 C4
Letterston Pembs 44 C4
Lettoch Highld 139 C6
Lettoch Highld 151 H13
Letton Hereford 48 E5
Letton Hereford 49 B5
Letton Green Norf 68 D2
Letty Green Herts 41 C5
Letwell S Yorks 89 F6
Leuchars Fife 129 B6
Leuchars Ho. Moray 152 B2
Leumrabhagh W Isles 155 F8
Levan Invclyd 118 B2
Levaneap Shetland 160 G6
Levedale Staffs 62 C2
Leven E Yorks 97 E7
Leven Fife 129 D5
Levencorroch N Ayrs 143 F11
Levens Cumb 99 F6
Levens Green Herts 41 B6
Levenshulme Gtr Man 87 E6
Levenwick Shetland 160 L6
Leverburgh = An t-Ob W Isles 154 J5
Leverington Cambs 66 C4
Leverton Lincs 79 E7
Leverton Highgate Lincs 79 E7
Leverton Lucasgate Lincs 79 E7
Leverton Outgate Lincs 79 E7
Levington Suff 57 F6
Levisham N Yorks 103 E6
Levishie Highld 137 C7
Lew Oxon 38 D3
Lewannick Corn 8 F4
Lewdown Devon 9 F6
Lewes E Sus 17 C8
Leweston Pembs 44 C4
Lewisham London 28 B4
Lewiston Highld 137 B8
Lewistown Bridgend 34 F3
Lewknor Oxon 39 E7
Leworthy Devon 8 D5
Leworthy Devon 21 F5
Lewtrenchard Devon 9 F6
Lexden Essex 43 B5
Ley Aberds 140 C4
Ley Corn 5 C6
Leybourne Kent 29 D7
Leyburn N Yorks 101 E6
Leyfields Staffs 63 D6
Leyhill Bucks 40 D2
Leyland Lancs 86 B3
Leylodge Aberds 141 C6
Leymoor W Yorks 88 C2
Leys Aberds 153 C10
Leys Perth 134 F2
Leys Castle Highld 151 G9
Leys of Cossans Angus 134 E3
Leysdown-on-Sea Kent 30 B4
Leysmill Angus 135 E6
Leysters Pole Hereford 49 C7
Leyton London 41 F6
Leytonstone London 41 F6
Lezant Corn 5 B8
Leziate Norf 67 C6
Lhanbryde Moray 152 B2
Liatrie Highld 150 H5
Libanus Powys 34 B3
Libberton S Lanark 120 E2
Liberton Edin 121 C5
Liceasto W Isles 154 H6
Lichfield Staffs 62 D5
Lickey Worcs 50 B4
Lickey End Worcs 50 B4
Lickfold W Sus 16 B3
Liddel Orkney 159 K5
Liddesdale Highld 130 D1
Liddington Swindon 38 F2
Lidgate Suff 55 D8
Lidget S Yorks 89 D7
Lidget Green W Yorks 94 F4
Lidgett Notts 77 C6
Lidlington C Beds 53 F7
Lidstone Oxon 38 B3
Lieurary Highld 158 D2
Liff Angus 134 F3
Lifton Devon 9 F5
Liftondown Devon 9 F5
Lighthorne Warks 51 D8
Lightwater Sur 27 C7
Lightwood Stoke 75 E6
Lightwood Green Ches E 74 E3
Lightwood Green Wrex 73 E7
Lilbourne Northants 52 B3
Lilburn Tower Northumb 117 B6
Lilleshall Telford 61 C7
Lilley Herts 40 B4
Lilley W Berks 26 B2
Lilliesleaf Borders 115 B8
Lillingstone Dayrell Bucks 52 F5
Lillingstone Lovell Bucks 52 E5
Lillington Dorset 12 C4
Lillington Warks 51 C8
Lilliput Poole 13 E8
Lilstock Som 22 E3
Lilyhurst Shrops 61 C7
Limbury Luton 40 B3
Limebrook Hereford 49 C5
Limefield Gtr Man 87 C6
Limekilnburn S Lanark 119 D7
Limekilns Fife 128 F2
Limerigg Falk 119 B8
Limerstone IoW 14 F5
Limington Som 12 B3
Limpenhoe Norf 69 D6
Limpley Stoke Wilts 24 C2
Limpsfield Sur 28 D5
Limpsfield Chart Sur 28 D5
Linby Notts 76 D5
Linchmere W Sus 27 F6
Lincluden Dumfries 107 B6
Lincoln Lincs 78 B2
Lincomb Worcs 50 C3
Lincombe Devon 6 D5
Lindal in Furness Cumb 92 B2
Lindale Cumb 99 F6
Lindean Borders 121 F7
Lindfield W Sus 17 B7
Lindford Hants 27 F6
Lindifferon Fife 128 C5
Lindley W Yorks 88 C2
Lindley Green N Yorks 94 E5
Lindores Fife 128 C4
Lindridge Worcs 49 C8
Lindsell Essex 42 B2
Lindsey Suff 56 E3
Linford Hants 14 D2
Linford Thurrock 29 B7
Lingague IoM 84 E2
Lingards Wood W Yorks 87 C8
Lingbob W Yorks 94 F3
Lingdale Redcar 102 C4
Lingen Hereford 49 C5
Lingfield Sur 28 E4
Lingreabhagh W Isles 154 J5
Lingwood Norf 69 D6
Linicro Highld 149 B8
Linkenholt Hants 25 D8
Linkhill Kent 18 C5
Linkinhorne Corn 5 B8
Linklater Orkney 159 K5
Linksness Orkney 159 H3
Linktown Fife 128 E4
Linley Shrops 60 E3
Linley Green Hereford 49 D8
Linlithgow W Loth 120 B3
Linlithgow Bridge W Loth 120 B2
Linshiels Northumb 116 D4
Linsiadar W Isles 154 D7
Linsidemore Highld 151 B8
Linslade C Beds 40 B2
Linstead Parva Suff 57 B7
Linstock Cumb 108 D4
Linthwaite W Yorks 88 C2
Lintlaw Borders 122 D4
Lintmill Moray 152 B5
Linton Borders 116 B3
Linton Cambs 55 E6
Linton Derbys 63 C6
Linton Hereford 36 B3
Linton Kent 29 E8
Linton N Yorks 94 C2
Linton Northumb 117 E8
Linton W Yorks 95 E6
Linton-on-Ouse N Yorks 95 C7
Linwood Hants 14 D2
Linwood Lincs 90 F5
Linwood Renfs 118 C4
Lionacleit W Isles 148 D2
Lional W Isles 155 A10
Liphook Hants 27 F6
Liscard Mers 85 E4
Liscombe Som 21 F7
Liskeard Corn 5 C7
L'Islet Guern 16
Liss Hants 15 B8
Liss Forest Hants 15 B8
Lissett E Yorks 97 D7
Lissington Lincs 90 F5
Lisvane Cardiff 35 F5
Liswerry Newport 35 F7
Litcham Norf 67 C8
Litchborough Northants 52 D4
Litchfield Hants 26 D2
Litherland Mers 85 E4
Litlington Cambs 54 E4
Litlington E Sus 18 E2
Little Abington Cambs 55 E6
Little Addington Northants 53 B7
Little Alne Warks 51 C6
Little Altcar Mers 85 D4
Little Asby Cumb 100 D1
Little Assynt Highld 156 G4
Little Aston Staffs 62 D4
Little Atherfield IoW 15 F5
Little Ayre Orkney 159 J4
Little-ayre Shetland 160 G5
Little Ayton N Yorks 102 C3
Little Baddow Essex 42 D3
Little Badminton S Glos 37 F5
Little Ballinluig Perth 133 D6
Little Bampton Cumb 108 D2
Little Bardfield Essex 55 F7
Little Barford Bedford 54 D2
Little Barningham Norf 81 D7
Little Barrington Glos 38 C2
Little Barrow Ches W 73 B8
Little Barugh N Yorks 96 B3
Little Bavington Northumb 110 B2
Little Bealings Suff 57 E6
Little Bedwyn Wilts 25 C7
Little Bentley Essex 43 B7
Little Berkhamsted Herts 41 D5
Little Billing Northants 53 C6
Little Birch Hereford 49 F7
Little Blakenham Suff 56 E5
Little Blencow Cumb 108 F4
Little Bollington Ches E 86 F5
Little Bookham Sur 28 D2
Little Bowden Leics 64 F4
Little Bradley Suff 55 D7
Little Brampton Shrops 60 F3
Little Brechin Angus 135 C5
Little Brickhill M Keynes 53 F7
Little Brington Northants 52 C4
Little Bromley Essex 43 B6
Little Broughton Cumb 107 F7
Little Budworth Ches W 74 C2
Little Burstead Essex 42 E2
Little Bytham Lincs 65 C7
Little Carlton Lincs 91 F7
Little Carlton Notts 77 D7
Little Casterton Rutland 65 D7
Little Cawthorpe Lincs 91 F7
Little Chalfont Bucks 40 E2
Little Chart Kent 30 E3
Little Chesterford Essex 55 E6
Little Cheverell Wilts 24 D4
Little Chishill Cambs 54 F5
Little Clacton Essex 43 C7
Little Clifton Cumb 98 B2
Little Colp Aberds 153 D7
Little Comberton Worcs 50 E4
Little Common E Sus 18 E4
Little Compton Warks 51 F7
Little Cornard Suff 56 F2
Little Cowarne Hereford 49 D8
Little Coxwell Oxon 38 E2
Little Crakehall N Yorks 101 E7
Little Cressingham Norf 67 D8
Little Crosby Mers 85 D4
Little Dalby Leics 64 C4
Little Dawley Telford 61 D6
Little Dens Aberds 153 D10
Little Dewchurch Hereford 49 F7
Little Downham Cambs 66 F5
Little Driffield E Yorks 97 D6
Little Dunham Norf 67 C8
Little Dunkeld Perth 133 E7
Little Dunmow Essex 42 B2
Little Easton Essex 42 B2
Little Eaton Derbys 76 E3
Little Eccleston Lancs 92 E4
Little Ellingham Norf 68 E3
Little End Essex 41 D8
Little Eversden Cambs 54 D4
Little Faringdon Oxon 38 D2
Little Fencote N Yorks 101 E7
Little Fenton N Yorks 95 F8
Little Finborough Suff 56 D4
Little Fransham Norf 68 C2
Little Gaddesden Herts 40 C2
Little Gidding Cambs 65 F8
Little Glemham Suff 57 D7
Little Glenshee Perth 133 F6
Little Gransden Cambs 54 D3
Little Green Som 24 E2
Little Grimsby Lincs 91 E7
Little Gruinard Highld 150 C2
Little Habton N Yorks 96 B3
Little Hadham Herts 41 B7
Little Hale Lincs 78 E4
Little Hallingbury Essex 41 C7
Little Hampden Bucks 40 D1
Little Harrowden Northants 53 B6
Little Haseley Oxon 39 D6
Little Hatfield E Yorks 97 E7
Little Hautbois Norf 81 E8
Little Haven Pembs 44 D3
Little Hay Staffs 62 D5
Little Hayfield Derbys 87 F8
Little Haywood Staffs 62 B4
Little Heath W Mid 63 F7
Little Hereford Hereford 49 C7
Little Horkesley Essex 56 F3
Little Horsted E Sus 17 C8
Little Horton W Yorks 94 F4
Little Horwood Bucks 53 F5
Little Houghton Northants 53 D6
Little Houghton S Yorks 88 D5
Little Hucklow Derbys 75 B8
Little Hulton Gtr Man 86 D5
Little Humber E Yorks 91 B5
Little Hungerford W Berks 26 B3
Little Irchester Northants 53 C7
Little Kimble Bucks 39 D8
Little Kineton Warks 51 D8
Little Kingshill Bucks 40 E1
Little Langdale Cumb 99 D5
Little Langford Wilts 25 F5
Little Laver Essex 41 D8
Little Leigh Ches W 74 B3
Little Leighs Essex 42 C3
Little Lever Gtr Man 87 D5
Little London Bucks 39 C6
Little London E Sus 18 D2
Little London Hants 25 E8
Little London Hants 26 D4
Little London Lincs 66 B2
Little London Lincs 66 B4
Little London Norf 81 E7
Little London Powys 59 F7
Little Longstone Derbys 75 B8
Little Lynturk Aberds 140 C4
Little Malvern Worcs 50 E2
Little Maplestead Essex 56 F2
Little Marcle Hereford 49 F8
Little Marlow Bucks 40 F1
Little Marsden Lancs 93 F8
Little Massingham Norf 80 E3
Little Melton Norf 68 D4
Little Mill Mon 35 D7
Little Milton Oxon 39 D6
Little Missenden Bucks 40 E2
Little Musgrave Cumb 100 C2
Little Ness Shrops 60 C4
Little Neston Ches W 73 B6
Little Newcastle Pembs 44 C4
Little Newsham Durham 101 C6
Little Oakley Essex 43 B8
Little Oakley Northants 65 F5
Little Orton Cumb 108 D3
Little Ouseburn N Yorks 95 C7
Little Paxton Cambs 54 C2
Little Petherick Corn 4 B4
Little Pitlurg Moray 152 D4
Little Plumpton Lancs 92 F3
Little Plumstead Norf 69 C6
Little Ponton Lincs 78 F2
Little Raveley Cambs 54 B3
Little Reedness E Yorks 90 B2
Little Ribston N Yorks 95 D6
Little Rissington Glos 38 C1
Little Ryburgh Norf 81 E5
Little Ryle Northumb 117 C6
Little Salkeld Cumb 109 F5
Little Sampford Essex 55 F7
Little Sandhurst Brack 27 C6
Little Saxham Suff 55 C8
Little Scatwell Highld 150 F6
Little Sessay N Yorks 95 B7
Little Shelford Cambs 54 D5
Little Singleton Lancs 92 F3
Little Skillymarno Aberds 153 C9
Little Smeaton N Yorks 89 C6
Little Snoring Norf 81 D5
Little Sodbury S Glos 36 F4
Little Somborne Hants 25 F8
Little Somerford Wilts 37 F6
Little Stainforth N Yorks 93 C8
Little Stainton Darl 101 B8
Little Stanney Ches W 73 B8
Little Staughton Bedford 54 C2
Little Steeping Lincs 79 C7
Little Stoke Staffs 75 F6
Little Stonham Suff 56 C5
Little Stretton Leics 64 D3
Little Stretton Shrops 60 E4
Little Strickland Cumb 99 C7
Little Stukeley Cambs 54 B3
Little Sutton Ches W 73 B7
Little Tew Oxon 38 B3
Little Thetford Cambs 55 B6
Little Thirkleby N Yorks 95 B7
Little Thurlow Suff 55 D7
Little Thurrock Thurrock 29 B7
Little Torboll Highld 151 B10
Little Torrington Devon 9 C6
Little Totham Essex 42 C4
Little Toux Aberds 152 C5
Little Town Cumb 98 C4
Little Town Lancs 93 F6
Little Urswick Cumb 92 B2
Little Wakering Essex 43 F5
Little Walden Essex 55 E6
Little Waldingfield Suff 56 E3
Little Walsingham Norf 80 D5
Little Waltham Essex 42 C3
Little Warley Essex 42 E2
Little Weighton E Yorks 97 F5
Little Weldon Northants 65 F6
Little Welnetham Suff 56 C2
Little Wenlock Telford 61 D6
Little Whittingham Green Suff 57 B6
Little Wilbraham Cambs 55 D6
Little Wishford Wilts 25 F5
Little Witley Worcs 50 C2
Little Wittenham Oxon 39 E5
Little Wolford Warks 51 F7
Little Wratting Suff 55 E7
Little Wymington Bedford 53 C7
Little Wymondley Herts 41 B5
Little Wyrley Staffs 62 D4
Little Yeldham Essex 55 F8
Littlebeck N Yorks 103 D6
Littleborough Gtr Man 87 C7
Littleborough Notts 90 F2
Littlebourne Kent 31 D6
Littlebredy Dorset 12 F3
Littlebury Essex 55 F6
Littlebury Green Essex 55 F5
Littledean Glos 36 C3
Littleferry Highld 151 B11
Littleham Devon 9 B6
Littleham Devon 10 F5
Littlehampton W Sus 16 D4
Littlehempston Devon 7 C6
Littlehoughton Northumb 117 C8
Littlemill Aberds 140 E2
Littlemill E Ayrs 112 C4
Littlemill Highld 151 F12
Littlemill Northumb 117 C8
Littlemoor Dorset 12 F4
Littlemore Oxon 39 D5
Littleover Derby 76 F3
Littleport Cambs 67 F5
Littlestone on Sea Kent 19 C7
Littlethorpe Leics 64 E2
Littlethorpe N Yorks 95 C6
Littleton Ches W 73 C8
Littleton Hants 26 F2
Littleton Perth 134 F2
Littleton Som 23 F6
Littleton Sur 27 C8
Littleton Sur 27 E7
Littleton Drew Wilts 37 F5
Littleton-on-Severn S Glos 36 F2
Littleton Pannell Wilts 24 D5
Littletown Durham 111 E6
Littlewick Green Windsor 27 B6
Littleworth Bedford 53 E8
Littleworth Glos 37 D5
Littleworth Oxon 38 E3
Littleworth Staffs 62 C4
Littleworth Worcs 50 D3
Litton Derbys 75 B8
Litton N Yorks 94 B2
Litton Som 23 D7
Litton Cheney Dorset 12 E3
Liurbost W Isles 155 E8
Liverpool Mers 85 E4
Liverpool Airport Mers 86 F2
Liversedge W Yorks 88 B3
Liverton Devon 7 B6
Liverton Redcar 103 C5
Livingston W Loth 120 C3
Livingston Village W Loth 120 C3
Lixwm Flint 73 B5
Lizard Corn 3 E6
Llaingoch Anglesey 82 C2
Llaithddu Powys 59 F7
Llan Powys 59 D5
Llan Ffestiniog Gwyn 71 C8
Llan-y-pwll Wrex 73 D7
Llanaber Gwyn 58 C3
Llanaelhaearn Gwyn 70 C4
Llanafan Ceredig 47 B5
Llanafan-fawr Powys 47 D8
Llanallgo Anglesey 82 C4
Llanandras = Presteigne Powys 48 C5
Llanarmon Gwyn 70 D5
Llanarmon Dyffryn Ceiriog Wrex 73 F5
Llanarmon-yn-Ial Denb 73 D5
Llanarth Ceredig 46 D3
Llanarth Mon 35 C7
Llanarthne Carms 33 B6
Llanasa Flint 85 F2
Llanbabo Anglesey 82 C3
Llanbadarn Fawr Ceredig 58 F3

Manar Ho. Aberds 141 B6
Manaton Devon 10 F2
Manby Lincs 91 F7
Mancetter Warks 63 E7
Manchester Gtr Man 87 E6
Manchester Airport Gtr Man 87 F6
Mancot Flint 73 C7
Mandally Highld 137 D5
Manea Cambs 66 F4
Manfield N Yorks 101 C7
Mangaster Shetland 160 F5
Mangotsfield S Glos 23 B8
Mangurstadh W Isles 154 D5
Mankinholes W Yorks 87 B7
Manley Ches W 74 B2
Mannal Argyll 146 G2
Mannerston W Loth 120 B3
Manningford Bohune Wilts 25 D6
Manningford Bruce Wilts 25 D6
Manningham W Yorks 94 F4
Mannings Heath W Sus 17 B6
Mannington Dorset 13 D8
Manningtree Essex 56 F4
Mannofield Aberdeen 141 D8
Manor London 41 F7
Manor Estate S Yorks 88 F4
Manorbier Pembs 32 E1
Manordeilo Carms 33 B7
Manorhill Borders 122 F2
Manorowen Pembs 44 B4
Mansel Lacy Hereford 49 E6
Manselfield Swansea 33 F6
Mansell Gamage Hereford 49 E5
Mansergh Cumb 99 F8
Mansfield E Ayrs 113 C6
Mansfield Notts 76 C5
Mansfield Woodhouse Notts 76 C5
Mansriggs Cumb 98 F4
Manston Dorset 13 C6
Manston Kent 31 C7
Manston W Yorks 95 F6
Manswood Dorset 13 D7
Manthorpe Lincs 65 C7
Manthorpe Lincs 78 F2
Manton N Lincs 90 D3
Manton Notts 77 B5
Manton Rutland 65 D5
Manton Wilts 25 C6
Manuden Essex 41 B7
Maperton Som 12 B4
Maple Cross Herts 40 E3
Maplebeck Notts 77 C7
Mapledurham Oxon 26 B4
Mapledurwell Hants 26 D4
Maplehurst W Sus 17 B5
Maplescombe Kent 29 C6
Mapleton Derbys 75 E8
Mapperley Derbys 76 E4
Mapperley Park Nottingham 77 E5
Mapperton Dorset 12 E3
Mappleborough Green Warks 51 C5
Mappleton E Yorks 97 E8
Mappowder Dorset 12 D5
Mar Lodge Aberds 139 E6
Maraig W Isles 154 G6
Marazanvose Corn 4 D3
Marazion Corn 2 C4
Marbhig W Isles 155 F9
Marbury Ches E 74 E2
March Cambs 66 E4
March S Lanark 114 C2
Marcham Oxon 38 E4
Marchamley Shrops 61 B5
Marchington Staffs 75 F8
Marchington Woodlands Staffs 62 B5
Marchroes Gwyn 70 E4
Marchwiel Wrex 73 E7
Marchwood Hants 14 C4
Marcross V Glam 21 C8
Marden Hereford 49 E7
Marden Kent 29 E8
Marden T&W 111 B6
Marden Wilts 25 D5
Marden Beech Kent 29 E8
Marden Thorn Kent 29 E8
Mardy Mon 35 C7
Marefield Leics 64 D4
Mareham le Fen Lincs 79 C5
Mareham on the Hill Lincs 79 C5
Marehay Derbys 76 E3
Marehill W Sus 16 C4
Maresfield E Sus 17 B8
Marfleet Hull 90 B5
Marford Wrex 73 D7
Margam Neath 34 F1
Margaret Marsh Dorset 13 C6
Margaret Roding Essex 42 C1
Margaretting Essex 42 D2
Margate Kent 31 B7
Margnaheglish N Ayrs 143 E11
Margrove Park Redcar 102 C4
Marham Norf 67 C7
Marhamchurch Corn 8 D4
Marholm Pboro 65 D8
Mariandyrys Anglesey 83 C6
Marianglas Anglesey 82 C5
Mariansleigh Devon 10 B2
Marionburgh Aberds 141 D6
Marishader Highld 149 B9
Marjoriebanks Dumfries 114 F3
Mark Dumfries 104 D5
Mark S Ayrs 104 B4
Mark Som 23 E5
Mark Causeway Som 23 E5
Mark Cross E Sus 17 C8
Mark Cross E Sus 18 B2
Markbeech Kent 29 E5
Markby Lincs 79 B7
Market Bosworth Leics 63 D8
Market Deeping Lincs 65 D8
Market Drayton Shrops 74 F3
Market Harborough Leics 64 F4
Market Lavington Wilts 24 D5
Market Overton Rutland 65 C5
Market Rasen Lincs 90 F5
Market Stainton Lincs 78 B5
Market Warsop Notts 77 C5
Market Weighton E Yorks 96 E4
Market Weston Suff 56 B3
Markethill Perth 134 F2
Markfield Leics 63 C8
Markham Caerph 35 D5
Markham Moor Notts 77 B7
Markinch Fife 128 D4
Markington N Yorks 95 C5
Marks Tey Essex 43 B5
Marksbury Bath 23 C8
Markyate Herts 40 C3
Marland Gtr Man 87 C6
Marlborough Wilts 25 C6
Marlbrook Hereford 49 D7
Marlbrook Worcs 50 B4
Marlcliff Warks 51 D5
Marldon Devon 7 C6
Marlesford Suff 57 D7
Marley Green Ches E 74 E2
Marley Hill T&W 110 D5
Marley Mount Hants 14 E3
Marlingford Norf 68 D4
Marloes Pembs 44 E2
Marlow Bucks 39 F8
Marlow Hereford 49 B6
Marlow Bottom Bucks 40 F1
Marlpit Hill Kent 28 E5
Marlpool Derbys 76 E4
Marnhull Dorset 13 C5
Marnoch Aberds 152 C5
Marnock N Lanark 119 C7
Marple Gtr Man 87 F7
Marple Bridge Gtr Man 87 F7
Marr S Yorks 89 D6
Marrel Highld 157 H13
Marrick N Yorks 101 E5
Marrister Shetland 160 G7
Marros Carms 32 D3
Marsden T&W 111 C6
Marsden W Yorks 87 C8
Marsett N Yorks 100 F4
Marsh Devon 11 C7
Marsh W Yorks 94 F3
Marsh Baldon Oxon 39 E5
Marsh Gibbon Bucks 39 B6
Marsh Green Devon 10 E5
Marsh Green Kent 28 E5
Marsh Green Staffs 75 D5
Marsh Lane Derbys 76 B4
Marsh Street Som 21 E8
Marshall's Heath Herts 40 C4
Marshalsea Dorset 11 D8
Marshalswick Herts 40 D4
Marsham Norf 81 E7
Marshaw Lancs 93 D5
Marshborough Kent 31 D7
Marshbrook Shrops 60 F4
Marshchapel Lincs 91 E7
Marshfield Newport 35 F6
Marshfield S Glos 24 B2
Marshgate Corn 8 E3
Marshland St James Norf 66 D5
Marshside Mers 85 C4
Marshwood Dorset 11 E8
Marske N Yorks 101 D6
Marske-by-the-Sea Redcar 102 B4
Marston Ches W 74 B3
Marston Hereford 49 D5
Marston Lincs 77 E8
Marston Oxon 39 D5
Marston Staffs 62 B3
Marston Staffs 62 C2
Marston Warks 63 E6
Marston Wilts 24 D4
Marston Doles Warks 52 D2
Marston Green W Mid 63 F5
Marston Magna Som 12 B3
Marston Meysey Wilts 37 E8
Marston Montgomery Derbys 75 F8
Marston Moretaine C Beds 53 E7
Marston on Dove Derbys 63 B6
Marston St Lawrence Northants 52 E3
Marston Stannett Hereford 49 D7
Marston Trussell Northants 64 F3
Marstow Hereford 36 C2
Marsworth Bucks 40 C2
Marten Wilts 25 D7
Marthall Ches E 74 B5
Martham Norf 69 C7
Martin Hants 13 C8
Martin Kent 31 E7
Martin Lincs 78 C5
Martin Lincs 78 D4
Martin Dales Lincs 78 C4
Martin Drove End Hants 13 B8
Martin Hussingtree Worcs 50 C3
Martin Mill Kent 31 E7
Martinhoe Devon 21 E5
Martinhoe Cross Devon 21 E5
Martinscroft Warr 86 F4
Martinstown Dorset 12 F4
Martlesham Suff 57 E6
Martlesham Heath Suff 57 E6
Martletwy Pembs 32 C1
Martley Worcs 50 D2
Martock Som 12 C2
Marton Ches E 75 C5
Marton E Yorks 97 F7
Marton Lincs 90 F2
Marton Mbro 102 C3
Marton N Yorks 95 C7
Marton N Yorks 103 F5
Marton Shrops 60 B4
Marton Shrops 60 D2
Marton Warks 52 C2
Marton-le-Moor N Yorks 95 B6
Martyr Worthy Hants 26 F3
Martyr's Green Sur 27 D8
Marwick Orkney 159 F3
Marwood Devon 20 F4
Mary Tavy Devon 6 B3
Marybank Highld 150 F7
Maryburgh Highld 151 F8
Maryhill Glasgow 119 C5
Marykirk Aberds 135 C6
Marylebone Gtr Man 86 D3
Marypark Moray 152 E1
Maryport Cumb 107 F7
Maryport Dumfries 104 F5
Maryton Angus 135 D6
Marywell Aberds 140 E4
Marywell Aberds 141 E8
Marywell Angus 135 E6
Masham N Yorks 101 F7
Mashbury Essex 42 C2
Masongill N Yorks 93 B6
Masonhill S Ayrs 112 B3
Mastin Moor Derbys 76 B4
Mastrick Aberdeen 141 D7
Matching Essex 41 C8
Matching Green Essex 41 C8
Matching Tye Essex 41 C8
Matfen Northumb 110 B3
Matfield Kent 29 E7
Mathern Mon 36 E2
Mathon Hereford 50 E2
Mathry Pembs 44 B3
Matlaske Norf 81 D7
Matlock Derbys 76 C2
Matlock Bath Derbys 76 D2
Matson Glos 37 C5
Matterdale End Cumb 99 B5
Mattersey Notts 89 F7
Mattersey Thorpe Notts 89 F7
Mattingley Hants 26 D5
Mattishall Norf 68 C3
Mattishall Burgh Norf 68 C3
Mauchline E Ayrs 112 B4
Maud Aberds 153 D9
Maugersbury Glos 38 B2
Maughold IoM 84 C4
Mauld Highld 150 H7
Maulden C Beds 53 F8
Maulds Meaburn Cumb 99 C8
Maunby N Yorks 102 F1
Maund Bryan Hereford 49 D7
Maundown Som 11 B5
Mautby Norf 69 C7
Mavis Enderby Lincs 79 C6
Maw Green Ches E 74 D4
Mawbray Cumb 107 E7
Mawdesley Lancs 86 C2
Mawdlam Bridgend 34 F2
Mawgan Corn 3 D6
Mawla Corn 3 B6
Mawnan Corn 3 D6
Mawnan Smith Corn 3 D6
Mawsley Northants 53 B6
Maxey Pboro 65 D8
Maxstoke Warks 63 F6
Maxton Borders 122 F2
Maxton Kent 31 E7
Maxwellheugh Borders 122 F3
Maxwelltown Dumfries 107 B6
Maxworthy Corn 8 E4
May Bank Staffs 75 E5
Mayals Swansea 33 E7
Maybole S Ayrs 112 D3
Mayfield E Sus 18 C2
Mayfield Midloth 121 C6
Mayfield Staffs 75 E8
Mayfield W Loth 120 C2
Mayford Sur 27 D7
Mayland Essex 43 D5
Maynard's Green E Sus 18 D2
Maypole Mon 36 C1
Maypole Scilly 2 E4
Maypole Green Essex 43 B5
Maypole Green Norf 69 E7
Maypole Green Suff 57 C6
Maywick Shetland 160 L5
Meadle Bucks 39 D8
Meadowtown Shrops 60 D3
Meaford Staffs 75 F5
Meal Bank Cumb 99 E7
Mealabost W Isles 155 D9
Mealabost Bhuirgh W Isles 155 B9
Mealsgate Cumb 108 E2
Meanwood W Yorks 95 F5
Mearbeck N Yorks 93 C8
Meare Som 23 E6
Meare Green Som 11 B8
Mears Ashby Northants 53 C6
Measham Leics 63 C7
Meath Green Sur 28 E3
Meathop Cumb 99 F6
Meaux E Yorks 97 F6
Meavy Devon 6 C3
Medbourne Leics 64 E4
Medburn Northumb 110 B4
Meddon Devon 8 C4
Meden Vale Notts 77 C5
Medlam Lincs 79 D6
Medmenham Bucks 39 F8
Medomsley Durham 110 D4
Medstead Hants 26 F4
Meer End W Mid 51 B7
Meerbrook Staffs 75 C6
Meers Bridge Lincs 91 F8
Meesden Herts 54 F5
Meeth Devon 9 D7
Meggethead Borders 114 B4
Meidrim Carms 32 B3
Meifod Denb 72 D4
Meifod Powys 59 C8
Meigle N Ayrs 118 C1
Meigle Perth 134 E2
Meikle Earnock S Lanark 119 D7
Meikle Ferry Highld 151 C10
Meikle Forter Angus 134 C1
Meikle Gluich Highld 151 C9
Meikle Pinkerton E Loth 122 B3
Meikle Strath Aberds 135 B6
Meikle Tarty Aberds 141 B8
Meikle Wartle Aberds 153 E7
Meikleour Perth 134 F1
Meinciau Carms 33 C5
Meir Stoke 75 E6
Meir Heath Staffs 75 E6
Melbourn Cambs 54 E4
Melbourne Derbys 63 B7
Melbourne E Yorks 96 E3
Melbourne S Lanark 120 E3
Melbury Abbas Dorset 13 B6
Melbury Bubb Dorset 12 D3
Melbury Osmond Dorset 12 D3
Melbury Sampford Dorset 12 D3
Melby Shetland 160 H3
Melchbourne Bedford 53 C8
Melcombe Bingham Dorset 13 D5
Melcombe Regis Dorset 12 F4
Meldon Devon 9 E7
Meldon Northumb 117 F7
Meldreth Cambs 54 E4
Meldrum Ho. Aberds 141 B7
Melfort Argyll 124 D4
Melgarve Highld 137 E7
Meliden Denb 72 A4
Melin-y-coed Conwy 83 E8
Melin-y-ddôl Powys 59 D7
Melin-y-grug Powys 59 D7
Melin-y-Wig Denb 72 E4
Melinbyrhedyn Powys 58 E5
Melincourt Neath 34 D2
Melkinthorpe Cumb 99 B7
Melkridge Northumb 109 C7
Melksham Wilts 24 C4
Melldalloch Argyll 145 F8
Melling Lancs 93 B5
Melling Mers 85 D4
Melling Mount Mers 86 D2
Mellis Suff 56 B5
Mellon Charles Highld 155 H13
Mellon Udrigle Highld 155 H13
Mellor Gtr Man 87 F7
Mellor Lancs 93 F6
Mellor Brook Lancs 93 F6
Mells Som 24 E2
Melmerby Cumb 109 F6
Melmerby N Yorks 95 B6
Melmerby N Yorks 101 F5
Melplash Dorset 12 E2
Melrose Borders 121 F8
Melsetter Orkney 159 K3
Melsonby N Yorks 101 D6
Meltham W Yorks 88 C2
Melton Suff 57 D6
Melton Constable Norf 81 D6
Melton Mowbray Leics 64 C4
Melton Ross N Lincs 90 C4
Meltonby E Yorks 96 D3
Melvaig Highld 155 J12
Melverley Shrops 60 C3
Melverley Green Shrops 60 C3
Melvich Highld 157 C11
Membury Devon 11 D7
Memsie Aberds 153 B9
Memus Angus 134 D4
Menabilly Corn 5 D5
Menai Bridge = Porthaethwy Anglesey 83 D5
Mendham Suff 69 F5
Mendlesham Suff 56 C5
Mendlesham Green Suff 56 C4
Menheniot Corn 5 C7
Mennock Dumfries 113 D8
Menston W Yorks 94 E4
Menstrie Clack 127 E7
Menthorpe N Yorks 96 F2
Mentmore Bucks 40 C2
Meoble Highld 147 C10
Meole Brace Shrops 60 C4
Meols Mers 85 E3
Meonstoke Hants 15 C7
Meopham Kent 29 C7
Meopham Station Kent 29 C7
Mepal Cambs 66 F4
Meppershall C Beds 54 F2
Merbach Hereford 48 E5
Mere Ches E 86 F5
Mere Wilts 24 F3
Mere Brow Lancs 86 C2
Mere Green W Mid 62 E5
Mereclough Lancs 93 F8
Mereside Blackpool 92 F3
Mereworth Kent 29 D7
Mergie Aberds 141 F6
Meriden W Mid 63 F6
Merkadale Highld 149 E8
Merkland Dumfries 106 B4
Merkland S Ayrs 112 E2
Merkland Lodge Highld 156 G7
Merley Poole 13 E8
Merlin's Bridge Pembs 44 D4
Merrington Shrops 60 B4
Merrion Pembs 44 F4
Merriott Som 12 C2
Merrivale Devon 6 B3
Merrow Sur 27 D8
Merrymeet Corn 5 C7
Mersham Kent 19 B7
Merstham Sur 28 D3
Merston W Sus 16 D2
Merstone IoW 15 F6
Merther Corn 3 B7
Merthyr Carms 32 B4
Merthyr Cynog Powys 47 F8
Merthyr-Dyfan V Glam 22 C3
Merthyr Mawr Bridgend 21 B7
Merthyr Tudful = Merthyr Tydfil M Tydf 34 D4
Merthyr Tydfil = Merthyr Tudful M Tydf 34 D4
Merthyr Vale M Tydf 34 E4
Merton Devon 9 C7
Merton London 28 B3
Merton Norf 68 E2
Merton Oxon 39 C5
Mervinslaw Borders 116 C2
Meshaw Devon 10 C2
Messing Essex 42 C4
Messingham N Lincs 90 D2
Metfield Suff 69 F5
Metheringham Lincs 78 C3
Methil Fife 129 E5
Methlem Gwyn 70 D2
Methley W Yorks 88 B4
Methlick Aberds 153 E8
Methven Perth 128 B2
Methwold Norf 67 E7
Methwold Hythe Norf 67 E7
Mettingham Suff 69 F6
Mevagissey Corn 3 B9
Mewith Head N Yorks 93 C7
Mexborough S Yorks 89 D5
Mey Highld 158 C4
Meysey Hampton Glos 37 E8
Miabhag W Isles 154 G5
Miabhag W Isles 154 H6
Miabhig W Isles 154 D5
Michaelchurch Hereford 36 B2
Michaelchurch Escley Hereford 48 F5
Michaelchurch on Arrow Powys 48 D4
Michaelston-le-Pit V Glam 22 B3
Michaelston-y-Fedw Newport 35 F6
Michaelstow Corn 5 B5
Michealston-super-Ely Cardiff 22 B3
Micheldever Hants 26 F3
Michelmersh Hants 14 B4
Mickfield Suff 56 C5
Mickle Trafford Ches W 73 C8
Micklebring S Yorks 89 E6
Mickleby N Yorks 103 C6
Mickleham Sur 28 D2
Mickleover Derby 76 F3
Micklethwaite W Yorks 94 E4
Mickleton Durham 100 B4
Mickleton Glos 51 E6
Mickletown W Yorks 88 B4
Mickley N Yorks 95 B5
Mickley Square Northumb 110 C3
Mid Ardlaw Aberds 153 B9
Mid Auchinlech Invclyd 118 B3
Mid Beltie Aberds 140 D5
Mid Calder W Loth 120 C3
Mid Cloch Forbie Aberds 153 C7
Mid Clyth Highld 158 G4
Mid Lavant W Sus 16 D2
Mid Main Highld 150 H7
Mid Urchany Highld 151 G11
Mid Walls Shetland 160 H4
Mid Yell Shetland 160 D7
Midbea Orkney 159 D5
Middle Assendon Oxon 39 F7
Middle Aston Oxon 38 B4
Middle Barton Oxon 38 B4
Middle Cairncake Aberds 153 D8
Middle Claydon Bucks 39 B7
Middle Drums Angus 135 D5
Middle Handley Derbys 76 B4
Middle Littleton Worcs 51 E5
Middle Maes-coed Hereford 48 F5
Middle Mill Pembs 44 C3
Middle Rasen Lincs 90 F4
Middle Rigg Perth 128 D2
Middle Tysoe Warks 51 E8
Middle Wallop Hants 25 F7
Middle Winterslow Wilts 25 F7
Middle Woodford Wilts 25 F6
Middlebie Dumfries 108 B2
Middleforth Green Lancs 86 B3
Middleham N Yorks 101 F6
Middlehope Shrops 60 F4
Middlemarsh Dorset 12 D4
Middlemuir Aberds 141 B8
Middlesbrough Mbro 102 B2
Middleshaw Cumb 99 F7
Middleshaw Dumfries 107 B8
Middlesmoor N Yorks 94 B3
Middlestone Durham 111 F5
Middlestone Moor Durham 110 F5
Middlestown W Yorks 88 C3
Middlethird Borders 122 E2
Middleton Aberds 141 C7
Middleton Argyll 146 G2
Middleton Cumb 99 F8
Middleton Derbys 75 C8
Middleton Derbys 76 D2
Middleton Essex 56 F2
Middleton Gtr Man 87 D6
Middleton Hants 26 E2
Middleton Hereford 49 C7
Middleton Lancs 92 D4
Middleton Midloth 121 D6
Middleton N Yorks 94 E4
Middleton N Yorks 103 F5
Middleton Norf 67 C6
Middleton Northants 64 F5
Middleton Northumb 117 F6
Middleton Northumb 123 F7
Middleton Perth 128 D3
Middleton Perth 133 E8
Middleton Shrops 49 B7
Middleton Shrops 60 B3
Middleton Shrops 60 E2
Middleton Suff 57 C8
Middleton Swansea 33 F5
Middleton W Yorks 88 B3
Middleton Warks 63 E5
Middleton Cheney Northants 52 E2
Middleton Green Staffs 75 F6
Middleton Hall Northumb 117 B5
Middleton-in-Teesdale Durham 100 B4
Middleton Moor Suff 57 C8
Middleton-on-Leven N Yorks 102 D2
Middleton-on-Sea W Sus 16 D3
Middleton on the Hill Hereford 49 C7
Middleton-on-the-Wolds E Yorks 96 E5
Middleton One Row Darl 102 C1
Middleton Priors Shrops 61 E6
Middleton Quernham N Yorks 95 B6
Middleton Scriven Shrops 61 F6
Middleton St George Darl 101 C8
Middleton Stoney Oxon 39 B5
Middleton Tyas N Yorks 101 D7
Middletown Cumb 98 D1
Middletown Powys 60 C3
Middlewich Ches E 74 C3
Middlewood Green Suff 56 C4
Middlezoy Som 23 F5
Middridge Durham 101 B7
Midfield Highld 157 C8
Midge Hall Lancs 86 B3
Midgeholme Cumb 109 D6
Midgham W Berks 26 C3
Midgley W Yorks 87 B8
Midgley W Yorks 88 C3
Midhopestones S Yorks 88 E3
Midhurst W Sus 16 B2
Midlem Borders 115 B8
Midmar Aberds 141 D5
Midsomer Norton Bath 23 D8
Midton Invclyd 118 B2
Midtown Highld 155 J13
Midtown Highld 157 C8
Midtown of Buchromb Moray 152 D3
Midville Lincs 79 D6
Midway Ches E 87 F7
Migdale Highld 151 B9
Migvie Aberds 140 D3
Milarrochy Stirling 126 E3
Milborne Port Som 12 C4
Milborne St Andrew Dorset 13 E6
Milborne Wick Som 12 B4
Milbourne Northumb 110 B4
Milburn Cumb 100 B1
Milbury Heath S Glos 36 E3
Milcombe Oxon 52 F2
Milden Suff 56 E3
Mildenhall Suff 55 B8
Mildenhall Wilts 25 C7
Mile Cross Norf 68 C5
Mile Elm Wilts 24 C4
Mile End Essex 43 B5
Mile End Glos 36 C2
Mile Oak Brighton 17 D6
Milebrook Powys 48 B5
Milebush Kent 29 E8
Mileham Norf 68 C2
Milesmark Fife 128 F2
Milfield Northumb 122 F5
Milford Derbys 76 E3
Milford Devon 8 B4
Milford Powys 59 E7
Milford Staffs 62 B3
Milford Sur 27 E7
Milford Wilts 14 B2
Milford Haven = Aberdaugleddau Pembs 44 E4
Milford on Sea Hants 14 E3
Milkwall Glos 36 D2
Milkwell Wilts 13 B7
Mill Bank W Yorks 87 B8
Mill Common Suff 69 F7
Mill End Bucks 39 F7
Mill End Herts 54 F4
Mill Green Essex 42 D2
Mill Green Norf 68 F4
Mill Green Suff 56 E3
Mill Hill London 41 E5
Mill Lane Hants 27 D5
Mill of Kingoodie Aberds 141 B7
Mill of Muiresk Aberds 153 D6
Mill of Sterin Aberds 140 E2
Mill of Uras Aberds 141 F7
Mill Place N Lincs 90 D3
Mill Side Cumb 99 F6
Mill Street Norf 68 C3
Milland W Sus 16 B2
Millarston Renfs 118 C4
Millbank Aberds 153 D11
Millbank Highld 158 D3
Millbeck Cumb 98 B4
Millbounds Orkney 159 E6
Millbreck Aberds 153 D10
Millbridge Sur 27 E6
Millbrook C Beds 53 F8
Millbrook Corn 6 D2
Millbrook Soton 14 C4
Millburn S Ayrs 112 B4
Millcombe Devon 7 E6
Millcorner E Sus 18 C5
Milldale Staffs 75 D8
Millden Lodge Angus 135 B5
Milldens Angus 135 D5
Millerhill Midloth 121 C6
Miller's Dale Derbys 75 B8
Miller's Green Derbys 76 D2
Millgreen Shrops 61 B6
Millhalf Hereford 48 E4
Millhayes Devon 11 D7
Millhead Lancs 92 B4
Millheugh S Lanark 119 D7
Millholme Cumb 99 E7
Millhouse Argyll 145 F8
Millhouse Cumb 108 F3
Millhouse Green S Yorks 88 D3
Millhousebridge Dumfries 114 F4
Millhouses S Yorks 88 F4
Millikenpark Renfs 118 C4
Millin Cross Pembs 44 D4
Millington E Yorks 96 D4
Millmeece Staffs 74 F5
Millom Cumb 98 F3
Millook Corn 8 E3
Millpool Corn 5 B6
Millport N Ayrs 145 H10
Millquarter Dumfries 113 F6
Millthorpe Lincs 78 F4
Millthrop Cumb 100 E1
Milltimber Aberdeen 141 D7
Milltown Corn 5 D6
Milltown Derbys 76 C3
Milltown Devon 20 F4
Milltown Dumfries 108 B3
Milltown of Aberdalgie Perth 128 B2
Milltown of Auchindoun Moray 152 D3
Milltown of Craigston Aberds 153 C7
Milltown of Edinvillie Moray 152 D2
Milltown of Kildrummy Aberds 140 C3
Milltown of Rothiemay Moray 152 D5
Milltown of Towie Aberds 140 C3
Milnathort Perth 128 D3
Milner's Heath Ches W 73 C8
Milngavie E Dunb 119 B5
Milnrow Gtr Man 87 C7
Milnshaw Lancs 87 B5
Milnthorpe Cumb 99 F6
Milo Carms 33 C6
Milson Shrops 49 B8
Milstead Kent 30 D3
Milston Wilts 25 E6
Milton Angus 134 E3
Milton Cambs 55 C5
Milton Cumb 109 C5
Milton Derbys 63 B7
Milton Dumfries 105 D6
Milton Dumfries 106 B5
Milton Dumfries 113 F8
Milton Highld 150 F6
Milton Highld 150 H7
Milton Highld 151 D10
Milton Highld 151 G8
Milton Highld 158 E5
Milton Moray 152 B5
Milton N Som 22 C5
Milton Notts 77 B7
Milton Oxon 38 E4
Milton Oxon 52 F2
Milton Pembs 32 D1
Milton Perth 127 C8
Milton Ptsmth 15 E7
Milton Stirling 126 D4
Milton Stoke 75 D6
Milton W Dunb 118 B4
Milton Abbas Dorset 13 D6
Milton Abbot Devon 6 B2
Milton Bridge Midloth 120 C5
Milton Bryan C Beds 53 F7
Milton Clevedon Som 23 F8
Milton Coldwells Aberds 153 E9
Milton Combe Devon 6 C2
Milton Damerel Devon 9 C5
Milton End Glos 37 D8
Milton Ernest Bedford 53 D8
Milton Green Ches W 73 D8
Milton Hill Oxon 38 E4
Milton Keynes M Keynes 53 F6
Milton Keynes Village M Keynes 53 F6
Milton Lilbourne Wilts 25 C6
Milton Malsor Northants 52 D5
Milton Morenish Perth 132 F3
Milton of Auchinhove Aberds 140 D4
Milton of Balgonie Fife 128 D5
Milton of Buchanan Stirling 126 E3
Milton of Campfield Aberds 140 D5
Milton of Campsie E Dunb 119 B6
Milton of Corsindae Aberds 141 D5
Milton of Cushnie Aberds 140 C4
Milton of Dalcapon Perth 133 D6
Milton of Edradour Perth 133 D6
Milton of Gollanfield Highld 151 F10
Milton of Lesmore Aberds 140 B3
Milton of Logie Aberds 140 D3
Milton of Murtle Aberdeen 141 D7
Milton of Noth Aberds 140 B4
Milton of Tullich Aberds 140 E2
Milton on Stour Dorset 13 B5
Milton Regis Kent 30 C3
Milton under Wychwood Oxon 38 C2
Miltonduff Moray 152 B1
Miltonhill Moray 151 E13
Miltonise Dumfries 105 B5
Milverton Som 11 B6
Milverton Warks 51 C8
Milwich Staffs 75 F6
Minard Argyll 125 F5
Minchinhampton Glos 37 D5
Mindrum Northumb 122 F4
Minehead Som 21 E8
Minera Wrex 73 D6
Minety Wilts 37 E7
Minffordd Gwyn 58 C4
Minffordd Gwyn 71 D6
Minffordd Gwyn 83 D5
Miningsby Lincs 79 C6
Minions Corn 5 B7
Minishant S Ayrs 112 C3
Minllyn Gwyn 59 C5
Minnes Aberds 141 B8
Minngearraidh W Isles 148 F2
Minnigaff Dumfries 105 C8
Minnonie Aberds 153 B7
Minskip N Yorks 95 C6
Minstead Hants 14 C3
Minsted W Sus 16 B2
Minster Kent 30 B3
Minster Kent 31 C7
Minster Lovell Oxon 38 C3
Minsterley Shrops 60 D3
Minsterworth Glos 36 C4
Minterne Magna Dorset 12 D4
Minting Lincs 78 B4
Mintlaw Aberds 153 D9
Minto Borders 115 B8
Minton Shrops 60 E4
Minwear Pembs 32 C1
Minworth W Mid 63 E5
Mirbister Orkney 159 F4
Mirehouse Cumb 98 C1
Mireland Highld 158 D5
Mirfield W Yorks 88 C3
Miserden Glos 37 D6
Miskin Rhondda 34 F4
Misson Notts 89 E7
Misterton Leics 64 F2
Misterton Notts 89 E8
Misterton Som 12 D2
Mistley Essex 56 F5
Mitcham London 28 C3
Mitchel Troy Mon 36 C1
Mitcheldean Glos 36 C3
Mitchell Corn 4 D3
Mitcheltroy Common Mon 36 D1
Mitford Northumb 117 F7
Mithian Corn 4 D2
Mitton Staffs 62 C2
Mixbury Oxon 52 F4
Moat Cumb 108 B4
Moats Tye Suff 56 D4
Mobberley Ches E 74 B4
Mobberley Staffs 75 E7
Moccas Hereford 49 E5
Mochdre Conwy 83 D8
Mochdre Powys 59 F7
Mochrum Dumfries 105 E7
Mockbeggar Hants 14 D2
Mockerkin Cumb 98 B2
Modbury Devon 6 D4
Moddershall Staffs 75 F6
Moelfre Anglesey 82 C5
Moelfre Powys 59 B8
Moffat Dumfries 114 D3
Moggerhanger C Beds 54 E2
Moira Leics 63 C7
Mol-chlach Highld 149 G9
Molash Kent 30 D4
Mold = Yr Wyddgrug Flint 73 C6
Moldgreen W Yorks 88 C2
Molehill Green Essex 42 B1
Molescroft E Yorks 97 E6
Molesden Northumb 117 F7
Molesworth Cambs 53 B8
Moll Highld 149 E10
Molland Devon 10 B3
Mollington Ches W 73 B7
Mollington Oxon 52 E2
Mollinsburn N Lanark 119 B7
Monachty Ceredig 46 C4
Monachylemore Stirling 126 C3
Monar Lodge Highld 150 G5
Monaughty Powys 48 C4
Monboddo House Aberds 135 B7
Mondynes Aberds 135 B7
Monevechadan Argyll 125 E7
Monewden Suff 57 D6
Moneydie Perth 128 B2
Moniaive Dumfries 113 E7
Monifieth Angus 134 F4
Monikie Angus 135 F4
Monimail Fife 128 C4
Monington Pembs 45 E3
Monk Bretton S Yorks 88 D4
Monk Fryston N Yorks 89 B6
Monk Sherborne Hants 26 D4
Monk Soham Suff 57 C6
Monk Street Essex 42 B2
Monken Hadley London 41 E5
Monkhopton Shrops 61 E6
Monkland Hereford 49 D6
Monkleigh Devon 9 B6
Monknash V Glam 21 B8
Monkokehampton Devon 9 D7
Monks Eleigh Suff 56 E3
Monk's Gate W Sus 17 B6
Monks Heath Ches E 74 B5
Monks Kirby Warks 63 F8
Monks Risborough Bucks 39 D8
Monkseaton T&W 111 B6
Monkshill Aberds 153 D7
Monksilver Som 22 F2
Monkspath W Mid 51 B6
Monkswood Mon 35 D7
Monkton Devon 11 D6
Monkton Kent 31 C6
Monkton Pembs 44 E4
Monkton S Ayrs 112 B3
Monkton Combe Bath 24 C2
Monkton Deverill Wilts 24 F3
Monkton Farleigh Wilts 24 C3
Monkton Heathfield Som 11 B7
Monkton Up Wimborne Dorset 13 C8
Monkwearmouth T&W 111 D6
Monkwood Hants 26 F4
Monmouth = Trefynwy Mon 36 C2
Monmouth Cap Mon 35 B7
Monnington on Wye Hereford 49 E5
Monreith Dumfries 105 E7
Monreith Mains Dumfries 105 E7
Mont Saint Guern 16
Montacute Som 12 C2
Montcoffer Ho. Aberds 153 B6
Montford Argyll 145 G10
Montford Shrops 60 C4
Montford Bridge Shrops 60 C4
Montgarrie Aberds 140 C4
Montgomery = Trefaldwyn Powys 60 E2
Montrave Fife 129 D5
Montrose Angus 135 D7
Montsale Essex 43 E6
Monxton Hants 25 E8
Monyash Derbys 75 C8
Monymusk Aberds 141 C5
Monzie Perth 127 B7
Monzie Castle Perth 127 B7
Moodiesburn N Lanark 119 B6
Moonzie Fife 128 C5
Moor Allerton W Yorks 95 F5
Moor Crichel Dorset 13 D7
Moor End E Yorks 96 F4
Moor End York 96 D2
Moor Monkton N Yorks 95 D8
Moor of Granary Moray 151 F13
Moor of Ravenstone Dumfries 105 E7
Moor Row Cumb 98 C2
Moor Street Kent 30 C2
Moorby Lincs 79 C5
Moordown Bmouth 13 E8
Moore Halton 86 F3
Moorend Glos 36 D4
Moorends S Yorks 89 C7
Moorgate S Yorks 88 E5
Moorgreen Notts 76 E4
Moorhall Derbys 76 B3
Moorhampton Hereford 49 E5
Moorhead W Yorks 94 F4
Moorhouse Cumb 108 D3
Moorhouse Notts 77 C7
Moorlinch Som 23 F5
Moorsholm Redcar 102 C4
Moorside Gtr Man 87 D7
Moorthorpe W Yorks 89 C5
Moortown Hants 14 D2
Moortown IoW 14 F5
Moortown Lincs 90 E4
Morangie Highld 151 C10
Morar Highld 147 B9
Morborne Cambs 65 E8
Morchard Bishop Devon 10 D2
Morcombelake Dorset 12 E2
Morcott Rutland 65 D6
Morda Shrops 60 B2
Morden Dorset 13 E7
Morden London 28 C3
Mordiford Hereford 49 F7
Mordon Durham 101 B8
More Shrops 60 E3
Morebath Devon 10 B4
Morebattle Borders 116 B3
Morecambe Lancs 92 C4
Morefield Highld 150 B4
Moreleigh Devon 7 D5
Morenish Perth 132 F2
Moresby Cumb 98 B1
Moresby Parks Cumb 98 C1
Morestead Hants 15 B6
Moreton Dorset 13 F6
Moreton Essex 41 D8
Moreton Mers 85 E3
Moreton Oxon 39 D6
Moreton Staffs 61 C7
Moreton Corbet Shrops 61 B5
Moreton-in-Marsh Glos 51 F7
Moreton Jeffries Hereford 49 E8
Moreton Morrell Warks 51 D8
Moreton on Lugg Hereford 49 E7
Moreton Pinkney Northants 52 E3
Moreton Say Shrops 74 F3
Moreton Valence Glos 36 D4
Moretonhampstead Devon 10 F2
Morfa Carms 33 C6
Morfa Carms 33 E6
Morfa Bach Carms 32 C4
Morfa Bychan Gwyn 71 D6
Morfa Dinlle Gwyn 82 F4
Morfa Glas Neath 34 D2
Morfa Nefyn Gwyn 70 C3
Morfydd Denb 72 E5
Morgan's Vale Wilts 14 B2
Moriah Ceredig 46 B5
Morland Cumb 99 B7
Morley Derbys 76 E3
Morley Durham 101 B6
Morley W Yorks 88 B3
Morley Green Ches E 87 F6
Morley St Botolph Norf 68 E3
Morningside Edin 120 B5
Morningside N Lanark 119 D8
Morningthorpe Norf 68 E5
Morpeth Northumb 117 F8
Morphie Aberds 135 C7
Morrey Staffs 62 C5
Morris Green Essex 55 F8
Morriston Swansea 33 E7
Morston Norf 81 C6
Mortehoe Devon 20 E3
Mortimer W Berks 26 C4
Mortimer West End Hants 26 C4
Mortimer's Cross Hereford 49 C6
Mortlake London 28 B3
Morton Cumb 108 D3
Morton Derbys 76 C4
Morton Lincs 65 B7
Morton Lincs 77 C8
Morton Lincs 90 E2
Morton Norf 68 C4
Morton Notts 77 D7
Morton S Glos 36 E3
Morton Shrops 60 B2
Morton Bagot Warks 51 C6
Morton-on-Swale N Yorks 101 E8
Morvah Corn 2 C3
Morval Corn 5 D7
Morvich Highld 136 B2
Morvich Highld 157 J10
Morville Shrops 61 E6
Morville Heath Shrops 61 E6
Morwenstow Corn 8 C4
Mosborough S Yorks 88 F5
Moscow E Ayrs 118 E4
Mosedale Cumb 108 F3
Moseley W Mid 62 E3
Moseley W Mid 62 F4
Moseley Worcs 50 D3
Moss Argyll 146 G2
Moss Highld 147 E9
Moss S Yorks 89 C6
Moss Wrex 73 D7
Moss Bank Mers 86 E3
Moss Edge Lancs 92 E4
Moss End Brack 27 B6
Moss of Barmuckity Moray 152 B2
Moss Pit Staffs 62 B3
Moss-side Highld 151 F11
Moss Side Lancs 92 F3
Mossat Aberds 140 C3
Mossbank Shetland 160 F6
Mossbay Cumb 98 B1
Mossblown S Ayrs 112 B4
Mossbrow Gtr Man 86 F5
Mossburnford Borders 116 C2
Mossdale Dumfries 106 B3
Mossend N Lanark 119 C7
Mosser Cumb 98 B3
Mossfield Highld 151 D9
Mossgiel E Ayrs 112 B4
Mosside Angus 134 D4
Mossley Ches E 75 C5
Mossley Gtr Man 87 D7
Mossley Hill Mers 85 F4
Mosstodloch Moray 152 B3
Mosston Angus 135 E5
Mossy Lea Lancs 86 C3
Mosterton Dorset 12 D2
Moston Gtr Man 87 D6
Moston Shrops 61 B5
Moston Green Ches E 74 C4
Mostyn Flint 85 F2
Mostyn Quay Flint 85 F2
Motcombe Dorset 13 B6
Mothecombe Devon 6 E4
Motherby Cumb 99 B6
Motherwell N Lanark 119 D7
Mottingham London 28 B5
Mottisfont Hants 14 B4
Mottistone IoW 14 F5
Mottram in Longdendale Gtr Man 87 E7
Mottram St Andrew Ches E 75 B5
Mouilpied Guern 16
Mouldsworth Ches W 74 B2
Moulin Perth 133 D6
Moulsecoomb Brighton 17 D7
Moulsford Oxon 39 F5
Moulsoe M Keynes 53 E7
Moulton Ches W 74 C3
Moulton Lincs 66 B3
Moulton N Yorks 101 D7
Moulton Northants 53 C5
Moulton Suff 55 C7
Moulton V Glam 22 B2
Moulton Chapel Lincs 66 C2
Moulton Eaugate Lincs 66 C3
Moulton Seas End Lincs 66 B3
Moulton St Mary Norf 69 D6
Mounie Castle Aberds 141 B6
Mount Corn 4 D2
Mount Corn 5 C6
Mount Highld 151 G12
Mount Bures Essex 56 F3
Mount Canisp Highld 151 D10
Mount Hawke Corn 3 B6
Mount Pleasant Ches E 74 D5
Mount Pleasant Derbys 63 C6
Mount Pleasant Derbys 76 E3
Mount Pleasant Flint 73 B6
Mount Pleasant Hants 14 E3
Mount Pleasant W Yorks 88 B3
Mount Sorrel Wilts 13 B8
Mount Tabor W Yorks 87 B8
Mountain W Yorks 94 F3
Mountain Ash = Aberpennar Rhondda 34 E4
Mountain Cross Borders 120 E4

226 Mou – Nor

Mountain Water Pembs 44 C4
Mountbenger Borders 115 B6
Mountfield E Sus 18 C4
Mountgerald Highld 151 E8
Mountjoy Corn 4 C3
Mountnessing Essex 42 E2
Mounton Mon 36 E2
Mountsorrel Leics 64 C2
Mousehole Corn 2 D3
Mousen Northumb 123 F7
Mouswald Dumfries 107 B7
Mow Cop Ches E 75 D5
Mowhaugh Borders 116 B4
Mowsley Leics 64 F3
Moxley W Mid 62 E3
Moy Highld 137 F7
Moy Highld 151 H10
Moy Hall Highld 151 H10
Moy Ho. Moray 151 E13
Moy Lodge Highld 137 F7
Moyles Court Hants 14 D2
Moylgrove Pembs 45 E3
Muasdale Argyll 143 D7
Much Birch Hereford 49 F7
Much Cowarne Hereford 49 E8
Much Dewchurch Hereford 49 F6
Much Hadham Herts 41 C7
Much Hoole Lancs 86 B2
Much Marcle Hereford 49 F8
Much Wenlock Shrops 61 D6
Muchalls Aberds 141 E8
Muchelney Som 12 B2
Muchlarnick Corn 5 D7
Muchrachd Highld 150 H5
Muckernich Highld 151 F8
Mucking Thurrock 42 F2
Muckleford Dorset 12 E4
Mucklestone Staffs 74 F4
Muckleton Shrops 61 B5
Muckletown Aberds 140 B4
Muckley Corner Staffs 62 D4
Muckton Lincs 91 F7
Mudale Highld 157 F8
Muddiford Devon 20 F4
Mudeford Dorset 14 E2
Mudford Som 12 C3
Mudgley Som 23 E6
Mugdock Stirling 119 B5
Mugeary Highld 149 E9
Mugginton Derbys 76 E2
Muggleswick Durham 110 E3
Muie Highld 157 J9
Muir Aberds 139 F6
Muir of Fairburn Highld 150 F7
Muir of Fowlis Aberds 140 C4
Muir of Ord Highld 151 F8
Muir of Pert Angus 134 F4
Muirden Aberds 153 C7
Muirdrum Angus 135 F5
Muirhead Angus 134 F3
Muirhead Fife 128 D4
Muirhead N Lanark 119 C6
Muirhead S Ayrs 118 F3
Muirhouselaw Borders 116 B2
Muirhouses Falk 128 F2
Muirkirk E Ayrs 113 B6
Muirmill Stirling 127 F6
Muirshearlich Highld 136 F4
Muirskie Aberds 141 E7
Muirtack Aberds 153 E9
Muirton Highld 151 E10
Muirton Perth 127 C8
Muirton Perth 128 B3
Muirton Mains Highld 150 F7
Muirton of Ardblair Perth 134 E1
Muirton of Ballochy Angus 135 C6
Muiryfold Aberds 153 C7
Muker N Yorks 100 E4
Mulbarton Norf 68 D4
Mulben Moray 152 C3
Mulindry Argyll 142 C4
Mullardoch House Highld 150 H5
Mullion Corn 3 E5
Mullion Cove Corn 3 E5
Mumby Lincs 79 B8
Munderfield Row Hereford 49 D8
Munderfield Stocks Hereford 49 D8
Mundesley Norf 81 D9
Mundford Norf 67 E8
Mundham Norf 69 E6
Mundon Essex 42 D4
Mundurno Aberdeen 141 C8
Munerigie Highld 137 D5
Muness Shetland 160 C8
Mungasdale Highld 150 B2
Mungrisdale Cumb 108 F3
Munlochy Highld 151 F9
Munsley Hereford 49 E8
Munslow Shrops 60 F5
Murchington Devon 9 F8
Murcott Oxon 39 C5
Murkle Highld 158 D3
Murlaggan Highld 136 E3
Murlaggan Highld 137 F6
Murra Orkney 159 H3
Murrayfield Edin 120 B5
Murrow Cambs 66 D3
Mursley Bucks 39 B8
Murthill Angus 134 D4
Murthly Perth 133 F7
Murton Cumb 100 B2
Murton Durham 111 E6
Murton Northumb 123 E5
Murton York 96 D2
Musbury Devon 11 E7
Muscoates N Yorks 102 F4
Musdale Argyll 124 C5
Musselburgh E Loth 121 B6
Muston Leics 77 F8
Muston N Yorks 97 B6
Mustow Green Worcs 50 B3
Mutehill Dumfries 106 E3
Mutford Suff 69 F7
Muthill Perth 127 C7
Mutterton Devon 10 D5
Muxton Telford 61 C7
Mybster Highld 158 E3
Myddfai Carms 34 B1
Myddle Shrops 60 B4
Mydroilyn Ceredig 46 D3
Myerscough Lancs 92 F4
Mylor Bridge Corn 3 C7
Mynachlog-ddu Pembs 45 F3
Myndtown Shrops 60 F3
Mynydd Bach Ceredig 47 B6
Mynydd-bach Mon 36 E1
Mynydd Bodafon Anglesey 82 C4
Mynydd-isa Flint 73 C6
Mynyddygarreg Carms 33 D5
Mynytho Gwyn 70 D4
Myrebird Aberds 141 E6
Myrelandhorn Highld 158 E4
Myreside Perth 128 B4
Myrtle Hill Carms 47 F6
Mytchett Sur 27 D6
Mytholm W Yorks 87 B7
Mytholmroyd W Yorks 87 B8
Myton-on-Swale N Yorks 95 C7
Mytton Shrops 60 C4

N

Na Gearrannan W Isles 154 C6
Naast Highld 155 J13
Naburn York 95 E8
Nackington Kent 31 D5
Nacton Suff 57 E6
Nafferton E Yorks 97 D6
Nailbridge Glos 36 C3
Nailsbourne Som 11 B7
Nailsea N Som 23 B6
Nailstone Leics 63 D8
Nailsworth Glos 37 E5
Nairn Highld 151 F11
Nalderswood Sur 28 E3
Nancegollan Corn 2 C5
Nancledra Corn 2 C3
Nanhoron Gwyn 70 D3
Nannau Gwyn 71 E8
Nannerch Flint 73 C5
Nanpantan Leics 64 C2
Nanpean Corn 4 D4
Nanstallon Corn 4 C5
Nant-ddu Powys 34 C4
Nant-glas Powys 47 C8
Nant Peris Gwyn 83 F6
Nant Uchaf Denb 72 D4
Nant-y-Bai Carms 47 E6
Nant-y-cafn Neath 34 D2
Nant-y-derry Mon 35 D7
Nant-y-ffin Carms 46 F4
Nant-y-moel Bridgend 34 E3
Nant-y-pandy Conwy 83 D6
Nanternis Ceredig 46 D2
Nantgaredig Carms 33 B5
Nantgarw Rhondda 35 F5
Nantglyn Denb 72 C4
Nantgwyn Powys 47 B8
Nantlle Gwyn 82 F5
Nantmawr Shrops 60 B2
Nantmel Powys 48 C2
Nantmor Gwyn 71 C7
Nantwich Ches E 74 D3
Nantycaws Carms 33 C5
Nantyffyllon Bridgend 34 E2
Nantyglo Bl Gwent 35 C5
Naphill Bucks 39 E8
Nappa N Yorks 93 D8
Napton on the Hill Warks 52 C2
Narberth = Arberth Pembs 32 C2
Narborough Leics 64 E2
Narborough Norf 67 C7
Nasareth Gwyn 82 F4
Naseby Northants 52 B4
Nash Bucks 53 F5
Nash Hereford 48 C5
Nash Newport 35 F7
Nash Shrops 49 B8
Nash Lee Bucks 39 D8
Nassington Northants 65 E7
Nasty Herts 41 B6
Nateby Cumb 100 D2
Nateby Lancs 92 E4
Natland Cumb 99 F7
Naughton Suff 56 E4
Naunton Glos 37 B8
Naunton Worcs 50 F3
Naunton Beauchamp Worcs 50 D4
Navenby Lincs 78 D2
Navestock Heath Essex 41 E8
Navestock Side Essex 42 E1
Navidale Highld 157 H13
Nawton N Yorks 102 F4
Nayland Suff 56 F3
Nazeing Essex 41 D7
Neacroft Hants 14 E2
Neal's Green Warks 63 F7
Neap Shetland 160 H7
Near Sawrey Cumb 99 E5
Neasham Darl 101 C8
Neath = Castell-Nedd Neath 33 E8
Neath Abbey Neath 33 E8
Neatishead Norf 69 B6
Nebo Anglesey 82 B4
Nebo Ceredig 46 C4
Nebo Conwy 83 F8
Nebo Gwyn 82 F4
Necton Norf 67 D8
Nedd Highld 156 F4
Nedderton Northumb 117 F8
Nedging Tye Suff 56 E4
Needham Norf 68 F5
Needham Market Suff 56 D4
Needingworth Cambs 54 B4
Needwood Staffs 63 B5
Neen Savage Shrops 49 B8
Neen Sollars Shrops 49 B8
Neenton Shrops 61 F6
Nefyn Gwyn 70 C4
Neilston E Renf 118 D4
Neinthirion Powys 59 D6
Neithrop Oxon 52 E2
Nelly Andrews Green Powys 60 D2
Nelson Caerph 35 E5
Nelson Lancs 93 F8
Nelson Village Northumb 111 B5
Nemphlar S Lanark 119 E8
Nempnett Thrubwell N Som 23 C7
Nene Terrace Lincs 66 D2
Nenthall Cumb 109 E7
Nenthead Cumb 109 E7
Nenthorn Borders 122 F2
Nerabus Argyll 142 C3
Nercwys Flint 73 C6
Nerston S Lanark 119 D6
Nesbit Northumb 123 F5
Ness Ches W 73 B7
Nesscliffe Shrops 60 C3
Neston Ches W 73 B6
Neston Wilts 24 C3
Nether Alderley Ches E 74 B5
Nether Blainslie Borders 121 E8
Nether Booth Derbys 88 F2
Nether Broughton Leics 64 B3
Nether Burrow Lancs 93 B6
Nether Cerne Dorset 12 E4
Nether Compton Dorset 12 C3
Nether Crimond Aberds 141 B7
Nether Dalgliesh Borders 115 D5
Nether Dallachy Moray 152 B3
Nether Exe Devon 10 D4
Nether Glasslaw Aberds 153 C8
Nether Handwick Angus 134 E3
Nether Haugh S Yorks 88 E5
Nether Heage Derbys 76 D3
Nether Heyford Northants 52 D4
Nether Hindhope Borders 116 C3
Nether Howecleuch S Lanark 114 C3
Nether Kellet Lancs 92 C5
Nether Kinmundy Aberds 153 D10
Nether Langwith Notts 76 B5
Nether Leask Aberds 153 E10
Nether Lenshie Aberds 153 D6
Nether Monynut Borders 122 C3
Nether Padley Derbys 76 B2
Nether Park Aberds 153 C10
Nether Poppleton York 95 D8
Nether Silton N Yorks 102 E2
Nether Stowey Som 22 F3
Nether Urquhart Fife 128 D3
Nether Wallop Hants 25 F8
Nether Wasdale Cumb 98 D3
Nether Whitacre Warks 63 E6
Nether Worton Oxon 52 F2
Netheravon Wilts 25 E6
Netherbrae Aberds 153 C7
Netherbrough Orkney 159 G4
Netherburn S Lanark 119 E8
Netherbury Dorset 12 E2
Netherby Cumb 108 B3
Netherby N Yorks 95 E6
Nethercote Warks 52 C3
Nethercott Devon 20 F3
Netherend Glos 36 D2
Netherfield E Sus 18 D4
Netherhampton Wilts 14 B2
Netherlaw Dumfries 106 E4
Netherley Aberds 141 E7
Netherley Mers 86 F2
Nethermill Dumfries 114 F3
Nethermuir Aberds 153 D9
Netherplace E Renf 118 D5
Netherseal Derbys 63 C6
Netherthird E Ayrs 113 C5
Netherthong W Yorks 88 D2
Netherthorpe S Yorks 89 F6
Netherton Angus 135 D5
Netherton Devon 7 B6
Netherton Hants 25 D8
Netherton Mers 85 D4
Netherton Northumb 117 D5
Netherton Oxon 38 E4
Netherton Perth 133 D8
Netherton Stirling 119 B5
Netherton W Mid 62 F3
Netherton W Yorks 88 C2
Netherton W Yorks 88 C3
Netherton Worcs 50 E4
Nethertown Cumb 98 D1
Nethertown Highld 158 C5
Netherwitton Northumb 117 E7
Netherwood E Ayrs 113 B6
Nethy Bridge Highld 139 B6
Netley Hants 15 D5
Netley Marsh Hants 14 C4
Netteswell Essex 41 C7
Nettlebed Oxon 39 F7
Nettlebridge Som 23 E8
Nettlecombe Dorset 12 E3
Nettleden Herts 40 C3
Nettleham Lincs 78 B3
Nettlestead Kent 29 D7
Nettlestead Green Kent 29 D7
Nettlestone IoW 15 E7
Nettlesworth Durham 111 E5
Nettleton Lincs 90 D5
Nettleton Wilts 24 B3
Neuadd Carms 33 B7
Nevendon Essex 42 E3
Nevern Pembs 45 E2
New Abbey Dumfries 107 C6
New Aberdour Aberds 153 B8
New Addington London 28 C4
New Alresford Hants 26 F3
New Alyth Perth 134 E2
New Arley Warks 63 F6
New Ash Green Kent 29 C7
New Barn Kent 29 C7
New Barnetby N Lincs 90 C4
New Barton Northants 53 C6
New Bewick Northumb 117 B6
New-bigging Angus 134 E2
New Bilton Warks 52 B2
New Bolingbroke Lincs 79 D6
New Boultham Lincs 78 B2
New Bradwell M Keynes 53 E6
New Brancepeth Durham 110 E5
New Bridge Wrex 73 E6
New Brighton Flint 73 C6
New Brighton Mers 85 E4
New Brinsley Notts 76 D4
New Broughton Wrex 73 D7
New Buckenham Norf 68 E3
New Byth Aberds 153 C8
New Catton Norf 68 C5
New Cheriton Hants 15 B6
New Costessey Norf 68 C4
New Cowper Cumb 107 E8
New Cross Ceredig 46 B5
New Cross London 28 B4
New Cumnock E Ayrs 113 C6
New Deer Aberds 153 D8
New Delaval Northumb 111 B5
New Duston Northants 52 C5
New Earswick York 96 D2
New Edlington S Yorks 89 E6
New Elgin Moray 152 B2
New Ellerby E Yorks 97 F7
New Eltham London 28 B5
New End Worcs 51 D5
New Farnley W Yorks 94 F5
New Ferry Mers 85 F4
New Fryston W Yorks 89 B5
New Galloway Dumfries 106 B3
New Gilston Fife 129 D6
New Grimsby Scilly 2 E3
New Hainford Norf 68 C5
New Hartley Northumb 111 B6
New Haw Sur 27 C8
New Hedges Pembs 32 D2
New Herrington T&W 111 D6
New Hinksey Oxon 39 D5
New Holkham Norf 80 D4
New Holland N Lincs 90 B4
New Houghton Derbys 76 C4
New Houghton Norf 80 E3
New Houses N Yorks 93 B8
New Humberstone Leicester 64 D3
New Hutton Cumb 99 E7
New Hythe Kent 29 D8
New Inn Carms 46 F3
New Inn Mon 36 D1
New Inn Pembs 45 F2
New Inn Torf 35 E7
New Invention Shrops 48 B4
New Invention W Mid 62 D3
New Kelso Highld 150 G2
New Kingston Notts 64 B2
New Lanark S Lanark 119 E8
New Lane Lancs 86 C2
New Lane End Warr 86 E4
New Leake Lincs 79 D7
New Leeds Aberds 153 C9
New Longton Lancs 86 B3
New Luce Dumfries 105 C5
New Malden London 28 C3
New Marske Redcar 102 B4
New Marton Shrops 73 F7
New Micklefield W Yorks 95 F7
New Mill Aberds 141 F6
New Mill Herts 40 C2
New Mill W Yorks 88 D2
New Mill Wilts 25 C6
New Mills Ches E 87 F5
New Mills Corn 4 D3
New Mills Derbys 87 F7
New Mills Powys 59 D7
New Milton Hants 14 E3
New Moat Pembs 32 B1
New Ollerton Notts 77 C6
New Oscott W Mid 62 E4
New Park N Yorks 95 D5
New Pitsligo Aberds 153 C8
New Polzeath Corn 4 B4
New Quay = Ceinewydd Ceredig 46 D2
New Rackheath Norf 69 C5
New Radnor Powys 48 C4
New Rent Cumb 108 F4
New Ridley Northumb 110 D3
New Road Side N Yorks 94 E2
New Romney Kent 19 C7
New Rossington S Yorks 89 E7
New Row Ceredig 47 B6
New Row Lancs 93 F6
New Row N Yorks 102 C4
New Sarum Wilts 25 F6
New Silksworth T&W 111 D6
New Stevenston N Lanark 119 D7
New Street Staffs 75 D7
New Street Lane Shrops 74 F3
New Swanage Dorset 13 F8
New Totley S Yorks 76 B3
New Town E Loth 121 B7
New Tredegar = Tredegar Newydd Caerph 35 D5
New Trows S Lanark 119 F8
New Ulva Argyll 144 E6
New Walsoken Cambs 66 D4
New Waltham NE Lincs 91 D6
New Whittington Derbys 76 B3
New Wimpole Cambs 54 E4
New Winton E Loth 121 B7
New Yatt Oxon 38 C3
New York Lincs 78 D5
New York N Yorks 94 C4
Newall W Yorks 94 E4
Newark Orkney 159 D8
Newark Pboro 66 D2
Newark-on-Trent Notts 77 D7
Newarthill N Lanark 119 D7
Newbarns Cumb 92 B2
Newbattle Midloth 121 C6
Newbiggin Cumb 92 C2
Newbiggin Cumb 98 E2
Newbiggin Cumb 99 B6
Newbiggin Cumb 99 B8
Newbiggin Cumb 109 E5
Newbiggin Durham 100 B4
Newbiggin N Yorks 100 E4
Newbiggin N Yorks 100 F4
Newbiggin-by-the-Sea Northumb 117 F9
Newbiggin-on-Lune Cumb 100 D2
Newbigging Angus 134 F4
Newbigging Angus 134 F4
Newbigging S Lanark 120 E3
Newbold Derbys 76 B3
Newbold Leics 63 C8
Newbold on Avon Warks 52 B2
Newbold on Stour Warks 51 E7
Newbold Pacey Warks 51 D7
Newbold Verdon Leics 63 D8
Newborough Anglesey 82 E4
Newborough Pboro 66 D2
Newborough Staffs 62 B5
Newbottle Northants 52 F3
Newbottle T&W 111 D6
Newbourne Suff 57 E6
Newbridge Caerph 35 E6
Newbridge Ceredig 46 D4
Newbridge Corn 2 C3
Newbridge Corn 5 C8
Newbridge Dumfries 107 B6
Newbridge Edin 120 B4
Newbridge Hants 14 C3
Newbridge IoW 14 F5
Newbridge Pembs 44 B4
Newbridge Green Worcs 50 F3
Newbridge-on-Usk Mon 35 E7
Newbridge on Wye Powys 48 D2
Newbrough Northumb 109 C8
Newbuildings Devon 10 D2
Newburgh Aberds 141 B8
Newburgh Aberds 153 C9
Newburgh Borders 115 C6
Newburgh Fife 128 C4
Newburgh Lancs 86 C2
Newburn T&W 110 C4
Newbury W Berks 26 C2
Newbury Park London 41 F7
Newby Cumb 99 B7
Newby Lancs 93 E8
Newby N Yorks 93 B7
Newby N Yorks 102 C3
Newby N Yorks 103 E8
Newby Bridge Cumb 99 F5
Newby East Cumb 108 D4
Newby West Cumb 108 D3
Newby Wiske N Yorks 102 F1
Newcastle Mon 35 C8
Newcastle Shrops 60 F2
Newcastle Emlyn = Castell Newydd Emlyn Carms 46 E2
Newcastle-under-Lyme Staffs 74 E5
Newcastle Upon Tyne T&W 110 C5
Newcastleton or Copshaw Holm Borders 115 F7
Newchapel Pembs 45 F4
Newchapel Powys 59 F6
Newchapel Staffs 75 D5
Newchapel Sur 28 E4
Newchurch Carms 32 B4
Newchurch IoW 15 F6
Newchurch Kent 19 B7
Newchurch Lancs 93 F8
Newchurch Mon 36 E1
Newchurch Powys 48 D4
Newchurch Staffs 62 B5
Newcott Devon 11 D7
Newcraighall Edin 121 B6
Newdigate Sur 28 E2
Newell Green Brack 27 B6
Newenden Kent 18 C5
Newent Glos 36 B4
Newerne Glos 36 D3
Newfield Durham 110 F5
Newfield Highld 151 D10
Newford Scilly 2 E4
Newfound Hants 26 D3
Newgale Pembs 44 C3
Newgate Norf 81 C6
Newgate Street Herts 41 D6
Newhall Ches E 74 E3
Newhall Derbys 63 B6
Newhall House Highld 151 E9
Newhall Point Highld 151 E10
Newham Northumb 117 B7
Newham Hall Northumb 117 B7
Newhaven Derbys 75 D8
Newhaven E Sus 17 D8
Newhaven Edin 121 B5
Newhey Gtr Man 87 C7
Newholm N Yorks 103 C6
Newhouse N Lanark 119 C7
Newick E Sus 17 B8
Newingreen Kent 19 B8
Newington Kent 19 B8
Newington Kent 30 C2
Newington Kent 31 C7
Newington Notts 89 E7
Newington Oxon 39 E6
Newington Shrops 60 F4
Newland Glos 36 D2
Newland Hull 97 F6
Newland N Yorks 89 B7
Newland Worcs 50 E2
Newlandrig Midloth 121 C6
Newlands Borders 115 E8
Newlands Highld 151 G10
Newlands Moray 152 C3
Newlands Northumb 110 D3
Newland's Corner Sur 27 E8
Newlands of Geise Highld 158 D2
Newlands of Tynet Moray 152 B3
Newlands Park Anglesey 82 C2
Newlandsmuir S Lanark 119 D6
Newlot Orkney 159 G6
Newlyn Corn 2 D3
Newmachar Aberds 141 C7
Newmains N Lanark 119 D8
Newmarket Suff 55 C7
Newmarket W Isles 155 D9
Newmill Borders 115 C7
Newmill Corn 2 C3
Newmill Moray 152 C4
Newmill of Inshewan Angus 134 C4
Newmills of Boyne Aberds 152 C5
Newmiln Perth 133 F8
Newmilns E Ayrs 118 F5
Newnham Cambs 54 D5
Newnham Glos 36 C3
Newnham Hants 26 D5
Newnham Herts 54 F3
Newnham Kent 30 D3
Newnham Northants 52 D3
Newnham Bridge Worcs 49 C8
Newpark Fife 129 C6
Newport Devon 20 F4
Newport E Yorks 96 F4
Newport Essex 55 F6
Newport Highld 158 H3
Newport IoW 15 F6
Newport = Casnewydd Newport 35 F7
Newport Norf 69 C8
Newport = Trefdraeth Pembs 45 F2
Newport Telford 61 C7
Newport-on-Tay Fife 129 B6
Newport Pagnell M Keynes 53 E6
Newpound Common W Sus 16 B4
Newquay Corn 4 C3
Newsbank Ches E 74 C5
Newseat Aberds 153 D10
Newseat Aberds 153 E7
Newsham N Yorks 101 C6
Newsham N Yorks 102 F1
Newsham Northumb 111 B6
Newsholme E Yorks 89 B8
Newsholme Lancs 93 D8
Newsome W Yorks 88 C2
Newstead Borders 121 F8
Newstead Northumb 117 B7
Newstead Notts 76 D5
Newthorpe N Yorks 95 F7
Newton Argyll 125 F6
Newton Borders 116 B2
Newton Bridgend 21 B7
Newton Cambs 54 E5
Newton Cambs 66 C4
Newton Cardiff 22 B4
Newton Ches W 73 C8
Newton Ches W 74 B2
Newton Ches W 74 D2
Newton Cumb 92 B2
Newton Derbys 76 D4
Newton Dorset 13 C5
Newton Dumfries 108 B2
Newton Dumfries 114 E4
Newton Gtr Man 87 E7
Newton Hereford 48 F5
Newton Hereford 49 D7
Newton Highld 151 E10
Newton Highld 151 G10
Newton Highld 156 F5
Newton Highld 158 F5
Newton Lancs 92 F4
Newton Lancs 93 B5
Newton Lancs 93 D6
Newton Lincs 78 F3
Newton Moray 152 B1
Newton Norf 67 C8
Newton Northants 65 F5
Newton Northumb 110 C3
Newton Notts 77 E6
Newton Perth 133 F5
Newton S Lanark 119 C6
Newton S Lanark 120 F2
Newton S Yorks 89 D6
Newton Staffs 62 B4
Newton Suff 56 E3
Newton Swansea 33 F7
Newton W Loth 120 B3
Newton Warks 52 B3
Newton Wilts 14 B3
Newton Abbot Devon 7 B6
Newton Arlosh Cumb 107 D8
Newton Aycliffe Durham 101 B7
Newton Bewley Hrtlpl 102 B2
Newton Blossomville M Keynes 53 D7
Newton Bromswold Northants 53 C7
Newton Burgoland Leics 63 D7
Newton by Toft Lincs 90 F4
Newton Ferrers Devon 6 E3
Newton Flotman Norf 68 E5
Newton Hall Northumb 110 C3
Newton Harcourt Leics 64 E3
Newton Heath Gtr Man 87 D6
Newton Ho. Aberds 141 B5
Newton Kyme N Yorks 95 E7
Newton-le-Willows Mers 86 E3
Newton-le-Willows N Yorks 101 F7
Newton Longville Bucks 53 F6
Newton Mearns E Renf 118 D5
Newton Morrell N Yorks 101 D7
Newton Mulgrave N Yorks 103 C5
Newton of Ardtoe Highld 147 D9
Newton of Balcanquhal Perth 128 C3
Newton of Falkland Fife 128 D4
Newton on Ayr S Ayrs 112 B3
Newton on Ouse N Yorks 95 D8
Newton-on-Rawcliffe N Yorks 103 E6
Newton-on-the-Moor Northumb 117 D7
Newton on Trent Lincs 77 B8
Newton Park Argyll 145 G10
Newton Poppleford Devon 11 F5
Newton Purcell Oxon 52 F4
Newton Regis Warks 63 D6
Newton Reigny Cumb 108 F4
Newton Solney Derbys 63 B6
Newton St Cyres Devon 10 E3
Newton St Faith Norf 68 C5
Newton St Loe Bath 24 C2
Newton St Petrock Devon 9 C6
Newton Stacey Hants 26 E2
Newton Stewart Dumfries 105 C8
Newton Tony Wilts 25 E7
Newton Tracey Devon 9 B7
Newton under Roseberry Redcar 102 C3
Newton upon Derwent E Yorks 96 E3
Newton Valence Hants 26 F5
Newtonairds Dumfries 113 F8
Newtongrange Midloth 121 C6
Newtonhill Aberds 141 E8
Newtonhill Highld 151 G8
Newtonmill Angus 135 C6
Newtonmore Highld 138 E3
Newtown Argyll 125 E6
Newtown Ches W 74 B2
Newtown Corn 3 D6
Newtown Cumb 107 E7
Newtown Cumb 108 C5
Newtown Derbys 87 F7
Newtown Devon 10 B2
Newtown Glos 36 D3
Newtown Glos 50 F4
Newtown Hants 14 B4
Newtown Hants 14 C3
Newtown Hants 15 C6
Newtown Hants 15 C7
Newtown Hants 15 D5
Newtown Hants 26 C2
Newtown Hereford 49 E8
Newtown Highld 137 D6
Newtown IoM 84 E3
Newtown IoW 14 E5
Newtown Northumb 117 B6
Newtown Northumb 117 D6
Newtown Northumb 123 F5
Newtown Poole 13 E8
Newtown = Y Drenewydd Powys 59 E8
Newtown Shrops 73 F8
Newtown Staffs 75 C6
Newtown Staffs 75 C7
Newtown Wilts 13 B7
Newtown Linford Leics 64 D2
Newtown St Boswells Borders 121 F8
Newtown Unthank Leics 63 D8
Newtyle Angus 134 E2
Neyland Pembs 44 E4
Niarbyl IoM 84 E2
Nibley S Glos 36 F3
Nibley Green Glos 36 E4
Nibon Shetland 160 F5
Nicholashayne Devon 11 C6
Nicholaston Swansea 33 F6
Nidd N Yorks 95 C6
Nigg Aberdeen 141 D8
Nigg Highld 151 D11
Nigg Ferry Highld 151 E10
Nightcott Som 10 B3
Nilig Denb 72 D4
Nine Ashes Essex 42 D1
Nine Mile Burn Midloth 120 D4
Nine Wells Pembs 44 C2
Ninebanks Northumb 109 D7
Ninfield E Sus 18 D4
Ningwood IoW 14 F4
Nisbet Borders 116 B2
Nisthouse Orkney 159 G4
Nisthouse Shetland 160 G7
Niton IoW 15 G6
Nitshill Glasgow 118 C5
No Man's Heath Ches W 74 E2
No Man's Heath Warks 63 D6
Noak Hill London 41 E8
Noblethorpe S Yorks 88 D3
Nobottle Northants 52 C4
Nocton Lincs 78 C3
Noke Oxon 39 C5
Nolton Pembs 44 D3
Nolton Haven Pembs 44 D3
Nomansland Devon 10 C3
Nomansland Wilts 14 C3
Noneley Shrops 60 B4
Nonikiln Highld 151 D9
Nonington Kent 31 D6
Noonsbrough Shetland 160 H4
Norbreck Blackpool 92 E3
Norbridge Hereford 50 E2
Norbury Ches E 74 E2
Norbury Derbys 75 E8
Norbury Shrops 60 E3
Norbury Staffs 61 B7
Nordelph Norf 67 D5
Norden Gtr Man 87 C6
Norden Heath Dorset 13 F7
Nordley Shrops 61 E6
Norham Northumb 122 E5
Norley Ches W 74 B2
Norleywood Hants 14 E4
Norman Cross Cambs 65 E8
Normanby N Lincs 90 C2
Normanby N Yorks 103 F5
Normanby Redcar 102 C3
Normanby-by-Spital Lincs 90 F4
Normanby by Stow Lincs 90 F2
Normanby le Wold Lincs 90 E5
Normandy Sur 27 D7
Norman's Bay E Sus 18 E3
Norman's Green Devon 11 D5
Normanstone Suff 69 E8
Normanton Derby 76 F3
Normanton Leics 77 E8
Normanton Lincs 78 E2
Normanton Notts 77 D7
Normanton Rutland 65 D6
Normanton W Yorks 88 B4
Normanton le Heath Leics 63 C7
Normanton on Soar Notts 64 B2
Normanton-on-the-Wolds Notts 77 F6
Normanton on Trent Notts 77 C7
Normoss Lancs 92 F3
Norney Sur 27 E7
Norrington Common Wilts 24 C3
Norris Green Mers 85 E4
Norris Hill Leics 63 C7
North Anston S Yorks 89 F6
North Aston Oxon 38 B4
North Baddesley Hants 14 C4
North Ballachulish Highld 130 C4
North Barrow Som 12 B4
North Barsham Norf 80 D5
North Benfleet Essex 42 F3
North Bersted W Sus 16 D3
North Berwick E Loth 129 F7
North Boarhunt Hants 15 C7
North Bovey Devon 10 F2
North Bradley Wilts 24 D3
North Brentor Devon 9 F6
North Brewham Som 24 F2
North Buckland Devon 20 E3
North Burlingham Norf 69 C6
North Cadbury Som 12 B4
North Cairn Dumfries 104 B3
North Carlton Lincs 78 B2
North Carrine Argyll 143 H7
North Cave E Yorks 96 F4
North Cerney Glos 37 D7
North Charford Wilts 14 C2
North Charlton Northumb 117 B7
North Cheriton Som 12 B4
North Cliff E Yorks 97 E8
North Cliffe E Yorks 96 F4
North Clifton Notts 77 B8
North Cockerington Lincs 91 E7
North Coker Som 12 C3
North Collafirth Shetland 160 E5
North Common E Sus 17 B7
North Connel Argyll 124 B5
North Cornelly Bridgend 34 F2
North Cotes Lincs 91 D7
North Cove Suff 69 F7
North Cowton N Yorks 101 D7
North Crawley M Keynes 53 E7
North Cray London 29 B5
North Creake Norf 80 D4
North Curry Som 11 B8
North Dalton E Yorks 96 D5
North Dawn Orkney 159 H5
North Deighton N Yorks 95 D6
North Duffield N Yorks 96 F2
North Elkington Lincs 91 E6
North Elmham Norf 81 E5
North Elmshall W Yorks 89 C5
North End Bucks 39 B8
North End E Yorks 97 F8
North End Essex 42 C2
North End Hants 26 C2
North End Lincs 78 E5
North End N Som 23 C6
North End Ptsmth 15 D7
North End Som 11 B7
North End W Sus 16 D5
North Erradale Highld 155 J12
North Fambridge Essex 42 E4
North Fearns Highld 149 E10
North Featherstone W Yorks 88 B5
North Ferriby E Yorks 90 B3
North Frodingham E Yorks 97 D7
North Gluss Shetland 160 F5
North Gorley Hants 14 C2
North Green Norf 68 F5
North Green Suff 57 C7
North Greetwell Lincs 78 B3
North Grimston N Yorks 96 C4
North Halley Orkney 159 H6
North Halling Medway 29 C8
North Hayling Hants 15 D8
North Hazelrigg Northumb 123 F6
North Heasley Devon 21 F6
North Heath W Sus 16 B4
North Hill Cambs 55 B5
North Hill Corn 5 B7
North Hinksey Oxon 38 D4
North Holmwood Sur 28 E2
North Howden E Yorks 96 F3
North Huish Devon 6 D5
North Hykeham Lincs 78 C2
North Johnston Pembs 44 D4
North Kelsey Lincs 90 D4
North Kelsey Moor Lincs 90 D4
North Kessock Highld 151 G9
North Killingholme N Lincs 90 C5
North Kilvington N Yorks 102 F2
North Kilworth Leics 64 F3
North Kirkton Aberds 153 C11
North Kiscadale N Ayrs 143 F11
North Kyme Lincs 78 D4
North Lancing W Sus 17 D5
North Lee Bucks 39 D8
North Leigh Oxon 38 C3
North Leverton with Habblesthorpe Notts 89 F8
North Littleton Worcs 51 E5
North Lopham Norf 68 F3
North Luffenham Rutland 65 D6
North Marden W Sus 16 C2
North Marston Bucks 39 B7
North Middleton Midloth 121 D6
North Middleton Northumb 117 B6
North Molton Devon 10 B2
North Moreton Oxon 39 F5
North Mundham W Sus 16 D2
North Muskham Notts 77 D7
North Newbald E Yorks 96 F5
North Newington Oxon 52 F2
North Newnton Wilts 25 D6
North Newton Som 22 F4
North Nibley Glos 36 E4
North Oakley Hants 26 D3
North Ockendon London 42 F1
North Ormesby Mbro 102 B3
North Ormsby Lincs 91 E6
North Otterington N Yorks 102 F1
North Owersby Lincs 90 E4
North Perrott Som 12 D2
North Petherton Som 22 F4
North Petherwin Corn 8 F4
North Pickenham Norf 67 D8
North Piddle Worcs 50 D4
North Poorton Dorset 12 E3
North Port Argyll 125 C6
North Queensferry Fife 128 F3
North Radworthy Devon 21 F6
North Rauceby Lincs 78 E3
North Reston Lincs 91 F7
North Rigton N Yorks 95 E5
North Rode Ches E 75 C5
North Roe Shetland 160 E5
North Runcton Norf 67 C6
North Sandwick Shetland 160 D7
North Scale Cumb 92 C1
North Scarle Lincs 77 C8
North Seaton Northumb 117 F8
North Shian Argyll 130 E3
North Shields T&W 111 C6
North Shoebury Southend 43 F5
North Shore Blackpool 92 F3
North Side Cumb 98 B2
North Side Pboro 66 E2
North Skelton Redcar 102 C4
North Somercotes Lincs 91 E8
North Stainley N Yorks 95 B5
North Stainmore Cumb 100 C3
North Stifford Thurrock 42 F2
North Stoke Bath 24 C2
North Stoke Oxon 39 F6
North Stoke W Sus 16 C4
North Street Hants 26 F4
North Street Kent 30 D4
North Street Medway 30 B2
North Street W Berks 26 B4
North Sunderland Northumb 123 F8
North Tamerton Corn 8 E5
North Tawton Devon 9 D8
North Thoresby Lincs 91 E6
North Tidworth Wilts 25 E7
North Togston Northumb 117 D8
North Tuddenham Norf 68 C3
North Walbottle T&W 110 C4
North Walsham Norf 81 D8
North Waltham Hants 26 E3
North Warnborough Hants 26 D5
North Water Bridge Angus 135 C6
North Watten Highld 158 E4
North Weald Bassett Essex 41 D7
North Wheatley Notts 89 F8
North Whilborough Devon 7 C6
North Wick Bath 23 C7
North Willingham Lincs 91 F5
North Wingfield Derbys 76 C4
North Witham Lincs 65 B6
North Woolwich London 28 B5
North Wootton Dorset 12 C4
North Wootton Norf 67 B6
North Wootton Som 23 E7
North Wraxall Wilts 24 B3
North Wroughton Swindon 38 F1
Northacre Norf 68 E2
Northallerton N Yorks 102 E1
Northam Devon 9 B6
Northam Soton 14 C5
Northampton Northants 53 C5
Northaw Herts 41 D5
Northbeck Lincs 78 E3
Northborough Pboro 65 D8
Northbourne Kent 31 D7
Northbridge Street E Sus 18 C4
Northchapel W Sus 16 B3
Northchurch Herts 40 D2
Northcott Devon 8 E5
Northdown Kent 31 B7
Northdyke Orkney 159 F3
Northend Bath 24 C2
Northend Bucks 39 E7
Northend Warks 51 D8
Northenden Gtr Man 87 E6
Northfield Aberdeen 141 D8
Northfield Borders 122 C5
Northfield E Yorks 90 B4
Northfield W Mid 50 B5
Northfields Lincs 65 D7
Northfleet Kent 29 B7
Northgate Lincs 65 B8
Northhouse Borders 115 D7
Northiam E Sus 18 C5
Northill C Beds 54 E2
Northington Hants 26 F3
Northlands Lincs 79 D6
Northlea Durham 111 D7
Northleach Glos 37 C8
Northleigh Devon 11 E6
Northlew Devon 9 E7
Northmoor Oxon 38 D4
Northmoor Green or Moorland Som 22 F5
Northmuir Angus 134 D3
Northney Hants 15 D8
Northolt London 40 F4
Northop Flint 73 C6
Northop Hall Flint 73 C6
Northorpe Lincs 65 C7
Northorpe Lincs 78 F5
Northorpe Lincs 90 E2
Northover Som 12 B3
Northover Som 23 F6
Northowram W Yorks 88 B2
Northport Dorset 13 F7
Northpunds Shetland 160 L6
Northrepps Norf 81 D8
Northtown Orkney 159 J5
Northway Glos 50 F4
Northwich Ches W 74 B3
Northwick S Glos 36 F2
Northwold Norf 67 E7
Northwood Derbys 76 C2
Northwood IoW 15 E5
Northwood Kent 31 C7
Northwood London 40 E3
Northwood Shrops 73 F8
Northwood Green Glos 36 C4
Norton E Sus 17 D8
Norton Glos 37 B5
Norton Halton 86 F3
Norton Herts 54 F3
Norton IoW 14 F4
Norton Mon 35 C8
Norton Northants 52 C4
Norton Notts 77 B5
Norton Powys 48 C5
Norton S Yorks 89 C6
Norton Shrops 60 F4
Norton Shrops 61 D5
Norton Shrops 61 D7
Norton Stockton 102 B2
Norton Suff 56 C3
Norton W Sus 16 D3
Norton W Sus 16 E2
Norton Wilts 37 F5
Norton Worcs 50 D3
Norton Worcs 50 E5
Norton Bavant Wilts 24 E4
Norton Bridge Staffs 75 F5
Norton Canes Staffs 62 D4
Norton Canon Hereford 49 E5
Norton Corner Norf 81 E6
Norton Disney Lincs 77 D8
Norton East Staffs 62 D4
Norton Ferris Wilts 24 F2
Norton Fitzwarren Som 11 B6
Norton Green IoW 14 F4
Norton Hawkfield Bath 23 C7
Norton Heath Essex 42 D2
Norton in Hales Shrops 74 F4
Nor'on-in-the-Moors Stoke 75 D5
Norton-Juxta-Twycross Leics 63 D7
Norton-le-Clay N Yorks 95 B7
Norton Lindsey Warks 51 C7
Norton Malreward Bath 23 C8
Norton Mandeville Essex 42 D1
Norton-on-Derwent N Yorks 96 B3
Norton St Philip Som 24 D2
Norton sub Hamdon Som 12 C2
Norton Woodseats S Yorks 88 F4

Norwell Notts 77 C7
Norwell Woodhouse Notts 77 C7
Norwich Norf 68 D5
Norwick Shetland 160 B8
Norwood Derbys 89 F5
Norwood Hill Sur 28 E3
Norwoodside Cambs 66 E4
Noseley Leics 64 E4
Noss Shetland 160 M5
Noss Mayo Devon 6 E3
Nosterfield N Yorks 101 F7
Nostie Highld 149 F13
Notgrove Glos 37 B8
Nottage Bridgend 21 B7
Nottingham Nottingham 77 F5
Nottington Dorset 12 F4
Notton W Yorks 88 C4
Notton Wilts 24 C4
Nounsley Essex 42 C3
Noutard's Green Worcs 50 C2
Novar House Highld 151 E9
Nox Shrops 60 C4
Nuffield Oxon 39 F6
Nun Hills Lancs 87 B6
Nun Monkton N Yorks 95 D8
Nunburnholme E Yorks 96 E4
Nuncargate Notts 76 D5
Nuneaton Warks 63 E7
Nuneham Courtenay Oxon 39 E5
Nunney Som 24 E2
Nunnington N Yorks 96 B2
Nunnykirk Northumb 117 E6
Nunsthorpe NE Lincs 91 D6
Nunthorpe Mbro 102 C3
Nunthorpe York 96 D2
Nunton Wilts 14 B2
Nunwick N Yorks 95 B6
Nupend Glos 36 D4
Nursling Hants 14 C4
Nursted Hants 15 B8
Nutbourne W Sus 15 D8
Nutbourne W Sus 16 C4
Nutfield Sur 28 D4
Nuthall Notts 76 E5
Nuthampstead Herts 54 F5
Nuthurst W Sus 17 B5
Nutley E Sus 17 B8
Nutley Hants 26 E4
Nutwell S Yorks 89 D7
Nybster Highld 158 D5
Nyetimber W Sus 16 E2
Nyewood W Sus 16 B2
Nymet Rowland Devon 10 D2
Nymet Tracey Devon 10 D2
Nympsfield Glos 37 D5
Nynehead Som 11 B6
Nyton W Sus 16 D3

O

Oad Street Kent 30 C2
Oadby Leics 64 D3
Oak Cross Devon 9 E7
Oakamoor Staffs 75 E7
Oakbank W Loth 120 C3
Oakdale Caerph 35 E5
Oake Som 11 B6
Oaken Staffs 62 D2
Oakenclough Lancs 92 E5
Oakengates Telford 61 C7
Oakenholt Flint 73 B6
Oakenshaw Durham 110 F5
Oakenshaw W Yorks 88 B2
Oakerthorpe Derbys 76 D3
Oakes W Yorks 88 C2
Oakfield Torf 35 E7
Oakford Ceredig 46 D3
Oakford Devon 10 B4
Oakfordbridge Devon 10 B4
Oakgrove Ches E 75 C6
Oakham Rutland 65 D5
Oakhanger Hants 27 F5
Oakhill Som 23 E8
Oakhurst Kent 29 D6
Oakington Cambs 54 C5
Oaklands Herts 41 C5
Oaklands Powys 48 D2
Oakle Street Glos 36 C4
Oakley Bedford 53 D8
Oakley Bucks 39 C6
Oakley Fife 128 F2
Oakley Hants 26 D3
Oakley Oxon 39 D7
Oakley Poole 13 E8
Oakley Suff 57 B5
Oakley Green Windsor 27 B7
Oakley Park Powys 59 F6
Oakmere Ches W 74 C2
Oakridge Glos 37 D6
Oakridge Hants 26 D4
Oaks Shrops 60 D4
Oaks Green Derbys 75 F8
Oaksey Wilts 37 E6
Oakthorpe Leics 63 C7
Oakwoodhill Sur 28 F2
Oakworth W Yorks 94 F3
Oape Highld 156 J7
Oare Kent 30 C4
Oare Som 21 E7
Oare W Berks 26 B3
Oare Wilts 25 C6
Oasby Lincs 78 F3
Oathlaw Angus 134 D4
Oatlands N Yorks 95 D6
Oban Argyll 124 C4
Oban Highld 147 C11
Oborne Dorset 12 C4
Obthorpe Lincs 65 C7
Occlestone Green Ches W 74 C3
Occold Suff 57 B5
Ochiltree E Ayrs 112 B5
Ochtermuthill Perth 127 C7
Ochtertyre Perth 127 B7
Ockbrook Derbys 76 F4
Ockham Sur 27 D8
Ockle Highld 147 D8
Ockley Sur 28 F2
Ocle Pychard Hereford 49 E7
Octon E Yorks 97 C6
Octon Cross Roads E Yorks 97 C6
Odcombe Som 12 C3
Odd Down Bath 24 C2
Oddendale Cumb 99 C7
Odder Lincs 78 B2
Oddingley Worcs 50 D4
Oddington Glos 38 B2
Oddington Oxon 39 C5
Odell Bedford 53 D7
Odie Orkney 159 F7
Odiham Hants 26 D5
Odstock Wilts 14 B2
Odstone Leics 63 D7
Offchurch Warks 51 C8
Offenham Worcs 51 E5
Offham E Sus 17 C7
Offham Kent 29 D7
Offham W Sus 16 D4
Offord Cluny Cambs 54 C3
Offord Darcy Cambs 54 C3
Offton Suff 56 E4
Offwell Devon 11 E6
Ogbourne Maizey Wilts 25 B6
Ogbourne St Andrew Wilts 25 B6
Ogbourne St George Wilts 25 B7
Ogil Angus 134 C4
Ogle Northumb 110 B4
Ogmore V Glam 21 B7
Ogmore-by-Sea V Glam 21 B7
Ogmore Vale Bridgend 34 E3
Okeford Fitzpaine Dorset 13 C6
Okehampton Devon 9 E7
Okehampton Camp Devon 9 E7
Okraquoy Shetland 160 K6
Old Northants 53 B5
Old Aberdeen Aberdeen 141 D8
Old Alresford Hants 26 F3
Old Arley Warks 63 E6
Old Basford Nottingham 76 E5
Old Basing Hants 26 D4
Old Bewick Northumb 117 B6
Old Bolingbroke Lincs 79 C6
Old Bramhope W Yorks 94 E5
Old Brampton Derbys 76 B3
Old Bridge of Tilt Perth 133 C5
Old Bridge of Urr Dumfries 106 C4
Old Buckenham Norf 68 E3
Old Burghclere Hants 26 D2
Old Byland N Yorks 102 F3
Old Cassop Durham 111 F6
Old Castleton Borders 115 E8
Old Catton Norf 68 C5
Old Clee NE Lincs 91 D6
Old Cleeve Som 22 E2
Old Clipstone Notts 77 C6
Old Colwyn Conwy 83 D8
Old Coulsdon London 28 D4
Old Crombie Aberds 152 C5
Old Dailly S Ayrs 112 E2
Old Dalby Leics 64 B3
Old Deer Aberds 153 D9
Old Denaby S Yorks 89 E5
Old Edlington S Yorks 89 E6
Old Eldon Durham 101 B7
Old Ellerby E Yorks 97 F7
Old Felixstowe Suff 57 F7
Old Fletton Pboro 65 E8
Old Glossop Derbys 87 E8
Old Goole E Yorks 89 B8
Old Hall Powys 59 F6
Old Heath Essex 43 B6
Old Heathfield E Sus 18 C2
Old Hill W Mid 62 F3
Old Hunstanton Norf 80 C2
Old Hurst Cambs 54 B3
Old Hutton Cumb 99 F7
Old Kea Corn 3 B7
Old Kilpatrick W Dunb 118 B4
Old Kinnernie Aberds 141 D6
Old Knebworth Herts 41 B5
Old Langho Lancs 93 F7
Old Laxey IoM 84 D4
Old Leake Lincs 79 D7
Old Malton N Yorks 96 B3
Old Micklefield W Yorks 95 F7
Old Milton Hants 14 E3
Old Milverton Warks 51 C7
Old Monkland N Lanark 119 C7
Old Netley Hants 15 D5
Old Philpstoun W Loth 120 B3
Old Quarrington Durham 111 F6
Old Radnor Powys 48 D4
Old Rattray Aberds 153 C10
Old Rayne Aberds 141 B5
Old Romney Kent 19 C7
Old Sodbury S Glos 36 F4
Old Somerby Lincs 78 F2
Old Stratford Northants 53 E5
Old Thirsk N Yorks 102 F2
Old Town Cumb 99 F7
Old Town Cumb 108 E4
Old Town Northumb 116 E4
Old Town Scilly 2 E4
Old Trafford Gtr Man 87 E6
Old Tupton Derbys 76 C3
Old Warden C Beds 54 E2
Old Weston Cambs 53 B8
Old Whittington Derbys 76 B3
Old Wick Highld 158 E5
Old Windsor Windsor 27 B7
Old Wives Lees Kent 30 D4
Old Woking Sur 27 D8
Old Woodhall Lincs 78 C5
Oldany Highld 156 F4
Oldberrow Warks 51 C6
Oldborough Devon 10 D2
Oldbury Shrops 61 E7
Oldbury W Mid 62 F3
Oldbury Warks 63 E7
Oldbury-on-Severn S Glos 36 E3
Oldbury on the Hill Glos 37 F5
Oldcastle Bridgend 21 B8
Oldcastle Mon 35 B7
Oldcotes Notts 89 F6
Oldfallow Staffs 62 C3
Oldfield Worcs 50 C3
Oldford Som 24 D2
Oldham Gtr Man 87 D7
Oldhamstocks E Loth 122 B3
Oldland S Glos 23 B8
Oldmeldrum Aberds 141 B7
Oldshore Beg Highld 156 D4
Oldshoremore Highld 156 D5
Oldstead N Yorks 102 F3
Oldtown Aberds 140 B4
Oldtown of Ord Aberds 152 C6
Oldway Swansea 33 F6
Oldways End Devon 10 B3
Oldwhat Aberds 153 C8
Olgrinmore Highld 158 E2
Oliver's Battery Hants 15 B5
Ollaberry Shetland 160 E5
Ollerton Ches E 74 B4
Ollerton Notts 77 C6
Ollerton Shrops 61 B6
Olmarch Ceredig 46 D5
Olney M Keynes 53 D6
Olrig Ho. Highld 158 D3
Olton W Mid 62 F5
Olveston S Glos 36 F3
Olwen Ceredig 46 E4
Ombersley Worcs 50 C3
Ompton Notts 77 C6
Onchan IoM 84 E3
Onecote Staffs 75 D7
Onen Mon 35 C8
Ongar Hill Norf 67 B5
Ongar Street Hereford 49 C5
Onibury Shrops 49 B6
Onich Highld 130 C4
Onllwyn Neath 34 C2
Onneley Staffs 74 E4
Onslow Village Sur 27 E7
Onthank E Ayrs 118 E4
Openwoodgate Derbys 76 E3
Opinan Highld 149 A12
Opinan Highld 155 H13
Orange Lane Borders 122 E3
Orange Row Norf 66 B5
Orasaigh W Isles 155 F8
Orbliston Moray 152 C3
Orbost Highld 148 D7
Orby Lincs 79 C7
Orchard Hill Devon 9 B6
Orchard Portman Som 11 B7
Orcheston Wilts 25 E5
Orcop Hereford 36 B1
Orcop Hill Hereford 36 B1
Ord Highld 149 G11
Ordhead Aberds 141 C5
Ordie Aberds 140 D3
Ordiequish Moray 152 C3
Ordsall Notts 89 F7
Ore E Sus 18 D5
Oreton Shrops 61 F6
Orford Suff 57 E8
Orford Warr 86 E4
Orgreave Staffs 63 C5
Orlestone Kent 19 B6
Orleton Hereford 49 C6
Orleton Worcs 49 C8
Orlingbury Northants 53 B6
Ormesby Redcar 102 C3
Ormesby St Margaret Norf 69 C7
Ormesby St Michael Norf 69 C7
Ormiclate Castle W Isles 148 E2
Ormiscaig Highld 155 H13
Ormiston E Loth 121 C7
Ormsaigbeg Highld 146 E7
Ormsaigmore Highld 146 E7
Ormsary Argyll 144 F6
Ormsgill Cumb 92 B1
Ormskirk Lancs 86 D2
Orpington London 29 C5
Orrell Gtr Man 86 D3
Orrell Mers 85 E4
Orrisdale IoM 84 C3
Orroland Dumfries 106 E4
Orsett Thurrock 42 F2
Orslow Staffs 62 C2
Orston Notts 77 E7
Orthwaite Cumb 108 F2
Ortner Lancs 92 D5
Orton Cumb 99 D8
Orton Northants 53 B6
Orton Longueville Pboro 65 E8
Orton-on-the-Hill Leics 63 D7
Orton Waterville Pboro 65 E8
Orwell Cambs 54 D4
Osbaldeston Lancs 93 F6
Osbaldwick York 96 D2
Osbaston Shrops 60 B3
Osbournby Lincs 78 F3
Oscroft Ches W 74 C2
Ose Highld 149 D8
Osgathorpe Leics 63 C8
Osgodby Lincs 90 E4
Osgodby N Yorks 96 F2
Osgodby N Yorks 103 F8
Oskaig Highld 149 E10
Oskamull Argyll 146 G7
Osmaston Derby 76 F3
Osmaston Derbys 76 E2
Osmington Dorset 12 F5
Osmington Mills Dorset 12 F5
Osmotherley N Yorks 102 E2
Ospisdale Highld 151 C10
Ospringe Kent 30 C4
Ossett W Yorks 88 B3
Ossington Notts 77 C7
Ostend Essex 43 E5
Oswaldkirk N Yorks 96 B2
Oswaldtwistle Lancs 86 B5
Oswestry Shrops 60 B2
Otford Kent 29 D6
Otham Kent 29 D8
Othery Som 23 F5
Otley Suff 57 D6
Otley W Yorks 94 E5
Otter Ferry Argyll 145 E8
Otterbourne Hants 15 B5
Otterburn N Yorks 93 D8
Otterburn Northumb 116 E4
Otterburn Camp Northumb 116 E4
Otterham Corn 8 E3
Otterhampton Som 22 E4
Ottershaw Sur 27 C8
Otterswick Shetland 160 E7
Otterton Devon 11 F5
Ottery St Mary Devon 11 E6
Ottinge Kent 31 E5
Ottringham E Yorks 91 B6
Oughterby Cumb 108 D2
Oughtershaw N Yorks 100 F3
Oughterside Cumb 107 E8
Oughtibridge S Yorks 88 E4
Oughtrington Warr 86 F4
Oulston N Yorks 95 B8
Oulton Cumb 108 D2
Oulton Norf 81 E7
Oulton Staffs 75 F6
Oulton Suff 69 E8
Oulton W Yorks 88 B4
Oulton Broad Suff 69 E8
Oulton Street Norf 81 E7
Oundle Northants 65 F7
Ousby Cumb 109 F6
Ousdale Highld 158 H2
Ousden Suff 55 D8
Ousefleet E Yorks 90 B2
Ouston Durham 111 D5
Ouston Northumb 110 B3
Out Newton E Yorks 91 B7
Out Rawcliffe Lancs 92 E4
Outertown Orkney 159 G3
Outgate Cumb 99 E5
Outhgill Cumb 100 D2
Outlane W Yorks 87 C8
Outwell Norf 66 D5
Outwick Hants 14 C2
Outwood Sur 28 E4
Outwood W Yorks 88 B4
Outwoods Staffs 61 C7
Ovenden W Yorks 87 B8
Ovenscloss Borders 121 F7
Over Cambs 54 B4
Over Ches W 74 C3
Over S Glos 36 F2
Over Compton Dorset 12 C3
Over Green W Mid 63 E5
Over Haddon Derbys 76 C2
Over Hulton Gtr Man 86 D4
Over Kellet Lancs 92 B5
Over Kiddington Oxon 38 B4
Over Knutsford Ches E 74 B4
Over Monnow Mon 36 C2
Over Norton Oxon 38 B3
Over Peover Ches E 74 B4
Over Silton N Yorks 102 E2
Over Stowey Som 22 F3
Over Stratton Som 12 C2
Over Tabley Ches E 86 F5
Over Wallop Hants 25 F7
Over Whitacre Warks 63 E6
Over Worton Oxon 38 B4
Overbister Orkney 159 D7
Overbury Worcs 50 F4
Overcombe Dorset 12 F4
Overgreen Derbys 76 B3
Overleigh Som 23 F6
Overley Green Warks 51 D5
Overpool Ches W 73 B7
Overscaig Hotel Highld 156 G7
Overseal Derbys 63 C6
Oversland Kent 30 D4
Overstone Northants 53 C6
Overstrand Norf 81 C8
Overthorpe Northants 52 E2
Overton Aberdeen 141 C7
Overton Ches W 74 B2
Overton Dumfries 107 C6
Overton Hants 26 E3
Overton Lancs 92 D4
Overton N Yorks 95 D8
Overton Shrops 49 B7
Overton Swansea 33 F5
Overton W Yorks 88 C3
Overton = Owrtyn Wrex 73 E7
Overton Bridge Wrex 73 E7
Overtown N Lanark 119 D8
Oving Bucks 39 B7
Oving W Sus 16 D3
Ovingdean Brighton 17 D7
Ovingham Northumb 110 C3
Ovington Durham 101 C6
Ovington Essex 55 E8
Ovington Hants 26 F3
Ovington Norf 68 D2
Ovington Northumb 110 C3
Ower Hants 14 C4
Owermoigne Dorset 13 F5
Owlbury Shrops 60 E3
Owler Bar Derbys 76 B2
Owlerton S Yorks 88 F4
Owl's Green Suff 57 C6
Owlswick Bucks 39 D7
Owmby Lincs 90 D4
Owmby-by-Spital Lincs 90 F4
Owrtyn = Overton Wrex 73 E7
Owslebury Hants 15 B6
Owston Leics 64 D4
Owston S Yorks 89 C6
Owston Ferry N Lincs 90 D2
Owstwick E Yorks 97 F8
Owthorne E Yorks 91 B7
Owthorpe Notts 77 F6
Oxborough Norf 67 D7
Oxcombe Lincs 79 B6
Oxen Park Cumb 99 F5
Oxenholme Cumb 99 F7
Oxenhope W Yorks 94 F3
Oxenton Glos 50 F4
Oxenwood Wilts 25 D8
Oxford Oxon 39 D5
Oxhey Herts 40 E4
Oxhill Warks 51 E8
Oxley W Mid 62 D3
Oxley Green Essex 43 C5
Oxley's Green E Sus 18 C3
Oxnam Borders 116 C2
Oxshott Sur 28 C2
Oxspring S Yorks 88 D3
Oxted Sur 28 D4
Oxton Borders 121 D7
Oxton Notts 77 D6
Oxwich Swansea 33 F5
Oxwick Norf 80 E5
Oykel Bridge Highld 156 J6
Oyne Aberds 141 B5

P

Pabail Iarach W Isles 155 D10
Pabail Uarach W Isles 155 D10
Pace Gate N Yorks 94 D4
Packington Leics 63 C7
Padanaram Angus 134 D4
Padbury Bucks 52 F5
Paddington London 41 F5
Paddlesworth Kent 19 B8
Paddock Wood Kent 29 E7
Paddockhaugh Moray 152 C2
Paddockhole Dumfries 115 F5
Padfield Derbys 87 E8
Padiham Lancs 93 F7
Padog Conwy 83 F8
Padside N Yorks 94 D4
Padstow Corn 4 B4
Padworth W Berks 26 C4
Page Bank Durham 110 F5
Pagelsham Eastend Essex 43 E5
Pagham W Sus 16 E2
Paglesham Churchend Essex 43 E5
Paibeil W Isles 148 B2
Paible W Isles 154 H5
Paignton Torbay 7 C6
Pailton Warks 63 F8
Painscastle Powys 48 E3
Painshawfield Northumb 110 C3
Painsthorpe E Yorks 96 D4
Painswick Glos 37 D5
Pairc Shiaboist W Isles 154 C7
Paisley Renfs 118 C4
Pakefield Suff 69 E8
Pakenham Suff 56 C3
Pale Gwyn 72 F3
Palestine Hants 25 E7
Paley Street Windsor 27 B6
Palfrey W Mid 62 E4
Palgowan Dumfries 112 F3
Palgrave Suff 56 B5
Pallion T&W 111 D6
Palmarsh Kent 19 B8
Palnackie Dumfries 106 D5
Palnure Dumfries 105 C8
Palterton Derbys 76 C4
Pamber End Hants 26 D4
Pamber Green Hants 26 D4
Pamber Heath Hants 26 C4
Pamphill Dorset 13 D7
Pampisford Cambs 55 E5
Pan Orkney 159 J4
Panbride Angus 135 F5
Pancrasweek Devon 8 D4
Pandy Gwyn 58 D3
Pandy Mon 35 B7
Pandy Powys 59 D6
Pandy Wrex 73 F5
Pandy Tudur Conwy 83 E8
Panfield Essex 42 B3
Pangbourne W Berks 26 B4
Pannal N Yorks 95 D6
Panshanger Herts 41 C5
Pant Shrops 60 B2
Pant-glâs Powys 58 E4
Pant-glas Carms 33 B6
Pant-glas Gwyn 71 C5
Pant-glas Shrops 73 F6
Pant-lasau Swansea 33 E7
Pant Mawr Powys 59 F5
Pant-teg Carms 33 B5
Pant-y-Caws Carms 32 B2
Pant-y-dwr Powys 47 B8
Pant-y-ffridd Powys 59 D8
Pant-y-Wacco Flint 72 B5
Pant-yr-awel Bridgend 34 F3
Pantgwyn Carms 33 B6
Pantgwyn Ceredig 45 E4
Panton Lincs 78 B4
Pantperthog Gwyn 58 D4
Pantyffynnon Carms 33 C7
Pantymwyn Flint 73 C5
Panxworth Norf 69 C6
Papcastle Cumb 107 F8
Papigoe Highld 158 E5
Papil Shetland 160 K5
Papley Orkney 159 J5
Papple E Loth 121 B8
Papplewick Notts 76 D5
Papworth Everard Cambs 54 C3
Papworth St Agnes Cambs 54 C3
Par Corn 5 D5
Parbold Lancs 86 C2
Parbrook Som 23 F7
Parbrook W Sus 16 B4
Parc Gwyn 72 F2
Parc-Seymour Newport 35 E8
Parc-y-rhôs Carms 46 E4
Parcllyn Ceredig 45 D4
Pardshaw Cumb 98 B2
Parham Suff 57 C7
Park Dumfries 114 E2
Park Corner Oxon 39 F6
Park Corner Windsor 40 F1
Park End Mbro 102 C3
Park End Northumb 109 B8
Park Gate Hants 15 D6
Park Hill N Yorks 95 C6
Park Hill Notts 77 D6
Park Street W Sus 28 F2
Parkend Glos 36 D3
Parkeston Essex 57 F6
Parkgate Ches W 73 B6
Parkgate Dumfries 114 F3
Parkgate Kent 19 B5
Parkgate Sur 28 E3
Parkham Devon 9 B5
Parkham Ash Devon 9 B5
Parkhill Ho. Aberds 141 C7
Parkhouse Mon 36 D1
Parkhouse Green Derbys 76 C4
Parkhurst IoW 15 E5
Parkmill Swansea 33 F6
Parkneuk Aberds 135 B7
Parkstone Poole 13 E8
Parley Cross Dorset 13 E8
Parracombe Devon 21 E5
Parrog Pembs 45 F2
Parsley Hay Derbys 75 C8
Parson Cross S Yorks 88 E4
Parson Drove Cambs 66 D3
Parsonage Green Essex 42 D3
Parsonby Cumb 107 F8
Parson's Heath Essex 43 B6
Partick Glasgow 119 C5
Partington Gtr Man 86 E5
Partney Lincs 79 C7
Parton Cumb 98 B1
Parton Dumfries 106 B3
Parton Glos 37 B5
Partridge Green W Sus 17 C5
Parwich Derbys 75 D8
Passenham Northants 53 F5
Paston Norf 81 D9
Patchacott Devon 9 E6
Patcham Brighton 17 D7
Patching W Sus 16 D4
Patchole Devon 20 E5
Pateley Bridge N Yorks 94 C4
Paternoster Heath Essex 43 C5
Path of Condie Perth 128 C2
Pathe Som 23 F5
Pathhead Aberds 135 C7
Pathhead E Ayrs 113 C6
Pathhead Fife 128 E4
Pathhead Midloth 121 C6
Pathstruie Perth 128 C2
Patna E Ayrs 112 C4
Patney Wilts 25 D5
Patrick IoM 84 D2
Patrick Brompton N Yorks 101 E7
Patrington E Yorks 91 B7
Patrixbourne Kent 31 D5
Patterdale Cumb 99 C5
Pattingham Staffs 62 E2
Pattishall Northants 52 D4
Pattiswick Green Essex 42 B4
Patton Bridge Cumb 99 E7
Paul Corn 2 D3
Paulerspury Northants 52 E5
Paull E Yorks 91 B5
Paulton Bath 23 D8
Pavenham Bedford 53 D7
Pawlett Som 22 E5
Pawston Northumb 122 F4
Paxford Glos 51 F6
Paxton Borders 122 D5
Payhembury Devon 11 D5
Paythorne Lancs 93 D8
Peacehaven E Sus 17 D8
Peak Dale Derbys 75 B7
Peak Forest Derbys 75 B8
Peakirk Pboro 65 D8
Pearsie Angus 134 D3
Pease Pottage W Sus 28 F3
Peasedown St John Bath 24 D2
Peasemore W Berks 26 B2
Peasenhall Suff 57 C7
Peaslake Sur 27 E8
Peasley Cross Mers 86 E3
Peasmarsh E Sus 19 C5
Peaston E Loth 121 C7
Peastonbank E Loth 121 C7
Peat Inn Fife 129 D6
Peathill Aberds 153 B9
Peatling Magna Leics 64 E2
Peatling Parva Leics 64 F2
Peaton Shrops 60 F5
Peats Corner Suff 57 C5
Pebmarsh Essex 56 F2
Pebworth Worcs 51 E6
Pecket Well W Yorks 87 B7
Peckforton Ches E 74 D2
Peckham London 28 B4
Peckleton Leics 63 D8
Pedlinge Kent 19 B8
Pedmore W Mid 62 F3
Pedwell Som 23 F6
Peebles Borders 121 E5
Peel IoM 84 D2
Peel Common Hants 15 D6
Peel Park S Lanark 119 D6
Peening Quarter Kent 19 C5
Pegsdon C Beds 54 F2
Pegswood Northumb 117 F8
Pegwell Kent 31 C7
Peinchorran Highld 149 E10
Peinlich Highld 149 C9
Pelaw T&W 111 C5
Pelcomb Bridge Pembs 44 D4
Pelcomb Cross Pembs 44 D4
Peldon Essex 43 C5
Pellon W Yorks 87 B8
Pelsall W Mid 62 D4
Pelton Durham 111 D5
Pelutho Cumb 107 E8
Pelynt Corn 5 D7
Pemberton Gtr Man 86 D3
Pembrey Carms 33 D5
Pembridge Hereford 49 D5
Pembroke = Penfro Pembs 44 E4
Pembroke Dock = Doc Penfro Pembs 44 E4
Pembury Kent 29 E7
Pen-bont Rhydybeddau Ceredig 58 F3
Pen-clawdd Swansea 33 E6
Pen-ffordd Pembs 32 B1
Pen-groes-oped Mon 35 D7
Pen-llyn Anglesey 82 C3
Pen-lon Anglesey 82 E4
Pen-sarn Gwyn 71 C5
Pen-sarn Gwyn 71 E6
Pen-twyn Mon 36 D2
Pen-y-banc Carms 33 B7
Pen-y-bont Carms 32 B4
Pen-y-bont Gwyn 58 D4
Pen-y-bont Gwyn 71 E7
Pen-y-bont Powys 60 B2
Pen-Y-Bont Ar Ogwr = Bridgend Bridgend 21 B8
Pen-y-bryn Gwyn 58 C3
Pen-y-bryn Pembs 45 E3
Pen-y-cae Powys 34 C2
Pen-y-cae-mawr Mon 35 E8
Pen-y-cefn Flint 72 B5
Pen-y-clawdd Mon 36 D1
Pen-y-coedcae Rhondda 34 F4
Pen-y-fai Bridgend 34 F2
Pen-y-garn Carms 46 F4
Pen-y-garn Ceredig 58 F3
Pen-y-garnedd Anglesey 82 D5
Pen-y-gop Conwy 72 E3
Pen-y-graig Gwyn 70 D2
Pen-y-groes Carms 33 C6
Pen-y-groeslon Gwyn 70 D3
Pen-y-Gwryd Hotel Gwyn 83 F6
Pen-y-stryt Denb 73 D5
Pen-yr-heol Mon 35 C8
Pen-yr-Heolgerrig M Tydf 34 D4
Penallt Mon 36 C2
Penally Pembs 32 E2
Penalt Hereford 36 B2
Penare Corn 3 B8
Penarlâg = Hawarden Flint 73 C7
Penarth V Glam 22 B3
Penbryn Ceredig 45 D4
Pencader Carms 46 F3
Pencaenewydd Gwyn 70 C5
Pencaitland E Loth 121 C7
Pencarnisiog Anglesey 82 D3
Pencarreg Carms 46 E4
Pencelli Powys 34 B4
Pencoed Bridgend 34 F3
Pencombe Hereford 49 D7
Pencoyd Hereford 36 B2
Pencraig Hereford 36 B2
Pencraig Powys 59 B7
Pendeen Corn 2 C2
Penderyn Rhondda 34 D3
Pendine Carms 32 D3
Pendlebury Gtr Man 87 D5
Pendleton Lancs 93 F7
Pendock Worcs 50 F2
Pendoggett Corn 4 B5
Pendomer Som 12 C3
Pendoylan V Glam 22 B2
Pendre Bridgend 34 F3
Penegoes Powys 58 D4
Penfro = Pembroke Pembs 44 E4
Pengam Caerph 35 E5
Penge London 28 B4
Pengenffordd Powys 48 F3
Pengorffwysfa Anglesey 82 B4
Pengover Green Corn 5 C7
Penhale Corn 3 E5
Penhale Corn 4 D4
Penhalvaen Corn 3 C6
Penhill Swindon 38 F1
Penhow Newport 35 E8
Penhurst E Sus 18 D3
Peniarth Gwyn 58 D3
Penicuik Midloth 120 C5
Peniel Carms 33 B5
Peniel Denb 72 C4
Penifiler Highld 149 D9
Peninver Argyll 143 F8
Penisarwaun Gwyn 83 E5
Penistone S Yorks 88 D3
Penjerrick Corn 3 C6
Penketh Warr 86 F3
Penkill S Ayrs 112 E2
Penkridge Staffs 62 C3
Penley Wrex 73 F8
Penllergaer Swansea 33 E7
Penllyn V Glam 21 B8
Penmachno Conwy 83 F7
Penmaen Swansea 33 F6
Penmaenan Conwy 83 D7
Penmaenmawr Conwy 83 D7
Penmaenpool Gwyn 58 C3
Penmark V Glam 22 C2
Penmarth Corn 3 C6
Penmon Anglesey 83 C6
Penmore Mill Argyll 146 F7
Penmorfa Ceredig 46 D2
Penmorfa Gwyn 71 C6
Penmynydd Anglesey 82 D5
Penn Bucks 40 E2
Penn W Mid 62 E2
Penn Street Bucks 40 E2
Pennal Gwyn 58 D4
Pennan Aberds 153 B8
Pennant Ceredig 46 C4
Pennant Denb 72 D4
Pennant Denb 72 F4
Pennant Powys 59 E5
Pennant Melangell Powys 59 B7
Pennar Pembs 44 E4
Pennard Swansea 33 F6
Pennerley Shrops 60 E3
Pennington Cumb 92 B2
Pennington Gtr Man 86 E4
Pennington Hants 14 E4
Penny Bridge Cumb 99 F5
Pennycross Argyll 147 J8
Pennygate Norf 69 B6
Pennygown Argyll 147 G8
Pennymoor Devon 10 C3
Pennywell T&W 111 D6
Penparc Ceredig 45 E4
Penparc Pembs 44 B3
Penparcau Ceredig 58 F2
Penperlleni Mon 35 D7
Penpillick Corn 5 D5
Penpol Corn 3 C7
Penpoll Corn 5 D6
Penpont Dumfries 113 E8
Penpont Powys 34 B3
Penrherber Carms 45 F4
Penrhiw goch Carms 33 C6
Penrhiw-llan Ceredig 46 E2
Penrhiw-pâl Ceredig 46 E2
Penrhiwceiber Rhondda 34 E4
Penrhos Gwyn 70 D4
Penrhos Powys 34 C1
Penrhosfeilw Anglesey 82 C2
Penrhyn Bay Conwy 83 C8
Penrhyn-coch Ceredig 58 F3
Penrhyndeudraeth Gwyn 71 D7
Penrhynside Conwy 83 C8
Penrice Swansea 33 F5
Penrith Cumb 108 F5
Penrose Corn 4 B3
Penruddock Cumb 99 B6
Penryn Corn 3 C6
Pensarn Carms 33 C5
Pensarn Conwy 72 B3
Pensax Worcs 50 C2
Pensby Mers 85 F3
Penselwood Som 24 F2
Pensford Bath 23 C8
Penshaw T&W 111 D6
Penshurst Kent 29 E6
Pensilva Corn 5 C7
Penston E Loth 121 B7
Pentewan Corn 3 B9
Pentir Gwyn 83 E5
Pentire Corn 4 C2
Pentlow Essex 56 E2
Pentney Norf 67 C7
Penton Mewsey Hants 25 E8
Pentraeth Anglesey 82 D5
Pentre Carms 33 C6
Pentre Powys 48 B4
Pentre Powys 60 E2
Pentre Rhondda 34 E3
Pentre Shrops 60 C3
Pentre Wrex 72 F5
Pentre Wrex 73 E6
Pentre-bâch Ceredig 46 E4
Pentre-bach Powys 47 F8
Pentre Berw Anglesey 82 D4
Pentre-bont Conwy 83 F7
Pentre-celyn Denb 72 D5
Pentre-Celyn Powys 59 D5
Pentre-chwyth Swansea 33 E7
Pentre-cwrt Carms 46 F2
Pentre Dolau-Honddu Powys 47 E8
Pentre-dwr Swansea 33 E7
Pentre-galar Pembs 45 F3
Pentre-Gwenlais Carms 33 C7
Pentre Gwynfryn Gwyn 71 E6
Pentre Halkyn Flint 73 B6
Pentre-Isaf Conwy 83 E8
Pentre Llanrhaeadr Denb 72 C4
Pentre-llwyn-llŵyd Powys 47 D8
Pentre-llyn Ceredig 46 B5
Pentre-llyn cymmer Conwy 72 D3
Pentre Meyrick V Glam 21 B8
Pentre-poeth Newport 35 F6
Pentre-rhew Ceredig 47 D5
Pentre-tafarn-y-fedw Conwy 83 E8
Pentre-ty-gwyn Carms 47 F7
Pentrebach M Tydf 34 D4
Pentrebach Swansea 33 D7
Pentrebeirdd Powys 59 C8
Pentrecagal Carms 46 E2
Pentredwr Denb 73 E5
Pentrefelin Carms 33 B6
Pentrefelin Ceredig 46 E5
Pentrefelin Conwy 83 D8
Pentrefelin Gwyn 71 D6
Pentrefoelas Conwy 83 F8
Pentregat Ceredig 46 D2
Pentreheyling Shrops 60 E2
Pentre'r Felin Conwy 83 E8
Pentre'r-felin Powys 47 F8
Pentrich Derbys 76 D3
Pentridge Dorset 13 C8
Pentyrch Cardiff 35 F5
Penuchadre V Glam 21 B7
Penuwch Ceredig 46 C4
Penwithick Corn 4 D5
Penwyllt Powys 34 C2
Penybanc Carms 33 C7
Penybont Powys 48 C3
Penybontfawr Powys 59 B7
Penycae Wrex 73 E6
Penycwm Pembs 44 C3
Penyffordd Flint 73 C7
Penyffridd Gwyn 82 F5
Penygarnedd Powys 59 B8
Penygraig Rhondda 34 E3
Penygroes Gwyn 82 F4
Penygroes Pembs 45 F3
Penyrheol Caerph 35 F5
Penysarn Anglesey 82 B4
Penywaun Rhondda 34 D3
Penzance Corn 2 C3
Peopleton Worcs 50 D4
Peover Heath Ches E 74 B4
Peper Harow Sur 27 E7
Perceton N Ayrs 118 E3
Percie Aberds 140 E4
Percyhorner Aberds 153 B9
Periton Som 21 E8
Perivale London 40 F4
Perkinsville Durham 111 D5
Perlethorpe Notts 77 B6
Perranarworthal Corn 3 C6
Perranporth Corn 4 D2
Perranuthnoe Corn 2 D4
Perranzabuloe Corn 4 D2
Perry Barr W Mid 62 E4
Perry Green Herts 41 C7
Perry Green Wilts 37 F6
Perry Street Kent 29 B7
Perryfoot Derbys 88 F2
Pershall Staffs 74 F5
Pershore Worcs 50 E4
Pert Angus 135 C6
Pertenhall Bedford 53 C8
Perth Perth 128 B3
Perthy Shrops 73 F7
Perton Staffs 62 E2
Pertwood Wilts 24 F3
Peter Tavy Devon 6 B3
Peterborough Pboro 65 E8
Peterburn Highld 155 J12
Peterchurch Hereford 48 F5
Peterculter Aberdeen 141 D7
Peterhead Aberds 153 D11
Peterlee Durham 111 E7
Peter's Green Herts 40 C4
Peters Marland Devon 9 C6
Petersfield Hants 15 B8
Peterston super-Ely V Glam 22 B2
Peterstone Wentlooge Newport 35 F6
Peterstow Hereford 36 B2
Petertown Orkney 159 H4
Petham Kent 30 D5
Petrockstow Devon 9 D7
Pett E Sus 19 D5
Pettaugh Suff 57 D5
Petteridge Kent 29 E7
Pettinain S Lanark 120 E2
Pettistree Suff 57 D6
Petton Devon 10 B5
Petton Shrops 60 B4
Petts Wood London 28 C5
Petty Aberds 153 E7
Pettycur Fife 128 F4
Pettymuick Aberds 141 B8
Petworth W Sus 16 B3
Pevensey E Sus 18 E3
Pevensey Bay E Sus 18 E3
Pewsey Wilts 25 C6
Philham Devon 8 B4
Philiphaugh Borders 115 B7
Phillack Corn 2 C4
Philleigh Corn 3 C7
Philpstoun W Loth 120 B3
Phocle Green Hereford 36 B3
Phoenix Green Hants 27 D5
Pica Cumb 98 B2
Piccotts End Herts 40 D3
Pickering N Yorks 103 F5
Picket Piece Hants 25 E8
Picket Post Hants 14 D2
Pickhill N Yorks 101 F8
Picklescott Shrops 60 E4
Pickletillem Fife 129 B6
Pickmere Ches E 74 B3
Pickney Som 11 B6
Pickstock Telford 61 B7
Pickwell Devon 20 E3
Pickwell Leics 64 C4
Pickworth Lincs 78 F3
Pickworth Rutland 65 C6
Picton Ches W 73 B8
Picton Flint 85 F2
Picton N Yorks 102 D2
Piddinghoe E Sus 17 D8
Piddington Northants 53 D6
Piddington Oxon 39 C6
Piddlehinton Dorset 12 E5
Piddletrenthide Dorset 12 E5
Pidley Cambs 54 B4
Piercebridge Darl 101 C7
Pierowall Orkney 159 D5
Pigdon Northumb 117 F7
Pikehall Derbys 75 D8
Pilgrims Hatch Essex 42 E1
Pilham Lincs 90 E2
Pill N Som 23 B7
Pillaton Corn 5 C8
Pillerton Hersey Warks 51 E8
Pillerton Priors Warks 51 E7
Pilleth Powys 48 C4
Pilley Hants 14 E4
Pilley S Yorks 88 D4
Pilling Lancs 92 E4
Pilling Lane Lancs 92 E3
Pillowell Glos 36 D3
Pillwell Dorset 13 C5
Pilning S Glos 36 F2
Pilsbury Derbys 75 C8
Pilsdon Dorset 12 E2
Pilsgate Pboro 65 D7
Pilsley Derbys 76 B2
Pilsley Derbys 76 C4
Pilton Devon 20 F4
Pilton Northants 65 F7
Pilton Rutland 65 D6
Pilton Som 23 E7
Pilton Green Swansea 33 F5
Pimperne Dorset 13 D7
Pin Mill Suff 57 F6
Pinchbeck Lincs 66 B2
Pinchbeck Bars Lincs 65 B8
Pinchbeck West Lincs 66 B2
Pincheon Green S Yorks 89 C7
Pinehurst Swindon 38 F1
Pinfold Lancs 85 C4
Pinged Carms 33 D5
Pinhoe Devon 10 E4
Pinkneys Green Windsor 40 F1
Pinley W Mid 51 B8
Pinminnoch S Ayrs 112 E1
Pinmore S Ayrs 112 E2
Pinmore Mains S Ayrs 112 E2
Pinner London 40 F4
Pinvin Worcs 50 E4
Pinwherry S Ayrs 112 F1
Pinxton Derbys 76 D4
Pipe and Lyde Hereford 49 E7
Pipe Gate Shrops 74 E4
Piperhill Highld 151 F11
Piper's Pool Corn 8 F4
Pipewell Northants 64 F5
Pippacott Devon 20 F4
Pipton Powys 48 F3
Pirbright Sur 27 D7
Pirnmill N Ayrs 143 D9
Pirton Herts 54 F2
Pirton Worcs 50 E3
Pisgah Ceredig 47 B5
Pisgah Stirling 127 D6
Pishill Oxon 39 F7
Pistyll Gwyn 70 C4
Pitagowan Perth 133 C5
Pitblae Aberds 153 B9
Pitcairngreen Perth 128 B2
Pitcalnie Highld 151 D11
Pitcaple Aberds 141 B6
Pitch Green Bucks 39 D7
Pitch Place Sur 27 D7
Pitchcombe Glos 37 D5
Pitchcott Bucks 39 B7
Pitchford Shrops 60 D5
Pitcombe Som 23 F8
Pitcorthie Fife 129 D7
Pitcox E Loth 122 B2
Pitcur Perth 134 F2
Pitfichie Aberds 141 C5
Pitforthie Aberds 135 B8
Pitgrudy Highld 151 B10
Pitkennedy Angus 135 D5
Pitkevy Fife 128 D4
Pitkierie Fife 129 D7
Pitlessie Fife 128 D5
Pitlochry Perth 133 D6
Pitmachie Aberds 141 B5
Pitmain Highld 138 D3
Pitmedden Aberds 141 B7
Pitminster Som 11 C7
Pitmuies Angus 135 E5
Pitmunie Aberds 141 C5
Pitney Som 12 B2
Pitscottie Fife 129 C6
Pitsea Essex 42 F3
Pitsford Northants 53 C5
Pitsmoor S Yorks 88 F4
Pitstone Bucks 40 C2
Pitstone Green Bucks 40 C2
Pittendreich Moray 152 B1
Pittentrail Highld 157 J10
Pittenweem Fife 129 D7
Pittington Durham 111 E6
Pittodrie Aberds 141 B5
Pitton Wilts 25 F7
Pittswood Kent 29 E7
Pittulie Aberds 153 B9
Pity Me Durham 111 E5
Pityme Corn 4 B4
Pityoulish Highld 138 C5
Pixey Green Suff 57 B6
Pixham Sur 28 D2
Pixley Hereford 49 F8
Place Newton N Yorks 96 B4
Plaidy Aberds 153 C7
Plains N Lanark 119 C7
Plaish Shrops 60 E5
Plaistow W Sus 27 F8
Plaitford Wilts 14 C3
Plank Lane Gtr Man 86 E4
Plas-canol Gwyn 58 C2
Plas Gogerddan Ceredig 58 F3
Plas Llwyngwern Powys 58 D4
Plas Nantyr Wrex 73 F5
Plas-yn-Cefn Denb 72 B4
Plastow Green Hants 26 C3
Platt Kent 29 D7
Platt Bridge Gtr Man 86 D4
Platts Common S Yorks 88 D4
Plawsworth Durham 111 E5
Plaxtol Kent 29 D7
Play Hatch Oxon 26 B5
Playden E Sus 19 C6
Playford Suff 57 E6
Playing Place Corn 3 B7
Playley Green Glos 50 F2
Plealey Shrops 60 D4
Plean Stirling 127 F7
Pleasington Blackburn 86 B4
Pleasley Derbys 76 C5
Pleckgate Blackburn 93 F6
Plenmeller Northumb 109 C7
Pleshey Essex 42 C2
Plockton Highld 149 E13
Plocrapol W Isles 154 H6
Ploughfield Hereford 49 E5
Plowden Shrops 60 F3
Ploxgreen Shrops 60 D3
Pluckley Kent 30 E3
Pluckley Thorne Kent 30 E3
Plumbland Cumb 107 F8
Plumley Ches E 74 B4
Plumpton Cumb 108 F4
Plumpton E Sus 17 C7
Plumpton Green E Sus 17 C7
Plumpton Head Cumb 108 F5
Plumstead London 29 B5
Plumstead Norf 81 D7
Plumtree Notts 77 F6
Plungar Leics 77 F7
Plush Dorset 12 D5
Plwmp Ceredig 46 D2
Plymouth Plym 6 D2
Plympton Plym 6 D3

Ros – Shi 229

Rosehall Highld 156 J7
Rosehaugh Mains Highld 151 F9
Rosehearty Aberds 153 B9
Rosehill Shrops 74 F3
Roseisle Moray 152 B1
Roselands E Sus 18 E3
Rosemarket Pembs 44 E4
Rosemarkie Highld 151 F10
Rosemary Lane Devon 11 C6
Rosemount Perth 134 E1
Rosenannon Corn 4 C4
Rosewell Midloth 121 C5
Roseworth Stockton 102 B2
Roseworthy Corn 2 C5
Rosgill Cumb 99 C7
Roshven Highld 147 D10
Roskhill Highld 149 D7
Roskill House Highld 151 F9
Rosley Cumb 108 E3
Roslin Midloth 121 C5
Rosliston Derbys 63 C6
Rosneath Argyll 145 E11
Ross Dumfries 106 E3
Ross Northumb 123 F7
Ross Perth 127 B6
Ross-on-Wye Hereford 36 B3
Rossett Wrex 73 D7
Rossett Green N Yorks 95 D6
Rossie Ochill Perth 128 C2
Rossie Priory Perth 134 F2
Rossington S Yorks 89 E7
Rosskeen Highld 151 E9
Rossland Renfs 118 B4
Roster Highld 158 G4
Rostherne Ches E 86 F5
Rosthwaite Cumb 98 C4
Roston Derbys 75 E8
Rosyth Fife 128 F3
Rothbury Northumb 117 D6
Rotherby Leics 64 C3
Rotherfield E Sus 18 C2
Rotherfield Greys Oxon 39 F7
Rotherfield Peppard Oxon 39 F7
Rotherham S Yorks 88 E5
Rothersthorpe Northants 52 D5
Rotherwick Hants 26 D5
Rothes Moray 152 D2
Rothesay Argyll 145 G9
Rothiebrisbane Aberds 153 E7
Rothienorman Aberds 153 E7
Rothiesholm Orkney 159 F7
Rothley Leics 64 C2
Rothley Northumb 117 F6
Rothley Shield East Northumb 117 E6
Rothmaise Aberds 153 E6
Rothwell Lincs 91 E5
Rothwell Northants 64 F5
Rothwell W Yorks 88 B4
Rothwell Haigh W Yorks 88 B4
Rotsea E Yorks 97 D6
Rottal Angus 134 C3
Rotten End Suff 57 C7
Rottingdean Brighton 17 D7
Rottington Cumb 98 C1
Roud IoW 15 F6
Rough Close Staffs 75 F6
Rough Common Kent 30 D5
Rougham Norf 80 E4
Rougham Suff 56 C3
Rougham Green Suff 56 C3
Roughburn Highld 137 F6
Roughlee Lancs 93 E8
Roughley W Mid 62 E5
Roughsike Cumb 108 B5
Roughton Lincs 78 C5
Roughton Norf 81 D8
Roughton Shrops 61 E7
Roughton Moor Lincs 78 C5
Roundhay W Yorks 95 F6
Roundstonefoot Dumfries 114 D4
Roundstreet Common W Sus 16 B4
Roundway Wilts 24 C5
Rous Lench Worcs 50 D5
Rousdon Devon 11 E7
Routenburn N Ayrs 118 C1
Routh E Yorks 97 E6
Row Corn 5 B5
Row Cumb 99 F6
Row Heath Essex 43 C7
Rowanburn Dumfries 108 B4
Rowardennan Stirling 126 E2
Rowde Wilts 24 C4
Rowen Conwy 83 D7
Rowfoot Northumb 109 C6
Rowhedge Essex 43 B6
Rowhook W Sus 28 F2
Rowington Warks 51 C7
Rowland Derbys 76 B2
Rowlands Castle Hants 15 C8
Rowlands Gill T&W 110 D4
Rowledge Sur 27 E6
Rowlestone Hereford 35 B7
Rowley E Yorks 97 F5
Rowley Shrops 60 D3
Rowley Hill W Yorks 88 C2
Rowley Regis W Mid 62 F3
Rowly Sur 27 E8
Rowney Green Worcs 50 B5
Rownhams Hants 14 C4
Rowrah Cumb 98 C2
Rowsham Bucks 39 C8
Rowsley Derbys 76 C2
Rowstock Oxon 38 F4
Rowston Lincs 78 D3
Rowton Ches W 73 C8
Rowton Shrops 60 C3
Rowton Telford 61 C6
Roxburgh Borders 122 F3
Roxby N Lincs 90 C3
Roxby N Yorks 103 C5
Roxton Bedford 54 D2
Roxwell Essex 42 D2
Royal Leamington Spa Warks 51 C8
Royal Oak Darl 101 B7
Royal Oak Lancs 86 D2
Royal Tunbridge Wells Kent 18 B2
Roybridge Highld 137 F5
Roydhouse W Yorks 88 C3
Roydon Essex 41 D7
Roydon Norf 68 F3
Roydon Norf 80 E3
Roydon Hamlet Essex 41 D7
Royston Herts 54 E4
Royston S Yorks 88 C4
Royton Gtr Man 87 D7
Rozel Jersey 17
Ruabon = Rhiwabon Wrex 73 E7
Ruaig Argyll 146 G3
Ruan Lanihorne Corn 3 B7
Ruan Minor Corn 3 E6
Ruarach Highld 136 B2
Ruardean Glos 36 C3
Ruardean Woodside Glos 36 C3
Rubery Worcs 50 B4
Ruckcroft Cumb 108 E5
Ruckhall Hereford 49 F6
Ruckinge Kent 19 B7
Ruckland Lincs 79 B6
Ruckley Shrops 60 D5
Rudbaxton Pembs 44 C4
Rudby N Yorks 102 D2
Ruddington Notts 77 F5
Rudford Glos 36 B4
Rudge Shrops 62 E2
Rudge Som 24 D3
Rudgeway S Glos 36 F3
Rudgwick W Sus 27 F8
Rudhall Hereford 36 B3
Rudheath Ches W 74 B3
Rudley Green Essex 42 D4
Rudry Caerph 35 F5
Rudston E Yorks 97 C6
Rudyard Staffs 75 D6
Rufford Lancs 86 C2
Rufforth York 95 D8
Rugby Warks 52 B3
Rugeley Staffs 62 C4
Ruglen S Ayrs 112 D2
Ruilick Highld 151 G8
Ruishton Som 11 B7
Ruisigearraidh W Isles 154 J4
Ruislip London 40 F3
Ruislip Common London 40 F3
Rumbling Bridge Perth 128 E2
Rumburgh Suff 69 F6
Rumford Corn 4 B3
Rumney Cardiff 22 B4
Runcorn Halton 86 F3
Runcton W Sus 16 D2
Runcton Holme Norf 67 D6
Rundlestone Devon 6 B3
Runfold Sur 27 E6
Runhall Norf 68 D3
Runham Norf 69 C7
Runham Norf 69 D8
Runnington Som 11 B6
Runsell Green Essex 42 D3
Runswick Bay N Yorks 103 C6
Runwell Essex 42 E3
Ruscombe Wokingham 27 B5
Rush Green London 41 F8
Rush-head Aberds 153 D8
Rushall Hereford 49 F8
Rushall Norf 68 F4
Rushall W Mid 62 D4
Rushall Wilts 25 D6
Rushbrooke Suff 56 C2
Rushbury Shrops 60 E5
Rushden Herts 54 F4
Rushden Northants 53 C7
Rushenden Kent 30 B3
Rushford Norf 68 F2
Rushlake Green E Sus 18 D3
Rushmere Suff 69 F7
Rushmere St Andrew Suff 57 E6
Rushmoor Sur 27 E6
Rushock Worcs 50 B3
Rusholme Gtr Man 87 E6
Rushton Ches W 74 C2
Rushton Northants 64 F5
Rushton Shrops 61 D6
Rushton Spencer Staffs 75 C6
Rushwick Worcs 50 D3
Rushyford Durham 101 B7
Ruskie Stirling 126 D5
Ruskington Lincs 78 D3
Rusland Cumb 99 F5
Rusper W Sus 28 F3
Ruspidge Glos 36 C3
Russell's Water Oxon 39 F7
Russel's Green Suff 57 B6
Rusthall Kent 18 B2
Rustington W Sus 16 D4
Ruston N Yorks 103 F7
Ruston Parva E Yorks 97 C6
Ruswarp N Yorks 103 D6
Rutherford Borders 122 F2
Rutherglen S Lanark 119 C6
Ruthernbridge Corn 4 C5
Ruthin = Rhuthun Denb 72 D5
Ruthrieston Aberdeen 141 D8
Ruthven Aberds 152 D5
Ruthven Angus 134 E2
Ruthven Highld 138 E3
Ruthven Highld 151 H11
Ruthven House Angus 134 E3
Ruthvoes Corn 4 C4
Ruthwell Dumfries 107 C7
Ruyton-XI-Towns Shrops 60 B3
Ryal Northumb 110 B3
Ryal Fold Blackburn 86 B4
Ryall Dorset 12 E2
Ryarsh Kent 29 D7
Rydal Cumb 99 D5
Ryde IoW 15 E6
Rye E Sus 19 C6
Rye Foreign E Sus 19 C5
Rye Harbour E Sus 19 D6
Rye Park Herts 41 C6
Rye Street Worcs 50 F2
Ryecroft Gate Staffs 75 C6
Ryehill E Yorks 91 B6
Ryhall Rutland 65 C7
Ryhill W Yorks 88 C4
Ryhope T&W 111 D7
Rylstone N Yorks 94 D2
Ryme Intrinseca Dorset 12 C3
Ryther N Yorks 95 F8
Ryton Glos 50 F2
Ryton N Yorks 96 B3
Ryton Shrops 61 D7
Ryton T&W 110 C4
Ryton-on-Dunsmore Warks 51 B8

S

Sabden Lancs 93 F7
Sacombe Herts 41 C6
Sacriston Durham 110 E5
Sadberge Darl 101 C8
Saddell Argyll 143 E8
Saddington Leics 64 E3
Saddle Bow Norf 67 C6
Saddlescombe W Sus 17 C6
Sadgill Cumb 99 D6
Saffron Walden Essex 55 F6
Sageston Pembs 32 D1
Saham Hills Norf 68 D2
Saham Toney Norf 68 D2
Saighdinis W Isles 148 B3
Saighton Ches W 73 C8
St Abbs Borders 122 C5
St Abb's Haven Borders 122 C5
St Agnes Corn 4 D2
St Agnes Scilly 2 F3
St Albans Herts 40 D4
St Allen Corn 4 D3
St Andrews Fife 129 C7
St Andrew's Major V Glam 22 B3
St Anne Ald 16
St Annes Lancs 85 B4
St Ann's Dumfries 114 E3
St Ann's Chapel Corn 6 B2
St Ann's Chapel Devon 6 E4
St Anthony-in-Meneage Corn 3 D6
St Anthony's Hill E Sus 18 E3
St Arvans Mon 36 E2
St Asaph = Llanelwy Denb 72 B4
St Athan V Glam 22 C2
St Aubin Jersey 17
St Austell Corn 4 D5
St Bees Cumb 98 C1
St Blazey Corn 5 D5
St Boswells Borders 121 F8
St Brelade Jersey 17
St Breock Corn 4 B4
St Breward Corn 5 B5
St Briavels Glos 36 D2
St Bride's Pembs 44 D3
St Brides Major V Glam 21 B7
St Bride's Netherwent Mon 35 F8
St Brides super Ely V Glam 22 B2
St Brides Wentlooge Newport 35 F6
St Budeaux Plym 6 D2
St Buryan Corn 2 D3
St Catherine Bath 24 B2
St Catherine's Argyll 125 E7
St Clears = Sanclêr Carms 32 C3
St Cleer Corn 5 C7
St Clement Corn 3 B7
St Clements Jersey 17
St Clether Corn 8 F4
St Colmac Argyll 145 G9
St Columb Major Corn 4 C4
St Columb Minor Corn 4 C3
St Columb Road Corn 4 D4
St Combs Aberds 153 B10
St Cross South Elmham Suff 69 F5
St Cyrus Aberds 135 C7
St David's Perth 127 B8
St David's = Tyddewi Pembs 44 C2
St Day Corn 3 B6
St Dennis Corn 4 D4
St Devereux Hereford 49 F6
St Dogmaels Pembs 45 E3
St Dogwells Pembs 44 C4
St Dominick Corn 6 C2
St Donat's V Glam 21 C8
St Edith's Wilts 24 C4
St Endellion Corn 4 B4
St Enoder Corn 4 D3
St Erme Corn 4 D3
St Erney Corn 5 D8
St Erth Corn 2 C4
St Ervan Corn 4 B3
St Eval Corn 4 C3
St Ewe Corn 3 B8
St Fagans Cardiff 22 B3
St Fergus Aberds 153 C10
St Fillans Perth 127 B5
St Florence Pembs 32 D1
St Genny's Corn 8 E3
St George Conwy 72 B3
St George's V Glam 22 B2
St Germans Corn 5 D8
St Giles Lincs 78 B2
St Giles in the Wood Devon 9 C7
St Giles on the Heath Devon 9 E5
St Harmon Powys 47 B8
St Helen Auckland Durham 101 B6
St Helena Warks 63 D6
St Helen's E Sus 18 D5
St Helens IoW 15 F7
St Helens Mers 86 E3
St Helier Jersey 17
St Helier London 28 C3
St Hilary Corn 2 C4
St Hilary V Glam 22 B2
Saint Hill W Sus 28 F4
St Illtyd Bl Gwent 35 D6
St Ippollytts Herts 40 B4
St Ishmael's Pembs 44 E3
St Issey Corn 4 B4
St Ive Corn 5 C8
St Ives Cambs 54 B4
St Ives Corn 2 B4
St Ives Dorset 14 D2
St James South Elmham Suff 69 F6
St Jidgey Corn 4 C4
St John Corn 6 D2
St John's IoM 84 D2
St John's Jersey 17
St John's Sur 27 D7
St John's Worcs 50 D3
St John's Chapel Durham 109 F8
St John's Fen End Norf 66 C5
St John's Highway Norf 66 C5
St John's Town of Dalry Dumfries 113 F6
St Judes IoM 84 C3
St Just Corn 2 C2
St Just in Roseland Corn 3 C7
St Katherine's Aberds 153 E7
St Keverne Corn 3 D6
St Kew Corn 4 B5
St Kew Highway Corn 4 B5
St Keyne Corn 5 C7
St Lawrence Corn 4 C5
St Lawrence Essex 43 D5
St Lawrence IoW 15 G6
St Leonard's Bucks 40 D2
St Leonards Dorset 14 D2
St Leonards E Sus 18 E4
Saint Leonards S Lanark 119 D6
St Levan Corn 2 D2
St Lythans V Glam 22 B3
St Mabyn Corn 4 B5
St Madoes Perth 128 B3
St Margaret's Hereford 49 F5
St Margarets Herts 41 C6
St Margaret's at Cliffe Kent 31 E7
St Margaret's Hope Orkney 159 J5
St Margaret South Elmham Suff 69 F6
St Mark's IoM 84 E2
St Martin Corn 5 D7
St Martins Corn 3 D6
St Martin's Jersey 17
St Martins Perth 134 F1
St Martin's Shrops 73 F7
St Mary Bourne Hants 26 D2
St Mary Church V Glam 22 B2
St Mary Cray London 29 C5
St Mary Hill V Glam 21 B8
St Mary Hoo Medway 30 B2
St Mary in the Marsh Kent 19 C7
St Mary's Jersey 17
St Mary's Orkney 159 H5
St Mary's Bay Kent 19 C7
St Maughans Mon 36 C1
St Mawes Corn 3 C7
St Mawgan Corn 4 C3
St Mellion Corn 5 C8
St Mellons Cardiff 35 F6
St Merryn Corn 4 B3
St Mewan Corn 4 D4
St Michael Caerhays Corn 3 B8
St Michael Penkevil Corn 3 B7
St Michael South Elmham Suff 69 F6
St Michael's Kent 19 B5
St Michaels Worcs 49 C7
St Michael's on Wyre Lancs 92 E4
St Minver Corn 4 B4
St Monans Fife 129 D7
St Neot Corn 5 C6
St Neots Cambs 54 C2
St Newlyn East Corn 4 D3
St Nicholas Pembs 44 B3
St Nicholas V Glam 22 B2
St Nicholas at Wade Kent 31 C6
St Ninians Stirling 127 E6
St Osyth Essex 43 C7
St Osyth Heath Essex 43 C7
St Ouens Jersey 17
St Owens Cross Hereford 36 B2
St Paul's Cray London 29 C5
St Paul's Walden Herts 40 B4
St Peter Port Guern 16
St Peter's Jersey 17
St Peter's Kent 31 C7
St Petrox Pembs 44 F4
St Pinnock Corn 5 C7
St Quivox S Ayrs 112 B3
St Ruan Corn 3 E6
St Sampson Guern 16
St Stephen Corn 4 D4
St Stephen's Corn 8 F5
St Stephens Corn 6 D2
St Stephens Herts 40 D4
St Teath Corn 8 F2
St Thomas Devon 10 E4
St Tudy Corn 5 B5
St Twynnells Pembs 44 F4
St Veep Corn 5 D6
St Vigeans Angus 135 E6
St Wenn Corn 4 C4
St Weonards Hereford 36 B1
Saintbury Glos 51 F6
Salcombe Devon 6 F5
Salcombe Regis Devon 11 F6
Salcott Essex 43 C5
Sale Gtr Man 87 E5
Sale Green Worcs 50 D4
Saleby Lincs 79 B7
Salehurst E Sus 18 C4
Salem Carms 33 B7
Salem Ceredig 58 F3
Salen Argyll 147 G8
Salen Highld 147 E9
Salesbury Lancs 93 F6
Salford C Beds 53 F7
Salford Gtr Man 87 E6
Salford Oxon 38 B2
Salford Priors Warks 51 D5
Salfords Sur 28 E3
Salhouse Norf 69 C6
Saline Fife 128 E2
Salisbury Wilts 14 B2
Sallachan Highld 130 C3
Sallachy Highld 150 H2
Sallachy Highld 157 J8
Salle Norf 81 E7
Salmonby Lincs 79 B6
Salmond's Muir Angus 135 F5
Salperton Glos 37 B7
Salph End Bedford 53 D8
Salsburgh N Lanark 119 C8
Salt Staffs 62 B3
Salt End E Yorks 91 B5
Saltaire W Yorks 94 F4
Saltash Corn 6 D2
Saltburn Highld 151 E10
Saltburn-by-the-Sea Redcar 102 B4
Saltby Leics 65 B5
Saltcoats Cumb 98 E2
Saltcoats N Ayrs 118 E2
Saltdean Brighton 17 D7
Salter Lancs 93 C6
Salterforth Lancs 93 E8
Salterswall Ches W 74 C3
Saltfleet Lincs 91 E8
Saltfleetby All Saints Lincs 91 E8
Saltfleetby St Clements Lincs 91 E8
Saltfleetby St Peter Lincs 91 F8
Saltford Bath 23 C8
Salthouse Norf 81 C6
Saltmarshe E Yorks 89 B8
Saltney Flint 73 C7
Salton N Yorks 96 B3
Saltwick Northumb 110 B4
Saltwood Kent 19 B8
Salum Argyll 146 G3
Salvington W Sus 16 D5
Salwarpe Worcs 50 C3
Salwayash Dorset 12 E2
Sambourne Warks 51 C5
Sambrook Telford 61 B7
Samhla W Isles 148 B2
Samlesbury Lancs 93 F5
Samlesbury Bottoms Lancs 86 B4
Sampford Arundel Som 11 C6
Sampford Brett Som 22 E2
Sampford Courtenay Devon 9 D8
Sampford Peverell Devon 10 C5
Sampford Spiney Devon 6 B3
Sampool Bridge Cumb 99 F6
Samuelston E Loth 121 B7
Sanachan Highld 149 D13
Sanaigmore Argyll 142 A3
Sanclêr = St Clears Carms 32 C3
Sancreed Corn 2 D3
Sancton E Yorks 96 F5
Sand Highld 150 B2
Sand Shetland 160 J5
Sand Hole E Yorks 96 F4
Sand Hutton N Yorks 96 D2
Sandaig Highld 149 H12
Sandal Magna W Yorks 88 C4
Sandale Cumb 108 E2
Sandbach Ches E 74 C4
Sandbank Argyll 145 E10
Sandbanks Poole 13 F8
Sandend Aberds 152 B5
Sanderstead London 28 C4
Sandfields Glos 37 B6
Sandford Cumb 100 C2
Sandford Devon 10 D3
Sandford Dorset 13 F7
Sandford IoW 15 F6
Sandford N Som 23 D6
Sandford S Lanark 119 E7
Sandford Shrops 74 F2
Sandford on Thames Oxon 39 D5
Sandford Orcas Dorset 12 B4
Sandford St Martin Oxon 38 B4
Sandfordhill Aberds 153 D11
Sandgate Kent 19 B8
Sandgreen Dumfries 106 D2
Sandhaven Aberds 153 B9
Sandhead Dumfries 104 E4
Sandhills Sur 27 F7
Sandhoe Northumb 110 C2
Sandholme E Yorks 96 F4
Sandholme Lincs 79 F6
Sandhurst Brack 27 C6
Sandhurst Glos 37 B5
Sandhurst Kent 18 C4
Sandhurst Cross Kent 18 C4
Sandhutton N Yorks 102 F1
Sandiacre Derbys 76 F4
Sandilands Lincs 91 F9
Sandilands S Lanark 119 F8
Sandiway Ches W 74 B3
Sandleheath Hants 14 C2
Sandling Kent 29 D8
Sandlow Green Ches E 74 C4
Sandness Shetland 160 H3
Sandon Essex 42 D3
Sandon Herts 54 F4
Sandon Staffs 75 F6
Sandown IoW 15 F6
Sandplace Corn 5 D7
Sandridge Herts 40 C4
Sandridge Wilts 24 C4
Sandringham Norf 67 B6
Sandsend N Yorks 103 C6
Sandside Ho. Highld 157 C12
Sandsound Shetland 160 J5
Sandtoft N Lincs 89 D8
Sandway Kent 30 D2
Sandwell W Mid 62 F4
Sandwich Kent 31 D7
Sandwick Cumb 99 C6
Sandwick Orkney 159 K5
Sandwick Shetland 160 L6
Sandwith Cumb 98 C1
Sandy C Beds 54 E2
Sandy Carms 33 D5
Sandy Bank Lincs 79 D5
Sandy Haven Pembs 44 E3
Sandy Lane Wilts 24 C4
Sandy Lane Wrex 73 E7
Sandycroft Flint 73 C7
Sandyford Dumfries 114 E5
Sandyford Stoke 75 D5
Sandygate IoM 84 C3
Sandyhills Dumfries 107 D5
Sandylands Lancs 92 C4
Sandypark Devon 10 F2
Sandysike Cumb 108 C3
Sangobeg Highld 156 C7
Sangomore Highld 156 C7
Sanna Highld 146 E7
Sanndabhaig W Isles 148 D3
Sanndabhaig W Isles 155 D9
Sannox N Ayrs 143 D11
Sanquhar Dumfries 113 D7
Santon N Lincs 90 C3
Santon Bridge Cumb 98 D3
Santon Downham Suff 67 F8
Sapcote Leics 63 E8
Sapey Common Hereford 50 C2
Sapiston Suff 56 B3
Sapley Cambs 54 B3
Sapperton Glos 37 D6
Sapperton Lincs 78 F3
Saracen's Head Lincs 66 B3
Sarclet Highld 158 F5
Sardis Carms 33 D6
Sarn Bridgend 34 F3
Sarn Powys 60 E2
Sarn Bach Gwyn 70 E4
Sarn Meyllteyrn Gwyn 70 D3
Sarnau Carms 32 C4
Sarnau Ceredig 46 D2
Sarnau Gwyn 72 F3
Sarnau Powys 48 F2
Sarnau Powys 60 C2
Sarnesfield Hereford 49 D5
Saron Carms 33 C7
Saron Carms 46 F2
Saron Denb 72 C4
Saron Gwyn 82 E5
Saron Gwyn 82 F4
Sarratt Herts 40 E3
Sarre Kent 31 C6
Sarsden Oxon 38 B2
Sarsgrum Highld 156 C6
Satley Durham 110 E4
Satron N Yorks 100 E4
Satterleigh Devon 9 B8
Satterthwaite Cumb 99 E5
Satwell Oxon 39 F7
Sauchen Aberds 141 C5
Saucher Perth 134 F1
Sauchie Clack 127 E7
Sauchieburn Aberds 135 C6
Saughall Ches W 73 B7
Saughtree Borders 115 E8
Saul Glos 36 D4
Saundby Notts 89 F8
Saundersfoot Pembs 32 D2
Saunderton Bucks 39 D7
Saunton Devon 20 F3
Sausthorpe Lincs 79 C6
Saval Highld 157 J8
Savary Highld 147 G9
Savile Park W Yorks 87 B8
Sawbridge Warks 52 C3
Sawbridgeworth Herts 41 C7
Sawdon N Yorks 103 F7
Sawley Derbys 76 F4
Sawley Lancs 93 E7
Sawley N Yorks 94 C5
Sawston Cambs 55 E5
Sawtry Cambs 65 F8
Saxby Leics 64 C5
Saxby Lincs 90 F4
Saxby All Saints N Lincs 90 C3
Saxelbye Leics 64 B4
Saxham Street Suff 56 C4
Saxilby Lincs 77 B8
Saxlingham Norf 81 D6
Saxlingham Green Norf 68 E5
Saxlingham Nethergate Norf 68 E5
Saxlingham Thorpe Norf 68 E5
Saxmundham Suff 57 C7
Saxon Street Cambs 55 D7
Saxondale Notts 77 F6
Saxtead Suff 57 C6
Saxtead Green Suff 57 C6
Saxthorpe Norf 81 D7
Saxton N Yorks 95 F7
Sayers Common W Sus 17 C6
Scackleton N Yorks 96 B2
Scadabhagh W Isles 154 H6
Scaftworth Notts 89 E7
Scagglethorpe N Yorks 96 B4
Scaitcliffe Lancs 87 B5
Scalasaig Argyll 144 D2
Scalby E Yorks 90 B2
Scalby N Yorks 103 E8
Scaldwell Northants 53 B5
Scale Houses Cumb 109 E5
Scaleby Cumb 108 C4
Scaleby Hill Cumb 108 C4
Scales Cumb 92 B2
Scales Cumb 99 B5
Scales Lancs 92 F4
Scalford Leics 64 B4
Scaling Redcar 103 C5
Scallastle Argyll 124 B2
Scalloway Shetland 160 K6
Scalpay W Isles 154 H7
Scalpay Ho. Highld 149 F11
Scalpsie Argyll 145 H9
Scamadale Highld 147 B10
Scamblesby Lincs 79 B5
Scamodale Highld 130 B2
Scampston N Yorks 96 B4
Scampton Lincs 78 B2
Scapa Orkney 159 H5
Scapegoat Hill W Yorks 87 C8
Scar Orkney 159 D7
Scarborough N Yorks 103 F8
Scarcliffe Derbys 76 C4
Scarcroft W Yorks 95 E6
Scarcroft Hill W Yorks 95 E6
Scardroy Highld 150 F5
Scarff Shetland 160 E4
Scarfskerry Highld 158 C4
Scargill Durham 101 C5
Scarinish Argyll 146 G3
Scarisbrick Lancs 85 C4
Scarning Norf 68 C2
Scarrington Notts 77 E7
Scartho NE Lincs 91 D6
Scarwell Orkney 159 F3
Scatness Shetland 160 M5
Scatraig Highld 151 H10
Scawby N Lincs 90 D3
Scawsby S Yorks 89 D6
Scawton N Yorks 102 F3
Scayne's Hill W Sus 17 B7
Scethrog Powys 35 B5
Scholar Green Ches E 74 D5
Scholes W Yorks 88 B2
Scholes W Yorks 88 D2
Scholes W Yorks 95 F6
School Green Ches W 74 C3
Scleddau Pembs 44 B4
Sco Ruston Norf 81 E8
Scofton Notts 89 F7
Scole Norf 56 B5
Scolpaig W Isles 148 A2
Scone Perth 128 B3
Sconser Highld 149 E10
Scoonie Fife 129 D5
Scoor Argyll 146 K7
Scopwick Lincs 78 D3
Scoraig Highld 150 B3
Scorborough E Yorks 97 E6
Scorrier Corn 3 B6
Scorton Lancs 92 E5
Scorton N Yorks 101 D7
Scotbheinn W Isles 148 C3
Scotby Cumb 108 D4
Scotch Corner N Yorks 101 D7
Scotforth Lancs 92 D4
Scothern Lincs 78 B3
Scotland Gate Northumb 117 F8
Scotlandwell Perth 128 D3
Scotsburn Highld 151 D10
Scotscalder Station Highld 158 E2
Scotscraig Fife 129 B6
Scots' Gap Northumb 117 F6
Scotston Aberds 135 B7
Scotston Perth 133 E6
Scotstoun Glasgow 118 C5
Scotstown Highld 130 C2
Scotswood T&W 110 C4
Scottas Highld 149 H12
Scotter Lincs 90 D2
Scotterthorpe Lincs 90 D2
Scottlethorpe Lincs 65 B7
Scotton Lincs 90 E2
Scotton N Yorks 95 D6
Scotton N Yorks 101 E6
Scottow Norf 81 E8
Scoughall E Loth 129 F8
Scoulag Argyll 145 H10
Scoulton Norf 68 D2
Scourie Highld 156 E4
Scourie More Highld 156 E4
Scousburgh Shetland 160 M5
Scrabster Highld 158 C2
Scrafield Lincs 79 C6
Scrainwood Northumb 117 D5
Scrane End Lincs 79 E6
Scraptoft Leics 64 D3
Scratby Norf 69 C8
Scrayingham N Yorks 96 C3
Scredington Lincs 78 E3
Scremby Lincs 79 C7
Scremerston Northumb 123 E6
Screveton Notts 77 E7
Scrivelsby Lincs 79 C5
Scriven N Yorks 95 D6
Scrooby Notts 89 E7
Scropton Derbys 75 F8
Scrub Hill Lincs 78 D5
Scruton N Yorks 101 E7
Sculcoates Hull 97 F6
Sculthorpe Norf 80 D4
Scunthorpe N Lincs 90 C2
Scurlage Swansea 33 F5
Sea Palling Norf 69 B7
Seaborough Dorset 12 D2
Seacombe Mers 85 E4
Seacroft Lincs 79 C8
Seacroft W Yorks 95 F6
Seadyke Lincs 79 F6
Seafield S Ayrs 112 B3
Seafield W Loth 120 C3
Seaford E Sus 17 E8
Seaforth Mers 85 E4
Seagrave Leics 64 C3
Seaham Durham 111 E7
Seahouses Northumb 123 F8
Seal Kent 29 D6
Sealand Flint 73 C7
Seale Sur 27 E6
Seamer N Yorks 102 C2
Seamer N Yorks 103 F8
Seamill N Ayrs 118 E2
Searby Lincs 90 D4
Seasalter Kent 30 C4
Seascale Cumb 98 D2
Seathorne Lincs 79 C8
Seathwaite Cumb 98 C4
Seathwaite Cumb 98 E4
Seatoller Cumb 98 C4
Seaton Corn 5 D8
Seaton Cumb 107 F7
Seaton Devon 11 F7
Seaton Durham 111 D6
Seaton E Yorks 97 E7
Seaton Northumb 111 B6
Seaton Rutland 65 E6
Seaton Burn T&W 110 B5
Seaton Carew Hrtlpl 102 B3
Seaton Delaval Northumb 111 B6
Seaton Ross E Yorks 96 E3
Seaton Sluice Northumb 111 B6
Seatown Aberds 152 B5
Seatown Dorset 12 E2
Seave Green N Yorks 102 D3
Seaview IoW 15 E7
Seaville Cumb 107 D8
Seavington St Mary Som 12 C2
Seavington St Michael Som 12 C2
Sebergham Cumb 108 E3
Seckington Warks 63 D6
Second Coast Highld 150 B2
Sedbergh Cumb 100 E1
Sedbury Glos 36 E2
Sedbusk N Yorks 100 E3
Sedgeberrow Worcs 50 F5
Sedgebrook Lincs 77 F8
Sedgefield Durham 102 B1
Sedgeford Norf 80 D3
Sedgehill Wilts 13 B6
Sedgley W Mid 62 E3
Sedgwick Cumb 99 F7
Sedlescombe E Sus 18 D4
Sedlescombe Street E Sus 18 D4
Seend Wilts 24 C4
Seend Cleeve Wilts 24 C4
Seer Green Bucks 40 E2
Seething Norf 69 E6
Sefton Mers 85 D4
Seghill Northumb 111 B5
Seifton Shrops 60 F4
Seighford Staffs 62 B2
Seilebost W Isles 154 H5
Seion Gwyn 82 E5
Seisdon Staffs 62 E2
Seisiadar W Isles 155 D10
Selattyn Shrops 73 F6
Selborne Hants 26 F5
Selby N Yorks 96 F2
Selham W Sus 16 B3
Selhurst London 28 C4
Selkirk Borders 115 B7
Sellack Hereford 36 B2
Sellafirth Shetland 160 D7
Sellibister Orkney 159 D8
Sellindge Kent 19 B7
Sellindge Lees Kent 19 B8
Selling Kent 30 D4
Sells Green Wilts 24 C4
Selly Oak W Mid 62 F4
Selmeston E Sus 18 E2
Selsdon London 28 C4
Selsey W Sus 16 E2
Selsfield Common W Sus 28 F4
Selsted Kent 31 E6
Selston Notts 76 D4
Selworthy Som 21 E8
Semblister Shetland 160 H5
Semer Suff 56 E3
Semington Wilts 24 C3
Semley Wilts 13 B6
Send Sur 27 D8
Send Marsh Sur 27 D8
Senghenydd Caerph 35 E5
Sennen Corn 2 D2
Sennen Cove Corn 2 D2
Sennybridge = Pont Senni Powys 34 B3
Serlby Notts 89 F7
Sessay N Yorks 95 B7
Setchey Norf 67 C6
Setley Hants 14 D4
Setter Shetland 160 E6
Setter Shetland 160 H5
Setter Shetland 160 J7
Settiscarth Orkney 159 G4
Settle N Yorks 93 C8
Settrington N Yorks 96 B4
Seven Kings London 41 F7
Seven Sisters Neath 34 D2
Sevenhampton Glos 37 B7
Sevenoaks Kent 29 D6
Sevenoaks Weald Kent 29 D6
Severn Beach S Glos 36 F2
Severn Stoke Worcs 50 E3
Severnhampton Swindon 38 E2
Sevington Kent 30 E4
Sewards End Essex 55 F6
Sewardstone Essex 41 E6
Sewardstonebury Essex 41 E6
Sewerby E Yorks 97 C7
Seworgan Corn 3 C6
Sewstern Leics 65 B5
Sezincote Glos 51 F6
Sgarasta Mhor W Isles 154 H5
Sgiogarstaigh W Isles 155 A10
Shabbington Bucks 39 D6
Shackerstone Leics 63 D7
Shackleford Sur 27 E7
Shade W Yorks 87 B7
Shadforth Durham 111 E6
Shadingfield Suff 69 F7
Shadoxhurst Kent 19 B6
Shadsworth Blackburn 86 B5
Shadwell Norf 68 F2
Shadwell W Yorks 95 F6
Shaftesbury Dorset 13 B6
Shafton S Yorks 88 C4
Shalbourne Wilts 25 C8
Shalcombe IoW 14 F4
Shalden Hants 26 E4
Shaldon Devon 7 B7
Shalfleet IoW 14 F5
Shalford Essex 42 B3
Shalford Sur 27 E8
Shalford Green Essex 42 B3
Shallowford Devon 21 E6
Shalmsford Street Kent 30 D4
Shalstone Bucks 52 F4
Shamley Green Sur 27 E8
Shandon Argyll 145 E11
Shandwick Highld 151 D11
Shangton Leics 64 E4
Shankhouse Northumb 111 B5
Shanklin IoW 15 F6
Shanquhar Aberds 152 E5
Shanzie Perth 134 D2
Shap Cumb 99 C7
Shapwick Dorset 13 D7
Shapwick Som 23 F6
Shardlow Derbys 76 F4
Shareshill Staffs 62 D3
Sharlston W Yorks 88 C4
Sharlston Common W Yorks 88 C4
Sharnbrook Bedford 53 D7
Sharnford Leics 63 E8
Sharoe Green Lancs 92 F5
Sharow N Yorks 95 B6
Sharp Street Norf 69 B6
Sharpenhoe C Beds 53 F8
Sharperton Northumb 117 D5
Sharpness Glos 36 D3
Sharpthorne W Sus 28 F4
Sharrington Norf 81 D6
Shatterford Worcs 61 F7
Shaugh Prior Devon 6 C3
Shavington Ches E 74 D4
Shaw Gtr Man 87 D7
Shaw W Berks 26 C2
Shaw Wilts 24 C3
Shaw Green Lancs 86 C3
Shaw Mills N Yorks 95 C5
Shawbury Shrops 61 B5
Shawdon Hall Northumb 117 C6
Shawell Leics 64 F2
Shawford Hants 15 B5
Shawforth Lancs 87 B6
Shawhead Dumfries 107 B5
Shawhill Dumfries 108 C2
Shawton S Lanark 119 E6
Shawtonhill S Lanark 119 E6
Shear Cross Wilts 24 E3
Shearington Dumfries 107 C7
Shearsby Leics 64 E3
Shebbear Devon 9 D6
Shebdon Staffs 61 B7
Shebster Highld 157 C13
Sheddens E Renf 119 D5
Shedfield Hants 15 C6
Sheen Staffs 75 C8
Sheepscar W Yorks 95 F6
Sheepscombe Glos 37 C5
Sheepstor Devon 6 C3
Sheepwash Devon 9 D6
Sheepway N Som 23 B6
Sheepy Magna Leics 63 D7
Sheepy Parva Leics 63 D7
Sheering Essex 41 C8
Sheerness Kent 30 B3
Sheet Hants 15 B8
Sheffield S Yorks 88 F4
Sheffield Bottom W Berks 26 C4
Sheffield Green E Sus 17 B8
Shefford C Beds 54 F2
Shefford Woodlands W Berks 25 B8
Sheigra Highld 156 C4
Sheinton Shrops 61 D6
Shelderton Shrops 49 B6
Sheldon Derbys 75 C8
Sheldon Devon 11 D6
Sheldon W Mid 63 F5
Sheldwich Kent 30 D4
Shelf W Yorks 88 B2
Shelfanger Norf 68 F4
Shelfield W Mid 62 D4
Shelfield Warks 51 C6
Shelford Notts 77 E6
Shellacres Northumb 122 E4
Shelley Essex 42 D1
Shelley Suff 56 F4
Shelley W Yorks 88 C3
Shellingford Oxon 38 E3
Shellow Bowells Essex 42 D2
Shelsley Beauchamp Worcs 50 C2
Shelsley Walsh Worcs 50 C2
Shelthorpe Leics 64 C2
Shelton Bedford 53 C8
Shelton Norf 68 E5
Shelton Notts 77 E7
Shelton Shrops 60 C4
Shelton Green Norf 68 E5
Shelve Shrops 60 E3
Shelwick Hereford 49 E7
Shenfield Essex 42 E2
Shenington Oxon 51 E8
Shenley Herts 40 D4
Shenley Brook End M Keynes 53 F6
Shenley Church End M Keynes 53 F6
Shenleybury Herts 40 D4
Shenmore Hereford 49 F5
Shennanton Dumfries 105 C7
Shenstone Staffs 62 D5
Shenstone Worcs 50 B3
Shenton Leics 63 D7
Shenval Highld 137 B7
Shenval Moray 139 B8
Shepeau Stow Lincs 66 C3
Shephall Herts 41 B5
Shepherd's Green Oxon 39 F7
Shepherd's Port Norf 80 D2
Shepherdswell Kent 31 E6
Shepley W Yorks 88 D2
Shepperdine S Glos 36 E3
Shepperton Sur 27 C8
Shepreth Cambs 54 E4
Shepshed Leics 63 C8
Shepton Beauchamp Som 12 C2
Shepton Mallet Som 23 E8
Shepton Montague Som 23 F8
Shepway Kent 29 D8
Sheraton Durham 111 F7
Sherborne Dorset 12 C4
Sherborne Glos 38 C1
Sherborne St John Hants 26 D4
Sherbourne Warks 51 C7
Sherburn Durham 111 E6
Sherburn N Yorks 97 B5
Sherburn Hill Durham 111 E6
Sherburn in Elmet N Yorks 95 F7
Shere Sur 27 E8
Shereford Norf 80 E4
Sherfield English Hants 14 B3
Sherfield on Loddon Hants 26 D4
Sherford Devon 7 E5
Sheriff Hutton N Yorks 96 C2
Sheriffhales Shrops 61 C7
Sheringham Norf 81 C7
Sherington M Keynes 53 E6
Shernal Green Worcs 50 C4
Shernborne Norf 80 D3
Sherrington Wilts 24 F4
Sherston Wilts 37 F5
Sherwood Green Devon 9 B7
Shettleston Glasgow 119 C6
Shevington Gtr Man 86 D3
Shevington Moor Gtr Man 86 C3
Shevington Vale Gtr Man 86 D3
Sheviock Corn 5 D8
Shide IoW 15 F5
Shiel Bridge Highld 136 C2
Shieldaig Highld 149 A13
Shieldaig Highld 149 C13
Shieldhill Dumfries 114 F3
Shieldhill Falk 119 B8
Shieldhill S Lanark 120 E3
Shielfoot Highld 147 E9
Shielhill Angus 134 D4
Shielhill Invclyd 118 B2
Shifford Oxon 38 D3
Shifnal Shrops 61 D7
Shilbottle Northumb 117 D7
Shildon Durham 101 B7
Shillingford Devon 10 B4
Shillingford Oxon 39 E5
Shillingford St George Devon 10 F4
Shillingstone Dorset 13 C6
Shillington C Beds 54 F2
Shillmoor Northumb 116 D4
Shilton Oxon 38 D2
Shilton Warks 63 F8
Shilvington Northumb 117 F7
Shimpling Norf 68 F4
Shimpling Suff 56 D2
Shimpling Street Suff 56 D2
Shincliffe Durham 111 E5
Shiney Row T&W 111 D6
Shinfield Wokingham 26 C5
Shingham Norf 67 D7
Shingle Street Suff 57 E7
Shinner's Bridge Devon 7 C5
Shinness Highld 157 H8
Shipbourne Kent 29 D6
Shipdham Norf 68 D2
Shipham Som 23 D6
Shiphay Torbay 7 C6
Shiplake Oxon 27 B5
Shipley Derbys 76 E4
Shipley Northumb 117 C7
Shipley Shrops 62 E2
Shipley W Sus 16 B5
Shipley W Yorks 94 F4
Shipley Shiels Northumb 116 E3
Shipmeadow Suff 69 F6
Shippea Hill Station Cambs 67 F6
Shippon Oxon 38 E4
Shipston-on-Stour Warks 51 E7
Shipton Glos 37 C7
Shipton N Yorks 95 D8
Shipton Shrops 61 E5
Shipton Bellinger Hants 25 E7
Shipton Gorge Dorset 12 E2
Shipton Green W Sus 16 D2
Shipton Moyne Glos 37 F5
Shipton on Cherwell Oxon 38 C4
Shipton Solers Glos 37 C7
Shipton-under-Wychwood Oxon 38 C2
Shiptonthorpe E Yorks 96 E4
Shirburn Oxon 39 E6
Shirdley Hill Lancs 85 C4
Shirebrook Derbys 76 C5

Stoke sub Hamdon Som 12 C2
Stoke Talmage Oxon 39 E6
Stoke Trister Som 12 B5
Stoke Wake Dorset 13 D5
Stokeford Dorset 13 F6
Stokeham Notts 77 B7
Stokeinteignhead Devon 7 B7
Stokenchurch Bucks 39 E7
Stokenham Devon 7 E6
Stokesay Shrops 60 F4
Stokesby Norf 69 C7
Stokesley N Yorks 102 D3
Stolford Som 22 E4
Ston Easton Som 23 D8
Stondon Massey Essex 42 D1
Stone Bucks 39 C7
Stone Glos 36 E3
Stone Kent 19 C6
Stone Kent 29 B6
Stone S Yorks 89 F6
Stone Staffs 75 F6
Stone Worcs 50 B3
Stone Allerton Som 23 D6
Stone Bridge Corner Pboro 66 D2
Stone Chair W Yorks 88 B2
Stone Cross E Sus 18 E3
Stone Cross Kent 31 D7
Stone-edge Batch N Som 23 B6
Stone House Cumb 100 F2
Stone Street Kent 29 D6
Stone Street Suff 56 F3
Stone Street Suff 69 F6
Stonebroom Derbys 76 D4
Stoneferry Hull 97 F7
Stonefield S Lanark 119 D6
Stonegate E Sus 18 C3
Stonegate N Yorks 103 D5
Stonegrave N Yorks 96 B2
Stonehaugh Northumb 109 B7
Stonehaven Aberds 141 F7
Stonehouse Glos 37 D5
Stonehouse Northumb 109 D6
Stonehouse S Lanark 119 E7
Stoneleigh Warks 51 B8
Stonely Cambs 54 C2
Stoner Hill Hants 15 B8
Stone's Green Essex 43 B7
Stonesby Leics 64 B5
Stonesfield Oxon 38 C3
Stonethwaite Cumb 98 C4
Stoney Cross Hants 14 C3
Stoney Middleton Derbys 76 B2
Stoney Stanton Leics 63 E8
Stoney Stoke Som 24 F2
Stoney Stratton Som 23 F8
Stoney Stretton Shrops 60 D3
Stoneybreck Shetland 160 N8
Stoneyburn W Loth 120 C2
Stoneygate Aberds 153 E10
Stoneygate Leicester 64 D3
Stoneyhills Essex 43 E5
Stoneykirk Dumfries 104 D4
Stoneywood Aberdeen 141 C7
Stoneywood Falk 127 F6
Stonganess Shetland 160 C7
Stonham Aspal Suff 56 D5
Stonnall Staffs 62 D4
Stonor Oxon 39 F7
Stonton Wyville Leics 64 E4
Stony Cross Hereford 50 E2
Stony Stratford M Keynes 53 E5
Stonyfield Highld 151 D9
Stoodleigh Devon 10 C4
Stopes S Yorks 88 F3
Stopham W Sus 16 C4
Stopsley Luton 40 B4
Stores Corner Suff 57 E7
Storeton Mers 85 F4
Stornoway W Isles 155 D9
Storridge Hereford 50 E2
Storrington W Sus 16 C4
Storrs Cumb 99 E5
Storth Cumb 99 F6
Storwood E Yorks 96 E3
Stotfield Moray 152 A2
Stotfold C Beds 54 F3
Stottesdon Shrops 61 F6
Stoughton Leics 64 D3
Stoughton Sur 27 D7
Stoughton W Sus 16 C2
Stoul Highld 147 B10
Stoulton Worcs 50 E4
Stour Provost Dorset 13 B5
Stour Row Dorset 13 B6
Stourbridge W Mid 62 F3
Stourpaine Dorset 13 D6
Stourport on Severn Worcs 50 B3
Stourton Staffs 62 F2
Stourton Warks 51 F7
Stourton Wilts 24 F2
Stourton Caundle Dorset 12 C5
Stove Orkney 159 E7
Stove Shetland 160 L6
Stoven Suff 69 F7
Stow Borders 121 E7
Stow Lincs 78 F3
Stow Lincs 90 F2
Stow Bardolph Norf 67 D6
Stow Bedon Norf 68 E2
Stow cum Quy Cambs 55 C6
Stow Longa Cambs 54 B2
Stow Maries Essex 42 E4
Stow-on-the-Wold Glos 38 B1
Stowbridge Norf 67 D6
Stowe Shrops 48 B5
Stowe-by-Chartley Staffs 62 B4
Stowe Green Glos 36 D2
Stowell Som 12 B4
Stowford Devon 9 F6
Stowlangtoft Suff 56 C3
Stowmarket Suff 56 D4
Stowting Kent 30 E5
Stowupland Suff 56 D4
Straad Argyll 145 G9
Strachan Aberds 141 E5
Stradbroke Suff 57 B6
Stradishall Suff 55 D8
Stradsett Norf 67 D6
Stragglethorpe Lincs 78 D2
Straid S Ayrs 112 E1
Straith Dumfries 113 F8
Straiton Edin 121 C5
Straiton S Ayrs 112 D3
Straloch Aberds 141 B7
Straloch Perth 133 C7
Stramshall Staffs 75 F7
Strang IoM 84 E3
Stranraer Dumfries 104 C4
Stratfield Mortimer W Berks 26 C4
Stratfield Saye Hants 26 C4
Stratfield Turgis Hants 26 D4
Stratford London 41 F6
Stratford St Andrew Suff 57 C7
Stratford St Mary Suff 56 F4
Stratford Sub Castle Wilts 25 F6
Stratford Tony Wilts 13 B8
Stratford-upon-Avon Warks 51 D6
Strath Highld 149 A12
Strath Highld 158 E4
Strathan Highld 136 E2
Strathan Highld 156 G3
Strathan Highld 157 C8
Strathaven S Lanark 119 E7
Strathblane Stirling 119 B5
Strathcanaird Highld 156 J4
Strathcarron Highld 150 G2
Strathcoil Argyll 124 B2
Strathdon Aberds 140 C2
Strathellie Aberds 153 B10
Strathkinness Fife 129 C6
Strathmashie House Highld 137 E8
Strathmiglo Fife 128 C4
Strathmore Lodge Highld 158 F3
Strathpeffer Highld 150 F7
Strathrannoch Highld 150 D6
Strathtay Perth 133 D6
Strathvaich Lodge Highld 150 D6
Strathwhillan N Ayrs 143 E11
Strathy Highld 157 C11
Strathyre Stirling 126 C4
Stratton Corn 8 D4
Stratton Dorset 12 E4
Stratton Glos 37 D7
Stratton Audley Oxon 39 B6
Stratton on the Fosse Som 23 D8
Stratton St Margaret Swindon 38 F1
Stratton St Michael Norf 68 E5
Stratton Strawless Norf 81 E8
Stravithie Fife 129 C7
Streat E Sus 17 C7
Streatham London 28 B4
Streatley C Beds 40 B3
Streatley W Berks 39 F5
Street Lancs 92 D5
Street N Yorks 103 D5
Street Som 23 F6
Street Dinas Shrops 73 F7
Street End Kent 30 D5
Street End W Sus 16 E2
Street Gate T&W 110 D5
Street Lydan Wrex 73 F8
Streethay Staffs 62 C5
Streetlam N Yorks 101 E8
Streetly W Mid 62 E4
Streetly End Cambs 55 E7
Strefford Shrops 60 F4
Strelley Notts 76 E5
Strensall York 96 C2
Stretcholt Som 22 E4
Strete Devon 7 E6
Stretford Gtr Man 87 E6
Strethall Essex 55 F5
Stretham Cambs 55 B6
Strettington W Sus 16 D2
Stretton Ches W 73 D8
Stretton Derbys 76 C3
Stretton Rutland 65 C6
Stretton Staffs 62 C2
Stretton Staffs 63 B6
Stretton Warr 86 F4
Stretton Grandison Hereford 49 E8
Stretton-on-Dunsmore Warks 52 B2
Stretton-on-Fosse Warks 51 F7
Stretton Sugwas Hereford 49 E6
Stretton under Fosse Warks 63 F8
Stretton Westwood Shrops 61 E5
Strichen Aberds 153 C9
Strines Gtr Man 87 F7
Stringston Som 22 E3
Strixton Northants 53 C7
Stroat Glos 36 E2
Stromeferry Highld 149 E13
Stromemore Highld 149 E13
Stromness Orkney 159 H3
Stronaba Highld 136 F5
Stronachlachar Stirling 126 C3
Stronchreggan Highld 130 B4
Stronchrubie Highld 156 H5
Strone Argyll 145 E10
Strone Highld 136 F4
Strone Highld 137 B8
Strone Involyd 118 B2
Stronmilchan Argyll 125 C7
Strontian Highld 130 C2
Strood Medway 29 C8
Strood Green Sur 28 E3
Strood Green W Sus 16 B4
Strood Green W Sus 28 F2
Stroud Glos 37 D5
Stroud Hants 15 B8
Stroud Green Essex 42 E4
Stroxton Lincs 78 F2
Struan Highld 149 E8
Struan Perth 133 C5
Strubby Lincs 91 F8
Strumpshaw Norf 69 D6
Strutherhill S Lanark 119 E7
Struy Highld 150 H6
Stryt-issa Wrex 73 E6
Stuartfield Aberds 153 D9
Stub Place Cumb 98 E2
Stubbington Hants 15 D6
Stubbins Lancs 87 C5
Stubbs Cross Kent 19 B6
Stubb's Green Norf 69 E5
Stubbs Green Norf 69 E6
Stubhampton Dorset 13 C7
Stubton Lincs 77 E8
Stuckgowan Argyll 126 D2
Stuckton Hants 14 C2
Stud Green Windsor 27 B6
Studham C Beds 40 C3
Studland Dorset 13 F8
Studley Warks 51 C5
Studley Wilts 24 B4
Studley Roger N Yorks 95 B5
Stump Cross Essex 55 E6
Stuntney Cambs 55 B6
Sturbridge Staffs 74 F5
Sturmer Essex 55 E7
Sturminster Marshall Dorset 13 D7
Sturminster Newton Dorset 13 C5
Sturry Kent 31 C5
Sturton N Lincs 90 D3
Sturton by Stow Lincs 90 F2
Sturton le Steeple Notts 89 F8
Stuston Suff 56 B5
Stutton N Yorks 95 E7
Stutton Suff 57 F5
Styal Ches E 87 F6
Styrrup Notts 89 E7
Suainebost W Isles 155 A10
Suardail W Isles 155 D9
Succoth Aberds 152 E4
Succoth Argyll 125 E8
Suckley Worcs 50 D2
Suckquoy Orkney 159 K5
Sudborough Northants 65 F6
Sudbourne Suff 57 D8
Sudbrook Lincs 78 E2
Sudbrook Mon 36 F2
Sudbrooke Lincs 78 B3
Sudbury Derbys 75 F8
Sudbury London 40 F4
Sudbury Suff 56 E2
Suddie Highld 151 F9
Sudgrove Glos 37 D6
Suffield N Yorks 103 E7
Suffield Norf 81 D8
Sugnall Staffs 74 F4
Suladale Highld 149 C8
Sulaisiadar W Isles 155 D10
Sulby IoM 84 C3
Sulgrave Northants 52 E3
Sulham W Berks 26 B4
Sulhamstead W Berks 26 C4
Sulland Orkney 159 D6
Sullington W Sus 16 C4
Sullom Shetland 160 F5
Sullom Voe Oil Terminal Shetland 160 F5
Sully V Glam 22 C3
Sumburgh Shetland 160 N6
Summer Bridge N Yorks 94 C5
Summer-house Darl 101 C7
Summercourt Corn 4 D3
Summerfield Norf 80 D3
Summergangs Hull 97 F7
Summerleaze Mon 35 F8
Summersdale W Sus 16 D2
Summerseat Gtr Man 87 C5
Summertown Oxon 39 D5
Summit Gtr Man 87 D7
Sunbury-on-Thames Sur 28 C2
Sundaywell Dumfries 113 F8
Sunderland Argyll 142 B3
Sunderland Cumb 107 F8
Sunderland T&W 111 D6
Sunderland Bridge Durham 111 F5
Sundhope Borders 115 B6
Sundon Park Luton 40 B3
Sundridge Kent 29 D5
Sunipol Argyll 146 F6
Sunk Island E Yorks 91 C6
Sunningdale Windsor 27 C7
Sunninghill Windsor 27 C7
Sunningwell Oxon 38 D4
Sunniside Durham 110 F4
Sunniside T&W 110 D5
Sunnyhurst Blackburn 86 B4
Sunnylaw Stirling 127 E6
Sunnyside W Sus 28 F4
Sunton Wilts 25 D7
Surbiton London 28 C2
Surby IoM 84 E2
Surfleet Lincs 66 B2
Surfleet Seas End Lincs 66 B2
Surlingham Norf 69 D6
Sustead Norf 81 D7
Susworth Lincs 90 D2
Sutcombe Devon 8 C5
Suton Norf 68 E3
Sutors of Cromarty Highld 151 E11
Sutterby Lincs 79 B6
Sutterton Lincs 79 F5
Sutton C Beds 54 E3
Sutton Cambs 54 B5
Sutton Kent 31 E7
Sutton London 28 C3
Sutton Mers 86 E3
Sutton N Yorks 89 B5
Sutton Norf 69 B6
Sutton Notts 77 F7
Sutton Notts 89 F7
Sutton Oxon 38 D4
Sutton Pboro 65 E7
Sutton S Yorks 89 C6
Sutton Shrops 61 F7
Sutton Shrops 74 F3
Sutton Som 23 F8
Sutton Staffs 61 B7
Sutton Suff 57 E7
Sutton Sur 27 E8
Sutton W Sus 16 C3
Sutton at Hone Kent 29 B6
Sutton Bassett Northants 64 E4
Sutton Benger Wilts 24 B4
Sutton Bonington Notts 64 B2
Sutton Bridge Lincs 66 B4
Sutton Cheney Leics 63 D8
Sutton Coldfield W Mid 62 E5
Sutton Courtenay Oxon 39 E5
Sutton Crosses Lincs 66 B4
Sutton Grange N Yorks 95 B5
Sutton Green Sur 27 D8
Sutton Howgrave N Yorks 95 B6
Sutton In Ashfield Notts 76 D4
Sutton-in-Craven N Yorks 94 E3
Sutton in the Elms Leics 64 E2
Sutton Ings Hull 97 F7
Sutton Lane Ends Ches E 75 B6
Sutton Leach Mers 86 E3
Sutton Maddock Shrops 61 D7
Sutton Mallet Som 23 F5
Sutton Mandeville Wilts 13 B7
Sutton Manor Mers 86 E3
Sutton Montis Som 12 B4
Sutton on Hull Hull 97 F7
Sutton on Sea Lincs 91 F9
Sutton-on-the-Forest N Yorks 95 C8
Sutton on the Hill Derbys 76 F2
Sutton on Trent Notts 77 C7
Sutton Scarsdale Derbys 76 C4
Sutton Scotney Hants 26 F2
Sutton St Edmund Lincs 66 C3
Sutton St James Lincs 66 C3
Sutton St Nicholas Hereford 49 E7
Sutton under Brailes Warks 51 F8
Sutton-under-Whitestonecliffe N Yorks 102 F2
Sutton upon Derwent E Yorks 96 E3
Sutton Valence Kent 30 E2
Sutton Veny Wilts 24 E3
Sutton Waldron Dorset 13 C6
Sutton Weaver Ches W 74 B2
Sutton Wick Bath 23 D7
Swaby Lincs 79 B6
Swadlincote Derbys 63 C7
Swaffham Norf 67 D8
Swaffham Bulbeck Cambs 55 C6
Swaffham Prior Cambs 55 C6
Swafield Norf 81 D8
Swainby N Yorks 102 D2
Swainshill Hereford 49 E6
Swainsthorpe Norf 68 D5
Swainswick Bath 24 C2
Swalcliffe Oxon 51 F8
Swalecliffe Kent 30 C5
Swallow Lincs 91 D5
Swallowcliffe Wilts 13 B7
Swallowfield Wokingham 26 C5
Swallownest S Yorks 89 F5
Swallows Cross Essex 42 E2
Swan Green Ches W 74 B4
Swan Green Suff 57 B6
Swanage Dorset 13 G8
Swanbister Orkney 159 H4
Swanbourne Bucks 39 B8
Swanland E Yorks 90 B3
Swanley Kent 29 C6
Swanley Village Kent 29 C6
Swanmore Hants 15 C6
Swannington Leics 63 C8
Swannington Norf 68 C4
Swanscombe Kent 29 B7
Swansea = Abertawe Swansea 33 E7
Swanton Abbott Norf 81 E8
Swanton Morley Norf 68 C3
Swanton Novers Norf 81 D6
Swanton Street Kent 30 D2
Swanwick Derbys 76 D4
Swanwick Hants 15 D6
Swarby Lincs 78 E3
Swardeston Norf 68 D5
Swarister Shetland 160 E7
Swarkestone Derbys 63 B7
Swarland Northumb 117 D7
Swarland Estate Northumb 117 D7
Swarthmoor Cumb 92 B2
Swathwick Derbys 76 C3
Swaton Lincs 78 F4
Swavesey Cambs 54 C4
Sway Hants 14 E3
Swayfield Lincs 65 B6
Swaythling Soton 14 C5
Sweet Green Worcs 49 C8
Sweetham Devon 10 E3
Sweethouse Corn 5 C5
Sweffling Suff 57 C7
Swepstone Leics 63 C7
Swerford Oxon 51 F8
Swettenham Ches E 74 C5
Swetton N Yorks 94 B4
Swffryd Caerph 35 E6
Swiftsden E Sus 18 C4
Swilland Suff 57 D5
Swillington W Yorks 95 F6
Swimbridge Devon 9 B8
Swimbridge Newland Devon 20 F5
Swinbrook Oxon 38 C2
Swinderby Lincs 77 C8
Swindon Glos 37 B6
Swindon Staffs 62 E2
Swindon Swindon 38 F1
Swine E Yorks 97 F7
Swinefleet E Yorks 89 B8
Swineshead Bedford 53 C8
Swineshead Lincs 78 E5
Swineshead Bridge Lincs 78 E5
Swiney Highld 158 G4
Swinford Leics 52 B3
Swinford Oxon 38 D4
Swingate Notts 76 E5
Swingfield Minnis Kent 31 E6
Swingfield Street Kent 31 E6
Swinhoe Northumb 117 B8
Swinhope Lincs 91 E6
Swining Shetland 160 G6
Swinithwaite N Yorks 101 F5
Swinnow Moor W Yorks 94 F5
Swinscoe Staffs 75 E8
Swinside Hall Borders 116 C3
Swinstead Lincs 65 B7
Swinton Borders 122 E4
Swinton Gtr Man 87 D5
Swinton N Yorks 94 B5
Swinton N Yorks 96 B3
Swinton S Yorks 88 E5
Swintonmill Borders 122 E4
Swithland Leics 64 C2
Swordale Highld 151 E8
Swordland Highld 147 B10
Swordly Highld 157 C10
Sworton Heath Ches E 86 F4
Swydd-ffynnon Ceredig 47 C5
Swynnerton Staffs 75 F5
Swyre Dorset 12 F3
Sychtyn Powys 59 D6
Syde Glos 37 C6
Sydenham London 28 B4
Sydenham Oxon 39 D7
Sydenham Damerel Devon 6 B2
Syderstone Norf 80 D4
Sydling St Nicholas Dorset 12 E4
Sydmonton Hants 26 D2
Syerston Notts 77 E7
Syke Gtr Man 87 C6
Sykehouse S Yorks 89 C7
Sykes Lancs 93 D6
Syleham Suff 57 B6
Sylen Carms 33 D6
Symbister Shetland 160 G7
Symington S Ayrs 118 F3
Symington S Lanark 120 F2
Symonds Yat Hereford 36 C2
Symondsbury Dorset 12 E2
Synod Inn Ceredig 46 D3
Syre Highld 157 E9
Syreford Glos 37 B7
Syresham Northants 52 E4
Syston Leics 64 C3
Syston Lincs 78 E2
Sytchampton Worcs 50 C3
Sywell Northants 53 C6

T

Taagan Highld 150 E3
Tabost W Isles 155 A10
Tabost W Isles 155 F8
Tackley Oxon 38 B4
Tacleit W Isles 154 D6
Tacolneston Norf 68 E4
Tadcaster N Yorks 95 E7
Taddington Derbys 75 B8
Taddiport Devon 9 C6
Tadley Hants 26 C4
Tadlow C Beds 54 E3
Tadmarton Oxon 51 F8
Tadworth Sur 28 D3
Tafarn-y-gelyn Denb 73 C5
Tafarnau-bach Bl Gwent 35 C5
Taff's Well Rhondda 35 F5
Tafolwern Powys 59 D5
Tai Conwy 83 E7
Tai-bach Powys 59 B8
Tai-mawr Conwy 72 E3
Tai-Ucha Denb 72 D4
Taibach Neath 34 F1
Taigh a Ghearraidh W Isles 148 A2
Tain Highld 151 C10
Tain Highld 158 D4
Tainant Wrex 73 E6
Tainlon Gwyn 82 F4
Tairbeart = Tarbert W Isles 154 G6
Tai'r-Bull Powys 34 B3
Tairgwaith Neath 33 C8
Takeley Essex 42 B1
Takeley Street Essex 41 B8
Tal-sarn Ceredig 46 D4
Tal-y-bont Ceredig 58 F3
Tal-y-bont Conwy 83 E7
Tal-y-bont Gwyn 71 E6
Tal-y-bont Gwyn 83 D6
Tal-y-cafn Conwy 83 D7
Tal-y-llyn Gwyn 58 D4
Tal-y-wern Powys 58 D5
Talachddu Powys 48 F2
Talacre Flint 85 F2
Talardd Gwyn 59 B5
Talaton Devon 11 E5
Talbenny Pembs 44 D3
Talbot Green Rhondda 34 F4
Talbot Village Poole 13 E8
Tale Devon 11 D5
Talerddig Powys 59 D6
Talgarreg Ceredig 46 D3
Talgarth Powys 48 F3
Talisker Highld 149 E8
Talke Staffs 74 D5
Talkin Cumb 109 D5
Talla Linnfoots Borders 114 B4
Talladale Highld 150 D2
Tallarn Green Wrex 73 E8
Tallentire Cumb 107 F8
Talley Carms 46 F5
Tallington Lincs 65 D7
Talmine Highld 157 C8
Talog Carms 32 B4
Talsarn Carms 34 B1
Talsarnau Gwyn 71 D7
Talskiddy Corn 4 C4
Talwrn Anglesey 82 D4
Talwrn Wrex 73 E6
Talybont-on-Usk Powys 35 B5
Talygarn Rhondda 34 F4
Talyllyn Powys 35 B5
Talysarn Gwyn 82 F4
Talywain Torf 35 D6
Tame Bridge N Yorks 102 D3
Tamerton Foliot Plym 6 C2
Tamworth Staffs 63 D6
Tan Hinon Powys 59 F5
Tan-lan Conwy 83 E7
Tan-lan Gwyn 71 C7
Tan-y-bwlch Gwyn 71 C7
Tan-y-fron Conwy 72 C3
Tan-y-graig Anglesey 82 D5
Tan-y-graig Gwyn 70 D4
Tan-y-groes Ceredig 45 E4
Tan-y-pistyll Powys 59 B7
Tan-yr-allt Gwyn 82 F4
Tandem W Yorks 88 C2
Tanden Kent 19 B6
Tandridge Sur 28 D4
Tanerdy Carms 33 B5
Tanfield Durham 110 D4
Tanfield Lea Durham 110 D4
Tangasdal W Isles 148 J1
Tangiers Pembs 44 D4
Tangley Hants 25 D8
Tanglwst Carms 46 F2
Tangmere W Sus 16 D3
Tangwick Shetland 160 F4
Tankersley S Yorks 88 D4
Tankerton Kent 30 C5
Tannach Highld 158 F5
Tannachie Aberds 141 F6
Tannadice Angus 134 D4
Tannington Suff 57 C6
Tansley Derbys 76 D3
Tansley Knoll Derbys 76 C3
Tansor Northants 65 E7
Tantobie Durham 110 D4
Tanton N Yorks 102 C3
Tanworth-in-Arden Warks 51 B6
Tanygrisiau Gwyn 71 C7
Tanyrhydiau Ceredig 47 C6
Taobh a Chaolais W Isles 148 G2
Taobh a Thuath Loch Aineort W Isles 148 F2
Taobh a Tuath Loch Baghasdail W Isles 148 F2
Taobh a'Ghlinne W Isles 155 F8
Taobh Tuath W Isles 154 J4
Taplow Bucks 40 F2
Tapton Derbys 76 B3
Tarbat Ho. Highld 151 D10
Tarbert Argyll 143 C7
Tarbert Argyll 144 E5
Tarbert Argyll 145 G7
Tarbert = Tairbeart W Isles 154 G6
Tarbet Argyll 126 D2
Tarbet Highld 147 B10
Tarbet Highld 156 E4
Tarbock Green Mers 86 F2
Tarbolton S Ayrs 112 B4
Tarbrax S Lanark 120 D3
Tardebigge Worcs 50 C5
Tarfside Angus 134 B4
Tarland Aberds 140 D3
Tarleton Lancs 86 B2
Tarlogie Highld 151 C10
Tarlscough Lancs 86 C2
Tarlton Glos 37 E6
Tarnbrook Lancs 93 D5
Tarporley Ches W 74 C2
Tarr Som 22 F3
Tarrant Crawford Dorset 13 D7
Tarrant Gunville Dorset 13 C7
Tarrant Hinton Dorset 13 C7
Tarrant Keyneston Dorset 13 D7
Tarrant Launceston Dorset 13 D7
Tarrant Monkton Dorset 13 D7
Tarrant Rawston Dorset 13 D7
Tarrant Rushton Dorset 13 D7
Tarrel Highld 151 C11
Tarring Neville E Sus 17 D8
Tarrington Hereford 49 E8
Tarsappie Perth 128 B3
Tarskavaig Highld 149 H10
Tarves Aberds 153 E8
Tarvie Highld 150 F7
Tarvie Perth 133 C7
Tarvin Ches W 73 C8
Tasburgh Norf 68 E5
Tasley Shrops 61 E6
Taston Oxon 38 B3
Tatenhill Staffs 63 B6
Tathall End M Keynes 53 E6
Tatham Lancs 93 C6
Tathwell Lincs 91 F7
Tatling End Bucks 40 F3
Tatsfield Sur 28 D5
Tattenhall Ches W 73 D8
Tattenhoe M Keynes 53 F6
Tatterford Norf 80 E4
Tattersett Norf 80 D4
Tattershall Lincs 78 D5
Tattershall Bridge Lincs 78 D4
Tattershall Thorpe Lincs 78 D5
Tattingstone Suff 56 F5
Tatworth Som 11 D8
Taunton Som 11 B7
Taverham Norf 68 C4
Tavernspite Pembs 32 C2
Tavistock Devon 6 B2
Taw Green Devon 9 E8
Tawstock Devon 9 B7
Taxal Derbys 75 B7
Tay Bridge Dundee 129 B6
Tayinloan Argyll 143 D7
Taymouth Castle Perth 132 E4
Taynish Argyll 144 E6
Taynton Glos 36 B4
Taynton Oxon 38 C2
Taynuilt Argyll 125 B6
Tayport Fife 129 B6
Tayvallich Argyll 144 E6
Tealby Lincs 91 E5
Tealing Angus 134 F4
Teangue Highld 149 H11
Teanna Mhachair W Isles 148 B2
Tebay Cumb 99 D8
Tebworth C Beds 40 B2
Tedburn St Mary Devon 10 E3
Teddington Glos 50 F4
Teddington London 28 B2
Tedstone Delamere Hereford 49 D8
Tedstone Wafre Hereford 49 D8
Teeton Northants 52 B4
Teffont Evias Wilts 24 F4
Teffont Magna Wilts 24 F4
Tegryn Pembs 45 F4
Teigh Rutland 65 C5
Teigncombe Devon 9 F8
Teigngrace Devon 7 B6
Teignmouth Devon 7 B7
Telford Telford 61 D6
Telham E Sus 18 D4
Tellisford Som 24 D3
Telscombe E Sus 17 D8
Telscombe Cliffs E Sus 17 D7
Templand Dumfries 114 F3
Temple Corn 5 B6
Temple Glasgow 118 C5
Temple Midloth 121 D6
Temple Balsall W Mid 51 B7
Temple Bar Carms 33 C6
Temple Bar Ceredig 46 D4
Temple Cloud Bath 23 D8
Temple Combe Som 12 B5
Temple Ewell Kent 31 E6
Temple Grafton Warks 51 D6
Temple Guiting Glos 37 B7
Temple Herdewyke Warks 51 D8
Temple Hirst N Yorks 89 B7
Temple Normanton Derbys 76 C4
Temple Sowerby Cumb 99 B8
Templehall Fife 128 E4
Templeton Devon 10 C3
Templeton Pembs 32 C2
Templeton Bridge Devon 10 C3
Templetown Durham 110 D4
Tempsford C Beds 54 D2
Ten Mile Bank Norf 67 E6
Tenbury Wells Worcs 49 C7
Tenby = Dinbych-Y-Pysgod Pembs 32 D2
Tendring Essex 43 B7
Tendring Green Essex 43 B7
Tenston Orkney 159 G3
Tenterden Kent 19 B5
Terling Essex 42 C3
Ternhill Shrops 74 F3
Terregles Banks Dumfries 107 B6
Terrick Bucks 39 D8
Terrington N Yorks 96 B2
Terrington St Clement Norf 66 C5
Terrington St John Norf 66 C5
Teston Kent 29 D8
Testwood Hants 14 C4
Tetbury Glos 37 E5
Tetbury Upton Glos 37 E5
Tetchill Shrops 73 F7
Tetcott Devon 8 E5
Tetford Lincs 79 B6
Tetney Lincs 91 D7
Tetney Lock Lincs 91 D7
Tetsworth Oxon 39 D6
Tettenhall W Mid 62 E2
Teuchan Aberds 153 E10
Teversal Notts 76 C4
Teversham Cambs 55 D5
Teviothead Borders 115 D7
Tewel Aberds 141 F7
Tewin Herts 41 C5
Tewkesbury Glos 50 F3
Teynham Kent 30 C3
Thackthwaite Cumb 98 B3
Thainston Aberds 135 B6
Thakeham W Sus 16 C5
Thame Oxon 39 D7
Thames Ditton Sur 28 C2
Thames Haven Thurrock 42 F3
Thamesmead London 41 F7
Thanington Kent 30 D5
Thankerton S Lanark 120 F2
Tharston Norf 68 E4
Thatcham W Berks 26 C3
Thatto Heath Mers 86 E3
Thaxted Essex 55 F7
The Aird Highld 149 C9
The Arms Norf 67 E8
The Bage Hereford 48 E4
The Balloch Perth 127 C7
The Barony Orkney 159 F3
The Bog Shrops 60 E3
The Bourne Sur 27 E6
The Braes Highld 149 E10
The Broad Hereford 49 C6
The Butts Som 24 E2
The Camp Glos 37 D6
The Camp Herts 40 D4
The Chequer Wrex 73 E8
The City Bucks 39 E7
The Common Wilts 25 F7
The Craigs Highld 150 B7
The Cronk IoM 84 C3
The Dell Suff 69 E7
The Den N Ayrs 118 D3
The Eals Northumb 116 F3
The Eaves Glos 36 D3
The Flatt Cumb 109 B5
The Four Alls Shrops 74 F3
The Garths Shetland 160 B8
The Green Cumb 98 F3
The Green Wilts 24 F3
The Grove Dumfries 107 B6
The Hall Shetland 160 D8
The Haven W Sus 27 F8
The Heath Norf 81 E7
The Heath Suff 56 F5
The Hill Cumb 98 F3
The Howe Cumb 99 F6
The Howe IoM 84 F1
The Hundred Hereford 49 C7
The Lee Bucks 40 D2
The Lhen IoM 84 B3
The Marsh Powys 60 E3
The Marsh Wilts 37 F7
The Middles Durham 110 D5
The Moor Kent 18 C4
The Mumbles = Y Mwmbwls Swansea 33 F7
The Murray S Lanark 119 D6
The Neuk Aberds 141 E6
The Oval Bath 24 C2
The Pole of Itlaw Aberds 153 C6
The Quarry Glos 36 E4
The Rhos Pembs 32 C1
The Rock Telford 61 D6
The Ryde Herts 41 D5
The Sands Sur 27 E6
The Stocks Kent 19 C6
The Throat Wokingham 27 C6
The Vauld Hereford 49 E7
The Wyke Shrops 61 D7
Theakston N Yorks 101 F8
Thealby N Lincs 90 C2
Theale Som 23 E6
Theale W Berks 26 B4
Thearne E Yorks 97 F6
Theberton Suff 57 C8
Theddingworth Leics 64 F3
Theddlethorpe All Saints Lincs 91 F8
Theddlethorpe St Helen Lincs 91 F8
Thelbridge Barton Devon 10 C2
Thelnetham Suff 56 B4
Thelveton Norf 68 F4
Thelwall Warr 86 F4
Themelthorpe Norf 81 E6
Thenford Northants 52 E3
Therfield Herts 54 F4
Thetford Lincs 65 C8
Thetford Norf 67 F8
Theydon Bois Essex 41 E7
Thickwood Wilts 24 B3
Thimbleby Lincs 78 C5
Thimbleby N Yorks 102 E2
Thingwall Mers 85 F3
Thirdpart N Ayrs 118 E1
Thirlby N Yorks 102 F2
Thirlestane Borders 121 E8
Thirn N Yorks 101 F7
Thirsk N Yorks 102 F2
Thirtleby E Yorks 97 F7
Thistleton Lancs 92 F4
Thistleton Rutland 65 C6
Thistley Green Suff 55 B7
Thixendale N Yorks 96 C4
Thockrington Northumb 110 B2
Tholomas Drove Cambs 66 D3
Tholthorpe N Yorks 95 C7
Thomas Chapel Pembs 32 D2
Thomas Close Cumb 108 E4
Thomastown Aberds 152 E5
Thompson Norf 68 E2
Thomshill Moray 152 C2
Thong Kent 29 B7
Thongsbridge W Yorks 88 D2
Thoralby N Yorks 101 F5
Thoresway Lincs 91 E5
Thorganby Lincs 91 E6
Thorganby N Yorks 96 E2
Thorgill N Yorks 103 E5
Thorington Suff 57 B8
Thorington Street Suff 56 F4
Thorlby N Yorks 94 D2
Thorley Herts 41 C7
Thorley Street Herts 41 C7
Thorley Street IoW 14 F4
Thormanby N Yorks 95 B7
Thornaby-on-Tees Stockton 102 C2
Thornage Norf 81 D6
Thornborough Bucks 52 F5
Thornborough N Yorks 95 B5
Thornbury Devon 9 D6
Thornbury Hereford 49 D8
Thornbury S Glos 36 E3
Thornbury W Yorks 94 F4
Thornby Northants 52 B4
Thorncliffe Staffs 75 D7
Thorncombe Dorset 11 D8
Thorncombe Dorset 13 D6
Thorncombe Street Sur 27 E8
Thorncote Green C Beds 54 E2
Thorncross IoW 14 F5
Thorndon Suff 56 C5
Thorndon Cross Devon 9 E7
Thorne S Yorks 89 C7
Thorne St Margaret Som 11 B5
Thorner W Yorks 95 E6
Thorney Notts 77 B8
Thorney Pboro 66 D2
Thorney Crofts E Yorks 91 B6
Thorney Green Suff 56 C4
Thorney Hill Hants 14 E2
Thorney Toll Pboro 66 D3
Thornfalcon Som 11 B7
Thornford Dorset 12 C4
Thorngumbald E Yorks 91 B6
Thornham Norf 80 C3
Thornham Magna Suff 56 B5
Thornham Parva Suff 56 B5
Thornhaugh Pboro 65 D7
Thornhill Cardiff 35 F5
Thornhill Cumb 98 D2
Thornhill Derbys 88 F2
Thornhill Dumfries 113 E8
Thornhill Soton 15 C5
Thornhill Stirling 127 E5
Thornhill W Yorks 88 C3
Thornhill Edge W Yorks 88 C3
Thornhill Lees W Yorks 88 C3
Thornholme E Yorks 97 C7
Thornley Durham 110 F4
Thornley Durham 111 F6
Thornliebank E Renf 118 D5
Thorns Suff 55 D8
Thorns Green Ches E 87 F5
Thornsett Derbys 87 F8
Thornthwaite Cumb 98 B4
Thornthwaite N Yorks 94 D4
Thornton Angus 134 E3
Thornton Bucks 53 F5
Thornton E Yorks 96 E3
Thornton Fife 128 E4
Thornton Lancs 92 E3
Thornton Leics 63 D8
Thornton Lincs 78 C5
Thornton Mbro 102 C2
Thornton Mers 85 D4
Thornton Northumb 123 E5
Thornton Pembs 44 E4
Thornton W Yorks 94 F4
Thornton Curtis N Lincs 90 C4
Thornton Heath London 28 C4
Thornton Hough Mers 85 F4
Thornton in Craven N Yorks 94 E2
Thornton-le-Beans N Yorks 102 E1
Thornton-le-Clay N Yorks 96 C2
Thornton-le-Dale N Yorks 103 F6
Thornton le Moor Lincs 90 E4
Thornton-le-Moor N Yorks 102 F1
Thornton-le-Moors Ches W 73 B8
Thornton-le-Street N Yorks 102 F2
Thornton Rust N Yorks 100 F4
Thornton Steward N Yorks 101 F6
Thornton Watlass N Yorks 101 F7
Thorntonhall S Lanark 119 D5
Thorntonloch E Loth 122 B3
Thorntonpark Northumb 122 E5
Thornwood Common Essex 41 D7
Thornydykes Borders 122 E2
Thoroton Notts 77 E7
Thorp Arch W Yorks 95 E7
Thorpe Derbys 75 D8
Thorpe E Yorks 97 E5
Thorpe Lincs 91 F8
Thorpe N Yorks 94 C3
Thorpe Norf 69 E7
Thorpe Notts 77 E7
Thorpe Sur 27 C8
Thorpe Abbotts Norf 57 B5
Thorpe Acre Leics 64 B2
Thorpe Arnold Leics 64 B4
Thorpe Audlin W Yorks 89 C5
Thorpe Bassett N Yorks 96 B4
Thorpe Bay Southend 43 F5
Thorpe by Water Rutland 65 E5
Thorpe Common Suff 57 F6
Thorpe Constantine Staffs 63 D6
Thorpe Culvert Lincs 79 C7
Thorpe End Norf 69 C5
Thorpe Fendykes Lincs 79 C7
Thorpe Green Essex 43 B7
Thorpe Green Suff 56 D3
Thorpe Hesley S Yorks 88 E4
Thorpe in Balne S Yorks 89 C6
Thorpe in the Fallows Lincs 90 F3
Thorpe Langton Leics 64 E4
Thorpe Larches Durham 102 B1
Thorpe-le-Soken Essex 43 B7
Thorpe le Street E Yorks 96 E4
Thorpe Malsor Northants 53 B6
Thorpe Mandeville Northants 52 E3
Thorpe Market Norf 81 D8
Thorpe Marriot Norf 68 C4
Thorpe Morieux Suff 56 D3
Thorpe on the Hill Lincs 78 C2
Thorpe Salvin S Yorks 89 F6
Thorpe Satchville Leics 64 C4
Thorpe St Andrew Norf 69 D5
Thorpe St Peter Lincs 79 C7
Thorpe Thewles Stockton 102 B2
Thorpe Tilney Lincs 78 D4
Thorpe Underwood N Yorks 95 D7
Thorpe Waterville Northants 65 F7
Thorpe Willoughby N Yorks 95 F8
Thorpeness Suff 57 D8
Thorrington Essex 43 C6
Thorverton Devon 10 D4
Thrandeston Suff 56 B5
Thrapston Northants 53 B7
Thrashbush N Lanark 119 C7
Threapland Cumb 107 F8
Threapland N Yorks 94 C2
Threapwood Ches W 73 E8
Threapwood Staffs 75 E7
Three Ashes Hereford 36 B2
Three Bridges W Sus 28 F3
Three Burrows Corn 3 B6
Three Chimneys Kent 18 B5
Three Cocks Powys 48 F3
Three Crosses Swansea 33 E6
Three Cups Corner E Sus 18 C3
Three Holes Norf 66 D5
Three Leg Cross E Sus 18 B3
Three Legged Cross Dorset 13 D8
Three Oaks E Sus 18 D5
Threehammer Common Norf 69 C6
Threekingham Lincs 78 F3
Threemile Cross Wokingham 26 C5
Threemilestone Corn 3 B6
Threemiletown W Loth 120 B3
Threlkeld Cumb 99 B5
Threshfield N Yorks 94 C2
Thrigby Norf 69 C7
Thringarth Durham 100 B4
Thringstone Leics 63 C8
Thrintoft N Yorks 101 E8
Thriplow Cambs 54 E5
Throckenholt Lincs 66 D3
Throcking Herts 54 F4
Throckley T&W 110 C4
Throckmorton Worcs 50 E4
Throphill Northumb 117 F7
Thropton Northumb 117 D6
Throsk Stirling 127 E7
Throwleigh Devon 9 E8
Throwley Kent 30 D3
Thrumpton Notts 76 F5
Thrumster Highld 158 F5
Thrunton Northumb 117 C6
Thrupp Glos 37 D5
Thrupp Oxon 38 C4
Thrushelton Devon 9 F6
Thrussington Leics 64 C3
Thruxton Hants 25 E7
Thruxton Hereford 49 F6
Thrybergh S Yorks 89 E5
Thulston Derbys 76 F4
Thundergay N Ayrs 143 D9
Thundersley Essex 42 F3
Thundridge Herts 41 C6
Thurcaston Leics 64 C2
Thurcroft S Yorks 89 F5
Thurgarton Norf 81 D7
Thurgarton Notts 77 E6
Thurgoland S Yorks 88 D3
Thurlaston Leics 64 E2
Thurlaston Warks 52 B2
Thurlbear Som 11 B7
Thurlby Lincs 65 C8
Thurlby Lincs 78 C2
Thurleigh Bedford 53 D8
Thurlestone Devon 6 E4
Thurloxton Som 22 F4
Thurlstone S Yorks 88 D3
Thurlton Norf 69 E7
Thurlwood Ches E 74 D5
Thurmaston Leics 64 D3
Thurnby Leics 64 D3
Thurne Norf 69 C7
Thurnham Kent 30 D2
Thurnham Lancs 92 D4
Thurning Norf 81 E6
Thurning Northants 65 F7
Thurnscoe S Yorks 89 D5
Thurnscoe East S Yorks 89 D5
Thursby Cumb 108 D3
Thursford Norf 81 D5
Thursley Sur 27 F7
Thurso Highld 158 D3
Thurso East Highld 158 D3
Thurstaston Mers 85 F3
Thurston Suff 56 C3
Thurstonfield Cumb 108 D3
Thurstonland W Yorks 88 C2
Thurton Norf 69 D6
Thurvaston Derbys 76 F2
Thuxton Norf 68 D3
Thwaite N Yorks 100 E3

Thwaite Suff 56 C5
Thwaite St Mary Norf 69 E6
Thwaites W Yorks 94 E3
Thwaites Brow W Yorks 94 E3
Thwing E Yorks 97 B6
Tibbermore Perth 128 B2
Tibberton Glos 36 B4
Tibberton Telford 61 B6
Tibberton Worcs 50 D4
Tibenham Norf 68 F4
Tibshelf Derbys 76 C4
Tibthorpe E Yorks 97 D5
Ticehurst E Sus 18 B3
Tichborne Hants 26 F3
Tickencote Rutland 65 D6
Tickenham N Som 23 B6
Tickhill S Yorks 89 E6
Ticklerton Shrops 60 E4
Ticknall Derbys 63 B7
Tickton E Yorks 97 E6
Tidcombe Wilts 25 D7
Tiddington Oxon 39 D6
Tiddington Warks 51 D7
Tidebrook E Sus 18 C3
Tideford Corn 5 D8
Tideford Cross Corn 5 C8
Tidenham Glos 36 E2
Tideswell Derbys 75 B8
Tidmarsh W Berks 26 B4
Tidmington Warks 51 F7
Tidpit Hants 13 C8
Tidworth Wilts 25 E7
Tiers Cross Pembs 44 D4
Tiffield Northants 52 D4
Tifty Aberds 153 D7
Tigerton Angus 135 C5
Tigh-na-Blair Perth 127 C6
Tighnabruaich Argyll 145 F8
Tighnafiline Highld 155 J13
Tigley Devon 7 C5
Tilbrook Cambs 53 C8
Tilbury Thurrock 29 B7
Tilbury Juxta Clare Essex 55 E8
Tile Cross W Mid 63 F5
Tile Hill W Mid 51 B7
Tilehurst Reading 26 B4
Tilford Sur 27 E6
Tilgate W Sus 28 F3
Tilgate Forest Row W Sus 28 F3
Tillathrowie Aberds 152 E4
Tilley Shrops 60 B5
Tillicoultry Clack 127 E8
Tillingham Essex 43 D5
Tillington Hereford 49 E6
Tillington W Sus 16 B3
Tillington Common Hereford 49 E6
Tillyarblet Angus 135 C5
Tillybirloch Aberds 141 D5
Tillycorthie Aberds 141 B8
Tillydrine Aberds 140 E5
Tillyfour Aberds 140 C4
Tillyfourie Aberds 140 C5
Tillygarmond Aberds 140 E5
Tillygreig Aberds 141 B7
Tillykerrie Aberds 141 B7
Tilmanstone Kent 31 D7
Tilney All Saints Norf 67 C5
Tilney High End Norf 67 C5
Tilney St Lawrence Norf 66 C5
Tilshead Wilts 24 E5
Tilstock Shrops 74 F2
Tilston Ches W 73 D8
Tilstone Fearnall Ches W 74 C2
Tilsworth C Beds 40 B2
Tilton on the Hill Leics 64 D4
Timberland Lincs 78 D4
Timbersbrook Ches E 75 C5
Timberscombe Som 21 E8
Timble N Yorks 94 D4
Timperley Gtr Man 87 F5
Timsbury Bath 23 D8
Timsbury Hants 14 B4
Timsgearraidh W Isles 154 D5
Timworth Green Suff 56 C2
Tincleton Dorset 13 E5
Tindale Cumb 109 D6
Tingewick Bucks 52 F4
Tingley W Yorks 88 B3
Tingrith C Beds 53 F8
Tingwall Orkney 159 F4
Tinhay Devon 9 F5
Tinshill W Yorks 95 F5
Tinsley S Yorks 88 E5
Tintagel Corn 8 F2
Tintern Parva Mon 36 D2
Tintinhull Som 12 C3
Tintwistle Derbys 87 E8
Tinwald Dumfries 114 F3
Tinwell Rutland 65 D7
Tipperty Aberds 141 B8
Tipsend Norf 66 E5
Tipton W Mid 62 E3
Tipton St John Devon 11 E5
Tiptree Essex 42 C4
Tir-y-dail Carms 33 C7
Tirabad Powys 47 E7
Tiraghoil Argyll 146 J6
Tirley Glos 37 B5
Tirphil Caerph 35 D5
Tirril Cumb 99 B7
Tisbury Wilts 13 B7
Tisman's Common W Sus 27 F8
Tissington Derbys 75 D8
Titchberry Devon 8 B4
Titchfield Hants 15 D6
Titchmarsh Northants 53 B8
Titchwell Norf 80 C3
Tithby Notts 77 F6
Titley Hereford 48 C5
Titlington Northumb 117 C7
Titsey Sur 28 D5
Tittensor Staffs 75 F5
Tittleshall Norf 80 E4
Tiverton Ches W 74 C2
Tiverton Devon 10 C4
Tivetshall St Margaret Norf 68 F4
Tivetshall St Mary Norf 68 F4
Tividale W Mid 62 E3
Tivy Dale S Yorks 88 D3
Tixall Staffs 62 B3
Tixover Rutland 65 D6
Toab Orkney 159 H6
Toab Shetland 160 M5
Toadmoor Derbys 76 D3
Tobermory Argyll 147 F8
Toberonochy Argyll 124 E3
Tobha Mor W Isles 148 E2
Tobhtarol W Isles 154 D6
Tobson W Isles 154 D6
Tocher Aberds 153 E6
Tockenham Wilts 24 B5
Tockenham Wick Wilts 37 F7
Tockholes Blackburn 86 B4
Tockington S Glos 36 F3
Tockwith N Yorks 95 D7
Todber Dorset 13 B6
Todding Hereford 49 B6
Toddington C Beds 40 B3
Toddington Glos 50 F5
Todenham Glos 51 F7
Todhills Cumb 108 C3
Todlachie Aberds 141 C5
Todmorden W Yorks 87 B7
Todrig Borders 115 C7
Todwick S Yorks 89 F5
Toft Cambs 54 D4
Toft Lincs 65 C7
Toft Hill Durham 101 B6
Toft Hill Lincs 78 C5
Toft Monks Norf 69 E7
Toft next Newton Lincs 90 F4
Toftrees Norf 80 E4
Tofts Highld 158 D5
Toftwood Norf 68 C2
Togston Northumb 117 D8
Tokavaig Highld 149 G11
Tokers Green Oxon 26 B5
Tolastadh a Chaolais W Isles 154 D6
Tolastadh bho Thuath W Isles 155 C10
Toll Bar S Yorks 89 D6
Toll End W Mid 62 E3
Toll of Birness Aberds 153 E10
Tolland Som 22 F3
Tollard Royal Wilts 13 C7
Tollbar End W Mid 51 B8
Toller Fratrum Dorset 12 E3
Toller Porcorum Dorset 12 E3
Tollerton N Yorks 95 C8
Tollerton Notts 77 F6
Tollesbury Essex 43 C5
Tolleshunt D'Arcy Essex 43 C5
Tolleshunt Major Essex 43 C5
Tolm W Isles 155 D9
Tolpuddle Dorset 13 E5
Tolvah Highld 138 E4
Tolworth London 28 C2
Tomatin Highld 138 B4
Tombreck Highld 151 H9
Tomchrasky Highld 137 C5
Tomdoun Highld 136 D4
Tomich Highld 137 B6
Tomich Highld 151 D9
Tomich House Highld 151 G8
Tomintoul Aberds 139 E7
Tomintoul Moray 139 C7
Tomnaven Moray 152 E4
Tomnavoulin Moray 139 B8
Ton-Pentre Rhondda 34 E3
Tonbridge Kent 29 E6
Tondu Bridgend 34 F2
Tonfanau Gwyn 58 D2
Tong Shrops 61 D7
Tong W Yorks 94 F5
Tong Norton Shrops 61 D7
Tonge Leics 63 B8
Tongham Sur 27 E6
Tongland Dumfries 106 D3
Tongue Highld 157 D8
Tongue End Lincs 65 C8
Tongwynlais Cardiff 35 F5
Tonna Neath 34 E1
Tonwell Herts 41 C6
Tonypandy Rhondda 34 E3
Tonyrefail Rhondda 34 F4
Toot Baldon Oxon 39 D5
Toot Hill Essex 41 D8
Toothill Hants 14 C4
Top of Hebers Gtr Man 87 D6
Topcliffe N Yorks 95 B7
Topcroft Norf 69 E5
Topcroft Street Norf 69 E5
Toppesfield Essex 55 F8
Toppings Gtr Man 86 C5
Topsham Devon 10 F4
Torbay Torbay 7 D7
Torbeg N Ayrs 143 F10
Torboll Farm Highld 151 B10
Torbrex Stirling 127 E6
Torbryan Devon 7 C6
Torcross Devon 7 E6
Tore Highld 151 F9
Torinturk Argyll 145 G7
Torksey Lincs 77 B8
Torlum W Isles 148 C2
Torlundy Highld 131 B5
Tormarton S Glos 24 B2
Tormisdale Argyll 142 C2
Tormitchell S Ayrs 112 E2
Tormore N Ayrs 143 E9
Tornagrain Highld 151 G10
Tornahaish Aberds 139 D8
Tornaveen Aberds 140 D5
Torness Highld 137 B8
Toronto Durham 110 F4
Torpenhow Cumb 108 F2
Torphichen W Loth 120 B2
Torphins Aberds 140 D5
Torpoint Corn 6 D2
Torquay Torbay 7 C7
Torquhan Borders 121 E7
Torran Argyll 124 E4
Torran Highld 149 D10
Torran Highld 151 D10
Torrance E Dunb 119 B6
Torrans Argyll 146 J7
Torranyard N Ayrs 118 E3
Torre Torbay 7 C7
Torridon Highld 150 F2
Torridon Ho. Highld 149 C13
Torrin Highld 149 F10
Torrisdale Highld 157 C9
Torrisdale-Square Argyll 143 E8
Torrish Highld 157 H12
Torrisholme Lancs 92 C4
Torroble Highld 157 J8
Torry Aberdeen 141 D8
Torry Aberds 152 E4
Torryburn Fife 128 F2
Torterston Aberds 153 D10
Torthorwald Dumfries 107 B7
Tortington W Sus 16 D4
Tortworth S Glos 36 E4
Torvaig Highld 149 D9
Torver Cumb 98 E4
Torwood Falk 127 F7
Torworth Notts 89 F7
Tosberry Devon 8 B4
Toscaig Highld 149 E12
Toseland Cambs 54 C3
Tosside N Yorks 93 D7
Tostock Suff 56 C3
Totaig Highld 148 C7
Totaig Highld 149 F13
Tote Highld 149 D9
Totegan Highld 157 C11
Tothill Lincs 91 F8
Totland IoW 14 F4
Totnes Devon 7 C6
Toton Notts 76 F5
Totronald Argyll 146 F4
Totscore Highld 149 B8
Tottenham London 41 E6
Tottenhill Norf 67 C6
Tottenhill Row Norf 67 C6
Totteridge London 41 E5
Totternhoe C Beds 40 B2
Tottington Gtr Man 87 C5
Totton Hants 14 C4
Touchen End Windsor 27 B6
Tournaig Highld 155 J13
Toux Aberds 153 C9
Tovil Kent 29 D8
Tow Law Durham 110 F4
Toward Argyll 145 G10
Towcester Northants 52 E4
Towednack Corn 2 C3
Tower End Norf 67 C6
Towersey Oxon 39 D7
Towie Aberds 140 C3
Towie Aberds 153 B8
Towiemore Moray 152 D3
Town End Cambs 66 E4
Town End Cumb 99 F6
Town Row E Sus 18 B2
Town Yetholm Borders 116 B4
Townend W Dunb 118 B4
Towngate Lincs 65 C8
Townhead Cumb 108 F5
Townhead Dumfries 106 E3
Townhead S Ayrs 112 D2
Townhead S Yorks 88 D2
Townhead of Greenlaw Dumfries 106 C4
Townhill Fife 128 F3
Townsend Bucks 39 D7
Townsend Herts 40 D4
Townshend Corn 2 C4
Towthorpe York 96 D2
Towton N Yorks 95 F7
Towyn Conwy 72 B3
Toxteth Mers 85 F4
Toynton All Saints Lincs 79 C6
Toynton Fen Side Lincs 79 C6
Toynton St Peter Lincs 79 C7
Toy's Hill Kent 29 D5
Trabboch E Ayrs 112 B4
Traboe Corn 3 D6
Tradespark Highld 151 F11
Tradespark Orkney 159 H5
Trafford Park Gtr Man 87 E5
Trallong Powys 34 B3
Tranent E Loth 121 B7
Tranmere Mers 85 F4
Trantlebeg Highld 157 D11
Trantlemore Highld 157 D11
Tranwell Northumb 117 F7
Trapp Carms 33 C7
Traprain E Loth 121 B8
Traquair Borders 121 F6
Trawden Lancs 94 F2
Trawsfynydd Gwyn 71 D8
Tre-Gibbon Rhondda 34 D3
Tre-Taliesin Ceredig 58 E3
Tre-vaughan Carms 32 B4
Tre-wyn Mon 35 B7
Trealaw Rhondda 34 E4
Treales Lancs 92 F4
Trearddur Anglesey 82 D2
Treaslane Highld 149 C8
Trebanog Rhondda 34 E4
Trebanos Neath 33 D8
Trebartha Corn 5 B7
Trebarwith Corn 8 F2
Trebetherick Corn 4 B4
Treborough Som 22 F2
Trebudannon Corn 4 C3
Trebullett Corn 5 B8
Treburley Corn 5 B8
Trebyan Corn 5 C5
Trecastle Powys 34 B2
Trecenydd Caerph 35 F5
Trecwn Pembs 44 B4
Trecynon Rhondda 34 D3
Tredavoe Corn 2 D3
Tredegar Bl Gwent 35 D5
Tredegar = Newydd New Tredegar Caerph 35 D5
Tredington Glos 37 B6
Tredington Warks 51 E7
Tredinnick Corn 4 B4
Tredomen Powys 48 F3
Tredunnock Mon 35 E7
Tredustan Powys 48 F3
Treen Corn 2 D2
Treeton S Yorks 88 F5
Tref-Y-Clawdd = Knighton Powys 48 B4
Trefaldwyn = Montgomery Powys 60 E2
Trefasser Pembs 44 B3
Trefdraeth Anglesey 82 D4
Trefdraeth = Newport Pembs 45 F2
Trefecca Powys 48 F3
Trefechan Ceredig 58 F2
Trefeglwys Powys 59 E6
Trefenter Ceredig 46 C5
Treffgarne Pembs 44 C4
Treffynnon = Holywell Flint 73 B5
Treffynnon Pembs 44 C3
Trefgarn Owen Pembs 44 C3
Trefil Bl Gwent 35 C5
Trefilan Ceredig 46 D4
Trefin Pembs 44 B3
Treflach Shrops 60 B2
Trefnanney Powys 60 C2
Trefnant Denb 72 B4
Trefonen Shrops 60 B2
Trefor Anglesey 82 C3
Trefor Gwyn 70 C4
Treforest Rhondda 34 F4
Trefriw Conwy 83 E7
Trefynwy = Monmouth Mon 36 C2
Tregadillett Corn 8 F4
Tregaian Anglesey 82 D4
Tregare Mon 35 C8
Tregaron Ceredig 47 D5
Tregarth Gwyn 83 E6
Tregeare Corn 8 F4
Tregeiriog Wrex 73 F5
Tregele Anglesey 82 B3
Tregidden Corn 3 D6
Treglemais Pembs 44 C3
Tregole Corn 8 E3
Tregonetha Corn 4 C4
Tregony Corn 3 B8
Tregoss Corn 4 C4
Tregoyd Powys 48 F4
Tregroes Ceredig 46 E3
Tregurrian Corn 4 C3
Tregynon Powys 59 E7
Trehafod Rhondda 34 E4
Treharris M Tydf 34 E4
Treherbert Rhondda 34 E3
Trekenner Corn 5 B8
Treknow Corn 8 F2
Trelan Corn 3 E6
Trelash Corn 8 E3
Trelassick Corn 4 D3
Trelawnyd Flint 72 B4
Trelech Carms 45 F4
Treleddyd-fawr Pembs 44 C2
Trelewis M Tydf 35 E5
Treligga Corn 8 F2
Trelights Corn 4 B4
Trelill Corn 4 B5
Trelissick Corn 3 C7
Trellech Mon 36 D2
Trelleck Grange Mon 36 D1
Trelogan Flint 85 F2
Trelystan Powys 60 D2
Tremadog Gwyn 71 C6
Tremail Corn 8 F3
Tremain Ceredig 45 E4
Tremaine Corn 8 F4
Tremar Corn 5 C7
Trematon Corn 5 D8
Tremeirchion Denb 72 B4
Trenance Corn 4 C3
Trenarren Corn 3 B9
Trench Telford 61 C6
Treneglos Corn 8 F4
Trenewan Corn 5 D6
Trent Dorset 12 C3
Trent Vale Stoke 75 E5
Trentham Stoke 75 E5
Trentishoe Devon 20 E5
Treoes V Glam 21 B8
Treorchy = Treorci Rhondda 34 E3
Treorci = Treorchy Rhondda 34 E3
Tre'r-ddôl Ceredig 58 E3
Trerule Foot Corn 5 D8
Tresaith Ceredig 45 D4
Tresawle Corn 3 B7
Trescott Staffs 62 E2
Trescowe Corn 2 C4
Tresham Glos 36 E4
Tresillian Corn 3 B7
Tresinwen Pembs 44 A4
Treskinnick Cross Corn 8 E3
Tresmeer Corn 8 F4
Tresparrett Corn 8 E3
Tresparrett Posts Corn 8 E3
Tressait Perth 133 C5
Tresta Shetland 160 D8
Tresta Shetland 160 H5
Treswell Notts 77 B7
Trethosa Corn 4 D4
Trethurgy Corn 4 D5
Tretio Pembs 44 C2
Tretire Hereford 36 B2
Tretower Powys 35 B5
Treuddyn Flint 73 D6
Trevalga Corn 8 F2
Trevalyn Wrex 73 D7
Trevanson Corn 4 B4
Trevarren Corn 4 C4
Trevarrian Corn 4 C3
Trevarrick Corn 3 B8
Trevaughan Carms 32 C2
Treveighan Corn 5 B5
Trevellas Corn 4 D2
Treverva Corn 3 C6
Trevethin Torf 35 D6
Trevigro Corn 5 C8
Treviscoe Corn 4 D4
Trevone Corn 4 B3
Trewarmett Corn 8 F2
Trewassa Corn 8 F3
Trewellard Corn 2 C2
Trewen Corn 8 F4
Trewennack Corn 3 D5
Trewern Powys 60 C2
Trewethern Corn 4 B5
Trewidland Corn 5 D7
Trewint Corn 8 E3
Trewint Corn 8 F4
Trewithian Corn 3 C7
Trewoofe Corn 2 D3
Trewoon Corn 4 D4
Treworga Corn 3 B7
Treworlas Corn 3 C7
Treyarnon Corn 4 B3
Treyford W Sus 16 C2
Trezaise Corn 4 D4
Triangle W Yorks 87 B8
Trickett's Cross Dorset 13 D8
Triffleton Pembs 44 C4
Trimdon Durham 111 F6
Trimdon Colliery Durham 111 F6
Trimdon Grange Durham 111 F6
Trimingham Norf 81 D8
Trimley Lower Street Suff 57 F6
Trimley St Martin Suff 57 F6
Trimley St Mary Suff 57 F6
Trimpley Worcs 50 B2
Trimsaran Carms 33 D5
Trimstone Devon 20 E3
Trinafour Perth 132 C4
Trinant Caerph 35 D6
Tring Herts 40 C2
Tring Wharf Herts 40 C2
Trinity Angus 135 C6
Trinity Jersey 17
Trisant Ceredig 47 B6
Trislaig Highld 130 B4
Trispen Corn 4 D3
Tritlington Northumb 117 E8
Trochry Perth 133 E6
Trodigal Argyll 143 F7
Troed-rhiwdalar Powys 47 D8
Troedyraur Ceredig 46 E2
Troedyrhiw M Tydf 34 D4
Tromode IoM 84 E3
Trondavoe Shetland 160 F5
Troon Corn 3 C5
Troon S Ayrs 118 F3
Trosaraidh W Isles 148 G2
Trossachs Hotel Stirling 126 D4
Troston Suff 56 B2
Trottiscliffe Kent 29 C7
Trotton W Sus 16 B2
Troutbeck Cumb 99 B5
Troutbeck Cumb 99 D6
Troutbeck Bridge Cumb 99 D6
Trow Green Glos 36 D2
Trowbridge Wilts 24 D3
Trowell Notts 76 F4
Trowle Common Wilts 24 D3
Trowley Bottom Herts 40 C3
Trows Borders 122 F2
Trowse Newton Norf 68 D5
Trudoxhill Som 24 E2
Trull Som 11 B7
Trumaisgearraidh W Isles 148 A3
Trumpan Highld 148 B7
Trumpet Hereford 49 F8
Trumpington Cambs 54 D5
Trunch Norf 81 D8
Trunnah Lancs 92 E3
Truro Corn 3 B7
Trusham Devon 10 F3
Trusley Derbys 76 F2
Trusthorpe Lincs 91 F9
Trysull Staffs 62 E2
Tubney Oxon 38 E4
Tuckenhay Devon 7 D6
Tuckhill Shrops 61 F7
Tuckingmill Corn 3 B5
Tuddenham Suff 55 B8
Tuddenham St Martin Suff 57 E5
Tudeley Kent 29 E7
Tudhoe Durham 111 F5
Tudorville Hereford 36 B2
Tudweiliog Gwyn 70 D3
Tuesley Sur 27 E7
Tuffley Glos 37 C5
Tufton Hants 26 E2
Tufton Pembs 32 B1
Tugby Leics 64 D4
Tugford Shrops 61 F5
Tullibardine Perth 127 C8
Tullibody Clack 127 E7
Tullich Argyll 125 D6
Tullich Highld 138 B2
Tullich Muir Highld 151 D10
Tulliemet Perth 133 D6
Tulloch Aberds 135 B7
Tulloch Aberds 153 E8
Tulloch Perth 128 B2
Tulloch Castle Highld 151 E8
Tullochgorm Argyll 125 F5
Tulloes Angus 135 E5
Tullybannocher Perth 127 B6
Tullybelton Perth 133 F7
Tullyfergus Perth 134 E2
Tullymurdoch Perth 134 D1
Tullynessle Aberds 140 C4
Tumble Carms 33 C6
Tumby Woodside Lincs 79 D5
Tummel Bridge Perth 132 D4
Tunga W Isles 155 D9
Tunstall E Yorks 97 F9
Tunstall Kent 30 C2
Tunstall Lancs 93 B6
Tunstall N Yorks 101 E7
Tunstall Norf 69 D7
Tunstall Stoke 75 D5
Tunstall Suff 57 D7
Tunstall T&W 111 D6
Tunstead Derbys 75 B8
Tunstead Gtr Man 87 D8
Tunstead Norf 81 E8
Tunworth Hants 26 E4
Tupsley Hereford 49 E7
Tupton Derbys 76 C3
Tur Langton Leics 64 E4
Turgis Green Hants 26 D4
Turin Angus 135 D5
Turkdean Glos 37 C8
Turleigh Wilts 24 C3
Turn Lancs 87 C6
Turnastone Hereford 49 F5
Turnberry S Ayrs 112 D2
Turnditch Derbys 76 E2
Turners Hill W Sus 28 F4
Turners Puddle Dorset 13 E6
Turnford Herts 41 D6
Turnhouse Edin 120 B4
Turnworth Dorset 13 D6
Turriff Aberds 153 C7
Turton Bottoms Blackburn 86 C5
Turves Cambs 66 E3
Turvey Bedford 53 D7
Turville Bucks 39 E7
Turville Heath Bucks 39 E7
Turweston Bucks 52 F4
Tushielaw Borders 115 C6
Tutbury Staffs 63 B6
Tutnall Worcs 50 B4
Tutshill Glos 36 E2
Tuttington Norf 81 E8
Tutts Clump W Berks 26 B3
Tuxford Notts 77 B7
Twatt Orkney 159 F3
Twatt Shetland 160 H5
Twechar E Dunb 119 B7
Tweedmouth Northumb 123 D5
Tweedsmuir Borders 114 B3
Twelve Heads Corn 3 B6
Twemlow Green Ches E 74 C4
Twenty Lincs 65 B8
Twerton Bath 24 C2
Twickenham London 28 B2
Twigworth Glos 37 B5
Twineham W Sus 17 C6
Twinhoe Bath 24 D2
Twinstead Essex 56 F2
Twinstead Green Essex 56 F2
Twiss Green Warr 86 E4
Twiston Lancs 93 E8
Twitchen Devon 21 F6
Twitchen Shrops 49 B5
Two Bridges Devon 6 B4
Two Dales Derbys 76 C2
Two Mills Ches W 73 B7
Twycross Leics 63 D7
Twyford Bucks 39 B6
Twyford Derbys 63 B7
Twyford Hants 15 B5
Twyford Leics 64 C4
Twyford Lincs 65 B6
Twyford Norf 81 E6
Twyford Wokingham 27 B5
Twyford Common Hereford 49 F7
Twyn-y-Sheriff Mon 35 D8
Twynholm Dumfries 106 D3
Twyning Glos 50 F3
Twyning Green Glos 50 F4
Twynllanan Carms 34 B1
Twynmynydd Carms 33 C7
Twywell Northants 53 B7
Ty-draw Conwy 83 F8
Ty-hen Carms 32 B4
Ty-hen Gwyn 70 D2
Ty-mawr Anglesey 82 C4
Ty Mawr Carms 46 E4
Ty Mawr Cwm Conwy 72 E3
Ty-nant Conwy 72 E3
Ty-nant Gwyn 59 B6
Ty-uchaf Powys 59 B7
Tyberton Hereford 49 F5
Tyburn W Mid 62 E5
Tycroes Carms 33 C7
Tycrwyn Powys 59 C8
Tydd Gote Lincs 66 C4
Tydd St Giles Cambs 66 C4
Tydd St Mary Lincs 66 C4
Tyddewi = St David's Pembs 44 C2
Tyddyn-mawr Gwyn 71 C6
Tye Green Essex 41 D7
Tye Green Essex 42 B3
Tye Green Essex 55 F6
Tyldesley Gtr Man 86 D4
Tyler Hill Kent 30 C5
Tylers Green Bucks 40 E2
Tylorstown Rhondda 34 E4
Tylwch Powys 59 F6
Ty'n-y-celyn Wrex 73 F5
Ty'n-y-coed Shrops 60 B2
Tyn-y-fedwen Powys 72 F5
Ty'n-y-ffridd Powys 72 F5
Ty'n-y-graig Powys 48 D2
Ty'n-y-groes Conwy 83 D7
Ty'n'-y-maes Gwyn 83 E6
Tyn-y-pwll Anglesey 82 C4
Ty'n'-yr-eithin Ceredig 47 C5
Tyncelyn Ceredig 46 C5
Tyndrum Stirling 131 F7
Tyne Tunnel T&W 111 C6
Tyneham Dorset 13 F6
Tynehead Midloth 121 D6
Tynemouth T&W 111 C6
Tynewydd Rhondda 34 E3
Tyninghame E Loth 122 B2
Tynron Dumfries 113 E8
Tynygongl Anglesey 82 C5
Tynygraig Ceredig 47 C5
Ty'r-felin-isaf Conwy 83 E8
Tyrie Aberds 153 B9
Tyringham M Keynes 53 E6
Tythecott Devon 9 C6
Tythegston Bridgend 21 B7
Tytherington Ches E 75 B6
Tytherington S Glos 36 F3
Tytherington Som 24 E2
Tytherington Wilts 24 E4
Tytherleigh Devon 11 D8
Tywardreath Corn 5 D5
Tywyn Conwy 83 D7
Tywyn Gwyn 58 D2

U

Uachdar W Isles 148 C2
Uags Highld 149 E12
Ubbeston Green Suff 57 B7
Ubley Bath 23 D7
Uckerby N Yorks 101 D7
Uckfield E Sus 17 B8
Uckington Glos 37 B6
Uddingston S Lanark 119 C6
Uddington S Lanark 119 F8
Udimore E Sus 19 D5
Udny Green Aberds 141 B7
Udny Station Aberds 141 B8
Udston S Lanark 119 D6
Udstonhead S Lanark 119 E7
Uffcott Wilts 25 B6
Uffculme Devon 11 C5
Uffington Lincs 65 D7
Uffington Oxon 38 F3
Uffington Shrops 60 C5
Ufford Pboro 65 D7
Ufford Suff 57 D6
Ufton Warks 51 C8
Ufton Nervet W Berks 26 C4
Ugadale Argyll 143 F8
Ugborough Devon 6 D4
Uggeshall Suff 69 F7
Ugglebarnby N Yorks 103 D6
Ughill S Yorks 88 E3
Ugley Essex 41 B8
Ugley Green Essex 41 B8
Ugthorpe N Yorks 103 C5
Uidh W Isles 148 J1
Uig Argyll 145 E10
Uig Highld 148 C6
Uig Highld 149 B8
Uigen W Isles 154 D5
Uigshader Highld 149 D9
Uisken Argyll 146 K6
Ulbster Highld 158 F5
Ulceby Lincs 79 B7
Ulceby N Lincs 90 C5
Ulceby Skitter N Lincs 90 C5
Ulcombe Kent 30 E2
Uldale Cumb 108 F2
Uley Glos 36 E4
Ulgham Northumb 117 E8
Ullapool Highld 150 B4
Ullenhall Warks 51 C6
Ullenwood Glos 37 C6
Ulleskelf N Yorks 95 E8
Ullesthorpe Leics 64 F2
Ulley S Yorks 89 F5
Ullingswick Hereford 49 E7
Ullinish Highld 149 E8
Ullock Cumb 98 B2
Ulnes Walton Lancs 86 C3
Ulpha Cumb 98 E3
Ulrome E Yorks 97 D7
Ulsta Shetland 160 E6
Ulva House Argyll 146 H7
Ulverston Cumb 92 B2
Ulwell Dorset 13 F8
Umberleigh Devon 9 B8
Unapool Highld 156 F5
Unasary W Isles 148 F2
Underbarrow Cumb 99 E6
Undercliffe W Yorks 94 F4
Underhoull Shetland 160 C7
Underriver Kent 29 D6
Underwood Notts 76 D4
Undy Mon 35 F8
Unifirth Shetland 160 H4
Union Cottage Aberds 141 E7
Union Mills IoM 84 E3
Union Street E Sus 18 B4
Unstone Derbys 76 B3
Unstone Green Derbys 76 B3
Unthank Cumb 108 F4
Unthank Cumb 109 E6
Unthank End Cumb 108 F4
Up Cerne Dorset 12 D4
Up Exe Devon 10 D4
Up Hatherley Glos 37 B6
Up Holland Lancs 86 D3
Up Marden W Sus 15 C8
Up Nately Hants 26 D4
Up Somborne Hants 25 F8
Up Sydling Dorset 12 D4
Upavon Wilts 25 D6
Upchurch Kent 30 C2
Upcott Hereford 48 D5
Upend Cambs 55 D7
Upgate Norf 68 C4
Uphall W Loth 120 B3
Uphall Station W Loth 120 B3
Upham Devon 10 D3
Upham Hants 15 B6
Uphampton Worcs 50 C3
Uphill N Som 22 D5
Uplawmoor E Renf 118 D4
Upleadon Glos 36 B4
Upleatham Redcar 102 C4
Uplees Kent 30 C3
Uploders Dorset 12 E3
Uplowman Devon 10 C5
Uplyme Devon 11 E8
Upminster London 42 F1
Upnor Medway 29 B8
Upottery Devon 11 D7
Upper Affcot Shrops 60 F4
Upper Ardchronie Highld 151 C9
Upper Arley Worcs 61 F7
Upper Arncott Oxon 39 C6
Upper Astrop Northants 52 F3
Upper Badcall Highld 156 E4
Upper Basildon W Berks 26 B3
Upper Beeding W Sus 17 C5
Upper Benefield Northants 65 F6
Upper Bighouse Highld 157 D11
Upper Boddington Northants 52 D2
Upper Borth Ceredig 58 F3
Upper Boyndlie Aberds 153 B9
Upper Brailes Warks 51 F8
Upper Breakish Highld 149 F11
Upper Breinton Hereford 49 E6
Upper Broadheath Worcs 50 D3
Upper Broughton Notts 64 B3
Upper Bucklebury W Berks 26 C3
Upper Burnhaugh Aberds 141 E7
Upper Caldecote C Beds 54 E2
Upper Catesby Northants 52 D3
Upper Chapel Powys 48 E2
Upper Church Village Rhondda 34 F4
Upper Chute Wilts 25 D7
Upper Clatford Hants 25 E8
Upper Clynnog Gwyn 71 C5
Upper Cumberworth W Yorks 88 D3
Upper Cwm-twrch Powys 34 C1
Upper Cwmbran Torf 35 E6
Upper Dallachy Moray 152 B3
Upper Dean Bedford 53 C8
Upper Denby W Yorks 88 D3
Upper Denton Cumb 109 C6
Upper Derraid Highld 151 H13
Upper Dicker E Sus 18 E2
Upper Dovercourt Essex 57 F6
Upper Druimfin Argyll 147 F8
Upper Dunsforth N Yorks 95 C7
Upper Eathie Highld 151 E10
Upper Elkstone Staffs 75 D7
Upper End Derbys 75 B7
Upper Farringdon Hants 26 F5
Upper Framilode Glos 36 C4
Upper Glenfintaig Highld 137 F5
Upper Gornal W Mid 62 E3
Upper Gravenhurst C Beds 54 F2
Upper Green Mon 35 C7
Upper Green W Berks 25 C8
Upper Grove Common Hereford 36 B2
Upper Hackney Derbys 76 C2
Upper Hale Sur 27 E6
Upper Halistra Highld 148 C7
Upper Halling Medway 29 C7
Upper Hambleton Rutland 65 D6
Upper Hardres Court Kent 31 D5
Upper Hartfield E Sus 29 F5
Upper Haugh S Yorks 88 E5
Upper Heath Shrops 61 F5
Upper Hellesdon Norf 68 C5
Upper Helmsley N Yorks 96 D2
Upper Hergest Hereford 48 D4
Upper Heyford Northants 52 D4
Upper Heyford Oxon 38 B4
Upper Hill Hereford 49 D6
Upper Hopton W Yorks 88 C2
Upper Horsebridge E Sus 18 D2
Upper Hulme Staffs 75 C7
Upper Inglesham Swindon 38 E2
Upper Inverbrough Highld 151 H11
Upper Killay Swansea 33 E6
Upper Knockando Moray 152 D1
Upper Lambourn W Berks 38 F3
Upper Leigh Staffs 75 F7
Upper Lenie Highld 137 B8
Upper Lochton Aberds 141 E5
Upper Longdon Staffs 62 C4
Upper Lybster Highld 158 G4
Upper Lydbrook Glos 36 C3
Upper Maes-coed Hereford 48 F5
Upper Midway Derbys 63 B6
Upper Milovaig Highld 148 D6
Upper Minety Wilts 37 E7
Upper Mitton Worcs 50 B3
Upper North Dean Bucks 39 E8
Upper Obney Perth 133 F7
Upper Ollach Highld 149 E10
Upper Padley Derbys 76 B2
Upper Pollicott Bucks 39 C7
Upper Poppleton York 95 D8
Upper Quinton Warks 51 E6
Upper Ratley Hants 14 B4
Upper Rissington Glos 38 C2
Upper Rochford Worcs 49 C8
Upper Sandaig Highld 149 G12
Upper Sanday Orkney 159 H6
Upper Sapey Hereford 49 C8
Upper Saxondale Notts 77 F6
Upper Seagry Wilts 37 F6
Upper Shelton C Beds 53 E7
Upper Sheringham Norf 81 C7
Upper Skelmorlie N Ayrs 118 C2
Upper Slaughter Glos 38 B1
Upper Soudley Glos 36 C3
Upper Stondon C Beds 54 F2
Upper Stowe Northants 52 D4
Upper Stratton Swindon 38 F1
Upper Street Hants 14 C2
Upper Street Norf 69 C6
Upper Street Norf 69 C6
Upper Street Suff 56 F5
Upper Strensham Worcs 50 F4
Upper Sundon C Beds 40 B3
Upper Swell Glos 38 B1
Upper Tean Staffs 75 F7
Upper Tillyrie Perth 128 D3
Upper Tooting London 28 B3
Upper Tote Highld 149 C10
Upper Town N Som 23 C7
Upper Treverward Shrops 48 B4
Upper Tysoe Warks 51 E8
Upper Upham Wilts 25 B7
Upper Wardington Oxon 52 E2
Upper Weald M Keynes 53 F5
Upper Weedon Northants 52 D4
Upper Wield Hants 26 F4
Upper Winchendon Bucks 39 C7
Upper Witton W Mid 62 E4
Upper Woodend Aberds 141 C5
Upper Woodford Wilts 25 F6
Upper Wootton Hants 26 D3
Upper Wyche Hereford 50 E2
Upperby Cumb 108 D4
Uppermill Gtr Man 87 D7
Uppersound Shetland 160 J6
Upperthong W Yorks 88 D2
Upperthorpe N Lincs 89 D8
Upperton W Sus 16 B3
Uppertown Derbys 76 C3
Uppertown Highld 158 C5
Uppertown Orkney 159 J5
Uppingham Rutland 65 E5
Uppington Shrops 61 D6
Upsall N Yorks 102 F2
Upshire Essex 41 D7
Upstreet Kent 31 C6
Upthorpe Suff 56 B3
Upton Cambs 54 B2
Upton Ches W 73 C8
Upton Corn 8 D4
Upton Dorset 12 F5
Upton Dorset 13 E7
Upton Hants 14 C4
Upton Hants 25 D8
Upton Leics 63 E7
Upton Lincs 90 F2
Upton Mers 85 F3
Upton Norf 69 C6
Upton Northants 52 C5
Upton Notts 77 B7
Upton Notts 77 D7
Upton Oxon 39 F5
Upton Pboro 65 D8
Upton Slough 27 B7
Upton Som 10 B4
Upton W Yorks 89 C5
Upton Bishop Hereford 36 B3
Upton Cheyney S Glos 23 C8
Upton Cressett Shrops 61 E6
Upton Cross Corn 5 B7
Upton Grey Hants 26 E4
Upton Hellions Devon 10 D3
Upton Lovell Wilts 24 E4
Upton Magna Shrops 61 C5
Upton Noble Som 24 F2
Upton Pyne Devon 10 E4
Upton Scudamore Wilts 24 E3
Upton St Leonard's Glos 37 C5
Upton Snodsbury Worcs 50 D4
Upton upon Severn Worcs 50 E3
Upton Warren Worcs 50 C4
Upwaltham W Sus 16 C3
Upware Cambs 55 B6
Upwell Norf 66 D4
Upwey Dorset 12 F4
Upwood Cambs 66 F2
Uradale Shetland 160 K6
Urafirth Shetland 160 F5
Urchfont Wilts 24 D5
Urdimarsh Hereford 49 E7
Ure Shetland 160 F4
Ure Bank N Yorks 95 B6
Urgha W Isles 154 H6
Urishay Common Hereford 48 F5
Urlay Nook Stockton 102 C1
Urmston Gtr Man 87 E5
Urpeth Durham 110 D5
Urquhart Highld 151 F8
Urquhart Moray 152 B2
Urra N Yorks 102 D3
Urray Highld 151 F8
Ushaw Moor Durham 110 E5
Usk = Brynbuga Mon 35 D7
Usselby Lincs 90 E4
Usworth T&W 111 D6
Utkinton Ches W 74 C2
Utley W Yorks 94 E3
Uton Devon 10 E3
Utterby Lincs 91 E7
Uttoxeter Staffs 75 F7
Uwchmynydd Gwyn 70 E2
Uxbridge London 40 F3
Uyeasound Shetland 160 C7
Uzmaston Pembs 44 D4

V

Valley Anglesey 82 D2
Valley Truckle Corn 8 F2
Valleyfield Dumfries 106 D3
Valsgarth Shetland 160 B8
Valtos Highld 149 B10
Van Powys 59 F6
Vange Essex 42 F3
Varteg Torf 35 D6
Vatten Highld 149 D7
Vaul Argyll 146 G3
Vaynor M Tydf 34 C4
Veensgarth Shetland 160 J6
Velindre Powys 48 F3
Vellow Som 22 F2
Veness Orkney 159 F6
Venn Green Devon 9 C5
Venn Ottery Devon 11 E5
Vennington Shrops 60 D3
Venny Tedburn Devon 10 E3
Ventnor IoW 15 G6
Vernham Dean Hants 25 D8
Vernham Street Hants 25 D8
Vernolds Common Shrops 60 F4
Verwood Dorset 13 D8
Veryan Corn 3 C8
Vicarage Devon 11 F7
Vickerstown Cumb 92 C1
Victoria Corn 4 C4
Victoria S Yorks 88 D2
Vidlin Shetland 160 G6
Viewpark N Lanark 119 C7
Vigo Village Kent 29 C7
Vinehall Street E Sus 18 C4
Vine's Cross E Sus 18 D2
Viney Hill Glos 36 D3
Virginia Water Sur 27 C8
Virginstow Devon 9 E5
Vobster Som 24 E2
Voe Shetland 160 E5
Voe Shetland 160 G6
Vowchurch Hereford 49 F5
Voxter Shetland 160 F5
Voy Orkney 159 G3

W

Wackerfield Durham 101 B6
Wacton Norf 68 E4
Wadbister Shetland 160 J6
Wadborough Worcs 50 E4
Waddesdon Bucks 39 C7
Waddingham Lincs 90 E3
Waddington Lancs 93 E7
Waddington Lincs 78 C2
Wadebridge Corn 4 B4
Wadeford Som 11 C8
Wadenhoe Northants 65 F7
Wadesmill Herts 41 C6
Wadhurst E Sus 18 B3
Wadshelf Derbys 76 B3
Wadsley S Yorks 88 E4
Wadsley Bridge S Yorks 88 E4
Wadworth S Yorks 89 E6
Waen Denb 72 C3
Waen Denb 72 C5
Waen Fach Powys 60 C2
Waen Goleugoed Denb 72 B4
Wag Highld 157 G13
Wainfleet All Saints Lincs 79 D7
Wainfleet Bank Lincs 79 D7
Wainfleet St Mary Lincs 79 D8
Wainfleet Tofts Lincs 79 D7
Wainhouse Corner Corn 8 E3
Wainscott Medway 29 B8
Wainstalls W Yorks 87 B8
Waitby Cumb 100 D2
Waithe Lincs 91 D6
Wake Lady Green N Yorks 102 E4
Wakefield W Yorks 88 B4
Wakerley Northants 65 E6
Wakes Colne Essex 42 B4
Walberswick Suff 57 B8
Walberton W Sus 16 D3
Walbottle T&W 110 C4
Walcot Lincs 78 F3
Walcot N Lincs 90 B2
Walcot Shrops 60 F3
Walcot Swindon 38 F1
Walcot Telford 61 C5
Walcot Green Norf 68 F4
Walcote Leics 64 F2
Walcote Warks 51 D6
Walcott Lincs 78 D4
Walcott Norf 69 A6
Walden N Yorks 101 F5
Walden Head N Yorks 100 F4
Walden Stubbs N Yorks 89 C6
Waldersey Cambs 66 D4
Walderslade Medway 29 C8
Walderton W Sus 15 C8
Walditch Dorset 12 E2
Waldley Derbys 75 F8
Waldridge Durham 111 D5
Waldringfield Suff 57 E6
Waldringfield Heath Suff 57 E6
Waldron E Sus 18 D2
Wales S Yorks 89 F5
Walesby Lincs 90 E5
Walesby Notts 77 B6
Walford Hereford 36 B2
Walford Hereford 49 B5
Walford Shrops 60 B4

County and unitary authority boundaries

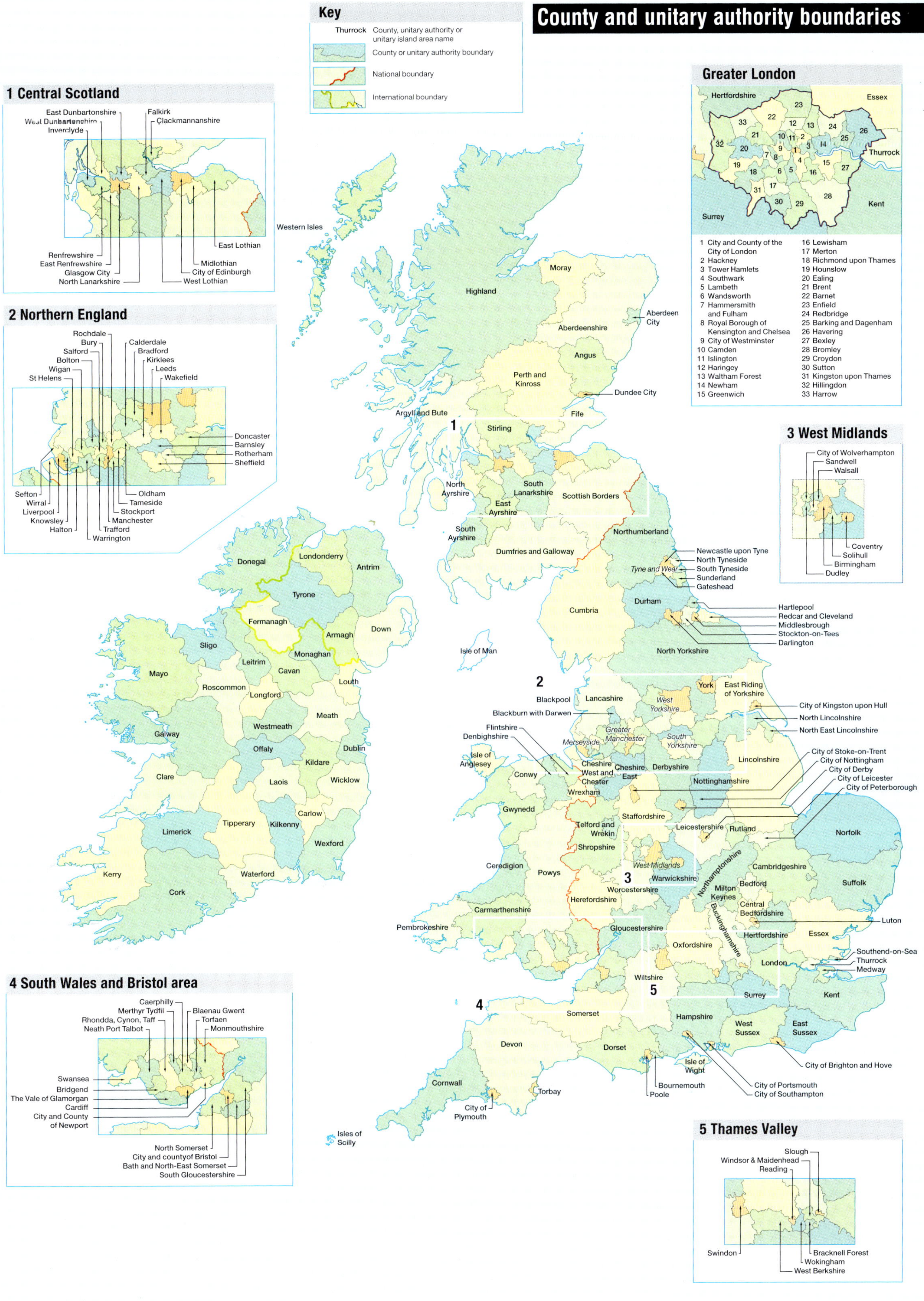

Key

Thurrock — County, unitary authority or unitary island area name

County or unitary authority boundary

National boundary

International boundary

Greater London

Hertfordshire
Essex
Surrey
Kent
Thurrock

1 City and County of the City of London
2 Hackney
3 Tower Hamlets
4 Southwark
5 Lambeth
6 Wandsworth
7 Hammersmith and Fulham
8 Royal Borough of Kensington and Chelsea
9 City of Westminster
10 Camden
11 Islington
12 Haringey
13 Waltham Forest
14 Newham
15 Greenwich
16 Lewisham
17 Merton
18 Richmond upon Thames
19 Hounslow
20 Ealing
21 Brent
22 Barnet
23 Enfield
24 Redbridge
25 Barking and Dagenham
26 Havering
27 Bexley
28 Bromley
29 Croydon
30 Sutton
31 Kingston upon Thames
32 Hillingdon
33 Harrow

1 Central Scotland

East Dunbartonshire
West Dunbartonshire
Inverclyde
Falkirk
Clackmannanshire

Renfrewshire
East Renfrewshire
Glasgow City
North Lanarkshire
East Lothian
Midlothian
City of Edinburgh
West Lothian

2 Northern England

Rochdale
Bury
Salford
Bolton
Wigan
St Helens
Calderdale
Bradford
Kirklees
Leeds
Wakefield

Doncaster
Barnsley
Rotherham
Sheffield

Sefton
Wirral
Liverpool
Knowsley
Halton
Oldham
Tameside
Stockport
Manchester
Trafford
Warrington

3 West Midlands

City of Wolverhampton
Sandwell
Walsall
Coventry
Solihull
Birmingham
Dudley

4 South Wales and Bristol area

Caerphilly
Merthyr Tydfil
Rhondda, Cynon, Taff
Neath Port Talbot
Blaenau Gwent
Torfaen
Monmouthshire

Swansea
Bridgend
The Vale of Glamorgan
Cardiff
City and County of Newport

North Somerset
City and county of Bristol
Bath and North-East Somerset
South Gloucestershire

5 Thames Valley

Windsor & Maidenhead
Reading
Slough
Swindon
Bracknell Forest
Wokingham
West Berkshire

Scotland

Highland
Moray
Aberdeenshire
Aberdeen City
Angus
Perth and Kinross
Dundee City
Fife
Stirling
Argyll and Bute
North Ayrshire
South Lanarkshire
East Ayrshire
South Ayrshire
Scottish Borders
Dumfries and Galloway
Western Isles

Ireland

Donegal
Londonderry
Antrim
Tyrone
Fermanagh
Down
Armagh
Monaghan
Sligo
Leitrim
Cavan
Louth
Mayo
Roscommon
Longford
Meath
Westmeath
Offaly
Dublin
Galway
Kildare
Wicklow
Clare
Laois
Carlow
Limerick
Tipperary
Kilkenny
Kerry
Waterford
Wexford
Cork

England & Wales

Northumberland
Newcastle upon Tyne
North Tyneside
South Tyneside
Sunderland
Gateshead
Tyne and Wear
Cumbria
Durham
Hartlepool
Redcar and Cleveland
Middlesbrough
Stockton-on-Tees
Darlington
North Yorkshire
York
East Riding of Yorkshire
City of Kingston upon Hull
North Lincolnshire
North East Lincolnshire
Blackpool
Lancashire
West Yorkshire
Greater Manchester
South Yorkshire
Blackburn with Darwen
Merseyside
Isle of Anglesey
Conwy
Flintshire
Denbighshire
Cheshire West and Chester
Cheshire East
Derbyshire
Wrexham
Lincolnshire
City of Stoke-on-Trent
City of Nottingham
City of Derby
City of Leicester
City of Peterborough
Gwynedd
Staffordshire
Nottinghamshire
Telford and Wrekin
Shropshire
Leicestershire
Rutland
Norfolk
Ceredigion
Powys
West Midlands
Warwickshire
Northamptonshire
Cambridgeshire
Bedford
Suffolk
Worcestershire
Herefordshire
Milton Keynes
Central Bedfordshire
Carmarthenshire
Gloucestershire
Buckinghamshire
Hertfordshire
Essex
Luton
Pembrokeshire
Oxfordshire
Southend-on-Sea
Thurrock
Medway
London
Wiltshire
Surrey
Kent
Somerset
Hampshire
West Sussex
East Sussex
Devon
Dorset
Isle of Wight
City of Brighton and Hove
Cornwall
Torbay
City of Plymouth
Bournemouth
Poole
City of Portsmouth
City of Southampton
Isles of Scilly
Isle of Man

Notes